Handbook of Research on Teaching the English Language Arts

Now in its third edition, the *Handbook of Research on Teaching the English Language Arts* — sponsored by the International Reading Association and the National Council of Teachers of English — offers an integrated perspective on the teaching of the English language arts and a comprehensive overview of research in the field. Prominent scholars, researchers, and professional leaders

- provide historical and theoretical perspectives about teaching the language arts
- focus on bodies of research that influence decision making within the teaching of the language arts
- explore the environments for language arts teaching
- reflect on the methods and materials for instruction

Reflecting important recent developments in the field, the Third Edition is restructured, updated, and includes many new contributors. More emphasis is given in this edition to the learner, multiple texts, learning, and sharing one's knowledge.

A Companion Website, new for this edition, includes among other features

- interactive tools, such as organizing questions and essay prompts, that connect chapters with one another
- PowerPoint® slides for highlighting the main points of each chapter
- several videos that readers can use to analyze chapters from the multiple perspectives provided in the book

The *Handbook of Research on Teaching the English Language Arts, Third Edition* is an essential resource for all professional educators, researchers, curriculum designers, students, and prospective and practicing teachers across the field of the English language arts.

Diane Lapp is Distinguished Professor of Education in the Department of Teacher Education at San Diego State University.

Douglas Fisher is Professor of Language and Literacy Education in the Department of Teacher Education at San Diego State University.

www.routledge.com/textbooks/9780415877367

D1158563

HANDBOOK
OF RESEARCH ON
TEACHING THE
ENGLISH LANGUAGE ARTS

THIRD EDITION

Sponsored by the International Reading Association
and the National Council of Teachers of English

EDITED BY
DIANE LAPP
San Diego State University
DOUGLAS FISHER
San Diego State University

Routledge
Taylor & Francis Group

NEW YORK AND LONDON

First published 1991 by Macmillan Publishing Company

Second edition published 2003 by Lawrence Erlbaum Associates, Inc.

This edition published 2011
by Routledge
711 Third Avenue, New York, NY 10017

Simultaneously published in the UK
by Routledge
2 Park Square, Milton Park, Abingdon, Oxon OX14 4RN

Routledge is an imprint of the Taylor & Francis Group, an informa business

Typeset in Times by EvS Communication Networx, Inc.

Library of Congress Cataloging in Publication Data
Handbook of research on teaching the English language arts / edited by Diane Lapp, Douglas Fisher. — 3rd ed.
p. cm.
1. Language arts. 2. English language—Study and teaching. I. Lapp, Diane. II. Fisher, Douglas, 1965-
LB1576.H234 2010
428.0071073—dc22
2010018988

ISBN 13: 978-0-415-87735-0 (hbk)
ISBN 13: 978-0-415-87736-7 (pbk)
ISBN 13: 978-0-203-83971-3 (ebk)

Contents

Preface

Until 1991 when the first edition of this handbook became a reality, the profession had seen reviews of research on reading, research studies on writing, studies on response to literature, and many on specialized topics such as spelling, punctuation, handwriting, and listening. While these studies occurred throughout the grades and in a variety of settings, the need to compile a comprehensive research handbook that would address all of the language arts components and also other topics related to teaching of the English language arts, while challenging, was obvious to my colleague and dear friend Jim Flood. He suggested that we should invite Jim Squire and Julie Jensen to discuss the possibility of compiling a comprehensive volume that would address all topics related to the English language arts.

Together the four of us agreed that the isolated appearance of reading studies in the International Reading Association (IRA) journals, and those related to listening, speaking, and writing in the National Council of Teachers of English (NCTE) journals, were indicative of the separateness of both professional organizations and also the existing non-integrated classroom teaching of these language arts components. We contacted decision makers at NCTE and IRA, as well as Lloyd Chilton of Macmillan Publishing, to begin discussing a proposal for developing the first Handbook of Research on Teaching the English Language Arts that would be jointly sponsored by each organization and published by Macmillan.

Prominent scholars and professional leaders were invited to compile and evaluate the significance of existing research on a specified topic, identify relationships with related fields, note possible conflicts, controversies, and issues that appeared as hindrances to language arts instruction. Each author was tasked with addressing diverse perspectives regarding theoretical, historical, contextual, research, and contemporary influences on how the English language arts were taught and learned. They were also tasked with identifying next step priorities for teaching the English language arts.

What resulted was 888 pages or 39 chapters organized into five sections which addressed historical and theoretical perspectives, methods of research, language learners, instructional environments, and, aspects affecting instruction. Our goal in compiling the volume was to testify to the need for the unification of language arts research and practice as a way to go beyond data to inform teaching which continues to be central to the success of schools and all members of society.

Second Edition

The same goal applied to the second edition of the handbook, published in 2003. The second edition was designed as an extension and expansion of the topics addressed in the first edition. Presented as a compilation of research driven information, readers were invited to utilize these as a frame to assess the success occurring via English language arts instruction for all learners from kindergarten beyond grade twelve and the factors influencing this instruction.

What continued to be obvious was that the degree of attention paid by researchers to various areas and components of the language arts continued to differ. While listening and handwriting were again scarcely studied, both language acquisition and development, comprehension, writing, vocabulary, spelling, phonics, learning environments, and diversity among learners had received much attention. In fact these topics had received so much attention that multiple chapters offering insights from various contexts were compiled.

Many of the same scholars updated their chapters and several others wrote new chapters on topics that pertained to the original five sections. The result was a second edition containing 75 chapters and 1098 pages. The new topics reflected the growth of the research areas that had gained prominence in the intervening years. These clustered within themes such as the significance of teacher inquiry, ethnographic, qualitative, and case studies as authentic voices of investigation, learners in middle grades and those who were bilingual, English learners, or speakers of African American Vernacular English, the power of multicultural literature on establishing classroom equilibrium and student engagement, implications on learning via the expanding technologies, impacts of high-stakes assessment, and the need for balanced literacy programs and instruction.

The range of these additions confirmed our understanding as editors that research was only one of the forces that affected classroom practice. The art as well as the science of teaching and student learning was, and continues to be, influenced by theories emerging and converging from many fields including anthropology, psychology, sociology, linguistics, literary theory, and information technology. Diversity across and among communities of researchers, theorists, policymakers, and practitioners continues to define English language arts research and practice.

Third Edition

During the years between editions two and three, both Jim Flood and Jim Squire died and Julie Jensen retired. In 2008, I was asked by Naomi Silverman at Routledge to develop the third edition that would have a 2011 publication date. Before I share the contents of this edition I would like to pay a special tribute to my former coeditors.

James Flood, with his keen intellect and gentle heart, dreamed of a world of literacy as totally inclusive; where all children would have equal opportunity to receive the best education, or as he labeled it, "a first-class education," from the finest prepared teachers who viewed themselves as able to implement instructional practice that demonstrated an awareness and appreciation of all aspects of diversity. These teachers would be prepared to study their practice in ways that tested, refined, confirmed, or elaborated research on teaching, with the results providing learning experiences designed to encourage intellectual, emotional, and personal growth for every student in their classrooms.

James Squire contextualized the first two editions of the handbook by the questions he never ceased to ask; questions such as: What is English? Why can't all students learn to read and write? Are all teachers being equally prepared to teach the language arts? What role will technology play in language arts teaching and learning? How will diverse communities of researchers define language arts instruction? and, Even if research isn't perfect what alternative, more effective ways are there to provide a sound knowledge base? He had quite an inquiring mind.

By including a wide variation of views from the chapter contributors, **Julie Jensen** reminded us that these handbooks would have the potential to impact a larger readership of language arts educators and the resulting instruction that would occur in their classrooms. She viewed these volumes as a way to preserve an historical snapshot of what was occurring in English language arts research and instruction during a given time period. Reflecting on Julie's belief that knowing this history means not just knowing the ideas, but also the people who conceived the ideas, I feel exceptionally fortunate to have known and to have worked closely with these three giants in the field of the English language arts.

Having enjoyed a professional history of collegiality, I invited my colleague and friend Doug Fisher to co-edit this third edition because I knew that he had a combination of factors such as keen intellect, valuing of history, sensitivity to diversity, and insightful questioning that had been so characteristic of Jim, Jim, and Julie. Doug agreed and what follows is an overview of the third edition, which we dedicate to Jim Flood who first conceived of an English language arts research to practice handbook.

Diane Lapp

Overview

The major themes that have received much attention between editions two and three have been the potential of assessments to reflect student performance across the language arts, and the power of technology to bridge the worlds of school and home for a diverse population of students through expanded literacies. To address these topics we have increased the five original sections of the handbook to seven in order to fully explore the many faces of texts existing today, and the assessment frameworks and practices being experienced in English language arts classrooms.

Each of the 61 chapters in this volume can be conceived of more as an encyclopedic entry than an exhaustive review of the literature on a specific topic. This change of format was intentional since we feel that the comprehensive topical reviews have been previously shared in editions one and two. We also invited a trio of scholars renowned or becoming renowned for their knowledge in a particular area, to serve as section editors. Together we selected the topics and authors for each chapter, with the goal of presenting a comprehensive update within each section.

Ways of studying language arts related questions also changed between editions. Scholars from different disciplines now converge to forge conversations about issues related to language arts teaching and learning. Encouraging more teacher voice while honoring their overwhelming schedules has also begun to add a universality of balance to the conversations that must occur if the intricacies of the learner and language arts instruction are to be fully comprehended.

The approach to studying these questions, while still primarily advancing either a quantitative or qualitative framework, has also broadened to include mixed methodology and process or formative assessment designs. We predict this trend toward the use of even more synergistic designs to study language arts related questions by scholars across disciplines will be common practice by the time we edit the fourth edition. Our belief is based on observing, in our own work, the power of these combinations of design and voices to increase our understanding about the complexities of the issues and also the participants.

As the editors of the third edition we welcome your voices as participants in the ongoing study of the English language arts. There are many questions remaining to be answered and unearthed. The possibility of continuing "to know" can only occur as we work together, poised to see, examine, and act on countless possibilities that will affect learning opportunities for all students and their teachers.

Diane Lapp
Douglas Fisher

Section I

The Language Learner

SECTION EDITORS
NANCY ROSER, MARÍA E. FRÁNQUIZ, AND ALLISON SKERRETT

Introduction to Section One: The Language Learner

The opening section of this volume focuses on the linguistic diversity that contemporary students bring to language arts classrooms. The chapters examine the richness of talent and complexities of need within the group of students called "language learners," as well as the implications of language diversity for teaching and learning the English language arts.

Callahan and Valdez portray the remarkable racial, cultural, linguistic, and socioeconomic diversity represented by students in U.S. schools today, offering demographic trends for students for whom English is a second language. In particular, they discuss two defining factors that should be considered in teaching and supporting these students: (a) their statuses related to immigration, citizenship, and transnationalism; and (b) the role of language(s) and literacies in their lives.

Cazden points toward sociocultural factors that affect learners acquiring languages. Focusing on the intersection of language learning and identity development, for example, Cazden argues that learners are actively navigating and developing multiple identities as they become socialized into multiple linguistic communities.

Escamilla and Hopewell propose a more robust understanding of bilingualism, whereby English Language Learners are not treated as a single research subgroup,

nor the acquisition of languages assumed as sequentially acquired. They advocate for comprehensive and long-term programs to improve the quality of language instruction in bilingual settings.

Ball, Skerrett, and Martínez describe culturally and linguistically complex classrooms (CLCCs) in which the varieties of English students bring to school (such as African American Vernacular English and Spanglish), as well as the sophisticated linguistic abilities students possess can be used as resources for teaching and learning the language arts. They also consider how teachers may be more effectively prepared to recognize, value, and use linguistic diversity as generative tools for teaching and learning.

Fránquiz and Pratt provide a description of local literacy practices and challenges for teachers in Spanish-English bilingual educational contexts in Puerto Rico and Central Texas. Among other methods, the authors explore videoconferencing as a professional development communicative tool for improving language arts instruction for this student population.

Taken together, these chapters offer a portrait of the students entering today's language arts classrooms, and implicate optimal opportunities for these students' learning of the English language arts that both acknowledges and builds on the repertoires of language, literacies, and identities they bring.

1

Who Is Learning Language(s) in Today's Schools?

VERÓNICA E. VALDEZ AND REBECCA M. CALLAHAN

U.S. schools traditionally serve students who bring rich cultural and linguistic resources. The past three decades have brought an upsurge in linguistic and cultural diversity in the classroom not experienced since the 1920s (Capps et al., 2005). Often culturally and linguistically diverse (CLD) students bring resources that may go undetected or underutilized by mainstream teachers. Language arts educators have been asked to examine current instructional practices to build upon the heterogeneity of students and the resources they bring to learning (Gutiérrez, 2001; Gutiérrez, Baquedano-López, & Tejeda, 2000). Educators are to look to pedagogical practices which connect to students' local cultural and linguistic knowledge and practices (funds of knowledge), personal experiences, and varied ways of showing their abilities (González, Moll, & Amanti, 2005; Ladson-Billings, 2001; Zentella, 2005), rather than students' language designation. Ultimately, good instruction begins with knowing one's students. This chapter paints a demographic portrait of language learners, illustrating the complexity of issues underlying the resources they bring and their achievement patterns. We focus on English Learners (ELs) in particular—language minority students who require linguistic support in English—as they represent the fastest growing segment of the student population.

Demographic Trends[1]: In the U.S, in Our Public Schools

In 2008, 74 million children aged birth to 17 comprised 24% of the total U.S. population (Federal Interagency Forum, 2009). That same year, 20% of the U.S. population over the age of 5 reported speaking one or more languages other than English; the most common being Spanish (61.9%) and Chinese (4.4%) (Terrazas & Batalova, 2009). In addition, between 1970 and 2000, the population of school-age children speaking Spanish at home doubled from 3.5 to 7

million, while those who spoke Asian languages tripled from 0.5 to 1.5 million (Capps et al., 2005). Without a doubt, our schools contain multiple languages and literacies; what may not be as evident is that ELs negotiating two or more languages may bring linguistic abilities distinct from those of their monolingual English-speaking peers. Language(s) play a defining role in the development and negotiation cultural and linguistic identities (Genesee, Paradis, & Crago, 2004). Among ELs, variation occurs in the development and ability to use their home language(s) and English. In addition, immigration occurs across the grades and across the life course, with greater numbers of first generation ELs in secondary schools (44%) than elementary (24%) (Capps, et al., 2005). Although it may take 5 to7 years to develop literacy in a second language (Collier, 1987), not all ELs enter in kindergarten; it is critical to explore language(s) and literacies in the lives of EL students in the context of the elementary and secondary education demands they encounter.

Although the majority of children live in two-parent households, 67% in 2006 (Federal Interagency Forum, 2009), the patterns vary greatly by race/ethnicity and socio-economic status (SES). In addition poverty, also associated with race/ethnicity, presents one of the biggest challenges for 17% of school-age children shaping where families live, the schools children attend, the resources allocated to schools, and student mobility (Planty et al., 2008). Forty-three percent of households experiencing poverty reported housing that was physically inadequate, crowded, or cost more than half the family income. Additionally, regardless of ethnicity, single-mother households were more likely to live in poverty (43%) than two-parent households (9%) (Planty et al., 2008). Latino/a and Black children are more likely than their White counterparts to come from low-income families (26% and 33%, respectively, compared to 10% for Whites and single-mother households (Capps et al., 2005; Planty et al., 2008). Although poverty rates across all ethnicities have decreased from their 1995 peak of 21% among school-age children (Planty et al, 2008), the current global economic recession threatens to reverse this trend.

National trends in poverty and household composition coincide with a numerical increase in children in the United States, and increased diversity among youth. Currently, the youth population is comprised of 22% Latina/o, 15% Black, 4% Asian, and 5% "all other races" (Federal Interagency Forum, 2009). Perhaps the most significant population growth has been among Latino/a children, a 9% to 22% increase in the share between 1980 and 2008. It is projected that by 2021 one in four U.S. children will be of Latina/o origin (Federal Interagency Forum, 2009). Linguistic diversity has increased as well; 20% of the U.S. population 5 years and older spoke a language other than English at home in 2008, with 66% reporting speaking English "very well" (U.S. Census Bureau, 2008a). Of the other-language speakers, 62% spoke Spanish and 38% spoke another language (U.S. Census Bureau, 2008a).

Nowhere is the shifting racial and ethnic distribution of the United States more evident than in K–12 public schools. Over 47.5 million K–12 students enrolled in U.S. public schools in 2008, adding public prekindergarten enrollment increases the total by 2.7 million (U.S. Census Bureau, 2008b). Public school enrollment will likely continue to rise through 2017, reaching an estimated high of 54.1 million students, with culturally and linguistically diverse (CLD)[2] students comprising the fastest growing segment (43%) of the K–12 student population, a 12% increase over the last two decades (Planty et al., 2008). In 2006, 57% of students enrolled in U.S. schools were White, down from 78% in 1972, while Latinas/os increased to 20%, Blacks to 16%, Asian, Pacific Islander, American Indian/Alaskan Natives, and students of more than one race together to just over 7% (Planty et al., 2008).

Although the past three decades show evidence of an increase in CLD student enrollment across the U.S, the distribution has varied by region. The South and West enroll more CLD students than the Midwest and Northeast; the Midwest enrolls the fewest and the West the most (CLD enrollment exceeds Whites by 10%). Regional variation occurs among the CLD population as well; Latina/o student numbers exceed those of Blacks in the West, while Black enrollment exceeds that of Latinas/os in the South and Midwest (Planty et al., 2008). In addition, the proportion of students who speak a language other than English at home is increasing faster than the general K–12 population. Between 1995 and 2005, enrollment of language minority students designated ELs by the public schools grew by 56% while the entire student population grew by less than 3% (National Clearinghouse for English Language Acquisition [NCELA], 2007). Research indicates that many ELs have not been well served by the U.S. educational system (Callahan, 2005; Harklau, 1994a; Valenzuela, 1999), suggesting a need for research to better understand EL instruction and achievement.

English Learners in U.S. Schools: Characteristics, Experiences, and Needs

ELs represent a diverse group of K–12 students nationally at various stages of learning English. The lack of a uniform identification process presents perhaps the greatest challenge to defining the EL population and ultimately meeting student needs; states and Local Education Agencies (LEAs) have specific definitions of what it means to be designated an EL, whereas the U.S. Census reports the number of individuals who speak languages other than English in the home, with adult respondents reporting English-speaking ability within the household. State education agency (SEA) definitions draw from student's English oral proficiency, as well as academic competency (test scores and grade-level achievement) (Ragan & Lesaux, 2006; U.S. Department of Education, 2005). As a result, Census data may underreport EL numbers compared to state and school district reports. For example, 2000 SEA EL numbers prove 15% higher than those of Census 2000. The 2006 Survey of U.S. SEAs reports enrollment of over 5 million ELs, double the 1990 enrollment (NCELA, 2008). The EL representation varies with ethnicity as well; in 2007, 64% of Asian and 68% of Latina/o children spoke a language other than English at home, compared to 6% of White and 5% of Black children (Planty et al., 2008). Not surprisingly, Spanish, Chinese, and Vietnamese lead the list of non-English languages spoken by ELs in U.S. schools (Capps et al., 2005).

Of the overall U.S.population, 12% is foreign-born or first generation[3] (35 million); 11% is second-generation with at least one of foreign-born parent (31 million), and 77% is third-plus generation, children of U.S.-born parents (226 million) (Dixon, 2006). Among the school-age population, these numbers are lower for first generation (5%) and higher for second-generation (22%) (Planty et al., 2008; U.S. Census Bureau, 2008b). First- and second-generation children of immigrants represent the majority of the EL population. Prior research suggest that the generational status and the country of origin of students makes a difference in their educational trajectories with second-generation students achieving at higher levels than first generation or third-plus generations (Dixon, 2006; Rumbaut & Portes, 2001). Student background characteristics, including parental education level and socio-economic status also play a role. Research found lower levels of achievement and higher levels of retention among Central American and Mexican-origin immigrant children compared to other immigrant groups (Dixon, 2006). While immigrant and language minority students may present linguistic, academic and social challenges to our schools, they also bring vast resources in their transnational ties and ready access to multiple linguistic supports.

Children of immigrants comprise the fastest-growing segment of the U.S. youth population—one out of every five children is born to immigrant parents (Levitt & Waters, 2002). Primarily from Asia and Latin America (Ruiz-de-

Velasco, Fix, & Clewell, 2000), today's immigrant parents are documented and undocumented; their children are either foreign-born as well (first generation), or U.S.-born second generation. As immigrant parents leave their countries of origin for a number of reasons—economic, familial, political, and religious—the educational trajectories of immigrant children in U. S. schools often reflect their parents' immigration context.

Although important, the demographic information regarding CLD students, especially ELs, illustrates general trends yet tells us little about the unique issues and challenges shaping ELs' identities and resources. In the following section, we discuss two critical constructs key the EL experience: (a) immigration, citizenship, and transnationalism, and (b) language(s) and literacies. Together, cultural and linguistic factors contribute to the heterogeneity of EL experiences and the importance of these factors in shaping ELs' academic and linguistic trajectories.

Immigration, Citizenship, & Transnationalism: Shaping the EL Experience

ELs, frequently children of immigrants, simultaneously draw from the culture of the home and their parents, as well as that of the school (Suárez-Orozco & Suárez-Orozco, 2001); in many cases their social and academic development also draws from transnational experiences—where they remain connected and strongly influenced by two countries (Sánchez & Machado-Casas, 2009). ELs in public school classrooms draw from a range of immigration experiences; they can be refugees, migrants (U.S. born or foreign-born); temporary visitors, or immigrants (documented or undocumented foreign-born immigrants, or U.S.-born children of immigrants). As we identify each student groups' defining characteristics, we highlight challenges associated with each status and provide examples of resources or "funds of knowledge" that said learners may bring to the classroom (Gonzalez et al., 2005).

Refugees. Individuals who were forced to flee their countries of origin for political and/or economic reasons and were granted legal entry and support services in the United States are considered refugees. Since the 1980s, more than 1.8 million refugees have resettled in the United States (Office of Refugee Resettlement, 2005), many of whom experienced traumatic events (e.g., bodily harm, death of loved ones, and/or long-term experiences in temporary refugee camps). Many refugee experiences may present challenges to children's adaptation to U.S. schools; however, they also bring a wealth of information about global events gained through lived experiences, events often unfamiliar to many of their classmates. The geographic and personal transition may prove unsettling to refugee students, now tasked with handling the vast differences between their origins and their present situation; a classroom where they must sit still for an extended period of time (Birman, 2002). Refugees' experiences overcoming extreme conditions often result in resilience and survival skills that may go unrecognized in the contemporary classroom.

Temporary Visitors: Human Capital. Individuals with temporary U.S. residency due to employment and/or educational pursuits (e.g., exchange or international post-secondary students) comprise one type of temporary visitor. Japan, South Korea, China (including Taiwan), India, and Germany send the most *human capital* temporary visitors (Batalova, 2006). Many visiting families generally display strong efforts to maintain the home language and literacy abilities of their children as well as social and professional connections. These patterns are supported by the grade-level continuous schooling common among children of visiting families.

Temporary Visitors: Migrants. A second type of temporary visitor, migrants, are workers motivated by economic survival who move following available agricultural or fishing/poultry opportunities. Foreign-born or U.S.-born immigrants, students from migrant families often experience interruptions in their schooling as their families pursue employment across states and regions. Interrupted schooling can lead to gaps in language and academic content, especially among foreign-born migrants who may have difficulty speaking English. Migrant life brings economic challenges that require children to work and bear family responsibilities at the expense of school attendance (Salínas & Fránquiz, 2004). Yet, many migrant students demonstrate high levels of responsibility, translate for their parents, and possess knowledge of their families' trade—such as the names, geographic locations, and planting and harvesting seasons of different crops.

Legal Status. Although immigrants who enter the country legally may face struggles acquiring English and adjusting to U.S. schools their integration may be facilitated by the stability of their legal status, a security lacking among the undocumented, constantly aware of the threat of deportation. Legal status may speak to immigrants' access to strong social networks and supports which facilitate navigation of the complex U.S. immigration process. Immigrant youth whose parents or who themselves entered the country without legal documentation face perhaps the most daunting social, academic, and personal challenges to their educational trajectories. For undocumented children, their entry into the country may have been filled with risk and danger, or they may have entered so young that that the U.S. has become the only home they know. An estimated 11.9 million undocumented immigrants lived in the U.S. in 2008, a figure more or less stable since 2006 (Passel & Cohn, 2009). In 2008 it was estimated that 5.5 million children in 2008 had at least one undocumented immigrant parent (Passel & Cohn, 2009). Many undocumented immigrants report witnessing and or surviving traumatic events in their journeys to the United States (Valdez, 2006). Once here, their presence is tenuous; they remain aware that exposure could mean a return to their home and separation from family members. Thus, many learn to navigate the United States and its systems, often declining social supports so as not to call attention to themselves. Undocumented adolescent ELs not only must persevere to succeed in high school, but upon graduation, they must also determine what, if any, higher education or employment options are available.

Transnationalism. Due to the relatively low-cost technology and communication tools available such as the Internet, texting, email, cell phones, and low cost airfares, transnationalism is relatively prominent among immigrant youth today (Sánchez & Machado-Casas, 2009). Thus, even U.S.-born second-generation children who have never visited their parents' countries of origin may be raised in homes where the home countries' values, languages, and people are very visible (Levitt & Glick Schiller, 2004). For example, Yi (2009) found that online community provided a critical social context in which Korean American adolescents engaged in transnational literacy practices and constructed transnational identities. Also, Sanchez (2007) found that adolescent girls' transnational learning communities build dual local cultural knowledge, cultural flexibility, and notions of global citizenship tied to an awareness of the social disparities in society. Transnational experiences represent untapped resources for ELs in U.S. schools, as do students' linguistic experience as members of multiple language communities.

Primary Language Development Bilingualism research has explored simultaneous language development among children from birth to age 3, and sequential language development within educational settings (Bialystok, 2001). Whether a child experiences sequential or simultaneous bilingualism, each language is used with different people, in unique contexts, and for distinct purposes, leading to variation in proficiency across contexts and languages, with competencies evolving over time (Baker, 2006). ELs born in the United States often quickly develop conversational proficiency in English, but take longer to develop the academic English proficiency necessary to master the core content. In the early grades, children continue to develop their primary language skills, even as they acquire English. It is during this time that complex language skills such as syntactic and semantic systems, inference, and figurative understandings are acquired (Crutchley, 2007). Older children and adolescents who enter the U.S. system already having developed literacy in the primary language, must transfer these understandings to English while developing the English proficiency necessary to master academic content.

L1 and English Acquisition. The rate at which ELs develop conversational and academic English proficiency often depends on how much the primary language (L1) is allowed to continue to develop. Research has shown that a strong base in the primary language not only facilitates the acquisition of English and additional languages, but also continued and parallel gains in the primary language (Cummins, 1981). In particular, Thomas and Collier (1997, 2002) found that children who developed high levels of primary language proficiency while acquiring English demonstrated comparable levels of academic success and literacy compared to native English speakers after 4 to 7 years of schooling. In contrast, children schooled in an English–only context from an early age took 7 to 10 years to approximate the academic success of their native English-speaking peers. In fact, many may never reach this point; that approximately 60% of secondary ELs in California have been in the state's schools more than 5 years (Callahan, 2005) suggests that many ELs schooled in English-only never acquire the skill set necessary to exit EL status.

Despite such evidence, many schools continue to advocate earlier and greater exposure to English for ELs, signaling a preference for English; a message reinforced with the passage of English-only legislation in California, Massachusetts, and Arizona. Immigrant ELs' language choices quickly shift to English in such contexts; however, there are powerful consequences to these shifts. Wong-Fillmore (2000) documents the Chen family's immersion in an English school environment across the course of a decade. English-only instruction ultimately resulted in language loss and cultural distance for all four Chen children, negatively influencing their identity formation and relations with Chinese family members. For one son, these processes culminated in his decision to drop-out of high school, highlighting the critical importance of primary language maintenance for academic, economic, and societal reasons.

Benefits to Bilingualism. Bilingualism itself brings multiple advantages including linguistic and metalinguistic abilities; cognitive flexibility; heightened concept formation, divergent thinking, general reasoning, and verbal abilities; better problem solving and higher order thinking skills (Bialystok, 2001; Hakuta, 1986). Two unique linguistic abilities exhibited by bilingual ELs are *oral codeswitching* and *language interpreting/ brokering* (Baker, 2006). *Oral codeswitching* or the switching between languages is typical in bilinguals varies with the content and context of the conversation, and with the language skills of the individuals involved. Code switching tends to be used purposefully by highly proficient bilingual ELs able to use the full extent of their linguistic resources (Meisel, 2004). ELs use oral codeswitching to: emphasize a point, substitute a word, express a concept for which there is no equivalent, reinforce or clarify a request, express identity, recount a conversation in its original language, interject, inject humor, signify a change in attitude or relationship, exclude people from a conversation, or discuss a subject based principally in the other language (Baker, 2006). Many ELs also demonstrate language interpreting/brokering—translating a conversation for parents and others, simultaneously negotiating responses (Valdés, 2003). The benefits to bilingual ELs of participating in language interpreting/brokering include, but are not limited to: improved status within the family, early maturity, personal initiative, family closeness, metalinguistic awareness, paraphrasing skills, and character formation (Baker, 2006). Overall, primary language development simultaneous with English acquisition brings many advantages to ELs that are overlooked in the classroom.

Bilingual ELs' Literacies. ELs often possess a range of literacy skills across the primary language and English. Primary language literacy can be a major advantage in terms of linguistic and content area achievement (Collier, 1987). However, the schooling and background knowledge ELs have prior to entering U.S. schools helps determine students' literacy levels and academic achievement (Callahan, 2005). Some ELs enter U.S. schools with age and grade-level skills, while others have limited or no literacy due to limited prior schooling experiences, interrupted schooling, and other circumstances (Freeman, Freeman, & Mercuri, 2002; Suárez-Orozco & Suárez-Orozco, 2001). Even when schooled primarily in the United States, ELs may not have sufficient academic preparation for post-secondary success. Callahan (2005) found that 98% of the EL students she sampled had not enrolled in the coursework necessary to apply to a 4-year university. The academic content provided to high school ELs, more than their English language proficiency, appears to determine their overall achievement; prior research exploring the secondary English as a Second Language (ESL) context (Dillon, 2001; Ek, 2009; Harklau, 1994b, 1999; Katz, 1999), suggests a need to improve ELs' literacy experiences.

Adolescent ELs continue to develop academic English proficiency throughout secondary school, simultaneously mastering core content in English, all the while being held to the same accountability standards which presume academic literacy in English (Short & Fitzsimmons, 2007). In fact, while proficiency in English certainly influences ELs' performance in U.S. schools, prior research suggests that academic preparation and track placement play a greater role in predicting their academic success (Callahan, 2005). Likewise, some first generation ELs, schooled in the home country, nonetheless struggle to transition into the U.S. secondary school system. These ELs may lack content area knowledge, or the content itself may be specific to the U.S. context, new and unfamiliar to the immigrant EL. Background knowledge is critical to the development of new knowledge and understanding; its absence isespecially problematic in middle and high school where content area gaps may constrain attainment and achievement.

New Literacies and the English Learner

Literacies are embedded in social practices that include ways of acting, thinking, and speaking, as well as the use of various non-linguistic symbols and tools (Gee, 2007). Explorations into multiple literacy practices have produced insights into the complexity involved and the abilities gained in becoming literate in two or more languages (Gee, 2007; Hornberger, 2003; Martin-Jones & Jones, 2000). Recognizing students' multiple literacies requires acknowledging the range of meaning-making strategies ELs explore with different forms of texts and tools—books, musical instruments, Web-based data, video cameras, canvas, or even social networking venues like Facebook. As access to technology has increased, more ELs are using the Internet, reading its contents, sending emails, instant messaging, text messaging, listening to music, and watching videos for large segments of their day in and out-of-school settings (Espinoza, Laffey, & Whittaker, 2006). The wide range of out-of-classroom literacy experiences of the growing bilingual EL population merits exploration.

Linguistic Skills and Strategies. Interrelated language processes that can develop in a parallel fashion with one enriching the other (Moll & Dworin, 1996; Reyes, 2006), bilingualism and biliteracy shape the academic and social development of immigrant ELs. Moll and Dworin (1996) argue no single path to developing biliteracy exists; ELs' pathways to biliteracy are shaped by students' histories, learning and social contexts, and opportunities to use each language. Despite these multiple pathways, literacy development among ELs exposed to two languages maintains several key characteristics (Valdez & Fránquiz, 2010). For example, prior research points to the *bidirectionality* of bilingualism and biliteracy between parents and students, and students and their peers (Dworin, 2003; Reyes, 2006); *interliteracy* where linguistic elements of the primary language are applied to a second (Gort, 2006); *strategic codeswitching*, the purposeful alternation of languages for instructional purposes (Gort, 2006); use of *codeswitching* as a routine language practice (Reyes, 2006); and *spontaneous biliteracy* when literacy is developed in the second language for which you are not receiving instruction (De La Luz Reyes, 2000). ELs able to access linguistic resources for academic and personal purposes demonstrate each, if not all, of the aforementioned characteristics.

Bi-Literacy Resources. EL students who gain English proficiency at school while maintaining the primary language are often asked assume greater responsibilities on behalf of their families and communities. Reflecting their complex literacy skills, they may be asked to go with family members to various appointments with doctors, landlords, social services, etc., to translating written materials for family members from English to the home language as well as paraphrasing the content of information provided to the family in English (Moje, Ciechanowski, Kramer, Ellis, Carillo, & Callazo, 2004; Orellana, Reynolds, Dorner, & Meza, 2003). Many ELs assist their families in other ways as well; working to contribute financially, caring for younger siblings, cooking and cleaning when their parents go to work, and getting their school work done. Gained from these experiences are maturity, responsibility, and organizational and decision-making skills. ELs bring these resources gained in out-of-school settings into their schools and classrooms schools. A beginning level EL may have limited English skills compared to classmates, but at home may be the only one who can speak any English.

Reflections and Conclusions

We wrote this chapter to emphasize the importance of knowing the whole student; it is not sufficient to know an EL's language proficiency level, but a good teacher will know her prior academic preparation, her family characteristics, her out-of-school skill-set, as well. The engaged teacher will ask; *Who* is my student? *How* can I best nurture her gifts and highlight her resources? ELs are not a monolithic population; educators cannot assume that all ELs share the same needs, backgrounds, and perspectives. De La Luz Reyes (2000) found that the teacher's ability to set up a respectful environment which fostered both languages allowed the development biliteracy among the young ELs. EL achievement can only be enhanced with a renewed focus on student's histories, language, experiences, and values in classroom activities (Au, 1993; Fránquiz & Reyes, 1998). Literature exploring funds of knowledge in Latino/a ELs' homes, communities, and classrooms (Gonzalez et al., 2005); the range of language and literacy practices exhibited by Latina/o families (Zentella, 2005); and Els' varied expressions of language and literacy practices (Purcell-Gates, 2007) all reflect the depth of knowledge available to educators from ELs and their families.

There is no doubt that many ELs face daunting challenges, especially high school age immigrants and refugees with limited prior schooling. Yet, Newcomer and similar programs designed to facilitate the secondary experience, staffed by committed educators, programs that combine closer contact and follow-up with these students, and promote academic and linguistic rigor hold promise (Boyson & Short, 2003; Short, 2002). Educators need to talk with and know their students, especially ELs who come with unique linguistic and academic profiles. Educators have the ability to help students discover and utilize linguistic resources and abilities, to assist them as they learn to make associations between their lived experiences and the academic material presented to them. For the growing EL population, it is a journey worth taking.

Notes

1. The demographic data available to describe the U.S. school-age population, student enrollment information, and English Learner populations vary considerably in the way those reporting the data define their populations and in how and when they collect their data. Thus, these demographic datasets and reported findings present some challenges and limitations, particularly in their ability to be compared with each other. Therefore, we have attempted to use these data in ways that complement each source's contributions to the topic described providing a general, if imprecise, representation of the demographic trends.

2. We use culturally and linguistically diverse (CLD) students to refer to students who are identified as non-White and includes students who may speak languages other than English at home.

3. In accordance with prior immigration literature (e.g., Rumbaut & Portes, 2001), we define generational status as follows: first generation: student is foreign-born with foreign-born parents, living in United States; second generation, student is U.S.-born with at least one foreign-born parent; third-plus generation, both student and parents are U.S.-born.

References

Au, K. H. (1993). *Literacy instruction in multicultural settings*. New York: Harcourt Brace.

Baker, C. (2006). *Foundations of bilingual education and bilingualism* (4th ed.). Tonawanda, NY: Multilingual Matters.

Batalova, J. (2006). *Foreign students and exchange visitors.* Washington, DC: Migration Policy Institute. Retrieved from http://www.migration-information.org/feature/display.cfm?ID=489

Bialystok, E. (2001). *Bilingualism in development: Language, literacy, and cognition.* Cambridge, UK: Cambridge University Press.

Birman, D. (2002). *Refugee mental health in the classroom: A guide for the ESL teacher.* Denver, CO: Spring Institute for Intercultural Learning. Retrieved from http://www.spring-institute.org

Boyson, B. A., & Short, D. J. (2003). *Secondary school newcomer programs in the United States* (Research Report 12). Santa Cruz, CA: Center for Research on Education Diversity & Excellence.

Callahan, R. (2005). Tracking and high school English learners: Limiting opportunities to learn. *American Educational Research Journal, 42*(2), 305–328.

Capps, R., Fix, M., Murray, J., Ost, J., Passel, J. S., & Herwantoro, S. (2005). *The new demography of America's schools: Immigration and the No Child Left Behind act.* Washington, DC: Urban Institute.

Collier, V. P. (1987). Age and rate of acquisition of language for academic purposes. *TESOL Quarterly, 21*(4), 677–741.

Crutchley, A. (2007). Comprehension of idiomatic verb + particle constructions in 6- to 11-year-old children. *First Language, 27*(3), 203–226.

Cummins, J. (1981). The role of primary language development in promoting educational success for language minority students. In California State Department of Education (Ed.), *Schooling and language minority students: A theoretical framework.* Los Angeles, CA: California State Department of Education.

De La Luz Reyes, M. (2000). Unleashing possibilities: Biliteracy in the primary grads. In M. De La Luz, Reyes & J. Halcón (Eds.), *The best for our children: Critical perspectives on literacy for Latino students* (pp. 96–121). New York: Teachers College Press.

Dillon, P. W. (2001). Labeling and English language learners: Hearing recent Iimmigrants' needs. In *Labeling: Pedagogy and politics* (pp. 93–105). London: Routledge Falmer.

Dixon, D. (2006). *The second generation in the United States.* Washington, DC: Migration Policy Institute. Retrieved from http://www.miigration-information.org/USfocus/print.cfm?ID=446

Dworin, J. E. (2003). Insights into biliteracy development: Toward a bi-directional theory of bilingual pedagogy. *Journal of Hispanic Higher Education, 2*(2), 171–186.

Ek, L. D. (2009). Language and literacy in the pentecostal church and the public high school: A case study of a Mexican ESL student. *The High School Journal, 92*(2), 1–13.

Espinosa, L., Laffey, J., & Whittaker, T. (2006). *Language minority children analysis: Focus on technology use* (Final Report). Washington, DC: CRESST/National Center for Education Statistics.

Federal Interagency Forum on Child and Family Statistics [Federal Interagency Forum]. (2009). *America's children: Key national indicators of well-being, 2009.* Washington, DC: U.S. Government Printing Office.

Fránquiz, M., & Reyes, M. (1998). Creating inclusive learning communities through English-language arts: From chanclas to canicas. *Language Arts, 75*(3), 211–220.

Freeman, Y. S., Freeman, D. E., & Mercuri, S. (2002). *Closing the achievement gap: How to reach limited-formal-schooling and long-term English learners.* Portsmouth, NH: Heinemann.

Gee, J. P. (2007). *Social linguistics and literacies: Ideology in discourses.* London: Falmer Press.

Genesee, F., Paradis, J., & Crago, M. (2004). *Dual language development and disorders: A handbook on bilingualism and second language learning.* Baltimore, MD: Paul H. Brookes.

González, N., Moll, L., & Amanti, C. (Eds.). (2005). *Funds of knowledge: Theorizing practices in households, communities, and classrooms.* Mahwah, NJ: Erlbaum.

Gort, M. (2006). Strategic codeswitching, interliteracy, and other phenomena of emergent bilingual writing: Lessons from first grade dual language classrooms. *Journal of Early Childhood Literacy, 6*(3), 323–354.

Gutiérrez, K., Baquedano-López, P., & Tejeda, C. (2000). Rethinking diversity: Hybridity and hybrid language practices in the third space. *Mind, Culture, and Activity, 6*(4), 286–303.

Gutiérrez, K. D. (2001). What's new in the English language arts: Challenging policies and practices, ¿y qué? *Language Arts, 78*(6), 564–569.

Hakuta, K. (1986). *Mirror of language: The debate on bilingualism.* New York: Basic Books.

Harklau, L. (1994a). ESL versus mainstream classes: Contrasting L2 learning environments. *TESOL Quarterly, 28*(2), 241–272.

Harklau, L. (1994b). Tracking and linguistic minority students: Consequences of ability grouping for second language learners. *Linguistics and Education, 6,* 217–244.

Harklau, L. (1999). The ESL learning environment in secondary school. In C. J. Faltis & P. Wolfe (Eds.), *So much to say: Adolescents, bilingualism and ESL in the secondary school* (pp. 42–60). New York: Teachers College Press.

Hornberger, N. (2003). *Continua of biliteracy an ecological framework for educational policy, research, and practice in multilingual settings.* Clevedon, UK: Multilingual Matters.

Katz, S. R. (1999). Teaching in tensions: Latino immigrant youth, their teachers and the structures of schooling. *Teachers College Record, 100*(4), 809–840.

Ladson-Billings, G. J. (2001). *Crossing over to Canaan: The journey of new teachers in diverse classrooms.* San Francisco: Jossey-Bass.

Levitt, P., & Glick Schiller, N. (2004). Conceptualizing simultaneity: A transnational social field perspective on society. *International Migration Review, 38*(3), 1002–1039.

Levitt, P., & Waters, M. (Eds.). (2002). *The changing face of home: The transnational lives of the second generation.* New York: Russell Sage Foundation.

Martin-Jones, M., & Jones, K. (2000). *Multilingual literacies: Reading and writing different worlds.* Philadelphia: John Benjamins.

Meisel, J. M. (2004). The bilingual child. In T. K. Bhatia & W. C. Ritchie (eds.), *The handbook of bilingualism.* Malden, MA: Blackwell.

Moje, E. B., Ciechanowski, K. M., Kramer, K., Ellis, L., Carrillo, R., & Collazo, T. (2004). Working toward third space in content area literacy: An examination of everyday funds of knowledge and discourse. *Reading Research Quarterly, 39*(1), 38–69.

Moll, L. C., & Dworin, J. (1996). Biliteracy development in classrooms: Social dynamics and cultural possibilities. In D. Hicks (Ed.), *Discourse, learning, and schooling* (pp. 221–246). Cambridge, UK: Cambridge University Press.

National Clearinghouse for English Language Acquisition (NCELA). (2007). *The growing numbers of limited English proficient students: 1995/96–2005/06.* Washington, DC: Author. Retrieved from http://www.ncela.gwu.edu/policy/states/reports/statedata/2005LEP/GrowingLEP_0506.pdf

National Clearinghouse for English Language Acquisition (NCELA). (2008). *How has the English language learner (ELL) population changed in recent years? Ask An Expert: NCELA frequently asked questions.* Retrieved from http://www.ncela.gwu.edu/files/rcd/BE021773/ How_Has_The_Limited_English.pdf

Office of Refugee Resettlement (ORR). (2005). *Annual ORR Report to Congress -2005.* Washington, DC: Author. Retrieved from http://www.acf.hhs.gov/programs/ orr/data/arc_05.htm

Orellana, M. F., Reynolds, J., Dorner, L., & Meza, M. (2003). In other words: Translating or "paraphrasing" as a family literacy practice in immigrant households. *Reading Research Quarterly, 38*(1), 12–34.

Passel, J. S., & Cohn, D. (2009). *A portrait of unauthorized immigrants in the United States.* Washington, DC: Pew Hispanic Center.

Planty, M., Hussar, W., Snyder, T., Provasnik, S., Kena, G., Dinkes, R., et al. (2008). *The condition of education 2008* (NCES 2008-031). Washington, DC: National Center for Education Statistics, Institute of Education Sciences, U.S. Department of Education.

Purcell-Gates, V. (2007). *Cultural practices of literacy: Case studies of language, literacy, social practice, and power.* Mahwah, NJ: Erlbaum.

Ragan, A., & Lesaux, N. (2006). Federal, state, and district level English Language Learner program entry and exit requirements: Effects on the education of language minority students, *Education Policy Analysis Archives, 14,* 1–29.

Reyes, I. (2006). Exploring connections between emergent biliteracy and bilingualism. *Journal of Early Childhood Literacy, 6*(3), 267–292.

Ruiz-de-Velasco, J., Fix, M., & Clewell, B. C. (2000). *Overlooked & underserved: Immigrant students in U.S. secondary schools.* Washington, DC: The Urban Institute.

Rumbaut, R. G., & Portes, A. (2001). *Ethnicities: Children of immigrants in America.* Berkeley: University of California Press.

Salínas, C., & Fránquiz, M. E. (Eds.). (2004). *Scholars in the field: The challenges of migrant education.* Charlston, WV: AEL, Inc.

Sánchez, P. (2007). Urban immigrant students: How transnationalism shapes their world learning. *The Urban Review, 39*(5), 489–517.

Sánchez, P., & Machado-Casas, M. (2009). Introduction: At the intersection of transnationalism, Latino youth, and education. *High School Journal, 92*(4), 3–15.

Short, D. J. (2002). Newcomer programs: An educational alternative for secondary immigrant students. *Education and Urban Society, 34*(2), 173–198.

Short, D., & Fitzsimmons, S. (2007). *Double the work: Challenges and solutions to acquiring language and academic literacy for adolescent English language learners—A report to Carnegie Corporation of New York.* Washington, DC: Alliance for Excellent Education.

Suárez-Orozco, C., & Suárez-Orozco, M. M. (2001). *Children of immigration.* Cambridge, MA: Harvard University.

Terrazas, A., & Batalova, J. (2009). Frequently requested statistics on immigrants and immigration in the United States. Washington, DC: Migration Policy Institute. Retrieved from http://www.migrationinformation.org/USfocus/print.cfm?ID=747

Thomas, W. P., & Collier, V. (1997). *School effectiveness for language minority students.* Washington, DC: National Clearinghouse for Bilingual Education.

Thomas, W. P., & Collier, V. (2002). *A national study of school effectiveness for language minority students' long-term academic achievement.* Santa Cruz, CA: Center for Research on Education, Diversity and Excellence.

U.S. Census Bureau. (2008a). Selected social characteristics in the United States: 2006–2008. *2006–2008 American community survey–3 year estimates.* Retrieved from http://factfinder.census.gov/servlet/ADPTable?_bm=y&-geo_id=01000US&-ds_name=ACS_2008_3YR_G00_&-_lang=en&-_caller=geoselect&-format=

U.S. Census Bureau. (2008b). S1401. School enrollment. *2008 American community survey—1 year estimates.* Retrieved October 18, 2009 from http://factfinder.census.gov/servlet/STTable?_bm=y&geo_id=01000US&qr_name=ACS_2008_1YR_G00_S1401&ds_name=ACS_2008_1YR_G00_&-_lang=en&-redoLog=false&-format=&-CONTEXT=st

U.S. Department of Education. (2005). *The nation's report card: An introduction to the National Assessment of Educational Progress (NAEP).* Washington, DC: U.S. Department of Education, Institute of Education Sciences, National Center for Education Statistics.

Valdés, G. (2003). *Expanding definitions of giftedness: The case of young interpreters from immigrant communities.* Mahwah, NJ: Erlbaum.

Valdez, V. E. (2006). *Mothers of Mexican origin within day-to-day parent involvement: Agency & Spanish language maintenance* (Unpublished doctoral dissertation, The University of Texas at Austin, 2005) (Proquest No. AAT 3217626).

Valdez, V. E., & Fránquiz, M. E. (2010). Latin@s in early childhood education: Issues, practices, and future directions. In E. G. Murillo, Jr., S. A. Villenas, R. T. Galván, J. S. Muñoz, C. Martínez, & M. Machado-Casas (Eds.), *Handbook of Latinos and education: Theory, research, and practice* (pp. 474–487). New York: Routledge.

Valenzuela, A. (1999). *Subtractive schooling: U.S.-Mexican youth and the politics of caring.* Albany: State University of New York.

Wong-Fillmore, L. (2000). Loss of family languages: Should educators be concerned? *Theory into Practice, 39*(4), 203–210.

Yi, Y. (2009). Adolescent literacy and identity construction among 1.5 generation students: From a transnational perspective. *Journal of Asian Pacific Communication, 19*(1), 100–129.

Zentella, A. C. (2005). *Building on strength: Language and literacy in Latino families and communities.* New York: Teachers College Press.

2

As Learners Acquire Language

Courtney B. Cazden

The title of this chapter, "As Learners Acquire Language," was assigned in these words by the editors. At first glance, their wording may seem just an unusual way of expressing a focus on the learners who are both agents and beneficiaries of the life-long process of language acquisition. What makes the title unusual is the fact that its form is a dependent clause that begs the question of "So what else is happening? What else is being acquired along with language?" An answer would normally be supplied by the immediately following main clause; instead, supplying it is the topic of this chapter.

I will argue that learners acquire the language forms and culturally appropriate uses, first of their family and immediate face-to-face community, then of increasingly diverse communities of practice (Lave & Wenger, 1991), in modes written as well as oral. In addition, for most people around the world and the increasing number of foreign-born Americans, learners acquire additional languages as well. Finally, and most significantly for this chapter, during this complex life-long process, language learners are also gaining new identities—initially singular, later increasingly multiple. This chapter does not attempt a literature review of either language learning or identity learning; its focus is only on their intersection.

Identity has been defined in various ways. James Gee, for example, gives "four ways to view identity." Here are Gee's categories, with my application to learners for each (2001, p. 100):

1. Nature (N)—identity as states given by nature: Learners as visually identifiable as by race or gender;
2. Institution (I)—identity as officially authorized: Learners as students in a certain school, grade, track, assigned class (e.g., Advanced Placement or Special Education);
3. Discourse (D)—identity as speakers (and writers) of a certain kind: learners audibly identifiable by accent, dialect, or as English language learner;

4. Affinity (A)—identity as experiences shared with specific groups: Learners in each particular classroom or, on a shorter time scale, in an ad hoc smaller group around a book or hobby, or as participants in a particular new media (e.g., Crystal, 2008).

In a later book, Gee (2008) explains in more detail his conception of relationships between discourses, as conventionalized variations in language forms and uses, and what he considers *identities*:

> Discourses are ways of behaving, interacting, valuing, thinking, believing, speaking, and often reading and writing, that are accepted as instantiations of particular identities (or "types of people") by specific groups, whether families of a certain sort, lawyers of a certain sort,... church members of a certain sort, African Americans of a certain sort, and so on and so forth through a very long list. Discourses are ways of being "people like us." They are "ways of being in the world";... they are socially-situated identities. (p. 3)

All of Gee's above four categories of identities are "socially situated." The first, Gee's Nature (N)—identity, may seem an exception, but how much of a difference any visible mark of differentiation makes is indeed socially situated (Bourdieu, 1991). Race, institutional labels, and speaking style interact in complex ways in influencing teachers' expectations and how they routinely position students for opportunities to learn. See, for example, Australian Jennifer Miller's (2003) *Audible Difference: ESL and Social Identity in Schools*.

In the Beginning

Consider the language/identity relationship in its beginning. Here are examples from the child-parent conversations of the first two children in Roger Brown's now-classic study of the development of *A First Language* (1974). Given pseudonyms as Adam and Eve, both children were from educated graduate-student families. They differed in age— Adam 27 months old, Eve 18 months at the beginning of the research—but the quality of their utterances and parental responses were similar.

The first article reporting that research (Brown & Bellugi, 1964) called attention to one frequent maternal response to the child's not yet fully formed utterances, which they named "expansions" (from Table 3, p. 141):

	Child	Mother
Adam:	Sat wall	He sat on the wall
	Throw Daddy	Throw it to Daddy
	Pick glove	Pick the glove up
Eve:	Baby highchair	Baby is in the highchair
	Eve lunch	Eve is having lunch
	Mommy sandwich	Mommy'll have a sandwich

Each expansion retains the exact order of the content words in the child's utterance, adds in the necessary function words to express more explicitly relationships of place (on, to, in, up) time ('ll have), whether action is completed or ongoing (is having), particular object vs. an example of a class (the vs. a). In Brown and Bellugi's words, "It seems to us that a mother in expanding [her child's] speech may be teaching more than grammar; she may be teaching something like a world view" (1964, 143). The "world view" they glimpse in its developmental beginnings Gee would consider a beginning identity. Adam and Eve are being socialized through language to be the appropriate kind of person in their family. We now can see a continuum in language socialization between these particular parent-child conversations and later teacher-student socialization in schools. Both families with educated parent families like Adam and Eve's and most classrooms are communities of practice in which explicit expression of meaning is valued.

But there is also an importance difference between families and classrooms. In most families, the child is considered what Lave and Wenger (1991) call a "legitimate peripheral participant"—not yet a full participant, but fully expected to become one and supported all along the way. The result is virtually universal acquisition of "a first language." .In school, however, some learners—for reasons that often include audible (D), visual (N), or institutional (I) features of their identity—may be marginalized and not positioned with full opportunities to learn.

Language Socialization

Language socialization has come to be a widely used term for this reciprocal language/identity relationship. During the 1960s, two new research traditions were initiated. A psychological tradition (e.g., Brown & Bellugi) studied children's language development by longitudinally following a very small sample of young children. This tradition is sometimes referred to as "developmental psycholinguistics."

In 1964, the same year that Brown and Bellugi published their first article, the second tradition was also initiated. Two linguistic anthropologists, John Gumperz and Dell Hymes (1964), issued a programmatic call for a new field that would bridge linguistics and anthropology, to which they gave the name Ethnography of Communication. Among others, two younger anthropologists, Elinor Ochs and Bambi Schieffelin, answered this call and, in the then-typical anthropological tradition, went to study the development of children's language in non-Western societies (Ochs in Samoa, Schieffelin in Papua New Guinea). They have now co-authored "an historical overview" of the language socialization literature that they helped to initiate (Ochs & Schieffelin, 2008).

Ochs and Schieffelin (2008) point out the limitations of the earlier tradition. First, it was limited in focus to the acquisition of grammar and phonology, ignoring the crucial fact that children were simultaneously gaining implicit knowledge of more than language. Second, Ochs and Schieffelin realized from their own research that, although the South Pacific children whose development they followed were learning the language of their home and face-to-face community as successfully as were the American children like Adam and Eve, they were doing so despite significant cultural differences in the language of their caregivers. In both Samoa and Papua New Guinea, caregivers did not talk like mothers in the United States research, limited as it then still was to families from the same academic communities as the researchers. Since Miller's (1981) study of three children in working-class Baltimore, neither of these limitations holds true.

Outside the scope of this chapter is a continuing controversy within the developmental psycholinguistic literature about "the source of linguistic competence as located either in innate structures, as the product of verbal input from the child's environment, or some combination of both" (Ochs and Schieffelin, 2008, p. 5). They point out that, even though their research was initiated in response to the limitations of the pro-nature tradition, it turns out to offer one resolution of the nature/nurture controversy:

> Paradoxically, these observations about baby talk register at once support a rigorous biological capacity for children's acquisition of phonology and grammar, flourishing independent of extensive grammatical simplification and clarification in the communicative environment, and an equally rigorous requirement for children's sociocultural attunement to language-mediated acts, activities, genres, stances, meanings, roles, relationships, and ideologies through the process of language socialization. (p. 6)

Of course, like language learning, identity learning does not end in childhood. Few people remain members of only the culture of their family and earliest face-to-face community. We become members of additional social groups, ideally learning additional language variations and/or additional languages appropriate in each, and thereby become able to shift successfully with varying degrees of self-consciousness among multiple identities as, in Gee's (2008) words, various "types of people."

Socialization involves two fundamental processes: immersion of learners within communities of practice plus variable frequencies of more explicit teaching, as we will see in examples below. Sometimes the terms "acquisition" and "learning" are used to differentiate these forms of socialization—acquisition in contexts of immersion; learning in contexts of explicit teaching, especially in school. But all three terms—acquisition, learning, and socialization--are used variously by different authors, and readers should be careful to discern the intended referents in each context.

Language Variations

Language variations can be roughly differentiated as dialects, registers, and genres. (See entries for socialization, identity, register, and genre in the reference book, *Key Terms in Language and Culture*, Duranti, 2001.) Learning an additional language, so important in the educational biography of an increasing number of students in most classrooms, has had to be omitted from this chapter because of space limits.

Dialects Dialects are varieties of a language associated with regionally or socially defined groups of people, marked by syntax and pronunciation or accent. The dialect that is now referred to in educational discourse as Standard English started out as the regional speech of people in southeastern England; when they gained political dominance, so did their speech. Now, Standard English is a collection of the socially preferred dialects from various parts of the United States and other English-speaking countries (Adger, Wolfram, & Christian, 2007).

Regional dialects in the United States can still mark their speakers in ways perceived negatively by hearers. Shirley Brice Heath, author of the now classic *Ways with Words* (1983/1996), grew up in rural Virginia where her grandmother ran the store in an otherwise Black community. When she applied for graduate school, she was admonished to replace her southern accent with "general American pronunciation" (personal communication).

For reasons that have more to do with ethnocentric attitudes of hearers or readers than with linguistic differences themselves, the dialect most discussed in education is African American Vernacular English, and several times in the last 45 years local controversies about its use in schools have erupted into the national media (historical summary in Cazden, 2001, 174–177).

The most recent episode started in Oakland, California, in 1996–97. Concerned about the achievement gap between Black and White children, the Oakland School Board passed a well-intentioned resolution designed to guide teachers in helping African American students learn Standard English. Calling their African American dialect "Ebonics," the resolution recognized it as a language system that should be taken into account in teaching the students to speak Standard English. Controversy over interpretations of the resolution quickly went national: for and against; from educators, linguists, politicians, parents; Black and White alike.

Some years before that 1996 resolution, Ogbu, a Nigerian-born Black anthropologist at the University of California, Berkeley, himself a resident of Oakland and member of the School Board Task Force that suggested the resolution, had conducted a 2-year ethnographic study of language attitudes among Black members of one Oakland public school community that he called Lafayette. In the aftermath of the controversy, he published a research report, "Beyond Language: Ebonics, Proper English and Identity in a Black-American Speech Community" (1999). Its importance then and now is that while the resolution and most of the ensuing controversy focused on linguistic differences between dialects per se, what Ogbu documented was the important influence of speakers' dialect attitudes of which they were largely unaware.

In 2 years of ethnographic observations, and interviews with 33 adults and 76 students in elementary through high school, Ogbu's research team documented strong mixed emotions of ambivalence and resistance. His summary adopts the terms most often used in the Lafayette community: proper English and slang English.

> The problem which the people of this community are not aware of I will call their *dialect dilemma*. The dilemma is that Lafayette Blacks hold incompatible beliefs about proper English: (a) They believe on the one hand that it is necessary to master it for education and job success, (b) but they also believe that mastering proper English threatens their slang English, *their bona fide* membership in their community and social solidarity; furthermore, mastering proper English for education and jobs is a requirement imposed on Black people by their White American oppressors. These incompatible beliefs raise the question of how to succeed in school and in the job market, both requiring proper English, and yet retain slang English identity, bona fide membership in Lafayette community and racial solidarity as Black people in America. (Ogbu, 1999, p. 168, emphasis in the original)

In an endnote to that paragraph, Ogbu cites evidence of such attitudes in other Black U.S. communities. Cazden, Bryant, and Tillman (1970) found similarly ambivalent attitudes in an earlier interview-only study of parents, teachers, and community leaders in a Black preschool community in Boston. The report's title, taken from one of the interviews, was "Making It and Going Home."

School is one of the few places that can provide opportunities for non-standard dialect speakers to not only learn but have opportunities for using proper English. Yet, at the same time, it is a social situation in which student speakers have the challenge of a dual audience: teacher representing one speech community, peers representing another. In one small example, White linguist Roger Shuy remembers himself responding to a teacher in the give and take of classroom recitation with a hybrid utterance:

> Personally, I can remember very clearly my school conflicts between peer pressure and teacher expectations. One strategy to avoid this conflict is to give the right answer to

the teacher but to do so in either nonstandard or informal English. (1981)

For teaching suggestions, see two post-Ebonics-controversy books: one edited by two African American educators (Perry & Delpit, 1998, the other by a bi-racial trio of linguists (Adger, Christian, & Taylor, 1999).

Genres Genres are types of multi-sentence oral or written text structures that have become conventionalized for particular purposes with expected organizational patterns, as well as language features that are described below under register. Whenever children first encounter formal schooling, they have to learn the special ways of speaking. and the all-important rules, more implicit than explicit, for staying silent in voice and body (Shultz, 2009). One well-researched primary-grade oral genre focuses individual Sharing Time narratives. See Michaels (1981) for a detailed linguistic analysis of conflicts between teacher and African American students over appropriate narrative form, and Cazden (2001, chapter 2,for subsequent research).

There are also group oral genres into which students become socialized. One familiar oral genre in formal schooling around the world is what is often referred to as the default option of classroom recitation: the IRE/F of teacher Initiation, student(s) Response, teacher Evaluation/Feedback (Cazden, 2001, chapter 3). Some reading comprehension interventions require socialization into carefully designed oral genres for both teacher and students: e.g., Questioning the Author for non-fiction texts, Shared Inquiry for fiction. Michaels and Cazden (in press) report a comparative description of the two programs, each with fourth-grade students).

Explicit genre teaching is more commonly involved in helping students write individual compositions. One recent American guidebook for teachers, *Reading and Writing with Understanding* (Hampton & Resnick, 2009) describes five genres that fourth and fifth graders should become able to read and write: informational, argument, narrative, poetic, and blended (called elsewhere multi-genre) texts.

Australian educational linguists have been influential in offering English-medium schooling detailed analyses of both genre structures and their linguistic features, drawing on Michael Halliday's linguistics (2004). Derewianka (1990) succinctly describes seven text types: recount, narratives, reports, procedures, arguments, discussions, and explanations. Christie and Derewianka (2008) provide more detailed analyses of genres for language arts/English, history, and the sciences. They also provide a valuable chronological chart of the "Developmental trajectory in writing." While this Australian work has been criticized as overly prescriptive, we can learn from it more rigorous analytical categories, while retaining a more critical stance toward implications for pedagogy (as Ivanic suggests below).

Registers Registers refer to the language features with which people speak or write in specific recurring situations.

Children's earliest socialization often includes some register variations—for example, learning the modifications expected when talking to grandparents. Surprisingly, even preschool children also gain knowledge of how people speak in certain adult roles they have observed but not enacted in reality. Anderson (1978), for example, reports experimental research in which 4- to 7-year-old children demonstrate their knowledge of relational identities—giving a doctor puppet lower pitch and more imperatives and questions when talking to the nurse puppet, and the nurse more polite requests back to the doctor. Through their puppets' speech, the children are displaying common gender stereotypes of roles but accurate role relationships of power.

Well known to teachers are the different registers in different curriculum subjects, most obviously in specialized terminology. For language arts teachers, grammatical terms are needed for discussing the multiple expressive options available to writers. Because the standards set by the National Council of Teachers of Mathematics include a focus on being able to communicate about problem-solving processes, math discourse research more often identifies features of the math register. Two examples exemplify the complementary socialization processes of immersion in a community of practice plus explicit teaching.

One example quotes two third graders' responses to the problem posed by their teacher to "find the difference between the height of two children, Jorge and Paolo...." Several children offered answers before the teacher gave any comment:

> Roberto: I shrunk the big guy down by taking away the little guy from him [pointing to his drawing of Paolo and Jorge]....
>
> Maria: I subtracted Paolo from Jorge like Roberto did, but....
>
> Ms. Hudson: Can someone tell how Roberto's and Maria's methods are alike?.... (Heibert et al., 1996).

Both children's formulations accurately describe what they (correctly) had done, but only Maria uses the mathematical term "subtracted", thereby shortening her description from Roberto's 14 words to 5. The teacher chose to discuss how the answers were functionally alike, rather than call attention to one child's use of a technical term, at least not at this time—thus providing only a situated immersion experience for Roberto and the rest of the class.

The second example comes from the fifth-grade teacher who is also the first author of the research report (Lampert, Rittenhouse, & Crumbaugh, 1996). Here the problem posed was to state the rule for getting from the numbers in the first column to their corresponding "outputs" in the second column: $8 - ? = 4$ (first of 4 equations).

Ellie was the first to speak:

> Um, well, there were a whole bunch of—a whole bunch of rules you could use, um, divided by two. And you could do, um, minus one half.

An immediate gasp after Ellie's answer led to an extended discussion, facilitated by probing questions from T. Finally, the teacher (T) concludes by explaining to Ellie and the class the importance of language conventions in mathematics:

T: One of the things that is kind of a convention in mathematics is that when we just talk about numbers and we don't associate them with any object or group of objects, that the symbol means half of one whole. So if, if you were gonna communicate with the rest of the world who uses mathematics, they would take this [pointing to the expression "8 – ½" on the chalkboard] to mean eight wholes minus one-half of a whole. OK, Ellie?…

Ellie: That's what I meant, but I couldn't put it in there, but that's what was in my mind.

In this example, the teacher decided to use this immersion moment for some explicit teaching about the conventions of mathematical language. Note especially that she explained the reasons for the conventionalized usage. One can imagine that the preceding extended discussion implicitly demonstrating the communication problems that can otherwise result should make that teaching most likely to be understood and internalized.

In a later interview, Ellie expressed her discomfort at being the focus of extended student discussion that included reasoned civil argument, a group oral discourse genre the teacher had carefully socialized her students into (Lampert et al, 1996, p. 742). Ellie did not express discomfort with the teacher's suggested terminology per se, but another example shows that learning unfamiliar language, or simply using the preferred academic term, can awaken identity issues for the learner.

One semester in my graduate course on Classroom Discourse, Alaskan Native teacher Martha Demientieff introduced her take-home exam with an unusually thoughtful reflection:

> As I began work on this assignment, I thought of the name of the course and thought I had to use the word *discourse*. The word felt like an intruder in my mind, displacing my word *talk*. I could not organize my thoughts around it, It was like a pebble thrown into a still pond disturbing the smooth water. It makes all the other words in my MIND out of sync. When I realized that I was using too much time agonizing over how to write the paper, I sat down and tried to analyse my problem. I realized that in time I will own the word and feel comfortable using it, but until that time my own words were legitimate. Contrary to some views that exposure to the dominant culture gives an advantage in learning, in my opinion it is the ownership of words that gives one confidence. I must want the word, enjoy the word, and use the word to own it. (Demientieff, 1988, term paper, Harvard Graduate School of Education, emphasis in the original)

Unfortunately, we don't have information on Demientieff's educational and language development. We can only admire the positive strength of her identity in all of Gee's aspects:

as an indigenous woman (N), as a speaker and writer of both her indigenous language (that she demonstrated for us in class discussions) and of English (D), in her temporary position as a Harvard graduate student (I), and a much admired older classmate in this particular community of practice (A).

As all students advance through the grades, and some continue on to college, written assignments become increasingly important. The required types of writing become increasingly distant from the way we speak, and the stakes become higher for how well teacher expectations are met. Relationships between learning to write and issues of identity are most widely discussed with respect to the more general category of academic writing, especially at the college/university level, where writing assignments may form the sole basis for course grades. Whatever the assignment, writers have to decide how to express their ideas about academic topics, while at the same time and with the same words, whether intentionally or not, they express a particular presentation of self. I will depend here on two researchers in the college composition field, one British and one American.

British Ivanic stresses the problem of presentation of self: "Although dilemmas about self representation in relation to readers are rarely made explicit, they are at the heart of most acts of writing" (Ivanic, 1998, p. 2). American Bartholomae's (1985) diagnosis emphasizes the novice academic writer's combined dilemma of expressing a stance toward the assigned topic and toward the self in relation to it:

> I think that all writers, in order to write, must imagine for themselves the privilege of being 'insiders'—that is, the privilege of being inside an established and powerful discourse and of being granted a special right to speak (143). To speak with authority [student writers] have to speak not only with another's voice but with another's code;… they have to speak in the voice and through the codes of those of us with power;… and they have to do it before they know what they are doing. (p. 156)

As Ivanic paraphrases Bartholomae, "students have to adopt a voice which they do not yet own" (1998, p .86).

Ivanic selected for her "co-researchers" eight older, non-traditional students, women and men who were beginning university in diverse fields of study with the aid of special grants for mature students. All had entered the university after years away from their earlier schooling. Both their relative unfamiliarity with the academic expectations they confronted, and their fears about failing to meet them, were therefore in the extreme.

Her book-length research report, "Writing and Identity: The Discoursal Construction of Identity in Academic Writing" (1998), provides a list of features of the academic writing register they were being socialized to use:

- density of clause structure,
- verbs about relationships between abstract entities and mental activities,

- complex nominalizations and nominal groups,
- present tense for timeless truths, declarative mood, and modality expressing certainty,
- vocabulary with high frequency of Graeco-Latin words. (Ivanic, pp. 259–273)

Among additional features Ivanic found, three can carry implications for the writer's expressed identity. First-person pronouns are rare. Citations to other literature can be used to define one's reference group. And most interestingly, putting quotation marks around some terms can mark them as somehow atypical to the writer(s) familiar idiom, as Dementieff put the term "discourse" in italics. (Quotation marks not used for direct speech are sometimes appropriately called "scare quotes.")

In another study, Freeman and Cazden (1991) analyzed both quantitatively and qualitatively such quotation marks in 20 papers by students in a master's program in foreign language teaching. Here they seemed to express a shared positive reflexive attention to language use that was highly valued in the program, and thus demonstrated their developing membership in that community of practice. (In this study Freeman was the teacher-researcher, analyzing the professional development program he helped design, while Cazden was an outsider researcher. Cazden, 2003, argues for the beneficial complementarity of these two writing positions for research on racial issues in schooling.)

Ivanic's language analyses derive from Michael Halliday's functional grammar that is less well known in the United States than in England and Australia. But she makes clear her ambivalent stance toward Hallidayan theories of language:

> While I have adopted Halliday's functional grammar as an analytical tool, I am not adopting along with it his view that particular contexts of situation require or prescribe particular linguistic features. Rather I want to show … that some discourse practices, with their associated values and beliefs, are extremely pervasive in the academic community, and … that there is, nonetheless, variation in these practices, and that they are open to contestation and change. (1998, pp. 259–260)

A Final Consideration

Consider once more the two common terms in this chapter's assigned title, *learning* and *acquiring*, plus the more recent umbrella term, *socialization*. Think of the agents of the verbs: *acquire, learn,* and *socialize.* The grammatical subject of the first two, acquire and learn, is the learner; but the grammatical subject of socialize is the parent, teacher, or community of practice, whose actions can help or hinder the learner(s) further language development.

There can be a danger in the shift to thinking of pedagogy in terms of socializing practices, the danger of implicitly assuming that what socializing agents do determines the effects—that, in a word, teaching produces learning. We may forget that the true agents of acquiring new forms and uses of language are, inevitably, in the end the students themselves. It couldn't be otherwise when language use, and therefore language learning, are so intimately related to identity.

References

Adger, C. T., Christian, D., & Taylor, O. (Eds.). (1999). *Making the connection: Language and academic achievement among African American students.* McHenry, IL: Delta Systems.

Adger, C. T., Wolfram, W., & Christian, D. (2007). *Dialects in schools and communities* (2nd ed.). Mahwah, NJ: Erlbaum.

Anderson, E. A. (1978). *Learning to speak with style: A study of the sociolinguistic skills of children.* Doctoral dissertation, Stanford University. University Microfilm #78-8755.

Bartholomae, D. (1985). Inventing the university. In M. Rose (Ed.), *When a writer can't write.* New York: Guilford.

Bourdieu, P. (1991). *Language and symbolic power.* Cambridge, MA: Harvard University Press.

Brown, R. (1974). *A first language.* Cambridge, MA: Harvard University Press.

Brown, R., & Bellugi, U. (1964). Three processes in the child's acquisition of syntax. *Harvard Educational Review, 34,* 133–151.

Cazden, C. B. (2001). *Classroom discourse: The language of teaching and learning* (2nd ed.). Portsmouth, NH: Heinemann.

Cazden, C. B. (2003). Teacher and student attitudes on racial issues: The complementarity of practitioner research and outsider research. In S. Greene & D. Abt-Perkins (Eds.), *Making race visible: Literacy research for cultural understanding* (pp. 35–50). New York: Teachers College Press.

Cazden, C. B., Bryant, B. H., & Tillman, M. A. (1970). "Making it and going home": The attitudes of Black people toward language education. *Harvard Graduate School of Education Association Bulletin, 14*(3), 3, 9.

Christie, F., & Derewianka, B. (2008). *School discourse: Learning to write across the years of schooling.* London: Continuum.

Crystal, D. (2008). *Txtng: The gr8 DB8.* Oxford, UK: Oxford University Press.

Derewianka, B. (1990). *Exploring how texts work.* Portsmouth NH: Heinemann.

Duranti, A. (Ed.). (2001). *Key terms in language and culture.* Oxford, UK: Blackwell.

Freeman, D., & Cazden, C. (1991). Learning to talk like a professional: Some pragmatics of foreign language teacher training. In L. F. Bouton & Y. Kachru (Eds.), *Pragmatics and language learning* (Vol. 2). Urbana: University of Illinois: Division of English as an International Language.

Gee, J. P. (2001). Identity as an analytic lens for research in education. *Review of Research in Education, 25,* 99–125.

Gee, J. P.. (2008). *Social linguistics and literacies: Ideology in discourses* (3rd ed.). New York: Routledge.

Gumperz, J., & Hymes, D. (1964). The ethnography of communication. *American Anthropologist* (Special Issue), *66*(6).

Halliday, M. (2004). *An introduction to functional grammar.* New York: Oxford University Press.

Hampton, S., & Resnick, L. B. (2008). *Reading and writing with understanding: Comprehension in fourth and fifth grades.* Washington, DC: The National Center for Education and the Economy.

Heath, S. B. (1983/1996). *Ways with words: Language, life, and work in communities and classrooms.* Cambridge, UK: Cambridge University Press.

Heibert, J., Carpenter, T. P., Fennema, E., et al. (1996, May). Problem-solving as a basis for reform in curriculum and instruction: The case of mathematics. *Educational Researcher, 23,* 12–21.

Ivanic, R. (1998). *Writing and identity: The discoursal construction of identity in academic writing.* Amsterdam: John Benjamins.

Lampert, M., Rittenhouse, P., & Crumbaugh, C. (1996). Agreeing to disagree: Developing sociable mathematical discourse. In D. R. Olson & N. Torrance (Eds.), *The handbook of education and human development: New models of learning, teaching, and schoolingteaching and schooling* (pp. 731–764). Cambridge, UK: Blackwell.

Lave, J., & Wenger, E. (1991). *Situated learning: Legitimate peripheral participation.* Cambridge, UK: Cambridge University Press.

Michaels, S. (1981). Sharing Time: Children's narrative style and differential access to literacy. *Language in Society, 10,* 423–442.

Michaels. S., & Cazden, C. B. (in press). Reading comprehension in class discussions.

Miller, J. (203). *Audible difference: ESL and social identity in schools.* Clevedon, UK: Multilingual Matters.

Miller, P. (1981). *Amy, Wendy, and Beth: A study of early language development in South Baltimore.* Austin: University of Texas Press.

Ochs, E., & Schieffelin, B. (2008). Language socialization: An historical overview. In N. H. Hornberger (Ed.), *Encyclopedia of language and education* (2nd ed., Vol. 8, pp. 3–15). New York: Springer.

Ogbu, J. U. (1999). Beyond language: Ebonics, proper English, and identity in a Black-American speech community. *American Educational Research Journal, 36,* 147–184.

Perry, T., & Delpit, L. (Eds.). (2009). *The real Ebonics debate: Power, language, and the education of African American children.* Boston: Beacon Press.

Shultz, K. (2009). *Rethinking classroom participation: Listening to silent voices.* New York: Teachers College Press.

Shuy, R. (1981). Learning to talk like teachers. *Language Arts, 58,* 168–174.

3

When Learners Speak Two or More Languages

Kathy Escamilla and Susan Hopewell

Effective implementation of research-based instructional practices for learners who speak two or more languages requires that we understand who our bilingual learners are, and that we differentiate amongst practices found to be effective for these students. Historically, pedagogies designed for bilingual learners were predicated upon the idea that it was advantageous to develop one language in isolation of another. Additionally, research practices found to be effective with one population were assumed to be effective with all populations. As we will outline below, such practices rely upon faulty premises that should be reshaped into more robust and appropriate learning paradigms for students who speak two or more languages. Current research indicates that we are better able to describe the population of learners who speak two or more languages than we are to design pedagogies and programs to teach them.

Briefly, English Language Learners (ELLs) are considered to be students who speak little or no English and/or whose knowledge of English is limited to the extent that they cannot participate meaningfully in a classroom where English is the sole language of instruction (Crawford, 2004). This student population has grown dramatically during the past 20 years. In 1990, 2 million K–12 public school students, or one in 20, was an ELL. By 2005, there were more than 5 million such students, or 1 in 9. This growth is especially notable when considered in light of the fact that the overall K–12 population grew by less than 4% during the same time period (NCELA, 2006). Demographers estimate that in 20 years the number off ELLs may be as high as 1 in 4 (NCELA, 2008; Capp et al., 2005). Importantly, 60% of ELLs were born in the United States. They are U.S. citizens entitled to all the rights and privileges therein. Conversely, 80% of their parents are immigrants who were born outside of the country (Capp et al., 2005). This is just one of a number of contradictions that describes this student population.

Consider, for example, the oft celebrated linguistic heterogeneity of the ELL population. Although ELLs speak over 400 languages; it is critical to recognize that 80% speak Spanish and that the majority of Spanish speakers are from Mexico (Kindler, 2002). After Spanish, Vietnamese, Hmong, Chinese, Korean, Khmer, Laotian, Hindi, and Tagalog *together* comprise only about 8% of the ELL population. Thus, while the ELL population is diverse, it is overwhelmingly represented by Spanish-speaking students.

A further contradiction relates to the socio-economic status of ELLs. It is widely reported that the majority of ELLs are poor and/or economically disadvantaged (Larsen, 2004). While this is generally true for Spanish speaking ELLs, as well as for Cambodians, Laotians, and Hmongs, it does not describe the economic situation of Filipino, Indian, and Taiwanese ELLs, who often come from families with college degrees and middle class mores (Larsen, 2004). It is inappropriate to dismiss the socioeconomic diversity within the ELL population, and researchers and practitioners would be wise to consider the impact of this variable when drawing conclusions about effective practices. The Taiwanese, for example, who are represented less in the overall ELL population and who may be privileged with educational and economic backgrounds more aligned to the norms and expectations of middle-class U.S. schooling, are not an appropriate point of comparison for Spanish speaking ELLs who arrive to school with different economic and educational circumstances.

Currently, many research studies and syntheses lump ELLs into a single category without a detailed description of who these learners are, what language and cultural groups they belong to, how proficient they are in English or whether or not they are part of a majority/minority language group or a language group less numerous. It is quite likely that different populations of ELLs may have different instructional needs, yet ELLs are frequently treated in the research as if they are a homogeneous group. Add to this very serious shortcoming, the fact that the vast majority of identified ELLs are in school programs where English is the sole medium of instruction, thereby making it difficult for researchers to identify and to document instructional programs and practices that may be efficacious for some groups of ELLs, but not for others (Zehler et al., 2003). Given that the population of ELLs is heterogeneous, but not numerically equivalent with regard to national origin, language, and socioeconomic status, it is critical that researchers carefully define their populations when doing research on ELLs. It is also important that the research include a great variety of school programs and instructional interventions for the burgeoning population of K–12 learners that are tailored to specific language and cultural groups.

We begin this chapter, therefore, with a caution to the reader that when learners speak two or more languages it is incumbent upon the research community to define precisely the population of learners who are being labeled ELL and to delineate the contexts in which these students are speaking and learning two or more languages. Further, given the uneven distribution of the ELL population, it is important that consumers of research understand that studies conducted on one ethnolinguistic group may not be generalizable to another, and that the current "one size fits all" English medium programs for ELLs is likely limiting our ability to design research that develops and implements more efficacious and innovative programs for these students. With this realistic, albeit discouraging, introduction, the remainder of this chapter will summarize briefly what we know from the extant research about K–12 ELLs and will outline some issues we still need to address to better serve this population.

We have divided our discussion into two parts. The first highlights the need to create more robust paradigms for understanding bilingual development, including more appropriate labels. The second discusses what we know about effective practices for students who speak and are learning two or more languages.

Beyond ELL: Toward a More Robust Understanding of Bilingualism

As stated above, there is a great need in the field for researchers to define the populations of ELLs that they are studying. Lumping ELLs into a single research sub-group does little to improve our understanding of these learners. In addition to better defining the population of ELLs in the United States, we must broaden our understanding of bilingual growth. Research and program development for ELLs in this country has focused for too long on the acquisition of English as the major and/or only educational outcome for ELLs, and has situated understandings of acquiring two languages within frameworks of sequential bilingualism. We need to expand our understandings and change our labels to reflect the desirability of bilingualism and biliteracy as academic outcomes within K–12 U.S. schooling.

For this reason, the term "English Language Learner" is problematic. It focuses solely on English acquisition without acknowledging the value of a learner's additional languages and/or the value of becoming bilingual. At all levels of the educational spectrum, from the federal government to university researchers to policy makers and practitioners, emerging bilingual (García, Skutnabb-Kangas, & Torres-Guzmán, 2006) children are routinely labeled ELL as if learning English is their single most (or only) defining characteristic. It communicates an assimilationist outlook and the desire to mask the vast linguistic, cultural, and national diversity discussed above. Its ubiquitous use is evidenced by its prevalence even in schools where bilingual or dual language approaches are implemented. In sum, the term "ELL" enables researchers and program developers to dismiss and/or ignore the role that students' native languages play both in learning English and in becoming bilingual.

It is worth noting that the last five meta-analyses examining what the research is telling us about how best to teach learners who speak two or more languages to read have all reached the same conclusion that teaching students to read in their first language promotes higher levels of reading achievement *in English,* not to mention that learning to read in two languages promotes biliteracy (August & Shanahan, 2006; Genesee, Lindholm-Leary, Saunders, & Christian, 2006; Greene, 1997; Rolstad, Mahoney, & Glass, 2005a, 2005b; Slavin & Cheung, 2005). The research is conclusive that children who speak two languages can become literate in two languages and that biliteracy instruction results in higher achievement in English. Changing our definition from English Language Learner to emerging bilingual learner begins the process of moving researchers and practitioners toward an understanding that reflects this research finding. Two languages are not competing for space in a student's brain, but are mutually supportive and reinforcing. Bilingual practices, in fact, improve English acquisition. Changing the label from ELL to emerging bilingual learner might also enable us to broaden the goals of schooling from only English acquisition to that of bilingualism and biliteracy as desired outcomes of K–12 schooling.

Related to the limiting and problematic nature of the term ELL is the fact that our understandings of bilingual development in the past few decades have been focused on only one type of bilingual development known as sequential bilingual development. Frameworks of sequential bilingualism promote the notion that languages develop in isolation and that all students must have an identifiable first language which will be used only until students can be immersed in English medium instruction. This framework demands that languages be strictly separated and that literacy instruction be limited to one language at a time (Cloud, Genesee, & Hamayan, 2000; Lessow-Hurley, 2000). Given that the vast majority of students speaking two or more languages was born in the United States (Capp et al., 2005) and has been learning two languages since birth, the sequential bilingual paradigm is less applicable to understanding their bilingual development than is the simultaneous bilingual framework. Briefly defined, simultaneous bilingual children are those who, from the ages of 0–5, have been exposed to and are acquiring two languages (Baker, 2001). In contrast to the above, sequential bilinguals are persons who began the process of second language acquisition after the age of 6 with a well established first language base (Baker, 2001).

The distinction between sequential and simultaneous bilingualism is not minor as simultaneous bilinguals have attributes and behaviors that are commonly misunderstood by teachers, policy makers, and researchers who have heretofore relied solely upon sequential bilingual theories. Among the important characteristics of simultaneous bilinguals that lead to misunderstanding and misinterpretation by researchers and practitioners are: (a) Simultaneous bilingual learners may know some concepts in one language and some in another language, therefore monolingual assessments may capture only some of what a learner knows and can do. When assessment only measures a portion of what a learner knows, it is easy to conclude that the learner has limited knowledge linguistically and/or conceptually; (b) Simultaneous bilingual learners have differing and often idiosyncratic patterns of language development particularly with regard to grammar and vocabulary that is different from monolinguals in each of their languages, and that may be interpreted as signs that two languages are confusing the learner. Rather, the simultaneous acquisition and development of two languages can be expected to have a unique and quite normal trajectory that differs in predictable ways from monolingual language and literacy growth; and (c) Simultaneous bilinguals often code-switch (deliberative use of two languages to communicate) leading to the conclusion that the learner does not know either language well. Misunderstanding the characteristics of simultaneous bilingual development have lead some to conclude that many 'English Language Learners' are deficient in both of their two languages; therefore it is important to focus solely on English since the learner does not have a well developed first language. While recent research has challenged the idea that simultaneous bilinguals are limited in both of their languages (McSwan, Rolstad, & Glass, 2002; Escamilla, 2006; Zentella, 2005), changing an ingrained paradigm is difficult.

The following examples more fully illustrate misinterpretations of simultaneous bilingual learner behavior. Simultaneous bilingual children may know some words or concepts in one language, and an alternative set of concepts in a different language because they come from homes where a language other than English is dominant, but attend a pre-school where English is the medium of instruction. These children learn concepts related to their families, food, games etc. in one language while they learn concepts related to school in English. To understand what these learners know across both of their languages requires a type of bilingual assessment that is virtually non-existent in the field today, but is very much needed if we are to gain a more complete picture of bilingual development.

With regard to grammar and vocabulary, simultaneous bilinguals may borrow verbs in one language and conjugate them regularly in their second language (e.g., *estoy eskipeando/* I am skipping). The verb *eskipear* (to skip) was borrowed from the verb to skip in English and then conjugated in Spanish. While some might consider this borrowing to be a sign of language confusion, we argue a different perspective. Young, monolingual children frequently over generalize grammar rules. It is common to hear 4-year-olds say, "We goed to the store." In the case of monolinguals, there is little concern about this grammar error as it is thought to be an over generalization and evidence that the child is internalizing the rule governed nature of language. The same can be said for the simultaneous bilingual. The learner has borrowed a word from English, and generalized its use in a grammatically correct way in Spanish. Rather than being a sign of cross-language confusion, we propose that this is a sign of normal simultaneous bilingual development. Currently, we lack a robust theory of simultaneous bilingual development that includes a comprehensive description of these phenomena.

With regard to code-switching, it should be noted that there is a large and growing body of research that concludes that contrary to being a linguistic deficit, it is in fact highly rule governed behavior, and symptomatic of a learner who has a very sophisticated understanding of how to communicate using two languages (Escamilla & Hopewell, 2007; Kenner, 2004; Zentella, 1997). As members of bilingual communities, many have learned to draw on all of their linguistic resources when communicating with other bilinguals. As a field, our research on students who speak two or more languages has been limited by the use of the term ELL and by the prevailing sequential bilingual paradigms. More robust understandings of bilingualism must be added to our knowledge base particularly for K–12 students who speak two or more languages and have resided in the United States since birth.

Is Good Teaching Really Just Good Teaching? Issues in Quality Instruction for Emerging Bilingual Learners

The final section of this chapter deals with issues of quality of instruction for emerging bilingual Learners. While much has been written and/or debated about the language of instruction for speakers of two or more languages, much less has been written about the quality of language instruction for these students. We submit that both are important. As stated above, the results of five major meta-analyses and research syntheses have concluded that teaching emerging bilingual students to read in their first language promotes higher levels of reading achievement in English (August & Shanahan, 2006; Genesee et al., 2006; Greene, 1997; Rolstad et al., 2005a, 2005b; Slavin & Cheung, 2005). However, it is important to note that this conclusion is based largely on work with Spanish/English emerging bilingual students whose first and second languages share an alphabetic principle and whose languages are both major world languages spoken by millions of people. This finding may or may not apply to less common languages and/or to languages that do not have a written orthographic system. Further, it is apparent that the effects of learning to read in two languages are cumulative; that is, greater benefits are derived if the bilingual reading instruction is carried out over a longer period of time (e.g., 5 years is more beneficial than 1; Goldenberg, 2008). This suggests that if bilingual reading instruction is to benefit reading achievement in English, more is better. Finally, cross language transfer needs to be taught explicitly. Not all students infer and can apply orthographic, phonemic, syntactic, and semantic similarities across languages without direct instruction. Moreover, the greatest benefit of learning to read and write in two languages is the obvious benefit of biliteracy.

While research strongly supports the use of students' native languages (especially Spanish) as a part of a comprehensive instructional program for students learning two or more languages, the fact is that there are situations where it is not possible to implement this type of program and/or where state or local educational policies prohibit or limit the use of languages other than English in instruction. Unfortunately, many believe that if non-English languages cannot be used for content and language arts instruction, they should not be used at all, and in some contexts students' native languages are banned from use in classrooms, on playgrounds and in the overall school environment.

It is noteworthy that there is no research evidence to support that banning non-English languages accelerates English language acquisition, in fact, such practices may serve to decrease motivation thereby having a negative impact. What the research indicates is that using students' native languages can enhance learning even if they are not used as a medium of instruction. For example, students' native languages can be used in clarifying information and concepts, in classroom management, in communicating with parents, in encouraging students to make cross-language connections, and in promoting the value of bilingualism (August & Shanahan, 2006; Goldenberg, 2008). The research is clear that bilingualism is a cultural, intellectual, cognitive, vocational, and economic advantage. Further, it is also clear that banning or forbidding learners to use their native languages in schools is counter-productive and does *not* accelerate English acquisition.

Due to the generic nature of the research on emerging bilingual learners (e.g. lumping all language groups into a single sub-category), it has been postulated too often that teachers really do not need to modify instruction in any significant way for learners who speak two or more languages, and that good teaching is good teaching. In fairness, the research indicates that this platitude is somewhat accurate, and *some* of what we know about good instruction and curriculum in general holds true for emerging bilingual learners (August & Shanahan, 2006; Goldenberg, 2008). Research indicates, for example, that all students benefit from: predictable and consistent classroom routines; well-designed, clearly structured and appropriately paced instruction; active engagement and participation; opportunities to practice, apply, and transfer new learning; feed-back

on correct and incorrect responses; frequent and periodic assessment of progress; and feeling that they belong to a classroom and school community. In this regard good teaching is good teaching.

However, it is equally clear in the research that when instructing emergent bilingual learners in English, teachers must modify instruction to take into account students' developing English skills especially in teaching literacy. Emerging bilingual learners benefit from direct and explicit instruction in the components of literacy (Genesee et al, 2006), further studies of vocabulary instruction also show these students are more likely to learn words when they are directly taught *and* when the words are embedded in meaningful contexts with ample opportunities for repetition. However, there are no studies documenting the benefits of direct teaching of phonemic awareness and subsequent comprehension of text for emerging bilingual learners; and there is a dearth of research on reading comprehension strategies for emerging bilingual learners. In fact, strategies that have been found to be effective for monolingual English learners have not had the same results for learners who speak two or more languages (August & Shanahan, 2006).

Finally, there is emerging evidence that there is no need to delay the teaching of literacy in English to learners speaking two or more languages until some level of oral language proficiency is achieved in English, that literacy and language arts teaching should focus on productive as well as receptive skills and that teaching writing is likely as important as teaching reading (Slavin & Cheung, 2005). Finally, for speakers of two or more languages, the role of oral language development is critical to English language acquisition. Contrary to previous assumptions, the English language arts and literacy program should not be thought to be the same for second language learners as for monolingual English learners only delivered in a delayed structure. The language arts program needs significant modification. These results indicate that good teaching is *not* good teaching in many aspects of language arts and literacy teaching and K–12 instructional programs.

Aside from language arts and literacy, the research seems to indicate that emerging bilingual learners *must* have time to learn English as a language, and that there is a need for separate ELD time (Saunders, Foorman, & Carlson, 2006). Content based approaches to teaching English as a second Language, such as Sheltered Instruction Observation Protocol (SIOP) or sheltered English instruction, assist students in acquiring content in English, but these content based approaches alone are insufficient.

The research seems to be clear that learners who speak two or more languages need comprehensive long-term programs to become fully proficient in English, and ideally to become bilingual and biliterate. Such programs need to teach both academic and social language, they need to be delivered using a variety of instructional techniques and approaches, and they need to be built upon the assumption that learning a second language, like learning a first takes a life-time. Sadly, for the 5 million students who are speakers of two or more languages, the more we know about how to best teach them, the less it seems we want to do.

Conclusion

We conclude this chapter with a brief summary of what we know and what we still need to learn. We know how diverse our population is and yet we still need to better define it in research studies. We need a more robust understanding of and value for bilingual development. Finally, and perhaps more importantly, we need a will to implement quality, comprehensive, and long-term programs for learners who speak two or more languages that consider their unique strengths and needs.

References

August, D., & Shanahan, T. (Eds.). (2006). *Developing literacy in second-language learners: Report of the national literacy panel on language-minority children and youth.* Mahwah, NJ: Erlbaum.

Baker, C. (2001). *Foundations of bilingual education and bilingualism* (3rd ed.). Clevedon, UK: Multilingual Matters.

Capp, R., Fix, M., Murray, J., Ost, J., Passel, J. S., & Herwantoro, S. (2005). *The new demography of America's schools: Immigration and the No Child Left Behind Act.* Washington DC: Urban Institute.

Cloud, N., Genesee, F., & Hamayan, E. (2000). *Dual language instruction: A handbook for enriched education.* Boston, MA: Heinle.

Crawford, J. (2004). *Educating English learners: Language diversity in the classroom* (5th ed.). Los Angeles: Bilingual Education Services.

Escamilla, K. (2006). Semilingualism applied to the literacy behaviors of Spanish-speaking emerging bilinguals: Bi-iliteracy or emerging biliteracy? *Teachers College Record, 108*(11), 2329–2353.

Escamilla, K., & Hopewell, S. (2007, April 10). *The role of code-switching in the written expression of early elementary simultaneous bilinguals.* Paper presented at the annual conference of the American Educational Research Association, Chicago.

García, O., Skutnabb-Kangas, T., & Torres-Guzman, O. (2006). Weaving spaces and (De) constructing ways for multilingual schools: The actual and the imagined. In O. García, T. Skutnabb-Kangas, & O. Torres-Guzman (Eds.), *Imagining multilingual schools* (pp. 3–50). Clevedon, UK: Multilingual Matters.

Genesee, F., Lindholm-Leary, K., Saunders, W. M., & Christian, D. (2006). *Educating English language learners.* New York: Cambridge University Press.

Goldenberg, C. (2008). Teaching English language learners: What the research does — and does not — say. *American Educator*, 8–44.

Greene, J. (1997). A meta-analysis of the Rossell and Baker review of bilingual research. *Bilingual Research Journal, 21*(2&3), 103–122.

Kenner, C. (2004). Living in simultaneous worlds: Difference and integration in bilingual script-learning. *Bilingual Education and Bilingualism, 7*(1), 43-61.

Kindler, A. (2002). *Survey of the states' limited English proficient students and available educational programs and services: 2000-2001 summary report.* Prepared for OELA by National Clearinghouse for English Language Acquisition and Language Instruction Programs. Washington, DC: National Clearinghouse for English Language Acquisition and Language Instruction Programs.

Larsen, L. J. (2004). The foreign-born population in the United States: 2003. *Current Population Reports.* Washington DC: U.S. Census Bureau.

Lessow-Hurley, J. (2000). *The foundations of dual-language instruction.* New York: Longman.

MacSwan, J., Rolstad, K., & Glass, G. V. (2002). Do some school-age children have no language? Some problems of construct validity in the Pre-LAS Español. *Bilingual Research Journal, 26*(2), 395–420.

National Clearinghouse for English Language Acquisition. (2006). The growing numbers of Limited English Proficient Students 1995/96–2005/06. Washington, DC: Author. Retrieved August 25, 2009, from http://www.ncela.gwu.edu/files/uploads/4/GrowingLEP_0506.pdf

National Clearinghouse for English Language Acquisition. (2008). *ELL Demographics by State.* Washington DC: NCELA. Retrieved August 27, 2009, from http://www.ncela.gwu.ed/stats/3_bystate.htm

Rolstad, K., Mahoney, K., & Glass, G. (2005a). The big picture: A meta-analysis of program effectiveness research on English language learners. *Educational Policy, 19*(4), 572–594.

Rolstad, K., Mahoney, K., & Glass, G. (2005b). Weighing the Evidence: A meta-analysis of bilingual education in Arizona. *Bilingual Research Journal, 29*(1), 43–67.

Saunders, W., Foorman, B., & Carlson, C. (2006). Is a separate block of time for English language development in programs for English learners needed? *Elementary School Journal, 107*(2), 181–198.

Slavin, R., & Cheung, A. (2005). A synthesis of research on language of reading instruction for English language learners. *Review of Educational Research, 75*(2), 247–284.

Zehler, A. M., Fleischman, H. L., Hopstock, P. J., Stephenson. T. G., Pendzick, M. L., & Sapru, S. (2003). *Descriptive study of services to LEP students and LEP students with disabilities. Volume 1: Research report.* Arlington, VA: Development Associates, Inc.

Zentella, A. C. (1997). *Growing up bilingual.* Oxford, UK: Blackwell.

Zentella, A. C. (2005). *Building on strength: Language and literacy in Latino families and communities.* New York: Teachers College Press.

4

Research on Diverse Students in Culturally and Linguistically Complex Language Arts Classrooms

Arnetha F. Ball, Allison Skerrett, and Ramón Antonio Martínez

This chapter reports on research pertaining to African American, Latina/o, and other students from linguistically diverse backgrounds who receive language arts instruction in what Ball (2009) termed culturally and linguistically complex classrooms (CLCCs). Our goals in preparing this chapter were to locate empirical research that illuminates effective and innovative curriculum, instructional, and teacher preparation approaches to improving teaching and learning in CLCCs.

Culturally and Linguistically Complex Classrooms

Rapid changes in student demographics and continuing underachievement of a disproportionate number of students from linguistically diverse backgrounds have increased the need for more critical attention from the research community and improved instruction for these students. The National Center for Educational Statistics (NCES, 2006) reported that by 2020, over 50% of the U.S. public school population will be classified as students of color—from Latina/o, African American, Pacific Islander, and American Indian backgrounds. Concern about the linguistic complexity these students bring to the language arts classroom is a nationwide phenomenon. Table 4.1 below illustrates the prevalence of language diversity in some of the nation's largest urban school districts and lists some of the many languages spoken in these districts.

The districts listed below serve students from over 170 different language groups and all are faced with the challenge of teaching the language arts to students in CLCCs.

In keeping with these national trends, classrooms around the globe are faced with this challenge. The UNESCO Institute for Statistics (2005) reported that, while half of our linguistically diverse global populations now live in urban areas, that figure is expected to rise to two-thirds—or about 6 billion people—by 2050. Urban classrooms around the globe are experiencing the largest influx of students from diverse backgrounds since the beginning of the 20th cen-

tury. As Ball (2009) points out, by the time these students reach the secondary grades, previously segregated groups often come together in linguistically diverse classrooms with teachers who feel under-prepared to teach students from culturally and linguistically diverse backgrounds. Low academic achievement, high dropout rates, and low college graduation rates among low income, culturally and linguistically diverse students are far too frequent in these classrooms (UNESCO Institute for Statistics, 2005). Yet a growing body of research demonstrates how linguistic diversity among African American, Latina/o, and other students can be recruited as a resource for teaching and learning in language arts classrooms.

Research on African American Students Studies of African American Vernacular English (AAVE) speakers have provided foundational understandings about teaching and learning the language arts in CLCCs. An ERIC search for peer-reviewed studies published from 2000 to 2009 using the key terms "African American Vernacular" or "Black Dialects" and "Language Arts" or "Reading" or "Literacy" or "Writing" or "Curriculum" or "Instruction" or "Assessment" or "Technology" resulted in only 35 studies, 13 of which were directly related to using AAVE as a resource in teaching and learning the language arts in K–16 classrooms. An additional expanded search of Education Full Text using identical parameters resulted in 71 studies, an additional seven of which focused on our topic. Overall, the majority of the studies documented the benefits of encouraging AAVE in instructional talk (e.g., Lee, 2006; Sealey-Ruiz, 2007); exploring with students scholarship about language ideologies and sociolinguistics (e.g., Godley & Minnici, 2008); using literature and popular culture materials written in AAVE or hybrid language texts (e.g., Lee); and teaching African American students to code switch both orally and in writing to promote meaning making and communication while maintaining their cultural and linguistic identities (e.g., Williams, 2006).

TABLE 4.1
Language Diversity in Largest U.S. School Districts[1]

District	% English Learners	# of Languages Spoken	Example of Languages Spoken
New York City Public Schools http://schools.nyc.gov	14.1% (148, 401)	166	Spanish (68%); Chinese (11.2%); Bengali (2.9%); Arabic (2.5%); Haitian Creole (2.3%); Russian (1.9%); Urdu (1.8%); French (1.3%); Korean (0.9%); Albanian (0.9%); Polish (0.7%); Punjabi (0.7%); Other (5.2%)
Los Angeles Unified School District http://notebook.lausd.net	35.3% (240,249)	92	Spanish (94%); Korean (1.1%); Armenian (1%); Tagalog (0.9%); Cantonese (0.4%); Farsi (0.3%); Vietnamese (0.3%); Russian (0.2%); Other (1.8%)
Chicago Public Schools http://www.cps.edu	13.3% (54,425)	100	Spanish (79.9%); Polish (2.7%); Cantonese (1.6%); Arabic (1.3%); Urdu (1.1%); Vietnamese (0.7%); Tagalog (0.6%); Bosnian/Serbian (0.5%); Assyrian (0.3%); French (0.27%); Ukrainian (0.27%); Gujarati (0.26%); Other (10.5%)
Miami-Dade County Public Schools http://www.dadeschools.net	15% (51,772)	100+	Spanish (54.5%); Haitian Creole (5.1%); French (0.6%); Portuguese (0.5%); Other Chinese languages—i.e., not Mandarin or Cantonese (0.2%); Arabic (0.1%); Russian (0.1%); Urdu (0.1%); Vietnamese (0.07%); Hebrew (0.07%); Other (39.9%)
Houston Independent School District http://www.houstonisd.org	30.87% (61,809)	100	Spanish, Vietnamese, French, Farsi, Mandarin, Arabic, Urdu
School District of Philadelphia http://www.phila.k12.pa.us	6.7% (10,925)	113	Spanish, Chinese, Khmer, Vietnamese, Arabic, Russian, Creole, Albanian, Malayalam, French, Portuguese, Ukrainian

1 These data were retrieved in July, 2009 from the pertinent school districts' websites as indicated in the table. The percentage of students speaking each of the various languages in the Houston and Philadelphia school districts was not available.

Using AAVE in Instructional Talk. Some studies have linked AAVE to the secondary language arts curriculum and instructional discourse and interactions (Ball & Lardner, 2005; Lee, 2006; Sealey-Ruiz, 2007). Lee documented the benefits of this approach in her longitudinal curriculum project on Cultural Modeling, which she defined as "a framework for the design of curriculum and learning environments that links everyday knowledge with learning academic subject matter, with a particular focus on racial/ethnic minority groups, especially youth of African descent" (p. 308). Lee described, for instance, a literature unit on symbolism that drew on students' cultural data sets, or everyday cultural knowledge, that included rap lyrics and short films that were steeped in symbolism. In this form of instruction, she posited, classroom talk and participation structures necessarily change as students, who are experts of their cultural data sets, educate their teachers about cultural concepts with which they may be unfamiliar. Teachers then scaffold students' transfer of discourse about local knowledge into academic language. Lee described the genre African-American English improvisational argumentation and documented how students' reasoning is highest when they dominate classroom talk. She found that sanctioning students' use of AAVE in classroom talk encouraged high levels of engagement and participation that facilitated learning (see also Cooks & Ball, 2009; Sealey-Ruiz, 2007). In their review of literature on AAVE and adolescents' literacy learning, Cooks and Ball reported that teachers' positive attitudes toward students' use of AAVE in the classroom

encourages students' positive self-concepts about using AAVE and supports their school achievement.

Curriculum and Instruction in Language Ideologies and Linguistics. In their review, Cooks and Ball (2009) noted several strategies for educating students about the linguistic resources they possessed and making them critically aware of language ideologies. These included: making explicit connections between the home/community language and that of the school; incorporating literacy community practices into classroom learning; facilitating students' work as critical ethnographers of their individual and community literacy practices; and implementing critical language pedagogy where students examine language ideologies that stigmatize their home languages. Drawing from their synthesis of research on Black English and dialect shift, Greene and Walker (2004) laid out several strategies through which teachers can support AAVE-speaking students' acquisition and use of Standard English (SE) while recognizing and embracing the value of AAVE. One strategy entailed teachers demonstrating an understanding and respect of Black English and learning and teaching students the history of AAVE and its development in relation to SE.

Sealey-Ruiz (2005, 2007) experienced how validating the language backgrounds of her African American students served as a catalyst for the students' writing. Sealey-Ruiz engaged students, all of whom spoke AAVE, in conversations about their language varieties and their language ideologies. They also read scholarship about AAVE as a rule governed language. Her intent was for students to recognize that their goal of becoming better writers could only be achieved by using all their language resources. In one strategy, she encouraged students to use AAVE to sound out and write words for which they were unsure of the SE English pronunciation or spelling. Another strategy entailed using a range of curriculum materials that represented students' languages and sociocultural experiences. Godley and Minnici (2008) implemented what they called critical language pedagogy with African American students in a 10th-grade language arts classroom to encourage them to develop critical perspectives on language. This pedagogy involved (a) critiquing dominant language ideologies, (b) emphasizing the diversity of dialects spoken in the United States and in the students' communities, and (c) raising students' awareness of the ways that they used language for different purposes and audiences.

Instruction in Code Switching.   Godley and Minnici (2008) designed instructional activities where students practiced code switching in writing and other linguistic tasks. They found that such exercises improved students' understandings about the grammatical patterns of privileged and stigmatized dialects while helping them apprehend underlying issues of power that privileged SE. Williams (2006) and Wheeler and Swords (2006) also recommended using students' AAVE speech patterns to teach SE grammatical conventions. And Greene and Walker (2004) recommended that teachers themselves code switch to promote students' engagement in effective code switching and that they model for students how meaning can be affected by language choice.

Assessment.   Research stresses the importance of including teachers from diverse cultural backgrounds in assessing the work of AAVE-speaking youth (Cooks & Ball, 2009). Ball found that African American teachers, more so than European American teachers, emphasized the content and quality of students' ideas and balanced these with writing conventions and forms (Ball, 1997, in Cooks & Ball). Ball also argued that teachers should learn about the language patterns of their students, communicate and negotiate with them about writing expectations, and intensively support them in meeting writing objectives (Ball, 1999, in Cooks & Ball). Greene and Walker (2004) also recommended communicating expectations for language use in the classroom including explaining which varieties of English are appropriate for different classroom occasions or activities.

Standardized assessments provide a limited account of AAVE-speaking youth's knowledge and abilities; alternative and more multifaceted assessments should be explored (Champion, Hyter, McCabe, & Bland-Stewart, 2003; Cooks & Ball, 2009; Greene & Walker, 2004; Thomas-Tate, Washington, Craig, & Packard, 2006). Greene and Walker encouraged teachers to use criteria such as appropriate language use, organization of thoughts and ideas, delivery,

and other communications competencies when developing assessments. Assessments, they proposed, should be structured and incorporated over the scope of the course. The authors further suggested creating culturally reflective assignments such as tribute speeches that allow students opportunities to further develop proficiency in code switching while affirming their cultural identities. Implementing some of these strategies, Sealey-Ruiz (2007) noticed her students distinguishing and choosing between writing in either AAVE and SE and using AAVE to support their understanding and use of SE. Students, she reported, also used AAVE or a combination of AAVE and SE for creative writing assignments thus enriching their written work.

AAVE and Technology.   Studies related to AAVE and technology are limited. However, existing studies show that technology can be used to improve AAVE-speakers' development of literacy skills (Hall & Damico, 2007; Judge, 2005; Redd, 2003). Hall and Damico concluded that using culturally relevant pedagogy with African American youth facilitated their production of digital texts that contained complex meanings. The students employed various features of AAVE: tonal semantics, sermonic tone, call and response, and signifying in producing their digital texts. In her U.S.-based composition course, Redd encouraged her students to use AAVE in online discussions. She also initiated expansion of their literacy communities to include South African students so that her students could discuss South African literature with these cultural insiders. Redd's students also engaged in culturally relevant multimodal literacy activities, for example, collaboratively building an African American literature website with students from another university. They also utilized various informational websites to foster their understanding of literature throughout the course.

Teacher Preparation.   Teacher educators need to provide in-depth instruction in AAVE and address teachers' attitudes toward it if teachers are to value and draw on the language variety in teaching diverse students (Dixson & Dingus 2006; Fogel & Ehri, 2006). Fogel and Ehri familiarized a group of predominantly White SE-speaking teachers with AAVE to see whether their attitudes toward this language variety and their dispositions toward teaching with it in their classrooms would improve. Across three subgroups that received varying amounts of exposure to and instruction in AAVE, the researchers concluded that all teachers improved their knowledge about and positive attitude toward AAVE. However, teachers who received the most training in AAVE exhibited the greatest attitude shifts. Additionally, these teachers were less likely than other teachers to advocate a teacher-directed rather than a student-directed instructional approach and less likely to favor correcting dialect-based errors in students' reading and writing assignments. This work suggests the potential of teachers studying AAVE and exploring their language ideologies.

Research on Latina/o Students   Over the past 10 years, researchers have increasingly drawn attention to the various linguistic resources—or linguistic *repertoires of practice* (Gutiérrez & Rogoff, 2003)—that Latina/o students bring to our nation's classrooms. The review that follows highlights recent studies that emerged in our search of the Educational Resources Information Center (ERIC) and Social Sciences Index databases from 2000 to 2009 using key word descriptors that included *language diversity, Latina/o students, Spanish-speaking students, literacy,* and *language arts.*

Latina/o Students' Linguistic Repertoires.   Compton-Lilly (2008), Orellana, Reynolds, Dorner, and Meza (2003), Sánchez (2007), and Sayer (2008) have all conducted research that illuminates the linguistic repertoires that Latina/o students bring to the classroom. Taken together, this research underscores the fact that this supposedly monolithic group of students exhibits diverse and expansive linguistic repertoires, which include "standard" English, "standard" Spanish, regional, and vernacular dialects of both languages, various indigenous languages, *Spanglish/* Spanish-English code-switching, and interpreting/translating, among other everyday language practices. Noting that such resources are often overlooked in schools, these scholars have emphasized the potential for leveraging Latina/o students' language practices and experiences as resources for teaching and learning in English language arts classrooms. Orellana et al., for example, suggested that bilingual Latina/o students' experiences translating and interpreting between languages can be used to support the within-language paraphrasing that is valued as an academic literacy skill in schools. Sayer argued that there is value in using Spanglish—a hybrid mixture of English and Spanish—as a tool for academic content learning. Similarly, Martínez (in press) identified parallels between the specific skills embedded in middle school students' use of Spanglish and the skills that these students were expected to master according to California's sixth-grade English language arts standards. He argued that students' skillful use of Spanglish could be leveraged as a resource for helping them to develop these academic literacy skills.

Leveraging Spanish as a Resource.   While there is no shortage of research literature on the *potential* for leveraging Latina/o students' linguistic resources, few studies have explicitly addressed the issue of *how* such resources might be practically leveraged in the classroom. Some studies have approximated this focus by highlighting how Latina/o students draw on Spanish as a resource within English Language Arts classrooms and related learning contexts. Michael, Andrade, and Bartlett (2007), for example, studied curricular and instructional arrangements at a New York City high school that served first-generation Latina/o immigrant students. The authors argued that one of the key determinants of the school's success was the way in which faculty, staff, and students "treated Spanish language and literacy proficiency as a resource" (p. 173) and worked

together to "culturally construct the Spanish language as a resource to be developed and supported through the curriculum" (p. 174). Similarly, Gort (2006) examined the writing processes of emergent bilingual Latina/o students during writing workshops at an elementary school in the northeastern United States, noting that students successfully drew on their knowledge of Spanish to compose monolingual texts in both English and Spanish. These studies suggest that students' knowledge and use of Spanish can serve as powerful resources for learning English language arts.

Drawing on Everyday Language and Discourse Practices.   Other studies have broadened their focus on Latina/o students' linguistic resources to include attention to discourse style and hybridity. Herrero (2006) studied the use of Dominican oral literature and discourse as a resource for literacy learning among "low-achieving" students from the Dominican Republic. She found that students produced more elaborate writing in both English and Spanish when they were allowed to draw on patterns of language and discourse used in their everyday language practices. In a similar study, Martínez-Roldán and Sayer (2006) explored how bilingual third-grade students used language during story retellings. They found that students demonstrated greater comprehension of the stories when they used Spanglish to mediate their retellings than they did when retelling stories using only English.

Translating and Interpreting Practices.   Finally, some studies have focused on Latina/o students' everyday engagement in the practices of translating and interpreting. Borrero (2007) studied middle school students' involvement in a program designed to promote their academic success by training them in the skills of translation and interpreting. His analysis of standardized test scores, observational data, and interview data revealed an overall positive impact on students' academic achievement. Similarly, Martínez, Orellana, Pacheco, and Carbone (2008) worked with a group of Chicana/o sixth graders at a middle school in East Los Angeles. The authors found that, when engaged in lessons and activities that leveraged their translating skills and experiences, students could successfully apply those same skills and experiences to academic writing tasks that required them to shift voices for different audiences.

Preparing Teachers to Leverage Students' Linguistic Repertoires.   Most of the studies cited above have focused on how *students* drew on their own linguistic repertoires within English language arts contexts. Although these studies have contributed a great deal to our understanding of Latina/o students' linguistic repertoires, there is a need for more empirical studies that deliberately and explicitly examine (a) how teachers can leverage these various resources for English language arts instruction, and (b) how teacher education programs can prepare teachers to recognize and effectively leverage Latina/o students' linguistic resources. Some studies have begun to move in this direction. Vacca-Rizopoulos and Nicoletti (2009), for example, explored pre-service teachers' reflections on working with Latina/o English learners. Analyzing these pre-service teachers' observations in urban classrooms and their conversations with in-service teachers, the authors emphasized the lack of preparedness that many teachers felt, and they underscored the critical importance of building on students' linguistic resources. Similarly, Cadiero-Kaplan and Rodriguez (2008) critiqued the context of teacher preparation in light of No Child Left Behind legislation. Noting the lack of responsiveness implicit in this legislation, they described alternative efforts in California towards preparing teachers to recognize and build on English learners' linguistic strengths. Future research in this area should explore what happens when teachers deliberately leverage specific language practices as resources for learning in English language arts classrooms and when teacher education programs deliberately prepare teachers to recognize and leverage these resources.

Research on Students in Linguistically Complex Classrooms Recent increases in the incidence of CLCCs are a result of changing birth rates, migration, and immigration patterns that result in a growing number of students whose language backgrounds include not only African American and Latina/o, but also Arabic, Hmong, Tagalog, Cantonese, Urdu, Vietnamese, Bosnian/Serbian, Gujarati, Haitian Creole, and other language groups in the same classrooms. The review that follows highlights studies conducted within the last decade on teaching students who bring multiple linguistic backgrounds into CLCCs. Our recent search of the Educational Resources Information Center (ERIC) database from 2000 to the present used the descriptors *language diversity, linguistic diversity,* and *language arts* to generate 83 entries. Additional database searches included the Social Science Research Index and the table of contents of relevant journals on teaching the English language arts. A review of the entries that emerged revealed that research on CLCCs falls primarily into two categories: (a) research on *curriculum,* instructional strategies, and pedagogical approaches in classroom and/or community *contexts* and (b) *teacher education,* professional development, and the preparation of teachers to work with diverse student populations. Using these two categories to organize the information, this review focuses on the major findings that have emerged.

Curriculum, Instructional Strategies, and Pedagogical Approaches Lotherington's (2007) study took place in a school in Toronto where more than two thirds of the students spoke a language other than English or French at home and where over 30 languages were spoken in the community. The participants in Lotherington's study included Tamil, Vietnamese, Turkish, English, and Guyanese Creole speaking students across six classes. The students used digital technologies to rewrite traditional children's literature from localized cultural and linguistic perspectives as a means of inexpensively supporting home language maintenance,

fostering language awareness, and aiding learning English as a second language in the community. Lotherington and her colleagues successfully guided students in creating a variety of multilingual stories although they encountered some problems such as unequal support for the many languages students spoke. Students also experienced some difficulty producing linguistically personalized texts.

Moore-Hart (2004) investigated students' literacy learning using multicultural literature and information technology within a reading/writing curriculum. The students in two classes came from African American, European American, Native American, Chinese, Japanese, Latino, Hmong, and Indian backgrounds. The use of multicultural literature and links to a hypermedia program allowed students to access information related to other cultures about which they were reading. Moore-Hart learned, however, that access to multicultural books, resources, and technology was not enough for deep student learning. She found that teachers must use a *process approach* to learning that provides meaningful learning contexts based in the students' cultural and personal experiences.

Dagenais, Walsh, Armand, and Maraillet's (2008) study in Montreal and Vancouver, Canada, examined how collaborative language awareness activities encouraged students to draw on collective language resources to approach languages unknown by the majority. The researchers found that these language arts activities enabled teachers to engage students in focused discussions about language diversity and fostered the emergence of a community of learners who had access to a repertoire of languages that expanded beyond the official languages. Valuing and sharing knowledge of diverse languages in classroom discussions fostered the discursive co-construction of new knowledge about the evolution of languages, relationships between languages, as well as a critical stance on the relative status of languages.

Teacher Preparation. During our review of the research literature, several studies emerged that focused on the development and support of teachers' abilities to draw on students' rich linguistic repertoires when they enter CLCCs. Ball (2006) investigated the use of writing as a pedagogical tool to motivate and facilitate teacher ideological change as they participated in a teacher education course. She also investigated the use of writing as a pedagogical tool for documenting the changing perspectives of transitioning teachers as they began to envision themselves becoming effective teachers in CLCCs. Several other studies have investigated the use of specific writing strategies in teacher education programs to prepare teachers to teach in CLCCs (e.g., Abbate-Vaughn, 2006; Moore & Ritter, 2008). Moore and Ritter engaged pre-service teachers in a homogenous university location with a classroom of linguistically diverse learners at various stages of writing development. The project afforded the pre-service teachers rich understandings of the children's diversity and reshaped their perceptions of their roles as teachers in supporting and responding to each child's individual strengths.

Ball (2009) reported on research designed to advance our knowledge concerning *what* and *how* teachers must learn from professional development programs in order to successfully teach in CLCCs. Ball concluded that *generativity* plays a critical role in the preparation of teachers to meet the educational needs of their students in CLCCs. By generativity, Ball means that teachers must have the ability to add to their understanding by connecting their personal and professional knowledge with their students' knowledge in ways that allow them to produce new knowledge that is useful to them in curricular planning and pedagogical problem solving. She argued that teachers must envision their classrooms as "communities of change" where transformative learning and emancipatory teaching take place. Such learning, she asserted, can educate not only a generation of teachers who are generative thinkers, but also a new generation of students who will themselves become generative in their thinking and literacy practices as well. Such learning requires the incorporation of critical consciousness pedagogy as a crucial part of teacher and student knowledge. This work requires a research agenda that focuses specifically on preparing teachers for work in CLCCs and for pre-service and in-service programs that envision CLCCs as communities of change. To accomplish this, Ball proposed a model of generative change that can be used in the restructuring of teacher education programs and replicated in the classrooms of teachers working in CLCCs (see Ball for a full discussion).

Conclusions and Implications for Future Research

Our review of the literature points to the need for more research that undergirds the development of pedagogical strategies that allow students in linguistically heterogeneous classrooms to learn from each other and about each other concerning the rich linguistic heritage that makes up our pluralistic society. In reporting research findings, researchers should share more detailed information on the data and analytical approaches. Doing so would allow other researchers to see the explicit processes through which teachers can draw on students' linguistic resources to achieve particular instructional goals, the challenges encountered, how those challenges were addressed, and the degree to which instructional goals were met (see Williams, 2006, for a good example). For example, while many researchers recommend drawing on AAVE as a resource, much more research is needed on *how* to draw on AAVE as a resource for teaching and learning in the English language arts classroom. In addition, more large scale, longitudinal studies are needed that document the substantive value and the long-term effects of using particular strategies that leverage AAVE as a linguistic resource for teaching and learning. Primarily due to the lack of sufficient funding to support the work, there is very little recent research that systematically supports the leveraging of AAVE as a linguistic resource for academic learning or for teaching and learning within the disciplines.

Our review of the research also revealed that we need to hear more from the students themselves about their experiences and understanding of how curriculum and instructional practices can help them achieve not only the instructor's learning goals but their own academic, social, and personal goals. Much of the research on how to use linguistic diversity as a resource in English language arts classrooms is occurring in college composition classrooms. More research is needed at the elementary and secondary levels where students must develop the confidence, motivation, and academic skills to pursue higher education. We also found that studies related to language diversity and technology were very limited. In the burgeoning field of digital literacy, it is critical that serious attention be paid to how linguistic diversity can be leveraged to support the development of linguistically diverse students' competencies.

There is also a need for more studies that examine how teacher educators and pre-service teachers engage with available research on using language diversity as a teaching and learning resource, the impact of professional development on teachers' subsequent practices within CLCCs, and how teachers develop curriculum and instructional resources with and for their students. Furthermore, more collaborative studies are needed where researchers work alongside teachers and students to produce knowledge for the wider education community about how to draw on diverse students' linguistic backgrounds. And, as Ball (2009) argues, we need to study closely how teachers' generativity can be fostered so that they can continuously innovate effective teaching and learning approaches in the evolving linguistic landscapes of their classrooms.

Finally, we close this chapter by noting that teaching the English language arts to multiple language groups at the same time within the same educational context is indeed a very complex task. The vast majority of research on language diversity has been small scale, single site studies that have taken place with one minority language group. Perhaps this is understandable because there are many communities where monoethnic, monolingual communities remain the norm. However, with rapidly changing classroom demographics, we urgently need large scale, longitudinal, systematic studies to update our understanding of linguistic diversity and how to meet the needs of students in CLCCs. The international research community seems to be providing leadership in the area of studies on CLCCs; however studies are needed from the U.S. context as well. There is much that we can learn from the international community, but there is much that we can contribute to the conversation as well.

References

Abbate-Vaughn, J. (2006). "Not writing it out but writing it off": Preparing multicultural teachers for urban classrooms. *Multicultural Education, 13*(4), 41–48.

Ball, A. F. (2006). *Multicultural strategies for education and social change: Carriers of the Torch in the US and South Africa.* New York: Teachers College Press.

Ball, A. F. (2009). Toward a theory of generative change in culturally and linguistically complex classrooms. *American Educational Research Journal, 46*(1), 45–72.

Ball, A. F., & Lardner, T. (2005). *African American literacies unleashed: Vernacular English and the composition classroom.* Carbondale: Southern Illinois University Press.

Borrero, N. (2007). Promoting cultural and linguistic diversity in American public schools: Fostering the assets of bilingual adolescents. *The International Journal of Diversity in Organizations, Communities and Nations, 7*(1), 195–204.

Cadiero-Kaplan, K., & Rodriguez, J. L. (2008). The preparation of highly qualified teachers for English Language Learners: Educational responsiveness for unmet needs. *Equity & Excellence in Education, 41*(3), 372–387.

Champion, T. B., Hyter, Y. D., McCabe, A., & Bland-Stewart, L. M. (2003). "A matter of vocabulary": Performances of low-income African American Head Start children on the Peabody Picture Vocabulary Test—III. *Communication Disorders Quarterly, 24*(3), 121–127.

Compton-Lilly, C. (2008). Teaching struggling readers: Capitalizing on diversity for effective learning. *Reading Teacher, 61*(8), 668–672.

Cooks, J., & Ball, A. F. (2009). Research on the literacies of AAVE-speaking adolescents. In L. Christenbury, R. Bomer, & P. Smagorinsky (Eds.). *Handbook of adolescent literacy research* (pp. 140–152). New York: Guilford Press.

Dagenais, D., Walsh, N., Armand, F., & Maraillet, E. (2008). Collaboration and co-construction of knowledge during language awareness activities in Canadian elementary school. *Language Awareness, 17*(2), 139–155.

Dixson, A. D., & Dingus, J. E. (2006). Personal investments, professional gains: Strategies of African American women teacher educators. *Mid-Western Educational Researcher, 19*(2), 36–40.

Fogel, H., & Ehri, L. C. (2006). Teaching African American English forms to standard American English-speaking teachers: Effects on acquisition, attitudes, and responses to student use. *Journal of Teacher Education, 57*(5), 464–480.

Godley, A. J., & Minnici, A. (2008). Critical language pedagogy in an urban high school English class. *Urban Education, 43*(3), 319–346.

Gort, M. (2006). Strategic code-switching, interliteracy, and other phenomena of emergent bilingual writing: Lessons from first grade bilingual classrooms. *Journal of Early Childhood Literacy, 6*(3), 323–354.

Greene, D. M., & Walker, F. R. (2004). Recommendations to public speaking instructors for the negotiation of code-switching practices among black English-speaking African American students. *Journal of Negro Education, 73*, 435–442.

Gutiérrez, K. D., & Rogoff, B. (2003). Cultural ways of learning: Individual traits or repertoires of practice. *Educational Researcher, 32*(5), 19–25.

Hall, D. T., & Damico, J. (2007). Black youth employ African American vernacular English in creating digital texts. *Journal of Negro Education, 76*(1), 80–88.

Herrero, E. A. (2006). Using Dominican oral literature and discourse to support literacy learning among low-achieving students from the Dominican Republic. *International Journal of Bilingual Education and Bilingualism, 9*(2), 219–238.

Judge, S. (2005). The impact of computer technology on academic achievement of young African American children. *Journal of Research in Childhood Education, 20*(2), 91–101.

Lee, C. D. (2006). "Every good-bye ain't gone": Analyzing the cultural underpinnings of classroom talk. *International Journal of Qualitative Studies in Education (QSE), 19*(3), 305–327.

Lotherington, H. (2007). Rewriting traditional tales as multilingual narratives at elementary school: Problems and progress. *Canadian Journal of Applied Linguistics, 10*(2), 241–256.

Martínez, R. A. (in press). Spanglish as literary tool: Toward an understanding of the potential role of Spanish-English code switching in the development of academic literacy. *Research in the Teaching of English.*

Martínez, R. A., Orellana, M. F., Pacheco, M., & Carbone, P. (2008). Found in translation: Connecting translating experiences to academic writing. *Language Arts, 85*(6), 421–431.

Martínez-Roldán, C., & Sayer, P. (2006). Reading through linguistic borderlands: Latino students' transactions with narrative texts. *Journal of Early Childhood Literacy, 6*(3), 294–322.

Michael, A., Andrade, N., & Bartlett, L. (2007). Figuring "success" in a bilingual high school. *Urban Review: Issues and Ideas in Public Education, 39*(2), 167–189.

Moore-Hart, P. (2004). Creating learning environments that invite all students to learn through multicultural literature and information technology: The intermingling of cultures, religions, and languages across the United States enriches classrooms, while presenting new challenges to teaching and learning. *Childhood Education, 81*(2), 87.

Moore, R. A., & Ritter, S. (2008). "Oh Yeah, I'm Mexican. What Type Are You?" Changing the Way Preservice Teachers Interpret and Respond to the Literate Identities of Children. *Early Childhood Education Journal, 35*(6), 505–514.

National Center for Educational Statistics (NCES). (2006). *Characteristics of the 100 largest public elementary and secondary school districts in the United States: 2003–04 statistical analysis report.* Washington, DC: U.S. Department of Education.

Orellana, M. F., Reynolds, J., Dorner, L., & Meza, M. (2003). In other words: Translating or "para-phrasing" as a family literacy practice in immigrant households. *Reading Research Quarterly, 38*(1), 12–34.

Redd, T. M. (2003). "Tryin to make a dolla outa fifteen cent": Teaching composition with the Internet at an HBCU. *Computers and Composition, 20*(4), 359–373.

Sánchez, P. (2007). Cultural authenticity and transnational Latina youth: Constructing a meta-narrative across borders. *Linguistics and Education, 18*(3–4), 258–282.

Sayer, P. (2008). Demystifying language mixing: Spanglish in school. *Journal of Latinos and Education, 7*(2), 94–112.

Sealey-Ruiz, Y. (2005). Spoken soul: The language of black imagination and reality. *The Educational Forum, 70*(1), 37–46.

Sealey-Ruiz, Y. (2007). Wrapping the curriculum around their lives: Using a culturally relevant curriculum with African American adult women. *Adult Education Quarterly: A Journal of Research and Theory, 58*(1), 44–60.

Thomas-Tate, S., Washington, J., Craig, H., & Packard, M. (2006). Performance of African American preschool and kindergarten students on the expressive vocabulary test. *Language, Speech, and Hearing Services in Schools, 37,* 143–149.

UNESCO Institute for Statistics. (2005). *Global education digest 2005: Comparing education statistics across the world.* Montreal, Canada: Author.

Vacca-Rizopoulos, L. A., & Nicoletti, A. (2009). Preservice teachers' reflections on effective strategies for teaching Latino ESL students. *Journal of Latinos and Education, 8*(1), 67–76.

Wheeler, R. S., & Swords, R. (2006). *Code-switching: Teaching standard English in urban classrooms.* Urbana, IL: National Council of Teachers of English.

Williams, C. H. (2006). "You gotta reach 'em": An African American teacher's multiple literacies approach. *Theory Into Practice, 45*(4), 346–351.

5

Crossing Borders with Language

Teachers and the Transformative Potential
of Professional Development Opportunities

MARÍA E. FRÁNQUIZ AND ELLEN PRATT

In this chapter we argue that the MayaWest Writing Summer Institute offered at the University of Puerto Rico in Mayagüez and the Proyecto Maestría program offered at the University of Texas in Austin provides professional development spaces where contested discourses on languages and literacies can safely and comfortably take place. In order to revision themselves and their classroom pedagogies, the teachers participating in both of these professional development projects planned to cross borders, including but not limited to linguistic, cultural, political, and technological borders. Teacher participation in these projects assumes teachers are serious about addressing inequalities in schooled literacy achievement. It also assumes teachers are willing to "try on" new forms of language use in order to learn about pedagogies that may better serve students whose repertoires put them at greater risk of failure to thrive within the larger society and dominant culture. The "trying on" of new ways of teaching was simply stated by a teacher during a "mock" demonstration of what occurred at the inaugural MayaWest Writing Project Summer Institute in 2008; "estamos aquí por ellos, los estudiantes/we are here for them, the students."

In this chapter we highlight particular literacy events in the two professional development programs because these events provided varied transformative experiences for teachers. We index these two programs and events as cases that applaud teachers for seeking the additive characteristics of sociocultural competence (Moll & Arnot-Hopffer, 2005) to precipitate change in the way language and the language arts are taught to students becoming biliterate (Pérez, 2003) in Puerto Rico and in Texas.

According to Heath's (1983) classic study, a literacy event refers to what people do with their language. She defines a literacy event as "any occasion in which a piece of writing is integral to the nature of participants' interactions and their interpretive processes" (p. 93). She highlighted that these literacy events ought to be interpreted in relation to the larger sociopolitical patterns of society at large. Street (1984, 1988) employed the phrase "literacy practices" focusing upon everyday uses and meanings of literacy that participants bring to bear upon literacy events. Barton and Hamilton (2000) added that texts are central to literacy events. These texts arise from practices that, in many ways, are shaped by the very events in which they take place. Therefore, if literacy events are shaped by texts, and, literacy practices shape the literacy events themselves, then the organization of our chapter should capture how this recursive cycle worked for the teachers participating in the MayaWest Summer Writing Institute and Proyecto Maestría Program. Toward this end, we first present descriptions of the history, goals, and participants of both of these professional development opportunities as well as our relationship to these two programs. Next, we provide an overview of a third space transformative framework that highlights teachers navigating familiar and unfamiliar literacy practices within literacy events. Examples illustrate how teachers perceived shifts in their pedagogical stances as a result of the authoring practices provided and taken up by them in literacy events. Finally, we close with implications related to our work with teachers who choose to be, in the words of Aronowitz and Giroux (1985), transformative intellectuals.

Professional Development for Teachers of Bilingual Students

History of MayaWest Writing Project (MWWP) The goal of the MayaWest Writing Project is to provide teachers with professional development in the teaching of writing and literacy at all levels. It is based on the core values of many writing project sites of the National Writing Project (NWP). These values include the following premises: writing is critical to learning across all disciplines and grade levels; working as partners, universities and schools can improve student writing; teachers are the best teachers of teachers; when teachers are given time to write and reflect on their writing, their teaching is enhanced. When these values are embodied the teachers reflect the additive personality documented by Moll and Arnot-Hopffer (2005) in Arizona. In their longitudinal study the teachers of a case study school built an environment that cultivates the development of biliteracy, establishes *confianza* (mutual trust) with colleagues and administrators, and becomes vigilant of their own political and ideological clarity (Bartolomé & Balderrama, 2001) related to the language rights and responsibilities of the children they teach.

What makes the NWP program different than other professional writing approaches is the fact that teachers teach teachers in order to take on responsibilities as skilled consultants/coaches who serve as mentors for best practices in literacy instruction in their regions. Initially, the teacher leaders in-the-making, participate in an intensive 4-week summer institute and immerse themselves in reading, writing, and demonstrating to each other literacy lessons that have been successful with their students. Writing in several genres is a central literacy practice to the institute and teachers, themselves, go through the process of composing and revising their own writing and then searching out publishing possibilities. The unique characteristic of the MayaWest Writing Project is that the teaching, learning, demonstrating, and publishing are accomplished through two languages, Spanish and English.

When the project began in 2008, there was one NWP site in Puerto Rico on the campus of Sagrado Corazón, a private university. It is named the Borinquen Writing Project and serves the San Juan metropolitan area and the eastern part of the Island. The MayaWest Writing Project serves school districts from Ponce on the southwest side of the Island and as far as Arecibo on the northwest side of the Island. While the University of Puerto Rico at Mayagüez is primarily a polytechnic university offering degrees in engineering, sciences, agriculture, and business it also houses an English department. The university does not have a college of Education. Instead, the English and Spanish departments work in conjunction with the Continuing Education program to prepare its K–16 teachers. Unlike other universities, a Bilingual Writing Center offers trained tutors to assist students requiring English as a second language (ESL) and writing services, and they offer presentations available to all interested members of the campus community.

Puerto Rico has a unique language context that contributes to a public school that is plagued with many challenges. Since 1898 when Puerto Rico was ceded by Spain to the United States, the status of Spanish and English has varied. In 1917 when Puerto Ricans were made U.S. citizens, the majority of residents were monolingual Spanish-speaking; by 1952, when the Island became an associated Commonwealth, most residents had studied English as a subject in school. The 2000 census reported 3,800,000 Puerto Ricans living on the Island and almost as many living stateside with the largest concentrations living in the urban areas of New York, New Jersey, Massachusetts, Pennsylvania, and Illinois. Educators on the Island estimate that more than 50%

of the Puerto Rican population is abroad at any one time, and the constant state of seasonal movement or circulatory migration between the Island and the mainland has had an impact on language teaching and literacy learning (Tucker, 2005). According to Nieto (2000), "[F]or many Puerto Ricans migration has tended to be a series of periodic movements to and from the Island. Consequently, what Puerto Ricans as a group expect of U.S. schools is not assimilation, but rather accommodation to and even the protection and maintenance of their language and culture" (p. 11). However, the educators associated with the MayaWest writing project in 2008 lamented the impact of current educational policies on what students know and don't know about their Puerto Rican culture, history, and traditions.

For the inaugural MayaWest Writing Project, 18 teachers were selected for the intensive summer institute of 2008. This first group of teachers set the foundation for future projects and became the founding teacher consultants. They represented private and public schools, grades K–16 and taught in English, Spanish, or bilingual classrooms. For the second year, another 18 teachers were selected and 4 teacher consultants from the inaugural group joined in the directorship of the summer institute of 2009. Ellen Pratt is a professor of English and was acting Director for both summer institutes. María Fránquiz is a professor of Bilingual-Bicultural Education and provided support during the application process for MWWP in 2007 and visited on-site during the latter week of the summer institutes of 2008 and 2009. María became a teacher consultant of the SouthCoast Writing Project (SCWriP) at the University of California at Santa Barbara in the summer of 1993. She was born in Puerto Rico but has not been a full time resident of the Island since her third year of schooling. Ellen was born stateside but has been a full time resident of the island for over three decades.

History of Proyecto Maestria Proyecto Maestría Collaborative for Teacher Leadership in Bilingual and ESL Education is the product of a grant from the U.S. Dept of Education, Office of English Language Acquisition. Proyecto Maestría provides scholarship money for current, certified bilingual teachers with 5 years experience from the local Central Texas area to pursue a Masters degree in Curriculum and Instruction with specialization in bilingual education. Its purpose is to improve the quality and increase the quantity of highly skilled bilingual and ESL teachers in the metropolitan area, promote teacher retention, and improve the educational outcome for the region's growing population of English Language Learners (ELLs). Because the majority ELL enrollment is of Mexican heritage, the teachers selected to participate in the program teach in elementary school Spanish/English bilingual classrooms.

The 2008 Proyecto Maestria cohort was comprised of nine teachers and the 2009 cohort was comprised of twelve teachers. The majority of teachers in each cohort are of Mexican origin and some have deep generational ties to when Texas was part of Mexico. During two summers, the exemplary bilingual teachers selected to participate in Proyecto Maestría attend university classes full-time; during the 9 months of the academic calendar year they are enrolled in classes part-time. Upon completion of the Masters program, the graduates serve as mentor teachers on their campuses and provide leadership related to bilingual and ESL education to their districts.

Professors Pratt and Fránquiz agreed to have the teachers participating in the MayaWest Writing Summer Institute and the teachers participating in session I of Proyecto Maestría (a four course intensive summer session) to meet via videoconferencing. The purpose of the videoconference was to learn about literacy events and practices and what they mean to language teachers in bilingual educational settings of various schools in Puerto Rico and in Central Texas. The meeting was expected to become an articulation of teacher identity, or what Holland, Lachicotte, Skinner, and Cain (1998) call identity in practice. The connections across the two groups of teachers provided "one way of naming the dense interconnections" of personhood, not as "independent from but webbed within historical social worlds" (p. 270). When the teachers met via digital technologies they were immersed in their second week of their summer professional development projects. They were reading and writing in Spanish, English, or bilingually and making sense of social, cultural, historical, political, and economic practices of which they were a part.

Transformative Framework for Teacher Development

Studies that acknowledge, enhance, and develop the existing strengths, or funds of knowledge, of teachers are few. Chicana feminist thought is helpful in the study of bilingual educators because these perspectives promote a focus on bilingualism, biculturalism, and coalition building. This frame can also be influenced by teacher experiences with dual languages and border crossings.

To use border theory and third space Chicana feminist theories of identity, the work of Gloria Anzaldúa (1987) is critical. She explored how the structures of culture can both bind and deter bonding with the group. In her seminal work, *Borderlands La Frontera: The New Mestiza,* Anzaldúa, as a lesbian, identified the structures that forced her to resist the group culture of homophobia (pp. 41–42). At the same time, she claimed that the music and *corridos* (pp. 82–83) and many other cultural expressions helped her form an allegiance to and a loyalty to that cultural group. Thus, she suggested the metaphor of a bridge across differences and situated the process as movement inside the in-between border spaces and liminal places—*nepantla* (the Aztec concept for the third space). While Anzaldua's ideas are grounded in her South Texas lived reality, they transcend across borders and address issues found in the greater sociocultural world. For this reason we found it pertinent to our work with teachers who were predominantly of Mexican or Puerto Rican origin because the linguistic resources students bring into classroom literacy events can be effectively used as mate-

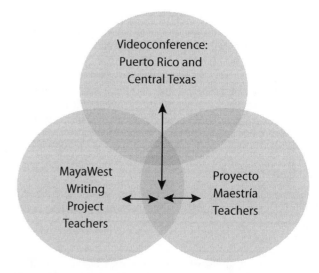

Figure 5.1 Digital technology as third space for teacher professional development.

rial resources for communicating, making meaning and constructing one's identity as a bilingual person (Fránquiz & Salazar, 2004).

Videoconferencing as a Third Space for Teacher Professional Development A visual representation of what happened when we brought the bilingual language teachers from the two professional groups together into a dialogical space is shown in Figure 5.1. The videoconference between MayaWest Writing Project teachers and Proyecto Maestría teachers served as a meditational tool to promote a zone of expanded learning (Bhabha, 1994; Gutierrez, Baquedano-López, & Tejeda, 1999; Soja, 1996) through dialogue. Although the visual representation in Figure 5.1 does not reflect the dynamics of movement in a third dimensional space, it does provide an idea of the third space for transformation in the videoconference literacy event.

Some of the themes that emerged in the space of videoconferencing were: teachers overcoming the fear of writing, a common worry about standardized writing measures for their students, concerns about stronger family involvement practices, needing more pedagogy for including children with special needs, addressing resistant language learners, *manteniendo corazones abiertos a nuevas ideas*/maintaining hearts open to new ideas, painting pictures of possibilities, among other themes.

Transcripts of each videoconference and teachers' subsequent written reflections of the literacy event were used to cull these themes. Transcripts indicate that during 2008 the teachers used more English and in 2009 they used more Spanish in their dialogue. One of the Proyecto Maestría teachers wrote in her reflection, "I feel this was my very first step of becoming a teacher of teachers" which is actually a primary goal of the MayaWest Writing Project. Another Proyecto Maestría teacher raised an important question in her written reflection of the videoconference literacy event.

The comment that surprised me the most was that teachers felt that in Puerto Rico the public schools are failing to prepare students in academic English sufficient to be successful with the primary language of texts at the University or College level. They expressed how public and private schools are attracting new students by providing English as the primary language of instruction. This issue is similar to the challenges of the bilingual programs in public schools throughout the United States. The question in both cases is: Are we providing equitable and adequate education for our second language learners to meet the challenges of higher education?

Interestingly, a teacher from the MayaWest Project expressed this same new consciousness when she wrote in her journal:

> Learning about the struggles other teachers have in their classrooms regarding writing skills in a multilingual setting provided us with a clear understanding of what teachers go through. The tendency in Puerto Rico is to live inside a bubble, perhaps a characteristic many islanders feel at times. The opportunity to share "live" with teachers beyond our land is just an example of how far we can go with technology. At the end, teachers have the same passion, interests, and motivations, and through these resources, we are truly blessed to share strategies and successful stories that enrich us all, *rompiendo las barreras de la distancia, uniendonos a traves de un fin común, una educación dinámica de cambios y transformación social* [breaking distance barriers, uniting together toward a common goal, a dynamic education for change and social transformation].

Another digital technology that provided a "third space" for teachers occurred within the MayaWest Writing Project itself. Teachers tested out and expanded their changing beliefs about languages and literacies by posting their writing on the E-Anthology, a space maintained by NWP. In this space there were no directors or leaders monitoring what people wrote. In the absence of hierarchy there were four locations for contributions: Guestbook, Classroom Matters, A Day in the Life, and Open Mike. At first, English was recognized as the language of communication on the E-Anthology so initially the Puerto Rican teachers introduced themselves in English, including the Spanish teachers among them. Slowly they began to introduce Spanish words and phrases in their writing; then entire pieces written in Spanish were posted on the E-Anthology. By the end of the institute, eloquent pieces incorporated both languages as expressions of their dual language identities. Interestingly, their audience was overwhelmingly monolingual English speaking. The crossing of borders on the E-Anthology raised all sorts of issues related to past training and experiences. For example, for some teachers their first contacts with code switching had been negative. Also, their pedagogical training viewed the teaching of English as separate from the teaching of Spanish. Additionally, Spanish teachers were blamed for not teaching writing and English teachers were blamed for placing too much emphasis on English. Contentions ended with a call for a hybridized

curriculum (Gutierrez et al., 1999). We wondered if the changed attitudes were a result of the audience on the online forum provided by the E-Anthology; the audience had been accepting of the Spanish postings. For example, one bilingual teacher stateside wrote:

> *Gracias por presentar un día típico. He aprendido mucho de ustedes este verano. Son un grupo dinámico. Me encantó la última linea que dice, "El escribir se ha convertido en vicio, pero si este vicio es gratificante, seguiremos con este vicio." Seguramente este es un vicio muy bueno.*

> Thank you for describing a typical day. I have learned much from you this summer. You are a dynamic group. I loved the last line that stated, "Writing has turned into a vice, but if this vice is so gratifying, on with it!" Surely this is a good vice to have.

It was the third space of Web-based technology that had created a supportive environment for the development of biliteracy, *confianza*, and ideological clarity regarding the use of all linguistic resources, including code switching, for writing. Clearly, a more critical understanding of the role of language in the construction of their own and students' identities and an awareness of how linguistic ideology can serve to maintain rigid borders contributed to the sociocultural competence of teachers participating in the MayaWest Writing Project Summer Institute. Researchers such as Hornberger (1989, 2000) published a comprehensive review of the literature on biliteracy development because she asserts that the most productive settings for developing biliteracy exemplify a balance between attention to receptive and productive skills, between oral and written languages, and between the use of native language and second language. What isn't totally clear in this research is the plurality of texts associated with multimedia technologies (New London Group, 1996) and the semiotic toolkit (Dyson, 2001; Jewitt & Kress, 2003) needed to access the literacy practices of the contemporary social landscape (Luke, 2000). For example, when one of the Proyecto Maestría teachers commented on the resources available in her district for students' composing of multimodal texts the scarcity of material resources in Puerto Rico became evident. Nonetheless, Reyes (2001) states that teachers should "unleash students' potential by creating classrooms where English and Spanish are promoted, modeled, valued, nurtured, legitimized and utilized" (p.119) even if the shift from page to screen is limited. Nevertheless, the experience the teachers had using technology to communicate across borders in two languages awakened them to the possibilities for how they could use technology in their classrooms. After the 2009 Summer Institute, a writing project teacher found a classroom stateside that her students could communicate with through the Internet and Skype. She recognized her experience in the summer as the motivating force for this endeavor.

Cultivating authors in MayaWest Writing Project and in Proyecto Maestría By achieving a measure of ideological clarity regarding crossing linguistic borderlands

the MayaWest Writing Project Summer Institute teachers were provided opportunities to experience the unleashing of their own potential as writers of two languages. Besides the videoconference there were regular events nurtured through literacy practices that became ordinary to participants. Many of these literacy practices are promoted by NWP across their 200+ sites and are also writing process routines in many K–16 classrooms. In that sense they are literate practices not invented by the practitioners of the local context (Brandt & Collins, 2002) except for a hybridization of language use. The literate practices included scribe for the day, author's chair, book talk, I-search (replaced Research Paper of Summer 2008), Demonstration, Writing to a Prompt or Quote, Memoirs, and other Freewriting activities. When one of the teachers from Proyecto Maestría asked the Puerto Rican teachers participating in summer 2009, *¿Cúal es su favorita parte del día?*/What is your favorite part of the day? a teacher from the MayaWest Summer Writing Institute answered, *"El día...la parte favorita del día es cuando se lee el "scribe." Nosotros narramos lo que sucedió y así podemos ver lo que hemos completado durante todo el día. Esa es la parte favorita del día mío.*/The day…the favorite part of the day is when the scribe reads. We narrate what happened and that way we can know what we have completed during the whole day. That's my favorite part of the day." Another teacher answered, *"Disfruto mucho el momento en que vamos a la silla del autor ya que entiendo...que todos dejamos expresar nuestra emoción, nuestro sentimiento, y a veces entre risas y lagrimas disfrutamos todos el día.*/I enjoy the moment of the author's chair now that I understand… that we all express our emotion, our feeling, and at times between laughs and tears we enjoy the day together."

The literate practice of a scribe sharing ethnographic notes regarding the accomplishments of the previous day in the writing project took many different and creative forms—one day a poem, one day a narrative, one day a recipe, one day a song, and much more. Another literate practice, Author's Chair, requires active listening to the author who is sharing; this event is designed to help teachers and students better understand literacy processes. In the case of the scribe, Mercado and Moll (2000) discuss the transformative powers middle school children in New York experienced linguistically, relationally, and academically while documenting life in their local Puerto Rican community. Writing about the life around them was empowering. Equally satisfying is sharing writing with those who belong to the local community. With the Author's Chair writers assume the various roles of reader, writer, listener, and critic/editor (Graves & Hansen, 1983; Graves, 1983). Author's Chair grows out of writing process pedagogy and authors use this public occasion as a means to receive affirmative feedback and/or for revising. In these interactive literacy practices group members share writing with each other through high levels of participation. For teachers in the project, the experience of sharing what they had written during the day also allowed them to hear their own voices,

thus providing a sense of self-affirmation and empowerment through their writing.

For the Proyecto Maestría teachers, classrooms were set up as safe dialogic spaces for the co-construction of a community that discloses, reflects, conceptualizes, and transforms former monocultural ways of being. As such, they are encouraged to use the language and language varieties from home and community in the learning process. Since many of the teachers have grown up along the U.S./ Mexico border with many internalized majoritarian tales (Delgado & Stefancic, 1993; Chapman, 2007) such as, "Speak Spanish at home and English at school" or "Speak Spanish correctly, and cut out that Tex Mex language," the invitation to express thoughts through all available linguistic resources is often liberating. The writing project was also set up to provide similar spaces for their teachers, and the use of English and Spanish and Spanglish alternated throughout the day with bilingual teachers code switching often. Given the tumultuous history of the island and the United States, language is closely tied to issues of Puerto Rican identity (Zentella, 1997), and the project provided the desirable space to share language identities in English and Spanish through their writing.

In order to provide opportunities for Proyecto Maestría teachers to author their autobiographies, Fránquiz presents an assignment the first day of class that is an exercise to "trigger both negative and positive memories" (Tello, 1994, p. 59) of past language and literacy experiences. The act of eliciting *memorias/memories* about oppressive moments in personal and collective educational histories serves at least two purposes: (a) becoming conscious of one's cultural and linguistic oppression makes visible the impact of majoritarian tales such as "Forget your native language and culture, and become part of the great American melting pot" and, (b) raises questions such as, "Does the American dream have to be dreamt in English-only?" This assignment is intended to deconstruct tales of a single path to Americanization and also begins the journey toward libratory pathways so that the teachers are not left behind in sync with the totalizing effects of majoritarian tales.

Memorias were elicited from all the Proyecto Maestría teachers of summers 2008 and 2009. The assignment was simply called "My Literacy Journey Box." In the research literature a journey box is "literally a box (e.g., suitcase, trunk, chest, cardboard container) that contains a themed set of photographs, selected artifacts, texts, journal entries, and an index that together tell a first-hand story of time and place" (Labbo & Field, 1999, p. 177). It is a typical way to understand the use of primary documents in the field of social studies. For example, to construct the life of a heroine, a president, or a civil rights leader. In the journey box project, the heroine or hero is the teacher and the *memoria* is the story of her/his subordinated knowledge first represented in the journey box, then in a timeline, and finally in an autobiography. This assignment requires a few more modalities than a typical memoir, and the teachers typically share the contents of their journey box in English, Spanish, or bilingually with the whole class whereas the autobiography is shared in a dyad. Following is the influence this assignment had on one of the Proyecto Maestría teachers.

The teacher whom I will call Liliana was born in South Texas at the Suntex Farms ranch right outside of Rio Grande City, Texas. She is first generation U.S. born of migrant farm workers. In summer of 2008, during her initial summer in Proyecto Maestría, Liliana wrote in her autobiography:

> When I was introduced to researching in my science and social studies classes I came to the realization that I loved to write about facts. Reading history books and writing reports about my learning became a favorite past time of mine. This type of writing together with my poetry writing and letter writing really gave me an outlet to express the thoughts, feelings, emotions and learning that I was experiencing at school and at home. Writing provided me with the consciousness of thinking about my thinking and putting it on paper. I guess in my literary life the one thing I always tried to find was my own voice. In the chaos of child poverty and migrant working, it became very important. It was an outlet away from the realities of life and a place to contemplate on what life should become for me in the future.

The search for her writer's voice both in disciplinary and social writing provided Liliana with the tools necessary to deal with the mobility that was ordinary to her bilingual migrant family and Mexican-American community. She was acutely aware of the benefits of the funds of knowledge (Vélez-Ibañez & Greenberg, 1992; Moll, Amanti, Neff, & González, 1992) at home as can be seen by another passage in her auto-narrative.

> Today, I am bilingual because of the fact my environment provided me with an enriched life filled with bilingualism and biculturalism that I wouldn't have otherwise. If it had been up to my educational system they would have stripped me of it all. I find myself today as a teacher struggling with the fact that my students could experience this stripping away of their language and culture. The only thing I pray for is that I give them some tools to defend themselves and to protect themselves from it all.

Liliana's writing illustrates deep critical reflection regarding her own education whereby maintenance of her Spanish heritage language had typically been seen as a problem to be expunged from her and other Mexican heritage students. Instead, Liliana knew that her bilingualism should have been seen as a resource for her learning (Fránquiz & Reyes, 1998) or acknowledged as her fundamental human right (Ruiz, 1984). The desire to equip her students with the same bilingual and bicultural tools that had been passed to her by family and community was evident across the weeks that she participated in the foundational courses of Proyecto Maestría.

Conclusion

The collaborative study described in this chapter encompasses our ethnographic musings through which we imagine new possibilities for teachers and their students. We emphasize the resource that hybridity in multimodal literacy events offer and the literate practices that sustain life in linguistically diverse classrooms. The teachers in Puerto Rico and Central Texas shared common concerns and took risks as users of language in order to develop characteristics of sociocultural competence.

Because little is known about the preparation of teachers of color generally (Elenes, González, Delgado Bernal, & Villenas, 2001; Sheets, 2004) and bilingual education teachers in particular (Arce, 2004; Clark & Flores, 2001), the two projects reported in this chapter heed the call of Darling-Hammond, French, and Garcia-Lopez (2002) and Darling-Hammond and Baratz-Snowden (2005) who argue that teacher education must assist all teachers in acquiring the necessary knowledge and skills to teach language and literacy for social justice. As the effort of a collaborative team of university teacher educators, we offered important insights based on the privilege we share in working with educators from K–16, many who are teachers of color seeking guidance in understanding and responding to learner diversity in ways appropriate to local contexts. It is fitting to close with the words of one of the teachers who experienced a transformation during her professional development opportunity at the MayaWest Writing Summer Institute. In her own words she describes a new found language of solidarity with the other teachers.

> *We were one... porque compartimos diferencias y complementamos pensamientos. Adoptamos una misma misión y disfrutamos la riqueza de nuestra identidad como un solo cuerpo. Fuimos, somos y seremos historia para contar, llena de recuerdos para revivir y saborear.*

> We were one… because we shared differences and complemented thoughts. We adopted the same mission and enjoyed the richness of our identity as if we were one body. We went, we are, and we will be, a story ready for telling, full of memories to relive and taste.

References

Anzaldúa, G. (1987). *Bordelands/La frontera: The new mestiza*. San Francisco: Aunt Lute.

Arce, J. (2004). Latino bilingual teachers: The struggle to sustain an emancipatory pedagogy in public school. *International Journal of Qualitative Studies in Education, 17*(2), 227–246.

Aronowitz, S., & Giroux, H. A. (1985). *Education under siege: The conservative, liberal and radical debate over schooling*. South Hadley, MA: Bergin & Garvey.

Bhabha, H. (1994). *The location of culture*. London: Routledge

Bartolomé, L. I., & Balderrama, M.V. (2001). The need for educators with political and ideological clarity: Providing our children with "the best". In J. J. Halcón & M. de la Luz Reyes (Eds.), *The best for our children: Critical perspectives on literacy for Latino students* (pp. 48–64). New York: Teachers College Press.

Barton, D., & Hamilton, M. (2000). Literacy practices. In D. Barton, M. Hamilton, & R. Ivanic (Eds.), *Situated literacies: Reading and writing in context* (pp. 7–15). London: Routledge.

Brandt, D., & Collins, K. (2002). Limits of the local: expanding perspectives on literacy as a social practice. *Journal of Literacy Research, 34*(3), 337–356.

Chapman, T. (2007). Interrogating classroom relationships and events: Using portraiture and critical race theory in education research. *Educational Researcher, 36*(3), 156–162.

Clark, E. R., & Flores, B. B. (2001). Who am I? The social construction of ethnic identity and self-perceptions in Latino preservice teachers. *The Urban Review, 33*(2), 69–86.

Darling-Hammond, L., & Baratz-Snowden, J. (2005). *A good teacher in every classroom: Preparing the highly qualified teachers our children deserve.* San Francisco: Jossey-Bass.

Darling-Hammond, L., French, J., & Garcia-Lopez, S. P. (Eds.). (2002). *Learning to teach social justice.* New York: Teachers College Press.

Delgado, R., & Stefancic, J. (1993). Critical race theory: An annotated bibliography. *Virginia Law Review, 79*(2), 461–516.

Dyson, A. H. (2001). Writing and children's symbolic repertoires: Development unhinged. In S. B. Neuman & D. Dickinson (Eds.), *Handbook of early literacy research* (pp. 126–141). New York: Guilford.

Elenes, C. A., González, F. E., Delgado Bernal, D., & Villenas, S. A. (2001). Introduction: Chicana/Mexicana feminist pedagogies: *Consejos, respeto, y educación* in everyday life, *International Journal of Qualitative Studies in Education, 14*(5), 595–602.

Fránquiz, M. E., & Salazar, M. (2004). The transformative potential of humanizing pedagogy: Addressing the diverse needs of Chicano/Mexicano students. *The High School Journal, 87*(4), 36–53.

Fránquiz, M. E., & Reyes de la Luz (1998). Creating inclusive learning communities through English language acts. *Language Arts 75*(3), 210–220.

Graves, D. H. (1983). *Writing: Teachers and children at work.* Portsmouth, NH: Heinemann.

Graves, D., and Hansen, J. (1983). The author's chair. *Language Arts, 60*, 176–183.

Gutierrez, K. D., Baquedano-López, P., & Tejeda, C. (1999). Rethinking diversity: Hybridity and hybrid language practices in the third space. *Mind, Culture, and Activity, 6*(4), 286–303.

Heath, S. B. (1983). *Ways with words: Language, life, and work in communities and classrooms.* New York: Cambridge University Press.

Holland, D., Lachicotte, W., Skinner, D., & Cain, C. (1998). *Identity and agency in cultural worlds.* Cambridge, MA: Harvard University Press.

Hornberger, N. (1989). Continua of biliteracy. *Review of Educational Research, 59*, 271–296.

Hornberger, N. H., & Skilton-Sylvester, E. (2000). Revisiting the continua of biliteracy: International and critical perspectives. *Language and Education, 14*(2), 96–122.

Jewitt, C., & Kress, G. (Eds.). (2003). *Multimodal literacy.* New York: Peter Lang.

Labbo, L. D., & Field, S. L. (1999). Journey boxes: Telling the story of place, time and culture with photographs, literature and artifacts. *The Social Studies, 90*(4), 177–182.

Luke, A. (2000). Critical literacy in Australia. *Journal of Adolescent and Adult Literacies, 43*(5), 448–461.

Mercado, C., & Moll, L. C. (2000). Student agency through collaborative research in Puerto Rican communities. In S. Nieto (Ed.), *Puerto Rican students in U.S. schools* (pp. 297–329). Mahwah, NJ: Erlbaum.

Moll, L. C., Amanti, C., Neff, D., & González, N. (1992). Funds of knowledge for teaching: Using a qualitative approach to connect homes and classrooms. *Theory into Practice, 31,* 132–141

Moll, L. C., & Arnot-Hopffer, E. A. (2005). Sociocultural competence in teacher education. *Journal of Teacher Education, 56*(3), 242–247.

New London Group. (1996). A pedagogy of multiliteracies: Designing social futures. *Harvard Educational Review, 66*(1), 60–92.

Nieto, S. (2000). Puerto Rican students in U.S. schools: A brief history. In S. Nieto (Ed.), *Puerto Rican students in U.S. schools* (pp. 5–37). Mahwah, NJ: Erlbaum.

Pérez, B. (2003). *Becoming biliterate: A study of two-way bilingual immersion education.* New York: Routledge.

Reyes, M. de la Luz (2001). Unleashing possibilities: Biliteracy in the primary grades. In M. de la Luz Reyes & J. Halcon (Eds.), *The best for our children: Critical perspectives on literacy for Latino students* (pp. 96–121). New York: Teachers College Press.

Ruiz, R. (1984). Orientations in language planning. *The Journal for the National Association of Bilingual Education, 8*(2), 15–34.

Sheets, R. H. (2004). Preparation and development of teachers of color. *International Journal of Qualitative Studies in Education, 17*(2),163–166.

Soja, E. W. (1996). *Thirdspace: Journeys to Los Angeles and other real-and-imagined places.* Malden, MA: Blackwell.

Street, B. (1984). *Literacy in theory and practice.* New York: Cambridge University Press.

Street, B. (1988). Literacy practices and literacy myths. In R. Saljo (Ed.), *The written word: Studies in literate thought and action* (pp. 59–72). New York: Springer-Verlag Press.

Tello, J. (1994). *Cara y corazón, face and heart: A family-strengthening, rebalancing and community mobilization process.* San Antonio, TX: National Latino Children's Institute.

Tucker, G. R. (2005). Innovative language education programmes for heritage language students: The special case of Puerto Ricans. *The International Journal of Bilingual Education and Bilingualism, 8*(2&3), 188–195.

Vélez-Ibañez, C. G., & Greenberg, J. B. (1992) Formation and transformation of funds of knowledge among U.S.-Mexican households. *Anthropology & Education Quarterly, 23*(4), 313–335.

Zentella, A. C. (1997). Returned migration, language and identity; Puerto Rican bilinguals in dos worlds/two mundos. In A. Darder, D. Torres, & H. Gutierrez (Eds.), *Latinos and education: A critical reader* (pp. 302–318). New York: Routledge.

Section II

Contexts for Language Learning

SECTION EDITORS
DONNA E. ALVERMANN, CHRISTINE A. MALLOZZI, AND CHERYL A. McLEAN

Context matters. Though not a new idea, it is one that bears special attention in an audit culture, or audit society, such as the one in which we presently live and work. In the few short years between the appearance of the second edition of the *Handbook of Research on Teaching the English Language Arts* and this third edition, public and private sectors worldwide have witnessed a persistent rise in calls for accountability and objectivity in measurement. These calls engulf us as a field, and, regardless of our personal values and purposes, they earmark what will count as language and literacy education in any given context. As Hodkinson (2004) noted, an audit culture "thrives upon the assertion that subjectivity can be tamed, so that research quality, teaching quality, the effectiveness of learning and 'value for money' can be objectively determined and un-problematically demonstrated" (p. 17). Cognizant of the demands of an audit culture, the chapter authors in this section provide varying degrees of critique and enthusiasm for "what works" in the current context of teaching the English language arts. Their nuanced understandings of the range of contexts that shape and are shaped by an audit culture provide diversity in reflecting the communities of practice they call home or simply represent. Regardless of the perspective taken, the chapter authors in this section are clear on one point: undeniably, context matters.

Lesley Mandel Morrow and Susan Dougherty explore the bases for their argument that a child-centered approach and a skills-based approach to early literacy education are neither separate nor distinct from one another. Drawing from philosophical and research literatures steeped in developmental psychology, linguistics, sociocultural interaction, and human cognition, they offer a comprehensive literacy instruction model that in their words "might be satisfactory" to adherents of both approaches.

Dorothy Strickland and Dianna Townsend describe how learners develop as readers and writers in the early and middle elementary years. They acknowledge that literacy development is more inclusive than reading and writing,

but for the purpose of this chapter, they concentrate on the challenges that readers and writers face as they engage with varied types of texts. Their recommendations for policy and practice are informed by the interplay of individual differences and varied text offerings.

Joyce Many, Mary Ariail, and Dana Fox focus their attention on English language arts teaching and learning in the middle grades. Emphasizing the need for teachers to take into account that school-based literacy is mediated in part by young people's ability to make connections to their lives outside of school, the three co-authors draw implications from the research on social practices affecting literacy learning, and in particular, the importance of young adult literature.

Tom Bean and Helen Harper explore historical and contemporary factors that influence the teaching of English language arts in the high school years. The untimely passing of Helen Harper has left a void in the literacy research community. Fortunate are those who have acces to Helen's co-authored chapter in this handbook—a chapter that was very special to her, according to her partner and co-author, Tom Bean. In this chapter, they illustrate through research and policy initiatives how certain factors (e.g., demographic changes, changes in English as a subject, and multiple literacies) both constrain and enable a teacher's ability to reach today's students. They also explore the tensions and ambivalences that define what is and is not possible in teaching high school English.

Ernest Morrell explores how educators have accounted for various demographic influences in their efforts to design and implement context specific literacy instruction. Using popular culture, sociocultural language pedagogies, and youth participatory action research, educators have successfully accommodated these demographic influences. However, as Morrell points out, the challenge is to engage in what he calls "powerful teaching" as a means of addressing the age-old issue of low expectations.

William Muth and Kristen Perry describe the social,

economic, and cultural flux that situates certain adult literacy practices in order to demonstrate the role that literacy plays in mediating this unrest. They intentionally mark the duality of two stances—a reductive one and a holistic one—and then map three sub-fields (literacy-proficiency discourse, workplace literacy, and English language learners) as a means of putting both stances to work.

Cynthia Brock, Fenice Boyd, and Julie Pennington, examine how variations in spoken and written language influence teachers' attitudes, beliefs, literacy practices, and, ultimately, students' learning. Tabled data on the studies they review along with the types of positioning (accountive, second order, and self) reflected in the studies provide insight into various contexts for teaching the English language arts. Among other implications, the authors call for teachers and students to develop bi-dialectical expertise.

Jeanne Paratore and David Yaden use the U.S. Department of Education's Even Start program as both an entry point and backdrop for their review of the literature on family literacy. After discussing the national evaluations of Even Start, they examine the impact of different types of home literacy activities on children's early and later literacy development, as well as the impact of other home literacy programs that contain some but not all of Even Start's components.

Lalitha Vasudevan and Kelly Wissman explore the communicative, composing, interactional, and dissemination practices in "out-of-school literacies"—a term they question but use to frame research involving young people whose literate identities in school often belie their out-of-school literate lives. Although they discuss bridging in- and out-of-school literacies, they caution against doing so uncritically. They also reflect on ways of re-imagining and transforming institutional contexts for learning.

Allan Luke, Radha Iyer, and Catherine Doherty establish that print and digital literacies set conditions for globalization that challenge the teaching of language. The authors use the paradigms of development, hegemony, and New Literacies to analyse the increasingly complex explanations of literacy and globalization in relation to the other. They find that not only is globalization linked to literacy as context, globalization is an object of literacy and a means for literacy.

In sum, the authors in this section invite us to consider a range of sites for teaching and learning (contemporary classrooms and grade levels, workplaces, and out-of-school communities), approaches (child-centered, skills-based), learners (language learners, children, youth, and adults), and communities (literacy, ethnic/racial, and immigrant). They remind us that context matters and that, ultimately, an audit culture is only as successful as its ability to tap into situated contexts and effectively respond to the society it is intended to serve.

Reference

Hodkinson, P. (2004). Research as a form of work: Expertise, community and methodological objectivity. *British Educational Research Journal, 30*(1), 9–26.

6

Early Literacy Development

Merging Perspectives That Influence Practice

LESLEY MANDEL MORROW AND SUSAN DOUGHERTY

This chapter reviews the issues surrounding the types of literacy instruction deemed appropriate in preschool and kindergarten. We will discuss two major perspectives and how their practice evolved influenced by research, theory and policy. We will identify the characteristics of each perspective. Then we explore whether the two could blend to create a comprehensive model that might be satisfactory to the different groups.

The *child-centered* approach in early childhood literacy education has been the most widely accepted. Within this approach preschool and kindergarten are viewed as places for social, emotional, physical growth, and natural intellectual development. Those who adhere to the child-centered approach think that learning is best prompted by exploring and experimenting in playful environments. Children also learn to self-regulate to prepare for more formal school. The proponents of the child-centered approach refer to their instruction as "developmentally appropriate practice."

The second approach, which we refer to as a *skills-based* model, involves systematic explicit teaching of literacy. This approach views preschool and kindergarten as a time when children are ready to learn the early reading and writing skills that will improve literacy achievement in the future (Hart & Risley, 1999; Barnett, 1998). Those who follow the child-centered model find it difficult to embrace a skills-based approach with young children. They view explicit teaching of skills in early literacy as a push down curriculum where kindergarten becomes first grade and preschool like kindergarten. Those who embrace the skills-based model view the child-centered approach as wasting precious time for learning.

Child-Centered Models

Philosophers, theorists, psychologists, and educators have addressed learning in early childhood and what is appropriate educational practice. Their ideas respond to the question of whether learning is primarily a result of nature or nurture or a combination of both. All have implications for planning early literacy instruction. Jean-Jacques Rousseau (1962/1762) and Johann Heinrich Pestalozzi (Rusk & Scotland, 1979) strongly recommended that a child's early education be natural; this meant avoiding contrived instruction and instead allowing children to learn through their own interest and curiosity. Pestalozzi did however combine natural elements for learning with a bit of informal instruction since he felt that it was necessary for teachers to create conditions in which the learning process would grow. Friedrich Froebel (1974) specified the importance of playing-to-learn, but it required adult guidance and a planned environment. He designed a curriculum for young children, which included materials involving sensory experiences that children would have the opportunity to manipulate. When playing with these materials, children learned about them by using psychomotor skills and language to discuss shape, color, size, smell, measurement and comparison. He coined the term "kindergarten," which means children's garden. He viewed the child as a seed that needed to be tended to by the gardener, or in this case the teacher and then he/she would thrive.

John Dewey's (1966) philosophy of early childhood education led to the concept of the child-centered curriculum built around the interests of children. He agreed with Froebel that children learn best through play and in real-life settings. He maintained that social interactions encourage learning. Dewey rejected the idea of teaching skills as an end unto themselves. He also believed that learning is maximized through integrating content areas. Dewey influenced programs in early childhood throughout the twentieth-century and his influence is seen in classrooms today. Perhaps the most salient example of the Deweyian philosophy is the "center." Early childhood classrooms often have different content area centers where children experiment with the materials there. For example, a science center might have a water-play table, plants, and magnets. The math center could have a scale, tactile numbers, and counting rods. The centers were based on a theme that children chose to study such as animals. As a result, materials in art, music, play, math, science, social studies and the language arts would revolve around the topic of animals. The instruction of reading and writing was embedded in activities such as stories written and read were about animals. There would be discussion and conversation about animals, and art and music related to the theme. Classrooms organized based on Dewey's philosophy lacked formal skill instruction. Instead, these classrooms were rich with materials and activities allowing children to explore their interests and learn through purposeful play.

These philosophers and theorists strongly influenced what preschools and kindergartens look like. During the time they developed their ideas, there was little controversy about the child-centered approach.

Policies Effecting Preschool and Kindergarten Instruction The first federal policy that had an impact on preschool education was passed in 1965 under President Johnson as part of extensive legislation related to education (see Shanahan's chapter 22, this volume). This legislation, which was passed during the civil rights movement, provided funding for preschools for disadvantaged children. The program was called Head Start, and the guidelines followed the child-centered model. The program was established to help children become ready for school socially, emotionally, and physically. The curriculum emphasized good nutrition, general health habits such as brushing teeth and hand washing as well as learning self-regulation. At the same time the National Association for the Education of Young Children (NAEYC) became the main accreditation organization for independent preschools in the United States. Those within the organization coined the phrase Developmentally Appropriate Practice. Their philosophy for preschool was also child centered.

Social Constructivist Influences Prominent from the 1960s through the 1980s, the work of social constructivists brought about many changes in instructional practice in early childhood literacy development. Investigators looked at the cognitive development of the child using varied research methodologies. The research was done in diverse cultural, racial, and socioeconomic settings. It was field based, taking place in classrooms and homes rather than in laboratories. This qualitative research where children's literacy behaviors were observed and described enabled us to understand more of the processes involved in becoming literate. It was recognized that in order to acquire skill in oral language, early reading, and writing, children need models to emulate. They needed the support of their families and teachers.

The term "emergent literacy" first used by Marie Clay (1966) changed attitudes and ideas about early childhood strategies for literacy development. Emergent literacy assumes that the child acquires some knowledge about language, reading, and writing before coming to school. Under this view, literacy development is recognized as beginning in the first year of life. There is a dynamic relationship among the communication skills (reading, writing, oral language, and listening) since each influences the other in the course of development. Development occurs in everyday contexts of the home, community, and school through meaningful and functional experiences that require the use of literacy in natural settings. Children at every age possess certain literacy skills, although these skills are not as fully developed or "conventional" in the sense that they match mature use of literacy skills (Baumann, Hoffman, Duffy-Hester, & Ro, 2000). For example, emergent literacy acknowledges a child's scribble marks on a page as rudimentary writing, even if not one letter is discernible. The child who knows the difference between scribble writing and drawings has some sense of the difference between writing and illustrating. Literacy development approached in this manner accepts children at any level of literacy they are functioning and provides a program for instruction based on individual needs. The emergent literacy perspective exposes children to books and writing early; it is a child-centered approach with more emphasis on problem solving than on direct instruction of skills. The emergent literacy perspective is similar to the whole language philosophy of how children learn to read. Whole language addresses all children at all ages; emergent literacy is only addressing beginning readers. The similarities are evident however.

In both whole-language and emergent literacy, learning is designed to be meaningful and functional. The purpose and significance are drawn from the child's life experiences at home or those created in school. Commercial materials do not dictate the instructional program. Literacy learning is consciously embedded throughout the curriculum in the whole school day (Collins & Shaeffer, 1997; Dunn, Beach, & Konto, 1994; Fingon, 2005). Literacy activities are purposefully integrated into the learning of content-area subjects such as art, music, social studies, science, math, and play. Equal emphasis is placed on teaching reading, writing, listening, and oral language, because all help to create a literate individual. Varied genres of children's literature are the main source of reading material for instruction. Teachers create literacy-rich classrooms environments with materials for reading and writing in centers. Learning is individualized, with self-selection and choices of literacy activities. Rather than teaching lessons in literacy, teachers are more likely to provide models of literacy activities for children to emulate. Children learn through practice by engaging in long periods of independent reading and writing. In classrooms using a holistic approach, skills are taught when they are relevant; for example, when studying a theme such as "Healthy Habit," the teacher may focus on the initial consonant "h" since it is being used in context. Some who used whole language thought that skills were not to be taught in any systematic way and that children would acquire them by being immersed in experiences with writing and the reading of children's literature. This did cause some problems for children who needed more explicit instruction (Morrow, 2009).

Jean Piaget's theories (Piaget & Inhelder, 1969) had a strong influence on early childhood eduction. Piaget believed that a child acquires knowledge by interacting with the world and constantly changing and reorganizing their own knowledge. Piaget stressed that learning occurs when children engage with peers and adults in a social setting. Educators who incorporated Piaget's theories in curricula for early childhood education have designed child-centered programs that look very much like what Pestalozzi or Froebel might have created. The setting has real-life materials, including the opportunities to play, experiment, and use language. A Piagetian preschool curriculum emphasizes decision-making, problem-solving, using self-discipline, goal-setting, planning and evaluating one's own activities with teachers and peers. Piaget's theory interpreted into classroom practice advocates using centers that involve children in the following cognitive activities: *Language Development*: talking, listening to stories, describing, etc.; *Classifying*: children describe attributes of objects, notice sameness and differences, sort, match, etc.; *Seriating*: children arrange objects by color, size, shape, etc.; *Representing in Different Modalities*: learning about something in many different ways (For example, to learn about an apple the child can eat it, make it into apple sauce, draw it, write and read the word apple, and sing a song about apples, etc.); and *Spatial Relations*: children are asked to put things together, take things apart, rearrange things, reshape things, see things from a different point of view, describe direction, and distance.

Piaget agreed that young children should use their curiosity and spontaneity to learn. Lev S. Vygotsky's general theory of intellectual development, like Piaget's, suggests that learning occurs as children acquire new concepts or schemas. A schema is a mental structure in which we store information we know. We store information about concepts or schemas and call them to mind to predict, generalize, and infer. According to Vygotsky, mental functions are acquired through social relationships. To extend or learn new tasks children must interact with others. Children need to talk about new ideas in order to understand them. Parents and teachers provide the language children need to help them solve a problem and internalize new concepts. The child needs a more knowledgeable person to scaffold and model the new ideas by showing children how to complete the task. Scaffolding discussions give information about finishing a task, provide advice, and directs a child's attention to what they need to know. Vygotsky speaks of the time when the child is almost capable of performing the new task alone as the "zone of proximal development." This is when a child can do some parts of a task, but not all. This is a sensitive time for learning and gowth. It is important for the adult to step back at this time and allow the child to perform and practice the new skill so it becomes internalized (Vygotsky, 1978).

Skills-Based Models

The idea of a skills-based model for literacy instruction in preschool and kindergarten is a difficult concept for those who believe in a child-centered approach. The two models in their extreme form deal with literacy instruction in completely different ways.

Judging from the professional literature from the early 1900s, little attention was paid to a child's literacy development before he or she entered first grade. A strong influence on reading instruction came from developmental psychologists like Gesell (1925) who suggested that maturation was the most important factor in learning to read. Preschool and kindergarten teachers generally ignored reading instruction. Instead, the influences of Pestalozzi and Froebel were evident in their classrooms with stories read to them, play, exploration, songs and discussions based on themes. Methods were child centered with great concern for the social, emotional, and physical development.

Influenced by the climate of the times, Morphett and Washburne (1931) supported the postponement of reading instruction until a child was developmentally "old enough." Their research concluded that children with a mental age of 6 years 6 months made better progress on a test of reading achievement than younger children. This correlational study was taken as support for the postponing of reading instruction until a child was "old enough." But although many educators believed that maturation was the precursor to literacy, others grew uncomfortable with simply waiting for children to become ready to read. They didn't advocate formal reading instruction in early childhood, but they did begin providing experiences they believed would help children become ready for reading.

Reading Readiness The growing popularity of testing during the 1930s and 1940s affected early childhood reading instruction. Generally, the standardized tests served the prevailing concept of maturation by indicating if a child had reached the maturity he or she needed to learn to read. The skills tested were thought to be elements that would help children become ready to read. Instead of waiting for a child's natural maturation to unfold, educators focused on nurturing that maturation through instruction with a set of skills identified as prerequisites for reading. The concept gained strength when publishers of reading materials capitalized on the idea of reading readiness skills and began to prepare materials for preschool and kindergarten that would make children ready to read. Skills associated with reading readiness include: (a) *auditory discrimination*: the ability to identify and differentiate familiar sounds, similar sounds, rhyming words, and the sounds of letters; (b) *visual discrimination*: including color recognition, shape, and letter identification; (c) *visual motor skills*: such as left to right eye progression, cutting on a line with scissors and coloring within the lines of a picture; and (d) *large motor skills*: such as skipping, hopping, and walking on a line.

Early childhood literacy instruction based on the reading

readiness implies that one prepares for literacy by acquiring a set of prescribed skills. These skills are taught systematically on the assumption that all children are at a similar level of development when they come to preschool or kindergarten. The system does not consider experiences or information that a child may already have about literacy.

Slavin, a well-known behaviorist, fostered skill-based models of direct instruction for young children (1977). His research had a strong effect on classroom practice. He suggested that we learn through imitation, association and through conditioning. The conditioning consists of a series of systematic steps that are repeated so that the response becomes automatic. Skinner (1954) hypothesized that human learning is not automatic and unintentional. People themselves operate on their environment to produce learning and when given positive reinforcement for a desired behavior the frequency of use of that behavior increased. Skinner's point of view emphasized that skills are acquired in a series of steps, small enough to avoid failure and frustration, with rewards at each level.

Learning with a behaviorist perspective includes an organized program presented in a systematic and direct manner. Learning requires direct instruction, time on task, structure, routines, and practice. Behaviorist programs are concerned about the acquisition of skills, with little time or concern for social, emotional, or physical development. The material used in behaviorist programs are rated according to difficulty, can include programmed sequential lessons, and can have guides for teachers which include objectives for learning, the outcomes expected and a script that the teacher recites to students.

Maria Montessori (1965) believed that children needed early, orderly, systematic training in mastering one skill after another. She created and supplied her teaching environment with materials for learning specific objectives. The use of the materials is modeled by the teacher and then provides the source of learning for the child. Children use the manipulatives to learn and because the materials are self- correcting, the children are able to determine their own errors and make corrections independently. All materials in the classroom are stored in their own containers, on a particular shelf, and in order of difficulty. In the Montessori curriculum, children's natural curiosity and exploration are of less concern than their ability to work with specific materials to achieve a particular goal done correctly. Unstructured play is not important in the Montessori model, instead work is very important for achieving goals. However, the materials that Montessori created are manipulative. As the children work at accomplishing a goal, the tasks are interesting and playful.

By the turn of the 21st century, the explicit teaching approach in kindergarten classrooms was bolstered by research dealing with phonics and phonological awareness. Research by Juel (1989), determined that as children first begin to experiment with reading and writing, they need to focus on the sounds that make up words. Children need to know that words are made up of individual sounds. The ability to segment these sounds out of the words and blend them together is called phonemic awareness. Studies found that phonemic awareness instruction in preschool, kindergarten and first grade strengthens reading achievement. Phonemic awareness is also thought to be a precursor to phonics instruction (Byrne & Fielding-Barnsley, 1993, 1995; Stanovich, 1986). With phonemic awareness, children then learn phonics which includes:

1. alphabetic understanding (knowing that words are composed of letters), and
2. Cryptoanalytic intent or sound–symbol relationships (knowing that there is a relationship between printed letters and spoken sound).

Research also suggests that knowledge of sound–symbol relationships, or phonics, is necessary for success in learning to read and write (Anthony & Lonigan, 2004; Lonigan, 2006). Those who propose a behaviorist or explicit-skills approach for literacy instruction have argued for a strong phonemic awareness program in preschool and both phonemic awareness and beginning phonics in kindergarten. The materials for instruction are systematic and provide direct instruction with scripted manuals for teachers to use.

Based on the research discussed, changes in early literacy instruction occurred in the mid-1990s. Some moved away from a totally child-centered spontaneous approach and learning to read and write became more systematic. Meeting standards, and accounting for skills acquired became a major concern. It is apparent that success in early literacy is crucial for survival. Those who are literate earn more than those who aren't. Those who are literate are less likely to have social problems or get in trouble with the law. Those who are literate are less likely to be chronically ill. If a child's language is not appropriately developed at age 3 and he/she does not attend a quality preschool with a language and literacy focus, it is likely that this child will have trouble learning to read. If a child does not learn to read in by the end of third grade, we can predict that this youngster is likely to drop out of school. Ninety percent of the children who do not read on level at the end of grade 3 will never reach grade level. Preschool and kindergarten are the time when literacy gaps can be closed and those who are at risk can catch up. As a result of these facts, early childhood is increasingly seen as a vitally important time for learning phonemic awareness, beginning phonics, listening and beginning reading comprehension, increasing vocabulary and concept development (Hart & Risley, 1999).

The Influence of No Child Left Behind and Scientifically Based Research

The results from the National Reading Panel Report (2000, NRP) and the National Early Literacy Report (2008, NELP) are from scientifically based research. The federal government called for states to create rigorous standards for literacy development for kindergarten to Grade 3, and in many states preschool literacy standards are created or are still being created. The standards are based on the NRP report (2002) and the NELP report (2008).

The NELP report (2008) and the NRP report (2000) present findings about the most effective strategies for teaching children to read. The NRP panel reviewed more than 100,000 studies to come up with their results. The results of the report indicate that teaching the following elements are crucial to learn for reading success in kindergarten through Grade 3:

- Phonemic awareness
- Phonics
- Vocabulary
- Comprehension
- Fluency

The NELP report also studied existing scientifically based research to identify the skills and abilities of young children from birth through age 5 that predict later achievement in reading. The variables the panel identified include:

- Oral language development: expressive, receptive, and vocabulary
- Alphabetic code: alphabet knowledge, phonological and phonemic awareness, invented spelling
- Print knowledge: environmental print, concepts about print, writing one's name
- Other skills: rapid naming of letters and numbers, visual memory, and visual perceptual abilities

As a result of the NRP report, the NELP report models for preschool and kindergarten instruction are still being discussed. Many advocates of the child-centered models find the new guidelines inappropriate for preschool and kindergarten programs. Several large scales studies that observed and described what was happening in child-centered preschools found that in preschools where social, emotional, physical and language development and the learning of self regulation skills were considered important: 35% of the time was spent in routines such as lining up, meals, bathroom, cleaning up, etc.; 32% of the children's time was spent in free choice activities and center time; 23% of the time was spent in whole group instruction and 6% of the time was used for small group instruction. These findings were considered indicative of a lack of focus on the development of academic skills, which are typically best addressed in small groups, particularly with young children. Studies that examined the time spent on the development of skills found the following: 12% of time was spent on literacy; 6% on math; 1% on writing; 8% on science; 13% on social studies; 9% on art and music; 7% on large motor activities, and the remaining 44% of time was spent on activities that related to none of the skill areas. In a study that looked at the extent of teacher-child verbal interaction in preschool, which is important in the fostering of language development, it was found that: 8% of verbal interaction was elaborated; 18% minimal; 1% routine and the remaining 73% of the time no teacher-child verbal interactions occurred (Bowman, Donovan, & Burns, 2000; Shonkoff & Phillips, 2000; Dickinson & Tabors, 2001). Those concerned with the academic preparation of children in preschools view this data as highly problematic.

Do the theories and research discussed contribute to a way we could look at literacy development in early childhood that would satisfy those who hold a child-centered orientation and those who are in favor of a skills-based model?

We believe this is possible when we look at the most important elements from each model.

1. Concern for individual needs and level of development: physical, social, emotional, and intellectual
2. Concern for prepared environments in which learning can take place
3. Emphasis on learning and on teaching
4. Emphasis on social interaction with supportive adults who scaffold learning
5. Focus on learning through real experiences in meaningful and natural settings
6. Focus on learning in settings with explicit but appropriate teaching
7. Focus on actively engaging students in learning using manipulative materials and experiences that are functional and interesting
8. Practicing and repeating skills learned

A Comprehensive Literacy Instruction Model

The following documents help to define a combination of child-centered and skills-based instruction for young children. One is published by the International Reading Association and the National Association for the Education of Young Children entitled *Learning to Read and Write: Developmentally Appropriate Practices* (1998), the other two are position statement by the International Reading Association, one entitled *Using Multiple Methods of Beginning Reading Instruction* (1999) and the other, *Literacy Development in the Preschool Years* (2005). These documents suggest that no single method or single combination of methods can successfully teach all children to read. Teachers must know the children they teach from a social, emotional, physical, and intellectual perspective. They also must know about the many methods for reading and writing instruction. Only then can they develop a comprehensive plan for teaching reading to meet individual needs. A comprehensive approach or one that blends the two models discussed includes careful selection of the best theories available and use of learning strategies matched to the learning styles of individual children (Morrow & Tracey, 1997). According to Pressley (1998), skills-based, explicit teaching is a good start for constructivist problem-solving activities, and constructivist activities permit consolidation and elaboration of skills. One method does not preclude or exclude the other. A comprehensive perspective is not a random combination of strategies. A teacher may select strategies from different learning theories. One child, for example, may be an auditory learner and benefit from instruction in phonemic awareness and phonics; another child, whose strength may be kinesthetic, needs manipulatives to learn. A comprehensive approach is a thoughtful and mature approach. It focuses more on what is important for individual children than on the latest fad in literacy instruction. Comprehensive instruction is grounded in a rich model of literacy learning that encompasses both the elegance and complexity of the reading and language arts processes. Such a model acknowledges the importance of both forms (phonemic awareness, phonics, mechanics, etc.) and function (comprehension, purpose, meaning) of the literacy processes and recognizes that learning occurs most effectively in a whole–part–whole context. This type of instruction is characterized by meaningful literacy activities that provide children with both the skill and desire to become proficient and lifelong literacy learners.

In a preschool that fosters a comprehensive model, a rich literacy environment and content area centers filled with interesting materials for exploration and experimentation will be present. Books and paper and writing utensils will be provided in the centers. In addition to times for problem solving and play there will be a time during the day when children meet with teachers in small groups for explicit instruction based on need. The instruction will however be developmentally appropriate, for example, learning letters will begin with letters in the child's name. The child will be given magnetic letters that match those in his/her name and will be shown how to put them into the right order. The child might also find a letter in their name that is in his/her friend's name or copy the letter. For a child who is not yet phonologically aware, instruction might involve clapping the number of syllables in his/her name and of others in the classroom. Similarly, children learn sight words by having a collection of their favorite "Very Own Words" that are drawn from the child's environment. One child's words might include his Mom's name with her picture, the word *football* with a picture since it is his favorite sport, and McDonald's since he likes to eat there. While these types of small group, explicit lessons are congruent with the skills-based approach to early education, other parts of the day in the comprehensive preschool program will be drawn from the traditional child-centered approach. Thematic teaching, art, music and play will be incorporated throughout the day. During these times of the day, the teacher will continue to seek opportunities to purposefully teach literacy skills.

Final Comments

The research, theory, philosophies, and methods that have influenced early education through the years have helped us to understand that children learn in situations that are purposeful. They develop literacy in social contexts and through interaction with adults and other children. The instruction they receive should reflect upon their background knowledge and be sensitive to a child's stage of development socially, emotionally, physically, and intellectually. We have also learned that skill-based literacy instruction or the systematic teaching of skills in an organized fashion is a necessary for literacy development. When teaching, the following features are essential if learning is to occur:

- Explicit modeling and scaffolding of lessons to be learned
- Guided practice
- Independent practice
- Time on task
- Structure and routines
- Differentiation of instruction to meet individual needs
- Feedback for children
- Time to explore
- Time to experiment
- Time to collaborate in social settings
- Time for problem-solving

Literacy development begins at birth and continues throughout the early childhood years. The philosophies, theories, research and policy presented here suggest there is no one best approach to literacy instruction in the early years. Selecting the right format for each child is how we will be successful. We learn from this review that quality instruction takes place in literacy-rich environments, with social interaction, peer collaboration, and whole-class, small-group, and individual learning experiences. Those from the skills-based tradition have shown us that children must be taught explicitly during small group instruction to meet individual needs. On the other hand, those from the child-centered tradition have demonstrated the benefits of exploration and problem solving. The work of child-centered theorists and educators suggest that literacy needs to be taught in an integrated fashion—therefore, oral language, reading, writing, listening and viewing should be taught in an integrated system. Learning must be functional for children and related to real-life experiences so it is meaningful. Finally, it is clear that literacy activities that are integrated into content areas through thematic instruction create enthusiasm. We advocate, then, a comprehensive approach to literacy instruction in the early childhood years. This approach will incorporate aspects of both the child-centered and skills-based tradition and, thus, will support both the social and emotional growth and academic preparation of young children.

References

Anthony, J. L., & Lonigan, C. J. (2004). The nature of phonological awareness: Converging evidence from four studies of preschool and early grade school children. *Journal of Educational Psychology*, *96*(1), 1–18.

Barnett, W. S. (1998). Long-term effects on cognitive development and school success. In W. S. Barnett & S. S. Boocock (Eds.), *Early care and education for children in poverty: Promise, programs, and long-term results* (pp. 11–44). Albany: State University of New York Press.

Baumann, J. F., Hoffman, J. V., Duffy-Hester, A. M., & Ro, J. M. (2000). The first R: Reading in the early grades. *Reading Teacher, 54*, 84–98.

Bowman, B. T., Donovan, S., & Burns, M. S. (2000). *Eager to learn: Educating our preschoolers.* Washington, DC: National Academies Press.

Byrne, B., & Fielding-Barnsley, R. (1993). Evaluation of a program to teach phonemic awareness to young children: A one-year follow-up. *Journal of Educational Psychology, 85*, 104–111.

Byrne, B., & Fielding-Barnsley, R. (1995). Evaluation of a program to teach phonemic awareness to young children: A two- and three-year follow-up and a new preschool trial. *Journal of Educational Psychology, 87*, 488–503.

Clay, M. M. (1966). *Emergent reading behavior.* Unpublished doctoral dissertation, University of Auckland, New Zealand.

Collins, N. L. D., & Shaeffer, M.B. (1997). Look, listen, and learn to read. *Young Children, 52*(5), 65–67.

Dewey, J. (1966). *Democracy and education.* New York: First Press.

Dickinson, D. K., & Tabors, P. O. (2001). *Beginning literacy with language: Young children learning at home and school.* Baltimore: Paul H. Brookes.

Dunn, L., Beach, S., & Konto, S. (1994). Quality of early literacy environment in day care and children's development. *Journal of Research in Childhood Education, 9*(1), 24–34.

Fingon, J. (2005). The words that surround us. *Teaching PreK-8, 35*, 54–56.

Froebel, F. (1974). *The education of man.* Clifton, NJ: Augustus M. Kelly.

Gesell, A. (1925). *The mental growth of the preschool child.* New York: Macmillan.

Hart, B., & Risley, T. R. (1999). *The social world of children learning to talk.* Baltimore: Paul H. Brookes.

International Reading Association and the National Association for the Education of Young Children. (1998). *Learning to Read and Write: Developmentally Appropriate Practices.* Newark, DE: International Reading Association.

International Reading Association. (1999). Position statement: *Using multiple methods of beginning reading instruction.* Newark, DE: International Reading Association

International Reading Association. (2005). Position statement: *Literacy-Instruction in the preschool years.* Newark, DE: International Reading Association.

Juel, C. (1989). The role of decoding in early literacy instruction and assessment. In L. Morrow & J. Smith (Eds.), *Assessment for instruction in early literacy* (pp. 135–154). Upper Saddle River, NJ: Prentice Hall.

Lonigan, C. (2006). Conceptualizing phonological processing skills in prereaders. *Handbook of Early Literacy Research, 2*, 77–89.

Montessori, M. (1965). *Spontaneous activity in education.* New York: Schocken Books.

Morrow, L. M. (2009). *Literacy development in the early years: Helping children read and write* (6th ed.). Needham, MA: Allyn and Bacon/Pearson.

Morrow, L. M., & Tracey, D. (1997). Strategies for phonics instruction in early childhood classrooms. *Reading Teacher, 50*(8), 2–9.

Morphett, M. V., & Washburne, C. (1931). When should children begin to read? *Elementary School Journal, 31*, 496–508.

National Center for Family Literacy. (2004). Report of the *National Early Literacy Panel.* Washington DC: National Institute for Literacy.

National Reading Panel Report. (2000). *Teaching children to read.* Washington, DC: National Institute of Child Health and Human Development.

Piaget, J., & Inhelder, B. (1969). *The psychology of the child.* New York: Basic Books.

Pressley, M. (1998). *Reading instruction that works: The case for balanced teaching.* New York: Guilford Press.

Rousseau, J. (1962). *Emile* (Ed. & Trans. William Boyd). New York: Columbia University Teachers College. (Original work published 1762)

Rusk, R., & Scotland, J. (1979). *Doctrines of the great educators.* New York: St. Martin's Press.

Shonkoff, J. P., & Phillips, D. A. (Eds.). (2000). *From neurons to neighborhoods: The science of early childhood development. A report of the National Research Councils.* Washington, DC: National Academies Press.

Slavin, R. E. (1997). *Educational psychology: Theory and practice* (5th ed.). Boston: Allyn and Bacon.

Skinner, B. F. (1954). The science of learning and the art of teaching. *Harvard Educational Review, 24*, 86–97.

Stanovich, K. E. (1986). Mathew effects in reading: Some consequences of individual differences in the acquisition of literacy. *Reading Research Quarterly, 21*, 360–407.

Vygotsky, L. S. (1978). *Mind in society: The development of psychological processes.* Cambridge, MA: Harvard University Press.

7

The Development of Literacy in the Elementary School

Dorothy Strickland and Dianna Townsend

Children's literacy development during the elementary school years is the foundation for their academic success and, to an extent, their life success in their later years. While this chapter focuses on reading and writing, we would like to acknowledge the multifaceted nature of literacy development. Speaking, listening, reading and writing are integrated, communicative processes (Langer, 1986; Teale & Yokota, 2000). Contemporary researchers also conceive of literacy as text mediated social practices, which consist of many literacies in many identifiable forms within varying social contexts and under varying conditions, including new technologies (Knobel & Lankshear, 2005). Within these varying social contexts and technologies, oral language is intricately related to reading and writing development. While a rich examination of oral language development is beyond the scope of this chapter, we would be remiss in not emphasizing that oral language functions both as precursor and ongoing support for literacy development across the elementary years.

With this acknowledgement of the complex and multi-layered process that is literacy development, we now turn to reading and writing in the early elementary years. Both kindergarten and early primary grade learners (grades 1–2) and learners in the middle elementary grades that immediately follow (grades 3–5) view reading and writing as being both purposeful and cognitive activities used to help them conceptualize personal experience and world knowledge. This chapter reports what the research says about how children in the early elementary school years develop as readers and writers and what that means for classroom teachers and policy makers. First, we present theory and research on reading and writing in the kindergarten and early primary grades and then in the early middle grades. Next, we explore two critical themes in the research on literary development, individual differences in literacy development, and the challenges that readers and writers face as they confront varied types of texts. Finally, we offer implications and recommendations for policy and practice.

The Primary Years (K–2)

Perspectives on Literacy Learners in the Primary Grades Until the late 1980s, reading readiness was the approach used by most early literacy teachers to provide a foundation for formal literacy instruction, which typically began in first grade. Even then, Teale and Yokota (2000) suggested that reading readiness was pursued by educators along two different paths. Down one path went educators who were convinced that readiness was essentially a result of maturation or "neural ripeness." Down the other path were those who believed that appropriate experiences created readiness or came to accelerate it.

Several decades ago, Lapp and Flood (1978) defined reading readiness as the necessary level of preparation children should attain before beginning formal reading instruction. Alphabet and word recognition, vocabulary knowledge, and visual discrimination were cited as possible predictors of reading readiness. More recently, *Developing Early Literacy: The Report of the National Early Literacy Panel* (National Institute for Literacy, 2008) confirmed that alphabet knowledge, phonological awareness, oral language, and writing/name writing in 4- and 5–year-old children are among the best predictors of later success in literacy achievement. In traditional readiness programs, prescribed skills in these areas are directly taught to get children "ready" to read.

Emergent literacy, on the other hand, looks at both reading and writing (literacy) as they are in the process of emerging in the everyday lives of children from their earliest years (Teale & Sulzby, 1986; Teale & Yokota, 2000). More recent research on the phonological skills of young children indicates that the developmental origins of learning to read begin prior to the onset of formal reading instruction in school (Lonigan, 2006). Thus, when researchers and teachers use the term emergent literacy they are usually referring to children from infancy through kindergarten or first grade (Chapman, 2006).

Writing in the Primary Grades Emergent writing most often refers to both written texts and to other representational forms (Chapman, 2006). There is a strong body of foundational research in this area. According to Sulzby (1985a) and Temple, Nathan, Burris, & Temple (1988), most kindergarteners begin to write by drawing and scribbling. They will write such things as messages, grocery lists, stories and notes, and "pretend read" them to parents, teachers, or peers. As soon as they can write a few letters (e.g., those in their name), they begin to add these and other letter-like marks to their drawings/scribbles, showing that they know writing is not completely arbitrary but that it involves certain kinds of special marks (Clay, 1975). Temple et al. (1988) call this the prephonemic stage. Gentry (1981) notes that the scribbling stage parallels the babbling stage in oral language development.

When their informal exposure to written language through environmental print is augmented by more direct experiences with print such as group composing of text (Hall, 1981) and shared reading interventions (Wasik, 2001; Zevenbergen, Whitehurst, & Zevenbergen, 2003), children begin to internalize the alphabetic principle. They may use one or two letters, usually consonants, to stand for whole words. Temple et al. (1988) call this the early phonemic stage and give the following example: RCRBKDN = Our car broke down. With an accompanying illustration, the message is perfectly understandable, thereby indicating children's early development of the alphabetic principle.

With daily meaningful reading/writing experiences, children move into the letter-name stage in which vowels begin to appear along with prominent consonants (Read, 1986; Temple et al., 1988). By now they know the names of the letters but not necessarily which letters represent which sounds. As active learners, they invent spellings according to their own phonemic rules, for example, "chran" for "train,""yet/yent" for "went," and "pan" for "pen." Soon standard spellings are mixed with invented spellings, and children are said to be in a transitional stage. Throughout the elementary school years, spelling tends to become more standard, but invented spellings can be found at all levels. Furthermore, invented spelling is related to learning to read; Ouellette and Senechal (2008) found that kindergarteners who participated in an invented spelling intervention that included developmentally-appropriate feedback made greater gains in learning to read new words than their peers who participated in a phonological awareness intervention.

However, children do not move through these suggested developmental phases evenly. Some may skip and appear to go from drawing directly to invented spelling. According to Teale and Sulzby (1986), writing development is best thought of as a sociocognitive constructivist process. Rather than being an invariant sequence, children vary in their experiential backgrounds, approaches to learning, abilities, and overall rates of development. Furthermore, different purposes, tasks, and discourse forms also influence children's writing processes.

The interdependence of oral language and literacy development is evident from the earliest years and continues through the grades. Both talking and drawing are necessary adjuncts to writing in kindergarten and Grade 1 (Dyson, 1983; Calkins, 1986). By Grade 2, drawing becomes less necessary, but talking with others, as rehearsal for writing and for feedback on drafts, becomes even more important. Bodrova and Leong (2006) suggest that private speech seems to support young children's writing in several ways. It helps them remember the words they wish to write, to practice voice-to-print correspondence, and to concentrate in ways that promote accurate phonemic representations.

As children mature, their sense of themselves as writers broadens. Seven-year-olds find emotional support in peer review. Manning, Manning, and Hughes (1987) found that personal content dominated the journals of first graders, who wrote about themselves and their feelings and their families and pets. However, given the opportunity, young children can write informational texts and stories and are aware of how they are different (Donovan, 2001; Wollman-Bonilla 2000).

Reading in the Primary Grades Smith (1985) describes reading as an active, constructive process in which one applies different kinds of knowledge (knowledge of the world, the language system, and the content) to make meaning from written language. Ashby and Rayner (2006) agree that reading is much more than an automatic act of object perception. Children come to school able to understand and respond to thousands of spoken words, but their ability to recognize words in print relates to their preschool activities with written language. Most will be able to recognize their names and can quickly learn to read the names of their classmates, signs and labels in their classroom, and a basic vocabulary of common words from language experience and shared book activities (Mason & Au, 1986; Roskos & Christie, 2000). There are, however, significant gaps in vocabulary knowledge among students from different socio-economic status (SES) groups in the elementary years (Hart & Risley, 1995). One model for addressing this gap is Beck and McKeown's (2006) program *Text Talk*; in the context of this program using read-alouds, Beck and McKeown found that rich vocabulary instruction can significantly enhance low-income kindergarteners' and first graders' oral vocabulary knowledge.

In addition to vocabulary knowledge, research has clearly established phonemic awareness as significant in early reading development (e.g., Adams, 1990) and in literacy achievement throughout the elementary school years (Torgeson, Morgan, & Davis, 1992; Schatschneider, Fletcher, Francis, Carlson, & Foorman, 2004). While reading development can indeed be idiosyncratic, stages of reading development have been identified by several scholars. Chall (1983) distinguished between learning to read and reading to learn, two sets of stages that explain children's reading development. In the learning to read stages, children are learning to decode fluently; in the reading to learn stages, children are learning new information from independent reading. Additionally, Weaver (1988) suggested phases that children may go through, similar to those noted in spelling development. In the schema emphasis phase stage, which is compared with the pre-phonemic stage in spelling, children exhibit reading-like behavior, turning pages and "reading" from prior knowledge of story and picture clues. In the semantic/syntactic emphasis phase, which is like the phonemic or invented spelling stage in writing, they continue to use schematic knowledge and picture clues but begin to read some words in context. Miscues at this stage are likely to fit the context semantically and syntactically but may not reflect the actual words on the page, for example "bird" for "canary." Researchers found developmental progressions as children rely on grapho-phonemic cueing systems (Weaver, 1988); engage in quasi-reading (Bussis, Chittenden, Amarel, & Klausner, 1985) and eventually engage in independent reading (Sulzby, 1985b).

The Middle Elementary Years (Grades 3–5)

Perspectives on Literacy Learners in the Middle Elementary Grades Most middle-grade students have mastered the basic skills required to cope with relatively simple texts, such as narratives and uncomplicated informational books. Most can read and carry out simple directions contained in recipes and procedures for constructing models. As they move through the grades, however, intermediate grade children encounter more abstract, complex, and unfamiliar content (Schleppegrell, 2004). At the same time, high stakes tests are often implemented in these grades to hold teachers and children "accountable" for achievement and success (Alvermann, 2002). Ivey (2002) reviewed the research on the literacy needs of middle elementary grade and adolescent learners. The research reveals inconsistencies throughout this grade range between the literacy skills of these young learners and the literacy demands of the school, including: (a) a mismatch between instruction and students' needs, (b) a tension between school literacy versus out-of- school literacy, (c) and a focus on the teaching of content versus the teaching of content literacy. These inconsistencies generally begin at Grade 4.

Writing in the Middle Elementary Grades At the onset of the middle elementary years (i.e., around Grade 3), writing become increasingly more important in the everyday lives of children. Key findings of research on intermediate grade writers indicate that they gradually gain awareness and control of their writing process, draw on multiple sources of information as they write, and include their own experiences, repertoires of knowledge, and social worlds (Calkins, 1994). Intermediate writers focus more on meaning and making connections among ideas (Langer, 1986) and they use writing as a vehicle for personal exploration of ideas and growth (McGinley & Kamberelis, 1992). Children's conceptions of writing also change with age and experience. Bradley (2001) investigated first-grade children's conceptions of writing, concluding that their perceptions

and actions are greatly influenced by what their teachers say about writing. Children defined "good writing" as making sense, demonstrating conventional correctness, and having an acceptable appearance. Likewise, the second-grade children interviewed by Kos and Maslowski (2001) focused on the conventions of writing as qualities of good writing. McCarthey (2001) examined fifth-grade students' notions of good writing; these students focused on the use of imagination, expressiveness, and capacity for a variety of genres. This research, although cross-sectional rather than longitudinal, suggests students' increasing sensitivity to the multiple purposes and genres of writing throughout the elementary school years.

By the age of 10, children can view their writing through the eyes of a reader. Their writings become more multidimensional, and they can shift between narrative and description and narrative and dialogue in one piece. Calkins (1986) suggests that children begin to be able to reread to revise in grades 4 to 6, especially if they are in instructional environments in which they read their pieces to others for reaction and response. She suggests that children gradually move toward holding their own internal conferences as they shift from the concrete approach taken by younger children, who write everything out, to write out only portions of alternative leads, endings, and titles, and simply think about others as they move toward more representational thought. Thus, writing becomes a means of thinking and rethinking. In addition, the ability to comfortably use and combine print, spoken, visual and digital processes in composing a piece of writing is an important aspect of the writing development of today's primary and middle-grade students (Yancey, 2000). Children's enthusiasm for writing with computers is a relatively consistent finding, though researchers suggest that more studies are needed in this area (Kamil, Intrator, & Kim, 2000).

Reading in the Middle Elementary Grades Despite the wide difference in abilities and experiences and the idiosyncratic nature of literacy development itself, research suggests some trends in reading development for children in the middle elementary years. Third graders exhibit a growing independence in reading. Relying heavily on cues in the text, they can figure things out for themselves. However, they see print as literal truth and think that what the text says is correct. Although they can read orally with meaning and expression, they like to read to themselves both for pleasure and information. By this time, most children have internalized several print grammars, both narrative and simple expository, to help them make sense of written language appropriate to their experiential background (Cochrane, Cochrane, Scalena, & Buchanan, 1984; Van Sluys & Tropp Laman, 2006).

Middle-grade students are faced with the task of comprehending an increasing variety of texts in a variety of forms, formats, and genres. In their report on the knowledge base on reading comprehension, the RAND Reading Study Group (RRSG; 2002) defines the term reading comprehension as "the process of simultaneously extracting and constructing meaning through interaction and involvement with written language" (p. 9). The RRSG explains that learning to read well is a long-term developmental process. As they move through the elementary school years, children's ability to comprehend written language may be limited by their prior knowledge or their knowledge of text structures and topics (Mason & Au, 1986). Readers are actively constructing meaning from text, based on what they already know and what the author has written. Serving many purposes, student's background knowledge help them make inferences, summarize, remember, add new knowledge, and make decisions about what is important (McNeil, 1970; National Institute of Child Health and Human Development, 2000).

Vocabulary knowledge is also essential for successful comprehension. Although children do build their vocabulary from explicit instruction, they also add thousands of words each year from their reading of trade books and content area texts. Students learn most new words incidentally through repeated exposures; only about 10% of new words are learned from explicit instruction (Carlisle, 2007). Incidental word learning can occur in many contexts, including independent reading (Nagy, Anderson, & Herman, 1987), but there must be sufficient understanding of other words in the text for students to learn new words (Blachowicz and Fisher, 2000). Biemiller and Slonim (2001), in their seminal work on the size and sequence of vocabulary development, found that typically-achieving students know about 8,400 root words by the fifth grade.

Finally, besides being active readers, children in the middle grades are strategic readers. Meyers and Paris (1978) found that these children are aware of a variety of reading strategies and know how to use them, acquiring metacognitive capabilities as they go through the grades. Babbs and Moe (1983) define metacognition as the ability to monitor one's own thinking. Teachers can actively promote metacognition by modeling comprehension strategies, having children practice them in a variety of situations and content areas, and encouraging students to teach each other about the reading process (Garner, 1987; Pressley, 2002).

Literary Development

Galda, Ash, and Cullinan (2000) suggest that most research on children's literature in the classroom has focused on children's ability to recognize literary elements or to use those elements in their speech or writing. For example, researchers studying children's concepts of story have noted that children's early notions of story are gradually modified and refined as they continue to encounter new stories in a variety of situations (McNeil, 1987). Stadler and Ward (2005), using earlier models of narrative development in children, found that children in the early grades follow a predictable sequence characterized by the following actions: labeling, listing, connecting, sequencing, and narrating. Similarly, Whaley (1981) found evidence of a developmental trajectory in that, when reading stories,

older children were better at predicting events than younger children. She concluded that the expansion of a story sense in older students enabled them to predict more of the story structures. With respect to young children, Sutton-Smith (1981), and Long and Bulgarella (1985) report that they organize their stories around basic pairs of actions such as chase and escape and that they tend to repeat these actions in their written stories. However, Mandler (1978) found that as children mature, their story retellings appear to move away from a simple, ideal concept of story toward a more complex adult model. Analyses of children's written stories reveal the same developmental patterns. Sipe (1996, 2008) created a typology of children's literary understandings based on their oral responses to picture books. He describes three dimensions through which children's understandings can be seen: (a) Stance: How children situate themselves in relation to texts; (b) Action: What children do with texts; (c) Function: How texts function. This typology suggests that even first and second graders analyze stories and consider the characteristics of books. Indeed, the ability to identify and focus on literary elements after a reading appears to be enhanced by the stance the reader takes at the time of the reading (Many & Wiseman, 1992). Students asked to take an aesthetic stance prior to reading were more likely to identify literary elements in their response than those given an efferent stance, and this ability increased with age. In general, young children talk about plots and story endings, link stories to other literary works, and describe connections across authors or genres.

In addition to text structure, texts can also differ in respect to multicultural perspectives. Some researchers have looked at children's literary experiences as multicultural and global education (Au, 2003). For example, Bishop (1994) suggests that children's literature provides both a "mirror and a window," an illuminating metaphor for thinking about this aspect of children's literary development and their developing understanding of diversity. Consequently, as Hade (1997) suggests, children can learn to read either multiculturally or "against a text" (Nodelman, 1996). As such, it is important for authors to provide authentic representations of cultures in their writing. And, as readers develop, it becomes their responsibility to recognize and question the author's implicit assumptions.

Implications for Policy and Practice

Research on children's written language development provides evidence that learning to listen, speak, read, and write is complex and multidimensional. No single approach is likely to be appropriate for all children. Yet, there is a convergence of research evidence that can be applied to both policy and practice. Following is a set of recommendations for policy and practice related to the classroom environment and to learner attributes.

Classroom and Instructional Environment First, a print rich environment is essential. Classroom environments that support language and literacy are filled with appropriate literature, meaningful environmental print, prominent reading and writing centers, and opportunities for students to discuss what they read, write and experience (Feeley, 1982; Chapman, 2006). In addition, instruction should include a variety of texts and modalities, including technology and traditional print sources.

Meaning should be at the center of language and literacy activities in the classroom. Both language and literacy are best taught within the context of topics and situations of interest and importance to children. Moreover, such practice will likely increase motivation (Alvermann, 2002). Attention to motivation, particularly in the middle grades, is extremely important for both policy and practice. Efforts to address demands for accountability need not result in an over emphasis on the results of standardized tests, which may serve to foster less effective teaching and decrease student motivation.

Reading and writing should not be isolated from each other or from other aspects of the curriculum, including the content areas. Additionally, there should be increasing attention to expanding children's knowledge about text structures and literary genres (McNeil, 1987; Mason & Au, 1986). Given the unique text structures and literacy demands of the content areas (Schleppegrell, 2004; Achugar, Schleppegrell, & Oteiza, 2007), professional development should be provided to teachers to heighten their sensitivity to content-area demands and to employ scaffolds to support students of varying linguistic backgrounds with these demands.

Learner Attributes Attention to cultural and linguistic differences should be integral to all language and literacy activities. Policy, and funding, should support students' access to books that reflect a range of cultures and encourage respect for cultural and linguistic differences. Similarly, special attention needs to be given to the needs of linguistically diverse learners. What we know about good instruction and curriculum in general holds true for English learners as well (August & Shanahan, 2006). When possible, bilingual education for ELLs should be supported because of its positive effects on reading and achievement in English (Francis, Lesaux, & August, 2006).

Building background knowledge and vocabulary are critical to literacy development. Children should be encouraged to make use of what they know about topics to aid in meaning making and to broaden their experiential background. As their conceptual base grows, so will their vocabulary for oral and written language (Langer, 1986). Because background knowledge and vocabulary are most effectively employed when students are purposeful in their literacy habits, children should be encouraged to be reflective and metacognitive about their reading and writing. Students should be taught to plan, evaluate, and regulate their own comprehension and to be more aware of strategies that improve their reading comprehension (Paris, Cross, & Lipson, 1984; Pressley & Woloshyn, 1995).

Conclusion

The literacy development of elementary students is influenced by a variety of social, instructional, and intra-individual factors. Understanding the interplay of these factors is essential to best support children's early literacy development and to provide the foundation that will serve them in all later academic endeavors. Policy and practice decisions should be informed by research and implemented in ways that directly support the literacy development of young children.

References

Achugar, M., Schleppegrell, M. J., & Oteiza, T. (2007). Engaging teachers in language analysis: A functional linguistics approach to reflective literacy. *English Teaching: Practice and Critique, 6*, 8–24.

Adams, M. J. (1990). *Beginning to read: thinking and learning avout print.* Cambridge, MA: MIT Press.

Alvermann, D. E. (2002). Effective literacy instruction for adolescents. *Journal of Literacy Research, 34*, 189–208.

Ashby, J., & Rayner, K. (2006). Literacy development: Insights from research on skilled reading. In D. Dickinson & S. Neuman (Eds.), *Handbook of early literacy research* (Vol. 3, pp. 52–63). New York: Guilford Press.

Au, K. H. (2003). Literacy research and students of diverse backgrounds: What does it take to improve achievement? In C. Fairbanks, J. Worthy, B. Maloch, J. V. Hoffman, & D. L. Schallert (Eds.), *52nd yearbook of the National Reading Conference* (pp. 85–91). Oak Creek, WI: National Reading Conference.

August, D., & Shanahan, T. (Eds.). (2006). *Developing literacy in second-language learners: Report of the National Literacy Panel on language-minority children and youth.* Mahwah, NJ: Erlbaum.

Babbs, P. J., & Moe, A. J. (1983). Metacognition: A key for independent learning from text. *The Reading Teacher, 32*, 422–426.

Beck, I. L., & McKeown, M. G. (2006). Increasing young low-income children's oral vocabulary repertoires through rich and focused instruction. *The Elementary School Journal, 107*, 251–271.

Biemiller, A., & Slonim, N. (2001). Estimating root word vocabulary growth in normative and advantaged populations: Evidence for a common sequence of vocabulary acquisition. *Journal of Educational Psychology, 93*, 498–520.

Bishop, R. S. (1994). Multicultural literature for children: Making informed choices. In V. Harris (Ed.), *Teaching multicultural literature in grades K-8* (pp. 37–54). Norwood, NJ: Ablex.

Blachowicz, C. L. Z., & Fisher, P. (2000). Vocabulary instruction. In M. L. Kamil, P. B. Mosenthal, P. D. Pearson, & R. Barr (Eds.), *Handbook of reading research* (Vol. 3, pp. 503–523). Mahwah, NJ: Erlbaum.

Bodrova, E., & Leong, D. J. (2006). Vygotskian perspectives on teaching and learning early literacy. In D. Dickinson & S. Neuman (Eds.), *Handbook of early reading research* (Vol. 2, 243–256). New York: Guilford Press.

Bradley, D. (2001). How beginning writers articulate and demonstrate their understanding of the act of writing. *Journal of the College Reading Assocaition, 40*, 273–296.

Bussis, A. M., Chittenden, E. A., Amarel, M., & Klausner, E. (1985). *Inquiry into meaning: An investigation of learning to read.* Hillsdale, NJ: Erlbaum.

Calkins, L. M. (1986). *The art of teaching writing.* Portsmouth, NH: Heinemann.

Calkins, L. M. (1994). *The art of teaching writing.* Portsmouth, NH: Heinemann.

Carlisle, J. F. (2007). Fostering morphological processing, vocabulary development, and reading comprehension. In R. K. Wagner, A. E. Muse, & K. R. Tannenbaum (Eds.), *Vocabulary acquisition: Implications for reading comprehension* (pp. 78–103). New York: Guilford Press.

Chall, J. S. (1983). *Stages of reading development*. New York: McGraw-Hill.

Chapman, M. (2006). Research on composition: Preschool through elementary writing. In P. Smagorinsky (Ed.), *Research on compostion: Multiple perspectives on two decades of change* (pp. 15–47). New York: Teachers College Press.

Clay, M. (1975). *What did I write?* Exeter, NH: Heinemann.

Cochrane, O., Cochrane, D., Scalena, S., & Buchanan, E. (1984). *Reading, writing, and caring*. New York: Richard C. Owens.

Donovan, C. (2001). Children's development and control of written story and informational genres: Insights from one elementary school. *Research in the teaching of English, 35,* 394–447.

Dyson, A. H. (1983). *The role of oral language in early writing processes. Research in the Teaching of English, 17(1),* 1–30.

Feeley, J. T. (1982). A print environment for beginning readers. *Reading, 16,* 23–50.

Francis, D. J., Lesaux, N. K., & August, D. (2006). Language of instruction. In D. August & T. Shanahan (Eds.), *Developing literacy in second-language learners* (pp. 365–413). Mahwah, NJ: Erlbaum.

Galda, L., Ash, G., & Cullinan, B. (2000). In M. Kamil, P. Mosenthaal, P. D. Pearson, & R. Barr (Eds.), *Handbook of reading research* (Vol 3, pp. 361–380). White Plains, NY: Longman.

Garner, R. (1987). *Metacognition and reading comprehension*. Norwood, NJ: Ablex.

Gentry, J. R. (1981). *Learning to spell developmentally. The Reading Teacher, 34,* 378–381.

Hade, D. D. (1997). *Reading multiculturally*. In V. Harris (Ed.), *Using multiethnic literature in the K-8 classroom* (pp. 233–256). Norwoood, MA: Christopher-Gordon.

Hall, M. A. (1981). *Teaching reading as a language experience*. Columbus, OH: Merrill.

Hart, B., & Risley, T. R. (1995). *Meaningful differences in the everyday experiences of young American children*. Baltimore: Paul H. Brookes.

Ivey, G. (2002, Spring). Meeting not ignoring teen literacy needs. *Middle Matters, 10,* 1–2, 6.

Kamil, M. L., Intrator, S. M., & Kim, H. S. (2000). The effects of other technologies on literacy and literacy learning. In M. L. Kamil, P. B. Mosenthal, P. D. Pearson, & R. Barr (Eds.), *Handbook of reading research* (Vol. 3, pp. 771–790). Mahwah, NJ: Erlbaum.

Knobel, M., & Lankshear, C. (2005). New literacies: Research and social practice. In B. Malock, J. Hoffman, D. Schallert, C. Fairbanks, & J. Worthy (Eds.), *54th yearbook of the National Reading Conference* (pp. 22–50). Oak Creek, WI: National Reading Conference.

Kos, R., & Maslowski, C. (2001). Second graders' perceptions of what is important in writing. *The Elementary School Journal, 101,* 567–584.

Lapp, D., & Flood, J. (1978). *Teaching reading to every child*. New York: Macmillan.

Langer, J. A. (1986). *Children reading and writing*. Norwood, NJ: Ablex.

Long, R., & Bulgarella, L. K. (1985). Social interaction and the writing process. *Language Arts, 62,* 166–172.

Lonigan, C. (2006). Conceptualizing phonological processing skills in prereaders. In D. Dickinson & S. Neuman (Eds.), *Handbook of early reading research* (Vol. 2, 77–89). New York: Guilford Press.

Mandler, J. (1978). A code in the node: The use of story schema in retrieval. *Discourse Processes, 1,* 1–13.

Manning, M., Manning, G., & Hughes, J. (1987). Journals in first grade: What children write. *The Reading Teacher, 41,* 311–315.

Many, J. E., & Wiseman, D. L. (1992) The effect of teaching approach on the third grade students" response to literature. *Journal of Reading Behavior, 24,* 265–287.

Mason, J. M., & Au, K. H. (1986). *Reading instruction for today*. Glenview, IL: Scott, Foresman.

McCarthey, S. (2001). Identity construction in elementary readers and writers. *Reading Research Quarterly, 36,* 122–151.

McGinley, W. J., & Kamberelis, G. (1992). Transformative functions of children's writing. *Language Arts, 69,* 330–338.

McNeil, J. (1970). *The acquisition of language: The study of development psycholinguistics*. New York: Harper & Row.

McNeil, J. D. (1987). *Reading comprehension: New directions for classroom practice* (3rd ed.). Glenview, IL: Scott, Foresman.

Meyers, M., & Paris, S. G. (1978). Children's metacognitive knowledge about reading. *Journal of Educational Psychology, 70,* 680–690.

Nagy, W., Anderson, R. C., & Herman, P. A. (1987). Learning word meanings from context during normal reading. *American Educational Research Journal, 24,* 237–270.

National Institute for Literacy. (2008). *Developing early literacy: Report of the National Early Literacy Panel*. Washington, DC: National Institute for Literacy.

National Institute of Child Health and Human Development (NICHD). (2000). *Report of the National Reading Panel: Teaching children to read: An evidence-based assessment of the scientific research literature on reading and its implications for reading instruction* (NIH Publication No. 00-4769). Washington, DC: U.S. Government printing Office.

Nodelman, P. (1996). The pleasures of children's literature (2nd ed.). White Plains, NY: Longman.

Ouellette, G. P., & Senechal, M. (2008). Pathways to literacy: A study of invented spelling and its role in learning to read. *Child Development, 79,* 899–913.

Paris, S. G., Cross, D. R., & Lipson, M. Y. (1984). Informed strategies for learning: A program to improve childrens reading awareness and comprehension. *Journal of Educational Psychology, 76,* 1239–1252.

Pressley, M., & Woloshyn, V. (Eds.). (1995). *Cognitive strategy instruction that really improves children's academic performance* (2nd ed.). Cambridge, MA: Brookline.

Pressley, M. (2002). Metacognition and self-regulated comprehension. In A. Fartstrup & S. J. Samuels (Eds.), *What research has to say about reading instruction* (pp. 291–309). Newark, DE: International Reading Association.

RAND Reading Study Group. (2002). *Reading for understanding: Toward a R&D program in reading comprehension*. Arlington, VA: RAND.

Read, C. (1986). *Children's creative spelling*. Boston, MA: Routledge & Kegan Paul Books.

Roskos, K. A., & Christie, J. F. (Eds.). (2000). *Play and literacy in early childhood: Research from multiple perspectives*. Mahwah, NJ: Erlbaum.

Schatschneider, C., Fletcher, J. M., Francis, D. J., Carlson, C. D., & Foorman, B. R. (2004). Kindergarten prediction of reading skills: A longitudinal comparative analysis. *Journal of Educational Psychology, 96,* 256–282.

Schleppegrell, M. J. (2004). *The language of schooling: A functional linguistics perspective*. Mahwah, NJ: Erlbaum.

Sipe, L. (1996). *The construction of literary understandings by first and second graders in response to picture storybook readalouds*. Unpublished doctoral dissertation, The Ohio State University, Columbus.

Sipe, L. (2008). *Storytime*. New York: Teachers College Press.

Smith, F. (1985). *Reading without nonsense*. New York: Teachers College Press.

Stadler, M. A., & Ward, G. C. (2005). Supporting the narrative development of young children. *Early Childhood Education Journal, 33,* 73–80.

Sulzby, E. (1985a). Kindergartens as writers and readers. In M. Farr (Ed.), *Advances in writing research: Vol. 1. Children's early writing development* (pp. 127–199). Norwood, NJ: Ablex.

Sulzby, E. (1985b). Children's emergent reading of favorite storybooks: A development study. *Reading Research Quarterly, 20,* 458–481.

Sutton-Smith, B. (1981). *The folkstories of children*. Philadelphia: University of Pennsylvania Press.

Teale, W., & Sulzby, E. (Eds.). (1986). *Emergent literacy: Writing and reading*. Norwood, NJ: Ablex.

Teale, W. & Yokota, J. (2000). D. S. Strickland & L. M. Morrow (Eds.), *Beginning reading and writing* (pp. 3–21). Newark, DE: International Reading Association.

Temple, C. A., Nathan, R. G., Burris, N. A., & Temple, F. (1988). *The beginnings of writing*. Boston, MA: Allyn & Bacon.

Torgesen, J. K., Morgan, S. T., & Davis, C. (1992). Effects of two types of phonological training on word learning in kindergarten children. *Journal of Educational Psychology, 84*, 364–370.

Van Sluys, K., & Tropp Laman, T. (2006). Learning about language: Written conversations and elementary language learners. *The Reading Teacher, 60*, 222–233.

Weaver, C. (1988). *Reading process and practice.* Portsmouth, NH: Heinemann.

Whaley, J. (1981). Story grammar and reading instruction. *The Reading Teacher, 34,*762–771.

Wollman-Bonilla, J. (2000). Teaching science writing to first graders: Genre learning and recontextualization. *Research in the Teaching of English, 35*, 35–65.

Yancey, K. B. (2000). Using multiple technologies to teach writing. *Educational Leadership, 62*, 38–40.

Zevenbergen, A. A., Whitehurst, G. J., & Zevenbergen, J. A. (2003). Effects of a shared-reading intervention on the inclusion of evaluative devices in narratives of children from low-income families. *Journal of Applied Developmental Psychology, 24*, 1–15.

8

Language Arts Learning in the Middle Grades

Joyce E. Many, Mary Ariail, and Dana L. Fox

The middle-grade years, which frame a context for language arts learning for young adolescents, have garnered substantial attention both historically and in recent years. During the period between elementary and high school, readers and writers encounter increasing demands presented by disciplinary literacy. They begin to participate in diverse discourse communities in and out of schools and use multiple literacies for social and political purposes. Middle-grade students' engagement in school-based literacy is mediated in part by their ability to connect themselves, their lives, and their cultures to the literature and the experiences they encounter in language arts classrooms (NCTE, 2007).

Historically, attention to the cognitive, psychosocial, emotional, physical, and moral changes experienced by adolescents led to the conceptualization of the middle school philosophy articulated in *Turning Points* by the Carnegie Council on Adolescent Development (1989). The report emphasized the uniqueness of adolescence and the need to reform schools in ways to address developmental needs through interdisciplinary teams, flexible organization, advisory experiences, and heterogeneous instruction with cooperative groups. Subsequently, the middle school movement guided the classroom instruction of language arts teachers through the turn of the century, as evidenced by increased cooperative learning experiences, reading/writing workshops, and interdisciplinary planning and instruction (Simmons & Carroll, 2003).

With the dawn of the 21st century, adolescent literacy has continued to garner both attention and concern. The National Council of Teachers of English 2006 policy research brief on adolescent literacy reform emphasized that today's adolescents lack the literacy skills needed to be successful in information-driven societies. The middle-school concept's emphasis on meeting the developmental needs of early adolescents has drawn criticism, with particular concern focused on whether the middle school philosophy shifts attention away from academics (Yecki, 2005). Even proponents of the middle-school movement stress the need for academic rigor while maintaining an emphasis on adolescents' social, emotional, and physical needs (Cooke, Faulkner, & Kinne, 2009).

In this chapter, we endeavored to understand recent research addressing the middle grades as a context for language arts learning. We began with attention to recent theoretical writings focusing on development from childhood to adolescence. Next, we examined peer-reviewed research published from 2000–2009 that was conducted with participants in grades 4 through 9. The selected studies characterize trends associated with (a) changes in language arts instruction at the middle-grade levels related to changes in learners, (b) social practices which affect literacy in middle grades, and (c) uses of adolescent and young adult literature in the middle-level years.

Theories of Childhood Into Adolescence

The publication of G. Stanley Hall's (1904) *Adolescence* marked the beginning of widespread awareness of adolescence as a pivotal period in children's lives. Hall portrayed adolescence as a time of *sturm* and *drang* (storm and stress) corresponding to the turbulence and transition in the history of human evolution. In the 1960s–1980s, others also described the dramatic physical (Tanner, 1972), social (Manning & Allen, 1987), and cognitive (McCall, 1990) changes experienced by children between ages 10 and 14. Eichhorn (1966) coined the term "transescence" to describe changes that occur in the period of development that begins with the onset of puberty and extends through the early stages of adolescence, later positing that transcescence "delineates the essence of middle schools" (1984, p. 31).

During this period, perspectives on adolescent identity development were heavily influenced by psychoanalytic theories (Malmquist, 1978), such as those proposed by Erik Erickson (1968), who argued that the major task of adolescence was to establish a sense of personal identity. In the early 1990s, however, discourses related to adolescent development began to reflect a growing interest in sociocultural and poststructural theories, leading to more pluralistic views of the self. Hillman (1991), for example, wrote, "Though youngsters in early adolescence are often thought to be quite homogeneous, nothing could be further from the truth. They are a group characterized by great variability and diversity" (p. 4). Earlier research related to adolescent identity, which was typically quantitative and drew heavily on psychoanalytic theories (e.g., Freud, 1961), shifted toward more qualitative studies, focusing on the ways in which adolescents position themselves and are positioned by others in social and academic contexts (Cherland, 2008; Fairbanks & Ariail, 2006). This shift was heavily influenced by the development of poststructuralist thought which suggests that the self is never stable, but constantly improvising (Holland, Lachicotte, Skinner, & Cain, 1998, p.18). The notion of shifting identities (or subjectivities) is consistent with a sociocultural view of learning; thus, the positioning of the self is always contingent upon the sociocultural (Johnson & Cowles, 2009) and sociopolitical (Lewis & Ketter, 2008) context.

Changes in Middle-Grades Language Arts Instruction with Changes in Learners While early adolescents experience developmental changes across the middle-level years, the literacy tasks early adolescents encounter are also considerably different from those they experienced in elementary grades. Text structure, vocabulary, and the nature of reading and writing can vary considerably across the disciplines. As a result, young adolescent readers and writers must develop and be able to regulate a repertoire of language and literacy strategies. Personal interests and motivation also become increasingly important factors. Accordingly, language arts instruction must reflect an awareness of students' development as young adolescents and as language users while also taking into account the increasingly complex demands of texts in English classes and other disciplines. In the following section, we examine trends in language arts instruction in the middle-level years in light of the changes middle-grade learners experience.

While research in the 2000s continued to document the effectiveness of integrating reading and writing processes, research examining middle-grades language arts integration in the early 21st century did not follow the 1970s–1990s emphasis on interdisciplinary teaming for instruction (Simmons & Carroll, 2003). Instead of focusing on team-teaching or interdisciplinary units, recent middle-level studies have focused on the effectiveness of integrating reading and writing processes in the English/reading curriculum and how explicit strategy instruction might impact performance in the content areas.

Integration of the reading and writing curriculum was evident in Stevens' (2006) urban middle school investigation of the Student Team Reading and Writing (STRW) model to engage young adolescents in meaningful learning. The STRW model consisted of research-based instructional practices with cooperative learning processes and with extended opportunities to learn to read, to read to learn, and to write to express what one has learned. The STRW approach combined reading and English across a two class block utilizing high quality literature as texts for reading and as models for writing. Results indicated the STRW students performed significantly better than students in a traditional program on standardized achievement tests for vocabulary, reading comprehension, and language expression.

The goal for Ivey and Broaddus's study (2007) was for seventh- to eighth-grade immigrant students to be engaged in reading and writing in ways that addressed their personal needs and their motivations to learn. Making meaningful connections across reading, writing, and content was vital for English language learners, with supports such as writing scaffolds, use of language experience activities, and explicit discussion of unfamiliar concepts found to be particularly effective. An integrated reading/writing approach was also found to be effective in Thames et al.'s research (2008) with struggling middle-school readers. In this study, preservice teachers taught weekly lessons with fourth- to eighth-grade students who were reading below grade level. Lessons incorporated fiction and non-fiction and emphasized listening, speaking, reading, writing, viewing, visual representation, and metacognitive activities. Involvement in the integrated language arts experiences significantly impacted students' silent comprehension of both narrative and expository passages in comparison to the performance of similar students in a control group.

When middle-level language teachers integrate reading into the English language arts classroom, they take on responsibility for understanding and supporting young adolescents' continued development as readers. While difficulties experienced by early adolescents have often been associated with the increased demands of content area texts, reading fluency or a need for effective reading strategies may also contribute to the struggles middle-grade readers may face. Rasinski and Padak (2005) argue that adolescents who lack fluency may redirect cognitive resources needed for comprehension to the task of word decoding. Their work with ninth graders indicated a substantial portion of the students' reading performance could be attributed to their fluency or their lack of fluency. To support students' fluency development, language arts teachers could use repeated readings (Raskinski & Padak), 5- to 6-minute supplemental fluency instruction by paraprofessionals (Mercer, Campbell, Miller, Mercer, & Lane, 2000), and independent reading (Reis et al., 2007) to positively impact middle-grade students' fluency and reading achievement.

In order to comprehend complex texts encountered in middle school, young adolescents also need to develop strategic reading skills. Teaching students to decode multisyllabic words or content vocabulary has been found to impact adolescents' word attack, word identification, and/or reading comprehension (Bryant et al., 2000; Diliberto, Beattie, Flowers, & Algozzine, 2009). In addition, explicit introduction, modeling, and guided practice of reading strategies can be effective in improving reading achievement and students' confidence in learning from text (Manset-Williamson & Nelson, 2005; Schorzman & Cheek, 2004).

Research focusing on the strategy instruction within language arts also indicates such an emphasis can have important role in developing writing competencies that can improve disciplinary literacy in specific content areas. Aulls' (2003) 2-year study demonstrated that intensive reading and writing with a focus on text structure significantly impacted the quality of seventh graders' English essays. In addition, skills addressed in the reading/writing curriculum transferred to the content areas, significantly impacting students' expository writing in seventh-grade geography and their strategic use of text properties in eighth-grade social studies assignments.

When middle-grades language arts teachers plan contexts for learning, they not only need to consider the demands of texts and how to support students' developing abilities, they also must consider how to design experiences to which young adolescents can relate. When instruction does not address students' needs, motivation and engagement can be diminished (NCTE, 2006). Opportunities for early adolescents to be involved in independent thought and analysis seems to be closely linked to their motivation for and engagement in literacy activities.

In an observational study, Raphael, Pressley, and Mohan (2008) described instructional behaviors associated with engaging and non-engaging middle-grade teachers. In classes where 90% or more of the students were engaged in tasks that required thinking at least 90% of the time, teachers used supportive practices such as scaffolding, modeled problem solving and strategy use, and encouraged students' independent strategy use. Ivey and Broaddus (2007) found English language learners showed increased engagement and understanding when teachers provided structure in the form of read alouds, explanations of unfamiliar content, writing patterns, and language experience approaches. They also found, however, choral reading and echo reading to be ineffective. Finally, Kelly and Turner (2009) examined the structure of instructional activities to understand classroom discourse and the effects of whole class instruction on student engagement. Their findings indicate that the quality that impacts engagement is the degree to which instruction is focused on the goal of developing independent critical thinking, with students' opinions taken seriously.

The importance of recognizing students' opinions was also seen in research highlighting student choice in reading and writing. Ivey and Broaddus (2001) investigated aspects of instruction that motivated sixth graders to read. Students valued independent reading as an integral component of reading/language arts instruction and appreciated reading for personal uses. Others have found that when students are given opportunities to read self-selected texts in school, they are more likely to be involved in voluntary reading and to show an increase in intrinsic motivation, vocabulary, reading comprehension and attitudes toward reading (Edwards, 2009; Reis et al., 2007). Choice has also been found to impact young adolescents' writing behaviors (Abbott, 2000), where opportunities to choose genre, style, ownership, and length led to fifth graders' flow experiences and increased engagement in writing.

In this section we have examined research trends related to changes that young adolescents experience in the time between elementary and secondary school. In addition, changes in literacy practices in today's society also impact language and literacy learning in today's middle schools. We turn next to research on social practices affecting language and literacy education for early adolescents.

Social Practices Affecting Middle-Grades Literacy The most dramatic changes in early adolescent literacy education within the last decade are indisputably linked to digital technologies and online communications, or *new literacies* (Leu, 2002; Tierney, Bond, & Bresler, 2006). In addition to digital technologies, new literacies also include multimodal representations (Albers & Harste, 2007). Multimodal literacies transcend written and spoken language for communications and include other sign systems that carry meaning, such as visual and spatial.

With the expanded uses of these modes of communication has come a proliferation of social practices that seem to have rendered antiquated the notion of traditional reading and writing as the only legitimate forms of literacy. Consider, for example, the following: blogging, emailing, podcasting, instant messaging, texting, wikis, tweeting, threaded discussion groups, Kindles, Facebook, MySpace, and YouTube. These artifacts of social practices call for a vocabulary that is used fluently by early adolescents but may be a foreign language to some adults. Although Moje (2009) challenges educators to consider whether these are "new" literacies or simply old literacies that employ new media, the fact remains that changes in technology use have significantly influenced the ways adolescents interact with others.

Recognition of the popularity of new literacies among early adolescents has encouraged many middle-school teachers to consider a curriculum more appealing to students than a traditional curriculum (MacGillivray & Curwen, 2007). Bridging the spaces between their positions as children toward their positions as adults, early adolescents seek opportunities to explore new ways of interacting socially with others and negotiating their sense of self in their social worlds. Social networking spaces on the Internet such as MySpace and Facebook provide arenas in which young adolescents can construct and reconstruct social identities as they negotiate their changing sense of self.

Interest in new literacies has resulted in studies suggesting that students exhibit greater levels of student engagement when using digital technologies. For example, in a 2-year study of seventh- and eighth-grade struggling readers, O'Brien, Beach, and Scharber (2007) found that participants perceived new literacies practices that focused on digital media to be more engaging than traditional practices. Larson (2009) also found higher levels of engagement in fifth-grade students who explored technology integration in the context of a reading workshop. Opportunities for asynchronous conversations on a message board elicited insightful and heartfelt responses and encouraged group members to think deeply about the literature. Grisham and Wolsey (2006) also found that the students were more engaged when using digital technologies, learned to examine literature through a more critical lens, and socially constructed knowledge while creating an authentic learning community.

At the same time, some educators have expressed concerns about possible negative effects on students' cognition and literacy skills that may be attributed to increased use of computer mediated communications (CMC's; Jacobs, 2008). For example, CMC's such as Instant Messaging and texting, which encourage quick writing in a limited space, call for condensed forms of text (e.g., LOL, CU@8). Many parents and teachers fear that students' frequent use of abbreviations will undermine their knowledge of conventional spelling patterns and lead to fragmentation of thought (Turner, 2009). However, research suggests that children's knowledge of texting is not associated with poor written language outcomes (Plester, Wood, & Bell, 2008). Furthermore, Jacobs (2006) argues that students who are adept at Instant Messaging are preparing themselves as members of a fast capitalist workforce which itself is a result of increases in Internet use.

Uses of Adolescent and Young Adult Literature in the Middle Grades

Early adolescents' motivation for language learning in the middle grades relates not only to their ability to use the multiple literacies, but also the extent to which they encounter texts to which they can relate. In the final section, we review research on trends in adolescent and young adult literature, early adolescents' reading interests, and the use of and the study of young adult literature in the middle-level years.

Critical Analyses of Adolescent and Young Adult Literature. The number and variety of books published for adolescents and young adults grew considerably in recent years (Donelson & Nilsen, 2005). Koss and Teale (2009) found a distinct lack of cultural diversity in quality YA literature from 1999 to 2005; in fact, the majority of the books represented only one general cultural group, most often European American. Categorized as predominately fiction, these books represented a shift in content from the "problem" or coming-of-age novel to youth finding themselves/ their identities or grappling with everyday situations.

While Koss and Teale focused on general trends in young adult (YA) publishing, Fox and Short's (2003) and Short and Fox's (2004) review of a decade of research on cultural authenticity revealed multiple, complex layers regarding definitions of cultural authenticity in literature for young people. Their reviews noted research has underscored the importance of authors' own cultural backgrounds and experiences, ways that authors develop an "insider" perspective,

authors' intentions in writing a particular book, and the relationship between authorial freedom and authors' social responsibilities. Even though an accuracy of details, lack of stereotyping, and lack of misrepresentation were evident in the literature, they also found that culturally sensitive images and illustrations and the strategic, skillful use of two or more languages represented in a book contributed to a book's cultural authenticity.

Diverse Text Choices and Reading Interests of Adolescents. Themes in research related to adolescents' reading interests reveal strong connections among a sense of choice and ownership in text selection, interest in a diversity of text types, and motivation to read. For example, in a 2-year ethnographic study, Moss and Hendershot (2002) found that adolescents chose nonfiction titles for six reasons: curiosity or the "need to know," engaging visual features, knowledge of authors and intertextuality, knowledge of book awards and genre, personal connections, and others' recommendations. Moje, Overby, Tysvaer, and Morris (2008) found that Latino/a urban youth preferred to read books about people like them (e.g., race, ethnicity, age, class, or gender) as well as those who are working through relationships, staying resilient through struggles, and trying to figure out who they are.

Other research revealed adolescents' preferences for magazines, comic books, graphic novels, information books, mysteries, manga, and Internet texts (Ivey & Broaddus, 2001; Hughes-Hassell & Pradnya, 2007). Newkirk (2002) and Smith and Wilhelm (2002) found that boys preferred texts that are short, visual, humorous, and realistic. Smith and Wilhelm also learned boys sought texts that were storied, that sustain engagement (such as series and collections), and that are edgy or subversive. Cavazos-Kottke (2006) found that gifted middle school boys preferred series and imaginative fiction, science fiction/fantasy, and mystery/thriller novels.

Critical Discussions, Adolescent Identities, and Young Adult Literature. Many researchers studied how middle-level students engaged in critical discussions of young adult literature. Research tended to focus on how adolescents interrogated critical social issues through whole-class literature discussion or small book clubs. While researchers acknowledged the complexity of orchestrating productive literature discussion on controversial topics, they also argued for safe spaces for such talk and suggested strategies to promote learning through critical talk about multicultural literature.

In a case study of one middle-school class' response to Taylor's *Roll of Thunder, Hear My Cry*, Brooks and Hampton's (2005) study showed how the author's creative mix of history and fiction, the teacher's instructional approaches and attention to student responses, and the development of the classroom context offered students a safe space or "laboratory for studying the complexity of racism" (p. 98). They found that students gained historical knowledge, sought to understand racist behaviors, vented anger productively, and appreciated productive responses to racism. Brooks' (2006) study also explored how one middle school class responded to three culturally conscious, African American adolescent novels, noting that (a) recurring cultural themes, linguistic patterns, and ethnic group practices were identified as African American text features; and (b) readers used cultural knowledge, their own experiences, and African American textual features to develop literary understandings.

Brooks, Browne, and Hampton (2008) found that an after-school book club for middle school students reading Flake's *The Skin I'm In* provided a setting for discussions of *colorism* as well as female body image, status, and cultural identity. While the African American female participants were able and willing to discuss these sensitive topics, their responses did not reveal a highly sophisticated understanding of colorism and its historical roots. The researchers pointed out the need for teachers to familiarize themselves with related cultural and historical issues before engaging students in such contemporary multicultural literature for young adults.

Working with middle school girls in their discussion of multicultural female representations in four young adult novels, Johnson (2000) explored how girls-only literature circles helped to disrupt girls' silencing. Given time (almost 1 year), the girls were able to discuss complex issues of race, ethnicity, class, and gender openly and with relative ease. Johnson found, however, that it was easier for the seventh-grade girls to transcend their silence and talk across cultural groups than their eighth-grade counterparts. In a girls-only book discussion group focused on strong female protagonists, Carico (2001) found that girls needed to employ "real talk" in order to try out ideas and interpretations, their talk was sometimes inappropriate for school contexts, and some participants exerted power or positions of privilege in the group. She argued that the teacher's role in orchestrating many voices is critical for meaning making to flourish. Smith (2005) studied sixth-grade girls' responses to multicultural young adult novels and found an informal, out-of-school setting to be important as a safe space for inviting exploratory talk and racial identity construction through responses to the characters and events in the novels.

Other studies suggested complexities related to early adolescents' engagement in the discussion of young adult literature, the performance of identities, and the shaping of classroom culture. Broughton (2002) found that a book club discussion group offered adolescent girls a safe space to perform and construct themselves (or their "subjectivities") through participation in story worlds, engagement in social interaction with peers, and critical reflections/questionings of the self. Blackford's (2004) research challenged the notion that girls use fictional texts to struggle with their own identities. Through her interviews with 33 racially, socioeconomically, and geographically diverse girls (only a few of whom were avid readers), she found that the literature they most appreciated had very little to do with their own lives. Blackford argued that her research goes against the grain, since she found that girls do not read to see themselves or their experiences reflected in books; instead, using their aesthetic imaginations, they read for pleasure in order to lose themselves in books.

Other middle-level research has examined how the contexts surrounding literary experiences may be sites for young adolescents to grapple with how they define themselves and their relationships with others. McCarthy's (2002) nine ethnographic case studies demonstrated the ways linguistically and culturally diverse students appropriated, resisted, or transformed their classroom contexts. The cases showed how students' conformity or resistance within the power struggles of school literacy events influenced their identities. In her qualitative study of the social codes and practices that shaped a combined fifth-/sixth-grade classroom, Lewis (2001) found that young adolescents negotiated their social roles and identities in peer-led literature discussions in ways that both sustained and challenged the status and power hierarchies and cultural norms of the classroom community. Through these studies, the researchers demonstrated how issues of power and cultural norms influence students' identity construction in the context of literature discussion and literacy events.

Summary In summary, while the period of early adolescence may be marked by *sturm* and *drang* (Hall, 1904), this does not necessarily lead to negative outcomes for middle-grades students. Middle-level language arts teachers must be knowledgeable about the changing literacy demands of middle-grades years and continue to develop students' ability to navigate complex texts. Educators must also recognize the social capital that early adolescents bring to the classroom and use students' new literacies to build a foundation upon which understandings of disciplinary content can occur. Finally, educators should ensure that young people have regular, meaningful engagements with high-quality literature that is culturally authentic and accurate. Having access to such literature, freedom to make choices regarding what they read, and safe spaces for conversations about such literature is critical for young adolescents' motivation to read and their engagement in literary activities. By being aware of and sympathetic to the diverse needs of pre-adolescents, educators can help students direct their energies into highly productive, educational experiences during the middle-grade years.

References

Abbott, A. J. (2000). Blinking out and having the touch: Two fifth-grade boys talk about flow experiences in writing. *Written Communication, 17,* 53–92.

Albers, P., & Harste, J. (2007). The arts, new literacies, and multimodality. *English Education, 40*(1), 6–20.

Aulls, W. M. (2003). The influence of a reading and writing curriculum on transfer learning across subject and grades. *Reading Psychology, 24,* 177–215.

Blackford, H. V. (2004). *Out of this world: Why literature matters to girls.* New York: Teachers College Press.

Brooks, W. (2006). Reading representations of themselves: Urban youth use culture and African American textual features to develop literary understandings. *Reading Research Quarterly, 41*, 372–392.

Brooks, W., & Hampton, G. (2005). Safe discussions rather than first hand encounters: Adolescents examine racism through one historical fiction text. *Children's Literature in Education, 36*(1), 83–98.

Brooks, W., Browne, S., & Hampton, G. (2008). "There ain't no accounting for what folks see in their own mirrors": Considering colorism within a Sharon Flake narrative. *Journal of Adolescent and Adult Literacy, 51*, 660–669.

Broughton, M. A. (2002). The performance and construction of subjectivities of early adolescent girls in book club discussion groups. *Journal of Literacy Research, 34*, 1–38.

Bryant, D. P., Vaughn, S., Linan-Thompson, S., Ugel, N., Hamff, A., & Hougen, M. (2000). Reading outcomes for students with and without reading disabilities in general education middle-school content area classes. *Learning Disability Quarterly, 23*, 238–252.

Carico, K. M. (2001). Negotiating meaning in classroom literature discussions. *Journal of Adolescent and Adult Literacy, 44*, 510–518.

Carnegie Council on Adolescent Development. (1989). *Turning points: Preparing American youth for the 21st century.* Washington, DC: Carnegie Corporation.

Cavazos-Kottke, S. (2006). Five readers browsing: The reading interests of talented middle school boys. *Gifted Child Quarterly, 50*(2), 132–147.

Cherland, M. (2008). Harry's girls: Harry Potter and the discourse of gender. *Journal of Adolescent & Adult Literacy, 52*, 273–282.

Cooke, C. M., Faulkner, S. A., & Kinne, L. J. (2009). Indicators of middle school implementation: How do Kentucky's Schools to Watch measure up? *Research in Middle Level Education Online, 32*(6), 1–10. Retrieved July 12, 2009, from http://www.nmsa.org/Publications/RMLEOnline/Articles/Vol32No6/tabid/1865/Default.aspx

Diliberto, A. J., Beattie R. J., Flowers P. C., & Algozzine F. R. (2009). Effects of teaching syllable skills instruction on reading achievement in struggling middle school readers. *Literacy Research and Instruction, 48*, 14–27.

Donelson, K. L., & Nilsen, A. P. (2005). *Literature for today's young adults* (7th ed.). Boston, MA: Pearson.

Edwards B. (2009). Motivating middle school. *School Library Media Activities Monthly, 25*(8), 56–58.

Eichhorn, D. (1966). *The middle school.* New York: Center for Applied Research in Education.

Eichhorn, D. (1984). The nature of transcescents. In D. H. Lounsbury (Ed.), *Perspectives: Middle school education* (pp. 30–37). Columbus, OH: National Middle School Association.

Erikson, E. H. (1968). *Identity, youth, and crisis.* New York: Norton.

Fairbanks, C. M., & Ariail, M. (2006). The role of social and cultural resources in literacy and schooling: Three contrasting cases. *Research in the Teaching of English, 40*, 310–354.

Fox, D. L., & Short, K. G. (Eds.). (2003). *Stories matter: The complexity of cultural authenticity in children's literature.* Urbana, IL: National Council of Teachers of English.

Freud, S. (1961). *The ego and the id.* (Standard Edition, 19). London: Hogarth. (Original work published 1923)

Grisham, D. L., & Wolsey, T. D. (2006). Recentering the middle school classroom as a vibrant learning community: Students, literacy, and technology intersect. *Journal of Adolescent and Adult Literacy, 48*, 648–660.

Hall, G. S. (1904). *Adolescence, its psychology and its relations to physiology, anthropology, sociology, sex, crime, religion and education* (2 vols.). New York: Appleton.

Hillman, S. B. (1991, September). What developmental psychology has to say about early adolescence. *Middle School Journal,* 3–8.

Holland, D., Lachicotte, W., Skinner, D., & Cain, C. (1998). *Identity and agency in cultural worlds.* Cambridge, MA: Harvard University Press.

Hughes-Hassell, S., & Pradnya, R. (2007). The leisure reading habits of urban adolescents. *Journal of Adolescent and Adult Literacy, 51*, 22–33.

Ivey, G., & Broaddus, K. (2001). "Just plain reading": A survey of what makes students want to read in middle school classrooms. *Reading Research Quarterly, 36*, 350–377.

Ivey, G., & Broaddus, K. (2007). A formative experiment investigating literacy engagement among adolescent Latina/o students just beginning to read, write, and speak English. *Reading Research Quarterly, 42*, 512–545.

Jacobs, G. (2006). Fast times and digital literacy: Participation roles and portfolio construction within instant messaging. *Journal of Literacy Research, 38*, 171–196.

Jacobs, G. (2008). People, purposes, and practices: Insights from cross-disciplinary research into instant messaging. In J. Coiro, M. Knobel, C. Lankshear, & D. J. Leu (Eds.), *Handbook of research on new literacies* (pp. 469–493). New York: Routledge.

Johnson, A., & Cowles, L. (2009). Orlonia's literacy-in-persons: Expanding notions of literacy through biography and history. *Journal of Adolescent & Adult Literacy, 52*, 410–420.

Johnson, H. (2000). "To stand up and say something": "Girls only" literature circles at the middle level. *The New Advocate, 13*, 375–389.

Kelly S., & Turner J. (2009). Rethinking the effects of classroom activity structure on the engagement of low-achieving students. *Teachers College Record Volume, 111*, 1665–1692.

Koss, M. D., & Teale, W. H. (2009). What's happening in YA literature? Trends in books for adolescents. *Journal of Adolescent and Adult Literacy, 52*, 563–572.

Larson, L. C. (2009). Reader response meets new literacies: Empowering readers in online learning communities. *The Reading Teacher, 62*, 638–648.

Leu, D. J., Jr. (2002). The new literacies: Research on reading instruction with the internet. In A. E. Farstrup & S.J. Samuels (Eds.), *What research has to say about reading instruction* (pp. 310–336). Newark, DE: International Reading Association.

Lewis, C. (2001). *Literacy practices as social acts: Power, status, and cultural norms in the classroom.* Mahwah, NJ: Erlbaum.

Lewis, C., & Ketter, J. (2008). Encoding youth: Popular culture and multicultural literature in a rural context. *Reading & Writing Quarterly, 24*, 283–310.

MacGillivray, L., & Curwen, M. S. (2007). Tagging as a social literacy practice. *Journal of Adolescent and Adult Literacy, 5*, 354–369.

Malmquist, C. P. (1978). *Handbook on adolescence.* New York: Aronson.

Manning, M. L., & Allen, M. G. (1987). Social development in early adolescence. *Childhood Education, 63*, 172–176.

Manset-Williamson, G., & Nelson, J. M. (2005). Balanced, strategic reading instruction for upper-elementary and middle school students with reading disabilities: A comparative study of two approaches. *Learning Disability Quarterly, 28*, 59–74.

McCall, R. B. (1990). The neuroscience of education: More research is needed before application. *Journal of Educational Psychology, 82*, 885–888.

McCarthy, S. J. (2002). *Students' identities and literacy learning.* Newark, DE: International Reading Association.

Mercer, C. D., Campbell, K. U., Miller, M. D., Mercer, K. D., & Lane, H. B. (2000). Effects of a reading fluency intervention for middle schoolers with specific learning disabilities. *Learning Disabilities Research & Practice, 15*, 179–189

Moje, E. B. (2009). A call for new research on new and multi-literacies. *Research in the Teaching of English, 43*, 348–362.

Moje, E. B., Overby, M., Tysvaer, N., & Morris, K. (2008). The complex world of adolescent literacy: Myths, motivations, and mysteries. *Harvard Educational Review, 78*(1), 107–280.

Moss, B., & Hendershot, J. (2002). Exploring sixth graders' selection of nonfiction trade books. *The Reading Teacher, 56*, 6–16.

National Council of Teachers of English. (2006). *NCTE principles of adolescent literacy reform: A policy research brief.* Urbana, IL: NCTE.

National Council of Teachers of English. (2007). *Adolescent literacy: A policy research brief.* Urbana, IL: NCTE.

Newkirk, T. (2002). *Misreading masculinity: Boys, literacy, and popular culture.* Portsmouth, NH: Heinemann.

O'Brien, D., Beach, R., & Scharber, C. (2007). "Struggling" middle schoolers: Engagement and literate competence in a reading writing intervention class. *Reading Psychology, 28,* 51–73.

Plester, B., Wood, C., & Bell, V. (2008). Txt msg n school literacy: Does texting and knowledge of text abbreviations adversely affect children's literacy attainment? *Literacy, 42*(3), 137–144.

Raphael, L. M., Pressley, M., & Mohan, L. (2008). Engaging instruction in middle school classrooms: An observational study of nine teachers. *The Elementary School Journal, 109*(1), 61–81.

Rasinski, T., & Padak, N. D. (2005). Fluency beyond the primary grades: Helping adolescent struggling readers. *Voices from the Middle, 13*(1), 34–41.

Reis, S. M., McCoach, D. B., Coyne, M., Schreiber, F. J., Eckert, R. D., & Gubbins, E. J. (2007). Using planned enrichment strategies with direct instruction to improve reading fluency, comprehension, and attitude toward reading: An evidence-based study. *The Elementary School Journal, 108*(1), 3–23.

Schorzman, E. M., & Cheek Jr., E. H. (2004). Structured strategy instruction: Investigating an intervention for improving sixth-graders' reading comprehension. *Reading Psychology, 25,* 37–60.

Short, K. G., & Fox, D. L. (2004). The complexity of cultural authenticity in children's literature: A critical review. In J. Worthy, B. Maloch, J. V. Hoffman, D. L. Schallert, & C.M. Fairbanks (Eds.), *53rd yearbook of the National Reading Conference* (pp. 373–384). Oak Creek, WI: National Reading Conference.

Simmons, J., & Carroll, P. S. (2003). Today's middle grades: Different structures, students, and classrooms. In J. Flood, D. Lapp, J. R. Squire, & J. M. Jensen (Eds.). *Handbook of research on the teaching of the English language arts* (pp. 357–392). Mahwah, NJ: Erlbaum.

Smith, M.W., & Wilhelm, J. D. (2002). *"Reading don't fix no chevys": Literacy in the lives of young men.* Portsmouth, HN: Heinemann.

Smith, S. A. (2005). "We feel like we're separating us": Sixth grade girls respond to multicultural literature. In B. Maloch, J. V. Hoffman, D. L. Schallert, C. M. Fairbanks, & J. Worthy (Eds.), *54th yearbook of the National Reading Conference* (pp. 362–375). Oak Creek, WI: National Reading Conference.

Stevens, R. J. (2006). Integrated reading and language arts instruction. *Research in Middle Level Education Online, 30*(3), 1–12.

Tanner, J. M. (1972). Sequence, tempo, and individual variation in growth and development of boys and girls aged twelve to sixteen. In J. Kagan & R. Coles (Eds.), *Twelve to sixteen: Early adolescence* (pp. 1–24). New York: W.W. Norton.

Thames, D. G., Reeves, C., Kazelskis, R., York, K., Boling, C., Newell, K., & Wang, Y. (2008). Reading comprehension: Effects of individualized, integrated language arts as a reading approach with struggling readers. *Reading Psychology, 29,* 86–115.

Tierney, R. J., Bond, E., & Bresler, J. (2006). Examining literate lives as students engage with multiple literacies. *Theory into Practice, 45,* 359–367.

Turner, K. H. (2009). Flipping the switch: Code-switching from text speak to standard English. *English Journal, 98*(5), 60–65.

Yecki, C. P. (2005). *Mayhem in the middle: How middle schools have failed America — and how to make them work.* Washington, DC: Thomas B. Fordham Institute.

9

The Context of English Language Arts Learning

The High School Years

THOMAS W. BEAN AND HELEN HARPER

In the United States, the English Language Arts (ELA) classroom can be seen as a highly dynamic site: one in transition as it shifts curricular practices and policies to meet the changing social, economic, and demographic conditions of the 21st century (Burke, 2008). At the same time, and perhaps more often, the ELA classroom can be seen as a deeply conservative context, imbued with history, highly resistant to change, and continuing to maintain at its core, values, beliefs, and practices formed during the industrial age (Luke, 2004a, 2004b). Perhaps it is best described as a complex context where the conflicting forces of 'tradition and reform play out in the everyday of classroom life (Applebee, 1974; see also Sperling & DiPardo, 2008). Although this may be true for all school subjects, the dreams of the past, demands of the present, and possibilities for a soon-to-be-realized future would seem to collide with particular force in the high school ELA classroom.

In this chapter we will explore the historical and contemporary factors that currently shape the ELA high school years and its context in new and not so new ways, creating the tensions and ambivalences that come to define what is and is not possible in the ELA classroom. We begin with one of the most pressing factors affecting the context of ELA: a changing student population.

A Changing Population of High School English Language Arts Students

One of the most powerful and certainly most visible changes in the American educational context is the nature of the student population. Over the last 30 years, the student population has become more racially, culturally, and ethnically diverse. As noted in the U.S. Department of Education National Center for Education Statistics (NCES, 2009), between 1972 and 2007 the percentage of White students decreased from 78% to 56% while the minority population increased from 22% to 44%. In the Western states increasing racial and ethnic diversity is particularly evident: as of 2004,

minority enrollment exceeded white enrollment in Alaska, Arizona, California, Colorado, Hawai'i, Idaho, Montana, Nevada, New Mexico, Oregon, Utah, Washington, and Wyoming (NCES, 2009). The increase in minority enrollment mirrors changes in population in general. As of 2005, Hispanics, African Americans, Asians, Pacific islanders/Native Americans made up 33% of the U.S. population with Hispanics the largest minority group at 14%t (NCES, 2007; Pilonieta & Medina, 2009). The U.S. Bureau of Statistics (2009) predicts that by 2042 no one racial or ethic group will constitute a clear majority. The increasing diversity of the population is due in part to accelerated immigration rates brought about by globalization and the intensification of global capitalism. As noted by Gibson and Rojas (2006), globalization and the rapid social and economic changes it has engendered "is as much about deterritorialization and the displacement of a large and growing number of peoples, as it is about the free movement of capital, information and services" (p. 69). In the United States current estimates place the total number of foreign born at around 12% of the total population. School enrollment figures suggest that 20% (1 in 5) of all children in the United States are either foreign born or have at least one immigrant parent (NCES, 2009; Hernandez, Denton, & Macartney, 2009. This number is expected to double within the next twenty years (Jimenez & Teague, 2009; NESC, 2005). This is not the first time that there has been a large influx of immigrants to the United States, but families immigrating in these times originate not from Europe but predominantly from Latin America (62%), and Asia (22%), and, to a lesser extent, from Africa (2%). This shift, together with existing minority groups has dramatically increased the racial, ethnic, religious, cultural, and linguistic diversity of the country as a whole, and thus, the population of students in our schools. One of the effects of increasing and changing immigration patterns is that large numbers of students speak a language other than English at home. According to U.S. Department of Education National Centre for Education Statistics (NCES,

2008), the number of these students doubled from 3.8 to 10.8 million between 1979 and 2006. The vast majority of these students require English language instruction. Lee Gunderson (2008), drawing on statistics from The National Clearinghouse for English Language Acquisition and Language Instruction, reports that the percentage of English Language Learners (ELLs) in the United States has risen by 57% since 1995 and that ELLs now comprise over 10% of the total student population. In some states the increase in the number of ELLs has been nothing short of dramatic. North Carolina reports a 500% increase in the number of ELLs; Colorado, Nevada, Oregon, Nebraska, Georgia, and Indiana, over 200% (Pilonieta & Medina, 2009; Batalova, Fix, & Murray, 2005). Of particular interest to high school English teachers is the fact that the greatest increase in the number of ELLs is occurring in grades 7–12 (Gunderson, 2008, p.185). This increase reflects only those students who are classified as ELL, but not the whole range of students of second language learners who may still require English language support during the 5 to 7 years it takes to become proficient in academic English (Cummins, 2009). Changing immigrant patterns and increasing diversity suggests that more than ever a wider range of linguistic and cultural backgrounds and a wider range of English language proficiencies exist in the high school ELArts classroom. While this has always been true in urban schools, in some border communities, and in Native American/Alaskan/Hawaiian communities, it is now the rule rather than the exception. English language learning is thus becoming part and parcel of everyday life in high school ELA classes across the nation. More generally, growing awareness of the cultural, social, and linguistic diversity that exists across but also within groups, along with the acknowledgement of individual differences, makes it increasingly evident that heterogeneity rather than homogeneity characterizes the high school ELA classroom.

In light of this increasing diversity, ELA theory and practice needs to assume heterogeneity in the student population. For example, we need more research on how best to make academic instruction in English approachable for ELL and indeed, all students (Jimenez & Teague, 2009). Based on a review of curricular practices for ELL students, Jimenez and Teague argued that "any school that serves these students needs to analyze both instruction and content from the students' perspectives" (p. 130). In the English classroom, this means careful attention to mapping and gauging the demands of academic vocabulary and related concepts in planning instruction. The increasingly diverse and heterogenous nature of contemporary students means that the nature and educational needs of youth are not easily generalizable, if indeed they ever were. Recent scholarship suggests that the assumptions and generalizations that have historically named "youth" and "adolescence" do not and perhaps never have captured the dynamic, complex, and diverse nature of this population and their various skills and knowledges which may or may not be shared by adults (e.g., computer skills; Alvermann, 2009; Bean & Harper, 2009;

Lesko, 2001; Vadeboncoeur & Stevens, 2005). Acknowledging the complexity and diversity of youth, their skills, abilities, and knowledges can enrich classroom life, but, at the same time, requires rethinking curricular practices and policies that have been constructed rightly or wrongly on the assumption that students share a social, cultural, and linguistic background, and, collectively, have only limited or deficient skills and knowledges compared to adults. At the very least it can be said that the changing nature of the student population and its increasing diversity factors strongly in the 21st-century context of teaching and learning. It is one force among many in this era of contemporary globalization demanding response in the context of high school ELA classes.

Changing Subject English: Adolescent Literacy

Related to the changing nature of the student body, another factor affecting the high school ELA classroom has been the increasing attention to the basic literacy skills of adolescents. Evidence from a variety of sources indicates that ELA students as a whole are not doing well in this area. Statistics from the U.S. Department of Education are particularly alarming. Although the average reading and mathematics scores on the long-term trend National Assessment of Educational Progress (NAEP) were higher in 2008 than in the early 1970s for 9- and 13-year-olds, the scores for 17-year-olds were not measurably different over the same period (NCES, 2009).

One can speculate that this trend will continue and possibly escalate if ELA teachers are not adequately prepared to teach a diverse group of students, including the growing population of ELL students. Tracking and marginalizing ELL students contributes to maintaining the status quo in students' performance on high-stakes tests and reduces access and opportunities to acquire mainstream cultural capital (Jimenez & Teague, 2009).

Simply put, there has been no improvement in the reading scores of adolescent students over some 30 years. While the Program for International Student Assessment (PISA), which measures the academic performance of 15-year-old students from across 30 industrialized nations, indicates that U.S. students' literacy achievement is at average with students from the other countries, students from Finland, Canada, and New Zealand clearly outperformed their American counterparts. The National Governors Association 2005 reports that only 3 out of 10 eighth-grade students are proficient readers, and almost 40% of high school graduate lack the reading and writing skills those employers seek (National Governors Association, 2005). Language diversity in the United States may well contribute to this difference. Nevertheless, some findings suggest only 50% of high school graduates have acquired the reading skills necessary to succeed in college (Lewin, 2005).

Considering the increase in the diversity of the student body nationally, there is also growing concern over the persistent underachievement of ELLs, racial and ethnic minority students, and students from lower socioeconomic backgrounds (PISA, 2003; NCES, 2009, 2008, 2005). As reported by Short and Fitzsimmons (2007), English language learners are among the nation's lowest performing students with 71% of students identified as ELL performing below grade level. Although there are exceptions, as a group ELLs are less likely to succeed in school, often have low reading scores, and greater difficulty passing state high school literacy exit exams and thus, not surprisingly, have one of the highest drop-out rates of any group (Duran, 2008; Gunderson, 2008; PISA, 2003). As stated by Jimenez and Teague (2009), "It is clear that the number of ELLs in the secondary grades is sizable, is growing, and that this population is not currently being well served" (p.114).

In addition to the ELL population, speakers of various dialects including African American Vernacular English (AAVE) also deserve attention in the ELA classroom (Brock, McMillan, Pennington, Townsend, & Lapp, 2009). Valuing students' linguistic diversity involves treating language as dynamic and contextualized with an emphasis on code shifting across contexts. For example, knowing when and how to move from AAVE to standard English (e.g., in writing a formal paper) is crucial (Brock et al., 2009). Using literature that features and respects linguistic diversity, including AAVE, demonstrates valuing multiple language forms (Brock et al., 2009).

Others have emphasized the need to explore language as directly related to the tensions of power (Fecho, Davis, & Moore, 2006). These researchers had their adolescent students in English create questions surrounding language and power. For example, how do people react to a Black English (AAVE) speaker who fluidly code shifts into standard English? Students conducted interviews, kept journals, and made audio recordings that began to probe the power dimensions in play for their various questions. Fecho et al. (2006) argue that all stakeholders in an ELA classroom should engage in language inquiry that exposes how power operates to permit or disrupt access to cultural capital. "All stakeholders need to acknowledge the oppressive nature of mainstream power codes while affording students the opportunity to become fluent in those codes" (p. 200).

By incorporating multiple language codes into the ELA classroom, students whose language and dialect might, in the past, be excluded from the center of instruction can become a focal point for exploring the complex and nuanced way language operates to chart or derail possible futures. The stakes are high as recent analyses show.The achievement gap between African American and Hispanic students, and Caucasian students is such that according to the National Centre for Education Statistics reports "a 13 year old dominant-majority student's academic performance matches or exceeds that of a 17 year old black or Latino high school senior" (Portes & Salas, 2009, p. 97). Teale, Paciga, and Hoffman (2007) among others, point to the literacy achievement gap that continues to exist between low-income and middle-/high-income students. The results from PISA confirm this gap, and indicate further that the portion of American students with low socioeconomic status and low test scores is higher than in all but one other country (PISA, 2003). As David Moore (2009) states, "This means that the United States is among the least effective industrialized countries in ameliorating the results of low social and economic status on academic performance" (p. 19). Considering that approximately 40% of Hispanic, African American and Native America children, along with 14% of White, non-Hispanic children live in poverty, there is a strong need for reform (Portes & Salas, 2009). Finally, although evidence continues to show a gender difference in literacy achievement with female students outperforming males across the spectrum (PISA, 2003), there is a growing concern that a substantial portion of girls and many boys are not proficient readers and writers (Brozo & Gaskins, 2009; NAEP, 2005; Sprague & Keeling, 2009). In light of these various findings, the Alliance for Excellent Education (2006) boldly states, "American adolescents face a literacy crisis" (p.1). With no measurable improvement in literacy scores for high school students over the last 30 years, with current measures confirming significant segments of the high school population struggling with reading and writing, adolescent literacy is receiving greater attention than at any other time in the past (Cassidy, Valadez, Garrett, & Barrera, 2010).

As will be outlined in the policy section of this chapter, local, state, and federal governments, agencies, and associations along with various advocacy groups have promoted a variety of initiatives aimed at improving ELA practices and policy. In the past, initiatives focused almost exclusively on improving literacy learning in elementary grades, as noted by Carol Santa in 1999, then president of the International Reading Association, "In the United States, most Title 1 budgets are allocated for early interventions—little is left over for the struggling adolescent reader" (Moore et. al., 1999, p.1). In addition to some change in funding, there is an expanding body of research now focused on a wide spectrum of topics falling under the rubric of adolescent literacy (see, for example, Alvermann, Hinchman, Moore, Phelps & Waff, 2006; Christenbury, Bomer, & Smagorinsky, 2009; Guzzetti, 2007; Lewis, 2009; Wood & Blanton, 2009; Lewis & Moorman, 2007; see also Journal of Adolescent & Adult Literacy). Of course, there has always been a concern for and interest in the reading and writing abilities of high school students, but at this time improving the literacy performance of high school students seems particularly urgent. This urgency is due in part to various assessments mentioned earlier, but underlying these tests, their development and the reactions to their findings, are more general concerns and fears that reside well beyond the classroom doors.

As mentioned earlier, intensifying globalization and the development of global capitalism has accelerated the movement of people across borders. At times the efforts to improve the literacy education of the large and increasingly diverse population of adolescents who are new to the country and those historically underserved and underachieving groups of adolescents (African Americans, Native Americans, Hispanics, etc.) have been framed within a notion of social justice and a need to insure the opportunities and possibilities of American democratic and economic life are available to all. Ensuring such opportunities increases the political and economic involvement of all citizens, which in turn supports the ongoing development and security of American life.

Although these are important goals, they may be too narrowly focused on national interest to the exclusion of global, transnational needs and circumstances. The Internet offers adolescents and migrant adolescents borderless contact with peers around the globe. As we reconceptualize the ELA classroom to acknowledge the importance of national goals situated in a global context, research on transnational communication will also be increasingly important. For example, Lam (2009), in an in-depth case study of the instant messaging practices of an adolescent girl who migrated from China to the United States, argued for a curriculum that accounts for the fluidity of communication practices across and beyond national borders. Lam posed the following question: "In other words, how may we envisage literacy education that recognizes the affiliations that young people of migrant backgrounds have with diverse linguistic and cultural communications and promote their ability to draw from the social and textual resources in these communities for their learning?" (p. 394).

A combination of advanced Internet based communication skills and more traditional literacy skills meet head on in our contemporary ELA classrooms to meet both national interests and transnational global circumstances. Both are important elements as we think about how best to frame ELA curriculum for the 21st century. A number of significant challenges to teachers' incorporation of new literacies practices in secondary English remain. For example, Lewis and Chandler-Olcott (2009) explored 16 secondary English teachers' experiences and perspectives as they sought to incorporate digital literacies in students' literature responses. In one instance, a teacher wanted to have her students compose text messages between two characters in Arthur Miller's play, The Crucible. Because students were only allowed to create simulated text messages (not online) by having to handwrite their messages, they complained that their cell phones would have facilitated this process. As a result, the creative potential of the assignment was derailed by an odd mix of old and new literacies practices. These hybrid practices were at least a nod to new literacies potentials but, clearly, the obstacles to engaging students in realistic digital literature responses ran head on into district policies concerning access to the Internet. In addition, issues surrounding students' basic literacy development also conspired to limit students' code shifting from creative text messaging forms (e.g., LOL) to formal language.

Since the beginnings of the nation, basic literacy skills have been considered part of what is necessary to secure full economic and political involvement (Shannon, 2007, 2001). Possessing strong literacy skills provides cultural capital that can result in better job prospects and better communication and thus greater harmony and unity across the difference and diversity that comprises the nation.

However, another argument concerns the nation in the world and suggests that the improvement of literacy scores of adolescents, who will soon be voting citizens and domestic/global workers, is necessary in order to ensure and secure America's economic and political standing in the world. In particular, a sound literacy education is considered essential to developing a strong labor force that will help to ensure America's global competitiveness.

In these new times the need to develop adolescents' literacy skills serves in fact or in fiction to alleviate the fears of a changing world, a changing nation, and a changing community and the fears that Americans will not be able to seize the new and emerging opportunities brought about by globalization. However it is understood, basic literacy is now a factor in the context of the high school ELA program. At the very least the teaching of basic literacy is no longer considered the exclusive responsibility of the elementary school teacher.

While the improvement of basic literacy skills is a strong concern, the new communication technologies are also a factor in the high school ELA context. Globalization has brought not only the accelerated movement of people and capital, but because of the new technologies, the rapid movement of ideas, images, and information (Spring, 2008). Many adolescents (with the resources to do so) have embraced technology as an integral part of their world, logging many hours writing, composing videos, and communicating on Internet sites with enthusiasm (Considine, Horton, & Moorman, 2009; Lam, 2009; Tapscott, 2009). Indeed, these new modalities and new literacies practices are changing the form and nature of communication locally and globally; and are factoring into the high school ELA context.

Changing Subject English: New and Multiple Literacies

The terms "new literacies" and "multiple literacies" are umbrella categories that attempt to name the fast-moving flows of the Internet and other non-print media, and the literacies, practices, and competencies such media require. In addition, new and multiliteracies has the potential to change in thinking about knowledge, communication and education, particularly with respect to the value of collaboration, inquiry in learning, and creativity in knowledge construction, and as will be discussed, literacy itself (Bean, 2010; Coiro, Knobel, Lankshear, & Leu, 2008; Knobel & Lankshear, 2009).

The new technologies and the new literacies that result are dynamic. The Internet, for example, has shifted from an information storage and retrieval site (i.e., a site of consumption) to one where users can produce and display an array of multimedia texts (i.e., a site of production). Adolescents have taken to the new communication technologies, embracing the new and emerging possibilities offered; for example, using Web 2.0's interactive properties to engage in wiki writing, online book clubs, and other ever-evolving forums for collaboration. Current estimates vary but in general suggest that over 1.3 billion people worldwide are using the Internet, the vast majority of these users, adolescents and young adults (Tapscott, 2009).

In a large-scale study of Net Generation students (born between January 1977 and December 1997), Tapscott found adolescents and young adults using the new technologies for work and for play, both producing and consuming ideas, information, images; constructing themselves and their worlds. These findings are supported by other research; for example, in a review of research in new literacies and the English classroom, Snyder and Bulfin (2008) noted that more than half of American teenagers have created material for the Internet.

Researchers and educators have been exploring the pedagogical potential in the new communication technologies (Coiro, Knobel, Lankshear, & Leu, 2008; Considine, Horton, & Moorman, 2009; Walker, Bean, & Dillard, 2010). The pedagogical possibilities of the new and multiliteracies, in addition to the intense engagement of adolescents in new multiliteracies practices, suggest that teachers need to better tailor in-school curriculum that taps into these practices (Tierney, 2009). And certainly educators, particularly those whose schools and districts provide technological support and access, have been quick to develop classrooms activities that involve the new and multiple literacies for their students including minority and ELLs. In a recent article, West (2008) noted that Weblogs (blogging) offer a vehicle for student writing and collaborative interpretation in the English classroom where students can weigh in to critically comment on novels, films, poetry, essays, and a host of other literature. Similarly, Scharber (2009) explored online book clubs as a way of integrating old and new literacies practices. Judith Rance-Roney (2010) has developed "digital jumpstarts" for English language learners that provide much needed content background knowledge using the new technologies.

The new communication technologies are redefining the "basic" literacies needed for 21st-century life, and therefore literacy instruction in the English language arts classroom. In a 2008 document from the National Council of Teachers of English (NCTE), the link between literacy instruction and technology is notes: "As society and technology change so does literacy. Because technology has increased the intensity and complexity of literate environments, the twenty-first century demands that a literate person possess a wide range of abilities and competencies, [thus] many literacies" (NCTE, 2008, n.p.). Specific skills and competencies listed involve developing proficiency with the tools of technology, the ability to individually and collaboratively design and share information, images and ideas across culture, the abilities to manage, analyze and evaluate multimedia texts, and to attend to the ethically responsibilities required by new and expanding communication environments.

More generally, the new technologies challenge traditional notions and value of print-based school literacies. They challenge the dominance of print literacy, shift authority over reading and writing norms away from a central institution or individual, broaden and diversify the audiences and purposes, and stress, not individual ownership or authorship of a work, but, instead encourage collaboration, sharing, and collective production (Alvermann, 2009; Kress, 2003). With these challenges, the new literacies have the potential to change the subject of English language dramatically.

However, whether the schools, the teachers or the students are fully, deeply, or not at all engaged in the new literacies, and the challenge the new communication technologies present to print-based literacy instruction, the impact of new and emerging technology will be felt by all for better or worse, both now and in the future (Hull, Zacher, & Hibbert, 2009; Luke, 2004a, 2004b; Tapscott, 2009). At the very least the ELA classroom is and will be redefined by the new literacies, if only in terms of its relevance (or not) to the soon-to-be-realized futures of 21st-century adolescents.

In addition to the new and multiliteracies, an increased emphasis on policy is also factoring into the context of 21st-century ELA classroom. We turn now to these developments.

Policy Developments and the ELA Classroom

Unlike the recent past, today high school English teachers and university educators have access to numerous research reports, position papers, and policy documents, along with state and district standards and guidelines pertaining specifically to the literacy of adolescents. Donna Alvermann (2009) notes that in the year 2007, no fewer than eight major reports on adolescent literacy, commissioned by highly respected professional organizations and private foundations, were released to school boards and districts as well as the general public.

Most recently, the National Governors Association (2009) has proposed a set of Common Core State Standards in English language arts to replace the highly diverse current state standards. Centered on developing students work in a global, digitally influenced world, the core standards for reading, writing, and speaking and listening recommend that "English language arts teachers not only must engage their students in a rich array of literature but also must help their students' ability to read complex works of nonfiction independently" (p. i).

In recognition of the need for policies that drive teacher support through professional development, Hinchman (2009), writing on behalf of the Literacy Research Association Board of Directors, noted that "The proposed standards represent expectations for reading comprehension and oral language that very few secondary teachers are now prepared to meet" (p. 2). In addition, Hinchman argued that more emphasis on digital literacies versus the overwhelming attention to traditional print literacy skills needs to be represented in any final version of the core standards.

Undoubtedly, the one private foundation that has spearheaded the call to improve literacy instruction for adolescents is the Carnegie Corporation of New York. Pointing to high school dropout rates of 3000 students-per-day, the Carnegie often-cited document: Reading Next: A Vision for Action and Research in Middle and High School Literacy (Biancarosa & Snow, 2006), focused on struggling adolescent readers. Various strategies shown to be effective with adolescent learners (e.g., graphic organizers, summarization, question asking), were viewed as crucial for preparing high school students "to become productive citizens in the workplace" (The State of Adolescent Literacy, n.d.). Citing meta-analytic studies of well-established and successful strategies like graphic organizers, and concept mapping, Reading Next directs the attention of educators to instructional practice and reaffirms the importance of improving adolescent literacy in the ELA classroom.

In addition to an ongoing concern with high school students' reading development, writing has its own call to action. *Writing Next* (Graham & Perin, 2007) is a sister report to *Reading Next,* and, while acknowledging the reciprocal relationship between reading and writing, argues for dedicated writing instruction as an end in itself. In a meta-analytic review of writing instruction, Graham and Perrin found that teaching students planning, revising, and editing strategies specific to various genres (e.g., persuasive writing), improved secondary students' writing. This carefully scaffolded, dedicated writing instruction was most beneficial for low achieving writers. Teaching summarization through a gradual fading of teacher support, along with collaborative writing also showed significant impact on students' compositions. Computer support for writing was helpful in constructing multiple drafts.

The National Writing Project, with many years of support for teachers' professional development in writing instruction and a long track record of success (e.g., Olson, in press, welcomed attention to writing and the focus on the research findings found in *Writing Next*. In their response to the report, Coyle and Bennett of the National Writing Project (2006) noted that "When students are given opportunities to write throughout the day, they sharpen their writing, their reading, and their learning, leading to higher achievement levels in courses across the curriculum" (p. 1). Taken together the *Reading Next* and *Writing Next* focus the high school English language arts teacher on improving literacy through the deployment of specific pedagogical strategies and practices. An instrumental focus dominates the discourse in both documents.

In a similar way the International Reading Association in conjunction with other professional associations including the National Council of Teachers of English, has developed *Standards for Middle and Secondary High School Literacy Coaches* (2006) calling for collaboration between English language arts teachers and literacy coaches. Such collaboration is aimed at helping high school students' literacy, by ensuring among other things, that students can identify the main and supporting ideas in text passages, understand text structures, and read for deeper and critical understanding. Although not directed at the English language arts teacher, the standards for literacy coaches, shifts the work of the ELA teacher to include collaboration with other specific literacy professionals to improve students' literacy performance.

In addition to these three reports, the National Council of Teachers of English, the International Reading Association, and the National Reading Conference (recently renamed the Literacy Research Association), have developed position papers and statements that address broader aims and directions for adolescent literacy. These and other documents are now widely available and indicate the strong interest and concern about ELA curriculum, the details of which evidently cannot be left to individual teachers or school departments. In addition there is a question as to whether these policy documents are affecting the ELA classroom, as noted by Donna Alvermann (2009), "Given all of this top-down attention to adolescent literacy, I have to wonder when the high profile that the field [of adolescent literacy] is presently experiencing will have a major impact on classroom instruction at the secondary level or for that matter, at the postsecondary/tertiary level" (p. 99). Policy documents, whether the vast majority of teachers are specifically aware of them or not, have become part of the context of high school ELA. We anticipate that more and more ELA teachers will be required to know and use these documents in their curriculum planning and delivery. What we do know is that high-stakes testing and the thinking that supports these tests is a factor currently affecting the ELA classroom. The provisos of No Child Left Behind with its emphasis on high-stakes testing remain largely in place and are a part of the everyday of the ELA context.

High-Stakes Testing

Many states have instituted state literacy examines that all students at the secondary level must pass in order to receive their high school diploma (Tierney, 2009). Typically, and relevant to the ELA classroom, these standardized assessments aim to measure print-based literacy achievement with a focus on vocabulary and relatively low level comprehension questions on selected passages. Despite the prominence of new literacies in adolescents' lives, the ELA classroom must naturally accommodate federal mandates by narrowly defining what counts as literacy.

Indeed, in a qualitative metasynthesis of 49 studies, Au (2007) found that high-stakes testing tended to narrow subject area content into easily testable items. Creative thinking, reflection, and thoughtful analysis take a back seat in order to accommodate high-stakes tests. Unfortunately, many of the current policies mitigate against progressive, creative, forward thinking teaching of high school English. Sadly, if these policies persist, we are likely to see a continuing trend in high school dropout rates and a population of citizens well trained in answering narrow, testable questions but ill prepared to participate in a cosmopolitan, global world (Tierney, 2009).

The ELA Past: The ELA Future

In addition to high-stakes testing and the continuing curriculum focus on print-based literacies in English, in our view, what seems to be missing is a realization that high school students are entering a global world. As we suggested earlier, preparation as world citizens with dispositions to function fluidly and intelligently across nation-state borders and cultures should be a centerpiece of curriculum design. There are a few beacons on the horizon that deserve attention. For example, the NCTE (2008) document cited earlier that aims to chart 21st-century literacies specifically mentions ensuring that students develop facility with technology, engage in collaboration, participate in global communities, and create multimedia texts (Alvermann, 2009). This document and ongoing research and discussion in ELAs' professional communities has the potential to chart a new course that better serves contemporary adolescents. As noted earlier, our diverse population of students demands a course change that balances public interest in accountability with the talents and dispositions needed to function in a global world.

Our well-documented diversity both locally and nationally is matched by increasing interconnectedness and interdependency of people globally. There is a concomitant need for communication skills and global sensibilities that will ensure creative and productive workers and citizens. Diversity and changing socioeconomics brought about by globalization, but also by technological changes should be driving changes in our ELA curriculum that acknowledges and capitalizes upon students' local and international funds of knowledge (i.e., their unique literatures and cultures). Attention to reading means also attending to the changing literacy needs of the 21st century. In essence, English teaching can keep one foot rooted in the past with enduring canonical literature while expanding into global literature and digital spaces that afford students an opportunity to produce their own unique responses to these works.

There are some instances where high school English is embracing a more contemporary model that acknowledges diversity, globalization, and the fast-moving nature of text in new literacies Internet-based multimedia (Prosek, 2007). But these classrooms seem to be an oasis in the larger landscape of secondary English where canonical literature and traditional writing conventions are privileged.

Tapscott (2009, p. 126) argued that "Students need to be able to think creatively, critically, and collaboratively" to function in a global world. However, he also noted that the prevailing model of education remains sadly mired in the Industrial Age with an emphasis of the teacher at the center of learning, delivering information.

There are exceptions. For example, Scott Prosek, an Alaskan English teacher decided to teach English in an international school context where his students came from 20 different nations (Prosek, 2007). In thinking about his English curriculum in this setting, he began to examine "What constitutes being literate as a citizen of the world"

(p. 99). Based on a discussion of "cultural literacy," Prosek asked his students to create lists reflecting what it means to be literate in their various cultures. He then challenged students to think about what it might be like to step out of the comfort zone of their own culture's literature to reflect on global citizenship. "In broadening what it means to study English, we can do much to broaden what it means to be culturally literate" (Prosek, p. 101). Having students translate poems from various languages into English provokes the question, "what is gained and what is lost?"

To a great extent, adolescents playing multiplayer worldwide video games and communicating on social networks about immigration policy, the economy, and other issues are already many steps ahead of our standards based curriculum, forged to fit high-stakes testing but diminish deep, intellectual thought.

Since the second edition of the *Handbook of Research on Teaching the English Language Arts* and Thomas Newkirk's (2003) chapter on the high school, the structural features of high schools have changed very little in terms of their departmental organization, sheer size, and narrow high-stakes assessments.

Therefore, in many ways, Newkirk accurately predicted a high school model that persists and impedes the very talents and skills students need for 21st-century life. At the close of Newkirk's (2003) chapter, the then predominant model of big high schools with predictable single subject department structures was viewed as a model that the public wanted to retain, despite documented problems with attrition. Newkirk concluded that "It is a system where a majority of students fail to develop the habits of mind central to reflective thought" (p. 402).

As the demographic data in this chapter illustrate, these are new times that call for an equally revolutionary English curriculum that combines wisdom from the past with the rich resources multiliteracies offer. Amidst Adequate Yearly Progress (AYP), No Child Left Behind (NCLB), and the continuing emphasis on high-stakes testing, such a change will require courage and professional collaboration across NCTE, International Reading Association, and other organizations that give voice to the field and directly inform practice.

References

Alliance for Excellent Education. (2006, June). Why the crisis in adolescent literacy demands a national response: Policy brief. Washington, DC: Author. Retrieved September 1, 2009, from http://www.all4ed.org/publication_material/fact_sheets/crisis

Alvermann, D. (2009). Research//Teaching adolescents: Literacies with a history. In J. Hoffman & Y. Goodman (Eds.), *Changing literacies for changing times: An historical perspective on the future of reading research, public policy and classroom practices* (pp. 98–107). New York: Routledge.

Alvermann, D., Hinchman, K., Moore, D., Phelps, S., & Waff, D. (Eds.). (2006). *Reconceptualizing the literacies in adolescents' Lives* (2nd ed.). Mahwah, NJ: Erlbaum.

Applebee, A. (1974). *Tradition and reform in the teaching of English: A history.* Urbana, IL: National Council of Teachers of English.

Au, W. (2007). High-stakes testing and curricular control: A qualitative metasynthesis. *Educational Researcher*, 36, 258–267.

Batalova, J., Fix, M., & Murray, J. (2005). *Measures of change: The demography and literacy of adolescent English language learners—a report to the Carnegie Corporation of New York*. New York: Migration Policy Institute.

Bean, T. W. (2010). *Multimodal learning for the 21st century adolescent*. Huntington Beach, CA: Shell Education.

Bean, T. W., & Harper, H. (2009). The "Adolescent" in adolescent literacy: A preliminary review. In K. Woods & W. Blanton (Eds.), *Literacy instruction for adolescents: Research-based practice* (pp. 37–53). New York: Guilford.

Biancarosa, G., & Snow, C. (2006). *Reading next: A vision for action and researchin middle and high school literacy: A report to the Carnegie Corporation of New York* (2nd ed.). Washington, DC: Alliance for Excellent Education. Retrieved January 8, 2007, from http://www.all4ed.org/publications/ReadingNext/ReadingNext.pdf

Brock, C. H., McMillan, G. T., Pennington, J. L., Townsend, D., & Lapp, D. (2009). Academic English and African American Vernacular English. In L. M. Morrow, R. Rueda, & D. Lapp (Eds.), *Handbook of research on literacy and diversity* (pp. 137–157). New York: Guilford Press.

Brozo, W., & Gaskins, C. (2009). Engaging texts and literacy practices for adolescentboys. In K. Wood & W. Blanton (Eds.), *Literacy instruction for adolescents: Research-based practice* (pp. 170–186). New York: Guilford Press.

Burke, J. (2008). *The English teacher's companion* (3rd ed.). Portsmouth, NH: Heinemann.

Carnegie Corporation of New York. (n.d.). *The state of adolescent literacy today: Why adolescent literacy matters*. Retrieved June 16, 2009 from http://www.carnegie.org/literacy/why.html

Cassidy, J., Valadez, C., Garrett, S. D., & Barrera, E. (2010, March). Adolescent & adult literacy: What's hot, what's not. *Journal of Adolescent & Adult Literacy*, 53, 448–456.

Christenbury, L., Bomer, R., & Smagorinsky, P. (2009). *Handbook of adolescent literacy research*. New York: Guilford Press.

Coiro, J., Knobel, M., Lankshear, C., & Leu, D. J. (Eds.). (2008). *Handbook of research on new literacies*. New York: Erlbaum/Taylor Francis.

Considine, D., Horton, J., & Moorman, G. (2009). Teaching and reaching the millennial generation through media literacy. *Journal of Adolescent & Adult Literacy*, 52, 471–481.

Coyle, J., & Bennett, G. (2006). *National Writing Project responds to Writing Nextreport*. Retrieved February 28, 2007, from http://www.writingproject.org/cs/nwpp/1pt/nwpr/2359

Cummins, J. (2009). Literacy and English-Language Learners: A shifting landscape for students, teachers, researchers, and policy makers. *Educational Researcher*, 38, 382–384.

Duran, R. (2008). Assessing English-Language learners' achievement. In G. Kelly, A. Luke, & J. Green (Eds.), *Review of research in education, 32* (pp. 292–327). Thousand Oakes, CA: Sage.

Fecho, B., Davis, B., & Moore, R. (2006). Exploring race, language, and culture in critical literacy classrooms. In D. E. Alvermann, K. A. Hinchman, D. W. Moore, S. F. Phelps, & D. R. Waff (Eds.), *Reconceptualizing the literacies in adolescents' lives* (2nd ed., pp. 187–204). Mahwah, NJ: Erlbaum.

Gibson, M. A., & Rojas, A. R. (2006). Globalization, immigration, and the education of "new" immigrants in the 21st century. *Current Issues in Comparative Education, 9*(1), 69–76.

Graham, S., & Perin, D. (2007). *Writing next: Effective strategies to improve writing of adolescents in middle and high schools: A report to the Carnegie Corporationof New York*. Washington, DC: Alliance for Excellent Education. Retrieved February 12, 2007, from http//www.all4ed.org/publications/WritingNext/WritingNext.pdf

Gunderson, L. (2008). The state of art of secondary ESL teaching and learning. *Journal of Adolescent & Adult Literacy, 52*(3), 184–187.

Guzzetti, B. (2007). *Literacy for the new millennium: Adolescent literacies* (Vol. 3). Westport, CT: Praeger/Greenwood.

Hernandez, D., Denton, N., & Macartney, S. (2009). School-age children in immigrant families: Challenges and opportunities for America's schools. *Teachers College Record, 11*, 616–658.

Hinchman, K. (2009, October). *Letter to the National Governors Association Center for Best Practices from the Board of Directors, Literacy Research Association*. Oak Creek, WI: Literacy Research Association.

Hull, G., Zacher, Z., & Hibbert, L. (2009). Youth, risk, and equity in a global world. *Review of Research in Education, 33*, 117–159.

Jimenez, R., & Teague, B. (2009). Language, literacy, and content: Adolescent English language learners. In L. Morrow, R. Reuda, & D. Lapp (Eds.), *The handbook of research on literacy and diversity* (pp. 114–136). New York: Guilford Press.

Knobel, M., & Lankshear, C. (2009). Wikis, digital literacies, and professional growth. *Journal of Adolescent & Adult Literacy, 52*, 632–634.

Kress, G. (2003). *Literacy in the new media age*. London: Routledge.

Lam, W. S. E. (2009). Multiliteracies on instant messagingin negotiating local, transnational affiliations: A case of an adolescent immigrant. *Reading Research Quarterly, 44*, 377–397.

Lesko, N. (2001). *Act your age: A cultural construction of adolescence*. New York: Routledge Falmer.

Lewin, T. (2005, August 17). Many going to college are not ready, report says. *New York Times*, 8.

Lewis, E. C., & Chandler-Olcott, K. (2009). From screen to page: Secondary English Teachers' perspectives on redesigning their teaching of literature in a new literacies era. In K. M. Leander, D. W. Rowe, D. K. Dickenson, M. K. Hundley, R. T. Jimenez, & V. J. Risko (Eds.), *58th yearbook of the National Reading Conference* (pp. 205–217). Oak Creek, WI: National Reading Conference.

Lewis, J. (2009). *Essential questions in adolescent literacy*. New York: Guilford Press.

Lewis, J., & Moorman, G. (2007). *Adolescent literacy instruction: Policies and promising practices*. Newark, DE: International Reading Association.

Luke, A. (2004a). The trouble with English. *Research in the Teaching of English, 39*(1), 85–95.

Luke, A. (2004b). Teaching after the market: From commodity to cosmopolitan. *Teachers College Record, 106*, 1422–1433.

Moore, D. (2009). Advocating reading instruction in middle and high school classrooms. In K. Wood & W. Blanton (Eds.), *Literacy instruction for adolescents: Research-based practice* (pp. 13–33). New York: Guilford Press.

Moore, D. W., Bean, T. W., Birdyshaw, D., & Rycik, J. A. (1999). *Adolescent literacy: A position statement for the Commission on Adolescent Literacy of the International Reading Association*. Newark, DE: International Reading Association.

National Center for Educational Statistics (NCES). U. S. Department of Education. Retrieved August 10, 2009, from http://cnces.ed.gov

National Council of Teachers of English Executive Committee. (2008). *Toward a definition of 21st-century literacies*. Retrieved August 13, 2009, from http://www.ncte://www.ncte.org/announce/129117.htm

National Governors Association Center for Best Practices. (2005). *Reading to achieve: A governor's guide to adolescent literacy*. Washington, DC: Author. Retrieved from http://www.nga.org

National Governors Association Center for Best Practices Core Standards. (n.d.). Washington, DC: Retrieved December 4, 2009, from http://www.corestandards.org

Newkirk, T. (2003). The learner develops: The high school years. In J. Flood, D. Lapp, J. R. Squire, & J. M. Jensen (Eds.), *Handbook of research on teaching the English language arts* (2nd ed., pp. 393–404). Mahwah, NJ: Erlbaum.

Olson, C. (in press). Teaching secondary English language learners to understand, analyze, and write interpretive essays about theme. *Journal of Adolescent & Adult Literacy*.

Organisation for Economic Co-operation and Development. (n.d.). The PISA 2003 assessment framework—mathematics, reading, science and problem solving knowledge and skills. Retrieved September 1, 2009, from http://www.pisa.oecd.org

Pilonieta, P., & Medina, A. (2009). Meeting the needs of English language learners in middle and secondary classroom. In K. Wood & W. Blanton

(Eds.), *Literacy instruction for adolescents: Research-based practice* (pp. 125–143). New York: Guildford Press.

Portes, P., & Salas, S. (2009). Poverty and its relation to development and literacy. In L. Morrow, R. Reuda, & D. Lapp (Eds.), *The handbook of research on literacy and diversity* (pp. 97–113). New York: Guilford Press.

Prosek, S. (2007). Rethinking English and literacy: A view from overseas. *English Journal, 96*(5), 98–101.

Rance-Roney, J. (2010, Feb.). Jumpstarting language and schema for English language learners: Teacher-composed digital jumpstarts for academic reading. *Journal of Adolescent & Adult Literacy, 53*, 386–395.

Scharber, C. (2009). Online book clubs: Bridges between old and new literacies practice. *Journal of Adolescent & Adult Literacy, 52*, 433–437.

Shannon, P. (2001). *Becoming political, too.* Portsmouth, NH: Heinemann.

Shannon, P. (2007). *Reading against democracy: The broken promises of reading instruction.* Portsmouth, NH: Heinemann.

Short, D. J., & Fitzsimmons, S. (2007). *Double the work: Challenges and solutions to acquiring language and academic literacy for adolescent English language learners—a report to Carnegie Corporation of New York.* Washington, DC: Alliance for Excellent Education. Retrieved August 10, 2009, from http://www.all4ed.org/adolescent_literacy/index.html

Snyder, I., & Bulfin, S. (2008). Using new media in the secondary English classroom. In J. Coiro, M. Knobel, C. Lankshear, & D. J. Leu (Eds.), *Handbook of research on new literacies* (pp. 805–837). New York: Erlbaum/Taylor & Francis.

Sperling, M., & DiPardo, A. (2008). English Education research and classroom practice: New directions for new times. In G. Kelly, A. Luke,

& J. Green (Eds.), *Review of research in education, 32* (pp. 62–108). Thousand Oakes, CA: Sage.

Sprague, M., & Keeling, K. (2009). Paying attention to girls' literacy needs. In K. Wood & W. Blanton (Eds.) *Literacy instruction for adolescents: Research-based practice* (pp. 187–209). New York: Guilford Press.

Spring, J. (2008). Research on globalization and education. *Review of Educational Research, 78*, 330–363.

Standards for middle and high school literacy coaches. (2006). Newark, DE: International Reading Association.

Tapscott, D. (2009). *Grown up digital: How the net generation is changing your world.* New York: McGraw-Hill.

Teale, W. H., Paciga, K. A. & Hoffman J. L. (2007). Beginning reading instruction in urban schools: The curriculum gap ensures a continuing achievement gap. *Reading Teacher, 61*, 344–348.

Tierney, R. J. (2009). Literacy education 2.0: Looking through the rear vision mirror as we move ahead. In J. V. Hoffman, & Y. M. Goodman (Eds.), *Changing literacies for changing times* (pp. 282–303). New York: Routledge.

United States Bureau of Statistics. Department of Educational Statistics. (2009). Retrieved August 10, 2009, from http://nces.ed.gov/programs/coe

Vadeboncoeur, J. A., & Patel Stevens, L. (2005). *Re/constructing "the adolescent."* New York: Peter Lang.

Walker, N., Bean, T. W., & Dillard, B. (2010). *When textbooks fall short: New ways, new texts, new sources of information in the content areas.* Portsmouth, NH: Heinemann.

West, K. C. (2008). Weblogs and literacy response: Socially situated identities and hybrid social language in English class blogs. *Journal of Adolescent & Adult Literacy, 51*, 588–598.

Wood, K. D., & Blanton, W. E. (2009). *Literacy instruction for adolescents: Research-based practice.* New York: The Guilford Press.

10

Context Specific Literacy Instruction

Ernest Morrell

At a time when literacy is more important than ever to citizenship, professional employment, and future life pathways, we see persistent gaps in literacy achievement between various cultural groups in the United States. Throughout the years literacy research has progressed from deficit explanations of the "literacy" crisis to more culturally and socially oriented research that revealed disconnects between home and school literacy practices. Linguists and literacy theorists have helped us to reconsider literacy as "literacies" that are multiple, socially situated cultural practices (Barton & Hamilton, 1998; Hymes, 1974; New London Group, 1996; Street 1984). Through ethnographic case studies informed by the cross cultural and sociocultural traditions, we learned that valuable language and literacy practices in homes and communities have been largely unnoticed, ignored, or misunderstood by schools and formal institutions (Heath, 1983; Purcell-Gates, 1997; Scribner & Cole, 1981; Mahiri, 1998).

While we have been able to theorize literacy as a cultural practice (instead of an autonomous one) and we have been able to document the existence of non-school literacies, what we need now is to establish a research-base that demonstrates how culturally accommodating literacy practices are improving literacy learning and literacy achievement for historically underserved groups. Toward this end, this chapter explores how educators have effectively accommodated to demographic influences in their literacy instruction. From my own research and from examining existing literature I will share powerful examples of how educators have been able to achieve remarkable results by accounting for demographic influences when designing and implementing literacy pedagogy.

I begin with the assumption that all successful learning is the result of meaningful connection and therefore all successful literacy teaching will draw connections between the worlds of students and the world of academic literacy. Therefore I include work from ethnographies of literacy where scholars have documented powerful literacy practices in out of school settings from groups that have traditionally been labeled as non-literate in school settings. I then show how researchers have built upon this work to establish practices in school that draw upon these out of school language and literacy practices. I conclude with a call to educators to become social theorists and social scientists that continually explore the lives of their students in search of making positive and powerful connections to literacy pedagogy.

New Literacy Studies: The Importance of Context to Literacy Learning

Shirley Brice Heath, in *Ways With Words* (1983), reports the findings of her longitudinal study of the language and literacy practices of families in the Piedmont Carolinas. The study showed that students often fail in school literacy even though they engage in legitimate literacy practices in the home. The study revealed the power of ethnography as an additive tool when studying communities that have been historically underserved by schools. I say additive because through ethnography we are able to unpack the logic of cultural practice. Rather than looking for deficits in students, families, and communities, ethnography allows us to understand how communities make sense of the world on their own terms. The assumption in ethnography is that cultures have a logic and intelligence all of their own and they exist on a relative equal footing of legitimacy and sophistication when viewed through a relatively objective lens (Geertz, 2000). Heath's study and other ethnographers from the New Literacy Studies (e.g., Barton & Hamilton, 1998; Street, 1984; Purcell-Gates, 1997) have had tremendous substantive and methodological impact on the field of literacy studies. These studies have shown us that literacies are multiple, they have taken us into the literate lives of people who have struggled in school, and they have shown us the power of cultural study to inform educational practice.

The question for this chapter is how have teachers

learned about their local contexts in ways that allowed them to develop powerful and relevant literacy pedagogies? The best way to understand this question is to study what successful language arts teachers have done across contexts. Toward this end I have identified studies that show how teachers adapted to the specific needs and concerns of the students to create rigorous and relevant English Language Arts instruction. I focus on three primary areas of scholarship; popular culture, sociocultural language pedagogies, and youth participatory action research. From a meta-analysis of these studies my goal is to offer both a general theory of English Language Arts Teaching in context and an approach to learning about students and incorporating student's lives into literacy teaching.

Youth Popular Culture

Over the past decade a host of scholars have examined the use of popular culture to make connections with students who have struggled in English. Through critical ethnographies and action research projects conducted in classrooms these scholars have shown the positive outcomes associated with literacy practices that adapt to local contexts. One of the pioneers in this work is Donna Alvermann (Alvermann, Moon, & Hagood, 1999) whose work in the late 1990s is really the first to connect the worlds of popular culture and English teaching. Like many of us would later come to do, Alvermann and her colleagues recognized in students' budding interest in media technologies a possible entry point into academic work. Alvermann's work has explored the myriad ways that children and adolescents make meaning of the world through their explorations of popular culture. Alvermann shows students generating excitement and participating in traditional academic activities of reading and writing as a result of their interest in video games and hip-hop music. Her scholarship provides many examples of ways that classroom teachers draw upon students' interest in popular culture to learn academic content. In one example a teacher collaboratively developed a unit on Pokemon with her sixth graders (Alvermann & Xu, 2003). Together they created a unit that met standards for science, math, and reading language arts. In the reading/language arts portion of the unit, the students brought Gameboys to class and wrote how-to essays that would explain to strangers how to play the Pokemon game. The students were enthusiastic and the teacher ended up playing a game by reading instructions written by a student who, until that time, had written very little in her class. In distinguishing between more effective and less effective approaches to she advocates for:

> Developing students' ability to be self-reflexive in their uses of popular culture. Teachers working from this perspective provide opportunities for students to explore issues such as "how media and the mass-produced icons of popular culture situate us into relations of power by shaping our emotional, political, social, and material lives. (Alvermann & Xu, 2003, p. 149)

Fisher (2007) conducted an ethnographic investigation of the Power Writers, an after school writing program for students of color in the Bronx, New York. Through writing poems that spoke to their everyday experiences growing up in the city, these young people also developed a passion for writing that translated to conversations about academic language and literacy. Similarly Jocson (2008) examined the literacy learning of urban high school youth in June Jordan's Poetry for the People program. Jocson's study included seven students who, over a multi-year period, developed empowering literacies as they read, wrote, published, and performed poetry in and outside of school. Using a sociocultural and critical framework on literacy and pedagogy, her study focused on the experiences of urban youth to understand the changes in their identity and literacies associated with becoming critical poets.

For years Elizabeth Moje has studied the out of school literacy experiences of youth of color in attempts to inform content area literacy instruction. Her early work in Utah explored the literacy practices of gangs (Moje & Thompson, 1996), and her recent work has examined the outside of school popular reading practices of Latino youth in Southwestern Detroit in attempts to make connections to their literacy development in social studies and science classrooms. In 2000 Moje authored *All the Stories We Have* in which she demonstrates ways that adolescents' lived experiences can serve as the focal point of secondary curricula. Moje argues that, in order to maximize literacy learning, educators need strategies to facilitate their own learning about students both in and out of the classroom. To emphasize this point, and to offer explicit strategies, Moje draws from adolescents' stories to highlight what students need from teachers. Moje's work combines sociocultural learning theory, youth popular culture, and adolescent literacy to advocate for interdisciplinary, project-based pedagogies that build outward from youth's lived experience to content area pedagogies.

Employing a New Literacy Studies framework that draws methodologically from the work of Heath, Street, Moll, and others, I have conducted a series of ethnographic studies exploring the possible connections between pedagogies of popular culture and the development of academic and critical literacies. For example, I have conducted studies that investigate the potential of drawing upon youth engagement with hip-hop culture to teach critical reading, literary analysis, and the production of expository and creative writing (Morrell, 2004). Along with a colleague (Morrell & Duncan-Andrade, 2002), I developed a curriculum that explored the role of poets in history and in the present day. As a class we read classic poets such as Shakespeare and the Romantic poets, but we also read hip-hop texts and discussed the role that hip-hop artists play as the spokespersons for urban youth. At the culmination of the unit we had the students compare and contrast hip-hop songs with canonical poems. Students were able to draw upon their knowledge of hip-hop culture to develop sophisticated analyses of both the hip-hop texts and canonical poems. From interviews we also learned that the students had an increased motivation to study the hip-hop texts and they gained an appreciation for canonical poetry. In the analysis of the discourse and the written artifacts, we had ample evidence that students were also developing the academic literacy skills of argument and textual analysis.

In more recent work I have investigated the potential of critical media pedagogies with urban youth, assessing the way that a critical media education can make youth better consumers and producers of media (Morrell, 2008). For example I have documented the ways that young people can be taught to decipher negative and stereotypical images in popular media and I have also documented the process involved in young people becoming producers of short documentary films covering issues of inequality in their schools and communities (Morrell, 2008). This work has shown that youth are capable of producing high-level digital films and this process of becoming digital filmmakers involves multiple traditional and new media literacies.

Other notable scholars in popular culture have looked at the intersection of hip-hop and academic literacy. Some of these scholars include Jamal Cooks, David Kirkland, and Marc Lamont Hill. Hill (2009), for example, conducted an ethnography of a hip-hop centered English class at a Philadelphia High School. Hill's goal was to use hip-hop as a strategy for helping students to gain textual analysis skills, but also to challenge students to explore the relationships between mainstream popular culture and their own identity development. Hill's in-depth study of classroom life shows that the use of a critical hip-hop lens enabled students to open up to one another and develop a powerful community where they were able to share their stories while also learning valuable literacy and analytic skills. He also reported increased engagement and attendance from students as a result of the Hip-Hop Based Education (HHBE).

Sociocultural Language Pedagogies

Drawing on the cultural historical psychology of Vygotsky (1978), Luis Moll (Moll, Amanti, Neff, & Gonzalez, 1992) and his colleagues at the University of Arizona began conducting research on the funds of knowledge possessed in Spanish-speaking communities where students were underperforming on traditional literacy measures. His research team found considerable funds of knowledge that could be drawn upon by educators to make links between these local language and literacy practices and the worlds of the classroom. They also began to work with local teachers both helping them understand how to engage in community ethnography and how to transform their classroom practice to make it more relevant, more connected, and more affirming of their literate lives outside of the classroom.

Near this same time in Southside Chicago, Carol Lee (1993, 1995) was drawing many of the same conclusions as Moll and his research team, except her population consisted primarily of African-American students and the discipline was English. Lee, also drawing from Vygotsky, found that the language practice of signifyin' contained many of the sophisticated cognitive skills that could be applied to the interpretation of literary texts. According to Lee:

> Signifying, a form of discourse in the African American community, is full of irony, double entendre, satire, and metaphorical language. Participation in this form of discourse is highly prized in many circles within the Black community. (1995, p. 612)

Lee's study involved a culturally based cognitive apprenticeship where students first became aware of their unconscious use of signifying in social discourse and then learned to use these cultural skills to analyze canonical literature. In several units, Lee was able to draw upon her students' implicit knowledge of signifying to improve students' reading comprehension.

For 15 years Kris Gutierrez has served as the principal investigator of an after school computer learning club for low-income elementary students in Southern California. This project (Las Redes) has produced path-breaking scholarship on the application of sociocultural theory to the literacy development of English Language Learners. Through countless studies Gutierrez and her colleagues (i.e., Gutiérrez, Baquedano-Lopez, Alvarez, & Chiu, 1999) have been able to document how a culturally appropriate computer video game can engage and motivate students to develop academic language and literacy. The video game taps into students growing connection to popular culture and technology as well as their desire to learn through play. The central character El Maga an androgynous cyber entity that asks the students to write to him/her about their experiences at the learning center and specifically, their challenges playing the computer games. Gutiérrez and her colleagues state that:

> The children and El Maga continuously engage in problem-solving exchanges in which they pose questions to one another hoping to achieve their own individual and shared goals. For example, El Maga often asks questions to help the children elaborate on statements made in previous e-mail texts. It is important to note that the children do not always answer Maga's questions. While this is one goal of the activity, the larger learning goal is to promote ongoing communication and collaboration between the children and El Maga en route to literacy development. The larger database illustrates how this evolving relationship becomes the stimulus for elaborated writing and problem solving. (1999, p. 88)

Gutiérrez has shown that the hybrid literacy practices promote a culture of collaboration, joint participation, and literacy learning as the students work together and individually through the game. Gutiérrez has drawn on this sociocultural research to fundamentally challenge contemporary approaches to literacy teaching that are developed out of marketplace priorities rather than a true understanding of how students learn. She argues for more culturally relevant pedagogies that honor the students' sociohistorical literacies, that allow for hybrid literacies to exist alongside dominant literacy practices, and the creation of a Third Space where work and play and sanctioned and non-sanctioned discourses can co-exist in vibrant and authentic learning environments.

Youth Participatory Action Research

A third area of literacy teaching that pays attention to contest is an approach to instruction that actually engages youth as researchers of their own environment. Several scholars, myself included, have contended that working with youth as researchers of their own environments allows the youth to tap into expertise in a way that also encourages them to act in powerful ways as civic agents.

In their 2006 *Harvard Educational Review* article, Veronica Garcia and a team of high school researchers (Garcia, Agbemakplido, Abdella, Lopez, & Registe) describe the experiences of Boston-area high school students involved in a student leadership and social justice class. The course, which focused on student research and social justice aimed to get students more involved in exploring social issues while also developing academic skills. This particular article explores the student group that investigated high school students' perspectives on the 2001 No Child Left Behind Act's definition of a highly qualified teacher. Garcia, who was also an instructor in the course, worked with the students to develop action research projects where they examined their high school experiences with teachers. Students' research suggested that highly qualified teachers should cultivate safe, respectful, culturally sensitive, and responsive learning communities, establish relationships with students' families and communities, express their high expectations for their students through instructional planning and implementation, and know how students learn. This article speaks to the need to reconsider our policies and practices around teacher development, but it also speaks to the power of working with youth as researchers of their experiences. The youth, through sharing their personal stories and conducting research, were able to speak back to a policy that they felt had a negative impact on their educational experiences. They were also able to use this experience to develop academic research and presentation skills that are useful for academic advancement as well as professional membership and civil life. Finally, the youth became co-authors publishing an article in one of the most respected journals for educational research.

In a similar effort Michelle Fine and a team of high school co-researchers published an article in *Teachers College Record* in 2005 (Fine et al., 2005) outlining their impressive multi-method participatory research project. Written as a letter to Zora Neale Hurston, author, anthropologist, and part of the Harlem Renaissance, the students use research to describe the victories and challenges they have faced in the 50 years following the *Brown v. Board of Education* decision. While there have been some gains, the students' research points out the impact of negative

policies that help to maintain a persistent opportunity gap that affects countless youth in U.S. schools. Fine's work with youth in New York City is yet another example of the power of participatory action research to engage students critically and academically. Her 2008 co-edited a book with Julio Cammarota entitled *Revolutionizing Education: Youth Participatory Action Research in Motion* chronicles successful YPAR projects across the county.

In *Becoming Critical Researchers* (Morrell, 2004), I explored a community of practice where high school students learned to research their educational conditions as part of a process to learn how to more effectively navigate a school where they had traditionally not done well. The school population was fairly evenly split along racial and class lines and the program with which I worked focused primarily on students who were lower income and African American and Latino. While the affluent students performed well academically and attended prestigious public and private universities, the African American and Latino students' performance more resembled that of the urban high schools in the area with below average test scores, low grade point averages, and low completion rates. The district superintendent, the principal at the time, and several other stakeholders wanted to understand how two different schools could exist on the same campus. They also wanted to know what to do about it so, in 1997, the Pacific Beach project was created to explore these issues through following a randomly selected cohort of ninth graders, members of that "second school" by virtue of their race, their family income, and their performance in grades K–8. My role in the project as a graduate student at a nearby university became to work with the lead teacher at Pacific Beach High (also a graduate student) and to create a summer program at the university where students would learn more about the process of becoming critical researchers. My focus then, was on creating a powerful learning community, one that would develop a critical consciousness of the inequitable schooling conditions they were experiencing, but also one that would develop a motivation to develop college-ready academic skills. At the time we were framing our work around a triangular approach that included Paulo Freire's pedagogy of liberation (Freire, 1970), John Dewey's education for civic engagement, and Jean Lave and Etienne Wenger's (1991) learning through joint participation in changing communities of practice. What all of these works had in common was a focus on the learning context and a keen interest in building learning from the immediate social contexts of the students. Our response was to center the curriculum around the life of young people attending poor and failing schools.

For obvious reasons the students were motivated to participate in the research. They were greatly affected by the schooling conditions they were studying and they recognized that they could collect, analyze, and share information that would bring attention to these problems in ways that might generate conversations and actions leading to change. My findings showed that the process of becoming a participant in this research community had lasting effects on students' identities as scholars and their development of academic and critical literacies.

Teachers as Social Scientists and Social Theorists of Language and Literacy

At the conclusion of this chapter I would advocate that, rather than thinking about a particular type of instruction, we need to focus more on how teachers learn effectively about students' lives in ways that allow them to incorporate this powerfully into their standards-based curricula. How can teachers facilitate academic development without sacrificing cultural sensitivity? How can teachers facilitate the development of traditional literacies while also imparting important 21st-century literacy skills? These are the questions of our time.

One of the biggest decisions we can make as educators is to work more closely with the families and neighborhoods where we teach, but one of the first challenges we face is attempting to learn more about students, their families, the neighborhoods, and the cities in which we teach. I know as a student I learned a great deal about ancient civilizations, I even learned a great deal about the United States government and American history, but I learned very little in my formal schooling about the local cultures in my neighborhood or even about the cities where I grew up. For teachers to learn about local cultural practices and the history of the neighborhoods and communities where they teach, they must become, in a sense, cultural anthropologists.

Generally, anthropologists use participant observation a methodology where they record field notes, conduct interviews, and collect every day artifacts that reveal something about the practices in a particular culture; they do this for an extended amount of time to learn something about how that particular group makes sense of the world on their own terms (Geertz, 2000) and, from this information, they create *ethnographies* or extended narratives that describe life as it typically happens inside of a particular cultural community at a particular moment in time. Granted, teachers have busy full lives just trying to plan and stay on top of life inside of their classrooms and they cannot spend all of their days involved in ethnographic observation, but I will try to show some ways that teachers can develop their ethnographic and sociological sensibilities that may enhance what they do inside of classrooms.

Studying culture means studying everyday ways of life for historically marginalized populations within and against the institutions that constrain them. The study of culture requires a combination of anthropology, sociology, and social theory in order to understand the whole picture. I will say more about this in a moment, for now, back to the simple definition of the term. Culture is a frequently used, but seldom-defined term in the educational landscape. Sometimes culture can be used to refer to a national way of life (i.e., American culture). Sometimes culture is used as a politically correct euphemism to replace the problematic

and more volatile and sensitive term of race; sometimes it is used to mean ethnicity. Multiculturalism, for example, is usually a term used in reference to honoring diverse ethnic cultures. These grand narratives of culture are generally the domain of sociology, or philosophy, or ethnic studies and are valuable but generally not the way that we primarily envision culture in schools and classrooms. Of course, students come as members of nations and races and religions; however, educators are also interested in cultural practices inside of homes and communities. This idea of culture as a local practice comes to us from anthropology, a discipline of the social sciences that is interested in the study of human beings and their beliefs, values, and activities in their local contexts. The primary method of anthropology is participant observation or ethnography, where the researcher spends long amounts of time with members of a particular group and writes detailed field notes of what he or she sees in addition to collecting photographs and other cultural artifacts. Some of the more famous anthropologists of the early 20th century (i.e., Franz Boas, Ruth Benedict, Bronislaw Malinowski, and Margaret Mead) studied "exotic" cultures in far away places (from Europe and the U.S.) like Samoa and the Trobiand Islands. Of course, this is tied to the evolution of anthropology as a largely Western discipline developed at a time (the early 20th century) when the United States and Europe held imperialist relationships with other regions of the globe. India was still a colony of Britain, most African nations were then colonies of European nations, and Islands such as Samoa and the Phillipines were commonwealths under the watchful eye of the United States or some other global power. This colonial-colonized underpinning of anthropological research has drawn its necessary criticism and, while there is still some of the exotic tied to anthropological research, we now have many more examples in education of anthropological work being used to help us understand how people in local neighborhoods make meaning of the world on their own terms so that we can better make connections between their worlds and the world of education. In its most positive and pure sense, cultural anthropology is an additive form of research that is respectful and honoring of the sophisticated logic that is at the heart of everyday life and membership in communities (Moll, 2000).

Not everyone who studies culture, however, comes from the anthropological tradition. Others, for example, come from sociology and look at the relationship between local cultures and the larger society. From the sociological perspective, culture is understood as a relationship between local practices and the global institutions. Studying what it means to be African American inside of a nation with a history of racism and inequity may require a different set of tools than what an anthropologist would use during an extended stay within an African American community in the Mississippi Delta. In addition to fieldwork or interviews, sociologists would also look at demographic data on educational attainment, employment, residential segregation, incarceration rates, life expectancy, and political participation, to name a few. They might also look at these data over extended periods of time to gain a more historical understanding of life within a particular cultural community. An anthropologist might miss the global or historical context for specific local practices. However, the tradeoff is that anthropologists usually have more thick description (Geertz, 2000) of a few local events about which they are able to say a great deal. Sociologists will have more broad data, but it may not have the specific details of day to day life for a particular group.

People in the field of cultural studies would take an even different tack and explore the practices of everyday subcultures like skaters, or MySpace users and understand the consumption and production associated with these practices. Those in cultural studies are more interested in culture as popular culture than culture as ethnic affiliation per se. Each of these perspectives is unique and important and they will all inform how we think about cultures, communities, and practices in language and literacy.

There are many ways to build upon the work of social theorists and social scientists to develop our capacities to learn meaningful information about life in communities that we can then incorporate into our classroom instruction and just the general life of the schools. There are many spaces inside of schools that are not only class-based that can also show ties to the communities that surround them. I can think of several schools where I have worked that have murals and other artwork that reflects the history of the surrounding communities; parents and other residents have come into schools to plant gardens; schools have held weekend events where local citizens share food and arts and crafts with students, teachers, and staff. Even less formally, schools can invite local community members to visit and share a little about what they do. I was recently at a school assembly where a local author and bookstore owner addressed the entire ninth-grade class. He talked about his past, life in the neighborhood, read passages from his book, and invited the students to visit him at his bookstore.

All of these activities are worthwhile and go a long way in establishing good will between a school and its surrounding community. I still contend that the most important outcomes, though, will be on a more local and immediate scale; and that will be the comfort and affirmation that students will feel seeing and hearing themselves in the everyday activities that happen in the classrooms of individual teachers.

Conclusion: Powerful Teaching is Powerful Teaching

This chapter taps into research and scholarship that reveal the important knowledge base that teachers have developed in order to ensure success across contexts. It helps to have knowledge of sociocultural theory, especially as it relates to learning and to multiple literacies. It also helps to have an anthropological and sociological understanding of the literacy practices embedded in local community participation. We have further explored several ways that educators have moved from theory to practice in including popular culture, sociocultural language pedagogies, and youth participatory action research into classroom literacy instruction.

I would like to conclude, though, with a return to the basic transaction between teachers and students that is at the heart of any meaningful pedagogy. None of the sociocultural theory matters if students and their families are not viewed as competent and capable individuals who in most cases want very badly to succeed in school and in life. Literacy education is always tied to civic agency, to professional employability, and to power and access. Those who have the privilege of being literacy educators, then, wield great power; a power we can often choose to share or withhold from students, families, and communities. And we have to admit that inequities in literacy education stem from low expectations and not just a lack of knowledge about cultural contexts or learning theory. If we pretend that the issue is a lack of knowledge, then we do not have to confront ugly issues like racism that may have an impact on literacy achievement. Powerful teaching is an act of love. It is, when working with historically marginalized groups, also an act of resistance. When we talk about the knowledge base needed for powerful literacy instruction, we also have to talk about anti-racism and critical consciousness so that we can remember why we have the inequity that exists and so that we can be vigilant about remedying these problems for future generations.

References

Alvermann, D. E., Moon, J. S., & Hagood, M. C. (1999). *Popular culture in the classroom: Teaching and Researching critical media literacy.* Newark, DE: International Reading Association and the National Reading Conference.

Alvermann, D. E., & Xu, S. H. (2003). Children's everyday literacies: Intersections of popular culture and language arts instruction. *Language Arts, 81*(2), 145–155.

Barton, D., & Hamilton, M. (1998). *Local literacies: Reading and writing in one community.* New York: Routledge.

Fine, M., Bloom, J., Burns, A., Chajet, L., Guishard, M., Payne, Y., et al. (2005). Dear Zora: A letter to Zora Neale Hurston 50 years after Brown. *Teachers College Record, 107*(3), 496–528.

Fisher, M. T. (2007). *Writing in rhythm: Spoken word poetry in urban classrooms.* New York: Teachers College Press.

Freire, P. (1970). *Pedagogy of the oppressed.* New York: Continuum.

Garcia, V., Agbemakplido, W., Abdella, H, Lopez, O., & Registe, R. (2006). High school students' perspectives on the 2001 No Child Left Behind act's definition of a highly qualified teacher. *Harvard Educational Review, 76*(4), 698–724.

Geertz, C. (2000). *Local knowledge: Further essays in interpretive anthropology.* New York: Basic Books.

Gutiérrez, K. D., Baquedano-López, P., Alvarez, H. H., & Chiu, M. M. (1999). Building a culture of collaboration through hybrid language practices. *Theory into Practice, 38*(2), 87–92.

Heath, S. B. (1983). *Ways with words: Language, life and work in communities and classrooms.* Cambridge, UK: Cambridge University Press.

Hill, M. L. (2009). *Beats, rhymes, and classroom life: Hip-hop pedagogy and the politics of identity.* New York: Teachers College Press.

Hymes, D. H. (1974). *Foundations in sociolinguistics: An ethnographic approach (conduct and communication).* Philadelphia: University of Pennsylvania Press.

Jocson, K. (2008). *Youth poets: Empowering literacies in and out of schools*. New York: Peter Lang.

Lave, J., & Wenger, E. (1991). *Situated learning: Legitimate peripheral participation*. Cambridge, UK: Cambridge University Press.

Lee, C. D. (1993). *Signifying as a scaffold for literary interpretation: The pedagogical implications of an African-American discourse genre*. Urbana, IL: NCTE.

Lee, C. D. (1995). A culturally based cognitive apprenticeship: Teaching African American high school students skills in literary interpretation. *Reading Reseach Quarterly, 30*(4) 608–630.

Mahiri, J. (1998). *Shooting for excellence: African American and youth culture in new century schools*. New York: Teachers College Press.

Moje, E. B., & Thompson, A. (1996, September). *Sociocultural practices and learning to write in school: Exploring the communicative and transformative potential of gang literacies*. Paper presented at the Second Conference for Socio-cultural Research: Vygotsky-Piaget, Geneva, Switzerland.

Moje, E. B. (2000). *All the stories that we have: Adolescent's insights about literacy and learning in secondary schools*. Newark, DE: International Reading Association.

Moll, L. (2000). Inspired by Vygotsky: Ethnographic experiments in education. In C. Lee & P. Smagorinsky (Eds.), *Vygotskian perspectives on literacy research: Constructing meaning through collaborative inquiry* (pp. 256–268). Cambridge, UK: Cambridge University Press.

Moll, L. C., Amanti, C., Neff, D., & Gonzalez, N. (1992). Funds of knowledge for teaching: Using a qualitative approach to connect homes and classrooms. *Theory into Practice, 31*, 132–141.

Morrell, E. (2004). *Becoming critical researchers: Literacy and empowerment for urban youth*. New York: Peter Lang.

Morrell, E. (2007). Youth Participatory Action Research, Civic Engagement, and Educational Reform: Lessons from the IDEA Seminar. In J. Camarrota & M. Fine (Eds.), *Revolutionizing education: Youth participatory action research in motion*. New York: Routledge.

Morrell, E. (2008). *Critical literacy and urban youth: Pedagogies of access, dissent, and liberation*. New York: Routledge.

Morrell, E., & Duncan-Andrade, J. (2002). Toward a critical classroom discourse: Promoting academic literacy through engaging hip-hop culture with urban youth. *English Journal, 91*, 6, 88–94.

New London Group. (1996). A pedagogy of multiliteracies: Designing social futures. *Harvard Educational Review, 66*(1), 60–92.

Purcell-Gates, V. (1997). *Other people's words: The cycle of low literacy*. Cambridge, MA: Harvard University Press.

Scribner, S., & Cole, M. (1981). *The psychology of literacy*. Cambridge, MA: Harvard University Press.

Street, B. (1984). *Literacy in theory and practice*. Cambridge, UK: Cambridge University Press.

Vygotsky, L. (1978). *Mind in Society*. Cambridge, MA: Harvard University Press.

11

Adult Literacy

A Review from Two Perspectives

BILL MUTH AND KRISTEN H. PERRY

The problem…is accommodating these two sets of concerns—the need to acknowledge existing language, knowledge, practices and organizations in a society, and the need…to develop highly literate, bureaucratic national institutions and the competence to fully participate in them. (Olson & Torrance, 2009, p. 12)

Consider the following from an adult literacy perspective: Exiled Afghan women NGOs use the Afghan Women Network to negotiate new gender roles, arguing that access to education and full economic participation will support Islam and reduce ethnic division (Rostami-Povey, 2007); prisoners in Ireland are given voting rights and responsibilities (Behan & O'Donnell, 2008); children of Sudanese refugees act as brokers to help parents understand the purpose of a school yearbook (Perry, 2009); the President's Council of Economic Advisors identifies skills needed for emerging jobs in healthcare and green technologies (PCEA, 2009). These phenomena illustrate the social, economic and cultural flux that situates adult literacy practices. Conversely, as a cultural tool for reading the world and sharing understandings, literacy mediates this flux.

Like any field of study, adult literacy needs to be understood from multiple perspectives. In this chapter we draw an intentionally sharp line between two research stances: a reductive one that isolates variables from context to establish generalizable truths, and a holistic one that describes literacy practices in context to understand their complex social, psychological and cultural purposes (Bredo, 2009). We agree with literacy and mixed methods scholars who press to move beyond this duality. But the duality serves two purposes here. First, most of the studies cited in the chapter can be aligned with one or the other stance. Second, the duality helps highlight the strengths and limits of both approaches.

In this chapter we describe these two stances, which we refer to as epistemic and phronetic, based on the work of

Bent Flyvbjerg, and summarize key characteristics of each. Then we report on three adult literacy sub-fields—related to the literacy-proficiency discourse, literacy and work, and English language learners—and observe the shifts between episteme and phronesis along the way. Our intent is to put both perspectives on even footing, while illustrating distinct advantages of each way of knowing about adult literacy.

From Flesch to Flyvbjerg

In 1955, Rudolf Flesch reignited the debate over the primacy of code-versus-meaning approaches to early reading instruction. Since then, "code-side" adult literacy scholars have studied the roles of reading components and cognitive processes such as phonological processing and short-term memory (Read, 1988), decoding and prior knowledge (Adams, 1990), vocabulary (Curtis, 2006), and processing speed (Sabatini, 2002). Contemporary scholars (e.g., Alamprese, 2009) attempted to apply these insights to adult literacy instruction.

Growing knowledge about component-level reading processes provides a practical framework for understanding diverse cognitive strengths and needs of adult learners (Kruidenier, 2002). However, researchers have struggled to demonstrate the effects of component approaches on learning. Their work is hampered by ethical and practical problems related to random assignment (see Reder & Bynner, 2009), weak interventions driven by persistence problems, and intervention fidelity (e.g., Hurry, Brazier, & Wilson, 2009). Experimental research is reductive in nature. To the extent it is possible to isolate variables, control for complexity, and generalize instructional rules across contexts, controlled experiments are the gold standard of adult literacy research.

Other researchers take interest in literacy events that are intuitive and holistic rather than rule-governed and context-free. The Danish urban planner Bent Flyvbjerg (2001) argued for a social science that makes sense of context-dependent events. He cited Dreyfus and Dreyfus' (1986) description of expert chess players shifting from rule-based to non-linear, intuitive ways of "reading" chessboards. They seemed to judge new situations in their entirety, based on cumulative past experiences, rather than adhere to a set of rules. Flyvbjerg argued that, like these chess players, adults become experts (or virtuosos) at routine tasks such as reading itemized bill statements and shopping for bargains at the grocery store. Rule-governed activity is important at beginning stages of learning. As learning proceeds to mastery, context-independent rules become less important, and judgment—about when, how, and why to use skills— becomes increasingly so. Through multiple, *situated* experiences learning transcends mastery and approaches virtuosity. In new situations virtuosity relies almost exclusively on intuitive, holistic *judgment* rather than rule-governed behavior. Situated literacy practices— whether at beginner or advanced levels (Barton, Ivanic, Appleby, Hodge, & Tusting, 2007)—often involve virtuosity in that they require holistic and multi-dimensional ways of knowing that might require understanding code, genre, and cultural values (Perry, 2009). Thus, literacy learners often act as virtuosos and beginners simultaneously.

Flyvbjerg (2001) argued that the situatedness of human behavior is difficult to study through experimentation because each context presents uncontrollable variance. Using Aristotelian categories, he viewed *episteme*—analytical scientific knowledge such as that gained from controlled experiments—as suited to natural science's search for general rules. Although he acknowledged episteme's capacity to address technical questions raised in social science, he saw another Aristotelian form of knowledge, *phronesis*, as necessary to study social (human) activity precisely because it resists reduction. Phronesis attends to contingencies of experiences to produce a practical, applied wisdom. Thus liberated from "physics envy" (Sennett, 1995, p. 43), the social sciences, in Flyvbjerg's view, should no longer be held to an exclusively *epistemic* standard of truth. He posited an equally rigorous *phronetic* standard that concerns irreducible understandings of complex, power-infused practices. Flyvbjerg saw social science's primary role as igniting debate and informing policy by bringing power relationships and social practices to light, the way, for example, ethnography sometimes reveals the virtuosity of non-dominant discourses despite their de-valuation in mainstream cultures.

The exclusivity of the epistemic gold standard for social science is rightly challenged. (This may sound like an old argument; nevertheless all six adult literacy studies approved by NICHD's Adult Literacy Research Network from 2001–2007 employed experimental designs [NICHD, 2004]). We agree with Flyvbjerg that episteme has an important role in social science and adult literacy research. Epistemic knowledge is needed to inform instruction in rule-governed skills. Metalinguistic awareness, for example, requires language learners to step out of context, sometimes through comparison across language systems (Nagy & Anderson, 1999). When skills are taught progres-

sively, episteme helps identify best practices and calibrate standards. But literacy classrooms are host to situated practices where literacy events are infused with meanings that impede and enhance instruction in idiosyncratic ways. Thus we advocate for a tempered and pragmatic use of episteme (Green, 2007).

There is an interplay between epistemic and phronetic ways of knowing. Epistemic study can help a society formulate general proficiency levels of literacy, while phronesis provides the means to set the bar at levels consistent with its values and aspirations (Chall, 1990). See, for example, Smith (2009), Sticht (2001, 2005), and Strucker, Yamamoto, and Kirsch (2007) for a lively debate around the criterion— an .80 response probability—used in the National Adult Literacy Study (NALS), the Adult Literacy and Lifeskills (ALL) survey, and the International Adult Literacy Survey to gauge proficiency level.

Researchers study adult literacy within contexts (phronesis) and across them (episteme). Table 11.1 summarizes attributes of both approaches. In the remaining sections, we comment on studies in terms of the episteme-phronesis dichotomy, and the interplay between them or the lopsided way one approach dominates the discussion. We have not attempted an exhaustive review of both stances. Rather, our purpose is two-fold: (a) to provide an update in three sub-fields of adult literacy, and (b) to champion the unique contributions of phronetic and epistemic approaches to social science research.

Literacy and Proficiency Three notions about literacy have been shifting over the past 40 years (Wagner, Venezky & Street, 1999): (a) literacy is a singular system cultivated by an

TABLE 11.1
Two Adult Literacy Research Stances

	Episteme	Phronesis
Foci:	component level "variables" generalizable skills	literacy-in-use; context situated practices
Ways of Knowing:	analysis of parts	judgment based on holisms
Literacy as:	rule-based skills component-level processes	communication practices that involve intention, power-relationships, values
Learners as:	students at various proficiency levels	beginner-virtuosos participants in community
Instruction as:	a-political, neutral	ideological
Knowledge as:	received, instrumental	constructed, transformative
Major Contributions:	measure behavior against standards determine best interventions	examine complexity, power, agency, identities, narratives
Limitations:	difficult to establish rigor needed for controlled experiments	difficult to generalize, difficult to build theory across studies

elite class; (b) it is a unidirectional cause of economic pros-
perity; and (c) people are either literate or not. The discussions
of literacy proficiency that follow implicate these ideas.

Illiteracy Myths.   Scribner and Cole's (1981) study
of the psychological effects of print literacy debunked the
widely accepted belief that literacy *per se* improved cognition. The economic benefits of literacy are also contested.
Illiteracy is often blamed for poor productivity, but others
complain that the term is over applied (Mikulecky, 1978),
blames the worker for complex institutional problems
(Graff, 1979), privileges independence over interdependence (Fingeret & Drennon, 1997), and perpetuates a
discourse of privilege (Street, 1984). Robinson-Pant (2004)
critiqued the agendas of literacy campaigns in developing
countries and identified unintended consequences such as:
(a) valuing women's roles as mothers but not as individuals;
(b) blaming 'illiterate' women for economic underdevel-
opment and ignoring the motives of aid organizations; (c)
devaluing the parenting role of men; (d) privileging autonomous social structures; (e) discounting women's everyday
literacy and orality; and (f) seeking technical solutions to
deep political problems.

The term "illiteracy" became a discursive battleground
of adult literacy, sometimes pitting champions of day-to-
day virtuosity (and situated literacy) against proponents of
conventional approaches. Deconstructing illiteracy's ideologies constituted a phronetic corrective, yet episteme, too,
provided correctives, as the following section illustrates.

Proficiency Scales.   Policy discourses have shifted from
a literacy/illiteracy dichotomy to degrees of proficiency
(Wagner et al., 1999). Reflecting this shift, the 2003 ALL
survey measured the proficiency levels of adults from six
countries (Bermuda, Canada, Italy, Norway, Switzerland,
and the United States). Kirsch, Braun, Yamamoto, and
Sum (2007) found a "perfect storm" (p. 1) of disturbing
findings: (a) the proficiency of U.S. adults declined from
1992 to 2003; (b) Blacks, Hispanics, and Asians were more
likely than Whites to perform at lowest levels; and (c) of six
countries with complete data, U.S. adults scored lower in
literacy and numeracy than all but Italy. Higher proficiency
was associated with higher employment and wages. For
example, only 49% of level one (lowest proficiency level)
performers were working or looking for work, compared to
91% of those at level five (highest proficiency level).

The picture is bleak, but not entirely. A comparison of
the 1992 NALS with the 2003 National Assessment of Adult
Literacy (NAAL; White & Dillow, 2005), revealed U.S. proficiency trends in three areas: prose, document, and quantitative. In 2003 only 13% performed at the proficient level
on prose and document tasks, down from 15% in 1992, but
fewer adults performed at below basic levels in document
and quantitative literacy tasks—a drop from 14% to 12%
in document, and from 26% to 22% in quantitative. Since
1992, more U.S. adults perform at basic and intermediate
levels and fewer at below basic or proficient levels.

Becoming Proficient.   The NAAL-NALS comparison
provides snap shots of two points in time, but does not
explain how adults acquire knowledge and skills over time.
Reder (2009) filled some gaps by monitoring the literacy
development of 658 adults from 1998 to 2005. During this
span some participants attended literacy programs while
others did not. Reder found that White, U.S. born males had
the highest proficiency levels at entry. However, over time
learners who were younger or born outside of the United
States achieved proficiency at higher rates. Reder did not
find that participation in programs increased proficiency,
but did improve "engagement in literacy and numeracy
practices" (p. 79). He also found a relationship between
practice and literacy development.

Alamprese (2009) studied the progress of adults continuously enrolled in Adult Basic Education (ABE) programs
over 2 years. She found younger adults made greater gains
in comprehension, and non-U.S. born adults had greater
gains in decoding and word recognition. But all participants
made very small gains in vocabulary and comprehension in
the first year. She criticized the National Reporting System
(NRS) for not being sensitive to component-level gains: "…
the use of general literacy measures may not be adequate
to document gains…Rather, instruments that measure
decoding as a discrete skill may need to be included in…
NRS reporting" (p. 127). (We might suggest another NRS
outcome measure—literacy practice—based on Reder's
findings above.)

Strucker (1997) argued that a single measure—such as
a comprehension score—can mask important differences
at the component level of reading. Alamprese (2009) demonstrated this by showing how a phonics program did not
improve comprehension of learners with low decoding/
low comprehension profiles, but did for low-decoders with
medium-high comprehension.

These epistemic studies provide nuanced descriptions of
populations. They suggest: (a) U.S. adults have more basic
skills but less proficiency than in 1992; (b) proficiency correlates with economic growth; (c) gains in comprehension
may take more than a year to demonstrate; and (d) instruction may need to be tailored to learner characteristics such
as reading profiles.

Work-Related Literacy Adults integrate literacy practices
into their lives in many ways—parenting, community life,
etc. In this chapter we focus on one: work-related practices.
Kirsch et al.'s (2007) perfect storm called for intense adult
literacy resources, given the growing sophistication of the
workplace. The studies that follow—largely using phronetic
approaches—examine the nature of these on-the-job demands. We then present epistemic and phronetic approaches
to integrating literacy and work skill instruction.

Literacy on the Job.   Mikulecky (2009) enumer-
ated the functional literacy practices of receptionists and
paramedics—such as taking phone messages or reading
Do Not Resuscitate orders—and noted the "pervasiveness

of literacy in daily work and how different these materials and tasks are from what most students experience in the classroom" (p. 148). The PCEA (2009) also identified non-academic literacy practices. In an analysis of emerging occupations—especially health care and green technology—PCEA concluded, "…while many…jobs in the past required only proficiency in well-defined tasks—e.g., operating a rotary drill—the…jobs [now involve] tasks that are uncertain and interactive" (p. 9). These practices were anticipated by the U.S. Secretary of Labor's Commission on Achieving Necessary Skills (SCANS) in 1991, with its emphasis on "…critical thinking, problem solving, decision making, knowing how to learn…working productively with others" (Rockman, 2004, p. 13).

Hull and Grubb (1999) found literacy practices "woven throughout the fabric" (p. 312) of a circuit-board manufacturing plant; but they questioned the extent to which rhetoric of higher-level skills was reflected on the factory floor:

> …frontline workers…were…engaged in tasks [which] were quite constrained…limited to describing to management what was happening on the shop floor. In effect, the literacies that workers acquired served to put them even more securely under the thumb of manage[ment]. (p. 312)

Conversely, Hart-Lansberg and Reder (1997) described production teams' sophisticated social literacy practices such as collective agenda setting and problem solving. The extent to which higher-level literacy practices are actually embedded in the "good jobs," defined as "those that pay high wages and provide a ticket to the middle class" (PCEA, 2009, p. 9), remains to be determined.

Integrated Instruction. Instructional approaches that integrate literacy and technology learning are gaining popularity. However, divisions remain about what should be integrated, and how. We review integrated instruction from two perspectives: (a) a functional-context perspective that fuses academic and vocational skill learning and seeks replicable instructional models; and (b) a situated practice critique of the unintended consequences of work-place literacy policies.

The PCEA (2009) identified problems with the adult education system, including: (a) low completion rates (only 53% of community college students earned or still pursued a degree within 6 years); (b) high rates of first year students in remedial courses (one-third); and (c) widespread use of drill and skill instruction. PCEA cited Washington State's Integrated Basic Education and Skills Training (I-BEST) program as a model that "blends basic skills and occupational training to generate more contextualized learning, where traditionally these have been segregated into distinct programs" (p. 18). The Council reported that I-BEST students were more likely than others to "improve basic skills and earn college-level credits" (p. 18). Functional-context approaches like I-BEST and others (see Reder & Bynner, 2009), frame literacy as discrete skills that can be woven into the vocational curriculum (Grubb, 1997; Hull & Grubb, 1999).

These approaches draw on experiential learning to the extent they include realia (e.g., medical charts, job applications). But they have been criticized for not drawing on learners' *lived* experiences and their layered ways of knowing. Note, for example, Hull's (1995, p. 19) description of a lived workplace literacy event:

> To be literate in the workplace means being a master of a complex set of rules and strategies which govern who uses texts, and how, and for what purposes…[to know] when to speak, when to be quiet, when to write, when to reveal what was written, and when…to respond to texts already written.

In this situated view of literacy, the learner must simultaneously apprehend purpose, culture, code, and one's agency and make judgments about how to act. This integration goes beyond discrete skills—whether basic or advanced, functional or academic—and involves the actor as both a virtuoso with accumulated life experience and a learner. Belfiore, Defoe, Folinsbee, Hunter, and Jackson (2004) stated that integrated approaches work "only when skills are learned and used in a manner that is integrated with understanding and action" and suggested that teachers, "not…treat them as isolated…skills…but as integral parts of everyday cultural knowledge…" (p. 8).

The Grameen Bank study (Khan, 1994) illustrated the way economic development can precede literacy development, as impoverished Bangladeshi women (identified as illiterate) were given collateral-free loans to improve their families' welfare or start micro-businesses. The women became members of a new economic community. Although literacy was not the goal of the project, Hull and Grubb (1999, p. 316) noted:

> [the women] began to engage in…literacy practices… [which] transform[ed] their ways of thinking about themselves and their relationship with others…The women acquired rudimentary reading and writing practices in the face of tremendous odds because these activities were part…of their emerging identities as providers.

In situated approaches such as this, literacy learning is integrated with vocational training. But unlike functional-context models, literacy skills are learned on the job and are often by-products of participation in collective experience.

The integrated approaches above reflect two perspectives—functional-context and situated practice. Functional-context approaches may have advantages over traditional literacy instruction, including increased motivation, content learning, social interaction, and modeling of real work tasks through simulations (Grubb, 1997). Functional-context curricula emphasize discrete skills that can be evaluated epistemically. On the other hand phronesis-oriented studies exposed hidden agendas and unintended side effects of some functional-content approaches and contributed important correctives, such as: viewing learners as virtuosos as well as students; illuminating genres and other overlooked dimensions of learning, raising awareness of power relationships, supporting learner agency, and reflecting on literacy as a by-product. Still, others have complained that deconstructing existing practices is insufficient, and argue for concrete models that help practitioners move beyond academic workplace instruction.

Phronesis and English Language Learners (ELLs) ELLs represent the fastest growing sector of adult education in the United States (Strucker, 2007). This group's great diversity is often poorly understood by adult literacy practitioners and oversimplified in policy, despite the fact that much research in this field reflects a situated perspective offering rich ethnographic data. We therefore emphasize studies that reveal the great diversity of adult ELLs, the nuances of literacy as it is practiced in day-to-day contexts, and the characteristics of programs that embrace complexity as a learning resource. Thus, the studies cited in this section are more likely to make phronetic arguments than epistemic ones.

ELLs—A Diverse Group.   ELLs are far from homogeneous—they represent a great range of backgrounds, including a wide variety of prior experiences with languages, literacy practices, and formal schooling. Some ELLs are international migrants, such as refugees, legal and illegal immigrants, while others represent groups that are native to the United States but grow up speaking languages other than English. While some may share characteristics with native English-speaking learners, they also have distinct characteristics. For example, one group of researchers in the U.K. found that

> There is a marked difference between many ESOL students, particularly refugees and asylum seekers, and other literacy and numeracy students. This group has, on the whole, higher levels of confidence in educational settings… Compared with other learners, people in this group are often experiencing downward mobility. Many are well qualified or have high academic potential, yet even 'fast tracking' will not lead to jobs of the financial and social status they had or could expect in the countries they came from. (Barton et al., 2007, pp. 102–103)

However, the opposite can also be true of some ELLs from certain backgrounds. For example, participants in one intergenerational literacy program for low-English-literate adults represented a great range of educational experiences; nearly all at one of the two research sites were African refugees who were unschooled in their own countries and could neither speak English nor read or write in any language (Anderson, Purcell-Gates, Gagne, & Jang, 2009). Yet, even within a single cultural community, educational experiences may vary widely; Perry's (2009) study of southern Sudanese refugee families included adults with educational experiences ranging from some elementary school to professional degrees.

As a result, educators must not assume that adult English language learners all require the same type of learning. Some learners, who may be well-educated and literate in

their own languages, require only English language development. Others, particularly those who had limited (or no) opportunities to attend school or become literate, may require both English and literacy instruction. Still others may represent some sort of middle ground, such as those who already are literate in a different script but must still develop facility with the Roman alphabet. Despite this diversity, programs often treat learners as though all had the same learning needs—and that those needs are the same as those of English-speaking adult literacy learners (McKenna & Fitzpatrick, 2004).

Issues Facing Adult ELL Instruction.   Adult and intergenerational literacy programs often encounter struggles not faced by educators in K–12 or higher education settings. Adult ELL educators often are volunteers or employed part-time and may have little (if any) professional training or experience. They may lack training in language acquisition theories, effective methods for teaching reading and writing, and/or pedagogical content knowledge related to ELLs (Anderson et al., 2009; McKenna & Fitzpatrick, 2004). As McKenna and Fitzpatrick (2004) note, "The volunteer ethos in most countries…has created a tradition of a teaching workforce with minimal professionalism…and a lack of clear training and career pathways" (p. 7).

Additional special challenges are associated with teaching ELLs who may be non-schooled, non- or low-literate. For example, many adult ELL programs must accommodate a range of English language and literacy levels within one class (Anderson et al., 2009; Mingkwan et al., 1995). Suda (2002) argued that the literacy needs of ELLs are highly specific and are generally not well-addressed in either English language or adult basic literacy courses. Although classes organized by ability, language, and culture are ideal, this organization rarely is possible.

Another challenge facing both learners and teachers is the perceived need for students to rapidly become a productive part of the workforce, often an explicit goal of some programs. However, English for employment purposes only is not sufficient (Mingkwan et al., 1995); it fails to account for the full range of students' survival needs, educational aspirations, and life goals (Perry, 2008). While seeking employment may be some students' primary goal (Barton et al., 2007), others hope to gain English language and literacy skills for purposes such as pursuing higher education, helping their children in school, or participating in the community life of their new contexts (Burgoyne & Hull, 2007; Perry, 2008). As a result, adult ELL instruction must be grounded in a "broader framework of wellbeing" (Suda, 2002) that also connects to practical real-world skill areas outside of work (Burgoyne & Hull, 2007).

Students' diverse personal and community histories greatly matter in adult ELL instruction, and educators can be more successful when they get to know their learners well. For example, researchers found that teachers in one program for Sudanese refugees were not aware that their students came from a highly oral culture and that this might have certain implications for the students' learning of English literacy (Burgoyne & Hull, 2007). Educators' values also can be greatly at odds with those of their students, which may impact the quality and effectiveness of instruction (Anderson et al., 2009; Suda, 2002). Experts, therefore, advocate for dialogic models of instruction, such as those based on Freirean educational models, in which practitioners get to know their students' histories and goals, and in which learners have a "say" in the process (Anderson et al., 2009; Barton et al., 2007; Suda, 2002).

Conclusions

The chapter provided an update on the field of adult literacy and illustrated two ways adult literacy researchers frame their work based on Flyvbjerg's (and Aristotle's) episteme/phronesis distinction. We recognize that our framework perpetuates what some would consider an unhelpful dichotomy, and we share Olson and Torrance's (2009) desire to unify the field. Nevertheless, we believe the dichotomy does a reasonable job of juxtaposing major research traditions. Further, duality can call attention to double standards—such as the privileging of epistemic over phronetic ways of doing research by powerful U.S. research institutes. Our argument for the second standard—phronesis—which tempers precise understandings of general instructional truths with the practical wisdom to judge when and how learning in context is optimized, is based on our desire to see both research stances privileged.

The complex issue of how to move past the duality remains. We do not believe there is necessarily one way for the adult literacy field to move forward, as illustrated by the different approaches of this two-person author team. Muth adopts a bicultural stance (Kidder & Fine, 1987) that attempts to make sense of pragmatic convergences and dialectical (and irreconcilable) differences across paradigms. Perry advocates for a more strongly phronetic stance, emphasizing that context matters a great deal, and anything—whether it be an individual learner, a cultural community, a learning process, or an educational program—must be understood from the perspective of the multiple layers of context that shapes it. However the field advances, we hope resolution of tensions between these world views is no longer achieved by privileging one over the other.

References

Adams, M. J. (1990). *Beginning to read. Thinking and learning about print.* Cambridge. MA: MIT Press.

Alamprese, J. A. (2009). Developing learners' reading skills in ABE Programs. In S. Reder & J. Bynner (Eds.), *Tracking adult literacy and numeracy skills: Findings from longitudinal research.* New York: Routledge.

Anderson, J., Purcell-Gates, V., Gagne, M., Jang, K. (2009). *Implementing an intergenerational literacy program with authentic literacy instruction: Challenges, responses, and results.* Vancouver, BC: University of British Columbia.

Barton, D., Ivanič, R., Appleby, Y., Hodge, R., & Tusting, K. (2007). *Literacy lives and learning.* London: Routledge.

Behan, C., & O'Donnell, I. (2008). Prisoners, politics and the polls. *British Journal of Criminal Justice, 48,* 319–336.

Belfiore, M. E., Defoe, T., Folinsbee, S. Hunter, J., & Jackson, N. S. (2004). *Reading work. Literacies in the new workplace.* Mahwah, NJ: Erlbaum.

Bredo, E. (2009). Getting over the methodology wars. *Educational Researcher, 38,* 441–448.

Burgoyne, U., & Hull, O. (2007). *Classroom management strategies to address the needs of Sudanese refugee learners.* Adelaide, ustralia: The National Centre for Vocational Education Research.

Chall, J. S. (1990). Policy implications of literacy definitions. In R. L. Venzky, D. A. Wagner, & B. S. Ciliberti (Eds.), *Toward Defining Literacy.* (pp. 54–62). Newark, DE: IRA.

Curtis, M. E. (2006). The Role of Vocabulary Instruction in Adult Basic Education. *Annual Review of Adult Learning and Literacy, 6,* 43–69. NCSALL.

Dreyfus H., & Dreyfus, S. (1986). *Mind over matter. The power of human intuition and expertise in the era of the computer.* New York: Free Press.

Fingeret, H. A., & Drennon, C. (1997). *Literacy for life: Adult learners, new practices.* New York: Teachers College Press.

Flyvbjerg, B. (2001). *Making social science matter. Why social inquiry fails and how it can succeed again.* Cambridge, UK: Cambridge University Press.

Graff, H. J. (1979). *The illiteracy myth. Literacy and social structure in the nineteenth century city.* New York: Academic Press.

Green, J. C. (2007). *Mixed methods in social inquiry.* San Francisco: Wiley.

Grubb, W. N. (1997). Dick and Jane at work: The new vocationalism and occupational literacy programs. In G. Hull (Ed.), *Changing work, changing workers. Critical perspectives on language, literacy and skills* (pp. 159–188). Albany: State University of New York Press.

Hart-Landsburg, S., & Reder, S. (1997). Teamwork and literacy: Teaching and learning at Hardy Industries. In G. Hull (Ed.), *Changing work, changing workers. Critical perspectives on language, literacy and skills* (pp. 350–382). Albany: State University of New York Press.

Hull, G. (1995). Controlling literacy: The place of skills in 'high performance' work. *Critical Forum, 3,* 3–26.

Hull, G., & Grubb, W. N. (1999). Literacy, skills, and work. In D. A. Wagner, R. L. Venezky, & B. Street (Eds.), *Literacy: An international handbook* (pp. 311–317). Boulder, CO: Westview.

Hurry, J., Brazier, L., & Wilson, A. (2009). Improving the literacy and numeracy of young offenders. In S. M. Reder & J. M. Bynner (Eds.), *Tracking adult literacy and numeracy skills: Findings from longitudinal research* (pp. 261–280). New York: Routledge.

Khan, Z. R. (1994). Bangladesh in 1993: Values, identity, and development. *Asian Survey, 34,* 160–167.

Kidder, L. H., & Fine, M. (1987). Qualitative and quantitative methods: When stories converge. In M. M. Mark & R. L. Shotland (Eds.), *Multiple methods in program evaluation. New directions in program evaluation, 35* (pp. 57–75). San Francisco: Jossey-Bass.

Kirsch, I., Braun, H., Yamamoto, K., & Sum, A. (2007). *America's perfect storm: Three forces changing our nation's future.* Princeton, NJ: Educational Testing Service.

Kruidenier, J. R. (2002). *Research-based principles for Adult Basic Education reading instruction.* Washington, DC: National Institute for Literacy.

McKenna, R., & Fitzpatrick, L. (2004). *Building sustainable adult literacy provision: A review of international trends in adult literacy policy and programs.* Adelaide, Australia: The National Centre for Vocational Education Research.

Mikulecky, L. (1978). *Aliteracy and a changing view of reading goals.* Paper presented at Annual Meeting of International Reading Association, Houston, Texas, May 1–5.

Mikulecky, L. (2009). Workplace literacy. In B. J. Guzzetti (Ed.), *Literacy for the new millennium, Volume 4* (pp. 139–156). Westport CT: Praeger.

Mingkwan, B., Kuehn, P., Baker, A., Le, V., Pen, P., Rickert, J., et al. (1995). *California Refugee Language Training Task Force final evaluation report.* Sacramento: California State Department of Social Services.

National Institute of Child Health and Human Development (NICHD). (2004). *Adult and family literacy: Current research and future directions: A workshop summary.* Washington, DC: U.S. Government Printing Office.

National Research Council. (2002). *Scientific research in education.* Washington, DC: National Academies Press.

Nagy, W. E., & Anderson, R. C. (1999). Metalinguistic awareness and literacy acquisition in different languages. In D. A. Wagner, R. L. Venezky, & B. Steet (Eds.), *Literacy: An international handbook* (pp. 155–160). Boulder CO: Westview.

Olson, D. R., & Torrance, N. (Eds.). (2009). *The Cambridge handbook of literacy.* Cambridge,UK: Cambridge University Press.

Perry, K. (2008, December). "More of the people want to know English": Sudanese Refugee Adults' Participation in ESL Programs. In B. Teague (Chair), *The second language and literacy development of adult English language learners.* Symposium conducted at the meeting of the National Reading Conference, Orlando, Florida.

Perry, K. (2009). Genres, Contexts, and Literacy Practices: Literacy Brokering among Sudanese Refugee Families. *Reading Research Quarterly, 44*(3), 256–276.

President's Council of Economic Advisors (PCEA). (2009, July). *Preparing the workers of today for the jobs of tomorrow.* Washington DC: Executive Office of the President.

Read, C. (1988). *Adults who read like children. The psycholinguistic bases. Report to the US Department of Education.* Madison, WI: Center for Educational Research.

Reder, S. M. (2009). The development of literacy and numeracy in adult life. In S. M. Reder & J. M. Bynner (Eds.), *Tracking adult literacy and numeracy skills: Findings from longitudinal research* (pp. 59–84). New York: Routledge.

Reder, S. M., & Bynner, J. M. (Eds.). (2009). *Tracking adult literacy and numeracy skills: Findings from longitudinal research.* New York: Routledge.

Robinson-Pant, A. (Ed.). (2004). *Women, literacy, and development: Alternative perspectives.* London: Routledge.

Rockman, I. F. (2004). *Integrating information literacy into the higher education curriculum: Practical models for transformation.* San Francisco: Jossey-Bass.

Rostami-Povey, E. (2007). *Afghan women. Identity and invastion.* London: Zed Books.

Sabatini, J. P. (2002). Efficiency in word reading of adults: Ability group comparisons. *Scientific Studies of Reading, 6,* 267–298.

Scribner, S., & Cole, M. (1981). *The psychology of literacy.* Cambridge MA: Harvard University Press.

Sennett, R. (1995, May 25). Sex, lies and social science: An exchange. *The New York Review of Books.*

Smith, M. C. (2009). Literacy in adulthood. In M. C. Smith & N. DeFrates-Densch (Eds.), *Handbook of research on adult learning and development* (pp. 601–635). New York: Routledge.

Sticht, T. G. (2001). The International Adult Literacy Survey: How well does it represent the literacy of adults? *The Canadian Journal for the Study of Adult Education, 15,* 19–36.

Sticht, T. G. (2005, May). *ALL wrong again! Can adult literacy assessments be fixed?* National Adult Literacy Database. Retrieved August 10, 2009, from http://www.nald.ca/index.htm

Street, B. V. (1984). *Literacy in theory and practice.* Cambridge, UK: Cambridge University Press.

Strucker, J. (1997). What silent reading tests alone can't tell you: Two case studies in adult reading differences. *Focus on Basics, 1,* 13–17.

Strucker, J. (2007). Adult ESL in the United States. In B. J. Guzzetti (Ed.), *Literacy for the new millennium, Volume 4* (pp. 73–90). Westport CT: Praeger.

Strucker, J., Yamamoto, K., & Kirsch, I. (2007). *Component skills of reading: Tipping points and five classes of adult learners* (Report #29). Cambridge, MA: National Center for the Study of Adult Learning and Literacy.

Suda, L. (2002). *Discourses of greyness and diversity: Revisiting the ALBE and ESL interface.* Victoria, Australia: Adult Literacy and Numeracy Australian Research Consortium.

Wagner, D. A., Venezky R. L., & Street, B. (Eds.). (1999). *Literacy: An international handbook.* Boulder, CO: Westview .

White, S., & Dillow, S. (2005). *Key concepts and features of the 2003 National Assessment of Adult Literacy* (NCES 2006-471). U.S. Department of Education.Washington, DC: National Center for Education Statistics.

12

Variation in Language and the Use of Language Across Contexts

Implications for Literacy Teaching and Learning

CYNTHIA H. BROCK, FENICE B. BOYD, AND JULIE L. PENNINGTON

In this chapter, we examine how variation in spoken and written language, as well as variation in the use of language across contexts, impacts (a) students' literacy learning, and (b) the attitudes, beliefs, and practices of teachers and teacher educators. In the first part of this chapter we explore theoretical conceptions of language, literacy, and learning. This background frames our later discussion of empirical work. Next, we articulate the data sources and procedures we drew on for this chapter. Finally, we introduce, discuss, and analyze pertinent empirical studies that were conducted in the past decade since we wrote a previous handbook chapter on this topic (i.e., Brock, Boyd, & Moore, 2002).

Literacy, Learning, and Language Variation

Our goals in this section are twofold. First, we present positioning theory as the lens we use to interpret the studies we review in this chapter. Second, we explicate key language-related concepts that we draw on as we analyze and interpret the studies we present in this chapter.

Positioning Theory According to sociocultural theorists, human learning in general, and literacy learning, in particular, is facilitated through effectively mediated social interactions (Cole, 1996; Moll, 1997; Wertsch, 1998). Vygotsky (1978) argued that higher psychological processes, such as those involved in literacy learning, occur first in interactions with others. Then, over time, they are appropriated within an individual. That is, learning does not happen merely "in the head" of the learner. Rather, interactions with others shape the very nature of the unique knowledge and ideas about the world that learners can construct. Since these interactions occur through language, language plays a central role in shaping the literacy learning opportunities that are constructed in social interactions.

Positioning theory—a theory within the broader family of sociocultural theories—draws attention to the manner in which conversants use sign systems, in general, and

language, in particular, to act and interact together (Harré & van Langenhove, 1999). According to Harré and Gillett (1994), *a position* is "a set of rights, duties, and obligations as a speaker" (p. 35). Davies and Harré (1990) suggest that positioning in oral and written conversations must be understood in terms of: (a) conversants' purposes and what they say and do in relation to the social context in which they converse, (b) culturally-determined ways of perceiving interactions among people in different settings across different time frames, and (c) the ways conversants conceive of themselves and of the other participants within a conversation.

According to Harré and his colleagues (1991), there are many different modes of positioning that can occur in written and/or oral conversational encounters. For example, *second order positioning* is the explicit questioning of storylines such as questioning what the role of teacher or student should be in any given context. *Intentional positioning* is striving to position oneself or others in intentional ways. Modes of positioning are worth examining because they indicate who says what, who listens, and various consequences of interactions for speakers and listeners. Because the manner in which varieties of language are positioned plays an important role in understanding the speakers of language varieties, we use positioning theory, in general, and modes of positioning, in particular, to interpret the studies we review for this chapter (Davies & Harré, 1990; Harré & van Langenhove, 1999).

Social/Cultural Conceptions of Language and Language Variation Halliday (1993) suggests that "learning is learning to mean, and to expand one's meaning potential" (p. 113). Learners "learn to mean" about any given phenomenon through language. Since language plays a central role in learning, we explore some of the many complexities of language. However, because we are interested in factors that impact the language that children and teachers speak and write as well as the ways that the language backgrounds of children and teachers impact their literacy learning and teaching, we draw on the work of scholars (e.g., Gee, 1996; Halliday, 1993; Wardhaugh, 1998; Wolfram & Schilling-Estes, 2006) who stress the importance of studying how language is used in social contexts.

Language scholars have long maintained that language variation refers to the non-uniform nature of language (Hymes, 1974; Wardhaugh, 1998; Wolfram, Adger, & Christian, 1999; Wolfram & Schilling-Estes, 2006). Language varies with respect to "sociocultural characteristics of groups of people such as their cultural background, geographical location, social class, gender, or age" (Wolfram et al., 1999, p. 1). When a variety of language is shared by a group of speakers, linguists refer to the language variety as a dialect (Wolfram & Schilling-Estes, 2006). According to Wolfram and Schilling-Estes (2006):

> Languages are invariably manifested through their dialects, and to speak a language is to speak some dialect of that language. In this technical usage, there are no particular social or evaluative connotations to the term—that is, there are no inherently "good" or "bad" dialects; dialect is simply how we refer to any language variety that typifies a group of speakers within a language. (p. 2)

When defining dialects, or language varieties, Wolfram and Schilling-Estes (2006) emphasize that linguists strive to use the term in a "neutral" (p. 2) way emphasizing how social groups use language varieties in shared ways. However, Wolfram and Schilling-Estes (2006) are quick to point out that non-language scholars in the general public often have misconceptions about dialects. For example, a popular non-academic myth is that a "dialect is something that someone else speaks"; however, linguists argue that "everyone who speaks a language speaks some dialect of the language because it is not possible to speak a language without speaking a dialect of the language" (Wolfram & Schilling-Estes, 2006, pp. 8–9). In short, dialects, and perceptions of dialects, are social constructions; different individuals and groups—depending on their motives and beliefs—*position* dialects, and the people who speak them, in different ways (e.g., positive, neutral, or negative) (Alim & Baugh, 2007; Wolfram et al., 1999).

Background and Methods

A decade ago when we wrote our chapter on language variation and literacy for the previous edition of the *Handbook of Research on Teaching English Arts* (e.g., Brock, Boyd, & Moore, 2002), we conducted large data based searches using key words such as "language variation and literacy" and "dialect and literacy." Additionally, we hand-searched through almost a dozen of the most prominent language and literacy-related journals (e.g., *Reading Research Quarterly*, *Linguistics & Education*, etc.) for studies relating to language variation and literacy. Our extensive search yielded very few studies pertaining specifically to language variation as it relates directly to literacy; however, because

linguists attribute variation in people's language and ways of communicating to socioeconomic status, social and cultural background, gender, geographical location, and ethnicity (Connell, 1994; Wardhaugh, 1998; Wolfram & Schilling-Estes, 1998; Wolfram et al., 1999), we collected and analyzed literacy studies that related to these linguistic categories.

As we began our search for studies for this present chapter, we sought the studies in a manner similar to our last review of literature for this topic. We searched for studies published in the last 10 years in three databases: ERIC, EbscoHost, and Psych Info. Like our last search 10 years ago, we used the following descriptors: "literacy and language variation," and "literacy and dialect." We noticed several studies pertaining to literacy, dialect, and teacher education during this first round of searching, so we entered the descriptors "literacy, language variation, and teacher education" and "literacy, dialect, and teacher education" in the same three data bases. We culled through the lists of studies from all of these database searches using the following criteria: empirical work, prioritization of peer-reviewed journals, and international studies that focused on preK through high school, and teacher education.

Results and Discussion

Our current search yielded 16 studies pertaining specifically to the topics of dialect/language variation, literacy, and teacher education. (Recall that during our last search 10 years ago, there were only a few studies pertaining specifically to literacy and dialect/language variation.) We grouped the current studies into the following four categories: early and upper-level literacy and dialect/language variation (five studies), adolescent literacy and dialect/language variation (four studies), teacher education, literacy, and dialect/language variation (five studies), and large-scale reform efforts pertaining to literacy and dialect/language variation (two studies).

Using positioning theory (e.g., Harré & Van Langenhove, 1999) as a theoretical lens[1] to analyze this body of studies, we address the following questions: (a) How do the researchers of the focus studies position the students and the language varieties they speak in their work? and (b) How do the researchers of the focus studies position the teachers with whom the students work? This section is divided into four major sub-sections. First, we examine the studies that focus on the students and their language varieties. Then, we use positioning theory to critique those studies. Second, we examine the studies that focus on the teachers with whom the students work. Then, we use positioning theory to critique those studies.

The Studies: How Students and their Language Varieties Were Positioned Of the 16 studies we reviewed, six did not focus specifically on PreK through Grade 12 students; the five teacher education studies and one of the large-scale reform studies pertained more specifically to teacher learning. We placed the 10 remaining studies into two broad categories based on our interpretation of how students and their varieties of language in the studies were viewed by the researchers who conducted the studies. That is, researchers in six of the studies viewed the students and their language varieties in highly contextualized ways in their classrooms and/or communities. Researchers in the other four studies viewed students in relation to their use of language features.

Research that Viewed Students and Their Language Varieties as Contextualized in Their Classrooms and/or Communities. We discerned two general themes with respect to the findings of the six studies in this category. First, student learning is promoted when teachers examine and critique their own beliefs and practices with respect to language variation and literacy (Fox, 2005; Godley, Carpenter, & Werner, 2007; Grote, 2006; & Jones, 2006). All four of the studies that reached this conclusion involved in-depth, long-term examinations of students' learning. Jones's (2006) 3-year ethnography focused on the literacy learning of seven White girls from "working-poor" background in grades 2 through 4. Fox (2005) took a retrospective look at a 1980s large-scale language reform project—which included numerous studies of the reform process over several years—on an island in the Caribbean. Grote (2006) and Godley et al. (2007) each conducted yearlong qualitative investigations that involved hundreds of hours of participant observation and interviewing of six girls who spoke Aboriginal English (Grote, 2006) and 31 students who spoke African American English (Godley et al., 2007).

A second theme we discerned as we analyzed the studies in this category is that teachers must understand and build on students' home language practices in their literacy instruction (Blake & Van Sickle, 2001; Bryan, 2004; Fox, 2005; & Jones, 2006). For example, in their in-depth case study of a small group of African American children who lived on an island off the coast of South Carolina and spoke an island dialect, Blake and Van Sickle (2001), began their study with the underlying premise: The teachers/researchers would need to learn the island dialect and use their knowledge of it to help the adolescents in their literacy class learn to speak and write a more standard version of English. Thus, not only did Blake and Van Sickle provide meaningful instruction to their students (e.g., writing workshop, dialogue journals, etc.), they learned about the children's island language and culture and drew upon what they learned to help their students learn a version of Standard English. In a similar vein, Fox (2005) reported a series of four studies that took place on a Caribbean island nation that changed the medium of instruction in the nation's schools from English to Creole (the native language of most of the islanders). Fox (2005) found that when Creole-speaking children started their formal education in Creole rather than English and then began learning a dialect of Standard English they were much more successful academically than their Creole-speaking counterparts who began their instruction learning Standard English *even when the latter group had significantly more instruction in Standard English.*

Research that Viewed Students in Relation to Their Use of Language Features. Researchers in four of the studies we reviewed looked at the students in their studies less holistically and more in terms of how they used particular language features (Clacher, 2004; McDonald, Connor, & Craig, 2006; Terry, 2006; Thompson, Craig, & Washington, 2004). All four have several features in common; they all involve researchers administering standardized language assessments to large numbers of students. A common thread across all four of the studies (e.g., Clacher, 2004; McDonald et al., 2006; Terry, 2006; & Thompson et al., 2004) is that children in all of these studies demonstrated flexibility and metalinguistic awareness in their language use. For example, testing 92 African American first through third graders who spoke African American Vernacular English (AAVE), Terry found that students had difficulty spelling dialect-sensitive orthographic patterns. Terry (2006) posited that this might have been because students had not seen—or studied in written form at school—the oral AAVE forms and patterns that were familiar to them. Like Terry, Thompson et al. (2004) noted differences in the ways that the 50 African American third grade students in their study used oral and written language; most students' use of AAVE decreased from the oracy to the written literacy tasks in which they engaged. The researchers posited that this was because the students had likely not seen AAVE in written form at school; thus, they may have been likely to assume that written AAVE is neither used nor sanctioned at school.

Theoretical Critique: How Researchers Positioned Students and their Language Varieties Figure 12.1 provides an overview of the nature of positioning relative to the 10 focus studies of students and their dialects. The first column in Figure 12.1 provides an overview of the 10 studies in this section. The second column lists the types of positioning relative to the focus studies, and the third column provides a brief definition of the types of positioning listed in the second column.

The researchers in the first six studies listed in Figure 12.1 (i.e., Bryan, 2004; Blake & Van Sickle, 2001; Fox, 2005; Godley et al., 2007; Grote, 2006; & Jones, 2006) engage in *second order positioning* of the students and their language varieties. All question the status quo that it is the responsibility of parents to send children to school speaking a standard variety of the sanctioned language (whether it be Standard Australian English, Standard American English, Standard Modern Greek, or Standard Jamaican English) and with a White, middle-class upbringing. Researchers in these first six studies argue that is the responsibility of educators to value and honor all students and to learn the language varieties that they bring to their classrooms.

The researchers in these first six studies also engage in *accountive positioning* with respect to the language varieties the students in their studies speak. That is, these

Studies	Types of Positioning	Definitions of Types of Positioning
1. Bryan, 2004 2. Blake & Van Sickle, 2001 3. Fox, 2005 4. Godley et al., 2007 5. Grote, 2006 6. Jones, 2006	*Second order positioning* of the students and their language varieties *Accountive positioning* with respect to the language varieties the students speak	Second order positioning involves the explicit questioning of "typical" storylines Accountive positioning refers to examining the positioning that occurs in a specific context
7. Clacher, 2004 8. McDonald et al. 2006 9. Terry, 2006 10. Thompson et al., 2004	*Tacit positioning* of the students and their language varieties	Tacit positioning is not striving to position oneself or others in an intentional way

Figure 12.1 Positioning relative to ten focus studies of students and their dialects.

researchers assert that the language varieties the students in their studies speak are stigmatized negatively, but they also argue that they should not be viewed in this manner. For example, Bryan (2004) argued that progress is being made in Jamaican schools towards understanding the value of Jamaican Creole as a viable, rule-governed language variety. An important implication of viewing the students and their languages as the researchers in these studies view them is that this work is additive (Valenzuela, 1999). These researchers advocate valuing the languages and cultures that children bring to school and building upon them in positive ways.

We see much more *tacit positioning* with respect to the students and their languages in the last four studies listed in Figure 12.1 (i.e., Clacher, 2004; McDonald, Connor, & Craig, 2006; Terry, 2006; Thompson et al., 2004). While the students were positioned explicitly as speakers of different language varieties who were metalinguistically aware, they were *tacitly positioned* as language users in classroom contexts. That is, because the students were discussed only with respect to isolated language tasks, the reader does not have a clear sense of how the researchers viewed students in the broader communicative contexts of their classrooms or how the findings of these studies might impact classroom teaching and learning. AAVE was also *tacitly positioned* as inferior to Standard English by several researchers. For example, the stated goal of McDonald et al. (2006) was to examine why African American students are not as successful as their White peers. Because the researchers only viewed the students' isolated use of AAVE, it seems logical that these researchers viewed AAVE as "the problem." If they felt that there were other reasons for the African American students' lack of success, they would likely have directed the focus of their work to explore something else. They might, for example, have studied the ways that the teachers of the students in the study scaffolded (or not) the students' learning of Standard English. They could also have studied whether or not the schools in their work prioritized the use of Standard English at the expense of other language varieties that students speak.

The Studies: How Researchers Positioned Teachers of Students who Speak Different Language Varieties Nine of the 16 studies focused on some aspect of teacher learning

(Blake & Van Sickle, 2001; Bryan, 2004; Cahill & Collard, 2003; Fogel & Ehri, 2006; Godley et al., 2007; LeMoine & Hollie, 2007; Papapavlou & Pavlos, 2005; Pavlos & Papapavlou, 2004; Vriend Van Duinen & Wilson, 2008).

We divided these nine studies into two general categories. One category included six of the nine studies that documented teachers' learning, and their changing instructional practices across time, with respect to language variation and literacy learning as that work was contextualized in classrooms and/or school districts (i.e., Blake & Van Sickle, 2001; Bryan, 2004; Cahill & Collard, 2003; & Godley et al., 2007; LeMoine & Hollie, 2007; Vriend Van Duinen & Wilson, 2008). The second category included three studies that explored isolated aspects of teacher learning and/or beliefs (i.e., Fogel & Ehri, 2006; Papapavlou & Pavlou, 2005; Pavlou & Papapavlou, 2004).

Research that Viewed Teachers' Work as Contextualized in Classrooms and/or School Districts. We discerned two general themes as we analyzed the six studies in this category. First, three of the studies highlighted teachers' understandings of important relationships between language, identity, and broader cultural contexts and practices (Bryan, 2004; Vriend Van Duinen & Wilson, 2008; Cahill & Collard, 2003). For example, Vriend Van Duinen includes study of the topic of language variation in her pre-service teacher education course. She uses children's literature with authentic dialects (e.g., Appalachian English & AAVE) as one way to help the pre-service teachers in her classes come to understand language variation. In the context of their work together, the author and her students came to realize important relationships between language and identity; they learned that dialects are more than merely "different words and grammatical patterns… [T]hey involve discourse patterns impossible to mimic by those who don't understand the language as part of their identity" (Vriend Van Duinen & Wilson, 2008, p. 33).

A second theme we discerned relative to teacher learning about language variation and literacy was the importance of exploring instructional practices in-depth and across time (Blake & Van Sickle, 2001; Godley et al., 2007; LeMoine & Hollie, 2007). For example, working with teachers and students over a 3-year period of time on one of South Carolina's Sea Islands where many students spoke a dialect of AAVE, Blake and Van Sickle (2001) found that a combination of meaningful instruction implemented across a significant period of time—while honoring and learning children's dialect and culture in the process—brought about the most positive student learning outcomes. LeMoine and Hollie (2007) noted similar results in their work studying a vast and in-depth professional development project in Los Angeles that included a two-pronged approach to facilitating teacher learning about literacy and language variation (a) extensive instruction in quality literacy instructional practices (e.g., effective use of writing workshop, dialogue journals, reader response, etc.), and (b) systematic instruction in linguistics and language variety drawing on the work of language scholars such as Geneva Smitherman. In short, teacher learning was most significant when instruction was meaningful, in-depth, and conducted over time.

Research that Viewed Teachers in Less Contextualized Ways.   The three studies in this category viewed teacher attitude and learning in much more isolated ways. For example, two researchers (i.e., Papapavlou & Pavlos, 2005; Pavlos & Papapavlou, 2004) administered surveys to 133 elementary teachers randomly selected from 14 elementary schools to explore their attitudes towards Greek Cypriot Dialect (GCD)[1] as compared to Standard Modern Greek (SMG). They found that Cypriot children entering school have certain literacy practices that are neither appreciated nor utilized by teachers in the schools, and more than half of the teachers surveyed do not have negative attitudes towards GCD.

Fogel and Ehri (2006) sought to explore ways to teach teachers about AAVE dialect forms so that they could more effectively work with dialect speakers in their classrooms. Participants (73 teachers currently enrolled in 3 master's-level teacher education programs) were divided into one of three conditions: (a) exposure to text written in AAVE,

(b) instruction in dialect transformation strategies, and (c) guided practice with feedback in the use of these strategies. Perhaps, not surprisingly, the teachers in the third condition showed the most gains in post-tests.

Theoretical Critique: How Researchers Positioned Teachers of Students Who Speak Non-Standard Dialects Figure 12.2 provides an overview of the nature of the positioning relative to the nine focus studies of teachers of students who speak non-standard dialects. The first column in Figure 12.2 provides an overview of the nine studies in this section. The second column lists the types of positioning relative to the focus studies. Note in the second column that studies 1 through 6 all involve accountive and second-order positioning. However, only studies 4, 5, and 6 involve self-positioning. The third column provides a brief definition of the types of positioning listed in the second column.

We noted three kinds of positioning in the first six studies we reviewed in this sub-section that were highly contextualized in classrooms, schools, and/or districts (i.e., Blake & Van Sickle, 2001; Bryan, 2004; Cahill & Collard, 2003; & Godley et al., 2007; LeMoine & Hollie, 2007; Vriend Van Duinen & Wilson, 2008). First, all six of these studies involved *accountive positioning* because all of them involved talking about, or examining, the ways that teachers were positioned (either by themselves or others) to do their work. Second, all six studies in the first sub-section involved *second order positioning* because the teachers (and/or the teachers' colleagues involved in the studies) questioned the ways the teachers had been teaching their children about language variation and literacy. Moreover, the teachers in all of these studies sought to make positive changes in their practices, and part of the goal of the research—in all six cases—was to document the nature of those changes to discern what worked and what did not

Studies	Types of Positioning		Definitions of Types of Positioning
1. Blake & Van Sickle, 2001 2. Bryan, 2004 3. LeMoine & Hollie, 2007 4. Cahill & Collard, 2003 5. Godley et al., 2007 6. Vriend Van Duinen & Wilson, 2008	*Accountive positioning* with respect to the teachers who work with students who speak non-standard language varieties *Second order positioning* of the teachers who work with students who speak non-standard language varieties	 Studies 4, 5, & 6: *Self-positioning* of teachers who work with students who speak non-standard language varieties	Accountive positioning refers to examining the positioning that occurs in a specific context Second order positioning involves the explicit questioning of "typical" storylines *self positioning* refers to situating oneself in a conversational encounter
7. Fogel & Ehri, 2006 8. Papapavlou & Pavlou, 2005	*Intentional positioning* of teachers who work with students who speak non-standard language varieties *Other positioning* of teachers who work with students who speak non-standard language varieties		*Other positioning* refers to situating someone else in a conversational exchange *Intentional positioning* is striving to position oneself or others in an intentional way

Figure 12.2 Positioning relative to nine focus studies of teachers of non-standard dialect speakers.

work to promote student learning. Finally, three of the studies involved *self-positioning* because they were teacher research studies whereby the teachers positioned themselves as researchers exploring, critiquing, and commenting on their own practice.

The two primary kinds of positioning we noted in the last category of three less-contextualized studies were *intentional positioning* and *other positioning* (i.e., Fogel & Ehri, 2006; Papapavlou & Pavlos, 2005; Pavlou & Papapavlou, 2004). All three studies involved *intentional positioning* because the researchers in two studies (i.e., Papapavlou & Pavlos, 2005; Pavlos & Papapavlou, 2004) sought to understand teachers' beliefs and instructional practices pertaining to Greek Cypriot, and the teachers in the Fogel and Ehri (2006) study were intentionally positioned because the researchers sought to determine which of three conditions was most effective. All three of these studies also involved *other positioning* because the researchers positioned the teachers and their beliefs and actions in their studies.

What immediately stands out to us as we look across these two sets of studies is that much more agency is present in the first six studies as compared to the latter three. That is, the teachers in the first six studies are positioning themselves to enter scholarly conversations about language variation and literacy learning. Moreover, these teachers (and the researchers with whom they work) seek to explore how they can change their instructional practices to more effectively teach all of the children in their classrooms. The positioning in the second set of three studies is much more passive; it reports what teachers currently think about language variation and literacy learning (Papapavlou & Pavlos, 2005; Pavlou & Papapavlou, 2004) as well as what can be done with teachers (i.e., the third treatment condition outlined in Fogel & Ehri, 2006) to promote their learning about literacy and language variation. In short, the first set of six studies is more dynamic and agentive; these studies explore changing practices across time side-by-side with the teachers in the work. The second set of three studies is more passive and static; the researchers look at teachers (rather than working with them) and explore what is (rather than would could or might be).

Concluding Comments

As we conducted this review of literature 10 years after our first literature review on this topic, we were heartened to see more studies pertaining specifically to language variation and literacy learning. We are especially excited to see scholarship whereby teacher educators are studying issues of language variation and literacy learning in their pre- and in-service courses. While progress has clearly been made in our field in the last decade, much work remains to be done in at least four general areas. First, given that teachers in most of the schools in the studies we reviewed from around the world speak and write versions of the standard dialects in those societies, teachers (and teacher educators,

too, of course) have much to learn about the structures of different dialects and their relationships to varieties of standard dialects. Second, all of us as educators, teacher educators, and researchers have much to learn about how we can foster not only an understanding of—but the valuing of—the multiple dialects used in schools and society. The work of Cahill and Collard (2003) is helpful in this regard. Their objective is not just for all students and teachers to learn Standard Australian English, but also for students and teachers to develop bi-dialectical expertise. They, like other scholars such as Vriend Van Duinen and Wilson (2008) recognize the complex interplay between language (and language varieties) and culture in shaping identity. Third, all of us still have much to learn about how we can provide meaningful richly contextualized instructional practices that foster bi-dialecticalism. Finally, our theoretical bent is studying the teaching and learning of language variation and literacy is its social and cultural contexts. We believe that the work we reviewed for this chapter that is contextualized in meaningful social and cultural contexts provides richer answers to the complex questions we face about quality literacy instruction as it relates to issues of language variation.

Notes

1. Please note that Greek Cypriot Dialect (GCD) is considered the stigmatized dialect in this context and Standard Modern Greek (SMG) is considered the "standard" dialect in this context. That is, GCD tends to be viewed negatively by those who speak SMG.

References

Alim, H. S., & Baugh, J. (Eds.). (2007). *Talkin black talk: Language, education, and social change.* New York: Teachers College Press.

Blake, M. E., & Van Sickle, M. (2001). Helping linguistically diverse students share what they know. *Journal of Adolescent & Adult Literacy, 44*(5), 468–475.

Brock, C. H., Boyd, F., & Moore, J. (2002). Variation in language and the use of language across contexts: Implications for literacy learning. In J. Flood, D. Lapp, J. Squire, & J. Jensen (Eds.), *Handbook of research on teaching the English language arts.* Mahwah, NJ: Erlbaum.

Bryan, B. (2004). Language and literacy in a Creole-speaking environment: A study of primary schools in Jamaica. *Language, Culture, and Curriculum, 17*(2), 87–96.

Cahill, R., & Collard, G. (2003). Deadly ways to learn…a yarn about some learning we did together. *Comparative Education, 39*(2), 211–219.

Clacher, A. (2004). The construction of creole-speaking students' linguistic profile and contradictions in ESL literacy programs. *TESOL Quarterly, 38*(1), 153–165.

Cole, M. (1996). *Cultural psychology; A once and future discipline.* Cambridge, MA: Harvard University Press.

Connell, R. W. (1994). Poverty and education. *Harvard Educational Review, 64,* 125–129.

Davies, B., & Harré, R. (1990). Positioning the discursive production of selves. *Journal for the Theory of Social Behaviour, 20*(1), 43–63.

Fogel, H., & Ehri, L. (2006). Teaching African American English forms to standard American English-speaking teachers: Effects on Acquisition, Attitudes and responses to student use. *Journal of Teacher Education, 57*(5), 464–480.

Fox, J. (2005). Revisiting the storied landscape of language policy impact over time: A case of successful educational reform. *Curriculum Inquiry, 35*(3), 261–293.

Gee, J. P. (1996). *Social linguistics and literacies: Ideology in discourses.* Bristol, PA: Taylor and Francis.

Godley, A. J., Carpenter, B. D., & Werner, C. A. (2007). "I'll speak in proper slang": Language ideologies in a daily editing activity. *Reading Research Quarterly, 42*, 100–131.

Grote, E. (2006). Challenging the boundaries between school-sponsored and vernacular literacies: Urban indigenous teenage girls writing in an 'at risk' programme. *Language and Education, 20*(6), 478–492.

Halliday, M. A. K. (1993). Towards a language-based theory of learning. *Linguistics and Education, 5*, 93–116.

Harré, R., & van Langenhove, L. (1991). Varieties of positioning. *Journal for the Theory of Social Behavior, 21*(4), 393–407.

Harré, R., & van Langenhove, L. (1999). *Positioning theory.* Malden, MA: Blackwell.

Hymes, D. (1974). *Foundations in sociolinguistics.* Philadelphia: University of Pennsylvania Press.

Jones, J. (2006). Language with an attitude: White girls performing class. *Language Arts, 84*(2), 114–124.

LeMoine, N., & Hollie, S. (2007). Developing Academic English for Standard English Learners, In H. S. Alim & J. Baugh (Eds.), *Talkin black talk: Language, education and social change* (pp. 43–55). New York: Teachers College Press.

McDonald, Connor, C., & Craig, H. K. (2006). African American preschoolers' language, emergent literacy skills, and use of African American English: A complex relation. *Journal of Speech, Language, and Hearing Research, 49*, 771–792.

Moll, L. (1997). The creation of mediating settings. *Mind, Culture, and Activity, 4*, 191–200.

Papapavlou, A., & Pavlos, P. (2005). Literacy and language-in-education policy in bidialectal settings. *Current Issues in Language Planning.* 6(2). 164–181.

Pavlos, P., & Papapavlou, A. (2004). Issues of dialect use in education from the Greek Cypriot perspective. *International Journal of Applied Linguistics, 14*(2), 243–258.

Terry, N. P. (2006). Relations between dialect variation, grammar, and early spelling skills. *Reading and Writing, 19*, 907–931.

Thompson, C. A., Craig, H. K., & Washington, J. A. (2004). Variable production of African American English across oracy and literacy contexts. *Language, Speech, and Hearing Services in Schools, 35*, 269–282.

Valenzuela, A. (1999). *Subtractive schooling: U. S. Mexican youth and the politics of caring.* Albany: State University of New York Press.

Vriend Van Duinen, D., & Wilson, M. J. (2008). Holding the words in our mouths: Responses to dialect svariations in oral reading. *English Journal, 97*(3), 31–37.

Vygotsky, L. (1978). *Mind in society: The development of higher psychological processes.* Cambridge, MA: Harvard University Press.

Wardhaugh, R. (1998). *An introduction to sociolinguistics.* Malden, MA: Blackwell.

Wertsch, J. (1998). *Mind as action.* New York: Oxford University Press.

Wolfram, W., Adger, C., & Christian, D. (1999). *Dialectics in school and communities.* Mahwah, NJ: Erlbaum.

Wolfram, W., & Schilling-Estes, N. (1998). *American English.* Malden, MA: Blackwell.

Wolfram, W., & Schilling-Estes, N. (2006). *American English* (2nd ed.). Malden, MA: Blackwell.

13

Family Literacy on the Defensive

The Defunding of Even Start—Omen or Opportunity?

JEANNE R. PARATORE AND DAVID B. YADEN, JR.

In the second edition of *the Handbook of Research on Teaching the English Language Arts*, we argued that strengthening the state of family literacy research required three fundamental steps: (a) increasing the methodological complexity of research, (b) changing the field's deficit-oriented research terminology to recognize families as capable partners rather than victims, and (c) broadening the theoretical framework of literacy to reflect a bio-ecological stance (cf. Bronfenbrenner, 1979, 2005) that recognizes societal, cultural, political, and institutional (e.g., workplace) influences upon parents' and children's choices and behaviors (Yaden & Paratore, 2002, pp. 537–541).

Despite the passage of time and a fair amount of additional research, we continue to believe that these prior recommendations remain fundamentally important to the discussion of the current state of family literacy research, perhaps more so in view of the decision to eliminate funding by fiscal year 2010 of the U. S. Department of Education's Even Start Family Literacy program (Office of Management and Budget, 2009), the nation's largest family literacy effort.

Given that Even Start has provided the general framework for nearly all federally funded family literacy programs for the past 20 years, we have chosen it as both a starting point and as a backdrop for our review. First, we examine the national evaluations of Even Start. In the next two sections, we examine and discuss the evidence regarding (a) investigations that measure the impact of different types of home literacy activities on children's early and later literacy development, and (b) studies of other family literacy programs which include some, but not all, of Even Start's major components. Finally, we offer some interpretations which differ, we think, from the current discussions of Even Start's general failure to produce lasting outcomes for children and their families and we speculate on the future of "family literacy" as a field.

Even Start and its Outcomes

The Even Start Family Literacy Program was first authorized in 1988 as part of the *Elementary and Secondary Education Act of 1965* (ESEA) and grew from a small set of demonstration projects to "more than 1,000 projects serving 40,000 families in all fifty states" (St. Pierre, Ricciuti, & Rimdzius, 2005, p. 955) with total funding over its 20-year existence exceeding 2.5 billion. Even Start was established to "improve the educational opportunities of the nation's children and adults by integrating early childhood education and adult education for parents into a unified program" (P.L. 100-297, Sec. 1051). Numerous qualitative studies (e.g., Love & Thayer, 2004; Seaman & Yoo, 2001) and small, experimental studies (e.g., Ryan, 2005) have documented the efficacy of Even Start in local or statewide implementations. However, in each case, the design of the study (e.g., non-experimental), the nature of the data sources (e.g., primarily self-report), or a small or homogenous sample size limited generalizability of the findings. To find generalizable evidence of overall effects of Even Start, we turned to the three national evaluations and follow-up studies.

In the first national evaluation, St. Pierre, Swartz, Murray, Deck, and Nickel (1993) collected descriptive data of existing projects and conducted an In-Depth Study (IDS) of 10 projects (179 children) to determine short-term effects for parents and children. The IDS projects were set across five sites (all demographically similar and with poverty levels at or above 60%), and families were randomly assigned either to an Even Start or a comparison group. Results were mixed. On a test of cognitive development, Even Start children's scores increased at more than double the expected rate. However, on vocabulary and early literacy measures, no program effects were found. Adult measures showed small or no effects on measures of reading growth. There was, however, a positive effect on Graduate Equivalency Degree (GED) attainment when compared with adults in other adult education programs, but the percentage of adults who achieved this outcome was small. There were no program effects on parents' use of reading and writing at home, on learning activities in the home, amount of parent-child talk, on parent-child reading interactions, or on parents' personal skills thought to affect parenting behaviors (e.g., depressive symptoms, self-efficacy). Small, significant effects ($d = .30$) were found on the number of different types of reading materials in the home, favoring Even Start families. In a follow-up study of "medium-term effects" (p. 15) of the same families, Gamse, Conger, Elson, and McCarthy (1997) found no differences between Even Start and comparison group students on measures of school attendance, grades, achievement test scores, grade retention, and participation in special services.

In the second national Even Start evaluation, Tao, Gamse, and Tarr (1998) examined programs from 1993–97. Fifty-seven projects (representing approximately 10% of total number of projects) provided data on program outcomes (with no control group). Data sources documented child cognitive development, adult education, and parenting. Data were collected from participants who remained in Even Start for a period long enough to allow collection of two rounds of data, and analyses indicated that these families differed from those who participated for a shorter period of time. Families who participated long enough to have both pretest and posttest data were more likely to be employed, to have higher incomes, and to speak languages other than English at home. Fewer of these families were headed by a single parent, and mothers' education was almost a grade higher than those with pretest only. Accordingly, as the researchers noted, the sample represented a biased subgroup of the population served.

Individual growth modeling indicated that, on tests of cognitive development, children made progress greater than expected on the basis of development alone; moreover, the longer the length of participation, the greater the gain. Adult outcomes were similar to those reported in the first evaluation: gains on tests of adult learning were comparable to those achieved by adults in other programs; and again, a small percentage earned the GED. There were also small gains (3.5 points from pretest to posttest) on a measure of cognitive stimulation and emotional support in the home environment for parents of children from birth to 3 years of age and of children between 3 and 6 years of age.

The third national evaluation (St. Pierre et al., 2003; Ricciuti, St. Pierre, Lee, Parsad, & Rimdzius, 2004) included an experimental design study of 18 projects implemented between 1999 and 2001 that met criteria for fidelity of implementation and also agreed to random assignment of eligible participants. Of approximately 750 funded projects, 115 met these criteria, and of these, 18 volunteered to participate, yielding 309 families randomly assigned to an Even Start group and 154 families to a control group. (Control group families were also participating in some form of adult education and early childhood education services.)

On every measure, Even Start and control group children and parents made similar gains. Moreover, Even Start families under-used services, participating for fewer months and fewer hours "relative to the amount of instruction received by children in other programs that have generated large effects on child development" (St. Pierre et al., 2003, p. 5). Further, according to quality of instruction indicators, in the early childhood classrooms "there was not sufficient emphasis on language acquisition and reasoning" (St. Pierre et al., 2003, p. 7) to enable Even Start youngsters to outperform their peers in the control group or other early childhood programs.

A follow-up study (Ricciuti, St. Pierre, Lee, Parsad, & Rimdzius, 2004) in which posttest data were collected 9 months later (n = 239 Even Start families and n = 115 Control Group families) yielded similar outcomes: gains of Even Start children and adults did not differ from those made by children and parents in the control group.

Finally, Judkins et al. (2008) studied a subgroup of 120 Even Start projects serving 3- to 5-year-old children that incorporated "research-based" early childhood curricula and parent-child literacy activities into their overall intervention structure. Despite projects' reasonable fidelity of implementation to the prescribed early childhood curricula and parenting program over the 2 years of implementation, there were no significant advantages for any of the treatment groups on any of the language and literacy outcomes in Spanish or English. Regarding the overall efficacy of Even Start, St. Pierre et al. (2005) concluded,

> The fact that two experimental studies of Even Start show similar results, even though they were done at different times, one in the early 1990s at the very beginning of the program (St. Pierre et al., 1995) and a second after a decade of program implementation and many amendments to the program (St. Pierre et al., 2003), lead us to question the theoretical model underlying Even Start and most other family literacy programs. (p. 965)

Evidence of Facilitative Family Literacy Events

Despite the convergent evidence of few programmatic effects attributable to participation in Even Start programs, unlike St. Pierre et al. (2005), we are unwilling as yet to generalize the outcomes to all family literacy initiatives and interventions. There are three reasons for our reticence. First, the reported outcomes are a clear contradiction of research on the effectiveness of literacy-focused parent involvement, and as such demand further examination. Second, critiques of the third national evaluation (e.g., Espinosa, 2006; National Council of La Raza, 2006) point out that nearly all of the measures used for children were in English only and have little validity for dual language learners, a group that comprises the majority of Even Start's child population. Third, independent evaluations (Appel & Russell, n.d.) have documented that Even Start participants outscored other English language learners on statewide tests of achievement through second grade.

To understand the discrepant findings yielded by the national evaluations and other studies, we looked back at the programs included in the national evaluations to determine the particular family literacy events that were common across programs. According to St. Pierre et al. (2003), parent-child activities varied widely among the projects studied in the third national evaluation. Activities included arts and crafts, making toys or books, making food or play materials, playing active games, story reading, group singing, and at times, volunteering in their child's classroom. In some projects, parents were taught how to use a toy or game at home, how to support children's language development, and how to read to their children. Although the amount of time spent on particular literacy activities is undocumented, the range in types of activities specified suggests a lack of intensive focus on parent-child literacy interactions. In instances when projects described weekly routines, only one to two of the five days of the week focused on parent-child literacy interactions. With this description as a backdrop, we examined evidence of home literacy interventions in other studies that found positive changes in children's literacy and language knowledge.

We turned first to Sénéchal's and Young's (2008) meta-analytic review of the effects of various types of family literacy interventions. They identified 16 studies (representing 1,340 families) that met five characteristics: they were experimental or quasi-experimental in design, published in a peer-reviewed journal, tested effects of parent involvement on children's literacy learning, included at least five participants, and either reported effect sizes or reported statistics that allowed the calculation of effect sizes.

Meta-analyses yielded a mean weighted effect size of 0.65, which "would correspond to a 10-point gain on a standardized test (with a standard deviation of 15) for the intervention children as compared to the control children" (p. 889). However, Sénéchal and Young also noted the large variability in the effect sizes across studies (0.07 to 2.02). To test their hypothesis that particular types of interventions might explain the differences, they classified interventions as: (a) parents read to child, (b) parents listen to child read books, and (c) parents tutor specific literacy skills (e.g., alphabet naming, letter-sound association, word or sentence reading, with activities). Tutoring children in specific literacy activities (7 studies) resulted in the most positive outcomes, yielding an effect size of 1.15. Listening to children read books (6 studies) yielded an effect size of .52, a significant outcome, but also significantly less effective that tutoring children in specific activities. Reading to children (3 studies) yielded an effect size of 0.18, indicating small or no effect. Effect sizes did not vary according to length of intervention or inclusion of supportive feedback, nor did effects vary according to age of children (kindergarten or grades 1–3), children's reading facility (above or below grade level), or family background (working, middle, or high economic class).

The outcome related to positive effects of direct teaching of emergent and early literacy skills are largely consistent with other studies (Baker, Fernandez-Fein, Scher, & Williams, 1998; Sénéchal & LeFevre, 2002; Sénéchal, LeFevre, & Thomas, 1998; Sénéchal, 1997); the finding of positive effects of listening to children read is also validated by previous work (e.g., Toomey, 1993; Hindin & Paratore, 2007). Toomey (1993) noted, however, that achieving positive results requires more than simply listening to children read; training parents to listen and to scaffold and reinforce effective reading behaviors leads to significant achievement gains. Likewise, Hindin and Paratore (2007) found that children whose parents provided the most help decoding unknown words made the largest gains.

The finding that parent-child book reading has little or no effect on children's reading achievement differed from the findings of two previous meta-analyses (Bus, van IJzendoorn, & Pellegrini, 1995; Scarborough & Dobrich, 1994), both of which yielded evidence of positive, significant effects of storybook reading on children's language and reading achievement. Although these analyses yielded effect sizes that differed in strength (for further discussion, see Bus et al., 1995; Dunning, Mason, & Stewart, 1994), for the most part, there is convergence around a conclusion that parent-child book reading positively affects preschool children's literacy and language development but to a smaller degree than previously thought, partially because the process of shared book reading is more complex than generally assumed (Stahl, 2003; van Kleeck, Stahl, & Bauer, 2003; Yaden, 2003).

So, how do we make sense of the evidence and relate it to family literacy interventions? In a nutshell, we know that literacy learning is a complex enterprise, and different types of events and interactions influence its development in different ways at different points in time. Designing effective family literacy interventions, then, is fundamentally dependent on a clear understanding of the theory of change (see W. K. Kellogg Foundation, 2004; Organizational Research Services, 2004) and a clear statement of desired outcomes, followed by selection of activities and tasks that will prompt parent-child interactions that are associated with achievement of the specified goal. For those outcomes to have both short-term and long-term effects on children's literacy achievement, the data tell us the following:

First of all, parents' involvement in literacy instruction that is meaningfully embedded within authentic play settings, sufficiently repetitive, and of an appropriate duration has been shown to prepare children for the types of early literacy tasks that characterize kindergarten and first-grade classroom reading and writing demands.

Second, teaching parents to listen to children read books has positive effects on children's reading accuracy, fluency, and comprehension, and even more so when parents receive instruction in how to mediate children's word reading difficulty and how to reinforce and support children's successful reading behaviors.

Finally, helping parents to engage their children in shared book reading has the potential to support interest and engagement in reading and accelerate vocabulary and concept knowledge, knowledge about print and words, and comprehension development.

Aligning Research on Facilitative Parent-Child Activities with Family Literacy Interventions

As we reflected on the findings of research related to family literacy interventions that effectively prepare children for school success and the description of parent-child activities provided by St. Pierre et al. (2003), we concluded that there is little evidence that Even Start policy requirements resulted in systematic and routine attention to the types of events and interactions that make a difference in children's early and later reading achievement. But we wondered about effects of interventions based on family literacy models varying from Even Start. There are numerous reports of such programs having positive effects on language or literacy knowledge of young children (e.g., Brooks, Gorman, Harman, Hutchinson, & Wilkin, 1996; Neuman, 1996; Rodriguez-Brown & Meehan, 1998); however these studies did not include a comparison group. Since we wanted to make direct comparisons to the outcomes of Even Start's national evaluations, we delimited our search to include only those that included control group comparisons.

Jordan, Snow, and Porche (2000) studied 248 kindergarten students and families (177 in an intervention group and 71 in a control group). The setting was a suburban school district of mostly middle-income European American and mostly English speaking (as a first language) families. Parents of children in the intervention group attended five training sessions, each dedicated to a 1-month unit focused on a particular theme. At each session, the trainer provided parents information about the importance of a particular skill or ability (e.g., vocabulary knowledge); described ways parents could support children's development of the skill or ability; provided activities for parents to use; and engaged parents with their children in modeled activities. During each of the next 3 weeks, teachers sent home scripted activities that built on the focal skill or ability for parents to use with their children.

Children in the intervention group outperformed control group children on several language-related measures. Moreover, children with the lowest scores at pretest experienced the greatest benefit. There was also a positive relationship between amount of participation (defined as number of completed book activities) and the effect size.

Yaden and colleagues (Yaden & Brassell, 2002; Yaden & Martinez, 2008; Yaden, Tam, & Madrigal, 2003; Yaden et al., 2000) examined effects of an intervention that engaged urban, preschool Latino children in routine storybook reading both at home and at school as compared to children in an affiliated center experiencing a toy intervention during play time. The intervention was based on a multilayered fundamental premise: children need and deserve challenging, meaningful tasks, adults who respect their intellectual ability and their cultural capital, and frequent opportunities to share their ideas and opinions in both their native language and English. Children participated in a 2- to 3-hour language and literacy community-based program which included an infusion of over 1,000 high-quality children's books, a Big Book shared reading program, and participation in writing centers. In addition, the intervention included a book-lending library for families coupled with parent workshops on reading at home and other strategies for encouraging children's engagement in literacy activities.

At the beginning of kindergarten, 55 children who had enrolled in the preschool program as 4-year-olds outscored their peers from other preschool programs on tests of upper- and lower-case letter identification and vowel and consonant recognition. At the end of first grade, these same children outscored all other first-grade children in the school district in reading, language, and math on the Stanford Achievement Test; at the end of second grade, they outscored all other English language learners (ELL) in the district on these same subtests. Data also indicate that participants became proficient in English twice as fast as other ELLs in the district and had a far smaller referral rate to special programs than any other population of students.

Paratore, Krol-Sinclair, David, and Schick (2010) examined long-term effects of children whose parents participated in the Intergenerational Literacy Program (ILP), a family literacy program that has three purposes: to help parents develop their own literacy, to support the practice of family literacy in the home, and, in turn, to support children's school-based success. The ILP provides direct service to parents, and through parents, to children. During each week (for a minimum of 12 weeks) parents participate in 6–8 hours of instruction, half of which focuses on reading and writing texts of adult interest. These texts are typically timely and consequential, informing parents about current events in their neighborhoods or communities, in their children's schools, or information about their home lands and cultural groups. The other half of the time is spent on texts of importance to child development and learning and on engaging and motivating children's books.

Each day, teachers provide explicit instruction to help parents improve their own English literacy and to help them support their children's literacy development. A cornerstone of daily and weekly routines is family storybook reading. Each week teachers introduce a focal book, model the types of read-aloud strategies parents might use when sharing the book with children, and parents practice reading the book aloud in preparation for reading at home with their children.

Earlier studies have documented the short-term effectiveness of the ILP on parent and child literacy (Paratore, 1993, 1994; Paratore, Melzi, & Krol-Sinclair, 1999). In this latest study, data were collected on 120 students who had participated in the ILP and remained in the school system for the next 10 years (or through the end of their school careers). These students served as the treatment group sample: 86% qualified for free or reduced lunch; 87% spoke Spanish as a first language; others spoke either Bosnian, Cape Verdean Creole, Haitian Creole, Khmer, Somali, and Vietnamese. Average number of years of parent education was 7.8 years, slightly lower than the program population mean. Families had completed an average of 3.6 cycles in the ILP (above the program mean of 2 cycles). Twenty-nine percent were identified for Special Education services (with 10% of these enrolled in substantially separate settings). At the time that data were collected grade placements ranged from Grade 4 to 3 years post graduation. The general school population served as a comparison group (N = 5,627). Demographically, these students were similar to those in the treatment group: 87% qualified for free or reduced lunch and 81% spoke a first language other than English (mostly Spanish). However, a far smaller percentage (13%) was identified for special education services (with 4% of these enrolled in substantially separate settings). Children whose parents had participated in the literacy program had significantly higher rates of school attendance than their comparison group peers, consistently higher grade-point averages, consistently higher scores on both English Language Arts and Mathematics subtests of the state assessment, and higher rates of enrollment in post-secondary education.

This collection of non-Even Start studies is small in number, and two of the three have small sample sizes. Nonetheless, the consistently positive outcomes stand in contrast to the outcomes of the Even Start national evaluations, but not in contrast to the larger body of literature on effects of parent-child literacy interventions. The analysis of what these programs had in common is important: they were all intensively focused on literacy activities. Moreover, in each case, they used allocated time to explain, model, and guide parents in implementation of the types of literacy events and interactions that are known to prepare children for school success. Further, the literacy events were embedded in engaging, high quality texts and in motivating, interesting, and playful games and activities, and often within contexts that had social import for family members. Finally, in all cases, emphasis was placed on both development of emergent literacy abilities (e.g., phoneme awareness, alphabet knowledge) and language knowledge (vocabulary, concepts, linguistic and text structures).

Discussion

There is wide theoretical and empirical agreement regarding the important role that parents play in their children's school success, especially in the area of literacy learning. However, attempts to interpret and apply theory and research to practical models have met with uneven levels of success. We believe that the unevenness is explained, at least partially, by the mismatch between what we know about parent-child interactions that influence literacy learning and the ways time and resources are allocated in particular programs.

At least for now, our review causes us to reject the conclusion of St. Pierre et al. (2003) that the findings of the national evaluations call into question the "theoretical model" (p. 965) underlying "most" (p. 965) family literacy models. Rather, we believe that a model that builds on families' existing literacy knowledge and family routines, introduces, explains, models, and supports implementation of new literacy knowledge and routines, and maintains focused, intensive support to deepen knowledge and facilitate routines can be predicted to yield positive outcomes.

Moreover, as Bronfenbrenner (2005) described, it is not so much a matter of the number of hours spent in several activities that fosters development in an individual—or in our case, a family—but an ever-increasing complex relationship which grows in reciprocity, commitment, and trust between and among the people involved in the relationship. Bronfenbrenner's description of the key aspects of development are relevant to a family's engagement in any program that purports to increase social, economic, and intellectual capital, as Even Start claimed to do:

> In order to develop—intellectually, emotionally, socially, morally—a child requires, for all these, the same thing: participation in *progressively more complex activities*, on a regular basis over an extended period of time in the child's life, with one or more persons with whom the child develops *a strong, mutual emotional attachment, and who are committed to the child's well-being and development, preferably for life*. (Bronfenbrenner, 2005, p. 9)

We suspect that large-scale programs such as Even Start, perhaps impersonally implemented, using a plethora of existing community-based resources with varying quality, goals, and even conflicting or unspecified theories of change (cf. Walker & Kubisch, 2008) actually work against the type of personal and professional cohesion that must take place between consortium partners and family literacy participants to produce substantial gains in children's cognitive development or parents' abilities to access resources.

Our concern also is with the absence of descriptions of specific logic models of cause and effect indicating the exact mechanisms to be put to work and effectively monitored so that the desired outcomes for families and children can be expected. In the last half decade, in particular, organizations such as the W. K. Kellogg and Anne E. Casey Foundations have commissioned work on developing theories of change documents (Organizational Research Services, 2004; W. K. Kellogg Foundation, 2004) as an aid to their grantees and others in specifying just what the links are between and among organizational goals, the full range of factors likely to contribute to goal achievement (social, economic, cultural, cognitive, linguistic), and the pertinent service networks that must be engaged for goal attainment. We have yet to see a process of this type described in any evaluation study of Even Start, or any family literacy program for that matter. Factors such as the *delivery* of the service, number of participants, and number of hours spent in an activity often suffice as indices of success. It might come as no surprise, then, that absent sufficient attention to the full network of possible causes, mediators, and effects of actions and investments, the deeper, more difficult-to-achieve outcomes are not realized.

There remains much to learn and understand about effective family literacy interventions, especially as they relate to families who are economically, socially, culturally, and linguistically different from the mainstream. However, existing theory and research should, at a minimum, teach us that as we seek to improve children's and family's literacy learning opportunities, we must maintain a clear understanding of the importance of attending to the broader context—the social, emotional, cultural, intellectual, and economic networks in which the families function day in and day out—even as we remain relentlessly focused on activities and events that have been proven to support literacy learning.

References

Appel, E., & Russell, M. (n.d.). *California W.F.G. Goodling Even Start Family Literacy: Summary report: 2004–2005 evaluation findings related to performance indicators and 2001–2005 comparison of evaluation findings*. Retrieved from http://www.nclr.org/content/resources/detail/42607/

Baker, L., Fernandez-Fein, S., Scher, D., & Williams, H. (1998). Home experiences related to the development of word recognition. In J. L. Metsala & L. C. Ehri (Eds.), *Word recognition in beginning literacy* (pp. 263–288). Mahwah, NJ: Erlbaum.

Bronfenbrenner, U. (1979). *The ecology of human development: Experiments by nature and design*. Cambridge, MA: Harvard University Press.

Bronfenbrenner, U. (2005). *Making human beings human: Bioecological perspectives on human development*. Thousand Oaks, CA: Sage.

Brooks, G., Gorman, T., Harman, J., Hutchinson, D., & Wilkin, A. (1996). *Family literacy works*. London: The Basic Skills Agency.

Bus, A. G., van IJzendoorn, M. H., & Pellegrini, A. D. (1995). Joint book reading makes for success in learning to read: A meta-analysis in intergenerational transmission of literacy. *Review of Educational Research, 65*, 1–21.

Dunning, D. B., Mason, J. M., & Stewart, J. P. (1994). Reading to preschoolers: A response to Scarborough and Dobrich (1994) and recommendations for future research. *Developmental Review, 14*, 324–339.

Espinosa, L. M. (2006). *The third national Even Start evaluation and Latinos: Do the data distort reality?* Retrieved from http://www.nclr.org/content/resources/detail/42608/

Gamse, B. C., Conger, D., Elson, D., & McCarthy, M. (1997). *Follow-up study of families in the even start in-depth study* (Final Report No. ED 413 099). Cambridge, MA: Abt Associates.

Hindin, A., & Paratore, J. R. (2007). Supporting young children's literacy learning through home-school partnerships: The effectiveness of a home repeated-reading intervention. *Journal of Literacy Research, 39*(3), 307–333.

Jordan, G. E., Snow, C. E., & Porche, M. V. (2000). Project EASE: The effect of a family literacy project on kindergarten students' early literacy skills. *Reading Research Quarterly, 35*, 524–546.

Judkins, D., St. Pierre, R., Gutmann, B, Goodson, D., von Glatz, A., Hamilton, J., et al. (2008). A *study of classroom literacy interventions and outcomes in Even Start* (NCEE 2008-4028). Washington, DC: National Center for Education Evaluation and Regional Assistance, Institute of Education Sciences, U.S. Department of Education.

Love, C. T., & Thayer, M. (2004). Even start improves literacy in Colorado. *Journal of Family and Consumer Sciences, 96*(4), 63–64.

National Council of La Rasa. (2006). *NCLR briefing panelists urge congress to restore Even Start funding* [NCLR News Release]. Retrieved from http://www.nclr.org/content/news/detail/42612/

Neuman, S. B. (1996). Children engaging in storybook reading: The influence of access to print resources, opportunity, and parental interaction. *Early Childhood Research Quarterly, 11*, 495–513.

Office of Management and Budget (2009). *Terminations, reductions, and savings: Budget of the U.S. Government, fiscal year 2010*. Retrieved from http://www.whitehouse.gov/omb/budget/TRS/

Organizational Research Services. (2004). *Theory of change: A practical tool for action, results and learning* [Report prepared for the Anne E. Casey Foundation]. Seattle, WA: Organizational Research Services. Retrieved from http://www.organizationalresearch.com/publications_and _resources.htm#ocm

Paratore, J. (1993). Influence of an intergenerational approach to literacy on the practice of literacy of parents and their children. In C. Kinzer & D. Leu (Eds.), *Examining central issues in literacy, research, theory, and practice. Forty-second yearbook of the National Reading Conference* (pp. 83–91). Chicago: National Reading Conference.

Paratore, J. (1994). Parents and children sharing literacy. In D. Lancy (Ed.), *Emergent literacy* (pp. 193–216). New York: Praeger Press.

Paratore, J. R., Krol-Sinclair, B., David, B., & Schick, A. (2010). Writing the next chapter in family literacy: Clues to long-term effects? In D. Fisher & K. Dunsmore (Eds.), *Family literacy: Research and practice* (pp. 265–288). Newark, DE: International Reading Association.

Paratore, J. R., Melzi, G., & Krol-Sinclair, B. (1999). *What should we expect of family literacy: Home and school literacy experiences of Latino children whose parents participate in an intergenerational literacy project*. Newark, DE: International Reading Association.

Ricciuti, A. E., St. Pierre, R. G., Lee, W., Parsad, A., & Rimdzius, T. (2004). *Third national even start evaluation: Follow-up findings from the experimental study design*. Washington, DC: US Department of Education, Institute of Education Sciences, National Center for Education Evaluation and Regional Assistance. Retrieved from http://ies.ed.gov/ncee/pdf/20053002.pdf

Rodriguez-Brown, F., & Meehan, M. A. (1998). Family literacy and adult education:; Project FLAME. In M. C. Smith (Ed.), *Literacy for the twenty-first century* (pp. 175–194). Westport, CT: Praeger.

Ryan, A. M. (2005). The effectiveness of the Manchester even start program in improving literacy outcomes for preschool Latino students. *Journal of Research in Childhood Education, 20*(1), 15–26.

Scarborough, H. S., & Dobrich, W. (1994). On the efficacy of reading to preschoolers. *Developmental Review, 14*, 245–302.

Seaman, D. F., & Yoo, C. Y. (2001). The potential for even start family literacy programs to reduce school dropouts. *Preventing School Failure, 46*(1), 42–46.

Sénéchal, M. (1997). The differential effect of storybook reading on preschoolers' acquisition of expressive and receptive vocabulary. *Journal of Child Language, 24*, 123–138.

Sénéchal, M., & Young, L. (2008). The effect of family literacy interventions on children's acquisition of reading from kindergarten to grade 3: A meta-analytic review. *Review of Educational Research, 78*, 880–907.

Sénéchal, M., & LeFevre, J. (2002). Parental involvement in the development of children's reading skill: A five-year longitudinal study. *Child Development, 73*(2), 445–460.

Sénéchal, M., LeFevre, J., & Thomas, E. M. (1998). Differential effects of home literacy experiences on the development of oral and written language. *Reading Research Quarterly, 33*, 96–116.

Stahl, S. A. (2003). What do we expect storybook reading to do? How storybook reading impacts word recognition. In A. van Kleeck, S. A. Stahl, & E. B. Bauer (Eds.), *On reading books to children: Parents and teachers* (pp. 363–384). Mahwah, NJ: Erlbaum.

St. Pierre, R. G., Ricciuti, A. E., & Rimdzius, T. A. (2005). Effects of a family literacy program on low-literate children and their parents: Findings from an evaluation of the even start family literacy program. *Developmental Psychology, 41*(6), 953–970.

St. Pierre, R. G., Swartz, J. P., Gamse, B., Murray, S., Deck, D., & Nickel, P. (1995). *National evaluation of the even start family literacy program: Final report*. Cambridge, MA: Abt Associates.

St. Pierre, R., Ricciuti, A., Tao, F., Creps, C., Swartz, J., Lee, W., et al.

(2003). *Third national even start evaluation: Program impacts and implications for improvement*. Washington, DC: U.S. Department of Education.

St. Pierre, R., Swartz, J., Murray, S., Deck, D., & Nickel, P. (1993). *National evaluation of even start's family literacy program: Report on effectiveness* (Congressionally mandated interim report). Washington, DC: U. S. Department of Education, Office of Policy and Planning.

Tao, F., Gamse, B., & Tarr, H. (1998). *National evaluation of even start family literacy program, 1994–1997, final report*. Washington, DC: U. S. Department of Education, Planning and Evaluation Service.

Toomey, D. (1993). Parents hearing their children read: A review. Rethinking the lessons of the Haringey Project. *Educational Research, 35*, 223–236.

Walker, G., & Kubisch, A. C. (2008). Evaluating complex systems-building initiatives: A work in progress. *American Journal of Evaluation, 29*, 494–499. Retrieved from http://aje.sagepub.com at the University of Arizona Library. DOI: 10.1177/1098214008326200

W. K. Kellogg Foundation. (2004). Using logic models to bring together planning, evaluation, and action: Logic model development guide. Battle Creek, MI: W.K. Kellogg Foundation.

van Kleeck, A., Stahl, S. L., & Bauer, E. (2003). *On reading books to children: Parents and teachers*. Mahwah, NJ: Erlbaum.

Yaden, D. B. (2003). Parent-child storybook reading as a complex adaptive system: Or "An igloo is a house for bears." In A. van Kleeck, S. A. Stahl, & E. B. Bauer (Eds.), *On reading books to children: Parents and teachers* (pp. 336–362). Mahwah, NJ: Erlbaum Associates.

Yaden, D. B., Jr., & Brassell, D. (2002). Enhancing emergent literacy with Spanish-speaking preschoolers in the inner-city: Overcoming the odds. In. C. Roller (Ed.), *Comprehensive reading instruction across grade levels* (pp. 20–39). Newark, DE: International Reading Association.

Yaden, D. B., Jr., & Martinez, C. (2008, July). *The emergent literacy project*. Paper presentation at the World Congress of Reading, San Jose, Costa Rica.

Yaden, D. B., Jr., Madrigal, P., & Tam, A. (2003). Access to books and beyond: Creating and learning from a book lending program for Latino families in the inner city. In G. Garcia (Ed.), *English learners: Reaching the highest level of English literacy* (pp. 357–386). Newark, DE: International Reading Association.

Yaden, D. B., Jr., & Paratore, J. (2002). Family literacy at the turn of the century: The costly future of maintaining the status quo. In J. Flood, D. Lapp, J. S. Squire, & J. Jensen (Eds.), *Handbook of research on teaching the English language arts* (2nd ed., pp. 532–545). Mahwah, NJ: Erlbaum.

Yaden, D. B., Jr., Tam, A., Brassell, D., Massa, J., Altamirano, S., & Armendariz, J. (2000). Early literacy for inner-city children: The effects of reading and writing interventions in English and Spanish during the preschool years. *The Reading Teacher, 56*, 186–189.

14

Out-of-School Literacy Contexts

Lalitha Vasudevan and Kelly Wissman

A young woman takes out her smartphone while waiting for the subway and begins reading an article for class that she downloaded earlier.

A garage has been transformed into a makeshift music studio and a teenage girl mixes beats while her friend recites his latest lyrics.

Two girls sit at home and text each other while watching a popular television program.

At a local park, a group of adolescent boys meets weekly to participate in an alternate reality game mediated by handheld GPS technology.

These brief examples suggest the range and variation of literacy outside of school walls, images that are in contrast to the daily experiences of many youth as they sit in classrooms. In this chapter, we examine the complex and shifting terrain of literacies beyond classroom and school contexts. Our definition of literacy is informed by studies that primarily employ sociocultural lenses to explore literacies as social, multiple, and imbued with the political, cultural, and historical meanings of particular contexts. We also draw on theorizing about literacy as multimodal (engaging multiple modes of expression to communicate meaning) and moving across space and time to frame our discussion of the range of literacy practices that are engaged across contexts.

The term "out-of-school" is often used to denote particular literacy practices by virtue of where and when—geographically, spatially, and temporally—they occur and their perceived distance from school expectations and routines. By understanding out-of-school literacies, the argument goes, educators can create better bridges to academic goals. Tethering an understanding of out-of-school literacies to material spaces, however, can be problematic. Whereas sociocultural lenses crystallized the significance of *multiple* contexts of literacy, theories of space and spatiality invite us to consider contexts as dynamic and lived spaces. Rather than overemphasizing the material and physical na-

ture of context, we might explore how spaces are informed and shaped by the participants in that space (Leander & Lovvorn, 2006; Leander & Sheehy, 2004). For example, a 10' × 15' room that functions as a classroom populated by tenth graders and a chemistry teacher from 10:00 to 11:15 a.m. is a different kind of space than the same room organized as a makeshift theater for an after-school, multi-grade drama club. Furthermore, students often appropriate in-school spaces for their own purposes and literacy work. In a high school history class, for example, adolescents might surreptitiously be engaged in reading texts that are not necessarily sanctioned in school such as "street fiction" or updated video game maneuvers.

An attention to spatial understandings of literacies therefore has implications for how we study literacies and how we incorporate and live new spaces in our literacy pedagogy. Most pointedly, it encourages an interrogation and disruption of the in and out-of-school literacy binary. Studies of out-of-school literacies are often characterized by descriptions of how they allow for experimentation, for expressions of affinity with other likeminded people, and for the pursuit of a variety of purposes, including searches for meaning, self-authoring, and political action. In contrast, many descriptions of in-school literacies reflect Street's (1995) notion of the "autonomous" model of literacy that understands literacy as a primarily cognitive process, as an act of de-coding, and as disconnected from the social context and relations of power. Hull and Schultz (2002), however, question tendencies to "...build and reify a great divide between in school and out of school," arguing that "this dichotomy relegates all good things to out-of-school contexts and everything repressive to school" (p. 3). Given the recent emergence of digital artifacts and electronic tools that mark communication practices, and the corresponding research about the new ways of communicating and composing in this landscape, the in/out-of-school binary is further complicated (Stornaiuolo, Hull, & Nelson, 2009). With new spaces and new modalities come new social arrangements that are generative of different teaching and learning relationships and expectations about the form and function of literacy practices, possibilities that far eclipse simple classifications of "in" or "out" of school (Kirkland, 2009).

Our purpose in this chapter is to explore the range and variation of the communicative, composing, interactional, and dissemination practices encompassed within the term "out-of-school literacies" and to consider the implications for classroom practice. First, we explore how multiple studies of young people's out-of-school literacies provide a framing image of adolescent literate identities as engaged, shape-shifting, and socially conscious. Next, we review literature that presents new ways to think about what it means to be engaged in literacy and learning, particularly for young people whose identities in school belie the robust nature of their out-of-school literate lives. We continue a discussion of learning in the third section by focusing on the possibilities of bridging in-school and out-of-school literacies. In our fourth section, we raise cautions about doing so uncritically. We conclude by calling for a re-imagining of institutional spaces of learning by engaging the rich landscape of out-of-school literacies research. While we recognize the plurality of literacies research situated outside of school that explores the experiences of preschool children to adults, in this review we focus on the out-of-school literacies of adolescents.

Adolescents' Out-of-School Literate Lives

Alvermann and Eakle (2007) argue that young people actively "dissolve" the traditional boundaries of time, space, and in/out-of-school literacies, characterizing their work as "completing projects to help explain themselves, their interests, their pleasures, and the worlds they inhabit or would like to inhabit" (p. 164). Given our awareness of how young people are continually inhabiting multiple spaces at any given time and how their literacy practices are continually moving across multiple contexts and modalities, we seek to highlight the complexity and dynamism found in the literacies in which youth engage outside of school walls. In this section, we explore some of the out-of-school spaces—physical locations and virtual domains—in which literacies flourish through the multi-layered image of an engaged, shape-shifting, and socially conscious adolescent. This lens is shaped by studies that depict adolescents as engaged participants, whose involvement in spaces such as after-school programs and spoken word venues is visible in their textual as well as embodied performances. In these spaces, youth enact "agentive identities" (Hull & Katz, 2006) through acts of (re)authoring themselves in ways and in spaces of their choosing. Just as youth can be understood as engaged and agentive, we also see them as "shape shifting portfolio people" (Gee, 2002) whose acts of authoring and communication are not confined to a limited scope of local sites, but exist across networks with global reach. This shape shifting contrasts the shape-fitting that is required

of many adolescents in their in-school lives. Finally, we understand that adolescents engage multiple modalities, literacies, and digitally mediated spaces of expression in order to seek social change through social critique of their lived realities and their surrounding contexts.

Youth media organizations such as the Educational Video Center (EVC) and HarlemLIVE in New York City and Appalshop in Eastern Kentucky are representative of organizations populated by young people who seek opportunities to compose narratives outside of school and to be heard in their role as media producers. Youth Radio, located in Oakland, California, was founded with the intention of helping underserved youth to develop technical skills and to cultivate their identities as multi-media producers and mentors to their peers. These young broadcasters contribute much needed youth voices to adult-dominated discourses such as international conflicts and unemployment, as well as topics to which they have personal affinity, including standardized testing, the Iraq war, and the youth vote in the most recent election (Soep, 2006). In these spaces, youth are held to professional and artistic standards (Heath, 2001) and they embark on social critique and analysis from the position of storyteller via the medium of radio or documentary film.

Whereas these youth media programs exist as spaces where youth intentionally engage in social issue media production, there is also evidence of youth whose incidental and everyday literacy practices reflect an ongoing social critique in response to the world around them (Alim, 2007; Blackburn, 2003; Kinloch, 2010). From self-initiated documentary making to the writing of poetry and lyrics, the five African American youth in Mahiri's (2004) study composed out-of-school texts known as "street scripts." These literacies were motivated in response to personal experiences and ongoing analysis of their worlds. For these young people, and many others (e.g., Gutierrez, 2008; Hull & Katz, 2006), the practices of writing and composing multimodally were themselves spaces in which to assert authorial power and perform social critique.

Sablo Sutton (2004) also shares accounts of youth seeking social action through their language and literacy practices. She studied the spoken word practices and performances among youth she describes as "young magicians," youth whose connection with their community and lived realities are transformed through this practice. The spoken word performances Sablo Sutton attended took place in a setting she calls "The Basement," where candlelight and an eager crowd await the poets' latest musings on topics ranging from sociopolitical issues to personal relationships. Unlike most school writing, authoring in this space was intimately tied to a connection with the audience; the poets viewed their texts and performances as acts of truth-telling to a room of engaged listeners.

Still other compositions across a variety of spaces highlight different aspects of the performative nature of out-of-school literacies. Lewis (2007) suggests that in this current digital climate, performative practice might very well be "built into digital technology with multiple windows, synchronicity, graphical possibilities, and what Ito (2006, p. 3) calls 'hypersociality'" (p. 232). Today's youth, more than in any time previously, are writing prolific amounts and with an especially acute awareness of audience. Adolescents are active participants in online sites for video sharing, blogging, and social networking in which their participation is mediated through a range of literacy practices necessary for creating online profiles, commenting on others' profiles, and communicating with known and unknown audiences (e.g., Livingstone, 2008; Wilber, 2007). Youth are aware of and writing to *multiple* audiences and adapting the form and content of their writing to meet the diverse demands and expectations of those audiences (Lunsford, 2006). For instance, instant messaging (IM) and its communicative cousin, texting, are two literacy practices that are ubiquitous in adolescents' communications. Lewis and Fabos's (2005) research, along with Jacobs's (2008), highlights the multivocality of their participants' IM practices, suggesting layered and simultaneous authoring occurring during any one IM session.

Multivocality and audience motivated the adolescent girls with whom Pleasants (2008) worked at a community center to craft digital stories that allowed them "to tell stories in their own voices, and render these stories visually" (p. 230). As both a form of text and a space of composing, digital storytelling afforded these and other youth opportunities to assert discursive agency as they made themselves known on their own terms (Vasudevan, 2006). The work of Hull and her colleagues (2006) echoes Pleasants's discussion of the unexpected and agentive affordances of digital storytelling. They find community-based sites to be especially fertile ground for adolescents to assume new roles and identities through their multimodal composing.

Such forms of textual remixing (Knobel & Lankshear, 2008), in which "original" material is cut, copied, edited, and rearranged to create new texts, have led literacy researchers to inquire into the motivations and rationales behind the production of online content (Alvermann, 2008). Researchers studying various forms of digital remixing— e.g., anime music videos (AMVs) (Ito, 2006), fan fiction (Black, 2005, Thomas, 2007)—find that adolescents take on roles that allow for multiple forms of participation in communities to which these remixing practices are connected. Portable technologies and a reliable Internet connection make it possible to leverage these practices more readily for entry into a variety of virtual spaces, including virtual worlds and online gaming sites. In the next section, we consider the implications of these engaged, shape-shifting, and socially conscious identities that youth assume outside of school for rethinking what it means to be engaged in literacy and learning across contexts.

Re-Envisioning Literacies and Literacy Learners

Research that considers literacies in the lives of youth across a range of contexts provides compelling portraits of students who are engaged in literacies outside of school, but who are considered "struggling" inside of school. Many students have school histories that reflect low test scores, placements in remedial classes, and labels such as "reluctant readers," "below grade level," and "at-risk"; however, ethnographic research provides contrasting images of these very same young people successfully navigating a range of sign systems, including print, outside of school. In her study of 13-year-old Jacques, Knobel (2001) found that his involvement in his family's church community and family business called upon a range of sophisticated practices related to reading, writing, listening, and speaking. These literacies were marked by a clear sense of audience and utility, e.g., to create flyers to attract potential customers for the family's lawn care business, to provide a compelling testimony of faith. His out-of-school literacies were not recognized in what Knobel (2001) calls the "impoverished conceptions of literacy in national curricula and benchmarks" (p. 409).

Other researchers have also found students who were considered based on test scores and teacher perception as "struggling" readers to be especially adept at moving across sign systems, particularly when tied to popular culture. O'Brien (2006) provides vivid portraits of young people who thrived in the "mediacentric" atmosphere supported by a literacy lab that differed from the "printcentric" attributes of school classrooms. Within opportunities to conduct multimodal research on a range of topics from music, to historical events, to local issues, students drew upon a range of sources to find information and to present their perspectives. Given the students were both active consumers and producers of multimodal and multigenre texts, O'Brien (2006) develops the term "multimediating" to suggest how young people orchestrate a range of literacies to construct knowledge, identities, and meaning-making with and through multiple media. In these inquiry projects, students used such practices as Instant Messaging, Internet searches, and video games—practices that were not condoned in classrooms and were in fact often seen as detracting from school sanctioned literacies. O'Brien (2006) claims, however, that these practices were in fact more sophisticated than those valued in school and allowed students to claim agency in their own learning, arguing, "These multimediating adolescents are developing a very clear *self*-regulation of complex linguistic, cognitive, technical, and social skills and strategies" (emphasis in original, p. 44).

Staples (2008) describes the affordances of non-school spaces to open up new ways of being for youth who are laden with disparaging identity markers inside the school walls. In her description of her work with African American young men and women who met with her for an afterschool media literacy club, she recounts how the students had been identified by their teachers as having low literacy proficiency and in need of remediation. Staples, however, details richly layered and analytical conversations and resultant texts that were the hallmarks of her interactions with and observations of the same youth.

These studies and others that inquire into the distinctions

between the literacy cultures inside and outside of classrooms illustrate the ways in which the institution of school itself, whose practices of labeling and categorization coupled with missed opportunities to really know youth, plays a significant role in the bifurcation of youths' lives and literacies in and out of school. They suggest that a recognition of the nature of the literacy practices pursued across contexts could expand not only our understandings of students and their literacies (Moje, 2002), but also our understanding of the literacies we value and promote in schools, an area of inquiry we explore further in the next section.

Bridging In and Out-of-School Literacies

In their review of research on out-of-school literacies, Hull and Schultz (2001) ask two questions that are reflected in the inquiries of subsequent studies exploring the possibilities of incorporating out-of-school literacies into school-based pedagogies, asking "[h]ow might out-of-school identities, social practices, and the literacies that they recruit be leveraged in the classroom?" (p. 603) and "[h]ow might teachers incorporate out-of-school interests and predilections but also extend the range of the literacies with which [students] are conversant?" (p. 603). These questions and the studies that are informed by them attempt to explore and disrupt the in and out-of-school divide.

A number of studies explore how literacy practices typically viewed as being pursued outside of school have been incorporated inside of school to build on existing curricula to promote academic literacies. These studies reflect the calls of such organizations as the National Council of Teachers of English and the International Reading Association to respond to the evolving nature of adolescent literacies and to suggest how "new literacies are in a synergistic, reciprocal, and constantly evolving relationship with older literacies" (Swenson, Young, McGrail, Rozema, & Whitin, 2006, p. 357). Digital media and software, for example, have been found to complement progressive writing process principles and traditional print-based approaches to literature response. In her discussion of the insights she gained from studying her middle school students' out-of-school blogging, Read (2006) argues that she incorporates the practice into her writing instruction in order to extend her instructional goals related to raising student awareness of the importance of audience, drafting, and revising. Davis and McGrail (2009) engage their fifth-grade bloggers in "proof-revising" the stories posted to their classroom blogs. Teachers create podcasts that encourage students not only to look for surface errors and sentence-level revisions, but also to consider the narrative impact of their work across the semiotic domains. Even the study of Shakespeare has been shaped by literacy practices hardly imaginable in his time. Desmet (2009) discusses using YouTube within the study of the bard, while Shamburg and Craighead (2009) draw on a repertoire of practices informed by out-of-school praxis to extend the study of his plays, including the incorporation of nonprint texts, the creation of a participatory culture within the classroom, and the principles of remixing to invite a range of student responses.

Another related line of inquiry explores how the practices traditionally considered out-of-school can play a role not only in revitalizing English education to reflect the emerging reading and writing practices of today's adolescents, but also how these practices could be used in the service of social justice. Morrell calls for the recognition of popular culture and youth cultural production to inform school practice. Arguing for a "critical English education," Morrell (2005) contends that students need "skills to deconstruct dominant texts carefully (i.e., canonical literature, media texts) while also instructing them in skills that allow them to create their own critical texts that can be used in the struggle for social justice" (p. 313). Lee (2007) argues for the use of cultural models drawing from African American language practices, music, film, and literature to facilitate academic literacies. Hip-hop (Alexander-Smith, 2004; Hill, 2009); spoken word and slam poetry (Fisher, 2007) and "digital DJing" (Mahiri, 2006) all proceed from the premise that the cultural practices that have relevance and significance to youth outside of school can be pursued within school to enhance critical literacies, engage with academic texts, and provide opportunities to work toward social change.

Lost in Translation? Considerations and Challenges

As we consider further what are or what could be relationships between in and out-of-school literacies, and as we consider the possibilities of infusing classroom practices with out-of-school perspectives, we wonder what happens when out-of-school literacies are *not* in a "synergistic, reciprocal, and constantly evolving" (Swenson et al., 2006, p. 357) relationship with the values, definitions, outcomes, and purposes of school-based literacy education or schooling in general? How do we think about the seemingly intractable "deep grammar of schooling" (Lankshear & Knobel, 2003, p. 30) that shapes how knowledge is constructed within schools and for what purposes? How do we consider the fate of critical, culturally relevant, and multimodal pedagogies within schools that adopt scripted curricula aimed at teaching basic skills and preparing students for standardized exams? How do we consider the institutional constraints that shape not only access to the digital media tools in schools, but also how structures of power and authority within schools can limit students' freedom and agency in pursuing online literacies?

Questions therefore emerge about attempts to import out-of-school literacies without sufficient attention to how the context of schooling necessarily shapes the literacies that can emerge within in-school spaces. As Sheehy (2009) contends, we need additional work "examining the social processes that hinder or facilitate the mobility of specific literacies across contexts" (pp. 144–145). O'Brien and Bauer (2005) describe the challenges of bringing new literacies into what they term "Institutions of Old Learning," suggesting that we need to "to consider the broader social, cultural, and political ecology within which schools exist" (p. 126), an ecology shaped by an emphasis on the value of print literacies and the pressures on schools to raise test scores. Lankshear and Knobel (2007) contend that a particular set of conditions, what they call "technical stuff" (the affordances of new technologies) and "ethos stuff" (characteristics of literacies as "participatory" or "distributed"), are needed to foster the affordances of online learning. This "ethos stuff," however, is not at all easy to foster, even within well-resourced schools. In Leander's (2007) study of a school where students had ample access to laptops and a wireless network, classroom practices emerged that began to exert increasing control over students' access to online sources, over the processes they were allowed to pursue once online, and over the purpose of the students' learning. Leander (2007) argues that in contrast to the ways in which young people engage in online literacies on their own terms, "In official school practice, the wireless network was 're-wired' or closed off and anchored in ways that reproduced traditional school space-time" (p. 25).

Thus, the ways that time and space are organized within schools influence and are in a shaping and reciprocal relationship to how learning is pursued and knowledge is constructed. In practices associated with gaming literacies it is possible to see how this phenomena can cause particular threats to out-of-school literacies once they move into school (Squire, 2008). The complexity of the learning and participation involved in gaming, Gee (2003) argues, is in stark contrast to the "skill and drill" and "back to basics" approaches that shape many approaches to literacy pedagogies. Gee's (2003) work highlights how video game players display habits of being and ways of participating that allow them to take on distinctive identities, assert agency, tackle challenging problems, think sequentially and holistically about issues, assemble resources and players to address meet goals, and pursue competence through trial and error. Gee (2003) approaches the research less from an impetus to consider how video games themselves might be incorporated into school-based curricula; instead, he considers how young people's engagement with video games can provide insight into theories of learning.

These kinds of approaches to exploring the in and out-of-school literacies relationship suggest the need to move away from an importation model. Gustavson (2007), in his study of the creative practices of three adolescent boys, argues for a "process-based understanding of youth" and their art forms through which educators might more effectively appropriate the "ritual, routines, and skills that youth within these and other practices employ in order to do the work" (p. 136). He calls for teachers to take on the perspective of inquiring amateurs and ethnographers, to pursue exploration with students, and to encourage multiple forms of performance and experimentation. These kinds of principles, as we contend in our conclusion, have potential for moving the field forward in considering what we can learn from the out-of-school literacies of adolescents to inform in-school practice.

Conclusion: Re-Imagining In-School Spaces and Literacies

We conclude our review by reflecting on how institutional contexts for learning might be re-imagined and transformed through critical and thoughtful engagement with the knowledge gleaned from studies of spaces outside of school in which adolescents are participating in meaningful literacy engagements. When teachers create opportunities to engage the out-of-school commitments, histories, and bodies of knowledge that students bring with them to school, classrooms can become more permeable, less bounded, and more inclusive (cf. Fisher, 2007; Kajder, 2004; Kinloch, 2005; Medina & Campano, 2006; Larson & Marsh, 2005; Mahar, 2003; Pahl & Rowsell, 2006). Such blurring of the in/out-of-school divide is evident in Wissman's (2009) research with adolescent girls of color in an urban high school who participated in a photography and poetry elective course. As a teacher researcher, Wissman pursued a critical and multimodal pedagogy (Janks, 2006), co-constructing this in-school course with the young women with the aim to give the students "the space and support to communicate critically, aesthetically, lovingly, and agentively" (Hull, 2003, p. 230). The texts that were explored and composed within the course illustrate the ways in which the students' literacies circulated across the multiple contexts of home, school, and community. Like the course Wissman taught, the Power Writers program located within a Bronx high school was envisioned as a space where the literacies of adolescents were viewed through the lenses of possibility and transformation (Fisher, 2007). Here, adolescents and their dedicated teachers came together to engage in deep critical inquiry, language exploration, and personal reflection. Fisher writes, "Power Writing was more than a class. It was a job, a sacred space, a home, a functional—or sometimes 'dysfunctional,' as one student wrote in a poem—family" (p. 3). Fisher urges educators to recognize that "young people are yearning to be chosen and to be claimed" as part of something bigger and that educators have a privileged role to "help young people develop the tools to transform this yearning into words and actions that chart the future they desire and deserve" (p. 101).

We contend that maintaining the in/out-of-school binary has detrimental effects on how we understand youth and consequently what kinds of educational spaces we construct with and for them. While we recognize that opportunities for expansive literacies are often more readily evident outside of boundaries of the classroom, we argue that it is not predetermined or preordained what can happen within schools, as evidenced by the growing number of examples that reflect re-imagined purposes of literacy teaching, learning, and research within and across contexts.

References

Alexander-Smith, A. C. (2004). Feeling the rhythm of the critically conscious mind. *English Journal, 93*(3), 58–63.

Alim, H. S. (2007). Critical Hip-Hop language pedagogies: Combat, consciousness, and the cultural politics of communication. *Journal of Language, Identity, and Education, 6*(2), 161–176.

Alvermann, D. E. (2008). Why bother theorizing adolescents' online literacies for classroom practice and research? *Journal of Adolescent & Adult Literacy, 52*(1), 8–19.

Alvermann, D. E., & Eakle, A. J. (2007). Dissolving learning boundaries: The doing, re-doing, and undoing of school. In D. Thiessen & A. Cook-Sather (Eds.), *International handbook of student experience in elementary and secondary school* (pp. 143–166). Dordrecht, The Netherlands: Springer.

Black, R. W. (2005). Access and affiliation: The literacy and composition practices of English-language learners in an online fanfiction community. *Journal of Adolescent and Adult Literacy, 49*(2), 118–128.

Blackburn, M. (2003). Exploring literacy performances and power dynamics at the Loft: Queer youth reading the world and the word. *Research in the Teaching of English, 37*(4), 467–490.

Davis, A., & McGrail, W. (2009). "Proof-revising" with podcasting: Keeping readers in mind as students listen to and rethink their writing. *The Reading Teacher, 62*(6), 522–529.

Desmet, C. (2009). Teaching Shakespeare with YouTube. *English Journal, 99*(1), 65–70.

Fisher, M. T. (2007). *Writing in rhythm: Spoken word poetry in urban classrooms.* New York: Teachers College Press.

Gee, J. (2002). Millennials and Bobos, Blue's Clues and Sesame Street: A story for our times. In D. E. Alvermann (Ed.), *Adolescents and literacies in a digital world* (pp. 51–67). New York: Peter Lang.

Gee, J. P. (2003). *What video games have to teach us about learning and literacy.* New York: Palgrave.

Gustavson, L. (2007). *Youth learning on their own terms: Creative practices and classroom teaching.* New York: Routledge.

Gutierrez, K. (2008). Developing a sociocritical literacy in the third space. *Reading Research Quarterly, 43*(2), 148–164.

Heath, S. B. (2001). Three's not a crowd: Plans, roles, and focus in the arts. *Educational Researcher, 30*(7), 10–17.

Hill, M. L. (2009). *Beats, rhymes, and classroom life: Hip-hop pedagogy and the politics of identity.* New York: Teachers College Press.

Hull, G. A. (2003). Youth culture and digital media: New literacies for new times. *Research in the Teaching of English, 38*(2), 229–233.

Hull, G., & Katz, M. L. (2006). Crafting an agentive self: Case studies of digital storytelling. *Research in the Teaching of English, 41*(1), 43–81.

Hull, G., Kenney, N. L., Marple, S., & Forsman-Schneider, A. (2006). *Many versions of masculine: An exploration of boys' identity formation through digital storytelling in an afterschool program.* New York: The Robert Bowne Foundation.

Hull, G., & Schultz, K. (2001). Literacy and learning out of school: A review of theory and research. *Review of Educational Research, 71,* 575–611.

Hull, G., & Schultz, K. (Eds.). (2002). *School's out!: Bridging out-of-school literacies with classroom practice.* New York: Teachers College Press.

Ito, M. (2006). Japanese media mixes and amateur cultural exchange. In D. Buckingham & R. Willett (Eds.), *Digital generations: children, young people, and new media* (pp. 49–66). London: Routledge.

Jacobs, G. (2008). We learn what we do: Developing a repertoire of writing practices in an instant messaging world. *Journal of Adolescent and Adult Literacy, 52*(3), 203–211.

Janks, H. (2006). Games go abroad. *English Studies in Africa, 49*(1), 115–138.

Kajder, S. B. (2004). Enter here: Personal narrative and digital storytelling. *English Journal, 93*(3), 64–68.

Kinloch, V. F. (2005). Poetry, literacy, and creativity: Fostering effective learning strategies in an urban classroom. *English Education, 37*(2), 96–114.

Kinloch, V. F. (2010). *Harlem on our minds: Place, race, and the literacies of urban youth.* New York: Teachers College Press.

Kirkland, D. E. (2009). Researching and teaching English in the digital dimension. *Research in the Teaching of English, 44*(1), 8–22.

Knobel, M. (2001). "I'm not a pencil man": How one student challenges

our notions of literacy "failure" in school. *Journal of Adolescent and Adult Literacy, 44*(5), 404–419.

Knobel, M., & Lankshear, C. (2008). Remix: The art and craft of endless hybridization. *Journal of Adolescent & Adult Literacy, 52*(1), 22–33.

Lankshear, C., & Knobel, M. (2003). *New literacies: Changing knowledge and classroom learning.* Buckingham, UK: Open University Press.

Lankshear, C., & Knobel, M. (2007). Sampling "the new" in new literacies. In M. Knobel & C. Lankshear (Eds.), *A new literacies sampler* (pp. 1–24). New York: Peter Lang.

Larson, J., & Marsh, J. (2005). *Making literacy real.* Thousand Oaks, CA: Sage.

Leander, K. M. (2007). "You won't be needing your laptops today": Wired bodies in the wireless classroom. In M. Knobel & C. Lankshear (Eds.), *A new literacies sampler* (pp. 25–48). New York: Peter Lang.

Leander, K. M., & Lovvron, J. F. (2006). Literacy networks: Following the circulation of texts, bodies, and objects in the schooling and online gaming of one youth. *Cognition and Instruction, 24*(3), 291–340.

Leander, K. M., & Sheehy, M. (Eds.). (2004). *Spatializing literacy research and practice.* New York: Peter Lang.

Lee, C. (2007). *Culture, literacy, and learning: Taking bloom in the midst of the whirlwind.* New York: Teachers College Press.

Lewis, C. (2007). New literacies. In M. Knobel & C. Lankshear (Eds.), *A new literacies sampler* (pp. 229–237). New York: Peter Lang.

Lewis, C., & Fabos, B. (2005). Instant Messaging, literacies, and social identities. *Reading Research Quarterly, 40*(4), 470–501.

Livingstone, S. (2008). Taking risky opportunities in youthful content creation: Teenagers' use of social networking sites for intimacy, privacy and self-expression. *New Media & Society, 10*(3), 393–411.

Lunsford, A. A. (2006). Writing, technologies, and the fifth canon. *Computers and Composition, 23,* 169–177.

Mahar, D. (2003). Bringing the outside in: One teacher's ride on the anime highway. *Language Arts, 81*(2), 110–117.

Mahiri, J. (2004). Street scripts: African American youth writing about crime and violence. In J. Mahiri (Ed.), *What they don't learn in school: Literacy in the lives of urban youth* (pp. 19–24). New York: Peter Lang.

Mahiri, J. (2006). Digital DJ-ing: Rhythms of learning in an urban school. *Language Arts, 84*(1), 55–62.

Medina, C. L., & Campano, G. (2006). Performing identities through drama and teatro practices in multilingual classrooms. *Language Arts, 83*(4), 332-341.

Moje, E. B. (2002). But where are the youth? Integrating youth culture into literacy theory. *Educational Theory, 52,* 97–120.

Morrell, E. (2005). Critical English education. *English Education, 37*(4), 312–321.

O'Brien, D. (2006). "Struggling" adolescents' engagement in multimediating: Countering the institutional construction of incompetence. In D. E. Alvermann, D. W. Moore, S. F. Phelps, & D. R. Wolf (Eds.), *Reconceptualizing the literacies in adolescents' lives* (2nd ed., pp. 29–46). Mahwah, NJ: Erlbaum.

O'Brien, D. G., & Bauer, B. B. (2005). New literacies and the institution of old learning. *Reading Research Quarterly, 40*(1), 120–131.

Pahl, K., & Rowsell, J. (Eds.). (2006). *Travel notes from the New Literacy Studies: Instances of practice.* Clevedon, UK: Multilingual Matters.

Pleasants, H. (2008). Negotiating identity projects: Exploring the digital storytelling experiences of three African American girls. In M. L. Hill & L. Vasudevan (Eds.), *Media, learning, and sites of possibility* (pp. 205–233). New York: Peter Lang.

Read, S. (2006). Tapping into students' motivation: Lessons from young adolescents' blogs. *Voices from the Middle, 14*(2), 38–46.

Sablo Sutton, S. (2004). Spoken word: Performance poetry in the Black community. In J. Mahiri (Ed.), *What they don't learn in school: Literacy in the lives of urban youth* (pp. 213–233). New York: Peter Lang.

Shamburg, C., & Craighead, C. (2009). Shakepeare, our digital native. *English Journal, 99*(1), 74–78.

Sheehy, M. (2009). Can the literacy practices in an after-school programme be practised in school? A study of literacies from a spatial perspective. *Pedagogy, Culture, & Society, 17*(2), 141–160.

Soep, E. (2006). Youth media citizenship: Beyond "youth voice." *After-school Matters, 5,* 1–11.

Squire, K. (2008). Video-game literacy: A literacy of expertise. In J. Coiro, M. Knobel, C. Lankshear, & D. J. Leu (Eds.), *Handbook of research on new literacies* (pp. 635–670). New York: Erlbaum.

Staples, J. M. (2008). "Hustle & Flow": A critical student and teacher-generated framework for re-authoring a representation of Black masculinity. *Educational Action Research, 16*(3), 377–390.

Stornaiuolo, A., Hull, G., & Nelson, M. E. (2009). Mobile texts and migrant audiences: Rethinking literacy and assessment in a new media age. *Language Arts, 86*(5), 382–392.

Street, B. (1995). *Social literacies*. New York: Longman Group.

Swenson, J., Young, C., McGrail, E., Rozema, R., & Whitin, P. (2006). Extending the conversation: New technologies, new literacies, and English education. *English Education, 38*(4), 351–369.

Thomas, A. (2007). Blurring and breaking through the boundaries of narrative, literacy, and identity in adolescent fan fiction. In M. Knobel & C. Lankshear (Eds.), *A new literacies sampler* (pp. 137–165). New York: Peter Lang.

Vasudevan, L. (2006). Making known differently: Engaging visual modalities as spaces to author new selves. *E-Learning, 3*(2), 207–216.

Wilber, D. (2007). MyLiteracies: Understanding the net generation through LiveJournals and literacy practices. *Innovate: Journal of Online Education, 3*. Retrieved from http://www.innovateonline.info/index.php?view=article&id=384

Wissman, K. (2009). Reading and becoming living authors: Urban girls pursuing a poetry of self-definition. *English Journal, 98*(3), 39–45.

15

Literacy Education in the Context of Globalisation

ALLAN LUKE, RADHA IYER, AND CATHERINE DOHERTY

Harvey Graff's (1979) history of the "literacy myth" and Brian Street's (1984) ethnographic case for an "ideological model" of literacy set the grounds for a three decade revision of the core premises of literacy education. The shapes and consequences of literacy are not universal. They depend on historical and cultural context: on political ideologies and disciplinary discourses, systems of governance, ownership and control of texts and information, and local functions and uses of literacy. Institutions like schools, religions, and media/Internet corporations provide selective sociohistorical scripts for its acquisition and use. These institutions stand in complex and contested relationships with the traditions and practices of vernacular and indigenous cultures and languages (Hornberger, 2002).

Economic and cultural globalisation has, in effect, put these relationships on steroids, with accelerated patterns of contact, change and disruption. New cultural, technological and economic conditions have generated what are referred to in this volume as "new literacies" (Lankshear & Knobel, 2003). Digital culture and economic globalisation are grounded in shifts in dominant modes of communication, spatial relocations of industrial means of production, and transnational economies of ownership and control, censorship and access to information (Graham, 2002). The print publishing and media industries (e.g., Newscorp) are rapidly moving towards hybrid print/digital markets; the next wave of cross-marketing structures and alliances for the consolidation and expansion of media is underway (e.g., Apple, Sony, Google). Autocratic governments and authors alike face issues of the control and censorship of information and intellectual property, free and paid access, and the ownership of texts.

While book sales remain robust and newspapers shift to digital delivery, there are significant changes in the everyday modes and genres of reading and writing: from e-reading to social networking and videogaming. While much of this is via expanded corporate markets, the Internet has also created openings for non-profit, activist, local and regional social, cultural, and political work and for new, rogue forms of criminal action and black economies.

Researchers are theorising and examining emergent identities and textual practices in a multiplicity of spaces and temporalities beyond the print "classroom-as-container" (Leander, Phillips, & Taylor, 2010). A wave of research on youth and digital culture has documented new patterns of agency, identity, and exchange, remixing and reappropriation of texts, often in ways that escape corporate and government control (e.g., Lam, 2006; Pinkard, Barron, & Martin, 2008).

Yet debates over the policy and practices of schools continue to work from 20th-century hierarchical and linear models that assume a universal individual development from alphabetic "basics" to "higher order" reading skills. School curriculum maintains a focus on canonical print genres. Current curriculum debates in Australia, Japan, the United States, and UK feature a resurgence of traditional literature study. In the United States, UK, and Australia, national education policies focus on high stakes pencil-and-paper testing of basic print skills. Simply, schools do not know what to do with digital culture or transnational identities, relations and practices.

Cultural and economic globalisation requires a dual optics: (a) a focus on new textual and linguistic practices and "semiotic social spaces" (Gee, 2005), and affiliated issues of ownership, access and control, surveillance, and censorship; and (b) a focus on persistent inequitable access to traditional reading and writing. Teachers and researchers work in non-synchronous educational contexts where print and digital cultures sit side-by-side and exist simultaneously, where new literacies and print literacy sit in close social, geographical, and cultural proximity. These conditions require cogent analysis of the effects of the global on educational media, youth identities and cultures, and literate practices and epistemologies and a deliberate, reflexive making of global flows, forces and exchange the objects of literate practices, as the very substantive curriculum content of literacy. Our case is that researchers, teachers, and students require a critical analysis of this new global information order, its possibilities and problems, its local, regional, and transnational effects and synergies, and its contradictions and inequities. These are the new fields for literate power and exchange.

The global exchange of information, discourse, economic, and symbolic capital, material resources, cultural artefacts, manufactured goods, and people has been enabled, enhanced, and accelerated by communications technologies (Innis, 1950). Literacy and globalisation thus stand in a complex and dynamic relationship. Globalisation depends upon the compression of time and space via transportation and communications technologies (Harvey, 1989). Increased literacy in dominant lingua francae (e.g., English, Mandarin) is viewed by nations as prerequisite for economic growth and late modernity, its collateral effects on Indigenous cultures and languages notwithstanding (Phillipson, 2004). Print and digital literacies, then, are both means and ends, subjects and objects of transnational economic, cultural, and semiotic exchange. The effects of literacy remain, pace Graff (1979) and Street (1984), mixed, local, and contingent on the "push/pull" effects (Burbules & Torres, 2000) of global exchange. Literacy enables economic participation and political enfranchisement, and, often in the same contexts, sets the conditions for new forms of hegemony and social stratification.

This chapter examines the implications of technologically driven globalisation for the teaching of English language arts. Our aim is to provide an overview of: (a) challenges and issues for those literacy educators and researchers who work in North America, the UK, Australia, and New Zealand; (b) challenges and issues for educational systems in selected 'Other' postcolonial countries and regions where English holds a powerful and contested space. We propose three contemporaneous frames for considering literacy in transnational and global contexts:

The Development Paradigm: focusing on the spread of basic literacy, its economic and social effects;
• The Hegemony Paradigm: focusing on the ideological and cultural effects of 'official' literacy formalised by schools, media and the state;
The New Literacies Paradigm: focusing on the emergent cultures, identities and practices of multimodal and digital literacies.

Throughout we refer to developments in China and India as key reference points, due in part to their acknowledged geopolitical and economic significance. With complex histories of colonisation, nationalism, socialism and capitalism, China and India were technically classified as 'third-world' and 'developing' countries in postwar development models. Both countries have complex multilingual and multiethnic histories. Both have emerged as nexuses of capital exchange, cultural and linguistic influence, intellectual and technological innovation—albeit with very different political and economic structures. They also illustrate the non-synchronous character of literacies in current conditions: where problems of universal access to basic literacy coexist, often uncomfortably, with new digital exchange.

The Development Paradigm

International comparisons on standardised achievement testing systems like PISA (OECD, 2000) indicate the overall achievement bands tend to locate the same cluster of wealthy countries (e.g., UK, EU, United States, Canada, Japan, Korea, Singapore, Australia, New Zealand) in achievement levels above those still developing compulsory educational provision. China and India have expanded educational provision and increased levels of literacy in the context of expanding economic and geopolitical power, and domestic poverty amelioration. Yet, there are over 25 million adults and youth unable to read in these same countries (UNESCO, 2008). While there has been an increase in literacy rates with over 9% reported in East Asia, there is "below-global-average increase of over 5%" in Sub-Saharan Africa (p. 34). UNESCO concludes that policies of "the last half century have not reduced inequalities" (p. 48). This pattern has been exacerbated during the 'boom' period of globalisation: with increased stratification of wealth within even 'successful' economies (Stiglitz, 2002), and deteriorating conditions for the poor globally (Cohen, 2006).

Since World War II, work in the field of language planning set thresholds for literacy in terms of a number of years of primary/elementary schooling achieved (Kaplan & Baldauf, 2003). These thresholds exclude recognition of informal education in community, rural and village settings (Farrell, 2008). Given wide variability in curriculum and school infrastructure, national comparisons offer at best a notional sense of the spread of literacy They also reflect ideological, religious and political economic divisions, especially in those countries where the universal educational provision for girls and women has lagged (UN Millenium Project, 2005) where religious and traditional practice has enabled or constrained access to particular sub-groups (Rosowsky, 2008), where state censorship of print and digital texts continues, and where cultural and linguistic minorities have been educationally marginalised (Hornberger, 2009).

The general assumption of postwar language planning experts and of non-government organisations (e.g., the World Bank), then, has been that levels of literacy are robust predictors of economic and social development. Debates around the spread and distribution of literacy are based upon human capital models of education and social development. There are several key issues here. First, as noted, levels of formal schooling have been taken as proxies for actual facility with print. Second, the model was premised on a 'thermometer' model, with a focus on more or less literacy per se, as a singular entity, rather than as on the diverse and stratified spread of specialised practices with print and other media (Freebody, 2007). While the United States, UK,

Canada, and Australia have over 95+% levels of functional literacy, by the school-attainment proxy, young adults leave school with stratified levels of textual capacity, and differential histories of engagement and access to canonical, specialised and 'high stakes' texts and discourses. Despite legislated school reform, persistent gaps between upper and lower socioeconomic groups, between dominant and minority linguistic and cultural communities persist—with a persistent Indigenous achievement gap (OECD, 2000). Recent reviews of U.S. data have indicated that high stakes testing and accountability systems have failed to close and, in some states, increased gaps in achievement (Nichols, Glass, & Berliner, 2005). In the United States and the UK, these gaps increased during periods of increased income disparity and declining social mobility (Jantti et al., 2006).

Since the 1960s universal literacy has been a key Indian national goal (Bordia & Kaul, 1992). Yet legislation for universal, compulsory, and free elementary education is still under consideration as this volume goes to press. Literacy levels vary from as high as 90% in Kerala, 70% in Tamil Nadu at one end of the continuum to a low 45% in states such as Bihar and Rajasthan—and reflect differences in regional economic development and political stability. In many poor communities, children are carers for siblings and do domestic and paid labor; in other communities, girls' education has low community and family priority (Rampal, 2007). In remote areas, health, sanitation, and basic services have taken precedence over schooling. At the same time, a burgeoning market economy, corporate services, manufacturing and technology, industrial and digital sectors have set the conditions for a "commercialisation of education" (NCERT, 2005, p. 9) and an expansion of the tertiary sector for urban middle and upper classes.

Using school proxy measures, literacy amongst youth aged 15–24 in India overall is 79.8% (UNESCO, 2007) with 84.4% males and 74.8% females reported as literate. Literacy instruction is influenced by century-old politicised debates of mother tongue versus official languages. Combined with caste, religion, class, geographic, and political issues, this complicates any coordinated national or regional literacy policy. In parts of the country, regional languages are the medium of instruction at the elementary level (e.g., Hindi, Marathi, Tamil) (Petrovic & Majumdar, 2010). These are second languages for those who speak a variety of dialects, and for many students English is a third language (Kamal, 1991). Yet, in India, as throughout Asia, English literacy is viewed by government, the corporate sector, and educated elites as necessary for economic success, class mobility, and, increasingly, regional and transnational educational and occupational mobility.

In China, the proxy measure of literacy among youth aged 15–24 is 99%, with, notably, little significant differences between genders (UNESCO, 2007). Since 1949, the Chinese government has successfully expanded the provision of universal, compulsory schooling with the target of universal literacy. In the aftermath of the Cultural Revolution, education and literacy became a central focus of the school reform movement in the 1970s and 1980s (Peterson, 1997). These targets have been achieved with an official policy of "digraphic" (Liu, 2005) and "bi-scriptal literacy" (Wang, Perfetti, & Liu, 2005), with school children receiving instruction in Putonghua alphabetic and character systems. The result is the largest extant population cohort with mastery of two writing systems. As in other historical cases, the press for a national, compulsory literacy in an official language—in this case, Mandarin—has had collateral effects on the intergenerational transmission and use of regional dialects and Indigenous languages (Lin & Man, 2009).

The 1979 Open Door Policy set English as a compulsory college entry subject, affiliating English with ideologies of modernity and progress. Since that period, China has grown into the world's largest market for private and government, formal and informal, face-to-face, and online English as a 'foreign' language teaching. In this millennium the number of English speakers in countries like China and India is likely to exceed that of the total populations of the United States and the UK (Crystal, 2003). Yet at the same time, the enthusiasm of educated youth for English has been described in the state-run China Daily (Zuo, 2010) as "English idolatry", with youth caught up in a "mimicry" of Hollywood culture, fashion, and identity.

The spread of literacy to the rural and urban poor in developing countries is a pressing matter of human rights and redistributive social justice. Many governments in Africa, Asia, and the Americas are struggling to provide basic educational infrastructure that would enhance economic, social and political participation. However, as the cases of India and China suggest, the development paradigm offers at best a partial explanation of literacy in the context of globalisation. Since their inception in the 15th century, national literacy campaigns have stressed standardisation and monolingualism (Arnove & Graff, 1987), with direct impacts on regional dialectal and linguistic variation, and Indigenous language loss. In both countries, governments have supported the expansion of World Language English as a medium of multinational capital and transnational cultural exchange (Lin & Martin, 2005).

The Hegemony Paradigm

A primary assumption of the hegemony paradigm is that mass literacy enables transmission and reproduction of ideological systems that serve dominant social classes. From a postcolonial perspective, Western literacy has been a vehicle for ideological indoctrination, linguistic imperialism and the eradication of Indigenous cultures (Pennycook, 1998). Yet literacy also is a means of power: as a critical, counter-hegemonic tool with the potential to analyse, critique and contest neo-colonialism and global economic and cultural forces.

European colonisation of Africa, the Americas and Asia entailed the symbolic, physical, and bodily imposition of colonial religion, governance, and education. The transplantation of colonial literacy education was a central strategy, eradicating or overwriting indigenous languages and cultures, and yielding, however intentionally, hybrid languages, cultural styles, identities, and practices (e.g., Stroud & Wee, 2005). Schooled literacy in a colonial language and knowledge of Western scientific and literary canons became the Eurocentric benchmarks and measures of 'civilisation' and elite culture in many countries in the Middle East, Africa, the Americas, and Asia. Colonial textbooks, pedagogies, and examination systems were the educational means for the spread of imperial ideologies, for linguistic and cultural imposition, and for the subordination and eradication of Indigenous languages and knowledges (Nozaki, Openshaw, & Luke, 2005). With decolonisation, new nationalist curriculum settlements were forged, entailing new languages of instruction and postcolonial textbook ideologies (e.g., Wong, 2007). In East Asian countries like Malaysia, Indonesia, and Vietnam, literacy instruction was seen as a primary means for the building of a new social imaginary in languages suppressed by colonial powers.

Yet in many of these same postcolonial countries, English language literacy is now viewed as a material prerequisite for participation in global flows of capital and discourse, bodies and workers across borders (Wiley & Artiles, 2007). In these contexts, the extension of mass literacy, the spread of English, the loss of vernacular language and culture, and the engagement with economic globalisation is a site for cultural conflict and political dispute. The case for a direct 'hypodermic' relationship between literacy and economic development is vexed by questions of literacy in which language, for whom, in whose interests, and to what ends.

In India, the politics of English language education has become a de facto struggle over the push-pull relationships between transnational and vernacular cultural politics (Sonntag, 1996). In the 2005 National Curricular Framework (NCERT, 2005) of India, English is promoted as "a global language" and "a political response to people's aspirations" (p. 380). An educational focus on English language literacy has set the conditions for the emergence of a domestic and transnational middle class that services multinational export industries (e.g., call centres, software development). This has enhanced economic growth and the expansion of the middle class, increased the number of Indian students and scientists engaged in transnational work and study, and expanded the scope and power of the Indian diaspora. However, within India the attainment of English literacy has become a fault line between rich and poor in the country (Ramanathan, 2005).

Paulo Freire (1970) and other educators working in colonial and postcolonial contexts argued for a reinvention of literacy instruction to encourage political critique, cultural and economic analysis and social action. Critical models of literacy education build literacy from vernacular knowledge and local problems, interrogating background knowledge and issues, and encouraging the critical analysis of material conditions and social relations (Freire & Macedo, 1987).

This requires a "micro-social analysis" sensitive to the "everyday strategies of linguistic negotiation of the local people" (Canagarajah, 2000, p. 123), as well as pedagogic dialogue about the social fields and relations where texts are used (Fairclough, 1990). Principles of critical education have shaped literacy education in postcolonial contexts (e.g., Mozambique, Venezuela, South Africa, Peru) (e.g., Janks, 2010), the education of migrant and second language learners (e.g., Norton & Toohey, 2004), and the teaching of English, reading and language arts (e.g., Comber & Simpson, 2001; Luke & Carrington, 2002).

American critical education has focused on setting the grounds for a critique of popular culture and media, curricular representations of history and culture, and dominant state ideologies. Current work has moved towards an examination of how critical educational approaches can entail a critique of the dominant technocratic discourses and taken-for-granted assumptions about current material and cultural conditions. This would entail both an engagement with local effects of globalisation—on language uses, cultural practices, work, identity and everyday social relations—and with the texts and master discourses that explain, rationalise, and justify the expansion of multinational corporations across borders. It would also entail students working with digital technology to access information and generate an analysis of transnational relations and effects of cultural and economic flows, a focus on global and local power on students' communities, and the possibilities of indigenous knowledges and alternative epistemological stances.

The New Literacies Paradigm

The 2010 decision by Google to suspend operations in China highlighted the contentious issues raised by digital access to texts, discourses and information. China has become a global "superpower … in information acquisition and dissemination" (Srikantaiah & Xiaoying, 1998). Spires, Morris, and Zhang (2008) report that while Chinese students (2.4 hours per week) tended to spend less time than their American counterparts (4.3 hours per week) on the Internet, their preferred practices were similar. Estimates of the number of Internet users in China range from 250 to 400 million. Their practices include: business and commercial exchanges, social networking and blogging, videogaming, music and media downloads, accessing of news outside of officially controlled print media, online English learning and university study, and participation in the flourishing artistic and political underground. Chinese and English search engines are under close government monitoring and censorship, with corporations like Newscorp and Google negotiating filters and firewalls, with government authorities. Internet use accelerates the shift towards dominant languages—English and Chinese. Many language communities with smaller transnational populations (e.g., Tamil speakers in India, Sri Lanka, and Singapore) have made Web resources available, and Internet resources have served Indigenous language revitalisation programs (see, for example, http://www.ojibwemowin.com/learnOjibwe/index.html)—but vernacular languages do not feature prominently in transnational exchange.

Chinese users are concentrated amongst emergent middle class in urban centres (e.g., Beijing, the Pearl River Delta), while rural communities in Western and Northern China and an older generation of Chinese continue to have limited patterns of access and use. Increasing numbers of Chinese Internet users, like their Japanese and Korean counterparts, have urban access and sufficient income to participate in the consumption of cross-marketed goods and 'styles' of hybridised media cultures. These cultures are not unidirectional impositions from America. Bollywood, Japanese Manga cultures, Cantopop, Korean soap operas, and other non-American influences are at work across Asia (Lin & Tong, 2008). Chinese, Japanese, Korean, and Indian brands and media images feature in print and online marketing in Asia and in the West. Unlike print and broadcast media, new media practices have generated hybrid, transcultural social and cultural practices and affiliated youth identities (Kraidy, 2005). Digital technologies have resulted in cultural convergence (Jenkins, 2006) and remixing "combining elements of R/O [read/only] culture; it succeeds by leveraging the meaning created by reference to build something new" (Lessig, 2008, p. 76).

The shift from "R/O" [read/only] culture to a widely accessible remix digital production culture marks out a major conceptual shift in literacy practices. 'Users' do not simply encode messages broadcast by central sources and authorities, but engage in potentially less regulable and recombinatory coding of new and blended messages. In effect, Youtube, blogs, and online e-publishing have disrupted publishers' and media corporations' late 20th century monopolies on production. New media forms have created new discourses, hybrid languages, and conventions of exchange based on peer networks and affinity groups (Gee, 2004). This has altered longstanding relationships of power in communications models of 'dominant' and interpellating ideology (Hammer & Kellner, 2009), between encoders and decoders, writers and readers, commercial/state messages and text consumers—a matter well understood by government authorities attempting to surveil and control Internet access and use.

These shifts have implications for schooling and print literacy teaching and learning, the institutions at the core of the development paradigm. How adequate is traditional print literacy curricula for preparing students to deal with the borderless flow of texts, practices, and discourses? Currently, national and state standards and curricula refer to digital or Internet competence as cross-curricular competencies for integration into traditional school subjects. The policy focus on traditional print literacy is premised on the assumption that basic reading and writing developmentally precede digital cultural engagement, despite evidence that children's use of digital technology may precede initial print education (e.g., Marsh, 2005). There is, further, a liberal humanist position that print literacy

and literature can act as a moral and ideological defence against the messages of new media (e.g., Postman, 1993). This complements a growing atmosphere of moral panic around the Internet as a means for terrorism, bullying, pedophilia, fraud, and a limitless list of potential criminal acts (Luke & Luke, 2000).

Approaches to critical literacy based on critical linguistics have focused on ideology critique and the analysis of dominant discourses and texts (Muspratt, Luke, & Freebody, 1997), with an increasing focus on visual and multimodal texts (Jewitt & Kress, 2003). Other work has focused on assisting students to navigate complex and multiple sources of information, taking account of the "uncertainty and theoretical disarray" (Selfe, 1999, p. xvi), non-traditional concepts of knowledge (Rantala & Korhonen, 2008), and incorporating multiple view points (Lankshear & Knobel, 2003). As the 2008 U.S. election campaigns and the current issues around state censorship in China illustrate, the new media has the potential to mark out a shift towards media production and networking as forms of social agency and political action, locally based but taking up the themes and issues raised by transnational relations. The shift from decoding to encoding, from critical analysis of texts to the production of new textual forms has the potential to reconnoitre Freire's (1970) original conceptions of education for cultural and political action.

Making Globalisation an Object of Study

We began from the premise that the conditions of cultural and economic globalisation have created non-synchronous conditions for print and digital literacies. Our intent here has been to 'make the familiar strange' for North American readers by showing a contrasting but converging picture of literacy. In Delhi and Shanghai, Los Angeles and Phoenix, we find parallel worlds of literacy and education in close geographic and cultural proximity and contact. Urban poor, migrants, agricultural workers and indigenous families and their children continue to struggle for equitable access to basic print literacy, within kilometres of office buildings where educated workers busy themselves with the transnational exchange of capital, information and discourse. Where they have access, youth of diverse cultural and economic backgrounds communicate with others globally and locally in new textual forms—creating local and transnational new identities, communities and textual forms (Warriner, 2007; Hull, Zacher, & Hibbert, 2009; McGinnis, Goodstein-Stolzenberg, & Costa Saliani, 2007).

This is nothing less than a new global "eduscape" (C. Luke, 2006), however uneven and inequitable its spread, depth, and breath may be. It is characterised by population movement and cultural contact, ubiquitous everyday engagement with new modes of sound and image, an unprecedented proliferation of the archive of available texts and discourses, and the global spread of a text-saturated, multimediated culture. This educational 'reality' is set in complex and, at times, incomprehensible corporate and state political economies which, ironically, are not the objects of study in school (Luke, Luke, & Graham, 2007).

English language arts educators face a complex array of new challenges for the everyday work of curriculum, instruction and assessment in classrooms. Globalised economies and cultures have destabilised the core assumptions of 20th-century education: about the cultural and linguistic homogeneity of student bodies; about the stability of curriculum knowledge; about the centrality of face-to-face classroom interaction, and about the pre-eminence of print. This is a new space for conflict and struggle over whose languages, texts, and discourses will count, over who will produce, use, and own them, over whose voices will count and be heard, and over who will be excluded and marginalised.

Many education systems have responded with "back to the basics" policies, a curriculum fundamentalism based on a restoration of educational conditions, student identities, and cultural conditions past (Luke & Luke, 2000). For literacy researchers and educators, however, there are immediate practical ways forward. Historically, literate societies have inducted youth to selective cultural scripts about how the technologies of writing work, where they can be used, with what social and cultural effects, and in whose human interests. This is what the traditional study of literature sets out to achieve on behalf of print. We can begin by making these new conditions—of transnationalism, cosmopolitanism, and globalism—focal objects of study for literacy education. This would not amount to a simple inclusion of print and digital literacies qua skills—but a full consideration of their possibilities and limits, an analysis of their communities, and a considered examination of how they can be used for development and hegemony alike. It would entail the generation of new texts, designs, and worlds by students and teachers, youth and elders, masters and apprentices. Given the rapidity, volatility. and uncertainty of these new worlds, this will require nothing less than a critical literacy of the 'global.'

References

Arnove, R., & Graff, H. (Eds.). (1987). *National literacy campaigns: historical and comparative perspectives.* New York: Plenum Press.

Bordia, A., & Kaul, A. (1992). Literacy efforts in India. *Annals of the American Academy of Political and Social Science, 520,* 151–162.

Burbules, N. C., & Torres, C. A. (Eds.). (2000). *Globalization and education: Critical perspectives.* New York; London: Routledge.

Canagarajah, S. (2000). Negotiating ideologies through English: Strategies from the periphery. In T. Ricento (Eds.), *Ideology, politics, and language policies: Focus on English* (pp. 121–132). Amsterdam, The Netherlands: John Benjamins.

Cohen, D. (2006). *Globalization and its enemies* (translated by Jessica B. Baker). Cambridge, MA: MIT Press.

Comber, B., & Simpson, A. (Eds.). (2001). *Negotiating critical literacies in classrooms.* Mahwah, NJ: Erlbaum.

Crystal, D. (2003). *English as a global language.* Cambridge, UK: Cambridge University Press.

Fairclough, N. (Ed.). (1990). *Critical language awareness.* London: Longman.

Farrell, J. (2008). Community education in developing countries: The quiet revolution in schooling. In F. M. Connolly, M. He, & J. Phillon

(Eds.), *Sage handbook of curriculum and instruction* (pp. 343–360). London: Sage.

Freebody, P. (2007). *Literacy education in school: Research perspectives from the past, for the future.* Camberwell, Victoria, Australia: ACER Press.

Freire, P. (1970). *Pedagogy of the oppressed.* New York: Continuum.

Freire, P., & Macedo, D. (1987). *Literacy: Reading the word & the world.* London: Routledge & Kegan Paul.

Gee, J. P. (2004). *Situated language and learning: A critique of traditional schooling.* New York: Routledge.

Gee, J. P. (2005). Semiotic social space and affinity spaces. In D. Barton & K. Trusting (Eds.), *Beyond communities of practice: Language, power and social context* (pp. 214–232). Cambridge, UK: Cambridge University Press.

Graff, H. J. (1979). *The literacy myth: Literacy and social structure in the nineteenth-century city.* New York: Academic Press.

Graham, P. (2002). Hypercapitalism: Language, new media and social perceptions of value. *Discourse & Society, 13*(20), 227–249.

Hammer, R., & Kellner, D. (Eds.) (2009). *Media/cultural studies: Critical approaches.* New York: Peter Lang.

Harvey, D. (1989). *The condition of postmodernity.* Oxford, UK: Blackwell.

Hornberger, N. H. (Ed.). (2002). *Continua of biliteracy.* Clevedon, UK: Multilingual Matters.

Hornberger, N. (2009). Multilingual language policy and school linguistic practice: globalization and English-language teaching in India, Singapore and South Africa. *Compare: A Journal of Comparative & International Education, 39*(3), 305–320.

Hull, G., Zacher, J., & Hibbert, L. (2009). Youth, risk and equity in a global world. *Review of Research in Education, 33,* 117–159.

Innis, H. (1950). *Empire and communications.* Oxford, UK: Clarendon Press.

Janks, H. (2010). *Literacy and power.* New York: Routledge.

Jantti, M., Bratsberg, B., Roed, K., Raaum, O., Naylor, R., Osterbacka, E., et al. (2006). *American exceptionalism in a new light: A comparison of intergenerational earning mobility in the Nordic countries, the United Kingdom and the United States.* Turku, Finland: Nordic Council of Ministers. Retrieved January 3, 2010, from http://www.ne.su.se/research/seminars/pdf/060907.pdf

Jenkins, H. (2006). *Convergence culture: Where old and new media collide.* New York: New York University Press.

Kamal, S. K. (1991). *Language and literacy: The case of India.* Retrieved on July 27, 2009, from http://www.eric.ed.gov/ERICDocs/data/ericdocs2sql/content_storage_01/0000019b/80/23/f1/98.pdf

Kaplan, R., & Baldauf, R. (2003). *Language and language-in-education: Planning in the Pacific basin.* Dordrecht, The Netherlands: Kluwer.

Kraidy, M. (2005). *Hybridity or the cultural logic of globalization.* Philadelphia: Temple University Press.

Jewitt, C., & Kress, G. (2003). *Multimodal literacy.* New York: Peter Lang.

Leander, K. M., Phillips, N. C., & Taylor, K. H. (2010). The changing social spaces of learning: Mapping new mobilities. *Review of Research in Education, 34,* 329–394.

Lam, W. S. E. (2006). Culture and learning in the context of globalization: Research Directions. *Review of Research in Education, 30,* 213–237.

Lankshear, C., & Knobel, M. (2003). *New literacies: Changing knowledge and classroom learning.* Buckingham, UK: Open University Press.

Lessig, L. (2008). Remix: Making art and commerce thrive in the hybrid economy. New York: Penguin Press.

Lin, A., & Man, E. (2009). *Bilingual education: Southeast Asian perspectives.* Hong Kong: Hong Kong University Press.

Lin, A., & Martin, P. (Eds.). (2005). *Decolonisation, globalisation: Language in education policy and practice.* Clevedon, UK: Multilingual Matters.

Lin, A., & Tong, A. (2008). Re-imagining a cosmopolitan 'Asian us': Korean media flows and imaginaries of Asian modern femininities. In C. Beng Huat & K. Iwabuchi (Eds.), *East Asian pop culture: Analysing the Korean wave.* Hong Kong: Hong Kong University Press.

Liu, Y. B. (2005). A pedagogy for digraphia: An analysis of the impact of Pinyin on literacy teaching in China and implications for curricular and pedagogical innovations in a wider Community. *Language and Education, 19,* 400–414.

Luke, A., & Carrington, V. (2002). Globalisation, literacy, curriculum practice. In R. Fisher, M. Lewis & G. Brooks (Eds.), *Language and Literacy in Action.* New York: Routledge.

Luke, A., & Luke, C. (2000) Adolescence lost/childhood regained: On early intervention and the emergence of the techno-subject. *Journal of Early Childhood Literacy, 1,* 92–120.

Luke, A., Luke, C., & Graham, P. (2007). Globalization, corporatism, and critical language education. *International Multilingual Research Journal, 1*(1), 1–13.

Luke, C. (2006). Eduscapes: Knowledge, capital and cultures. *Language and Capitalism, 1,* 97–120.

Marsh, J. (Ed.). (2005). *Popular culture, new media and digital literacy in early childhood.* London: Routledge.

McGinnis, T., Goodstein-Stolzenberg, A., & Costa Saliani, E. (2007). Indnpride: Online spaces of transnational youth as sites of creative and sophisticated literacy and identity work. *Linguistics and Education, 18*(1), 283–304.

Muspratt, S., Luke, A., & Freebody, P. (Eds.). (1997). *Constructing critical literacies.* New York: Hampton.

National Council of Educational Research and Training (NCERT). (2005). *National curricular framework.* New Delhi, India: Author

Nichols, S. L., Glass, G. V., & Berliner, D. C. (2005, September). *High-stakes testing and student achievement: Problems for the No Child Left Behind act.* Retrieved March 15, 2010, from Arizona State University Web Site: http:// epsl.asu. edu/epru/ documents/EPSL-0509-105-EPRU.pdf

Norton, B., & Toohey, K. (Eds.). (2004). *Critical pedagogies and language learning.* New York: Cambridge University Press.

Nozaki, Y., Openshaw, R., & Luke, A. (Eds.). (2005). *Struggles over difference: Curriculum, texts, and pedagogy in the Asia-Pacific.* Albany: State University of New York Press.

Organisation of Economic Cooperation and Development (OECD). (2000) *School factors related to quality and equity: Results from PISA 2000.* Paris: OECD. Retrieved March 10, 2010, from http://www.pisa.oecd.org/dataoecd/15/20/34668095.pdf

Pennycook, A. (1998). *English and the discourses of colonialism.* London: Routledge.

Peterson, G. (1997). *Power of words: Literacy and revolution in South China, 1949–96* (Vol. 1). Vancouver, Canada: University of British Columbia Press.

Petrovic, J., & Majumdar, S. (2010). Language planning for equal educational opportunity in multilingual states of India. *International Multilingual Research Journal, 4*(1), 1–19.

Phillipson, R. (2004). English in globalization: Three approaches. *Journal of Language, Identity and Education, 3*(1), 73–84.

Pinkard, N., Barron, B., & Martin, C. (2008). Digital youth network: Fusing school and after-school networks to develop youth's new media literacies. In *Proceedings of the 8th International Conference for the Learning Sciences* (Vol. 3, pp. 113–114). Utrecht, The Netherlands: International Society of the Learning Sciences Publications.

Postman, N. (1993). *Technopoly: The surrender of culture to technology.* New York: Vintage Books.

Rampal, A. (2007). Ducked or bulldozed? Education of deprived urban children of India. In W. Pink & G. Noblilt (Eds.), *International handbook of urban education, Vol. 1* (pp. 285–304). Dordrecht, The Netherlands: Springer.

Ramanathan, V. (2005). *The English-vernacular divide: Postcolonial language politics and practice.* Clevedon, UK: Multilingual Matters.

Rantala, L., & Korhonen, V. (2008). New literacies as a challenge for traditional knowledge conceptions in school: A case study from fifth graders digital media production. *SIMILE: Studies in Media and Information Literacy Education, 8*(2), 1–15.

Rosowsky, A. (2008). *Heavenly readings: Liturgical literacy in a multilingual context.* Bristol, UK: Multilingual Matters.

Selfe, C. L. (1999). *Technology and literacy in the twenty-first century: The importance of paying attention.* Carbondale: National Council of Teachers of English and Southern Illinois University Press.

Sonntag, S. (2003). *The local politics of global English: Case studies in linguistic globalization.* Lanham, MD: Lexington Books.

Spires, H. A., Morris, G., & Zhang, J. (2008, March). *New literacies in the US and China: Middle grade teachers confront the issues.* Paper presented at the American Educational Research Association, New York, NY. Retrieved March, 13, 2010, from http:// www. fi.ncsu.edu/ assets/research_papers

Srikantaiah, T. K., & Xiaoying, D. (1998). The Internet and its impact on developing countries: Examples from China and India. *Asian Libraries, 7*(9). Retrieved March 13, 2010, from http://gateway.library. qut. edu.au/login?url=http://proquest.umi.com.ezp01.library.qut.edu.au/pqdweb?did=115725015&sid=1&Fmt=3&clientId=14394&RQT=3 09&VName=PQD

Stiglitz, J. E. (2002). *Globalization and its discontents.* London: Penguin.

Street, B. V. (1984). *Literacy in theory and practice.* Cambridge, UK: Cambridge University Press.

Stroud, C., & Wee, L. (2005). Style, identity and English language literacy. *Linguistics and Education 16,* 319–337.

UN Millennium Project. (2005). *Taking action: Achieving gender equity and empowering women.* London: Earthscan. Retrieved March 14, 2010, from http://www. unmillenniumproject.org/ documents/Gender-frontmatter.pdf

UNESCO Institute of Statistics. (2007). *UIS statistics in brief.* Retrieved March 13, 2009, from http://stats. uis.unesco.org/ unesco/ TableViewer/document.aspx?ReportId=124&IF_Language=eng&BR_Country=1560&BR_Region=40515

UNESCO Institute of Statistics. (2008). *International literacy statistics: A review of concepts, Methodology and current data.* Retrieved March 14, 2010, from http://www.uis.unesco.org/template/pdf/Literacy/LiteracyReport2008.pdf

Wang, M., Perfetti, C. A., & Liu, Y. (2005). Chinese-English biliteracy acquisition: Cross language and writing system. *Cognition, 97,* 67–88.

Warriner, D. (2007). Transnational literacies: Immigration, language learning and identity. *Linguistics and Education, 18*(3-4), 201–214.

Wiley, T., & Artiles, A. (2007). The antinomies of global English and national pedagogies. *International Multilingual Research Journal, 1*(2), 57–60.

Wong, T. H. (2007). Education and state formation reappraised — Chinese school identity in postwar Singapore and Hong Kong. *International Studies in Sociology of Education, 17*(1/2), 63–78.

Zuo, L. (2010, October 3). *China's English idolatry.* China Daily. Retrieved from: http://www.chinadaily.com.cn/opinion/2010-03/16/content_9596880.htm

Section III
History and Theoretical Perspectives

Section Editors
Lesley Mandel Morrow, Robert Rueda, and Douglas K. Hartman

In Section III the authors focus on historical influences and theoretical perspectives that language arts models are grounded in. The chapters offer a breadth of information that has influenced instruction in the English language arts from the past to the present. Each chapter identifies a critical historical, theoretical, or policy issue and reviews research about it. In addition the authors analyze critical issues related to their topic.

Using a historical perspective, Douglas Hartman and Jennifer Monaghan document the uneven progress we have made in integrating the language arts (listening/reading, speaking/writing, and now viewing/visually representing) at the elementary school level. Continuing a long educational tradition, Europeans who immigrated to the American colonies required children to "listen" to them by teaching them to read from books that represented the community's religious, ethical, and social values. Today, after a long and uneven journey along the road of integrating the language arts of reading and writing, teachers are encouraging children to "speak" and express themselves as early as the first grade by nurturing their composition.

Henry Levin suggests in his chapter that costs of programs to improve literacy are usually not salient in the concerns of literacy scholars or practitioners. He explains how to understand costs and their measurement. There are some surprising results on the large differences in costs found in implementing literacy projects.

John Guthrie, Ana Taboada, and Allan Wigfield portray the cognitive science of thinking proposed by Nobel prize winner Daniel Kahneman as it relates to reading. In addition, diverse motivations for reading align with our cognition. One motivation powers our automatic processes, and a different motivation energizes our more deliberate aspects of thinking and reading. This alignment is a powerful synthesis of the heart and mind in reading.

Patricia Enciso analyzes foundations for contemporary language arts education. She uses Vygotsky's sociocultural-historical principles of social mediation, joint problem-solving, and language as mediating sign for imagining possible worlds. Commitments and challenges to equity and diversity in school and community-based literacy research are foregrounded through reference to theories of dialogism, authorship, and identity.

Robert Jimenez, Brian Rose, Mikel Cole, and Tanya Flushman examine the notion of "best practices" in language and literacy with English language learners. Drawing from a sociocultural framework, they argue for broadening the notion of "best practice" from the simple mechanics of specific instructional practices, which they acknowledge is important. They propose one critical dimension that bears consideration, namely the quality of meaningful teacher-student relationships, which form the foundation for effective classroom instruction. They conclude by arguing for broadening current perspectives about what effective teachers should be able to do to promote high quality classroom environments.

Richard Beach and Thomas Swiss trace the history of how four basic types of literary theories influenced the purpose and practices of English language arts instruction since the 1950s. Text-based theories (New/formalist Criticism) promoted close-reading analysis of the autonomous text by acquiring knowledge of literary conventions constituting text meaning. Reader-based literary theories valued individual readers' aesthetic experiences of texts, leading to an emphasis sharing or enactment of students' unique responses. Sociocultural literary theories fostered the need for instruction based on creating critical classroom contexts and stances for analysis of literary representations of race, class, and gender. New Media literary theories promote teaching interpretive strategies to interpret the interactive, multimodal, and hypertextual aspects of digital literature.

In the final chapter in this section, Timothy Shanahan provides a summary of literacy policy at the federal level in the United States during the past 50 years. This analysis shows how literacy policy has changed during that period from Title I to Race to the Top, with particular attention to the forces that operate on literacy education policy making.

16

Integrating the Elementary Language Arts

An Historical Perspective

E. Jennifer Monaghan and Douglas K. Hartman

In 1996 the International Reading Association (IRA) and the National Council of Teachers of English (NCTE) combined forces—not, it must be said, without considerable professional strain—to issue *Standards for the English Language Arts* for educators, students, parents, curriculum designers, and policy makers in the United States (IRA/NCTE, 1996). The document was a milestone in the nearly four-century-long journey to connect the traditional four arts of listening, speaking, reading, and writing. But the *Standards* did more than recapitulate the arts of language. It broadened and extended the conception of language arts by adding "viewing" and "visually representing" to the mix of communication modes. In nearly every respect, it represented a revised destination.

In this chapter, we examine the long, winding road that led to the 1996 *Standards* document, with a special focus on the elementary years. Nelson and Calfee (1998) conducted an extensive review of two language arts (reading-writing connections) that included secondary and college education (see also Lindemann, 2010; Shanahan, 2006). But given the very different paths that elementary, secondary, and collegiate curricula followed in integrating the English language arts, we trace the road that has received less attention historically—the elementary age years—and is marked by more potholes, dips, and curves. Far from moving in a straight line toward a more perfect integration, travelers have veered off course more than once. Several questions form a backdrop to our discussion. At any point in time, who had ownership over what was being taught in the language arts? Why was the pedagogical and even national focus directed for so long at reading instruction rather than writing instruction? What kept instruction in reading and writing, those two sides of the literacy coin, apart for all those decades?

Here we concentrate on seven milestones on the way toward integrating the elementary language arts in the American context. These milestones—which take the form of a book, person, practice, or construct—represent significant changes of direction in the journey toward the 1996 *Standards* document: (a) *The New England Primer*; (b) Noah Webster's spelling books; (c) Pestalozzianism and child-centered schoolbooks; (d) Francis Wayland Parker and progressive education; (e) the whole word approach; (f) reintegrating the language arts in the 1980s; and finally (g) where we are now, in the era of No Child Left Behind.

The New England Primer: Sequential Teaching of Reading and Writing, 1620s to 1780s

One immediate answer to the question of why reading instruction has been favored over writing instruction is that it is through reading materials that a culture conveys its value system to the young. The Protestantism of the early immigrants to New England in the 1620s and later naturally emphasized reading instruction, which would enable the young to read biblical texts for themselves. The traditional reading instructional sequence in the American colonies, as in England, was a fast course in Christianity: It began with the hornbook (which featured the Lord's Prayer) and continued with a primer, the psalter (book of Psalms), New Testament, and finally the entire Bible. In New England, reading instruction was usually mandatory: By the 1670s, most New England colonies had passed legislation that required families to teach the children under their roof to read—but not to write (E. J. Monaghan, 2005, pp. 31–43).

A text indigenous to New England was the famous *New England Primer*, whose first extant edition is a Boston imprint of 1727. In its picture alphabet, the letter A is for Adam, and its accompanying couplet plunges straight into the doctrine of original sin: "In *Adam's* Fall / We sinned all." The next letter, B, for Bible, offers redemption through reading, not writing. Its woodcut depicts a large book labeled "BIBLE," and the young reader is advised, "Thy Life to Mend / This *Book* Attend" (E. J. Monaghan, 2005, pp. 100–102).

The integration of reading and writing was not even a goal during the colonial period, for the order of the "three R's" as "reading, 'riting, and 'rithmetic" faithfully represented the actual order and separation of instruction for two of the language arts. Reading instruction invariably preceded writing instruction, partly because of the difficulty of handling a quill pen. Writing was defined as penmanship, the mastery of a series of ever more challenging scripts (E. J. Monaghan, 1987; Thornton, 1996). The only evidence of composition instruction in colonial America, other than Latin composition in grammar schools, came from British letter-writing manuals, reprinted in the colonies (Dierks, 2009, pp. 72–73, 143–152).

Noah Webster's Spelling Books: Integrating Speaking and Spelling with Reading Instruction, 1780s to 1840s

Except for the syllabary ("ab eb ib ob ub," etc.) and a few pages of syllabified words, the *New England Primer* does not present any full exposition of the relationship between the written and spoken language. To explicate this link, a genre of schoolbook emerged known as a spelling book (speller). It was not until the 1730s that spellers designed to teach *young* children were imported, reprinted in the American colonies, and added to the reading instructional sequence between the primer and psalter, where they became the most important text used to teach reading (E. J. Monaghan, 2005, pp. 213–231). Embodying the alphabet method, they presupposed that the alphabetical letter was the foundation of all learning. The task of the instructor was to teach children how to pronounce words (what we would call decoding) by naming the letters of the word aloud, syllable by syllable, in order to pronounce the entire word (E. J. Monaghan, 2005, pp. 386–387). The alphabet method was therefore a rare example of a unified approach to speaking, reading, and spelling at a time when reading was still largely an oral exercise.

After the Revolutionary War, the future lexicographer Noah Webster decided to write his own spelling book to replace English ones. Published in 1783, his first speller became a huge success, particularly after he revised it in 1787 and retitled it *An American Spelling Book* (E. J. Monaghan, 1983). Since the purpose of spellers was to teach pronunciation, the work succeeded in part because it was a genuine improvement over earlier spelling books. For instance, Webster helped children pronounce vowels by placing numerical superscripts over them. When he published a drastically revised version of his speller in 1829 (1829/1843), he improved his pronunciation scheme further by using the diacritical marks (such as macrons and breves) that most dictionaries still use today.

Pestalozzianism and Child-Centered Schoolbooks: Parallel Shifts in Reading and Writing Materials, 1820s to 1880s

Dating from the 1820s, a profound change was occurring in

some educational circles in the perception of children and the vision of how they should be taught. The source for this change was the work of Johann Pestalozzi, a Swiss educator. Pestalozzi deplored harsh discipline and rote learning. He believed that children learned globally before they zeroed in on particulars and that teachers should begin where the child was and shape their instruction accordingly. His opinions, which received widespread coverage in the *American Journal of Education,* begun in 1826, influenced many schoolbook authors (Carr, Carr, & Schultz, 2005; C. Monaghan & E. J. Monaghan, 2010). Since the alphabet method was the quintessential part-to-whole pedagogical approach, both the method itself and the spellers embodying, it came under harsh criticism from reformers, who emphasized that children needed to understand what they were reading.

The most successful reading series to incorporate Pestalozzian principles was that of William Holmes McGuffey, who won almost instant success with the first and second readers of his *Eclectic* series in 1836. Breaking sharply with the past, his readers offered simple stories about children, printed in a comparatively large font and adorned with plenty of illustrations. As a cohesive and carefully planned set of six readers, the series set the stage for almost all future reading series (Lindberg, 1976. For McGuffey's alleged plagiarism of Samuel Worcester's readers, see Venezky, 1987, pp. 251–252).

Pestalozzian principles also had an impact, briefly, on 19th-century writing instruction. During that period, composition instruction, variously defined, was largely the province of colleges and high schools (Schultz, 1999). But in the 1830s, for the first time, authors began writing schoolbooks on composition that focused on young children's writing and on their practice rather than on their learning grammatical or rhetorical rules. John Frost (1839) asked his young readers to draw on their own experiences for their writing: "Describe your own idea of a pleasant summer holiday" (Schultz, 1999, p. 52). Within certain guidelines, therefore, children took control, at least briefly, of their own writing, possibly for the first time in American educational history.

Francis Wayland Parker: Progressivism and the Integration of Literacy Instruction, 1880s to 1930s

One theoretical approach that always favored integrating children's reading and writing was the constantly reinvented progressive movement (Shannon, 1990), which resurfaced in the late 19th century. By the 1880s, the progressive mantle had passed to Francis Wayland Parker, who in 1899 opened an experimental school in Chicago. His approach was based on meaningfulness: "Reading should be first of all interesting to the learner," he wrote (quoted in Kline, Moore, & Moore, 1987, p. 143). Children would read what they themselves had dictated or written while teachers provided the spelling until children could do so for themselves. Once they had learned sight words, Parker encouraged phonics from his 21-page book of word families—onsets and rimes such as *flour, hour, sour* (Kline et al., p. 147).

Parker died in 1902, but when Edmund Burke Huey (Hartman & Davis, 2008; Reed & Meyer, 2007) reviewed reports on progressive schools for his 1908 book (discussed below), he identified Parker's Chicago Institute as one of the best of them. It embraced the philosophy of John Dewey, the leading figure in progressive education. Dewey had declared that play was the child's work and school a preparation for adult life. "Thus reading and writing and drawing ['visually representing,' as the *Standards* would put it]," Huey wrote of the Chicago Institute, "are learned in the service of what the children are doing as a social community" (1908/1913, p. 300).

Huey linked progressive education directly to the whole word method, suggesting that the latter was "very little used in America until 1870, when progressive teachers began using it in various parts of the country" (1908/1913, p. 272). The widespread acceptance of the whole word as the basic unit of instruction was surely encouraged by Huey's book, *The Pedagogy and Psychology of Reading* (1908/1913). Updated several times during his life, it continued to be republished yearly even after his untimely death in 1913 (Hartman & Davis, 2008). The whole word approach was also accepted by adherents of the scientific movement in education (Israel & E. J. Monaghan, 2007; N. Smith, 1965/2002). As the field of reading differentiated itself from educational psychology, the measurement work of Edward Lee Thorndike (Sears, 2007), who virtually invented educational psychology, became ever more influential.

The Whole Word Approach: Disintegrating the Language Arts, 1930s to 1970s

Adherents of the scientific movement believed strongly that basal reading series were the most appropriate instructional tools for teaching reading. Yet they and progressives at least shared one feature in common: a preference for the whole word as the basic unit of instruction. Both groups found the whole word approach liberating. Gone was the need to present only those words that could be decoded from the elements taught up to any given point. Gone were the restrictions on syllabic length that had been such a feature of the alphabetic method. Now any word of any length that had meaning to children was acceptable. For the new scientific researchers, whole words had an additional benefit. As the scientific movement began to quantify everything in sight, it was easy to tabulate, on the basis of their frequency, the words that children most needed to be taught. Between about 1870 and 1930, the date at which William S. Gray (Lauritzen, 2007) began serving as an author of the Scott, Foresman series, the whole word became fully accepted by adherents of both philosophies.

From the perspective of integrated instruction, the whole word had a harmful impact on integrating reading and writing, for it implicitly discouraged a key aspect of spelling acquisition—the ability to break down the spoken word into

its constituent syllables and phonemes. Few people noticed that the whole word method embodied in basal reading series, even with the addition of Gates's (see Sailors, 2007) analytic phonics, altered the teaching of spelling as well as reading instruction. It had long been known (e.g., Gates, 1922, pp. 69–73) that recognizing whole words from their context was not powerful enough to guarantee the accurate reproduction of their letters in spelling. But now the new spelling books, as they organized their content by word frequency or semantic groupings, unintentionally disguised the link between sound and symbol. Phonic "rules" were frowned on after a much cited study by Clymer (1963) found an accuracy rate of over 75% in only two-fifths of 45 common phonic "rules." So in most public school classrooms across the country, teachers postponed the teaching of writing, other than having children form letters for copying purposes, until at least the second grade. Not until the research of Hanna, Hodges, and Hanna (1971) did it become acceptable among reading experts to talk of spelling as a rule-governed enterprise. Yet, theoretically, the link between grapheme and phoneme (phonics) is where we could reasonably expect the integration of reading and writing to begin. Moreover, while the whole word methodology integrated reading and viewing ("look and say"), it did a disservice to language arts integration—by again focusing so much attention on reading instruction alone. Claims that the approach also ignored phonics led to fierce attacks from outsiders such as Rudolf Flesch (1955). (For details, see Pearson, 2002; Pressley, Allington, Wharton-McDonald, Block, & Morrow, 2001, pp. 10–31).

Old and New Theories of Language Acquisition, 1970 to 1980

Throughout all this, behaviorism, still in fashion since Thorndike, continued to be the prevailing theory in education. It reappeared on the reading scene with renewed vigor in the late 1960s (Pearson, 2002). Despite its prominence in the 1970s, however, the days of behaviorism were numbered. From 1957 on, Noam Chomsky published works that were to transform formal linguistics (1957/1969) by reintroducing mentalism to the study of language. This reintroduction reached the wider reading research community in 1970 with the publication of Harry Levin and Joanna Williams' *Basic Studies in Reading*. Researchers turned from studying reading methodology to examining children's comprehension. Investigators made striking advances in identifying practices, such as scaffolding, that would aid teachers to teach comprehension (Israel & Duffy, 2009; Pearson, 1985). But valuable as this work was, only some of its aspects, such as promoting written summarizing, fostered a closer integration between reading and writing instruction.

Reintegrating the Language Arts, 1980s to 1990s

In short, until the 1970s, approaches to integrating all the language arts in the elementary grades never became the pedagogical mainstream. Up to this point it was the teaching of reading that had been the major focus of pedagogy, research, and public money (E. J. Monaghan & Saul, 1987). Yet important conceptual, political, and structural efforts toward integrating reading and writing instruction had already been made by several organizations. Even as early as the 1930s, a small group of educators had attempted to develop ways to integrate the language arts more fully (Hatfield, 1935; Weeks, 1936). The most prominent and persistent of these efforts at integration was NCTE's *Commission on the English Curriculum*, which between 1952 and 1965 published five volumes on integrating the language arts (National Council of Teachers of English, 1952, 1954, 1956, 1963, 1965). Other organizations, such as the National Education Association (NEA) and the National Society for the Study of Education (NSSE) were part of the effort as well: NEA focused its 30th *Yearbook* on language arts in the elementary school (Hudson, 1941) while NSSE's 43rd *Yearbook* concentrated on teaching the integrated language arts in the elementary school (Henry, 1944). The University of Chicago's 23rd Conference on Reading focused exclusively on the language arts (Robinson, 1963). Each of these efforts embraced social conceptions of language and explored how the various language functions could be holistically embraced when teaching. Their impact was only limited and usually brief, but one of their strongest features was their encouragement of the integration of reading, writing, speaking, and listening.

In the late 1960s and 1970s, however, a novel line of work contributed to illuminating the development of children's literacy acquisition: research on emergent literacy. Language acquisition studies of children before they were exposed to formal schooling indicated that they were active in their acquisition of the written language (e.g., E. V. Clark, 1978). Precocious reader studies focused on the experiences of children who came to school already reading (e.g., Durkin, 1966; M. M. Clark, 1976). And literacy acquisition studies described in detail the emerging reading and writing behaviors of children (e.g., Clay, 1967; Ferreiro, 1978). Emergent literacy (Mavrogenes, 1989) received its first full explication in the seminal volume edited by Teale and Sulzby (1986), who notably concluded that "Listening, speaking, reading, and writing abilities (as aspects of language—both oral and written) develop concurrently and interrelatedly, rather than sequentially" (p. xviii). This realization suggested that curricular and instructional designs should be shaped to support the complementary ways in which these aspects of language influence each other as they develop. In time, more detailed and extensive research suggested that children's literate behaviors and artifacts included non-linguistic elements too (e.g., Yaden, Rowe, & MacGillivray, 2000; Short, 1992). These additional elements of communication—sometimes called "semiotic" tools (e.g., drawings, photographs, objects, graphs, videos)—were found to be integral to spoken and written communication, developing concurrently with print elements (Dyson, 1986; Suhor & Little, 1988). As we have seen, their importance

was formalized in IRA's and NCTE's *Standards for the English Language Arts* (IRA/NCTE, 1996), which redefined the language arts as "viewing" and "visually representing" in addition to reading, writing, listening, and speaking. This extension of the language arts to other aspects and tools of communication came to be named, most recently, "multimodal literacy" (Lancaster & Rowe, 2009).

Drawing in part on the insights of emergent literacy research, three movements in the 1980s and 1990s became, synergistically, dominant forces in the discourse and practice of integrating the elementary language arts curriculum: *process writing*, *whole language*, and *literature-based reading* (Gavelek, Raphael, Biondo, & Wang, 2000; Pearson, 1992).

The concept of process writing worked its way downward from the high school level. The new research interest in writing may be dated back to Janet Emig's classic study of 12th-graders as they composed (1971). Interest in researching the processes of writing mounted fast. In 5-year intervals, as recorded in the Educational Resources Information Center (ERIC), we can compare the number of reading research studies with those of writing (E. J. Monaghan & Saul, 1987, p. 101):

	1976–80	1981–85		1976–80	1981–85
Reading Research	2,795	2,394	Reading Processes	896	605
Writing Research	147	882	Writing Processes	154	1,073

The rise in studies on writing in the early 1980s is striking. As Pearson put it, "In the middle 1980s, writing achieved a stronghold in the elementary language arts curriculum that it had never before held" (2002, pp. 446–447). Indeed, during the 1980s process writing became the "primary paradigm" for writing instruction in many states (Pritchard & Honeycutt, 2006, p. 277). Key figures in this transformation were Donald Graves (e.g., 1983) and Lucy Calkins (e.g., 1983).

The whole language movement was another powerful force for integration. Its most visible leaders were Kenneth Goodman (e.g., 1989) and Frank Smith (e.g., 1971). Advocates and observers of the whole language movement described it as a curriculum "integrated in the sense that artificial boundaries are not set up between any two of the four language functions...All are regarded as supportive facets of the same underlying cognitive and linguistic phenomenon" (Pearson, 1989, p. 233; Watson, 1989; Wilson, 1997).

And the literature-based reading movement drew together the four arts of language through means of policy and practice. The 1988 California Reading Framework, more than any other policy initiative, united authentic literature, activities to write about it, and opportunities to speak and listen to others when discussing it. Nancy Atwell's (1987) *In the Middle: Writing, Reading, and Learning with Adolescents* provided for a generation of teachers an image of how to integrate the language arts through reading workshops.

Similarly, literature circles and book clubs rose in visibility, providing a means by which students could "interact using oral and written language to construct meaning about what they have read" (Raphael & McMahon, 1994, p. 103; Raphael, Florio-Ruane, & George, 2001).

Where We Are Now in the Era of NCLB: 1990s to 2010

A major blow to language arts integration could have occurred with the fall from grace of both the whole language and literature-based movements. The late 1990s, however, saw an important professional shift. New voices (particularly the voice of Michael Pressley, 1998/2006) within the reading profession called for "balanced" reading instruction, arguing that the principles of whole language and explicit phonics instruction were not mutually exclusive. One important study observed six "exemplary" teachers uniting the two approaches as they taught their first-grade students to write as well as read, in classrooms that were models not only of language arts integration but of individualized teaching and cross-curricular connections (Pressley, Allington, Wharton-McDonald, Block, Morrow, 2001).

Just how far reading and writing researchers and instructors have come in viewing literacy acquisition as an integrated and constructive activity, one that demands integrated teaching, is illustrated by a review of the latest research on instruction in the elementary grades. Studies support the authors' recommendation that "reading and writing instruction should not be isolated from each other" or from the content areas (Strickland & Townsend, this volume). Moreover, some researchers have taken a new look at reintegrating spelling into the curriculum. Bear and his colleagues have identified different layers of the orthographic system (such as alphabet, pattern, and meaning layers) on which they base their teaching of spelling with games that enable children, including non-native speakers of English, to infer graphic rules (Bear, Templeton, Helman, & Baren, 2003; Bear, Invernizzi, Templeton, & Johnston, 2005/2010).

Yet a countervailing tendency to these integrating forces comes from another direction: national and state testing. The passage of the federal act known as No Child Left Behind (NCLB, 2002)—actually a reauthorization of the Elementary and Secondary Education Act of 1965--signaled an unprecedented increase in federal involvement in state education (see Shanahan, this volume) and an emphasis on high-stakes testing. Its major focus was once again on reading—just as it had been in the federal legislation of the 1960s (Hayes, 2008, p. 45; E. J. Monaghan & Saul, 1987)—not writing. The act's requirement of state testing of all students from grades three to eight threatened to deprive teachers of their control of the curriculum. The consequences of their students not making the "adequate yearly progress" required by the act were so dire, even threatening teachers' own jobs, that "teaching to the test"

became inevitable (Valli, Croninger, Chambliss, Graeber, & Buese, 2008, especially chapter 6). Meanwhile, state testing of writing has also evoked criticism (e.g., Mabry, 1999). And it is still unclear whether the new Secretary of Education in the Obama administration will throw his weight behind the more repressive aspects of NCLB or favor a more progressive formulation (Price, 2009).

Conclusion

If we return to our initial questions, several answers emerge from taking a historical perspective. Ownership of methodology and content in teaching literacy was implicitly denied to both teachers and students in most of the periods we have discussed. Because reading instructional texts convey the values of a given culture and because we are responsible for conveying those values to our children, pedagogy had overwhelmingly favored an emphasis upon reading instruction over writing instruction. Not until we were prepared to value children's self-expression (speaking/writing) as much as their listening to/reading the words of adults was the way opened to nurturing children's presentation of self. We can glimpse this shift in the early 19th-century composition instruction of authors like John Frost, but more powerfully in Francis Parker's schools at the turn of the 20th century, and in the "exemplary" first-grade classrooms of our own day. The consensus of IRA and NCTE that we should aim at integrating the four language arts and two visual ones involves a radical change of assumptions, perhaps the most radical in the history of American literacy instruction. These new assumptions, however, face recent and powerful external pressures like those of NCLB. Whether, therefore, the desired destination will be reached remains to be seen.

Notes

1. Short biographies of the following persons may be found in Israel & E. J. Monaghan (2007): A. I. Gates, by M. Sailors (pp. 327–346); W. S. Gray, by C. Lauritzen (pp. 307–326); E. B. Huey, by J. B. Reed & R. . Meyer (pp. 101–139); and E. L. Thorndike, by L. A. Sears (pp. 119–139).
2. The National Council of Teachers of English (NCTE) published five volumes on integrating the language arts, all printed by Appleton-Century Crofts of New York: NCTE (1952), *The English language arts* [NCTE Curriculum Series, Vol. I]; NCTE (1954), *Language arts for today's children* [NCTE Curriculum Series, Vol. II]; NCTE (1956), *The English language arts in the secondary school* [NCTE Curriculum Series, Volume III]; NCTE (1963), *The education of teachers of English for American schools and Colleges* [NCTE Curriculum Series, Vol. V]; NCTE (1965), *The college teaching of English* [NCTE Curriculum Series, Vol. VI].

References

Atwell, N. (1987). *In the middle: Writing, reading, and learning with adolescents*. Portsmouth, NH: Heinemann.

Bear, D. R., Invernizzi, M., Templeton, S., & Johnston, F. (2010). *Words their way: Word study for vocabulary, and spelling instruction* (3rd ed.). New York: Pearson.

Bear, D. R., Templeton, S., Helman, L. A., & Baren, T. (2003). Orthographic development and learning to read in different languages. In

G. G. Garcia (Ed.), *English learners: Reaching the highest level of English literacy* (pp. 71–95). Newark, DE: International Reading Association.

Calkins, L. M. (1983). *Lessons from a child: On the teaching and learning of writing*. Portsmouth, NH: Heinemann.

Carr, J. F., Carr, S. L., & Schultz, L. M. (2005). *Archives of instruction: Nineteenth-century rhetorics, readers, and composition books in the United States*. Carbondale: Southern Illinois University Press.

Chomsky, N. (1969). *Syntactic structures*. The Hague, Netherlands: Mouton. (Original work published 1957)

Clark, E. V. (1978). Awareness of language: Some evidence from what children say and do. In A. Sinclair, R. J. Jarvella, & W. M. Levelt (Eds.), *The child's conception of language* (pp. 17–43). New York: Springer-Verlag.

Clark, M. M. (1976). *Young fluent readers: What can they teach us?* London: Heinemann.

Clay, M. M. (1967). The reading behavior of five-year-old children: A research report. *New Zealand Journal of Educational Studies, 2,* 11–31.

Clymer, T. (1963). The utility of phonic generalizations in the primary grades. *The Reading Teacher, 19,* 252–258.

Dierks, K. (2009). *In my power: Letter writing and communications in early America*. Philadelphia: University of Pennsylvania Press.

Durkin, D. (1966). *Children who read early*. New York: Teachers College Press.

Dyson, A.H. (1986). The imaginary worlds of childhood: A multimedia presentation. *Language Arts, 63*(8), 799–808.

Emig, J. A. (1971). *The composing processes of twelfth graders*. Urbana, IL: National Council of Teachers of English.

Ferreiro, E. (1978). What is written in a written sentence? A written answer. *Journal of Education, 160,* 25–39.

Flesch, R. (1955). *Why Johnny can't read—and what you can do about it*. New York: Harper & Row.

Frost, J. (1839). *Easy exercises in composition: Designed for the use of beginners*. Philadelphia: W. Marshall.

Gates, A. I. (1922). *The psychology of reading and spelling with special reference to disability*. New York: Teachers College, Columbia University Press.

Gavelek, J. R., Raphael, T. E., Biondo, S.M ., & Wang, D. (2000). Integrated literacy instruction. In M. L. Kamil, P. Mosenthal, P. D. Pearson, & R. Barr (Eds.), *Handbook of reading research* (Vol. 3, pp. 587–607). Hillsdale, NJ: Erlbaum.

Goodman, K. S. (1989). Whole language research: Foundations and development. *Elementary School Journal, 90,* 208–221.

Graves, D. H. (1983). *Writing: Teachers and children at work*. Exeter, NH: Heinemann.

Hanna, P. R., Hodges, R. E., & Hanna, J. S. (1971). *Spelling: Structure and strategies*. Boston: Houghton Mifflin.

Hartman, D. K., & Davis, D.H . (2008). Edmund Burke Huey: The formative years of a scholar and field. In R. W. Rowe, R. T. Jimenez, D. L. Compton, D. K. Dickinson, Y. Kim, K. M. Leander, & V. J. Risko (Eds.), *57th Yearbook of the National Reading Conference* (pp. 41–55). Oak Creek, WI: National Reading Conference.

Hatfield, W. W. (1935). *An experience curriculum in English: A report of the curriculum commission of the National Council of Teachers of English*. New York: Appleton-Century.

Hayes, W. (2008). *No Child Left Behind: Past, present and future*. New York: Rowman & Littlefield Education.

Henry, N. B. (1944). *Teaching language in the elementary school. The forty-third yearbook of the National Society for the Study of Education, Part II*. Chicago: University of Chicago Press.

Hudson, J. S. (1941). *Language arts in the elementary school* [The National Elementary Principal, Bulletin of the Department of Elementary School Principals, National Education Association], *20*(6). Washington, DC: National Education Association.

Huey, E. B. (1913). *The psychology and pedagogy of reading*. New York: Macmillan. (Original work published 1908)

International Reading Association/National Council of Teachers of English (IRA/NCTE). (1996). *Standards for the English language arts*. Newark, DE: International Reading Association/National Council of Teachers of English.

Israel, S. E., & Duffy, G. G. (Eds.). (2009). *Handbook of research on reading comprehension*. New York: Routledge.

Israel, S. E., & Monaghan, E. J. (Eds.). (2007). *Shaping the reading field: The impact of early reading pioneers, scientific research, and progressive ideas*. Newark, DE: International Reading Association.

Kline, E., Moore, D. W., & Moore, S. A. (1987). Colonel Francis Parker and beginning reading instruction. *Reading Research and Instruction, 26,* 141–150.

Lancaster, L., & Rowe, D. (2009). Editorial [Themed Issue on Multimodal Literacy]. *Journal of Early Childhood Literacy, 9,* 114–116.

Lauritzen, C. (2007). William Scott Gray (1885–1960). In S. E. Israel & E. J. Moriaghan (Eds.), *Shaping the reading field: The impact of early reading pioneers, scientific research, and progressive ideas* (pp. 307–326). Newark, DE: International Reading Association.

Levin, H., & Williams, J.P. (1970). *Basic studies in reading*. New York: Basic Books.

Lindberg, S. W. (1976). *The annotated McGuffey: Selections from the McGuffey Eclectic Readers, 1836–1920*. New York: Van Nostrand Reinhold.

Lindemann, E. (Ed.). (2010). *Reading the past, writing the future: A century of American literacy education and the National Council of Teachers of English*. Urbana, IL: National Council of Teachers.

Mabry, L. (1999). Writing to the rubric: Lingering effects of traditional standardized testing on direct writing assessment. *Phi Delta Kappan, 80*(9), 673–679.

Mavrogenes, N. A. (1987). Young children composing then and now: Recent research on emergent literacy. *Visible Language, 21,* 271–297.

McGuffey, W. H. (1836). *The eclectic first reader, for young children, consisting of progressive lessons in reading and spelling mostly in easy words of one and two syllables*. Cincinnati, OH: Truman & Smith.

Monaghan, C., & Monaghan, E. J. (2010). Schoolbooks. In R. A. Gross & M. Kelley (Eds.), *History of the book in America. Vol. 2. An extensive republic: Print, culture, and society in the new nation, 1790–1840* (pp. 304–318). Chapel Hill: Univ. of North Carolina Press and the American Antiquarian Society.

Monaghan, E. J. (1983). *A common heritage: Noah Webster's blue-back speller*. Hamden, CT: Archon Books.

Monaghan, E. J. (1987). Readers writing: The curriculum of the writing schools of eighteenth-century Boston. *Visible Language, 21,* 167–213.

Monaghan, E. J. (2005). *Learning to read and write in colonial America*. Amherst: University of Massachusetts Press.

Monaghan, E. J., & Saul, E. W. (1987). The reader, the scribe, the thinker: A critical look at the history of American reading and writing instruction. In T. S. Popkewitz (Ed.), *The formation of school subjects: The struggle for creating an American institution* (pp. 85–122). Philadelphia: Falmer.

National Council of Teachers of English. Commission on the the English Curriculum. (1952). *The English language arts* (NCTE Curriculum Series, Vol. 1). New York: Appleton-Century-Crofts.

National Council of Teachers of English. Commission on the the English Curriculum. (1954). *Language arts for today's children* (NCTE Curriculum Series, Vol. 2). New York: Appleton-Century-Crofts.

National Council of Teachers of English. Commission on the the English Curriculum. (1956). *The English language arts in the secondary school* (NCTE Curriculum Series, Vol. 3). New York: Appleton-Century-Crofts.

National Council of Teachers of English. Commission on the the English Curriculum. (1963). *The education of teachers of English for American schools and colleges* (A. H. Grammon, ed.) (NCTE Curriculum Series, Vol. 5). New York: Appleton-Century-Crofts.

National Council of Teachers of English. Commission on the the English Curriculum. (1965). *The college teaching of English* (J. C. Gerber, ed.) (NCTE Curriculum Series, Vol. 1). New York: Appleton-Century-Crofts.

Nelson, N., & Calfee, R.C. (1998). The reading-writing connection viewed historically. In N. Nelson & R. C. Calfee (Eds.), *The reading-writing connection. Ninety-seventh yearbook of the National Society for the Study of Education, Part II* (pp. 1–52). Chicago: National Society for the Study of Education.

No Child Left Behind (NCLB). (2002). Public Law 107-110. Retrieved January 2, 2010, from http://www.gpo.gov/fdsys/pkg/PLAW-107-publ110/pdf/PLAW-107publ110.pdf

Pearson, P. D. (1985). Changing the face of reading comprehension instruction. *Reading Teacher, 38,* 724–738.

Pearson, P. D. (1989). Reading the whole language movement. *Elementary School Journal, 90,* 231–241.

Pearson, P. D. (1992). RT remembrance: The second 20 years. *Reading Teacher, 45,* 378–385.

Pearson, P. D. (2002). American reading instruction since 1967. In N. B. Smith (Ed.), *American reading instruction* (pp. 419–472). Newark, DE: International Reading Association.

Pressley, M. (2006). *Reading instruction that works: The case for balanced reading* (3rd. ed.). New York: Guilford Press.

Pressley, M., Allington, R. L., Wharton-McDonald, R., Block, C. C., & Morrow, L. M. (2001). *Learning to read: Lessons from exemplary first-grade classrooms.* New York: Guilford Press.

Price, A. U-L. (2009, November 13). Can progressive education thrive under Arne Duncan? Retrieved February 12, 2010, from http://www.tikkun.org/tikkundaily/2009/11/13/can-progressive-education-thrive-under-arne-duncan

Pritchard, R. J., & Honeycutt, R.L. (2006). The process approach to writing instruction: Examining its effectiveness. In C. A. MacArthur, S. Graham, & J. Fitzgerald (Eds.), *Handbook of writing research* (pp. 275–290). New York: Guilford Press.

Raphael, T. E., Florio-Ruane, S., & George, M. (2001). Book club plus: A conceptual framework to organize literacy instruction. *Language Arts, 79*(2), 159–168.

Raphael, T. E., & McMahon, S. I. (1994). Book club: An alternative framework for reading instruction. *Reading Teacher, 48*(2), 102–116.

Reed, J. B., & Meyer, R. J. (2007). Edmund Burke Huey (1870–1913): A brief life with an enduring legacy. In S. E. Israel & E. J. Monaghan (Eds.), *Shaping the reading field: The impact of early reading pioneers, scientific research, and progressive ideas* (pp. 159–175). Newark, DE: International Reading Association.

Robinson, H. A. (1963). *Reading and the language arts.* Proceedings of the annual conference on reading held at the University of Chicago, Supplementary Educational Monographs, Number 93. Chicago: University of Chicago Press.

Sailors, M. (2007). Arthur Irving Gates (1890–1972); Educational psychology and the study of reading. In S. E. Israel & E. J. Monaghan (Eds.), *Shaping the reading field: The impact of early reading pioneers, scientific research, and progressive ideas* (pp. 327–346). Newark, DE: International Reading Association.

Schultz, L. M. (1999). *The young composers: Composition's beginnings in nineteenth-century schools.* Carbondale: Southern Illinois University Press.

Sears, L. A. (2007). Edward Lee Thorndike (1874–1949): A look at his contributions to learning and reading. In S. E. Israel & E. J. Monaghan (Eds.), *Shaping the reading field: The impact of early reading pioneers, scientific research, and progressive ideas* (pp. 119–139). Newark, DE: International Reading Association.

Shanahan, T. (2006). Relations among oral language, reading, and writing development. In C. A. MacArthur, S. Graham, & J. Fitzgerald (Eds.), *Handbook of writing research* (pp. 171–183). New York: Guilford Press.

Shannon, P. (1990). *The struggle to continue: Progressive reading instruction in the United States.* Portsmouth, NH: Heinemann.

Short, K. G. (1992). Intertextuality: The search for connections. In D. Leu & C. Kinzer (Eds.), *The forty-first yearbook of the National Reading Conference.* Chicago: National Reading Conference.

Smith, F. (1971). *Understanding reading: A psycholinguistic analysis of reading and learning to read.* New York: Holt, Rinehart and Winston.

Smith, W. B. (2002). *American reading instruction.* Special edition. Newark, DE: International Reading Association. (Original work published 1965)

Suhor, C., & Little, D. (1988). Visual literacy and print literacy—Theoretical considerations and points of contact. *Reading Psychology, 9*(4), 469–481.

Teale, W. H., & Sulzby, E. (1986). *Emergent literacy: Writing and reading.* Norwood, NJ: Ablex.

Thornton, T. P. (1996). *Handwriting in America: A cultural history.* New Haven, CT: Yale University Press.

Valli, L., Croninger, R. G, Chambliss, M. H., Graeber, A. O., & Buese, D. (2008). *Test driven: High-stakes accountability in elementary schools.* New York: Teachers College Press.

Venezky, R L. (1987). A history of the American reading textbook. *Elementary School Journal, 87,* 247–265.

Watson, D. J. (1989). Defining and describing whole language [Special Issue: Whole Language]. *The Elementary School Journal, 90*(2), 129–141.

Webster, N. (1843). *The elementary spelling book; being an improvement on the American Spelling Book.* New York: Cooledge & Brother. (Original work published 1829)

Weeks, R. W. (1936). *A correlated curriculum: A report of the committee on correlation of the National Council of Teachers of English.* New York: Appleton-Century.

Wilson, L. (1997). Defining whole language in a postmodern age. *Australian Journal of Language and Literacy, 20*(2), 116–122.

Yaden, D. B. Jr., Rowe, D. W., & MacGillivray, L. (2000). Emergent literacy: A matter (polyphony) of perspectives. In M. L. Kamil, P. B. Mosenthal, P. D. Pearson, & R. Barr (Eds.), *Handbook of reading research* (Vol. 3, pp. 425–454). Mahwah, NJ: Erlbaum.

17

The Consideration of Costs in Improving Literacy

Henry M. Levin

Several decades ago, I courted a young woman who had latched on to the "new" feminism. We went on dates and enjoyed each other's company. But, she warned me there was no future because: "A woman needs a man like a fish needs a bicycle." At first I thought this was an item she was repeating from the Miller Analogy test, but I eventually got her point. From the perception of educators, there are probably no two subjects as distant from each other as the English language arts and economics. Nevertheless, just as I tried to convince my prospective paramour that the two genders were hardly as estranged as fish and bicycles, I will contend that the economics of education can be usefully mated with the English language arts.

In this chapter I will begin by providing a brief introduction to the challenge in choosing programs and interventions that might improve student learning in the English language arts. I will proceed to point out that program selection must be assessed not only by its effectiveness, but what it can achieve within a given cost constraint. I will then endeavour to provide a brief picture of why costs are important, how they can be measured, and how they can be used as one dimension of program choice. Finally, I will provide a presentation of costs of program interventions for struggling adolescent readers with some surprising results and the lessons that they might hold.

Why Worry?

Why worry about costs of programs? That is something that administrators and accountants do, and educational professionals try to avoid. Many professionals in the English language arts believe that their principal goal is to infuse school personnel and students with enthusiasm for and proficiency in the many dimensions of the English language arts. They wish to focus single-mindedly on empowering the young as critical readers, writers, listeners of and contributors to our common language.

Certainly, this is an idealized view of the world. Edu-cational professionals have made a lofty commitment to education, and it is up to those who value what they can accomplish to fund it. Sadly, we cannot escape the fact that we live in a world of limited resources relative to demands. Not only do the English language arts compete with other subjects and school activities for resources, but education must further compete for resources with health care, housing, transportation, public assistance, defense, natural resources, the environment, justice system, and other public goods. And, in the larger sense, public activities compete for resources with the needs of families who must pay taxes to fund the public sector. Thus we are confronted with how to allocate available resources to a plethora of competing ends to obtain the highest level of wellbeing for society,

In the more limited framework of the English language arts we must seek to attain the best results with the resources that are provided to us. We may believe that the resources are inadequate and that expanding them is justified. But, whatever the resource limits that we work with, it is important that they be used most effectively. And, it is productive and efficient use of resources that is often the best argument for increased resources.

Pursuing this quest has two components. The first is that educators seek to develop and promote instructional approaches that are demonstrably effective. Much of this volume is devoted to that goal. It is clear that not everything works and that even among those interventions that are effective, some are superior to others in improving knowledge, use, and appreciation of the English language. We want to identify these strategies, focusing especially on the contextual conditions that promote results for particular approaches.

But, knowing that a particular intervention yields better results relative to the status quo or another intervention is not enough. One of the greatest flaws in educational evaluation policy has been recommending any alternative that seems to do better without consideration of costs. For example, a pioneering use of computer-assisted instruction in the 1960s showed strong positive results on mathematics achievement for educationally at-risk students. On that basis it was recommended strongly as an educational reform. But, within the experiment were data that showed that additional teacher focus on the same mathematics goals could produce equivalent results for less than one fifth of the cost of this early version of computer-assisted instruction. Nevertheless, the evaluators argued for the use of computers over teachers. The fact that costs were not included in the article imparted a policy gloss to the computer strategy, despite the fact that it would have bankrupted most school systems.

Cost-effectiveness analysis compares not only the effectiveness of educational alternatives in terms of what they might achieve, but also the cost of obtaining such results. The goal of this approach is to ascertain how to obtain the largest educational impact for any given budgetary and non-budgetary assistance such as support from sources outside the schools. Cost-effectiveness analysis has only rarely been applied in educational policy, in part, because educational administrators and policy makers are not trained in the subject and, in part, because program and instructional decisions are often based upon ideologies and politics rather than costs and effectiveness. Nevertheless, the use of cost-effectiveness analysis in education is growing rapidly with a considerable number of studies emerging (Levin & McEwan, 2001, pp. 265–284).

Application to English Language Arts

The practice of cost-effectiveness analysis in the English language arts comprises a number of steps. First, it is important to consider goals and how they should be measured. For example, a school may perceive that its performance on a standard assessment of writing is lacking. If it accepts that system of assessment—and in some cases it will have little choice because of district or state adoption—it may seek ways to improve student writing within that format. Among the alternatives are the adoption of a new writing curriculum, training all subject matter teachers in how to assist students in writing assignments, computer-based approaches to writing improvement, increased writing requirements, and teacher professional development in writing instruction. These are only examples of the many possible alternatives that might be considered.

The second step is to consider the potential effectiveness of each alternative for improving the writing of the students in the school. Obviously, this will entail an evaluation of typical student challenges in writing as identified in both the external assessments such as analysis of results on district or state tests and in teacher evaluations of their own students' work. Detailed scrutiny of student writing may identify strengths and weaknesses of students on particular types of writing. This type of careful analysis can help to set priorities with regard to what specific needs should be addressed by the writing intervention with priorities given to the greatest challenges.

Data should be gathered on each alternative under consideration to ascertain its likely effectiveness. Of course, particular attention should be focused on addressing effectiveness of alternatives for the particular types of students in the school and particular areas of weakness. Information might be derived from research reports, experiences of districts with similar students who have adopted the intervention, and evaluations by independent agencies such as the What Works Clearinghouse, a federally sponsored effort (http://ies.ed.gov/ncee/wwc/). Although publishers and developers of specific interventions can also be sources of data, one must be cautious with their claims which are often self-serving and promotional rather than objective. A systematic analysis of the information should be assembled so that the probability of success of each can be viewed according to the same criteria, for example, those used in the rubric for writing assessment. A numerical rating system can be used such as a scale from 1 to 10 where 1 might be a ranking for no evidence of success to 10 where the evidence suggests high effectiveness on a criterion. These ratings can then be used to assess the probability of success in adopting specific writing interventions, either by adding the ratings for each alternative or possibly weighting those more heavily where the dimension is of higher priority. It is obvious that while some of the evaluation process can rely on relatively objective information, some must necessarily be subjective and based upon the theory of action behind interventions and the experiences of the educational professionals making the judgments.

In some cases it might be possible to project effectiveness from formal evaluations in the research literature which compare interventions using experimental or quasi-experimental designs (Shadish, Cook, & Campbell, 2002). Such evaluations are becoming increasingly available over time because of the importance given these methods in the research community. The What Works Clearinghouse considers only these types of evaluations in making its assessments of effectiveness.

Once one has obtained a comparative evaluation of the specific alternatives that are under consideration, one needs to evaluate their costs (Levin & McEwan, 2001). The proper method for evaluating costs of interventions is to assess what additional resources will be required and what their cost is in the marketplace. This cost analysis can answer two questions. (a) Which interventions can be implemented within the resources that are available? This is a feasibility question in determining if the costs can be accommodated. Those interventions that are substantially more costly than available resource provision need to be omitted from consideration or subjected to a major effort to obtain additional budgetary and other support to implement. (b) Which of the interventions is most promising in terms of effectiveness relative to its cost? That is, information on effectiveness of each alternative can be combined with cost to determine which alternatives promise the largest writing improvement per dollar of investment. Clearly, much more can be accomplished by investing in programs that are highly effective relative to their costs than ones that have high costs relative to their effectiveness.

Determining Costs of Interventions

Although there is a common belief that the business office of a school district can identify the potential cost of an intervention, that is rarely the case. School accounting methods are designed for purposes other than the costs of instructional interventions. It is usually necessary for those considering program innovation to assist the business office and consultants with estimating the costs of alternative interventions as discussed in detail in Levin and McEwan (2001).

Fortunately, there are relatively simple tools to identify the resources and costs that are needed to implement reforms. The basic model used to evaluate costs of alternatives is what is known as the "ingredients method" (Levin & McEwan, 2001). The first step is to identify the "ingredients" or resources that will be required (Levin & McEwan, 2001, pp. 43–58). This must be done in a systematic way and entails participation by both school and district staff. School leadership and teachers need to understand what it takes to implement the reform. Most of this type of analysis can be done by using a financial spread sheet such as EXCEL. Personnel positions are listed according to their qualifications and the portion of time that will be needed. At the same time it is important to begin to identify where these personnel will come from. Will substitute teachers be needed to free-up time for professional development and teacher discussions and deliberations? If so, how many positions will be needed and with what qualifications?

Facilities needs and specific furnishings and equipment are also identified. If additional classroom space is needed for reductions in class size, that space should be specified. If computers, software, instructional materials, and other equipment are required, these also need to be specified. Ultimately, all of the ingredients will be listed with sufficient detail on qualities and characteristics. The compiling of the needed ingredients is important for developing a complete list of resources associated with the intervention. It also gives school and district personnel a better understanding of planning needs and enlists broader support in obtaining resources. Specific sources of information in identifying ingredients include the descriptive materials on the reform and interviews with the sponsor or developer of the intervention; articles and reports on experiences of other schools in adopting the intervention; and observations and interviews (often by email or telephone) with personnel in other schools or districts that have adopted the intervention.

The second stage in using the ingredients method is to determine their costs. These methods are well-developed in the literature (Levin & McEwan, 2001, pp. 59–76). A complete listing of the ingredients and their costs will provide an estimate of the overall cost of the intervention. This step also clarifies the resources that must be in place to promise success.

With systematic estimates of costs of the different types of interventions, it is possible to compare these with their predicted effectiveness. Those with the highest effectiveness per unit of cost are those that should have priority for consideration. However, when cost-effectiveness among alternatives does not differ substantially, it is important to bring other considerations to bear as well. For example, schools might consider issues of implementation, differences in the ability to accommodate specific alternatives and use them effectively. Clearly, if teaching staff have specific skills and professional development experience that is supportive of some of the alternatives, this should be taken into account.

Costs of Programs for Struggling Adolescent Readers

One of the pressing challenges for educators in the English language arts is the challenge of low adolescent literacy and struggling readership. The Carnegie Advisory Council on Advancing Adolescent Literacy has studied the challenge of improving adolescent literacy and has found a large number of interventions that address that goal (Deshler, Palincsar, Biancarosa, & Nair, 2007). The purpose of the Carnegie effort was to assist school decision makers and schools to select strategies to improve literacy among their students.

To demonstrate how costs might be assessed in making these decisions, Levin, Caitlin, and Elson (2007) used the method described above to estimate costs for three proposed interventions: Read 180, Question the Author, and Reading Apprenticeship. Because of space limitations here, the reader should refer to the backgrounds and descriptions of each of these approaches in Deshler et al. (2007) which also comprises reviews of evidence on effectiveness. Detailed reviews of evidence are also found in Slavin, Cheung, Groff, and Lake (2008) and Shanahan (2005) illustrating that different studies of the evidence may draw somewhat different conclusions. Many of the interventions that are reviewed use cooperative learning or computers, curriculum reform or specific instructional approaches. From the perspective of resource use, a common element found across many of the interventions is increasing instructional time on reading to 90 minutes a day and limiting reading groups to no more than 15 students. These substantial increases in time devoted to reading in combination with large reductions in the size of reading groups could account for most of the gains in effectiveness, despite the fact that advocates herald the other features of their interventions as accounting for the gains.

For estimating costs we sought information from program developers, program reports, and interviews with school personnel at both district and school sites. From these we assembled ingredients lists for the interventions and national costs for each ingredient. These were converted to cost per student for the intervention at each site as well as costs based upon the recommended ingredients of the developer or publisher.

Read 180 Read 180 is a widely used intervention sponsored by Scholastic. Lessons consist of whole group, small group, and individualized literacy instruction. During whole group instruction teachers read aloud, engage students in shared and choral reading, and model fluent reading and the use of reading strategies. The class is then divided into three groups that rotate through three reading stations: small group instruction, computerized instruction, and independent reading. In small group instruction, the teacher gives more personalized reading instruction to a small group of students. At the computer station which has access to Read 180 courseware, students receive individualized instruction via a program that advances to new text only after students demonstrate mastery in fluency, word recognition, spelling and comprehension. Read 180 recommends a minimum of 90 minutes a day devoted to reading and reading groups no larger than 15, both requiring substantial additional resources.

Ingredients were compiled for three Read 180 sites with considerable assistance from school personnel at these sites, and costs were evaluated in detail (Levin, Caitlin, & Elson, 2007). The cost per student at the three sites varied widely from the estimate of about $1,100 per student that we constructed from the developer's ingredients recommendations. At the three sites the costs varied from $285 per student to $611 to $1,514 per student. Differences were mainly due to differences in implementation and the extent of modifications in time devoted to reading instruction and reading group size. The low cost site lacked the available resources to adopt the smaller groups and greater reading time recommendations.

Questioning the Author Questioning the Author is a professional development program developed by Isabel Beck, Margaret McKeown and colleagues at the University of Pittsburgh that aims to equip teachers with new tools for engaging students in text and curriculum (Beck, McKeown, Sandora, Kucan, & Worthy, 1996). Students are taught to attempt what an author is trying to express to construct a representation. It does not require additional materials or modifications to the school day. Because there are very broad guidelines for class size and no recommendations for period length, it is extremely unlikely that schools will hire additional staff for the express purpose of implementing QtA; however, it is suggested that a minimum of two teachers per school are trained so that they can plan lessons and provide support to each other.

We were able to obtain detailed information from only a single site. Almost all of the cost is attributable to professional development, a relatively low cost ingredient when compared to additional personnel to reduce group size and obtain more reading instructional time. The cost of ingredients for the developer's recommendation was only $11 per student per year. The cost at the site was about $35 per student reflecting investment in more professional development time than the developer requires.

Reading Apprenticeship Reading Apprenticeship (RA) was developed by the research and development organization, WestED, an intervention that trains teachers to think

and teach in a new way (Jordan, Jensen, & Greenleaf, 2001). Subject-area teachers attempt to inculcate among their students the skills and strategies that expert readers of their subjects use. There are no facilities or equipment costs associated with implementation nor instructional time nor group size requirements. The program is delivered by the existing content-area teachers in their content-area classes. While the personnel costs for teachers do not change with RA, the program does incur costs for the time of school and district level administrators.

The developer did not have a specific estimate of ingredients, so we relied on our evaluators for the two sites using RA. Both sites had very low costs consisting primarily of the costs of administration and coordination and professional development. At one site the annual cost per student was only about $9, and at the other $31.

Some Conclusions

The policy implications of costs and cost differences of interventions for an English language arts program or intervention are fairly obvious. Differences in costs among interventions are enormous, from about $9 per student to more than $1,500 per student. Even within interventions, site-based costs can differ by large magnitudes. It is rare that differences in effectiveness among interventions vary so substantially. Moreover, the differences in resource implementation are substantial, raising questions about whether the effectiveness of a "model" implementation should be generalized to all sites and situations without consideration of resource use.

It is clear that differences in costs among interventions must be taken account of rather than simply examining effectiveness ratings. By no means does this suggest that costs be considered in the absence of educational impacts. Costs and effectiveness need to be considered jointly. But, Questioning the Author and Reading Apprentice account for only 1%–3% of the estimate of more than $1,000 per student for Read 180 based upon the ingredients required by its developer. Even if Read 180 were 10 times as effective overall as these other two interventions (and we have no such evidence), the difference in costs would make it considerably less effective per dollar of cost. Costs and effectiveness must be considered jointly in making professional and policy decisions in the English language arts as in other areas of education if we are to use resources in their most effective manner.

References

Beck, I., McKeown, M., Sandora, C., Kucan, L., & Worthy, J. (1996). Questioning the Author: A yearlong classroom implementation to engage students with text. *The Elementary School Journal, 96*(4), 385–414.

Deshler, D., Palincsar, A. S., Biancarosa, G., & Nair, M. (2007). *Informed choices for struggling adolescent readers: A research-based guide to instructional programs and practices.* Newark, DE: International Reading Association.

Jordan, M., Jensen, R., & Greenleaf, C. (2001). "Amidst familial gatherings": Reading apprenticeship in a middle school classroom. *Voices from the Middle, 8*(4), 15–24.

Levin, H., Caitlin, D., & Elson, A. (2007). Costs of implementing adolescent literacy programs. In D. Deshler, A. S. Palincsar, G. Biancarosa, & M. Nair (Eds.), *Informed choices for struggling adolescent readers: A research-based guide to instructional programs and practices* (pp. 61–91). Newark, DE: International Reading Association.

Levin, H., & McEwan, P. (2001). *Cost-effectiveness analysis: Methods and applications.* Thousand Oaks, CA: Sage Publications and Cambridge University Press.

Shadish, W., Cook, T., & Campbell, D. (2002). *Experimental and quasi-experimental designs for generalized causal inference.* Boston: Houghton-Mifflin.

Shanahan, C. (2005). *Adolescent literacy intervention programs.* Napierville, IL: Learning Point Associates. Retrieved from http://www.learningpt.org/literacy/adolescent/intervention.pdf

Slavin, R., Cheung, A., Groff, C., & Lake, C. (2008, July/August/September). Effective reading programs for middle and high school students. *Reading Research Quarterly*, pp. 290–322.

18

Alignment of Cognitive Processes in Reading with Motivations for Reading

John T. Guthrie, Ana Taboada, and Allan Wigfield

Within the discipline of psychology two prominent domains of inquiry into reading are cognitive science and motivation theory. From the vast variety of investigations in cognitive science that include studies of the brain, language, speech, and thinking, we focus on one salient contribution made by Daniel Kahneman. He was awarded the Nobel Prize in 2002 for his work with Amos Tversky, emphasizing how our intuition and reasoning work together. Remarkably, two theories of reading comprehension, developed from cognitive perspectives, show striking parallels with the inner workings of intuition and reasoning portrayed in Kahneman's research. Specifically, the landscape theory of van den Broek and the compensatory encoding theory of Walczyk both reveal intuitive qualities as well as reasoning processes in reading comprehension. Understanding the interplay of these processes can inform our viewpoints about the development of mature reading comprehension.

Central to our message in this chapter is the proposal that the motivations of readers align with the cognitive processes of intuition and reasoning to form an integrated system. In this alignment, intrinsic motivation is a major contributor to intuitive reading, while motivations related to self-discipline are the prominent forces driving reasoning in reading. We provide evidence for this alignment from both experimental and correlational investigations with students from grades four to college level. The significance of this alignment is that it reveals the interplay of cognition and motivation during reading and permits us to envision educational innovations that foster integrated development.

Intuition and Reasoning

The Kahneman and Tversky Perspective On December 8, 2002, the Nobel Prize was awarded to Daniel Kahneman in Stockholm. Based on Kahneman's lecture upon receiving the award, he wrote an article published in the *American Psychologist* (Kahneman, 2003). From that article and

others, we extract his perspective on the two-tier system of the processes and contents in human cognition. In a lecture in 2008 at Harvard University Kahneman noted, "Most of the time we run at very low effort and people don't check themselves as much as they should." He was referring to the human tendency to judge things quickly, to go with the familiar and easy perceptions instead of giving a question or a problem sufficient attention, reflection, and thought. In the article and the lecture, Kahneman outlined two distinct systems of thinking which have an ancient history in psychology. The first cognitive system relies on perception, intuition, and emotion and is often performed unconsciously. The second system is a guided, controlled set of thinking operations. Both systems contribute to our intelligence and mental acuity.

A graphic display of intuition and reasoning is shown in Figure 18.1. On the intuition side, we are talking about our perceptions of the world such as seeing a tree, hearing a word, or feeling a flight of steps with our feet as we climb them. Our processes of seeing, hearing, or feeling in these situations share a cluster of attributes. As part of the intuitive system these processes are typically fast, automatic, effortless, associative, implicit (not available to introspection) and they may be emotionally salient. When we see a tree we do not make a decision about whether we are seeing the tree. Rather, it is fast, automatic, and effortless. As we hear a familiar word in an understandable sentence the meaning is brought to mind quickly, associated with other meanings automatically, and may bring laughter or tears. These processes all occur without our intentions or conscious attempts to make them happen. As we shall see, there are crucially important, similar processes in reading at several levels of sophistication.

On the reasoning side of our cognitive systems, the contents are conceptual and language based. We reason about concepts, problems, and decisions such as how to make an investment, whether to trust a neighbor, and how to program the digital recorder. As Figure 18.1 depicts, the

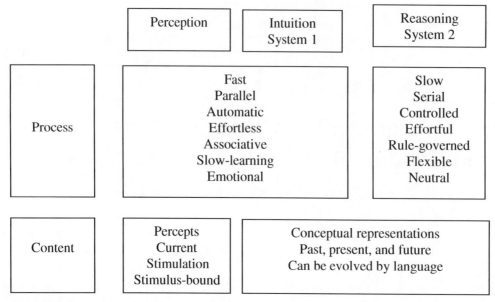

Figure 18.1 Process and content in two cognitive systems.

processes of reasoning are slower, sequential, effortful, and governed by standards or criteria of satisfaction.

As Kahneman (2003) observed summarizing his own research and that of others, we may use the anthropomorphic phrase that reasoning monitors the activities of intuition. Of course, the monitoring is loose and allows many intuitive judgments to be accepted, although some may be incorrect. The flow of intuitive information is so fast and rich that it all cannot be checked. Intuitive processing is often powerful and accurate. For example, studies show that nurses who intuitively detect subtle signs of illness may often be correct in important matters. Likewise, chess masters may play several chess games simultaneously making rapid, intuitive judgments about complex chess patterns and winning many games. A core quality of intuitive thoughts is that they come to mind spontaneously and effortlessly. In this sense, Kahneman refers to the contents of intuition as accessible. Some accessible perceptions are visible, like a brilliant red, whereas other accessible perceptions are emotional, like kind words from a significant other. The problem with many perceptions is that we may be inaccurate about them. We may simplify them, reduce them to categories, ignore important details, omit inconsistent information, or make rapid inferences that are incorrect. Occasionally, our inaccurate perceptions conflict with each other, collide with our conscious goals, or alert us to danger. When such incorrect perceptions imperil our well being, we retrieve our forces of reasoning to monitor intuition and bail us out.

When the intuitive system is inaccurate or threatening in some way, the reasoning system kicks in. We evaluate information that seems inconsistent or incomprehensible. In evaluating we compare, relate, reassess, organize, transform, and otherwise reconfigure our inputs from the intuitive perceptions.

In his writing, Kahneman (2003) provides a plethora of examples for intuition and reasoning. Consider this basic math problem:

A bat and a ball cost $1.10 in total.
The bat costs $1.00 more than the ball.
How much does the ball cost?

According to Kahneman, the neat and quick answer that so many come up with is $.10. But the correct answer is $.05. As Kahneman says, "[Intuition] determines an answer, and it's immediate and it's wrong." Here, intuition is misleading because people see two things, a bat and a ball, with two monetary figures, $1.00 in one case and $.10 in the other case. So we assign $.10 to the ball. Only by reasoning mathematically do we determine $.05 for the ball (plus $1.05 for the bat) yield a total of $1.10.

The reasoning system may be disrupted by many sources. The corrective operations of reasoning are impaired by time pressure, by being required to perform a competing task simultaneously, by performing the task in the evening for morning people or in the morning for evening people, and by distracting stimuli such as noise. As we all know, reasoning is delicate and decidedly not foolproof.

Cognitive Theories of Reading Comprehension

Landscape Theory   In an extensive program of experimental cognitive research, Paul van den Broek of the University of Minnesota promotes the landscape theory to illuminate and explain text comprehension. At the center of his formulation are twin processing systems; one called "memory based" and one termed "constructionist." These processes are both crucial and operate in conjunction during reading comprehension (van den Broek, Rapp, & Kendeou, 2005).

In the memory-based view, the comprehender, say a fourth grader reading on grade level, encounters new information in reading a text. As each word appears, the meaning of that word is brought to mind; it appears rapidly and automatically and accurately (for a substantial majority of words). The meaning of these words is said to come forth "free." We do not usually put effort to understand the meaning of a simple word. In addition, the word evokes associations with other words in the sentence and the surrounding text. These associations also come effortlessly. These memory-based processes related to word meanings are autonomous and passive. As van den Broek says, they are "dumb" in the sense that meaning activation for these words is not a conscious goal of the reader; it is merely happening.

On the other side of the coin are constructionist processes. These are initiated by explicit or implicit goals of the reader. The most general goal is a search/effort after meaning that readers bring to a text. Van den Broek and colleagues (2005) report that readers hold internal standards for coherent meanings during reading. They try to meet "standards of coherence" by integrating, organizing, connecting to background knowledge, and inferring sufficient to build a knowledge structure that makes sense to them. Constructionist-based processes prominently include activating knowledge that has been recently acquired from previous sections of text. Activations may also occur for background knowledge from long-term memory and for connections formed during recent reading. Many other constructionist processes may occur such as seeking key words, and most essentially, building causal inferences that enable the reader to formulate new knowledge structures that are integrated.

Most vitally, the memory-based and constructionist processes interact with each other. An example of the interaction is shown in research using an inconsistency paradigm. In this research approach, readers encounter information early in a paragraph (e.g., Bill was old and weak. [sentence 1]). That sentence is inconsistent with later information (Bill ran quickly and picked up the boy. [sentence 2]). Alternatively, a sentence may be given which is consistent with the prior such as (Bill was unable to reach the boy in time. [sentence 3]). Readers who encounter sentence 2 slow down and spend much longer reading the sentence than readers who encounter sentence 3. The increased reading time reflects the inconsistency. As the student perceives the inconsistent sentence, she needs to engage in some inferential processes and knowledge activation processes to establish the coherence of the two sentences. The rapid reading of sentence 3 was due to its predictability from sentence 1 and high level of similarity and meaning. Thus, the constructionist processes kick into gear to cope with memory-based processes that are inaccurate or incompatible with the quest for meaning. These constructionist processes are much slower, more conscious, and more deliberate, as well as being more goal driven, than the memory-based processes which are fast, automatic, and accurate most of the time for most readers.

In addition to traditional laboratory experiments, the landscape model has been investigated using computer simulations in artificial intelligence. The simulations contain predictions about word meanings, coherence of text, and ease of comprehension for particular paragraphs. From the model, authors can predict which sentences will be easily recalled by students. The computer simulation accurately predicts which sentences will be easily read aloud during a verbal protocol tasks or will be recalled accurately in free recall tasks following a text reading activity. Thus, the landscape model has been operationally defined precisely enough that it can be programmed into a computer and make accurate predictions about students' level of reading comprehension.

Although landscape theory explains comprehension for narrative and expository text, a powerful application of landscape theory has been made in explaining the positive benefits of refutational text in science. Previous investigators have shown that text which contains alerts to potentially confusing information or to information that conflicts with students' background knowledge is more effective than text that does not include the alerts. Such alerts may include phrases such as notice that, or you may think….but actually… Although alerts are valuable, previous research had not attempted to explain the source of benefit for refutational text over traditional passages (van den Broek & Kendeou, 2008).

In a verbal protocol study, van den Broek and Kendeou (2008) asked students to read refutational text while thinking aloud, as well as read traditional text while thinking aloud. In the students' verbal protocols the investigators observed that during the reading of refutational text students simultaneously activated text-based information that was incompatible with prior knowledge (subject to misconceptions), as well as text that was compatible with prior knowledge. Thus, the verbal protocols revealed *co-activation* of consistent and inconsistent knowledge during reading. After this co-activation, students performed inferences and reasoning processes that enabled them to resolve the conflict between the consistent and inconsistent information. Thus, the co-activation during refutational text reading brought up constructionist processes that enable students to build coherent knowledge. In contrast, verbal protocols for reading traditional text did not show the inferencing and integration efforts of students and did not result in highly coherent knowledge constructions after reading. The authors interpreted the benefits of refutational text which contained the alerts to be attributable to *co-activation* of memory-based information that is inconsistent with each other, which elicited constructionist-based processes of inferencing and reasoning that were sufficient to build an organized set of interrelated information that satisfied the readers' standards of coherence.

The similarities of Kahneman's framing of intuition and reasoning with van den Broek's landscape model of reading comprehension are substantial. Van den Broek's memory-based processes are very much like the intuitive processes Kahneman proposes for many of our perceptions. In other words, like intuition, the memory-based processes are rapid, automatic, effortless, and may be effective. They may also be inaccurate. In contrast, the constructionist processes are akin to reasoning in the sense that they are slower, higher effort, logic driven, and may be used to monitor their counterparts. Thus, although memory-based processes do the vast bulk of the work in basic reading just as intuitive processes do the vast majority of cognitive enablement of our behavior, we have backup systems. When memory processes are insufficient or inaccurate we invoke complex, difficult, but more reliable constructionist systems to improve comprehension just as we invoke reasoning to give corrective action to misguided intuitions.

Compensatory Encoding Theory Proposed by Jeffrey Walczyk, compensatory encoding theory is a framework for understanding the interplay between automatic processes and strategic resources in reading (Walczyk et al., 2007). The theory describes how readers compensate for poorly automated skills and identifies a list of compensatory actions that serve to mend misinformation or misunderstandings generated by these skills.

For readers at the third-grade level and above, there are many automatic elements to the reading process. For example, letter identification is essentially automatic and rapid. Most 8-year-old students reading at Grade 3 grade equivalent and above do not stop at a single letter and ask, "Shall I recognize this letter?" Their letter recognition is free and automatic. Furthermore, as letters are embedded in words, words become the object of immediate perception and may be read accurate without seeing or requiring all of the letters. Even phrases may become objects of immediate perception based on our abilities to predict syntactically. Third graders will recognize a phrase "red, white, and b_____" as ending with "blue" based on knowledge of the flag and syntactic predictions. Few would read "red, white, and black," much less "red, white, and but." Students may also automatically process a genre, such as the beginning of a story, initiated by "Once upon a time…" Thus, automatic processes include letter recognition, lexical access, speech recoding, semantic encoding, prepositional encoding, and sentence integrations. In on-grade reading for students who do not possess cognitive challenges, Walczyk et al. (2007) proposed that several compensatory strategies may be used when these automatic processes fail to function adequately. The reader brings these compensatory processes to the rescue when the normally automatic ones let them down. For example, sounding out words methodically is a common compensatory strategy which may be applied to an inaccurate or unfamiliar word. Rereading text is also shown by think aloud studies that this is a deliberate strategy which often resolves confusions noted during previous reading. Walczyk and colleagues report that the strategies of compensation will be used if the text is unusually difficult, exceptionally verbose, or too abstract for the reader to easily assimilate. First, Walczyk et al. reported that with ample time students used compensation strategies to make up for inaccurate performance in automatic strategies. In other words, students used a large number of compensation strategies when their accuracy in word recognition and sentence comprehension was low. They did a lot of pausing, looking back, and sounding out successfully when they were

inaccurate in basic processes, but were less likely to pause, look back, and sound out when they were more accurate. However, when time restrictions were placed on readers, these correlations reduced to zero. In other words, students did not have an opportunity to perform compensatory actions to make up for inaccurate, automatic processing when they were hurried by severe time constraint. Despite its benefits, the compensatory system can be disrupted by interference such as a severe time constraint.

Walczyk et al. (2007) found that the effectiveness of the compensatory strategies increased from grades 3, 5, and 7. Although the accuracy of automatic processing determined the comprehension of text for third graders, the accuracy of these automatic processes was weakly related to comprehension for seventh graders. This was due to the efficiency and power of the compensatory strategies for accommodating low accuracies or slow times of automatic processing. In other words, the deliberate, conscious, corrective system among seventh graders was developed to the point that it vastly reduced the impact of the lower level automatic system on comprehension of text. In addition, seventh graders gained compensation strategies that did not interfere with their reading comprehension processes as much as lower level readers. For example, seventh graders were likely to use context to infer word meanings, to resolve anaphors by looking back rather than completely rereading the text. Older readers were likely to pause at phrase and sentence boundaries to integrate text. These compensatory strategies were less disruptive than jumping over words or completely rereading a paragraph as was more common for younger readers. The compensatory system itself becomes more efficient and less intrusive with growing expertise.

The compensatory encoding theory is relevant for students roughly in the 3–6 reading grade level range. It explains the transition from decoding and word reading focus of the early reader to fuller comprehension of the intermediate age reader. The landscape model of van den Broek, however, is more suitable for explaining the complex comprehension of high school and older readers. The two models are completely consistent with each other and do not conflict. Both of the sets of processes in both models may be occurring for some readers. They each depict intuitive and reasoning processes that emerge at different phases of mature comprehension development. It can be noted that neither model provides an account of how or when these appear in the developing reader.

The similarity of compensatory encoding theory to the framework of intuition and reasoning proposed by Kahneman is substantial. For skilled readers of Grade 3 and older, processes of letter recognition, word recognition, syntactic processing in sentences, and word meaning retrievals are rapid and automatic coming for "free" to the reader. This is remarkably similar to the intuitive nature of perception according to Kahneman (2003). Furthermore, just as the reasoning portion of our cognition monitors the automatically acquired perceptions, the strategic reading of students using compensatory strategies is a corrective force during reading comprehension. It is apparent that the intuition and reasoning that dominate adult decision making and thinking is appearing by third grade in reading and gaining strength in the reading comprehension processes of students through the intermediate grade years.

Motivations Align with Processes in the Cognitive System People vary in their approaches to reading and studying in school. Some students are self-disciplined in their approach. They read history, science, or literature that is assigned and are committed to being thorough and complete in their work. Taking pride in the accomplishment that their consistency affords them, these students often have a schedule for school reading or homework and are conscientious in meeting standards of their teachers. These students are gratified by being high achievers and believe their success will benefit them in future schooling or later in life.

Students' attributes of self-discipline have been studied recently by Angela Duckworth and her colleagues, including Martin Seligman, leader of the Positive Psychology Center at the University of Pennsylvania. One title from Duckworth's research is a mini abstract of her findings which is the following: "Self-discipline outdoes IQ in predicting academic performance of adolescents." In her study, Duckworth and Seligman (2005) studied 140 eighth-grade students in one investigation and 164 eighth graders in a follow up. Students took IQ tests and questionnaires about their study habits and their self-discipline based on work by Tangney, Baumeister, and Boone (2004). The questionnaire included 36 items with positive statements such as the following:

- I never allow myself to lose control.
- I keep everything neat.
- I am reliable.
- I eat healthy foods.

Negative indicators of self-discipline included the following:

- I have a hard time breaking bad habits.
- I change my mind fairly often.
- Sometimes I can't stop myself from doing something, even if I know it is wrong.
- Pleasure and fun sometimes keep me from getting work done.

This latter set was reverse coded to form a questionnaire where high scores reflected high self-discipline and low scores reflected low self-discipline.

The main finding of Duckworth and Seligman's study (2005) was that self-discipline predicted students' GPA at .52 and .66 in studies 1 and 2, whereas IQ predicted final grades at .34 in study 2. Even when IQ was accounted for statistically, self-discipline significantly predicted GPA in both the first and second marking periods. One reason that self-discipline correlated with grades higher than IQ was

that the very highest achievers showed remarkably high self-discipline, although their IQ was only moderately high. In addition, the very lowest achievers showed strikingly low self-discipline, even though their IQ was only moderately low. A limitation of the study was that this was a magnet school with relatively high performing students who were relatively talented. For this group of individuals in a slightly narrow range of talented individuals, self-discipline makes the big difference in GPA. Impacts of self-discipline on reading and achievement are well documented in other studies (Duckworth, Peterson, Matthews, & Kelly, 2007).

Alignment of Motivation Processes with Cognitive Systems

We propose that there is an alignment between the two sides of the cognitive system described previously—intuition and reasoning—and the two sides of the motivation system presented in the previous paragraphs—self-discipline and intrinsic motivation. That is, certain types of motivation occur primarily with intuitive reading processes. An example may be the reading processes of a skilled reader who is enjoying a favorite type of fiction. This individual is reading easily, meanings are appearing in the mind effortlessly, and it is rare that the individual corrects mistakes and checks his thinking during this form of reading. The motivation prevailing during intuitive reading is likely to be intrinsic motivation. For the individual enjoying fiction, it is the gratification of the moment that sustains the reading activity. This reading act is not performed for the purpose of attaining an external goal or acquiring information to be used at a later time.

In contrast to intuitive reading performed under conditions of intrinsic motivation, reasoning in reading is likely to be accompanied by motivational processes of self-discipline. For example, a student who is reading a science text in school is likely to have an explicit goal of comprehending the text for an explicit purpose such as writing answers to questions about the topic. The individual will bring standards of coherence to the activity, will use strategies such as identifying key points, organizing information, and linking to prior knowledge in order to build a knowledge structure and enter the material into long-term memory. In this reading of a science text, reasoning, or constructionist processes in van den Broeks's theory, is often required because the words are difficult, the sentences and information structures are complicated, and the burden on recently learned knowledge is heavy. Thus, self-discipline comes into play. The successful reader of this science text is likely to be self-disciplined in the sense that he subdivides broad aims into subgoals, frequently makes inferences deliberately to connect information within the text being read, and may take notes or organize ideas, placing concepts and relationships in his own words. Sustaining high effort and working to completion of tasks is key to success in this reading event and the persevering individual is most likely to attain the goals of building coherent understandings. Students who give up midcourse or neglect key points or fail to be resilient in the face of challenge will be less likely to achieve personal and classroom expectations for comprehending text. This may be called strategic reading and the use of strategies requires slow, deliberate, and methodical effort.

The two forms of reading may be contrasted both cognitively and motivationally. Intuitive reading is dominated by fluent flow of basic processes. It occurs quickly, effortlessly with positive affect, which suggests intrinsic motivation as a propelling force of this reading. On the other side, strategic reading is performed with cognitive awareness, deliberate use of strategies to build meanings according to standards of coherence, and constant attempts to integrate knowledge with background information. Motivations for this reading are characterized by persistent effort in attaining long-term goals. An individual performs the difficult operations to gain valued knowledge, to maintain the self-image as a high caliber student, to sustain a high GPA, and to be known as a successful student in the classroom and school.

We do not wish to make an inherent connection between genre and alignment. Although intrinsic motivation often occurs with fiction, intrinsic motivation may appear for information text that is familiar to a reader interested in the topic. However, intuitive reading is most likely to occur when the reader's disposition is to read for the absorption in text. In contrast, reasoning is most probable when the reader is seeking to gain knowledge that may be connected to prior knowledge about a topic. Frequently, but not necessarily, these varying reading dispositions are connected to different genres. Intuitive, intrinsic reading may occur for science text if the reader is expert in the topic and facile with the text's register. Likewise, reasoned, self-disciplined reading may occur with literature that challenges the reader to think methodically. These cases are slight exceptions to the general trend for 'light' fiction to be reading intuitively for intrinsic motivation and 'heavier' exposition to be read with self-disciplined reasoning.

Evidence for Alignment Our case for the alignment of the basic cognitive systems in reading and fundamental motivations in reading begins with simple cogency. It seems eminently sensible that intuitive reading, which is easy and propelled by automatic processes, should be performed when the individual is seeking enjoyment in the process. When the individual is seeking immediate gratification from reading she will find text that requires medium to low effort while it is rewarding her with events, characters, and experiences. On the other hand, when we face challenging texts that we read for the purposes of education or employment, we are unlikely to rely on intrinsic motivation as a propelling force. Rather, we tap our capacity for self-discipline by thinking of long-term goals, planning our approach to the reading challenge, and deploying our strategic resources as adeptly as possible.

Experimental Studies Compelling evidence favoring this alignment consists of experimental studies of these vari-

ables. Narvaez, van den Broek, and Ruiz (1999) attempted to determine whether students who were reading for intrinsic motivation performed reading processes differently than individuals who were reading for a typical school studying task which required self-discipline. They gave undergraduate students a narrative text consisting of a fictional story about a bellboy who hears strange sounds from a hotel room and breaks into the room to save a woman. They also gave them an expository text on the scientific theory and evidence concerning the causes of the eradication of dinosaurs. One group was instructed that they should read for pleasure as though they were reading for fun or recreation. They were to imagine they had music and a sunny day for their reading activity. The second group was instructed that they should attempt to gain as much information from the text as possible and that they should prepare for an examination over the content of the text. They should think of themselves as studying in a library or their room. Students read aloud and verbal protocol data were collected and coded into categories consisting of evaluations, repetitions, and coherence breaks which represented reflections about the integration of information in the text. Verbal protocols were also coded into associations, explanations, and predictions.

Students who read for the purpose of studying, which required self-discipline and reasoning, revealed in their verbal protocols that they were undergoing more evaluations, repetitions, and detection of coherence breaks in the text. However, the impacts of the two motivations on cognitive processing appeared for expository text significantly, but did not appear for narrative text (i.e., bellboy story). In other words, when reading the expository text (e.g., eradication of dinosaurs), students who were reading under the self-discipline that required them to gain knowledge, performed a large number of reasoning processes that were not performed by individuals who were reading for entertainment or intrinsic motivation. On the other hand, the motivational conditions did not significantly influence the evaluations, repetitions, or coherence breaks that appeared in the verbal protocols for those reading narrative texts.

This evidence supports the alignment of motivational processes and cognitive systems. When students face the task of building knowledge from text they employ their self-disciplinary competencies of reasoning during reading. These reasoning processes occur more dramatically in the presence of expository than narrative text. On the other hand, when students read for pleasure or reading to satisfy curiosity in a topic (e.g., bellboy story), they do not perform these reasoning processes as fully. They are less likely to report repetitions or breaks in the coherence of text as problems to be solved in the reading activity.

Because this evidence is based on true experiments, with individual students assigned to motivation treatment conditions, our conclusion from the data must be that the nature of the motivation impacted the nature of the reading process. Whether students were reading intuitively or strategically depended upon whether they were reading for intrinsic motivation, which led to intuitive reading, or knowledge building, which required self-discipline in the case of studying. Furthermore, this occurred irrespectively of students' working memory capacity. It should be noted that this striking alignment appeared for expository text and was not examined in this study for its possible occurrence with narrative text.

Conclusion

An educational implication of this alignment suggests that both intuitive and reasoning processes of reading should be fostered in schools. However, in school after about Grade 4, knowledge goals increase in importance. Texts that convey this knowledge are often complex, challenging, and may conflict with student naïve experience-based understandings. Information texts, although they are not popular with students, are pre-eminently valuable for students' knowledge acquisition, which is the main agenda of middle and secondary schooling. Teaching students the motivational processes of self-discipline and the cognitive systems of reasoning about text ascends in importance with advancements in schooling. At the same time, the powerhouses that drive both intuitive and reasoned reading, consisting of intrinsic motivation and self-discipline, should receive explicit attention from educators in order to assure that stu-

dents receive full support in becoming deep comprehenders and broadly engaged readers.

References

Duckworth, A. L., Peterson, C., Matthews, M. D., & Kelly, D. R. (2007). Grit: Perseverance and passion for long-term goals. *Journal of Personality and Social Psychology, 92,* 1087–1101.

Duckworth, A. L., & Seligman, M. E. P. (2005). Self-discipline outdoes IQ in predicting academic performance of adolescents. *Psychological Science, 16,* 939–944.

Kahneman, D. (2003). A perspective on judgment and choice: Mapping bounded rationality. *American Psychologist, 58,* 697–720.

Narvaez, D., van den Broek, P., & Ruiz, A. B. (1999). The influence of reading purpose on inference generation and comprehension in reading. *Journal of Educational Psychology, 91,* 488–496.

Tangney, J. P., Baumeister, R. F., & Boone, A. L. (2004). High self-control predicts good adjustment, less pathology, better grades, and interpersonal success. *Journal of Personality, 72,* 271–322.

van den Broek, P., & Kendeou, P. (2008). Cognitive processes in comprehension of science texts: The role of co-activation in confronting misconceptions. *Applied Cognitive Psychology, 22,* 335–351.

van den Broek, P., Rapp, D. N., & Kendeou, P. (2005). Integrating memory-based and constructionist processes in accounts of reading comprehension. *Discourse Processes, 39,* 299–316.

Walczyk, J. J., Wei, M., Grifith-Ross, D. A., Cooper, A. L., Zha, P., & Goubert, S. E. (2007). Development of the interplay between automatic processes and cognitive resources in reading. *Journal of Educational Psychology, 99,* 867–887.

19

Sociocultural Theory

Expanding the Aims and Practices of Language Arts Education

PATRICIA ENCISO AND CAITLIN RYAN

I begin this chapter with a brief description of five 12-year-old boys and girls as they discuss a life experience having to do with chickens. Their families are headed by adults who have lived in Appalachian towns and urban centers for several generations, or who have immigrated to the United States and Midwest during the past 3 years. The children and I met weekly in the school library to participate in what we called "story club," an informal gathering, where the children could tell stories to entertain one another, ask questions, describe their worldviews, and challenge social and academic rules about identities, learning, and living in a global society.

We are sitting around a rectangular table in their school library. Having finished their lunches, they are peering at a page in Carmen Lomas Garza's book, *Family Pictures: Cuadros de Familia* (2005), in which an older woman holds a chicken by the neck above her shoulder, while a man and several children look on. I had just opened the book to this page when Tomás leaned across the table, his head close to the book, and pointed to each figure in the picture, saying,

"That's my aunt, and that's my uncle. And those are my cousins."

"Wait!" says James, "That's your aunt?"

Tomás continues, "That's what we do. We swing it like this." He imitates the practiced motion of swinging the chicken overhead, using his wrist and lower arm, holding his shoulder in place. Chris joins in the motion, and also leans across the table toward the picture,

"Yeah. At my grandpa's that's what we did, too."

James repeats his question to Tomás, "That's your aunt? That's your family?"

Tomás responds, shrugging, "Could be."

Then James quietly asks, "Where are you *from*?"

But Chris continues an enactment of killing a chicken before Tomás can respond. I turned to Habib and Sara and asked if they have killed chickens too. They smile and

nod, and Habib says emphatically, "Oh yeah. And I don't like it."

In this brief excerpt, it is clear that, despite their diverse geographic origins, several of the children shared experiences of killing chickens, and they could proudly mimic adults' actions as depicted in the painting. In the midst of their descriptions, James and Tomás considered what it means to be "in a book" set in Southwest Texas and at the same time, live in the Midwest. "Could be," suggests Tomás. His own family experiences were so accurately represented they could have been, in his view, the subjects of Lomas Garza's painting.

Explaining oneself to others, especially in a highly diverse community where children are uncertain about the rules of belonging, requires selective use of language, cultural resources, and interpretive practices (Li, 2008; Campano, 2007; Orellana & Reynolds, 2008). Story club provided a regular time and place where children could figure out what to share in their stories and how they could listen to and question others' tales. Over 5 months of meetings, patterns of form and content unfolded in their tellings, and their recognition of one another's sense of place, history, and identity was formed and reformed through their talk, questions, related stories, and popular cultural references.

As these children participated in story telling events, they learned to structure their experiences for their particular audience of peers, to participate in story club practices, to select and use their cultural resources, multilingual resources, and to understand social relations to co-create new knowledge about story telling, their lives, and one another.

As I organized and planned for this club's regular meetings, I was informed by sociocultural theory, and its close relative, cultural historical activity theory (CHAT), as well as the extensive literacy research that has grown from these theories since the mid-1970s (Cole, 1996; Gutiérrez & Stone, 2000; Martínez-Roldán, 2005; Mehan, 1979;

Rogoff, 2003; Scribner & Cole, 1981). My research also relies on insights from cultural studies, poststructural theory, and theories of identity and globalization, but is always framed by overarching sociocultural principles of learning (Enciso, 2007). Literacy, in this view, develops through relationships within social practices, across locations, and is expressed and refined through participants' references to specific social histories, tacit knowledge, and opportunities for problem-solving (Moje & Lewis 2007; DeNicolo & Fránquiz, 2006; Gutiérrez, Morales, & Martinez, 2009; Orellana & Reynolds, 2008).

In this chapter I place the story club's practices and their implications for literacy education in the context of three principles of sociocultural theory (Vygotsky, 1972, 1978) that explain relationships among language, learning, and society: (a) thought is mediated by social, historical relations and activity, (b) the potential to learn is optimal within situations where a problem makes use of and extends the language, knowledge, motivation and relationships already available to learners, and (c) language and other sign systems are historically and culturally developed through social interaction but become available for individuals as a form of inner control over immediate and future activity. The first principle deals generally with the concept of mediation and the historically formed social activities that lend meaning, materials, and direction to conceptual understanding. The second principle builds on an understanding of mediation but focuses on the specific site and mechanism of teaching and learning as a "zone of proximal development" (ZPD; Vygotsky, 1978); that is, a site for problem-solving with others. The ZPD requires transformation of language, signs, and tools so that tacit knowledge or 'hunches' are extended and made explicit for new learning. The third principle of sociocultural theory posits language as the quintessential mediating resource or sign for learning which is, itself, mediated by the historical and political meanings circulating within social situations and societies. I conclude with a discussion of more recent interpretations and analyses of sociocultural theory—including Bakhtin's (1981) poststructural philosophy of language, identity, and authorship (Dyson, 2004; Juzwick, 2004; Wertsch, 1991)—and their implications for pedagogy, equity, and achievement in language arts education.

Social Mediation of Learning

In 1924, when Vygotsky joined Luria and Leontiev in Moscow at the Institute of Psychology, the field of psychology was dominated by behavioral theorists who assumed that stimuli-response research could explain the nature of human cognition. Vygotsky argued that mind and behavior could not be understood separately (Vygotsky & Luria, 1930; Luria, 1993; Vygotsky, 1978), and that complex thought could not be understood through behavioral training. Thus, Vygotsky established a new direction for the study of higher order thinking. He argued that conceptual development

requires awareness and control of ideas, not only repetition. Social interaction and use of materials enable extensions and connections of everyday or spontaneous knowledge to broader, more stable understandings of mathematical, literary, or scientific concepts. Without completely rejecting the effects of stimuli in concept development, Vygotsky argued that the world is constantly stimulating and, therefore, must be made meaningful and useful in the context of actions shared by people who develop and use historically developed cultural knowledge. Such goal-directed interaction, in his view, was not a matter of an individual making choices, detached from others' social practices, histories, or interests. Rather each person's understanding was *mediated by* socially-culturally developed tools and signs that could be used to interpret and act with others in the world.

Based on research with child-adult dyads, Vygotsky established the principle that development or conceptual change is enacted socially before it appears individually:

> Any function in the child's cultural development appears twice: First, on the social level, and later, on the individual level. First it appears between people (interpsychological), and then within the child (intrapsychological)...All the higher functions originate as actual relations between human individuals. (Vygotsky, 1978, p. 57)

He argued, further, that social interaction and signs are not static variables in a context, but are transformed as they are subsequently made available in new situations, creating a history of mediating signs and practices within social organizations and in each person. For Vygotsky, learning through the use of mediated signs is mutually constitutive of the social situation, the sign, and the individuals participating in an activity.

Many well-known ethnographic studies of relationships between home and classroom language and literacy practices (cf. Au, 1980; Heath, 1983; Wells, 1986; Cazden, 1988/2001; Mehan, 1979; McDermott, 1993) share the underlying assumptions of Vygotsky's argument that learning is inherently social. Descriptions of literacy learning, therefore, depend on close observations of social life involving mediating artifacts (e.g., books, letters, pictures, music) in formal and informal settings. Researchers have also shown how students' knowledge and participation in learning are selected and evaluated in school, and thus, how learning is invariably tied to the politics and biases of institutionalized literacy practices (Bloome & Egan-Robertson, 1993). Too often, the rich, distinctive interactions researchers documented in home settings were (and continue to be) dismissed as wrong or useless in school settings. Instead of understanding learning as socially mediated practice, schools are typically organized around the assumption that one monolithic, 'standardized' way of speaking, interacting, and building conceptual knowledge is natural and, therefore, meaningful and right for everyone. Thus, the forms of participation in learning that non-dominant children bring to school are viewed as suspect rather than as historically rich signs and practices for mediating new ideas.

The Politics of Social Mediation and Literacy Education

Extending Vygotsky's ideas, Street (1995) argues that social activities are culturally and historically produced, including how people interpret, share, and value texts. As such, literacy acts and materials are politically and historically constituted and therefore, ideological. In schools and communities, people use texts and literacy practices to accomplish social activities that often have implications for what—and who—will be regarded as meaningful, powerful, or worthwhile. In contrast to this ideological approach to literacy, an autonomous view makes no reference to social relationships or the historically formed practices associated with using texts (Street, 1995). Instead, it assumes a universal, neutral context for all participants' literacy and learning. From a sociocultural standpoint, an autonomous viewpoint disregards the cultural resources that inform and transform students' and their communities' literacy education.

The children in the story club were expected to conform to autonomous school policies that required them to focus on a district literacy curriculum. However, the story club research operated outside these restrictions, and could actively solicit children's histories with texts, tales, and languages and created new opportunities to express and examine inter-and intra-cultural knowledge.

Creating Mediating Contexts for Culturally Responsive Literacy Education

Sociocultural theorists argue, with Street, that learning and literacy development are not universal, but are mediated by and made evident in the transformation of participation in activity (Rogoff, 2003). Following these ideas as well as principles of cultural psychology (Cole 1996), González, Moll, and Amanti (2005) and a team of teachers initiated a study of the "funds of knowledge" in a community of Latino adults that they hoped could ground students' learning in classrooms. Their work documented the community's expertise, literacy practices, and social relations as forms of distributed knowledge and socially mediated learning. They then used this data for curricular designs that recognized and extended children's knowledge, forming *confianza* or mutual trust among members of the community, teachers, and researchers.

In the process of documenting and transforming community knowledge for their classrooms, teachers, working as members of the research team, redefined literacy as an inquiry process "for action, as situated by the nature of the activities developed by both teachers and students." Through their co-construction of a new culture of learning, teachers learned to view students as "…displaying competence, within the expanded possibilities for action made available by exceeding the limits of tightly prescribed lessons…" (Moll, 2005, p. 284).

The process of rethinking curricular and social networks also challenged and shaped teachers' perceptions of themselves, so that their identities shifted from an individual "teacher" to one of community member associated with families and a team of researchers. According to Moll (2005), teachers' professional identity development is crucial to sustaining long term change in literacy education in communities. By recognizing different ways of mediating knowledge, it was possible for participants to define and develop new social and conceptual relationships.

Mediating Systems and Contradictions: An overview of CHAT

Moll and his colleagues' research design and practices were located across communities that could be understood as historically formed *systems* of mediation (Leontiev, 1978). Similarly, in my research, the children's storytelling during story club, though located in the library during lunchtime, was not simply removed from the space, history, or practices of their school and community activity systems. The children often pointed out the differences between their literacy experiences in their regular classrooms and those they developed during story club. Following cultural historical activity theory (CHAT), a significant extension of Vygotsky's principle of social mediation (Luria, 1976, 1993; Leontiev, 1978; Engeström, 1996; Cole, 1996; Miettinen, 2006), our group's activity was shaped by attention to the contradictions and tensions we perceived between the practices of school, home life, and the story worlds they remembered and imagined. According to Engeström (1996), contradictory rules, materials, and goals can drive participants to seek new purposes, uses of materials, and forms of interaction. In addition, activities and their relation to other systems can achieve an expansive cycle of reflection and change as participants examine the sources of contradiction (Engeström, 1996). Disagreements about the facts often arose as the children's stories intersected with one another's histories and values, and with the history of rules, materials, divisions of labor and goals organized at the school, district, state, and national levels (Gutiérrez, Hunter, & Arzubiga, 2009).

Learning as Potential

The second principle of sociocultural theory proposes that change in individual development cannot be accounted for through biological or individually constructed concepts. Rather, social life, activity, tools, signs, and imagination drive learning; waiting for a child to be conceptually capable of developing more systematic control of ideas only isolates them from opportunities to use language and socially-mediated activity in new ways. Vygotsky argued that learning could *precede* development. He observed that when children and adults worked together, using available signs, especially language, they solved problems and developed concepts beyond the child's immediate capabilities, but within reach for future learning. Thus, learning is oriented to the child's potential in a changing world located within the social interaction established by participants in social situations.

Vygotsky's work on zones of proximal development (1978) often focused on children's engagement in imaginative play. In play, rules are borrowed from everyday life. That is, pretending to be a sister invites the players to find out what sister means. To find out what something means requires thinking beyond the given, concrete materials within a visual field and replacing "what is" with "what if." Similarly, reading and interpreting texts requires us to bring another world into view. A play-like approach creates a socially vibrant space for inventing and examining the meanings of words and worlds.

The ZPD also represents an optimistic space where a more capable other, whether a peer or adult, is able to guide a novice in the meaning and use of a concept that would otherwise be left to spontaneous learning. These guides or scaffolds for learning are intended to be "temporary, adjustable frameworks for construction-in-progress..." (Cazden, 1996, p. 168). Without this flexibility, the dynamic mediation of knowledge between individuals and social life might become a rigid structure that assumes knowledge in one participant can be transmitted to another.

Complicating the Zone While Vygotsky's theory introduces a mechanism for learning, it does not specify how participants should create such a space (Gee 1996a). In literacy education, many have argued that guided instruction is crucial for the development of metalanguages and meta-awareness of the ways texts work so that reading and writing can become internalized as natural, yet self-aware processes (Schoenbach, Greenleaf, Cziko, & Hurwitz, 1999). However, as Delpit (1988) and Willis (1995, 2008), among others (Bruner, 1996; Jiménez, 2000; Orellana, 2009; Tatum, 2008), have argued, metalanguages and meta-awareness are not culturally or politically neutral. What teachers count as good writing or proficient reading is likely to depend on normative assumptions, and, therefore, set teachers' and students' complex social practices and expectations in conflict with one another. Too often, teachers' implicit language practices are misunderstood by children and result in teachers' low assessments of children's knowledge and skills. And yet, as shown in a study of classroom discourse practices by Gutiérrez, Rymes, and Larson (1995) when teachers' and students' interactions are highly structured for explicit learning goals, "...participation in joint activity [can be] so restricted that fundamental educational goals are subsumed and often subverted to ensure the control associated with 'appropriate' socialization" (p. 445). In other words, the zone of proximal development is lost as classroom interaction is reduced to social control rather than negotiation of meaning and knowledge.

Indeed, for many urban African American and Latino students, their schools' primary focus is on surveillance of behavior rather than on disciplinary knowledge development. Carol Lee's theory of Cultural Modeling (2007) addressed this gap in the domain of literary study by applying Vygotskian principles of mediation and conceptual development. This model appropriates students' spontaneous knowledge resources (in this case, everyday linguistic practices using metaphor and imagery) for academic, non-

spontaneous understanding in the domain of literary reading and interpretation. Lee developed "cultural data sets" such as familiar metaphors, song lyrics, videos, and short stories recognizable and interesting to students that also held literary analogs for the novels they read and analyzed together. Through reference to cultural data sets and ongoing modeling of the forms of talk and questioning specific to literary understanding, Lee taught ninth grade students who were failing English to take risks with interpretation as they learned to identify and critique literary structures for thematic representations of human dilemmas represented in Morrison's *Beloved* (1987). Subsequently, many of these students were asked to enroll in Honors English. Lee's research exemplifies the kind of institutional, multicontextual, and culturally specific insights that are needed to create environments for learning complex disciplinary concepts and forms of participation. Based on her multi-year study, Lee argues that teachers should create the conditions for seeking and incorporating students' cultural knowledge, but with the intention of guiding their experience with and conceptualization of an academic discipline, not merely for the sake of motivating students' interest.

Creating a Dialogic Learning Zone Learning in a zone of proximal development requires teachers to give as much attention to students' culturally specific linguistic and knowledge resources as they do to intended disciplinary aims and concepts. When both teachers and students are interested in one another's ideas and knowledge, it is possible to create a dialogic zone. Based on Bakhtin's concepts of language and social experience, dialogism points to the many voices and histories of relationships formed through language that are always at play during any social interaction—including teaching and learning. Wells (1999), Wertsch (1991), and other scholars (Edmiston & Enciso, 2002; Smagorinsky, 2001) describe this dialogic zone as one that deliberately includes multiple perspectives, based on individuals' and communities' diverse experiences and relations, with attention given to the resulting contradictions and convergences among their ideas. Dialogism is not an end in itself. Rather, learning is most vital and transformative when it occurs as a hybrid intersection of teachers' and children's experiences in and out of school "...in which alternative and competing discourses and positionings transform conflict and difference into rich zones of collaboration and learning." (Gutiérrez & Stone, 2000, p. 157).

Story club functioned through dialogic discourse that was transformed by, and transformative of, children's viewpoints and knowledge as it also changed the meaning and practices within a school space that was generally viewed as a place to complete assignments. Although children were usually segregated from one another in school, based in part on English proficiency, in story club they could venture across divides to describe, for example, the ways their families required them to learn and memorize religious texts. As they told stories about memorizing the verses of the Qur'an or biblical Psalms, they recognized the differences in their cultural histories while commiserating over the additional work involved in complying with adults' expectations for their religious educations. Their efforts to understand one another reshaped the space imposed by school structures, so they could collaboratively describe and define their multilingual and multi-referential literacy knowledge.

Language as Mediational Sign

The third principle of sociocultural theory is based on Vygotsky's insight that language development is not supplementary to learning, but is crucial to engagement with the problems posed by new situations. Vygotsky believed that language is the "tool of tools" (1978; Vygotsky & Luria, 1994) for advancing and organizing higher order thought and transforming social relations. By using the symbolic power of language, children and adults are able to mediate the immediacy of a concrete, only-present world: "The creation of an imaginary situation is…the first manifestation of the child's emancipation from situational constraints" (Vygotsky, 1978, p. 99). Spoken and written language, especially in the context of play, create a zone of proximal development in which it is possible to rehearse ideas, formulate plans, imagine ourselves and others as a head taller, and reflect on actions and insights (cf. p.102). To return to story club, the children's storytelling created imagined worlds that required negotiations of meaning about characters, imagery, and plot trajectories. Through stories, the children were invited to inhabit one another's worlds which supported their ability to abstract from, and simultaneously reference, their social and linguistic knowledge.

In extensions of Vygotsky's theory of development and social change, language is viewed not only as a sign for building meaning and memory, but also as a profoundly social, political and personal means for shaping power, identity, and agency (Lewis, Enciso, & Moje, 2007; Jiménez, 2000; Ball & Freedman, 2008; Gee, 1996; Holland & Lachicotte, 2007; Volisinov, 1929/1973). Language mediates how and what we perceive, but its meaning and use are themselves mediated by cultural activity and historically formed relations with the world.

Holland, Lachicotte, Skinner, and Cain (1998) brought together Vygotsky's concept of language as meditational sign and Bakhtin's concepts of histories of meaning in language, to construct a more comprehensive view of activity, identity, improvisation in learning, and social change. Central to their synthesis is the concept of "authoring a self," put forward by Bakhtin (1981) as a way to explain the daily, ongoing experiences we have with language that address us ("That's your family?") and for which we are inevitably answerable ("Could be"). Every utterance, according to Bakhtin, is addressed to someone and has a history of relationships with other events, ideas, and identities that people interpret and use as meaningful. Thus, language is never static; it is constantly improvised in relation to new circumstances and configurations of people.

According to Bakhtin, relationships and identities can be altered—or at least questioned—through inversions, rephrasing, tonal, and stylistic shifts in language use. But changing relations of power and identity through face to face interactions requires attention to prevailing discourses or storylines about who people can and cannot be, and how people should and should not act in relation with others. Story club became a place of improvisation, allowing children to ask about each other's journeys within and outside the U.S., while they also elaborated on these stories with references to the shared language of video games, horror films, and television game shows. To be addressed and answerable as a storyteller, was also to author oneself as a curious and more fully humanized member of the school community.

Holland et al. (1998) argue that daily improvisations and shifts in how we answer or address others through larger, societal storylines can become "pivots" much like Vygotsky's mediating signs, and allow us to think and act beyond the immediately imposed constraints of everyday life. Once a pivot is established, it can serve as a future referent or sign; i.e., as a means for rethinking or refiguring discourses and relations of power that oppress, exclude, or diminish oneself and others. Authorship of self, then, has the potential to become available for mediating one's own and others' learning and authorship of social life.

Conclusion

Viewed through the lenses of Bakhtin's authorship, Holland et al.'s (1998) theory of refigured storylines and Vygotsky's principles of socially formed learning, literacy education is never only about learning to speak, listen, view, compose, interpret, and read a neutral, ahistorical language. Rather, literacy education entails the deliberate construction of mediating spaces, signs, and relationships that will enable all participants to author possible selves and possible worlds, in the service of adaptive, diverse, equitable communities (Freire, 1998).

If minds and texts are social, as Vygotsky suggests, literacy educators should develop a keen understanding of the cultural resources that inform students' thinking and forms of expression. As argued by the New London Group (1996), if the focus of learning is oriented to planning, problem solving, and building tools and concepts to serve new situations, then literacy education should emphasize students' use of language and other sign systems in settings where they can interact with other people and engage with increasingly complex needs and concerns. Further, Vygotsky's emphasis on the critical role of language as a mediating sign for focusing and planning *during* learning, means that literacy educators must develop pedagogies for interpreting and expanding students' language-in-use, as they solve problems in their local communities and within worlds they imagine through literature, drama, digital narratives, film, and creative writing.

References

Au, K. H. (1980). Participation structures in a reading lesson with Hawaiian children: Analysis of a culturally appropriate instructional event. *Anthropology and Education Quarterly, 11*(2), 91–115.

Bakhtin, M. M. (1981). *The dialogic imagination: Four essays* (M. Holquist, Ed.; C. Emerson & M. Holquist, Trans.). Austin, TX: University of Texas Press.

Ball, A. F. (1995). Text design patterns in the writing of urban African-American students: Teaching to the strengths of students in multicultural settings. *Urban Education, 30,* 253–289.

Ball, A., & Freedman, S. (Eds.). (2008). *Bakhtinian perspectives on language, literacy, and learning.* Cambridge, UK: Cambridge University Press.

Bloome, D., & Egan-Robertson, A. (1993). The social construction of intertextuality and classroom reading and writing. *Reading Research Quarterly, 28*(4), 303–333.

Bruner, J. (1996). *The culture of education.* Cambridge, MA: Harvard University Press.

Campano, G. (2007). *Immigrant students and literacy: Reading, writing and remembering.* New York: Teachers College Press.

Cazden, C. (1988; 2001). *Classroom discourse: The language of teaching and learning.* Portsmouth, NH: Heinemann.

Cazden, C. (1996). Selective traditions: Readings of Vygotsky in writing pedagogy. In D. Hicks (Ed.), *Discourse, learning, and schooling* (pp. 165–188). Cambridge, UK: Cambridge University Press.

Cole, M. (1996). *Cultural psychology: A once and future discipline.* Cambridge, MA: Harvard University Press.

Delpit, L. (1988). The silenced dialogue: Power and pedagogy in educating other people's children. *Harvard Educational Review, 58*(3), 280–293.

DeNicolo, C., & Fránquiz, M. (2006). "Do I have to say it?" Critical encounters with multicultural children's literature. *Language Arts, 14*(2), 157–170.

Dyson, A. H. (2004). Where are the childhoods in childhood literacy?: An exploration in outer (school) space. In T. Grainger (Ed.). *The RoutledgeFalmer reader in language and literacy* (pp. 84–106). London: RoutledgeFalmer.

Edmiston, B., & Enciso, P. (2002). Reflections and refractions of meaning: Dialogic approaches to classroom drama and reading. In J. Flood, D. Lapp, D., J. Squire, & J. Jensen (Eds.), *The handbook of research on teaching and the English language arts* (pp. 868–880). New York: Simon and Schuster.

Enciso, P. (2007). Reframing history in sociocultural theories: Toward an expansive vision. In C. Lewis, P. Enciso, & E. Moje (Eds.), *Reframing sociocultural research on literacy: Identity, agency, and power* (pp. 49–74). Mahwah, NJ: Erlbaum.

Engeström, Y. (1996). Activity theory and individual and social transformation. In Y. Engeström, R. Miettinen, & R-L. Punamäki (Eds.), *Perspectives on activity theory* (pp. 19–38). Cambridge, UK: Cambridge University Press.

Freire, P. (1998). *Teachers as cultural workers: Letters to those who dare teach.* Boulder, CO: Westview.

Garza, C. L. (2005). *Family Pictures: Cuadros de familia.* San Francisco: Children's Book Press.

Gee, J. P. (1996). *Social linguistics and literacies: Ideology in discourses* (2nd ed.). London: Taylor & Francis.

Gee, J. P. (1996a). Vygotsky and current debates in education: Some dilemmas as afterthoughts to *Discourse, Learning, and Schooling.* In D. Hicks (Ed.), *Discourse, learning, and schooling* (pp. 269–282). Cambridge, UK: Cambridge University Press.

González, N., Moll, L., & Amanti, C. (2005). *Funds of knowledge: Theorizing practices in households, communities, and classrooms.* Mahwah, NJ: Erlbaum.

Gutiérrez, K. (2008). Developing a sociocritical literacy in the third space. *Reading Research Quarterly, 43*(2), 148–164.

Gutiérrez, K., Rymes, B., & Larson, J. (1995). Script, counterscript, and underlife in the classroom: James Brown versus Brown v. Board of Education. *Harvard Educational Review, 65*(3), 445–471.

Gutiérrez, K., & Stone, L. (2000). Synchronic and diachronic dimensions of social practice: An emerging methodology for cultural-historical perspectives on literacy learning. In C. Lee & P. Smagorinsky (Eds.), *Vygotskian perspectives on literacy research: Constructing meaning through collaborative inquiry* (pp. 150–164). Cambridge, UK: Cambridge University Press.

Gutiérrez, K., Hunter, J. D., & Arzubiga, A. (2009). Re-mediating the university: Learning through sociocritical literacies. *Pedagogies: An International Journal, 4,* 1–23.

Gutiérrez, K., Morales, P. Z., & Martinez, D. (2009). Re-mediating literacy: Culture, difference, and learning for students from nondominant communities. In V. Gadsden, J. E. Davis, & A. Artiles (Eds.), *Review of research in education: Risk, schooling, and equity* (Vol. 33, pp. 212–245). Thousand Oaks, CA: Sage.

Heath, S. B. (1983). *Ways with words: Language, life, and work in communities and classrooms.* New York: Cambridge University Press.

Holland, D., & Lachiotte, W. (2007). Vygotsky, Mead, and the new sociocultural studies of identity. In H. Daniels, M. Cole, & J. Wertsch (Eds.), *The Cambridge companion to Vygotsky* (pp. 101–135). Cambridge, UK: Cambridge University Press.

Holland, D., Lachicotte, W., Skinner, D., & Cain, C. (1998). *Identity and agency in cultural worlds.* Cambridge, MA: Harvard University Press.

Holquist, M. (1990). *Dialogism: Bakhtin and his world.* London: Routledge.

Jiménez, R. (2000). Literacy and the identity development of Latina/o students. *American Educational Research Journal, 37*(4), 971–1000.

Juzwick, M. (2004). Towards an ethics of answerability: Reconsidering dialogism in sociocultural literacy research. *College Composition and Communication, 55*(3), 536–567.

Leander, K. M. (2002). Locating Latanya: The situated production of identity artifacts in classroom interaction. *Research in the Teaching of English, 37,* 198–250.

Lee, C. (2007). *Culture, literacy, and learning: Taking bloom in the midst of the whirlwind.* New York: Teachers College Press.

Lewis, C., Enciso, P., & Moje, E. (Eds.). (2007). *Reframing sociocultural research on literacy: Identity, agency, and power.* Mahwah, NJ: Erlbaum

Li, G. (2008). *Culturally contested literacies: America's "Rainbow Underclass" and urban schools.* New York: Routledge.

Leontiev, A. N. (1978). *Activity, consciousness, and personality.* Hillsdale, NJ: Prentice-Hall.

Luria, A. R. (1976). *Cognitive development: Its cultural and social foundations.* Cambridge, MA: Harvard University Press.

Luria, A. R. (1993). The child and its behavior (Trans. and ed. V. Golod & J. Knox). In L. S. Vygotsky & A. R. Luria, *Studies on the history of behavior: Ape, primitive and child* (pp. 140–231). Mahwah: New Jersey: Erlbaum.

Martínez-Roldan, C. (2005). The Interplay between context and students' self-regulation in bilingual literature discussions: A case study. In J. Cohen, K. McAlister, K. Roslstad, & J. MacSwan (Eds.), *ISB4: Proceedings of the 4th International Symposium on Bilingualism* (pp. 1501–1521). Somerville, MA: Cascadilla Press.

McDermott, R. (1993). Acquisition of a child by a learning disability. In S. Chaiklin & J. Lave (Eds.), *Understanding practice* (pp. 269–305). Cambridge, UK: Cambridge University Press.

Mehan, H. (1979). *Learning lessons: Social organization in the classroom.* Cambridge, MA: Harvard University Press.

Miettinen, R. (2006). The sources of novelty: A cultural and systemic view of distributed creativity. *Creativity and Innovation Management, 15*(2), 173–181.

Moje, E., & Lewis, C. (2007). Examining opportunities to learn literacy: The role of critical sociocultural literacy research. In C. Lewis, P. Enciso, & E. Moje (Eds.), *Reframing sociocultural research on literacy: Identity, agency, and power* (pp. 15–48). Mahwah, NJ: Erlbaum.

Moll, L. (Ed.). (1990). *Vygotsky and education: Instructional implications and applications of sociohistorical psychology.* Cambridge, UK: Cambridge University Press.

Moll, L. (2005). Reflections and possibilities. In N. González, L. Moll, & C. Amanti (Eds.), *Funds of knowledge: Theorizing practices in households, communities, and classrooms* (pp. 275–288). Mahwah, NJ: Erlbaum.

Morrison, T. (1987). *Beloved.* New York: Knopf.

New London Group. (1996). A pedagogy of multiliteracies: Designing social futures. *Harvard Educational Review, 66*(1), 60–92.

Orellana, M. F. (2009). *Translating childhoods: Immigrant youth, language, and culture.* New Brunswick, NJ: Rutgers University Press.

Orellana, M. F., & Reynolds, J. (2008). Cultural modeling: Leveraging bilingual skills for school paraphrasing tasks. *Reading Research Quarterly, 43*(1), 48–65.

Rogoff, B. (2003). *The cultural nature of human development.* Oxford, UK: Oxford University Press.

Schoenbach, R., Greenleaf, C., Cziko, C., & Hurwitz, L. (1999). *Reading for understanding.* San Francisco: Jossey-Bass

Scribner, S. (1997). Mind in action: A functional approach to thinking. In M. Cole, Y. Engeström, & O. Vasquez (Eds.), *Mind, culture, and activity: Seminal papers from the laboratory of comparative human cognition* (pp. 354–368). Cambridge, UK: Cambridge University Press.

Scribner, S., & Cole, M. (1981). *The psychology of literacy.* Cambridge, UK: Cambridge University Press.

Smagorinsky, P. (2001). If meaning is constructed, what is it made from? Toward a cultural theory of reading. *Review of Educational Research, 71*(1), 133–169.

Street, B. V. (1995). *Social literacies: Critical approaches to literacy development, ethnography, and education.* London: Longman.

Tatum, A. W. (2008). Toward a more anatomically complete model of literacy instruction: A focus on African American male adolescents and texts. *Harvard Educational Review, 78*(1), 155–182.

Volosinov, V. (1973). *Marxism and the philosophy of language* (L. Matejka & I. Titunik, Trans.). Cambridge, MA: Harvard University Press. (Original work published 1929)

Vygotsky, L. S. (1972). *Thought and language.* Cambridge, MA: MIT Press.

Vygotsky, L. S. (1978). *Mind in society: The development of higher psychological processes.* Cambridge, MA: Harvard University Press.

Vygotsky, L. S., & Luria, A. R. (1930). The function and fate of ego-centric speech. *Proceedings of the 9th International Congress of Psychology* (pp. 464–465). Princeton, NJ: The Psychological Review.

Vygotsky, L. S., & Luria, A. N. (1994). Tool and symbol in child development. In R. Van Der Veer & J. Valsiner (Eds.), *The Vygotsky reader* (pp. 99–174). Cambridge, UK: Blackwell.

Wells, G. (1986). *The meaning makers: Children learning language and using language to learn.* Portsmouth, NH: Heinemann.

Wells, G. (1999). *Dialogic inquiry: Toward a sociocultural practice and theory of education.* Cambridge, UK: Cambridge University Press.

Wertsch, J. V. (1991). *Voices of the mind: A sociocultural approach to mediated action.* Cambridge, MA: Harvard University Press.

Willis, A. I. (1995). Reading the world of school literacy: Contextualizing the experience of a young African American male. *Harvard Educational Review, 65*(1), 30–49.

Willis, A. I. (2008). *Reading comprehension research and testing in the US: Undercurrents of race, class, and power in the struggle for meaning.* Mahwah, NJ: Erlbaum.

20

English Language Learners

Language and Relationships

ROBERT T. JIMÉNEZ, BRIAN C. ROSE, MIKEL W. COLE, AND TANYA R. FLUSHMAN

In this chapter, we consider, on the basis of a select review of the literature, which issues matter most with respect to the academic achievement of English language learners. To do this, we begin by examining the notion of *best* practices for the instruction of English language learners (ELLs) with a particular focus on language and literacy, and we consider what our field gains and loses by foregrounding an approach to instruction that may obscure other more pressing concerns. For example, Valenzuela (1999) points out that far too often good or effective teaching is viewed solely in methodological terms and that such a perspective backgrounds what may be more influential, which is the development of meaningful relationships between young people and teachers. Valenzuela develops her thesis that teachers and other educators need to develop and communicate an ethic of caring before students are willing to invest in the process of schooling, or as she puts it, "many students ask to be cared for *before* they care about" (p. 24).

The fact that instructional methods have been foregrounded in the minds of many educators and policymakers may be an artifact of traditional academic perspectives and approaches to thinking about the schooling of ELLs. Traditional ways of thinking about ELLs and academic achievement tend to privilege discussion of factors that can be readily identified, measured, or counted. For example, Genesee, Lindholm-Leary, Saunders, and Christian (2006) offer a synthesis on this topic, and while they recognize that many factors influence these students' school experiences, they limit their discussion to only consider a particular set of issues that affect oral language, literacy, or other academic outcomes.

In contrast, Hawkins (2004) challenges the dominant discourses of current federal policy, suggesting that there is a good deal of disagreement within the educational research community about how to identify "best practices." Hawkins calls for a collaborative research agenda that acknowledges the sociocultural nature of language teaching and learning that focuses on communities of practice rather than the transmission of skills and knowledge. While we would argue that extensive knowledge of effective instructional practices and methodologies is absolutely necessary for teachers to be successful in providing equitable access to academic content for ELLs, this knowledge is in no way sufficient. Otherwise, teachers and students are overlooked as both the primary participants and determinants of what happens in classrooms. They engage or fail to engage in the tasks of teaching and learning to the degree that they view these activities as worthwhile investments of their time and energy (e.g., Pierce, 1995; Pittaway, 2004). Citing Bourdieu, Pierce (1995) suggests that individual learners exercise agency to the degree that they assert the right to be heard, and successful instruction consists in teachers structuring opportunities for learners to develop competency inside and outside of the classroom.

In addition, Reinking (2007) has argued that the notion of best practices needs critical examination. He contends that literacy researchers would be better served by the pursuit of *good* and *better* practices while simultaneously identifying and exposing malpractice. We agree with his analysis while at the same time we recognize and understand our responsibility to provide teachers with useful instructional tools. Here we examine literature that identifies critical *issues shown to play a role in the academic achievement of ELLs*. These issues begin with the recognition that far too many ELLs languish in classrooms where no cognitive challenge is present, where instruction consists of meaningless routines disconnected from the mainstream curriculum, and where students, for the most part, are tracked into academic dead ends far from the goals of either meaningful work or tertiary schooling (Valdés, 2001; Valenzuela, 1999; Reeves, 2006).

Narrative and ethnographic methods provide rich descriptions and in-depth explanations of what motivates ELLs to engage or disengage in communication, and these methodologies capture aspects of dynamic, shifting processes and subtleties of interaction that experimental studies alone cannot (Bell, 2002). McKay and Wong (1996) provide an outstanding example of an ethnographic study of four ELLs and four of their teachers in an English as a second language (ESL) program in a California middle school. Their careful observations allowed them to document the ways that learners were positioned by discourses of power and how they exerted agency in accepting or resisting these dominant discourses. For instance, one learner identified himself as an athlete and rejected the nerdy role suggested by the "model minority stereotype" to which he was subjected. Consequently, he focused his language learning efforts on listening and speaking skills and resisted efforts to focus on reading and writing.

While acknowledging that descriptive methodologies may not answer questions of causality, we foreground qualitative and ethnographic work in this chapter for the purpose of determining how teachers can build meaningful relationships through interactions with their students. "School success is created in educator-student interactions that simultaneously affirm student identities and provide a balance of explicit instruction focused on academic language, content, and strategies together with extensive opportunities for students to engage with literacy and collaborative critical inquiry" (Cummins, 2000, p. 268). We argue that ELLs are particularly vulnerable in schools because they lack sufficient proficiency in English, which limits access to and the ability to form relationships with their teachers. We begin this chapter with a brief critique of two of the main theoretical perspectives that guide the research done in the field of ELL instruction. We then identify problematic practices, and close the chapter by contextualizing useful instructional practices identified within this body of literature that lead to the academic achievement of ELLs. We assert that this focus on relationships should inform academic discourses regarding the quality of instructional practices for frequently marginalized students by emphasizing the fundamental nature of human interaction in the learning process.

Theoretical Perspectives

Cognitive theories, while not monolithic or inherently opposed to socially oriented perspectives such as sociocultural theory, are occasionally employed in ways that we find problematic. For instance, some cognitive theorists portray learning in a mechanistic manner that deemphasizes the role of a thinking, feeling human being actively engaged in the learning process (e.g., Rumelhart, 1980). Our concern is that such a perspective may further marginalize language learners who are already physically segregated and emotionally disenfranchised. Also, some cognitive theories portray thinking and learning processes as universal (e.g., Von Eckartd, 1995); that is, linguistic and cultural differences do not affect the "underlying" cognitive processes that are more fundamental to all human thought. Thus, the unique linguistic strengths and cultural resources that ELLs bring to the classroom are seen as irrelevant, or at least second-

ary, to the learning process. Related to this critique is the notion of "normal" development and thinking common to cognitive theories. However, conceptions of what is considered the norm exist in tension with understandings of diversity and difference, and as these tensions play out in the classroom, they tend to contribute to the "othering" and alienation frequently experienced by language learners (Jiménez, Handsfeld, & Fisher 2008).

To be fair to these authors, and to cognitive theory more broadly, there appears to be a tension between goal-oriented activity and the more mechanistic descriptions of reading that we critique. Moreover, we understand that a number of sociocognitive researchers recognize the central role of culture and social interaction in their research (e.g., Moll, Estrada, Díaz, & Lopes, 1980). Thus, it is not all cognitive theories and theorists that we critique; rather, we claim that an emphasis on automatic processes and universalist assumptions tend to reinforce inequities for ELLs in classrooms where everyone is simply "treated the same" and where the unique strengths that these students bring as a result of their cultural and linguistic heritages remain unacknowledged.

In contrast, sociocultural theory conceives of the mind and learning as firmly rooted in human interaction and activity (Vygotsky, 1978; Wertsch, 1985; Lantolf & Thorne, 2006) where learning is considered more than just in terms of the individual. It is necessary to understand emotional and social factors, as well as cognitive factors, when considering student achievement in schools. Lantolf and Thorne (2006) theorized that "humans are always and everywhere social entities" (p. 56), and that the development of higher order thinking requires social interaction. With this perspective, all meaning and understanding is both mediated and constructed by and through culture. Thinking is mediated by both the activities in which one participates (i.e., going to school), the artifacts used (i.e., textbooks), and the concepts considered therein (i.e., education). In this chapter, the role of language is considered as a key mediator. Teachers mediate learning for all of their students through building relationships through language, including ELLs. Much research argues that the relationships teachers build with ELLs serve to mediate ELLs' learning in schools (Flores-González, 2002; Valenzuela, 1999; Lee, 2005; Valdés, 2001; Farr, 2006). The centrality of teacher-student relationships is epitomized by those who advocate an ethic of caring, which involves authentic dialogue and the confirmation of individual students (Noddings, 2005).

Cummins (2000) adds that "human relationships are at the heart of schooling" (p. 40), and also that some groups of students, because of historic inequities present in certain contemporary societies such as the United States, require "identity negotiation" if patterns of failure are to be reversed (p. 263). Without a doubt, many students classified as ELL constitute at least one of these groups. Finally, we believe it is important to point out that building healthy relationships requires time, effort, and information. It is not enough to accept the notion that relationships matter, one must also recognize that histories of domination and marginalization involve institutions, societal structures, and various ethnic and cultural communities. These additional facets of relationships indicate a need to look beyond individual personalities and desires.

Recently, national reading assessments revealed that 70% of ELLs in fourth grade scored below basic levels of achievement (Pew Hispanic Center, 2007). In light of alarming results such as these, there is clear need to discover the essential and effective components of successful instruction for ELLs. We argue that the sociocultural framework offers a well-suited approach to investigating the issues that come into play in the academic success of ELLs. The work on teacher-student relationships will be further explored here as an example of the rich, informative, and valuable contributions it makes to the research field.

Finding Ways to Build Meaningful Relationships

Both Flores-González (2002) and Valenzuela (1999) emphasize the importance of building meaningful relationships with students. Flores-González argues that what happens in schools is more important than home and community life, and that for the urban high school students of Puerto Rican origin in her study, the nature of this relationship determined whether students completed high school or whether they dropped out. This researcher identified four contexts in which students can connect with meaningful adults: athletics, academics, social clubs, and support services (p. 76).

She points out that in contrast to the productive possibilities available in schools, gang activity also exerts a powerful influence on many youths because gangs offer an "extracurricular activity" in which many high school students can excel. She adds that many of these urban students experience personal problems due to poverty, negative relationships with parents, and family responsibilities. A recurring issue for many adolescents is their belief that no one, particularly their parents, loves them. Flores-González argues that informed and understanding school personnel willing to get involved in students' lives can ameliorate the problems faced by these students. Her argument is that if school personnel can find ways to address students' pain and other life concerns that they will then, in turn, be more willing to invest their time and effort in learning.

Taking a somewhat different tack, Valenzuela (1999) critically examines the common wisdom that Latino youths are inherently anti-school and that they reflexively assume an oppositional stance toward education. She rejects this notion and argues instead that these young people often end up rejecting a system that consistently and knowingly disrespects them. Her underlying thesis is that the typical schooling experience subtracts the cultural, linguistic and community-based knowledge and resources possessed by culturally and linguistically diverse student populations. This subtractive schooling has the effect of producing students that are suspicious of the school's agenda and who also often find themselves in conflict with teachers, even those with good intentions. Valenzuela concludes that teachers who sincerely want better relations with their Mexican American students must learn all that they can about this community and its history of subordination in the United States. In other words, she does not recommend that teachers need further professional development concerning instructional methods but rather that they learn how to build meaningful relationships with students. Even so, we recognize that good instructional methods are also part of what teachers need to build such relationships.

Lee (2005) comes to similar conclusions in her study of Hmong American high school students that she conducted in Wisconsin. She shows how many of the teachers in her study took no responsibility for students they considered to be culturally different. In other words, few teachers other than those designated as ESL instructors, believed that the school success of the Hmong students was their concern or something that they should monitor. On the other hand, students respected those teachers who knew something about their lives outside of school. Teachers and other school personnel who took the time to learn something about students' cultural backgrounds and who found ways to explain both school and general life issues were those trusted by the students. The Hmong American students also complained about being isolated from mainstream students, about the exclusion of their culture and language from the curriculum, and about the lack of opportunities to discuss and learn about topics such as racism, which they believed exerted negative impacts on their lives.

In her book, *Learning and not learning English*, Guadalupe Valdés (2001) recognized that in the middle school where she collected her data the Mexican-origin students highly preferred a teacher who was direct and gruff to another teacher who was pleasant and soft-spoken. The difference between the two teachers, however, went beyond their communicative styles. The gruff teacher, for example, went out of her way to ask about students' family members such as brothers and sisters, and she regularly sent greetings to their mothers and fathers. In other words, students felt much more closely connected to the teacher who seemed to care about their families and their lives outside the school. As a result, students made sure they introduced this teacher to their parents during open house and other evening functions.

In a 15-year ethnographic study of Mexican-origin, U.S. residents who refer to themselves as *rancheros*, which could be translated as ranchers, cowboys or even country people, Marcia Farr (2006) concluded that teachers and other educators have much more influence over students and their families than they realize. For rancheros, vigorous physical labor is highly valued as is a plain spoken, direct communication style that often seems rude and jarring to their fellow citizens from more urban backgrounds. Farr makes the case that stereotypes and misleading mainstream views of this population need to be replaced with more accurate and, often, much more positive portrayals, and that by doing so, educators can avoid unintended insults and condescension. She notes that teachers often unwittingly make seemingly inconsequential comments that end up devastating or even, on occasion, elating their students. Again, the point is that interpersonal relationships matter a great deal and they need careful handling that is grounded in informed understandings of the groups in question.

Approaches to Building Relationships with Students

Based on the preceding discussion and analysis of research on the experiences of ELLs, we recommend the following to educators who wish to improve these students' academic experiences and outcomes. Like Nel Noddings, whose scholarship on the centrality of caring in educational reform is widely cited, we agree that, "Personal manifestations of care are probably more important in children's lives than any particular curriculum or pattern of pedagogy." (Noddings, 1995, p. 676). Therefore, we offer the importance of building relationships through integration, engaging students in a rigorous curriculum and maintaining a culturally sensitive stance.

Integration Segregation is an issue that surfaces frequently within the ethnographic literature on schooling for English language learners (Flores-González, 2002; Lee, 2005; Valdés, 2001). For example, Lee (2005) reported that Hmong American students felt isolated from students in the general education program in a public high school. There was a split between what she called "Americanized" Hmong youth and those who were in the process of learning English. All of the Hmong youths complained about a lack of contact with mainstream, native-English speaking European American students. The Americanized Hmong students believed that White students refused to socialize with Hmong students. By allowing groups of students to be isolated from one another, the school communicated an implicit message of ethnic and linguistic segregation. Educators need to find ways to interrupt such isolation through integration. If not, they risk complicity with isolationist policies and the negative messages these practices communicates, not only to those found within the school but also in the wider community. On an individual level, teachers also risk alienating students and any relationships they might hope to have with English language learners.

We recommend that teachers work toward finding ways to integrate ELL students into the school community by beginning to build strong relationships with their students. One way to begin this process is to create spaces and times where students can interact with native English speakers or other individuals who occupy socially desirable positions. This will help students begin to develop social networks and provide them with access to English. The building of friendship networks with high achieving students in and of itself has been shown to contribute to school completion for students from minority backgrounds (Ream & Rum-

berger, 2008). These spaces and times can involve projects in which ELLs work alongside native English speakers on topics like neighborhood reporting, local political events, or service opportunities. In addition to a large literature of quantitative effectiveness studies, cooperative learning approaches have been broadly documented in descriptive research as well. Jacob, Rottenberg, Patrick, and Wheeler (1996) claim that the traditional experimental evaluations of cooperative interventions have not resulted in successful wide-scale replications because these evaluations fail to adequately capture contextually sensitive factors. Utilizing an ethnographic approach, they documented the numerous ways that differences in students and group composition, differences in tasks and perceptions of tasks, and participant roles and the structure of the interaction all affected differential outcomes. In particular, they suggest that close monitoring and careful, sensitive tailoring of the activities by teachers was the most crucial aspect of successful implementation.

Rigorous Instruction Another frequently cited problematic issue in the ethnographic literature on ELLs is that of a lack of instruction designed to move students toward the twin goals of learning English and necessary subject or content material. Valdés (2001) detailed the types of instruction provided to the middle school students she studied, and found teachers frequently engaged students in the game of hangman, coloring, and a practice referred to as daily oral language. Daily Oral Language is an activity with only a bit more intellectual challenge than hangman and coloring. Here students are faced with a sentence written on the board that contains many spelling, grammatical, or punctuation errors. Students typically go to the board and correct one error at a time taking turns until the sentence is in standard form. None of these activities, however, are linked to the mainstream curriculum, are at a very low level of challenge, and do not help students learn English, particularly the English required to perform well in content areas such as science, social studies, and literature classes. Moreover, we find these activities to be generic and unresponsive to individual academic ability.

To provide ELLs with rigorous instruction, teachers will need to ensure that all coursework is grade-level appropriate, or when this is not possible, at least determine how each lesson moves students toward the goal of access to the mainstream curriculum. Successful alignment of instruction with state standards and local curricula demands that teachers know more than which pages to read on any given day; rather, teachers must know the prior knowledge, academic strengths and weaknesses, and demonstrated mastery of the material of their students, as well as family and community resources that are available to support in-school learning. Providing adequate opportunity to learn the curriculum is an affirmative obligation for teachers of ELLs, and opportunity to learn demands that instruction and curricula objectives adequately represent the standards to which students and schools are held accountable.

Provision of Multicultural and Linguistically Sensitive Instruction Many of the researchers presented in this review emphasized the fact that ELLs received no instruction concerning their native language or any information about their national origin or their ethnic backgrounds. Valenzuela (1999), for example, noted that schooling in general, and many teachers in particular, failed to recognize the linguistic, cultural, and community-based knowledge of the students. She continues this line of reasoning by pointing out that this failure resulted in an active effort to subtract these resources from students' lives. For example, few students of Mexican origin are able to study Spanish for the purpose of becoming literate in the language. Valenzuela demonstrates how second and third generation Mexican origin students struggle when they cannot speak or read and write Spanish and how these linguistic differences cause conflicts with recent Mexican immigrant students.

Valenzuela (1999) provides a classroom vignette in which Chicano students try to explain their understanding of what it means to not speak Spanish when so many people assume that they do. She argues that this issue strikes at the very core of many Mexican origin students' identity and that it would not be a difficult issue for schools to address. For example, Spanish classes for Spanish speakers can be offered for full credit towards graduation, can provide students with literacy in the language, and could even be linked to students' mainstream classes in ways that support students' progress towards degree (Valdés, 2001; Potowski, 2004). Furthermore, a Spanish literature class could focus on providing students with necessary understandings and information needed to do well in English literature classes. These classes can even be offered in states that have effectively banned bilingual instructional approaches, as they would be considered foreign language instruction. Of course, there is no reason why these classes need to be limited to Spanish. Other languages could also be accommodated depending on the availability of personnel, local views toward minority languages, and legal restrictions. Teachers will also need to acquire relevant classroom and curricular materials that address the experiences of students and their communities and that meet local district and state standards. In other words, teachers should have access to as much information about as many immigrant groups served in their schools as is humanly possible. We understand that some schools serve many different groups but such a situation needs to be viewed as a potentially enriching experience for all students, not an insurmountable challenge. In other words, the oft heard objection that "we have so much diversity we cannot and should not do anything to address that diversity" is a canard that needs to be rejected. The selection of materials to address the existing diversity should include children's and young adult literature on topics that are culturally relevant and familiar, informational texts that help students learn about their own communities and countries of origin, and digital materials such as dvds and videos whose topics include information about students' cultures and languages.

Recommendations

1. Learn about your students, their families, and the communities they represent. At a minimum, such learning would include a brief overview of students' communities, their history in the United States, cultural distinctiveness, and contributions to U.S. society. More importantly, however, we recommend that teachers learn as much as they can about the specific students in their own classrooms. There are many ways educators could accomplish the goal but we recommend teachers read novels written by members of these communities and compare the obstacles faced by the protagonists to issues faced by students in their classrooms.

2. Provide opportunities for students to develop their voice and also give them opportunities to assess and evaluate their school experiences. Ask them to rate the social climate of the school and elicit their ideas for how to make the school a more welcoming environment. When confronted by new, different cultural practices like early marriage, work to develop a non-judgmental response. One does not need to condone a practice to understand it. Use the opportunity to learn about the practice in question and consider whether it is in fact a cultural practice or a response to the conditions faced by immigrant students and their communities. In other words, find ways to let students speak about and hear about the immigrant experience in an ongoing and re-occurring fashion. Finally, learn the names of students' family members and inquire about their well being as a regular practice.

Conclusion

There is much to be hopeful for when considering the academic outcomes for ELL students. To be sure, there are also important challenges yet to be met. In a very recent paper, Portes and Fernández-Kelly (2008) identify influential "significant others" or teachers as a major ingredient in the high academic achievement of some immigrant youths. Although meaningful cross-cultural relationships can be difficult to achieve, the literature that we reviewed provides useful and practical guidance to teachers and other educators willing to invest in the long-term success of their students who must learn English in addition to the various subject matters they encounter in U.S. schools.

References

Bell, J. S. (2002). Narrative inquiry: More than just telling stories. *TESOL Quarterly, 36*(2), 207–213.

Cummins, J. (2000). *Language, power, and pedagogy.* Tonawonda, NY: UTP.

Farr, M. (2006). *Rancheros in Chicagoacán.* Austin: University of Texas.

Flores-González, N. (2002). *School kids/street kids: Identity development in Latino students.* New York: Teachers College Press.

Genesee, F., Lindholm-Leary, K., Saunders, B., & Christian, D. (2006). *Educating English language learners: A synthesis of research evidence.* Cambridge, UK: Cambridge University Press.

144   Robert T. Jiménez, Brian C. Rose, Mikel W. Cole, and Tanya R. Flushman

Hawkins, M. R. (2004). Researching English language and literacy development in schools. *Educational Researcher, 33*(3), 14–25.

Jacob, E., Rottenberg, L., Patrick, S., & Wheeler, E. (1996). Cooperative learning: Context and opportunities for acquiring academic English. *TESOL Quarterly, 30*(2), 253–280.

Jiménez, R. T., Handsfield, L. J., & Fisher, H. (2008). Rethinking Cognitive Strategy Instruction and Multilingual Students: A Review and Critique. In K. Moktari & R. Sheorey (Eds.), *Studies in first and second language reading strategies* (pp. 113–130). Norwood, MA: Christopher-Gordon.

Lantolf, J. P., & Thorne, S. L. (2006). *Sociocultural theory and the genesis of second language development.* New York: Oxford University Press.

Lee, S. J. (2005). *Up against whiteness.* New York: Teachers College Press.

McKay, S. L., & Wong, S. C. (1996). Multiple discourses, multiple identities: Investment and agency in second-language learning among Chinese adolescent immigrant students. *Harvard Educational Review, 66*(3), 577–608.

Moll, L. C., Estrada, E., Díaz, E., & Lopes, L. M. (1980). The organization of bilingual lessons: Implications for schooling. *The Quarterly Newsletter of the Laboratory of Comparative Human Cognition, 2*(3), 53–58.

Noddings, N. (1995). Teaching themes of care. *Phi Delta Kappan, 76,* 675–679.

Noddings, N. (2005). *The challenge to care in schools: An alternative approach to education.* New York: Teacher's College Press.

Pew Hispanic Center. (2007). *How far behind in math and reading are English language learners?* Washington, DC: Pew Hispanic Center

Pierce, B. N. (1995). Social identity, investment, and language learning. *TESOL Quarterly, 29*(1), 9–31.

Pittaway, D. S. (2004). Investment and second language acquisition. *Critical Inquiry in Language Studies: An International Journal, 1*(4), 203–218.

Portes, A., & Fernández-Kelly, P. (2008). No margin for error: Educational and occupational achievement among disadvantaged children of immigrants. *The Annals of the American Academy of Political and Social Science, 620,* 255–275.

Potowski, K. (2004). Towards teacher-development and national standards for Spanish as a heritage language. *Foreign Language Annals, 37*(3), 427–437.

Ream, R. K., & Rumberger, R. W. (2008). Student engagement, peer social capital, and school dropout among Mexican American and non Latino White students. *Sociology of Education, 81*(2), 109–139.

Reinking, D. (2007). Toward a good or better understanding of best practices. *Journal of Curriculum and Instruction, 1*(1), 75–88.

Reeves, J. (2006). Secondary teacher attitudes toward including English language learners in mainstream classrooms. *The Journal of Educational Research, 99,* 131–142.

Rumelhart, D. E. (1980). Schemata: The building blocks of cognition. In R. J. Spiro, B. C. Bruce, & W. F. Brewer (Eds.), *Theoretical issues in reading comprehension* (pp. 33–58). Hillsdale, NJ: Erlbaum.

Valenzuela, A. (1999). *Subtractive schooling: U.S.-Mexican youth and the politics of caring.* Albany: State University of New York Press.

Valdés, G. (2001). *Learning and not learning English.* New York: Teachers College Press.

Von Eckardt, B. (1995). *What is cognitive science?* Cambridge, MA: MIT Press.

Vygotsky, L. S. (1978). *Mind in society.* Cambridge, MA: Harvard University Press.

Wertsch, J. (1985). *Vygotsky and the social formation of mind.* Cambridge, MA: Harvard University Press.

21

Literary Theories and Teaching of English Language Arts

RICHARD BEACH AND THOMAS SWISS

In this chapter, we review the historical development of literacy theories related to teaching English/language arts (ELA). These literary theories derive from notions about valued ways of reading or responding, for example, a transactional theory of response (Rosenblatt, 1938/1996) as well as particular literary critical approaches, for example, feminist, Marxist, or New Criticism literary criticism.

Literary theories have shaped literature curriculum and instruction in several ways: Literary theories have to do with more than just ways of analyzing literary texts; they have to do with the different ways people construct meanings of texts and language reflecting different beliefs or assumptions about what constitutes valued interpretations. And, they reflect larger cultural forces or models shaping ELA instruction and schooling. An analysis of two states' literature standards found that these standards reflected either a "cultural heritage model" (Applebee, 1974) valuing historical knowledge about literature reflecting neoconservative notions of schooling as imparting traditional values versus a New Criticism model of close-reading of the autonomous text, reading strategies that can be assessed on standardized reading tests that reflect a neo-liberal, auditing model of schooling (Caughlan, 2007). These cultural models of literature instruction reflecting current neoconservative versus neoliberal framing of schooling often serve to exclude other cultural models of literature as works of art affording aesthetic experience (Rosenblatt, 1938/1996); expressions of diverse ideologies (Appleman, 2009; Eagleton, 2008); as reflecting competing social worlds of characters and readers (Beach, Heartling-Thein, & Parks, 2008); or, as in the form of graphic novels or digital poetry, alternative ways of expressing cultural insights (Caughlan, 2007). Educators need to recognize how these competing theories and cultural models shape ELA curriculum in making decisions about instructional priorities.

Influences of Literary Theories: An Historical Perspective

The influence of literary theories reflects certain historical forces and philosophies of education related to the larger purposes of schooling. For much of the 18th and 19th centuries, the notion that classical works of literature provides moral training consistent with the larger didactic role of schooling served to not only define English as a subject but to also promote the centrality of literature in the school curriculum. Literary theories emphasizing the moral socialization and cultivation of readers through literature led to the framing and justification of a "cultural heritage model" (Applebee, 1974) consistent with the "political tradition" of using literature to inculcate certain desired values (Marshall, 2000) evident in the use of the didactic *New England Primer* and *McGuffey* readers. While much of the English curriculum prior to the mid-19th century focused on teaching grammar, rhetoric, oratory, and reading, in the 1850s and 1860s, there was the emergence of literature as subject matter based on acquiring information about literary history of British literature.

The importance of the didactic role of literature was evident in the British imperialist attempts to shape the English curriculum in the mid-1800s in India. While the British authorities and missionaries recognized that attempting to directly impose or convert Indian people to Christianity would be problematic, they turned to a more indirect means—the use of literature that contained what was perceived as Christian ideas that were equal to those in the Bible (Viswanathan, 1989), leading to the centrality of literature to the subject of English beginning in the mid-1800s not only in India but in other countries.

In the late 1800s the primary focus on the didactic role shifted towards the Romantics valuing of the artistic, aesthetic power of literature to foster cultural understanding and appreciation, as argued by Matthew Arnold (1993) in *Culture and Anarchy and Other Writings.*

At the turn of the century, the importance of literature as providing moral instruction served to elevate the role of drama or theater production in schools, moving away from an earlier suspicion about its corrupting influence, leading to the organization of the Drama League of America in 1910 and the increased use of oral reading of texts (Applebee, 1974). At the same time, while the focus of English instruction in higher education in the 18th and first part of the 19th century revolved around oratory and recitation as essential for preparation for becoming politicians or ministers, in the last part of the 19th century, with the need to prepare people for specialized work in an industrial society, higher education English shifted to a focus on written texts, leading to a long-term privileging of the written text over the oral (Selfe, 2009).

During the first half of the 20th century, the rise of Dewey's progressive and aesthetic educational philosophies resulted in an increased focus on transactional theory positing the value of the "lived-through" experience with texts (Dewey, 1925/1997) as highlighted by the publication of Louise Rosenblatt's, *Literature as Exploration* (1938/1996). Rosenblatt (1991), author of the literary theory chapter in the *Handbook of Research on Teaching the English Language Arts*, drew on Dewey's emphasis on the aesthetic experience as fostering ethical reflections on the complexity of human exience in opposition to habitual, conventional, cliched perceptions of the world, theory that lay the groundwork for the later rise of a reader-response approaches in the 1960s and 1970s.

At the same time, the increasing academic focus on literary studies, particularly in high education, led to the rise of a host of literary critical theories, for example, New Criticism/ formalist analysis in the 1940s and 1950s, followed by neo-Marxist, feminist, poststructualist/deconstruction list, New Historicism, and postcolonial critical theories (Eagleton, 2008). However, despite the prelevance of these theories, one survey study found that 72% of teachers reported little or no knowledge of literary theories (Applebee, 1993). However, in the 1980s and 1990s, literary theories did influence the framing of ELA curriculum, particularly in terms of focusing on literature as an autonomous text for analysis reflecting New Criticism/formalist theories, as well as a means of teaching critical reading/thinking skills or as an expression of common cultural heritage (Caughlan, 2007). More recently, secondary literature teachers have turned to explicit instruction in application of literary theories as competing perspectives or approaches for interpreting texts in which teachers model the application of particular perspectives associated with certain theories, for example, applying feminist criticism to analyze portrayal of gender roles in a text (Appleman, 2009; Carey-Webb, 2001; Eckert, 2006).

Different Types of Literary Theories To discuss the influence of these different literary theories since the 1920s, the rest of this chapter is organized around four basic types of literary theories influencing English language arts instruction: text-based, reader-based, socio-cultural, and New Media theories (Beach, 1993).

Text-Based Literary Theories Text-based theories focus primarily on linguistic or structural features of texts shaping literary meaning.

New Criticism. In the 1920s, theorists such as I. A. Richards (1929) began conducting studies of college students' actual responses to formulate theories of close reading practices in responding to literary language. This research on the value of attending to the language of the text led to a later formulation of New Criticism by Cleanth Brooks, William Empson, John Crowe Ransom, Allen Tate, Robert Penn Warren, W. K. Wimsatt, Rene Wellek, Austin Warren and others. These "New Critics" codified a set of principles that assumed that interpretation needed to focus on the text itself through braketing out one's subjective experiences ("the affective fallacy") as well as attempts to intuit authorial intent based on biographical or lived-world contexts. They privileged the need for systematic analysis of different types of figurative language and verbal structures "in" the text.

During the 1940s and 50s, at the university level, this emphasis on a rigorous "scientific" approach served to legitimatize the value of literature instruction as of equal worth with the growing prominence of the sciences and social sciences (Beach, 1993). Application of New Criticism also led to formalist instruction involving understanding and identifying instances of character types, point of view, setting, story development, and theme. More recent forms of close-reading involves a focus on having students assume a more central role in identifying instances of difficulties understanding texts, leading to re-reading and revising interpretations (Blau, 2003).

Analysis of classroom instruction in secondary schools conducted in the early 1990s found that teachers reported a focus on both uses of New Critical/formalist approaches of close-reading, and, at the same time, uses of reader-response approaches in fostering whole-group discussions of literature, reflecting somewhat contradictory set of purposes driving the curriculum (Applebee, 1993). The use of New Critical approaches was more prevalent in 11th and 12th grades than in junior high/middle schools and in college-bound/PA classes. This dualism was also evident in an analysis of 530 *English Journal* articles on teaching of poetry from 1912–2005 (Faust & Dressman, 2009). While many of the articles adopted a formalist, close-reading orientation of "great" poets, an equally large number adopted a reader-response approach that challenge formalist approaches and the limitation of privileging a traditional poetry canon.

Performative Theories. Performative literary theories drawing on speech-act theory (Austin, 1975) as formulated by Mary Louise Pratt, Stanley Fish, J. Hillis Miller, Jacques Derrida, and Paul de Man examine the meaning of utterances by and in literary texts. For example, they ask whether literature itself performs actions involving changes in lived-world situations such as that performed by the Declaration of Independence in declaring the colonies a in independent country (Culler, 2007). Students can apply performative theories in identifying the nature of characters' speech acts—ordering, praising, requesting, asserting, proposing, etc., leading to inferences about characters' traits, beliefs, and goals, as well as the social conventions constituting their worlds. For example, students may infer that characters who consistently issue orders are in positions of power in a text world.

Structuralists.   Structuralist literary theorists such as Roland Barthes, Tzvetan Todorov, Roman Jakobson, and Umberto Eco, were interested in linguistic and semotic systems that define the meanings of language and signs in texts as reflecting underlying cultural codes (Scholes, 1974). This structuralist focus led to an increased focus on teaching the conventions underlying consistent storyline patterns and language use, for example, how conflicts revolve around binary oppositions between good versus evil, male versus female, or dark versus light.

Poststructualist/Deconstructionist.   Poststructualist or deconstructionist theorists such as J. Hillis Miller, Jacques Derrida, Paul de Man, Jonathan Culler, Barbara Johnson, and later Roland Barthes challenged the limitations of structuralists' binary oppositions by perceiving how these uses of categories are shifting, unstable, problematic and contradictory—for example, that distinctions between male versus female perpetuates limited, essentialist notions of gender differences (Crowley, 1989). Poststructuralists/ deconstructionists also adopt a postmodern critique of modernist notions of master narratives with their defined storylines and resolutions as themselves limited representations of the complexity of contemporary life. In applying this approach in the classroom, students unpack problematic aspects of categories in texts, for example, noting that Donne's poem, "'Death Be Not Proud' '...is very contradictory. Donne attempts to dissect death and make it smaller, but the contradictions in the poem thwart the attempt and deals ends up staying powerful and frightening'" (Appleman, 2009, p. 105).

Limitations of Text-Based Theories.   Critics of these text-based theories argue that locating text meaning based primarily on textual cues implying authorial intent fails to consider individual differences in the influence of readers' own knowledge, beliefs, and purposes on their responses (Iser, 1980; Mailloux, 1982; Rabinowitz, 1997; Rosenblatt, 1978, 1938/1996). Assuming that meaning is located primarily in the text fail to consider how variations in meanings represents differences in what individual readers bring to text.

Reader-Based Theories   In the late 1960s, there was a reaction to New Criticism/formalist literature instruction voiced at the Dartmouth Conference by British and American educators, who, drawing on earlier transactional theory, wanted to focus more on students' aesthetic experiences with texts (Rosenblatt, 1978, 1938/1996). This led to a number of research studies of differences in types of students' response to literature (engagement, description, connection, interpretation, judgement) as varying according to differences in texts, genres, age, gender, instruction, and stances (Purves & Beach, 1972; Marshall, 2000). For example, given Rosenblatt's (1978) notions of aesthetic versus efferent stances, researchers focused on the extent to which certain kinds of instruction resulted in adopting certain stances, findings that suggest that instruction may have an influence depending on the types of prompts employed and when those prompts are provided (Many, Wiseman, & Altieri, 1996). Or, Janice Radway (1984) examined how female reader responded positively to portrayals of romance novel heroines' nurturing role in transforming impersonal males as a means of validating their own lived-world roles as nurturers. Teachers apply these reader-based theories to teaching by fostering students' "envisionments" with their "living-through" experience with texts or autobiographical connections with a text resulting in their reflections on that experience itself (Langer, 1995).

Researchers also examined how readers drew on knowledge of narrative conventions for example, how readers, through reading literature, learn to apply "rules of notice" to attend to certain text features—titles, first and last sentences, opening scenes, etc. (Rabinowitz, 1987). This led to a focus on instruction to make explicit knowledge of literary conventions for interpretating authorial intent (Rabinowitz & Smith, 1998), as well as making explicit the problem-solving heuristics for coping with difficulties in texts (Blau, 2003).

Psychoanalytic Theories.   Drawing on Freud and Lacan's psychoanalytical theories, theorists such as Norman Holland (1975) and David Bleich (1978) began to study how readers' own subconscious needs and desires reflecting their own identity styles influenced their responses. For example, students with a strong need for closure in their lives may respond differently to indeterminate, postmodern literature than students with a high tolerance for ambiguity. Or, students may describe how their identifications with characters reflect shared desires or needs, leading to self-reflection about those desires or needs.

Psychological Theories.   Theorists also drew on cognitive psychological theory of minds and theories of narrative processing (Bruner, 1990) to describe readers' mind-reading, perspective-taking ability to infer characters' mental states, emotions, and perspectives of other characters (Zunshine, 2006). For example, in responding to detective fiction, readers engage in mind-reading of the detective's thinking related to shifting through clues and recognizing instances of suspects' evasion of the truth. These mind-reading/perspective-taking practices are also acquired through engaging in drama enactments that foster students' perspective-taking through empathizing with, adopting to, and anticipating others' thoughts and feelings (Wilhelm & Edmiston, 1998).

Limitations of Reader-Based Perspectives. In promoting the value of expression of individual, divergent responses based on unique aesthetic experiences, one of the challenges facing the application of reader-based theories in the classroom is the issue as to how to determine the validity of competing responses (Connell, 2008). Given a range of quite different responses, are some responses more valid than others and how does one determine differences in validity? Another limitation is that locating meaning primarily within readers' individual differences may not always recognize the influence of social, institutional, or cultural forces shaping those responses.

Socio-Cultural Theories During the 1980s and 1990s, there was an increased interest in socio-cultural learning theories (Vygotsky, 1978; Wertsch, 1998) shaping literacy learning suggesting the importance of the influence of cultural and ideological forces constituting texts, readers, and contexts (Galda & Beach, 2001; Rogers & Soter, 1997). Theorists such as Stanley Fish (1980) argued for the need to focus on the influence of social or disciplinary communities on readers' stances, how for example, the meanings of a poem in a religion class will be different from the meanings of that poem in a literature class. In their research on readers' adoption of an "information-driven" (focus on retrieving information), "story-driven" (engagment in story), or "point-driven" (interpreting thematic meanings) stances, Hunt & Vipond (1991) found that reader stances were shaped by the social forces operating in a literacy event—that interpreting the point of a text involves the social construction of the point of a discussion. Socio-cultural theorists also argue that through the imaginative, aesthetic experience of alternative subjectivities and embodied experience, students experience different forms of ethical understanding leading to change in their social or cultural identities (Misson & Morgan, 2006; Sumara, 2002).

Drawing on Bakhtin's (1984) dialogic theories of the multiple, heterglossia voices in literary texts, researchers also examined how students "double-voiced" or mimicked alternative stances, discourses, or cultural models that created tensions leading to competing interpretations (Lewis, 1997; Knoeller, 1998). This focus on students' adoption of multiple voices also led to analysis of teachers' use of open-ended or authentic discussion questions resulting in certain student responses or uptakes (Lewis, 1997; Marshall, Smagorinsky, & Smith, 1995; Nystrand & Gamoran, 1997), as well as student use of intertextual links to build social relationships in discussions (Bloome & Egan-Robertson, 1993) or their socialization into a literary community of practice reflected in the practices of a highly engaged literary book club (Edel-

sky, Smith, & Wolfe, 2002). Researchers also examined how the use of drawings or diagrams serves as prompts for students' verbal descriptions of their response (Smagorinsky & O'Donnell-Allen, 1998), as well as how sharing written records of re-reading experiences leads to an appreciation of the complexity of literature (Samura, 2004). More recently, researchers have examined how sharing narratives enhances discussions by fostering dialogic, intertextual connections between texts and/or experiences (Juzwik, Nystrand, Kelly, & Sherry, 2008). There has also been an increased focus on the value of spoken-word performances of literary texts as building on students' cultural experiences with rap/oral language experiences (Fisher, 2007; Lee, 2007).

These socio-cultural/dialogic theoretic perspectives and research fostered teachers' attention to facilitating the social dynamics of classroom discussions as well as the need to build on students' cultural knowledge and identities (Beach, Appleman, Hynds, & Wilhelm, 2010). For example, in her work on use of "cultural modeling" for teaching literature in urban Chicago schools, Carol Lee (1993) fostered students' use of experiences in "playing the dozens" to infer symbolic language use in Shakespeare's plays. This led Lee (2007) to formulate ELA curriculum based on cultural modeling that serves to integrate language, writing, media, and literature with students' cultural funds of knowledge derived from their everyday experiences.

Teachers also encouraged students to reflect on how their stances are shaped and limited by larger cultural forces constituting characters' and their own race, class, gender, or age differences, leading students to challenge dominant/authoritative interpretations or status-quo identities (Fecho, 2004). For example, through responding to the dialogic tensions in multicultural literature, high school students began to interrogate their status-quo discourses of racial, class, and gender differences portrayed in literature, leading them to revise their beliefs about the prevalence of institutional racism (Beach, Heartling-Thein, & Parks, 2008).

Feminist Theories. Feminist literary critics such as Judith Butler, Judith Fetterley, Sandra Gilbert, Susan Gubar, Annette Kolodny, Anne Mellor, and Elaine Showalter focus attention on the representations of gender differences in texts as well as the status of women writers that often reflect patriarchal discourses, as well as the need to foster readers' awareness of how their stances are constituted by gender discourses (Schweickart & Flynn, 2004). In applying feminist theories to critiquing texts, students recognize instances of how institutional forces have historically limited women in achieving agency, as well as ways in which responding to and creating literature provide students with opportunities to express that agency (Appleman, 2009). For example, responding to and writing horror fiction afforded working-class early-adolescent females with ways to confront their experiences of poverty (Hicks & Dolan, 2003).

Neo-Marxism. Teachers have also drawn on contemporary neo-Marxist theorists such as Terry Eagleton,

Raymond Williams, Fredric Jameson, Walter Benjamin, Antonio Gramsci, and Gilles Deleuze who examine how political and economic forces shape both the production and reception of texts (Eagleton, 2008). In applying a Neo-Marxist approach to literary analysis, students focus on characters' practices as constituted by class differences. For example, in analyzing characters in Austin or Dickens' novels, students note the class hierarchies shaping characters' practices, as then linked to analysis of markers of class differences in their own lives.

Postcolonial Theory. Postcolonial literary theory critiques negative, Eurocentric, imperialist/colonialist representations of colonialist/third-world cultures that ignored the cultural differences and strengths of these cultures (Said, 1978; Spivak, 1988). Postcolonial theories highlight the hybrid tensions between dominant versus marginalized cultural practices, hybridity that leads to challenging hegemonic discourses (Grobman, 2006). The marginalization of Black writers has led them to grapple with their marginal positioning in society (Gordon, 2000). By adopting a postcolonial stance, mainstream high school students recognized the limitations of their cultural perspectives and learned to validate immigrant/non-dominant students' perspectives (Johnston, 2003).

New Historicism. New Historicist critics such as Catherine Gallagher and Stephen Greenblatt focus on identifying the events and forces operating in a particular historical period that shaped not only the writing of a text, but also its reception. This approach can encourage students to research the historical period in which a text was written. It can also lead student's to compare and contrast their own historical perspectives with those shaping the texts they are reading in the classroom (Gallagher & Greenblatt, 2001). Drawing on Foucault and other scholars who deal with and complicate history, many of these critics are particularly interested in issues of power within texts as influenced by institutional forces. Such an approach may encourage ELA teachers to engage in cross-disciplinary teaching with social studies teachers to provide students with social studies perspectives on texts.

Limitations of Socio-Cultural Theories. Applying socio-cultural theories to challenge students' status quo stances often results in resistance from students reluctant to entertain alternative perspectives (Appleman, 2009). It may also be difficult for younger students to adopt critical stances leading to rethinking their beliefs. All of this suggests the need for teacher scaffolding and support for student grappling with dialogic, hyrid tensions (Beach, Heartling-Thein, & Parks, 2008).

New Media Literary Theories The increasing use of multimodal, hyperlinked, hypermobile, and interactive New Media/digital literary texts require new, alternative literary theories that account for how readers and writers under-

Figure 21.1 "An Allegory of Ambition." Courtesy of William Poundstone.

stand and produce these texts. These texts (for examples, see Electronic Literature Collection at http://collection.eliterature.org/1) are Web-based, composed for and meant to be read on a computer screen or mobile device such as a cell phone, and characterized by multiple links from pages or sections, multi-linear structures, recursive loops, sound, images, animations, video, and data bases (Hayles, 2008; Morris & Swiss, 2006). These texts also include computer art installations; novels that take the form of emails and blogs; poems and stories that are generated by computers, either interactively or based on coded parameters given at the outset; or collaborative writing projects using wikis or listservs that allow readers to contribute to the text of a digital work. And, these texts are also highly performative as represented by William Poundstone's (2002) "Ambition" portraying moving letters and words on the screen based on the poet, Dylan Thomas's thoughts (see Figure 21.1).

To understand the learning involved in processing these texts, New Media theorists contrast print and digital technologies, arguing that educators need to rethink what it means to teach and learn New Media texts based on interactive, lateral, multimodal literacy practices defined by Gregory Ulmer (2002) as "electracy" in which readers are co-constructors of texts. Other theorists note that although readers may still draw on some print-based literacies and institutions in responding to digital texts, they are seduced by assuming that the screen seems to be like print, while still realizing that the screen is not equivalent to the printed page (Hayles, 2008).

Understanding and producing these texts involves perceiving patterns or networks based on hypertextual connections through selecting optional pathways, something that can be a challenge for students accustomed to linear, narrative text-processing (Dobson & Luce-Kapler, 2005). To help students acquire strategies for navigating New Media literary texts, teachers need to provide explicit instruction on processing hypertexts, have students contrast their experiences with print versus digital texts, share their frustrations in navigating textual pathways, bracket familiar print literary expectations in attempting to construct narratives or infer some primary interpretation, work collaboratively to share alternative mappings, draw on their gaming experiences to process virtual worlds, and formulate alternative aesthetic notions as to what constitutes engaging texts (Hayles, 2008; Mott, 2008). All of this requires both students and teachers to learn new literary conventions for understanding New Media literary texts through articulating the practices and features they may know only intuitively from direct experience with these texts as well as creating their own digital literature/poetry.

Conclusion

These four types of literary theories each position texts, readers, and contexts in different ways, resulting in different instructional approaches and priorities. Textual literary theories emphasize acquisition of literary conventions for interpreting texts, ways of applying knowledge of conventions that are often modeled by teachers as expert readers. Reader-based literary theories emphasize valuing individual differences in readers' aesthetic experiences of texts, leading to an emphasis on classroom sharing or enactment of students' unique responses. Socio-cultural literary theories highlight the importance of the social and cultural contexts shaping the text-reader transaction, resulting in a focus on critical analysis of social-cultural forces shaping both characters and readers' practices, for example, critical analysis of representations of race, gender, and class in texts. And, New Media literary theories emphasize the interactive, multimodal, and hypertextual aspects of digital literature requiring instruction in often-unfamiliar interpretive strategies specific to understanding these texts.

Just as literary theories prevalent in the 18th and 19th centuries valued literature as a means for cultural socialization of values, each of these four types of theories also reflect larger assumptions about purposes for and value of teaching literature (Caughlan, 2007). For example, while reader-based theories value fostering students' expression of their individual voice or ideas, socio-cultural theories value acquiring critical stances on the world. Thus, different theories of and approaches to teaching literature will always reflect the historical evolution of the functions of schooling in society.

References

Applebee, A. N. (1974). *Tradition and reform in the teaching of English: A history.* Urbana, IL: National Council of Teachers of English.

Applebee, A. N. (1993). *Literature in the secondary school.* Urbana, IL: National Council of Teachers of English.

Appleman, D. (2009). *Critical encounters in high school English: Teaching literary theory to adolescents.* New York: Teachers College Press.

Arnold, M. (1993). *Culture and anarchy and other writings.* New York: Cambridge University Press.

Austin, J. L. (1975). *How to do things with words.* Cambridge, MA: Harvard University Press.

Bakhtin, M. (1984). *Problems of Dostoevsky's poetics* (Ed. and Trans., Caryl Emerson). Minneapolis: University of Minnesota Press.

Beach, R. (1993). *A teacher's introduction to reader-response theories.* Urbana, IL: National Council of Teachers of English.

Beach, R., Appleman, D., Hynds, S., & Wilhelm, J. (2010). *Teaching literature to adolescents.* New York: Routledge.

Beach, R., Heartling-Thein, A., & Parks, D. (2008). *High school students' competing social worlds: Negotiating identities and allegiances in response to multicultural literature.* New York: Routledge.

Blau, S. (2003). *The literature workshop: Teaching texts and their readers.* Portsmouth, NH: Boynton/Cook.

Bleich, D. (1978). *Subjective criticism.* Baltimore, MD: Johns Hopkins University Press.

Bloome, D., & Egan-Robertson, A. (1993). The social construction of intertextuality in classroom reading and writing lessons. *Reading Research Quarterly, 28,* 305–333.

Bruner, J. (1990). *Acts of meaning.* Cambridge, MA: Harvard University Press.

Carey-Webb, A. (2001). *Literature and lives: A response-based, cultural studies approach to teaching English.* Urbana, IL: National Council of Teachers of English.

Caughlan, S. (2007). Competing cultural models of literature in state content standards. In D. W. Rowe et al. (Eds.), T*he 56th yearbook of the National Reading Conference* (pp. 178–190). Oak Creek, WI: National Reading Conference.

Connell, J. M. (2008). The emergence of pragmatic philosophy's influence on literary theory: Making meaning with texts from a transactional perspective. *Educational Theory, 58*(1), 103–122.

Crowley, B. (1989). *A teacher's introduction to deconstruction.* Urbana, IL: National Council of Teachers of English.

Culler, J. (2007). *The literary in theory.* Palo Alto, CA: Stanford University Press.

Dewey, J. (1997). *Experince and education.* New York: Free Press. (Original work published 1925)

Dobson, T. M., & Luce-Kapler, R. (2005). Stitching texts: Gender and geography in *Frankenstein* and *Patchwork Girl. Changing English, 12*(2), 265–277.

Eckert, L. S. (2006). How does it mean: Engaging reluctant readers through literary theory. Portsmouth, NH: Heinneman.

Eagleton, T. (2008). *Literary theory: An introduction.* Minneapolis: University of Minnesota Press.

Edelsky, C., Smith, K., & Wolfe, P. (2002). A discourse on academic discourse. *Linguistics and Education, 12*(1), 1–38.

Fecho, B. (2004). *"Is this English?": Race, language, and culture in the classroom.* New York: Teachers College Press.

Faust, M., & Dressman, M. (2009). The other tradition: Populist perspectives on teaching poetry, as published in *English Journal,* 1912–2005. *English Education, 41*(2), 114–134.

Fish, S. E. (1980). *Is there a text in this class? The authority of interpretive communities.* New York: Cambridge University Press.

Fish, S. E. (2001). Interpreting the *variorum.* In V. B. Leitch (Ed.), *The Norton anthology* of *theory and criticism* (pp. 2071–2089). New York: W.W. Norton.

Fisher, M. T. (2007). *Writing in rhythm: Spoken word poetry in urban classrooms.* New York: Teachers College Press.

Galda, L., & Beach, R. (2001). Theory and research into practice: Response to literature. *Reading Research Quarterly, 36*(1), 64–73.

Gallagher, C., & Greenblatt, S. (2001). *Practicing new historicism.* Chicago: University of Chicago Press.

Gordon, L. (2000). *Existentia Africana: Understanding Africana, existential thought.* New York: Routledge.

Grobman, L (2006). *Multicultural hybridity: Transforming American literary scholarship and pedagogy.* Urbana, IL: National Council of Teachers of English.

Hayles, N. K. (2008). *Electronic literature: New horizons for the literary.* South Bend, IN: Notre Dame University Press.

Hicks, D., & Dolan, T. (2003). Haunted landscapes and girlhood imaginations: The power of horror fictions for marginalized readers. *Changing English: Studies in Reading and Culture, 10*, 45–57.

Holland, N. (1975). *Five readers reading.* New Haven, CT: Yale University Press.

Iser, W. (1980). *The act of reading: A theory of aesthetic response.* Baltimore, MD: Johns Hopkins University Press.

Johnston, I. (2003). *Re-mapping literary worlds: Postcolonial pedagogy in practice.* New York: Peter Lang.

Juzwik, M. M., Nystrand, M., Kelly, S., & Sherry, M. B. (2008). Oral narrative genres as dialogic resources for classroom literature study: A contextualized case study of conversational narrative discussion. *American Educational Research Journal, 45*(4), 1111–1154.

Knoeller, C. (1998). *Voicing ourselves: Whose words we use when we talk about books.* Albany: State University of New York Press.

Langer, J. A. (1995). *Envisioning literature: Literary understanding and literature instruction* New York: Teachers College Press.

Lee, C. D. (1993). *Signifying as a scaffold for literary interpretation: The pedagogical implications of an African-American discourse genre.* Urbana, IL: National Council of Teachers of English.

Lee, C. D. (2007). *Culture, literacy, & learning: Taking bloom in the midst of the whirlwind.* New York: Teachers College Press.

Lewis, C. (1997). The social drama of literature discussions in 5th/6th grade classrooms. *Research in the Teaching of English, 31*(2), 163–204.

Mailloux, S. (1982). *Interpretive conventions: The reader in the study of American literature.* Ithaca, NY: Cornell University Press.

Many, J., Wiseman, D., & Altieri, J. (1996). Exploring the influences of literature approaches on children's stance when responding and their response complexity. *Reading Psychology: An International Quarterly, 17*(1), 1–42.

Marshall, J. (2000). Research on response to literature. In M. L. Kamil, P. B. Mosenthal, P. D. Pearson, & R. Barr (Eds.). *Handbook of reading research* (Vol. III., pp. 381–402). Mahwah, NJ: Erlbaum.

Marshall, J., Smagorinsky, P., & Smith, M. (1995). *The language of interpretation: Patterns of discourse in discussions of literature.* Urbana, IL: National Council of Teachers of English.

Misson, R., & Morgan, W. (2006). *Critical literacy and the aesthetic: Transforming the English classroom.* Urbana, IL: National Council of Teachers of English.

Morris, A., & Swiss, T. (Eds.). (2006). *New media poetics: Contexts/technotexts/theories.* Cambridge, MA: MIT Press.

Mott, C. (2008). Electronic literature pedagogy: A questionable approach. Retrieved August 19, 2009, from http://newhorizons.eliterature.org/essay.php?id=3

Nystrand, M., & Gamoran, A. (1997). *Opening dialogue: Understanding the dynamics of language and learning in the English classroom.* New York: Teachers College Press.

Poundstone, W. (2002). An allegory of ambition. Retrieved August 19, 2009, from http://www.williampoundstone.net/Ambition.html

Purves, A., & Beach, R. (1972). *Literature and the reader: Research on response to literature, reading interests, and the teaching of literature.* Urbana, IL: National Council of Teachers of English.

Rabinowitz, P. (1987). *Before reading: Narrative conventions and the politics of interpretation.* Ithaca, NY: Cornell University.

Rabinowitz, P., & Smith, M. (1998). *Authorizing readers: Resistance and respect in the teaching of literature.* New York: Teachers College Press.

Radway, J. (1984). *Reading the romance: Women, patriarchy, and popular literature.* Chapel Hill: University of North Carolina Press.

Richards, I. A. (1929). *Practical criticism.* New York: Harcourt Brace.

Rogers, T., & Soter, A. (1997). *Reading across cultures: Teaching literature in a diverse society.* New York: Teachers College Press.

Rosenblatt, L. (1938/1996). *Literature as Exploration, 5th ed.* New York: The Modern Language Association.

Rosenblatt, L. (1978). *The reader, the text, the poem.* Carbondale : Southern Illinois University Press.

Rosenblatt, L. (1991). Literary theory. In J. Flood, J. Jensen, D. Lapp, & J. Squire (Eds.), *Handbook of research on teaching the English language arts* (pp. 57–62). New York: Macmillan.

Said, E. W. (1978). *Orientalism.* New York: Pantheon Books.

Scholes, R. (1974). *Structuralism in literature: An introduction.* New Haven, CT: Yale University Press.

Schweickart, P., & Flynn, E. (Eds.). (2004). *Reading sites: Social difference and reader response.* New York: Modern Language Association.

Selfe, C. L. (2009). The movement of air, the breath of meaning: aurality and multimodal composing. *College Composition & Communication, 60*(4), 616–663.

Smagorinsky, P., & O'Donnell-Allen, C. (1998). Reading as mediated and mediating action: Composing meaning for literature through multimedia interpretive texts. *Reading Research Quarterly, 33*(2), 198–226.

Spivak, G. C. (1988). *Other worlds: Essays in cultural politics.* London: Methuen.

Sumara, D. J. (2002). *Why reading literature in school still matters: Imagination, interpretation, insight.* Mahwah, NJ: Erlbaum.

Ulmer, G. L., (2002). *Internet invention: From literacy to electracy.* New York: Longman.

Viswanathan, G. (1989). *Masks of conquest: Literary study and British rule in India.* New York: Columbia University Press.

Vygotsky, L. (1978). *Mind in society.* Cambridge, MA: Harvard University Press.

Wertsch, J. (1998). *Mind as action.* New York: Oxford University Press.

Wilhelm, J. D., & Edmiston, B. (1998). *Imagining to learn: Inquiry, ethics, and integration through drama.* Portsmouth, NH: Heinemann.

Zunshine, L. (2006). *Why we read fiction: Theory of mind and the novel.* Columbus: Ohio State University Press.

22

Education Policy and the Language Arts

Timothy Shanahan

Many variables affect English language arts teaching. Teachers have special talents and limitations, and make choices, even within highly regimented systems. Principals, coaches, specialists, and other educators can make a difference as well through their ability to decide on teacher placements, professional development, and supervision. At a district level, there are school boards, superintendents, and curriculum directors who are responsible for many of the decisions that affect classroom life, and state bureaucrats and educational publishers have played a role too. Until recently, that was the universe of influence in a language arts classroom.

More recently, the educational policies of the federal government have begun to reshape language arts teaching. The transformation from having no educational policy role to being a major influence has been nothing short of remarkable. This entry provides an analysis of the transformation of the federal role in education policy, particularly during the past half century—from the Great Society programs of the 1960s through No Child Left Behind and the Race to the Top efforts of the current decade.

This chapter only considers federal policy, and only policy making with direct implications for the English language arts. An issue like school funding, which has little specific bearing on the language arts is ignored, while anti-poverty legislation, though not about literacy and language teaching, is reviewed because of its implications for such teaching. Federal legislation has occasionally addressed writing, but such efforts have been circumscribed, and there have been no similar efforts with other parts of the language arts. Consequently, this chapter focuses mainly on federal reading instruction policies.

Federal education policy has become increasingly demanding and specific about literacy teaching during the past half century. This chapter describes major features of this transformation, including the nature of federal education funding, accountability, research role, and politics, and it will review the federal programs aimed at improving literacy, pre-school through Grade 12.

The Nature of Federal Involvement in Education

Most countries have a ministry responsible for that nation's educational policies. That has not been true in the United States. The Constitution makes no mention of education, and the Bill of Rights says that powers not expressly delegated to the federal government are reserved to the states. Consequently, state and local governments have had the major responsibility for education in the United States.

From the beginning, nevertheless, the federal government adopted policies to encourage education; for example, land grants were based on the recipient's willingness to build schools on a portion of the land, a policy eventually extended to universities. The federal role in education expanded following the Civil War. In 1867, a National Bureau of Education was formed in the Department of the Interior to formulate educational policy and coordinate educational activities at a national level, though this agency did little more than compile educational statistics (Jennings, 1999).

More relevant to educational policy was the Bureau of Refugees, Freedmen, and Abandoned Lands (the "Freedmen's Bureau"), established in 1865 to address the needs of the newly-freed slaves (Bentley, 1970). This bureau was to provide emergency food, medical support, and housing to the freed slaves, but it took steps to provide educational support, too. By 1870, it had established more than 1,000 schools for former slaves, including appropriating land and buildings, formulating curricula, and publishing reading textbooks (Smith, 1965). These efforts ended in 1872, but federal involvement in education during emergencies surfaced again during the Great Depression; Franklin Roosevelt's New Deal programs provided bailout money to prevent school closures and construction money for schools.

Thus, the federal government has played a recurring role in education, but that role was *categorical* rather than *general* (Graham, 1984). The federal government did not provide general education funding to the states, towards the states' own policies. Instead, it provided support for categorical activities or specific purposes (setting aside land for schools) or for particular groups of students, while authority for general education was maintained by the states.

After World War II, the federal government played an expanding role in almost every realm of American life, except education. The idea of providing general support for schools was debated during the Truman, Eisenhower, and Kennedy administrations, but to no avail (Graham, 1984). The idea of local control of schools ran too deep, and opposition from various groups who feared the implications of a federal takeover of schools blocked federal involvement.

This policy logjam was broken in the wake of the Kennedy assassination. Given the outpouring of support, in 1965 President Johnson pushed through Congress the most extensive federal education legislation in history (Graham, 1984). This legislation was categorical in nature, aimed at supporting disadvantaged children. Programs such as Head Start and Title I of the Elementary and Secondary School Act (ESEA) were meant more as anti-poverty or civil rights programs than educational ones (Graham, 1984; Jeffrey, 1978). Over the next three decades, these programs grew, with ESEA repeatedly receiving additional funding.

In 1983, the report, *A Nation at Risk,* set off a wave of school reform effort that continues to this day (Davies, 2007; National Commission on Excellence in Education, 1983). That report, issued by the White House, revealed that U.S. students were lagging their international counterparts despite a costly education system. The most enduring result of these reform efforts has been the "education standards movement." The idea was that schools needed to have more demanding learning goals, and that progress towards those standards could be monitored through testing. These efforts, led by the National Governors Association, with federal support, emphasized the need to improve reading levels, and instigated state efforts to improve test scores (Jennings, 1998). On a federal level, there were efforts to create national literacy standards, and experiments in the support of educational programming aimed at improving reading (such as the Reading Excellence Act—which attempted to get states to intensify their reading improvement efforts and to bring those efforts more in line with research findings).

In 2002, President George W. Bush signed into law No Child Left Behind, a reauthorization of ESEA (No Child Left Behind, 2001). This law increased federal education support, created major new literacy programs, and mandated compliance to accountability standards. What started in 1965 as assistance to local districts to meet the needs of poverty students has grown into a larger program with the power to require accountability reforms for all students. Critics have claimed the federal government provides too little funding to dictate local policies, but two decades of case law supports the idea that federal categorical support requires adherence to more general federal mandates. Thus, federal education policy is important with regard to literacy and language because of its ability to leverage local policies.

NCLB required that states meet educational standards, but allowed each state to define these standards locally. This preserved local control, but discouraged the establishment of high, competitive standards, since states could lose support if they failed to meet their standards. However, in 2009, 48 states agreed to adopt common standards, and Secretary of Education Arne Duncan pledged $350 million to develop new tests. He also pledged $4.5 billion for Race to the Top, an effort to increase accountability (by linking teacher salaries to test scores) and strengthen the federal role in education reform; at this time the criteria for Race to the Top have not been released, but states have been changing to state laws to ensure that they could compete, including expanding charter schools and making sure that teacher could be linked to student tests.

Federal policies have been a significant influence on literacy education. Because of the expansive definitions of eligibility devised to ensure wide political support, Title I programs have operated in most local school districts (more than $14 billion dollars are distributed through Title I to more than 50,000 schools). The broad distribution of this program has accustomed school districts to reliance on federal aid.

That ESEA funding has been so heavily aimed at elementary schools has focused these programs on literacy. Since ESEA had required separate educational programming for poverty children, Title I supported pull-out remedial reading programs, requiring the hiring of Title I teachers and the purchase of reading materials and assessments. Changes during the Clinton administration have made combinations of federal and local funds easier to enact if more than 60% of the students are living in poverty. This means that in such schools Title I money can be combined with general education money to support reading instruction for all students, without regard to poverty status.

These federal programs have had accountability requirements that will be discussed in the next section. It is sufficient to note that civil right laws gave the federal government power to withhold funding if states did not comply with policy standards. These powers were used to force the desegregation of local schools, and during the past decade these enforcement powers allowed the federal government to influence literacy education as well.

Accountability In 1965, the ESEA included accountability provisions. Senator Robert Kennedy asked that the law include evaluations that would allow the measurement of the effects of Title I due to concerns that school programs might not improve the achievement of disadvantaged children (Bailey & Mosher, 1968). Accordingly, legislation required the annual academic testing of children enrolled in Title I programs.

When ESEA was first revised, another testing provision was added establishing an assessment to promote a national benchmark of learning progress against which to measure learning in light of ESEA. As a result, the National Assessment of Educational Progress (NAEP) began monitoring reading achievement in 1969.

Thus, the use of tests as the measure of educational success and the monitoring of student learning by the federal government through tests were built into this legislation early on, though the federal government's enforcement powers were hampered. For example, since schools selected the ESEA-mandated tests and with no required criteria for success, no one could be held accountable for student progress. Similarly, the National Assessment results could not determine the success of schools or programs, and even state comparisons were proscribed.

However, the 1964 Civil Rights Act had enforcement provisions that allowed the federal government to use ESEA to require changes in local policies affecting general education programs (Civil Rights Act, 1964). The leveraging of ESEA in this way helped to desegregate schools, but also opened the way for the government to use categorical support as leverage to influence general education programs.

Title VI of the 1964 Civil Rights Act said, "no person in the United States shall, on the basis of race, color, or national origin, be excluded from participation in, be denied the benefits of, or be subjected to discrimination under any program or activity receiving federal financial assistance." This means that the feds could terminate funding to districts that were out of compliance with this federal law. Since many segregated school districts received ESEA funding, the threat to withhold these funds was serious, and the Department of Health, Education and Welfare that administered ESEA, took its enforcement responsibilities seriously, forcing districts to change polices (Davies, 2007). Some states resisted, arguing that the narrow stream of support did not entitle the federal government authority to require broader policy compliance. The courts supported the constitutionality of these enforcement powers.

Claiming literacy as "the new civil right," President George W. Bush put forth the No Child Left Behind (NCLB) legislation which amended the ESEA law in 2002 (Henry, 2001). NCLB required districts to test all students in reading, math, and science, and the tests were to evaluate the success of various racial, linguistic, and economic groups. If local standards were not achieved, then the schools had to allow students to transfer to other schools and provide afterschool tutoring. Claims that this represented an unfunded mandate were rejected by the courts based on the earlier desegregation rulings; literacy had truly become the new civil right. The link of literacy to civil rights was continued by the Obama administration. Secretary of Education Arne Duncan has declared that "Education is the civil rights issue of our generation" (Duncan, n.d.), and he has called for an expansion of a federal test-based accountability.

The Role of Research The role of research in education policy has changed over the years: "Research played a new role in influencing policy… In the past, research has been regarded just as one among many information sources consulted in policy formation…but those expectations were dramatically elevated in the late 1990s" (Schoenfeld & Pearson, 2009, p. 567).

During the period prior to the passage of ESEA, researchers from several fields explored the idea that intelligence was not a fixed ability predetermined by genes, but was influenced environmentally. These theories suggested that educational programming aimed at preschoolers and children growing up in "cultures of deprivation" could improve learning (Silver & Silver, 1991).

It is clear from the policy advice given at the time that empirical data played little role (Jeffrey, 1978). Data were used more as persuasive examples than scientific proof, which meant that single flawed studies could be influential. For example, the influence of the Banneker project in which a school district tried to improve reading achievement by changing teachers' attitudes towards poor children (but not curriculum or instruction) was used as evidence of the likely success of ESEA (Silver & Silver, 1991). Although the difficulty of improving the achievement of severely disadvantaged children was evident in existing research, neither policymakers nor the scholar-advisors gave attention to such data (Jeffrey, 1978).

The role of research changed quickly, however, as the Civil Rights Act of 1964 required the commissioning of a study, *Equality of Educational Opportunity* (Coleman, 1966), and the release of this study suggested the limited effectiveness of federal programs. "The important fact about the Coleman report…was not its detailed findings, but its contribution to a climate of opinion in which 'scientific' evaluation was coming to be expected" (Silver & Sliver, 1991, p. 119). During the decades following the Coleman report, educational evaluation studies had mixed results concerning the effectiveness of Title I and Head Start. These studies focused on variables such as IQ, but gradually shifted their attention to reading. Despite negative findings about the effectiveness of federal education efforts in improving reading achievement, these programs continued to be funded without much effort to reform the quality of these programs.

This began to change due to literacy debates that raged in states like California (McGill-Franzen, 2000; Schoenfeld & Pearson, 2009; Taylor, 1998). During the 1980s, California bureaucrats adopted state-level curricular policies. Critics began pushing back almost immediately, but their efforts gained little headway until NAEP began publishing state comparisons. In 1992, when NAEP placed California at the bottom of tested states in reading achievement, lawmakers imposed extensive curriculum reforms. These divisive debates over beginning reading (labeled the Reading Wars) were often marked by the rhetorical, partisan, and contradictory use of research.

As a result, the federal government intervened to determine what instructional practices were supported by research. In 1997, Congress requested the appointment of the National Reading Panel (NRP). NRP established criteria for evaluating research, requiring practices to have rigorous studies showing their effectiveness. The panel issued its controversial synthesis of 450 studies, concluding that some practices conferred learning benefits to children, including the teaching of phonemic awareness, phonics, oral reading fluency, vocabulary, reading comprehension, and professional development for teachers (NICHD, 2000). These findings were soon adopted as the basis of federal education policy. In 2002, President George W. Bush signed NCLB into law, which included provisions for Reading First and Early Reading First, requiring specific instructional efforts in the areas identified by NRP (No Child Left Behind, 2001). The law mentioned "scientific based reading research" more than 100 times.

Shifting Political Alliances Ultimately, electoral politics underlie government policy. In many areas of public interest, political alignments are well established and longstanding. With regards to education policy, however, there has been greater fluidity and, consequently, it is harder to predict which policy makers or parties will support particular positions.

The reason for such flexibility is that the federal role in education was minimal until recently, so there has not been much opportunity to develop a history of consistent policy support. Also, even though education groups endorse candidates and make donations to political campaigns, few voters make federal electoral choices on the basis of education. This gives candidates room to adjust positions, and education has been an ideal issue to draw attention to a quality of a candidate's character or policy such as bipartisanship, toughness, or altruism.

In the early 1960s, President John F. Kennedy, a Democrat, saw political advantage in moving federal dollars to schools, but strongly opposed general education support, and did little on the education agenda (Graham, 1984). He was succeeded by President Lyndon Johnson, a former school teacher and fellow Democrat, but who was a strong proponent of education. Johnson initiated the first major federal support for schools, but later in his term, he attempted to severely limit additional support (Graham, 1984).

Then came President Richard M. Nixon, a Republican, who wanted to reduce the federal education role, and ESEA and Head Start funding did not increase during his administration (Davies, 2007). However, though Nixon had campaigned on the idea of slowing school desegregation law enforcement, the federal role in education was strengthened greatly through his administration's strict enforcement of those laws. Nixon championed school literacy programs, and his policies and approaches were largely continued under presidents Gerald Ford and Jimmy Carter, a Republican and a Democrat (Davies, 2007). Carter wanted more education funding than his Republican predecessors, and he grudgingly supported the establishment of a cabinet level department of education, but otherwise there was little difference (Davies, 2007).

The only president to express strong opposition to federal involvement in education was Ronald Reagan, a Republican (Davies, 2007). He promised to close the new Department of Education, and tried to stop categorical support for schools, preferring block grants. As president, he did little to move his negative educational agenda, except opposing increases in funding. His position on block grants was contradictory of past conservative doctrine which had always opposed general education support. Interestingly, an important factor in expanding the federal role in education came from the *A Nation at Risk* report which was issued by the White House during his presidency.

The next two presidents, George H. W. Bush and Bill Clinton, a Republican and a Democrat, worked closely with the National Governors Association to establish national educational goals (Jennings, 1998). President Bush called for "a national crusade" to improve schools, and it was during his administration that national education goals were written into law, America 2000, including the idea that all students would demonstrate competency in English and that every adult would be literate. President Clinton continued these policies, and called for a national achievement test, an idea strongly opposed by Republicans who had supported national learning goals. Clinton also established the National Reading Panel and the Reading Excellence Act, legislation aimed at improving elementary reading achievement that required states to use "research based" approaches to teaching.

President George W. Bush, a Republican, worked closely with Senator Edward Kennedy, a Democrat, to craft NCLB (DeBray, 2006; Rudalevige, 2003). This legislation increased federal support, but also established accountability standards. This legislation provided more than $5 billion in support for the improvement of reading instruction in preschool and elementary school. Additionally, President Bush supported changes in Head Start to increase its emphasis on early literacy skills. Finally, President Barak Obama, a Democrat, supports extensive increases in federal support to schools, but with a tightening of accountability standards. President Obama is encouraging the development of common standards, with teacher salaries linked to student success on achievement tests.

What this brief chronology reveals is the striking lack of consistency in the support of education within the political parties, ideologies, or even some of the individuals themselves. There is no consistent literacy alignment, and future policies will likely show the same kind of flexibility or inconsistency.

Federal Literacy and Language Legislation Modern federal education policy making began in the mid-1960s, and those initial efforts exerted little specific impact on language arts teaching, except increasing the hiring of elementary reading teachers. This approach changed quickly, and by 1970, the federal government began addressing literacy directly.

Initially, federal support was neutral—including reading in national testing, and providing small amounts of grant money to improve reading instruction. Over time, as the national assessment revealed stagnant achievement, a growing concern since *A Nation at Risk*, federal involvement in literacy became more substantial, prescriptive, and accountability driven (see Table 22.1). Below is a description of each of these federal literacy policies and programs, arrayed in chronological order. This compendium of federal policies illustrates the increasing specificity and scope; and the consistency of this transformation across parties and ideologies, suggesting that the federal role is unlikely to abate until student literacy achievement improves.

National Assessment of Educational Progress. NAEP began in 1969, and was required to test the reading of samples of students in grades 4, 8, and 11. These tests were administered twice per decade, a schedule that now requires testing every 2 years. NAEP reports are the most influential of any regarding education policy, and the pattern of reading achievement has influenced federal law. In the 1970s and early 1980s, NAEP showed that students were steadily improving in reading, particularly children from low-income families. These gains were lost during the 1980s and early 1990s, a trend blamed, fairly or not, upon the whole language reforms that had swept reading education (Schoenfeld & Pearson, 2009). Since the early 1990s, fourth-grade reading achievement has regained the levels attained in earlier decades.

Right to Read. The first federal foray into literacy education in modern times was made in 1970, with the creation of Right to Read. Originally announced as a voluntary national effort, and intended to distract public attention from divisive issues, such as desegregation, this effort eventually grew into an annual $10 million expenditure for professional development efforts in ESEA schools (Allen, 1970).

Reading is Fundamental (RIF). In 1966, RIF began as a private organization to encourage reading by distributing books to children who had never owned books. The early success of this program led to the establishment, in 1975, of federal funding to help pay for book-giving nationwide (Inexpensive Book Distribution Program). Through this funding stream provided by the Department of Education, with RIF as sole contractor, local programs receive matching funds for the purchase and distribution of books to children, from preschool through high school. More than $24 million annually is provided to motivate reading.

National Research Centers. During the 1970s, the U.S. Department of Education provided support for a national research center in reading focused on reading comprehension. The Center for the Study of Reading opened in 1976 at the University of Illinois at Urbana-Champaign, and was funded until 1992. During that time, the center published hundreds of research papers and reports on the teaching of reading, including the influential research summaries, Becoming a Nation of Readers and Beginning Reading.

The federal government also supported a national writing center, from 1990 to 1995, at the University of California, Berkeley, and Carnegie Mellon University. The purpose of that center was to conduct research into how to teach writing effectively.

In 1992, the reading research funding was moved to support the National Reading Research Center at the universities of Maryland and Georgia, with an emphasis on studying reading motivation, and in 1997, the funds went to create the Center for the Improvement of Early Reading Achievement at the University of Michigan (which led a consortium of five universities). These research centers have published a plethora of work that has influenced literacy teaching. At this time, there are no federal research centers with this kind of focus.

National Writing Project. The National Writing Project began as a local effort at the University of California, Berkeley, towards improving professional development. The Writing Project expanded as affiliate groups received funding from their states, and in 1991, the federal government adopted the National Writing Project network providing funds for its activities since that time. That core grant, supplemented with state and local support, now funds approximately 200 sites where teachers can learn how to support student writing development.

William F. Goodling Even Start Family Literacy Programs. The Even Start program began in 1988 and distributes, through the states, more than $65 million annually to local family literacy programs. The purpose of Even Start is to offer assistance to families to help end the cycle of poverty by providing literacy education to parents and their children. Even Start supports coordinated adult literacy and early childhood education services.

National Voluntary English Language Arts Standards. In 1992, the National Governors Association proposed the adoption of rigorous and specific learning goals. Such standards would serve as the criteria for measuring accountability. To facilitate state efforts, the U.S. Department of Education provided funding for the creation of national "voluntary" standards. Accordingly, a contract was issued to the University of Illinois at Urbana-Champaign, International Reading Association (IRA), and National Council of Teachers of English (NCTE) to develop national language arts standards; about $1 million was spent before the government pulled the plug in 1994. The Department of Education criticized the standards saying they were not specific enough to "define what students should know and be able to do in the domains of language, literacy, and literature" (Diegmueller, 1994). IRA and NCTE later published the standards themselves (1996).

National Reading Panel (NRP). At the height of controversy in the 1990s over how to teach reading, the Congress required the appointment of a panel to determine what works in reading instruction through a formal review of research. NRP issued a report (NICHD, 2000) which was later adopted as the foundation of federal policy. NRP became the basis for the curricular requirements of Early Reading First and Reading First, and led to other federally-supported research reviews: the National Literacy Panel on Language Minority Children and Youth (August & Shanahan, 2006), considering research on teaching English learners, and the National Early Literacy Panel (NELP, 2008), which reviewed research on preschool and kindergarten literacy.

Reading Excellence Act (REA). REA became law in 1998, and provided funding for states to help upgrade literacy. This was the first education legislation to provide a definition of "scientifically based reading research" and to indicate that reading included "the understanding of how phonemes (speech sounds) are connected to print; the ability to decode unfamiliar words and read fluently; and the knowledge of sufficient background information and vocabulary to foster reading comprehension." States competed for this support.

Reach Out and Read (ROR). This private reading promotion provides books to infants and young children through their pediatricians. Parents are guided in reading to their children as an approach to improve language development and early literacy. First embraced by the federal government in 1997 at a White House conference on early reading, ROR began receiving federal support in 2000, about $5 million annually.

Early Reading First (ERF). ERF provides multiyear grants to schools to enhance the early language and literacy development of preschoolers from low income families. Schools that receive ERF funding are required to adopt strategies and professional development approaches consistent with scientifically based reading research. ERF distributes more than $100 million annually to improve preschool literacy and language teaching through programs that emphasize the teaching of phonological awareness, language development, alphabet knowledge, and print awareness.

Reading First. Established by NCLB in 2002, it represents the largest federal commitment to literacy education (about $1 billion per year), to improve reading achievement K–3. Reading First programs had to explicitly teach phonemic awareness, phonics, oral reading fluency, vocabulary, and comprehension, and the federal funds were for supporting such teaching through professional development, curriculum materials, reading assessments, and instructional interventions. The requirements for Reading First were more prescriptive than any prior federal policy, and it was plagued by claims that it was giving unfair advantages to particular commercial programs, charges later upheld by an investigation of the Inspector General (2006). Federal studies of the effectiveness of the program were not positive

(Gamse, Bloom, Kemple, & Jacob, 2008). Nevertheless, the program has exerted an important influence on all reading instruction provided through Title I (U.S. Department of Education, 2008).

Striving Readers. In 2005, the Department of Education began a small discretionary grant program to support efforts to improve the reading achievement of adolescents. These funds, about $30 million annually, are to be spent on the implementation of reading interventions for "striving readers" in middle and high schools. This program was expanded in 2009 and will be supported in all states.

Head Start. Head Start began in 1965 as a social service program for disadvantaged preschoolers to increase their health, encourage parental support, and enhance early cognitive functioning. This program, administered by the Department of Health and Human Services, was not designed to address academic skills. During the past decade, dissatisfaction with early literacy achievement has led to a revamping of Head Start (Improving Head Start Act, 2007). Head Start programs now must hire staff qualified to "promote the language skills and literacy growth of children and that provide children with a variety of skills that have been identified, through scientifically based reading research, as predictive of later reading achievement."

Conclusions

Federal policy making does not stand still, and many of these programs will end or change over time. As this is written, funding for Reading First has not been renewed and President Barack Obama has proposed an end to the funding of Reading is Fundamental, National Writing Project, and Even Start, and Congress is debating expansive new literacy legislation to combine Early Reading First, Reading First, and Striving Readers into a single larger program aimed at improving the teaching of reading and writing through the use of research-based instruction, preschool through high school. The Chief State School Officers and National Governors Association are hurrying to complete common core learning standards for the teaching of English language arts, which are likely to be de facto national education standards

TABLE 22.1
The Transformation of Federal Education Policy.

Federal Education Policy 1960	Federal Education Policy 2010
Mainly elementary grades	Preschool through high school
Voluntary	Compulsory
General, symbolic efforts	Specific, prescriptive efforts
Targeted involvement in federally-supported classrooms	Universal coverage
Local control	More centralized authority
No accountability	High accountability
Diversity	Standardization

that will exert an important influence on teachers of the English language arts.

Of course, no one has the crystal ball that will reveal which of these new efforts will come to fruition and which will be stillborn. However, what seems certain, is that until literacy attainment reaches the levels demanded by the public, an ever-shifting alignment of players, parties, and ideologies will promote research-based federal education legislation that will continue to exert extensive influences—by leveraging the power of targeted categorical investments in local schools—on the teaching of literacy and the English language arts.

References

Allen, J. E., Jr. (1970). Interview. *Harvard Educational Review, 40,* 533.

August, D., & Shanahan, T. (2006). *Developing literacy in second-language learners: Report of the National Literacy Panel on Language-Minority Children and Youth.* Mahwah, NJ: Lawrence Erlbaum Associates.

Bailey, S. K., & Mosher, E. K. (1968). *ESEA: The Office of Education administers a law.* Syracuse, NY: Syracuse University Press.

Bentley, G. R. (1970). *A history of the Freedmen's Bureau.* London: Octagon Books.

Civil Rights Act of 1964, P. L. 88-352, 78 Stat. 241.

Coleman, J. S. (1966). *Equality of educational opportunity.* Washington, DC: U.S. Department of Health, Education, and Welfare.

Davies, G. (2007). *See government grow: Education politics from Johnson to Reagan.* Lawrence: University of Kansas Press.

DeBray, E. H. (2006). *Politics, ideology, & education: Federal policy during the Clinton and Bush administrations.* New York: Teachers College Press.

Diegmueller, K. (1994, March 30). English group loses funding for standards. *Education Week.*

Duncan, A. (n.d.). Retrieved from U.S. Department of Education Web site, http://www.ed.gov/news/staff/bios/duncan.html

Elementary and Secondary Education Act (ESEA), 1965. (P. L. 89-10, 79 Stat. 27, 20 U.S.C. ch. 70).

Gamse, B. C., Bloom, H. S., Kemple, J. J., & Jacob, R. T. (2008). *Reading First Impact Study: Interim Report* (NCEE 2008-4016). Washington, DC: National Center for Education Evaluation and Regional Assistance, Institute of Education Sciences, U.S. Department of Education.

Graham, H. D. (1984). *The uncertain triumph: Federal education policy in the Kennedy and Johnson years.* Chapel Hill: University of North Carolina.

Henry, T. (2001, June 20). Lawmakers move to improve literacy, the 'new civil right'. *USA Today.* Retrieved from http://www.usatoday.com/news/nation/2001-06-11-literacy.htm

Improving Head Start for School Readiness Act of 2007. Retrieved from http://thomas.loc.gov/cgi-bin/query/F?c110:6:./temp/~c110fd7gF1:e1545:

Inspector General. (2006). *The Reading First program's grant application process.* Washington, DC: U.S. Department of Education.

International Reading Association/National Council of Teachers of English. (1996). *Standards for the English language arts.* Newark, DE: International Reading Association.

Jeffrey, J. R. (1978). *Education for children of the poor: A study of the origins and implementation of the Elementary and Secondary Education Act of 1965.* Columbus: Ohio State University Press.

Jennings, J. F. (1998). *Why national standards and tests? Politics and the quest for better schools.* Thousand Oaks, CA: Sage.

Jennings, J. F. (1999). *A brief history of the federal role in education: Why it began and why it's still needed.* Washington, DC: Center on Education Policy. (ED 438 335).

McGill-Franzen, A. (2000). Policy and instruction: What is the relationship? In M. L. Kamil, P. B. Mosenthal, P. D. Pearson, & R. Barr (Eds.), *Handbook of reading research* (Vol. III, pp. 889–908). Mahwah, NJ: Erlbaum.

National Commission on Excellence in Education. (1983). *A nation at risk: The imperative for educational reform.* Washington, DC: U.S. Department of Education.

National Early Literacy Panel. (2008). *Developing early literacy.* Washington, DC: National Institute for Literacy.

National Institute of Child Health and Human Development (NICHD). (2000). *Report of the National Reading Panel. Teaching children to read: An evidence-based assessment of the scientific research literature on reading and its implications for reading instruction* (NIH Publication No. 00-4769). Washington, DC: U.S. Government Printing Office.

No Child Left Behind Act, 2001. PL 107-110. Retrieved from http://www.ed.gov/policy/elsec/leg/esea02/index.html

Rudalevige, A. (2003). The politics of No Child Left Behind. *Education Next, 3*(4). Retrieved from http://www.hoover.org/publications/ednext/3346601.html

Schoenfeld, A. H., & Pearson, P. D. (2009). The reading and math wars. In G. Sykes, B. Schneider, & D. N. Plank (Eds.), *Handbook of education policy research* (pp. 560–580). New York: Routledge.

Silver, H., & Silver, P. (1991). *An educational war on poverty: American and British policy-making 1960–1980.* Cambridge, UK: Cambridge University Press.

Smith, N. B. (1965). *American reading instruction.* Newark, DE: International Reading Association.

Taylor, D. (1998). *Beginning to read and the spin doctors of science.* Urbana, IL: National Council of Teachers of English.

U.S. Department of Education. (2008). *Reading First implementation evaluation annual report.* Washington, DC: Office of Planning, Evaluation and Policy Development.

U.S. Department of Education. (2009). *Fiscal Year 2009 Budget Summary — February 4, 2008.* Retrieved from http://www.ed.gov/about/overview/budget/budget09/summary/edlite-section3.html

Section IV

The Many Faces of Texts

SECTION EDITORS
PEGGY ALBERS, VIVIAN VASQUEZ, AND JEROME C. HARSTE

Section IV focuses on research methods, theoretical frameworks, and methodologies found in research concerning digital, visual, and media texts. The following chapters describe, analyze, and critique these current research trends in the field of literacy education.

Beach, Hull, and O'Brien open this section with an examination of research related to the various ways in which English language arts (ELA) teachers are beginning to incorporate into their instruction the uses of Web 2.0 tools (e.g., digital video/storytelling, social networking sites, cell phones, blogs, wikis, podcasts, etc.) that involve both accessing *and* producing knowledge in ways that move beyond passive consumption to active construction of knowledge mediated by hyperlinks, interactivity, multimodality, and social networking. They conclude that educators need to rethink current spatial and temporal boundaries that emphasize face-to-face classroom spaces in which the teacher is the primary arbiter/audience of learning, and transform ELA instruction in which students assume more control of their learning through communicating with immediate, local, national, and world-wide audiences.

Levy and Marsh present an overview of three key areas of research on literacy and information and communication technologies (ICT) in the early years of schooling, children aged zero to 8. They examine research related to the role of digital literacy practices in homes in which children, from birth, are immersed in a technological world, experiences that have profound consequences for their literacy development. This is followed by a discussion of research that has shown how new technologies are informing pedagogical practice with regard to literacy in early years settings and classrooms. Lastly, they examine recent research that has illuminated the continuities and discontinuities in digital literacy practices across home and school domains. They conclude the chapter by articulating implications for further research in this field.

Rowsell and Pahl review recent research on multimo-

dality and New Literacies Studies which suggest that text-making is as much about material qualities of texts and their relationship to the meaning-maker as they are about the literacy practices being shaped by context and the identities of meaning makers. They follow this discussion with the significance that these two lenses can play in understanding texts as situated within the contexts of students' worlds, as multimodal, and as sedimenting identities. They conclude that these lenses can open up new spatial and ecological research methods, such as mapping, as powerful ways to articulate new visions of communities.

Tate presents an overview of research surrounding the definition, implementation, and future of media literacy in the English language arts. She begins by presenting how media literacy has been defined by a range of scholars. This is followed by a presentation of how media literacy has been integrated into English language arts classrooms and teacher education programs, and articulates the importance of developing critical media literacy. She then concludes with a discussion of the future of media literacy, the need for equity and access for all students, and that issues of power, access, and privilege are kept in mind.

Wohlwend and Lewis examine critical literacy within an evolving digital and global landscape in their chapter. They present two dimensions of critical literacy that take into account the multimodal affordances of digital technologies, convergence, and embodiment. Rather than present a comprehensive review of studies, they present several key studies within each dimension that they deem to be important in understanding critical engagement and technology. Their focus is on critical literacy in transition and the promise of new directions at a time that demands a critically literate public in the face of changing economic and informational flows brought on by globalization.

Albers, Vasquez, and Harste review some of the breakthroughs that have been made in the analysis of visual texts in the context of telling their own stories presented as extended discussions within the larger frameworks of visual literacy and critical literacy. Within their review of this research, they present theirs and other scholars' research, research that situates the role that Discourses play in the reading, interpreting, and analysis of visual texts, how visual analysis significantly implicates the textmaker and the viewer as active and critical makers and readers of visual texts, and the importance of critical analysis of visual media in English language arts classes and teacher education programs.

Siegel and Rowe outline the major semiotic traditions and their contributions to defining, theorizing, and analyz-ing texts. They begin with an overview of Charles Sanders Peirce and Ferdinand de Saussure, the two figures most closely associated with the development of semiotic thought in modern times. This is followed by their examination of the work of Vygotsky, Bakhtin, Voloshinov, Kress, and Scollon and Scollon, all of whom give signs a central place in their theories of human thought, language, and literacy. Their review suggests the importance of these ideas as essential both to understanding texts and to imagining new possibilities for designing, interpreting, embodying, and questioning texts in school literacy curricula.

23

Transforming English Language Arts in a Web 2.0 World

Richard Beach, Glynda Hull, and David O'Brien

In California a group of middle school youth attend an after-school program whose centerpiece is Web 2.0 technologies. Creating digital music and digital stories, as well as t-shirts, logos, greeting cards, and drawings, these youth exchange multiple, inventive creative products with youth in South Africa and India via a private social networking site called space2cre8. Through blogs, wall postings, emails, and photos, they represent themselves, their friends, families, school, and communities, taking tentative steps toward imagining and connecting with kids who are physically, linguistically, and culturally on the other side of the world. An Oakland, California, boy named De'Von posted a photo of himself accompanied by a blog called "hello world": "ive finally got a pic and im online and anybody on the cre8 hit up mr. man of the year [his profile name] ya dig." "My three wishes are: I want to take all my cousins to Great America. I want to be an astronaut. I want my mom to get the job she is interviewing for today." Kassandra's blog posting followed, and subtly indexed, a group discussion of a digital story by a girl in India, in which was paired a photograph of an outdoor cooking pot with a voiceover that "we don't have a proper kitchen."

Youth in South Africa viewed this story too, and one boy summarized the effect of its depiction of Bakhti's economic circumstances in India, in juxtaposition to the constraints experienced in his own village, simply but eloquently: "It moved me." De'Von back in California observed about the young Indian author: "I think she's a person who will be blessed along the road." To be sure, not all of the communicative exchanges among this digitally connected group of young people proceeded so smoothly or resulted automatically in shared or hospitable understandings. A South African youth found himself pondering how to respond to a forthright query from an Indian girl about his decision to use as his profile picture, not his own photograph, but an Internet image of the rap artist Lil' Wayne. This girl did not share his sense of aesthetics or appropriateness or his enagement in American-origin popular culture: "Hello Kelvin, I am Maya. You don't have a picture of yourself? Why do you use this photo. I don't like your profile picture. Please use your photo." Kelvin's considered response turned out to be much delayed, however, due to frequent Internet problems at his school, which provided his only access to computers or Web-based tools, and had in fact been technologically outfitted for the first time only in the past year.

As a Web 2.0 tool, this social neworking site, like many others, has the potential to mediate a range of different "language arts" literacy practices. These practices include cross-cultural, cross-geographic, cross-linguistic exchanges; the making and sharing of meanings and knowledge through multiple modes; the representation of self, to not only friends and acquaintances, but also to imagined others and audiences afar; the exploration and negotiation of a wealth of textual and platform affordances and constraints; exposure to and interaction with divergent and sometimes vastly different lifeworlds; the creation of additional and alternative social spaces and the intersection and interweaving of online and offline experience; and the reversal of "polarities of interpretation" (Silverstone, 2007), whereby persons who are accustomed only to being interpreted get their turn at the wheel. With such practices and their affordances come considerable challenges, including a still inequitable distribution of tools, resources, and capital, and at this historical moment, a mismatch between them and the ideologies, goals, and participant structures of schooling.

It is widely agreed that Web 2.0 technologies, and related literate, semiotic, and social practices, have transformative potential for communication, identity formation, and knowledge construction in our global world. We see that potential played out daily in the informal digital practices of youth evident in the space2cre8 intercontinental exchanges. Yet, the question that remains is whether educational institutions should, can, and will follow suit. It is not inconsequential that the space2cre8 project described above takes place in U.S. contexts during out-of-school time rather than during the school day, where traditional—uni-modal, non-digital, decontextualized, test-directed, and teacher-centric—versions of literacy at this writing still dominate classrooms.

In this chapter, we examine research related to the various ways in which English language arts (ELA) teachers are beginning to incorporate these uses of Web 2.0 tools into their instruction. By Web 2.0 tools, we mean those digital tools—digital video/storytelling, social networking sites, cell phones, blogs, wikis, podcasts, etc., that involve both accessing *and* producing knowledge in ways that move beyond passive consumption to active construction of knowledge mediated by hyperlinks, interactivity, multimodality, and social networking (Carrington & Robinson, 2009; Davies & Merchant, 2009; Richardson, 2009; for a comparison of Web 1.0 and Web 2.0 environments, see Rosen & Nelson, 2008). In contrast to much of print-based ELA instruction, Web 2.0 tools also allow students to communicate to multiple audiences within and beyond their classrooms, enhancing their sense of engagement and agency in constructing and sharing their ideas. And, because students and teachers use Web 2.0 tools to communicate with each other at any time and from any place, educators need to rethink current spatial and temporal boundaries long associated with schooling to transform familiar face-to-face classroom spaces in which the teacher is the primary arbiter/audience of learning so that students assume more control of their learning through communicating with immediate, local, national, and worldwide audiences.

Redefining Learning in ELA Classrooms Through Uses of Web 2.0 Tools

We signal the importance of moving beyond a framing of Web 2.0 tools as simply a matter of "learning technologies" or "digital literacies" to a conceptualization of these tools as harbingers and prime movers in fundamentally different patterns of knowledge construction, communication, and identity formation, and hopefully in teaching too, via mediated participation in the global community (Knobel & Lankshear, 2008; Leu, O'Byrne, Zawilinski, McVerry, & Everett-Cacopardo, 2009). The most desirable and most helpful relationship between quickly evolving mediational tools and more conventional understandings of literacy as print-dominant, non-digital, and essay-centric is currently much debated in the field. Leander (2009), for example, has helpfully identified four stances toward this relationship: "resistance" to new literacies, "replacement" of old literacies with new, using new literacies to validate or "return" to the old, and "remediation" in which new media alongside old forms are assessed according to their affordaces for expression and learning. Leander further advocates a "parallel pedagogy" in which print literacies exist side-by-side, and are considered comparatively to, uses of Web 2.0 tools—for instance, print-based memories in Leander's course for pre-service teachers are explored for their affordances in juxtaposition to digital stories (see below).

In this chapter, we propose a transformation of ELA around two basic ideas—that uses of Web 2.0 tools are redefining what it means to *construct knowledge*, and that students are using Web 2.0 tools to *explore and enact alternative identities*. Web 2.0 tools have transformed knowledge construction from a system of top-down, vetted control of knowledge as reflected in the *Encyclopedia Britannica* or academic journal dissemination to one of bottom-up collaborative, social construction of knowledge mediated by links as reflected in Wikipedia (Weinberger, 2007). Knowledge is also represented in highly multimodal ways through images, videos, digital mapping, etc. (Hull & Nelson, 2005). In the latter, knowledge construction becomes transparent through documentation of vetting, voicing of alternative perspectives, rules of evidence, and related links. Students therefore can acquire not simply information, but can also experience the modeling of meta-knowledge or heuristics for constructing their own understandings. This involves a major shift from passive consumption to active, shared construction of knowledge—from top-down, vertical acquisition of information—learning *that*, to horizontal learning *how*, as well as from acquiescing to knowledge authorities to collective construction and judgments about the credibility of knowledge through networked "many-to-multitudes" interaction (Davidson & Goldberg, 2009, pp. 27–35). Web 2.0 tools mediate this collaborative, social construction of knowledge through sharing of links, RSS feeds, tags, as well as collaboration tools such as wikis, social networking sites, or Google Docs., etc., so that connections build on connections (Donath & boyd, 2004).

Such online sharing leads to our second focus: the construction of online identities within specific social communities or "participatory cultures" (Greenhow, Robelia, & Hughes, 2009; Jenkins, 2009). Research on how youth in the United States use digital tools in their everyday lives outside of school suggests that they construct their identities as active members of online communities through "hanging out" with peers, "messing around" by experimenting with online media use and production, and "geeking out" through participation in networks or communities focusing on specific tool uses such as the writing fanfiction (Ito et al., 2009). Accoding to boyd (2009, p. 9), engagement in these "networked publics" are constituted by "persistence" (communication is recorded and stored); "searchability" (people can readily locate each other and information); "replicability" (material can be copied and moved); and "invisible audiences" (it is difficult to identify one's potential viewers or readers). Because they are no longer limited by physical proximity in local face-to-face community interactions defined by race, gender, class, age, or language markers (Davies & Merchant, 2009), youth can experiment with constructing alternative, "projective identities" (Gee, 2007) through, for example, creating avatars and employing different language styles (Kafai, Peppler, & Chapman, 2009; Thomas, 2007). They also can experience a sense of agency through the sharing of their expertise as part of situated knowledge construction (Gee, 2007). For example, given that 31% of adolescents play games on a daily basis, and 76% play games with others, they share knowledge of game cheat strategies, enhancing their sense of agency as contributing to a community (Lenhart et al., 2008).

Other examples of youthful agency derive from the experience of attracting viewers (sometimes in the thousands) to online video or photo-shares (Willet, 2009) or experiencing the influence of their postings on participants in social networking sites, such as was the case for Bakti from India in relation to the circulation of her digital story on space2cr8. In constructing digital content, youth are also engaged in producing or remixing multimodal material based on certain aesthetic design principles that constitute a visual rhetoric for combining images, audio, video, and texts (Black, 2008). For example, in designing a fan site for a punk rock band, one teen was aware of how altering, modifying, sharing, and remixing images projects certain aspects of their own identities in ways that will appeal to teen audiences, again, enhancing their sense of agency as digital artists (Leander & Frank, 2006; cf. Hull & Nelson, 2010).

These online learning experiences involving public, social display of visual rhetoric are redefining what it means to learn ELA. Students are constructing meaning as negotiated and knowledge as relational, generative, engaged, and dilemma-driven within specific communities (boyd, 2009). In doing so, they are moving from uses of signs as words, images, sounds, and gestures to uses of signs as part of sign systems with multiple modes and genres (Finnegan, 2002). In traditional educational research, linguistic systems and cognitive systems are central to learning: writing and reading print, talking about print, formulating concepts, activating schema, assimilating and accommodating information. In contrast, new semiotic systems explore multimodality by looking at how all resources (linguistic, visual, audio, actional/performance) can be selected, organized, and produced to make meaning (Jewitt & Kress, 2003). Further, an attention to play, pleasure, and performance in online communicative environments calls attention to the often neglected place of emotion and desire in identity formation and learning.

Transforming ELA Instruction through Use of Web 2.0 Tools

These changes in uses of Web 2.0 for constructing knowledge and identities require transforming ELA instruction (Beach, Anson, Kastman-Breuch, & Swiss, 2009; Carrington & Robinson, 2009; Davies & Merchant, 2009; Lankshear & Knobel, 2008; Richardson, 2009). A transformed ELA curriculum builds on a range of social practices: play, performance, simulation, appropriation, multitasking, distributed cognition, collective intelligences, judgment, transmedia navigation, networking, negotiation, and awareness (MIT New Media Literacy Center, 2008). Unfortunately, analysis of current school instruction finds little evidence of students using Web 2.0 tools for engaging in critical inquiry or for producing/publishing digital content for audiences outside the school (Luckin et al., 2009). Students are not exploiting the full potential for uses of Web 2.0 tools because their schools' ELA curriculums remain organized around print-based paradigms

that perceive digital tools as merely an add-on rather than as a transformation of ELA. Moreover, uses of Web 2.0 tools continues to mirror lived-world social and economic inequalities. For example, White middle-class adolescents perceive MySpace as more appropriate for working-class/ non-dominant adolescents while Facebook is considered to be more for middle-class adolescents (boyd, 2009). And, disparities in broadband access, particularly in the home or school, leads to disparities in skills in using Web 2.0 tools based on in race, class, and gender differences (Hargittai & Hinnant, 2008).

Despite these challenges, we remain hopeful that Web 2.0 tools can serve as levers to transform ELA instruction, as illustrated by examples to follow in five areas: digital storytelling, social networking/use of mobile devices, text processing, and text construction. These illustrations lead to recommendations for reimagining schooling, teacher preparation, and conceptions of development.

Digital Storytelling. "Let's make a movie." This seemingly simple invitation is a staple in the digital storytelling workshops where participants' audio-video stories are rendered into movies driven by a subversive, empowerment motive of what some have called a global "social movement" (Hartley & McWilliam, 2009): to put in the hands of everyday people, as opposed to an elite mass media or cadre of film experts, the power of narrative and self-expression through the creation of personal movies. Digital storytelling, fostered by organizations such as the Center for Digital Storytelling (http://www.storycenter. org/), ranges from the efforts of individual educators to introduce the practice to their students to a large, multi-year effort sponsored by the British Broadcasting Corporation to "Capture Wales" (http://www.bbc.co.uk/wales/audiovideo/ sites/galleries/pages/capturewales.shtml). With the advent of Web-based video-sharing capabilities such as YouTube and more generally the explosion of social networking sites, the possibilities for distributing digital stories and for increasing their reach have similarly expanded. Now it is possible, for example, for the BBC to post the hundreds of stories collected in Wales on its Web site, and a girl in India can have the experience through her participation in a social network of influencing youth in the United States and South Africa through her digitalized narrative depiction of a day in her life.

Researchers have focused on how digital storytelling functions as a "technology of the self," to use Foucault's term, or a powerful kind of cultural tool that fosters and shapes the enactment of identities (Lundby, 2008). Out-of-school programs that focus on digital storytelling have served as alternative spaces for identity formation that allow students labelled as unsuccessful during the school day to reinvent their biographies as learners (Hull, Kenney, Marple, & Forsman-Schneider, 2006). To understand students' aesthetic considerations in constructing digital stories, researchers examine the semiotic affordances of multi-modal combinations of print, image, voice, and music that appeal to peer audiences (Hull & Nelson, 2005; Leander, 2009). The ease via Web 2.0 tools of constructing multimodal artifcats, and the importance of what Willis (1990) has called "symbolic creativity" among youth, suggest the need for an "aesthetic turn" (Hull & Nelson, 2010) in literacy studies. As they engage in multimodal production, students are acquiring aesthetic stances as to what constitutes effective forms of visual rhetoric through performance, the production of artifacts, and the stylization of bodies that constitute new ways of knowing and enacting identities. In their study of music in Columbian youth cultures, Muñoz and Marín (2006) find that participation in an artistic process, such as music-making, "leads young people towards self-creation, to the production of new subjectivities—to the search for, and generation of, something else in the domains of ethics, politics, art and forms of knowledge converted into praxis" (p. 132). They describe what they term the "motor forces of creation" (p. 132) that drive or liberate creativity in youth cultures.

Research on digital storytelling and a range of semiotic systems suggests the need to transform ELA instruction such that it includes a focus on multimodal construction that also draws on informal personal learning experiences (Carrington & Robinson, 2009; Siegel, 2006). Future research needs to address the tensions between attempts to implement digital storytelling in schools dominated by incompatible accountability systems and print-based ideologies and practices. While most work on digital storytelling focuses on its potential and the positive effects of authoring personal mediated stories, other commentators have begun to document the cultural, social, and institutional constraints that work against giving voice to marginalized populations, and indeed, the contradictions within that very impulse (Taub-Pervizpour, 2009). Similarly, while most research focuses on the social practices that characterize youthful engagement in creating multimodal texts, there has been less attention to the consequences of the circulation of those texts, which can take on an unexpected agency of their own (Nelson, Hull, & Roche-Smith, 2008). And, given the aesthetic dimensions of multimodal production, researchers could helpfully consider what constitutes effective visual rhetoric in uses of genre conventions associated with online narrative forms (Couldry, 2008).

Social-Networking Sites/Mobile Devices. Social networking sites such as Facebook and Myspace allow users to represent themselves by creating a profile that includes text, images, and video; to create and continually add to a list of friends within the network; and to correspond publicly with those friends by posting greetings, news, photos, status updates, etc. Social networks are currently theorized as prime sites for experimentation with self-presentation; the maintenance of social ties and real-time connection; and the creation and exchange of social capital (Tu, Blocher, & Roberts, 2008). Such sites are viral among young people: a now dated estimate is that 55% of U.S. teens online have online profiles (Lenhart & Madden, 2007). Indeed, the

practice has spread around the world, and even in countries with fewer ICT resources, such as many on the African continent, there is nonetheless growing participation. As social networks (and other Web 2.0 tools) migrate from computers to mobile phones, they will achieve greater prominence in such countries still, where the inventive use of cell phones has long trumped computers with their expensive band width requirements.

Much research on social networking currently relies soley on large-scale surveys, small-scale interviews, and analyses of content found online, almost always without benefit of participant observation and cross-site comparisons, both online and offline. Research on educational or literacy-related applications are just beginning (see, for example, Beach & Doerr-Stevens, 2009; Hull & Nelson, 2010; Kirkland, 2009; Knobel & Lankshear, 2008). Educators and organizations have begun to use social networking tools in their classroom, even as schools and governments wrestle with concerns about privacy, access, and safety, choosing sometimes to ban the sites or regulate their usage severely. Through their participation in these sites, students are acquiring literacies involved in socially recognizing ways/or practices for presenting themselves by customizing their profile pages, creating meaningful content valued by their network group, employing discourses constituting their online identity, and using encoded texts such as images or videos to communicate in multimodal ways (Knobel & Lankshear, 2008).

ELA teachers also use online asynchronous and synchronous discussions sites using Moodle, WebCT/Vista, Drupal, Ning, Tappedin.org, etc., for interactions across schools or countries on sites such as Youth Voices (http://youthvoices. net/elgg) or TakingItGlobal (http://discuss.tigweb.org). For example, high school students used a Ning to engage in an online role-play debate on the issue of blocking web sites in their school by creating profiles and adopting pro-con roles, material they used to convince their school administrators to unblock sites (Beach & Doerr-Stevens, 2009).

Among the uses of social networking sites that teachers could exploit is its potential to erase traditional face-to-face boundaries and to create new virtual spaces that allow for global, cross-cultural interaction (Appadurai, 1996). Social networking sites are currently used most typically to connect to friendship networks that already exist offline; research shows as well that racial, class, and geographic boundaries that exist offline are usually maintained on digital sites (Hargittai & Hinnant, 2008). Yet, Silverstone (2007) has called eloquently for the creation of a moral sphere in the use of media, whereby we all become more attentive to responsible representations and interpretations of others. The Youth Voices, Taking it Global, and space2cre8 projects are examples of how teachers can reconceptualize language arts activities in ways that encourage children to bridge cultural, linguistic, geographic, and ideological divides.

Text Processing: Informational Literacies. Increased uses of online text production (Lenhart, Arafeh, Smith, &

Macgill, 2008) also involves informational literacies of processing, accessing, subscribing to, and tagging online material. The multimodality of online texts serves to accelerate and bootstrap lower-level processes like decoding from the surface and propositional levels of a text involving bridging processes that build on readers' prior knowledge and experiences with print texts (Kress, 2003). In contrast to print texts, processing online texts requires readers to formulate purposes for reading that guides attention to certain signaling cues, text structure, and authorial intentions (Kress, 2003), as well as knowing how to select certain links as both semantic and navigational elements (Burbules, 2007). Links are read as presenting potential meaningful associations between web pages or web page elements; as such, the links are read critically to help one construct meaning one way or the other, depending on how readers suppose the links connect pages. In reading online texts, readers also adopt scan-and-skip processing without reading every word, requiring students to know how to highlight and vary their processing rate (Coiro & Dobler, 2007). Given this scan-and-skip reading process, in constructing texts, students need to know how to employ an "inverted pyramid" organizational structure by initially stating their overall topic summary in the beginning of their text.

In addition, online settings change the roles of readers and texts. In agent-based literacy theory, (McEneaney, 2006) an online environment, which is more interactive than a traditional print-based environment, enables text to "act on" readers. When reading online, readers encounter texts that, unlike static documents in print, are more accurately depicted as networks of nodes and links that define a virtual structure—the new textuality and intertextuality. The virtual structure, which is unfolding rather than the static, fixed, structure ascribed by traditional theories of text and comprehension enables many possible readings, depending on how readers choose links (McEneaney, 2006).

Researchers have also examined how students construct their own implicit theories about reading online (Coiro & Dobler, 2007). For example, sixth-grade students perceived online reading as faster than print-based reading, involving a "snatch and grab" approach to obtain immediate results (Sutherland-Smith, 2002). Students also had difficulty with web authorship and assessing the credibility of online information. Determining the credibility of multimodal texts, especially on/within the Internet with its "vast network of relations of credibility" (Burbules & Callister, 2000), is particularly challenging because these texts mix images, music, graphic arts, video, and print to make sophisticated claims supported by various forms or types of evidence. The identification of literacy practices unique to online text processing requires new theories of how knowledge domains are represented in texts and the flexible reassembly of existing knowledge with new knowledge needed, as well as new approaches to reading instruction (Coiro & Dobler, 2007). Students need to acquire a cognitive flexibility to process online knowledge as ill-structured, random, or contradictory by knowing how to frame their searches in

terms of specific purposes, select relevant links, monitor their pursuit of information, assess the credibility of information, tag or categorize material for later use, and reflect on subsequent next moves. All of this points to the need to transform current print-based "reading" instruction in ways that account for new ways of processing online texts.

Constructing Texts. ELA teachers are also using Web 2.0 tools such as blogs, wikis, collaborative writing tools, and e-portfolios to construct texts (Beach, Anson, Kastman-Breuch, & Swiss, 2009 [http://digitalwriting.pbworks. com]; Carrington & Robinson, 2009; Davies & Merchant, 2009; Richardson, 2009). Students can use these tools to communicate with a wider range of audiences than simply the teacher, leading students to engage in self-initiated blog writing based on their sense of responsibility to their audiences—the fact that they can share their writing with audiences enhances their enjoyment of writing in school (Lenhart et al., 2008). For example, fifth-grade students who received comments from peers and people outside of their class were motivated to improve their writing because they enjoyed receiving comments, which they used to further explore the topics being addressed (Davis & McGrail, 2009). Given their interaction with peers' ideas, students engage in summarizing, "forwarding" or "extending" those ideas for constructing new knowledge (Harris, 2006) or used fictional blogs to collaboratively construct ongoing narratives across different posts (Thomas, 2007). Students also learn to use wikis or tools such as Google Docs for collaborative writing; students can also create or edit Wikipedia entries.

As is the case with processing texts, learning to create multimodal, interactive, hyperlinked texts also requires transforming print-based "writing" instruction to foster uses of these features. For example, learning to engage in effective wiki writing requires modeling of use of wiki features, providing strategies for collaboration, fostering a sense of ownership, and evaluating according to achieving one's intended goals (Cleary, Sanders-Betzold, Hoover, & St. John, 2009).

Uses of Web 2.0 Tools To Transform English Language Arts and Schooling

While these use of Web 2.0 tools are challenging status quo conceptions of what counts as language arts, their broader implications push us to rethink status quo spatial and temporal boundaries that have defined schooling as occuring in particular locations during set periods of time, blurring in-school and out-of-school contexts in ways that go beyond the dichotomies of the past. There is also a potential change in the locus of agency for learning, as students take on productive and interpretive authority. New conceptions of learning in Web 2.0 environments emphasize sociality: collective intelligence; interactions among peers and distant audiences; and a new consciousness of and facility with always being connected to information, people, and places. In addition to solitary confrontations with texts and abstractions, there is the possibility of play, performance, joint problem-solving, and interaction. Such notions imply very different conceptions of educational institutions, as illustrated by a school opened in 2009 in New York City that is organized around the design principles associated with games. At the Quest to Learn school (http://q2l.org/), youth not only use Web 2.0 tools, they learn to design them. And in fact, design and innovation are the school's calling cards, along with the underpinning assumption that youth in our new century learn in different ways via interactions with digital tools.

Redefining ELA and rethinking schooling and notions of childhood and development also require transforming ELA teacher preparation so that preservice and inservice teachers acquire technological pedagogical content knowledge (TPACK), the integration of ELA content, ELA pedagogical content knowledge, and Web 2.0 tools (Mishra & Koehler, 2006, p. 1029), not simply to change instruction, but also to focus on changes in student learning (Hughes & Scharber, 2008). Teachers can also use Web 2.0 tools such as digital portfolios or annotations of videos of their teachers to engage in self-reflection leading to change, particularly through publicly sharing of work with colleagues on teacher research network.

References

Appadurai, A. (1996). *Modernity at large: Cultural dimensions of globalization.* Minneapolis: University of Minnesota Press.

Beach, R., Anson, C., Kastman-Breuch, L., & Swiss, T. (2009). *Teaching writing using blogs, wikis, and other digital tools.* Norwood, MA: Christopher-Gordon.

Beach, R., & Doerr-Stevens, C. (2009). Learning argument practices through online role-play: Toward a rhetoric of significance and transformation. *Journal of Adolescent & Adult Literacy, 52*(6), 460–468.

Black, R. W. (2008). *Adolescents and online fan fiction.* New York: Peter Lang.

boyd, d. (2009). Living and learning with social media. *Penn State Symposium for Teaching and Learning with Technology.* State College: Pennsylvania State University. Retrieved August 22, 2009, from http://www.danah.org/papers/talks/PennState2009.html

Burbules, N. C. (2007). E-lessons learned. In L. Smolin, K. Lawless, & N. C. Burbules (Eds.), *Information and communication technologies* (pp. 207–216). Malden, MA: Blackwell.

Burbules, N. C., & Callister, T. A., Jr. (2000). *Watch IT: The risks and promises of information technologies for education.* Oxford, UK: Westview Press.

Carrington, V., & Robinson, M. (Eds.). (2009). *Digital literacies: Social learning and classroom practices.* Los Angeles: Sage.

Cleary, M. N., Sanders-Betzold, S., Hoover, P., & St. John, P. (2009). Working with wikis in writing-intensive classes. *Kairos, 14*(1). Retrieved August 22, 2009, from http://kairos.technorhetoric.net/pmwiki/pmwiki.php/WikiResearch/Home

Couldry, N. (2008). Mediatization or mediation? Alternative understandings of the emergent space of digital storytelling. *New Media and Society, 10*(3), 373–391.

Coiro, J., & Dobler, E. (2007). Exploring the online comprehension strategies used by sixth-grade skilled readers to search for and locate information on the Internet. *Reading Research Quarterly, 42,* 214–257.

Davies, J., & Merchant, G. (2009). *Web 2.0 for schools: Learning and social participation.* New York: Peter Lang.

Davidson, C. N., & Goldberg, D. T. (2009). *The future of learning institutions in a digital age.* Cambridge, MA: MIT Press.

Davis, A. P., & McGrail, E. (2009). The joy of blogging. *Educational Leadership, 66*(6), 74–77.

Donath, J., & boyd, d. (2004). Public display of connections. *BT Technological Journal, 22*(4), 71–82.

Finnegan, R. (2002). *Communicating: The multiple modes of human interconnection.* London: Routledge.

Gee, J. P. (2007). *What video games have to teach us about learning and literacy.* New York: Palgrave Macmillan.

Greenhow, C., Robelia, B., & Hughes, J. E. (2009). Learning, teaching, and scholarship in a digital Age: Web 2.0 and classroom research: What path should we take Now? *Educational Researcher, 38*(4), 246–259.

Hargittai, E., & Hinnant, A. (2008). Digital inequality: Differences in young adults' use of the Internet. *Communication Research, 35*(5), 602–621.

Hartley, J., & McWilliam, K. (Eds.). (2009). *Story circle: Digital storytelling around the world.* New York: Wiley-Blackwell.

Harris, J. (2006). *Rewriting: How to do things with texts.* Logan: Utah State University Press.

Hughes, J. E., & Scharber, C. M. (2008). Leveraging the development of English TPCK within the deictic nature of literacy. In AACTE Committee on Innovation and Technology (Ed.)., *Handbook of technological pedagogical content knowledge (TPCK) for educators* (pp. 87–106). New York: Routledge/AACTE.

Hull, G., Kenney, N., Marple, S., & Forsman-Schneider, A. (2006). *Many versions of masculine: Explorations of boys' identity formation through multimodal composing in an after-school program.* The Robert F. Bowne Foundation's Occasional Papers Series. New York: Robert F. Bowne Foundation.

Hull, G., & Nelson, M. (2005). Locating the semiotic power of multimodality. *Written Communication, 22*(2), 224–262.

Hull, G., & Nelson, M. (2010). Literacy, media, and morality: Making the case for an aesthetic turn. In M. Baynham & M. Prinsloo (Eds.), *The future of literacy studies* (pp. 199–228). New York: Palgrave Macmillan.

Ito, M., Baumer, S., Bittanti, M., Boyd, D., Cody, R., Herr, B., et al. (2009). *Hanging out, messing around, geeking out: Living and learning with New Media.* Cambridge, MA: MIT Press.

Jenkins, H. (2009). *Confronting the challenges of participatory culture: Media education for the 21st century.* Cambridge, MA: MIT Press.

Jewitt, C., & Kress, G. (Eds.). (2003). *Multimodal literacy.* New York: Peter Lang.

Kafai, Y. B., Peppler, K. A., & Chapman, R. N. (2009). *The computer clubhouse: Constructionism and creativity in youth communities.* New York: Teachers College Press.

Kirkland, D. (2009). Standpoints: Researching and teaching English in the digital dimension. *Research in the Teaching of English, 44*(1), 8–22.

Knobel, M., & Lankshear, C. (2008). Digital literacy and participation in online social networking spaces. In C. Lankshear & M. Knobel (Eds.). *Digital literacies: Concepts, policies and practices* (pp. 247–278). New York: Peter Lang.

Kress, G. (2003). *Literacy in a new media age.* New York: Routledge.

Lanskshear, C., & Knobel, M. (2008). *Digital literacies: Concepts, policies and practices.* New York: Peter Lang.

Leander, K. (2009). Composing with old and new media: Toward a parallel pedagogy. In V. Carrington & M. Robinson (Eds.), *Digital literacies: Social learning and classroom practices* (pp. 147–164). Los Angeles: Sage.

Leander, K., & Frank, A. (2006). The aesthetic production and distribution of image/subjects among online youth. *E–Learning, 3*(2), 185–206.

Lenhart, A., & Madden, M. (2007). *Social networking sites and teens.* Washington, DC: Pew Internet and American Family Project.

Lenhart, A., Arafeh, S. Smith, A. & Macgill, A. R. (2008). Writing, technology & teens: PEW Internet & American Life Project. Washington, DC: Pew Internet and American Life Project. Retrieved June 25, 2008, from http://www.pewinternet.org/PPF/r/247/report_display.asp

Lenhart, A., Kahne, J., Middaugh, E., Macgill, A., Evans, C., & Vitak, J. (2008). Teens, video games and civics. Washington, DC: Pew Internet and American Life Project. Retrieved August 23, 2009, from http://www.pewinternet.org/Reports/2008/Teens-Video-Games-and-Civics.aspx

Leu, D. J., O'Byrne, W. I., Zawilinski, L., McVerry, J. G., & Everett-Cacopardo, H. (2009). Expanding the New Literacies conversation. *Educational Researcher, 38*(4), 264–269.

Luckin, R., Clark, W., Graber, R., Logan, K., Mee, A., & Olive, M. (2009). Do Web 2.0 tools really open the door to learning? Practices, perceptions and profiles of 11-16-year-old students. *Learning, Media and Technology, 34*(2), 87–104.

Lundby, K. (Ed.). (2009). *Digital storytelling, mediated stories: Self-representations in New Media.* New York: Peter Lang.

McEneaney, J. E. (2006). Agent-based literacy theory. *Reading Research Quarterly, 41*(3), 352–371.

Mishra, P., & Koehler, M. J. (2006). Technological pedagogical content knowledge: A framework for teacher knowledge. *Teachers College Record, 108*(6), 1017–1054.

MIT New Media Literacy Center. (2008). Teaching new media literacies. Retrieved July 30, 2009, from http://newmedialiteracies.org

Muñoz, G., & Marín, M. (2006). Music is the connection: Youth cultures in Columbia. In P. Nilan & C. Feixa (Eds.), *Global youth? Hybrid identities, plural worlds* (pp. 130–148). London: Routledge.

Nelson, M. E., Hull, G., & Roche-Smith, J. (2008). Challenges of multimedia self-presentation: Taking, and mistaking, the show on the road. *Written Communication, 25*(4), 415–440.

Richardson, W. (2009). *Blogs, wikis, podcasts, and other powerful Web tools for the classroom* (2nd ed.). Los Angeles: Corwin Press.

Rosen, D., & Nelson, C. (2008). Web 2.0: A new generation of learners and education. *Computers in the Schools, 25*(3), 211–225.

Siegel, M. (2006). Rereading the signs: Multmodal tranformations in the field of literacy education. *Language Arts, 84*(1), 65–77.

Silverstone, R. (2007). *Media and morality: On the rise of the mediapolis.* Malden, MA: Polity Press.

Sutherland-Smith, W. (2002). Weaving the literacy web: Changes in reading from page to screen. *The Reading Teacher, 57*(7), 662–669.

Taub-Pervizpour, L. (2009). Digital storytelling with youth: Whose agenda is it? In J. Hartley & K. McWilliam (Eds.), *Story circle: Digital storytelling around the world* (pp. 245–251). Malden, MA: Wiley-Blackwell.

Thomas, A. (2007). *Youth online: Identity and literacy in the digital age.* New York: Peter Lang.

Tu, C.-H., Blocher, M., & Roberts, G. (2008). Constructs for Web 2.0 learning environments: A theatrical metaphor. *Educational Media International, 45*(4), 253–269.

Weinberger, D. (2007). *Everything is miscellaneous: The power of the new digital disorder.* New York: Times Books.

Willet, R. (2009). Young people's video productions as new sites of learning. In V. Carrington & M. Robinson (Eds.), *Digital literacies: Social learning and classroom practices* (pp. 13–25). Los Angeles: Sage.

Willis, P. (1990). *Common culture: Symbolic work at play in the everyday cultures of the young.* Boulder, CO: Westview Press.

24

Literacy and ICT in the Early Years

Rachael Levy and Jackie Marsh

In this chapter, we offer an overview of research on literacy and information and communication technologies (ICT) in the early years of schooling. The rationale for the focus on this age group is twofold. First, many of the reviews of ICT and literacy already in existence concentrate on children in the later stages of schooling (e.g., Andrews, 2004). Second, it is important for researchers in the field of ICT and literacy to be familiar with research that illuminates the practices of younger children, as this can inform approaches to work with older children and young people. The review therefore focuses on research relating to children aged from birth to 8 years.

The relationship between literacy and technology is a complex one. Marsh and Singleton (2009) suggested that:

> Technology has always been an essential part of literacy. In order to write, one needs tools and the nature of those tools inevitably shapes the writing process. In order to read, one also needs a technology—paper, print, computer screen, etc.—on which to present text, and the nature of that technology inevitably influences the literacy experience. (p. 1)

However, what is becoming increasingly obvious is that new technologies are fundamentally changing literacy practices and texts (Lankshear & Knobel, 2006). It is, therefore, timely to focus this review on literacy practices that are mediated by new technologies—what some have termed 'digital literacies' (Carrington & Robinson, 2009). This involves reading, writing and meaning-making with texts that are created using digital technologies and disseminated via a range of media such as computers, mobile phones, and televisions.

The chapter addresses three key areas of work. First, we consider research that has examined young children's digital literacy practices in homes. Many children are, from birth, immersed in a technological world and these experiences have profound consequences for their literacy development. We then move on to consider research that has illuminated

the way in which new technologies are informing pedagogical practice with regard to literacy in early years settings and classrooms. Finally, we examine recent research that has illuminated the continuities and discontinuities in digital literacy practices across home and school domains. We close the chapter by reflecting on the implications of our analysis for further research in this field.

ICT and Literacy in the Home

There is extensive evidence that young children are, from birth, immersed in a media and technology-rich environment. In the UK, Marsh, Brooks, Hughes, Ritchie, and Roberts (2005) conducted a survey of 1,852 parents of children aged from birth to 6 years in 10 Local Authorities in England in which young children's use of popular culture, media and new technologies was identified. The Digital Beginnings study concluded that many young children were competent users of technologies from an early age and that parents felt that children developed a wide range of skills, knowledge and understanding in this use. Plowman, McPake, and Stephen (2010) reported on a study conducted in Scotland in which they surveyed 346 families in Scotland and conducted 24 case studies of young children's use of technology in the home. This study identified that children and parents were active users of technology, that patterns of interaction differed across families due to a range of factors, such as parents' attitudes towards and experiences of technology, and that an increase in technological items in the home does not necessarily relate to amount of use of technology by children. This work resonates with a study conducted in the United States which indicated that children under the age of 6 are immersed in technology from birth (Rideout, Vandewate, & Wartella, 2003).

Much of this use of digital technology can be characterised as creative and playful in nature (Willet, Robinson, & Marsh, 2009) as it offers potential for children to engage as produsers (Bruns, 2006), to re-mix and mash-up cultural content in the production of new texts (Lankshear & Knobel, 2006). Media and digital cultures are arguably at the centre of leisure practices for many children in developed countries and this area of childhood culture has, more than any other, led to concerns regarding the commercialisation of childhood (Kenway & Bullen, 2001). However, what is frequently overlooked in these debates is the fact that commercial practices and childhood are mutually constitutive (Cook, 2008). Children are engaged in literacy practices linked to what Appadurai (1996) terms 'mediascapes'. Mediascapes reflect the global distribution of electronic media and images of the world created by media. These inter-relate to create narratives in which commodities and ideology are combined in complex ways and Appadurai argues that these mediascapes offer scripts for imagined lives. Globalised mediascapes are locally recontextualised in children's literacy practices, which are culturally situated in children's everyday lives.

Children undertake a range of reading and writing practices using digital technologies. Table 24.1 summarises the practices identified in a range of studies (Marsh, 2006, in press-a; Marsh et al., 2005).

Recent work (Marsh, in press-a) indicates that young children are becoming increasingly social in their reading and writing on the Internet. Whereas in previous eras children may have simply accessed favourite Internet sites, often media-related, to play games, there is now evidence that children are using social networking sites to interact with others in online play. This play sometimes takes place in virtual worlds, which are online simulations of offline spaces and involve the use of an avatar to represent individual users. Popular virtual worlds include sites such as *Club Penguin, Barbie Girls,* and *Webkinz.* What these kinds of activities offer is the opportunity for children to be engaged in social networks with both known and unknown interlocutors and they learn, from their earliest years, what is means to be involved in the participatory culture (Jenkins, Clinton, Purushotma, Robison, & Weigel, 2006) of the new media age.

There is, therefore, widespread evidence that young children are confident and competent users of a range of new technologies in the home and that, through this use, they develop understanding and knowledge relating to reading and writing on screens. In the next section of the chapter, we move on to consider how far ICT and literacy are integrated in early years classrooms.

ICT and Literacy in the Early Years Setting

It is now commonly expected that most children will encounter aspects of digital technology within the early years setting. Indeed, having gathered data from teachers and practitioners in four English cities, Bearne et al. (2007) discovered that young children are often exposed to computers, interactive whiteboards, televisions, videos, and digital cameras in their school or pre-school setting, while others also used mobile phones and games consoles in their role play situations. Yet what are the implications of this technology for pedagogic practice, particularly in relation to the teaching and learning of literacy?

As we suggested previously, it is becoming increasingly acknowledged that literacy and technology are

TABLE 24.1
Young Children's Digital Literacy Practices in Homes

Media	Texts read	Texts written
	Words and symbols on remote control	
	Electronic programming guide	
	Text included in games	
	Words, signs and symbols in programmes and advertisements	
Computer	Alphabet on keyboard	Random typing of letters
	Text on web sites	Writing of name
	Text instructions for programs	Writing lists, letters and stories
	Text in programs	Typing in words/ phrases in online sites such as games and virtual worlds
Handheld computers	Text instructions for programs	
	Text in programs	
Mobile phones/PDAs	Text on screen e.g. text messages	Pressing random letters
	Signs and symbols on the keypad	Choosing emoticons
Electronic games e.g. LeapPad	Alphabet on keyboards and text on screen e.g. alphabet games	Typing in letters and words
Console games	Text instructions for programs	
	Text in programs	
Musical hardware e.g. CD Players/ radios/karaoke machines	Words and symbols on operating systems	
	Words on screen with karaoke machines	
GPS technologies e.g. TomTom	Text on screen e.g. navigation page	
Other domestic electronic devices e.g. microwave, washer	Words, signs and symbols on the devices	

intrinsically related (Burnett, in press; Marsh & Singleton, 2009; Robinson & Mackey, 2003), but it is important that this relationship is understood within the context of the early years setting, if teachers and practitioners are able to effectively utilise such media within the classroom. As Marsh and Singleton (2009, p. 1) pointed out, research into literacy and technology has tended to follow two avenues of enquiry; the first seeking 'to determine the ways in which literacy needs to be redefined in a digital age', while the second has been concerned with investigating the ways in which 'technology can enhance learners' skills, knowledge and understanding in relation to the reading and writing of print'. Both of these strands of research have substantial implications for the early years setting. First, given the 'new textual landscapes' (Carrington, 2005) of modern communication systems, schools must acknowledge that definitions of literacy, and constructions of what it means to be 'literate', are indeed currently changing. But this raises questions about the extent to which the early years literacy curriculum has accommodated, or is attempting to accommodate these changes. Second, even though technology may be mediating change within the global discourse on literacy, it remains the case that children are expected to acquire a level of print literacy during their first years in school. Key questions relate to how far print literacy fits within this broader discourse on literacy and how effectively the early years curriculum allow children to develop understandings about print within this broader context.

To return to the first issue, it is clear from the research reviewed in the previous section that many children entering the formal education system today are already proficient in using a variety of digital media. Indeed Bearne et al. (2007, p. 11) reported that 'very young children show expertise in on-screen reading, even where homes have no computers', as the handling of such texts is now embodied within a culturally valued discourse. As a result, it appears that young children are developing the skills to become 'digitally literate' (Glister, 1997) before they come into the school setting. While this may mean that young children are developing strategies that allow them to access and read a variety of digital texts with fluency (Levy, 2009a), Merchant (2007) argued that the term should relate to more than a general confidence in handling screen texts, and should be orientated towards the 'study of written or symbolic representation that is mediated by new technology' (p. 121). In other words, the term 'digital literacy' can help to redefine conceptualisations of literacy as an ability to understand the many sign and symbol systems in existence within texts today as well as the ways in which children make sense of them within their home environments.

Many young children entering the school system today have therefore not only been exposed to a variety of digital and paper texts, but are already developing skills to help them make sense of complex multimodal features (Albers, Frederick, & Cowan, 2009). This has clear implications for the schooling of literacy. In a recent review of research into

technology and literacy in early childhood settings, Burnett (in press) cites nine studies which demonstrate 'the complex interactions that occur between children, technology, and their wide-ranging experiences of literacy'. For example, she noted how particular studies (Cohen, 2005; Teale & Gambrell, 2007) have shown how networked technologies, such as email, support children's on-going literacy development by creating new audiences for children's writing 'through engaging in new communities or managing existing communities in new ways' (Burnett, in press). Moreover, Burnett also explained that further research has shown that regular use of screen-based texts in early years settings has encouraged increasingly sophisticated interaction to occur between children themselves (Chung & Walsh, 2006; Hyun & Davis, 2005). This included skills of collaborative dialogue and exploratory communication.

It is clear that new media has much to offer the early years classroom, both in terms of children's day-to-day interaction with texts and as well as teaching approaches. Nevertheless it must be recognised that texts, whether they are paper-based or digital, carry particular affordances in terms of their value within the classroom. For example, the Interactive Whiteboard appears to be widely used in schools, however as Bearne et al. (2007, p. 23) point out, 'the large screen is not in itself a magic formula for transforming teaching. Its use can be stultifying if not planned as part of a varied approach to teaching.' It is possible that media such as the Interactive Whiteboard could end up being used in much the same way as a whiteboard or a flip chart if teachers do not recognise the potential of the resource, as the software does allow for considerable flexibility (given the features such as colour and sound effect) that can help teachers to meet the individual needs of children in their class. As Bearne et al. conclude, teachers can develop 'the potential afforded by the large screen in a new and exciting way' when they understand the possibilities within such texts (p. 23).

It therefore appears to be the case that rather than suggesting that young children should be exposed to digital texts in the early years setting to help them to 'do literacy', practitioners and policy makers need to recognise that digital texts 'are literacy'. Yet as Burnett (in press) points out, despite the fact that in England the government has published case studies demonstrating how technology can be used in the early years setting (DCSF, 2009), this does not translate into the curriculum. She stated that:

> The 'early learning goals' for 'communication, language and literacy', which establish expectations for what most children will achieve by the age of five (DCSF, 2008), contain no reference to children's engagement with digital texts. From age five onwards, the government currently recommends that children's literacy learning is structured by the primary National Strategy Framework for Literacy (PNS, 2006). Whilst this requires teachers to plan to use on-screen multimodal texts, assessment criteria still reflect the skills and knowledge associated with print-based alphabetic literacy.

This brings us to the second issue raised above. If schools are to acknowledge children's broader interactions with texts, as a consequence of the digital age, what are the implications for the teaching and learning of print-based alphabetic literacy? This issue was recently explored by Hassett (2006, p. 82) who argued that the reluctance for schools to accept new forms of reading 'has less to do with a "new" medium…and more to do with the way that alphabetic print literacy discourses are maintained in education.' Hassett goes on to claim that print-literacy skills need to become embedded within a broader discourse on reading that values the variety of sign and symbol systems in existence in texts today, including, but by no means confined to, the decoding of print.

What is more, further study has indicated that young children may already be developing not only understanding, but confidence in handling print through their interactions with screen texts in their own homes. In a recent longitudinal study of 12 young children (aged 3–6), Levy (2009a) discovered that these children were not only making meaning from iconic symbols and pictures within the context of the computer, but were making sense of printed prompts in much the same way. For example, many of the children appeared to understand the meaning of printed prompts such as '*Play*' or '*Play again?*', which they reported to mean 'Start' or 'Go'. The project data strongly suggested that the medium of the computer in particular allowed the children opportunities to make sense of print within a context that was meaningful and free from proficiency grading. Yet the study also indicated that this confidence in handling print was at risk of disruption by the demands of the school curriculum as the children moved to more formalised approaches to the teaching of reading in school.

As was indicated previously in our review of young children's use of virtual worlds, it is becoming increasingly clear that literacy in a new media age is leading to literacy practices that are embedded in social networks. Recent research in some early years classrooms has focused on the use of Web 2.0 sites and products and has indicated how powerful the adoption of some of these out-of-school practices can be for literacy learning. For example, blogging is now quite prevalent in many schools and in some early years settings, as it can offer valuable opportunities to connect with 'real-world' audiences outside of school (Marsh, 2009; Merchant, in press). Other Web 2.0 practices are becoming utilised in schools. In Marsh (in press-b), the work of a teacher of 6- and 7 year-olds in the north of England, Martin Waller, is outlined. He allows the children in 'Orange Class' to use the social networking system (SNS) Twitter to log their thoughts and activities over the course of a school day. Twitter enables users to upload to the Internet messages containing up to 140 characters, known as tweets. Twitter enables users to log accounts of their activities over the course of a day if they so wish, with some decrying this seemingly trivial use of technology (Sandy & Gallagher, 2009). However, others

suggest that these apparently mundane exchanges have the effect of thickening offline social ties and that there are numerous examples of the way in which SNS can have a positive impact on the lives of individuals (Dowdall, 2009; Ito et al., 2008). Martin enables the children to upload their photographs on Twitpic, which are then attached to one of their tweets and used to extend the children's communication, or reinforce their messages. Adults and other children using Twitter respond to 'Orange Class' and in this way, Martin ensures the children have an external audience for their work. As Merchant (in press) suggests:

> This raises questions about what happens as bounded classrooms are connected to diverse and fluid networked spaces with new possibilities for presenting, exchanging, and making meaning. Other studies (Burnett, 2009; Merchant, 2009) have suggested that teachers feel challenged once children move into fluid networked spaces and begin to explore their own paths.

This work suggests that it is fruitful for schools to find ways in which to develop children's own constructions of literacy practice, based on their everyday experiences, particularly in relation to the use of digital media. Unfortunately, these kinds of practices are not yet widespread. This means that sometimes, children have to resort to other measures in order to incorporate digital technologies into their school experience. This is wonderfully rendered in Karen Wohlwend's (2009) account of children who are located in print-centric early years classrooms, yet who long to play with the new technologies and media that are part of their everyday experiences outside of school. She details how one child, thwarted by the limitations of the toys on offer in the classroom, drew his own mobile phone:

> He gave an oblong piece of paper rounded corners and penciled a 3 by 3 array of squares below a much larger square to represent a numeric pad and an LCD screen. Additional phone features (receiver, compact size) were emphasized by adding play actions: he held the opened paper flat in the palm of his hand, raised his hand to his ear, talked into the paper for a few seconds, then snapped it shut with one hand, and tucked it into his pocket. (p. 125)

The 5-, 6-, and 7-year-old 'early adopters' in Wohlwend's (2009) study used paper and pencil to create mobile phones, ipods, and video games in order to bring their own cultural worlds into being in the face of technological neglect. This is a reminder that experiences of computer technology tend to be situated within the child's own unique social and cultural heritage (Facer, Furlong, Furlong, & Sutherland, 2003; Holloway & Valentine, 2003), and it seems that such digital 'funds of knowledge' (Moll, Amanti, Neff, & Gonzalez, 1992) appear to stem largely from the home setting. It is therefore important to consider the ways in which the literacy discourses of home and school relate to one another in terms of digital text use, which is the focus for the next section of the chapter.

ICT and Literacy: The Home, the School, and the Space in Between

In a study investigating 12 children's perceptions of reading, Levy (2008) describes how nursery school children were using aspects of their home experience, such as television texts, computer technology, popular culture, and play, to find continuity between home and school discourses on reading. For example, Shaun (aged 4) demonstrated confidence and skill when using unfamiliar computer texts in the classroom, even though his own experiences of interactive games within the home tended to be situated within television texts (interactive games on Sky television), handheld games consoles and games on his father's mobile phone. Yet even though Shaun had not been actively taught how to use a computer within either the home or school setting, he appeared to have developed a certain 'digital literacy' in handling technology that allowed him to access a variety of digital texts with fluency across the boundaries of home and school. This suggested that digital technology helped to create a comfortable space for Shaun in between the literacy discourses of home and school.

Yet the study indicated that for some of the children, discontinuities between home and school meant that they lost confidence in their own constructions of reading from their earliest years in school. As the domination of a 'schooled' discourse seemed to overrule their own constructions, some of the children began to devalue their own strategies to make sense from a variety of texts. For example, two girls in the study (Caitlyn and Kelly) were observed making regular use of the computer in their homes and were also described by their parents as displaying a substantial ability to navigate a variety of screen texts with independence. However, the nursery school teacher reported that both girls showed little interest in the computer within the school context, and rarely chose to use it when given a free choice of activity. Screen reading therefore became confined to the home setting for these children.

What is more, the study further revealed that aspects of the girls' book reading behaviour also became increasingly confined to the home setting. Having followed the children over the course of one academic year, changes were identified during the period of data collection. While Caitlyn in particular was observed creating detailed and sophisticated narratives based on the pictures in books, during her nursery year, by the time she was in the first year of elementary school she was claiming that this was not 'real' reading, because she now had to use the printed words to 'see if they sound' and make sure they are 'the right letters'. Similarly, in the final phase of the study, Kelly's mother reported that Kelly enjoyed reading her own books at home more than her schoolbooks. She went on to explain that Kelly 'is not reading word for word, but she'll look at the pictures' and will be 'putting quite a lot of expression in' when reading her own books at home, which contrasted with Kelly's reading of her schoolbooks which her mother described as being 'quite monotonous'.

In sum, this study revealed that these young children were developing broad constructions of reading literacy within their home settings, which allowed them to use a wide variety of multimodal cues, such as icon, colour, picture, sound, and print, in order to make sense of screen and paper based texts. Yet as the children moved into their first year of elementary school, definitions of reading became dominated by a 'schooled' discourse that focused on the need to decode printed text in books (and within schooled reading scheme texts in particular) (Levy, 2009b). As a consequence, many of the children in this study were seen to forsake their own strategies to make sense of text. Moreover, many of these children also lost confidence in themselves as readers, because their own 'home' constructions of reading did not match with those of the school. This strongly suggests that schools need to not only recognise the variety of literacy skills that children bring with them into school, but must find ways in which to build upon these valuable 'funds of knowledge' within the school context.

It now seems imperative that the prevalence of digital technology in modern society becomes more greatly reflected within the early years literacy curriculum. This does of course raise questions with regard to the implementation of the early years reading curriculum. In particular, what are the implications for assessment? First, as the above study has indicated, Bearne et al. (2007) also argue that young screen readers use a range of skills to access meaning from text, however they go on to claim that many of these skills can be described by the QCA Reading Assessment Focuses. When one reflects upon the specific targets for reading as outlined in the Foundation Curriculum, it is clear that young screen readers are meeting these targets by demonstrating a knowledge that print conveys meaning, recognition of familiar words, understandings of directionality, and the ability to access stories as well as displaying sequencing and information retrieval skills.

However, if early years settings are to show that they value children's home constructions of literacy, then it may be that they also need to recognise that some aspects of children's literacy skills cannot be described by assessment focuses. For example as Bearne et al. (2007) pointed out:

> Children's multimodal compositions, by their very nature, cannot be assessed in the same way as paper-based texts. The same is true of multimodal reading. The reading assessment focuses cannot capture the interpretation of sound, movement and colour as part of the reading process. (p. 20)

Perhaps the time has come to re-evaluate the role of assessment altogether within the early years literacy curriculum. Rather than focusing attention on formal literacy assessment, perhaps schools should concern themselves more solidly with finding ways to build young children's confidence in themselves as readers and writers of text. Given the issues covered in this chapter, this will include widening opportunities for young children to engage with a variety of different paper and screen based texts during their early years in school, and finding ways to encourage the development of individual literacy identity through the use of meaningful contexts.

Conclusion

In this chapter, we have considered ways in which literacy and ICT relate to each other across home and school domains. From this overview, we can identify a number of areas in which there is need for further research in the years ahead. First, much of the research considered here has been undertaken in the developed world and there is a need to extend this to ensure that literacy and ICT in a global context can be the site for analysis. Second, there is still much that needs to be understood about the way in which children's understanding of digital literacy is constructed through inter-generational practices as well as peer-to-peer interaction. Emergent research (Voida & Greenberg, 2009) on the inter-generational use of console games, such as Nintendo Wii, for example, indicates that the dynamics between family members are a rich site for further analysis in the development of an understanding of how family cultures shape practices. Third, the significant work that has been undertaken on young children's critical literacy practices (Vasquez, 2004) needs to be extended to include digital texts, so that young children can develop further their ability to analyse critically the range of online texts they encounter, which are often shaped by discourses of commercialisation. Finally, there is a need for research that can inform the development of innovative curricula and pedagogy that are relevant for a new media age. We need to understand issues relating to children's meaning-making across multiple modes, and what progression might look like in this regard. Given the pace of change due to the rapid development of technologies, this work needs to be undertaken urgently if we are to enable young children to join the digital 'literacy club' (Smith, 1987) of the 21st century.

References

Albers, P., Frederick, T., & Cowan, K. (2009). Features of gender: An analysis of the visual texts of third grade children. *Journal of Early Childhood Literacy, 9*(2), 234–260.

Andrews, R. (Ed.). (2004). *The impact of ICT on literacy education.* London: Routledge.

Appadurai, A. (1996). *Modernity at large: Cultural dimensions of globalization.* Minneapolis: University of Minnesota Press.

Bearne, E., Clark, C., Johnson, A., Manford, P., Mottram, M., & Wolstencroft, H. (2007). *Reading on screen.* Leicester: United Kingdom Literacy Association (UKLA).

Bruns, A. (2006). Towards produsage: Futures for user-led content production. In F. Sudweeks, H. Hrachovec, & C. Ess (Eds.), *Proceedings: Cultural attitudes towards communication and technology 2006* (pp. 275–284). Perth, Australia: Murdoch University. Retrieved August 22, 2007, from http://snurb.info/files/12132812018_towards_produsage_0.pdf

Burnett, C. (in press). Technology and literacy in early childhood educational settings: a review of research. *Journal of Early Childhood Literacy.*

Carrington, V. (2005). New textual landscapes, information and early literacy. In J. Marsh (Ed.), *Popular culture, new media and digital literacy in early childhood* (pp. 13–27). London: RoutledgeFalmer.

Carrington, V., & Robinson, M. (2009). *Digital literacies: Social learning and classroom practices.* London: Sage.

Chung, Y., & Walsh, H. D. (2006). Constructing a joint story-writing space: The dynamics of young children's collaboration at computers. *Early Education and Development, 17*(3), 373–420.

Cohen, R. (2005). An early literacy telecommunication exchange pilot project: The MMM project. *Educational Media International, 42* (2), 109–115.

Cook, D. (2008). The missing child in consumption theory. *Journal of Consumer Culture, 8,* 219–243.

Department for Children Schools and Families (DCSF). (2009). *ICT in the foundation stage: Case studies.* Retrieved July 31, 2009, from http://nationalstrategies.standards.dcsf.gov.uk/search/results/%22ICT+in+the+foundation+stage%22+nav%3A46398+facets%3A24315+args%3Asource%3Dlucene?solrsort=nav_idx_score_46398+desc%2C_type+asc

Dowdall, C. (2009). The texts of me and the texts of us: improvisation and polished performance in social networking sites. In R. Willett, M. Robinson, & J. Marsh (Eds.), *Play, creativities and digital cultures* (pp. 73–91). New York: Routledge.

Facer, K., Furlong, J., Furlong, R., & Sutherland, R. (2003). *Screenplay: Children and computing in the home.* London: RoutledgeFalmer

Glister, P. (1997). *Digital literacy,* New York: Wiley.

Hassett, D. (2006). Signs of the times: The governance of alphabetic print over "appropriate" and "natural" reading development. *Journal of Early Childhood Literacy, 6*(1), 77–103.

Holloway, S. L., & Valentine, G. (2003). *Cyberkids: Children in the information age.* London: RoutledgeFalmer.

Hyun, E., & Davis, G. (2005). Kindergartners' conversations in a computer-based technology classroom, *Communication Education, 54*(2), 118–135.

Ito, M., Horst, H. A., Bittanti, M., boyd, d., Herr-Stephenson, B., Lange, P. G., et al. (2008). *Living and learning with new media: Summary of findings from the digital youth project.* The John D. and Catherine T. MacArthur Foundation Reports on Digital Media and Learning. Retrieved May 2009 from http://digitalyouth.ischool.berkeley.edu/report

Jenkins, H., Clinton, K., Purushotma, R., Robison, A., & Weigel, M. (2006). *Confronting the challenges of participatory culture: Media education for the 21st century.* An occasional paper on digital media and learning. The John D. and Catherine T. MacArthur Foundation. Retrieved May 2009 from http://digitallearning.macfound.org/site/c.enJLKQNlFiG/b.2108773/apps/nl/content2.asp?content_id={CD911571-0240-4714-A93B-1D0C07C7B6C1}andnotoc=1

Kenway, J., & Bullen, E. (2001). *Consuming children: Education – entertainment – advertising.* Buckingham, UK: Open University Press.

Lankshear, C., & Knobel, M. (2006). *New literacies>: Everyday practices and classroom learning* (2nd ed.). Maidenhead, UK: Open University Press.

Levy, R. (2008). Third spaces' are interesting places; applying 'third space theory' to nursery-aged children's constructions of themselves as readers. *Journal of Early Childhood Literacy, 8*(1), 43–66.

Levy, R. (2009a). You have to understand words…but not read them'; Young children becoming readers in a digital age. *Journal of Research in Reading, 32*(1), 75–91.

Levy, R. (2009b). Children's perceptions of reading and the use of reading scheme texts. *Cambridge Journal of Education, 39*(3), 361–377.

Marsh, J. (2006). Global, local/ public, private: Young children's engagement in digital literacy practices in the home. In J. Rowsell & K. Pahl (Eds.), *Travel notes from the new literacy studies: Case studies in practice* (pp. 19–38). Clevedon, UK: Multilingual Matters.

Marsh, J. (2009). Productive pedagogies: Play, creativity and digital cultures in the classroom. In R. Willett, M. Robinson, & J. Marsh

(Eds.), *Play, creativity and digital cultures* (pp. 200–218). New York: Routledge.

Marsh, J. (in press-a). Young children's play in online virtual worlds. *Journal of Early Childhood Research.*

Marsh, J. (in press-b). 'The ghosts of reading past, present and future: material resources for reading in homes and schools . In K. Hall, U. Goswami, C. Harrison, S. Ellis, & J. Soler (Eds.), *Interdisciplinary perspectives on learning to read: Culture, cognition and pedagogy,* London: Routledge.

Marsh, J., Brooks, G., Hughes, J., Ritchie, L., & Roberts, S. (2005). *Digital beginnings: Young children's use of popular culture, media and new technologies.* Sheffield, UK: University of Sheffield. Retrieved January 2009, from http://www.digitalbeginings.shef.ac.uk/

Marsh, J., & Singleton, C. (2009). Editorial: Literacy and technology: Questions of relationship. *Journal of Research in Reading, 32*(1), 1–5.

Merchant, G. (2007). Writing in the future in the digital age, *Literacy, 41*(3), 118–128.

Merchant, G. (in press). Web 2.0, new literacies, and the idea of learning through participation. *English Teaching: Practice and Critique.*

Moll, L. C., Amanti, C., Neff, D., & Gonzalez, N. (1992). Funds of knowledge for teaching using a qualitative approach to connect homes and classrooms. *Theory into Practice, XXXI*(2), 132–141.

Plowman, L., McPake, J., & Stephen, C. (2010). The technologisation of childhood? Young children and technology in the home. *Children and Society, 24(1),* 63–74.

Rideout, V. J., Vandewater, E. A., & Wartella, E. A. (2003). *Zero to six: Electronic media in the lives of infants, toddlers and preschoolers.* Washington, DC: Kaiser Foundation.

Robinson, M., & Mackey, M. (2003). Film and television. In N. Hall, J. Larson, & J. Marsh (Eds.), *Handbook of early childhood literacy* (pp. 126–141). London: Sage.

Sandy, M., & Gallagher, I. (2009, January 3). How boring: Celebrities sign up to Twitter to reveal the most mundane aspect of their lives. *Mail Online.* Retrieved May 2009 from http://www.dailymail.co.uk/tvshowbiz/article-1104726/How-boring-Celebrities-sign-Twitter-reveal-mundane-aspect-lives.html

Smith, F. (1987). *Joining the literacy club: Further essays into education.* Portsmouth, NH: Heinemann.

Teale, W., & Gambrell, L. (2007). Raising urban students' literacy achievement by engaging in authentic, challenging work. *Reading Teacher, 60*(8), 728–739.

Vasquez, V. M. (2004). *Negotiating critical literacies with young children.* Mahwah, NJ: Erlbaum.

Voida, A., & Greenberg, S. (2009). Collocated intergenerational console gaming. Research Report 2009-932-11, Department of Computer Science, University of Calgary, Calgary, Alberta T2N 1N4, Canada. Retrieved November 2009 from http://grouplab.cpsc.ucalgary.ca/grouplab/uploads/Publications/Publications/2009-InterGenerational.Report2009-932-11.pdf

Willet, R., Robinson, M., & Marsh, J. (Eds.). (2008). *Play, creativity and digital cultures.* New York: Routledge.

Wohlwend, K. (2009). Early adopters: Playing new literacies and pretending new technologies in print-centric classrooms. *Journal of Early Childhood Literacy, 9*(2), 117–140.

25

The Material and the Situated

What Multimodality and New Literacy Studies Do for Literacy Research

JENNIFER ROWSELL AND KATE PAHL

Caught between discourses at home and school, deeply committed to the relations and values lived within his family, Jake struggled to negotiate a space for himself as a young reader and writer in the classroom. He practiced school literacies—sometimes giving himself up to the task of writing about car racing or family events, sometimes reading books reflective of his interests. Storylines voiced about him in his family, however, often seemed a stronger pull, a more powerful shaping of his boyhood identities. (Hicks, 2002, p. 123)

Introduction

Deborah Hicks' evocative depiction of the literacy worlds of two White, working-class children, their communities, and the implications of both for the future of other working-class children serves as an apt segue for a chapter on what multimodality and New Literacy Studies contribute to literacy education. Multimodal and ethnographic perspectives, together and separately, capture a liminal space between home and school and between beloved, familiar objects and pedagogic ones informing and making more explicit the discontinuities across domains of practice that can cause difficulties for students such as Jake. Jake's capacity to write about NASCAR miniatures alongside using a basal reader captures so well the subtle ways in which school literacy becomes relevant to learners like Jake in a detailed, situated, material way. Looking as much at the materiality of Jake's car and what value it has for the learner as we do at a set of practices used to incorporate the car into a writing activity gives a clear picture of a literacy learning moment and what it can tell us about a learner.

Over the past 10 years there has been a steady braiding of the fields of multimodality and New Literacy Studies. Part of reason for this interweaving of two related yet different fields of literacy research and education lies in the explosion of multimodal texts and engagement and participation with them across a wide range of sociocultural contexts.

From a paper crane that a middle school student makes, to a wiccan fanzine a high school student contributes to, to an adult's fascination about old friends on her Facebook page, each one of these texts and practices rely as much on the manipulation of modes to create an effect as it does on social practice and situated conditions of identity. There is more of a necessity than ever to look as much at material qualities of texts and their relationship to the meaning-maker as there is to look at literacy practice being shaped by context and the identities of meaning makers.

Literacy can be understood as being a situated social practice that has links to everyday life (Street, 1984; Barton & Hamilton, 1998). Texts are also multimodal and have material qualities, as they contain words and images and these both work together to create meaning (Kress, 1997; Kress & Van Leeuwen, 1996). In our work, we wanted to link literacy, multimodality, and material culture. When a child connects to literacy, and is asked to write a story, this is the end of a long process of meaning making that could begin in a different setting, in the everyday, for example; with Hicks in mind, a child could love cars, and be obsessed with collecting cars. This interest spills into a story about cars. This could then become crafted as a digital story, and or written or narrated as a narrative text. School is one domain of practice, home another (Barton & Hamilton, 1998). By linking together the material, everyday life of a child, with narrative, two things are brought together, and domains of practice, home and school, are then linked through text-making.

Multimodality and New Literacy Studies as a Heuristic

There are two truisms of literacy today. Number one, in Brian Street's words "literacy is always instantiated, its potential realized through local practices" (2003, p. 8). Number two, we cannot escape multiple modalities in texts and practices, beyond the written word. Returning to *Travel Notes From the New Literacy Studies* (Pahl & Rowsell, 2006) in which we first conflated multimodality with New Literacy Studies, we talked about focusing on the ethnographic dimension of multimodal communicative practices to lift out not only the identities and the habitus (Bourdieu, 1990) of individual meaning makers, but also locally and globally shaped practice. As a lens for practice, the ethnographic and the semiotic gives a more nuanced picture of meaning making in situated, textured contexts. Moments when meanings makers produced texts with traces of social practice, contexts, and sedimented identities, we argued, were instance of practice to be analyzed for broader implications. In this way, we understand the process of the local and the global as one of *instances*.

Multimodality takes its roots from the work of Gunther Kress (1997, 2003) and even further back to Michael Halliday (1978). Halliday wrote about locating language study in social context and using social context as a way of understanding text. Kress took the concept of texts in context and moved it into the direction of the notion of the motivated sign (Kress, 1997). Signs made or used by meaning makers are motivated by the interests of the sign-maker. The theory is and was groundbreaking because it opened up communicative events beyond a sole gaze on the written word to extend into other modalities. Taken up and used as an optic in other studies, multimodality increasingly becomes a way of breaking apart a literacy event. Today, multimodality is an accepted approach to literacy education and used as an informing principle in many studies (Harste & Albers, 2007; Jewitt, 2005; Lancaster, 2003; Leander, 2002; Marsh, 2005, 2006; Pahl, 2004; Schwartz & Rubinstein-Ávila, 2006). A main impetus for adopting a multimodal approach is to look at multimodal texts that children, adolescents, and adults use all of the time and to explain its design and content as visual, sound-based, animated, etc.

New Literacy Studies (NLS) grew out of the work of scholars such as Sylvia Scribner and Michael Cole (1981) and their anthropological work with the Vai people in Liberia to explore what represents literacy practices in day-to-day life. What they found at the time of their research was that literacy happens across communities and cannot be viewed as sets of ideas and practices solely tied to schooling. In 1983, Shirley Brice Heath conducted her 10-year study of literacy practices in three communities in the Carolinas establishing that literacy practices not only existed outside of school, but also that literacy practices were shaped by the context and identities in which and by which they are used. Shortly after Heath's study, Brian Street (1984) examined literacy practices in different parts of the same community in Iran, finding correspondingly that literacy practices are shaped by context and identity, and also that an ideological view of literacy takes account of practices, concepts, texts, identities, and contexts in which they take place. Instantiated into these perspectives is the issue of power in that Standard English was seen as happening in school, which rendered outside literacy practices as less powerful

and relevant. These international studies sparked a host of other studies that looked at ideological models of literacy practices in local and global contexts (Barton & Hamilton, 1998; Davies, 2006; Gee, 1996; Hull & Schultz, 2004; Hymes, 1996; Janks & Comber, 2006; Luke & Carrington, 2002). As researchers, it is important to be sensitized to the global as well as the local when analyzing literacy events and practices (Brandt & Clinton, 2006).

Behind both NLS and multimodality disciplines sit epistemologies and research methods: semiotics and ethnography. Semiotics is a grammar of sign systems, and with the dominance of multimodal texts, a semiotic perspective allows researchers to broaden the nature of text analysis. Ethnography provides the context and the tracing process to understand texts. We see ethnography in the context of a focus on meaning in context (Geertz, 1993). As researchers, we recognize that the richness of thick description is invaluable in unpacking how texts are created. Bringing semiotics and ethnography together provides a way of viewing texts as material and situated, as tracers of social practices and contexts. This method of analysis gives an ideological quality to multimodality and multimodality gives ethnography and New Literacy Studies an analytic tool to understand artifacts.

Multimodal Practice as Ideological

In light of our joint and separate research, we have found that the complementarity of New Literacy Studies and multimodality opens up new spaces for students. This accords with Street's (1993) notion of an ideological model of literacy as inextricably linked to cultural and power structures in society. Such a view of literacy is in stark contrast with an autonomous model which conceptualizes literacy in technical terms, treating it as independent of social context. Isolating literacy events as in particular events when literacy takes place and literacy practices which look at patterns within such events achieves what Janet Maybin (2000) talked about as a main goal of New Literacy Studies:

> I shall suggest that the taking on of more complex ideas about discourse and intertextuality in these studies of literacy enables the researchers to more clearly conceptualise the pivotal role of literacy practices in articulating the links between individual people's everyday experience, and wider social institutions and structures. (p. 197)

The key point here is the lifting out of everyday experiences and tying it to macro concerns such as issues of power and limits in power due to a mismatch between sanctioned literacy practices and contextualized literacy practices.

Where in the past we have blended New Literacy Studies with multimodality (Pahl & Rowsell, 2005, 2006; Rowsell & Pahl, 2007), in our more recent work we take New Literacy Studies and the ethnographic more into the multimodal and the material. A presiding claim is that NLS and multimodality as a heuristic more powerfully illustrates the everyday, the habitus in texts made and valued by meaning makers. Viewing the everyday and situated in the materiality of texts gives meaning makers more power as learners. As multimodal events unfold, in that process, it is possible to watch modes sedimenting identity (Rowsell & Pahl, 2007). The choice of mode is itself a trace of meaning-making as modes are infused with emotion. There is a felt connection with modes chosen during meaning-making which has a direct tie to habitus (Bourdieu, 1990) as an unfolding of the everyday. Bi-modal representation means that meaning-makers can merge different modes such as visuals and sounds to make complex artifacts. Multimodal events such as creating digital stories (Pahl & Rowsell, 2010), draw on multimodal practices. Given that multimodality gives the meaning maker more agency and more license to pull on habitus, it represents a more current, viable, and indeed ideological approach to literacy education.

Implications of NLS and Multimodality for Research

Over the past decade, we have adopted an NLS-multimodal lens for studies featured in Table 25.1. The aim of fore-grounding the chart is to illustrate the potential for New Literacy Studies and multimodality as a lens for practice. Each perspective spotlighted in the table represents a strand present in our research that can feed into new ways of using New Literacy Studies and multimodality.

Literacy as Situated In adopting an ethnographic-NLS lens to literacy research, researchers can uncover meanings of literacy to participants, the academic community, and themselves that suspend previous cultural constructs and narratives and acknowledge and listen to others' ways of making meaning. By focusing on listening as a methodology (Back, 2007), researchers can make sense of meanings that reside not only in texts, but in visual modes. For example, in Kate's project in Thirsk, North Yorkshire, UK, whereby parents made digital stories with their children about their favourite objects, a mother described to her 8-year-old daughter, who was filming her, what a pink crystal meant to her:

Lucy: I got this crystal off my friend because I have had a hard time in the last couple of years and she thought

TABLE 25.1
Many Faces of Multimodal and New Literacy Studies Work

Face	Timeframe	Researcher	Aim
Literacy as Situated	1999–2003 4 year study	Kate Pahl	**Three homes in London:** This study was an ethnographic study of three boys and their meaning making in three London homes.
	1998–2001 4 year study	Jennifer Rowsell	**Texts as Traces of Practice:** This study was an ethnographic-style study of the educational publishing industry.
Literacy as Multimodal	2008–2009 3 months	Kate Pahl Jenny Wells, The World of James Herriot Museum	**My Family, My Story:** This was a digital storytelling project that worked with five families to create five digital stories, together with a museum and a school.
	2009 3 months	Kate Pahl Steve Pool Sally Newham Gail Harrison	**A Reason to Write**: Using artifacts to create reasons to write in the classroom.
	2006–2009 3 year study	Jennifer Rowsell, Julie Dunham, Courtney Crane, Barbara O'Breza, and Doug Levandowskil	**Artifactual English:** This project is an ethnographic-style research study looking at the artifactual lives of sixty teenagers using interviews, observations, and artifactual collection and analysis as the main mode of data collection and analysis.
Literacy as Sedimenting Identities	2005–2007 2 year study	Kate Pahl Heads Together Sally Bean	**Capturing the Community:** The study was an ethnographic study of the impact of a group of artists on the work of children in a school in Barnsley.
	2006–2007 1 year 3 months	Kate Pahl Andy Pollard Zahir Rafiq	**Ferham Families:** This project created a museum exhibition, Ferham Families, from ethnographic interviews with five family members of families who migrated to the UK from Pakistan in the 1960s.
	2003–2005 2 year study	Jennifer Rowsell, Marianna Diiorio, Kathy Broad, Mary Lynn Tessaro	**Family Literacy Experiences:** The study was a focus group and interview-based study of family literacy practices of eight families and the stories of their grade four child.
Literacy as Ecological	2009–2011 2 years	Kate Pahl Margaret Lewis Louise Ritchie	**Inspire Rotherham:** An ecological study of the impact of a literacy initiative in Rotherham on parents' learning using visual and ecological methodologies.
	2006–2009 3 year study	Sue Nichols PI), Helen Nixon (PI), Jennifer Rowsell (Partner Investigator), Sophia Rainbird	**Parents Networks of Information:** This project takes an ethnographic, ecological, and geosemiotic perspective on how parents develop networks of information within three quite different communities in Australia and the United States.

it would help and because I had that one I collect a few little ones as well.

J: Does it help?

Lucy: No (long pause, laughter)...it looks nice! (long pause)

J: Does it feel special to you.

Lucy: Yes, because my very close friend gave me it.

Artifacts can become a tool for listening (Pahl & Rowsell, 2010) and can become imbued with wider meanings because of their complex modal properties. The crystal was pink, it was a natural stone, and her friend gave it to her. This connective node of representations plus history provided a place from which to tell a story. Literacy is situated within material culture and is it in itself a material cultural practice that links to storytelling in community contexts.

Jennifer's work with parents and their children and her work with teenagers lifted out valuable, naturalized practices that can be built upon in school. For example, in her high school project, Artifactual English, by harnessing canonical texts to familiar, digital texts such as Facebook, students built on their tacit understanding and appreciation of multimodal texts within more traditional, written texts. Student participants created Facebook profiles for characters in *Black Boy* such as Richard or Bessie and combined their digital practices such as doing a Google search on popular music in the 1920s and then speculating on the kinds of music, literature, and interests that characters in Wright's novel would enjoy (Wright, 1945). What the assignment compelled students to think about was what characters value, why they value them, who is in their inner circle, how to multimodally represent characters. Figure 25.1 illustrates

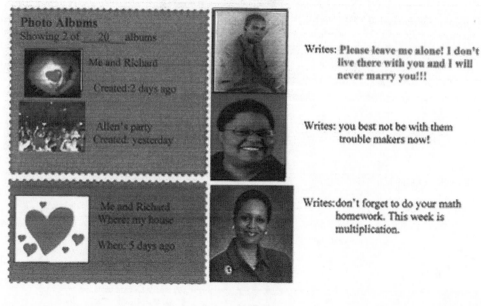

Figure 25.1

how students designed Facebook pages about characters in *Black Boy*. To create a Facebook profile, students had to choose a photo that resembles the character, create a typical dialogue that characters might have on their wall, and even choose particular games or applications that they might use. Grounding literacy in student worlds, lived experiences, and their community offers them more ways to appreciate its relevance in their lives.

Literacy as Multimodal A challenge for literacy researchers has been a growing recognition that we can no longer focus on alphabetic print as the unit of study in literacy education. The balance is shifting to the visual and other channels or modes of expression for literacy research and pedagogy to remain current and to less the gap between monomodal school policy and multimodal forms of living and communicating. By making an understanding of literacy multimodal, the affordances of meaning making open up. For example, children move swiftly from talk, to model making, and then to storying and writing (Pahl, 2009). In a small scale project Kate conducted called 'A Reason to Write' in an ex-mining community school in Yorkshire, UK, children aged 4–6 created models of a giant castle, worked with giant artifacts such as a giant shoe, and drew giant footprints on the playground (see Figure 25.2). This footprint was then followed up with writing, such as the inscribed 'big' beside the shoe, and stories about the giant. The affordances of the multimodal boxes to create the giant's castle, using the chalk to make the big words on the playground, and then the spilling over into talk from that experience widened the writing of the young children. When literacy is understood as multimodal, and the roughness of chalk on a playground is acknowledged, then the meanings are stretched.

In Jennifer's work, she has moved from print-based technologies and modal choice and its tie to meaning makers to digital spaces as pathways to understanding students' literacy practices (Rowsell & Burke, 2009; Rowsell, 2009; Sheridan & Rowsell, 2010). In a digital literacies study with Anne Burke, Jennifer found that middle school students have sophisticated understandings of interface design, story plots and structures, and intertextuality, but at the same time lack core academic literacies (Street, 2005). One case study, Peter, stands out for his in-depth understanding of Naruto and the concept of Chakra, yet he exhibits very little interest in reading and writing in-school (Rowsell & Burke, 2009).

Literacy as Sedimenting Identities The texts children, adolescents, adults make and value can tell us so much about how they learn, who features in their lives, and what events were pivotal. A consistent and powerful thread in our research draws from an interest in locating identities and even fractures of identities within texts (Rowsell & Pahl, 2007). For example, Kate observed how a group of girls sedimented fractal shards of identity in a multimodal text, creating an ocean environment in which stories of home and school, lining up and having babies, were sedimented over time in the course of the making of the boxes, and, then, as conversations shifted in context, the boxes themselves became differently understood and contextualised (Pahl, 2009).

Situating literacy practices and understanding identities and their connections to literacy can be achieved through observations and interviews, but if identified identities are fleeting and often ephemeral. Locating fractures of identities in texts and practices with texts is in some ways a more tangible and concrete way of locating meaning makers in contexts. Histories of particular localities and people in these localities, and individuated histories that accompany them, can be read off of texts. For this reason,

Figure 25.2

we have argued that ethnographies of literacy practices can yield powerful results. By situating literacy within a wider sociohistorical context, and making the connections alive between felt experience and textual practices, through an imaginative effort of ethnographic work, a more critical and nuanced understanding emerges of the relationship between literacy and identity in relation to social practice (Blackburn & Clark, 2007; Willis, 2000).

Literacy as Ecological Viewing communities and neighborhoods as ecologies is a way of isolating the situated nature of contexts and it imbues the locating effect of a study. As ecologies, communities have hubs or centres of activity and these hubs carry their own unique set of literacy practices. Taking an ecological approach to data collection means documenting commercial spaces, institutional spaces, places of worship, schools, and health clinics. Taking an NLS-multimodal research entails taking equal account of surroundings and practices in surroundings as it does interpreting the material quality and even geosemiotics of spaces. Kate is conducting a study in Rotherham that uses Google map to trace learning journeys of parents across the borough. By asking parents to use disposable cameras to map their encounters with literacy providers, she is creating a research space that is participatory and provides a way of accessing visual methods of hearing parents' voices. By looking at communities in relation to the contexts for interactions and mapping those contexts in spatial forms, the research gains an additional layer of 'thick description,' following Geertz' point that,

> No one lives in the world in general. Everybody, even the exiled, the drifting, the diasporic, or the perpetually moving, lives in some confined and limited stretch of it—'the world around here.' (1996, p. 262)

The ecologies of literacy make connections between lived experience, home, everyday life, and the ways in which literacy intersects with that, through letters, school newsletters, library and sports events, mother and toddler groups. These multifaceted literacy experiences can be perceived as spaces through which parents can traverse and experience in a community setting that is itself agentive and changing. This way of mapping literacies across neighborhoods links up individuals with contexts, community activist groups and literacy organisations with schools and families to enable new connections to be explored across these spaces that illuminate how parents perceive the agencies and literacy providers around them and how these providers impact upon home spaces.

In the multi-sited, international project Jennifer is involved in with Sue Nichols, Helen Nixon, and Sophia Rainbird at the University of South Australia, the research team takes an ecological approach to analyzing three neighborhoods in relation to parents' networks of information about children's literacy and development. Their study has three interconnecting dimensions as part of its ecological survey:

1. An environmental focus: artifact collection, mapping, visual documentation, and observation in three contrastive sites
2. An organizational focus: interviews with information workers, network tracing, and artifact collection.
3. A family focus: ethnographic participant observation, interviews, and artifact collection.

Part of the study involves using technological tools such as Google map to chart out key landmarks in communities, to document where case study participants go with their small children, to highlight areas with less access to information and materials, and so forth. Time-space grids are used as a part of the methodology to chart how parents talk about their networks of literacy information in relation to their own childhood and their child's past/more recent past juxtaposed with where these moments happen in space, whether it is at home, in the community, in cyberspace, etc. Finally, geosemiotics has provided a language for analyzing texts and discourses in such artifacts as signs, billboards, leaflets, and flyers (Scollon & Scollon, 2003).

Conclusion

Seeing literacy as materially situated enabled new kinds of connections to be made. Literacy can be mapped, as in the ecological studies described above, and thereby conceptualized differently in relation to contexts, activities, and practices and the connections between them. Literacy can be understood as linked to local practice but also these local practices can have diasporic, global contexts, such as the context of migration (Appadurai, 1996). We would argue that it is important 'to examine the relationship between the local and global from the perspective of the local' (Blackburn & Clark, 2007, p. 19). Listening to the local means an active focus on listening methodologies, from using digital stories, to community exhibitions, such as Kate's work for Ferham Families that resulted in a website and set of learning resources (www.everyobjecttellsastory.org.uk).

It can also result in creating new spatial and ecological research methods, such as using Google map, or using architects to work with children, as a powerful way to for articulate new visions of communities. For example, Barbara Comber's (2010) work has been focused on giving children the tools to articulate a lived vision of what their communities could look like as part of a critical literacies project. Rogers, Mosley, Kramer, and the Literacy for Social Justice Teacher Research Group (2009) have advocated a critical literacy pedagogy that engages with parents and children's lived experiences of inequality and then create spaces to argue for social change in practical ways. In our own work, we have suggested a pedagogy of artifactual critical literacies—that is, using artifacts to find out about the experiences students bring to schooling and to their narratives and explore, through imaginative ways, the links between lived experience and socio historical contexts (Pahl & Rowsell, 2010). This requires an ethnographic imagination (Willis, 2000) and a commitment to creating spaces for listening that are dialogic, open, and alive to how people's everyday life connects with the texts they make and the representations they produce (Back, 2007). If literacy is seen as materially situated, it looks different—it becomes something that reflects the reality of the lived world and its everyday-ness. It ceases to be autonomous (Street, 1993); instead it is ideological and can be linked to timescales, spaces, and places of lived experience, global identities and local concerns. By linking New Literacy Studies with multimodality, a lens appears that shifts literacy into a space that accounts for local practice, lived experience, and the imaginative and cultural spaces of the everyday.

References

Appadurai, A. (1996). *Modernity at large: Cultural dimensions of globalization.* Minneapolis: University of Minneapolis Press.

Back, L. (2007). *The art of listening.* London: Berg.

Barton, D., & Hamilton, M. (1998). *Local literacies: Reading and writing in one community.* London: Routledge.

Blackburn, M., & Clark, C. (Eds.). (2007). *Literacy research for political action and social change.* New York: Peter Lang.

Bourdieu, P. (1990). *The logic of practice* (R. Nice, Trans.). Cambridge, UK: Polity Press,

Brandt, D., & Clinton, K. (2006). Afterword. In K. Pahl & J. Rowsell (Eds.), *Travel notes from the new literacy studies: Instances of practice* (pp. 254–258). Clevedon, UK: Multilingual Matters.

Comber, B. (2010). Critical literacies in place: Teachers who work for just and sustainable communities. In J. Lavia & M. Moore (Eds.), *Decolonizing community contexts* (pp. 46–57). London: Routledge.

Davies, J. (2006). Escaping to the borderlands: An exploration of the internet as a cultural space for teenaged Wiccan girls. In K. Pahl & J. Rowsell (Eds.), *Travel notes from the new literacy studies: Instances of practice* (pp. 57–71). Clevedon, UK: Multilingual Matters.

Gee, J. P. (1996). *Social linguistics and literacies: Ideology in discourses* (2nd ed.). London: Taylor and Francis.

Geertz, C. (1993). *The interpretation of cultures.* London: Fontana Press. (Original work published 1973)

Geertz, C. (1996). Afterword. In S. Feld & K. H. Basso (Eds.), *Sense of place* (pp. 259–262). Santa Fe, NM: School of American Research Press.

Halliday, M. (1978). *Language as social semiotic: The social interpretation of language and meaning.* London: Arnold.

Harste, J., & Albers, P. (2007). The arts, new literacies, and multimodality. *English Education, 40*(1), 3–5.

Heath, S. B. (1983). *Ways with words: Language, life and work in communities and classrooms.* Cambridge, UK: Cambridge University Press.

Hicks, D. (2002). *Reading lives: Working-class children and literacy learning.* New York: Teachers College Press.

Hull, G., & Schultz, K. (2004). *School's out: Bridging out-of-school literacies with classroom practice.* New York: Teacher's College Press.

Hymes, D. (Ed.). (1996). *Ethnography, linguistics, narrative inequality: Towards an understanding of voice.* London: Routledge.

Janks, H., & Comber, B. (2006). Critical literacy across continents. In K. Pahl & J. Rowsell (Eds.), *Travel notes from the new literacy studies: Instances of practice* (pp. 95–117). Clevedon, UK: Multilingual Matters.

Jewitt, C. (2005). Multimodal 'reading' and 'writing' on screen. *Discourse: Studies in the Cultural Politics of Education* [Special edition: Digital childhood and youth: new texts, new literacies], *26*(3), 315–332.

Kress, G. (1997). *Before writing: Rethinking the paths to literacy.* London: Routledge.

Kress, G. (2003). *Literacy in the new media age.* London: Routledge.

Kress, G., & Van Leeuwen, T (1996). *Reading images: The grammar of visual design.* London: Routledge.

Lancaster, L. (2003). Beginning at the beginning: How a young child constructs time multimodally. In C. Jewitt & G. Kress (Eds.), *Multimodal literacy* (pp. 107–122). New York: Peter Lang.

Leander, K. M. (2002). Locating Letanya: The situated production of identity artifacts in classroom interaction. *Research in the Teaching of English, 37,* 198–248.

Luke, A. & Carrington, V. (2002). Globalisation, literacy, curriculum practice. In R. Fisher, M. Lewis, & G. Brooks (Eds.), *Language and literacy in action* (pp. 231–250). London: Routledge/Falmer.

Marsh, J. (Ed.). (2005). *Popular culture, new media and digital literacy in early childhood.* London: Routledge/Falmer.

Marsh, J. (2006). Popular culture and literacy: A Bourdieuan analysis. *Reading Research Quarterly, 46*(2), 160–174.

Maybin, J. (2000). The new literacy studies: Context, intertextuality, and discourse. In D. Barton, M. Hamilton, & R. Ivanic (Eds.), *Situated literacies: Reading and writing in context* (pp. 197–205). London: Routledge.

Pahl, K. (2004) Narratives, artifacts and cultural identities: An ethnographic study of communicative practices in homes. *Linguistics and Education, 15*(4), 339–358.

Pahl, K. (2009). Interactions, intersections and improvisations: Studying the multimodal texts and classroom talk of six to seven year olds. *Journal of Early Childhood Literacy, 9*(2), 188–210.

Pahl, K., & Rowsell, J. (2005). *Literacy and education: The new literacy studies in the classroom.* London: Paul Chapman.

Pahl, K., & Rowsell, J. (Eds) (2006). *Travel notes from the new literacy studies: Instances of practice.* Clevedon, UK: Multilingual Matters Ltd.

Pahl, K., & Rowsell, J. (2010). *Artifactual literacies: Every object tells a story.* New York: Teachers College Press.

Rogers, R. Mosley, M. Kramer, M. A., & the Literacy for Social Justice Teacher Research Group (2009). *Designing socially just learning communities.* London: Routledge

Rowsell, J. (2009). My life on Facebook: Assessing the art of online social networking. In A. Burke & B. Hammett (Eds.), *Assessing multimodal practice* (pp. 95–113). New York: Peter Lang.

Rowsell, J., & Burke, A. (2009). Reading by design: Two case studies of digital reading practices. *Journal of Adolescent and Adult Literacy, 52*(9) 106–118.

Rowsell, J., & Pahl, K. (2007). Sedimented identities in texts: Instances of practice. *Reading Research Quarterly, 42*(3), 388–401.

Schwartz, A., & Rubinstein-Ávila, E. (2006). Understanding the manga hype: Uncovering the multimodality of comic-book literacies. *Journal of Adolescent and Adult Literacy, 50*(1), 40–49.

Scribner, S., & Cole, M. (1981). The psychology of literacy. Cambridge, MA: Harvard University Press.

Scollon, R., & Scollon, S. (2003). *Discourses in place: Language in the material world.* London: Routledge.

Sheridan, M. P., & Rowsell, J. (2010). *Design literacies: Learning and innovation in the digital age.* London: Routledge.

Street, B. (2003). The limits of the local—'autonomous' or 'disembedding'? *International Journal of Learning, 10,* 2825–2830.

Street, B. V. (1984). *Literacy in theory and practice.* Cambridge, UK: Cambridge University Press.

Street, B. V. (Ed.). (1993). *Cross-cultural approaches to literacy.* Cambridge, UK: Cambridge University Press.

Street, B. V. (Ed.). (2005). *Literacies across educational context: Mediating teaching and learning.* Philadelphia: Caslon Publishers.

Willis, P. (2000). *The ethnographic imagination.* Cambridge, UK: Polity Press.

Wright, R. (1945). *Black boy.* New York: Bantam.

26

Media Literacy

Stacie L. Tate

The history and use of media in the classroom is rich and complex. Teachers have always used media to convey facts and information, however the form in which it is used is often for entertainment or as a way to reward, not necessarily for its literary value (NCTE, 2008, "Use of Media," para. 1). The growing importance of technology in society has increased what media means for the classroom. NCTE in its position statement about media in the 21st century states,

> Because technology has increased the intensity and complexity of literate environments, the twenty-first century demands that a literate person possess a wide range of abilities and competencies, many literacies." These literacies— from reading online newspapers to participating in virtual classrooms—are multiple dynamic and malleable. (NCTE, 2008, "Media Literacy Education," para. 1)

Media literacy continues to be an important curricular foundation for many classrooms. Given its goal to "access, analyze, evaluate and communicate messages in a wide variety of forms" (NCTE, 2008, "Media Literacy Education," para. 1), media literacy changes what it means to be literate within the 21st century. Due to the emergence of media literacy, we now understand that simply seeing literacy as a "book culture" is not an adequate way to educate students (Luke, 2000, p. 424). More importantly, media literacy in the classroom creates opportunities for students to examine the sociopolitical context of literacies that impact their everyday lives.

Given the importance of technology in developing literate environments, this chapter seeks to address how media literacy is defined, what media literacy means for teacher education and secondary English language arts classrooms, and its future given the national standardization of the school curriculum and the sociopolitical context often associated with the role of media in schools and society.

What is Media Literacy?

Media Literacy and Culture Since its inception, the definition of media literacy continues to transform. Currently, the National Council of Teachers of English (NCTE) defines media literacy as "the capacity to access, analyze, evaluate and communicate messages in a wide variety of forms" (NCTE, 2008, "Media Literacy Education," para. 1). Coined in 1964 by John Caulkin, the definition and practice of media literacy continues to evolve and expand as new technology leads to emerging insight about the effects of media on literacy and literacy education (National Association for Media Literacy Education [NAMLE], 2007, "Media Literacy," para. 1). Caulkin states,

> The attainment of (media) literacy involves more than mere warnings about the effects of the mass media and more even than constant exposure to the better offerings of these media. This [media literacy] is an issue demanding more than good will alone; it requires understanding. (Moody, 2007, para. 2)

This initial overview of media literacy was for teachers to think in new ways and understand the function of media in culture (Moody, 2007, para. 9). Culkin's original idea establishes the foundation of media literacy-culture. Culture according to Bruner (1996), "takes its inspiration from the evolutionary fact that the mind could not exist save for culture" (p. 3) and that "learning and thinking are always *situated* in a cultural setting and always dependent upon the utilization of cultural resources" (p. 4). To understand media literacy one must recognize its apparent and close relationship to culture and cultural studies. According to Giroux (1996),

> Cultural studies, with its ambiguous founding moments spread across multiple continents and diverse institutional spheres, has always been critically attentive to the changing conditions influencing the socialization of youth and the

social and economic context producing such changes. The self and social formation of diverse youth subcultures mediated by popular cultural forms remain prominent concerns of cultural studies. (p. 15)

Cultural studies offer a look into the changing conditions that influence the media. Since media is a condition of culture, according to Giroux, we must consider how media such as popular film and music are serious sites for social knowledge but more importantly how the two are inextricably linked.

Additionally, Bruner (1996) offers insight into how culture, "provides us with the toolkit to construct not only our worlds, but our very conceptions of ourselves and our powers" (p. 10). Clearly, media literacy is about the triangulation of culture, power and identity. Since Bruner sees culture as "a way in which we question about the making and negotiating of meanings [and] about the constructing of self and sense of agency" (p. 12), media literacy is about these same ideological perspectives. According to the National Association for Media Literacy Education, one of the core principles of media literacy is that it recognizes that media is a part of culture and it functions as an agent of socialization. In agreement, Bruner would see culture as key to media literacy because "learning and thinking are always situated in a cultural setting and always dependent upon the utilization of cultural resources" (p. 4). Media literacy relies on culture to provide students with what Luke (2000) states are "critical analytic tools to understand reader and viewer diversity of reading positions and sociocultural locations and differences that influence affinities to particular kinds of media forms and messages" (p. 425). Additionally, this takes into account Caulkin's initial idea about media literacy requiring "more than good will alone" but a true understanding of the sociocultural ideas associated with media literacy.

Hall (1999) also presents another overview about how the foundation of media literacy is linked to culture and cultural studies. Media literacy reflects the fluidity of cultural studies. This fluidity is both the intellectual and pragmatic enterprise of media literacy committed to a moral evaluation of modern society and a radical line of political action (Hall, 1999; Sarder & Van Loon, 1998). The same can be said of media literacy with its ever-changing definition due to its roots in culture. Hall asserts that cultural studies are "rooted in a profound tension between ideas of power, global reach, and the history making capacities of capital; the question of class and the complex relationships between power and exploitation" (p. 265). These ideas can be found in the guiding principles of media literacy. One of the principles of media literacy is that it develops "reflective and engaged students that are essential for a democratic society" and that students realize the "socially constructed messages of media" (NCTE, 2008, "Media Literacy Education," para. 1). Culture and cultural studies foregrounds media literacy by providing a platform in which to analyze the sociopolitical nature of media. Finally, Hall asserts that

cultural studies have multiple discourses and a number of different histories that speak to media literacies overall goal to access, analyze, evaluate, and communicate messages in a wide variety of forms (NCTE, 2008, "Media Literacy Education," para. 1).

Giroux, Bruner, and Hall provide the foundation of media literacy-culture. Each theorist sees culture as a link to defining what media literacy is and forefront the notion that culture encourages students to reflect and understand the critical and analytical tools to understand positions of power and sociocultural relations. These theorists provide insight into the notion that media literacy is a site for social knowledge built on the concept that media is a part of culture and a crucial agent in teaching and learning.

Core Principles of Media Literacy The National Association for Media Literacy Education (NAMLE, 2007, p. 4) believes there are core principles that articulate a common ground around what media literacy is. NAMLE found six core principles for media literacy:

1. Media literacy education requires active inquiry and critical thinking about the messages we receive and create
2. Media literacy education expands the concept of literacy (i.e. reading and writing to include all form of media
3. Media literacy education builds and reinforces skills for learners of all ages. Like print literacy, those skills necessitate integrated, interactive and repeated practice
4. Media literacy education develops informed, reflective and engaged participants essential for a democratic society
5. Media literacy education recognizes that media are a part of culture and functions as agents of socialization
6. Media literacy education affirms that people use their individual skills, beliefs and experiences to construct their own meanings from media messages.

Each principle according to NAMLE offers not only a definition of what media literacy is but also its implications for practice. Additionally, part of the core principles outlined by NAMLE is how people learn to think critically about their world. These principles speak to media literacy, culture and its functions in education. Media literacy according to NAMLE considers ideas such as how media messages are constructed and how these messages can influence beliefs, attitudes, values behaviors as well as the democratic progress. They also consider media literacies roots in culture. According to NAMLE media literacy integrates media text that present diverse voices and perspectives. Media literacy is not about teaching students what to think; it is about teaching them how they can arrive at informed choices that are most consistent with their own values. Finally, media literacy expands the concept of literacy. Pirie (1997) argues that we must begin to redefine the definition of literacy to include technology. According to the principles of media literacy, this practice takes into account that literacy can be defined in different ways. Media literacy encompasses both analysis and expression. It enables students to express their own ideas through multiple forms of media (e.g. traditional print, electronic, digital, user-generated and wireless). All of these can be considered as literacy. The National Council of Teachers of English sees media literacy in the same way.

According to NCTE media literacy education distinctively features the analytical attitude that teachers and learners, working together, adopt toward the media objects they study (NCTE). NCTE sees media literacy as:

1. All media messages are constructed
2. Each medium has different characteristics and strengths and a unique language of construction
3. Media messages are produced for particular purposes
4. All media messages contain embedded values and points of view
5. People use their individual skills, beliefs and experiences to construct their own meanings from media messages
6. Media and media messages can influence beliefs, attitudes, values, behaviors and the democratic process.

Each of these foundational ideas outlined by NCTE sees media literacy as a response to the demands of cultural participation in the 21st century. It includes both "receptive and productive dimensions that encompass critical analysis and communication skills" (NCTE, 2008, "Media Literacy Education," para. 1). More importantly, it "defines the relationship between literacy, mass media, popular culture and digital media" (NCTE, 2008, "Media Literacy Education," para. 1). Finally, NCTE makes the distinction between the use of media in education and media literacy in education. According to NCTE, films screened to reward the class are not media literacy education. If the media material used is for essentially the same purposes for which it originally was intended—to instruct or to entertain—this is not media literacy (NCTE, 2008, "Use of Media In Education," para. 13).

What is media literacy? There have been several ideas that define what media literacy is. It takes into account the cultural, historical and sociopolitical context of media and is comprised of concrete principles about how media literacy should be defined and used within K–12 settings. The next logical consideration is what media literacy looks like in the classroom.

Media Literacy in the Classroom

According to NCTE, media literacy education may occur as "a separate program or course but often it is embedded within other subject areas, including literature, history, anthropology, sociology, public health, journalism, communication, and education (NCTE, 2008, "Media Literacy Education," para. 1). The content of media literacy can vary to lessons designed to expose the mechanics of how language, images, sound, music, and graphic design operate

as a way of transmitting meaning to an exercise designed to reinforce these understandings through hands-on media making (NCTE, 2005, "Declarations Multimodal Literacies," para. 14).

Media literacy in the K–12 setting is deeply rooted in the notion that students are more inclined to develop literacy skills if they have a cultural frame that is connected to the material presented during instruction (Duncan-Andrade & Morrell, 2000). Given the belief that students are more inclined to develop literacy skills if they have a cultural frame of reference makes media literacy a necessary tool for the classroom. Additionally, the use of media literacy in the classroom provides different perspectives about what constitutes literacy. Consequently, NCTE advocates broadening the concept of literacy in order for students to apply the knowledge of their language conventions and structure to create, critique and discuss print and non-print texts (NCTE, 2005, "Declarations Multimodal Literacies," para. 10).

Because technology has increased the complexity of what we consider literate environments, the 21st-century classroom demands that students possess a wide range of abilities from reading on-line articles to participating in virtual classrooms. Currently, most classrooms use some form of media literacy. However, according to Pirie (1997) it is also about changing how literacy is seen in the classroom. There are several classrooms that effectively use media literacy not only helping students to become effective users and readers of text but also helping students derive meaning from traditional and canonical text that are often seen by students as distant and obscure from their everyday lives.

Media Literacy in the Teacher Education Classroom Luke (2000) contends that media, cultural, computer and technology studies can no longer be taught independently of one another (p. 424). She asserts that the development and new framework for media literacy begins in teacher education. Since media has a greater presence in the English language arts classroom, Luke believes that teacher education programs must contend with the current movement of class curriculums built around a book culture that is not adequately educating students in a changing environment (p. 424). Therefore, teacher education programs must provide the necessary tools for teachers to effectively incorporate media literacy into their curriculum.

Luke (2000) found that media use in the English language arts classrooms had been "reduced to add-on units to more mainstream literary content, or as a remedial strategy to capture reluctant readers or at-risk students for whom traditional literacy instruction has failed" (p. 426). But more importantly, she argued that there has been a confinement of media literacy to the English language arts classroom thereby reducing media literacy to the teaching of operational skills. In order to address the issue of media literacy in teacher education, Luke believes there are crucial components that must be included in media literacy courses for teachers.

First, there is the issue of multiliteracies (New London Group, 1996). Luke (2000) believes multilieracies should be studied in order to understand how people negotiate their lives using a diversity of literacies (p. 424). Luke argues that because of the many social, political, and cultural issues at stake, instruction on the shift from print to cybertextualiy is crucial in the education of teachers (p. 427). In her study Luke emphasized the need to move beyond the operational skills of technology and for teachers to understand and reflect on the social and cultural dynamics of teaching in virtual environments. Second, Luke believes that we have to understand issues of technology as it relates to "intercultural communication-that is a heightened meata-awareness (perhaps even self-censorship) of "others" in our communications…it is the kind of cultural literacy that is crucial for teachers and students" (p. 432). According to Luke this idea is vital because it requires teachers "to ensure that their students understand concepts of the social and cultural other" (p. 433).

Luke believed these components were important in order to deemphasize book-based curriculum resources as being the sole source of teaching and learning and a way to "remake" courses on media literacy in teacher education (p. 434). Luke asserts that it is about, "using IT as a tool with which to transform (a) the very relationships between student and teacher, among students, and between students and knowledge and (b) the very organization of school knowledge itself" (p. 435).

Media Literacy in the English Language Arts Classroom Duncan-Andrade and Morrell (2000) noticed that students who could critically analyze the complex and richly metaphoric and symbolic hip-hop music they listened to where failing to exhibit these same analytical skills when relating to canonical text (p. 2). Their hypothesis was that media literacy, or in this case, hip-hop music, could be used as a vehicle for urban youth to develop literary skills. The premise of their argument included the basic notion of media literacies connection to student's cultural frame of reference, in this case hip-hop music, to create and construct meaning from canonical texts.

One of the major principles of media literacy is the idea that students are able to understand how media messages can influence their beliefs, attitudes, values and behaviors in addition to offering students how media is a socialization tool often used to critique and understand society. According to Duncan Andrade and Morrell (2000), hip-hop music is one of the few modes of media that offers a useful approach when using media in the classroom in to provide cultural and academic relevance to students (p. 24).

Given the intention of media literacy to "access, analyze, evaluate and communicate messages in a wide variety of forms" (NCTE, 2008, "Media Literacy Education," para. 1). Duncan-Andrade and Morrell (2000) developed what they coined an "intervention project" that would enable students to critique the messages sent to them through a popular cultural medium (rap music) that permeates their everyday life (p. 24). The unit was "designed for both its cultural and academic relevance by incorporating rap music into a poetry unit" (p. 25). In addition to its social and cultural relevance, one of the main objectives of this unit was to create a space for urban youth to view elements of popular culture through a critical lens and critique message sent to them through popular media (p. 25). More importantly, this unit was about using media for literacy development.

The unit started with an overview of poetry and understanding the historical background of poetry for interpretation. For example, Elizabethan, Puritan Revolution, Romantics, and Post Industrial Revolution poetry were placed along side rap music so that students would be able to use a period and genre of poetry they were familiar with as a lens to examine other literary works and re-evaluate the manner in which they view elements of their popular culture (p. 26). After the initial overview of poetry and its relationship to rap music, the second part of the unit was for students to present a poem and rap song. The students prepared interpretations of a chosen poem and rap song with relation to its historical and literary period. For example students matched Walt Whitman's "O Me! O Life!" to the rap group Public Enemy's "Don't Believe the Hype" and Shakespeare's "Sonnet 29" to rapper Nas' "Affirmative Action."

Morrell and Duncan Andrade's (2000) unit was consistent with the ideas of media literacy. The unit provided cultural and social relevancy while exposing students to the literary canon. Additionally, this unit practiced the principles of media literacy because it was situated in the experiences of the students and called for a critical engagement of the text, by asking students to relate it to larger social and political issues. Media literacy calls for these basic tenets. More importantly this unit's use of media enabled students to develop a powerful connection to canonical texts (p. 30).

In addition to the use of rap music in the classroom, other forms of media that are popular within the English language arts classrooms provide spaces for students to see literacy in another form. According to Bell (2001), the study of popular culture offers the possibility of understanding how "politics of pleasure" address students in a way that shapes and sometimes secures the often contradictory relations they have to both schooling and the politics of everyday life (p. 241). In this study, Bell looked at how teachers could bring popular film texts into the classroom. Pre-service teachers evaluated and participated in discussions of films in order to develop their use of critical literacy and media the in their classrooms. Critical literacy practices were used with pre-service teachers in order to further their understanding of the possibilities of popular culture. The teachers not only saw how to turn this theory into practice, but also had the opportunity to become a part of critical literacy instruction by evaluating and critiquing popular movies and films. The teachers were not just instructed on the practice of critical literacy, but were also able to critically engage in the exercise of media literacy. According to Freebody and Luke (1990), text analysis, or in this case media analysis is a part of what successful readers of media do. This type of analysis provides a descriptive framework of a reader's role. They explain:

> A successful reader in our society needs to develop and sustain the resources to adopt four related roles: code breaker ("how do I crack this?"), text participant (what does this mean?"), text user (what do I do with this here and now?"), and the text analyst (what does all this do to me?"). (p. 10)

The "literacy" aspect of media literacy considers that there are other factors besides empowerment and emancipation of students, but students are ultimately interacting and creating texts. However, it is the student's ability to critically analyze texts that provides the literacy aspect of this term. The use of media literacy in the classroom goes beyond the idea of accessing, analyzing and evaluating communicate messages. Media literacy in the classroom is about how this practice can transform students and teachers not just socially and politically, but academically as well.

The Future of Media Literacy

Critical Media Literacy in the Classroom Inclusion of media literacy in teacher education and K–12 classrooms is not the only issue that should be considered when determining media literacy instruction. There is also the issue of "an unprecedented concentration of for-profit media into conglomerates, in alliance with the government and especially with the federal regulating agency—Federal Communications Commission-and other powerful institutions and corporations" (Torres & Mercado, 2006, p. 260). Since media literacy contemplates how media is constructed and the active inquiry and critical thinking of the messages we receive and create, issues of power, privilege and the sociopolitical context of media within the classroom must be considered.

Torres and Mercado (2006) argue that "corporate culture is taking over public education" (p. 270). While media literacy and education is important, there is still the notion that it must be "critical." Critical should not be viewed as just a pathological response or negative connotation, but a word that invokes a sense of hope and transformation. So, for this chapter, *critical* articulates the philosophy originally developed by the Frankfurt School. *Critical* presents the belief of emancipation, counter-hegemonic discourse and social justice. According to Torres and Mercado (2006), one of the dimensions of critical medial literacy is "understanding the educators' responsibility to help students become actively engaged in alternative media use and development" (p. 261). While media literacy is crucial, critical media literacy incorporates "the use and abuse of the power of media to control masses of people especially children, for the profit of those who own those media and their political allies" (p. 262). While there is a push for media in the classroom, there are still issues of hegemony and control. Critical media literacy makes explicit the need for alternative media and

advises teachers to "help students 'read between the lines' of the media messages, question the interest behind them, and learn how to look for alternative ways to be informed and/or entertained" (p. 273). While the general principles about media literacy defined by NCTE and NAMLE consider some of these aspects, the purposes of critical media literacy according to Torres and Mercado are:

1. To act as intellectual self-defense.
2. To discover and support the increase in number and in power of independent nonprofit media.
3. To develop alternative media networks among special interest groups using the new advanced media and multimedia technologies.
4. To make information available on the democratic premise of education for all. (p. 278)

Each of these ideas focuses on what Torres and Mercado deem "the use and abuse of mass media power by putting profit (economic and political) first and service to the public last" (p. 279). These ideas must also be considered when examining media literacy in the classroom.

Equity, Access, and Media Literacy

In discussing media literacy, I believe it is important to acknowledge the future of media literacy in the climate of No Child Left Behind (NCLB). While media literacy is an important trend that many educators and researchers believe is necessary to create multi-literate students, the reality for many students and schools is that standardize testing and resources leave little room for the incorporation of media in the classroom.

According to Noguera (2008), NCLB has forced many schools to eliminate subjects like art, music and science because they are not covered on standardized test (p. 179). If basic subjects such as art and science are being eliminated where does that leave media and media instruction? Many schools continue to struggle for basic resources. New textbooks, adequate school resources and test scores are often the priority, not the use of media in the classroom. While there continues to be a push for media literacy there is still a "digital divide." In a study conducted by Hess and Leal (2001), they found that students in districts with a larger percentage of African American students had less access to classroom computers. Additionally, since urban districts receive most of the their funding for technology initiatives from federal funds test scores attached to federal dollars means that under-achieving schools miss out on the funding necessary to address media and technology needs (p. 766). If media literacy argues that students must be "reflective and engaged participants essential for a democratic society," there must be initiatives in place to ensure "equitable and substantial access" to media (p. 766). While the role of technology continues to become a pressing issue, there is still the matter of access. With the cost and complexity of new technologies, how can we ensure that effective and efficient media literacy is provided to all students?

Conclusion

With the growing field of technology, media literacy continues to evolve. NCTE and others have continued to ensure that media literacy includes "both receptive and productive dimensions, encompassing critical analysis and communication skills, particularly in relationship to mass media, popular culture and digital media" (NCTE, 2008, "Media Literacy Education," para. 1). Subsequently, this evolvement has not always considered the cultural and political conventions of society. While the evolution of media literacy continues to grow, it must do so with issues of power, access and privilege in mind. For this chapter media literacy is more than the capacity to access, analyze, evaluate, and communicate messages, media literacy gives students and teachers the opportunity to examine the sociopolitical context of literacies that impact their everyday lives.

References

Bell, J. (2001). Building bridges/making meanings: Texts of popular culture and critical pedagogy in theory and practice. In B. Comber & A. Simpson (Eds.), *Negotiating critical literacies in classrooms* (pp. 229–244). Mahwah, NJ: Erlbaum.

Bruner, J. (1996). *The culture of education.* Cambridge, MA: Harvard University Press.

Duncan-Andrade, J., & Morrell, E. (2000, April 24). *Using hip-hop culture as a bridge to canonical poetry texts in an urban secondary English class.* Paper presented at the Annual Meeting of the American Educational Research Association, New Orleans, LA.

Freebody, P., & Luke, A. (1990). "Literacies" programs: Debates and demands in cultural context. *Prospect: The Australian Journal of TESOL, 5*(3), 7–16.

Giroux, H.A. (1996). *Fugitive cultures: race, violence, and youth.* New York: Routledge.

Hall, S. (1999). Cultural studies and its theoretical legacies. In S. During (Ed.), *The cultural studies reader* (pp. 97–112). New York: Routledge.

Hess, F., & Leal, D. (2001). A shrinking "digital divide"? The provision of classroom computers across urban school systems. *Social Science Quarterly, 82*(4), 765–778.

Luke, C. (2000). New literacies in teacher education. *Journal of Adolescent and Adult Literacy. 43*(5), 424–435.

Moody, K. (2007). *John Culkin: The man who invented media literacy: 1928–1993.* Center for Media Literacy. Retrieved from http://www.medialit.org/reading_room/article408.html

National Association for Media Literacy Education (NAMLE). (2007, November). Core principles of media literacy education in the United States. Retrieved from http://www.amlainfo.org/core-principles

National Council of Teachers of English (NCTE). (2003). Resolution on composing with nonprint media. Retrieved from http://www.ncte.org/positions/statements/composewithnonprint

National Council of Teachers of English (NCTE). (2005, November). Position Statement on Multimodal Literacies. Retrieved from http://www.ncte.org/positions/statements/multimodalliteracies

National Council of Teachers of English (NCTE). (2008, November). Code of best practices in fair use for media literacy education. Retrieved from http://www.ncte.org/positions/statements/fairusemedialiteracy

New London Group. (1996). A pedagogy of multiliteracies: Designing social futures. *Harvard Educational Review, 66*(1), 60–92.

Noguera, P. (2008). *The trouble with black boys...and other reflections on race, equity, and the future of public education.* San Francisco: Jossey-Bass.

Pirie, B. (1997). *Reshaping high school english.* Urbana, IL: National Council of Teachers of English.

Sarder, Z., & Van Loon, B. (1998). *Introducing cultural studies.* New York: Totem.

Torres, M., & Mercado, M. (2006). The need for critical media literacy in teacher education. *Educational Studies: A Journal of the American Educational Studies Association, 39*(3), 260–282.

27

Critical Literacy, Critical Engagement, and Digital Technology

Convergence and Embodiment in Glocal Spheres

KAREN E. WOHLWEND AND CYNTHIA LEWIS

This chapter examines critical literacy within an evolving digital and global landscape. The last decade has produced a steady stream of research focusing on digital literacy practices. Those who study these practices have been engaged in the making of a discipline as they explore how readers and writers negotiate the demands and affordances of literacy practices that employ digital technologies.[1]

With this theme of transition in mind—the changing landscape of literacy and the subsequent re-making of a field—it is no wonder that many researchers, too, have been operating in a transitional space, often studying digital literacies through the lens of print literacies. At the same time that researchers have marveled at the competence and engagement that research participants demonstrate in their use of new technologies, many studies have emphasized how digital technology can foster the development of print literacy skills such as comprehension (Coiro & Dobler, 2007), argumentation (Beach & Doerr-Stevens, 2009), and audience awareness (Lewis & Fabos, 2005). However, these studies show that skills traditionally associated with print literacy are accomplished through the construction of a new ethos (Lankshear & Knobel, 2007) that is "participatory," "collaborative," and "distributed," rather than "individuated" and "author-centric" (p. 9).

In some respects, critical literacy has never been a "traditional" print literacy in that it has been consistently associated with challenging dominant assumptions and inequities including, as Siegel and Fernandez (2000) argued, "the ways in which literacy instruction participates in the production" (p. 149) of unjust and inequitable schooling. Although perhaps not best classified as "traditional," a strand of research on critical literacy and technology focuses on building upon print approaches to achieve critical readings of online texts. Kellner (2004), argued for the importance of this approach to critical literacy in digital environments in which "traditional print literacy takes on increasing importance in the computer-mediated cyberworld as people need to critically scrutinize and scroll tremendous amounts of information, putting increasing emphasis on developing reading and writing abilities" (p. 17). One example of this focus on critical scrutiny is research conducted by Baildon and Damico (2009) which examined high school students' efforts to determine the credibility of the video *Loose Change* (http://www.loosechange911.com/), which argues that the U.S. government covered up the truth about 9/11. In this work and other related projects, Carter, Damico, and Kumasi-Johnson (2008) build on a model of print literacy that includes a critical lens for analyzing author manipulation. The research findings of the *Loose Change* study undercut facile comparisons between print and online literacies in that the students' search for credibility was deeply complicated by intertextual modes and discourses both within and outside the video. Thus, when students tried to draw upon prior knowledge about determining credibility, their efforts were confounded by the affordances and challenges of multimodality.

This chapter focuses on research—such as that by Baildon and Damico—that examines the changing nature of critical literacy within digital and global environments. What does critical literacy mean in relation to digital technology use? What does it look like? What are its properties? Our scope is limited to research involving children and adolescents—both in and out of school—with a focus on two dimensions of critical literacy that take into account the multimodal affordances of digital technologies:

convergence: the collision and merging of old and new media as well as corporate and user-driven media

embodiment: the immersion of bodies and emotions in digital spaces as well as the ways in which bodies and emotions are represented in and shaped by digital spaces

We have not attempted to be comprehensive in our review of literature, but rather have decided to draw on a few studies within each key category that we deem to be important in understanding critical engagement and technology. Our focus is on critical literacy in transition and the promise of new directions at a time that demands a critically literate public in the face of changing economic and informational flows brought on by globalization. Globalization is marked by increased movement of objects, images, persons, and discourses (Appadurai, 2000). The globalized citizen is imagined as enterprising (Apple, 2001), an ongoing project (Arnett, 2002), shape-shifting (Gee, 2004), and translocal (Appadurai, 2000). In turn, this redefinition of citizenship as fluid and translocal shapes young people's expectations for texts and the ways in which possible identities, discourses, relationships, and futures are represented and broadened by them (Lewis & Dockter, in press; Medina, 2010).

From Critical Literacy to Critical Engagement

Over a decade ago, Peters and Lankshear (1996) focused on the intersection of critical literacy and technology with an early analysis of the ways that digital texts reposition readers and writers, sometimes opening new spaces for criticality and reframing. These features include: interactivity, which disrupts reader-writer distinctions; multimodality, which reconfigures the relationship between word, image, and sound; emerging discourses, which interrupt the privileging of academic discourse; and easy dissemination, which deconstructs the hegemony of publishing, making the way for more participatory authorship. All of these features create opportunities for adopting a critical stance that, according to Peters and Lankshear, involve a combination of distance (for making critical evaluations) and closeness (for in-depth knowledge).

Few theorists in the intervening years have focused on the intersection of critical literacy and technology (see Fabos, 2008, for an exception). The practice of critical literacy, however, has received much attention, including discussions of its theoretical roots (Morgan, 1997), goals (Lewison, Flint, & Van Sluys, 2002), and dimensions (Lewis, Ketter, & Fabos, 2001; Janks, 2002). Lewison and colleagues (2002) identified four goals of critical literacy: disrupting the commonplace, interrogating multiple viewpoints, focusing on sociopolitical issues, and promoting social justice through action. Lewis et al. (2001) identified three dimensions of critical literacy: how texts position readers; how readers position texts; and how texts are positioned within sociopolitical contexts. Similarly, dimensions of critical literacy put forth by Janks—diversity, domination, access, and design—signal the complicated relationships that are necessary to enable critique of the hegemony of dominant texts in relation to diverse cultural and sociopolitical resources and with the possibility of agentic responses through productive design. Janks (2002) argued for alternatives to rationalized approaches to critical literacy in which we detach and coolly deconstruct lived language in ways that leave selves untouched:

We expose the faulty logic, look for the silences in the text, criticise the values that underpin the text and we reveal the underlying assumptions. When we have finished, students can produce a reasoned critique that is not in any way transformative. (p. 3)

The dimensions of engagement, emotion, and aesthetics are generally absent from accounts of critical literacy, as Misson and Morgan (2006) noted, but these absences are reason to revise rather than scrap critical literacy and its many strengths. In this chapter, we think of critical literacy in terms of critical distance *and* immersion, a process both analytic and playful, resistant and emotional. This process merges the seemingly contradictory stance toward literature that Toni Morrison (1992) described in her book *Playing in the Dark: Whiteness and the Literary Imagination*, when she discusses her process of reading a particular text as an illustration of "how each of us reads, becomes engaged in, and *watches* what is being read all at the same time" (p. x). It is this complicated enterprise—combining the presumably unselfconscious act of engagement with the decidedly self-conscious act of watching that interests us and moves us to use the term "critical engagement" when discussing the future of critical literacy.

We argue that the goals and dimensions of critical literacy remain important but require expansive definition to keep up with 21st-century literacy practices. Proliferating technologies and colliding global systems make it paradoxically easier and harder to track the echoes, emanations, and effects of widely dispersed, fleeting digital texts. Burbules (2004) asserted that virtual spaces are particularly conducive to engagement in that they potentially promote the interest, involvement, imagination, and interaction that result in immersion. Our challenge is to reinterpret critical literacy for the new commonplace: visual and embodied texts, digital technologies, interactive media, and virtual spaces circulated through global flows that are at once universalizing and fragmenting. We do so in the next sections of this chapter, focusing on critical engagement through the dimensions of convergence and embodiment that are foregrounded through the affordances of digital technology as they play out locally and in a global sphere.

Convergence

For those who can afford expensive gadgets and broadband connections, distinctions among social identities as consumers, producers, and learners blur and converge. Critical engagement with convergence unpacks dense meanings and social affordances created by overlapping and interconnected technologies but also makes transparent the motives and influence of information and communication providers concentrated in a few mass media conglomerates. In a commodified view of literacy and technology, production is a top-down process in which a small number of producers create and publish books and media to distribute and sell to mass markets. From this perspective, critical issues involve capital expenditures, hardware costs, and usage patterns, raising concerns about centralized ownership among producers and inequitable access or competence among consumers according to a digital divide that explains disparities along fault lines of class, education, gender, and age. Gounari (2009) viewed the Internet as a site for public pedagogy that is more often consumerist than democratic. With similar concerns, Burbules and Callister (2000) and Fabos (2004, 2008) argued for careful, critical readings of Internet sites and texts that uncover the politics of representation and commercial sponsorship. A few studies examine adolescents' uses of technology that involve this kind of critical practice. For example, Guzzetti and Gamboa (2004) studied adolescent girls' creation of zines that challenged oppressive gender representations, and Humphrey (2006) revealed the semiotic resources used to create solidarity in adolescents' weblogs created for the purpose of political activism, with an emphasis on how they vary depending on the size and familiarity of the audience.

Critical engagement considers how quality of participation enables or limits the ability to produce and not just consume and how participation affects life chances. Comber and Janks (2006) remind us that although digital artifacts zip around the globe, bodies remain stuck in the local. Mobility is especially limited for people in high-poverty communities, priced out of the possibility of global travel and confined to the operating hours of libraries, schools, and public sites for Internet access. In contrast, users with the latest technological resources enjoy interactive and converged technologies as facile pathways for consuming, producing, and representing selves and others within participatory cultures.

Participatory Cultures

> A participatory culture is a culture with relatively low barriers to artistic expression and civic engagement, strong support for creating and sharing one's creations, and some type of informal mentorship whereby what is known by the most experienced is passed along to novices. A participatory culture is also one in which members believe their contributions matter, and feel some degree of social connection with one another (at the least they care what other people think about what they have created). (Jenkins, Purushotma, Clinton, Robison, & Weigel, 2006, p. 3)

Participatory cultures enable individuals to connect with others with similar aesthetic, social, and political goals. Online groups who share a passion for the same media, products, or interests have been described variously as knowledge communities (Jenkins, 2006), affinity groups (Gee, 2004), or fan cultures (Beavis, 2009). A unifying aim of such groups is production of new content and circulation of commentary on insider issues that build group cohesiveness and legitimates members who contribute valued information.

Critical engagement with participatory cultures looks at the way digital literacy practices legitimate full membership in online communities within spheres of influence that ripple out from these groups. Jenkins (2006) identified four key forms of participation in online communities, each related to particular kinds of digital texts: affiliations (e.g., in social networks such as Facebook, nings), creative expressions (e.g., zines, mashups), collaborative problem-solving (e.g., wikis), and circulations (e.g., podcasts, blogs, tweets). Converged environments produce hypersociality (Ito, 2007) through interactions that are "wired, extroverted and…augmented by a dense set of technologies, signifiers, and systems of exchange" (p. 42). Hypersociality constitutes distant yet active social relationships that enable collective mentoring into each digital culture's interpretive, expressive, and strategic practices with new kinds of texts.

Power relations map onto the intersections of social relationships and digital literacies where expertise is measured by who reads whom and quantified by hits from Facebook friends, Twitter followers, or blog readers. Critical engagement considers how the desire to belong interacts with individual agency as well as members' complicity in circulating practices, media, and discourses with disparate social effects. Pascarella (2008) argued that although youth often have facility with new media environments, they may not be adept at the critical processes necessary for analyzing the cultural practices and institutional norms of these environments.

Collective Interactivity   Merchant (2007) offered a way to compare the "dispersed interactivity" of digital participation through a matrix that varies along two dimensions: timing and collectivity (p. 123). Synchronous forms range from instant messaging involving one-to-one relationships to chat rooms, virtual worlds, and online games involving "many-to-many" public relationships. Asynchronous forms vary in collectivity from "one-to-one" personal emails to "one-to-many" blogs to "many-to-many" wikis, discussion boards, and Flickr or YouTube sites. Massively multi-player video games are quintessential collective interactive texts, requiring sustained collaboration and collective cohesion embodied by multiple players cooperating with interactive media to sustain a fluid and reactive text. Such texts provide an opportunity for productive critical engagement through interactive, immersive texts that put more control over the narrative in the hands of multiple players/readers than one-player video games, films, or e-books.

Interactivity enabled by portable and ubiquitous connections between fans, electronic technologies, and media products support the development of collective imaginaries (Appadurai, 1996). Creativity is a function of collective action in wikis, fan sites, and online game communities where participants work together to produce content and influence media sources by buying, downloading, creating new uses for products, attracting more consumer-producer participants, and reshaping media to create new content. Hierarchies tend to flatten in interactive environments where knowledge is produced collaboratively and anonymously

(Black, 2009; Gee, 2004). Knowledge-building in participatory cultures fuels consumer interest and buying which prompt producer response and increased production which enable more buying, a cycle that intensifies the effects of productive consumption (de Certeau, 1984), creating global trends and fads.

Interdiscursivity Online knowledge production merges discourses from media, popular culture, and academic disciplines, creating intertexts and interdiscursivity that blur traditional distinctions among academic disciplines and popular culture. Tensions among overlapping technologies and literacy practices arise when the intertexts they produce bring discourses into contact with each other. Carrington (2005) described the case of a 13-year-old Scottish student who turned in the following back-to-school essay written in the abbreviated style of text messaging and submitted via her cell phone.

> My smmr hols wr CWOT. B4, we used 2go2 NY 2C my bro, his GF & thr 3 :- kids FTF. ILNY, it's a gr8 plc.

> Translation: My summer holidays were a complete waste of time. Before, we used to go to New York to see my brother, his girlfriend and their three screaming kids face to face. I love New York. It's a great place. (p. 161)

This "txt" traveled beyond the student's classroom and her teacher's response; it was picked up by BBC news service websites, reported in international newspapers, and discussed on Australian radio talk shows. Intertwined texts worked together to produce layered social constructions, "enmeshed in a discursive chain which linked txting to youth to declining standards to poor academic achievement to social breakdown" (p. 163). This intertext represented different social practices to different audiences when situated in discourses of standards and institutional accountability, teachers' integration of popular culture into school curricula, and economic fears about rapidly changing technologies and literacy practices.

Discursive clashes, prompted by text traversals, open opportunities for institutional discourse to reinforce the imperative of conventional standards and "proper" English. Similar discursive disciplinary effects can happen when popular media is imported into classrooms and educators end up domesticating out-of-school literacies by bringing them under the control of the institutional discourses, a phenomenon that Lankshear and Bigum termed "old wine in new bottles" (1999, p. 455). Converged texts capable of traversing disciplines and institutions across online and offline contexts require critical scrutiny of historical traces and trajectories as well as immediate screen content (Damico, Baildon, & Campano, 2005). Critical engagement tracks how meanings shift in traversals of print, image, audio, or video messages across pages, screens, and discourses and how convergence plays out in simultaneously expanding, conflating, and proliferating functions, sources, and modes (Myers, Hammett, & McKillop, 1998).

Embodiment

Immersion and Attachment Critical engagement is active engagement, embedded in physicality, emotion, and sensation, that reads bodies as sociopolitical texts and writes with bodies to produce identity texts. Identity texts in digital cultures take diverse forms that merge texts and bodies: gamers, bloggers, avatars, media characters, reality television programs, or fan fiction narratives. These converged texts blur distinctions between the virtual and the "real," between online projected identities and everyday selves (Leander & McKim, 2003).

> Avatars also maintain a sense of personal space to one another that mirrors that of offline practice. While it would be technically possible to walk an avatar through another one, avatars walk around one another... (p. 229)

Critical engagement attends to complicated relationships between children's and adolescents' popular media desires and gendered, raced, and classed identity expectations, whereas critical literacy teaching all too often ends in reproducing rather than transforming stereotypical identity performances despite curricular social justice goals. Media franchises and brand affiliations meld into identity performances and emotional attachments; desires, pleasures, and identities are expressed through embodied performances and displays with favorite video games, films, celebrities, or designer products. Gender performance is a prime feature of digital game play on media websites and social networks such as Barbie Girls—a virtual world steeped in "pink technologies" that merge the Barbie brand, hyperfeminine identities, enticements to consume, and electronic goods (Marsh, 2010, in press). Global distribution of hetero-normative gendered discourses through children's media Web sites (e.g., Bob the Builder, Disney Princesses) and social networks suggests the need for curricula that provides critical engagement with these glocalized identity texts.

Hull and Nelson (2005) argued that the power of multimodality lies in its co-present modes that work to achieve something larger than any of its parts, framing narrative elements and the audience-author relationship in a way that combines emotion, cognition, and learning. In their study of critical engagement and raced identities in an urban high school English class, Lewis and Dockter (2008) viewed emotion as structured through ideology (Boler, 1999) and, therefore, central to critical literacy. In their study of critical engagement in a high-poverty high school, they found that although the teacher framed a discussion of the film *Pocahontas* to contest dominant White culture and representations of native versus White female sexuality for two African American young women, the discussion was more than scholarly. Instead of engaging in critique, these students responded with strong emotion in the face of mediascapes and social worlds that cast them as hyper-sexual. Emotion often reveals underlying ideologies through an act of intensely involved participation or immersion that results in important understandings about texts and discourses. Zembylas and Vrasidas (2005) called this "critical emotional literacy."

In research on identity and positioning related to the media art produced by students in a Canadian alternative high school, Rogers and Schofield (2005) and Rogers, Winters, and LaMonde (in press), found that students moved explicitly from image to ideology, using their video and other multimodal productions to critique the discourses that marginalized youth—themselves and others. To create this critically conscious media art, students used what the researchers call "discursive resources" (Rogers et al., in press) to engage in "imaginative, biographical, and spatial practices" (Rogers & Schofield, 2005, p. 216). In all of the products described across the two reports of the study, students drew heavily on their own biographies and the socio-spatial worlds that shaped their lives. Critical engagement in multimodal representation flourished even after the course was over, as is evident in the comments of one student concerned, a year later, that her digital photography project may have contributed to stereotyping Aboriginal youth.

The inseparable nature of meaning and being in participatory cultures suggests the need to scrutinize how digital literacy practices recruit and immerse members in embodied ways of expressing passions, attachments, and affiliations. Embodied literacies such as play and drama evoke critical interpretations and digital representations that are deeply personal as well as fanciful, opportunistic, and improvisational. These "playful pedagogies" acknowledge the power of pleasure while problematizing dominant stereotypes through "irreverent play with meaning in which seriousness and rationality are replaced by irony and parody" (Buckingham, 2003, p. 162). Doerr-Stevens (2009) describes the strategic process of "glocal appropriation" used by a student in a university writing class to construct his online identity for an online role play. The student used both local and global resources—resulting in some contradictory identities related to race—in order to critique depictions of White American males and offer a more hybrid and fluid version of masculinity. Critical engagement taps into the performative and transformative power of multimedia identity texts, as in YouTube spoofs (Willett, 2008), student-produced films (Nelson, Hull, & Roche-Smith, 2008; Nixon & Comber, 2005; Wohlwend, 2009a), or fan fiction narratives (Black, 2009). These playful productions can be both an expression and criticism of affiliation. For example, fan fiction provides a way of spinning new storylines for favorite media or video game characters as a way to display fan knowledge and to remake pre-packaged storylines. Black (2009) showed the transformative potential of digital literacy practices in a study of three adolescent English language learners writing in a popular online fan fiction archive. "When creating fan fiction, fans extend storylines, create new narrative threads, develop romantic relationships between characters, and focus on the lives of undeveloped characters from various media" (Black, 2009, p. 398). Film-making combined with children's media play creates embodied fanfiction, a prime site for productive critique. Wohlwend (2009a) found that kindergarten film-makers and actors had to negotiate emotional attachments to beloved Disney Princess characters and their desires to enact performances that were more personally satisfying (e.g., playing a comatose Sleeping Beauty or fending off an attacking dragon). When girls enthusiastically took up commercial media narratives, they encountered social limitations in passive princess identities, improvised character actions, and revised storylines to produce their own counter-narratives.

Research Approaches for Critical Engagement

Critical engagement complicates research designs with needs for converged methods that coordinate multiple perspectives and nuanced interpretations that attend to the "curious cocktail of effects from cultural and economic flows" (Luke & Carrington, 2005, p. 244). Research methods for critical engagement must track traces and trajectories beyond here-and-now activity, analyse "many-to-many" (Merchant, 2007) collective literacy practices and relationships, and remediate productive-consumption relations with globalization. Some promising conceptual approaches include:

- *Literacy Networks.* The study of literacy flows across multiple contexts looks at converging bodies, objects, and texts to understand how we make use of and are used by technologies. Leander and Lovvorn (2006) used actor network theory to track how bodies are translated into texts that move across literacy networks. Actor network theory researches technologies as not mere extensions of selves but as mergers in which social agents are not easily distinguished from their tools. Similarly, mediated discourse analysis tracks embodied practices to see how power wielded through physical actions with multimedia and technologies shapes meanings and identities (T. Y. Lewis, in press; Wohlwend, 2009a).
- *Nexus and Activity Systems.* Expanded forms of activity theory provide ways to trace interaction and power relations within and across online communities of practice (Beavis, 2009). Nexus analysis (Scollon & Scollon, 2004) reveals how these communities are situated in global systems and maintained by webs of tacit literacy practices.
- *Semiotic Signs.* Digital media contain layers of sign-making and identity-construction: in games within games (Lemke, 2006), or internal and external semiotic perspectives (Gee, 2007; Wohlwend, 2009b) in video game play.
- *Multimodal Spaces.* Multimodal analysis examines convergences in overlapping modes, for example, in video texts (Jewitt, 2006) or embodied practices among children playing a computer game (Norris, 2002). Multimodal analysis coordinates multiple tactile, aural, and visual modes to understand how images, icons, gaze,

actions, and physical proximity constitute digital literacy practices and spaces.

Critical engagement is built upon the legacy of critical literacy and rational deconstruction of logical structures of text. Critical interpretation and production of embodied literacies in digital cultures provides a way to address the complexity and complicity of desires, pleasures, and sensations bound up with readings (Janks, 2002) and to attend to overlaps, disruptions, and affordances among convergences, embodiment, and global flows.

Note

1. We use two terms throughout the chapter: "digital technology(ies)," and "digital media." Our use of these terms depends on whether the emphasis is on the technology tool or the media. When we refer to published research, we use the term the authors employ.

References

Appadurai, A. (1996). *Modernity at large: Cultural dimensions of globalization.* Minneapolis: University of Minnesota Press.

Appadurai, A. (2000). Grassroots globalization and the research imagination. *Public Culture, 12*(1), 1–19.

Apple, M. (2001). Comparing neo-liberal projects and inequality in education. *Comparative Education, 37*(4), 409–423.

Arnett, J. J. (2002). The psychology of globalization. *American Psychologist, 57*(10), 774–783.

Baildon, M., & Damico, J.S. (2009). How do we know?: Students examine issues of credibility with a complicated multimodal web-based text. *Curriculum Inquiry, 39*(2), 265–285.

Beach, R., & Doerr-Stevens, C. (2009). Learning argument practices through online role-play: Toward a rhetoric of significance and transformation. *Journal of Adolescent & Adult Literacy, 52*(6), 460–468.

Beavis, C. (2009). Games within games: Convergence and critical literacy. In R. Willett, M. Robinson, & J. Marsh (Eds.), *Play, creativity, and digital cultures* (pp. 15–35). New York: Routledge.

Black, R. W. (2009). Online fan fiction, global identities, and imagination. *Research in the Teaching of English, 43*(4), 397–425.

Boler, M. (1999). *Feeling power: Emotions and education.* New York: Routledge.

Buckingham, D. (2003). *Media education: Literacy, learning, and contemporary culture.* Cambridge: Wiley-Blackwell.

Burbules, N. (2004). Rethinking the virtual. *E-Learning, 1*(1), 162–183.

Burbules, N. C., & Callister, T. A. (2000). *Watch it: The risks and promises of information technologies for education.* Boulder, CO: Westview Press.

Carrington, V. (2005). Txting: The end of civilisation (again)? *Cambridge Journal of Education, 35*(2), 161–175.

Carter, S., Damico, J. S., & Kumasi-Johnson, K. (2008). The time is now!: Talking to African American youth about college. *Voices in the Middle, 16*(2), 47–53.

Coiro, J., & Dobler, B. (2007). Exploring the online reading comprehension strategies used by sixth-grade skilled readers to search for and locate information on the Internet. *Reading Research Quarterly, 42,* 214–257.

Comber, B., & Janks, H. (2006). Critical literacy across continents. In K. Pahl & J. Rowsell (Eds.), *Travel notes from the new literacy studies: Instances of practice* (pp. 95–117). Clevedon, UK: Multilingual Matters.

Damico, J., Baildon, M., & Campano, G. (2005). Integrating literacy, technology and disciplined inquiry in social studies: The development and application of a conceptual model. *Technology, Humanities, Education and Narrative* [Electronic journal] Retrieved July 15, 2010, from http://thenjournal.org/feature/92/

de Certeau, M. (1984). *The practice of everyday life* (S. Rendall, Trans.). Berkeley: University of California Press.

Doerr-Stevens, C. (2009). Hybrid identity design online: Glocal appropriation as multiliterate practice for civic pluralism. In D. L. Pullen, M. Baguley, & C. Gitsaki (Eds.), *Technoliteracy, discourse and social practice: Frameworks and applications in the digital age* (pp. 36–54). Hershey, PA: IGA Global.

Fabos, B. (2004). *Wrong turn on the information superhighway: Education and commercialization of the Internet.* New York: Columbia University Teachers College Press.

Fabos, B. (2008). The price of information: Critical literacy, education and today's Internet. In D. J. Leu, J. Coiro, M. Knobel, & C. Lankshear (Eds.), *Handbook of research on new literacies* (pp. 839–870). Mahwah, NJ: Erlbaum.

Gee, J. P. (2004). *Situated language and learning: A critique of traditional schooling.* New York: Routledge.

Gee, J. P. (2007). *What video games have to teach us about learning and literacy.* New York: Palgrave Macmillan.

Gounari, P. (2009). Rethinking critical literacy in the new information age. *Critical Inquiry in Language Studies, 6*(3), 148–175.

Guzzetti, B. J., & Gamboa, M. (2004). Zines for social justice: Adolescent girls writing on their own. *Reading Research Quarterly, 39*(4), 408–436.

Hull, G. A., & Nelson, M. E. (2005). Locating the semiotic power of multimodality. *Written Communication, 22*(2), 224–261.

Humphrey, S. (2006). 'Getting the reader on side': Exploring adolescent online political discourse. *E-Learning, 3*(2), 143–156.

Ito, M. (2007). Technologies of the childhood imagination: Media mixes, hypersociality, and recombinant cultural form [Electronic Version]. *Médiamorphoses, 21.* Retrieved September 12, 2009, from http://documents.irevues.inist.fr/handle/2042/23561

Janks, H. (2002) 'Critical literacy: beyond reason'. *Australian Educational Researcher, 29*(1), 7–27. [Electronic version]. Retrieved September 13, 2009, from http://www.unisa.edu.au/hawkeinstitute/cslplc/documents/Beyond.pdf

Jenkins, H. (2006). *Convergence culture: Where old and new media collide.* New York: New York University Press.

Jenkins, H., Purushotma, R., Clinton, K., Robison, A. J., & Weigel, M. (2006). *Confronting the challenges of participatory culture: Media education for the 21st century.* Chicago: The John D. and Catherine T. MacArthur Foundation.

Jewitt, C. (2006). *Technology, literacy and learning: A multimodal approach.* London: Routledge.

Kellner, D. (2004). Technological transformation, multiple literacies, and the re-visioning of education. *E-Learning, 1*(1), 9–37.

Lankshear, C., & Bigum, C. (1999). Literacies and new technologies in school settings. *Pedagogy, Culture, & Society, 7*(3), 445–465.

Lankshear, C., & Knobel, M. (Eds.). (2007). *The new literacies sampler.* New York: Peter Lang.

Leander, K. M., & Lovvorn, J. F. (2006). Literacy networks: Following the circulations of texts, bodies, and objects in the schooling and online gaming of one youth. *Cognition and Instruction, 24*(3), 291–340.

Leander, K. M., & McKim, K. K. (2003). Tracing the everyday 'sitings' of adolescents on the Internet: A strategic adaptation of ethnography across online and offline spaces. *Education, Communication & Information, 3*(2), 211–240.

Lemke, J. L. (2006). Toward critical multimedia literacy: Technology, research, and politics. In M. McKenna, D. Reinking, L. Labbo, & R. Kieffer (Eds.), *The international handbook of literacy & technology* (pp. 3–14). Mahwah, NJ: Erlbaum.

Lewis, C., & Fabos, B. (2005). Instant messaging, literacies, and social identities. *Reading Research Quarterly, 40*(4), 470–501.

Lewis, C., & Dockter, J. (2008). *Mediascapes and social worlds: The discursive construction of critical engagement in an urban classroom.* San Antonio, TX: National Council of Teachers of English.

Lewis, C., & Dockter, J. (in press). Reading literature in secondary school: Disciplinary discourses in global times. In S. Wolf, K. Coats, P. Enciso, & C. A. Jenkins (Eds.), *Handbook of research on children's and young adult literature.* New York: Routledge.

Lewis, C., Ketter, J., & Fabos, B. (2001). Reading race in a rural context. *International Journal of Qualitative Studies in Education, 14*(3), 317–350.

Lewis, T. Y. (in press.) Digital literacies and stories: Artifacts of a motherboard. In K. Pahl & J. Rowsell (Eds.), *Literacy learning through artifacts: Every object tells a story.* New York: Teachers College Press.

Lewison, M., Flint, A. S., & Van Sluys, K. (2002). Taking on critical literacy: The journey of newcomers and novices. *Language Arts, 79*(5), 382–392.

Luke A. & Carrington, V. (2005). Globalisation, literacy, curriculum practice. In. R. Fisher, M. Lewis, & G. Brooks (Eds), *Raising standards in literacy* (pp. 231–250). London: RoutledgeFalmer.

Marsh, J. (2010). Young children's play in online virtual worlds. *Journal of Early Childhood Research, 8*(1), 23–29.

Marsh, J. (in press). New literacies, old identities: Young girls' experiences of digital literacy at home and school. In C. Jackson, C. Paechter, & E. Reynolds (Eds.), *Girls and education 3–16: Continuing concerns, new agendas.* Buckingham,UK: Open University Press.

Medina, C. (2010). Reading across communities in biliteracy practices: Examining translocal discourses and cultural flows in literature discussions. *Reading Research Quarterly 45*(1), 40–60.

Merchant, G. (2007). Writing the future in the digital age. *Literacy, 41*(3), 118–128.

Misson, R., & Morgan W. (2006). *Critical literacy and the aesthetic: Transforming the English classroom.* Urbana, IL: National Council of Teachers of English.

Morgan, W. (1997). *Critical literacy: The art of the possible.* New York: Routledge.

Morrison, T. (1992). *Playing in the dark: Whiteness and the literary imagination.* Boston, MA: Harvard University Press.

Myers, J., Hammett, R., & McKillop, A. M. (1998). Opportunities for critical literacy and pedagogy in student-authored hypermedia. In D. Reinking, M. C. McKenna, L. D. Labbo, & R. D. Kieffer (Eds.), *Handbook of literacy and technology: Transformations in a post-typographic world* (pp. 63–78). Mahwah, NJ: Erlbaum.

Nelson, M. E., Hull, G. A., & Roche-Smith, J. (2008). Taking, and mistaking, the show on the road: Challenges of multimedia self-presentation. *Written Communication, 25*(4), 415–440.

Nixon, H., & Comber, B. (2005). Behind the scenes: Making movies in early years classrooms. In J. Marsh (Ed.), *Popular culture, new media and digital literacy in early childhood* (pp. 219–236). New York: RoutledgeFalmer.

Norris, S. (2002). The implication of visual research for discourse analysis: Transcription beyond language. *Visual Communication, 1*(1), 97–121.

Pascarella, J. (2008). Confronting the challenges of critical digital literacy: An essay review of *Critical constructivism: A primer. Educational Studies, 43*(3), 246–255.

Peters, M., & Lankshear, C. (1996). Critical literacy and digital texts. *Educational Theory, 46*(1), 51–70.

Rogers, T., & Schofield, A. (2005). Things thicker than words: Portraits of youth multiple literacies in an alternative secondary program. In J. Anderson, M. Kendrick, T. Rogers, & S. Smythe (Eds.), *Portraits of literacy across families, communities and schools* (pp. 205–220). Mahwah, NJ: Erlbaum.

Rogers, T., Winters, K., & LaMonde, A. M. (in press). From image to ideology: Analyzing shifting identity positions of marginalized youth across the cultural sites of video production. *Pedagogies: An International Journal.*

Scollon, R., & Scollon, S. W. (2004). *Nexus Analysis: Discourse and the Emerging Internet.* New York: Routledge.

Siegel, M., & Fernandez, S. L. (2000). Critical approaches. In M. L. Kamil, P. D. Pearson, R. Barr, & P. B. Mosenthal (Eds.), *The handbook of reading research* (Vol. III, pp. 141–152). Mahwah, NJ: Erlbaum.

Willett, R. (2008). Consumption, production, and online identities: Amateur spoofs on YouTube. In R. Willett, M. Robinson, & J. Marsh (Eds.), *Play, creativity, and digital cultures* (pp. 54–72). London: Routledge.

Wohlwend, K. E. (2009a). Damsels in discourse: Girls consuming and producing gendered identity texts through Disney Princess play. *Reading Research Quarterly, 44*(1), 57–83.

Wohlwend, K. E. (2009b). Early adopters: Playing new literacies and pretending new technologies in print-centric classrooms. *Journal of Early Childhood Literacy, 9*(2), 119–143.

Zembylas, M., & Vrasidas, C. (2005). Globalization, information and communication technologies, and the prospect of a 'global village': promises of inclusion or electronic colonization? *Journal of Curriculum Studies, 37*(1), 65–83.

28

Making Visual Analysis Critical

Peggy Albers, Vivian Vasquez, and Jerome C. Harste

Within the past few years much attention has been paid to visual literacy. We are particularly excited about the research done examining the visual texts being produced in English language arts classrooms. Burnaford, Brown, Doherty, and McLaughlin reviewed this research (2007) and concluded that while literacy and the arts had obvious connections, the idea that literacy instruction should help students develop frames for talking about visual texts is new in all too many schools (Albers, Harste, Vander Zanden, & Felderman, 2008; Marsh, 2006; Rowsell & Pahl, 2007; Vasquez, Harste, & Albers, 2010). Ann Hass Dyson (2006) has gone so far as to argue that the ability to understand how visual literacy influences and constitutes one's cultural and linguistic experiences must be part of the school's everyday literacy practices.

For the past decade the three of us have studied how visual texts do the work they do from the perspectives of semiotics and critical literacy. We have worked with teachers in designing and researching literacy curricula for use in public schools and universities. We have worked hard to make the reading and the analysis of visual texts a significant part of our—and the teachers we work with—everyday literacy practices, including publications and at professional conferences. To illustrate how this stance positions our work, we start our chapter with a text that was generated by a teacher in a workshop we did in Toronto, Canada in response to our invitation to create a "counter text" to a set of advertisements we had been using with the class. We first taught teachers to use visual discourse analysis (Albers, 2007b) for purposes of unpacking the underlying messages being conveyed. We then asked them to design, create, and present their own counter-ad (Harste & Albers, 2008), talking back to the subliminal messages that encourage viewers to purchase and buy into the lifestyle that these ads promote. By participating in this curricular engagement, teachers learned to read visual media in public spaces like magazines, billboards, and newspapers from both a critical

and a semiotic perspective. In addition, they learned to understand the significance of reading, interpreting and interrogating everyday texts.

In this chapter we review some of the breakthroughs that have been made in the analysis of visual texts while telling our own stories of how we have been involved. These stories are presented as extended discussions and situate our work within the larger frameworks of visual literacy and critical literacy. Peggy shares her interest in the analysis of visual texts in light of "what else is being said." Vivian shares her work in early childhood education, critical literacy and digital technologies, and makes the case that it is never too early to begin. Jerry discusses his interest in understanding visual literacy as visual narratives that need to be interrogated. We suggest that although scholars have become more interested and receptive to the thinking of literacy as visual, much more work needs to be done.

Theoretical Frameworks

Kress (2003) argued that "the world told" is vastly different from "the world shown" (p. 1). Thus, our work is theoretically grounded in methods of visual analysis (Kress & van Leeuwen, 2006; Sonesson, 1988) and in visual discourse analysis (Albers, 2007b), all of which are located within the larger theory of semiotics. Semiotics is the study of how we use alternate sign systems (art, music, mathematics, dance) to mean, as well as the systems and processes underlying signification, expression, representation, and communication, and indicates the integral relationship between society and meaning (Harste, 1994; Peirce cited in Thayer, 1982).

In particular, we argue that messages within visual texts have particular structures that can be analyzed (Kress & van Leeuwen, 1996/2006) both in how something is said (grammar of visual texts: media, object placement, space, color, etc.), and within critical literacy or what is said (composition: messages conveyed and discourses). Identification

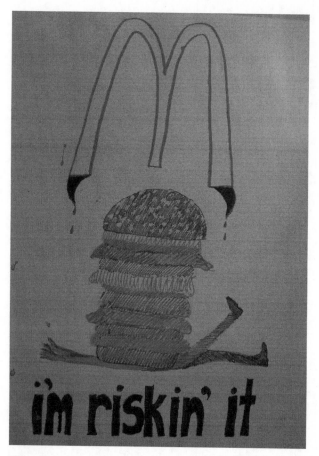

Figure 28.1

and location of these compositional and structural marks on the text offer insight into textmakers' definition and/or perception of the world and themselves as situated members, the social practices which sustain these ideas, and the pragmatic effects of ideas as "read" by others. Such work, as Teresa de Laurentis (1984) suggested, is a shift away from the classification of sign systems, their basic units, their levels of structural organization, and towards the exploration of the modes of production of signs and meanings, the ways in which systems and codes are used, transformed or transgressed in social practice. In congruence with these theories is the field of visual literacy, or "the ability to 'read,' interpret, and understand information presented in pictorial or graphic images" (Wileman, 1993, p. 114), further delineated by Sinatra (1986) as "the active reconstruction of past visual experience with incoming visual messages to obtain meaning" (p. 5). Visual literacy studies position the visual as a significant language through which we interpret and interact with our world, and suggest that we develop an ability to critically read and view images.

As scholars both of visual literacy and critical literacy, our work positions all textmaking as significant in terms of how it is read, interpreted, and interrogated, and how viewers are implicated in said visual messages. The next sections highlight our individual and collective work with visual texts as it is situated within a critical perspective.

Making Discourse Critical in Visual Texts

Informed by Elliot Eisner's (2002a, b) work in art education, Peggy's initial research evolved from a focus on integration of the arts to support strong literacy practices, including writing and reading, and into a more systematic analysis of visual texts in light of the organization of visual elements within these texts (Kress & van Leeuwen, 1996/2006) and Discourses (Gee, 2005) that emerged in visual messages. As Peggy has argued across writings (Albers, 2007a, b; 2008), analysis of visual texts, or a study of the relationships between and among objects within a visual text, along with a holistic reading of a visual text, provides information about the discourses that emerge in student-generated texts. Further, it leads to a more complete understanding of learners' literacy practices. Critical analysis of visual texts differentiates itself from arts-based literacy in that visual analysts are concerned with studying the systems of meaning that underpin the visual marks on the canvases of student-generated visual texts, while arts-based literacy understands the arts as supporting the reading and writing skills of students (Albers, 2006, 2007a, b).

In the early part of the 2000s, other researchers were focused on studying visual texts created by children (see Marsh, 1999, 2000; Moss, 2001; Rowsell & Pahl, 2007) and found links between children's identities and beliefs and their visual texts. At the same time, Peggy began to develop a method of analysis she called Visual Discourse Analysis (VDA; Albers, 2007b), to study the visual texts created by students in ELA classes in response to literature or those that accompanied original writings and the Discourses that informed these texts. Although a number of methods have been applied to professional-artworks (see Banks, 2001; Kress & van Leeuwen, 1996/2006; Pink, 2001; Rose, 2003), visual discourse analysis was applied to student-generated work, and addressed the discourses that emerged, the text itself, the macro and micro conversations surrounding the making and viewing of texts, and the visual text as a communicative event. Visual discourse analysis focuses not only on how visual elements relate within a text (Kress & van Leeuwen, 1996/2006), but also on how language is used to communicate and acts as a force on viewers to encourage particular actions or beliefs. Four principles guide visual discourse analysis. First, visual language is reflexive in that it both has the capacity to create and reflect the context and reality in which it was created. Second, language allows for situated meanings to occur, images or texts that are "assembled on the spot" (Gee, 2005, p. 94) in a given context (schools) and informed by signmakers and their interaction with other texts and conversations. Third, language is composed of many different social languages (Bahktin, 1981). How ELA students express their thoughts visually differs from how artists speak; students often have less knowledge about art as a discipline, and often default to structures and visual elements and objects that carry messages that society has defined and have become an accepted part of the social collective (Albers, 2007a). Fourth, there are cueing systems within visual texts, structural, semantic, artistic, tactile, and visual, that provide information regarding how, why and what students draw upon as they construct meaning (Albers, 2007b). Students often communicate more than what their oral or written narratives about a literary text say, and visual discourse analysis allows educators to understand what else students say about texts visually. This encourages a critical perspective, one which helps with the identification of political and social injustices and how social communities condone such inequalities, and to theorize our own visual productions of meaning and analyses of visual texts we see in public and/or in schools. Examined within a larger context, situated meanings, discourses, intertextuality, and structural features, visual discourse analysis offers insights into the beliefs, thoughts, and practices of the textmaker that otherwise lay hidden as "art."

Making Critical Visual Literacy in Early Childhood Settings

In schools, knowledge is predominantly created through language use, whether this is multimodal or specifically through print-based text. As children learn and use language, they learn different literacies. Embedded in the knowledge that literacies bring are learners' ways of doing and acting, what Gee (1997) refers to as "big 'D' discourse." In classrooms, children are only able to speak from the perspectives that are offered by the Discourses that have been made available to them. These ways of doing and acting are manifested in one's attitudes, actions, learning processes, and everyday life. They comprise forms of power that shape who one can be in a community. For the past 15 years, Vivian has worked with young children and how to support children as they learn to read, interpret and interrogate a range of texts critically (Vasquez, 2000, 2004; Vasquez & Wong-Kam, 2003). In this work, she focused on supporting students as they developed a critical stance towards literature, media, social issues, everyday texts such as candy wrappers and cereal boxes, and issues that arose in their own community and school.

A review of the literature reveals that teachers creating spaces for critical analysis of visual texts often frame their teaching from a critical literacy perspective (O'Brien, 1994, 1998; Marsh, 2000; Evans, 2004; Vasquez, 2000, 2005, 2010). Comber (2003) noted, "Critical literacy educators have drawn on perspectives from feminism, anti-racist education, critical discourse analysis, multiculturalism, theories of social justice and more" (p. 356). These perspectives in combination provide a powerful theoretical tool kit, with which to help young children understand that texts, including visual, are never neutral and are always socially constructed which means they can be deconstructed and re-constructed or re-designed to change inequitable representations such as stereotypes. Luke, O'Brien, and Comber (1994) explained, "By critical we mean ways that give students tools for weighing and critiquing, analyzing and appraising textual techniques and ideologies, values

and positions. The key challenge, then, is how to engage students with the study of how texts work semiotically and linguistically—while at the same time taking up how texts and their affiliated social institutions work politically to construct and position writers and readers in relations of power and knowledge"(p. 139). In 2001, Comber described three key moves in taking up critical literacies in classrooms with young children. These focused on recognizing and mobilizing children's analytic resources, examining existing critical texts, and offering children new discursive resources.

During the early 1900s, O'Brien (1994), while working with Comber in Australia, began creating opportunities for critical literacies in early childhood settings, breaking ground for future research on this topic. Comber (2003) described O'Brien as being "profoundly influenced by poststructuralist feminist theory, gender and literacy, critical discourse analysis and critiques of early childhood and progressive pedagogies" (p. 361). Such theories, according to Comber, suggested that children's capacities for literacy learning were being underestimated in the classroom. At the time when O'Brien was first imagining what critical literacy might be in early childhood settings, she drew primarily from demonstrations of practice in high school settings (Janks, 1993; Mellor, Patterson, and O'Neill, 1987). Her research focused on working with children to question and analyze the social worlds constructed in texts as a way of positioning them as readers who "could and should question the texts produced for them" (Comber, 2003, p. 362).

In a well-known study, O'Brien (1994) had her 5- to 7-year-old students critically analyze and re-design junk mail. This was a planned approach to critically analyzing visual images whereby O'Brien wanted to offer her students "a different way of looking at a ritual as taken-for-granted as Mother's Day and the advertising material that accompanies it" (p. 43). In doing so she had her students engage in analysis of the ads and catalogues creating spaces for discussions such as what groups of people get the most out of Mother's Day or how the mothers in the catalogues are like real mothers and how they are not like real mothers. The children then had an opportunity to create a new Mother's Day catalogue based on the information they had learned from their analysis of the ads and catalogues.

Having been influenced by the work of O'Brien (1994) as well as the work of Luke and Freebody (1990, 1997), Comber (1993), and Janks (1993), Vivian began to investigate negotiating spaces for critical literacies with 3- to 8-year-olds, in Ontario, Canada, in which she created opportunities for young children to critically analyze and re-design visual images found in books and everyday texts, such as posters and food packaging (Vasquez, 2003, 2004, 2007, 2010). However, rather than pre-determine what to study, Vivian took her cues from the children and created opportunities for critically analyzing visual images based on their inquiry questions. Vivian recounts in detail an experience in which children interrogated a visual text, a poster, while developing a critical stance towards gender.

While working with a group of pre-school children, Vivian created spaces to study issues of gender after hearing her students discuss a poster of the Royal Canadian Mounted Police (RCMP/Mountie; Vasquez, 2004). An RCMP officer who had come to visit the children had left the poster for display. While viewing the poster, her 4- and 5-year-old students initiated a conversation in which they began to discuss who could and could not be an RCMP. One young girl, Julia, declared that she wanted to be a Mountie when she grew up. In response, a young boy, Curtis, responded, "No, you can't! There are no girl Mounties in the poster" (Vasquez, 2010, p. 23). Upon closer inspection, Vivian discovered that the children were right. The poster, which depicted a group of RCMP on horseback, did not have a single female represented. From this poster, children developed conversations that critically analyzed the poster. The children began to tease out their perception of how boys and girls, and men and women, were positioned by everyday texts such as posters, especially posters designed for public spaces like schools. These children made problematic the absence of women in the RCMP poster, traditional notions of femininity were challenged, and traditional male and female roles destabilized.

In response to this conversation, Vivian and her students began an inquiry into Mounties, and with their information, they positioned themselves to engage in social action. They searched through their school library for information, with a particular eye for roles played by males and females and how these roles positioned people in particular ways. A number of other similar conversations took place as Vivian and these children continued to explore notions of gender including what they could to contribute to change the way certain groups such as girls and women are positioned in society. In response to these conversations, Andrea—whose parents were both in the RCMP—spoke up saying that if they (Mounties) "keep sending this poster out then some people, like girls, won't know that they can be Mounties too." As part of their decision to participate in social action, Jessica decided that she would redesign the Mountie poster and show what the poster should look like today, "because today, women are Mounties also." She thought that girls should be given not only the opportunity to become RCMP but, in fact, already are in position as RCMP officers; therefore, their presence should be recognized. She called her poster "My Poster of the Way the Mountie Poster Should Be." In Jessica's poster there was an equitable number of men and women represented. Once completed, she asked Vivian to help her with a cover letter to include with the revised poster, which was sent to the local RCMP office.

Such social action in response to visual media that is sent to schools and tacked to walls in public spaces evidenced children's interest in and critical response to messages sent visually. Common to both O'Brien's and Vivian's work are the ways in which children at a very young age were able to talk about textual ideologies, silences and absences, as well as notions of gender positioning. They learned that texts are not neutral and experienced disrupting taken for granted texts by participating in the re-design of such texts.

Making Critical the Analysis of Visual Texts

In an effort to develop a framework for the analysis of visual images, Jerry asked teachers in workshop settings to create a Jacob Lawrence-like painting addressing what they saw as an important social issue. To support them, Jerry showed a videotape of the painter, Jacob Lawrence, called *The Glory of Expression* (Irving, Feeman, & Davies, 1996), and invited teachers to use Lawrence's style as a model, even copying characters from his painting if need be. To develop an analyses system, Jerry created a research team and selected 40 teacher-created paintings from those he had collected. Jerry's team used Kress and van Leeuwen's (1996/2006) work on the grammar of visual design to read color, vectors, and the positioning of individuals and objects in the painting. Using Albers (2007b) visual discourse analysis procedures, Jerry's team also read the pictures in terms of pragmatics, specifically how the artist had positioned the viewer as well as the subjects being depicted in the art work. As a final step, the research team coded each picture in terms of what aspects of critical literacy were addressed, á la Janks' four dimensional model (2000, 2009) of critical literacy: dominance, diversity, access or design. To verify their reading of the visuals, they asked 3 different groups of 4 graduate students to give a one-line interpretation of the picture. These were propositionalized and compared in terms of meaning across interpretations. They also had the artist's reflection on his or her own production. These were used to lend further credence to the accuracy of the visual interpretation they had produced using Kress and van Leeuwen's, Albers', and Janks' procedures. While the analyses were complex, the research team was fortunate in having Kress, Albers, and Janks actually work with them in analyzing these data. What Jerry's team learned from this study was that visual images could be read with a good deal of accuracy by members of the same cultural group. While reviewers initially were concerned with, what they called, "over analysis" of the visual data, the cross analyzes performed showed this not to be the case; visual images were as straight-forward to analyze as was written text. Publishing this study raised new concerns. Reviewers felt Jerry's team had read too much into the visual texts. Reviewers wanted the artist's reflection to verify the researchers' interpretations of the pictures. So, in a study which argued that literacy researchers were too dependent on written language, Jerry's research team was forced to use written language to legitimize their analysis of the visual (see Harste, Leland, Grant, Chung, Enyeart, 2007).

Because this study suggested that participants came to both visual and critical literacy with some inherent analysis skills on which teachers could build curriculum, Jerry's second study was an attempt to investigate how inservice, preservice, and fifth-grade children read visual images. For this purpose, Jerry and his research teams used advertisements (Walmart, Barbie, The National Guard, fast foods, sports, among others) and invited participants to "unpack" them in terms of what details they noticed and what sense they made of what they noticed. In an effort to get at "desire" (a fifth dimension of critical literacy; Janks, 2009), Jerry and his research team asked each research group to identify which advertisements they really liked and why. Despite the fact that all three groups had been introduced to critical literacy, fifth graders were better at identifying stereotypes and questioning the major messages in advertisement than were practicing teachers and preservice teachers. Preservice teachers seemed to read advertisements as unproblematic, often saying things that suggested they saw the Barbie image as one worthy of emulation, had enjoyed playing with Barbie themselves, and hoped their children would do the same. More than anything these studies demonstrated that while everyone had some analytic abilities, as critical theorists and as persons interested in developing visual literacy, educators have their work cut out for them (see Albers, Harste, Vander-Zanden, & Felderman, 2008; Lewison, Leland, & Harste, 2008).

Although not written up, Jerry followed up this study by teaching groups of elementary children, preservice and inservice teachers Kress and van Leeuwen's (1996/2006) grammar of visual design. While all participants improved in their ability to unpack graphic images, progress was not as fast as expected. A review of the research at that time suggested that there was some evidence that having participants create "counter advertisements" (Figure 28.1) was more effective in supporting participants take-on a critical stance than was just asking participants to critically read advertisements.

Jerry's next study followed up on this finding. After showing some examples of "counter advertisements," Jerry, Vivian, and Peggy invited 90 inservice teachers to work in groups of 4 or 5 to create a "counter advertisement" to one of 4 ads that we had shown them and that had been used in our second set of studies. Using Kress and van Leeuwen (1996/2006), Albers (2007b), and Janks (2000), we read the 20 counter ads produced by this group of teachers in terms of what issues they took on, what messages were produced, and what stereotypes were questioned. We also studied these counter ads in terms of what was left unsaid, how the teacher-artists had positioned themselves as well as how they had positioned the subjects in their counter ad. This study showed that having the opportunity to produce a counter ad in collaboration with others—so participants could talk through aspects of visual literacy—supported teachers in taking on a critical stance as well as thinking semiotically about sign systems and how they mean (see Harste & Albers, 2008).

Our most recent study builds on these findings but asked teachers to unpack children's literature in terms of what they saw as significant sign systems (we asked them to identify 5) and, for each one, what work they saw these signs as doing (Harste, Vasquez, & Albers, 2009). Despite a year-long study of critical literacy with the two groups of 35 teachers

involved in this study, teachers had a great deal of trouble identifying stereotypes and questioning the underlying and often unspoken messages. One of the books we used was *Willy and Hugh* (Browne, 2000). While participants could identify significant signs and even generate counter messages, only 7% of the participants questioned the fact that boys not girls were positioned as bullies and in this book. Only 20% of the participants questioned the role of the church's involvement in segregation, one of the unspoken issues in the book, *Sister Anne's Hands* (Lorbiecki, 1998). While *Into the Forest* (Browne, 2004) plays around with several issues, one of the issues it addresses is the absent father in a household. When we read this to the children at the Center for Inquiry, a public option school in Indianapolis, the children were offended and saw it as racist, alluding to the much stigmatized absent Black father in the inner-city household. However, fewer than 14% of the teachers in our study questioned Anthony Browne's theme or saw it as problematic. While these data are not very encouraging, by repeatedly unpacking a children's picture book, participants became more and more astute and critical. Just recently, Jerry and Vivian started bringing to their workshop sessions with teachers picture books that are popular and cater to grandparents. These books often look innocent and do not seem to directly address social issues. *Pete and Pickles* (Breathed, 2008), for example, is the story of a little pig who saves a big elephant. The big elephant is fat and jolly, thus playing off of this common stereotype while the little pig is nerdy, smart, and studious, thus perpetuating another stereotype. While this study is still in progress, we can report that participants seem to be becoming more visual and critically literate with each experience.

Overall these studies are meant to support the critical examination of visual images. One of the things that has become clear is that literacy is semiotic, well beyond written language and visual images. As a children's book author, Jerry can report that children's books, for example, are written so they "sound" right; so they, in fact, roll off the tongue. In any oral reading of a book the gestures, voice changes, and rises and falls in pitch are all part of the performance. What this means is that the analysis of the semiotic nature of literacy has just begun. While it may make sense to focus on one sign system at a time, the orchestration of sign systems may be what really is important. Jerry is happy to report that some of this work is being done and worth following (see, for example, Beach, Enciso, Harste, Jenkins, Rains, Rogers, et al., 2009; Wohlwend, 2007).

Conclusion

This chapter encourages literacy researchers and educators to consider the role of analysis of visual texts as information that encourages a deeper discussion of what constitutes literacy. By knowing the role that Discourses play in the reading, interpreting, and analysis of visual texts, researchers and educators, alike, can more thoughtfully understand to what extent very young children through adults internalize messages that comprise these texts. Making critical the role of visual analysis significantly implicates the textmaker and the viewer as active and critical makers and readers of visual texts, rather than as a passive makers and viewers whose primary stance is aesthetic. The forms through which knowledge and understanding are constructed, remembered, and expressed must be wider than verbal or written language alone. If students, and educators, are to understand written, visual, musical, and dramatic texts (and so on) and be more able to express what they know through a range of media, they need to have the opportunity both to study structures, purposes, and qualities within their own visual texts, and to learn to read said texts.

References

Albers, P. (2006). Imagining the possibilities in multimodal curriculum design. *English Education, 38*(2), 75–101.

Albers, P. (2007a). *Finding the artist within: Creating and reading visual texts in English language arts classrooms.* Newark, DE: International Reading Association.

Albers, P. (2007b). Visual discourse analysis: An introduction to the analysis of school-generated visual texts. In D. W. Rowe, R. T. Jimenez, D. L. Compton, D. K. Dickinson, Y. Kim, K. M. Leander, et al. (Eds.), *56th yearbook of the National Reading Conference* (pp. 81–95). Oak Creek, WI: NRC.

Albers, P. (2008). Theorizing visual representation in children's literature. *Journal of Literacy Research, 40*(2), 163–200.

Albers, P., Harste, J. C., Vander Zanden, S., & Felderman, C. (2008). Using popular culture to promote critical literacy practices. In Y. Kim, V. J. Risko, D. L. Compton, D. K. Dickinson, M. Hundley, R. T. Jiménez, et al. (Eds.), *57th yearbook of the National Reading Conference* (pp. 70–83). Oak Creek, WI: NRC.

Bahktin, M. (1981). *The dialogic imagination.* Austin: University of Texas Press.

Banks, M. (2001). *Visual methods in social research.* London: Sage.

Beach, R., Enciso, P., Harste, J. C., Jenkins, C., Raina, S. A., Rogers, R., et al. (2009). Exploring the "critical" in critical content analysis of children's literature. In K. Leander, D. Rowe, D. Dickinson, M. Hundley, R. Jimenez, et al. (Eds.), *58th yearbook of the National Reading Conference* (pp. 129–143). Oak Creek, WI: NRC.

Burnaford, G., Brown, S., Doherty, J., & McLaughlin, H. J. (2007). *Arts integration frameworks, research & practice: A literature review.* Washington, DC: Arts Education Partnership.

Breathed, B. (2008). *Pete and Pickles.* New York: Philomel.

Browne, A. (2000). *Willy and Hugh.* New York: Red Fox.

Browne, A. (2004). *Into the forest.* Cambridge, UK: Candlewick Press.

Comber, B. (1993). Classroom explorations in critical literacy, *The Australian Journal of Language and Literacy, 16*(1), 73–83.

Comber, B. (2001). Negotiating critical literacies. *School Talk, 6*(3), 1–3.

Comber, B. (2003). Critical literacy: What does it look like in the early years? In N. Hall, J. Larson, & J. Marsh (Eds.), *Handbook of research in early childhood literacy* (pp. 355–368). London: Sage/Paul Chapman.

de Laurentis, T. (1984). *Alice doesn't: Feminism, semiotics, cinema.* Bloomington: Indiana University.

Dyson, A. H. (2006). On saying it right (write): "Fix-its" in the foundations of learning to write. *Research in the Teaching of English, 41,* 8–44.

Eisner, E. W. (2002a). *The arts and the creation of mind.* New Haven, CT: Yale University Press.

Eisner, E. W. (2002b). What can education learn from the arts about the practice of education? *Journal of Curriculum and Supervision, 18*(1), 4–16.

Evans, J. (2004). *Literacy moves on: Popular culture, new technolo-*

gies, and critical literacy in the primary classroom.* London David Fulton.

Gee, J. P. (1997). Meanings in discourses: Coordinating and being coordinated. In S. Muspratt, A. Luke, & P. Freebody (Eds.), *Constructing critical literacies: Teaching and learning textual practice* (pp. 273–302). Creskill, NJ: Hampton Press.

Gee, J. (2005). *An introduction to discourse analysis: Theory and method* (2nd ed.). Abingdon, UK: Routledge.

Harste, J. C. (1994). Literacy as curricular conversations. In R. B. Ruddell, M. R. Ruddell, & H. Singer, (Eds.), *Theoretical models and processes of reading* (pp. 1221–1242). Newark, DE: International Reading Association.

Harste, J. C., & Albers, P. (2008, December 3). *Teachers repackage consumerism* [Paper & PowerPoint available at mypage.harste.iu.edu] Presentation given at the annual meeting of the National Reading Conference, Orlando.

Harste, J. C., Leland, C. H., Grant, S., Chung, M., & Enyeart, J. (2007). Analyzing art in language arts research. In D. Rowe, R. Jimenez, D. Compton, D. Dickinson, Y. Kim, K. Leander, et al. (Eds.), *56th Yearbook of the National Reading Conference* (pp. 254–265). Oak Creek, WI: NRC.

Harste, J. C., Vasquez, V., & Albers, P. (2009, December 3). *Willy and Hugh get critical.* Presentation given at the annual meeting of the National Reading Conference, Albuquerque, NM.

Irving, D. (Writer & Director), Freeman, L. (Creator & Producer), & Davies, O. (Narrator). (1996). *Jacob Lawrence: The glory of expression* (VHS Video). New York: L&S Video, 28 minutes.

Janks, H. (Ed.) (1993). *Critical language awareness series.* Johannesburg, South Africa: Witswatersrand University Press and Hodder & Stoughton Educational.

Janks, H. (2000). Domination, access, diversity and design: A synthesis for critical literacy education. *Educational Review, 52*(1), 15–30.

Janks, H. (2009). *Language and power.* London: Routledge.

Kress, G. (2003). *Literacy in the new media age.* New York: Routledge.

Kress, G., & van Leeuwen, T. (1996/2006). *Reading images: The grammar of visual design* (1st and 2nd eds.). New York: Routledge.

Lewison, M., Leland, C., & Harste, J.C. (2008). *Creating critical classrooms: K-8 reading and writing with an edge.* Philadelphia: Erlbaum.

Lorbiecki, M. (1998). *Sister Anne's hands* (Ill. K. Wendy Popp). New York: Penguin.

Luke, A., & Freebody, P. (1990). Literacies programs: Debates and demands in cultural context. *Prospect: Australian Journal of TESOL, 5*(7), 7–16.

Luke A., & Freebody, P. (1997). Shaping the social practices of reading. In S. Muspratt, A. Luke, & P. Freebody (Eds.), *Constructing critical literacies* (pp. 185–223). Cresskill, NJ: Hampton Press.

Luke, A., O'Brien, J., & Comber, B. (1994). Making community texts objects of study. *Australian Journal of Language and Literacy, 17*(2), 139–149.

Marsh, J. (1999). Batman and batwoman go to school: Popular culture in the literacy curriculum. *International Journal of Early Years Education, 7*(2), 117–131.

Marsh, J. (2000). Teletubby tales: Popular culture in the early years language and literacy curriculum. *Contemporary Issues in Early Childhood, 1*(2), 119–136.

Marsh, J. (2006). Popular culture and literacy: A bourdieuan analysis. *Reading Research Quarterly, 46*(2), 160–174.

Mellor, B., Patterson, A. & O'Neill, M. (1987). *Reading stories.* Perth, Australia: Chalkface Press.

Moss, G. (2001). Seeing with the camera: Analysing children's photographs of literacy in the home. *Journal of Research in Reading, 24*(3), 279–292.

O'Brien, J. (1994). Show mum you love her: Taking a new look at junk mail. *Reading, 28*(1), 43–46.

O'Brien, J. (1998). Experts in Smurfland. In M. Knobel & A. Healy (Eds.), *Critical literacies in the primary classroom* (pp. 13–26). Newtown, Australia: PETA.

Pink, S. (2001). *Doing visual ethnography. Images, media, and representation in research.* London: Sage.

Rose, G. (2003). *Visual methodologies.* Thousand Oaks, CA: Sage.

Rowsell, J., & Pahl, K. (2007). Sedimented identities in texts: Instances of practice. *Reading Research Quarterly, 42*(3), 388–404.

Sinatra, R. (1986). *Visual literacy connections to thinking, reading and writing.* Springfield, IL: Charles C. Thomas.

Sonesson, G. (1988). *Methods and models in pictorial semiotics.* Report 3 from the Semiotics Project. Lund, Sweden: Institute of Art History.

Thayer, H. S. (1982). *Pragmatism: The classic writings.* Indianapolis, IN: Hackett.

Vasquez, V. (2000). Our way: Using the everyday to create a critical literacy curriculum. *Primary Voices, 9*(3), 8–13.

Vasquez, V. (2003). What engagement with Pokemon can teach us about learning and literacy. *Language Arts, 81*(1), 118–125.

Vasquez, V. (2004). *Negotiating critical literacies with young children.* Mahwah, NJ: Erlbaum.

Vasquez, V. (2005). Resistance, power-tricky, and colorless energy: What engagement with everyday popular culture texts can teach us about learning and literacy. In J. Marsh (Ed.), *Popular culture, media and digital literacies in early childhood* (pp. 201–219). New York: RoutledgeFalmer.

Vasquez, V. (2007). Using the everyday to engage in critical literacies with young children. *New England Reading Association Journal, 43*(2), 6–12.

Vasquez, V. (2010). *Getting beyond I like the book: Creating spaces for critical literacy in K-6 classrooms* (2nd ed.). Newark, DE: International Reading Association.

Vasquez, V., Harste, J., & Albers, P. (2010). Making new literacies critical. In B. Baker (Ed), *New literacies from multiple perspectives.* (pp. 265–285). New York: Guilford Press.

Vasquez, V., & Wong-Kam, J. (2003). Becoming critically literate. *School Talk, 8*(4), 1–2.

Wileman, R. E. (1993). *Visual communicating.* Englewood Cliffs, NJ: Educational Technology Publications.

Wohlwend, K. E. (2007). Reading to play and playing to read: A mediated discourse analysis of early literacy apprenticeship. In D. Rowe, R. Jimenez, D. Compton, D. Dickinson, Y. Kim, K. Leander, et al. (Eds.), *56th Yearbook of the National Reading Conference* (pp. 377–393). Oak Creek, WI: NRC.

29

Webs of Significance

Semiotic Perspectives on Text

MARJORIE SIEGEL AND DEBORAH WELLS ROWE

Why Semiotics Now?

Texts are not what they used to be. Consider the morning commute on a New York City subway. People still mark off their social boundaries by keeping their noses in a newspaper, or last night's homework, but it is more common to see people plugged into their mp3 players or tapping out text messages on their phones. Screens that used to take up entire desktops are now "personal, portable and pedestrian" (Ito, Okabe, & Matsuda, 2005) and dis/play images, music, and animation as well as writing. Much has been made of the shift "from page to screen" (Snyder, 1998) but with the rise of social networking sites, video gaming, fanfiction, blogging, and YouTube, texts have become part of a new web of signification—Web 2.0—a term that has come to signify the latest version of the Internet in which people are producers, not just consumers, of culture. Wikipedia and "WeMedia" (Bowman & Willis, 2003) capture this participatory ethos of interactivity and involvement. Expertise is under siege as anyone with time, interest, and digital access can contribute to deciding what counts as knowledge on Wikipedia, and what counts as news on websites serving as outlets for "citizen journalism" (e.g., blogs, Flickr, as well as media outlets such as http://www.cnn.com/ireport/). The emergence of Web 2.0 calls into question the conventional definition of a text as a static, monomodal, material surface that relays a writer's intended meaning to a reader.

The texts and practices characteristic of Web 2.0 point to the need for a theoretical lens broad enough to explain what counts as a text, how texts mean, and how to do things with texts in this new communicative landscape. Linguistic theories—even those that fuse language and social practice, such as Halliday's functional-systemic theory (1978) and Austin's speech act theory (1975)—can no longer suffice given the ease with which images, sounds, and movement can be tapped for signification. Semiotics—a broad field of studies that looks at "meanings and messages in all their forms and all their contexts" (Innis, 1985, p. vii)—provides

a rich conceptual palette for making sense of the "plurality of texts that circulate" (New London Group, 1996, p. 61) in a 21st-century social landscape. Until quite recently, semiotics has not been considered relevant to literacy theory and research, despite its long history within philosophical studies (see Deely, 1982). Yet, the basics of semiotics—the idea that signs are social forces and that anything can be taken as a sign—make semiotics uniquely suited for studying texts in the contemporary communicative landscape.

In this chapter, we outline the major semiotic traditions and their contributions to defining, theorizing, and analyzing texts. We begin with an overview of Charles Sanders Peirce (1839–1914) and Ferdinand de Saussure (1857–1913), the two figures most closely associated with semiotic thought in modern times. Of the two, Sausurre's definition of a sign as an arbitrary relationship between signifier and signified is more widely known, but we believe Peirce's theory of semiosis has a surprising resonance with contemporary literacy practice and thus offers greater potential for understanding texts. We then examine the work of Vygotsky, Bakhtin, Voloshinov, Kress, and Scollon and Scollon, all of whom give signs a central place in their theories of human thought, language, and literacy. Although our review will necessarily be limited in scope, we have selected those ideas we regard as essential both to understanding texts and to imagining new possibilities for designing, interpreting, embodying, and questioning texts in school literacy curricula.

To introduce these ideas, we turn to a setting that often appears immune to the changes in texts described earlier—school. Schools are the one place where texts appear to have undergone little change. Even more troubling is the way school literacy is shrinking to fit federal and state educational policies at the very moment that real world literacy is morphing into multiliteracies. Computers may be present in schools, but still cede center stage to books for reading and paper for writing. However, it doesn't take the click of a mouse to design and transform a text, Web 2.0 style; all you need is a child. Five-year-old Hector accomplished this with his reading partner, Beatriz, during independent reading time in their New York City kindergarten. Their joint participation in a reading event will serve to illustrate what each semiotic tradition can contribute to an understanding of texts.

Weaving Webs of Significance with Text: An Illustration

In a New York City kindergarten, the reader's workshop mini-lesson had just concluded, and children were directed to read their "little books" to themselves and then to their partners. Hector and Beatriz, two Dominican American children who had been reading partners for most of the school year, moved to the block corner with their book baggies, stuffed with books deemed just right for these two young readers. Beatriz selected *What Can Go Up?*—a book with a question-answer pattern describing items being placed in a tree house ("Can the rug go up? Yes, the rug can go up. Can the mat go up? Yes, the mat can go up.")—accompanied by a photograph depicting the action. As the children read the title, Beatriz inverted the title's meaning so it became *What Can Go Down?* and turned her book upside down as she did so. "This is my new book," she declared. Hector ignored this at first, reading the actual words quickly and in a robot-like voice. He finished his version before Beatriz, and declared, "I'm gonna get *What Can Go Down?*" He put his book back in his baggie, and pretended to look for the "new" book. "I found it!," he reported, and held his book upside down, so what appeared to go *up* in his first reading would go *down* in the second. He and Beatriz read the new version, turning the pages backwards and oftentimes pausing to check if they were on the same page. Suddenly, Hector started reading very fast, and Beatriz tried to catch up. He read the last page, "We can go down, too," closed his book quickly, and started singing while waiting for Beatriz to finish.

What does it mean to take a semiotic perspective on this literacy event, and what might such a lens contribute to educators' understandings of texts in these changing times? To address, these questions, we offer multiple readings of this event, each pursuing a different theoretical approach to semiotics.

Signs, Texts, and Meanings: Semiotic Traditions

We begin with a question that is basic to understanding texts: What is a sign? To answer this question, we must first assert, "nothing is a sign in and of itself" (Merrell, 1979, p. 150). As noted earlier, semiotics is the study of how acts and artifacts come to be interpreted as signs. Thus, signs do not have given meanings but, instead, have the *potential* to represent and generate meanings. Two distinct analytic traditions, emerging from the work of Saussure and Peirce, have addressed the problem of how signs work. Saussure, a Swiss linguist, considered linguistics a branch of what he called "semiology," yet his analysis of linguistic signs served as the model for all signs. Saussure's analysis of the

system by which linguistic signs achieve their meanings led to the development of an analytic approach known as structuralism (evident in the work of Piaget, Chomsky, and Levi-Strauss [Gardner, 1981]), that dominated the humanities to such an extent that semiotics and structuralism were regarded as synonymous.

Peirce, an American philosopher who had a long career as a scientist, may be best known for his taxonomy of icon, index, and symbol, signs that function by virtue of resemblance (icon), physical connection (index), or a cultural convention which has become a rule or habit (symbol). Peirce sought to develop an understanding of logic that could account for human thought and action. His starting point was the observation that there could be no direct knowledge of the world except as mediated by signs. In a well-known passage, Peirce wrote, "It seems a strange thing …that a sign should leave its interpreter to supply part of its meaning; but the explanation of the phenomenon lies in the fact that the entire universe…is perfused with signs" (cited in Sebeok, 1977, p. vi).

The most important idea semiotics contributes to the understanding of texts is how signs work, and the contrast between Saussure's explanation and that of Peirce amounts to the difference between structure and process. For Saussure, signs work only in relation to the structure of the sign system whereas for Peirce, signs work only when an interpreter brings one sign in relation to another, thus generating meaning through expansion as opposed to substitution. Saussure was interested in language as a system (langue) rather than the actual practice of speech (parole). He proposed that a sign is an association between form (signifier) and meaning (signified). This association is arbitrary (i.e., there is no resemblance between the word 'dog' and the concept of a dog). Thus, the signification that results from this association results from rules that govern the system. Key to understanding this system is the relation of signs to other signs in the system, rather than to their referents outside the system. Signs become meaningful on the basis of differences (typically oppositional differences) from other signs, so "house" acquires meaning in relation to apartment or vacation cottage or condo.

Peirce's description of sign-functioning, on the other hand, emphasizes process and generativity rather than structure. Peirce proposed that signs become meaningful through the enlargement and expansion of meaning, which he called "semiosis." In contrast to Saussure, who posited the relation of form and meaning as a two-term relation between signifier and signified, Peirce explained semiosis through his depiction of a semiotic triad. The sign (representamen) stands for the object in relation to a third element—another sign—which Peirce called an interpretant. For him, semiosis involved transformation, as in metaphor, and not simply the translation of a signifier into a signified. The meaning of one sign is expanded through the mediation of another sign. An important passage in Peirce's writing states "a sign is something by knowing which we know something more" (Hardwick, 1977, p. 31). The "something more" that we know is provided by the interpretant, which brings the object and representamen into relationship with another sign, and in this way, sets in motion an unending process of translation and interpretation that Peirce called "unlimited semiosis" (Eco, 1976). This is why Eco (1976) concludes, "the sign always opens up something new. No interpretant, in adjusting the sign interpreted, fails to change its borders to some degree" (p. 44).

Our discussion, thus far, suggests that a text cannot be a container of ready-made meanings; instead, a text is an "assemblage of signs" (Chandler, 2002, p. 2). Chandler adds that this assemblage is "constructed (and interpreted) with reference to the conventions associated with a genre and in a particular medium of communication" (p. 3). However, we would argue that any "assemblage of signs" has the potential to mean in ways not fully circumscribed by conventions of genre or medium. These aspects of the text are relevant but sometimes overemphasized and, especially in school, become a way to confine meaning by focusing on "appropriateness." Peirce's explanation of the interpretant in semiosis as a sign that both mediates and generates another sign is critical to understanding texts because it means that there are no single signs. The existence of a sign presupposes other signs: "the meaning of a sign inchoatively contains all the texts within which the sign can be inserted. A sign is a textual matrix" (Eco, 1976, p. 184). Thus, if a sign is a triadic relation that is part of a chain of semiosis, then a text can be understood as an assemblage of signs with the potential to produce and link to other texts.

These ideas may seem light-years away from Hector and Beatriz's reading of *What Can Go Up?* Yet, Peirce's explanation of semiosis can be useful in sorting out what is a text and how texts mean in this event. Given that a sign is anything that can be taken as a sign, and a text is an assemblage of signs, then this event incorporates multiple texts: the material text (*What Can Go Up?*); the invented text (*What Can Go Down?*); the children's textual performances (assemblages of linguistic, visual, kinesthetic, and musical signs); and, the discursive (practicing fluent reading of "just right" books with partners), temporal (during readers' workshop), and spatial (in the block corner) setting for the event. It is the children who decided to treat these materials and performances as texts, approaching them with the expectation that they could "stand to someone for something in some respect or capacity" (Peirce, cited in Eco, 1976, p. 180). From a sociocultural perspective on signs and texts, this expectation is regarded as a cultural achievement, and not a property of the material and embodied texts themselves. Hector's action of returning his copy of *What Can Go Up?* and pretending to search for his new book, *What Can Go Down?* illustrates two ideas usually masked by the familiar fiction that a text represents meanings to be reproduced: anything can be taken as a sign, and signs mean through their relation to other signs. Not only did the children decide what could be taken as a sign or a text, but, as Peirce observed, they also contributed part of the meaning of texts they read. With a participatory ethos as-

sociated with Web 2.0 practices, these sign-makers literally and metaphorically turned literacy on its head to generate a playful, imaginative, and embodied reading. The children violated text conventions by turning the book upside-down and reading back to front while generating a new meaning through the mediation of an interpretant such as "choice time" or "drama," two options during the school day. In doing so, they transformed the expected school reading of this text (fluently reading the words) into what Dyson (2003) would call a "textual toy." Thus, we would argue that Beatriz and Hector's "oppositional" reading of *What Can Go Up?* was not limited solely by the conventions associated with the genre of the "little book" or with reading as a practice in this classroom. They treated their classroom as "perfused with signs" and did the work assigned to them by the process of semiosis, generating meanings through the mediation of one sign with another.

Scollon and Scollon's (2003) recent work on geosemiotics extends Peirce's discussion of semiosis by highlighting the indexicality of signs—the ways that signs reflect or point to their locations in the concrete, spatial world. Rather than seeing texts/signs as autonomous artifacts, they argue that a significant part of the meaning of any sign is the way it is placed in the material world. Scollon and Scollon have highlighted two types of sign-functioning involving indexicality. Some signs (e.g., printed text, actions, objects) point to the physical spaces where they are located. For example, Beatriz and Hectors "little books" point to (index) the kinds of reading that kindergarteners are expected to do in the physical space of this classroom where they are taught to read using predictable language structures and illustrations as supports. Signs can also symbolically index spaces not physically present. For example, the children's reading of the text upside down and with the concept of *down* substituted for the text's printed word, *up,* likely indexed home spaces where they encountered the idea of "opposite day" through popular cartoon shows. In short, the signs produced by Hector and Beatriz in their reading performance, gained much of their meaning from their emplacement in the kindergarten classroom, but also from the ways they indexed the children's shared understanding of out-of-school spaces.

Signs gain their meaning not only from their emplacement in the material world, but also from the embodied practices (movements of bodies through space and in relation to one another) through with they are performed. Leander (2002) argues that embodied practices, as one type of material sign, are important semiotic resources offering possibilities for meaning-making different from those provided by language. Through gesture and the positioning of bodies, speakers create social spaces where certain identities are empowered or silenced. In our example, Hector and Beatriz not only link their talk, but also use gaze and coordinated physical action (page turning) to signal joint engagement. The embodied action of holding the books upside down signed collaborative engagement in both parodying and participating in a familiar school reading practice. Embodied practices are a critical part of complex, multimodal signs created through everyday social interaction. While the linguistic texts used or created in literacy events have been the usual focus of language arts researchers and educators, this work highlights the importance of broadening our semiotic lens to analyze the ways texts are created by the social geographies and embodied features of literacy events.

Sociocultural Perspectives

Mediation is as central to sociocultural theory as to Peirce's explanation of semiosis. However, when texts are viewed through a sociocultural lens, mediation fuses with human action to create an approach to signs, texts, and meanings that retains Peirce's focus on process while placing more emphasis on both the cultural and historical formation of signs and their power to shape external and internal worlds. Sociocultural theory, rooted in the illuminating essays of L. S. Vygotsky (1896–1934), has reshaped the way language educators understand thinking and learning. Yet, within the field of education, Vygotsky's notion of the zone of proximal development has overshadowed the centrality of semiotic mediation in his social theory of mind. Sociocultural theory foregrounds what human beings *do* as organized in *activities* that are *practiced* by *social* groups. Thus, the primary focus of sociocultural theory is human action, that is, culturally mediated social practices and their enactment through historical time.[1] As Wertsch (1991) notes, "When action is given analytic priority, human beings are viewed as coming into contact with, and creating, their surroundings as well as themselves through the actions in which they engage" (p. 8). Vygotsky's interest in how this transformation of external worlds and inner selves is accomplished led to his analysis of tools and signs, or what Wertsch calls "mediational means" (p. 12).

Vygotsky's distinction between tools and signs is fundamental to understanding semiotic mediation. He notes that both tools and signs serve a mediation function, but argues that the familiar analogy of signs as tools does not get at the important difference in how each orients human action. He writes, "A tool's function is to serve as the conductor of human influence on the object of activity; it is *externally* oriented" (Vygotsky, 1978, p. 55, emphasis in original). In contrast, the sign does not change the object of the action, but serves as "a means of internal activity aimed at mastering oneself" (p. 55). With these distinctions, Vygotsky argues that the "real tie between these activities" (p. 55) is their combined role in the development of higher psychological functioning, such that the use of signs "fundamentally changes all psychological operations just as the use of tools limitlessly broadens the range of activities within which the new psychological functions may operate" (p. 55).

Vygotsky recognized the varied forms of mediational means employed in human action (i.e., sign systems such as language, diagrams, and arithmetic), but tended to prefer verbal mediation and consider it natural even though his primary method was developmental, aimed at understanding the formation of what were thought to be natural mental processes (Wertsch, 1991). The use of the genetic, or developmental method, allowed Vygotsky to study how action changed—and thus how mental functioning changed—when mediational means were introduced. This preference for language is evident in much sociocultural analysis. However, some contemporary sociocultural scholars have shown that the variation in kinds of meanings to be represented have, historically, required the creation of multiple modes of representation, recognizing that language is neither the only mediational means available, nor the one best able to represent particular meanings (John-Steiner, 1985, 1995).

A sociocultural perspective on text, therefore, emphasizes "individual(s)-acting-with-mediational-means" (Wertsch, 1991, p. 12) within particular cultural, historical, and institutional settings. This implies a dynamic, reflexive relationship between text and context in which individuals-acting-with-text shape and are shaped by their participation in activities. The spotlight is on the actors and their actions with texts, rather than on the texts that are acted-upon. Moreover, Vygotsky's distinction between tool and sign suggests that texts can mediate action in both ways, that is, a text can be a tool that allows individuals to act on the world, and a text can be a sign that allows individuals to transform their mental functioning, consciousness, and identity.

Sociocultural theory takes us further in exploring Beatriz and Hector's reading by casting light on their actions with mediational means, including talk, gestures, and movements. We see how they use the text as a tool to act on the external world as well as a sign to act on their internal worlds. Understanding how the text becomes both a tool and a sign requires a consideration of the multiple goals of this activity. Despite the fact that their official reading spot is in the block corner, they are expected to accomplish an instructional goal—practicing fluent reading—by reading the text aloud to one another or in unison, a goal that is itself a cultural-historical artifact. But the children's actions suggest they have additional goals for this activity. One goal is relational in that the children are clearly eager to interact with one another as friends and reading partners. Another goal is play. These two goals are linked in action when Beatriz decides to turn the book upside-down and invent a new text, and Hector joins the play by pretending to find his own copy of the new book, *What Can Go Down?* He then launches into a fast-paced, robot-like reading that pays the barest attention to the conventions of "good reading," evidence of his collusion in Beatriz's reading game. Here we see how the children use text as a tool to act on each other and their world, transforming the activity from work to play. Their joint participation and shared knowledge is apparent in the words, gestures, and movements they use to make room for play in the course of their reading lesson. We cannot be certain how the text also became a sign for the children, transforming their inner selves, but we expect that their imaginative reading developed in Hector and Beatriz a greater control over, consciousness of, and identity as meaning-makers. Knowing that texts are meaning potentials and that even a text written in black and white can be re-mediated to generate a new and original meaning is a valuable, if unintended, outcome of this reading lesson.

In recent years, sociocultural theorists have turned to the work of M. M. Bakhtin (1895–1975) and V. N. Voloshinov (1884/5–1936) to extend Vygotsky's writings about the "social" in sociocultural. Wertsch (1991) argues that Vygotsky provided the outlines for the analysis of historically, culturally, and institutionally situated forms of mediated action, but his early death prevented a fuller rendering. The contributions of Bakhtin and Voloshinov are, thus, significant because they bring power and ideology to the analysis of the social through a focus on discourse rather than language as a system, as Saussure theorized. Indeed, their critiques of Saussure's structuralism led them to make the "living utterance" (Morris, 1994, p. 76) the basic unit of analysis in a theory of language. An utterance could be a word or a text, but "the living utterance, having taken meaning and shape at a particular historical moment in a socially specific environment, cannot fail to brush up against thousands of living dialogic threads…it cannot fail to become an active participant in the social dialogue" (p. 76).

Embedded in this quote are several essential ideas that have particular resonance for the way language arts educators think about texts. First, a text is dialogical, that is, socially situated and historically produced through its participation in multiple dialogues. As Bakhtin famously stated, "It is not, after all, out of the dictionary that the speaker gets his [sic] words!" (Morris, 1994, p. 77). Utterances are part of a chain of meaning; they respond to a prior dialogue and anticipate an answer. Second, a text is ideological in that it represents a particular view of the world. This is captured in Voloshinov's notion of the "evaluative accent" (p. 36) whereby "each element in a living utterance not only has a meaning but also has a value" (p. 37) that is always associated with a particular social group. The result is "a constant struggle of accents" (Morris, 1994, p. 37). Finally, this struggle of accents is evident in the heteroglossia that characterizes texts. If an utterance is part of an ongoing dialogue populated by other people's words, then a text carries the traces of multiple conflicting voices. Bakhtin referred to discourses within texts as "centripetal" and "centrifugal," terms he glossed as centralization and decentralization or unification and stratification. Thus, a text is a site for tension and conflict.

This brief description of Bakhtin and Voloshinov's contributions to a sociocultural approach to signs, text, and meanings allows us to revise our reading of Hector and Beatriz's event to acknowledge the ideology and power at work in what has, thus far, been represented as a playful interaction. What we observe in their reading of *What Can Go Up?* is the "struggle of accents" as they participate in an ongoing dialogue about what it means to be a reader and a child in this kindergarten class. In Hector's case, we can begin to hear his "evaluative accent" in his near-parody of school reading. Hector's super-fast reading, accomplished

with barely a look at the words and photographs and in the voice of a cartoon robot, bears traces of "other people's words," including the "unified" or official discourse of the lesson (good readers read fluently) and the unofficial discourse of their peer world (friendship, fun, and popular culture, especially Hector's favorite TV show, *SpongeBob SquarePants*, where "opposite" day regularly occurs). The heteroglossia of the children's own living utterances indicate their efforts to negotiate the tensions among multiple discourses and identities through mediated action.

A Social Semiotic Perspective

Semiotic traditions have always treated semiotics as social in that Sausurre defined signs as social conventions and Peirce claimed that signs do not exist without interpreters. However, social semiotics makes social practice the basis of sign, text, and meaning. M.A.K. Halliday (1978) first introduced the idea of language as social semiotic, rejecting Sausurre's autonomous, decontextualized system because it ignored the basic social fact that people talk to one another in particular sociocultural contexts. For Halliday, linguistic choices are social choices about how to represent the world (ideational function) and act out the social order (interpersonal function) through particular organizational means (textual function). Thus, "language as social semiotic" meant "interpreting language within a sociocultural context in which the culture itself is interpreted in semiotic terms" (p. 2). Hodge and Kress (1988) go further in their critique of Sausurre, proposing that the contents of Sausurre's "rubbish bin" constitute a semiotics of social practice in concrete social situations. This perspective would include what Saussure excluded: culture, society, and politics; semiotic systems beyond language; concrete signifying practices; time, history, process, and change; semiosic processes; the material nature of signs. Kress (1997, 2003) continues to elaborate these ideas by developing a social semiotic perspective on multimodal literacy practices. A central theme in his work on mulitmodality is the way each mode offers particular affordances of meaning. Kress and van Leeuwen (2006) analyze visual images to reveal that they, like language, are structured by a grammar rooted in social expectations for image construction. This work challenges language researchers to take seriously the semiotic notion that meaning making is not exclusively a linguistic enterprise—a fact that is increasingly apparent in a Web 2.0 environment.

Kress (1997) has also used the construct of interest to explain how the sign-maker's perspectives and preferences guide text construction including choices of meanings, modalities, and forms. He argues that sign-makers shape their texts in relation to their personal interpretations of the chosen topic and their preferences for modes of representation: "Signs arise out of our *interest* at a given moment, when we represent those features of the object which we regard as defining of that object at the moment (that is, *wheels* as defining of *car*). This interest is always complex and has physiological, psychological, emotional, cultural and social origins" (p.11). For Kress, interest is a personal frame bounding acts of sign-making (e.g., reading, writing, drawing) by identifying the criterial features of an object or event that sign-makers represent in the signs they create. Linking this idea to Peircian notions of semiosis, interest may, in part, guide sign-makers' choices of the second sign—the interpretant—they bring to an act of meaning-making.

While interest is, in some ways, individual, Kress points out that it is also social and cultural since an author's interests are shaped by the cultural practices and materials used in sign-making. He assumes that as sign-makers act out of their own interest they are influenced by their personal histories as well as the sociocultural affordances and constraints of their present location. Kress stresses the active and creative role of authors, who "act energetically, intelligently, perceptively, out of their *interest*, innovatively making for themselves their means of communication and representation (p. 113). Rowsell and Pahl (2007) have recently suggested that Kress' notion of interest can best be understood as a facet of a sign-maker's socioculturally situated identities. They describe interest as part of identity narratives constructed over time and expressed through the sign-maker's preferences for materials, topics, and actions during composing or reading. They argue that identities—and by extension, interests—are historically rooted in sign-makers' participation in the sociocultural practices of their communities and are evident—sedimented—in their actions and texts. Signs, then, are historical artifacts shaped by the sign-maker's performed identities that are in turn shaped by their histories of participation in the sociocultural practices of their Discourse communities. Beatriz and Hector's multimodal enactment of *What Can Go Up?* serves to illustrate how their histories of participation and socioculturally situated identities as engaged students, successful readers, friends, popular culture enthusiasts, and gender performers have become sedimented in their sign-making.

Conclusion

Semiotics provides us with a view of text and meaning making that is interpreted, multimodal, socially performed, emplaced, and embodied. Across the semiotic perspectives we have explored, there is a movement away from a Saussurian conception of texts as static signifying structures containing meaning, A Peircean view of signs as mediated by other signs contributed by the sign-maker meshes well with contemporary constructivist views of comprehension and textual interpretation. Further, Peirce's expansive view of sign-material provides a unified space for exploring the proliferation of sign systems that are part of new literacies. New directions in the semiotics of texts come at just the right time to provide the theoretical leverage needed to address literacy practices in a 21st-century landscape.

Note

1. We are indebted to Carolyn Panofsky for her clarifying insights into sociocultural theory.

References

Austin, J. L. (1975). *How to do things with words* (2nd ed.). Cambridge, MA: Harvard University Press.

Bowman, S., & Willis, C. (2003). *We media: How audiences are shaping the future of news and information.* Reston, VA: The Media Center at the American Press Institute.

Chandler, D. (2002). *Semiotics: The basics.* London: Routledge.

Deely, J. (1982). *Introducing semiotic.* Bloomington: Indiana University Press.

Dyson, A. H. (2003). *The brothers and sisters learn to write: Popular literacies in childhood and school culture.* New York: Teachers College Press.

Eco, U. (1976). *A theory of semiotics.* Bloomington: Indiana University Press.

Gardner, H. (1981). *The quest for mind* (2nd ed.). Chicago: University of Chicago Press.

Halliday, M. A. K. (1978). *Language as a social semiotic.* Baltimore, MD: University Park Press.

Hardwick, C. (Ed.). (1977). *Semiotics and signifies: The correspondence between Charles S. Peirce and Victoria Lady Welby.* Bloomington: Indiana University Press.

Hodge, R., & Kress, G. (1988). *Social semiotics.* Ithaca, NY: Cornell University Press.

Innis, R. (Ed.). (1985). *Semiotics: An introductory anthology.* Bloomington: Indiana University Press.

Ito, M., Okabe, D., & Matsuda, M. (Eds.). (2005). *Personal, portable, pedestrian: Mobile phones in Japanese life.* Cambridge, MA: MIT Press.

John-Steiner, V. (1985). *Notebooks of the mind.* Albuquerque: University of New Mexico Press.

John-Steiner, V. (1995). Cognitive pluralism: A sociocultural approach. *Mind, Culture, and Activity, 1*(2), 2–11.

Kress, G. (1997). *Before writing: Rethinking the paths to literacy.* London: Routledge.

Kress, G. (2003). *Literacy in the new media age.* London: Routledge.

Kress, G., & Van Leeuwen, T. (2006). *Reading images: The grammar of visual design.* London: Routledge.

Leander, K. (2002). Silencing in classroom interaction: Producing and relating social spaces. *Discourse Processes, 34*(2), 193–235.

Merrell, F. (1979). Some signs that preceded their times: Or, are we really ready for Peirce? *Ars Semeiotica, 2,* 149–172.

Morris, P. (Ed.). (1994). *The Bakhtin reader: Selected writings of Bakhtin, Medvedev, Voloshinov.* London: Edward Arnold.

New London Group. (1996). A pedagogy of multiliteracies: Designing social futures. *Harvard Educational Review, 66*(1), 60–92.

Rowsell, J., & Pahl, K. (2007). Sedimented identities in texts: Instances of practice. *Reading Research Quarterly, 42*(3), 388–404.

Scollon, R., & Scollon, S. W. (2003). *Discourses in place: Language in the material world.* London: Routledge.

Sebeok, T. (Ed.). (1977). *A perfusion of signs.* Bloomington: Indiana University Press.

Snyder, I. (Ed.). (1998). *Page to screen: Taking literacy into the electronic era.* New York: Routledge.

Vygotsky, L. S. (1978). *Mind in society: The development of higher psychological processes* (M. Cole, V. John-Steiner, S. Scribner, & E. Souberman, Eds.). Cambridge, MA: Harvard University Press.

Wertsch, J. V. (1991). *Voices of the mind: A sociocultural approach to mediated action.* Cambridge, MA: Harvard University Press.

Section V

Teaching the English Language Arts

SECTION EDITORS
KAREN WOOD, NANCY FREY, AND WEN MA

Section V focuses on the various composite skills, abilities, and curricular areas concerning teaching and learning the English language arts. The following 16 chapters describe, analyze, and critique current research trends and pedagogical issues in the field of literacy education in K–12 settings.

Hruby, Read, and Landon-Hays open the section with a brief review of the professional and scholarly stances on appropriate language arts instruction. Then they begin to explore the tensions in various areas: examining the opposition between methods and outcome; issues of student variability; the challenge of applying valid assessment measures for educative purposes; difficulties inherent in developmentally progressive curriculum design; the struggle between teacher expertise and specialist support, as well as influences of mandated policy and programs on educational effectiveness.

Tschannen-Moran and MacFarlane continue with an exploration of teacher self-efficacy in the ELA classrooms. Research suggests that ELA teachers may have differing self-efficacy across reading, writing, grammar and other areas. Tschannen-Moran and MacFarlane examine specific sources of teacher self-efficacy: vicarious experiences, social persuasion, physiological and emotional states, and mastery experiences. Teacher preparation programs may tap these sources to recruit, train, and retain teachers with these desirable qualities.

Edmiston reminds us of the arts in language arts with a review of the transformative nature of play in the lives of learners. Using Vygotsky's theory of play as a platform, the author provides an argument for the necessity of imagined and real experiences, and for the use of ensemble play in the form of dramatic interpretation. The exploration of situations in play and drama prepare learners for the circumstances they encounter in the lives of themselves and others. The remainder of the chapter explores the classroom pedagogy of inquiry, research, and literacy as tools for fostering and extending dramatic play.

Ehri sets the stage for the next chapters that examine aspects of English language arts curriculum in more detail. The author explains the nature of phonemic awareness and phonics using an instructional and curricular lens, and relates these to the development of early reading and writing skills. The chapter concludes with a discussion of the reciprocal nature of phonemic awareness and phonics with spelling development and instruction.

Rasinski follows with an overview of the role of fluency in reading, and its misapplication as a measure of reading proficiency. Reading fluency as a construct has had a tumultuous history, at times celebrated as the pinnacle of reading proficiency, at other times neglected. The author discusses the use of reading fluency as a tool for assessment, and as an element of instruction in the primary grades and with older students.

Templeton addresses another vital aspect of the English language arts curriculum with his review of spelling curriculum and instruction. The author provides a cogent discussion of the nature and development of spelling in English. A deep understanding of the ways words are known and constructed leads into a review of spelling instruction, and the interplay between spelling development and reading and writing.

Fisher, Blachowicz, and Watts-Taffe examine three contemporary issues in vocabulary instruction, with particular focus on students who come to school in need of additional assistance. Specifically they address questions related to the notion of approaching vocabulary comprehensively, how educators define dimensions of vocabulary, and what research-based resources are available to assist in vocabulary selection. They conclude with some practical thoughts for teachers on the topic of academic vocabulary and its varied contexts in the curriculum.

Lapp, Fisher, and Frey relate elements of the English language arts curriculum to reading comprehension. Although it is agreed that comprehension is the defining measure of reading proficiency, its instruction is debated. The chapter opens with a review of the research on the characteristics of the competent comprehender, then progresses to an historical perspective on reading comprehension instruction, including discussion on so-called "21st-century literacy" in a digital age. The chapter concludes with a deeper review of three prominent methods of comprehension instruction: reader response, gradual release of responsibility, and reciprocal teaching.

Roser, Martinez, and Wood review recent studies on students' literary responses describing changes over past decades in both scope and approach to research into literary meaning making. They examine the research through a broadened theoretical lens and a changing research methodology that includes more comprehensive ethnographic techniques and inductive analyses that investigate students' responses in a variety of settings including new technologies.

Hansen and Kissel focus on students as writers. After examining the processes student writers use in classrooms, homes, and other real-life settings, they discuss the evaluation processes that student writers and teachers follow respectively, and the processes writing instructors use when they focus on student's writing processes and on the texts are compared. The writing acts and the evaluation processes are multifaceted in schools in the advent of new literacies and the processing demands of writing.

McLaughlin and DeVoogd present a theoretical foundation for critical literacy discussing its recent acceptance within the context of a multiple literacies perspective. They explain the principles of critical literacy as a way of thinking that challenges texts and life and they connect this thinking to the current research. Lastly, they discuss common

contexts of critical literacy and the characteristics of critical readers while envisioning a world with more intellectual freedom and equality.

Hobbs and RobbGrieco discuss different purposes of media literacy and different theoretical perspectives related to media literacy education. These issues range from countering the negative effects of media, following critical perspectives of mass media, viewing media as tools or vehicles of communication, to using media in the cultivation of student agency, voice, and identity construction. In light of the educational potentials offered by media and media literacy, Hobbs and RobbGrieco suggest that teachers make active use of useful elements from these theoretical positions and teach while learning alongside their students.

Nelson defines rhetoric as a discipline and gives an overview of the major developmental stages in its history of over 2,000 years. Nelson explores not only broad rhetorical concerns such as rhetorical situations, rhetorical relations between author and audience, and rhetorical purposes and support for claims, but also more specific issues such as genre, audience, persona, and arguments. These topics will be helpful to school teachers as they develop effective pedagogy for literacy and rhetorical studies.

Gebhard and Martin conclude the section with an examination of three types of grammar: (a) traditional, (b) formal, and (c) functional. They use detailed text analysis of a 10th-grade Australian student's writing to highlight the relevance of functional grammar for literacy learning in schools. Drawing on Halliday's Systematic Functional Grammar, Gebhard and Martin discuss programs and studies of grammar instruction in the K–12 classrooms in an American context.

30

Tracing Instructional Tensions in the Teaching of the English Language Arts

A Primer

George G. Hruby, Sylvia Read, and Melanie Landon-Hays

Across the grade levels, teachers of the English language arts face many similar professional challenges. These can include unpredictable student variability; novel and often jarringly imposed administrative regimens, curricular mandates, and standardized assessments; disheartening political critiques in the media and naïve expectations from parents; unrequited quests for useful instructional material and helpful professional development; and the internecine crossfire between specialist and administrative turfdoms. Chief among these difficulties is the challenge of choosing appropriate and effective instructional methods to achieve pedagogic and curricular goals. Unfortunately, guidance from educational scholarship on how best to frame and make sense of these challenges can often seem puzzling, contradictory, or counter-intuitive.

The often chaotic nature of classroom teaching is regularly described in the practitioner literature through such complexity metaphors as juggling ("keeping a lot of balls in the air"), smorgasbords ("having a lot on one's plate"), or diplomacy ("negotiating the demands of numerous stake holders"). The metaphors employed in the scholarly literature, by contrast, are more likely to reduce this complexity to antagonistic dichotomies and vexing dilemmas, possibly enshrined in the image of counterweight scales, or in the framing of strawman arguments. To be fair, academics are quick to note the unsatisfactory simplicity of antagonistic binaries, but often address this through the expansion of their initial binaries with additional binaries: balance beams within balance beams (e.g., Pearson, Raphael, Benson, & Madda, 2007), or the numerous directions from which one may fall from the bifurcating line of a tight rope (e.g., Boyd & Bailey, 2009).

In this chapter we ourselves use a binary instructional continuum—that between the direct training of skills and the less direct structuring of educative experience—as a central filament around which other threads will be entwined to represent the knotty challenge of effective English language arts instruction. With the guidance of this metaphor we shall

interweave the opposition between instructional methods and curricular outcome; the tension inherent in addressing student variability within normative expectations; the challenge of applying valid assessment measures to educative purposes; the difficulty of designing a developmentally progressive curriculum across grade levels and content areas; the tension of redistributing teacher expertise and authority with specialist support; and, not least of all, the struggle between standardized educational programs and assessments on behalf of efficient administration of mandated policies, and responsible teacher autonomy warranted by reflective practice and professional development on behalf of educational effectiveness.

The Dichotomy of Trained Skills and Educative Experience

A long-standing instructional tension between skills training and experience-based pedagogy has manifested itself in school classrooms and educational theory alike in various ways since the early 19th-century. On the one hand, basic skills, identified through structuralist and behaviorist research, have been recommended as programmatic outcomes to be trained directly and discretely in piecemeal fashion (e.g., Thorndike, 1931; Watson, 1928), often requiring rote learning, lecture, or conditioned response, and typically for quick, targeted assessment. On the other hand, insights from functional and developmental psychology have inspired calls for learning through well-structured activities and environments (e.g., Dewey, 1938; Allen, 1976), preferably through carefully orchestrated experiences, purposeful inquiry, or independent discovery, typically for performative assessment. The tension between the didactic skills training and naturalistic experience-based development views of teaching and learning has been amply evident in the English language arts across decades. We will here consider it within three grade-level domains: (a) pre-elementary and early elementary classrooms, (b) upper elementary and middle school classrooms, (c) junior high and high school classrooms.

Pre-elementary and Early Elementary Language Arts Classrooms

In grades K–3, the tension between language arts training and experience is most obvious in the area of reading instruction, and in particular in the debate between skill training in phonics decoding (Adams, 1990) and methodologies for fostering reading comprehension proficiency through experience-driven pedagogy (Goodman & Goodman, 2004). This tension positions letter-based or serial processing models of reading against meaning-based or holistic views of literacy—the notorious "reading wars," a debate with an extensive history (Chall, 1967; Flippo, 1999). Theoretically, it has variously been framed as a debate between spelling vs. whole word recognition since the 19th century, the science of phonetics vs. principles of progressive education since the early 20th-century, and bottom-up/synthetic vs. top-down/analytic models of cognitive process since the late 20th-century. Yet, across the decades, the *instructional* implications have typically distilled to a recommendation for either efficient skill drilling or for literacy development through guided exploration within meaningful contexts.

Although there are numerous models that describe the reading process (see Ruddell & Unrau, 2004), a commonly employed way to articulate the reading debates is the so-called Simple View of Reading (Gough & Tunmer, 1986). In this view, R = D × L (*Reading* is the product of *Decoding* and *Linguistic comprehension*). Letters are said to be decoded to a language sound stream, and the sound stream is comprehended just as spoken language would be. Decoding skill and linguistic comprehension must both be developed to allow a student to read well. Moreover, decoding needs to be trained to non-conscious automaticity (LeBerge & Samuels, 1974) so that the multiple processes of decoding do not swamp the limited capacity of a child's working memory. If working memory is overloaded with sounding-out the print on a page, the theory goes, the reader will have insufficient cognitive capacity to make sense of the meaning, as well. Thus the developmental and instructional claim is often made that decoding must be mastered to fluency first so that comprehension can be allowed to occur subsequently. Limited to emergent and early reading, this view makes some intuitive sense.

However, whole language proponents (e.g., Goodman, 1994) have suggested just the opposite: that reading ability can be most effectively and individually developed through authentic reading experiences meant to support an understanding of the pragmatics of reading, and to develop the necessary motivation to drive linguistic development through ample encounters with text. This is deemed especially important for the development of syntactic and semantic processes central to language comprehension in reading. The development of decoding skills (in the form of graphophonemic processing or orthographic pattern recognition) is presumed to emerge naturally, just as phoneme perception does in speech, from meaningful encounters with text- and language-rich environments, with only minimal and focused phonics instruction provided as a particular student might require. It is posited that linguistic comprehension processes, such as syntactic and semantic processing, can bootstrap the development of decoding abilities.

It is important to distinguish two very different tensions at play in this phonics-whole language debate. The first is *developmental*, between either emphasizing decoding, in the belief that it will cause or facilitate the development of comprehension, or emphasizing comprehension, in the belief that it will cause or facilitate the development of decoding. The curricular implications of these two views are equally oppositional: either reading instruction in early elementary grades should be focused on decoding letters to sound, or should emphasize the making of meaning from texts.

But beneath this theoretical debate about reading *development* lies a different tension related to teacher practice, an *instructional* tension between drilling discrete skills in piece-meal, sequential fashion, or through student-centered experience-cued instruction. Decoding-first advocates generally recommend that decoding be taught through drilling phonemic awareness, phonics, and fluency skills, arguing that meaningful content and activity distracts students from mastering the code for fluent, phoneme-based word recognition (Moats, 2007). In truth, experience-based instruction can also be quite systematic, if not didactic (e.g., Allen, 1976). But instructional approaches that attend to student meaning-making typically argue the intrinsic motivation of the student on behalf of content or objective realization is crucial for well integrated and readily employed ability development (e.g., Harste, Short, & Burke, 1988).

The recent national experiment in the United States with universally mandated decoding drilling (e.g., Reading First, Institute of Educational Sciences, 2008), has demonstrated that emphatic skills instruction is a dependable way to foster decoding of decodable texts for most students, but that focusing solely on decoding to the exclusion of linguistic comprehension development does not appear to produce superior readers as measured by reading comprehension measures. Decoding skills are clearly a necessary prerequisite for making sense of print, but they are not sufficient. Many students pick up decoding relatively easily, and this is the case regardless of such school risk factors as socioeconomic status, verbal ability, or general intelligence measures (within the non-disabled range). Mandating 90 minutes of such skill drilling every day for all students for 3 to 4 years is not warranted given the results of Reading First. But *some* students, also regardless of risk factors, do require more structured instruction on the sound-letter code to facilitate their automatic word recognition. Programs, including reading remediation programs, that rule out the importance of explicit decoding instruction for students with poor phonological grain-size sensitivity or elemental acuity, are as worrisome as universally mandated phonics drills.

Thus, the debate between didactic vs. naturalistic instructional practice is one that too often demands a forced and false choice. Arguments are rationalized on the basis of scientific-proof and/or curriculum goals, but actually seem more driven by ideological devotion to an undemonstrated belief: that *how* a teacher teaches is as important a lesson for students as *what* a teacher teaches. This notion of a "hidden curriculum" goes back to the theoretical work of Horace Mann in the mid 19th-century on behalf of developing good citizens for the preservation of American democracy, and has been echoed by numerous educational theorists on both sides of the political spectrum ever since. Yet, to date, there is no empirical evidence that teaching students in a didactic fashion turns them into obedient fascists or that teaching them in a progressive fashion turns them into disruptive anarchists. Human development is not that simple. The belief that it should be seems an idée fix of policy advocates obsessed with the grandeur of their own authority—precisely the Napoleonic impulse warned against by Mann!

Over the years, attempts to tap the best of both instructional views have given rise to interactive, integrated, balanced, situated, and transactional models of instruction. For instance, a *balanced instruction* view (Pressley, 2006) would employ focused skills training to get discrete skills up and running within the instructional context of a highly active learning environment rich with language and authentic opportunities to apply the skills. In other words, authentic instructional activities and environments designed to promote curricular content become the purpose and context within which to develop and practice the authentic application of trained skills. Research on notably effective classrooms seems to support the balanced instruction view (e.g., Pressley, Wharton-McDonald, Allington, Block, & Morrow, 1998), although attempts to replicate such approaches in novel contexts have had only mixed success.

Although we have located our analysis so far in early reading instruction, similar tensions echo in early writing instruction. The balance among reading and writing in the early grade curriculum has favored reading and isolated skill development over the development of coherent written expression. Before the mid-20th century, early writing instruction was often little more than handwriting or grammar exercises. Starting in the 1960s, there was a recognition that students would learn to write only if they were encouraged in their oral expression and only if they had a meaningful purpose for writing (Darien Public Schools, 1971). An overemphasis on mechanical correctness in the early grades was discouraged, but nevertheless the time allotment for writing was scant: English language arts curriculum often consisted of literature selections paired with linguistic exercises, which were considered superior to traditional grammar instruction and which were the subject of experimental research (Martin, 1968). According to one curriculum guide from the era (Saporito, 1970), reading should receive 60–70 minutes of instruction time per day, spelling 15–20 minutes, handwriting 10–15 minutes, and English 30–35 minutes.

More recently, the writing curriculum has been sub-

merged into the basal, or core reading program, which is presumed to suffice as the entire early language arts curriculum. However, these programs offer very little on writing, and what they do offer arguably is not grounded in the research on effective writing instruction (Gleason & Isaacson, 2001). Even after decades of various types of school and curriculum reform efforts, writing instruction has been and continues to be subordinate to reading (Strickland et al., 2001).

To sum, in seeking guidance on the development of fundamental reading and writing abilities, early elementary language arts teachers must often confront strong scholarly stances, some of them concretized through policy mandates. These mandates often deny what classroom expertise and knowledge of effective instruction may suggest—that early reading and writing instruction requires positive and ample experience with a wide variety of developmentally appropriate and appealing text forms and practices to foster linguistic, cognitive, and creative skills.

Upper Elementary and Middle School Classrooms Additional language arts instructional issues, some merely forestalled, become manifest in grades 4–8. In this subsection we will focus primarily on those related to linguistic comprehension as a necessary compliment to decoding for language arts competence. We are not suggesting by any means that attention to language comprehension should wait until Grade 4, but it is typically at the middle elementary grades that a marked difference in students' linguistic ability correlates with literacy and scholastic success. We shall consider some reasons for this.

By Grade 4, the linguistic abilities of decoding-trained students demonstrate immense variability in part due to insufficient and well structured language experience in the context of schooling. Instead, language ability is carried forward only by informal linguistic experiences in schools, and with peers, family members, and the students' preferred media forms (often action-packed television cartoons and youth-glamour variety shows). Yet, with often ill-developed academic language competencies all students are expected to meet the following challenges as they enter Grade 4:

- Students are expected to learn the content of the texts they read—in other words, they must now read for meaning and learning, tasks about which they may have had little previous instruction or structured experience;
- Such reading-to-learn requires making use of context, purpose, and prior knowledge, precisely the components and skills use that had been eliminated from instruction with decodable texts;
- The assigned texts from which students are expected to learn content are more challenging in terms of vocabulary, syntactic complexity, and semantic construction than most students' oral language, or previous language experience;
- This challenging vocabulary and linguistic structure is increasingly married to subject-specific discourses and

text genres with which students may have little or no prior acquaintance;

- Students may lack the prior knowledge assumed of certain subject-specific discourses, particularly if this taken-for-granted "world knowledge" and "common sense" emanates from the purview of a middle-class living room;
- Increased use of new technologies in classrooms poses additional text genre and structure challenges requiring novel cognitive strategies, especially for the most at-risk students (Coiro & Dobler, 2007);
- The conceptual complexity of text content increases along assumptions of an average developmental trajectory, not necessarily the developmental trajectory of any particular student;
- Speed of oral recitation is no longer an indicator of good reading—indeed, learning to vary one's reading speed depending on purpose, or when comprehension is troubled, is an important skill for upper grade reading.

Similar challenges face teachers and students regarding the development of writing abilities. In the upper elementary grades, the expectation that students will be able to write a research report appears. Having gained some familiarity with narrative structure throughout the primary grades, students are suddenly asked to write in an expository mode (Duke, 2000; Flood, Lapp, Farnan, 1986). Also making an appearance in the upper grades is the statewide direct writing assessment, which has become prevalent, in part, as a way to promote writing in the curriculum (Calfee, 2000). However, direct writing assessments often have the unfortunate tendency to narrow the kinds of writing that teachers ask their students to do, and some have argued that students are encouraged to produce formulaic writing in response to prompts (Hillocks, 2002). For example, if the mode of writing demanded by a direct writing assessment is persuasion, the tendency is for teachers to neglect nearly all other forms of writing in order to prepare their students for the persuasive prompt they will encounter.

Here again, a tension emerges between the need for both basic and advanced skills, on the one hand, and authentic opportunities for their application on behalf of content learning, on the other. To foster the development of their professional expertise on this matter, teacher must confront a raft of questions that can only be effectively answered in context. For instance, when should vocabulary be taught through time-efficient rote memorization drills, training in morphemic analysis and context strategies, or through directed attention during meaningful reading with recourse to dictionaries, rich discussion, and ample opportunities for word use on behalf of world and concept knowledge development? When should syntax be parsed through grammatical sentence diagramming and prescriptive label and rule memorization, or through the kinds of experience that allow for the development of fluent syntactic pattern recognition? When should semantics be addressed through drilling in idioms and the avoidance of common errors of poor word choice, or through close examination, imitation, and rich discussion of how words interrelate in context and for purposes to indicate authorial intention and spark meaningful associations and responses in readers?

Further, should tone, style, and rhetoric be taught as technical attributes that require appropriate reader and authorial stances, or should they be taught as techniques for positioning readers and telling on authors and their narrators? Should subject-specific discourse and genre conventions be ignored as too abstract for pre-adolescent learners, or should students explicitly identify, discuss, and imitate these forms toward a comfortable familiarity with their semiotic conventions? Questions such as these almost always deserve the same general response: It depends! And although it depends on many factors, the needs of students, and the ability of teachers to identify and address them, are likely the paramount issue.

During the upper elementary years, increasing numbers of students begin to lag in their reading development, a phenomenon often referred to as the "fourth-grade slump" (Sanacore & Palumbo, 2009). This slump leaves them below grade-level as readers, leading to a widening achievement gap. For students in the middle and upper elementary grades, lower grade-level ability often means a K–3 reading level, where K–3 reading instruction and materials are presumed developmentally appropriate, including rudimentary decoding and fluency training. Thus, for teachers of such students, early elementary tensions in reading instruction continue to reverberate, compounded by the additional tension that the prior decoding curriculum have been ineffective. This leads to questions such as: was the student's early reading instruction competent? Had the student not been developmentally ready to take advantage of it? Does the student suffer from a reading disability? Were there (and are there still) ancillary factors that put the student at risk for reading failure? Should direct decoding and fluency drilling continue to be the focus of the students' reading instruction (as required in some state RTI models)? Will the student continue to (and does he/se even now) willingly participate in drilling for drilling's sake? What of the trade-off between time devoted to remedial drilling and time lost to grade-level content instruction?

In addition to reading ability differences, there are differences specific to English language proficiency. English language learners are an obvious case. However, native-born English speakers can also demonstrate this difficulty, which manifests itself in grade-inadequate linguistic comprehension. These deficiencies correlate strongly with socio-economic status (SES), and may have their origin in the variable quality of early childhood language experience (Hart & Risley, 1999). Depending on the literacy and language proficiencies of a child's parents, home-based language may offer little inkling of the lexical, syntactic, or semantic demands of the academic discourses. Such initial disparities may be exacerbated over time through a combination of instructional neglect and an absence of well-structured in-school language experience.

Given the large number of immigrant ELL students (English language learners) who are also of poverty, it is important to clarify when a proficiency issue is merely a language issue (ELL-factor), and when it is also a language ability development issue (SES-factor). Many low-SES ELL students could prove at-risk even in their native countries for the same reasons low-SES native English speakers often are. Teaching English as a second language may be insufficient for these ELL students and probably unhelpful for linguistically limited native English speakers. On the other hand, there may be value in effective second language teaching methods for improving English language proficiency for native speakers. More research is needed in this domain, where, too, the tension between skill drilling and immersion exists.

Finally, there is the tension in specialist support for these and other struggling readers. Classroom teachers, reading specialists, special educators, speech therapists, and ELL specialists may all lay claim to overlapping subpopulations of students. Regular classroom teachers, intending no disrespect to such specialists, may intuitively worry that the discrete skills focus of most specialist intervention programs may hamper more than help many struggling students, and deny sufficient participation in the mainstream curriculum. But without adequate professional development or training in how to address the issue of linguistic competence, the mid-level teacher may be at a loss for adequate intervention.

Junior High and High School Classrooms It could be fairly suggested that all of the previously described tensions deepen in the secondary grades, as language arts instruction is restricted to a particular subject domain classroom, and meaningful incorporation of good language, literacy, and learning skills across the content areas becomes increasingly difficult to manage or even inspire among faculty. Additionally, the academic diversity of the students grows broader, with some students lacking strong decoding skills, others with variable language comprehension deficits, still others with prior knowledge and vocabulary deficiencies, and many with ancillary personal issues (poor study skills, uneven reading habits, personal idiosyncrasies and personality traits mismatched to the reigning policy mandates, and extra-scholastic demands).

Motivation, student identity, self-efficacy, and the willingness of students to buy-in to curricular objectives all move front-and-center as instructional factors with adolescents, even with at-level and advanced students. At the same time, the curriculum becomes ever more varied and tightly packed with requirements that can seem culturally and personally irrelevant for many students. For adolescents, the world at large tempts with greater distraction, and exerts more vibrant engagement and inspiration than ever before.

Secondary English language arts instruction varies, too, driven by a curriculum that spans a literary canon featuring epic and modernist poetry, 19th- and early 20th-century novels, and plays by Shakespeare, O'Neil, and even Aristophanes. Increasingly, these works are abetted with young adult novels, the writings of traditionally marginalized peoples, and popular culture texts. Reading instruction is typically limited to the identification and explication of tropes, allusions, and obscure grammatical idioms in works of literature, often by way of simplified New Criticism or Reader Response analyses. Sentence diagramming makes the occasional appearance. Writing instruction is sparse, but spans from creative writing workshops, to reader response journals, student journalism, instruction in basic business writing, research report writing, and the notorious five-paragraph essay.

In spite of a recent emphasis on writing assessment, the results of a new national study on the state of writing instruction in middle and high schools indicates that students are not writing very much. Analysis of National Assessment of Educational Progress (NAEP) data shows that, in 1998, 14% of 12th-grade students did not write anything at all, even in their English classes. Between 2002 and 2007, the amount and kinds of writing that students were asked to do decreased, perhaps because of the pressures of high-stakes testing that emphasizes reading more than writing. Writing in other content areas besides English also decreased during the 2002–2007 period (Applebee & Langer, 2009).

Literacy for learning, or content area reading, is largely regarded as an unloved intruder to the secondary curriculum. It rarely makes an emphatic impact, perhaps due to the perception by content instructors in other subjects that literacy instruction is solely a language arts issue, and that reading instruction is a matter for elementary teachers. Of course, content area teachers do employ subject-specific literacies and discourses often without being aware of it—and are often equally unaware that lack of sufficient familiarity with these discourses can be an impediment to student learning (Moje & Speyer, 2008). However, content area literacy methods can be rare even in secondary English language arts classrooms, perhaps because many favored content area literacy strategies seem better suited for informational texts than literary ones.

The need for remedial reading services has traditionally gone unaddressed for want of time and money, and when employed often acted as a segregating mechanism. The potential for change in the years ahead is uncertain. Too quick reliance on simple reading rate measures of fluency can easily miscategorize struggling adolescent readers as needing decoding skills training, when many factors can impact reading rate in the secondary grades (Nichols, 2007). Traditionally, comprehension remediation instruction has focused on the instruction of cognitive strategies to improve students' generic reading comprehension skills for learning content across the subject domains (Dole, Nokes, & Drits, 2009). But an over-emphasis on cognitive strategies as discretely trainable skills—often presented as all-purpose "silver bullet" solutions—succeeds only in disappointing otherwise effective teachers and struggling students alike.

Tensions Extended into Professional Development Taking a developmental perspective, we note that as one moves across the grade levels, lower grade-level tensions are not displaced by, but are rather augmented and extended by, the tensions that grow more variegated yet pronounced in upper grade-level classrooms. It may be helpful, overall, for early grade teachers to consider the outcomes of their grade level instructional decisions on students' upper-grade success, and it may be equally helpful for upper grade teachers to consider the genesis of the challenges they face with a better understanding of the issues confronted by early grade teachers. But the value of a bird's-eye view and cross-grade generalizations must be weighed against being effectively within one's classroom at a particular moment with particular students under particular conditions.

The complexity of literacy acquisition and instruction for students across grade and developmental levels is mirrored in newer models of professional learning for teachers, which also reflect the dichotomy of trained skills and educative experience. Language arts teacher education has typically followed a skills-training and informational transmission approach to instructional professional development. Do-as-I-say lectures, "sit and gets," paint-by-number scripts, decontextualized instructor "modeling," or one-day workshops predominate in teacher in-service environments, yet these approaches have long been known to produce little lasting change in teacher's instructional practice, often leaving teachers frustrated as the promised generalized solutions fail to transfer to the specifics of their classrooms (Joyce & Showers, 2002).

Consequently, coaching has become a prevalent practice in many schools that are striving to enact long-term instructional change. This kind of professional development brings together experience-based learning with the need for generalized skills. Cantrell, Burns, and Callaway (2008) explain, "[s]uccessful approaches to teacher education de-emphasize teacher-centered transmission models in favor of engaging teachers in collaborative construction of knowledge that enables them to analyze the complexities of curricula, pedagogy, and school cultures" (p. 3). Joyce and Showers (2002) note, "where transfer to a classroom is the object, the full array [of staff development components] is needed—theory, demonstration, practice, and peer coaching" (p. 77).

As has been outlined, effective instruction differs across grade levels and is moreover specific to teacher preparation, school location, curricular requirements, student population, and the individual needs of learners. Studies on the effectiveness of classroom supports for student learning—and literacy skills, specifically—have shown "positive effects for programs that are designed to improve the core of classroom practice" (Slavin, Cheung, Groff, & Lake, 2008, p. 309). This approach to professional development is more firmly rooted in providing teachers with educative experience, while still accepting that many teachers may lack the knowledge and skills necessary to effectively negotiate instructional complexities.

Professional Tensions in Context: Standards, Assessments, and Mandates The instructional oppositions confronting teachers of the English language arts are comprehensively evident in the NCTE/IRA *Standards for Reading Professionals* (National Council of Teachers of English/International Reading Association, 1998–2010). For instance, decoding skills such as phonemic awareness, phonics, and fluency are explicitly identified in the standards for Pre-K and Elementary Classroom Teacher Candidates (2.2.3), as are language competency abilities such as vocabulary, comprehension, critical thinking, motivation, and writing. Drilling is not explicitly mentioned, but the emphasis on *evidence-based practices*, a now politically loaded term, suggests an openness to such methods. Standard 5, Literate Environment, is focused more on classroom management and use of space, than on contextualizing student constructions of meaning. But this is not ruled out. Similarly, the other standards cast a non-committal net over the previously reviewed tensions, offering no specific resolutions.

Standards, such as the NCTE/IRA Standards for the English Language Arts, should not be confused with standardization of the curriculum through state and federal mandates, which may work in opposition to teacher professionalization. Teacher knowledge and preparation is key to student achievement (Darling-Hammond, 2000), an insight that No Child Left Behind codified into law (Achinstein & Ogawa, 2006; Wills & Sandholtz, 2009). Educational policy has required standardized instructional programs because of the ease with which their application and efficacy can be inventoried through standardized high-stakes assessments. These political initiatives, although well-intentioned, cap the use of teachers' professional expertise by circumscribing their autonomy as competent and adaptively effective professionals. When the aforementioned curricular and instructional tensions are imposed by administrative fiat, the result is a new tension, one between a forced fidelity that often fails, and a provoked disloyalty that potentially dispirits.

Conclusion

We have attempted to trace several tensions entwined throughout the teaching of the English language arts. The difficulties seem perennial and beyond simple, abstractly formulated solution. They are tied to the unpredictable contingencies of real classrooms with particular students in specific moments in time. Moreover, the central tension between skills and contexts that we have traced here requires a more sophisticated notion of both, one that differentiates between basic and high level skills and more and less educative experiences. Finally, a tolerance for ambiguity and uncertainty, although anathema to popular politics, is requisite in effective instruction for literacy development. We would argue that attempts to standardize practice or professional development to preempt such uncertainty are unlikely to succeed. Other chapters in this section demonstrate in much greater detail the wealth of research and theory for effective practice in this regard.

References

Achinstein, B., & Ogawa, R. T. (2006). (In)Fidelity: What the resistance of new teachers reveals about professional principles and prescriptive educational policies. *Harvard Educational Review, 76*(1), 30–63.

Adams, M. J. (1990). *Beginning to read: thinking and learning about print*. Cambridge, MA: MIT Press.

Allen, R. V. (1976). *Language experiences in communication*. Boston: Houghton Mifflin.

Applebee, A. N., & Langer, J. A. (2009). What is happening in the teaching of writing? *English Journal, 98*(5), 18–28.

Boyd, F. B., & Bailey, N. M. (2009). Censorship in three metaphors. *Journal of Adolescent and Adult Literacy, 52*, 653–661.

Calfee, R. C. (2000). Writing portfolios: Activity, assessment, authenticity. In R. Indrisano & J. R. Squire (Eds.), *Perspectives on writing: Research, theory, and practice* (pp. 278–304). Newark, DE: International Reading Association.

Cantrell, S. C., Burns, L. D. & Callaway, P. (2008). Midlle- and high-school content area teachers' perceptions about literacy teaching and learning. *Literacy Research and Instruction, 48*(1), 76–94.

Chall, J. S. (1967). *Learning to read: The great debate*. New York: McGraw Hill.

Coiro, J. & Dobler, E. (2007). Exploring the online comprehension strategies used by sixth-grade skilled readers to search for and locate information on the Internet. *Reading Research Quarterly, 42*, 214-257.

Darien Public Schools, C. (1971). Curriculum guide for the language arts: Kindergarten-grade 6. (ERIC Document Reproduction Service No. ED068957) Retrieved September 26, 2009, from ERIC database.

Darling-Hammond, L. (2000). Teacher quality and student achievement: A review of state policy evidence. *Educational Policy Analysis Archives, 8*(1). Retrieved September 12, 2009, from http://epaa.asu.edu/epaa/v8n1

Dewey, J. (1938/1997). *Experience and education*. New York: Touchstone.

Dole, J. A., Nokes, J. D., & Drits, D. (2009). Cognitive strategy instruction. In S. E. Israel & G. G. Duffy (Eds.), *Handbook of research on reading comprehension* (pp. 347–372). New York: Routledge.

Duke, N. K. (2000). 3.6 minutes per day: The scarcity of informational texts in first grade. *Reading Research Quarterly, 35*(2), 202–225.

Flippo, R. F. (1999). Redefining the reading wars: The war against reading researchers. *Educational Leadership, 57*(2), 38–41.

Flood, J., Lapp, D., & Farnan, N. (1986). A reading-writing procedure that teaches expository paragraph structure. *The Reading Teacher, 39*(6), 556–562.

Gleason, M. M., & Isaacson, S. (2001). Using the new basals to teach the writing process: Modifications for students with learning problems. *Reading and Writing Quarterly, 17*(1), 75–92.

Goodman, K. A. (1994). Reading, writing, and written texts: A transactional sociopsycholinguistic view. In R. B. Ruddell, M. R. Ruddell, & H. Singer (Eds.), *Theoretical models and processes of reading* (4th ed., pp. 1093–1130). Newark, DE: International Reading Association.

Goodman, Y. M., & Goodman, K. S. (2004). To err is human: Learning about language processes. In R. B. Ruddell, & N. J. Unrau (Eds.), *Theoretical models and processes of reading* (5th ed., pp. 620–639). Newark, DE: International Reading Association.

Gough, P. B., & Tunmer, W. E. (1986). Decoding, reading, and reading disability. *Remedial and Special Education, 7*, 6–10.

Harste, J. C., Short, K., & Burke, C. (1988). *Creating classrooms for authors*. Porstmouth, NH: Heineman.

Hart, B., & Risley, T. R. (1999). *The social world of children learning to talk*. Baltimore, MD: Brookes.

Hillocks, G. (2002). *The testing trap: How state writing assessments control learning*. New York: Teachers College Press.

Institute of Educational Sciences. (2008). *Reading first impact study: Final Report* [NCEE 2009-4039]. Washington, DC: U. S. Department of Education.

Joyce, B., & Showers, B. (2002). *Student achievement through staff development* (3rd ed.). Alexandria, VA: Association for Supervision and Curriculum Development.

LeBerge, D., & Samuels, J. (1974). Toward a theory of automatic information processing in reading. *Cognitive Psychology, 6*, 293–323.

Martin, J. (1968). The development of sentence-writing skills at grades three, four, and five. (ERIC Document Reproduction Service No. ED041888) Retrieved September 26, 2009, from ERIC database.

Moje, E. B., & Speyer, J. (2008). The reality of challenging texts in high school science and social studies: How teachers can mediate comprehension. In K. A. Hinchman & H. K. Sheridan-Thomas (Eds.), *Best practices in adolescent literacy instruction* (pp. 185–211). New York: Guilford.

Moats, L. (2007). *Whole-language high jinks: How to tell when "scientifically-based reading instruction" isn't*. Washington DC: Thomas B. Fordham Institute.

National Council of Teachers of English/International Reading Association. (1998–2010). *NCTE/IRA Standards for the English Language Arts*. Newark, DE: International Reading Association/Urbana, IL: National Council of Teachers of English.

Nichols, W. D. (2007). Introduction to the adolescent reader [Special issue]. *Reading Psychology, 28*(1), 5–10.

Pearson, P. D., Raphael, T. E., Benson, V. L., & Madda, C. L. (2007). Balance in comprehensive literacy instruction: Then and now. In L. B. Gambrell, L. M. Morrow, & M. Pressley (Eds.), *Best practices in literacy instruction* (3rd ed., pp. 30–53). New York: Guilford.

Pressley, M. (2006). *Reading instruction that works: The case for balanced teaching*. New York: Guilford.

Pressley, M., Wharton-McDonald, R., Allington, R., Block, C. C., & Morrow, L. (1998). The nature of effective first-grade literacy instruction [CELA Research Report Number 11007]. Retrieved October 3, 2009, from http://www.albany.edu/cela/reports/pressley1stgrade11007.pdf

Ruddell, R. B., & Unrau, N. J. (Eds.). (2004). *Theoretical models and processes of reading* (5th ed.). Newark, DE: International Reading Association.

Sanacore, J., & Palumbo, A. (2009). Understanding the fourth-grade slump: Our point of view. *The Educational Forum, 73*, 63–74.

Saporito, L., & Vermilion Parish School Board, A. (1970). English language arts grades 1-2-3 curriculum guide, book one. (ERIC Document Reproduction Service No. ED079750) Retrieved September 26, 2009, from ERIC database.

Slavin, R.E., Cheung, A., Groff, C., & Lake, C. (2008). Effective reading programs for middle and high schools: A best evidence synthesis. *Reading Research Quarterly, 43*(3), 290–322.

Strickland, D. S., Bodino, A., Buchan, K., Jones, K. M., Nelson, A., & Rosen, M. (2001). Teaching writing in a time of reform. *The Elementary School Journal, 101*, 385–395.

Thorndike, E. L. (1931). *Human learning*. New York: Appelton.

Watson, J. B. (1928). *Psychological care of the infant and child*. New York: Norton.

Wills, J. S., & Sandholtz, J. H. (2009). Constrained professionalism: Dilemmas of teaching in the face of test-based accountability. *Teachers College Record, 111*(4), 1065–1114.

31

I Know I Can!

Teacher Self-Efficacy in the English Language Arts Classroom

Megan Tschannen-Moran and Bronwyn MacFarlane

Whether you think you can or you think you can't, you're right.

Henry Ford (1863–1947)

The function of education in English language arts (ELA) is to produce connoisseurs of language, people who enjoy and appreciate the written word and who can evaluate arguments, see logic, and appreciate the aesthetics of language (Piirto, 2007). Master ELA teachers not only possess passion for these subjects, they also have cultivated their skill in sharing their love of literary letters with young learners. Supporting the motivation for the continual professional learning required to maintain high-quality instruction are teachers' self-efficacy beliefs. Teacher self-efficacy beliefs are teachers' "conviction that they can influence how well students learn, even those who may be difficult or unmotivated" (Guskey & Passaro, 1994, p. 7). This chapter explores the role of teacher self-efficacy beliefs in English language arts instruction.

Teacher Self-Efficacy in the ELA Classroom

Bandura (1977) introduced the concept of self-efficacy beliefs as an assessment of one's capabilities to attain a desired level of performance in a given endeavor. He proposed that belief in one's abilities was a powerful driver influencing one's motivation to act, the effort one puts forth in the endeavor, persistence in that effort, and resilience in the face of setbacks. Bandura (1997) asserted that these beliefs were more powerful than one's actual abilities for the task at hand in influencing people's level of motivation, affective states, and actions (p. 2). Consequently, a teacher who did not expect to be successful in literacy instruction for certain students would likely put forth less effort in the preparation and delivery of instruction and would likely give up more readily as students struggled, even if she actually possessed teaching strategies that would likely assist these students if applied. Self-efficacy beliefs can therefore

become self-fulfilling prophesies, validating either beliefs of capability or of incompetence.

The study of teachers' sense of efficacy began in the mid-1970s with the RAND studies of reading instruction among low-income and minority students in Los Angeles (Armor et al., 1976). The RAND researchers, in search of variables that would explain differences in the effectiveness of certain teachers and methods, assessed the extent to which teachers believed they could influence student motivation and performance and whether teachers believed negative environmental factors overwhelmed the impact of their efforts in schools. The researchers found that teacher self-efficacy was positively related to variations in reading achievement among minority students, regardless of the reading curriculum used. Students taught by teachers who believed that they could influence students' motivation and learning showed significantly higher reading achievement than students whose teachers believed that there was little they could do in light of the impediments to learning posed by the environment.

The results of the RAND studies piqued interest in the construct of teachers' self-efficacy beliefs. Over the last three decades, researchers have repeatedly found teachers' sense of efficacy to be related to teachers' motivation, to the level of challenge in the goals to which teachers aspire, and the effort they invest in pursuit of those goals (Ross, 1998; Tschannen-Moran, Woolfolk Hoy, & Hoy, 1998). These, in turn, impact their instructional practices and their behavior in the classroom (Tschannen-Moran et al., 1998). Teachers with higher self-efficacy exhibit greater levels of planning, organization, commitment, enthusiasm for teaching, and persistence in assisting struggling learners (Allinder, 1994; Ashton & Webb, 1986; Gibson & Dembo, 1984; Tschannen-Moran et al., 1998). Teachers with strong self-efficacy are open to new ideas and more willing to experiment with new methods to better meet the needs of their students (Berman, McLaughlin, Bass, Pauly, & Zellman, 1977; Guskey, 1988; Stein & Wang, 1988). Teachers with stronger self-efficacy beliefs have greater commitment to teaching (Coladarci, 1992; Evans & Tribble, 1986; Trentham, Silvern, & Brogdon, 1985) and are more likely to stay in teaching (Glickman & Tamashiro, 1982). Teachers' self-efficacy beliefs are also related to important student outcomes. Teachers' self-efficacy predicts students' sense of self-efficacy and motivation (Midgley, Feldlaufer, & Eccles, 1989), as well as their achievement outcomes (Anderson, Greene, & Loewen, 1988; Ashton & Webb, 1986; Moore & Esselman, 1992; Pajares, 1996, Ross, 1992). An ELA instructor who judges herself capable of marshaling the complex set of knowledge and skills required to make instructional decisions based on student needs will likely exert greater effort, persistence, and resilience in the face of challenges. Teachers with a high sense of instructional efficacy tend to view difficult students as reachable and teachable and regard their learning problems as surmountable by ingenuity and extra effort. Teachers with low self-efficacy are inclined to invoke low student ability as an explanation for why their students cannot be taught (Ashton & Webb, 1986).

A teacher's sense of efficacy is not necessarily uniform across the different types of professional tasks that teachers perform, nor across different subject matter (Bandura, 1997). Teacher self-efficacy is context-specific, so that teachers who feel efficacious in one context may feel inefficacious in another. In fact, teachers may report different levels of self-efficacy for the different courses and student groups they encounter during the course of a school day (Ross, Cousins, & Gadalla, 1996). A growing number of scholars are conducting research on the influences of teacher self-efficacy as it relates specifically to language learning and teaching. Among a group of ELA preservice teachers, a positive relationship was found between language self-efficacy and the frequent use of a range of language-learning strategies in their preservice teaching (Wong, 2005). The self-efficacy beliefs of English teachers were found to differ across a range of English teaching tasks and competencies, revealing that teachers may purposefully select to teach specific components of the ELA curriculum for which they feel greater efficacy, while neglecting areas of the ELA curriculum in which they feel less confident (Hansen, 2006). The study of literature was found to be the strongest area of English teacher self-efficacy across a range of competencies.

Writing self-efficacy has been linked with writing performance and teacher beliefs about how to teach writing (Pajares, Johnson, & Usher, 2007; Graham, Harris, Fink, & MacArthur, 2001). In a study of preservice teachers in a graduate program, the relationship between teacher performance as a student and performance as an ELA teacher revealed a relationship between writing self-efficacy and the quality of their writing at the graduate level (Lavelle, 2006). In a study on the influence of self-efficacy beliefs on the teaching of writing, high self-efficacy teachers differed from low self-efficacy teachers in classroom writing instruction practices (Graham et al., 2001). Teachers in the highest quintile of self-efficacy reported spending significantly more time on writing each week, taught more writing processes, more grammar, and were more positive in the affect they displayed around writing. The language and writing self-efficacy of ELA teachers matters when it comes to their teaching practices.

Cultivating Teacher Self-Efficacy Beliefs With the well-documented link between teacher self-efficacy beliefs and a range of positive outcomes, it seems logical to investigate how these beliefs can be cultivated among ELA teachers. Teacher self-efficacy is determined in part, by the individual teacher's comparative judgment of whether their personal current abilities and strategies are adequate for the teaching task in question. Bandura (1997) proposed that self-efficacy beliefs emanate from four sources; vicarious experiences, social persuasion, physiological and emotional states, and mastery experiences. Each of these is explored below.

Vicarious Experiences. ELA teachers construct their beliefs in part from watching other educators teach. Teachers entering the field have typically experienced "apprenticeships" of at least 17 years as students. An ELA teacher may attribute the aspiration to become a teacher to a great ELA teacher whom they hoped to emulate. This modeling may continue during teacher preparation, as student teachers observe their cooperating teacher as well as their university instructors. Opportunities to observe colleagues teach are increasingly being structured into professional development for teachers. The degree to which the observer identifies with the model will influence the degree to which the performance of the model impacts the self-efficacy of the observer, such that when the model performs well self-efficacy is enhanced and when the model struggles with performance, self-efficacy beliefs decrease (Bandura, 1997). An ELA teacher who observes a literacy coach successfully model a particular reading strategy may experience an increase in self-efficacy if she views herself as similar to the model. However, if the literacy coach is observed having great difficulty with the lesson modeled, it may diminish the self-efficacy beliefs of the teacher observing the lesson.

Social Persuasion. Social persuasion involves receiving feedback from others about one's capabilities as a teacher. Self-efficacy is likely to increase when feedback is supportive, and diminish with criticism (Bandura, 1997). During teacher preparation, when the self-efficacy of a prospective ELA teacher is initially being developed, the feedback of supervisors is likely to have a strong impact on self-efficacy beliefs. Once in the field, supervisory or coaching conversations may play a role in either bolstering or undermining the teacher's self-efficacy. The finding that the support of their administrators was not a strong predictor of the self-efficacy beliefs of either novice or career teachers, however, may suggest the traditional practice of twice-a-year classroom visits from administrators with a preprinted evaluation form does not provide enough feedback to shape a teacher's belief about his or her professional capability (Tschannen-Moran & Woolfolk Hoy, 2007).

Teachers may also experience social persuasion during grade-level or department meetings or during informal conversations in the teachers' lounge. It is in these more informal settings that the role of the collective efficacy of the team may come into play. Collective efficacy is a group belief related to group performance. Collective efficacy beliefs may refer to the beliefs of an entire faculty or to smaller subcultures within the whole, such as departments of specific subject-area teachers. Collective efficacy may have a socialization effect shaped by the attitudes of other teachers about the task of teaching, the availability of resources, the challenges posed by the environment, and the prospects for student success (Goddard & Goddard, 2001). Individual teacher self-efficacy, collective teacher efficacy, and goals have been found to be related such that a change in one dimension can have an impact on the others (Kurz & Knight, 2004). Just as individual teacher self-efficacy impacts student performance, collective efficacy has been shown to affect student achievement as well (Goddard, Hoy, & Woolfolk Hoy, 2000; Tschannen-Moran & Barr, 2004).

Physiological and Emotional States. How teachers feel as they anticipate a teaching task also influences self-efficacy beliefs. Positive energy and emotions will contribute to a higher and more robust sense of self-efficacy while awareness of feelings of nervousness and anxiety will dampen self-efficacy beliefs. Physiological and emotional states may add to the feeling of mastery or incompetence, dependent upon whether the individual perceives their physiological response as positive or negative. Passion for the subject matter has not been studied as a source of self-efficacy but may be a factor for ELA teachers when it is experienced as a source of positive emotion.

Mastery Experiences. Mastery experiences are considered the most powerful source of self-efficacy. An individual perceives future success to be strongly linked to proficiency in past experiences. Conversely, the perception that one's own performance was a failure may lower self-efficacy beliefs contributing to an expectation for future poor performance. The self-efficacy beliefs of ELA teachers will likely be raised when they witness improvement in student performances as a result of their teaching. This belief subsequently contributes to optimism that future performances will also be proficient, resulting in greater effort and persistence. Repeated student failures, on the other hand, will likely lower self-efficacy beliefs and decrease motivation and resilience (Guskey, 1988; Ross, 1998; Tschannen-Moran et al., 1998).

Self-Fulfilling Prophesies. As we have seen, current self-efficacy beliefs contribute to current effort, which then creates a self-reinforcing cycle of success or failure. Teachers cognitively process information about their experience with the teaching task and assess the consequences; these assessments become new inputs of the four sources of self-efficacy information to repeat the cycle. Once teacher self-efficacy beliefs are established, such beliefs may be resistant to change. Contextual factors such as interpersonal support from colleagues, parents, and members of the community, and the availability of resources have been found to play a larger role in the self-efficacy beliefs of novice teachers than for career teachers (Tschannen-Moran & Woolfolk Hoy, 2007). Teachers who begin their careers with strong self-efficacy beliefs tend to build upon the motivation and persistence that those beliefs foster, fueling continued strong self-efficacy beliefs. Conversely, teachers who begin with weak self-efficacy beliefs are likely to engage in reinforcing action of those self-defeating beliefs and to persist in these beliefs as well. In this way, self-efficacy becomes both a product and a constructor of experiences (Tschannen-Moran et al., 1998).

Efficacy-Bolstering English Language Arts Interventions The research on teacher self-efficacy, in general, and on ELA teacher self-efficacy, in specific, has significant implications for teacher preparation programs and professional development initiatives for ELA teachers. In addition to concentrating on content and pedagogical skill development, teacher preparation programs would do well to attend to cultivating the self-efficacy beliefs of preservice teachers so that they enter the field with a robust sense of their capabilities. This would mean structuring preparation programs with an eye to the sources of self-efficacy, such as abundant opportunities for the observation of teaching strategies by successful role models and the provision of specific, useful, and encouraging feedback on early teaching experiences. Because mastery experiences are such a powerful source of self-efficacy, carefully structuring early teaching experiences to include gradually increasing levels of complexity and challenge to bolster a growing sense of proficiency would be important. These experiences would likely result in greater self-efficacy than the traditional practice of a long period of academic preparation followed by a short, intense period of full-immersion into teaching, which many novice teachers find daunting and discouraging. Finally, interpersonal support to find productive means to cope with the emotions attendant in beginning teaching would help support the fledgling self-efficacy beliefs of novice teachers.

An individual's self-efficacy beliefs are effected by whether the person believes that the abilities and strategies necessary for a certain task can or cannot be acquired through additional training (Bandura, 1993). Thus, preparation programs may seek to cultivate the conviction among their graduates that the skills they lack can be learned through professional development and practice. In exploring sources of teachers' self-efficacy beliefs for literacy instruction (TSELI), Johnson and Tschannen-Moran (2004) found that TSELI was significantly related to teachers' ratings of the perceived quality of university teacher preparation, ratings of the perceived quality of professional development, participation in a children's literature course, in a teachers-as-readers group, as well as participation in a book club. TSELI was unrelated to teacher characteristics such as race, the highest educational level achieved, or the years of teaching experience.

All four sources of self-efficacy are likely to be at play during preservice preparation and professional development initiatives. A study of undergraduate preservice teachers found that although the preservice teachers came to their reading methods class with fairly high self-efficacy scores, they increased their self-efficacy as a result of their increased knowledge and the application of that knowledge in practicum experiences (Shaw & Dvorak, 2007). The development of self-efficacy beliefs is not a linear progression, however, with new sources of self-efficacy adding incremental gains (Tschannen-Moran & McMaster, 2009). As teachers apply new learning, they may experience an "implementation dip" in self-efficacy as they begin to implement a change initiative (Ross, 1994; Stein & Wang, 1988; Woolfolk Hoy & Burke-Spero, 2005). These self-efficacy beliefs tended to rebound for teachers who were able to successfully implement the change initiative. In a quasi-experimental study, Tschannen-Moran and McMaster (2009) tested the potency of different sources of self-efficacy beliefs by structuring four professional development formats, presenting the same teaching strategy for beginning readers, with increasing levels of efficacy-relevant input. Results indicated that the professional development format that supported mastery experiences through follow-up coaching had the strongest effect on self-efficacy beliefs for reading instruction as well as for implementation of the new strategy. A substantial proportion of the teachers who participated in formats that included a demonstration with local students and a planning and practice session, but no follow-up coaching, experienced a decrease in their self-efficacy for reading instruction.

Meaningful professional development support is essential to ameliorating the "implementation dip" in self-efficacy beliefs common during the crucial early stages of change (Guskey, 1989; Joyce & Showers, 1988; Stein & Wang, 1988). In examining the effect of various components of professional development models, Joyce and Showers (1988) found a jump in effect sizes when practice feedback was added to information, theory, and demonstration components within professional development programs. There was further increase in effect size when coaching to support the implementation was added. Professional development programs that aim to support teachers' ongoing utilization of new knowledge of effective practice need to develop a delivery system characterized by the provision of continued support and follow-up after initial training (Guskey, 1989; Stein & Wang, 1988). Self-efficacy beliefs tended to rebound for teachers who successfully implemented the new instructional practices and continued the process of change.

Teacher self-efficacy and willingness to innovate are both a cause and an outcome of witnessing improvements in student achievement (Guskey, 1988, 1989). Teacher self-efficacy may impact the learning of diverse students dependent upon teacher perceptions of those students. Timperley and Phillips (2003) found generally low expectations and a low level of self-efficacy among teachers of students from disadvantaged backgrounds. After participating in a 6-month intervention in which teachers learned new and more powerful literacy teaching strategies and witnessed improved student outcomes as a result, teacher self-efficacy beliefs increased significantly. The teachers' expectations of both themselves and their students increased regardless of student backgrounds.

Current Issues in ELA Teacher Self-efficacy

In a challenge to the view that "more is better" when it comes to self-efficacy beliefs, Wheatley (2002) has proposed that doubts about one's efficacy can sometimes be beneficial in that uncertainty or doubt is crucial for teacher reflection that leads to new insights. Wheatley challenged Bandura's (1997) claim that it is difficult for a person to achieve while fighting self-doubt, stating instead that it is difficult for teachers to learn and improve without experiencing self-efficacy doubts. This disequilibrium and uncertainty may come about from a challenge to teachers' beliefs about their existing practices. Wheatley suggested that factors such as follow-up coaching might moderate the debilitating influence that teacher self-efficacy doubts may have on teachers, resulting in improved practice. Gregoire (2003) has proposed a model of teacher conceptual change based on whether teachers, when presented with an instructional reform initiative, appraise it as either a threat or a challenge. In this model, teachers who believe that they are already implementing the reform will assess that they are not implicated in the changes being proposed and will process the new content superficially. Teachers who do feel implicated by the reforms presented will experience stress and discomfort. Those with low self-efficacy are predicted to respond to the reform initiative as a threat, leading to an avoidance intention and superficial belief change. On the other hand, teachers with high self-efficacy who perceive that they have the resources, time, and support necessary to implement the proposed changes, would likely interpret the reform as a challenge and consequently engage in more systematic (and thus effortful) processing of the information presented. This model explicates the mechanisms through which teachers' self-efficacy mediates their response to instructional change.

An ongoing puzzle associated with teachers' self-efficacy is the accuracy of their self-assessments in terms of external standards of knowledge and skills. Few studies have tackled this issue, but there is evidence that teachers' calibration of the level of their content knowledge is not especially accurate, with teachers tending to overestimate their knowledge and skills. Cunningham, Perry, Stanovich, and Stanovich, (2004) asked primary teachers to assess their level of content knowledge of phonics, and found that teachers tended to overestimate their knowledge and skills. This overestimation of skill level may negatively affect self-efficacy beliefs in the face of evidence that personal knowledge and skills were not as strong as originally believed. Bandura (1997) suggested that a slight overestimation of skills may be beneficial in that it may lead to greater effort and persistence than a lower self-assessment might yield. On the other hand, grossly overestimating one's level of skill may lead to placing the blame for a lack of progress on students or of failing to engage in appropriate professional development opportunities. Several researchers have made use of observers' performance ratings of teachers in relation to self-report data of efficacy beliefs (Saklofske, Michaluk, & Randhawa, 1988; Trentham et al., 1985), and more studies of this kind would be useful.

Final Thoughts

Self-efficacy, the belief in one's abilities to accomplish desired outcomes, powerfully affects people's behavior, motivation and, ultimately, their success or failure (Bandura, 1997). Without self-efficacy, people do not expend effort in endeavors since they may perceive their efforts will be futile. Teachers with high self-efficacy may devote more classroom time to academic activities, provide all students with the guidance needed to succeed, and affirm academic accomplishments of students. In contrast, teachers with low self-efficacy may spend more time on nonacademic pastimes, readily give up on students who exhibit teaching challenges, or criticize students for performance failure (Ashton & Webb, 1986). Teacher preparation programs and ongoing professional development for practicing teachers that take seriously the impact of teacher self-efficacy will incorporate demonstrations, feedback, coaching, and monitoring of student progress. In addition to improved instruction, the results are likely to be teachers with greater commitment to teaching, who expend greater effort and persistence, and who remain in the field even in challenging circumstances. Bolstering the self-efficacy of ELA teachers is likely to contribute to their motivation in pursuit of the goal of every ELA teacher, that is, to develop proficient connoisseurs of the English language.

References

Allinder, R. M. (1994). The relationship between efficacy and the instructional practices of special education teachers and consultants. *Teacher Education and Special Education, 17*, 86–95.

Anderson, R., Greene, M., & Loewen, P. (1988). Relationships among teachers' and students' thinking skills, sense of efficacy, and student achievement. *Alberta Journal of Educational Research, 34*(2), 148–165.

Armor, D., Conroy-Oseguera, P., Cox, M., King, N., McDonell, L., Pascal, A., et al. (1976). *Analysis of the school preferred reading programs in selected Los Angeles minority schools* (Report No. R2007-LAUSD). Santa Monica, CA: Rand Corporation (ERIC Document Reproduction Service No. 130 243).

Ashton, P. T., & Webb, R. B. (1986). *Making a difference: Teachers' sense of efficacy and student achievement.* New York: Longman.

Bandura, A. (1977). Self-efficacy: Toward a unifying theory of behavioral change. *Psychological Review, 84*, 191–215.

Bandura, A. (1993). Perceived self-efficacy in cognitive development and functioning. *Educational Psychologist, 28*, 117–148.

Bandura, A. (1997). *Self-efficacy: The exercise of control.* New York: Freeman.

Berman, P., McLaughlin, M., Bass, G., Pauly, E., & Zellman, G. (1977). *Federal programs supporting educational change. Vol. VII: Factors affecting implementation and continuation* (Report No. R-1589/7-HEW). Santa Monica, CA: Rand Corporation (ERIC Document Reproduction Service No. 140 432).

Coladarci, T. (1992). Teachers' sense of efficacy and commitment to teaching. *Journal of Experimental Education, 60*, 323–337.

Cunningham, A. E., Perry, K. E., Stanovich, K. E., & Stanovich, P. J. (2004). Disciplinary knowledge of K-3 teachers and their knowledge calibration in the domain of early literacy. *Annals of Dyslexia, 54*, 139–167.

Evans, E. D., & Tribble, M. (1986). Perceived teaching problems, self-efficacy and commitment to teaching among preservice teachers. *Journal of Educational Research, 80*(2), 81–85.

Gibson, S., & Dembo, M. (1984). Teacher efficacy: A construct validation. *Journal of Educational Psychology, 76*, 569–582.

Glickman, C., & Tamashiro, R. (1982). A comparison of first-year, fifth-year, and former teachers on efficacy, ego development, and problem solving. *Psychology in Schools, 19*, 558–562.

Goddard, R. D., & Goddard, Y. L. (2001). A multilevel analysis of the relationship between teacher and collective efficacy in urban schools. *Teacher and Teacher Education, 17*, 807–818.

Goddard, R. D., Hoy, W. K., & Woolfolk Hoy, A. (2000). Collective teacher efficacy: Its meaning, measure, and impact on student achievement. *American Research Journal, 37*, 479–508.

Graham, S., Harris, K., Fink, B., & MacArthur, C. A. (2001). Teacher efficacy in writing: A construct validation with primary grade teachers. *Scientific Studies of Reading, 5*(2), 177–202.

Gregoire, M. (2003). Is it a challenge or a threat? A dual process model of teacher's cognition and appraisal processes during conceptual change. *Educational Psychology Review, 15*, 147–179.

Guskey, T. (1988). Teacher efficacy, self-concept, and attitudes toward the implementation of instructional innovation. *Teaching and Teacher Education, 4*(1), 63–69.

Guskey, T. (1989). Attitude and perceptual change in teachers. *International Journal of Educational Research, 13*, 439–454.

Guskey, T., & Passaro, P. (1994). Teacher efficacy: A study of construct dimensions. *American Educational Research Journal, 31*, 627–643.

Hansen, S. (2006). I can't do everything! English teachers' efficacy beliefs. *International Journal of Learning, 13*(7), 53–60.

Johnson, D. & Tschannen-Moran, M. (2004, April). *Exploring literacy teachers' self efficacy beliefs: Potential sources at play.* Paper presented at the annual meeting of the American Educational Research Association, San Diego.

Joyce, B., & Showers, B. (1988). *Student achievement through staff development.* White Plains, NY: Longman.

Kurz, T., & Knight, S. (2004). An exploration of the relationship among teacher efficacy, collective teacher efficacy, and goal consensus. *Learning Environments Research, 7*, 111–128.

Lavelle, E. (2006). Teachers' self-efficacy for writing. *Electronic Journal of Research in Educational Psychology, 8*(4), 73–84.

Midgley, D., Feldlaufer, H., & Eccles, J. (1989). Change in teacher efficacy and student self- and task-related beliefs in mathematics during the transition to junior high school. *Journal of Educational Psychology, 81*, 247–258.

Moore, W., & Esselman, M. (1992). *Teacher efficacy, power, school climate, and achievement: A desegregating district's experience.* Paper presented at the annual meeting of the American Educational Research Association, San Francisco.

Pajares, F. (1996). Self-efficacy beliefs in achievement settings. *Review of Educational Research, 66*, 543–579.

Pajares, F., Johnson, M., & Usher, E. (2007). Sources of writing self-efficacy beliefs of elementary, middle, and high school students. *Research in the Teaching of English, 42*(1), 104–120.

Piirto, J. (2007). *Talented children and adults: Their development and education.* Waco, TX: Prufrock Press.

Ross, J. (1992). Teacher efficacy and the effects of coaching on student achievement. *Canadian Journal of Education, 17*(1), 51–65.

Ross, J. (1994). The impact of an inservice to promote cooperative learning on the stability of teacher efficacy. *Teaching and Teacher Education, 10,* 381–394.

Ross, J. A. (1998). Antecedents and consequences of teacher efficacy, In J. Brophy (Ed.), *Advances in Research on Teaching* (Vol. 7, pp. 49–74). Greenwich, CT: JAI Press.

Ross, J. A., Cousins, J. B., & Gadalla, T. (1996). Within-teacher predictors of teacher efficacy. *Teaching and Teacher Education, 12,* 385–400.

Saklofske, D., Michaluk, B., & Randhawa, B. (1988). Teachers' efficacy and teaching behaviors. *Psychological Report, 63,* 407–414.

Shaw, D. M., & Dvorak, M. J. (2007). Promise and possibility: Hope for teacher education that pre-service literacy instruction can have an impact. *Reading Research and Instruction, 46*(3), 223–254.

Stein, M., & Wang, M. (1988). Teacher development and school improvement: The process of teacher change. *Teaching and Teacher Education, 4,* 171–187.

Timperley, H., & Phillips, G. (2003). Changing and sustaining teachers' expectations through professional development in literacy. *Teaching and Teacher Education, 19,* 627–641.

Trentham, L., Silvern, S., & Brogdon, R. (1985). Teacher efficacy and teacher competency ratings. *Psychology in Schools, 22,* 343–352.

Tschannen-Moran, M., & Barr, M. (2004). Fostering student learning: The relationship of collective teacher efficacy and student achievement. *Leadership & Policy in Schools, 3,* 189–209.

Tschannen-Moran, M., & McMaster, P. (2009). Sources of self-efficacy: Four professional development formats and their relationship to self-efficacy and implementation of a new teaching strategy. *The Elementary School Journal, 110,* 228–248.

Tschannen-Moran, M., & Woolfolk Hoy, A. (2007). The differential antecedents of self-efficacy beliefs of novice and experienced teachers, *Teaching and Teacher Education, 23,* 944–956.

Tschannen-Moran, M., Woolfolk Hoy, A., & Hoy, W. K. (1998). Teacher efficacy: Its meaning and measure. *Review of Educational Research, 68,* 202–248.

Wheatley, K. (2002). The potential benefits of teacher efficacy doubts for educational reform. *Teaching and Teacher Education, 18,* 5–22.

Wong, S. M. (2005). Language learning strategies and language self-efficacy: Investigating the relationship in Malaysia. *RELC Journal, 36*(3), 245–269.

Woolfolk Hoy, A., & Burke-Spero, R. (2005). Changes in teacher efficacy during the early years of teaching: A comparison of four measures. *Teaching and Teacher Education, 21,* 343–356.

32

Teaching for Transformation

Drama and Language Arts Education

BRIAN EDMISTON

If at present it isn't possible to merge the work of adults and the work of students because we don't value the contribution young children can bring to cultural development of the world's good, we can rely on proven drama systems to create 'the mirror to nature' and harness, through identification and empathy, the life knowledge which children will bring generously to meet us half-way. (Heathcote, 2006, p. xii)

Introduction

In this chapter I explore how adults can use drama to teach for transformation. I ground my analysis in the educational philosophy and drama pedagogy developed over half a century by Dorothy Heathcote (1984; Heathcote & Bolton, 2005) as well as in the synthesizing pedagogical model of transformative education, which includes language and literacy teaching, as presented by Mary Kalantzis and Bill Cope (2008) in *New Learning: Elements of a Science of Education*.

Transformative teaching requires adults as change agents focused both on designing, creating, and assessing collaborative critical learning situations as well as on strategic teaching interactions (Kalantzis & Cope, 2008). Teaching that promotes shifts in adults' and young people's identities is key so that all might become "collaborative researchers, designing and tracking purposeful, transformative interventions" in networks of collaborative inquiry (p. 37).

Heathcote (1984) envisions that drama, like the other arts, "could be a vehicle for changing the work of school" if teachers regarded themselves as "part of a recognized cultural power to influence [and shape] a society in action thinking, knowing, living human beings engaged with their culture" (pp. 192–193). As her biographer and colleague, Gavin Bolton (1984), notes, Heathcote not only, "brought drama back to the track of pursing knowledge" but her work has "challenged what a teacher *is*" (pp. 7–8, emphasis in original). Heathcote's "remarkable innovations"

center on creating dramatic representations with young people that can mediate their desires to examine and shape culture both in their schools and as active participants in society. Her pedagogy (1984) assumes the following: first, adult participation with young people in the process of creating and exploring imagined worlds, in contrast with a view of adults as only facilitators; second, a need for teachers to draw on extensive content knowledge as well as have high skills and standards in creating aesthetic form; third, ensemble- and inquiry-based learning rather than individualized or transmission-based approaches; grounded, fourth, by a core belief that teachers must always respectfully begin by accepting, and then using positively, students' energies, attitudes, interests, and existing understanding.

Heathcote's philosophy and pedagogy is echoed in Kalantzis and Cope's (2008) argument that ideally in classrooms, as in life, learning is social and distributed among collaborating, inquiring young people and adults who, over time, engage in the following interrelated shared processes: *experiencing* both the known and the new; *conceptualizing* not only by naming, as learners new to a topic do, but also, as more experienced learners do, by using cultural frameworks to theorize about the world; *analyzing* life experiences both functionally and critically; while always doing so through an appropriate, yet also creative, *application* of knowledge in authentic or life-like situations (pp. 178–186). These four inter-related pedagogical processes are used as organizational headings for this chapter.

Experiencing

For over a century, experiential learning has been considered the heart of educational practice and learning: young people should address real problems by making, actively doing, and experimenting with materials and ideas (Dewey, 1956). Yet, as literacy researchers applying spatial theory to classroom life have pointed out, the lived experiences of students are largely ignored in classroom spaces (Leander & Sheehy, 2004). Drama can address that absence.

James Moffett (1968) argues that all discourse is grounded by the "drama" of "present-tense" experiences. In "the universe of discourse" people build from, and toward, both direct lived felt experiences of events and their "projections" into the imagined experiences of literature and other narratives (p. 50). Moffett contrasts the drama of "what is happening" with people's stories of past events and other increasingly abstract and speculative uses of language they use to make ideational connections and construct understanding for themselves and others. Even in writing about abstract ideas for remote audiences, "experience is behind the discourse, buried in the processing and combined with other experiences" (p. 245). Moffett makes clear Kalantzis and Cope's pedagogical implication. Students learning to use language must, "abstract from the ground up" (p. 247): new understanding must be rooted in lived experiences.

Imagined-and-Real Experiences As Maxine Greene notes, "Imagining things being otherwise may be the first step toward acting on the belief that they can be changed" (1996, p. 22). A core difference between experiencing actions in everyday life and in socially imagined events is that the later occur in what Heathcote (1984, p. 128) calls a "no penalty zone" where young people, without fear of physical consequences, can experiment and improvise with how the world could be different. No one actually dies when they imagine the events of *Hamlet*. Yet, a group can explore and learn about how people's actions may affect another's life, and death, as they imagine together they are in Elsinore and explore each other's interpretations of the play. "I am concerned, in my teaching, with the difference in reality between the real world where we seem to 'really exist' and the 'as if' world where we can exist at will. I do live but I may also say, 'If it were like this, this is how I would live'" (Heathcote, 1984, p. 104).

As play theorists have argued, people know they are pretending, intend their imagined interactions, and have real social and emotional experiences as they play. Thus, the felt experiences of dramatic improvisation in imagined events, and the learning that occurs, always take place in spaces that can be considered imagined-and-real (Beach, Campano, Edmiston, & Borgmann, 2010). Players actively and intentionally transform objects and actions into imagined things and events that players use as tools to create abstract meaning different from their everyday meaning (Vygotsky, 1967). For example, a moving stick can become a horse or a chair can become a throne. Any socially imagined event may be used in conjunction with other semiotic representations (e.g., talking, moving, drawing, or writing) as social and cultural meaning-making tools. As Vygotsky (1967) stressed, it's the symbolic meaning of action rather than the literal act itself that predominates when people play. Vygotsky's play theory can be applied to all modes of dramatic improvisation ranging from spontaneous dramatic play to formal dramatic performance.

Life can be experienced in both the drama of everyday life and the drama of imagined lives whether in reading and writing, children's dramatic play, or teacher-led classroom uses of drama. Significantly for language arts educators, young people (often with adults) use and compose language to abstract meaning from their experiences of text-based or improvised representations of life. Whereas the projective imagination required in reading and writing texts is both individual and one step removed from actual interaction in the world of a text, any fictional dramatic experience, like that of everyday life, is social, emotional, and enacted; in drama young people move, talk, think, and feel as if events are actually happening to them in a world they collaboratively imagine that may include participating adults.

Ensemble-based Learning Given that theatre is "a quintessentially collaborative art form," Michael Boyd, the artistic director of the Royal Shakespeare Company has asked, "Can an ensemble…act in some sense as a…better version of the real world on an achievable scale which celebrates the virtues of collaboration?" (Neelands, 2009, p. 176). Leading drama education scholar, Jonothan Neelands reflecting on this question, has drawn parallels between the ensemble approach to theatre, the socially transformative power of the arts, and the possibility of creating and experiencing an ideal of participatory democracy in classrooms where drama is used.

An ensemble will not develop unless teachers can both be team-members as well as leaders who aren't domineering while assisting young people to focus and achieve in an exploratory workshop environment. As Heathcote (1984) has stressed, adults are needed to "keep the team together, work them to capacity, forwarding their projects efficiently, using their strengths, and helping them to know and overcome their weaknesses" (p. 44).

Applying

A situated view of language and literacy education recognizes that young people learn best in the sorts of everyday life "communities of practice" that provide people with supportive, extended, collaborative opportunities to apply past and new knowledge in authentic, practical, appropriate, social, and cultural situations (Wenger, 1998). In contrast, much of schooling is individualized and only focused on reports of other people's lives rather than sustained collaborative participation in communities where multiple literacies may be learned and practiced.

Adults who facilitate informal dramatic play and ensemble-based theatrical performances both create support for extensive application of situated uses of language. As Karen Wohlwend (2008) has convincingly shown, when young children's play is supported by adults providing resources that the children can transform into literacy tools, dramatic play becomes a collaborative "literacy of possibilities" grounded in children's passions and multimodal strengths. And as the research of Shirley Brice Heath and Shelby

Wolf (2005) has illustrated, students committed to dramatic performances will be prepared to explore competing interpretations, engage in background research, compose scripts, and express multiple representations as they collaboratively create and enact play scripts.

Imagined-and-Real Community Literacy Practices Teachers who engage with young people in extended dramatic inquiry create community social practices in which literacy applications may become more nuanced and complex. My term, "dramatic inquiry," privileges drama pedagogy that is a hybrid of dramatic play, dramatic performance, and inquiry-based education (Beach et al., 2010). As with informal dramatic play, an imagined world is formed and explored in multiple modes as participants experience and interact as if they are imagined people. Like dramatic performances, new views are shared as well as experienced: adults and/or young people may present ideas to others in the group. In dramatic inquiry teachers mediate students' inquiry and shape the work. Adults enter shared imagined spaces as a "teacher in role" (Heathcote, 1984) to negotiate and shape the creation of an imagined-and-real community in which, interacting as if they are fictional people, all may collaboratively engage in actual literacy practices.

Through dramatization, dramatic inquiry extends inquiry-based pedagogy (Short, Harste, & Burke, 1995; Beach & Myers, 2001). Young people engaged in classroom study organized around inquiry research and grapple with problems but they are limited by the tools actually available in the classroom. By contrast, in dramatic inquiry young people may investigate with the role and responsibility of people in a community that they identify with, having access to almost unlimited literacy tools made available through the use of social imagination. The following examples are all from central Ohio classrooms (Beach et al., 2010). In all cases, teachers took on roles alongside the young people. The students from mostly affluent households in Trish Russell's first-grade classroom identified as travel agents as they researched and planned a safe scuba diving vacation to a sunken wreck off Hawaii. Fifth-grade students in Sarah Higgins' mixed-income mostly White classroom designed a Thanksgiving memorial creating images from competing narratives of the events of 1610, and sixth-grade students at a middle school with a student population of high-poverty and a history of student violence, critiqued entries on a fictional Web site they created with Mary Ann Buchan, their student teacher, while reading Doug Wilhelm's *The Revealers*, a novel with a theme of bullying. High school students, in role as collaborative directors of a new movie adaptation of *Hamlet,* could choose words and actions from a possible script edited from Shakespeare's text in order to explore reasons for Hamlet's indecision. In each case, potential literacy events are embedded in the professional practices of a community in which the young people participate. Collaborating teachers can extend students' practices through interactions in imagined-and-real spaces: as a potential vacationer phoning travel agents for vacation ideas; as the historical character called Squanto, by Whites, being interviewed and giving factual information about how the peace treaty was broken; as a victim of bullying dictating a website entry; or as a fellow script writer collaboratively representing characters to create a text showing Hamlet's conflicting thoughts as he contemplates avenging his father's murder.

Dramatic Form The imagined-and-real social practices of dramatic inquiry shape and are shaped by its evolving aesthetic form: "everything irrelevant to the main issues must be lacking, and the relevant material [as considered by the group] must achieve order and style" (Heathcote, 1984, p. 55). As Susanne Langer (1953) states, in the arts, form is always more than shaping ideas with tools, form is experienced as "symbolic of human feeling". Visual artists create form using, for example, paints and clay, whereas dramatic artists primarily use people's words and movement. In addition, dramatic representations may incorporate the other arts, for example drawings, models, or soundscapes of imagined settings.

Heathcote (1984) clarifies the intended outcome of dramatic forming: "good drama for me is made up of the thoughts, the words and the gestures that are wrung from human beings on their way to, or in, or emerging from a state of desperation" (p. 80). Drama is always experienced with differing degrees of "dramatic tension" in "now and imminent time" (p. 161), as if events are actually happening. Learners are collaboratively engaged by their experience and the creation of dramatic tension in social and cultural spaces. For example, as a community of travel agents the first-grade children practiced what they would do if their clients encountered problems: children wanted to imagine the tension of a shark attack; the sixth-grade students-as-Web site-makers enacted the events and effects of bullying; and as *Hamlet* filmmakers the high school students could collectively select, represent, and experience, the dramatically conflicting deadly possibilities in Hamlet's mind. In each case, young people seamlessly participate in literacy practices when they compose and interpret the dramatic form of people in imagined-and-real "desperate" social situations and surrounding events.

Teacher participation, both as a member of the ensemble and as if people in any imagined world, both assists with the creation, and affects the experience of, dramatic form. The teacher must balance "structure and spontaneity" (O'Neill, 1995) to harness, on the one hand, playfulness that tends toward open-ended possibilities and lack of group cohesion and, on the other hand, theatricality that tends toward imposing predetermined representations of events. Operating like collaborative improvising playwrights, the teacher works with young people to negotiate the creation of dramatic form using the multimodal elements of theatre that include the dynamics of performance (movement and stillness, sound and silence, light and darkness) and conventions of representation e.g. using a chair with a draped cloth to represent a throne, a still person with a crown to represent a portrait of the dead king, or eerie music to evoke the feelings of those who saw the ghost (for more examples see Edmiston & Enciso, 2002).

Analyzing

As Dewey (1934) argued, personal experience and social participation alone is inadequate if people are to shape their learning and make changes in the world: young people must reflect on, and analyze, their own and others' experiences and they can do so via the arts. At the same time, though the application of knowledge in classroom communities of literacy practices builds cultural understanding, without critical analysis and inquiry into power relationships young people are more likely to become passive consumers than active citizens working for social justice (Comber & Simpson, 2001). Heathcote (1984) concurs: "In art we reflect upon nature, people's affairs, ideas and behaviour… the antiseptic and often sterile behaviour demonstrated in schools can be authenticated by [dramatic inquiry] another apparently unreal mode of communication in order to make school and society come into some form of [transformative] power for good influence" (p. 177).

Negotiating an Analytical Stance To be able to analyze any experience, as Heathcote (1984) argues, drawing on the seminal scholarship of James Britton (1970), young people must initially shift from the role of "participants" to that of "spectators". Writing and reading for meaning requires the ability to individually imagine oneself as both a participant in, and a spectator on, imagined events in a social world referenced only by the words and/or images of a particular text. However, when events are dramatized what would usually be abstracted literacy events can become enacted, visible, and thus more accessible for analysis. The performance dimension of dramatic inquiry means that as young people watch and listen to fictional presentations by peers, adults, or via electronic media, they may reflect for the possible meanings of what is being, or has been, represented. Without shifting to take up a spectator stance they cannot analyze events critically.

Young people may not readily take up a spectator stance. On the one hand, in spontaneous dramatic play young children tend to focus mostly on the experiences of participating in imagined events as if they are people in places they could never be in everyday life. Children seamlessly shift to a spectator stance in order to negotiate new roles and situations, for example "Let's not be travel agents, let's be divers now" but they spend little time analyzing. On the other hand, when students are asked to perform in front of their peers in everyday classroom spaces older students especially can be more focused on how they are being perceived by peers rather than on the ideas they are presenting (Leander, 2004).

Drawing on Erving Goffman's (1974) sociological theory of everyday performance, Heathcote (1984) conceptualizes a continuum ranging from life experiences mostly as participants, e.g., sharing an anecdote, to experience as spectators watching others show how life is lived, e.g., in ritualized events, like weddings or funerals, and highly crafted stage or screen performances.

Any performance may be the object of dramatic inquiry activities: anecdotes told in pairs about old king Hamlet; in a contemporary setting, a video news report of the marriage and coronation of King Claudius; or reenactments, using words from the text, of how Claudius poisoned his brother. At the same time, the ensemble nature of activities may similarly range from those closer to spontaneous dramatic play with a minimal spectator stance (e.g., pretending to be servants preparing for the wedding), through events improvised in different ways (e.g., practicing where, how, and by whom the crown will be presented), to a choreographed presentation (e.g., the critical selection of what will or will not be shown on the television news, given that the king will see the presentation).

Dramatizing inquiry activities may thus be regarded as on a continuum between those that are more playful to those that are more performative: the more playful the easier to shift viewpoints but the more performative the more a spectator stance is already assumed. When adults participate and reflect with students, as if they too are caught up by events in an imagined world, they can directly negotiate, or indirectly encourage, students' shift into a reflective stance.

Teachers can socially position young people as spectators of their actions as they interact with them in a dramatic role as if in a shared imagined-and-real space (Edmiston, 2003). If students are unable or unwilling to perform an episode, adults can always do so for the purpose of providing the young people with an object for their contemplation. As Heathcote (1984) puts it, "By taking up a role one offers not only a point of view to the others, but places them in a position from where it is assumed that they will also find a point of view…One cannot endow people with a commitment to a point of view, but often by placing them in the response position, they begin to hold a point of view, because they can see it has power" ranging from the crudest power of disagreeing with the role's position to agreement (pp. 164–165). At the same time, adults can introduce other material and conceptual objects for analytical reflection.

Inquiry Questions Frame Analysis Using Goffman's (1974) sociological theory of frame analysis, Heathcote (1984) proposed that every dramatic social role also provides potential "framings" of events. Teachers can negotiate with young people how they frame their analysis of imagined events. Whereas young people's framing of school topics tends to be from the viewpoint of their everyday role of "students", fictional roles provide them with framings that have much more responsibility for in-depth analysis than is usual in classrooms. In drama, "participants have to be framed into a position to influence…placed in a quite specific relationship to the action because this brings with it inevitably the responsibility, and more particularly the viewpoint which gets them into an affective [and analytical] involvement" (p. 168). Heathcote's (Heathcote & Bolton, 2005) "mantle of the expert approach" to dramatic inquiry illustrates how much young people may learn when over time they gradually take on a professional "mantle" of the responsibility and analysis that accompanies an area of expertise, for example as travel agents, as they carry out tasks for imagined clients. Shaffer's (2006) analysis of computer-game players similarly notes that players have a shared "epistemic frame" that provides "the ways of knowing, of deciding what is worth knowing, and of adding to the collective body of knowledge and understanding of a community of practice" (p. 161).

Negotiating the sort of inquiry questions that professionals are likely to grapple with focuses the analysis opened up by a particular epistemic framing. For example, the first graders in role as travel agents framed their analysis of potential vacations in terms of client safety as well as enjoyment. An ongoing inquiry question was negotiated by their teacher, embraced by the children, and displayed in their travel agency to guide enacted and text-based research: Are vacations going to be safe as well as fun? Negotiating a different role or asking a different inquiry question frames analysis of events differently. For example, as if they were members of the Florida Safety Commission the children, and their teacher, considered this additional critical inquiry question, "Should we shut down a travel agency if it's unsafe?" The children with great delight collectively represented the dangerous events of a "Swimming with Sharks" vacation run by Scuba Adventures when a vacationer was bitten and then, with their teacher-as-his-mother, the hospital where he was in intensive care. As commissioners they framed their analysis of the agency's actions in relation to enacted events exploring the consequences for the man and his family.

Inquiry becomes critical when students, "question the everyday world and consider actions that can be taken to promote social justice" especially as they "question and challenge the attitudes, values and beliefs that lie beneath the surface" (Lewison, Leland, & Harste, 2008, p. 8). Whereas classroom inquiry may dissipate into individual projects and uncritical concerns, dramatizing explorations can easily be quickly focused by an implicit or explicitly negotiated critical inquiry question framed by a fictional role's attitude in relation to a particular event that will likely engage the students if it illustrates an open, contested, ambiguous, or troubling aspect of whatever problem is under consideration. When adults engage with young people in the imagined-and-real events experienced and represented in dramatic improvisation, "there is the opportunity for one problem to be faced at a time" (Heathcote, 1984, p. 69). For example, should Hamlet kill his uncle, Claudius? This question could be posed by a teacher-as-Hamlet displaying uncertainty in recalling that the ghost of his dead father tells him he was murdered. The specific question and event illustrates a broader critical inquiry question relevant to both the multi-faceted world of *Hamlet* and young people's everyday lives: How do people know what to do if they're

unsure about the truth of what others' say? The question could be explored in social imagination from the multiple viewpoints of those affected, across any of the times and places of the imagined world: Ophelia unsure of the meaning of Hamlet's love letters and her father's belief that Hamlet is mad; Hamlet's mother Gertrude before the play opens, considering marriage to her brother-in-law; all in contrast with Laertes' impulse to immediately kill Hamlet to avenge his own father's death.

When inquiry is dramatic, different epistemic framings provide people with different degrees of emotional as well as analytical "distance" from events. Using another of Heathcote's (1984) terms, different framings allow young people to be "protected into" (p. 153) an analysis of a situation that in their everyday lives might feel emotionally too "hot" to analyze. For example, as advisors to the new King Fortinbras, at the end of *Hamlet*, students could be protected into an analysis of death, focused by an open inquiry question such as the following: Where should Hamlet, Gertrude, Claudius, and Laertes be buried in relation to the graves of King Hamlet, Polonius, and Ophelia and what should be written on their gravestones?

How people frame events in the moment of their participation can be contrasted with how people frame prior events when they analyze narrated experiences. There is dramatic tension for those at the end of *Hamlet* who must deal with an invading king and a collection of dead bodies. At the same time, the relationships among the dead and the living may be explored through dramatizations of memories, reports, records, and conjectures of past events. As soon as the conflicting views and attitudes of different characters are imagined and enacted to explore a critical inquiry question young people's analysis takes a critical turn.

Finally, as I have illustrated elsewhere in reference to longitudinal studies (Edmiston, 2008; Beach et al., 2010), adults using dramatic inquiry over time can support transformations in young people's identities. Young people, including those who may have had marginalized positions in classrooms, can be positioned to participate with higher authority and to draw on their social and cultural resources as they act and interpret events in spaces framed with shared responsibilities. Further, over time as they shift positions across events, relationships, possibilities, and perspectives young people may begin to view themselves and others differently as they dialogically evaluate their own and others' actions and experiences.

Conceptualizing

Transformative education requires learners not only to conceptualize by "naming" as they "clarify, classify, group and distinguish" but also "to be active theory makers" as they "consider their own lifeworld experiences, critically reflect on the knowledge they encounter, and apply that knowledge to real-world experiences" (Kalantizis & Cope, 2006, pp. 182–183). As teachers and young people collaboratively form, frame, and explore from different viewpoints inquiry questions about events in a drama world (O'Neill, 1995), their conceptualizing processes are significantly extended to include analysis of an evolving sequence of imagined-and-real events.

Dialogic Understanding

Bakhtin (1981) argues that creating any understanding always involves a "dialogic" intermingling of competing interpretations of the same event; people must be able to hold, and experience at the same time, the conflict between more than one perspective; new understanding requires that old views are "refracted" by new views. Participation in any type of drama inherently exposes people to a felt tension between conflicting viewpoints; teachers who intentionally and dialogically sequence dramatic inquiry activities mediate young people's creation of understandings that are more nuanced and complex (Edmiston & Enciso, 2002; Edmiston, 2008). As Heathcote (1984) puts it, "the realignment of…old experience [and attitudes] becomes useful when applied to the newer problem, thus enabling us to see new and deeper meanings" (p. 50). In comparison with everyday life, in imagined-and-real spaces there can be a greater "angle of refraction" between competing views and productive dissonance felt between competing views; there can be both more potential for deep change and more possibility of resisting change in understanding.

In Sarah Higgins' fifth-grade classroom, using dramatic inquiry for the first time, she initially focused a Thanksgiving inquiry by posing a critical question: from whose perspectives should the story be told? The students all agreed that indigenous perspectives had to be included. The inquiry questions were contextualized in the imagined task negotiated with her students: a group of sculptors were charged with designing a sculpture to commemorate Thanksgiving. Dramatic performances by her and two visiting adults presented alternative perspectives in relation to the stereotypical views assumed by the students' textbook and revealed in their initial drawings. The students encountered some of the voices in the Thanksgiving story silenced in their textbook, e.g., that the indigenous people kept the Pilgrims alive but were then attacked by the English who broke the 1621 peace treaty. However, it was only when the inquiry question was dramatically, and dialogically, tightened to focus on a more difficult question that the students-as-Wampanoag revisited their designs refracted their original views and began to comment on their assumption of their power to shape different interpretations: Should we continue to celebrate Thanksgiving as we have always done, or like many contemporary indigenous and non-indigenous people, should we participate in the National Day of Mourning?

Xavier: People think we got along and they want to put up a statue of us getting along, we did NOT get along.

John: You really can't change what happened in the past. The past is the past…. We're here and we're alive and that's all in the past and we're doing fine so we should just let it go.

Xavier: But you can change it now. You can change the past now so in the future…show a sculpture of a peace treaty but behind the sculpture a war scene.

John regarded the past as unchangeable events that should be let go whereas Xavier realized that he had some power to shape people's future interpretations about the meaning of the past. He became adamant that images of war should destabilize images based on the traditional discourse that Thanksgiving was an idyllic peace. The students-as-contemporary-Wampanoags were then asked to reinterpret their previous stereotypical drawings. Sarah noted that Xavier's ideas made a significant difference. His comments opened up a critical discussion about how the past dictates present-day actions.

Conclusion

The transformative and expansive tools of drama, which are available to whoever can imagine their use, may be used by adults and young people to harness dramatic imagination in order to create classroom spaces where collaborative, dialogic, and critical explorations of diverse social and cultural worlds becomes a norm.

Teachers who desire to use drama, and dramatic inquiry in particular, must be ready to create ensembles where young people and teachers take actions, grounded by playful collaboration, and shaped in the dialogic understanding made possible when people embrace, perform, and explore what they know of the world and how they imagine life might be different.

Like first-grade teacher Trish Russell, teachers are likely to begin a transformation in their identities. When reflecting on her experiences of learning over a year to use dramatic inquiry with her students her view of herself as a teacher had changed significantly from someone previously focused more on students' achievement of objective standards: "Not only do you teach them how to be creative and how to incorporate language arts but also how to be real people and to feel like they're going to be somebody in the world."

References

Bakhtin, M. M. (1981). *The dialogic imagination* (M. Holquist, Ed., C. Emerson, & M. Holquist, Trans.). Austin: Texas University Press.

Beach, R., Campano, G., Edmiston, B., & Borgman, M. (2010). *Literacy tools in the classroom: Teaching through critical inquiry grades 5–12.* New York: Teachers College Press.

Beach, R., & Myers, J. (2001). *Inquiry-based English instruction: Engaging students in life and literature.* New York: Teachers College Press.

Bolton, G. (1984). Introduction. In L. Johnston & C. O'Neill (Eds.), *Dorothy Heathcote: Collected writings on drama and education* (pp. 54–60). London: Hutchinson.

Britton, J. (1970). *Language and Learning.* Harmondsworth, Middlesex, UK: Penguin Books.

Comber, B., & Simpson, A. (2001). *Negotiating critical literacies in classrooms.* Mahwah, NJ: Erlbaum.

Dewey, J. (1934). *Art as Experience*. New York: Minton, Blach & Company.

Dewey, J. (1956). *The school and society & the child and the curriculum*. Chicago: Chicago University Press.

Edmiston, B. (2008). *Forming ethical identities in early childhood play*. London: Routledge.

Edmiston, B. (2003). What's my position? Role, frame, and positioning when using process drama. *Research in Drama Education, 8*(2), 221–229.

Edmiston, B., & Enciso, P. (2002). Reflections and refractions of meaning: dialogic approaches to classroom drama and reading. In J. Flood, D. Lapp, J. Squire, & J. Jensen (Eds.), *The handbook of research on teaching and the English language arts* (pp. 868–880). New York: Simon & Schuster Macmillan.

Goffman, E. (1974). *Frame analysis: An essay on the organization of experience*. New York: Harper & Row.

Greene, M. (1996). *Releasing the imagination: Essays on education, the arts, and social change*. San Francisco: Jossey-Bass.

Heath, S. B., & Wolf, S. (2005). *Dramatic learning in the primary school*. London: Creative Partnerships.

Heathcote, D. (1984). *Dorothy Heathcote: Collected writings on drama and education* (L. Johnston & C. O'Neill, Eds.). London: Hutchinson.

Heathcote, D. (2006). Foreword. In J. Carroll, M. Anderson, & D. Cameron. *Real players? Drama, technology, and education*. (pp. ix–xiii). Stoke on Trent, UK: Trentham.

Heathcote, D., & Bolton, G. (2005). *Drama for learning: Dorothy Heathcote's mantle of the expert approach to education*. Portsmouth, NH: Heinemann.

Kalantzis, M., & Cope, B. (2008). *New learning: elements of a science of education*. New York: Cambridge University Press.

Langer, S. (1953). *Feeling and form*. New York: Charles Scribner.

Leander, K. M. (2004). "They took out the wrong context": Uses of time–space in the practice of positioning. *Ethos, 32*, 188–213.

Leander, K., & Sheehy, M. (Eds.). (2004). *Spatializing literacy research and practice*. New York: Peter Lang.

Lewison, M., Leland. C., & Harste, J. (2008). *Creating critical classrooms: K-8 reading and writing with an edge*. New York: Erlbaum.

Moffett, J. (1965). I, you, and it. *College Composition and Communication, 16*(5), 243–248.

Moffett, J. (1968). *Teaching the universe of discourse*. Portsmouth, NH: Boynton/Cook.

Neelands, J. (2009). Acting together: Ensemble as a democratic process in art and life. *Research in Drama Education: the Journal of Applied Theatre and Performance, 14*(2), 173–190.

O'Neill, C. (1995). *Drama worlds: A framework for process drama*. Portsmouth, NH: Heinemann.

Schneider, J, Crumpler, T., & Rogers, T (2006). *Process drama and multiple literacies: Addressing social, cultural, and ethical issues*. Portsmouth, NH: Heinemann.

Shaffer, D. (2006). *How computer games help children learn*. New York: Palgrave Macmillan.

Short, K. G., Harste, J. C., & Burke, C. (1995). *Creating classrooms for authors and inquirers* (2nd ed.). Portsmouth, NH: Heinemann.

Vygotsky, L. (1967). Play and its role in the mental development of the child. *Soviet Psychology, 5*, 6–18.

Vygotsky, L. (1978). *Mind in society: The development of higher processes*. Cambridge. MA: Harvard University Press.

Wenger, E. (1998). *Communities of practice: Learning, meaning, and identity*. Cambridge, UK: Cambridge University Press.

Wohlwend, K. (2008). Play as a literacy of possibilities: Expanding meanings in practices, materials, and spaces. *Language Arts, 86*(2), 127–136.

33

Teaching Phonemic Awareness and Phonics in the Language Arts Classroom

A Developmental Approach

Linnea C. Ehri

When people read text, their eyes do not scan the rows of print like a moving camera but rather the eyes move and stop, move and stop (Rayner, Foorman, Perfetti, Pesetsky, & Seidenberg, 2001). Between stops, the eyes see nothing. The stops occur as each word is fixated and picked up by the brain. Even though readers might be able to predict upcoming words, their eyes land on them anyway. These findings reveal that words are the primary units of print processed by readers. Most of the words can be read quickly in one glance by retrieving them from memory because they are familiar and have been read before. Processing words automatically without attention or effort allows the reader to focus on the meaning of the text rather than upon identifying words. The purpose of phonemic awareness and phonics instruction is to teach the knowledge and strategies that enable students to become skilled at reading words automatically from memory in and out of text. In this chapter, these processes, their course of development, and instruction to promote progress are considered.

Phonemic Awareness. Phonemic awareness (PA) instruction teaches students to manipulate the smallest sounds or *phonemes* in spoken words, for example, segmenting and pronouncing the four phonemes in "s-t-o-p." Sometimes students confuse phonemes with letters. Letters symbolize phonemes in the writing system, but they can mislead. For example, CHECK has five letters but only three phonemes, /ch/ /e/ /ck/. The letter X symbolizes two phonemes, /k/ and /s/, for example, in FIX.

Phonemic awareness is important to teach, especially to beginners. Children are accustomed to paying attention to meanings in speech, not to phonemes. Separate phonemes are hard to distinguish because speech is continuous with phonemes folded together seamlessly. Learning to read in English requires PA because students must learn to form *connections* between phonemes and the letters that symbolize them, called *graphemes*, in order to decode words, to

spell words, and to build a vocabulary of words they can read from memory by sight.

Phonics. The term "phonics" is used in two ways: to refer to reading instruction that systematically teaches letter-sound relations and their use to read words, and to refer to the letter-sound knowledge and skills that are taught (Stahl, Duffy-Hester, & Stahl, 1998). Systematic phonics programs in the primary grades cover the major grapheme-phoneme relations following a scope and sequence. Students learn to use this knowledge by reading decodable texts, performing word study activities, and learning the spellings of words. Decodable texts are especially valuable early during acquisition when beginners have limited letter-sound knowledge (Juel & Roper-Schneider, 1985). In synthetic phonics programs, children are taught to read words by transforming graphemes into phonemes and blending them to form recognizable words. An especially effective approach at the outset is to teach blending and reading with a small set of grapheme-phonemes (GPs) and then gradually add new GPs to the blending and reading routine (Johnston & Watson, 2007). In analogy programs, children are taught to read and spell keywords and to use them to read new words sharing the same spelling patterns, for example, using NAME to read BLAME (Gaskins, Ehri, Cress, O'Hara, & Donnelly, 1996–97).

In the upper elementary grades, structural analysis is taught as an extension of phonics. Students learn to analyze spelling patterns within words, including syllabic and morphographic units. Morphemes are the smallest units of meaning in words, for example, the three morphemes in "un-happi-ness," so morpho-graphic refers to the spellings of morphemes. These include roots, affixes, compounds, and inflectional and derivational endings (e.g., -ED, -ING, -LY).

Ways that Words Are Read. Several strategies enable students to read words that are unfamiliar in print (Ehri,

1998, 2009). A decoding strategy involves sounding out and blending GP units or larger syllabic or morphographic chunks. An analogy strategy involves using parts of the spellings of known words to read new words. A prediction strategy involves using letters and context cues to predict an unfamiliar word, for example, "The doctor worked at the hos…."

When readers encounter new words and practice reading them, they are retained in memory to be read by sight. People used to think that sight words were read by remembering visual cues such as shape. However, evidence has shown that readers use their orthographic knowledge of grapheme-phoneme, syllabic, and morphographic units to build their sight vocabularies (Ehri, 1998, 2009). They remember how to read specific words by forming connections between letters in the words' spellings and sounds detected in their pronunciations. As a result, the spellings enter memory bonded to pronunciations along with meanings of the words. When readers encounter these words again, sight of them activates their spelling-pronunciation-meaning connections. Even irregularly spelled words are retained in memory by forming connections between the graphemes and phonemes that are regular within the word, for example, all but the W in SWORD, all but the S in ISLAND. In this way, all words that fit readers' orthographic knowledge and are practiced become sight words. The advantage of reading words from memory is that it takes less time, attention, and effort.

When readers read text, their attention needs to be free to focus on understanding the content, not on decoding, analogizing, or guessing unfamiliar words. The rule of thumb is that readers should be able to read over 90% of the words easily. Below this level, the text becomes frustrating. To maintain such a high level of accuracy, readers must be able to read most of the words from memory. So the major task of helping students learn to read is enabling them to enlarge their sight vocabularies to support the reading of increasingly higher levels of text. Phonemic awareness and phonics instruction provide teachers with the means of facilitating this growth.

Structure of the Writing System in English. English is an alphabetic system that consists of mappings between graphemes and phonemes within words. GP correspondences provide much of the regularity in words (Moats, 2000). One analysis revealed that GPs spelled about 50% of spoken words accurately, and an additional 36% were spelled with one error (Hanna, Hanna, Hodges, & Rudorf, 1966). One complexity of English is that GP mappings are variable. There are alternative ways to decode some graphemes and to spell some phonemes (Venezky, 1999). For example, G can symbolize /g/ or /j/; /k/ can be spelled with C, K, CH (as in *chorus*), Q (as in *queen*), or X (representing /k/ + /s/ as in *mix*). Vowel spellings are more variable than consonants.

Additional regularity is provided by multi-letter spelling patterns representing rimes, syllables, affixes, morphemes, and word families (Berninger, Abbott, Nagy, & Carlisle,

2009). Final silent E marks the preceding vowel as long in words such as *cake, dive, rope, cute*. Rime units consist of the vowel plus consonant such as -OT in "*hot,* -INK in *pink*. The spellings of 36 rime units map consistent pronunciations in over 500 words (Stahl, Osborn, & Lehr, 1990). In some cases, rimes impose regularity on GP units that appear irregular. For example, EA symbolizes long E in many words (e.g., *beak, cream*), but in the rime –EAD it symbolizes short E (e.g., *dead, head, bread*). Silent letters may become regular GPs when word families are considered, for example, the G in *sign* vs. *signature,* the B in *bomb* vs. *bombard*.

Although GPs are less transparent in English than in other languages such as Spanish or German, a system exists, and knowledge of this system makes it easier for students to read and spell individual words. Thus, it is important for teachers to learn about the sources of regularity and teach these to their students (see Moats, 2000, and Henry, 2003).

Course of Development

Chall (1983) provides a global picture of reading development. During the prereading or emergent literacy Stage 0, children prepare for learning to read by acquiring knowledge of spoken language and concepts about print from watching and listening to storybooks. During the initial reading or decoding Stage 1, children are formally taught alphabetic skills and their application to read words in simple text. During the confirmation and fluency Stage 2, the various processes involved in reading text become better integrated and reading speeds up. The reading-to-learn Stage 3 begins when children have learned to read and are ready to use reading to acquire new information. At this stage, texts become harder, the content is less familiar, and background knowledge, vocabulary, and reading comprehension strategies become important to teach.

Ehri (2005) proposes a theory of reading development focused on words. A series of phases are distinguished according to the alphabetic knowledge used by learners to read and spell words. The phases are: pre-alphabetic, partial alphabetic, full alphabetic, and consolidated alphabetic. The various phases differ in the predominant type of connections that are formed to remember how to read words and in the strategies available to read unfamiliar words and to spell words.

Pre-Alphabetic Phase. Children in this phase lack sufficient letter knowledge and phonemic awareness to process print using letter-sound relations. If they can read any words, their performance is prompted by visually or semantically salient cues, for example, tall posts in the middle of *yellow* or the tail at the end of *dog* (Gough, Juel, & Griffith, 1992). Words read in the environment are prompted by context cues rather than letters, for example, the golden arches cueing *McDonalds* (Masonheimer, Drum, & Ehri, 1984). Children who have learned to write some letters might refer to them by their shapes rather than their names, for example, the letter "t" as "the cross thing." In one study, when children were given practice learning to read words, pre-alphabetic phase children did better with words whose spellings were more distinctive visually than with words whose letters corresponded to sounds (Ehri & Wilce, 1985; Roberts, 2003). Children may appear to be reading a book but closer examination reveals that they have memorized it and are "pretend reading." Their inability to fingerpoint read by matching the words they say to the words in the text exposes their strategy.

Transition to the Partial Alphabetic Phase. Children move to the partial alphabetic phase when they learn the shapes and names or sounds of alphabet letters and phonemic awareness (PA). When measured upon entry to kindergarten, letter knowledge and PA are the two best predictors of how well children will learn to read during the next 2 years (Share, Jorm, Maclean, & Mathews, 1984). These are foundational skills that enable children to begin reading and spelling words using partial letter-sound cues.

Teaching children capital and lower-case letters takes time because there are many to learn and their visual forms, names and sounds are meaningless. Various mnemonics can speed up learning. The A-B-C song helps children learn letter names although they need further help to distinguish one name from the next in the sequence. Letter-sound associations are commonly taught using pictures whose labels begin with the sounds of the letters (e.g., *m-ouse* for M). Such pictures are especially effective when the letters are *embedded in and conform to* the shapes of the pictured objects, for example, a snake drawn in the shape of *S* symbolizing the sound /s/. Other examples are *a* drawn as an apple, *n* drawn as a nose on a face, *m* drawn as mountains, *v* drawn as a vase.

The effectiveness of embedded mnemonics rests on their ability to facilitate associative learning. The critical test is whether, when learners look at the bare letter, its shape easily reminds them of the object and its name so that they can retrieve its initial sound. In studies, children were found to learn letter shapes and sounds more rapidly, to remember them longer, and to apply them more effectively in reading and spelling tasks when they had learned with embedded picture mnemonics than with picture mnemonics that depicted the same objects and names but did not resemble letter shapes, referred to as disassociated mnemonics (Ehri, Deffner, & Wilce, 1984; Shmidman & Ehri, 2010). Inspection of A-Z alphabet friezes mounted in classrooms reveals that most are disassociated picture mnemonics. Embedded mnemonics can be found in programs such as Letterland (Wendon, 2007), Alphafriends (2001), and Zoo Phonics (2009).

Phonemic awareness has been taught using various tasks (Stahl & Murray, 1994). Easier tasks include segmenting initial and final sounds in words, or selecting from an array those objects whose names begin or end with the same sound. Harder tasks involve dividing words into separate phonemes, blending separately pronounced phonemes to form words, and deleting phonemes to say a different word. Studies have shown that when letters or tokens are used as concrete spatial markers to teach children to distinguish phonemes in speech, acquisition of PA is improved (Ehri, Nunes, Stahl, & Willows, 2001). For example, children are taught segmentation by sliding letters or tokens into drawings of squares arrayed horizontally as they pronounce the separate phonemes in words. This is essentially teaching children to spell the phonemes in words.

Although phonemes are commonly referred to as "sounds," what a listener hears in spoken words does not provide the necessary cues to distinguish phonemes. Monitoring articulation is more helpful. Whereas sounds are transitory, mouth positions are concrete and open to examination. Articulation awareness instruction involves drawing students' attention to their lips, teeth, and tongue as they analyze and manipulate phonemes in words. Results of a study by Boyer and Ehri (in press) showed that teaching 4- and 5-year-olds to segment words using eight mouth pictures to depict 15 different phonemes (e.g., drawing of lips closed to depict /m/, /p/, and /b/), and combining this with segmentation instruction using letters enhanced children's ability to acquire PA and spelling compared to a group taught to segment only with letters. Moreover, this combined training better enabled children to decode new words and to remember how to read words by sight. This suggests the added benefit of incorporating articulation into PA instruction taught with letters.

Children in the partial phase can read and spell words using partial alphabetic cues. They remember how to read words by forming connections between some of the graphemes and phonemes in words, for example, remembering connections between S and N and their sounds to read "spoon." Connections are partial because beginners lack full knowledge of the writing system, most often vowel spellings and consonant clusters. Studies have revealed how this limits their word reading (Ehri & Wilce, 1987; Mason, 1980). When reading words from memory, they mistake words having similar letters, especially the same initial and final letters. They may read words correctly one time but not the next. When given nonwords to read, they will misread them as familiar real words, for example, misreading KIG as "king." They are unable to sound out and blend letters to decode novel words. They cannot read new words by analogy to known words because they lack sufficient memory for full spellings to detect shared letter patterns.

Use of partial connections is also evident in their invented spellings, for example, BZ for buzz. Lacking knowledge of the conventional associations, they spell words by selecting letters whose names contain the relevant sounds, for example, YF for *wife* (name of Y contains /w/), HKN for *chicken* (name of H contains /ch/) (Read, 1971; Treiman, 1993). Consonant clusters are difficult to separate into two phonemes so only the more salient member is spelled, for example, SAT for *skate*, JUP for *jump*. Their detection of phonemes in words may not be conventional, for example, detecting affrication (i.e., turbulence in the air stream passing through the mouth) at the beginning of the letter name J and *dragon* and writing JRN. Although partial phase spellings may not be correct, they reveal that children are on the right track in attempting to map sounds with letters. They have difficulty remembering the correct spellings of words because they do not possess full knowledge of the conventional phoneme-grapheme associations that provide the glue to secure spellings bonded to their pronunciations in memory. Not only beginning readers but also older struggling readers show characteristics of the partial phase in their reading and spelling.

Transition to the Full Alphabetic Phase. The full alphabetic phase is attained when beginners' PA extends to all the phonemes in words, when they acquire more complete knowledge of the major GP relations, and when they apply these mapping relations to read and spell words. In systematic phonics programs, the GP relations are taught sequentially, with single consonants preceding consonant clusters (e.g., *bl, fr, st*) and digraphs (i.e., *sh, th, ch, wh*). Short vowel GPs are taught first (i.e., the vowels in *at, Ed, it, odd, up*) followed by long vowel spellings that consist of a vowel digraph or a final silent E marking the vowel as long (e.g., vowels in *bait, bake, beet, seat, bite, boat, cute*). Spellings of diphthongs such as *–oy, -oi, -ou,* and other vowels are taught after that (see Moats, 2000).

Movement into this phase involves learning to decode unfamiliar words by transforming letters into pronunciations that are recognized as meaningful words. Children apply their GP knowledge and decoding skill to build a sight vocabulary by forming complete connections between all the graphemes in spellings and phonemes in pronunciations to remember how to read specific words that they have practiced. Fully formed connections make their word reading more accurate because words have a unique address in memory so they are not confused with other words sharing some of the same letters. Also their GP knowledge enables children to remember the correct spellings of words having those GPs.

Systematic phonics instruction in the early grades provides a strong foundation enabling children to become full phase readers. A review of many studies revealed that this form of instruction boosted sight word reading, decoding, and reading comprehension among kindergartners and first graders more than beginning reading instruction that did not teach phonics systematically (Ehri et al., 2001).

Word reading and spelling skills are highly correlated indicating that they are part of the same underlying capability. Correlations have ranged from *rs* = .77 to .86 in samples of students from first through sixth grades (Ehri, 1997). Studies have shown that teaching beginners to spell strengthens their word reading ability (Boyer & Ehri, in press; Conrad, 2008; Ehri & Wilce, 1987; Uhry & Shepherd, 1993). However, to be effective, spelling instruction needs to be developmentally appropriate, that is, tailored to students' orthographic knowledge so that they possess the "glue" needed to retain specific spellings in memory (Schlagal, 2007). For example, if children do not know short vowel GP correspondences, then they will have much trouble remembering how to spell specific words with short vowels.

Spelling instruction in the form of word study (Bear, Invernizzi, Templeton, Johnston, 2007; Schlagal, 2007) helps children become full phase readers and spellers. The lists of words to be learned across weeks within and between grades are grouped by frequency, length, and contrastive spelling patterns. Spelling practice includes not only writing words but also reading words and analyzing spelling patterns in activities such as sorting words, and changing one letter or one sound at a time to read or spell words. Such activities teach children to process all of the letters and sounds in words. As a result, they remember how to read and spell specific words, and in addition, they learn about general spelling patterns.

Practice reading words in text is important for building a sight word vocabulary as well, especially for bonding the spellings of words to their pronunciations and meanings in memory. Share (2004) has shown that decoding functions as an effective self-teaching strategy during text reading. Processing all the GP mapping relations in the words enables readers to retain them in memory. Even if decoding results in a nonword, this indicates that the reader is attempting to fully analyze GPs to read words. This response is developmentally more advanced than one where readers slight letters and use context to guess the word. Context can aid the search for a word that fits the text graphically, syntactically, and semantically. Also it can confirm that a decoded word make sense. But contextual guessing should not replace attention to letters as the means of reading words in text (Tunmer & Chapman, 2006). Otherwise word learning suffers.

Transition to Consolidated Alphabetic Phase. Spelling units used to read words during the consolidated alphabetic phase begin to form during the full alphabetic phase. These consist of letter sequences that symbolize GP blends forming syllabic and subsyllabic units, for example, morphographs, rime spellings including patterns that are also sight words themselves (e.g., *at, it, on, up, ate, eat, ant, age*), and common syllable spellings. As readers learn to read different words that share letter patterns, these patterns become consolidated into units. This means that readers can pronounce the units as wholes. They do not need to sound out letters to read them. Being able to read letter chunks eases the task of reading and remembering multisyllabic words. For example, *in-ter-est-ing* can be read by decoding four syllabic units rather than nine GP units. The consolidated phase replaces the full alphabetic phase when the predominant connections for retaining sight words in memory are larger letter chunks.

As children accumulate a sight vocabulary of fully connected words in memory, they become able to use letter chunks in these words to read new words by analogy, especially if they are taught this strategy. In the Benchmark

Word Detectives program (Ehri, Satlow, & Gaskins, 2009; Gaskins et al., 1996–97), children are taught to fully analyze the GP connections in a set of 80 keywords during the year. Students practice segmenting, reading and spelling the words in order to get them into memory. They practice using them to read new words by analogy, not only single syllable words but multisyllabic words, for example, reading *interesting* by applying the keywords *in, her, nest, and king.*

Another source of consolidated units is provided by instruction in the Latin, Greek, and Anglo Saxon origins of spelling patterns (Henry, 2003). For example, PH for /f/ and CH for /k/ come from Greek. Many scientific terms have Greek origins and consist of combined morphemes in *microscope, hydrogen, chronometer, psychology.* Latin roots combined with prefixes or suffixes recur in many words, for example, *rupt, scrib, duct, tend.* There are many common Anglo Saxon suffixes such as *-able, -hood, -est, -ment.* Distinguishing among spellings in terms of their origins provides another source of regularity that helps students "glue" letter patterns within words in memory, particularly in the upper elementary grades where word origins help to explain important vocabulary words in the content areas.

Teaching students to analyze mappings between written and spoken syllables within words facilitates growth in their knowledge of spelling patterns as well as memory for specific words. In a study by Bhattacharya and Ehri (2004), struggling adolescent readers practiced reading and rereading 100 words, 25 per day, by dividing the words into spoken syllables and then matching them to written syllables. Another group practiced reading the same words as wholes without segmenting them. Results showed that the syllable-trained group remembered how to read and spell the words and to decode new words better than the whole word group. The explanation is that syllable training enabled students to recognize consolidated spelling patterns within the words to better retain them in memory.

Teacher Knowledge.   Although teachers may be skilled readers, this does not necessarily equip them with the knowledge needed to teach beginners how to read. Various studies have shown that unless teacher education students have received relevant instruction, they lack sufficient insight about how to segment words into phonemes and how graphemes in the spellings of words correspond to phonemes (Mather, Bos, & Balbur, 2001; McCutchen et al., 2002; Moats,1994; Scarborough, Ehri, Olson, & Fowler, 1998). Piasta, Connor, Fishman, and Morrison (2009) studied first-grade teachers with high and low knowledge of English phonology, orthography, morphology, and concepts of literacy acquisition and instruction. Among high knowledge teachers, the more time they spent teaching decoding skills, the greater were the gains of their students in reading words compared to students who received no decoding instruction. However, among teachers with low knowledge, the more time they spent teaching decoding skills, the *smaller* were their students' gains compared to the gains of students receiving *no*

decoding instruction. These findings indicate that teachers need a solid understanding of the alphabetic writing system to succeed in teaching phonemic awareness and phonics skills to elementary students.

Comprehensive Phonics Instruction.   In order for phonics instruction to be comprehensive, several components are needed and these need to be tailored to students' phase of development. Such components include: phonemic awareness instruction so that beginners learn to detect, segment, and blend the smallest sounds in spoken words; letter shapes and names so that children can identify them and write them from memory; the major grapheme-phoneme correspondences and their mapping function to connect graphemes to phonemes within specific words; decoding and analogizing strategies for reading unfamiliar words; spelling patterns forming consolidated units; practice in the application of GP knowledge and word-in-text reading strategies to develop sight vocabulary; spelling instruction that involves developmentally appropriate word study to build students' knowledge of spelling patterns as well as their memory for specific words. Although components are listed separately, their emergence is intertwined and interdependent as they contribute reciprocally to support the development of reading skill.

Although phonics programs are typically organized by grade level, it is important to recognize that at the beginning of kindergarten and first grade, students may vary in their phase of reading development. To enable each to make the greatest gains in learning to read during the year, students will need different levels and components of instruction (Connor, Morrison, & Katch, 2004; Juel & Minden-Cupp, 2000). This requires that teachers assess students' entering capabilities and then differentiate instruction accordingly. For example, Connor, Morrison, Fishman, Schatschneider, and Underwood (2007) have developed a computer program to help teachers identify the skills a child possesses or lacks in order to place them appropriately in beginning reading programs.

Summary and Conclusion.   Phonemic awareness instruction and phonics instruction are tools that enable knowledgeable teachers to enhance their effectiveness in teaching students to read words in and out of text and to spell words. Instruction is centered on systematically teaching the alphabetic system and its application. English is a variable system with alternative ways to read and spell letters and sounds. Its regularity resides in layers consisting of grapheme-phoneme correspondences and larger syllabic and morphographic letter patterns. Readers acquire knowledge of regularities and apply these to read unfamiliar words by decoding, analogy, or prediction, and to remember how to read and spell specific words. Specific word learning involves building a sight vocabulary by applying GP correspondences and spelling patterns to bond the spellings of specific words to their pronunciations and meanings in memory. As sight vocabularies grow, students are able to read and comprehend text at increasing levels of difficulty. Learning to read and spell words follows a course of development involving four phases that are characterized by the alphabetic knowledge readers use to build their sight vocabularies: pre-alphabetic, partial alphabetic, full alphabetic, and consolidated alphabetic. These phases indicate which components of phonics instruction are important to teach in order to facilitate growth and transition between the phases. It is essential that teachers in the elementary grades learn about these concepts to improve their effectiveness in carrying out reading instruction.

References

Alphafriends. (2001). *Houghton Mifflin Reading: A legacy of literacy.* Boston: Houghton Mifflin.

Bear, D., Invernizzi, M., Templeton, S., & Johnston, F. (2007). *Words their way: Words study for phonics, vocabulary, and spelling instruction.* Boston: Allyn & Bacon/Merrill.

Berninger, V., Abbott, R., Nagy, W. & Carlisle, J. (2009). Growth in phonological, orthographic, and morphological awareness in grades 1 to 6. *Journal of Psycholinguistic Research, 39,* 141–163.

Bhattacharya, A., & Ehri, L. (2004). Graphosyllabic analysis helps adolescent struggling readers read and spell words. *Journal of Learning Disabilities, 37,* 331–348.

Boyer, N., & Ehri, L. (in press). Contribution of phonemic segmentation instruction with letters and articulation pictures to word reading and spelling in beginners. *Scientific Studies of Reading.*

Chall, J. (1983). *Stages of Reading Development.* New York: McGraw Hill.

Connor, C., Morrison, F., Fishman, B., Schatschneider, C., & Underwood, P. (2007). The early years: Algorithm-guided individualized reading instruction. *Science, 315,* 464–465.

Connor, C., Morrison, F., & Katch, L. (2004). Beyond the reading wars: Exploring the effect of child-instruction interactions on growth in early reading. *Scientific Studies of Reading, 8,* 305–336.

Conrad, N. (2008). From reading to spelling and spelling to reading: Transfer goes both ways. *Journal of Educational Psychology, 100,* 869–878.

Ehri, L. (1997). Learning to read and learning to spell are one and the same, almost. In C. Perfetti, L. Rieben, & M. Fayol (Eds.). *Learning to spell* (pp. 237–270). Mawah, NJ: Erlbaum.

Ehri, L. (1998). Grapheme-phoneme knowledge is essential for learning to read words in English. In J. Metsala & L. Ehri (Eds.), *Word recognition in beginning literacy* (pp. 3–40). Mahwah, NJ: Erlbaum.

Ehri, L. (2005). Development of sight word reading: Phases and findings. In M. Snowling & C. Hulme (Ed.), *The science of reading, A handbook* (pp. 135–154). Oxford, UK: Blackwell.

Ehri, L. (2009). Learning to read in English: Teaching phonics to beginning readers from diverse backgrounds. In L. Morrow, R. Rueda, & D. Lapp (Eds.), *Handbook of research on literacy and diversity* (pp. 292–319). New York: Guilford.

Ehri, L., Deffner, N., & Wilce, L. (1984). Pictorial mnemonics for phonics. *Journal of Educational Psychology, 76,* 880–893.

Ehri, L., Nunes, S., Stahl, S., & Willows, D. (2001). Systematic phonics instruction helps students learn to read: Evidence from the National Reading Panel's meta-analysis. *Review of Educational Research, 71,* 393–447.

Ehri, L., Nunes, S., Willows, D., Schuster, B., & Yaghoub-Zabeh, Z., & Shanahan, T. (2001). Phonemic awareness instruction helps children learn to read: Evidence from the National Reading Panel's meta-analysis. *Reading Research Quarterly, 30,* 250–287.

Ehri, L., & Roberts, T. (2006). The roots of learning to read and write: Acquisition of letters and phonemic awareness. In D. Dickinson &

S. Neuman (Eds.), *Handbook of early literacy research* (Vol. 2, pp. 113–131). New York: Guilford.

Ehri, L., Satlow, E., & Gaskins, I. (2009). Grapho-phonemic enrichment strengthens keyword analogy instruction for struggling readers. *Reading and Writing Quarterly, 25,* 162–191.

Ehri, L., & Wilce, L. (1985). Movement into reading: Is the first stage of printed word learning visual or phonetic? *Reading Research Quarterly, 20,* 163–179.

Ehri, L. & Wilce, L. (1987). Cipher versus cue reading: An experiment in decoding acquisition. *Journal of Educational Psychology, 79,* 3–13.

Gaskins, I., Ehri, L., Cress, C., O'Hara, C., & Donnelly, K. (1996–97). Procedures for word learning: Making discoveries about words. *The Reading Teacher, 50,* 312–328.

Gough, P., Juel, C., & Griffith, P. (1992). Reading, spelling and the orthographic cipher. In In P. Gough, L. Ehri, & R. Treiman (Eds.), *Reading acquisition* (pp. 35–48). Hillsdale, NJ: Erlbaum.

Hanna, P., Hanna, J., Hodges, R., & Rudorf, E. (1966). *Phoneme-grapheme correspondences as cues to spelling improvement.* Washington, DC: U.S. Government printing Office.

Henry, M. (2003). *Unlocking literacy: Effective decoding and spelling instruction.* Baltimore, MD: Brookes.

Johnston, R., & Watson, J. (2007). *Teaching synthetic phonics.* UK: Learning Matters Ltd.

Juel, C., & Minden-Cupp. (2000). Learning to read words: Linguistic units and instructional strategies. *Reading Research Quarterly, 35,* 458–492.

Juel, C., & Roper-Schneider, D. (1985). The influence of basal readers on first grade reading. *Reading Research Quarterly, 20,* 134–152.

Masonheimer, P., Drum, P., & Ehri, L. (1984). Does environmental print identification lead children into word reading? *Journal of Reading Behavior, 16,* 257–272.

Mather, N., Bos, C., & Balbur, N. (2001). Perceptions and knowledge of preservice and inservice teachers about early literacy instruction. *Journal of Learning Disabilities, 34,* 472–482.

McCutchen, D., Abbott, R., Green, L., Beretvas, N., Cox, S., & Potter, N. (2002). Beginning literacy: Links among teacher knowledge, teacher practice, and student learning. *Journal of Learning Disabilities, 35,* 69–86.

Moats, L. (1994). The missing foundation in teacher education: Knowledge of the structure of spoken and written language. *Annals of Dyslexia, 44,* 81–102.

Moats, L. (2000). *Speech to print: Language essentials for teachers.* Baltimore, MD: Brooks.

Piasta, S., Connor, C., Fishman, B. & Morrison, F. (2009). Teacher knowledge of literacy concepts, classroom practices, and student reading growth. *Scientific Studies of Reading, 13,* 224–248.

Rayner, K., Foorman, B., Perfetti, C., Pesetsky, D., & Seidenberg, M. (2001). How psychological science informs the teaching of reading. *Psychological Science in the Public Interest, 2,* 31–74.

Read, C. (1971). Pre-school children's knowledge of English phonology. *Harvard Educational Review, 41,* 1–34.

Roberts, T. (2003). Effects of alphabet-letter instruction on young children's word recognition. *Journal of Educational Psychology, 95,* 41–51.

Scarborough, H., Ehri, L., Olson, R., & Fowler, A. (1998). The fate of phonemic awareness beyond the elementary school years. *Scientific Study of Reading, 2,* 115–142.

Schlagal, B. (2007). Best practices in spelling and handwriting. In S. Graham, C. Macarthur, & J. Fitzgerald (Eds.), *Best practices in writing instruction* (pp. 179–201). New York: Guilford.

Share, D. (2004). Orthographic learning at a glance: On the time course and developmental onset of self-teaching. *Journal of Experimental Child Psychology, 87,* 267–298.

Share, D., Jorm, A., Maclean, R., & Mathews, R. (1984). Sources of individual differences in reading acquisition. *Journal of Educational Psychology, 76,* 1309–1324.

Shmidman, A., & Ehri, L. (2010). Embedded picture mnemonics to learn letters. *Scientific Studies of Reading, 14,* 159–182.

Snow, C., Burns, M., & Griffin, P. (1998). *Preventing reading difficulties in young children.* Washington, DC: National Academy Press.

Stahl, S., Duffy-Hester, A., & Stahl, K. (1998). Everything you wanted to know about phonics (but were afraid to ask). *Reading Research Quarterly, 33,* 338–355.

Stahl, S., & Murray, B. (1994). Defining phonological awareness and its relationship to early reading. *Journal of Educational Psychology, 86,* 221–234.

Stahl, S., Osborn, J., & Lehr, F. (1990). *Beginning to read: Thinking and learning about print by Marilyn Jager Adams: A summary.* Urbana-Champaign, IL: Center for the Study of Reading.

Treiman, R. (1993). *Beginning to spell.* New York: Oxford University Press.

Tunmer, W., & Chapman, J. (2006). Metalinguistic abilities, phonological recoding skill, and the use of context in beginning reading development: A longitudinal study. In R. Joshi & P. Aaron (Eds.), *Handbook of orthography and literacy* (pp. 617–635). Mahwah, NJ: Erlbaum.

Uhry, J., & Shepherd, J. (1993). Segmentation/spelling instruction as a part of a first grade reading program: Effects on several measures of reading. *Reading Research Quarterly, 28,* 218–233.

Venezky, R. (1999). *The American way of spelling: The structure and origins of American English orthography.* New York: Guilford.

Wendon, L. (2007). *Letterland ABC.* Cambridge, UK: Letterland.

Zoo Phonics. (2009). Retrieved from http://www.zoo-phonics.com

34

The Art and Science of Teaching Reading Fluency

TIMOTHY RASINSKI

The construct of reading fluency has run a rather schizo-phrenic and tumultuous course (Rasinski, 2003). Early American reading instruction placed oral reading fluency (elocution) at the zenith of instructional goals. With the recognition in the late 19th century that silent reading was the most pervasive form of reading for most adults, oral reading fluency took a decidedly backseat in instruction. It remained at best a secondary reading goal, and gained further disrepute through the common practice of round robin reading. There fluency remained until the late 1970s and early 1980s when literacy scholars (e.g., Chomsky, 1976, 1978; LaBerge & Samuels, 1974) began to write theoretically and practically about the importance of read-ing fluency. Richard Allington (1983) consolidated the various emerging points of view related to fluency when he identified it as the "neglected reading goal." Rasinski and Zutell (1996) pointed out that instructional and professional development materials in reading of the time rarely, if at all, gave mention to reading fluency.

Yet, in the span of less than 20 years reading fluency has gone from neglected to "hot." Indeed, in its review of empirical research on effective literacy approaches, the National Reading Panel (2000) identified reading fluency as one of the critical components of effective reading pro-grams. A search of Amazon.com using *reading fluency* as key words resulted in over 3,000 titles listed, most published after 2000.

Still, a recent survey of reading experts of hot topics in reading has found that although fluency is hot, over 50% of the respondents indicated that it shouldn't be (Cassidy & Cassidy, 2009). The primary reason for this second decline in the status of reading fluency has been due to in large part to the way in which reading fluency has been assessed in students. The discovery of a relatively strong association between oral reading rate (also called oral reading fluency—ORF) and measures of reading compre-hension and overall reading achievement has led to the use of ORF as the primary tool for assessing reading fluency.

Recognizing the strength of this association, many in the reading practitioner community have created instructional approaches for teaching fluency by focusing on increasing students' oral reading rate. Scholars recognizing that this is a corruption of the notion of reading fluency, much in the same way as oral round robin reading had become an earlier corruption of reading fluency, have called for the de-emphasis of reading fluency in instructional settings.

Recent scholarly reviews of research in reading fluency (Kuhn & Rasinski, 2007, 2009; Kuhn, Schwanenflugel, & Meisinger, 2010; Rasinski, Reutzel, Chard, & Linan-Thompson, in press) have concluded that fluency is indeed an important theoretical and instructional construct in read-ing if viewed in the proper context. These articles provide a comprehensive review of research related to the theory and instructional practice related to reading fluency. Rather than merely reiterate the findings of these excellent reviews, in this article I attempt to provide a consensus definition and description of reading fluency, one that goes beyond mere reading rate, describe how reading fluency may be situated within a total literacy curriculum, identify instructional ap-proaches to fluency that are supported by the research, and explore contemporary issues in reading fluency that need to be addressed for the concept of fluency to move forward as a relevant construct in reading.

The previously mentioned reviews of research in fluency have identified various aspects of fluency—that it involves: the accurate and automatic recognition of words in writ-ten text; the expressive (oral) production of the text that reflects syntactic and semantic nature of the text (prosody); that it is an interactive process that involves the making of meaning (comprehension) and is itself influenced by the readers' comprehension; that it its properties are operative in authentic uses of silent as well as oral reading.

Although Huey (1908/1968) discussed the construct of fluency in his early and seminal volume on reading, the modern roots on automaticity in reading come from the work of LaBerge and Samuels (1974). In most human activities, LaBerge and Samuels argued, people can direct their attention to one task at a time. Multi-tasking can only be done successfully when humans alternate their attention between tasks or when one or more of the tasks have been learned so well that it can be performed automatically, effortlessly, or with minimal employment of attention. Reading is a multi-task operation. At the very least, successful reading requires readers to identify and understand words accurately and at same time construct or comprehend the meaning intended by the author of the text. Through plenty of practice of contextual reading proficient readers automatize the lower level word identification task in reading, allowing themselves to attend to the meaning of the text. Less proficient reading can result from an insufficient ability to decode the words in the text. It can also result from word identification that is not sufficiently automatized. Struggling readers may be able to decode words accurately. However, if they have to invest too much of their limited cognitive resources into that task, they will have less available for comprehension. As a result, comprehension will suffer.

Fluency, then, according to automaticity theory, is the ability to process the lower level task word identification task accurately and automatically so that the reader can devote his or her attention to the making of meaning. Other scholars have extended and elaborated on LaBerge and Samuels work (e.g., Logan, 1988, 1997; Perfetti, 1985; Stanovich, 1980, 1986). Logan (1988) posited that focused attention on a stimulus (word) encodes the features of the stimulus in memory. Repeated focused exposures results in stronger, more durable memory traces laid down in the brain to the point where retrieval of the stimuli in memory becomes automatized. Stanovich (1980) and Perfetti (1985) argued that if lower level processes in reading are not developed to an appropriate level of efficiency, higher level processes, those normally involved in comprehension, must compensate. As a result, comprehension is compromised.

Prosody is the area of phonology that focuses on the rhythmical and tonal features of speech that are layered upon individual phonological segments and include stress, pitch, and duration (Schreiber, 1991). Stress involves the prominence that is placed on individual syllables within words. Intonation is the rise and fall of voice pitch during speech or oral reading. Duration is the length of time employed in pronouncing a word or part of a word.

In reading, prosody refers to the ability to make oral reading sound like authentic oral speech. Referring to prosody in reading, Martin (1966) has stated that "much of the meaning of the sentence is in its sound, not necessarily in the words themselves" (p. 13). Prosody or prosodic reading has been identified by a number of reading scholars as an essential component of reading fluency (e.g., Allington, 1983; Kuhn & Stahl, 2000; National Reading Panel, 2000; Rasinski & Hoffman, 2003).

A distinct manifestation of fluent (and nonfluent) language production, including reading, lies in the language user's ability to parse texts into syntactical appropriate units or phrases. (The disfluent language user often processes oral language in a monotone, word by word manner or with nonconventional phrasing.) Phrasing plays an important role in oral language production and comprehension (Epstein, 1961; Johnson, 1965; Cooper & Paccia-Cooper, 1980). Schreiber (1980, 1987, 1991) and others (Coots, 1982; Dowhower, 1991) argue that prosody plays a role in oral and written language comprehension by assisting the reader in segmenting or chunking text into syntactically appropriate and meaningful phrasal groupings of words. Schreiber (1991) posits that the ability to chunk or phrase text into syntactically appropriate and meaningful multi-word units is a critical aspect of learning to read. In general, some but not all phrase boundaries in written text are marked by punctuation. When phrase boundaries are not explicitly marked in written texts readers must employ their prosodic sensitivity to parse written text into appropriate phrases. Research has shown that younger and less able readers are less able to employ prosodic elements in phrasing written texts (Clay & Imlach, 1971; Dowhower, 1987; Schreiber, 1980, 1987, 1991; Schreiber & Read, 1980). Although the role of prosody in reading has not been as extensively studied as automaticity (Dowhower, 1991), recent empirical research has demonstrated the relevance of prosody in reading (Miller & Schwanenflugel, 2006, 2008; Rasinski, Rikli, & Johnston, 2009; Whalley & Hansen, 2006).

Given these essential features of fluency, I propose the following comprehensive definition of fluency: Fluency is the component of the reading process that allows readers to decode the words in a text with sufficient accuracy and automaticity (efficiency) to allow for understanding the text and that reflect the prosodic features embedded in the text.

Within the definition of fluency used here, as well as those proposed in previous reviews of research, certain instructional approaches such as teaching fluency through an exclusive emphasis on word perfect oral reading production (i.e., round robin reading) or reading rate (ORF) must be excluded from any discussion of effective fluency instruction. Indeed, research has identified several productive instructional practices that are associated with reading fluency. In the following section, I discuss these practices within the context of the full reading curriculum.

An Effective Reading Curriculum

Although there is no one best approach for the effective teaching of reading, there is a recognition that certain areas of emphasis need to be part of any effective reading curriculum (National Reading Panel, 2000). Among these are word study (phonics and vocabulary), reading comprehension (guided reading), and reading fluency. In his model of effective literacy instruction, one that was implemented with some success in the Chicago Public Schools, Shanahan (2006) proposes a literacy curriculum of four distinct components—word knowledge, fluency, reading comprehension, and writing. Although fluency is only one part of the total literacy curriculum, according to various experts (e.g., Allington, 2005; National Reading

Panel, 2000; Rasinski, 2010; Shanahan, 2006) it is an essential component of that curriculum. Although there is no definitive estimate as to the amount of time within the school curriculum that should be devoted to reading fluency instruction, the less-than-5-minutes per day given to fluency in primary grade classrooms as reported by the recent review of Reading First programs (Gamse, Bloom, Kemple, & Jacob, 2008)) must certainly be considered insufficient. Accepting the notion that fluency must be taught, in this chapter I explore the instructional practices for fluency that are supported by the research.

The Science of Reading Fluency Instruction

Practice in Reading Fluency in any human endeavor is accomplished through practice. In reading instruction, practice is usually thought of in terms of wide silent reading. In wide silent reading students read a text and after an opportunity to respond to the text they move on to the next text. In their summary of research related to fluency Kuhn et al. (2010) suggest that this ubiquitous and widely accepted form of reading practice does indeed support fluency development. A recent study by Reutzel and colleagues (Reutzel, Fawson, & Smith, 2008; Reutzel, Jones, Fawson, & Smith, 2008) reported that silent scaffolded wide reading resulted in gains in elementary students' fluency and comprehension. Reutzel and colleagues argue that wide silent reading is most effective when students are held accountable for their reading and when teachers provide sufficient support and guidance to allow students to be successful in their wide reading.

Wide reading may be contrasted with deep reading, or reading that is practiced until the reader achieves a degree of mastery over the surface elements of the text practiced. Research supports this other form of practice—deep reading or guided repeated reading. Repeated reading is based on the assumption that readers need to develop some degree of mastery over one text before moving on to the next. If a reader reads a text one time in a mediocre manner and then moves on to another passage that is also read in a mediocre manner, it seems reasonable to assume that the ultimate results in terms of student growth and satisfaction in learning to read will also be mediocre.

In guided repeated reading a student will read a text of reasonable length several times until the student achieves an acceptable level of fluency before moving on to the next passage. The teacher plays a role in selecting appropriately leveled texts, modeling the reading of the texts, and providing students guidance and support in their own reading. The National Reading Panel (NRP; 2000) reported on 51 studies involving repeated reading and reported a mean effect size of 0.41 for repeated reading instruction on students' improvement of word recognition accuracy and rate (efficiency).

Subsequent to the report of the NRP several other studies have affirmed the effectiveness of guided repeated reading (e.g., Biggs, Homan, Dedrick, & Rasinski, 2008; Comp-

ton, Appleton, & Hosp, 2004; Daly, Bonfiglio, Mattson, Perampierie, & Foreman-Yate, 2006; Griffith & Rasinski, 2004; Hiebert, 2005, 2006; Musti-Rao, Hawkins, & Barkley, 2009; Rasinski & Stevenson, 2005; Sanders & Vadasy, 2008; Stahl & Heubach, 2006; Wickstrom, Jones, & Therrien, 2006; Vadasy & Sanders, 2008; Williams, Klubnik, & McCall, 2009). These studies have consistently found that repeated readings used with students at various grade and achievement levels, implemented by different forms of instructional delivery (e.g., teachers, para-educators, parents, technology), using various forms of texts (e.g., basal texts, informational, narrative, poetry, scripts, song lyrics) at various difficulty levels, and combined with various forms of support (e.g., modeling, choral reading) during and response after the readings (e.g., number of repetitions, word recognition instruction, comprehension follow-up) universally led to improvement in a variety of reading outcomes (e.g., word recognition, reading rate, comprehension, informal reading inventories) on passages practiced and on new passages not previously read.

Hiebert (2008) notes that text difficulty is a critical issue when it comes to learning to read. When texts are too difficult and long and accompanied with minimal differentiation of instruction and support, low-performing students are likely to attend to the text in a cursory manner and progress will be muted. Recent research suggests that the use of texts with deliberately controlled levels of difficulty and other text elements can provide optimal practice and learning conditions for developing reading fluency through practice (Hiebert, 2006; Menon & Hiebert, 2005). Interestingly, in their earlier review of research related to repeated readings, Kuhn and Stahl (2004) report that a significant number of studies in their review reported greater improvements in reading when the materials used for repeated reading was above students' instructional reading levels. Stahl and Heubach (2005), for example, reported that second-grade students made the greatest gains in achievement with materials at their frustration levels. One explanation for this anomalous finding is that the repetition and support offered in the repeated readings allowed students to expand their instructional reading level and work with more challenging materials. The more challenging materials allowed students to accelerate their progress in reading.

Clearly, the empirical research, then, supports fluency instruction that is based on both wide and repeated readings. Although issues related to various specific aspects of repeated readings are yet to be fully resolved (e.g., text difficulty, level of readers, provider of instruction, text type), it seems clear that repeated readings has been proven to be a positive instructional method, especially for students who struggle in achieving reading proficiency, and should be combined with wide reading for purposes of improving reading fluency and other aspects of reading proficiency.

Oral Assisted Reading Oral assisted reading refers to the practice of a student reading a text while simultaneously hearing it read to him or her. The roots of oral assisted reading go back to the Neurological Impress Method (Heckelman, 1969; Hollingsworth, 1978) that involved a struggling reader reading orally with a more proficient reader. As the less able reader visually tracked the text and simultaneously heard the text read in a relatively fluent manner, a neurological trace of the sight and sound of the words in the text would be laid out in the mind of the struggling reader that was similar to the trace that existed in the mind of the more advanced reader. Early research by Heckelman and Hollingsworth reported remarkably promising results.

Since this early research, a number of variations of oral assisted reading have been recognized or developed. These include reading simultaneously with a group (choral reading), with an adult partner (paired reading), with an older student, with a more advanced classmate, with prerecorded versions of the passages, closed-caption television, and with and without repetitions of the text (Biemiller & Shany, 1995; Carbo, 1978a, 1978b; Chomsky, 1976, 1978; Eldredge, 1990; Eldredge & Quinn, 1988; Feazell, 2004; Flood, Lapp, & Fisher, 2005; Fuchs, Fuchs, Mathes, & Simmons, 1997; Greenwood & Delquardri, 1995; Henk, Helfeldt, & Platt, 1986; King et al., 2001; Koskinen & Blum, 1986; Koskinen, Wilson, & Jensema, 1985; Labbo & Teale, 1990; Langford, Slade, & Burnett, 1974; Mathes, Simmons, & Davis, 1992; Mefferd & Pettegrew, 1997; Meisinger, Schwanenflugel, Bradley, & Stahl, 2004; Mikkelsen, 1981, Morgan & Lyon, 1979; Neuman & Koskinen, 1992; Pluck, 1995; Rasinski, 1990; Stahl & Heubach, 2005; Topping, 1987a, 1987b; Vaughn et al., 2000; Wright & Clearly, 2006). In general, all these forms of oral assisted reading have demonstrated positive results in terms of improvements in fluency and overall reading achievement.

Although the general concept of oral assisted reading seems to have strong support, questions concerning which form is best and the conditions under which oral assisted reading is optimized remain to be studied. Examinations of the nature of oral assisted reading with a peer age partner found that greater social cooperation between partners occurred when students could choose their partners (Meisininger, Schwanenflugel, Bradley, & Stahl, 2004). Moreover, Stahl and Heubach (2005) report that self-selection of partners led to more fluency practice, especially among primary-grade students, that instructional level materials seemed most appropriate for partner reading, and that a differential in reading achievement between partners seemed to facilitate practice and growth in reading.

Phrasing As was indicated earlier, it is well established that prosodic reading and sensitivity to phrasing is associated with proficient reading and speech. More proficient readers and speakers users tend to employ prosody in their oral reading and language—to segment text into meaningful phrases and perhaps in other ways to construct meaning. Methods used for developing readers' prosody such as guided oral and assisted repeated readings are known and have been shown to be effective in improving reading achievement.

Text segmenting (Dowhower, 1991) appears to be less well known in contemporary reading education. It refers to the explicit marking of phrase boundaries in written texts in order to assist readers in phrasing texts meaningfully and applying prosody during oral reading. Although research on the role of text phrasing as an approach to fluency instruction does not seem to be currently in vogue, Rasinski's (1990, 1994) reviews of research on instruction focused on text phrasing suggests that a focus on phrasing through explicit text marking has substantial potential for delivering positive outcomes on word recognition, fluency, and comprehension.

Synergistic Reading Fluency Instruction Synergistic fluency instruction refers to instructional approaches that integrate or combine various established methods of instruction for improving accuracy, automaticity, and prosody in reading into instructional wholes. Such models are based on the premise that the effects of an integrated lesson is greater than the sum of the parts and that such approaches would be easier to implement in classroom settings. Integrated approaches normally combine repeated readings and assisted readings with elements of phonics instruction.

Studies of the implementation of such approaches such as Fluency Oriented Reading Instruction (Kuhn et al., 2006; Stahl & Heubach, 2005, 2006; Stahl, Heubach, & Cramond, 1997), the Fluency Development Lesson (Rasinski, Padak, Linek, & Sturtevant, 1993), Fast Start (Padak & Rasinski, 2004; Rasinski, 1995; Rasinski & Stevenson, 2005), Oral Recitation Lesson (Hoffman, 1987; Reutzel & Hollingsworth, 1993; Reutzel, Hollingsworth, & Eldredge, 1994), the Shared Book Experience (Eldredge, Reutzel, & Hollingsworth, 1996), Retrieval, Automaticity, Vocabulary Elaboration, Orthography (RAVE-O; Wolf & Katzir-Cohen, 2001; Wolf, Miller, & Donnelly, 2000), and Read Naturally (De la Colina, Parker, Hasbrouck, & Alecio, 2001; Denton, Fletcher, Anthony, & Francis, 2006; Hasbrouck, Ihnot, & Rogers, 1999) have yielded promising results in measures of word recognition, fluency, reading comprehension, and overall reading achievement, especially for struggling readers.

English Language Learners Learning to read English can be particularly challenging for students whose first language is not English. Nevertheless, the Report of the National Literacy Panel on Language-Minority Children and Youth (August & Shanahan, 2006) indicated that reading fluency is a relevant instructional issue for ELL students. Lems (2006), for example, found significant correlations between measures of reading fluency and adult ELL students representing a number of different first languages. Other studies have demonstrated that instructional interventions in fluency can have positive impact on ELL students reading development (Da la Colina et al., 2001; Hiebert & Fisher, 2006).

The Art of Teaching Reading Fluency

The title of this volume is the *Handbook of Research on Teaching the English Language Arts.* Implied in this title is the notion that reading and instruction in reading is an art. The previous section of this chapter has examined the scientific evidence supporting the construct of fluency in reading and instruction in reading fluency. In this section I address some artistic issues involved in fluency instruction.

An important practical question that emerges from the research and practice of guided oral repeated and assisted readings previously reviewed revolve around the purpose for students to engage in such activities. Critics have argued that the over usage of reading rate (ORF scores) as a measure of fluency and progress in fluency has led to a primary emphasis on improving reading rate for fluency instruction with minimal regard for text comprehension (Rasinski, 2006; Samuels, 2007). Moreover, such an overt emphasis on improving reading rate may also lead to a disregard for the other critical aspect of reading fluency—prosody. When readers are focused on reading a text quickly, little regard is given to reading with appropriate expression that reflects the meaning of the text. Moreover, instruction that is aimed primarily at improving reading rate lacks authenticity. There are few instances in life where one is called on to read for the express purpose of speed.

Reading fluency is most often associated with oral reading (e.g., prosody is manifested in oral reading). An authentic (and artistic) use of oral reading is performance. Actors, singers, poets, orators, and others who perform regularly engage in repeated and assisted reading activities for the purpose of preparing to perform a text for an audience. Moreover, the purpose of the performance is often more than to inform. The purpose of oral performances by actors, singers, and poets are done to engender an aesthetic response (Rosenblatt, 1994). Art deals with aesthetics.

Certain text genres are meant to be performed (Rasinski, 2010). These include scripts, dialogues, monologues, poems, song lyrics, and speeches. When students are asked to perform such texts they have a natural reason to engage in rehearsal (i.e., guided oral assisted and repeated readings). The eventual performance provides an organic motivation for practice. Moreover, because the quality of the performance will, to a large extent, be judged on the expressiveness of the performer, the aim of the practice is not speed, but prosody—to be able to communicate meaning to an audience through the expressive interpretation of a text.

Alexander and Jetton (2000, p. 296) argue that reading is a "synthesis of skill, will, and thrill." A learner must have a commitment to read and the reading must have some form of personal gratification for reading. The oral performance of a text for an audience has great potential for increasing students' commitment and satisfaction in reading and the practice that precedes the performance.

A number of reading scholars (e.g., Rasinski, 2008; Worthy & Prater, 2002) have advocated the use of an artistic approach to fluency. Moreover, a growing body of research has examined the use of this artistic approach to reading fluency instruction. Matinez, Roser, and Strecker (1998/1999) studied second-grade students engaged in an instructional routine employing readers theater. Students received a short script at the beginning of each week which was then rehearsed over the course of the week and eventually performed. In a 3-month implementation the researchers reported that students in the readers theater program made greater gains in fluency and overall reading achievement than a control group of students in a more conventional form of instruction. Moreover, the gains exceeded the normal progress expected in such a time period. Students, teachers, and parents reported that high levels of engagement and motivation for the program.

Using a similar format of practice and performance of readers theater scripts with fourth-grade students, Griffith and Rasinski (2004) reported on 3 years of implementation,. Struggling readers made gains in reading achievement (2+ years growth in 1 year of instruction) and reading fluency (50+ words correct per minute gain in 1 year of instruction) well exceeding what would normally be expected. Other researchers have reported similar gains with implementations of readers theater with second-grade students (Young & Rasinski, 2009), fifth-grade students (Carrick, 2006), and high school students (Reese, 2005). Still other research has demonstrated improvements in confidence in and motivation for reading that results from performing scripts (Clark, Morrison, & Wilcox, 2009).

The use of poetry also suggests rehearsal and performance. Rasinski, Rupley, and Nichols (2008) suggest that the use of poetry with young children provides teachers and students with unique opportunities to teach and learn phonics as well as fluency since most poems for younger children make good use rhymes (rimes). Three reports of research using the repeated and assisted use and performance of poetry and nursery rhymes with primary-grade readers found very positive results, especially for the most at-risk students (Padak & Rasinski, 2004; Rasinski, 1995; Rasinski & Stevenson, 2005). Similarly positive results have been found with the use of song lyrics with struggling middle school readers (Biggs et al., 2008).

There is no reason why an artful and scientific approach to the teaching of reading fluency cannot complement one another to create instruction that nurtures and satisfies the "skill, will, and thrill" requisites of textual experiences.

Reading Fluency: Next Steps It has been nearly three decades since Allington (1983) called fluency the "neglected goal of the reading curriculum." Finally, fluency is recognized as an important part of the reading curriculum. Still, important questions remain to be answered by researchers and practitioners in positioning fluency in its optimal and appropriate place in the reading and language arts curriculum.

Various tensions between aspects of fluency and the reading curriculum require further attention. How does fluency fit into the overall reading curriculum? What is the optimal amount of time for fluency instruction, given the limitations to the school day? Should fluency be taught beyond the primary grades? Are the methods for fluency instruction appropriate in prereading environments and programs? Chall's (1996) model of reading development positions fluency in the primary grades. However, recent research has demonstrated that fluency is a concern for students in the upper elementary and middle school grades (Rasinski et al., 2009) as well as the secondary grade levels (Rasinski et al., 2005) and that fluency interventions can have a positive impact on older students' reading proficiency (Biggs et al., 2008; Rees, 2005).

The tension between automaticity and prosody is clearly an instructional issue that need resolution. Are these elements of fluency best addressed separately? Or can instruction be developed to promote both in an interactive manner? The tension between automaticity and prosody is especially present in the way that fluency is assessed. Automaticity is normally measured through reading rate; prosody through teacher ratings of the expressive nature of a student's oral reading. When speed is assessed, prosody is often neglected. Moreover, when readers interpret a text through oral reading, reading speed is usually not a major concern. Indeed, readers often slow their reading for purposes of text interpretation and to allow a listening audience more opportunities to digest or construct the meaning of the passage. Is it possible to develop assessments of fluency that integrate measures of automatic word recognition and prosodic reading?

A major tension in reading fluency lies in the relationship of oral to silent reading. Although fluency is most often associated with oral reading, the importance of fluency lies in the impact its development has on silent reading comprehension. What is the relationship between oral and silent reading fluency? And, is it possible to teach silent reading fluency directly?

Clearly, a tension exists in the nature of texts used for fluency instruction. Some researchers advocate the development of texts with highly controlled elements and difficulty levels to optimize students' fluency development. Such texts run the risk of limiting the authentic nature of reading texts. Some scholars suggest that informational texts are best suited for fluency and general reading development. Conversely, others have argued that informational texts are not generally meant to be performed, do not normally contain a compelling voice that would lend itself to prosodic reading, and thus are not well suited for fluency reading. At the same time, text length is an issue in fluency instruction. Most texts used for fluency instruction are relatively brief in order to allow for repeated readings. To what extent is fluency an issue for students on longer passages? Can fluency be fostered with longer texts? What features should teachers consider when choosing texts for fluency instruction?

Finally, the tension between wide and repeated reading is a major issue for reading scholars. Prior to fluency becoming an integral part of the school reading program, wide reading where students moved from one text to another after essentially one reading characterized most reading instruction. With the integration of fluency into the reading curriculum repeated readings must now be considered part of the instructional milieu. What is the appropriate balance between wide and repeated reading? What is the optimal number of readings of a passage as a function of the relative difficulty of the passage?

Unquestionably, many tensions need to be resolved and many questions remain to be answered in the realm of fluency. From a teaching viewpoint, however, perhaps no bigger tension, however, is the tension between the science and the art of teaching fluency. Fluency instruction is clearly important for developing readers, especially those who experience difficulty in learning to read. The challenge for researchers and practitioners is to develop reading fluency instruction that satisfies the scientific requisite to be effective in terms of increasing proficiency in the skill of reading and at the same time makes fluency instruction an authentic and engaging reading experience that satisfies the aesthetic needs of readers and teachers of reading.

References

Alexander, P. A., & Jetton, T. L. (2000). Learning from text: A multidimensional and developmental perspective. In M. Kamil, P. Mosenthal, P. D. Pearson, & R. Barr (Eds.), *Handbook of reading research* (Vol. III, pp. 285–310). Mahwah, NJ: Erlbaum.

Allington, R. L. (1983). Fluency: The neglected reading goal. *The Reading Teacher, 36*, 556–561.

Allington, R. L. (2005). *What really matters for struggling readers* (2nd ed.). New York: Allyn & Bacon.

August, D., & Shanahan, T. (2006). *Developing literacy in second-language learners: Report of the National Literacy Panel on language-minority children and youth.* Mahwah, NJ: Erlbaum.

Beimiller, A., & Shany, M. T. (1995). Assisted reading practice: Effects on performance for poor readers in grades 3 and 4. *Reading Research Quarterly 30*, 382–295.

Biggs, M., Homan, S., Dedrick, R., & Rasinski, T. (2008). Using an interactive singing software program: A comparative study of middle school struggling readers. *Reading Psychology, An International Quarterly, 29*, 195–213.

Carbo, M. (1978a). Teaching reading with talking books. *The Reading Teacher, 32*, 267–273.

Carbo, M. (1978b). A word imprinting technique for children with severe memory disorders. *Teaching Exceptional Children, 11*, 3–5.

Carrick, L., U.. (2006). Readers theatre across the curriculum. In T. Rasinski, C. Blachowicz, & K. Lems (Eds.), *Fluency instruction: Research-based best practices* (pp. 231–252). New York: Guilford Press.

Cassidy, J., & Cassidy, D. (2009). What's hot for 2009. *Reading Today, 26*(4), 1, 8, 9.

Chall, J. S. (1996). *Stages of reading development* (2nd ed.). Fort Worth, TX: Harcourt-Brace.

Chomsky, C. (1976). After decoding: What? *Language Arts, 53*, 288–296.

Chomsky, C. (1978). When you still can't read in third grade. After decoding, what? In S. J. Samuels (Ed.), *What research has to say about reading instruction* (pp. 13–30). Newark, DE: International Reading Association.

Clark, R., Morrison, T. G., & Wilcox, B. (2009). Readers' theater: A process of developing fourth-graders' reading fluency. *Reading Psychology, 30*, 359–385.

Clay, M. M., & Imlach, R. H. (1971). Juncture, pitch, and stress as reading behavior variables. *Journal of Verbal Learning and Verbal Behavior, 10*, 133–139.

Compton, D. L., Appleton, A. C., & Hosp, M. K. (2004). Exploring the relationship between text-leveling systems and reading accuracy and fluency in second-grade students who are average and poor decoders. *Learning Disabilities Research, 19*(3), 176–184.

Cooper, W. E., & Paccia-Cooper, J. (1980). *Syntax and speech*. Cambridge, MA: Harvard University Press.

Coots, J. H. (1982). *Reading comprehension: Instructional implications of SWRL research* (Tech Reports 052 and 120). Los Alamitos, CA: Southwest Regional Laboratory (ERIC Document Reproduction Service No. 241–902).

Daly III, E. J., Bonfiglio, C. M., Mattson, T., Persampieri, M., & Foreman-Yates, K. (2006). Refining the experimental analysis of academic skills deficits: Part II. Use of brief experimental analysis to evaluate reading fluency treatments. *Journal of Applied Behavior Analysis, 39*(3), 323–331.

De la Colina, M. G., Parker, R. I., Hasbrouck, J. E., & Alecio, R. (2001). Intensive intervention in reading fluency for at-risk beginning Spanish readers. *Bilingual Research Journal, 25*, 503–538.

Denton, C. A., Fletcher, J. M., Anthony, J. L., & Francis, D. J. (2006). An evaluation of intensive intervention for students with persistent reading difficulties. *Journal of Learning Disabilities, 39*(5), 447–466.

Dowhower, S. L. (1987). Effects of repeated reading on second-grade transitional readers' fluency and comprehension. *Reading Research Quarterly, 22*, 389–407.

Dowhower, S. L. (1991). Speaking of prosody: Fluency's unattended bedfellow. *Theory into Practice, 30*, 165–175.

Eldredge, J. (1990). Increasing reading performance of poor readers in the third grade by using a group assisted strategy. *Journal of Educational Research, 84*, 69–77.

Eldredge, J., & Quinn, W. (1988). Increasing reading performance of low-achieving second graders by using dyad reading groups. *Journal of Educational Research, 82*, 40–46.

Eldredge, J., Reutzel, D.., & Hollingsworth, P. (1996). Comparing the effectiveness of two oral reading practices: Round-robin reading and the shared book experience. *Journal of Literacy Research, 28*, 201–225.

Epstein, W. (1961). The influence of syntactical structure on learning. *American Journal of Psychology, 74*, 80–85.

Feazell, V. S. (2004). Reading acceleration program: A schoolwide intervention. *The Reading Teacher, 58*(1), 66–72.

Flood, J., Lapp, D., & Fisher, D. (2005). Neurological impress method plus. *Reading Psychology, 26*, 147–160.

Fuchs, D., Fuchs, L. S., Mathes, P., & Simmons, D. (1997). Peer-assisted learning strategies: Making classrooms more responsive to student diversity. *American Educational Research Journal, 34*, 174–206.

Gamse, B. C., Bloom, H. S., Kemple, J. J., & Jacob, R. T. (2008). *Reading First impact study: Interim report*. Washington DC: National Center for Education Evaluation and Regional Assistance, U.S. Department of Education.

Greenwood, C. R., & Delquardri, J. (1995). Class-wide peer tutoring and the prevention of school failure. *Preventing School Failure 39*, 21–25.

Griffith, L. W., & Rasinski, T. V. (2004). A focus on fluency: How one teacher incorporated fluency with her reading curriculum. *The Reading Teacher, 58*, 126–137.

Hasbrouck, J. E., Ihnot, C., & Rogers, G. (1999). Read Naturally: A strategy to increase oral reading fluency. *Reading Research and Instruction, 39*, 27–37.

Heckelman, R. G. (1969). A neurological impress method of reading instruction. *Academic Therapy, 4*, 277–282.

Henk, W. A., Helfeldt, J. P., & Platt, J. M. (1986). Developing reading fluency in learning disabled students. *Teaching Exceptional Children, 18*(3), 202–206.

Hiebert, E. H. (2005). The effects of text difficulty on second graders' fluency development. *Reading Psychology, 26*, 1–7.

Hiebert, E. H. (2006). Becoming fluent: Repeated reading with scaffolded texts. In S. J. Samuels & A. E. Farstrup (Eds.), *What research has to say about fluency instruction* (pp. 204–226). Newark, DE: International Reading Association.

Hiebert, E. H. (2008). The (mis)match between texts and students who depend on schools to become literate. In E. H. Hiebert & M. Sailors (Eds.), *Finding the right texts for beginning and struggling readers: Research-based solutions* (pp. 1–21). New York: Guilford Press.

Hiebert, E. H., & Fisher, C. W. (2006). Fluency from the first. In T. Rasinski, C. Blachowicz, & K. Lems (Eds.), *Fluency instruction: Research-based best practices* (pp. 279–295). New York: Guilford Press.

Hoffman, J. V. (1987). Rethinking the role of oral reading in basal instruction. *Elementary School Journal, 87*, 367–373.

Hollingsworth, P. M. (1978). An experimental approach to the impress method of teaching reading. *The Reading Teacher, 31*, 624–626.

Koskinen, P. S., & Blum, I. H. (1986). Paired repeated reading: A classroom strategy for developing fluent reading. *The Reading Teacher, 40*, 70–75.

Koskinen, P. S., Wilson, R. M., & Jensema, C. (1985). Closed-caption television: A new tool for reading instruction. *Reading World, 24*(4), 1–7.

Huey, E. B. (1968). *The psychology and pedagogy of reading*. Boston: MIT Press. (Original work published 1908)

Johnson, N. F. (1965). The psychological reality of phrase-structure rules. *Journal of Verbal Learning and Verbal Behavior, 4*, 469–475.

King, S., Yoon, E., Jernigan, M., Jaspers, J., Gilbert, T., Morgan, P., et al. (2001). Developing first-grade fluency through peer mediation. *Teaching Exceptional Children, 34*(2), 90–93.

Kuhn, M., & Rasinski, T. V. (2007). Best practices in fluency instruction. In L. Gambrell, L. M. Morrow, & M. Pressley (Eds.), *Best practices in literacy instruction, Volume 3*. New York: Guilford Press.

Kuhn, M., & Rasinski, T. V. (2009). Helping diverse learners to become fluent readers. In L. M. Morrow, R. Reuda, & D. Lapp (Eds.), *Handbook of research on literacy and diversity* (pp. 366–377). New York: Guilford Press.

Kuhn, M, R., Schwanenflugel, P. J., Morris, R. D., Morrow, L. M., Woo, D. G., Meisinger, E. B., et al. (2006). Teaching children to become fluent and automatic readers. *Journal of Literacy Research, 38*(4), 357–387.

Kuhn, M. R., Schwanenflugel, P. J., & Meisinger, E. B. (2010). Review of research: Aligning theory and assessment of reading fluency: Automaticity, prosody, and definitions of fluency. *Reading Research Quarterly, 45*(2), 230–251.

Kuhn, M. R., & Stahl, S. A. (2000). *Fluency: A review of developmental and remedial practices* (CIERA Rep. No. 2-008). Ann Arbor, MI: Center for the Improvement of Early Reading Achievement.

Kuhn, M. R., & Stahl, S. A. (2004). Fluency: A review of developmental and remedial practices. In R. B. Ruddell & N. J. Unrau (Eds.), *Theoretical models and processes of reading* (5th ed., pp. 412–451). Newark, NJ: International Reading Association.

Labbo, L. D., & Teale, W. H. (1990). Cross age reading: A strategy for helping poor readers. *The Reading Teacher, 43*, 363–369.

LaBerge, D., & Samuels, S. A. (1974). Toward a theory of automatic information processing in reading. *Cognitive Psychology, 6*, 293–323.

Langford, K., Slade, B., & Burnett, E. (1974). An examination of impress techniques in remedial reading. *Academic Therapy, 9*, 309–319.

Lems, K. (2006). Reading fluency and comprehension in adult English Language Learners. In T. Rasinski, C. Blachowicz, & K. Lems (Eds.). *Fluency Instruction: Research-based best practices* (pp. 231–252). New York: Guilford Press.

Logan, G. D. (1988). Toward an instance theory of automatization. *Psychological Review, 95*, 492–527.

Logan, G. D. (1997). TI: Automaticity and reading: Perspectives from the instance theory of automatization. *Reading and Writing Quarterly, 13*(2), 123–146.

Martin, B. (1966). *Sounds of language (teachers edition)*. New York: Holt Rinehart & Winston.

Martinez, M., Roser, N., & Strecker, S. (1998/1999). "I never thought I could be a star": A readers theatre ticket to reading fluency. *Reading Teacher, 52*(4), 326–334.

Mathes, P. G., Simmons, D. C., & Davis, B. I. (1992). Assisted reading techniques for developing reading fluency. *Reading Research and Instruction, 31*(4), 70–77.

Mefferd, P. E., & Pettegrew, B. S. (1997). Fostering literacy acquisition of student with developmental disabilities: Assisted reading with predictable trade books. *Reading Research and Instruction, 36,* 177–190.

Meisinger, E. B., Schwanenflugel, P. J., Bradley, B., & Stahl, S. A. (2004). Interaction quality during partner reading. *Journal of Literacy Research, 36*(2), 111–140.

Menon, S., & Hiebert, E. H. (2005). A comparison of first-graders' reading with little books or literature-based basal anthologies. *Reading Research Quarterly, 40*(1), 12–38.

Mikkelsen, V. P. (1981). *The effects of a modified neurological impress method on developing decoding skills.* Paper presented at East Carolina University, Greenville, NC. (ERIC Document Reproduction Service No. ED 209638).

Miller, J., & Schwanenflugel, P. J. (2006). Prosody of syntactically complex sentences in the oral reading of young children. *Journal of Educational Psychology, 98,* 839–853.

Miller, J., & Schwanenflugel, P.J. (2008). A longitudinal study of the development of reading prosody as a dimension of oral reading fluency in early elementary school children. *Reading Research Quarterly, 43*(4), 336–354.

Morgan, R., & Lyon, E. (1979). Paired reading: A preliminary report on a technique for parental tuition of reading-retarded children. *Journal of Child Psychology and Psychiatry and Allied Disciplines, 20,* 151–160.

Musti-Rao, S., Hawkins, R. O., & Barkley, E. (2009). Effects of repeated readings on the oral reading fluency of urban fourth-grade students: Implications for practice. *Preventing School Failure, 54*(1), 12–23.

National Reading Panel. (2000). *Report of the National Reading Panel: Teaching children to read. Report of the subgroups.* Washington, DC: U.S. Department of Health and Human Services, National Institutes of Health.

Neuman, S. B., & Koskinen, P. S. (1992). Captioned television as comprehensible input: Effects of incidental word learning from context for language minority students. *Reading Research Quarterly, 27*(1), 94–106.

Padak, N., & Rasinski, T. (2004). Fast Start: A promising practice for family literacy programs. *Family Literacy Forum, 3,* 3–9.

Perfetti, C. (1985). *Reading ability.* New York: Oxford University Press.

Pluck, M. (1995). Rainbow Reading Programme: Using Taped Stories. *Reading Forum, 1,* 25–29.

Rasinski, T. V. (1990). Effects of repeated reading and listening-while-reading on reading fluency. *Journal of Educational Research, 83,* 147–150.

Rasinski, T. V. (1990). *The effects of cued phrase boundaries in texts.* Bloomington, IN: ERIC Clearinghouse on Reading and Communication Skills. (ERIC Document Reproduction Service No. ED 313689)

Rasinski, T. V. (1994). Developing syntactic sensitivity in reading through phrase-cued texts. *Intervention in School and Clinic, 29,* 165–168.

Rasinski, T. V. (1995). Fast Start: A parental involvement reading program for primary grade students. In W. Linek & E. Sturtevant (Eds.), *Generations of literacy. Seventeenth Yearbook of the College Reading Association* (pp. 301–312). Harrisonburg, VA: College Reading Association.

Rasinski, T. V. (2003). *The fluent reader: Oral reading strategies for building word recognition, fluency, and comprehension.* New York: Scholastic.

Rasinski, T. V. (2006). Reading fluency instruction: Moving beyond accuracy, automaticity, and prosody. *The Reading Teacher, 59,* 704–706.

Rasinski, T. V. (2008). Teaching fluency artfully. In R. Fink & S. J. Samuels (Eds.), *Inspiring reading success: Interest and motivation in an age of high-stakes testing* (pp. 117–140). Newark, DE: International Reading Association.

Rasinski, T. V. (2010). *The fluent reader* (2nd ed.). New York: Scholastic.

Rasinski, T. V., & Hoffman, T. V. (2003). Theory and research into practice: Oral reading in the school literacy curriculum. *Reading Research Quarterly, 38,* 510–522.

Rasinski, T. V., Padak, N., Linek, W., & Sturtevant, E. (1993). The effects of fluency development instruction on urban second grader readers. *Journal of Educational Research, 87,* 158–164.

Rasinski, T., Padak, N., McKeon, C., Krug,-Wilfong, L., Friedauer, J., & Heim, P. (2005) Is reading fluency a key for successful high school reading? *Journal of Adolescent and Adult Literacy, 49,* 22–27.

Rasinski, T. V., Reutzel, C. R., Chard, D. & Linan-Thompson, S. (in press). Reading fluency. In M. L. Kamil, P. D. Pearson, P. Afflerbach, & E. B. Moje (Eds), *Handbook of reading research* (Vol. 4). New York: Routledge.

Rasinski, T. V., Rikli, A., & Johnston, S. (in press). Reading fluency: More than automaticity? More than an issue for the primary grades? *Journal of Literacy Research., 48,* 350–361.

Rasinski, T., Rupley, W. H., & Nichols, W. D. (2008). Two essential ingredients: Phonics and fluency getting to know each other. *The Reading Teacher, 62,* 257–260.

Rasinski, T., & Stevenson, B. (2005). The effects of Fast Start Reading, a fluency based home involvement reading program, on the reading achievement of beginning readers. *Reading Psychology: An International Quarterly, 26,* 109–125.

Rasinski, T. V., & Zutell, J. B. (1996). Is fluency yet a goal of the reading curriculum? In E. G. Sturtevant & W. M. Linek (Eds.), *Growing literacy. Eighteenth yearbook of the College Reading Association,* (pp. 237–246). Harrisonburg, VA: College Reading Association.

Reese, R. (2005). *The impact of participation in readers theater on reading attitudes and fluency skills among ninth grade students in an alternative program.* Unpublished doctoral dissertation. Akron, OH: University of Akron.

Reutzel, D. R., Fawson, P. C., & Smith, J. A. (2008). Reconsidering silent sustained reading: An exploratory study of scaffolded silent reading (ScSR). *Journal of Educational Research, 102*(1), 37–50.

Reutzel, D. R., & Hollingsworth, P. M. (1993). Effects of fluency training on second grader's reading comprehension. *Journal of Educational Research, 86*(6), 325–331.

Reutzel, D. R., Hollingsworth, P. M., & Eldredge, J. L. (1994). Oral reading instruction: The impact upon student reading development. *Reading Research Quarterly, 29*(1), 40–62.

Reutzel, D. R., Jones, C. D., Fawson, P. C., & Smith, J. A. (2008). Scaffolded silent reading (ScSR): An alternative to guided oral repeated reading that works! *The Reading Teacher, 62,* 194–207.

Rosenblatt, L. (1994). *The reader, the text, the poem: The transactional theory of the literary work.* Carbondale: Southern Illinois University Press.

Samuels, S. J. (2007). The DIBELS tests: Is speed of barking at print what we mean by fluency? *Reading Research Quarterly, 42,* 563–566.

Sanders, E. A., & Vadasy, P. F. (2008). Benefits of repeated reading intervention for low-achieving fourth- and fifth-grade students. *Remedial and Special Education, 29,* 235–249.

Schreiber, P. A. (1980). On the acquisition of reading fluency. *Journal of Reading Behavior, 12,* 177–186.

Schreiber, P. A. (1987). *Prosody and structure in children's syntactic processing.* In R. Horowitz & S. J. Samuels (Eds.), *Comprehending oral and written language* (pp. 243–270). New York: Academic Press.

Schreiber, P. A. (1991). Understanding prosody's role in reading acquisition. *Theory into Practice, 30,* 158–164.

Schreiber, P. A., & Read, C. (1980). Children's use of phonetic cues in spelling, parsing, and—maybe—reading. *Bulletin of the Orton Society, 30,* 209–224.

Shanahan, T. (2006). Developing fluency in the context of effective literacy instruction. In T. Rasinski, C. Blachowicz, & K. Lems (Eds.), *Fluency instruction: Research-based best practices.* New York: Guilford Press.

Stahl, S., & Heubach, K. (2005). Fluency-oriented reading instruction. *Journal of Literacy Research, 37,* 25–62.

Stahl, S. A., & Heubach, K. (2006). *Fluency-oriented reading instruction.* In K. A. D. Stahl & M. C. McKenna (Eds.), *Reading research at work: Foundations of effective practice* (pp. 177–204). New York: Guilford Press.

Stahl, S. A., Heubach, K., & Cramond, B. (1997). *Fluency-oriented reading instruction*, Reading research report no. 79. Athens, GA and College Park, MD: National Reading Research Center.

Stanovich, K. E. (1980). Toward an interactive-compensatory model of individual differences in the development of reading fluency. *Reading Research Quarterly, 16*(1), 32–71.

Stanovich, K. E. (1986). Matthew effects in reading: Some consequences of individual differences in the acquisition of literacy. *Reading Research Quarterly, 21,* 360–407.

Topping, K. (1987a). Paired reading: A powerful technique for parent use. *The Reading Teacher, 40,* 604–614.

Topping, K. (1987b). Peer tutored paired reading: Outcome data from ten projects. *Educational Psychology, 7,* 133–145.

Vadasy, P. F., & Sanders, E. A. (2008). Repeated reading intervention: outcomes and interactions with readers' skills and classroom instruction. *Journal of Educational Psychology, 100*(2), 272–290.

Vaughn, S., Chard, D. J., Bryant, D. P., Coleman, M., Tyler, B.J., Linan-Thompson, S., et al. (2000). Fluency and comprehension interventions for third grade students. *Remedial and Special Education, 21*(6), 325–335.

Whalley, K., & Hansen, J. (2006). The role of prosodic sensitivity in children's reading development. *Journal of Research in Reading. 29,* 288–303.

Wickstrom, K., Jones, K., & Therrien, W. J. (2006). Effect of a combined repeated reading and question generation intervention on reading achievement. *Learning Disabilities Research & Practice, 21*(2), 89–97.

Williams, J. C., Klubnik, C., & McCall, M. (2009). Three versus six rereadings of practice passages. *Journal of Applied Behavior Analysis, 42*(2), 375–380.

Wolf, M., & Katzir-Cohen, T. (2001). Reading fluency and its intervention. *Scientific Studies of Reading, 5*(3), 211–229.

Wolf, M., Miller, L., & Donnelly, K. (2000). Retrieval, automaticity, vocabulary, elaboration, orthography (RAVE-O): A comprehensive, fluency-based reading intervention program. *Journal of Learning Disabilities, 33*(4), 375–386.

Worthy, J., & Prater, K. (2002). "I thought about it all night": Readers theatre for reading fluency and motivation. *The Reading Teacher, 56,* 294–297.

Wright, J., & Cleary, K. S. (2006). Kids in the tutor seat: Building a schools' capacity to help struggling readers through a cross-age peer-tutoring program. *Psychology in the Schools, 43*(1), 99–107.

Young, C., & Rasinski, T. (2009). Implementing readers theatre as an approach to classroom fluency instruction. *The Reading Teacher, 63*(1), 4–13.

35

Teaching Spelling in the English/Language Arts Classroom

Shane Templeton

For almost 30 years educational researchers, developmental psychologists, and cognitive psychologists have established a fundamental insight about the role and importance of spelling knowledge: By examining the spellings of their students, teachers are able to gain the most direct information about the students' underlying word knowledge and how they apply that knowledge in writing *and* in reading; this in turn enables teachers better to determine the focus of their word-level instruction—both spelling and decoding. With respect to the spelling system itself, over the last several years a number of educators have emphasized what many linguists have pointed out for well over a century: The spelling system of American and British English is far more regular than traditionally assumed. The purpose of this chapter, therefore, is to explore the implications of and potential for a developmental approach to instruction that is informed by these two fundamental understandings: The regularities of the spelling system and the role of spelling or orthographic knowledge in literacy processes.

The Nature and Function of Orthographic Knowledge

For generations, educators and lay public alike have tended to focus on the most illogical examples of the spelling system of English, as if those exceptions proved a more general rule of widespread spelling irregularity. The pattern *ough*, for example, is often cited: It may be pronounced several different ways, as in *through*, *though*, *tough*, and *bough*. In reality, however, the spelling system is more logical and consistent in its representation of sound than often realized: There is a compelling consistency, for example, in the silent *e* marker to signal the difference between a short and a long vowel pattern, as in can/cane; the hard vs. soft sound of *c* as in voi*c*e/vo*c*alic; and the doubling of consonants at syllable junctures as in *dinner/diner* to signal a short vowel sound (closed syllable) vs. a long vowel sound (open syllable). Perhaps most significantly, the spelling system is quite consistent in its representation of *meaning* through mor-

phological or spelling-meaning relationships, as in *human/humanity*, *sign/insignia*, *custody/custodian*, and *paradigm/paradigmatic* (Templeton, 2003). While a number of years is required to master all of the conventions of the spelling system in English, the understanding that logic rather than whimsy and chance determines the conventions can be a reassuring guide—for teachers as well as for their students. As Venezky (1999) artfully and precisely observed, "English orthography is not a failed phonetic transcription system, invented out of madness or perversity" (p. 4) but one that reflects "a more complex and more *regular* relationship, wherein phonemes and morphemes play leading roles" (p. ix, emphasis added).

Most researchers concur that the acquisition of spelling or orthographic knowledge follows a developmental continuum. A debate continues regarding the degree to which this development may be described in terms of distinct developmental stages, phases, or statistical probabilities of particular spellings and the learner's degree of exposure to print (Chliounaki & Bryant, 2007; Deacon, Conrad, & Pacton, 2008; Sharp, Sinatra, & Reynolds, 2008; Templeton, 2003). There is agreement, however, on the fundamental observation that learning the conventional spellings of words in the English language and the processes that determine conventional spelling occur over the course of the school years; this knowledge evolves from productions at the alphabetic, pattern, and simpler morphological levels toward more complex productions reflecting primarily morphological relationships (Berninger, Abbott, Nagy, & Carlisle, 2009; Ehri & McCormick, 2004; Reed, 2008; Templeton & Bear, 1992). To determine where students fall along this developmental continuum, teachers may assess students' orthographic knowledge by administering a well-constructed spelling assessment (Morris, 2008; Templeton, Bear, & Madura, 2007). These assessments indicate (a) each student's hunch or "theory" of how orthography represents language, and (b) the types of orthographic or spelling information that are already secure, as well as information their theories are trying to accommodate: For both encoding and decoding, is a student drawing primarily upon alphabetic letter-sound relationships, clusters of letters that represent vowel patterns, syllable patterns, or spelling and meaning patterns in polysyllabic words (Conrad, 2008; Ehri, 2005; Templeton & Bear, 1992)? Looking at a student's spellings also provides insight, therefore, into what she attends to when she reads familiar words and decodes unfamiliar words in connected text. In addition, what she is able to perceive on the printed page is guided by her orthographic knowledge, which determines her eye movements during reading and the perceptual span during each fixation, that is, how many letters she perceives.

Figure 35.1 presents the developmental nature of orthographic knowledge as students learn, over time, the multi-layered relationships between letters in the printed word and the types of information the letters represent. As a function of level of literacy development, from Beginning Conventional Literacy through Skilled/Proficient Literacy, Figure 35.1 presents students' characteristic spelling errors. The errors also reflect the types of orthographic information to which developing learners attend, from alphabetic through a deeper understanding of the structure of single-syllable words, polysyllabic words, and morphological relationships. The significant orthographic features that represent this information are also presented. Grade level ranges are included as an approximation of where *most* students at these grade levels fall along the developmental continuum; at all grades, of course, there will be some students who are at an earlier phase of literacy development as well as those who are at a later phase; each will need to study words and patterns appropriate for their respective levels.

The Nature and Focus of Instruction

A developmental perspective on spelling instruction reveals

BEGINNING LITERACY	TRANSITIONAL LITERACY	INTERMEDIATE LITERACY	SKILLED/PROFICIENT LITERACY
Alphabetic	*Within-Syllable Patterns*	*Between-Syllable Patterns and Morphological Relationships I*	*Morphological Relationships II*
BAD – bed *SEP – ship* *LAP – lump* *JRIV – drive*	*TRANE – train* *FLOWT – float* *CATOL – cattle* *THOUT – throat*	*SHOPING – shopping* *HABBIT – habit* *CAPCHURE – capture* *MIDDEL – middle*	*APPEERENCE – appearance* *OPPISITION – opposition* *CONFRENCE – conference* *DEPRAVATION – deprivation* *FEASABLE – feasible*
[Grades K–1]	[Grades 2–3]	[Grades 3–5]	[Grades 6 and Above]
EMPHASIS IN SPELLING INSTRUCTION			

Early
– Beginning and ending single consonants
 	
Middle
– Short vowels
– Consonant digraphs
 	
Late
– Consonant blends
	Early–Middle
	– Common long vowel patterns
	
	Middle–Late
	– *r*- and *l*-influenced vowels
	– Three-letter consonant blends
	  str- scr-
	– Common spelling for diphthongs /ow/, /oi/
	– Complex consonants
	  Final sound of /k/
	  Final /ch/: -ch -tch
	  /j/: dge Vge
	– Compound words
	– Homophones
	  sail/sale beat/beet
		Early
		– Inflectional suffixes added to base -ed, -ing
		– Plural endings added to base -s -es
		– Base words + common prefixes and suffixes
		
		Middle
		– Syllable patterns
		  VCCV *bas/ket rab/bit*
		  VCV open: *hu/man*
		  VCV closed: *cab/in*
		– Less-frequent vowel patterns
		
		Late
		– Changing final *y* to *i*
		– Patterns in unaccented syllables
		– 2-syllable homophones
		  peddle/pedal dual/duel
		– 2-syllable homographs
		  PRESent/preSENT
		  REcord/reCORD
			Spelling/Meaning Relationships Related Words:
			sign music
			signal musician
			
			ignite reside mental
			ignition resident mentality
			
			Greek and Latin Roots
			-therm- -spect-
			-photo- -dic-
			
			"Absorbed" Prefixes
			in- + mobile = immobile
			ad- + tract = attract

	Students learn to apply their understanding of spelling patterns in single-syllable words to decoding polysyllabic words in their reading; for spelling purposes, these polysyllabic words will be studied more systematically during the Intermediate phase	*For vocabulary development, students learn about spelling-meaning relationships, including most-frequently-occurring Greek and Latin roots; for spelling purposes, these will be explored more systematically at the Skilled/Proficient phase.*	

Figure 35.1 The nature of spelling instruction in relation to level of literacy development.

that orthographic development does not occur simply through repetition and memorization. For most students, throughout the primary, intermediate, middle, and secondary grades, memory for words and patterns is supported by the development of underlying interrelationships among phonology, orthography, meaning, and morphology. This section examines hallmarks of the nature and focus of this development across the grades.

Spelling Knowledge at the Beginning and Transitional Levels of Literacy Development Learners exposed to an alphabetically-based writing system and who have at least partial phonemic awareness begin their examination of the written forms of words—their spellings—from a linear, left-to-right perspective, as in English and Spanish, or a right-to-left perspective, as in Arabic or Hebrew. For example, when native English- or Spanish-speaking children first become fully phonemically aware, defined as consciously attending to every consonant and vowel sound within a syllable, they encode spoken words primarily following a linear, left-to-right letter/sound matchup. This is usually their approach to the explicit analysis of words. Consider first-grader James's errors at mid-year: HEN/chin, JIM/drum. Because James's spelling provides our best insight into how he reads or decodes words, we know that he scans words left-to-right, matching each successive letter with a sound—very few letters are perceived during each fixation. And as he engages text, many words that he encounters in his reading correspond with his theory—for example, consonant/vowel/consonant patterns. Other words, however, contain features that do not "fit" his current theory—words with blends and digraphs, for example, and words with "silent" *e*. For example, when he encounters the word *make* he probably does not attend to the silent *e*—he would spell the work MAK—but his alphabetic-level knowledge and the context in which this new word occurs help him decode *make* and continue with his reading. As James continues to encounter the word *make* and other words that end in silent *e*, his theory of how spelling works begins to incorporate this information, as may be seen at the end of the year in his spelling of many words that contain a long vowel; for example, FRITE/fright and GRAEN/grain. Importantly, the teacher's phonics instruction has also targeted these elements, helping to raise them to a level of awareness. By this time James is also spelling most simple blends and digraphs correctly, as well as most short vowels. Such spellings suggest that James is picking up on the concept of *pattern* and is becoming a Transitional reader and writer. Invernizzi (1992) first noted that the correct representation of blends and digraphs usually signals the "rise of *conventional* spelling patterns to conscious attention" which afforded attention to "*the vowel and what follows as a frame for orthographic analysis*" (p. 118). This splitting of the orthographic representation of onset and rime allows the vowel and what follows to be perceived as a unit or chunk—the path to the exploration of additional short and long vowel patterns is now cleared and more negotiable.

Once students move from the alphabetic focus characteristic of Beginning Conventional Literacy to an increasing focus on pattern during the Transitional phase, their ability to read words accurately runs ahead of their ability to spell many of those words accurately. Research by Morris and his colleagues (summarized in Morris, 2008) has consistently demonstrated that, throughout most of the elementary school years, words to be examined for purposes of learning the correct spelling should be words that have first been encountered several times in reading. This is because it is easier to abstract and understand spelling patterns when students are examining *known* words—words they can read—than when they are examining words they do *not* yet know how to read. For example, Transitional level learners' "theory" of how spelling works includes the understanding that long vowel sounds are usually marked by silent letters, as in the orthographic patterns represented by vowel pairs and a vowel-consonant-silent *e*, and this understanding helps them decode words in their reading. More time is required, however, to learn the orthographic conventions that will determine accurate encoding: *Which* specific spelling patterns are used for *which* words (for example, is it *chane* or *chain*?), and the probability that some patterns will occur with greater frequency than others (the long *a* patterns of *ai* and vowel/consonant/silent *e*, for example, occur with far greater frequency than the long *a* patterns *ei* and *ea*). This latter expression of orthographic knowledge—accurate spelling of specific words—will result through continued reading of the words *and* exploration of the patterns that the words contain. In addition, as noted at the bottom of the Transitional Literacy column in Figure 35.1, although students' focus in spelling instruction is primarily on spelling patterns in single-syllable words, they should learn to apply their developing understanding of these patterns in decoding polysyllabic words in their reading. Teachers model how to apply knowledge of spelling patterns in decoding: "Look for patterns you know, and try them out," and model how the word *complaining*, for example, may be decoded by noting the single-syllable spelling patterns *com*, *plain*, and *ing*. While not holding students accountable for correctly spelling new vocabulary, it is important that teachers direct students' attention to the spellings of new words as part of their vocabulary instruction because, as Rosenthal and Ehri suggest (2008) "spellings activated graphophonemic connections to better secure pronunciations and meanings in memory" (p. 175).

Spelling Knowledge at the Intermediate and Skilled/Proficient Levels of Literacy Development The reciprocity between phonological awareness and orthographic awareness continues to develop throughout the more advanced developmental levels. The understanding that emerges from exploring short and long vowels in single-syllable words and their orthographic pattern representation grounds the developing awareness and understanding at the Intermediate level of orthographic conventions at syllable and/or morpheme junctures—whether a vowel is dropped or changed before a suffix is added (*glided*, *babies*) and whether consonants are doubled at these junctures (*hidden*) or left alone (*pilot*). These juncture conventions all depend on an awareness of the relationship between sound and spelling. Morphological analysis, the focused exploration of word-formation processes, is centered primarily on meaning, but also includes a phonological component and may in fact be facilitated by exploring and learning about orthographic structure. Just as the graphic representation of sounds facilitates young children's phonemic awareness, so may the orthographic representation of morphemes facilitate older students' morphological awareness, which in turn becomes a powerful pacemaker for vocabulary growth. As illustrated in Figure 35.1, for purposes of vocabulary development Intermediate level students may learn, and more deeply process, the identity and meaning of common Greek and Latin elements by attending to the spelling patterns that represent them. They may also explore a number of spelling-meaning patterns.

At the skilled/proficient level, students spell the vast majority of words they use correctly. In the middle- and secondary-English/language arts classrooms, words may be grouped according to spelling-meaning or morphological patterns and relationships and may be studied over a 1-, 2-, or 3-week period as an integral part of vocabulary instruction. Just as for Intermediate level students, spelling structure may be one of the most important factors in developing higher-order morphological knowledge, which is in turn a significant contributor to vocabulary development. The generative potential of Greek and Latin roots, identified by their spelling patterns, expands significantly. Different facets of spelling/meaning relationships may be explored, keyed by types of spelling errors that are common at the Skilled/Proficient level: for example, relating a known word to a misspelled word as with RESADENT / re*side*, VELUMINOUS / *vol*ume, NARR*I*TIVE/narr*a*tion, CRITI*SI*ZE/*critic*; and relating a similarly-spelled unknown word to a known misspelled word, thereby expanding students' vocabulary, as with PARADIME / *paradigm*atic. Occasionally these relationships involve discussing the core meanings underlying the different forms of a root or base to emphasize a relationship that is not immediately obvious to students; the misspelling EXILERATE is explained by pairing ex*hilar*ate and *hilar*ious.

Instructional Implications of a Developmental Approach

Most teachers may not be explicitly aware of the layers of information in the spelling system (Johnston, 2001) or of the specific features that they represent. This author (1979) first noted that "the theoretical position that a teacher adopts (consciously or not) with regard to English orthography—spelling—has direct influence on the way in which he or she perceives and teaches" spelling (p. 790), and in 1997 Hughes and Searle observed that "If we teachers do not believe that spelling has logical, negotiable patterns, how can we hope to help children develop that insight?" (p.

133). In part for this reason, a number of educators have called for a significant focus on the English spelling system and its instruction as part of preservice teacher education programs and inservice professional development (Fresch, 2007; Johnston, 2001). While teachers may increasingly indicate that they teach spelling developmentally, they do not appear to be differentiating instruction (Graham et al., 2008). Although reading levels are differentiated, spelling levels are not, so below-level students may be reduced to trying to memorize sequences of letters, and ironically, not receiving the supportive spelling instruction that would in turn better support their decoding.

What are the instructional implications for spelling of determining a student's level of literacy development? Because of the importance of ensuring strength and depth of word study, students should be afforded multiple exposures to words and patterns through reading words and writing words from a variety of perspectives, and there should be a balance of direct and exploratory instructional experiences. Through guided and independent comparison and contrast, the classification or sorting of words provides the strength and depth of processing that leads to fluent encoding and decoding (Carlo et al., 2004; Joseph, 2002; White, 2005). Some instructional materials published over the last several years in both the basal and the supplemental markets are including an emphasis on word sorting, although accommodation often is not made for students at different levels within the same classroom. In recent years a number of proposals for structuring curricular reforms in the teaching of vocabulary at the middle and secondary levels have been advanced that build on the relationship between spelling and meaning (Templeton, 2004), highlighting information represented in derivational relationships among words, and materials for students at the intermediate grades and above are more systematically and in some depth addressing the role of spelling-meaning connections, including Greek and Latin roots.

The developmental trend from primarily an alphabetic or sound-based analysis to a meaning-based analysis has been observed in a number of other languages as well (Bear, Templeton, Helman, & Baren, 2003; Joshi & Aaron, 2006), and a growing literature is supporting specific adjustments that teachers can effect in their word study to guide English learners' integration of meaning and phonological information with spelling as they acquire English. The spelling-meaning principle characteristic of English spelling exists to various degrees in other languages as well (*polygon / polígono*; *euphoric /eufórico / euphorique*), so that the exploration of cognates in other languages that share Latin and Greek elements may support English learners as well as native English speakers learning other languages (Templeton, 2010).

Conclusion

Because a common core of orthographic knowledge underlies both the encoding and decoding of words, a broader conception of spelling has emerged over the last few decades: The primary purpose of spelling instruction is to guide and support students' exploration of the structure of written words so that they will process deeply and understand more clearly the relationships between print and language at the alphabetic, pattern, and meaning levels. This characterization reflects the psychological and pedagogical interconnections among spelling, reading, and vocabulary instruction, while still addressing the traditional objective of spelling instruction: Helping students learn the conventional spellings of words so that they will need to devote less attention to basic encoding processes during the composing process, whether they are writing with pen and paper or digitally. And what of the role of orthographic knowledge in the digital age? While some opine that increasingly sophisticated voice recognition and spell check software may obviate the need for spelling instruction, because of the broader role that we now understand spelling or orthographic knowledge to play in the enterprise of literacy, there will probably not for the foreseeable future be an elimination of devoting instructional attention to the development of students' orthographic knowledge.

References

Bear, D., Templeton, S., Helman, L., & Baren, T. (2003). Orthographic development and learning to read in different languages. In G. C. Garcia (Ed.), *English learners: Reaching the highest level of English literacy* (pp. 71–95). Newark, DE: International Reading Association.

Berninger, V. W., Abbott, R. D., Nagy, W., & Carlisle, J. (2009). Growth in phonological, orthographic, and morphological awareness in grades 1 to 6. *Journal of Psycholinguistic Research – Online First*. Retrieved October 16, 2009.

Carlo, M. S., August, D., McLaughlin, B., Snow, C E., Dressler, C., Lippman, D. N., et al. (2004). Closing the gap: Addressing the vocabulary needs of English-language learners in bilingual and mainstream classrooms. *Reading Research Quarterly, 39*(2), 188–215.

Chliounaki, K., & Bryant, P. (2007). How children learn about morphological spelling rules. *Child Development, 78*(4), 1360–1373.

Conrad, N. J. (2008). From reading to spelling and spelling to reading: Transfer goes both ways. *Journal of Educational Psychology, 100*(4), 869–878.

Deacon, S. H., Conrad, N., & Pacton, S. (2008). Graphotactic and morphological regularities in spelling. *Canadian Psychology, 49*(2), 118–124.

Ehri, L. C., & McCormick, S. (2004). Phases of word learning: Implications for instruction with delayed and disabled readers. In R. B. Ruddell, M. R. Ruddell, & H. Singer (Eds.), *Theoretical models and processes of reading* (5th ed., pp. 365–389). Newark, DE: International Reading Association.

Ehri, L. C. (2005). Learning to read words: Theory, findings, and issues. *Scientific Studies of Reading, 9*(2), 167–188.

Fresch, M. (2007). Teachers' concerns about spelling instruction: A national survey. *Reading Psychology, 28*(4), 301–330.

Graham, S., Morphy, P., Harris, K. R., Fink-Chorzempa, B., Saddler, B., Moran, S., et al. (2008). Teaching spelling in the primary grades: A national survey of instructional practices and adaptations. *American Education Research Journal, 45*(3), 796–825.

Hughes, M., & Searle, D. (1997). *The violent e and other tricky sounds: Learning to spell from kindergarten through grade 6*. York, ME: Stenhouse Publishers.

Invernizzi, M. (1992). The vowel and what follows: A phonological frame of orthographic analysis. In S. Templeton & D. R. Bear (Eds.), *Development of orthographic knowledge and the foundations of literacy: A Memorial Festschrift for Edmund H. Henderson* (pp. 105–136). Hillsdale, NJ: Erlbaum.

Johnston, F. (2001). Exploring classroom teachers' spelling practices and beliefs. *Reading Research and Instruction, 40*, 143–156.

Joseph, L. M. (2002). Facilitating word recognition and spelling using word boxes and word sort phonic procedures. *School Psychology Review, 3*, 122–129.

Joshi, R. M., & Aaron, P. G. (Eds.). (2006). *Handbook of orthography and literacy*. Mahwah, NJ: Erlbaum.

Morris, D. (2008). *Diagnosis and correction of reading problems*. New York: Guilford Press.

Reed, D. K. (2008). A synthesis of morphology interventions and effects on reading outcomes for students in grades k-12. *Learning Disabilities Research & Practice, 23*(1), 36–49.

Rosenthal, J., & Ehri, L. C. (2008). The mnemonic value of orthography for vocabulary learning. *Journal of Educational Psychology, 100*(1), 175–191.

Sharp, A. C., Sinatra, G. M., & Reynolds, R. E. (2008). The development of children's orthographic knowledge: A microgenetic perspective. *Reading Research Quarterly, 43*(3), 206–226.

Templeton, S. (1979). The circle game of English spelling: A reappraisal for teachers. *Language Arts, 56*, 789–797.

Templeton, S. (2003). Spelling. In J. Flood, D. Lapp, J. R. Squire, & J. M. Jensen (Eds.), *Handbook of research on teaching the English language arts* (2nd ed., pp. 738–751). Mahwah, NJ: Erlbaum.

Templeton, S. (2004). The vocabulary-spelling connection: Orthographic development and morphological knowledge at the intermediate grades and beyond. In J. F. Baumann & E. J. Kame'enui (Eds.), *Vocabulary instruction: Research to practice* (pp. 118–138). New York: Guilford Press.

Templeton, S. (2010). Spelling-meaning relationships among languages: Exploring cognates and their possibilities. In L. Helman (Ed.), *Literacy development with English learners: Research-based instruction in grades K-6* (pp. 196–212). New York: Guilford Press.

Templeton, S., & D. R. Bear (Eds.). (1992). *Development of orthographic knowledge and the foundations of literacy: A memorial festschrift for Edmund H. Henderson*. Hillsdale, NJ: Erlbaum.

Templeton, S., Bear, D. R., & Madura, S. (2007). Assessing students' spelling knowledge: Relationships to reading and writing. In J. R. Paratore & R. L. McCormack (Eds.), *Classroom literacy assessment: Making sense of what students know and do* (pp. 113–134). New York: Guilford Press.

Venezky, R. L. (1999). *The American way of spelling: The structure and origins of American English orthography*. New York: Guilford Press.

White, T. G. (2005). Effects of systematic and strategic analogy-based phonics on grade 2 students' word reading and reading comprehension. *Reading Research Quarterly, 40*(2), 234–255.

36

Vocabulary Instruction

Three Contemporary Issues

PETER J. FISHER, CAMILLE L. Z. BLACHOWICZ, AND SUSAN WATTS-TAFFE

To write about vocabulary instruction and development in a handbook oriented towards teachers and researchers, authors have to answer the question, "What else is there to say?" Over the last three decades, numerous instructional investigations have taken place and rich summaries of research have been written. The second *Handbook of Reading Research* (Barr, Kamil, Mosenthal, & Pearson, 1991), contained two chapters on vocabulary, one dealing with vocabulary processes (Anderson & Nagy, 1991) and a second with vocabulary development (Beck & McKeown, 1991). These same topics were also addressed in the third *Handbook of Reading Research* (Blachowicz & Fisher, 2000; Nagy & Scott, 2000) in the *Handbook of Teaching the English Language Arts* (Baumann & Kame'enui, 1991), and in other comprehensive reviews (Farstrup & Samuels, 2008).

Further, several educators have surveyed this landscape of research and attempted to interpret it for practitioners in application volumes focused on instruction (Baumann & Kame'enui, 2004; Beck, McKeown, & Kucan, 2002; Blachowicz & Fisher, 2010; Graves, 2006; Hiebert & Kamil, 2005). At the same time, many articles on vocabulary have been published in instructional journals, and more than 400 dissertations on the topic of vocabulary have been abstracted in *Dissertation Abstracts* since the 1960s.

Rather than trying to replicate this fine historical and practical knowledge base, we will focus on the research related to three issues of current interest that are critical to advancing what we know about vocabulary instruction:

1. What does it mean to approach vocabulary comprehensively?
2. What are the dimensions of academic vocabulary?
3. What are some research-based resources to assist vocabulary selection?

What Does It Mean to Approach Vocabulary Comprehensively?

Throughout the years, theorists and researchers have studied vocabulary teaching and learning from a variety of perspectives. Key facets of study have included: the nature of vocabulary acquisition, including the wide array of information needed to truly "know" a word (Nagy & Scott, 2000), characteristics associated with effective instruction of individual word meanings (Mezynski, 1983; Stahl & Fairbanks, 1986), strategies that individuals use to determine the meanings of unknown words encountered in reading and the ways they can be successfully taught (Baumann, Font, Edwards, & Boland, 2005); characteristics of words that make them easier or harder to acquire and factors influencing the selection of words to teach (Nagy & Hiebert, in press); and differences in vocabulary acquisition across students (Biemiller & Slonim, 2001; White, Graves, & Slater, 1989; Hart & Risley, 1995). All of this information, and more, has brought us to the practical implication that in order to address the complex, multi-dimensional nature of word learning, we need to approach vocabulary comprehensively (Kamil & Hiebert, 2005; Stahl & Nagy, 2006; Watts-Taffe, Fisher, & Blachowicz, 2009).

Graves (2006) has summarized a comprehensive approach as one in which four components of vocabulary instruction are firmly in place for all students:

- *Rich and varied language experiences.* Students are immersed in words through listening, speaking, reading, and writing.
- *Instruction in individual words.* Students are taught the meanings of individual words through both definitional and contextual information, active engagement, and multiple practice opportunities over time.
- *Instruction in strategies for independent word learning.*

Students are taught how to use context, word structure, and outside resources such as the dictionary to independently determine the meanings of unknown words.

- *Fostering word consciousness.* Students are engaged in activities that promote their interest in and awareness of words, metacognition about words, and motivation to learn words.

A comprehensive approach is one in which vocabulary instruction is not an isolated event, confined to pre-teaching comprehension words before reading a new text during the time of day set aside for reading and language arts. Rather, vocabulary instruction is dispersed—across the school day, across the curricular areas, and across the grades, from pre-school through high school. Despite the fact that research and theory, taken collectively, provide strong support for a comprehensive approach, relatively few studies have directly investigated comprehensive approaches. Here, we describe two.

In a recent formative experiment in a diverse fifth-grade classroom, Baumann, Ware, and Edwards (2007) studied the impact of a year-long program of vocabulary instruction based on Graves' four components. Vocabulary instruction reflecting each of the four components occurred in a variety of ways across the school day. In addition to using a multifaceted approach to instruction, the researchers took a multifaceted approach to data collection including standardized tests, student writing samples, student interviews, parent questionnaires, and lesson plans. Results showed growth in students' use of sophisticated and challenging words, an increase in their interest and attitudes toward vocabulary learning, and demonstration of independent use of word learning strategies.

Lawrence, Snow, and White (2009) are working with the Boston Public Schools on the Word Generation Project, a comprehensive approach designed to increase middle school students' knowledge of academic words. The project is implemented either school-wide or, minimally, grade-wide, and involves teachers across content areas who focus on the same set of weekly words. Instruction reflects characteristics of effective instruction for individual words, the word learning strategies of morphological analysis and contextual analysis, and rich and varied language experiences. Preliminary findings show significant growth in word knowledge for project participants, and a higher rate of word learning for students engaged in the project compared with students not engaged in the project.

With increased emphasis on informational text and an emphasis on meeting state standards has come a focus on academic vocabulary required to comprehend informational texts and test passages across content areas (Marzano, 2004; Zwiers, 2008). Yet, as the term "academic vocabulary" is discussed in the literature, it is clear that there is no single, agreed-upon definition. In the next section, we examine some of the dimensions of academic vocabulary which must be an important component of any comprehensive approach to vocabulary instruction.

What Are the Dimensions of Academic Vocabulary?

One reason that vocabulary has become a hot issue in literacy instruction is that we know some students come to school knowing many fewer words than others (Hart & Risley, 1995), and that this has a major impact on school learning. It has been proposed that we may be able to help them succeed in school by teaching them the academic vocabulary needed to be successful (Marzano, 2004). Similarly, we know that many students, largely from low socio-economic backgrounds or non-mainstream cultural backgrounds, come to school unfamiliar with the discourse of school—school language. One dimension of school language is lexica—knowing the meaning of *line up, for example, when the class is getting ready for recess.* In a very broad definition of academic vocabulary, we might include these words simply because they occur in an academic setting, but it would not be what we would normally think of as being related to academic language.

Historically there has been a significant population of students who have also needed instruction in "school-based" vocabulary—English Language Learners (ELLs). To differentiate their vocabulary needs, one common term used in ELL instruction is CALP, or Cognitive Academic Language Proficiency. Cummins (2000) who was responsible for introducing the term, contrasts it with Basic Interpersonal Communication Skills (BICS), which a student may use in the playground. In this iteration, our students need to learn academic language, which is cognitively demanding and academic, and which includes school-based discourse patterns. However, within the ELL community there has been some debate about which vocabulary is academic and which is not (Aukerman, 2007). While the general distinction is clear, the particular instances of which words are academic may be contextually defined by their use in the classroom. The decision may be important to the extent that it impacts on what gets included on lists of words that should be taught as part of the curriculum—the words it is "necessary" for students to know.

Aside from the above considerations, an a priori definition of academic vocabulary would appear to be quite simple—the vocabulary of the content of a discipline, including those words that identify major concepts, such as *perimeter* or *osmosis,* and those that are related to processes within the discipline, such as *classify* or *differentiate.* It is apparent that each discipline has its own discourse, grammar, and lexicon (Yopp, Yopp, & Bishop, 2008). However, Nation (1990) suggested there may be a more general academic vocabulary—words that appear across content areas. Such a general academic vocabulary would have implications for instruction if these words have a general meaning that could be taught across disciplines (Bailey & Butler, 2007), and this has led to the generation of various word lists. These lists differ from Marzano's list (2004), for example, which is for developing students' background knowledge from the early grade levels. They are primarily for the use with upper elementary grade students and beyond (for example,

Hiebert & Lubliner, 2008) and are often morphemically based. In these grade levels there is still a considerable difference in the content area vocabulary knowledge of White students and Black and Hispanic students (Bravo, Hiebert, & Pearson, 2007). However, while teaching a general academic vocabulary may lead to less confusion, Fang (2006) reminds us that the structure of academic texts and other vocabulary, such as prepositions, conjunctions, and pronouns may also cause problems. For example, the conjunction *while* can also construe multiple logical relations. It can be temporal (*While the volcano erupted, the townspeople ...*), concessive (*While we know a lot about vocabulary learning, there is still ...*), or contrastive (*Some antonyms are polar, while others are scalar*).

Research on the teaching of content area vocabulary does not always make the distinction between content-specific and general academic vocabulary. Unfortunately, there is not much published research that is specifically about teaching vocabulary in the content areas (Harmon, Hedrick, & Wood, 2005). Some of the research focuses on analyzing content area texts. In mathematics and science texts, polysemy can be a source of difficulty (Fang, 2006; Harmon et al., 2005). Science texts also often contain multimorphemic words (*micro+organ+ism*) in conceptually dense sentences (Fang, 2006). However, one analysis found 76% of important words in a science curriculum were Spanish-English cognates (Bravo et al., 2007), which could be an important instructional and learning tool for Spanish speaking students.

Similar to the analytical work of Fang and colleagues in science, Schleppegrell (2007) reminds us that it is not just the technical vocabulary of mathematics that may pose difficulties for students, but long noun phrases with complex grammatical patterning that result in complex meaning relationships. In a detailed analysis of mathematics, science, and social studies texts at the fifth-grade level, Butler, Bailey, Stevens, and Hua (2004) found about 10% of the words in a mathematics text to be academic vocabulary (content-specific and general academic vocabulary), with content-specific vocabulary accounting for 7% For science texts the numbers were 21% and 14%, and for social studies 24% and 21%. So for these texts the number of general academic words accounted for between 3% and 7% of the text. Across all three subject areas only 15 out of 275 word types were found in common (for example, *equal, express,* and *products*). These results suggest that a general, cross-disciplinary academic vocabulary may be only a small part of the vocabulary that students need to learn in the content areas.

Some older studies indicate that discussion (Stahl & Clark 1987) and hands-on activities (Carlisle, Fleming, & Gudbrandsen, 2000; Lloyd & Contreras, 1985) help with vocabulary learning in science. Kossak (2007) found visual learning was better than traditional dictionary work for learning key terms in science. These, and other studies, mirror the findings of more general studies concerning the importance of engaging students in the active learning of

vocabulary. Similarly, Blachowicz & Obrochta (2007) have demonstrated that teachers using interactive methods and conceptually interesting materials can teach content area vocabulary even to primary grade students.

Observational research suggests that vocabulary instruction in the content areas is not always what it should be. For example, Bailey, Butler, LaFramenta, and Ong (2004) found that in upper elementary science classrooms "Students were rarely required to be actively involved in the acquisition of academic vocabulary" (p. 88), and Scott, Jamieson-Noel, and Asselin (2003) found that in upper-elementary classrooms in Canada only 1.4% of the time in core academic subject areas was spent developing vocabulary knowledge.

Teachers teach the content of the curriculum—we have always done so. That includes teaching the major concepts in the content areas and the vocabulary of the discourse of the discipline. We may not have always been very good at it, and now are much more aware of how many of our students are struggling with the vocabulary load in the content areas. The problem remains much as it has always been—it concerns the teaching of new terms for new concepts (which may be more likely to be content-specific), *and* new concepts for familiar terms (which may be more likely to be general academic vocabulary).

What Are Some Research-Based Resources for Academic and Content Vocabulary?

Regardless of definitions, there are several approaches that educators have used to choose appropriate words for instruction and for the construction of instructional materials. Suggested approaches include picking the words that are not well established in students' vocabularies and will be encountered frequently in the future (Beck et al., 2002), selecting words that are important to what is being read, and choosing words based on generativity, i.e., the ability to use this word or word parts to learn other words (Blachowicz & Fisher, 2009; Graves, 2006). Most educators would suggest that the words encountered most frequently in English are good candidates for learning, and that various word lists can help teachers select words appropriate to various grade levels and content areas. Hiebert and Lubliner (2008) have suggested that using content-focused materials with real-world referents can actually be more accessible to students from varying linguistic backgrounds.

Further, core reading programs, both commercial and locally constructed, have typically contained many genres of literature and have highlighted vocabulary from these selections to represent frequency, decodability, central selection content, and words needed for instruction in a particular skill or strategy (Ryder & Graves, 1994). Thus, with the exception of early literacy, when it is logical to focus on high-frequency vocabulary, the words selected for instruction may be highly variable from literature anthology to anthology, requiring a systematic appraisal by teachers to select the words most appropriate for their students (Beck et al., 2002). In the academic content areas, by contrast, the considerations of each domain require that certain words should be taught. Beyersdorfer (1991) reviewed studies of word choice, indicating that content area teachers produced word study lists with a high degree of overlap across teachers. The increase in the inclusion of content area materials in these core reading programs has necessitated a more careful look at words selected for instruction and has led to a reexamination and extension of research on word lists.

Some of the recent lists have specifically addressed academic vocabulary. Kendall and Marzano (2000) synthesized more than 100 national and state documents containing standards and benchmarks for K–12 education, and organized their content into 14 major categories. Marzano (2004) then went further and compiled a list of academic vocabulary for 11 subject areas, divided into four levels—K–2; 3–5; 6–8; 9–12. It resulted in 7,923 terms. He notes that history accounted for 2,579 of the terms, a consequence of the specificity of the standards in the subject area. A perusal of the lists shows what he means—we did not know *the Qing position on opium* or *the court of Heian.* That is not to say that we should not know them, but that seems to us to be a level of specificity that should be determined at a local level, which suggests one problem with lists such as this. Their value is dependent on the source and the compiler.

For the Academic Word List, produced by Coxhead (2000), words were selected from a range of over 400 advanced content area texts at the tertiary level of education. The audience was ELL students and the list was an attempt to identify families of words that would be useful across the disciplines. Coxhead eliminated sight words and frequent words and organized the remaining terms into a list containing 570 semantic fields divided into 10 sublists. The sublists are ordered such that the words in the first sublist are the most frequent words, such as *similar, compare, create,* which might be encountered in informational reading or television. Those in the last sublist are the least frequent. (These may be accessed online at a variety of locations including http://www.nottingham.ac.uk/~alzsh3/acvocab/wordlists.htm.) However, Hyland and Tse (2007) in an extensive analysis of the AWL using a new academic corpus of writing found that six word families (*analyze, consist, factor, indicate, period,* and *structure*) appeared in the top 60 of both Coxhead's list and their own. In addition they found that "individual items occur and behave in dissimilar ways in different disciplines…" (p. 251). For example, in engineering *analysis* tends to refer to the method of determining constituent parts, whereas in the social sciences it can have the more general meaning of considering something carefully. Further, they noted that the AWL was biased in favor of law and business and was thin in the area of the sciences and social sciences. They conclude that, at the university level, the search for a single collection of words that students can learn and transfer across disciplines is misguided. While this criticism may be true at the tertiary level, it is less clear that it may apply at lower levels of education. Hiebert and Lubliner (2008) are apparently aware of this analysis when

they use the AWL as the basis of their Core Academic Word List (CAWL). They describe academic vocabulary as consisting of four components: content-specific words (such as *equator),* school-task words (such as *learning log),* literary vocabulary (such as *flustered, rambunctious),* and general academic vocabulary (such as *features, reasons).* In other words, they include in their definition each of the types of academic vocabulary we have discussed so far, and add a fourth—the literary vocabulary. For their general academic vocabulary list, the CAWL, they chose 400 morphological families from Coxheads' 570 based on criteria related to frequency, morphological richness, and high-frequency Spanish cognates. This is the list currently being used as the basis for instructional research in middle schools in Boston (Lawrence et al., 2009).

Research on word frequency in speech and text has produced many lists of general vocabulary that can be informative to teachers. One of the earliest was The Ogden List of Basic English (Ogden, 1930; http://en.wiktionary.org/wiki/Appendix:Basic_English_word_list). This list contained 850 root words which could be affixed to produce other parts of speech. They are organized by category: operations, general things, picturable things, descriptive words, and a more opaque category of opposites. The list is dated and oriented towards Britishisms but has a remarkable overlap with later, better researched word lists and forms the basis for later lists. For older students and English language learners, lists constructed in England for TESOL, notably *The General Service List of English Words* (West, 1953), have had great utility. Later, more carefully researched corpuses for oral vocabulary include *The Living Word Vocabulary* (Dale & O'Rourke, 1976), which gives estimates of words known by school-age students, and it is a resource whose predictions seem, for the most part, valid today (Biemiller, 2004). The *Fry Instant Words* (Fry & Kress, 2006) contains 75% of the words that students will encounter in their school reading material. Other frequency lists include an early survey of elementary content vocabulary (Harris & Jacobson, 1982), the Zeno, Iven, Millard, and Duvvuri (1995) frequency study and two lists based on that compilation—the *First 4000 Words* (http://www.thefirst4000words.com/) and *Word Zones* (http://www.textproject.org/). White, Sowell, and Yanagihara (1989) also researched a list of the most useful prefixes and suffixes for instruction.

Vocabulary researchers agree on the major principles of vocabulary instruction, so the issue has become what it should look like in schools, particularly in relation to those populations who come to school needing additional help with word learning. In this chapter we have tried to address three contemporary issues with a similar theme: a comprehensive approach to instruction; the teaching of academic vocabulary to address the needs of students who are traditionally marginalized, and in particular the concept of a general academic vocabulary; and word lists as a source of words to teach. We would like to close with two thoughts for teachers. The first is that, while word lists have their place, the choice of which words to teach may sometimes be better contextualized in local curriculum, or even (especially in the early grades) in local classrooms. The second is that we are reminded by the researchers who analyzed texts (Fang, Scheleppegrell, & Cox, 2006; Schleppegrell, 2007) and word lists (Hyland & Tse, 2007) that academic vocabulary is situated in academic discourse, and each discipline has its own linguistic and grammatical features that may be as great a source of difficulty to students as the vocabulary. However, we are encouraged by early results of studies of comprehensive programs with general academic vocabulary (Lawrence et al., 2009). Future research will need to address whether mastering a general academic vocabulary actually results in improved learning in more than one content area.

References

Anderson, R. C., & Nagy, W. E. (1991). Word meanings. In R. Barr, M. L. Kamil, P. B. Mosenthal, & P. D. Pearson (Eds.), *Handbook of reading research* (Vol. 2, pp. 690–724). New York: Longman.

Aukerman, M. (2007). A culpable CALP: Rethinking the conversational/academic language proficiency distinction in early literacy instruction. *The Reading Teacher, 60*, 626–634.

Bailey, A. L., Butler, F. A., LaFramenta, C., & Ong, C. (2004). *Towards the characterization of academic language in upper elementary science classrooms.* Center for the Study of Evaluation Report 621, Graduate School of Education & Information Studies, University of California, Los Angeles.

Bailey, A. L., & Butler, F. A. (2007). A conceptual framework of academic English language for broad application to education. In A. L. Bailey (Ed.), *The language demands of school: Putting academic English to the test.* New Haven, CT: Yale University Press.

Barr, R., Kamil, M., Mosenthal, P., & Pearson, P. D. (Eds.). (1991). *Handbook of reading research* (Vol. 2). White Plains, NY: Longman.

Baumann, J. F., & Kame'enui, E. J. (1991). Research on vocabulary instruction: Ode to Voltaire. In J. Flood, J. J. D. Lapp, & J. R. Squire (Eds.), *Handbook of research on teaching the English language arts* (pp. 604–632). New York: Macmillan.

Baumann, J. F., & Kame'enui, E. J. (2004). *Reading vocabulary: Research to practice.* New York: Guilford Press.

Baumann, J., Font, Edwards, D. C., & Boland, (2005). Strategies for teaching middle grade students to use word parts and context clues to expand vocabulary. In E. H. Hiebert & M. L. Kamil (Eds.), *Teaching and learning vocabulary: Bringing research to practice* (pp. 179–205). Mahwah, NJ: Erlbaum.

Baumann, J., Ware, D., & Edwards, D.C. (2007). "Bumping Into Spicy, Tasty Words that catch your tongue": A Formative experiment on vocabulary instruction. *The Reading Teacher, 61*, 108–122.

Beck, I. L., & McKeown, M. G. (1991). Conditions of vocabulary acquisition. In R. Barr, M. L. Kamil, P. B. Mosenthal, & P. D. Pearson (Eds.), *Handbook of reading research* (Vol. 2, pp. 789–814). New York: Longman.

Beck, I. L., McKeown, M. G., & Kucan, L. (2002). *Bringing words to life: Robust vocabulary instruction.* New York: Guilford Press.

Beyersdorfer, J. M. (1991). *Middle school students' strategies for selection of vocabulary in science texts.* Unpublished doctoral dissertation, National-Louis University, Evanston, IL.

Biemiller, A. (2004). Teaching vocabulary in the primary grades: Vocabulary instruction needed. In J. F. Baumann & J. Kame'enui (Eds.), *Vocabulary instruction: Research to practice* (pp. 28–40). New York: Guilford Press.

Biemiller, A., & Slonim, N. (2001). Estimating root word vocabulary growth in normative and advantaged populations: Evidence for a common sequence of vocabulary acquisition. *Journal of Educational Psychology, 93*, 498–520.

Blachowicz, C. L. Z., & Fisher, P. (2010). *Teaching vocabulary in all classrooms* (4th ed.). Columbus, OH: Prentice-Hall.

Blachowicz, C. L. Z., & Fisher, P. J. L. (2000) Vocabulary instruction. In R. Barr, M. L. Kamil, P. B. Mosenthal, & P. D. Pearson (Eds.), *Handbook of reading research* (Vol 3, pp. 503–523). New York: Longman.

Blachowicz, C. L. Z., & Obrochta, C. (2007). "Tweaking practice": Modifying read-alouds to enhance content vocabulary learning in grade 1. In D. W. Rowe, R. Jimenez, D. Compton, D. Dickson, Y. Kim, K. Leander, & V. Risko (Eds.), *Fifty-sixth yearbook of the National Reading Conference yearbook* (pp. 111–121). Oak Creek, WI: National Reading Conference.

Bravo, M. A., Hiebert, E. H., & Pearson, P. D. (2007). In R. K. Wagner, A. E. Muse, & K. R. Tannenbaum (Eds.), *Vocabulary acquisition: Implications for reading comprehension* (pp. 140–156). New York: Guilford Press.

Butler, F. A., Bailey, A. L., Stevens, R., & Huang, B. (2004). *Academic English in fifth-grade mathematics, science, and social studies textbooks.* Center for the Study of Evaluation Report 642, Graduate School of Education & Information Studies, University of California, Los Angeles.

Carlisle, J. F., Fleming, J. E., & Gudbrandsen, B. (2000). Incidental word learning in science classes. *Contemporary Educational Psychology, 25*(2), 184–211.

Coxhead, A. (2000). A new academic word list. *TESOL Quarterly, 34*(2), 213–238.

Cummins, J. (2000). *Language, power and pedagogy: Bilingual children in the crossfire.* Buffalo, NY: Multilingual Matters.

Dale, E., & O'Rourke, J. P. (1976). *The living word vocabulary.* Chicago: Field Enterprises.

Fang, Z. (2006). The language demands of science reading in the middle school. *International Journal of Science Education, 28*(5), 491–250.

Fang, Z., Scheleppegrell, M. J., & Cox, B. E. (2006). Understanding the language demands of schooling: Nouns in academic registers. *Journal of Literacy Research, 38*(3), 247–273.

Farstrup, A., & Samuels, S. J. (Eds.). (2008), *What the research has to say about vocabulary instruction.* Newark, DE: International Reading Association.

Fry, E. B., & Kress, J. E. (2006). *The reading teacher's book of lists* (5th ed.). San Francisco: Jossey-Bass.

Graves, M. F. (2006). *The vocabulary book.* New York: Teachers College Press.

Harmon, J. M., Hedrick, W. B., & Wood, K. D. (2005). Research on vocabulary instruction in the content areas: Implications for struggling readers. *Reading and Writing Quarterly, 21*, 261–280.

Harris, A. J., & Jacobson, M. D. (1982). *Basic reading vocabularies.* New York: Macmillan.

Hart, B., & Risley, T. R. (1995). *Meaningful differences in the everyday experience of young American children.* Baltimore, MD: Brookes.

Hiebert, E. H., & Kamil, M. L. (Eds.). (2005). *Teaching and learning vocabulary: Bringing research to practice.* Mahwah, NJ: Erlbaum.

Hiebert, E. H., & Lubliner, S. (2008). The nature, learning, and instruction of general academic vocabulary. In A. E. Farstrup & S. J. Samuels (Eds.), *What research has to say about vocabulary instruction* (pp. 106–129). Newark, DE: International Reading Association.

Hyland, K., & Tse, P. (2007). Is there and academic vocabulary? *TESOL Quarterly, 41*(2), 235–253.

Kamil, M. L., & Hiebert, E. H. (2005). Teaching and learning vocabulary: Perspectives and persistent issues. In E. H. Hiebert & M. L. Kamil (Eds.), *Teaching and learning vocabulary: Bringing research to practice* (pp. 1–23). Mahwah, NJ: Erlbaum.

Kendall, J. S., & Marzano, R. J. (2000). *Content knowledge: A compendium of standards and benchmarks for K-12 education* (3rd ed.). Alexandria, VA: ASCD.

Kossak, S. (2007). Comparing the effects of high and low learning pathway instructional approaches on vocabulary mastery of middle school at-risk learners. *The International Journal of Learning, 14*(6), 199–206.

Lawrence, J., Snow, C. E., & White, C. (2009, April). *Results from year two of word generation.* Paper presented at the annual meeting of the American Educational Research Association, San Diego, CA.

Lloyd, C. V., & Contreras, N. J. (1985, December). *The role of experience in learning science vocabulary.* Paper presented at the 35th Annual Meeting of the National Reading Conference San Diego, CA.

Marzano, R. J. (2004). *Building background knowledge for academic achievement: Research on what works in schools.* Alexandria, VA: Association for Supervision & Curriculum Development.

Mezynski, K. (1983). Issues concerning the acquisition of knowledge. Effects of vocabulary training on reading comprehension. *Review of Educational Research, 53, 263–279.*

Nagy, W. E., & Hiebert, E. H. (in press). Toward a theory of word selection. In M. L. Kamil, P. D. Pearson, E. B. Moje, & P. Afflerbach (Eds.), *Handbook of reading research* (Vol. 4). New York: Longman.

Nagy, W., & Scott, J. (2000). Vocabulary processes. In M. L. Kamil, P. B. Mosenthal, P. D. Pearson, & R. Barr (Eds.), *Handbook of reading research* (Vol. 3, pp. 269–283). New York: Longman.

Nation, I. S. P. (1990). *Teaching and learning vocabulary.* Boston: Heinle & Heinle.

Ogden, C. K. (1930). *Basic English: A general introduction with rules and grammar.* London: Paul Treber.

Ryder, R. J., & Graves, M. F. (1994). Vocabulary instruction presented prior to reading in two basal readers. *Elementary School Journal, 95,* 139–153.

Schleppegrell, M. J. (2007). The linguistic challenge of mathematics teaching and learning: A research review. *Reading and Writing Quarterly, 23,* 139–159.

Scott, J. A., Jamieson-Noel, D., & Asselin, M. (2003). Vocabulary instruc-
tion throughout the day in twenty-three Canadian upper-elementary classrooms. *The Elementary School Journal, 103,* 269–286.

Stahl, S. A., & Clark, C. H. (1987). The effects of participatory expectations in classroom discussion on the learning of science vocabulary. *American Educational Research Journal. 24*(4), 541–555.

Stahl, S., & Fairbanks, M. (1986). The effects of vocabulary instruction. A model-based meta-analysis. *Review of Educational Research, 56,* 72–110.

Stahl, S., & Nagy, W. (2006). *Teaching word meanings.* Mahwah, NJ: Erlbaum.

Watts-Taffe, S., Fisher, P. J., & Blachowicz, C. L. Z. (2009). Vocabulary instruction for diverse students. In L. M. Morrow, R. Rueda, & D. Lapp (Eds.), *Handbook of research on literacy instruction: Issues of diversity, policy, and equity.* New York: Guilford Press.

West, M. (1953). *A general service list of English words.* London: Longmans, Green, and Company.

White, T. G., Graves, M. F., & Slater, W. H. (1989). Growth of reading vocabulary in diverse elementary schools. *Journal of Educational Psychology, 42,* 343–354.

White, T. G., Sowell, J., & Yanagihara, A. (1989). Teaching elementary students to use word-part clues. *The Reading Teacher, 42,* 302–308.

Yopp, H. K., Yopp. R. H., & Bishop, K. (2008). *Vocabulary instruction for academic success.* Huntington Beach, CA: Shell Education.

Zeno, S. M., Iven, S. H., Millard, R.T., & Duvvuri, R. (1995). *The educator's word frequency guide.* New York: Touchstone Applied Science Associates.

Zwiers, J. (2008). *Building academic language: Essential practices in content classrooms.* New York: Jossey-Bass.

37

Comprehension

The Cooperation of Many Forces

Douglas Fisher, Diane Lapp, and Nancy Frey

Throughout this volume, noted researchers have addressed various aspects of literacy. There have been discussions about learner characteristics, text characteristics, and literacy processes such as phonemic awareness and phonics, vocabulary, fluency, writing, and oral language development. Researchers in the area of reading comprehension maintain that comprehension is dependent on the interaction of four sets of critical variables: (a) reader variables (age, ability, affect, knowledge bases, and motivation); (b) text variables (genres, format, features, considerateness); (c) educational-context variables (environment, task, social grouping, purpose); and (d) teacher variables (knowledge, experience, attitude, and pedagogical approach) (Ganske & Fisher, 2009; Israel & Duffy, 2008; Snow, 2002).

Without taking each of these key variables into consideration, an adequate explanation of effective comprehension instruction is impossible. These variables have been considered independently thus far in this book, but it is worth noting again that each significantly impacts one's understanding or comprehension of a text. A breakdown in any one area compromises comprehension. And quite frankly, there's nothing more important than comprehension. Reading is comprehending; it isn't just decoding or reading fluently or defining words. While each of these tasks is an important component of comprehending, we would argue that if you don't comprehend, you haven't read.

As a profession, we've known this for a long time. In 1917, Edward Thorndike described reading as reasoning and argued that comprehension is "…a very complex procedure, involving the weighing of each of many elements in a sentence, their organization in the proper relations to one another, the selection of certain connotations and the rejection of others, and the cooperation of many forces to produce the final response" (p. 323). The complexity of comprehension has spurred more than a century's worth of research as we seek to understand this process.

What Researchers Know about the Competent Comprehender

Although research in reading comprehension instruction is still developing, most educators agree that competent comprehenders exhibit a set of discernible characteristics. Researchers have found that competent readers actively construct meaning through an integrative process in which they interact and transact with the words on the page, integrating new information with preexisting knowledge structures (Block & Pressley, 2001; Rosenblatt, 1982; Zwaan, 2004). Furthermore, a reader's prior knowledge, experience, attitude, and perspective determine the ways that information is perceived, understood, valued, and stored (Fisher & Frey, 2009; Gaskins, 1996).

In other words, competent comprehenders have developed automaticity with a set of cognitive processes, which are often called strategies. This is an important consideration in comprehension research. Our goal cannot be to create strategic readers who interrupt their reading to engage in cognitive processes but rather skilled readers who deploy these cognitive processes subconsciously and automatically; much in the same way they do while decoding. We agree with Afflerbach, Pearson, and Paris (2008) who note that the goal of comprehension instruction should be for students to use cognitive strategies with automaticity, applying them authentically as they read. As Afflerbach and colleagues, who place emphasis on the reader's actions, and whether they are automatic or deliberate, note, "reading skills operate without the reader's deliberate control or conscious awareness…[t]his has important, positive consequences for each reader's limited working memory" (p. 368). Strategies, on the other hand, are "effortful and deliberate" and occur during initial learning, and when the text becomes more difficult for the reader to understand (p. 369).

The Competent Comprehender: A Skilled Reader Skilled readers are those who actively and automatically construct meaning as they read; they are self-motivated and self-directed; they monitor their own comprehension by questioning, reviewing, revising, and rereading to enhance their overall comprehension (Block & Pressley, 2001). These readers understand that it is the *reader* in the reading process who creates meaning, not the text or even the author of the text. As Rosenblatt (1938) noted:

> The same text will have a very different meaning and value to us at different times or under different circumstances. Some state of mind, a worry, a temperamental bias, or a contemporary social crisis may make us either especially receptive or especially impervious to what the work offers. Without an understanding of the reader, one cannot predict what particular text may be significant to him or what may be the special quality of his experience. (p. 35)

There is some agreement among contemporary researchers about the mental processes that readers engage in while reading. Most agree that reading is essentially a thinking activity in which the reader engages in a series of complex processes (Anderson & Roit, 1996; Gillam, Fargo, & Robertson, 2009). First, the reader previews the text by noting its general features (print size, pictures, headings); then, as reading begins, the reader uses five different kinds of knowledge to comprehend the text, including:

1. Knowledge of letters and sound correspondences.
2. Knowledge of words and word forms.
3. Knowledge of syntax, i.e., the grammatical structures of sentences and their functions.
4. Knowledge of meanings and semantic relations.
5. Knowledge of the social ways in which language is used.

Throughout, the reader uses metacognitive processes to monitor, control, and advance the search for meaning. Flavell (1992) suggested that there were at least four components of metacognitive monitoring that readers use as they process texts. Competent comprehenders:

- establish learning goals;
- generate cognitive associations to achieve these goals;
- evaluate their own metacognitive experiences through questioning and reflections; and
- use their own metacognitive knowledge to monitor their own understanding.

There is also consensus among researchers that competent comprehenders have a plan for understanding and they use their metacognitive knowledge in an orderly way to implement their plan. Although the reader's approach varies for each text and task, the following aspects seem to be part of the competent reader's generalizable plan.

Before reading, the competent comprehender:
- *Previews* the text by looking at the title, the pictures, and the print in order to evoke relevant thoughts and memories.
- *Activates appropriate background knowledge* through self-questioning about what he/she already knows about the topic (or story), the vocabulary, and the form in which the topic (or story) is presented.
- *Sets a purpose* for reading by identifying what he/she wants to learn or experience during the reading episode.

During reading, the competent comprehender:
- *Checks understanding* of the text by paraphrasing the author's words.
- *Monitors comprehension* by using context clues to figure out unknown words and by imaging, imagining, inferencing, and predicting.
- *Integrates* new concepts with existing knowledge, continually revising the purpose for reading.
- *Obtains appropriate help* by adjusting pace, taking notes, creating a concept map, reading less difficult texts on the same topic, using the dictionary, or asking teachers, parents or peers for assistance.

After reading, the competent comprehender:
- *Summarizes* what has been read by retelling, or reflecting on, the plot of the story or the main idea of the text.
- *Evaluates* the ideas contained in the text against background knowledge.
- *Applies* the ideas in the text to unique situations, extending the ideas to broader perspectives.

What We Know about Reading Comprehension Instruction

If the preceding section accurately reflects the processes that the competent comprehender engages in, one might wonder, is there a role for the teacher or does comprehension ability merely occur as a result of practice, or extensive and frequent reading?

Historical Perspectives on Teaching Reading Comprehension in the United States The history of reading comprehension instruction in the United States is actually very brief. The term *comprehension* seems to first have been used by J. Russell Webb in the third reader of his series, *Normal Readers* in 1856 (Smith, 1965). Prior to that time, comprehension per se was not discussed—one presumes it was thought about but not researched or reported. Although it is dangerous to try to guess what our predecessors thought, there does seem to be evidence that comprehension was not included as a major thrust in reading instruction in the early years because it was thought to be a logical by-product of learning to read (Smith, 1965).

In the 19th century, the term *meaning* came into use, and in the early 20th century it evolved into *understanding what one reads*. The definition of comprehension in the late 19th century was one in which comprehension was thought to be the product of reading; the aggregated total of comprehending many small units. Perhaps the most significant shift in emphasis in reading comprehension instruction that is observable from published research reports occurred in the early part of the 20th century during which time educators shifted their emphasis from the improvement of oral reading as a means for "getting meaning" to an emphasis on improving comprehension during silent reading (Mathews, 1966).

This movement seems to have signaled (and foreshadowed) a growing interest in contemporary efforts that encourage students to be in control of their own comprehension processes. This early 20th century movement seems to have resulted in a contemporary concern to move the focus of learning from external control of comprehension (prescribed materials and predetermined activities) to internal control in which students generate their own perspectives, interpretations, and understandings.

And this is where comprehension research is focused today. In the 21st century, the definition of text has expanded to include digital collections. Flood and Lapp (1995) proposed a "broader conceptualization in which literacy is defined as the ability to function competently in the 'communicative arts,' which include the language arts as well as the visual arts of drama, art, film, video, and television" (p. 1). In traditional print, readers read in two dimensions: across and down. Now readers have to read a third dimension—into. With hyperlinks readers are provided a number of options for reading the text. Instead of a linear "front to back" experience, readers can click their way through an almost endless collection of related sites, never having to finish any of them to move on.

These new forms of visual and information literacy are changing the very nature of schooling. New literacies and digital literacy involves multiple forms of both text and media, including books, videos, life experiences, Web sites, CD-ROMs, illustrations, and the like. These multiple forms of media are significantly influenced by advances in technology and will have a direct and immediate impact on comprehension (Coiro, Knoebel, Lankshear, & Leu, 2008; Flood, Heath, & Lapp, 2008).

These shifts in practice over the years seem to reflect a growing understanding of the mental processes that are involved in comprehension and an understanding that these processes can be acquired and developed through instruction and practice. These radical changes over the years acknowledge the changing perspective of the teacher's role in fostering comprehension and the learner's role in controlling his or her own comprehension.

Instructional Methods in Reading Comprehension
There are a number of instructional methods that have been particularly successful in helping to develop competent comprehenders. Rather than focus on specific instructional routines such as Question-Answer Relationship (Raphael

& Au, 2005) or graphic organizers (Wood, Lapp, Flood, & Taylor, 2008), which are effective procedures to develop comprehension, we will focus on general approaches that provide a framework from which teachers can teach. There are any number of resources available on instructional routines that facilitate comprehension (e.g., Block, Parris, Reed, Whiteley, & Cleveland, 2009; Fisher, Brozo, Frey, & Ivey, 2007; Lapp & Fisher, 2009), so we will not focus on those for this chapter.

The first method, reader response to literature, is generally thought to be a method used for instruction with literary texts (narratives, poetry, drama), but it can also be used in some instances with certain forms of information texts. The second method, reciprocal teaching, has sometimes been classified as an instructional activity rather than a method of teaching. For our purposes in this review, we will classify it as a method because it is a comprehensive way to instruct students through an entire text. Reciprocal teaching has also sometimes been thought to be a method of instruction to be used with information texts exclusively. However, evidence suggests that it can be used effectively with many different forms of texts, including narrative pieces. The third method, gradual release of responsibility, is a way to organize instruction.

Before we turn our attention to these methods, we must acknowledge a few truisms that plague the comprehension instruction work. First, as students move through the grades the texts become more difficult. While this may seem obvious, it's worth attending to. Good comprehension instruction in the primary grades will not adequately prepare a student for high school reading tasks. Students must be taught to comprehend increasingly complicated texts. Unfortunately, after Grade 4, many teachers stop teaching reading comprehension, moving instead to content.

Second, comprehension instruction takes time. As evidenced from the three methods we will review here, instructional time must be devoted to helping students reach automaticity and become skilled readers. But, Durkin's data (1978–79) revealed that instruction designed to teach children to comprehend texts occurred in classrooms for approximately 20 minutes per day.

Third, comprehension instruction is not simply asking students questions about what they read. After approximately 4,500 hours of observation Durkin (1978–79) noted that few comprehension strategies were being taught; instead children were merely being questioned about what they had read. Yet 20 years after Durkin's study, studies suggest that students in at least some fourth- and fifth-grade classrooms are still answering questions rather than being taught how to read for comprehension (Pressley, Wharton-McDonald, Hampson, & Echevarria, 1998). When these three issues are addressed, the following three methods for developing comprehension will likely impact student understanding.

Reader Response Method for Teaching Literature.   As early as 1938, Rosenblatt proposed a "new" method for teaching literature; an essentially reader-based method that attended directly to what "real" readers thought of the literature they were reading. In more recent years, this method has become known as reader response. She argued that reader response instruction, in which readers' personal interpretations of texts were of primary importance, would provide for more meaningful and effective teaching than the critical interpretative methods that were traditionally used (Alazzi, 2008; Cai, 2008; Flood & Langer, 1994).

A reader-response-based method of teaching literature is a fundamental shift from the viewpoint that literary interpretation is a right–wrong entity to a view that perceives literary interpretation as a transaction between the reader and the text. Four basic assumptions underlie a response-based approach:

1. Literary meaning is a "transaction" between the reader and the text.
2. The meaning of literature is not contained in a static text.
3. Readers comprehend differently because every reader is unique.
4. Readers' personal responses to text are a critical element in meaning making.

In arguing for a shift to a reader response approach to the teaching of literature, which is essentially a constructivist process approach, Blau (1994) argued that such a change will take tremendous support because of the powerful and lasting effects of New Criticism on teaching and learning theory. In New Criticism theory, it is argued that meaning resides principally in the text, and students must be taught a great deal *about* literature before they can appropriately interpret a text. In advocating a reader response methodology, researchers are essentially arguing for a fundamental change in thinking and in teaching. Educators are being asked to alter their belief that each text has one, true accurate meaning to accepting what Rosenblatt (1982) and others (e.g., Commeyras & Sumner, 1998; Garber, 1999; Sipe, 1998) called transaction, or interrogation between text and reader.

Reader response methodology is not a new phenomenon; it has its roots in the work of Richards (1929) who believed that reader response was the only powerful route to literature teaching because readers are unique and their responses will always be individualistic, unique, and idiosyncratic. He believed in a process that allowed readers to interpret any way they want (provided that their responses adhere to principles of logical thought). Reader response has been investigated in many areas and it has been found to be affected by age, ability level, sex, and type of text that is read (Harkin, 2005; Laframboise & Griffith, 1998; Sipe, 1997; Spiegel, 1998; Totten, 1998).

For example, in Applebee's (1978) seminal study, he found that children at Piaget's preoperational stage (2 to 6 years of age) displayed step-by-step retellings; at the concrete stage (6 to 11 years of age) children used summarizations; at the formal stage, Level I (1 to 15 years of age), children displayed empathy in their responses and at Level II (16 years of age to adulthood) students were able to make generalizations.

The results of these studies taken collectively argue for the effectiveness of a response-based approach, but the researchers associated with these studies caution that there are factors that will impinge upon the effectiveness of the approach at various age levels, with various students and with various types of texts.

Reciprocal Teaching. Palincsar and Brown (1985) and Palincsar (1982, 1984, 1986) have developed a paradigm that has been effective for developing constructivist, process-oriented reading comprehension abilities. In their methodology, students and teachers take turns assuming the role of the teacher through a structured dialogue. The teacher models four distinct comprehension strategies and the students have opportunities to practice these strategies. Students are asked to (a) summarize the paragraph that was read in a simple sentence, (b) generate a question about the paragraph that was read to ask a fellow student, (c) ask for clarity (or resolution) of anything in the text that was unclear, and (d) make a prediction about what will happen next in the text. In their studies, students were shown how to do this by teacher modeling; adult support was withdrawn gradually as students exhibited their ability to perform the task independently.

Palincsar and Brown's (1985) original formulation was based on Vygotsky's (1978) notions about the zone of proximal development, which he described as "the distance between the actual developmental level as determined by independent problem solving and the level of potential development as determined through problem solving under adult guidance or in collaboration with more capable peers" (p. 117).

The foundation of reciprocal teaching rests on the premise that children can be taught to internalize rules for comprehending over a period of time through the gradual removal of supportive scaffolds (Alfassi, 1998; Klinger & Vaughn, 1996). This notion rests on the assumption that scaffolds are adjustable as well as temporary and that learning is a natural interactive process because it occurs in social contexts (King & Parent-Johnson, 1999; Myers, 2005). It is highly dependent upon discussions between students and teachers and relies on an interactive model as readers learn new information (Carter, 1997; Dermody & Speaker, 1999).

Gradual Release of Responsibility. A major movement in comprehension instruction is an instructional organization in which teachers intentionally develop student competence known as the gradual release of responsibility. This framework is designed to ensure that students are supported as they assume increased responsibility and that teachers refrain from doing all of the work for students. Or as Duke and Pearson (2002) suggested, teachers have to move from assuming "all the responsibility for performing a task...to a situation in which the students assume all of the responsibility" (p. 211). Research evidence suggests that systematic instruction in comprehension, such as is accomplished in a gradual release of responsibility framework, increases reading comprehension ability for specific texts (Baumann, 1983, 1986; Dole, Brown, & Trathen, 1996; Fisher & Frey, 2007). Successful reading comprehension instruction using this framework includes several stages in which responsibility gradually shifts from the teacher to the students (Fisher & Frey, 2008; Lapp, Fisher, & Wolsey, 2009):

1. *Establishing Purpose.* The teacher uses a structured overview to introduce the students to the task, including the purpose for the lesson. The purpose, or objective, is clearly communicated to the student and is based on the content standards appropriate for the grade level. The teacher assumes the major responsibility for this part of the instruction.
2. *Modeling.* The teacher demonstrates *how* comprehension occurs in his or her mind. Using "I statements" the teacher provides students with access to expert thinking in a brief lesson designed to highlight specific processes readers use to make sense of the text (Duffy, 2009; Fisher, Frey, & Lapp, 2008). The teacher again assumes the greatest responsibility for this part of the lesson.
3. *Guided Instruction.* The students attempt to follow the model provided by the teacher and are guided in this as the teacher uses cues, prompts, and questions to shift the cognitive work to the learner. Feedback and conferencing are an integral part of this step as students try on the procedures they have experienced during modeling. Students and teachers share the responsibility during this stage.
4. *Productive Group Work.* While some students are engaged in guided instruction with the teacher, the rest of the class works productively in small groups. As they do so, they consolidate their understanding and receive peer support to accomplish their tasks. The key to productive group work lies in the individual accountability students have as a component of the task (Frey, Fisher, & Everlove, 2009).
5. *Independent Practice.* The student practices independently with "novel" materials. The student accepts the major share of the responsibility for this part of the learning and applies what has been taught. Of course, the teacher is not uninvolved, but rather uses this as an opportunity to check for understanding and plan next steps instruction.

Conclusion The story of reading comprehension instruction has moved from a period of no awareness of the importance of instruction to a period of emphasis on the subskills that were thought to be the underpinnings of comprehension (Davis, 1944) to the present that views comprehension as a gradual, emerging process in which the reader constructs meaning through a transaction with the text.

Naturally, there are many unanswered questions and many questions unframed and unasked. Thankfully, the current climate in education argues well for continued research in comprehension because most educators agree that the fundamental purpose for reading instruction is to help develop lifelong, independent readers who understand, and can act on, what they've read.

References

Afflerbach, P., Pearson, P. D., & Paris, S. (2008). Clarifying differences between reading skills and reading strategies. *The Reading Teacher, 61,* 364–373.

Alazzi, K. (2008). Teacher candidates' emerging perceptions of reader response theory. *Essays in Education, 22,* 132–142.

Alfassi, M. (1998). Reading for meaning: The efficacy of reciprocal teaching in fostering reading comprehension in high school students in remedial reading classes. *American Educational Research Journal, 35,* 309–332.

Anderson, V., & Roit, M. (1996). Linking reading comprehension instruction to language development for language-minority students. *Elementary School Journal, 96,* 295–309.

Applebee, A. N. (1978). *The child's concept of story: Ages 2 to 17.* Chicago: University of Chicago Press.

Baumann, J. F. (1983). A generic comprehension instruction strategy. *Reading World, 22,* 284–294.

Baumann, J. F. (1986). Teaching third grade students to comprehend anaphoric relationships. The application of a direct instruction model. *Reading Research Quarterly, 21,* 70–90.

Blau, S. (1994). Transactions between theory and practice in the teaching of literature. In J. Flood & J. A. Langer (Eds.), *Literature instruction: Practice and policy* (pp. 19–52). New York: Scholastic.

Block, C., Parris, S., Reed, K., Whiteley, C., & Cleveland, M. (2009). Instructional approaches that significantly increase reading comprehension. *Journal of Educational Psychology, 101*(2), 262–281.

Block, C. C., & Pressley, M. (Eds.). (2001). *Comprehension instruction: Research-based best practices.* New York: Guilford.

Cai, M. (2008). Transactional theory and the study of multicultural literature. *Language Arts, 85*(3), 212–220.

Carter, C. J. (1997). Why reciprocal teaching? *Educational Leadership, 54*(6), 64–68.

Commeyras, M., & Sumner, G. (1998). Literature questions children want to discuss: What teachers and students learned in a second grade classroom. *Elementary School Journal, 99,* 129–152.

Coiro, J., Knoebel, M. Lankshear, C., & Leu, D. (2008). *The handbook of research in new literacies.* Mahwah, NJ: Erlbaum.

Davis, F. B. (1944). Fundamental factors of comprehension. *Reading Psychometrika, 9,* 185–197.

Dermody, M. M., & Speaker, R. B., Jr. (1999). Reciprocal strategy training in prediction, clarification, question generating and summarization to improve reading comprehension. *Reading Improvement, 36,* 16–23.

Dole, J. A., Brown, K. J., & Trathen, W. (1996). The effects of strategy instruction on the comprehension performance of at-risk students. *Reading Research Quarterly, 31,* 62–88.

Duffy, G. G. (2009). *Explaining reading: A resource for teaching concepts, skills, and strategies* (2nd ed.) New York: Guilford.

Duke, N. K., & Pearson, P. D. (2002). Effective practices for developing reading comprehension. In A. E. Farstup & S. J. Samuels (Eds.), *What research has to say about reading instruction* (pp. 205–242). Newark, DE: International Reading Association.

Durkin, D. (1978–79). What classroom observations reveal about reading comprehension instruction. *Reading Research Quarterly, XIV*(4), 481–533.

Fisher, D., Brozo, W. G., Frey, N., & Ivey, G. (2007). *50 content area strategies for adolescent literacy.* Upper Saddle River, NJ: Merrill Prentice Hall.

Fisher, D., & Frey, N. (2007). Implementing a schoolwide literacy framework: Improving achievement in an urban elementary school. *The Reading Teacher, 61*, 32–45.

Fisher, D., & Frey, N. (2008). *Better learning through structured teaching: A framework for the gradual release of responsibility.* Alexandria, VA: Association for Supervision and Curriculum Development.

Fisher, D., & Frey, N. (2009). *Background knowledge: The missing piece of the comprehension puzzle.* Portsmouth, NH: Heinemann.

Fisher, D., Frey, N., & Lapp, D. (2008). *In a reading state of mind: Brain research, teacher modeling, and comprehension instruction.* Newark, DE: International Reading Association.

Flavell, J. H. (1992). Cognitive development: Past, present, and future. *Developmental Psychology, 28*, 998–1005.

Flood, J., Heath, S. B., & Lapp, D. (Eds.). (2008). *Handbook of research on teaching literacy through the communicative and visual arts* (Vol. 2). Mahwah, NJ: Erlbaum.

Flood, J., & Langer, J. A. (Eds.). (1994). *Literature instruction: Practice and policy.* New York: Scholastic.

Flood, J., & Lapp, D. (1995). Broadening the lens: Toward an expanded conceptualization of literacy. In K. A. Hinchman, D. J. Leu, & C. K. Kinzer (Eds.), *The Forty-fourth yearbook of the National Reading Conference* (Vol. 44, pp. 1–16). Chicago: National Reading Conference.

Frey, N., Fisher, D., & Everlove, S. (2009). *Productive group work: How to engage students, build teamwork, and promote understanding.* Alexandria, VA: Association for Supervision and Curriculum Development.

Ganske, K., & Fisher, D. (Eds.). (2009). *Comprehension across the curriculum: Perspectives and practices K-12.* New York: Guilford.

Garber, S. (1999). Diamonds of thought: A reflection. *Language Arts, 76*, 401–403.

Gaskins, R. W. (1996). "That's just how it was": The effect of issue related emotional involvement on reading comprehension. *Reading Research Quarterly, 31*, 386–405.

Gillam, S., Fargo, J., & Robertson, K. (2009). Comprehension of Expository Text: Insights Gained From Think-Aloud Data. *American Journal of Speech-Language Pathology, 18*(1), 82–94.

Harkin, P. (2005). The reception of reader-response theory. *College Composition and Communication, 56*(3), 410–425.

Israel, S., & Duffy, G. (2008). (Eds.). *Handbook of research on reading comprehension.* New York: Taylor & Francis.

King, C. M., & Parent-Johnson, L. M. (1999). Constructing meaning via reciprocal teaching. *Reading Research and Instruction, 38*, 169–186.

Klinger, J. K., & Vaughn, S. (1996). Reciprocal teaching of reading comprehension strategies for students with learning disabilities who use English as a second language. *Elementary School Journal, 96*, 275–293.

Laframboise, K. L., & Griffith, P. L. (1998). Literature case studies: Case method and reader response come together in teacher education. *Journal of Adolescent and Adult Literacy, 41*, 364–375.

Lapp, D., & Fisher, D. (Eds.). (2009). *Essential readings on comprehension.* Newark, DE: International Reading Association.

Lapp, D., Fisher, D., & Wolsey, T. D. (2009). *Literacy growth for every child: Differentiating small-group literacy instruction.* New York: Guilford.

Mathews, M. (1966). *Teaching to read: Historically considered.* Chicago: University of Chicago Press.

Myers, P. (2005). The princess storyteller, Clara clarifier, Quincy questioner, and the wizard: Reciprocal teaching adapted for kindergarten students. *The Reading Teacher, 59*(4), 314–324.

Palincsar, A. S. (1982). Improving the reading comprehension of junior high students through the reciprocal teaching of comprehension monitoring strategies. *Dissertation Abstracts International, 43*, 3744A.

Palincsar, A. S. (1984). Reciprocal teaching of comprehension fostering and comprehension monitoring activities. *Cognition and Instruction, 2*, 117–175.

Palincsar, A. S. (1986). The role of dialogue in providing scaffolded instruction. *Educational Psychologist, 21*, 73–98.

Palincsar, A. S., & Brown, A. L. (1985). Reciprocal teaching activities to promote reading with your mind. In E. J. Cooper (Ed.), *Reading, thinking, and concept development: Interactive strategies for the class.* New York: The College Board.

Pressley, M., Wharton-McDonald, R., Hampson, J. M., & Echevarria, M. (1998). The nature of literacy instruction in ten grade 4/5 classrooms in upstate New York. *Scientific Studies of Reading, 2*, 159–191.

Raphael, T. E., & Au, K. H. (2005). QAR: Enhancing comprehension and test taking across grades and content areas. *The Reading Teacher, 59*, 207–221.

Richards, I. A. (1929). *Practical criticism: A study of literary judgment.* New York: Harcourt, Brace & World.

Rosenblatt, L. M. (1938). *The reader, the text, the poem: The transactional theory of the literary work.* Carbondale: Southern Illinois University Press.

Rosenblatt, L. M. (1982). The literary transaction: Evocation and response. *Theory Into Practice, 21*, 268–277.

Sipe, L. R. (1997). Children's literature, literacy, and literary understanding. *Journal of Children's Literature, 23*, 6–19.

Sipe, L. R. (1998). Individual literary response styles of first and second graders. *National Reading Conference Yearbook, 47*, 76–89.

Smith, N. B. (1965). *American reading instruction.* Newark, DE: International Reading Association.

Spiegel, D. L. (1998). Reader response approaches and the growth of readers. *Language Arts, 76*, 41–48.

Snow, C. E. (2002). *Reading for understanding: Toward a research and development program in reading comprehension.* Santa Monica, CA: RAND.

Thorndike, E. L. (1917). Reading as reasoning: A study in mistakes in paragraph reasoning. *Journal of Educational Psychology, 8*, 323–332.

Totten, S. (1998). Using reader-response theory to study poetry about the Holocaust with high school students. *Social Studies, 89*, 30–34.

Vygotsky, L. S. (1978). *Mind and society: The development of higher mental processes.* Cambridge, MA: Harvard University Press.

Wood, K. D., Lapp, D., Flood, J., & Taylor, D. B. (2008). *Guiding readers through text: Strategy guides for new times.* Newark, DE: International Reading Association.

Zwaan, R. (2004). The immersed experiencer: Toward an embodied theory of language comprehension. *The Psychology of Learning and Motivation, 44*, 35–62.

38

Students' Literary Responses

Nancy Roser, Miriam Martínez, and Karen Wood

Research into the reading responses of elementary and secondary students burgeoned in the 1970s, as more formalistic criticism lost favor, and Rosenblatt's (1978) transactional theory of reader response readily meshed with a cognitive-based revisioning of reading comprehension (Marshall, 2000; Pearson,1985). Rapidly, literacy researchers began to ask questions about how and under what circumstances readers constructed their interpretations of text. As the 21st century opened, Galda and Beach (2001) posited that the complex nature of response and new theoretical perspectives had contributed to even more "sophisticated questions about texts, readers, and contexts for response" (p. 64).

Since the publication of the second volume of the *Handbook for Research in Teaching the English Language Arts* in 2003 (in which Louise Rosenblatt contributed the chapter on literary theory), scholars have deliberated whether her transactional theory is comprehensive enough to enfold the sociocultural and critical perspectives that have characterized much inquiry in the last two decades (Cai, 2008; Dressman & Webster, 2001; Probst, 2002; Sumara, 2000). Rosenblatt (2003) contended that hers was a theory of *reading* that made room for each reader's history, circumstances, interpretations, and questions—"the matrix within which any critical approach is selected" (p. 70). Even so, in framing recent work, researchers have increasingly explained their theoretical bases as linking reader response theory with, for example, Vygotsky's (1978) sociocultural theory; Bahktinian (1986) perspectives on the dialogism of literacy events; Bourdieuian (1985) notions of social space, as well as critical perspectives on literacy, discourse, gender, class, and race. Whether a critical approach represents a unique stance or finds a place on an aesthetic-efferent continuum is not at stake here. That is, when a research perspective informs how literary understandings take shape (Van Sluys, Lewison, & Flint, 2006), the study became relevant to this review.

Along with a broadened theoretical lens, since the last edition of this *Handbook* was published researchers have drawn "different academic figurations of reading and interpreting literature" in a greater variety of settings, using a breadth of techniques for collecting and analyzing responses (Enciso, Coats, Jenkins, & Wolf, 2008, p. 220). For example, early research into how readers made sense of literary texts relied almost exclusively on writing or on interrupted readings to gain insight from informants (e.g., Purves & Rippere, 1968; Squire, 1964). In the years that followed, investigations turned to the naturally occurring talk of read-alouds, literature circles, and discussions, as well as readers' dramatic, and artistic representations of meanings (Adomat, 2007; Rowe, 1998; Sipe, 2008b; Whitin, 1996). Building from Hickman's (1981) pioneering work in elementary classrooms, investigators have frequently become observers or participant-observers (often teaming with the classroom teacher as co-inquirers) toward understanding the complexities of teacher moves and student responses to text invitations. Ethnographic techniques and inductive analyses, (e.g., McGinley & Kamberelis, 1996; Sipe, 2008a) have been more prevalent than empirical studies (e.g., Bobola, 2003). Further, recent shifts have involved researchers in collecting and analyzing students' responses gathered from new technologies, such as online book discussions, digital response journals, weblogs, wikis, and more (Larson, 2008; Love, 2002; Scharber, 2009; West, 2008).

Although there have been changes in both scope and approach to research into literary meaning making, we have chosen a traditional framework to organize this review—one that presents studies as primarily focused on the reader, on the text, or on the context—a frame through which we (Martinez & Roser, 1991, 2003), and others (e.g., Galda, Ash, & Cullinan, 2000; Marshall, 2000) have approached earlier syntheses. Although most inquiries cross these factors, we have nonetheless attempted to array studies to illustrate dominant themes, mindful of the interplay among reader, text, and context.

Reader-Centered Responses

Using a Literary Response Questionnaire, Dutch researchers (van Schootoen, Oostdam, & de Glopper, 2001) determined that grade, gender, education, vocabulary size, reading behavior, and cultural level of the home were among the best predictors of 600 upper grade students' literary response scores. More typically, however, researchers have used close lenses to describe the ways in which small groups or individual readers approach and interpret literary texts (e.g., Thein, 2009). In this section, we highlight selected studies that considered the influences of age, gender, and diversity on meaning making.

Young Children In a series of studies, Sipe (e.g., 2000, 2008a) investigated kindergarten through second grade children's discussions of texts read aloud in classrooms. Arguing from a Vygotskian perspective on the centrality of children's language use in social settings to their cognitive development, Sipe proposed a conceptual categorization system to describe children's responses to picturebooks as being primarily (a) analytical, (b) intertextual, (c) personal, (d) transparent, or (e) performative. The analytic category broadly subsumes children's talk of text structures and meanings, format features, narrative elements, references to the book as a crafted object, and more. The intertextual category collects conversational turns that relate the focus of the picturebook to other texts and products. Personal responses are those in which the children connect their own experiences to or from the text. Transparent responses are those in which children position themselves inside the narrative such that the story and the child's life merge. Finally, Sipe describes performative responses as those in which children use (or even subvert) the text as a platform for their own spontaneous playfulness. In his grounded theory of children's literary understanding, Sipe demonstrates the power of text to draw in young readers such that the barrier between story and life becomes permeable. Read-aloud time is construed as a space in which children thoughtfully and playfully receive, construct, elaborate, enact, and manipulate text toward greater literary understanding. For comprehensive reviews of young children's literary meaning making, see Sipe (2008b) and Martinez, Roser, & Dooley (2003).

Middle Elementary Through Adolescent Readers In their pioneering study of literature discussion in fifth grade, Eeds and Wells (1989) described features of the "grand conversation" that became possible when students (and teachers) worked together to construct and articulate meanings. Following their lead, other researchers have produced purposeful inspections of the ways in which readers collaborate to build defensible interpretations of text. In a year-long study of fifth-graders' perceptions of their own discussion groups, Evans (2002) found that students held clear notions of factors that contributed to effective student-led literature discussions. These included the gender make-up

of the group, respectful discussants, absence of a bossy group member, and a good text (with "good" defined as exciting, adventurous, or discussion-worthy). In a related inquiry, Almasi and O'Flahavan (2000) found that fourth-grade proficient peer discussions were marked by returns to prior topics, ability to sustain topics, and linkages compared to less proficient groups. Recent studies of middle grade and adolescent learners have led through literature to explorations of issues of identity, of personal and cultural connections, and the possibilities of one's own life (e.g., Broughton, 2002; Smith, 2005; Thein, 2005).

There is evidence that middle grade readers respond more positively and fully to literature that reflects their own cultural experiences (Brooks, 2006; Hicks, 2004). Dressel (2005) investigated the responses of middle school, dominant culture students to multicultural novels. In their dialogue journals, these students were able to "feel what it was like to be part of a non-dominant group" (p. 756); however, in post surveys, many of the students did not appear to recognize that characters from non-dominant cultures faced societal limitations. In a semester-long study, Beach, Thein, and Parks (2007) examined shifts in high school students' literary responses as they explored multicultural literature from a critical literacy perspective relating to issues of race, class, and gender. These researchers, along with many others (Alsup, 2003; Athanases, 1998; Bean & Rigoni, 2001; Knickerbocker & Rycik, 2006; Wood, Soares, & Watson, 2006), build a case for instructional methods that encourage students' discoveries that help to assault stereotypes, to remain open to diversity, and to take up text from multiple perspectives.

English Language Learners Drawing on findings from a second-grade bilingual classroom, Martinez-Roldán (2003) argued that the sharing of personal stories in literature circles may be especially important for readers from non-dominant cultures, enabling them to draw on their funds of knowledge in responding to literature. DeNicolo and Franquiz (2006) found that fourth-grade children in a bilingual classroom used time in literature circle to consider multiple perspectives and to think critically about the imprint of racism revealed through multicultural children's literature. Following a 2-year longitudinal study of adult/child story reading in the home of one Chinese American girl between the ages of 2 and 4, Wan (2000) concluded that such studies are critical for the understanding of children who are racially, linguistically, and culturally different from their teachers.

Gendered Readings Researchers have also inspected how reading particular texts serve to reveal and disrupt entrenched gender roles held by boy and girl readers. Dutro (2003) asked fifth-grade American boys to read a novel they had previously rejected as "for girls," arguing that boys must be encouraged to adopt a masculinity that is less oppositional to femininity. In a study of sixth-grade boys and girls reading a folktale containing both traditional and non-traditional gender roles, Rice (2000) uncovered traditional frames of references held by both boys and girls. Even so, girls registered more statements that reflected non-traditional female characteristics. Similarly, when investigators compared the responses of two groups of fourth graders across a span of 22 years to the picturebook, *William's Doll* (Zolotow, 1972), they found children separated by a generation held the same stereotypes for "appropriate" male toys. Girls, however, were more likely than boys to have favorable responses to a male character's desire for a doll (Greever, Austin, & Welhousen, 2000). In a study of home-schooled middle grade boys, Young (2000) showed how critical literacy activities (and participation in critical literacy discussions) sustained or disrupted the boys' awareness of gender inequities in their self-selected texts.

Race Other studies have described the effects of literature as launching points from which individuals analyze their own life experiences and ways of being positioned in the world by race. Often, gender and race conflate within inquiries. Sutherland (2005) highlighted the meaning making of 16-year-old Black girls reading *The Bluest Eye* (Morrison, 1994). She described how participants represented and co-constructed identities, as well as refuting the attempts of others to place limits on their lives. Similarly Brooks, Browne, and Hampton (2008) looked through participants' responses to what those responses suggested about readers' identification with a fictional hero whose status has been marked by peers based on skin color, clothes, and certain physical traits. In a study of first-grade children's responses to an African American version of *'Twas the Night Before Christmas* (Rosales, 1996), researchers described how a Black Santa character opened to conversation about race in the classroom (Copenhaver-Johnson, Bowman, & Johnson, 2007).

The composite reader emerging from these studies is one engaged, critically aware, and actively involved in identifying, analyzing, questioning, connecting with, and resisting a more diverse literature than ever before. The now extensive body of research on reader response suggests that readers become more thoughtful in the presence of particular texts and illustrations. The literature also suggests readers may cling to entrenched ways of responding even in the presence of texts that invite a critical stance.

Text-Centered Studies

Lewis (2000) has argued for engaging with literary texts in ways that meld "the personal, pleasurable, and critical in aesthetic response" (p. 257). Today's texts that invite the melding are written, oral, signed, digital, graphic, and enacted. Further, as mentioned above, there has been growing interest in texts described as critical literature—"risky" texts that can help to surface discussions of attitudes, assumptions, and beliefs. In classrooms researchers continued to examine the influence of particular genres on response, as well as respondents' awareness of the artistry of texts.

Genre Knowledge Elster and Hanauer (2002) found elementary aged children gave more attention to features of craft and genre during discussions of poetry than during discussion stories, adding evidence that children talk differently about different kinds of texts. Shine and Roser (1999) noted preschoolers assumed different stances and shared different kinds of responses to four literary genres—fantasy, realistic fiction, narrative nonfiction, and poetic narrative—underscoring an early sensitivity to text forms. Deep knowledge of a literary genre and its demands can be linked with exposure. That is, typically students spend more time with narrative structures than non-narrative, helping to explain why they may be less facile with the expository texts that dominate later schooling (Donovan & Smolkin, 2002; Yopp & Yopp, 2006). When students approach text genres (whether to read or write), their comfort may also be linked with their opportunities to explore and features of genre that can signal readers to adopt particular stances (Galda & Liang, 2003; Kamberelis, 1999; Maloch, 2008).

In a study of middle schoolers' responses to particular text features in culturally conscious African American children's books, Brooks (2006) found that students not only identified the text features, but actively used those features to develop literary understandings. Brooks's work suggests that culturally influenced textual features also have potential as pedagogical tools. Sipe (2000) argues that children's developing literary understandings are served by the intertextual connections they make. That is, intertextual connections help readers interpret language, narrative elements, and symbolic aspects of stories; and by comparing and contrasting stories, readers are able to make generalizations about story structure and genre.

Literary Understandings of Texts Literary readings require more than awareness of literary elements and story structures. Responsive readers, according to Nodelman and Reimer (2003) deploy knowledge of elements into a repertoire of strategies for responding to texts—strategies that include reading for character, experiencing plot, and exploring thematic structures. When researchers (Martinez, Keehn, Roser, Harmon, & O'Neal, 2002) read the same short story to nearly 300 students aged 6 to 14, the students revealed different understandings of character in their follow-up conversations. Overall, younger readers talked more extensively about external facets of character, describing a character's age, gender, or skin color. By contrast, older students rarely described characters' external attributes; rather, they talked about character traits, feelings, or the ways in which the character changed.

Young children demonstrate keen awareness of the crafting of the visual elements in both picture storybooks (Sipe, 2008b; Styles & Arizpe, 2001) and informational books (Maduram, 2000; Tower, 2002). In groundbreaking work, Sipe and Brightman (2009) inspected children's interpretations of the intervening action and events between page turns in a picturebook. Investigating young children's meaning making in postmodern picturebooks, Pantaleo (2002,

2004) found children actively collaborate to interpret these stories and attend, in particular, to the metafictive devices that distinguish postmodern picturebooks. Similarly, Mc-Clay (2000) found elementary students shared observations, extended one another's interpretations, and drew on their knowledge of other media in their collaborative reading of a postmodern picturebook.

Newer Text Forms Researchers have only begun to explore readers' responses within newer media. Online book clubs and literature discussions have been receiving much attention in professional journals, but systematic studies are fewer. For example, Larson (2008) introduces the electronic reading workshop (ERW) as a means of promoting online responses to literature discussion groups. Teachers have also invited video compositions, online book discussions, and Powerpoint interpretations of poetry as means of encouraging students' literate, cognitive, and social practices with new media, as well as preparing students for the multimodality of everyday life (Moje, 2009; Scharber, 2009).

Although print-based texts have had the longer run in garnering students' responses, newer media show the promise of providing different ways to understand. Popular texts (not just traditional literary ones) are also serving students' literate and composing lives (Dyson, 1997; Wohlwend, 2009).

The Context

Context—so widely and variantly defined (Rex, Green, Dixon, & the Santa Barbara Classroom Discourse Group, 1998)—has a potent impact on literary response. Beach (2000) nominated the social contexts of meaning construction (whether book club, computer chat, or classroom) as one of the primary contributions of Rosenblatt's transactional model of reader response. Even so, Beach contended that Rosenblatt's conception of context "needs more specificity regarding the various components shaping responding as a social event" (p. 238). In this section, we highlight studies in which context refers to the interacting influences of place, community, activity, purposes, discourses, practices, and conditions that support readers meeting and making sense of texts (Lewis, 2001).

Time/Space Möller and Allen (2000) describe the collective "response development zone" (p. 149) that emerged as an adult mentor and four fifth graders read Mildred Taylor's (1987) *The Friendship*, a story based on actual events in the deep south of the 1930s. The researchers contend the response development zone provides the time, the space, the guidance, and the dialectic that enable both connection and resistance to well-chosen texts with powerful central issues, such as racism. In their discussion, the four girls, described as struggling readers, used the provided time and support to understand characters and actions, to broaden their lens to the story's setting and tensions, to make deep connections that awakened present-day fears, and to lift the issues with

parents—in search of safer places. Both their "engaged connecting" and the "engaged resistance" were performed from places inside the story as they came together over a 2-week period to sort out their understandings. Arguing that the taking up of such texts entails risks and the opening to uncomfortable, resistant feelings, the authors point toward the necessity for a context for the conversations, support, and writing that such books and learners require.

Teacher Moves Researchers have also looked closely at the ways in which teachers' strategies and pedagogies shape and support literary meaning making, e.g., as teachers join a teen book club (Lapp & Fisher, 2009), or help children work out the vagaries of a text form (Evertson, 2004). At times, teachers support the reading experience by helping students build layers of meaning, as for example when a high school teacher uses simulation, lecture, poster analysis, and film to help students understand the context of a Chinese novella (Louie, 2005); or when a teacher introduces a mediator such as "body biographies"—life-sized human outlines to be filled with words, images, and phrases—to represent the character Laertes in Shakespeare's *Hamlet* (Smagorinsky & O'Donnell-Allen, 1998).

Others have investigated the nature of discussions in which teachers stretch and scaffold students' thought and talk. In describing the role of a primary-grade teacher whose children participated in rich discussion of information texts, Maloch (2008) found the teacher provided multiple opportunities to engage with information text, assurance of the text-child match, scaffolded meaning making, and explicit help with text features. Many (2002) also noted the nature of instructional scaffolding in conversations between teachers and students as they constructed meaning from literary and nonfiction texts. She presented her findings as "verbal tapestries" that provide images of the ways scaffolding weaves in and though the conversations.

At times, teachers work to make particular text forms more comprehensible and engaging. For example, Maloch and her colleagues (2008) studied third-grade children and their teachers as they read, thought about, discussed, and wrote fantasies during a six-week genre study unit. By exploring the classroom talk that surrounded the features and forms of fantasy, the researchers proposed three discursive moves that the teachers made to support students' understandings. The teachers (a) evoked and reframed shared experiences with texts, (b) revoiced students' contributions as a way of focusing and deepening insights, and (c) strengthened familiarity with a literary genre by nudging student talk between abstractions and specifics (and back again). In a study of how one first-grade teacher helped children navigate their first experience with a chapter book, Roser, Martinez, Fuhrken, and McDonnold (2007) described how she helped the children focus on character (traits, intentions, needs, and behaviors) as a way to both engage with the text and untangle the plot. Children were encouraged to enact, connect, link, revisit, write, draw, and puzzle out meanings together.

Conclusion

In the literature of response, the past decade has presented more attention to the diversity of readers; more and more critical types of texts to respond to (information text, graphic novels, multi-modal texts, and even picturebooks that break the mold); and more purposes, tool, activity, and outlets for response. With an eye to the diverse ways in which researchers work to make sense of disciplines and theories, we can point both to "the continuities in our practices" as well as "the edges and intersections" that could stretch our scholarship and open new conversations (Enciso et al., 2008, p. 220). When Galda and Beach (2001) examined research at the beginning of the decade, they pointed toward shifts in readers' interrogation of texts for the authenticity of the social norms they portray, in reader responses situated in social practices, and of teachers' influence on response within communities of social practice. Their review advocated the further blurring of boundaries among reader, text, and context, and they reminded researchers intent on describing changes in students' abilities to respond of the need to understand how "students acquire interpretive and social practices over time through participation in particular types of communities" (p. 67). The researchers represented in this review appear to have heard and heeded.

References

Adomat, D. S. (2007). Through characters' eyes: How drama helps young readers understand stories from the "inside out." In D. W. Rowe, R. Jimenez, D. Compton, D. Dickinson, Y. Kim, K. Leander, et al. (Eds.), *56th yearbook of the National Reading Conference* (pp. 68–80). Oak Creek, WI: National Reading Conference.

Almasi, J., & O'Flahavan, J. (2000). A comparative analysis of student and teacher deveopment in more and less proficient discussions of literature. *Reading Research Quarterly, 36*(2), 96–120.

Alsup, J. (2003). Politicizing young adult literature: Reading Anderson's "Speak" as a critical text. *Journal of Adolescent and Adult Literacy, 47*(2), 158–166.

Athanases, S. Z. (1998). Diverse learners, diverse texts: Exploring identity and difference through literary encounters. *Journal of Literacy Research, 30*(2), 273–296.

Bakhtin, M. M. (1986). *Speech genres and other late essays.* Austin: University of Texas Press.

Beach, R. (2000). Critical issues: Reading and responding to literature at the level of activity. *Journal of Literacy Research, 32*, 237–251.

Beach, R., Haertling Thein, A., & Parks, D. (2007). *High schools students' competing social worlds: Negotiating identities and allegiances in response to multicultural literature.* New York: Routledge.

Bean, T. W., & Rigoni, N. (2001). Exploring the intergenerational dialogue journal discussion of a multicultural young adult novel. *Reading Research Quarterly, 36*(3), 232–248.

Bobola, K. (2003). Children's minds at work. In C. Fairbanks, J. Worthy, B. Maloch, J. Hoffman, & D. Shallert (Eds.), *52nd yearbook of the National Reading Conference* (pp. 66–84). Oak Creek, WI: National Reading Conference.

Bourdieu, P. (1985). The social space and the genesis of groups. *Theory and Society, 14*(6), 723–744.

Brooks, W. (2006). Reading representations of themselves: Urban youth use culture and African American textual features to develop literary understandings. *Reading Research Quarterly, 41*(3), 372–392.

Brooks, W., Browne, S., & Hampton, G. (2008). "There ain't no accounting for what folks see in their own mirrors": Considering colorism within a Sharon Flake narrative. *Journal of Adolescent and Adult Literacy, 51*(8), 660–669.

Broughton, M. A. (2002). The performance and construction of subjectivities of early adolescent girls in book club discussion groups. *Journal of Literacy Research, 34*(1), 1–38.

Cai, M. (2008). Transactional theory and the study of multicultural literature. *Language Arts, 85*(3), 212–220.

Copenhaver-Johnson, J., Bowman, J., & Johnson, A. (2007). Santa stories: children's inquiry about race during picturebook read-alouds. *Language Arts, 84* (3), 234–244.

DeNicolo, C. P., & Franquiz, M. E. (2006). "Do I have to say it?": Critical encounters with multicultural children's literature. *Language Arts, 84*(2), 157–170.

Donovan, C. A., & Smolkin, L. B. (2002). Children's genre knowledge: an examination of K-5 students' performance on multiple tasks providing differing levels of scaffolding. *Reading Research Quarterly, 37*(4), 428–465.

Dressel, J. H. (2005). Personal response and social responsibility: Responses of middle school students to multicultural literature. *The Reading Teacher, 58*(8), 750–764.

Dressman, M., & Webster, J. (2001). Description, prescription, or cultural reproduction? Rosenblattian criticism in reader-response research and teaching. In J. Hoffman, E. Schallert, C. Fairbanks, J. Worthy, & B. Maloch (Eds.), *50th yearbook of the National Reading Conference* (pp. 164–177). Chicago: National Reading Conference.

Dutro, E. (2003). "Us boys like to read football and boy stuff: Reading masculinities, performing boyhood." *Journal of Literacy Research, 34*(4), 465–500.

Dyson, A. H. (1997). *Writing superheroes: Contemporary childhood, popular culture, and classroom literacy.* New York: Teachers College Press.

Eeds, M., & Wells, D. (1989). Grand conversations: An exploration of meaning construction in literature study groups. *Research in the Teaching of English, 23*(1), 4–29.

Elster, C. A., & Hanauer, D. I. (2002). Voicing texts, voices around texts: Reading poems in elementary school classrooms. *Research in the Teaching of English, 37*(1), 89–134.

Enciso, P., Coats, K., Jenkins, C., & Wolf, S. (2008). The Watsons go the NRC—2007: Crossing academic boundaries in the study of children's literature. In Y. Kim, V. Risko, D. Compton, D. Dickinson, M. Hundley, & R. Jimenez (Eds.), *57th yearbook of the National Reading Conference* (pp. 219–230). Oak Creek, WI: National Reading Conference.

Evans, K. S. (2002). Fifth grade students' perceptions of how they experience literature discussion groups. *Reading Research Quarterly, 37*(1), 46–69.

Evertson, J. W. (2004). Figuring out *mystery:* Young children's constructions of genre knowledge. *Language Arts, 81*(6), 491–501.

Galda, L., Ash, G. E., & Cullinan, B. E. (2000). Children's literature. In M. L. Kamil, P. B. Mosenthal, P. D. Pearson, & R. Barr (Eds.), *Handbook of reading research,* (Vol. 3, pp. 361–379). Mahwah, NJ: Erlbaum.

Galda, L., & Beach, R. (2001). Theory into practice: Response to literature as a cultural activity. *Reading Research Quarterly, 36*(1), 64–73.

Galda, L., & Liang, L. A. (2003). Literature as experience or looking for facts: Stance in the classroom. *Reading Research Quarterly, 38*(2), 268–275.

Greever, E. A., Austin, P., & Welhousen, K. (2000). *William's Doll* revisited. *Language Arts, 77*(4), 324–330.

Hickman, J. (1981). A new perspective on response to literature: Research in an elementary school setting. *Research in the Teaching of English, 15*(4), 343–354.

Hicks, D. (2004). Back to Oz? Rethinking the literary in a critical study of reading. *Research in the Teaching of English, 39*(1), 63–84.

Kamberelis, G. (1999). Genre development and learning: Children writing stories, science reports, and poems. *Research in the Teaching of English, 33*(4), 403–460.

Knickerbocker, J. L., & Rycik, J. (2006). Re-examining literature study in the middle grades: A critical response framework. *American Secondary Education, 34*(3), 43–56.

Lapp, D., & Fisher, D. (2009). Motivating teens to read. *Journal of Adolescent and Adult Literacy, 52*(7), 556–561.

Larson, L. C. (2008). Electronic reading workshop: Beyond books with new literacies and instructional technologies. *Journal of Adolescent and Adult Literacy, 52*(2), 121–131.

Lewis, C. (2000). Critical issues: Limits of identification: The personal, pleasurable, and critical in reader response. *Journal of Literacy Research, 32*(2), 253–266.

Lewis, C. (2001). *Literary practices as social acts: Power, status and cultural norms in the classroom.* Mahwah, NJ: Erlbaum.

Louie, B. (2005). Development of empathetic responses with multicultural literature. *Journal of Adolescent and Adult Literacy, 48*, 566–578.

Love, K. (2002). Mapping online discussion in senior English. *Journal of Adolescent and Adult Literacy, 45*(5), 382–396.

Maduram, I. (2000). "Playing possum": A young child's responses to information books. *Language Arts, 77*(5), 391–397

Maloch, B. (2008). Beyond exposure: The uses of information texts in a second grade classroom. *Research in the Teaching of English, 42*(3), 315–362.

Maloch, B., Roser, N., Martinez, M., Harmon, J., Burke, A., Duncan, D., et al. (2008). An investigation of learning to read and write fantasy. In Y. Kim, V. Risko, D. Compton, D. Dickinson, M. Hundley, & R. Jimenez (Eds.), *57th yearbook of the National Reading Conference* (pp. 256–270). Oak Creek, WI: National Reading Conference.

Many, J. E. (2002). An exhibition and analysis of verbal tapestries: Understanding how scaffolding is woven into the fabric of instructional conversations. *Reading Research Quarterly, 37*(4), 376–407.

Marshall, J. (2000). Research on response to literature. In M. L. Kamil, P. B. Mosenthal, P. D. Pearson, & R. Barr (Eds.), *Handbook of reading research* (Vol. 3, pp. 381–402) Mahwah, NJ: Erlbaum.

Martinez, M., Keehn, S., Roser, N., Harmon, J., & O'Neal, S. (2002). An exploration of children's understanding of character in grades 1–8. In D. Schallert, C. Fairbanks, J. Worthy, B. Malloch, & J. Hoffman (Eds.), *51st yearbook of the National Reading Conference* (pp. 310–320). Oak Creek, WI: National Reading Conference.

Martinez, M. G. & Roser, N. L. (1991). Children's responses to literature. In J. Flood, J. M. Jensen, D. Lapp, & J. R. Squire (Eds.), *Handbook of research on teaching the English language arts* (pp. 643–654). New York: Macmillan.

Martinez, M. G., & Roser, N. L. (2003). Children's responses to literature. In J. Flood, J. M. Jensen, D. Lapp, & J. R. Squire (Eds.), *Handbook of research on teaching the English language arts* (2nd ed., pp. 799–813). Hillsdale, NJ: Erlbaum.

Martinez, M. G., Roser, N. L., & Dooley, C. (2003). Young children's literary meaning making. In N. Hall, J. Larson, & J. Marsh (Eds.), *Handbook of early childhood literacy* (pp. 222–234). London: Sage.

Martinez-Roldán, C. (2003). Building worlds and identities: A case study of the role of narratives in bilingual literature discussion. *Research in the Teaching of English, 37*(4), 494–526.

McClay, J. K. (2000). "Wait a second…": Negotiating complex narratives in *Black and White. Children's Literature in Education, 31*(2), 91–106.

McGinley, W., & Kamberelis, G. (1996). *Maniac Magee* and *Ragtime Tumpie*: Children negotiating self and world through reading and writing. *Research in the Teaching of English, 30*(1), 75–113.

Moje, E. (2009). A call for new research on new and multi-literacies. *Research in the Teaching of English, 43*(4), 348–362.

Möller, K., & Allen, J. (2000). Connecting, resisting, and searching for safer places: Students respond to Mildred Taylor's *The Friendship. Journal of Literacy Research, 32*(2), 145–186.

Morrison, T. (1994). *The bluest eye.* New York: Knopf.

Nodelman, P., & Reimer, M. (2003). *The pleasures of children's literature* (3rd ed.). Boston: Allyn & Bacon.

Pantaleo, S. (2002). Grade 1 students meet David Wiesner's *three pigs. Journal of Children's Literature, 28*(2), 72–84.

Pantaleo, S. (2004). Young children interpret the metafictive in Anthony Browne's *voices in the park. Journal of Early Childhood Literacy, 4*(2), 211–233.

Pearson, P. D. (1985). Changing the face of reading comprehension instruction. *The Reading Teacher, 38*(8), 724–738.

Probst, R. E. (2002). Response to "reader response in perspective." *Journal of Children's Literature, 28*(1), 31.

Purves, A., & Rippere, V. (1968). *Elements of writing about a literary work: A study of response to literature.* Urbana, IL: National Council of Teachers of English.

Rex, L., Green, J., Dixon, C., & the Santa Barbara Classroom Discourse Group. (1998). What counts when context counts? The uncommon "common" language of literacy research. *Journal of Literacy Research, 30*(3), 405–433.

Rice, P. S. (2000). Gendered readings of a traditional "feminist" folktale by sixth-grade boys and girls. *Journal of Literacy Research, 32*(2), 211–236.

Rosales, M. (1996). *'Twas the night b'fore Christmas.* New York: Scholastic.

Rosenblatt, L. M. (1978). *The reader, the text, the poem: The transactional theory of the literary work.* Carbondale: Southern Illinois University Press.

Rosenblatt, L. M. (2003). Literary theory. In J. Flood, D. Lapp, J. R. Squire, & J. M. Jensen (Eds.), *Handbook of research on teaching the English language arts* (2nd ed., pp. 67–73). Mahwah, NJ: Erlbaum.

Roser, N., Martinez, M., Fuhrken, C., & McDonnold, K. (2007). Characters as guides to meaning. *The Reading Teacher, 60*(6), 548–559.

Rowe, D. (1998). The literate potentials of book-related dramatic play. *Reading Research Quarterly, 33*(1), 10–35.

Scharber, C. (2009). Online book clubs: Bridges between old and new literacies. *Journal of Adolescent and Adult Literacy, 52*(5), 433–437.

Shine, S., & Roser, N. (1999). The role of genre in preschoolers' response to picture books. *Research in the Teaching of English, 34*(2), 197–254.

Sipe, L. R. (2000). The construction of literary understanding by first and second graders in oral response to picture storybook read alouds. *Reading Research Quarterly, 35*(2), 252–275.

Sipe, L. R. (2008a). *Storytime: Young children's literary understanding in the classroom.* New York: Teachers College Press.

Sipe, L. R. (2008b). Young children's visual meaning making in response to picturebooks. In J. Flood, S. B. Heath, & D. Lapp (Eds.), *Handbook on teaching literacy through the communicative and visual arts* (Vol. 2, pp. 381–392). New York: Erlbaum.

Sipe, L. R., & Brightman, A. E. (2009). Young children's interpretations of page breaks in contemporary picture storybooks. *Journal of Literacy Research, 41*(1), 68–103.

Smagorinsky, P., & O'Donnell-Allen, C. (1998). Reading as mediated and mediating action: Composing meaning for literature through multimedia interpretive texts. *Reading Research Quarterly, 33*(2), 198–226.

Smith, S. (2005). "We feel like we're separating us": Sixth grade girls respond to multicultural literature. In B. Maloch, . Hoffman, D. Schallert, C. Fairbanks, & J. Worthy (Eds.), *54th yearbook of the National Reading Conference* (pp. 362–375). Oak Creek, WI: National Reading Conference.

Squire, J. R. (1964). *The responses of adolescents while reading four short stories* (NCTE Research Report No. 2). Urbana, IL: National Council of Teachers of English.

Styles, M., & Arizpe, E. (2001). A gorilla with 'Grandpa's eyes': How children interpret visual texts—A case study of Anthony Browne's *Zoo. Children's Literature in Education, 32*(2), 267–281.

Sumara, D. (2000). Critical issues: Researching complexity. *Journal of Literacy Research, 32*(2), 267–281.

Sutherland, L. M. (2005). Black adolescent girls' use of literacy practices to negotiate boundaries of ascribed identity. *Journal of Literacy Research, 37*(3), 365–406.

Taylor, M. (1987). *The friendship.* New York: Dial.

Thein, A. (2009). Identifying the history and logic of negative, ambivalent, and positive responses to literature: A case-study analysis of cultural models. *Journal of Literacy Research, 41*(3), 273–316.

Tower, C. (2002). "It's a snake, you guys!" The power of text characteristics on children's responses to information books. *Research in the Teaching of English, 37*(1), 55–88.

van Schootoen, E., Oostdam, R., & de Glopper, K. (2001). Dimensions and predictors of literary response. *Journal of Literacy Research, 33*(1), 1–32.

Van Sluys, K., Lewison, M., & Flint, A. S. (2006). Researching critical literacy: A critical study of analysis of classroom discourse. *Journal of Literacy Research, 38*(2), 197–233.

Vygotsky, L. (1978). *Mind in society: The development of higher psychological processes.* Cambridge, MA: MIT Press.

Wan, G. (2000). A Chinese girl's storybook experiences at home. *Language Arts, 77*(5), 398–405.

West, K. C. (2008). Weblogs and literary response: Socially situated identities and hybrid social languages in English class blogs. *Journal of Adolescent and Adult Literacy, 51*(7), 588–598.

Whitin, P. (1996). Exploring visual response to literature. *Research in the Teaching of English, 30*(1), 114–140.

Wohlwend, K. (2009). Damsels in discourse: Girls consuming and producing identity texts through Disney princess play. *Reading Research Quarterly, 44*(1), 57–83.

Wood, K. D., Soares, L., & Watson, P. (2006). Empowering adolescents through critical literacy. *Middle School Journal, 37*(3), 53–59.

Yopp, R. H., & Yopp, H. K. (2006). Informational texts as read-alouds at school and home. *Journal of Literacy Research, 38*(1), 37–51.

Young, J. P. (2000). Boy talk: Critical literacy and masculinities. *Reading Research Quarterly, 35*(3), 312–337.

Zolotow, C. (1972). *William's doll.* New York: Harper & Row.

39

K–12 Students as Writers

Research and Practice

Jane Hansen and Brian Kissel

We present this chapter in three sections: *The Processes Writers Use, The Evaluation Processes Writers and Writing Instructors Use*, and *The Processes Writing Instructors Use.* Initially, we present information about the processes writers use in classrooms, homes, and community centers when they are engaged in creating meaning of importance to them. Then we move into evaluation, an ongoing process used by writers and instructors as they review what they have done, are doing, and want to do next; they establish an ongoing evaluation loop driven by their determination to continuously improve. We end with views of instructors immersed in their craft, as they support and stretch the writers they teach.

The Processes Writers Use

What do writers do as they create texts? And how do their processes shift when they engage in online literacy? These questions undergird this section in which we examine *The New Literacies* and *The Processing Demands of Writing.* We see writers in the midst of what are fast becoming the *common literacies.* Then, we present the complicated nature of what writers do when they are in the process of writing, regardless of the task.

The Processes of New Literacies Yancy (2009) challenges the process model of writing as representative of what student writers do in the 21st century—or certainly whether it is applicable as often as it was in the latter decades of the 20th century when it emerged. Currently, what students do when they write is often a one-step process. A quick, first draft is off and read by millions on the Internet within minutes or seconds. And, if the student-writer is putting forth a call to action, action happens, as when one AP student called for, via Facebook, the injection of a particular phrase of humor in the AP exam. Thousands of students complied.

Our younger generation is redefining who we are as literacy creators and users (Leu, 2002; Williams, 2008).

Social networking sites such as Facebook and MySpace permit writers to create their identities and use them to connect to others. When writers create their own social networking page, they make continuous decisions about the identity they want to portray, redefining the notions of audience and voice.

Jacobs (2008) found this to be the case with Lisa, a 15-year-old girl who composed at home using Instant Messaging (IM). In doing so, Lisa adjusted her messages depending upon her audience and purposes. For conversational exchanges with friends, Lisa used abbreviations and alternative spelling patterns, and for more serious exchanges, she carefully modified her language.

In a 2-month study of Rosa, her 6-year-old daughter, Wollman-Bonilla (2003) didn't document differences within digital messages, but she did find differences between digital and print messages. When the study began, Rosa was familiar with creating handwritten letters, and email was new, but she learned the genre features associated with it. Rosa's emails were more telegraphic, and conversational. She largely ignored punctuation and capitalization in them, and learned to use type to express gestures.

The first-grade students of Brennan (Crafton, Brennan, & Silvers, 2007) took email a step farther. Angered by the plight of a homeless woman, the children used digital literacy to raise their voices in support of her, and sent their writings to the local newspaper. They received response and, importantly, the children continued, without prompting by Brennan, to write emails to support the woman's needs. This project marked a change in the writing processes of these children when they used computers. Previously, Brennan gave them programs designed for students, and the children were not in charge of the content. By deciding, on their own, to write about this real issue, the students were in control of the technology rather than being controlled by it.

Wanting to explore her students' 21st-century writing habits Kajder (2007) asked her 10th graders to list the tools they used for writing. They began with pen, paper, computers, and then, one student said, "Weblog." Another turned to Kajder and said, "That's not writing. You asked us for tools we use as writers. That means stuff from in here. That can't be on the list" (p. 150). As the conversation continued, the students listed many new literacies and Kajder was wise enough to change. The teens started to use their tools rather than hers in the classroom, and wrote, in part, via podcasts, wikis, and fan fiction, within the context of global, responsive communities. Importantly, Kajder realized they wanted to write well, and taught them within these new literacies.

Some students frequently immerse themselves in video games, which can be another source of inspiration. Raker (2006) studied an 8-year-old boy named Adrian who used videogames to inspire his writing topics and formats. Adrian developed plots, raising problems and quickly resolving them, only to develop other problems. These plot sequences in video games can parallel plot structures in chapters of narrative texts, but in videogames these sequences are often nonlinear and require the player to determine his/her own fate. This complicated structure worked for Adrian; for him this type of story is the one with which he is most familiar. To consider videogames as mentor texts is an option many students may value.

Zenkov and Harmon (2009) also capitalized on their students' at-home literacies. The authors provided each of their diverse students with a camera, they took pictures for several months and, by mixing media, they documented their answers to these questions: What are the purposes of school? What helps me succeed in school? What gets in the way of my school success? Importantly, the students shared their creations with younger members of the community; they felt a responsibility to provide guidance to the youth. And they shared with their elders to show their appreciation to those who had inspired them.

Digital writing in which students express controversial views can raise concerns, however (Witte, 2007). Cassandra, a middle school student of Witte wrote essays and poems on a blog and when Witte asked about this Cassandra replied, "That's online writing, not boring school writing." Witte decided to blend blogging with school writing. Her students responded to novels via a blog and other students provided comments, but district administrators asked her to cease the project because of their concerns about privacy. Reluctantly, Witte stopped, much to the students' dismay. They were incensed. They picked up their pens and wrote letters to the administration in protest.

In closing this section on *New Literacies* we see, overall, a change in the writing processes many K–12 students use. We began this section with Yancy (2009), who proposed plan, draft, revise, edit, publish as a writing process that must be reconsidered in this 21st century, and our review of students' engagement in *New Literacies* appears to support that challenge.

The Overall Processing Demands of Writing Increasingly large numbers of diverse students and technologies led Torrance and Galbraith (2008) to look at the many simultaneous processes engaged in by 21st-century writers. They monitor the coherence of their texts; revise, search for, and retrieve relevant content; identify search terms; create syntactic structure; inflect words; consider their audience; plan and locate Web sites; use visuals in various ways; and submit their creation for immediate response. Torrance and Galbraith, recognizing the complexity of students' writing tasks, hypothesize that part of their development involves developing writing-specific memory management strategies that involve the forgoing processes. This appears to tie in with the oft-held dictum that for students to become writers, they need to write frequently. As they gain fluency writers engage in dynamic writing processes that appear to be more true to what writers do, rather than engage in more simplified processes.

In studies of the writing processes of 15-year-olds, Rijlaarsdam and van den Bergh (2008) documented the decisions the adolescents made when they wrote. Via analysis of think-aloud protocols the researchers documented the frequency of eleven cognitive processes and found that the processes changed in frequency as a writer progressed through the task. And, the processes changed in nature. Thus, it would be simplistic to say that their writing processes were recursive. Instead, revision occurred at different times, for various reasons. Given that the writers engaged in the various aspects of writing repeatedly, in an unpredictable order, the question about processing demands of writing becomes: How do writers decide when to strategically engage in which process? This research shows that writers consciously decide whether and when to engage in particular processes, such as when to restructure or reread, leading to the possibility that procedural knowledge must be represented in models of writing.

Most learning processes are not linear. Lindfors (2008) explicates this when she writes about the processes children use when they talk, read, and write. With intention, they question, demand, and cajole. Children communicate with purpose. Their ability to express themselves depends, to a large degree, on the others with whom they interact; the responses they receive lead them forward (or not) as language users. Parallel notions apply to writing. Children who understand the power of writing experience it as a way to create texts that matter to them; their ability to express themselves depends, to a large degree, on the responses they receive. These evaluations lead them forward (or not) as writers.

Dyson (2008) writes about the children in a first-grade classroom who tried, unsuccessfully, to write texts that mattered to them. Their teacher, required to teach personal narratives by modeling events from her own life, wrote about going to movies and going out to dinner, but her students didn't identify with those ideas. During recess, the children created a world for themselves in which they used pine cones as weapons. When they returned to the classroom, their Pine Cone War became their personal narratives, despite their teacher's expressions of unease. Eventually, she banned "war" from the classroom, telling students about the real war (Iraq) going on and how people are dying. One student explained to Dyson that war was banned because Mrs. Kay was "thinking about real war, not fake war." Overall, the response of these children to their assignment to write personal narratives shows the problematic nature of an adult requirement that does not help children experience writing as a way to create texts that matter to them.

Response from peers and its influence on text construction, was noted by Kissel (2009) in his ethnographic study of pre-kindergarten writers. As children wrote about ideas of their choice (via image, movement, talk and/or print), interactions with peers influenced what they decided to put on the page. The young writers allowed others' suggestions and ideas to take their writing in surprising and unexpected directions. By listening to their conversations, watching interactions, and asking the children about their final products, their idiosyncratic, natural processes of creating meaning became clear.

Ray and Cleveland (2004) write about children as decision makers. Co-researchers in Cleveland's K–1 classroom, they show what her young authors do as they write books. We see the decisions the children make as they decide what to write about, what to illustrate, what to put on which page, and how to arrange their pages. As did the children in the above examples, these children engage in dynamic processes when they write.

In *Writing Now* (2008) the National Council of Teachers of English states that students need to engage in the kinds of writing shown above, and they provide three descriptors of the processes writers should engage in: *holistic, authentic,* and *variable.* In order to engage in *holistic* writing processes, their writing experiences must be multidirectional and multifaceted. They will not, in other words, progress through linear stages of a writing process. When they engage in *authentic* writing processes, student writers will create a wide variety of genres; address real, diverse audiences; identify their own strengths and weaknesses; and intentionally work to improve. They will seek and receive response while they are in the process of writing. Given that writers *vary,* the writers in a class will be at different points of expertise on any given day. They will write across the curriculum (WAC), and they will not do so by following formulas.

This provides us with a dynamic view of writers that guides us as we consider evaluation—by students and their instructors.

The Evaluation Processes Writers and Writing Instructors Use

In what ways do teachers and students find value in writing? This question undergirds this section as we review the evaluation processes writers continuously engage in as they compose, and then the evaluation processes writing instructors continuously engage in as they teach.

The Evaluation Processes of Writers The importance of students evaluating themselves is often lost in K–12 writing instruction. In our teacher education classes we continue to hear tales of *The Red Pen*—told by parents whose children currently bring home bled-upon papers accompanied by, "Mom, I don't know what to do!"

Student-writers can, however, be immersed in instruction that helps them figure out what to do. Their teachers learn about self-evaluation by writers in methods classes such as those taught by Delp (Freedman & Delp, 2007), based upon what she did with her eighth graders. The students played a large role in determining when, from whom, and what kind of assistance they needed. Through interactions with other students, the curriculum, and herself, her writers evaluated themselves and, in so doing, created opportunities for themselves. Delp supported them as they challenged themselves and, in accordance with what will become the theme of this section, the students' and Delp's evaluations drove instruction. Further evaluation informed additional instruction, and an evaluation-instruction loop became this classroom's signature. This loop, as we will see, serves as the central feature of classrooms in which students engage in dynamic writing processes and teachers welcome, support, and advise those processes.

Students, such as those in the above classroom, who learn to self-evaluate—see value in themselves—can become agentive authors (Hull & Katz, 2006). A case study of a young teen showed: the process of self-evaluation underlies the degree to which a writer intentionally becomes better. This writer's sense of self, her self-construction, was enhanced by supportive relationships and the opportunities for expression offered by a digital story. The young teen found it important, within the setting of this study in a community center, to negotiate what she wrote about and how she represented herself to the world. With these responsibilities, which she had seldom experienced in school, she worked hard. Hull and Katz close with a cry for teachers to support students "academically as learners, and socially as human beings.... And take seriously...their abilities to agentively engage in learning" (p. 73).

This research-based advice is, however, often not followed. In 2007, Pajaras, Johnson, and Usher studied the sources of students' self-efficacy beliefs about themselves as writers. Their analyses showed that students, especially middle school students, believe they are good writers if their teachers think they master their assignments. To rephrase, the students did not study their writing to acknowledge their strengths and weaknesses and intentionally work to improve—a necessary task if they are to become writers, as different from students who simply complete writing assignments.

If the above research paints a negative picture of students' reliance on teachers, NCLB has led us to paint an even more negative picture of our profession (Pearson, 2007). Whereas one cornerstone of evaluation is to value individual differences, federal policies "Have decreed that individual differences will not exist, either in the outcomes of education or in the means by which we attempt to achieve those outcomes" (p. 146). Within effective writing instruction, however, students send signals to their teachers about their strengths and needs, teachers read those signals, and provide feedback. This, however, is not possible within our current mandates that Pearson says are "hopelessly misguided and morally indefensible" (p. 158).

In order to shed light on evaluation within our culture of tests, Fu and Lamme (2002) studied two third graders and their portfolios. In each case, when the teacher, parent, and child sat down with the child's portfolio, they saw clear improvement in the work, and everyone, especially the children, articulated their changes in quality, length, and level of enjoyment. Tests don't provide as much information as the students' work and the collective perceptions of it.

Extending work on portfolios, a group of teacher-researchers at a Michigan National Writing Project site conducted a study of digital portfolios (Hicks et al., 2007). Their goal was to engage their students in the creation of them as a way to intentionally foster their self-evaluation and growth. The students constructed their own portfolios, but the public nature of their postings led to questions by other teachers about the students' evaluative decisions. One high school teacher noted spelling and editing issues raised by other faculty members, which left the teacher wondering whether she needed to pose standards on the students' portfolio choices. On a positive note, a fifth-grade teacher appreciated the comments students wrote to each other about their portfolio entries; their responses showed that they became more effective at evaluation over time. Overall, the importance of the decisions student-writers make when posting texts online becomes a topic to be addressed in our 21st century.

The Evaluation Processes of Teachers

Scott (2008) presents a brief history of assessment processes used by teachers, beginning with multiple-choice tests (1950s–1970s), holistically scored writing tests (1970s–mid-1980s), and portfolios (mid-1980s–90s). When writing teachers started to use portfolios, they used them as a means to honor their students' evaluations, but as larger numbers of teachers found portfolios useful, states started to collect writing data in the form of portfolios and, unfortunately, created ways to standardize them—defeating their purpose. This practice is part of the current assessment process most frequently engaged in by teachers—standardization.

As a probable way to enable useful standardization, rubrics arrived. To argue caution in their use, Wilson (2007), a high school English teacher, suggests that rubrics cheapen the language we use to respond to student writing. They are a form of standardization and our use of them can devalue our writers' work if feedback is prescriptive; writers need meaningful, specific, rich feedback. To support students' growth, however, teachers must know how to provide meaningful feedback. In a study of urban middle school teachers' written responses to students' drafts, researchers Patthey-Chavez, Matsumura, and Valdéz (2004) found that an overwhelming majority of the responses focused on conventions rather than content.

Further, even when the comments focused on content, the comments were not necessarily helpful in aiding the student to create a final product that would be more effective than the draft. In schools where students' academic scores are low, it is especially important that teachers learn what to say when they provide written responses to drafts. The difficulties of evaluation stem, at least to some degree, from the complicated nature of the dynamic processes writers use. And, similarly, the oft-uncertain results of evaluation, can only lead to uncertainty within instruction.

The Processes Writing Instructors Use

What do instructors do when they focus on *The Processes Students Use*? And, how do their instructional processes differ when they focus on *The Texts Students Create?* In this section we address each of these emphases.

Instructors Focus on the Processes Students Use "Studies of how writers work show them shuffling through phases of planning, reflection, drafting, and revision, rarely in a linear fashion" (National Writing Project & Nagin, 2003, p. 10). Teaching student-writers just what to do in order for their message to be compelling requires teachers who understand the idiosyncratic nature of the dynamic processes of writing.

Moher (2007), a high school English teacher-researcher, writes about what she does to accommodate her students' diverse processes when she holds writing conferences with them. She begins her essay, however, with hesitation, "After 25 years of practicing writing conferences, I hesitate to define what it is I do or what a conference should be. To attempt to do so diminishes the possibilities and capacities we might bring to our students, and them to us, in the paradoxical space between silence and dialogue" (p. 27). Her students often come with resistance—resistance they have learned in a school where autocratic methods of teaching prevail, where students seldom make decisions. Moher (2007) closes with her student Mark, details the conferences she held with him, and how her questions brought him to reconsider what he could write. Ultimately, the task of writing instructors is to give students leeway, offer options, focus on what they are learning rather than what they refuse to do, and help them find purpose.

Lassonde (2006) also focuses on the processes of a reluctant writer. In his second year in fifth grade he resisted writing, so Lassonde involved him in an after-school writing group, and encouraged him to confront his beliefs about school—within his writing. Then, Lassonde encouraged him to share his writing with peers, and when he received positive feedback, he gradually formed a more positive identity for himself, a difficult process for a student who is all-too-aware of his weaknesses. Writing forces students to form identities for themselves and is one of the few subjects that require this task. Many resistant writers come to upper-elementary classrooms with harrowing writing experiences; this boy talked about previous teachers who red-marked his papers, making him feel stupid. Lassonde (2006) found that he wrote when, most importantly, she made time to listen to him.

How to deeply engage writers is a common dilemma. Heffernan (Lewison & Heffernan, 2008) wanted to create the critical space in which her writers felt safe enough to use writing as a way to acquire agency in problematic social situations, a goal she hoped would engage them more deeply in writing than they appeared to be when they wrote personal narratives. To accomplish this, she immersed them in a study of bullying. She read books to them, they listened to each other's experiences, and wrote 10-minute quick-writes about their own experiences. Then, with Heffernan's encouragement to step out of their comfort zones—they wrote picture books. Everyone became committed.

Insights from the experienced writing teachers above become complicated in schools where literacy replaces reading and writing. Many literacy specialists are experienced in reading, and slight writing. To investigate the guidance literacy specialists need to provide in writing, McKinney and Giorgis (2009) studied several and found that those who had negative experiences as writers need extensive support in order to become literacy specialists—much more than they typically receive. In particular, when it comes to providing guidance in writing instruction, specialists "need to recognize the necessity of flexible approaches," especially today when "schools are being pushed toward a narrowing of tasks" in a "world that is becoming more global, requiring flexible skills and the ability to communicate with multiple audiences" (p. 145).

Cutler and Graham (2008) focused on the knowledge base of primary grade writing instructors, and only 20% of the teachers in the survey said they were prepared to teach writing when they entered the classroom. Seventy-two percent, however, said they attend to students' processes and skills when they teach, implying they try to create classrooms in which students actually engage in writing, and when they do, their writing processes are dynamic.

Instructors Focus on the Texts Students Create Teachers have not reached a consensus on how to teach writing, but a major point of agreement, documented by interviews (National Writing Project & Nagin, 2003), is that students need to write more in all subjects. Many content-area teachers, however, do not provide these opportunities, and when they do, the writing they request usually consists of brief responses rather than compositions seen as authentic by writers. Thus, writing across the curriculum (WAC), is now emerging as a discipline designed to include writing across subject areas, with the underlying notion that this will give students more time to write than if they only write in language arts and English classes. WAC encourages writers/learners in various disciplines to use writing as a way to learn about and show their knowledge about what they have learned, and WAC is based on a belief that student writers, regardless of their preferred discipline and genre, can learn from each other.

High school teachers in non-English fields who know their textbooks are poorly written, have started to use other genres for their students to learn from and create. A U.S. history teacher (Hansen, 2009) used centuries-old poetry from the Internet and songs to bring compassionate content into the course. Plus, her students wrote their own versions of U.S. history in the form of letters and scrapbooks. They learned, were engaged, and 27 out of 28 of these "general track" students passed their state history exam—a much higher average than that for their school at large. Younger students also benefit from WAC. At the middle school level, Ricklin (2006) writes about social studies students who wrote poems for two voices, showing the use of this genre in a field where many voices often play a role. And, Whitin (2007) writes about kindergarten children who engage in, and write about, a year-long scientific study.

Romano (2000) created multi-genre papers, and they continue to thrive, used by teachers at various grade levels (Allen & Swistak, 2004; Kissel, Wood, & Kiser, 2008) and in various curriculum areas. For these papers, students explore a topic or idea by writing about it in many genres, using the strength of each genre to provide insights. A finished paper shows, in kaleidoscope form, the impact of each format and, together, the writer and audience experience the overall impact of multi-ways of expressing and hearing the author's idea. Romano, in providing his students with this writing experience, repeatedly hears passion and compassion in their work. This format opens the doors to the world of writing for many of them.

Engaging their students in new literacies is, of course, what many teachers now try to do. Boling, Castek, Zawilinski, Barton, and Nierlich (2008) show the power of collaborative writing using Internet projects. In a fourth-grade classroom, students blogged about books with students miles away. The teacher noticed how the blogs encouraged her more reticent readers and writers, so she expanded their online experiences when she looped with her students to fifth grade, by having them co-create poems via Google Docs. Then, they uploaded them to another teacher's blog where others could hear the poems read aloud. Whereas these various aspects of online writing appealed to students, they especially appreciated receiving instant response from peers.

Alvermann (2008) and Gee (2003, 2004) write about the social draw that brings adolescents into online composing. Young people create content online for audiences who share common interests and spend copious amounts of time discussing this content, revising, and searching for more in the virtual world. Alvermann, in particular, reports on her own research in which a high school student transformed his computer into a virtual recording studio, composing songs and teaching others how to do the same. Overall, 93% of adolescents between 12 and 17 use the Internet as a vehicle for social interactions, a factor teachers consider when they provide writing experiences for their students.

Leander (2007), however, found "dueling discourses" between students and teachers when all were connected to laptops. In a school where every student had a laptop, teachers' attempts to honor students' online-created content challenged their centuries-old notions of the teacher as the authority. When students and teachers alike have access to a multitude of information and sort and blend it into their own coherent wholes, there is no top-down hierarchy; students are equal partners with teachers as they all construct knowledge together. Online literacies perpetuate a participatory culture in which students are active creators rather than passive learners.

Concluding Thoughts

In this information era, where the learner obtains and generates knowledge from multiple sources, while using multiple modalities, the teacher no longer bears all knowledge in the classroom. Through their engagement with online literacies, students access the many teachers who exist at their fingertips. And as they write across these literacies, authorship is neither a solitary, nor completely original enterprise (Alvermann, 2008). For teachers, instruction and evaluation of writers requires a pedagogical shift from "collection coded" to "connection coded" literacy acts (Luke, 2003).

In their evolutionary pedagogical processes, teachers may lose their status as all-knower, but gain by learning with, and from, their students. Teachers step out from behind their podiums into their classrooms. Amidst their writers, they notice, wonder, question, and challenge their students to think critically about online texts, the accuracy of the information, the possibilities of expression, and the potential pitfalls of creating online identities. All of these roles will become important as writing regains a foothold in schools.

Our profession, when we do teach writing, has one foot on the ground and the other hand in the Ethernet. The foot rests in a writing process grounded in paper and the hand gathers speed as dynamic processes race into the unknown. When writing reclaims its rightful place in our schools, *the processes writers use, the evaluation processes used by students and teachers,* and *the instructional processes teachers use* will gain a new life.

References

Allen, C., & Swistak, L. (2004). Multigenre research: The power of choice and interpretation. *Language Arts, 81*(3), 223–232.

Alvermann, D. (2008). Why bother theorizing adolescents' online literacies for classroom practice and research? *Journal of Adolescent & Adult Literacy, 52*(1), 8–19.

Boling, E., Castek, J., Zawilinski, L., Barton, K., & Nierlich, T. (2008). Collaborative literacy: Blogs and Internet projects. *Reading Teacher, 61*(6), 504–506.

Crafton, L., Brennan, M., & Silvers, P. (2007). Critical inquiry and multiliteracies in a first-grade classroom. *Language Arts, 84*(6), 510–518.

Cutler, L., & Graham, S. (2008). Primary grade writing instruction: A national survey. *Journal of Educational Psychology, 100*(4), 907–919.

Dyson, A. H. (2008). The pine cone wars: Studying writing in a community of children. *Language Arts, 85*(4), 305–315.

Freedman, S. W., & Delp, V. K. (2007). Conceptualizing a whole-class learning space: A Grand Dialogic Zone. *Research in the Teaching of English, 41*(3), 259–268.

Fu, D., & Lamme, L. (2002). Assessment through conversation. *Language Arts, 79*(3), 241–250.

Gee, J. P. (2003). *What video games have to teach us about learning and literacy.* New York: Palgrave Macmillan.

Gee, J. P. (2004). *Situated language and learning: A critique of traditional schooling.* New York: Routledge.

Hansen, J. (2009). Multiple literacies in the content classroom: High school students' connections to U.S. history. *Journal of Adolescent and Adult Literacy, 52*(7), 597–606.

Hicks, T., Russo, A., Autrey, T., Gardner, R., Kabodian, A., & Edington, C. (2007). Rethinking the purposes and processes for designing digital portfolios. *Journal of Adolescent & Adult Literacy, 50*(6), 450–458.

Hull, G. A., & Katz, M. (2006). Crafting an agentive self: Case studies of digital storytelling. *Research in the Teaching of English, 41*(1), 43–81.

Jacobs, G. (2008). We learn what we do: Developing a repertoire of writing practices in an instant messaging world. *Journal of Adolescent & Adult Literacy, 52*(3), 203–211.

Kajder, S. (2007). Plugging in to twenty-first century writers. In T. Newkirk & R Kent (Eds.), *Teaching the neglected "R": Rethinking writing instruction in secondary classrooms* (pp. 149–161). Portsmouth, NH: Heinemann.

Kissel, B. (2009). Beyond the page: Peers influence pre-kindergarten writing through talk, image, and movement. *Childhood Education, 85*(3), 160–166.

Kissel, B., Wood, K., & Kiser, K. (2008). Engaging adolescent learners in the multigenre life story project. *Middle School Journal, 39*(5), 59–69.

Lassonde, C. (2006). Listening for students' voices through positional writing practices. *Language Arts, 83*(5), 404–412.

Leander, K. M. (2007). "You won't be needing your laptops today": Wired bodies in the wireless classroom. In M. Knobel & C. Lankshear (Eds.), *A new literacies sampler* (pp. 25–48). New York: Peter Lang.

Leu, D. (2002). Internet workshop: Making time for literacy. *The Reading Teacher, 55*, 466–472.

Lewison, M., & Heffernan, L. (2008). Rewriting writers' workshop: Creating safe spaces for disruptive stories. *Research in the Teaching of English, 42*(4), 435–465.

Lindfors, J. W. (2008). *Children's language: Connecting reading, writing, and talk.* New York: Teachers College Press.

Luke, C. (2003). Pedagogy, connectivity, multimodality, and interdisciplinarity. *Reading Research Quarterly, 38*(3), 397–403.

McKinney, M., & Giorgis, C. (2009). Narrating and performing identity: Literacy specialists' writing identities. *Journal of Literacy Research, 41*, 104–149.

Moher, T. (2007). The writing conference: Journeys into not knowing. In T. Newkirk & R Kent (Eds.), *Teaching the neglected "R": Rethinking writing instruction in secondary classrooms* (pp. 26–38). Portsmouth, NH: Heinemann.

National Council of Teachers of English. (2008). *Writing now: A policy research brief.* Retrieved August 5, 2009, from http://www.ncte.org

National Writing Project & Nagin, C. (2003). *Because writing matters: Improving student writing in our schools.* San Francisco: Jossey-Bass.

Pajaras, F., Johnson, M. J., & Usher, E. L. (2007). Sources of writing self-efficacy beliefs of elementary, middle, and high school students. *Research in the Teaching of English, 42*(1), 104–120.

Patthey-Chavez, G. G., Matsumura, L. C., & Valdéz, R. (2004). Investigating the process approach to writing instruction in urban middle schools. *Journal of Adolescent & Adult Literacy, 47*(6), 462–477.

Pearson, P. D. (2007). An endangered species act for literacy education. *Journal of Literacy Research, 39*(2), 145–162.

Ray, K. W. with Cleveland, L. B. (2004). *About the authors: Writing workshop with our youngest writers.* Portsmouth, NH: Heinemann.

Ricklin, L. P. (2006). Poems for two voices: An interdisciplinary activity. *MLL: Middle Level Learning, 25,* 14–15.

Rijlaarsdam, G., & van den Bergh, H. (2008). Writing process theory: A functional dynamic approach. In C. A. MacArthur, S. Graham, & J. Fitzgerald (Eds.), *Handbook of writing research* (pp. 41–53). New York: Guilford Press.

Romano, T. (2000). *Blending genre, altering style: Writing multigenre papers*. Portsmouth, NH: Heinemann.

Scott, T. (2008). Happy to comply: Writing assessment, fast-capitalism, and the cultural logic of control. *Review of Education, Pedagogy & Cultural Studies, 30*(2), 140–161.

Torrance, M., & Galbraith, D. (2008). The processing demands of writing. In C. A. MacArthur, S. Graham, & J. Fitzgerald (Eds.), *Handbook of writing research* (pp. 67–80). New York: Guilford Press.

Whitin, P. (2007). The ties that bind: Emergent literacy and scientific inquiry. *Language Arts, 85*(1), 20–30.

Williams, B. (2008). Tomorrow will not be like today: Literacy and identity in a world of multiliteracies. *Journal of Adolescent & Adult Literacy, 51*(8), 682–686.

Wilson, M. (2007). Why I won't be using rubrics to respond to students' writing. *English Journal, 96*(4), 62–66.

Witte, S. (2007). That's online writing, not boring school writing: Writing with blogs and the Talkback Project. *Journal of Adolescent & Adult Literacy, 51*(2), 92–96.

Wollman-Bonilla, J. (2003). E-mail as genre: A beginning writer learns the conventions. *Language Arts, 81*(2), 126–134.

Yancy, K. B. (2009). *Writing in the 21st Century*. Urbana, IL: National Council of Teachers of English.

Zenkov, K., & Harmon, J. (2009). Picturing a writing process: Photovoice and teaching writing to urban youth. *Journal of Adolescent & Adult Literacy, 52*(7), 575–584.

40

Critical Literacy as Comprehension

Understanding at Deeper Levels

MAUREEN MCLAUGHLIN AND GLENN DEVOOGD

Our ever-changing world is causing us to rethink what constitutes comprehension of text. Critical educators suggest that readers should learn to comprehend at deeper levels—levels that require understanding beyond the printed page—to critically analyze the author's message. As Pearson (2001) describes it, we need to read "with a critical edge."

Reading from a critical literacy perspective is grounded in Freire's (1983) belief that reading is much more than decoding language—it is preceded by and intertwined with knowledge of the world. Because language and reality are dynamically interwoven, the understanding attained by the critical reading of a text implies perceiving the relation between text and context.

In this chapter, we begin by presenting a theoretical foundation for critical literacy. Next, we explain the principles of critical literacy and provide connections to current research. Finally, we discuss common contexts of critical literacy and the characteristics of critical readers.

Developing a Critical Stance

Although literacy has been commonly defined as the ability to read and write, we now live in an age of multiple literacies (Vogt & McLaughlin, 2004; McLaughlin, 2010). In recent years, the term *literacy* has expanded in meaning. The word itself has changed from *literacy* to *literacies*, because many different literacies have emerged over time. These *multiple literacies* are diverse, multidimensional, and learned in different ways (McLaughlin, 2010). Critical literacy, which has been in existence for decades, is now experiencing a wider range of acceptance. This has led to its inclusion in the list of literacies for the 21st century—the skills needed to flourish in today's society and in the future (Abilock, 2007).

Knoblauch and Brannon (1993) suggest that literacy should be defined by its purposes. The functionalist perspective focuses on ever higher levels of reading and writing skills for the purpose of communication, job competence, and self-improvement. Coming from this perspective, books emerge every few years to tell the public that students are not learning much. Similarly, the current emphasis on test scores appears to scold teachers and warn the public of the deteriorating state of public education. Cultural literacy focuses on the canon of common cultural understanding going beyond basic skills to obtain an aesthetic and philosophical appreciation for good literature and excellent writing. A third perspective on literacy comes from liberal ideology and centers more on literacy as a tool for voice and self-expression. While this perspective claims the importance of freedom and self-determination, it does not emphasize the importance of social aspects of literacy or the need for restructuring society. Critical literacy, a fourth perspective, makes power visible and uses language to exercise that power to transform society.

Critical literacy is not a teaching method but a way of thinking and a way of being that challenges texts and life as we know it. It envisions a world with more intellectual freedom and equality. Lewison, Flint, and Van Sluys (2002) suggest that, although there are many definitions of critical literacy, most have elements such as these in common: (a) disrupting the commonplace (stereotypes), (b) multiple viewpoints, (c) a focus on socio-political issues, and (d) action steps for social justice.

Freire (1970) suggests that instead of passively accepting the information presented, critical readers should not only read and understand the word, but "read the world" and understand the text's purpose to avoid being manipulated by it. "Reading the world" enables critically aware readers to comprehend beyond the literal level and think about the function and the production of texts. Reading the world means trying to understand *what* authors are trying to convey in their messages and *how* they are communicating those messages. It requires that readers not accept only superficial responses to the text; but rather reflect about the text's purposes and the author's style. This reasoning is often expressed through dialogue with others who are seeking to understand the hidden forces at work. This kind of reflection takes time and requires constant monitoring of the text.

In critical literacy, readers are active participants in the reading process, who move beyond passively accepting the text's message to question, examine, or dispute the power relations that exist between readers and authors—to ponder what the author wants readers to believe, take action, and promote fairness between people. It focuses on issues of power and promotes reflection, action, and transformation (Freire, 1970). Reading from a critical stance requires both the ability and the deliberate inclination to think critically about—to analyze and evaluate—texts (books, media, lyrics, life relationships), meaningfully question their origin and purpose, and take action by representing alternative perspectives (McLaughlin & DeVoogd, 2004b). Examples of the types of questions that promote reading from a critical stance appear in Figure 40.1.

Comber (2001) has observed that when teachers and students are engaged in critical literacy, they ask complicated questions about language and power, about people and lifestyle, about morality and ethics, about who is advantaged by the way things are and who is disadvantaged. In order to participate in such a classroom environment, readers must play not only the roles of code breakers, meaning makers, and text users, but also the role of text critics (Luke & Freebody, 1999). In other words, readers need to understand that they have the power to envision alternate ways of viewing the author's topic, and that they exert that power when they read from a critical stance.

Rosenblatt (2002) suggests that stances are "aspects of consciousness." Her Aesthetic-Efferent Continuum (1994) reflects the belief that readers transact with text from aesthetic and efferent stances. The aesthetic stance depicts a more emotional perspective; the efferent stance, a more factual one. Rosenblatt (2002) notes that no reading experience is purely aesthetic or purely efferent, but rather readers are always making choices about their thinking, focusing on both stances, and sometimes more on one than the other. A third stance—the critical stance—can be viewed as another component of that continuum. When reading from a critical stance, readers use their background knowledge to understand the power relationships between their ideas and the ideas presented by the author of the text. In this process, readers do exactly what Luke and Freebody (1999) suggest: They move beyond the roles of code breakers, meaning makers, and text users to become text critics. They exert their ability to question power relationships, problematize simplistic views, and explore perspectives other than the author's. This reflects what Durrant and Green (2001) describe as "a situated social practice model of language, literacy, and technology learning…authentic learning and cultural apprenticeships within a critical-sociocultural view of discourse and practice" (p. 151). Consequently, students reading from a critical stance raise questions about whose voices are represented, whose voices are missing, and who gains and who loses by the reading of a text.

Principles of Critical Literacy A number of essential understandings and beliefs about the power relationship that exists between the reader and the author underpin critical literacy (McLaughlin & DeVoogd, 2004a). These principles include the following.

Critical Literacy Focuses on Issues of Power and Promotes Reflection, Transformation, and Action. Whenever readers commit to understanding a text—whether narrative or expository, they submit to the right of the author to select the topic and determine the treatment of the ideas. Similarly, in conversations and social situations, the listener receives the ideas from the speaker, but upon reflection, the listener may decide the comments were unjust and act to promote equity. Young (2009) reported student reflections about Lesbian, Gay, Bisexual and Transgendered (LGBT)

Print (Books, newspapers, magazines, song lyrics, hypertext, etc.):

Whose viewpoint is expressed?

What does the author want us to think?

Whose voices are missing, silenced, or discounted?

How might alternative perspectives be represented?

How would that contribute to your understanding the text from a critical stance?

Where do the Internet links lead you and what does that mean?

What action might you take based on what you have learned?

Video/Photographs:

Who is in the video/photograph?

Why are they there?

What does the videographer/photographer want you to think?

Who/what is missing from the video/photograph? (silenced? discounted?)

What might an alternative video show?

What might an alternative photograph look like?

How would that contribute to your understanding the video or photograph from a critical stance?

What action might you take based on what you have viewed?

Figure 40.1 Questions that promote reading from a critical stance.

issues among high school students. The students identified comments like "that's so gay" as synonymous with "that is stupid." With the recognition that they and society in general marginalized people of LGBT orientation, students went on the identify ways in which they were privileged as heterosexuals with phrases such as: ability to discuss sexual issues openly, be approved by the church and family, experience stories about heterosexual love, and not being made fun of. Classroom dialogue about this topic led to transformation as university representatives from the LGBT community spoke to groups. Many students showed their solidarity with the LGBT panel by wearing white t-shirts and jeans and writing articles in the school newspaper. So after students reflected on power relationships among students of different sexual orientations, students acted to transform the attitudes of students in their school. In contrast to those who believe in the liberal ideology, critical students know that good intentions or awareness of an unjust situation will not transform it. They must act on their knowledge.

This dialogue, which represents a cycle of, "reflection and action upon the world in order to transform it" is what Freire (1970, p. 36) calls praxis. By nature, this process is not passive, but active, challenging and disrupting the ideal (Green, 2001) or commonplace (Lewison et al., 2002) for the purpose of relieving the inequity and injustice.

Critical Literacy Focuses on the Problem and its Complexity. Educational situations that are fairly intricate are often viewed from an essentialist—very simplistic— perspective. In critical literacy, rather than accepting an essentialist view, we would engage in problematizing— seeking to understand the problem and its complexity. In other words, we would raise questions and seek alternative explanations as a way of more fully acknowledging and understanding the complexity of the situation. For example, it would be essentialist to merely suggest that unmotivated students should receive an extrinsic reward for reading or be punished for not reading. Problematizing—or examining the complexity of this situation—would reveal that the lack of motivation is likely due to a variety of factors including poor quality texts, students' past reading experiences, classroom climate, self-efficacy, purpose, or limited opportunities to self-select, read, and discuss books in social settings.

Examining Multiple Perspectives Is an Important Aspect of Critical Literacy. Expressing ideas from a variety of perspectives challenges students to expand their thinking and discover diverse beliefs, positions, and understandings (McLaughlin, 2001). Examining texts from a variety of viewpoints is applicable in a wide range of classes including literature, social studies, science, and mathematics. Appreciation for and exploration of these alternative perspectives facilitates our viewing situations from a critical stance (Lewison et al., 2002; McLaughlin, 2001).

Techniques that Promote Critical Literacy are Dynamic and Adapt to the Contexts in Which They Are Used. There is no list of methods in critical literacy that works the same way in all contexts all the time. No technique that promotes critical literacy can be exported to another setting without adapting it to that context. As Freire (1998, p. xi) has observed, "It is impossible to export pedagogical practices without reinventing them." It is key to any exploration of critical literacy that the teacher constantly assess student responses to ensure that the experience is true to the philosophy and goals of critical literacy, but not necessarily consistent with the examples of others who practice critical literacy. For example, teachers might begin using an approach to critical literacy that is presented in this article or that they have seen working in another classroom. But upon reflecting on instructional goals and what is happening in their classes, they may adapt the method to make it more applicable—more meaningful—in that particular context. The dynamic nature of critical literacy supports this type of adaptation. There is a sense of empowerment and confidence in the act of creation that cannot be achieved by copying. Even when a method has been used, it is never quite the same. This is why those who are critically aware are fond of quoting Antonio Machado (1982, p. 142), the Spanish poet, who said, "Caminante, no hay camino, Se hace el camino al andar" (Traveler, there is no road. The road is made as you walk).

In the same way, teacher education of critical literacy and the formation of professional identity become deeper and more complex through dialogue (which serves as part of reflection) about student praxis in classroom situations (Rogers, Marshall, & Tyson, 2006). For example, upon reflection of their practice in classrooms, teacher education students who were struggling to implement critical literacy projects, decided to switch their practice and intermittently infuse critical moments in the regular curriculum (Rogers, 2007). In a 4-year study of two teacher education students, Jones and Enriquez (2009) reveal a complexity of uneven growth or no growth dependent upon the interweaving of formal learning and their personal, social, and political experiences. While the effectiveness of a student's growth in critical literacy is not guaranteed, they do caution professors: (a) not to assume that intellectual shifts in thinking will transfer to moral shifts in classroom practice, (b) not to make assumptions about students' ability to do critical literacy, (c) dialogue over an extended period of time is more productive than short term experiences. Though much of the dialogue that occurs to create changes in teacher educational practice is individual, small group, and whole class, Woodcock (2009) also found significant growth in dialogue occurring in online classes.

After a teacher understands the theoretical foundations of critical literacy and is committed to the cycle of praxis, some teachers take on a repertoire of pedagogical tools and adapt them to their classroom context. Many teachers like to use questions to interrogate text (see Figure 40.1). These questions used one at a time or in groups serve as catalysts toward deeper understanding of the text for dyad, small group, and whole group discussion. After reading a narrative, some teachers and students find it helpful to imagine alternative narratives by creating a new ending to the story or by substituting a different character for one in the story or by using a different setting. Discussion after making the switch may reveal power relationships or biases in the story. For example, using a gender switch, replace Snow White with a boy to see if it makes sense. Most likely students will find a need to change the part of the story in which the Queen looks at herself in the mirror and compares her looks to the beauty of Snow White. This leads to a discussion about differing expectations for women and men and their appearance. In the Bubble Project (http://thebubbleproject.com), for example, students switch texts by placing speech bubbles on pictures or in book illustrations and write an alternative narrative disrupting the ideas of the story.

Other teachers find that juxtaposing an image/story/movie that reflects a different theme/character/setting with the original text helps students raise issues that disrupt the text and reveal the hidden values implicit in the story. Teachers can also encourage students to read two different versions of informational text about the same topic to see what new understandings come to light. For example, they can read different perspectives on the Civil War to see that reality can be represented in diverse ways depending on the perspective of the author.

The principles of critical literacy help us understand what critical literacy is and how it functions. It is a dynamic process that examines power relationships, expands our thinking, and enlightens our perceptions as we read both the word and the world—as we read from a critical stance.

Critical literacy is partly an understanding that although we desire life and problems to be simple, they are actually more complex. So people often stereotype. Situations in the simplest form (and therefore untrue or distorted form) are referred to as *essentialist* or *reductionist*. In order to view a situation, which appears to be simple, in more sophisticated and complex ways, classroom teachers ask students to problematize the situation. To problematize, one asks lots of questions about the situation. For example, if one were to say, "Women are more sensitive than men." One might start asking questions to understand in more complex ways, such as, Who said that? Why did they say that? Is it always true? When is it not true? What does it mean to be sensitive? How do people become sensitive? After asking such questions, it becomes clear that the statement is too simplistic and needs to be revised.

Common Contexts of Critical Literacy The principles of critical literacy have been applied to a wide range of contexts to challenge social norms and oppressive status quo practices. Probably more than any other area, the literature reveals many articles on sex role stereotypes. While children occasionally cross the borders of status quo practices such as gender-segregated lunch rooms, primary school students often challenge storylines in fairy tales (Heffernan & Lewiston, 2005). For example, Bourke (2008) allows his first graders to speak freely about fairy tales; he finds

that they have no trouble expressing countertexts. One boy commenting on Sleeping Beauty told his teacher that he doesn't like kissing and that after being woken up, Sleeping Beauty argued that she didn't want to be kissed and would have been better off sleeping. Others report that girls who discover the limitations of their situation after they identify with female characters in fairy tales often create counter narratives that overcome the gender role stereotypes of the story (Wohlwend, 2009).

The second most common context in critical literacy addresses issues of culture and the content of the curriculum. In a history class in a segregated neighborhood, Duffy (2008) challenges the authority of the school sanctioned text to get students to investigate beyond the text and write essays concerning Thomas Jefferson's actions as a slave holder, which so drastically contradicts his words as a president. Other teachers find critical consciousness and cultural awareness important tools for students from traditionally oppressed cultures when they interrogate texts in school (Esposito & Swain, 2009). Lesley (2008) found her students interpreted a book about a White foster child from Long Island, *Hollis Woods,* in literal ways, but when reading poems from the recording artist Tupac Shakur's book, *The Rose That Grew from Concrete* (1999), her perspective of their reading ability shifted. Similarly, books like *Monster* by Walter Dean Meyers (2001), gave voice to the lives of urban teens, access to school, and opportunities to discuss the issues more deeply. In contrast, the setting and character of the text in *Hollis Woods* inhibited the students' desire to comprehend the text.

Becoming Critically Aware

It is important to note that we cannot just "become" critically literate. It is a process that involves learning, understanding, and changing over time. This includes developing theoretical, research, and pedagogical repertoires, changing with time and circumstance, engaging in self-critical practices, and remaining open to possibilities (Comber, 2001).

Readers who are critically aware become open-minded, active, strategic learners who are capable of viewing text from a critical perspective. They know the information they encounter has been authored from particular perspectives for particular purposes and they question it. They understand that meaning is "grounded in the social, political, cultural and historic contexts of the reading event" (Serafini, 2003), and they realize that when they read from a critical perspective, they not only become more engaged, but also comprehend at deeper levels.

References

Abilock, D. (2007). Building blocks of research: Overview of design, process, and outcomes. Retrieved from http://www.noodletools.com/debbie/projects/visual/LitProject.pdf

Bourke, R. T. (2008). First graders and fairy tales: One teacher's action research of critical literacy. *The Reading Teacher, 62*(4), 304–312.

Comber, B. (2001). Critical literacies and local action: Teacher knowledge and a "new" research agenda. In B. Comber & A. Simpson (Eds.), *Negotiating critical literacies in classrooms* (pp. 271–282). Mahwah, NJ: Erlbaum.

Duffy, J. (2008). Teaching for critical literacy and racial justice. *Democracy & Education, 17*(3), 38–45.

Durrant, C., & Green, B. (2001). Literacy and the new technologies in school education: Meeting the literacy challenge. In H. Fehring & P. Green (Eds.), *Critical literacy: A collection of articles from the Australian Literacy Educators' Association* (pp. 142–164). Newark, DE: International Reading Association.

Esposito, J., & Swain, A. (2009, Spring). Pathways to social justice: Urban teachers' uses of culturally relevant pedagogy as a conduit for teaching for social justice. *Perspectives on Urban Education, 28*–48.

Freire, P. (1970). *Pedagogy of the oppressed.* New York: Continuum.

Freire, P. (1983). The importance of the act of reading. *Journal of Education, 165,* 5–11.

Freire, P. (1998). *Teachers as cultural workers: Letters to those who dare to teach.* Boulder, CO: Westview.

Green, P. (2001). Critical literacy revisited. In H. Fehring & P. Green (Eds.), *Critical literacy: A collection of articles from the Australian Literacy Educators' Association* (pp. 7–14). Newark, DE: International Reading Association.

Heffernan, L., & Lewiston, M. (2005). What's lunch got to do with it? Critical literacy and the discourse of the lunchroom. *Language Arts, 83*(2), 107–117.

Jones, S., & Enriquez, G. (2009). Engaging the intellectual and the moral in critical literacy education: The four-year journeys of two teachers from teacher education to classroom practice. *Reading Research Quarterly, 44*(2), 145–168.

Knoblauch, C. H., & Brannon, L. (1993). *Critical teaching and the idea of literacy.* Portsmouth, NH: Boynton/Cook.

Lesley, M. (2008). Access and resistance to dominant forms of discourse: Critical literacy and "at risk" high school students. *Literacy Research & Instruction, 47*(3), 174–194.

Lewison, M., Flint, A. S., & Van Sluys, K. (2002). Taking on critical literacy: The journey of newcomers and novices. *Language Arts 79*(5), 382–392.

Luke, A., & Freebody, P. (1999). Further notes on the four resources model. *Reading Online.* Retrieved from http://www.reading.org/publications/ROL/

Machado, A. (1982). Proverbios y cantares (A. Trueblood, Trans.), *Antonio Machado: Selected poems.* Cambridge, MA: Harvard University Press.

McLaughlin, M. (2001, December). *Sociocultural influences on content literacy teachers' beliefs and innovative practices.* Paper presented at the 51st annual meeting of the National Reading Conference, San Antonio, Texas.

McLaughlin, M. (2010). *Content are reading: Teaching and learning in an age of multiple literacies.* Boston: Allyn & Bacon.

McLaughlin, M., & DeVoogd, G. (2004a). Critical literacy as comprehension: Expanding reader response. *Journal of Adolescent and Adult Literacy, 48*(1), 52–62.

McLaughlin, M., & DeVoogd, G. (2004b). *Critical literacy: Enhancing students' comprehension of text.* New York: Scholastic.

Meyers, W. D. (2001). *Monster.* New York: Amistad.

Pearson, P. D. (2001, December). *What we have learned in 30 years.* Paper presented at the 51st annual meeting of the National Reading Conference, San Antonio, TX.

Rogers, R. (2007). A case study of teaching for literacy acceleration within a critical literacy framework: Reconstructing pedagogical approaches. *Pedagogies, 4*(2), 233–250.

Rogers, T., Marshall, E., & Tyson, C. (2006). Dialogic narratives of literacy, teaching, and schooling: Preparing literacy teachers for diverse settings. *Reading Research Quarterly, 41*(2), 202–223.

Rosenblatt, L.M. (1994). The transactional theory of reading and writing. In R. B. Ruddell, M. R. Ruddell, & H. Singer (Eds.), *Theoretical models and processes of reading* (4th ed., pp. 1057–1092). Newark, DE: International Reading Association.

Rosenblatt, L. (2002, December). *A pragmatist theoretician looks at research: Implications and questions calling for answers.* Paper presented at the 52nd annual meeting of the National Reading Conference, Miami, FL.

Serafini, F. (2003, February). Informing our practice: Modernist, transactional, and critical perspectives on children's literature and reading instruction. *Reading Online, 6*(6). Retrieved from http://www.readingonline.org/articles/art_index.asp?HREF=serafini/index.html

Shakur, T. (1999). *The rose that grew from concrete.* New York: MTV.

Vogt, M. E., & McLaughlin, M. (2004). Teaching and learning in a global society: Examining changing definitions of literacy. In M. Pandis, A. Ward, & S. R. Mathews (Eds.), *Reading, writing, thinking: Proceedings of the 13th European Conference on Reading* (pp. 2–8). Newark, DE: International Reading Association.

Wohlwend, K. (2009). Damsels in discourse: Girls consuming and producing identity texts through Disney princess play. *Reading Research Quarterly, 44*(1), 57–83.

Woodcock, C. (2009). Fight the dragons: Using online discussion to promote critical literacy in teacher education. *Contemporary Issues in Technology & Teacher Education, 9*(2), 95–116.

Young, S. (2009). Breaking the silence: Critical literacy and social action. *English Journal, 98*(4), 109–115.

41

Passive Dupes, Code Breakers, or Savvy Users

Theorizing Media Literacy Education in English Language Arts

Renee Hobbs and Michael RobbGrieco

Dear reader: Before we begin, it's time for some self-reflection. How many movies do you watch in a weekend? How many hours do you spend in front of a screen of one sort or the other? How much of your waking activity is spent in using online media? Reading a newspaper? Reading a book? Listening to music? Watching TV shows or playing videogames? What role does pleasure play in these activities? How much of these activities support the escape function, providing a relief from the stress of daily life? How much supports your social interaction with the people who matter in your life? How much empowers you to act in relation to your work, your colleagues, and your community? How much informs your money and health decisions? Do you sometimes judge your life in relation to characters you see in the media? How much emphasis do you place on critical analysis when you read, listen, watch and view? How much time do you spend creating messages? How does your own use of mass media and popular culture shape the way you teach? How do your attitudes about newspapers, television, the Internet, videogames, and movies shape the way you teach?

In English language arts, educators who incorporate media texts, tools, and technologies have many different motives and purposes for doing so. Educators' perspectives often reflect an amalgam of theories from media studies scholarship and theories in the humanities. Each theory positions the user or audience in relationship to authorship, power, agency, and pleasure, and each theory suggests a particular approach to teaching and learning. In this chapter, we explore four theoretical perspectives about the role of mass media and communication on individuals and society, looking at the implication of these ideas on the shape of educators' instructional practices. As you read, we encourage you to position yourself, your students, their parents, and your colleagues among the theories as you consider how they may inform educational practice.

Media Literacy and the Digital Revolution

One longstanding goal of media literacy educators has been to develop "critical approaches which can apply to any text" (Masterman, 1985, p. xiv). These include strategic use of concepts like author, audience, message, meaning, representation, reality, purpose, subtext, and tone to understand the meaning-making process involving all kinds of texts, especially those that are meaningful to children and young people (National Association for Media Literacy Education, 2007).

But in the United States, the debate about how to give media literacy a meaningful place in elementary and secondary schools is still a robust and open issue, given the dominance of print literacy, the conservative nature of schooling and the institutional structures that control it. In the United States, media literacy education has become more visible in English language arts instruction through standards documents and curriculum materials (National Council of Teachers of English, 2009).

Today, there are many flavors of media literacy in English education, each corresponding to a different set of theoretical perspectives about the relationship between media, children and culture. The flavors reflect four types of general theoretical approaches which frame discussions of mass media and audiences: media effects, critical studies, media rhetoric, and cultural studies. Conceptualizations of audiences from each of these theoretical perspectives interact with institutional discourses about youth and adolescence, which together inform the various approaches to media literacy and media literacy education (Piette & Giroux, 1997; Livingstone, 2008; Scharrer, 2007).

Since the early 20th century, scholars in both education and communication have paid particular attention to children and adolescents based on a common view of the important and extensive role that mass media play in socialization, identity formation, and expression. Within each perspective, notions of audiences as more and less powerful in their relationships to mass media have evolved and fluctuated over time. Positioned in part by ideas from discourses in media studies, education and the humanities, media literacy educators see our students' relationships to media in diverse ways—from passive victims of media influence, to cultural dupes of dominant ideologies, to code breakers learning the symbol systems of mediated culture, to active users who construct their own meanings and social identities from the symbolic resources of popular mass media.

Within the term "media literacy," the notion of literacy suggests the necessity of this ability for participation in contemporary society while expanding the traditional typographic notion of literacy to include reading and writing across a wide range of genres and forms (Hobbs, 1998). However, literacy has also meant an appreciation of the "best" a culture has to offer (as in "literary" literacy), and literacy has been critiqued as a means of deepening social divisions rather than working towards overcoming them through greater civic and cultural participation (Livingstone, 2008).

English language arts educators are motivated to help students develop media literacy for diverse purposes: (a) to nurture students own authentic voices in composition; (b) to motivate learning by building on existing knowledge of popular culture; (c) to help young people understand and challenge dominant mass media power through critical thinking and social activism; (d) to develop marketable skills in using technology to access information and create effective messages; and (e) to develop strategies for managing one's own exposure to and processing of media messages in order to actively control media influence (Hobbs, 2004, 2007). Each of these purposes proceeds from particular views of children, media, teaching and learning. Each perspective also reflects theoretical conceptualizations of audiences from media effects, semiotics, critical and cultural studies.

Let's explore four of the theoretical perspectives that have informed approaches to media literacy and media literacy education with children and adolescents, considering their implications for K–12 educational practice. As you read, examine your own experience and knowledge to consider the questions: How do you and other stakeholders in education, from students and parents to other teachers, understand yourselves and students as media users in relation to authorship, power, agency, and pleasure? What purposes in teaching and learning can each of these theories be usefully put? What is omitted from each media theory that is important for teaching and learning?

Countering Negative Effects: Protecting the Vulnerable Audience

Media shape our understanding of ourselves and the world around us. Media effects approaches assume that media influence the behavior, beliefs, and attitudes of individuals in measurable, predictive ways (Bryant & Zillmann, 1994). As McLeod, Kosicki, and Pan (1991) point out, "there is a clear theoretical commitment, symbolized by the term 'effect' itself, to a predominant flow of influence from the media and its messages to the audience" (p. 236).

Cultivation theory, social cognitive theory, and uses and gratifications theories provide the foundation and current bases for discussions of media and adolescence from the media effects perspective (Bryant & Zillmann, 1994). Each of these theories work within the social scientific paradigm seeking to explain audience relationships to media in terms of media content, media exposure and individual differences, which predict behavior, attitudes and beliefs. Both cultivation and social cognitive theories posit the possibilities of powerful media effects on the attitudes and behavior of individuals. These theories have been used to address children and adolescent audiences as particularly vulnerable to media influence, which has informed approaches to media literacy as a means of managing one's own media exposure and processing in hopes of protecting young people from potentially harmful media effects.

Educators using this theoretical frame have developed innovative approaches to media literacy education: advertising and the representation of aggression and violence are common themes. In one project, Scharrer (2006) found that a 5-hour media literacy program helped Grade 6 students consider the ethical issues raised by rewarded violence, violence that goes unpunished, and violence perpetrated by likeable characters. Learning about the lack of consequences depicted in televised violence encouraged children to see media creators as irresponsible, believing that that they should portray realistic consequences more frequently. Lesson plans for elementary school students focus on how food advertising is constructed and how it influences attitudes and behaviors (Project Look Sharp, 2009); for middle school students, the focus is on how alcohol and tobacco advertisers manipulate people to "make you want the product" (New Mexico Media Literacy Project, 2006).

In this view, audiences are vulnerable to negative media messages and media users must gain knowledge and skills in order to resist media influence and attain a critical distance from the overwhelming symbolic environment of media. It's been claimed that this theoretical framework presents a deficit model of learners. But advocates for this position say it is responsive to the real needs of parents and educators as they see children's active imitation and uncritical acceptance of the values presented in mass media and popular culture.

Demystification and Resistance: Tools for the Dominated Audience

While media effects theories conceptualize media audiences as passive individuals, critical studies conceive of passive audiences at a macro-level of analysis as constructed by the media they consume. Adorno and Horkheimer (1972) theorize the audience of mass media as passive dupes of the culture industries. The mass audience consumes the products of the culture industries, which reproduce power relations in favor of those who control the means of production. In this Marxist formulation, the mass audience finds the products of the culture industry (movies, music, and the like) both irresistible and inescapable. Theorized as a monolithic mass, the audience cannot help but delight in seeing itself reproduced in the endless variation of representations in capitalist mass production.

Taken as the audience's own culture, these media products alienate the masses from the means of production of their own culture. The products of mass media suppress critical thinking on the part of the audience by producing a spectacular demand for automatic cognitive processing. Audiences may like the pleasures of feeling superior to mass media and popular culture. It makes them feel like experts. But critical theorists scorn this pleasure, positing that it produces a false consciousness in the mass audience (Bourdieu, 1993). The entertained masses rarely think to question the political economy and social relations that media texts produce by gratifying their audiences.

At the college level, media literacy courses using this theoretical position often include an awareness of, and concern for, issues of ideology and power, including issues of ownership and control, alternative media, and media activism and reform movements When these issues are valued by instructors, the focus of the pedagogy may become topic-centered, not learner-centered. Course syllabi underline just how much students need to know: the student must understand in detail the financial structure of media organizations, including who owns and controls the media, how media profits are made, who pays for content, and how economic considerations affect content (Duran, Yousman, Walsh, & Longshore, 2008).

Learning resistance can take many forms. One of the most popular is a form of counterpropaganda, offered as an alternative to replace students' existing uncritical perspective. In the videos distributed by the Media Education Foundation, video documentaries display experts offering their compelling critical readings of media texts including news programs, ads, and children's movies. Lesson plans encourage learners to identify stakeholders in public policy debates about media and join various advocacy groups.

In this approach, audiences are capable of resisting dominant discourses only through oppositional meaning-making by experts. Assuming that corporate media institutions perpetuate injustices, students are encouraged to identify sexist, racist, hetero-normative, and class-biased media messages and representations, and to create their own media messages to counter these representations (Kellner & Share, 2005). Students can also become "critical" through pursuing information and entertainment produced by independent and diverse sources.

In one Grade 4 classroom, teachers showed students examples of culture jamming, where advertising is disrupted through the use of speech bubbles which are used to promote an alternative reading or critical perspective. Students looked at fashion ads with speech bubbles reading, "I am hideously deformed" and health care ads with bubbles asking, "Why doesn't the government ensure our health?" Teachers showed students examples of outdoor ads that had been altered with speech bubbles, but also informed students that defacing outdoor advertising in this way is illegal. Then, students created their own projects, creating speech bubbles in response to magazine imagery (Ganier, Valdez-Gainer, & Kinard, 2009). Although most student-created responses were humorous and not critical in nature, the researchers consider this an important step towards creating citizens who can "disrupt, contest and transform media apparatuses" (Semali, 2003, p. 275).

This approach unabashedly assumes a social justice agenda from a liberal, pluralist point of view, which students inhabit in order to recognize and challenge the corporate media agenda, which privileges some groups and marginalizes others. Without addressing power in such ways, media studies can become a game of learning vocabulary to describe and demystify the functions of media without asking questions about who media serve and to what ends. By involving students in social activism through creating their own media representations and supporting independent media, and by inhabiting a particular point of view, critical media literacy educators may avoid the empty language game of demystifying media. However, contrary to the rhetoric of empowerment that often accompanies such efforts, students are seldom offered the opportunity to develop skills and knowledge of media and communication to strengthen and explore their own cultural positions and interests. Instead, this approach asserts a particular ideological position that students must take up.

The discourse of resistance in critical theory also contains another form of elitism, which sometimes devalues the mind-numbing content of popular cultural tastes in mass media and reveres high art as intellectually stimulating. A trace of this elitism is alive and well for many media educators who seek to develop cultural appreciation of critically-acclaimed or sophisticated popular media texts. Whereas once Adorno might have scoffed at media educators that proposed teaching Bob Dylan instead of Dylan Thomas, now, some media educators take up a similar view in choosing Bob Dylan over Spongebob Squarepants for study in the context of English education. As we have shown, critical media literacy approaches often work from the same deficit model of learners as approaches informed by media effects perspectives (Scharrer, 2007; Bragg, 2007).

Media literacy educators work from a position within critical theory in a more student-centered way when they encourage students to tackle the questions, "Who is telling the story?" and "What is omitted from the message?" (Hobbs, 2007). But the issue of teacher agency remains an inherent problematic embedded in this theoretical position. Conceptualizations of audience from critical theory perspectives clearly translate into specified roles for teacher and learner in the classroom. The English teacher inhabits the role of enlightened critic who must snap her class of cultural dupes out of false consciousness constructed by their passive relationships with media; a neat trick, simply performed (supposedly) by sharing some expert knowledge about the semiotic production of ideology and its base in the political economy of media institutions. However, this version of becoming critical often amounts to students playing a language game to gain caché with the teacher (Buckingham, 2003) as adolescents learn to "talk posh" about popular media (p. 110). There are dangers to a approach to media literacy that is positioned as counterpropaganda: much of it can become little more than a "superficial exercise in 'guessing what's in teacher's mind'" (Buckingham, 2007, p. 162).

The Rhetoric of Communication: Tools for the Code-Breaking Audience

Scholars in the humanities have long recognized the importance of language and other symbol systems as a structuring tool for human thought and action. People have been debating whether media emancipate us or are forms of social control for 2,500 years, beginning with the transition from oral to written culture (Provencal, 2004). The argument goes back to ancient times, with questions like these: How does our use of symbol systems like language and images shape social relationships? What is gained and what is lost with the strategic use of language and other symbols as tools for expression, persuasion and advocacy? How can symbol systems be used to express, distort or misrepresent our sense of personal identity, the value of social relationships, and our understanding of reality?

During the 20th century, the rise of structuralism and poststructuralism created renewed interest in these questions, exploring the relationship between language and other symbol systems as they relate to perception, cognition and meaning-making. Scholars working across a number of disciplines explored these issues in literature (Richards, Barthes), art history (Gombrich, Arnheim), linguistics (deSaussure, Peirce, Whorf, Ong), speech (Burke), developmental psychology (Bruner, Gardner), and film (Balazs).

In the field of communications, Marshall McLuhan was perhaps the foremost scholar within this tradition. A professor of literature with a specialty in British literature, he examined how changes in symbol systems of the electric age reshaped the nature of perception, knowledge, culture and values. In his view, electronic media disrupted the linear thought processes characteristic of Gutenberg man and replaced it with the simultaneous perception of electronic media man, just as phonetic literacy was a break boundary between oral culture and literate culture (McLuhan, 1964). Because new media create new environments, children grow up with a different set of skills, orientations, and ideas. For them, the perceptual environment of television influences "what kinds of facts are privileged as important and what type of stimuli are ignored or overlooked" (Fishman, 2006, p. 750). McLuhan's approach was based on the power of

metaphor as a playful means to gain insight on human experience. His most famous aphorism, "the medium is the message" called attention to the complex relationship between form and content. He wanted to explore the difference between reading a newspaper and watching a television news show, to consider how "the content of a medium is like the juicy piece of meat carried by the burglar to distract the watchdog of the mind" (McLuhan, 1964, p. 32). In this view, the effects of media are unnoticed because we focus on content and take the medium for granted. By practicing an inquiry approach to media, McLuhan theorized that we might shift our perspectives on our environs in order to assess what is gained and lost through our uses of media technologies—in order to ultimately act more strategically about our media use.

Often considered the grandfather of the media literacy movement, McLuhan created a media literacy syllabus for Grade 11 students under the rubric of a new approach to language and literature (Marchand, 1989), emphasizing the practice of interpretation not through an expert transmission model, but through student-centered practices of probing, deconstruction and close reading, using the media of communication as the text of study. Terms like genre, language, audience, message, medium, meaning, form, content, and context are central in this approach to critical analysis.

In the context of English education, media literacy educators aim to help students acquire a meta-language for analyzing their own responses to media texts. In the context of English education, students engaged in media literacy develop the ability to generalize about media texts, support assertions with evidence, appreciate context, develop more abstract ideas, and make reflexive judgments (Hobbs, 2007). This is most effective when students relate critical analysis to their own preferences as media users and audience members.

In exploring the language of media, visual designers have taken the canons of classical rhetoric (invention, arrangement, style, delivery, and memory) as a tool for analyzing the elements of visual and graphic design. In one media literacy textbook, students study how camera angles, transitions, camera movement are used in structuring a narrative, recognizing how point of view and tone are conveyed through skillful arrangement of visual and sound elements (Moses, 2008). Media literacy textbooks also use Barthes' notions of connotative and denotative meanings to help students develop an understanding about how media messages relate to cultural contexts of language and image use (Silverblatt, 2000). Core concepts in media literacy offer a way to compare how messages and their effects change when embodied in different media, which English educators often explore in comparing TV news to print, or the same narrative in a movie based on a book.

Critics contend that when formal analysis is emphasized over content, media literacy education can become formulaic, failing to incorporate critical perspectives on media institutions and ideologies (Lewis & Jhally, 1998); there is too much focus on the "what" of media languages and too little on the "who" and "what for." For English educators, a focus on identifying the many stylistic devices of film, photographic style, shot framing, advertising tactics, and types of interactivity may hark back to the debates between the Greeks about the aims of rhetoric. Does a focus on the medium itself come to trivialize and debase the power of language, the quest for truth and the search for meaning through the themes and concepts central to the humanities: ethics, identity, relationships and human values? Again, in the study of media rhetoric and semiotics, there are risks of learning becoming an empty language game of labeling functions and meaning-making devices. However, McLuhan and Barthes each saw their theoretical explorations of form and meaning as a way to heighten consciousness and inform strategic action around the uses of media and cultural power. English teachers who link studies of media grammar to decisions in students' own media production and consumption choices work towards embodying this vision.

Voice and Identity Play: Tools for the Powerful Audience

Audiences do creative work in the practice of meaning-making. Some scholars see critical theory as failing to consider the "multiple sets of discursive competencies" that media fans access "by virtue of more complex and contradictory places within the social formation" (Jenkins, 1992, p. 34). The American cultural studies tradition views critical and critical cultural perspectives as over-emphasizing the power of dominant media. Instead, readers of media texts are flexible and fluid in the reading, reception, and meaning-making process.

The study of media fandom has contributed to this argument. For example, in interviews with media fans about their favorite childhood television shows, Jenkins discusses how, typically, "The same person would shift between progressive and reactionary modes of thinking in the course of a single conversation, celebrating childhood resistance in one breath and demanding the regulation of childish pleasures in the next" (1992, p. 35). For Jenkins, media fans are cultural nomads who constantly move between various texts and identity positions to find and work on meanings to meet their social and personal needs and interests. This flexibility has made fans a model of the active audience for theorists working with the idea that culture is produced by the people from the bottom up as well as from the top down by powerful institutions like mass media.

There is significant experimentation underway in the use of technology to promote literacy, as English educators are using digital tools like blogs, wiki, and video to promote reading comprehension and composition skills (Kinszer & Leander, 2003; Lankshear & Knobel, 2007). Ironically, just as media literacy educators in the United States have begun the field's coalescence through the articulation of a shared set of key concepts and core principles developed primarily in relationship to mass media and popular culture (National Association for Media Literacy Education, 2007), the Inter-

net now stands at the center of the culture as a potentially decentralizing structure, obscuring and challenging the dominance of mass media corporations in popular culture. As the means to create and disseminate media messages extend to masses of connected users, media literacy educators must now consider how to help students participate with mass and digital media in addition to understanding and resisting its influence.

Media literacy educators use digital technology in cultivating student agency and voice in creating media, but the routines of school culture may interfere with these goals. Ratale and Korhonen (2008) developed a digital media production practice for Grade 5 students in Finland. In the 32-hour workshop, children experiment with software that enables them to create role-plays, storyboards, movies and animations on screen using drag and drop commands. They select from a themed library of resources including characters, sounds, backgrounds, and props. While students demonstrated high levels of creativity, the project was time-consuming. Teachers said, "There is never enough time. You always have to take it somewhere. Now it has been collected from here and there. Fifth grade is quite a demanding class. So even if you wished, it would not be possible to endlessly spend time with this" (p. 11).

Because it is associated with play, many children in the United States see the Internet primarily as an entertainment vehicle and not as a tool for learning (Kaiser Family Foundation, 2009). In many schools, digital media production stands as a real challenge to the traditional curriculum. Its novelty as an in-school activity can make it difficult to create organic connections between "school learning," "everyday life" and digital media. Talk about mass media, entertainment and popular culture in the English language arts classroom can also be perceived suspiciously by students, as children ask, "What does this have to do with school?" The strong framing of knowledge by the traditional school curriculum and the school's everyday order means "that children accept the truth of school knowledge as being within the logical space of the school world rather than having any relevance to life outside the school world" (Ratale & Korhonen, 2008, p. x).

Voice and identity play, as compelling as they are for supporting the creative development of children and young people, may run into difficulty in the context of K–12 teaching and learning, which is most often centered upon the decontextualized structure of the transmission model.

As we have shown, the notion of media audiences as powerful creators of meanings and culture presents new challenges and opportunities for integrating media literacy in English. The theory can be easily misappropriated to support a focus on tool acquisition at the expense of an emphasis on critical thinking about purposes and consequences of media use. English educators who support digital participation and interaction play an important role in helping students reflect on and share their online experiences. Such reflection on their new media use helps students to construct knowledge around the effective navigation and manipulation of information and media they find. By sharing experiences, students discuss ethics and their emerging skills for collaboration and collective action.

Conclusion

In the absence of survey research, it is difficult to know whether, at the K–12 practice level, English language arts educators include much more media literacy than the standard practices: an introduction to the difference between fact and opinion when reading a newspaper article, identifying persuasive strategies used in advertising, and instructional approaches to literary adaptation based on "read the book, watch the movie." These basic practices of media literacy education have been passed on generationally (from teacher to student who becomes teacher) since the beginning of the 20th century, beginning with early explorations in the use of film in English education and interest in language and propaganda (Hobbs & Jensen, 2009). When done as part of tradition and routine, they are likely to have little relevance and even less value to promote critical thinking and the robust development of communication skills.

However, because of our daily contact with children and young people, most English language arts educators do have an implicit or articulated philosophy about what matters when it comes to the inclusion of media texts, tools and technologies. As part of our job, educators see (more or less directly) how media and technology shape the experience of childhood and adolescence every day, in some many small (and some large) ways. We hear students using the catchphrases of popular songs in their own small talk, see how hairstyles and fashion change in relationship to the latest celebrity, and notice how students perk up when the talk turns to athletes, musicians, or the latest cell phone or videogame.

That's why we invited you, dear reader, to reflect on the nature of your own relationship with media and technology after considering the dynamic role these resources play in the lives of children and teens. Teacher educators can not assume that pre-service English teachers will integrate media and popular culture into their teaching plans even if they consider themselves "digital natives" and are interested in student-centered pedagogy, as research shows that new teachers are most likely to teach in the traditional ways they experienced as students (RobbGrieco, 2009). We believe that a theoretical foundation for educators' understandings of students as media users will provide useful support and bolster courage and conviction for teachers' efforts to integrate media literacy into English.

We see value in all four of the theoretical positions described in this chapter, even as we recognize the pitfalls and limitations of each. As media users, children and teens are still subject to mass media influence from within their own communities online and from the (still) powerful culture industries in digital, print, and broadcast media. While children and young people themselves create more and more media content, questioning and understanding the

ideological role of the cultural industries in shaping their tastes and values is as important as ever in order to afford young people the means to both resist and participate in dominant discourses as well as the means to transform them. As active audiences and users, children and adolescents both reproduce and exceed the preferred meanings of dominant ideology in their media use, but can always use help doing so in more reflective and strategic ways by engaging critical thinking. Furthermore, media literacy education should challenge students to confront issues of social justice in media representation and participation, building from the student's own social identifications and interests.

References

Adorno, T., & Horkheimer, M. (1972). *The culture industry: Enlightenment as mass deception. Dialectic of enlightenment* (pp. 120–167). New York: Herder & Herder.

Bourdieu, P. (1993). *The field of cultural production.* New York: Columbia University Press.

Bragg, S. (2007). What Kevin knows: Students' challenges to pedagogical thinking. In A. Nowak, S. Abel, & K. Ross (Eds.), *Rethinking media education: critical pedagogy and identity politics* (pp. 57–73). Cresskill, NJ: Hampton Press.

Bryant, J., & Zillmann, D. (1994). *Media effects: Advances in theory and research.* Hillsdale, NJ: Erlbaum.

Buckingham, D. (2003). *Media education: Literacy, learning, and contemporary culture.* Cambridge, UK: Polity.

Buckingham, D. (2007). *Beyond technology: Children's learning in the age of digital culture.* London: Polity.

Duran, R., Yousman, B., Walsh, K., & Longshore, M. (2008). Holistic media education: An assessment of the effectiveness of a college course in media literacy. *Communication Quarterly, 56*(1), 49–68.

Fishman, D. (2006). Rethinking Marshall McLuhan: Reflections on a media theorist. *Journal of Broadcasting and Electronic Media, 50*(3), 567–574.

Ganier, J. Valdez-Gainer, N., & Kinard, T. (2009). The elementary bubble project: exploring critical media literacy in a fourth grade classroom. *The Reading Teacher, 62*(8), 674–683.

Hobbs, R. (1998). The seven great debates in the media literacy movement. *Journal of Communication 44*(2), 16–32.

Hobbs, R. (2004). A review of school-based initiatives in media literacy education. *American Behavioral Scientist, 48*(1), 42–59.

Hobbs, R. (2007). *Reading the media: Media literacy in high school English.* New York: Teachers College Press.

Hobbs, R., & Jensen, A. (2009). The past, present and future of media literacy education. *Journal of Media Literacy Education, 1*(1), 1–11.

Jenkins, H. (1992). *Textual poachers: Television fans & participatory culture.* New York: Routledge.

Kaiser Family Foundation. (2010). Generation M2: Media in the lives of 8–18 year olds. Retrieved January 31, 2010, from http://www.kff.org/entmedia/mh012010pkg.cfm

Kellner, D., & Share, J. (2005). Towards critical media literacy: Core concepts, debates, organizations and policy. *Discourse: Studies in Ccultural Politics of Dducation, 26*(3), 369–386.

Kinzer, C., & Leander, K. M. (2003). Reconsidering the technology/language arts divide: Electronic and print-based environments. In D. Flood, D. Lapp, J. R. Squire, & J. M. Jensen (Eds.), *Handbook of research on teaching the English language arts* (pp. 546–565). Mahwah, NJ: Erlbaum.

Lankshear, C., & Knobel, M. (Eds.). (2007). *A new literacies sampler.* New York: Peter Lang.

Lewis, J., & Jhally, S. (1998). The struggle over media literacy. *Journal of Communication, 48,* 109–120.

Livingstone, S. (2008). Converging traditions of research on media and information literacies: Disciplinary, critical, and methodological issues. In J. Coiro, M. Knobel, C. Lankshear, & D. Leu (Eds.), *Handbook of research on new literacies* (pp. 103–132). New York: Taylor & Francis.

Marchand, P. (1989). *Marshall McLuhan: The medium and the messenger.* New York: Ticknor Fields.

Masterman, L. (1985). *Teaching the media.* London: Macmillan.

Mcleod, J., Kosicki, G., & Pan, Z. (1991). On understanding and misunderstanding media effects. In J. Curran & M. Gurevitch (Eds.), *Mass media and society* (pp. 235–266). London: Edward Arnold.

McLuhan, M. (1964). *Understanding media: The extensions of man.* New York: McGraw Hill.

Moses, L. (2008). *Introduction to media literacy.* New York: Kendall Hunt.

National Association for Media Literacy Education. (2007). Core principles of media literacy education in the United States. Retrieved August 29, 2009, from http://namle.net

National Council of Teachers of English. (2009). Pathways to 21st century literacies. Retrieved October 21, 2009, from http://www.ncte.org/pathways/21stcentury

Piette, J., & Giroux, L. (1997). Theoretical foundations of media education programs. In R. Kubey (Ed.), *Media literacy in the information age: Current perspectives* (pp. 89–134). New Brunswick, NJ: Transaction.

Provencal, J. (2004). Plato's dilemma and the media literacy movement. *Studies in Media & Information Literacy, 4*(3), 1–10.

Ratale, L., & Korhonen, V. (2008). New literacies as a challenge for traditional knowledge conception in school: A case study from fifth graders digital media production. *Studies in Media & Information Literacy, 8*(2), 1–15.

RobbGrieco, M. (2009, August 2). *Pre-service teachers' notions of texts and literacy practices for high school English.* Paper presented at National Association for Media Literacy Education conference in Detroit, MI.

Scharrer, E. (2007). Closer than you think: Bridging the gap between media effects and cultural studies in media education theory and practice. In A. Nowak, S. Abel, & K. Ross (Eds.), *Rethinking media education: Critical pedagogy and identity politics* (pp. 17–36). Cresskill, NJ: Hampton Press.

Scharrer, E. (2006). "I noticed more violence:" The effects of a media literacy program on critical attitudes toward media violence. *Journal of Mass Media Ethics, 21*(1), 69–86.

Silverblatt, A. (2000). *Media literacy: Keys to interpreting media messages.* New York: Praeger.

Semali, L. (2003). *Literacy in multimedia America.* New York: Falmer.

42

The Relevance of Rhetoric

Nancy Nelson

Rhetorical studies is an ever-changing field with deep historical roots dating back to Antiquity. This chapter is based on rich bodies of work from prior historical periods as well as the revived and revitalized rhetoric that has developed since mid-20th century. It begins with a consideration of referents for the term *rhetoric* and a brief historical overview of the discipline of rhetoric as it has developed and changed through the years. Then attention goes to rhetorical concerns that are most relevant to ongoing and emerging issues in the English language arts: rhetorical situations, author-audience relations, and rhetorical purposes and approaches. Within these general concerns are more specific matters that are central to teachers at all levels of education, such as genre, audience awareness and adaptation, persona, motives, appeals, and arguments.

The Term *Rhetoric*

Although different conceptions of rhetoric have different emphases, the focus of rhetoric, generally speaking, is on the uses of language in social contexts. Attention is on the linguistic means that are used to achieve agreement, as in Kenneth Burke's (1969) description of rhetoric as "the use of language as a symbolic means of inducing cooperation in beings that by nature respond to symbols" (p. 43). During the last few decades, during what some have called "the rhetorical turn," the domain of rhetoric has broadened beyond its former disciplinary boundaries in English and communication studies, as scholars in many areas have turned their attention to language and social practices.

Rhetoric is concerned with communicative acts, and thus attention has traditionally gone to author, audience, subject matter (or topic), and text. These four components can be positioned on a rhetorical triangle, as shown in Figure 42.1. The triangle highlights interconnections, such as that between author and audience, and also shows how, in one conception to be discussed later, a rhetorical aim, such as to persuade or to inform, can aligned with the component

receiving most emphasis. It is important to keep in mind that, even though the term *rhetoric* today is associated most often with the composing of texts, written and oral, it also includes response to texts. There is an approach to understanding texts that is being called *rhetorical reading*, and some also speak of *rhetorical listening*. Thus, rhetoric encompasses the four language arts of speaking, writing, listening, and reading. *Rhetoric* also refers to the discourse practices associated with particular groups, as in the phrases "Chicana rhetoric," "the rhetoric of science," and "the rhetoric of accountability."

Rhetoric encompasses the uses of language and the study of these uses by rhetoricians, and it also includes instruction in aspects of effective communication. It has played a role in the educational curriculum throughout history from ancient times to the present, and today the label is still used for a subject of study in higher education. Rhetorical principles are embedded in writing instruction in the K–12 curriculum.

In this discussion of referents, I must also acknowledge the use of the term *rhetoric* to refer to language that is flowery and without substance or is untruthful and intended to deceive and manipulate. Although this referent creates a complication for the scholars and educators whose work fits in the scholarly tradition discussed below, there is some historical justification for this use: At one point in the history summarized below, rhetoric focused only on eloquence apart from substance. That, however, was just one phase of a very long history dating back 26 centuries.

Rhetoric Through the Years

Historical treatments have presented major contributions and developments in rhetoric over time: Antiquity, Middle Ages, Renaissance, Enlightenment, and the subsequent centuries up to the present. In the following, I present a brief survey but refer the reader to more detailed histories (e.g., Herrick, 2009; Kennedy, 1994; Murphy & Katula, 2003;

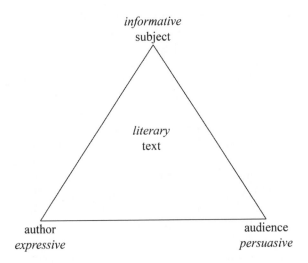

informative
subject

literary
text

author   audience
expressive   *persuasive*

Figure 42.1

Nelson & Kinneavy, 2003) as well a recent counter-history by Byron Hawk (2007), who critiqued the "metanarrative" used in many other treatments.

Classical to Modern Rhetoric In ancient times, persuasion was the focus of rhetoric, especially as persuasive discourse was used in legal and political contexts. Rhetoric had its beginnings in city-states of Greece and Sicily in the 6th century B.C. as governmental structures were changing and democracies were being formed. The Sophists and Plato made early contributions to rhetorical theory, but it was Aristotle who provided the works that would be most influential. Although Aristotle and the other Greeks provided the conceptual framework, it was the Romans, particularly Cicero and Quintilian, who developed a pedagogical approach grounded in Aristotelian theory. Major works by Cicero and Quintilian and also the *Rhetoric ad Herennium* by an anonymous author dominated rhetoric for centuries, and the Graeco-Roman conception had widespread influence as educators in other parts of Europe followed that model. In the classical education, students studied the five parts, or *canons*, of rhetoric—invention, arrangement, style, memory, and delivery. Today, English language arts educators tend to focus on three of the five—invention, arrangement, and style—often using the term *prewriting* for *invention* and *organization* for *arrangement*.

In the Middle Ages, rhetoric was the third of the seven liberal arts in education, and it followed grammar and logic. For years the major rhetorical texts were Cicero's *On Invention* and the anonymous *Rhetoric ad Herennium*, but by the 5th century, with the growth of Christianity, St. Augustine's *De Doctrina Christiana* became a major text as rhetorical principles were applied to Biblical study. The classical works on rhetoric received less attention in education, and some seemed to be lost.

During the European Renaissance, with the resurgence of interest in classical art and thought, rhetoric tended to return to the classical conception. This development was

supported by Petrarch, who located missing classical texts, and by Erasmus, who incorporated classical elements in his treatises. However, the 16th century saw some major changes in the relation between rhetoric and logic. Largely because of the efforts of the French rhetorician Ramus and his colleague Talon, invention and arrangement were moved from rhetoric to logic, and memory was collapsed into arrangement. These changes left rhetoric with only style and delivery—a focus on eloquence bereft of those elements that emphasize thought processes. The Ramist conception of rhetoric, without the classical emphasis on invention and arrangement, had some influence on the curriculum of the new American colleges formed by the colonists. When the Enlightenment brought new developments in science and technology in the 17th and 18th centuries, there was some questioning of classical rhetorical techniques: Could they accommodate the kinds of communication that were now required? Critics pointed to the seemingly superficial and even manipulative nature of rhetoric, with its emphasis on style.

There was some new life for rhetoric in the late 18th century when Scottish rhetoricians George Campbell (1776/1846) and Hugh Blair (1783/1867) offered interesting treatments of elements of rhetoric, including arrangement, and produced texts that were influential not only in Europe but also in the United States. Campbell incorporated insights from the associationist psychology of the day as he reclaimed arrangement for rhetoric and gave attention to modes and audience analysis, and Bair linked rhetoric to the belles lettres tradition. Then, in the 19th century, Richard Whately (1828) and Alexander Bain (1890) also produced influential textbooks.

The version of rhetoric that predominated in the last decades of the 19th century emphasized certain elements: the modes, especially exposition; abstract qualities for writing (unity, emphasis, coherence); and paragraph structure. This was the form of rhetoric that had become part of "English" as it was formed as a department in higher education in the United States. At this time American higher education was giving attention to the writing skills of entering students and considering them to be inadequate, and rhetoric was combined with new "remedial" composition courses to create what was sometimes called *rhetoric-composition*. Rhetoric persisted in this consolidated form in higher education, but as a subject of study it lost out at lower levels of American education. The concerns of classical rhetoric received little attention when the Committee of Ten established the school subject that was known as English at the turn of the century.

Current-traditional was the term Daniel Fogarty (1959) coined to describe the approach to composition instruction widely used during the first half of the 20th century. Although Fogarty was speaking of college instruction, his description also fit writing instruction at lower levels. Current-traditional pedagogy focused on arrangement with respect to modes, on paragraph development, and on mechanical correctness. This was a diminished form of rhetoric, and the term *current traditional* referred to what needed to be changed.

The "New" Rhetoric Rhetoric was being reinvented in various ways in the mid-20th century, as a number of people were talking about a *new rhetoric*. Although the *new* label caught on, there has been and is no single *new* rhetoric. Here my focus is on four approaches to rhetoric that have carried the "new" label. All developed over the past six decades and continue to have influence today: neoclassical rhetoric, expressivist rhetoric, cognitive rhetoric, and sociocultural rhetoric.

The *neoclassical rhetoric* label can be applied to the work of those rhetoricians who have attempted to center their theoretical work on the issues of classical rhetoric. Major contributors are Kenneth Burke (1969), who presented a biological, psychological, and sociological extension of Aristotelian rhetoric; James Kinneavy (1971), who focused on the aims of discourse in the liberal arts tradition; and Chaim Perelman and Lucie Olbrechts-Tyteca (1969), who brought a new conception of relation between author and audience by pointing to its situated nature. The *expressivist rhetoric* label goes to the work of a number of scholars, including Ken Macrorie (1970) and Don Murray (1972), who gave emphasis to individuals' processes of composing and their ownership of their own writing. Finally, the *cognitive rhetoric* label goes to a body of work that dates back to Janet Emig's (1971) inquiry into composing processes and numerous other process-oriented studies of writers. Predominant in this cognitive work is the problem-solving theory of writing developed by John R. Hayes and Linda Flower (1980). Finally, the label *sociocultural rhetoric* goes to a fourth major source of new life for rhetoric where attention is on productive and reproductive practices associated with groups or communities (e.g., Berkenkotter & Huckin, 1995). This work, which also began in the latter decades of the 20th century, explores the ways in which a community's values, norms, and worldviews are maintained but also transformed through social interaction by its members.

Rhetorical Concerns

Through the years, rhetoricians have pursued recurring issues and themes as they have contributed to rhetorical theory. Particularly relevant to English language arts are the matters of rhetorical situations and author-audience relations. After attention to both, I consider the rhetorical concepts of purposes and supports for claims that are relevant to the teaching of writing and speaking. Although discussed separately, all are interlinked. People experience rhetorical situations, and they produce texts to accomplish their purposes with their audiences. To have the desired effect, they must provide credible support for their claims.

Rhetorical Situations In the discipline of rhetoric, much attention has been given to the contexts in which people produce their texts, and much of the discussion of context has often centered on "rhetorical situation"—a notion that is certainly relevant today given the interest in situated practices (e.g., Lave & Wenger, 1991). Many English language arts educators seek to have students write texts for "real" audiences and "real" situations outside the classroom. The term *rhetorical situation* should be credited to Lloyd Bitzer (1968), who explained that a rhetorical situation is a "natural context of persons, events, objects, relations, and an exigence which strongly invites utterance" (p. 5). The *exigence*, or *exigency*, is the need to write or speak—the need to fill a gap, to communicate what the situation demands. A "correction" to Bitzer's notion came from Richard Vatz (1973), who argued that Bitzer had omitted something important from his description, the interpretive element. Vatz pointed out that the situations themselves are not rhetorical but, instead, the people interpreting them *make* them rhetorical. This was an important point: interpretation is required if one is to perceive a gap to fill.

But the concept of rhetorical situation has changed as the field of rhetoric itself has changed during the past decades. It has extended beyond the immediate context to include the larger sociocultural and historical context. Exigencies, or perceived invitations to produce discourse, fit within traditions and customs associated with social groups or communities. The nature of these invitations and their responses conform to the social practices in which people engage as members of the community (cf. Schmidt & vande Koppel, 1993). Community members experience recurring kinds of situations, and those who are immersed in their community "know" when responses are invited and what kinds of responses are expected. This point is relevant to English language arts educators, since they try to help students produce writing that is appropriate for a context.

This new emphasis on sociocultural and historical context is also relevant to the notion of genres, which have, in the past, been considered to be rather static text types to be chosen in somewhat arbitrary fashion by a writer or speaker. A major contribution to a reconceptualization was made by Carolyn Miller (1984) in her article, "Genre as Social Action," where she argued that genres are social *actions*—typified actions of members of a group or society in response to recurrent situations. For her, genre "acquires meaning from situation and from the social context in which that situation arose.... A genre is a rhetorical means for mediating private intentions and social exigence; it motivates by connecting the private with the public, the singular with the recurrent" (p. 163). Students experience "old" genres, such as reporting on a book, and new genres, such as blogging and texting.

A second and further broadening is the extension of the concept of the rhetorical situation to include the intertextual context as well, and the Russian theorist Mikhail Bakhtin (1981, 1986) can be credited for much of that expansion. In his dialogic theory of discourse, a writer (or speaker) is portrayed as entering and participating in a tradition that is tied to the past and is also oriented to present and future. Expanding the dialogue analogy beyond a single invitation and response, Bakhtin (1981) described a text as a response to a "background" of other texts, such as "contradictory opinions, points of view and value judgments" (p. 281). He was speaking not only of prior texts but also current and (possible) future texts. As he said, the writing is "determined by that which has not yet been said" (p. 280). This is a very interesting contribution to discourse theory: the claim that the text someone produces is influenced not only by texts that came before but also by texts that *might* or *might not* be produced in the future. It is another way of thinking about the importance of audience and the kind of reception that writers anticipate.

Rhetorical Relations Between Author and Audience

Central to rhetoric are the relations that exist, or are created, between authors and audiences. The discussion below considers first the relation that authors have with their audiences and then looks the other way to consider the relation that audiences have with authors of texts they experience.

Authors and Their Audiences. Authors produce texts for an audience, and that audience may be hypothetical or "real," individual or specific, single or multiple, immediate or distant, supportive or resistant; and among rhetoricians there has been much discussion of the nature of audience. In recent decades, the discourse community notion has complicated the notion of audience by emphasizing collective elements. A discourse community, as James Porter (1986) explained, can be seen as a group whose members share a common interest and whose discourse is socially regulated. In producing texts for their community, authors write for others who, to a great extent, share their values, knowledge, and beliefs and who are guided by similar conventions in communication. In this conception, the audience, in a sense, contributes to the authoring of a text because of the importance of community expectations as well as social interactions.

The classical Graeco-Roman conception emphasized the importance of audience, and audience analysis is where many rhetoricians through the years have put their attention. Composing texts entails "reading" one's readers, which means considering ways in which this audience will respond. Will they understand? Will they agree? Will they refute? There is epistemic value associated with audience, since an author wants to have knowledge of what the audience already knows, and there is also heuristic value, since an author generates material by thinking about what the audience would need to know.

Two concepts of importance to English language arts educators over the years are *audience awareness* and *audience adaptation*, both of which have been tied to individuals' social cognition (e.g., Rubin, 1984). Audience awareness is one's awareness that members of the audience may not have *all* the background or knowledge (or *the same* background or knowledge) that he himself or she herself has about the topic or that they have particular other needs; and audience adaptation is the ability to adjust one's writing or speech for the intended audience. Both awareness and adaptation are thought to develop as individuals mature, although there are situations in which all of us, even experienced writers, are unaware of audience needs and also of the means for adapting a text for them. Teachers encourage students to think about their audiences as they prepare to speak or write and, if writing, to attend to audience also in revising.

A third related concept at the intersection between author and audience is *persona* (from the Latin for "mask"). This is the "self" that a writer or speaker *projects* to an audience in a communication, or, from the other perspective, is the "self" for that author that the audience *interprets* from that communication. It is important to note that there is no singular persona for a particular individual; different personae are constructed and interpreted when situations and texts vary. This notion of persona continues to be relevant today, even with new technologies. For instance, writers seem to project personality attributes linked to persona through the typefaces they use for their texts (Brumberger, 2003). The notion of persona has become increasingly complex now that social factors are recognized to a greater extent, as in James Gee's (1989) discussion of *identity kits*—the "saying (writing)-doing-being-valuing-believing combinations" that identify people with a particular groups (p. 6).

Insights into rhetorical matters, including the author-audience relation, can be gained by considering something that Wayne Booth (1963) called the *rhetorical stance*. He explained that effective writing is a matter of "maintaining in any writing situation a proper balance among the three elements that are at work in any communicative effort: the available arguments about the subject itself, the interests and peculiarities of the audience, and the voice, the implied character, of the speaker" (p. 141). In his essay, Booth considered the challenge that individuals experience when they attempt to achieve a balance among author, audience, and subject matter—those elements located at the three points of the rhetorical triangle pictured above. Achieving a balance depends on the rhetorical situation itself, since there are no articulated "rules" that hold across situations. Writers must use their interpretations to make choices and try to give the various elements the emphasis appropriate for that situation. This notion of balance helps students understand the importance of the author and audience elements and see that there is more to writing than putting information together.

What features of writing help a writer connect with an audience? Rhetorical inquiry has focused on the devices—sometimes called *moves*—that writers use to connect with their audiences, and these insights are also relevant to students' writing. Although this body of work is too large to review here, I do want to mention, in particular, the research of Ken Hyland (2001), who has examined a large corpus of texts from a number of disciplines for what he called "addressee features." These features include using hedges to ward off objections while showing respect for readers' possible disagreement, first-person pronouns to mark inclusion, and references to shared knowledge to indicate social bonds.

Audiences and Their Authors. Although rhetoric has tended to focus, to a greater extent, on authors' interpretations of their audiences, the relations work the other way too. Audiences often "read" their authors, attributing motives, evaluating character, and assessing personae. Even though readers or listeners cannot know with any certainty what an author's intentions are, they do, at least sometimes, try to discern intent as they experience the text. The term *rhetorical reading* was coined by Chris Haas and Linda Flower (1988) for "readers actively trying to understand the author's intent, the context, and how other readers might respond" (p. 181). There is some evidence that people who have expertise in their field are more aware of these rhetorical aspects when they read (e.g., Wineburg, 2001) and that people become more rhetorical in their reading as they mature as writers.

For young students, a number of approaches are designed to develop what is called the *author concept*. Among them is Donald Graves and Jane Hansen's (1983) "Author's Chair," by means of which the children begin to see themselves as authors and to connect themselves with the authors of books they read. Another is Isabel Beck, Margaret McKeown, and Jo Worthy's (1995) approach called "Questioning the Author," in which the young people learn that authors of their textbooks had choices as they wrote and that the choices they made might not have been the best ones. The children would "question" the author about these choices and think of ways that the points may have been made more clearly. In addition to these specific instructional strategies, a more general example is the writing-workshop approach to writing instruction, in which students participate as authors in a *community of authors* (Atwell, 1998).

In this section thus far I have been discussing author-audience relations when a text is presented linearly and when an author attempts to guide the audience along that linear path. I conclude by asking: What happens to the author-audience relation when the text is nonlinear—when it is hypertext? Some theorists, including J. David Bolter (1991) and George Landow (2006), have argued that, when the text is hypertext, audience-author relations are changed. Authors lose some of their authorial control when the text is nonlinear and variable. (For a fuller discussion of this and other aspects of the audience-author relation, see Nelson, 2008; Nelson & Calfee, 1998.)

Rhetorical Purposes and Support for Claims

Today, in new conceptions of rhetoric, there is renewed emphasis on two classical concerns, purposes for writing or speaking and means of supporting claims. In what follows I discuss various classifications of purposes and then consider approaches for generating or for analyzing supports for claims.

Purposes. When people produce texts in rhetorical situations, they do so to accomplish their purposes (which might be called goals, aims, motives, or intentions), and, when understanding texts, they also can perform rhetorical reading and rhetorical listening, which entails attending to author's motives. This matter of purpose is complex and contested. Aristotle had conceptualized rhetoric as an art focused on one purpose, persuasion; and some rhetoricians have argued that, even though there may be other purposes, the basic intent is always to persuade. That has been countered by scholars who have discussed multiple purposes other than persuasion, such as an invitational purpose (inviting listeners or readers into one's world) (Foss & Griffith, 1995), or who focus on a particular realm of discourse that encompasses more specific purposes, such as "English for academic purposes" (e.g., Flowerdew & Peacock, 2001).

Some rhetoricians have attempted to come up with sets of general aims that are all-inclusive. These include Campbell's (1776/1846) "to enlighten the understanding, to please the imagination, to move the passions, and to influence the will" (p. 1). They also include Kinneavy's (1971) to persuade (persuasive), to inform (referential), to entertain (literary), and to express or to discover something about themselves (expressive). As mentioned above, these aims can be positioned on the rhetorical triangle of Figure 41.1, with expressive emphasizing the author; referential, or informative, emphasizing the subject; persuasive emphasizing the audience; and literary emphasizing features of the text itself. In any situation there are likely be multiple purposes, and purposes may change over the course of composing. Whereas in rhetorical theory purposes are differentiated from modes (the ways in which material is structured), some curriculum in the schools tends to conflate purpose and mode. For instance, narration and exposition might be presented as purposes instead of approaches to organizing texts.

Support for Claims. Invention, one of the five canons of classical rhetoric, is the means of generating material for accomplishing purposes through language. During the first half of the 20th century, invention received little attention as the emphasis was overwhelmingly on the arrangement of content. However, with the revival of rhetoric that began in the 1960s and 1970s, invention once more became a major focus. Classical rhetoric had treated invention in terms of *topoi*, or places, in accordance with the idea that there are mental places where certain kinds of material are stored. The topoi were a kind of heuristic for going to those "places" and seeing what might be said. In a neoclassical treatment, Edward P. J. Corbett (1971) provided a list that includes various means of development, including definition, comparison, cause-effect, antecedent-consequent, authority, and examples. It can be generative in considering a problem, for example, to think about how to define it, relate it to others with some similarity, to consider possible causes or effects, to consider past events, and so on. Because of their usefulness in helping writers think of relevant material, the topoi appear in instruction for young as well as older writers, even though they are not usually called topoi. They are also being used to analyze extant texts (e.g., Fahnestock, 2009).

Other approaches to generating material have also been developed. Well known among rhetoricians is *tagmemics*

(Young, Becker, & Pike, 1970), which provides different perspectives on a topic (particle, wave, and field). Also well known is Burke's (1969) pentad (act, scene, agent, agency, purpose), which has new life through its use in activity analysis (e.g., Ruth, 2009). Another major approach to generating and structuring material is based on Stephen Toulmin's (1964) model, which focuses on claims, data, and also warrants linking the claim and the data. This approach provides a way for individuals to examine their own arguments or those produced by others and see how strong and reasonable they are. For young writers or speakers, there are related approaches such as *cubing*, which is also a system for considering a topic from multiple perspectives.

Also relevant for producing and analyzing discourse are the appeals, a long-standing element of classical rhetorical theory. They include *logos,* the logical appeal that is associated with the subject matter itself; *ethos*, the appeal to one's own credibility; and *pathos*, the appeal to some quality of the audience, such as concern, feeling, passion. To have the desired impact, writers try to generate and organize ideas that seem logical, and they also want to reflect a suitable authorial persona and have the text resonate with their readers. Like the other approaches discussed above, consideration of appeals can be employed in analyzing as well as producing written and oral discourse.

Although discussed separately, this matter of making claims and supporting them is interlinked with the other elements. People write their texts to accomplish their purposes with their audiences; and, to have the desired effect, they must provide credible support for their claims.

Conclusion

In this chapter my attention has been on the relevance of rhetoric to issues in the English language arts. I have attempted to show how concerns dating back to the classical period of rhetoric are central to theory, research, and pedagogy in English language arts today. These matters have been discussed in terms of rhetorical situation, relations between author and audience, and rhetorical purposes and means of supporting claims. All have been and continue to be major foci of rhetorical pedagogy and scholarship.

The ancient Greeks spoke of rhetoric as *techne*—art, skill, craft—and placed emphasis on its situated, practical uses. "Useful" and "practical" are major descriptors today. As Charles Bazerman (1988) pointed out, rhetoric is "ultimately a practical study offering people greater control over their symbolic activity" (p 6). Rhetoric emphasizes the capacity of educators to teach effectiveness in the situated uses of language and of students to learn how to become more effective in their communications. It is important, in considering this relevance, to keep in mind that rhetoric, as a techne (art), is not a static kind of knowledge, is not a set of rules. Rhetoric is concerned with *doing*. Its concerns today lie in language used in particular situations or communities.

Although its roots were in oral uses of language, rhetoric it is best known among English educators today for its relevance to written communications. The link with writing is strong, so strong that often the labels *rhetoric* and *composition* seem synonymous. But rhetoric also has strong roots in other uses of language, and has a continued influence today in scholarship on analytic and critical reading, which in scholarly forms are called *rhetorical analysis* or *rhetorical criticism*. Because its territory is the social uses of language, rhetoric is relevant to all kinds of communicative acts in all kinds of contexts—is relevant to all the language arts.

References

Atwell, N. (1998). *In the middle: New understandings about writing, reading, and learning*. Portsmouth, NH: Heinemann.

Bain, A. (1890). *English composition and rhetoric: A manual* (enlarged ed.). New York: D. Appleton.

Bakhtin, M. M. (1981). *The dialogic imagination* (C. Emerson & M. Holquist, Eds., M. Holquist, Trans.). Austin: University of Texas Press.

Bakhtin, M. M. (1986). *Speech genres and other late essays* (C. Emerson & M. Holquist, Eds., V. W. McGee, Trans.). Austin: University of Texas Press.

Bazerman, C. (1988). *Shaping written knowledge: The genre and activity of the experimental article in science*. Madison: University of Wisconsin Press.

Beck, I. L., McKeown, M. G., & Worthy, J. (1995). Giving a text voice can improve students' understanding. *Reading Research Quarterly, 30*, 220–238.

Berkenkotter, C., & Huckin, T. (1995). *Genre knowledge in disciplinary communication: Cognition/culture/power*. Hillsdale, NJ: Erlbaum.

Bitzer, L. F. (1968). The rhetorical situation. *Philosophy and Rhetoric, 1*, 1–14.

Blair, H. (1867). *Lectures on rhetoric and belles lettres*. Philadelphia: Robert Aitken. (Original work published 1783)

Bolter, J. D. (1991). *Writing space: The computer, hypertext, and the history of writing*. Hillsdale, NJ: Erlbaum.

Booth, W. (1963). The rhetorical stance. *College Composition and Communication, 14*, 139–145.

Brumberger, E. R. (2003). The rhetoric of typography: The persona of typeface and text. *Technical Communication, 50*, 206–223.

Burke, K. (1969). *A rhetoric of motives*. Berkeley: University of California Press.

Campbell, G. (1846). *The philosophy of rhetoric*. New York: Harper & Brothers. (Original work published 1776)

Corbett, E. P. J. (1971). *Classical rhetoric for the modern student*. New York: Oxford University Press.

Emig, J. (1971). *The composing processes of twelfth graders*. Research Report No. 13. Urbana, IL: National Council of Teachers of English.

Fahnestock, J. (2009). Rhetorical analysis. In F. H. van Eemeren (Ed.), *Argumentation in context* (pp. 191–220). Philadelphia: John Benjamins.

Flowerdew, J., & Peacock, M. (2001). *Research perspectives on English for academic purposes*. Cambridge, UK: Cambridge University Press.

Fogarty, D. J. (1959). *Notes for a new rhetoric*. New York: Teachers College Press.

Foss, S. K., & Griffith, C. L. (1995). Beyond persuasion: A proposal for invitational rhetoric. *Communication Monographs, 62*, 2–18.

Gee, J. P. (1989). Literacy, discourse, and linguistics. *Journal of Education, 171*, 5–17.

Graves, D., & Hansen, J. (1983). The author's chair. *Language Arts, 60*, 176–183.

Haas, C., & Flower, L. (1988). Rhetorical reading strategies and the construction of meaning. *College Composition and Communication, 39*, 167–183.

Hawk, B. (2007). *A counter history of composition.* Philadelphia: University of Pennsylvania Press.

Hayes, J. R., & Flower, L. (1980). Identifying the organization of writing processes. In L. Gregg & E. R. Steinberg (Eds.), *Cognitive processes in writing* (pp. 3–28). Hillsdale, NJ: Erlbaum.

Herrick, J. A. (2009). *The history and theory of rhetoric* (4th ed.). New York: Allyn & Bacon.

Hyland, K. (2001). Bringing in the reader: Addressee features in academic writing. *Written Communication, 18,* 549–574.

Kennedy, G. A. (1994). *A new history of classical rhetoric.* Princeton, NJ: Princeton University Press.

Kinneavy, J. L. (1971). *A theory of discourse.* Englewood Cliffs, NJ: Prentice-Hall.

Landow, G. (2006). *Hypertext 3.0: Critical theory and new media in an era of globalization.* Baltimore, MD: Johns Hopkins University Press.

Lave, J., & Wenger, E. (1991). *Situated learning: Legitimate peripheral participation.* New York: Cambridge University Press.

Macrorie, K. (1970). *Uptaught.* Rochelle Park, NJ: Hayden.

Miller, C. R. (1984). Genre as social action. *Quarterly Journal of Speech, 70,* 151–167.

Murphy, J. J., & Katula, R. A. (2003). *A synoptic history of rhetoric* (3rd ed.). Mahwah, NJ: Erlbaum.

Murray, D. (1972, November). Teach writing as process not product. *Leaflet of the New England Association of Teachers of English,* 11–14.

Miller, C. R. (1984). Genre as social action. *Quarterly Journal of Speech, 70,* 151–167.

Nelson, N. (2008). The reading-writing nexus in discourse research. In C. Bazerman (Ed.), *Handbook of research on writing* (pp. 435–450). New York: Routledge.

Nelson, N., & Calfee, R. C. (Eds.). (1998). *The reading-writing connection: Ninety-seventh yearbook of the National Society for the Study of Education.* Chicago: University of Chicago Press.

Nelson, N., & Kinneavy, J. (2003). Rhetoric. In J. Flood, D. Lapp, J. R. Squire, & J. M. Jensen (Eds.), *Handbook of research on teaching the English language arts* (pp. 786–798). Mahwah, NJ: Erlbaum.

Perelman, C., & Olbrechts-Tyetca, L. (1969). *The new rhetoric: A treatise on argumentation* (J. Wilkinson & P. Weaver, Trans.). Notre Dame, IN: University of Notre Dame Press.

Porter, J. E. (1986). Intertextuality and the discourse community. *Rhetoric Review, 5,* 34–47.

Rubin, D. L. (1984). Social cognition and written communication. *Written Communication, 1,* 211–245.

Ruth, A. (2009). Computer-mediated learning applying Burke's pentad. In S. Kelsey & K. St. Amant (Eds.), *Handbook of research on computer mediated communication* (pp. 73–86). Hershey, PA: Information Science Reference.

Schmidt, G. D., & vande Koppel, W. J. (1993). *Communities of discourse.* Englewood Cliffs, NJ: Prentice-Hall.

Toulmin, S. E. (1964). *The uses of argument.* Cambridge, MA: Cambridge University Press.

Vatz, R. E. (1973). The myth of the rhetorical situation. *Philosophy and Rhetoric, 6,* 154–161.

Whately, R. (1828). *Elements of rhetoric.* Oxford, UK: Parker.

Wineburg, S. (2001). *Historical thinking and other unnatural acts.* Philadelphia: Temple University Press.

Young, R. E., Becker, A. L., & Pike, K. L. (1970). *Rhetoric: Discovery and change.* New York: Harcourt, Brace.

43

Grammar and Literacy Learning

MEG GEBHARD AND J. R. MARTIN

We begin this chapter by outlining three conceptions of grammar, which we term *traditional*, *formal*, and *functional* perspectives. We then focus on a *functional* perspective and how it can inform the work of literacy educators by providing an analysis of a text produced by an Australian tenth grader. We conclude with a brief discussion of how a functional perspective on grammar has been taken up in the United States as a way of supporting teachers and their students in negotiating the demands of changing social, political, and economic forces in education.

1. Which Grammar?

To talk about grammar, we first must establish what kind of grammar we are talking about. As educators, we have three choices: traditional school grammar, formal grammar, and functional grammar. Traditional grammar, inherited from the Greeks and Romans, was closely tied to the study of rhetoric and logic and enjoyed a scholarly tradition into the 19th century. The bare remnants of this tradition are what many of us would recognize as the grammar students study in English classes today (Christie, 1993). It consists of the study of parts of speech and prescriptive rules regarding correct usage. These parts of speech, or what linguists call categories or classes of words (e.g., noun, verb, preposition, adjective, adverb) are used in rules such as "Don't end a sentence with a preposition," "Don't begin a sentence with a conjunction," or "Never use the first person pronoun in academic writing." Some versions of school grammar, especially those used in teaching second languages, retain additional categorisation such as voice (active/passive), tense (present progressive, past progressive) and even more exotic phenomena such as gerunds and participles. In addition, relational categories such as Subject and Object are invoked to manage what is referred to as 'Subject verb agreement' (*I think, she thinks*). However, uncertainty about these additional categories can lead to nonsensical prescriptions such as "Avoid the passive tense."

School grammar of this kind has given the word "grammar" a bad name for a number of reasons. Students often find the experience of having their "grammar" corrected objectionable because it takes the focus off meaning; it imposes arbitrary rules that most people do not follow; it does not necessarily lead to more powerful ways of reading and writing; and it insults and discriminates against social or regional dialects. As a result of this bad name, many progressive educators and policymakers have worked to remove grammar instruction from state frameworks and teacher education programs altogether (Kollin & Hancock, 2005). This situation has created quite a challenge for educational linguists trying to get knowledge about language back into schools, since the only grammar that is less effective than traditional school grammar in fostering literacy development is no grammar at all. To this day, many debates about grammar polarize around school grammar of this sort, with conservatives arguing for prescriptive rules for language behavior, and liberals questioning the fairness and utility of these prescriptions.

Unlike traditional school grammar, which lost its footing in academe, both formal and functional grammar are based on work by theoretical linguists. One challenge for educators is that within these two broad traditions, there are many specialized theories with high levels of technicality. This diversification means care must be taken in choosing which models to adopt (Martin, 1999). As far as literacy learning is concerned, the choice has to do with selecting a model that best can inform studies of literacy development. In linguistics, especially in North America, formal grammar currently has more practitioners than functional grammar. Informed by Chomskian linguistics, the mission of formal grammar is to explore structures such as *Al wrote an essay* (Figure 43. 1) across languages to determine what all languages have in common. In addition, Chomskian linguists aim to propose universal constraints on the nature of constituent structures deriving ultimately from inferred neurological mutations allowing for just these structures

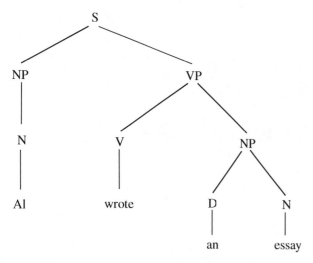

Figure 43.1 Phrase marker for the constituent structure in formal grammar.

and no others (e.g., *Al wrote an essay. What did Al write? Al wrote the beginning of an essay. What did Al write the beginning of? Al wrote an essay Bill published?* but not **Who did Al write an essay published.*)

A formal conception of grammar and associated scholarship continues across languages around the world today (Pinker, 1994). This research can be of relevance to literacy learning where it can be shown that certain syntactic structures develop before others and that structural configurations such as the one shown in Figure 43.1 can be used as evidence in measuring literacy development. For example, researchers such as Hunt (1970) in first language studies analyzed the syntactic complexity of students' writing samples to make claims about their stage of literacy devel-

opment. However, as Grabe and Kaplan (1996) make clear, "there has been an inability to demonstrate a clear relation between syntactic complexity measures and judgements of improved writing quality" (p. 45). The problem with trying to make such connections is, of course, that judgements of quality are not based on degrees of syntactic complexity alone, but on how aspects of syntax intersect with other meaning-making systems in particular contexts.

A question arises, therefore, as to what extent the study of grammar can be reoriented to the study of meaning (Coffin, 2006; Coffin, Donohue, & North, 2009). This in effect is the mission of functional linguists. One of the best known theorists of functional linguistics is M. A. K. Halliday, who from early in his career tuned his approach to grammar, known as systemic functional linguistics (SFL), to the needs of educators (e.g., Halliday, 2007). As a first step, Halliday's strategy relies on labelling the parts of a clause for grammatical function (e.g., Subject, Object) as well as class (for grammatical relations as well as categories in formalist terms). This information is left implicit in formal syntactic trees because it is argued that the shape of the tree can be used to infer functional relations: the Subject (S) is the Noun Phrase (NP) immediately dominated by S, while the Object (O) is the NP immediately dominated by Verb Phrase (VP) (see Figure 43.2).

Halliday prefers a flatter tree (because extra structure is not needed to show functions), with explicit function labels. Adopting his current terms for mood structure (Subject, Finite, Predicator, Complement), this graphically renders the clause structure illustrated in Figure 43.3. In this instance, there are two nominal groups immediately dominated by clause, distinguished by function labelling (the Finite and Predicator functions are conflated as Finite/Predicator

Figure 43.2 Implicit functional information in formal syntax.

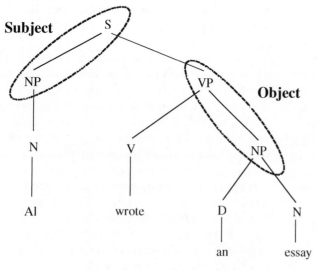

Figure 43.3 Clause structure with function and class labelling.

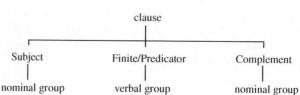

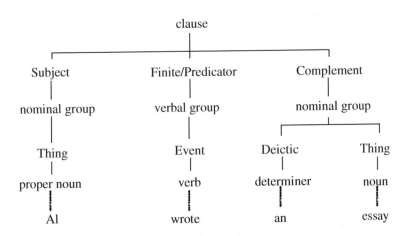

Figure 43.4 Function and class labelling at clause and group rank.

because they are realized by a single verb *wrote*; cf., *has written* or *will write* where they are separate constituents of the clause).

Whereas functional labels describe the role something is playing in a structure (e.g., Subject), class labels describe what it is (e.g., nominal group). The distinction is important because a function can be realized by more than one class (e.g., Subject realized by a nominal group or clause: *Al excited them/What Al said excited them*), and a class can realize more than one function (e.g., the nominal group as Subject and Complement above). Double labelling is also used for the next level of analysis of groups and phrases, as displayed in Figure 43.4. Once again, a group function can be realized by more than one class (e.g., Deictic by determiner or nominal group: *an essay, the student's essay*), and a class can realize more than one function (e.g., a noun as Classifier or Thing: *the student essay, the student*).

The additional function labelling allows us to be more specific about the work done by different classes, and thus infuses the grammatical description with more specific meanings. For example, in Figure 43.3 and 43.4, we have a Subject and Finite function. These functions give us the terms we need to describe the so-called Subject verb agreement noted above (i.e., Subject agreeing with Finite). In addition, they give us the categories we need to describe how English distinguishes between statements and questions (between declarative and interrogative mood):

Al has written an essay:
Has Al written an essay

And they further give us the terms we need to describe the formation of English tag questions:

All wrote an essay, didn't he?
And elliptical responses:
Has Al written an essay?
- He has.

The Complement 'complements' these terms by designating the part of the clause that can be made Subject though a change of voice from active to passive:

An essay has been written by Al.

This change potentially sets up a different kind of argument to that invited when Al is Subject:

Al has written an essay.
- No, he hasn't.
- Yes, he has.

An essay has been written by Al.
- No, it hasn't.
- Yes, it has.

The function labels in other words invest the analysis of clause structure with interpersonal meaning, focusing on how we position ourselves in dialogue and negotiate propositions with one another.

As a second step, Halliday develops the idea that classes can be labelled for function in more than one way, depending on the type of meaning we are orienting to. We could reconsider the example we are working with from the perspective of experiential meaning or what Halliday calls transitivity. Interpreted along these lines, the clause can be further labelled as Actor, Process, and Goal, so that we see explicitly who is doing what to what or whom:

Al	*has written*	*an essay*
Actor	Process	Goal
nominal group	verbal group	nominal group

Function labelling of this kind can be used to distinguish the grammatical construal of different types of experience from one another, for example the mental and verbal processes exemplified below:

Al	*liked*	*the essay*
Senser	Process	Phenomenon
nominal group	verbal group	nominal group

Al	*read*	*his essay*	*to Tipper*
Sayer	Process	Verbiage	Receiver
nominal group	verbal group	nominal group	prepositional phrase

The third aspect of Halliday's grammar is textual in nature. This permits us to re-label the clause as complementary waves of information. For English, this involves beginning with Theme, the function orienting us to what we are talking about, and typically ending with New, the function flagging newsworthy information. We'll show how his Theme analysis can be used to improve student writing in section 3 below.

Al	has written	an *essay*
Theme		New
nominal group	verbal group	nominal group

Space precludes further discussion of this kind of labelling in this chapter. Gee (2005) includes a beginners' appendix that provides a useful snapshot of Halliday's perspective. Derewianka (1998) provides accessible introductions for teachers. Halliday and Matthiessen (2004) provide the primary resource for research, and Martin, Painter, and Matthiessen's workbook (2010) supports these materials with grammar synopses, troubleshooting guides, and exercises. In considering taking up Halliday's functional metalanguage to support classroom literacy practices, educators need to balance the demands of introducing unfamiliar SFL terminology against the benefit of being able to work with students to analyze how grammar makes meaning in the texts they routinely read and write in school.

In describing these key differences between tradition, formal, and functional grammar in light of classroom practice, our main point is to reinforce the idea that when considering grammar and literacy, we must be clear about what kind of grammar we are talking about. Crucially, as educators, we have to ask how much insight a perspective on grammar gives us into meaning and meaning making in schools. For the reminder of this chapter we will focus on a Hallidayan perspective on grammar that maximizes this concern.

2. Functional Grammar in a Model of Literacy

The next step to take is to ask about the theoretical context of the grammar we are adopting. Traditional grammar, as we have noted, was once closely allied with rhetoric and logic as a resource for helping people use language more effectively, but its degeneration into school grammar shattered these connections, undermining its utility. Formal grammar is generally conceived as related to phonology, semantics, and pragmatics, which are studied separately using different methodologies. The study of formal syntax is not designed to help understand other levels of linguistic systems. In functional grammar, on the other hand, the relationship between levels is conceived as a coherent whole, with phonology/graphology, lexicogrammar, and discourse semantics designed to support one another in understanding and analysing meaning-making processes. As articulated by Martin and Rose (2008), SFL pushes this a step further by

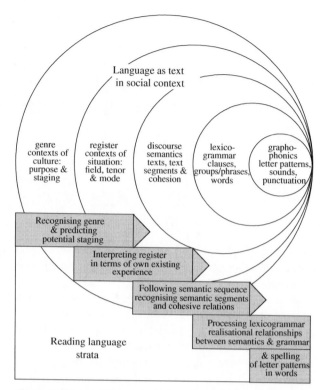

Figure 43.5 Rose's 2000 reading perspective on levels of language and context.

modelling social context along similar lines as genre and register (field, tenor, and mode). Rose's (2000) diagram for the relationship of these levels to grammar is presented in Figure 43.5, along with his glosses on its interpretation in relation to reading.

In this model grammar is positioned as realized by phonology (speaking) or graphology (writing) at the same time as it is realizing discourse semantics (i.e., the organization of grammatical units into texts). Turning to context, ideational meaning in language is interpreted as building field (institutional activity), interpersonal meaning as negotiating tenor (social relationships), and textual meaning as texturing information flow in relation to mode (the semiotic impact of channels of communication through speaking, writing, phoning, blogging, texting, or twittering); these three strands of meaning are then coordinated with one another at the level of genre.

As far as literacy is concerned, the critical issue centers on the relation of the grammar we are using to studying texts in context. Literacy, after all, is about successful communication, and this means getting all levels of language successfully working together in coherent texts that suit their social purposes. This makes a global fractal perspective on making meaning, including grammatical meaning, a key concern (Halliday & Matthiessen, 2009). A grammar that is theoretically decontextualized is going to be much less helpful for literacy educators than one that shows how grammar is related to all levels of the reading/writing process (Martin & Rose, 2003, 2008).

3. Context, Genre, and Grammar

What about context? How have functional linguists responded to literacy educators' concern with literacy as social process and the dynamics between texts and contexts? As reviewed by Hyland (2004), the most influential contributions have focused on *genre* and include the Sydney School, the New Rhetoric perspective, and English for Academic Purposes. Of these three, the Sydney School has drawn on SFL to push the furthest into language to show how graphological, lexicogrammatical, and discourse semantic resources construe genres.

As an example of the significance of an SFL perspective for literacy learning, consider the following text produced by an Australian 10th grader in a Geography class in an urban high school. The students have completed a unit on federal, state, and local government and have been assigned an essay question: "Are Governments necessary? Give reasons for your answer."

[1] I think Governments are necessary because if there wasn't any there would be no law people would be killing themselves. They help keep our economic system in order for certain things. If there wasn't no Federal Government there wouldn't have been no one to fix up any problems that would have occurred in the community. Same with the State Government if the SG didn't exist there would have been noone to look after the school, vandalism fighting would have occurred everyday. The local Government would be important to look after the rubbish because everyone would have diseases.

Dismayed though teachers might be by writing of this kind, if equipped with only the tools of traditional grammar, few can do more than edit the punctuation, spelling, and grammar "errors" in an effort to transform the text into standard written English (1' to 1" below):

[1'] I think Governments are necessary because if there [wasn't] any there would be no law [ ] [p]eople would be killing themselves. They help keep our economic system in order for certain things. If there wasn't [no] Federal Government there wouldn't have been [no one] to fix up any problems that would have occurred in the community. [ ] Same with the State Government [ ] if the SG didn't exist [ ] there would have been [noone] to look after the school[,] vandalism fighting would have occurred everyday. The local Government would be important to look after the rubbish because everyone would have diseases.

[1"] I think Governments are necessary because if there weren't any there wouldn't be any law: people would be killing themselves. They help keep our economic system in order for certain things. If there wasn't any Federal Government there wouldn't be anyone to fix up any problems that occur in the community. It's the same with the State Government — if the State Government didn't exist there wouldn't be anyone to look after the schools; vandalism and fighting would occur everyday. The local Government is important to look after rubbish, because otherwise everyone would have diseases.

Because this kind of editing concentrates on low-level features, the writing ends up looking more like standard written English, but it is still a bad essay—not the kind of writing that will allow students to pass high-stakes exams or gain entry to college.

Genre-based literacy programs would of course attend to editing issues, but starting from the other end of Rose's levels of language diagram—with genre. As the essay question flags, the text the student is working on is a proto-exposition. The student makes a statement regarding the necessity of government and supports his claim with three arguments:

[1'"] I think Governments are necessary because if there weren't any there wouldn't be any law: people would be killing themselves. They help keep our economic system in order for certain things.

If there wasn't any Federal Government there wouldn't be anyone to fix up any problems that occur in the community.

It's the same with the State Government - if the State Government didn't exist there wouldn't be anyone to look after the schools; vandalism and fighting would occur everyday.

The local Government is important to look after rubbish, because otherwise everyone would have diseases.

The local Government is important to look after rubbish, because otherwise everyone would have diseases.

So, how can grammar help? Halliday's (2007) theme analysis gives us one way in. His topical themes are underlined below, with marked Themes in bold. What this analysis reveals is the spoken counter-factual nature of the argumentation: 'I think x because if not a then b, if not c then d' and so on.

<u>I</u> think Governments are necessary
because if there weren't any <u>there</u> wouldn't be any law:
<u>people</u> would be killing themselves.
<u>They</u> help keep our economic system in order for certain things.

If there wasn't any Federal Government <u>there</u> wouldn't be anyone to fix up any problems that occur in the community.

<u>It</u>'s the same with the State Government -
if the State Government didn't exist <u>there</u> wouldn't be anyone to look after the schools;
<u>vandalism and fighting</u> would occur everyday.

<u>The local Government</u> is important to look after rubbish, because otherwise everyone would have diseases.

In academic writing, we typically organize our argument differently by using Theme to scaffold the structure of a written exposition genre. For this text, therefore, it would make sense to make governments Theme in the Thesis and

Reiteration stages of the exposition, and the appropriate level of government Theme is the Arguments.

[1"""]
Governments are necessary at different levels.
They make laws, without which people would be killing themselves,
and (they) help keep our economic system in order.

The Federal Government fixes up problems that occur in the community.

The State Government looks after schools, preventing vandalism and fighting.

The Local Government is important to look after rubbish: otherwise everyone would have diseases.

Governments at several administrative levels are necessary.

This structure could be further reinforced by adding textual Themes to the Arguments (italic below) and making use of circumstances of cause (italic bold below) in the Thesis and Reiteration stages. From the perspective of discourse semantics, what these grammatical resources do is organize the text's conjunctive structure (Martin & Rose, 2003).

[1""""]
Governments are necessary at different levels *for a number of reasons*.
They make laws, without which people would be killing themselves,
and (they) help keep our economic system in order.

To begin, the Federal Government fixes up problems that occur in the community.

Similarly, the State Government looks after schools, preventing vandalism and fighting.

Finally, the Local Government is important to look after rubbish: otherwise everyone would have diseases.

As a result of these factors, Governments at several administrative levels are necessary.

Pushing further, we could add nominal groups to the Thesis to predict the ideational orientation of each Argument (levels of government) and consolidate each Argument's news (problems, schooling, and waste disposal).

[1""""""]
Governments are necessary at different levels for a number of reasons. These have to do with the special responsibilities of Governments at different administrative levels - Federal, State and Local.

To begin, the Federal Government fixes up problems that occur in the community.

Similarly, the State Government looks after schools, preventing vandalism and fighting.

Finally, the Local Government is important to look after rubbish: otherwise everyone would have diseases.

As a result of their concern with general difficulties, schooling and waste disposal Governments at several levels of administrative organisation are necessary.

We are now in a position to elaborate each Argument, as we have done for the first Argument below, fleshing out the scaffold we have built thus far and moving the essay toward the advanced academic literacy functionality upon which upper secondary and college studies depend.

[1"""""""]
Governments are necessary at different levels for a number of reasons. These have to do with the special responsibilities of Governments at different administrative levels - Federal, State and Local.

To begin, the Federal Government is concerned with general difficulties faced by the community.

It organises armed forces to defend the country in case it is attacked and to help keep things peaceful in various parts of the world. It tries to improve the economy, helping businesses run more effectively and provide more jobs for people. And it collects taxes which it spends on Medicare, universities and airports.

Similarly, the State Government looks after schools, preventing vandalism and fighting.

Finally, the Local Government is important to look after rubbish: otherwise everyone would have diseases.

As a result of their concern with general difficulties, schooling and waste disposal Governments at several levels of administrative organisation are necessary.

Space precludes consideration of field, tenor, and mode here. But we have offered a glimpse of functional grammar interacting with discourse semantics in the interests of genre.

4. Using SFL in K–12 Contexts

A Hallidayan perspective was put to use in classrooms during the 1980s as a way of teaching academic literacies to linguistically and culturally diverse students in Sydney, Australia. Educational linguists, such as Christie, Derewianka, Kress, Martin, and Rotherty, drew on Halliday's theory of Systemic Functional Linguistics (SFL) to support teachers in making the workings of academic literacy practices transparent and potentially transformative for students, especially students from non-dominant linguistic and cultural communities (Cope & Kalantzis, 1993, Christie & Derewianka, 2008; Martin & Rose, 2003, 2008). Since then, a number of applied linguists in the United States have drawn on SFL scholarship as a way of supporting the academic literacies of English language learners (ELLs) and speakers of non-dominant varieties of English, particularly in the context of high-stakes school reforms such as No Child Left Behind legislation and English-only mandates (e.g., Brisk & Zisselsberger, in press; Gebhard, Demers, & Castillo-Rosenthal, 2008; Achugar, Schleppegrell, & Oteiza, 2007).

In California, for example, Schleppegrell (2003, 2004, 2005) collaborated with teachers to analyze the academic language demands placed on students by state curricular frameworks and aligned exams. As part of this project, they identified the genres California teachers were required to teach and their students were required to read and write in school (e.g., recounts, narratives, responses to literature, summaries, descriptions, explanations, reports, arguments, and analytic essays). In addition, they made recommendations regarding how state frameworks could be revised and aligned to support all students, not just ELLs, in developing "pathways" to academic literacy across disciplines as they transitioned from elementary to secondary schools (2003, p. 20; see also Christie & Derewianka, 2008). These pathways center on developing students' and teachers' metalinguistics awareness of genre and register features as they progress from reading and writing more everyday texts such as personal narratives, descriptions, and procedures to reading and writing more technical and grammatically denser texts in specific content areas, including, for example, scientific laboratory reports, mathematical proofs, explanations of historical events, and analyses of literature (Achugar & Schleppegrell, 2005; Fang, 2006; see also Fang, Schleppegrell, & Cox, 2006; Schleppegrell, 2007; Schleppegrell & Go, 2007; Schleppegrell & de Oliveira, 2006).

In regard to the teaching of History specifically, Schleppegrell and her colleagues developed summer professional development institutes for teachers. These institutes, called the California History Project (CHP), introduced teachers to SFL tools they could use to deconstruct the meaning of textbook passages and primary source documents. These tools included noticing how texts were structured and made coherent through the use of temporal markers and other cohesive devices; unpacking meaning clause by clause to see how participants were omitted or verbal processes transformed into nouns or became nominalized; and identifying participants, processes, and circumstances in key passages to become aware of how writers make agency explicit or not (Schleppegrell, Achugar, & Oteiza, 2007; Schleppegrell, & de Oliveira, 2006). Achugar and colleagues (2007) report that teachers planned lessons that incorporated this kind of language analysis and found that the approach enabled more in-depth discussion and understanding of history for the ELLs in particular:

> Students whose teachers participated in CHP institutes made significantly greater gains on the California History-Social Science test (a standardized measure) than students whose teachers had not participated in the workshops, and ELLs were among those who show great benefits from the approach....Students whose teachers used these strategies also wrote more effectively, developing a thesis and supporting it with evidence and analysis. (p. 15)

In Massachusetts, Gebhard, Willett, Jimenez, and Piedra (in press) have come to similar conclusions based on their work with elementary and middle school teachers and students in economically struggling school districts in former industrial cities in a project called the ACCELA Alliance (Access to Critical Content and English Language Acquisition). This project was established in 2002 with federal funds to support in-service teachers, administrators, teacher educators, and researchers in understanding and responding to the changing nature of literacy and schooling in the context of rapidly changing technologies, economies, and demographics (New London Group, 1996).

The broad goal of this on-going partnership has been to provide sustained and reciprocal professional development to all participants by engaging in collaborative research regarding the academic literacy development of non-dominant students in today's urban schools. A key feature of this collaboration has been that teachers, doctoral students, and faculty have used SFL tools to design curricular interventions aligned with state standards and student investments and to collect and analyze case study data (e.g., student writing samples, curricular materials, video and audio transcripts of classroom interactions, and formal and informal interviews with participants). For example, second graders created a class blog to share and respond to each others' recounts; third graders analyzed the genre of "show your thinking" in Math as a way of preparing for the state exam; fourth graders analyzed the genre and register features in Puerto Rican children's literature to create their own narratives; and fifth graders researched the benefits of recess to make an argument for reinstating recess in letters to their principal (Gebhard, Habana Hafner, & Wright, 2004; Gebhard, Harman, & Seger, 2007; Gebhard et al., in press; Shin, Gebhard, & Seger, in press).

Similar to the findings of Schleppegrell and her colleagues, ACCELA case studies suggest that participants developed a deeper understanding of both disciplinary content knowledge and associated language practices, both of which are essential components of teachers' knowledge base. Teachers also were supported in negotiating the imposition of scripted approaches to instruction and the language demands of high-stakes testing while making space for students to read and write about topics that mattered to them and their communities. The data also indicate that SFL-based pedagogy supported emergent ELL writers in analyzing and producing more coherent and autonomous texts reflective of written as opposed to oral discourse (e.g., greater use of *and* as a coordinating conjunction, greater use of temporal and logical connectives, a greater ability to manage new and given information). While these findings are promising, they would be strengthened by mix-method studies that would couple qualitative with quantitative methods to analyze changes in a greater number of students' texts over time. In addition, more research is needed to analyze how both micro and macro institutional practices opened and/or shut down critical discursive spaces for participants in the partnership (e.g., work intensification, institutional instability, unpredictable funding streams, and contradictory reform initiatives).

In sum, however, the work of the CPH and ACCELA, coupled with the robust scholarship of SFL scholars internationally (Unsworth, 2000), suggests that SFL-based pedagogy has the potential to support teachers and students in responding to the rapidly changing nature of schooling and ultimately the changing nature of work. Following the New London Group (1996), whose argument is rooted in a Hallidayan perspective of text and context dynamic, we argue that for non-dominant students to negotiate their way in a post-industrial world order (Gee, Hull, & Lankshear, 1996), they must be able to engage strategically and fluidly in the symbolic work of positioning and re-positioning themselves through their uses of texts. And students are better able to accomplish this task when they are in command of many, often hybrid, literacy practices and associated ways of knowing and being. Moreover, students are more likely to be prepared to engage in this kind of strategic semiotic work if they have been in classrooms with teachers who have a critical awareness of language and how to apprentice students to playing high-stakes language games (Wittgenstein, 1965).

References

Achugar, M., & Schleppegrell, M. (2005). Beyond connectors: The construction of cause in history textbooks. *Linguistics and Education: An International Research Journal, 16*(3), 298–318.

Achugar, M., Schleppegrell, M., & Oteíza, T. (2007). Engaging teachers in language analysis: A Functional linguistics approach to reflective literacy. *English Teaching: Practice and Critique, 6*(2), 8–24.

Brisk, M., & Zisselsberger, M. (in press). "We've let them in on a secret": Using SFL Theory to improve the teaching of writing to bilingual learners. In T. Lucas (Ed.), *Preparing all teachers to teach English language learners.* Mahwah, NJ: Erlbaum/Taylor & Francis.

Christie, F. (1993). The "received tradition" of English teaching: The decline of rhetoric and the corruption of grammar. In Bill Green (Ed.), *The insistence of the letter: Literary studies and curriculum theorizing* (pp. 75–106). London: Falmer Press.

Christie, F., & Derewianka, B. (2008). *School discourse: Learning to write across the years of schooling.* London: Continuum.

Coffin, C. (2006). *Historical discourse: The language of time, cause and evaluation.* London: Continuum.

Coffin, C., Donohue, J., & North, S. (2009). *Exploring English grammar: From formal to functional.* London: Routledge.

Cope, W., & Kalantzis, M. (1993). *The powers of literacy: A genre approach to teaching literacy.* London: Falmer.

Derewianka, B. (1998). *A grammar companion for primary teachers.* Sydney, Australia: Primary English Teaching Association.

Fang, Z. (2006). The language demands of science reading in middle school. *International Journal of Science Education, 28*(5), 491–520.

Fang, Z., Schleppegrell, M., & Cox, B. (2006). Understanding the language demands of schooling: Nouns in academic registers. *Journal of Literacy Research, 38*(3), 247–273.

Gee, J. (2005). *An introduction to discourse analysis.* London: Routledge.

Gee, J., Hull, G., & Lankshear, C. (1996). *The new work order: Behind the language of new capitalism.* Boulder, CO: Westview Press.

Gebhard, M., Demers, J., & Castillo-Rosenthal, Z. (2008). Teachers as critical text analysts: L2 literacies and teachers' work in the context of high-stakes school reform. *Journal of Second Language Writing, 17*(4), 274–291.

Gebhard, M., Habana Hafner, A., & Wright, M. (2004). Teaching English language learners the language game of math. Reprint. *The Harvard Letter, 20*(6), 5–7.

Gebhard, M., Harman, R., & Seger, W. (2007). Reclaiming recess in urban schools: The potential of systemic functional linguistics for ELLs and their teachers. *Language Arts, 84*(5), 419–430.

Gebhard, M., Willett, J., Jimenez, J., Piedra, A. (in press). Systemic functional linguistics, teachers' professional development, and ELLs' academic literacy practices. In T. Lucas (Ed.), *Preparing all teachers to teach English language learners.* Mahwah, NJ: Erlbaum/Taylor & Francis.

Grabe, W., & Kaplan, R. (1996). *Theory & practice of writing.* London: Longman.

Halliday, M. A. K. (2007). *Language and education.* London: Continuum.

Halliday, M. A. K., & Matthiessen, M. (2004). *An introduction to functional grammar.* London: Arnold.

Hunt, K. (1970). *Syntactic maturity in school children and adults.* Chicago: University of Chicago Press.

Hyland, K. (2004). *Genre and second language writing.* Ann Arbor: University of Michigan Press.

Kollin, M., & Hancock, C. (2005). The story of grammar in United States schools. *English Teaching: Practice and Critique, 4*(3), 11–31.

Martin, J. R. (1999). Linguistics and the consumer: Theory in practice. *Linguistics and Education, 9*(3), 409–446.

Martin, J. R., Painter, C., & Matthiessen, C. (2010). *Deploying functional grammar.* Beijing, China: Commercial Press.

Martin, J. R., & Rose, D. (2003). *Working with discourse: Meaning beyond the clause.* London: Continuum.

Martin, J. R., & Rose, D. (2008). *Genre relations: Mapping culture.* London: Equinox.

New London Group. (1996). A pedagogy of multiliteracies: Designing social features. *Harvard Educational Review, 66*(1), 60–92.

Pinker, S. (1994). *The language instinct.* New York: William & Marrow.

Rose, D. (2000, July). Discourse semantics of teaching reading. Paper presented at the *27th International Systemic Functional Linguistics Congress*, University of Melbourne, Australia.

Schleppegrell, M. (2003). *Grammar for writing: Academic language and the ELD Standards.* Santa Barbara: University of California's Linguistic Minorities Research Institute.

Schleppegrell, M. (2004). *The language of schooling: A functional linguistics perspective.* Mahwah, NJ: Erlbaum.

Schleppegrell, M. (2005). *Helping content area teachers work with academic language: Promoting English language learners' literacy in history.* Santa Barbara: University of California's Linguistic Minorities Research Institute.

Schleppegrell, M. (2007). The linguistic challenges of mathematics teaching and learning: A research review. *Reading & Writing Quarterly, 23*(2), 139–159.

Schleppegrell, M., & de Oliveira, L. (2006). An Integrated Language and Content Approach for History Teachers. *Journal of English for Academic Purposes, 5*(4), 254–268.

Schleppegrell, M., & Go, A. (2007). Analyzing the writing of English learners: A functional approach. *Language Arts, 84*(6), 529–538.

Shin, D. S., Gebhard, M., & Seger, M. (in press). Weblogs and English language learners academic literacy development: Expanding audiences, expanding identities. In S. Rilling & M. Dantas-Whitney (Eds.), *Authenticity in the classroom and beyond.* Alexandria, VA: TESOL, Inc.

Unsworth, L. (2000). *Researching language in schools and communities: Functional linguistics approaches.* London: Cassell.

Wittgenstein, L. (1965). *Philosophical investigations.* New York: Macmillan.

Section VI

Assessment of English Language Arts Teaching and Learning

SECTION EDITORS
JENNIFER D. TURNER, PATRICIA RUGGIANO SCHMIDT, AND PETER AFFLERBACH

Our dynamic world has produced new literacies that blur the boundaries between global and local, personal and social, and print and digital texts. Students bring a wide range of abilities and preferences, as well as multiple cultural, linguistic, ethnic, and economic identities, to the process of learning the English language arts. And educators must recognize, understand and appreciate this great range of differences in their classrooms and schools to help all students fulfill their potential. In light of these rapid changes, how can assessment materials, procedures, and systems honor the complexity of literacy development and achievement in 21st-century schools?

In response to this critical question, the chapters in this section explore the role of diversity in the assessment of the English language arts. Specifically, we conceptualize diversity broadly as a range of individual differences (e.g., needs, strengths, and interests).

Peter Afflerbach and Summer Clark examine diversity in assessment as it is situated in social contexts. They argue that functional and useful assessment of the English language arts is the result of careful alignment between teaching, learning, and assessment. Yet, this is not enough to guarantee good assessment. Their chapter describes the social, political, and economic influences on assessment choice, use, and advocacy.

Patricia Schmidt and Sunita Singh argue that language arts teacher assessment is embedded in teacher capacity, a term that explicates teachers' potential for increasing community understanding, gaining pedagogical content knowledge, and developing an awareness of their professional power.

Julie Coiro and Jill Castek describe the diverse skills and practices related to print and online literacy learning. Their chapter explores how educators can assess students' online literacy competencies, track progress over time, and identify strengths and weaknesses that can be addressed through English language arts instruction.

Jennifer D. Turner and Chrystine Hoeltzel advocate for purposeful assessment systems that provide comprehensive information about diverse students as learners of the English language arts. Their chapter outlines four critical purposes that teachers must consider in order to make responsive, data-driven instructional decisions in the language arts classroom.

In their chapter, Janette Klingner, KaiLonnie Dunsmore, and Patricia Edwards discuss the assessment of students with diverse academic needs. They describe recent changes in the assessment and identification of learning disabilities (LD), assessment in Response to Intervention (RTI) models, and provide a rationale for English language arts assessments in a special education system that attends to the cultural basis of school-based cognitive development and learning.

Lee Gunderson, Dennis Murphy Odo, and Reginald D'Silva focus on language diversity assessments and interpretation. They note the importance of careful and informed interpretations of assessment results, and explain the urgent need for improved assessment of English language learners.

In conclusion, the chapters in this section situate assessment among teachers, students, and classrooms. The chapters argue for the timely and valid measure of student and teacher accomplishment, and a clear theme emerges—the need to support teachers who make the commitment to teach and authentically assess their diverse groups of student in the English language arts. Accompanying the descriptions of teachers as pivotal in the development and use of effective assessment is the realization that teachers need time, knowledge, and resources for meaningful professional development. As well, students will benefit from assessment that supports their learning, reinforces their positive self-concepts, and leads them to further individual and academic understandings.

44

Diversity and English Language Arts Assessment

Peter Afflerbach and Summer Clark

In this chapter we address diversity and literacy assessment. We conceptualize diversity broadly, seeking to illustrate the complexities that are involved in conducting and using assessment in support of all students. It is critical to acknowledge the situated nature of literacy assessment, and the diversity of factors that influence the ways and means of assessment. To this end, we consider diversity in the purposes and audiences of assessment, and in the contexts of assessment. We examine the diverse manner in which the English language arts are defined and how related curriculum is conceptualized. We conclude with consideration of the diverse students and teachers whose lives are influenced by assessment, and the diverse array of assessments that contribute to effective teaching and student learning.

Diversity in the Audiences and Purposes of English Language Arts Assessment

Assessment must serve diverse audiences and purposes, and the overriding purpose of all English language arts assessment should be to foster students' learning and growth. However, different audiences have different purposes for assessment: Teachers want formative assessment that describes students' individual needs and accomplishments and guides instruction, while legislators want test scores to inform policy-making and allocation of funding. Parents want information that helps them understand both students' daily and weekly progress, as well as year-end standing in relation to standards and peers (Shepard & Bliem, 1995). The diverse audiences and purposes for literacy assessment are illustrated in Table 44.1. We note that the diversity of audiences is not always considered in a systematic or egalitarian manner when literacy assessment is planned, created, and implemented. This creates situations in which these audiences may be in competition with one another; addressing the needs of one audience takes limited school resources, and may narrow the diversity of assessments

used, and thus, of the particular audiences served by assessment. For example, funds spent on summative testing are funds that cannot be spent on helping students learn to use rubrics and performance assessments to evaluate complex classroom performances (Calkins, Montgomery, Santman, & Falk, 1998).

Assessment should serve diverse purposes, each contributing to students' English language arts growth. A classic distinction in the purpose of assessment is formative and summative assessment. Formative assessment provides information on individual students and their progress as they learn (Sadler, 1989), while summative assessment provides after-the-fact summaries of learning. The information yielded in formative assessment can be used by the teacher to maintain or revise a lesson, adjusting instruction to the student's needs. For example, teacher questioning can help us understand the effectiveness of a critical reading lesson as it takes place, with student responses to questions illustrating the nature of student understanding, or the locus of a student's difficulty. The teacher who conducts formative assessment during the critical reading lesson may determine that some students are able to identify claims and evidence in text, while others are not. Using this information, the teacher can adjust the lesson, re-teaching those students who need further instruction. Formative assessment, in the hands of talented teachers, provides information that can help shape diverse students' learning and achievement.

In contrast, summative assessment gives a summary statement of achievement and focuses on the products of students' literacy processes. Summative assessments are typically conducted at the end of lessons, units, marking periods and school years. They provide a gauge of students' learning in relation to daily goals, standards, benchmarks and longer term learning goals. Tests typically provide summative information—they are taken at the end of a learning episode, be it a chapter quiz, or a unit performance assessment. In some instances, an assessment may ably serve both purposes, as when performance assessments, with

TABLE 44.1

The Diverse Audiences and Purposes for Literacy Assessment

Audience	Purpose
Students	To report on learning and communicate progress
	To motivate and encourage
	To teach children about assessment and how to assess their own work and progress
	To build student independence
Teachers	To determine nature of student learning
	To inform instruction
	To construct grades and narrative reports
	To evaluate students
	To diagnose student strengths and weaknesses
Parents	To understand their child's achievement
	To help connect home and school efforts to support student
School administrators	To determine instructional program effectiveness
	To prove school and teacher accountability
	To allocate school resources
Politicians	To establish accountability of schools
	To inform the public of school progress
	To determine funding
Taxpayers	To demonstrate that tax dollars are well spent

Adapted from Afflerbach, Peter. (2007). *Understanding and using reading assessment, K-12*. Newark, DE: International Reading Association. Used by permission.

the use of scoring rubrics, guide teachers' understanding of student development in complex learning (formative), and also serve as the primary indicator of what a student was able to do and accomplish (summative). A functional literacy assessment system focuses on both formative and summative assessment.

A complementary perspective on assessment purpose focuses on the roles of *reporting, supporting* and *teaching*. Much of the assessment conducted in schools is used for *reporting*. For example, Running Records provides formative, process-oriented information to a classroom teacher on students' oral reading, fluency, decoding ability and comprehension. This information may be used to shape instruction: teaching the next lesson, or planning the next unit. A standardized test reports on a student's knowledge about reading or related school topics such as social studies or science, and this information is used typically to judge student, teacher and school achievement levels.

From a sociocultural perspective (Lewis, Enciso, & Moje, 2007) to learn literacy involves changes in student identity. Such shifts can be positive or negative, they can open up or shut out a learner from access to power, and they may be influenced by assessment. Learners may gain agency as they become recognized as members of a community of practice (Lave & Wenger, 1991), or they may perceive a lack of control as instructional practices and assessments communicate to them that they cannot effectively access, or participate fully in these communities. Thus, assessment's role in *reporting* can impact student identities; for example, weekly summative tests may communicate to students their

standing relative to peers. Students who have not been given sufficient opportunities or resources to learn may, in turn, internalize an identity, as defined by an assessment, as an incapable or less able learner. In this case the assessment may mask the true source of the economic and social inequities that shape the different assessment outcomes, in turn labeling the student as deficient rather than recognizing that societal power structures influence access to equitable educational experiences. In this case assessment serves to uphold rather than challenge social injustice. From a Bourdeian standpoint (Heller, 2008), such analyses of assessment's role in upholding hegemony is necessary for the educator concerned with educational equity.

Consider a second purpose for assessment: the *support* that assessment can provide for the diversity of students in a classroom. Some students receive consistently good news from assessment, some do not. The student whose assessment information consistently communicates "A," "94 percentile," and "Excellent work," is supported with positive feedback for successful performance. In contrast, a student whose assessment feedback includes "C," "36 percentile," "Needs improvement," or corrective, red ink on written work is less likely to feel supported. The supporting role of assessment may not exist for particular students, when students are regularly ranked in relation to one another. Thus, consideration of whether or not language arts assessment contributes to positive student self-concept and self-esteem is critical. Encouraging students in relation to assessment helps students understand that their effort leads to learning (Johnston, 2004), as when teacher feedback helps student writers focus on how their hard work contributes to increasingly compelling writing.

Assessments can be used to support student learning and insure marginalized students' access to power by holding teachers and schools accountable for student performance. Yet, as is evident in the percentile rankings mentioned in the above, assessment may promote what Pierre Bourdieu (1991) called "symbolic domination," Students' views of self are shaped by tests that label them as "deficient" or "slow." In some cases, the authoritative veneer of tests may mask the reality that student performance is influenced by conflicting cultural models (Lewis, Enciso, & Moje, 2007), differing forms of language or literacy (Heller, 2008), or lack of opportunity to learn. In contrast, assessment can be a tool of support and safe, constructive critique that encourages students to further develop positive identities and join diverse communities of practice.

A third, often unrealized purpose for assessment is *teaching* (Afflerbach, 2002). A hallmark of the successful student is independence, and this independence derives, in part, from the ability to assess one's self (Flavell, 1976; Pressley & Afflerbach, 1995). When we conceptualize language arts assessment as a means of teaching assessment, we can provide students with increasing opportunity (and related strategies and motivations) to work independently. Each of our diverse students must be encouraged to develop such independence and success. The student writer who receives consistent and supportive feedback can internalize the evaluative process as it is modeled. For example, attention to a student writer's use of descriptive detail in essay writing, initially provided by the teacher and peers in the writing conference, can become internalized by the student. When a student is asked "Does that make sense?" at key parts of an act of reading or listening, and the teacher highlights the need for the student to assume responsibility for asking such a question, the teaching of assessment is underway. The process is gradual, but all successful language users must become capable of careful assessment of their work. Moreover, by promoting diverse students' ability to self-assess, we may help them experience the transformative power of literacy in their lives; improving students' agency and access to power as they learn to take control over their own learning processes.

Diversity in the Contexts and Situations of English Language Arts Assessment

Assessment is always situated in relation to social, political, and economic forces that act, subtly or starkly, on students, teachers and classrooms (Afflerbach, Cho, Kim & Clark, 2010). There is great diversity in these forces, how they interact, and how they influence assessment. For example, current federal policy mandates testing in reading in grades 3 through 8. The imposed goal of Adequate Yearly Progress (AYP) is part of the No Child Left Behind legislation, which was passed by a vote of the United States Senate of 91 to 8. States' related Reading First programs are required by law to focus on the "five pillars" of reading, including phonemic awareness, phonics, fluency, vocabulary, and comprehension as the necessary components of reading development. Thus, national politics has considerable influence on how curriculum and assessment are conceptualized and enacted at all local levels.

Schools must dedicate resources to purchasing sanctioned, or authorized curriculum, and to administering, scoring, and reporting on annual tests. This economic obligation impacts the feasibility of using other types of assessment, for purposes other than examining school accountability. In addition, the value of an assessment is socially assigned. Standardized tests are viewed by many adults as scientific, fair, and reliable (Afflerbach, 2007), in spite of the minimal information they may provide about students' English language arts development. Habits and traditions of assessment may maintain, preventing consideration of innovative, possibly more useful assessments. That multiple-choice items with convergent "correct" responses continue to dominate tests of reading and content area literacy is due, in part, to widespread public acceptance of this class of assessment.

It is critical to consider the relationship between curriculum and assessment, as well as the nature of students' daily experiences in school (Crooks, 1988). School can be conceptualized as a set of psychological, sociocultural, and temporal/spatial spaces, in which complex interactions take place (Afflerbach et al., 2010). Assessment is always conducted in relation to the specific and diverse spaces of a classroom. Across the school year, requiring students to engage in inquiry based science, to identify and interrogate source texts in social studies, or to question the author of a persuasive text creates the need for the innovative and complex literacy assessments that are needed to accurately describe the levels of student achievement. In contrast, if student learning is restricted to learning reading skills and strategies, and to writing themed paragraphs, assessment will be similarly constrained.

A curriculum that focuses on attainment and mastery of language skills and strategies is different from one that encourages students to construct and examine meaning through language use. Assessment can be a tool that helps students learn to critique, challenge, imagine, and act rather than simply ingest prespecified pieces of knowledge. Assessments can provide opportunities for teachers to help students refine their skills of debate and their dispositions to question the status quo. As in the student-led writing conference, assessments can instill in students a sense of ownership over one's own ideas, actions, and decisions. Yet, assessment is often used in ways that restrict and limit the curriculum, especially as teachers are increasingly held accountable for their students' performance on tests that do not regularly assess higher-order forms of knowledge and thinking.

Diversity in How the English Language Arts Are Defined and How Curriculum Is Conceptualized

How are the English language arts conceptualized? The past century of educational research has broadly expanded definitions of reading, writing, speaking, and listening. Conceptualizations of language learning and its discrete, isolable, and universally applicable skills, have been replaced, in some quarters, with more complex descriptions of what literacy *is*. Constructivist theory, sociological and anthropological inquiry, critical literacy scholarship, and critical sociocultural theory have great potential to diversify how the English language arts are conceptualized, enacted and assessed. They reveal reading and writing instruction to be more than a science or a process but "language arts": diverse ways of using reading, writing, speaking, and listening to express and communicate.

Diverse theories of literacy demand a diverse understanding of curriculum and assessment. That students' literacy is situated within complex networks of language use, learning and power should encourage us to continually ask "Why"; "For whose benefit?"; "What for?"; and "With what consequences for whom?" when we consider both language arts curriculum and assessment. Taking this proactive stance with assessment allows us to determine, a priori, what assessments may be most useful. For example, asking "For whose benefit?" when we consider our assessment regimen may reveal a balance (or imbalance) in how teachers', students', and parents' assessment needs are met (or not met). Beneath particular assessment procedures may be conceptions of literacy that teach students that they are capable or incapable, that students can take action to transform society or passively accept things the way they are, that students' cultural ways of knowing count or don't count, and that literacy is or is not connected to their identities and their diverse understandings of the world (Moll, Amanti, Neff, & Gonzalez, 1992). Thus, assessments that help us understand our students in relation to their homes and communities, in addition to school curriculum, are necessary (Johnson, Willeke, & Steiner, 1998).

The diverse definitions of literacy that we embrace matter in relation to assessment because they limit or expand the construct that we would assess. For example, if the English language arts are viewed as tools for constructing meaning in relation to acts of reading, writing, speaking, and listening, then assessment might focus on students' constructed responses, allowing for divergent student language performances. If the English language arts are viewed as social practices that open up access to codes of power, then assessments should focus on literacy practices that empower students, as when making persuasive arguments. If the English language arts are viewed as tools of critical literacy, then assessments and assessment tasks should require students to take part in such critique, as when they are asked to evaluate claims and evidence in spoken and written text. In contrast, if a transmission model of English language arts is predominant, curriculum and instruction will focus on the delivery of course material, and assessment, particularly multiple-choice items and literal questions will focus on how well students learn, remember, and give back this course content. If the means and goals of language learning are considered dependent on skill and strategy instruction, then assessment of these discreet parts of language will follow.

Diversity in Teachers' Assessment Development and Expertise

Useful classroom assessment demands expertise. However, there is great diversity in teachers' knowledge of assessment and their ability to conduct valid and reliable assessment (Stiggins & Conklin, 1992). This is due, in part, to inconsistent initial training in effective classroom assessment, and inconsistent professional development opportunities to gain knowledge of assessment theory and practice. When the reliability and validity of teacher assessment of the processes and products of language learning are established, classroom assessment can be extremely useful, as demonstrated by Running Records (Clay, 2002), process approaches to writing instruction and assessment, and listening to students (Schultz, 2003). The success of such teacher assessment of the language arts revolves around rigorous initial teacher development and ongoing professional development.

Formative and summative assessments demand that teachers be evaluation experts (Johnston, 1987). This expertise helps teachers use assessments in the course of daily instruction to shape instruction for the diversity of students. For example, the teacher who is a reflective practitioner (Schon, 1983) regularly compares the goals of instruction with the status of student learning. Formative assessment provides the detailed information with which the teacher makes this comparison. Formative assessment plays a similar role in the classroom teacher's attempts to create teachable moments that benefit all students. Teachable moments are commonly associated with Vygotsky's (1978) zone of proximal development, in which students and teachers work to move from a current level of attainment to the next possible level of attainment. A teacher may scaffold instruction in relation to students' learning and strategies (Palincsar & Brown, 1984). The success of the scaffolding depends on the teachers' ability to assess and identify diverse students' current levels of capability and their next steps in ongoing achievement. For example, the teacher who in the midst of a lesson determines that a particular student has not yet learned an aspect of public speaking can modify the lesson, address the student's particular need for increased confidence and articulation, and then continue, with positive cognitive and affective outcomes. Lacking this information, the student will not learn, and may become frustrated, embarrassed and unmotivated.

Validity and Assessment

There are several forms of validity for assessment (Messick, 1989). Two of the most important forms are construct validity and consequential validity. Construct validity relates to how faithfully and comprehensively an assessment represents the thing we would measure (Pellegrino, Chudowsky, & Glaser, 2001). For example, a multiple-choice test can inform us about how well students are learning constrained skills of reading, such as sound-symbol correspondences, and determining literal meaning of text, but may be incapable of reporting on students' higher order thinking, given the constraints on multiple choice items (Afflerbach, Cho, Kim, & Clark, 2010). In such instances, the assessment may be "thin" (Davis, 1998), thereby accurately assessing a part of what it means to be a reader, but missing other important parts. If assessment includes tasks that require students to critically evaluate an author's claims, or to synthesize information from different sources, the construct of reading may be more fully sampled.

Consequential validity is a term originally coined to focus on the results of the use of test scores (Tittle, 2005), including the labeling of diverse students as "above average" or "below average," schools as "outperforming" or "underperforming" and teachers as "accountable" or "unaccountable," for students learning. However, we believe that a broader application of the term, including the consequences of conducting assessment and the use of all assessment information, is critical to establishing useful English language arts assessments. Assessment that helps teachers teach students how to conduct self-assessment has considerable positive consequence (Black & Wiliam, 1998), as does assessment that contributes to a student's positive self-image. In contrast, assessments that portray significant numbers of students as "below average" or "failing" may have negative consequence. In relation to the Hippocratic oath, we believe that assessment should do no harm: no assessment should have punitive consequences for any of the diverse students we teach.

Assessing the Diversity of Factors that Contribute to Students' English Language Arts Learning

The English language arts are central to students' cognitive, affective, and social growth, yet assessment focuses predominantly on cognitive skill and strategy development. Effective assessment can describe students' current affective and social characteristics, their ongoing growth in these areas, and this information complements the often-exclusive focus on cognitive achievement. Theories of teaching and learning increasingly describe the power and importance of positive affect and volition for student achievement (Corno & Mandinach, 2004). Student self-esteem and self-concept figure largely in motivation to participate in school, and engaged participation is central to academic achievement (Guthrie & Wigfield, 1997). Thus, it is important to consider the student characteristics that support (or work against) language use and growth, and to determine how assessment of these characteristics can contribute to successful school experiences. Extant assessments, including those that focus on motivation (Gambrell, Palmer, Codling, & Mazzoni, 1996), student reader self-concept (Chapman & Tunmer, 1995), and attitudes towards reading (McKenna & Kear, 1990) help us understand the multifaceted development of students' literacy.

Language use is social, and the development of students' social uses for literacy are worthy of assessment. Discussions of important issues, reading and reacting to reviews of books and movies, turn-taking in conversations, respect for others' ideas and opinions are important markers in an individual's language and social development. Without a related focus on how literacy is used, we may mistake students' skill and strategy development as the ability to use language to achieve diverse goals. The lesson is that the preponderance of current assessment that focuses on cognitive skills and strategies must be complemented by assessment that focuses on the situated use of skills and strategies (Baxter & Glaser, 1998), and on students' affective and social development in relation to literacy. Here, our ability to make detailed classroom observations of student growth, and to ask pertinent questions will enhance our full assessment of literacy development.

Assessing Diverse Students

There is no "average" student (Artley, 1981): each is a unique blend of cognitive, affective, and social characteristics, influenced by past experience and learning, and situated in complex cultural milieu. Our classrooms are comprised of students with diverse individual differences. Assessment must describe the diversity of student characteristics before, during and after instruction and learning, and it must do so with sensitivity to students' socio-cultural backgrounds, language experiences, strengths and needs. The influences on individual student's reading development are diverse, and reading assessment must recognize and measure these influences.

One approach to addressing diverse students' needs is to designate specific types of diversity, including English language learner (ELL) and learning disabled (LD). We believe that as each student is unique, and that attention to individual differences, as informed by assessment, is at the center of effective instruction and learning. Thus, we argue that the assessment attention given to students who are legally entitled to it should serve as a model and reminder: The model is one of collecting comprehensive and useful assessment information for each and every student, and the reminder is that each and every student is entitled to such assessment efforts. Accommodation is about knowing our students, gathering information that helps us best understand what assessment situations will provide us with the most useful information, and expertly using this information.

Literacy assessment must be conducted with sensitivity to the special nature of each student, and the general accommodations that can be afforded to groups and individuals. When we attend to diverse student characteristics in an a priori manner, all students may have productive assessment experiences and the assessment provides accurate accounts of their development and achievement. Zuriff (2000) claims that many unaccommodated students work at a maximum level of performance within the usual timeframe of a standardized test, while accommodated LD students demonstrate significantly better performance on untimed tests. Following, accommodation for LD students, including extra time to take tests, can provide students with a "differential boost" (Phillips, 1994), enhancing their performance more than the performance of unaccommodated students.

There is need for research that examines accommodation in classroom assessment, because most accommodation research focuses on standardized tests (Stansfield, 2002). Yet, the test-centric accommodation research base deserves consideration. Olson, Mead, and Payne (2002) found that the most common accommodations for LD students include testing in small groups, paraphrasing test instructions and contents, extending time to take tests, taking dictation from a student, and reading tests aloud to students. Assessment accommodation of ELL students includes the linguistic modification of test instructions and items (with the intent of making the language of the assessment more understandable), glossaries of key words and terms in tests' reading selections, and extra time to take the assessment (Abedi, Lord, & Plummer, 1997; Abedi, Lord, Hofstetter, & Baker, 2001).

Abedi and his colleagues (Abedi et al., 1997; Abedi et al., 2001) suggest four foci that can guide the accommodation of assessment, including *validity, effectiveness, differential impact* and *feasibility*. Attention to *validity* helps us discern if the provision of an accommodation alters the construct being measured—for example, when a reading test is read aloud to a student it transforms the reading test into a listening test (Stretch & Osborne, 2005). Should the accommodation change the construct, it is important to document the specifics of this change and to use this information in the interpretation of assessment results. *Effectiveness* focuses on what (and how) accommodations best diminish differences in the assessment performances of ELL and non-ELL students (or LD and non-LD students). *Differential impact* focuses on how accommodation may place some students at disadvantage, as when the provision of extra time benefits accommodated students, but gives them an advantage over unaccommodated students. *Feasibility* is a final consideration, as making accommodation of diverse students during assessment requires new resource distributions, and adds a new layer of adjustment, administration and analysis to the assessment enterprise.

We note that LD and ELL students are entitled to receive assessment accommodation, in accordance with Federal laws and mandates. As students meet specific criteria for inclusion, they are accommodated. Yet, this process may leave many diverse students who are deserving of some accommodation just beyond the reach of being accommodated, as if the student is not quite "ELL enough," or "LD enough." These students, as well as their legally designated peers, can be accommodated in literacy assessment routines that attend to individual differences. For example, the teacher who repeats assessment instructions, or provides varied wait time for students answering questions, based on an accurate appraisal of students' current level of competence, is practicing accommodation.

Characteristics of Effective Assessment

Given the range of diversities that successful assessment must negotiate, we are fortunate to have a broad array of assessment materials and procedures. In this section, we describe characteristics of successful assessment, including the ability to address students' formative and summative information, to describe students' cognitive, affective and social development. How is assessment useful? Those who use assessments and the information they yield are interested in better understanding their students. We conceptualize this process as constructing meaning with assessment information. Each teacher, parent, student and school administrator constructs understanding with assessment data. Thus, a goal for all users of assessment is the construction of an accurate and detailed mental model of the individual learner. This mental model must be dynamic. For example, a teacher's constructed understanding of a student's reading development must be continually updated with new information related to that development, else the assessment information grows stale and is not useful.

We obtain new assessment information through our strategic use of assessment resources. For example, when we ask questions in the classroom, administer a reading inventory, and examine students' test results, we can build an accurate and current sense of the student's reading development. The understanding of the student's development must also be situated—our understanding of motivation, affect, and cognitive skills and strategies must be in relation to the increasingly complex literacy contexts in which we expect matriculating students to participate. If the goal of assessment is to provide useful information that we can use to influence teaching and learning, and then to gauge students' products, we must have formative and summative information. If assessment is to help us understand how students learn and use literacy skills and strategies in increasingly complex contexts, the assessment venues must reflect this.

Conclusions

This is a time of great challenge and opportunity for assessment and the English language arts. Evolving theories of the English language arts, and of educational measurement suggest that our increased understanding of the complexity of language development and use can be complemented with assessments that provide valid and useful information. At the same time, assessment is situated in classrooms, schools and communities that are influenced by often-powerful economic, political and social factors. Effective literacy assessment is possible, and it is achieved when appropriate levels of will and resources are applied.

In this chapter we conceptualize diversity broadly, attempting to demonstrate that it is not enough to recognize how each of our students may differ. Assessment itself must be sensitive to the diverse contexts in which it is used, and the diverse audiences and purposes it serves. Our major point is that while it is common to frame student diversity in relation to particular characteristics of students, literacy assessment that is useful is the result of careful attention to the range of diversities that shape both the assessment environment, and our conceptualizations of students. The goal of assessment is to enhance the education, and attention to the cognitive, affective, and social dimensions of assessment for diverse students is critical.

References

Abedi, J., Lord C., & Plummer, J. R. (1997). *Final report of language background as a variable in NAEP mathematics performance*. Los Angeles, CA: Center for the Study of Evaluation, CSE Technical Report # 429.

Abedi, J., Lord, C., Hofstetter, C., & Baker, E. (2000). Impact of accommodation strategies on English language learners' test performance. *Educational Measurement: Issues and Practice, 19*, 16–26.

Afflerbach, P. (2002). Teaching reading self-assessment strategies. In C. C. Block & M. Pressley (Eds.), *Comprehension instruction: Research-based best practices* (pp. 96–111). New York, NY: Guilford Press.

Afflerbach, P. (2007). *Understanding and using reading assessment, K-12*. Newark, DE: International Reading Association.

Afflerbach, P., Cho, B., Kim, J., & Clark, S. (2010). Classroom assessment of literacy. In D. Wise, R. Andrews, & J. Hoffman (Eds.), *The international handbook of English, language and literacy teaching* (pp. 401–412). London: Routledge.

Artley, S. (1981). Individual differences and reading instruction. *Elementary School Journal, 82,* 142–151.

Baxter, G., & Glaser, R. (1998). Investigating the cognitive complexity of science assessments. *Educational Measurement: Issues and Practice, 17,* 37–45.

Black, P., & Wiliam, D. (1998). Inside the black box: Raising standards through classroom assessment. *Phi Delta Kappan, 80,* 139–148.

Bourdieu, P. (1991). *Language and symbolic power.* London: Polity Press.

Calkins, L., Montgomery, K., Santman, D., with Falk, B. (1998). *A teacher's guide to standardized reading tests: Knowledge is power.* Portsmouth, NH: Heinemann.

Chapman, J., & Tunmer, W. (1995). Development of young children's reading self-concepts: An examination of emerging subcomponents and their relationship with reading achievement. *Journal of Educational Psychology, 87,* 154–167.

Clay, M. (2002). *An observation survey of early literacy achievement, 2/e.* Portsmouth, NH: Heinemann.

Corno, L., & Mandinach, E. (2004). What we have learned about student engagement in the past twenty years. In D. McInerney & S. Van Etten (Eds.), *Big theories revisited, Vol. 4: Research on sociocultural influences on motivation and education* (pp. 299–328). Greenwich, CT: Information Age.

Crooks, T. (1988). The impact of classroom evaluation practices on students. *Review of Educational Research, 58,* 438–481.

Davis, A. (1998). *The limits of educational assessment.* Oxford, UK: Blackwell.

Flavell, J. (1976). Metacognitive aspects of problem solving. In L. B. Resnick (Ed.), *The nature of intelligence* (pp. 231–235). Hillsdale, NJ: Erlbaum.

Gambrell, L., Palmer, B., Codling, R., & Mazzoni, S. (1996). *Motivation to read profile (MRP).* Athens, GA: National Reading Research Center.

Guthrie, J., & Wigfield, A. (1997). *Reading engagement: Motivating readers through integrated instruction.* Newark, DE: International Reading Association.

Heller, M. (2008). Bourdieu and "literacy education.. In J. Albright & A. Luke (Eds.), *Pierre Bourdieu and literacy education* (pp. 50–67). New York: Routledge.

Johnson, R., Willeke, M., & Steiner, D. (1998). Stakeholder collaboration in the design and implementation of a family literacy portfolio assessment. *American Journal of Education, 19,* 339–353.

Johnston, P. (1987). Teachers as evaluation experts. *The Reading Teacher, 40,* 744–748.

Johnston, P. (2004). *Choice words.* Portland, ME: Stenhouse.

Lave, J., & Wenger, E. (1991). *Situated learning: Legitimate peripheral participation.* Cambridge, UK: Cambridge University Press.

Lewis, J., Enciso, P., & Moje, E. (2007). *Reframing sociocultural research on literacy: Identity, agency, and power.* Mahwah, NJ: Erlbaum.

McKenna, M., & Kear, D. (1990). Measuring attitude towards reading: a new tool for teachers. *The Reading Teacher, 43,* 626–639.

Messick, S. (1989). Validity. In R. L. Linn (Ed.), *Educational measurement* (3rd ed., pp. 13–104). New York, NY: Macmillan.

Moll, L., Amati, C., Neff, D., Gonzalez, N. (1992). Funds of knowledge for teaching: Using a qualitative approach to connect homes and classrooms. *Theory into Practice, 31,* 132–141.

Olson, B., Mead, R., & Payne, D. (2002). *A report of a standard setting method for alternate assessments for students with significant disabilities* (Synthesis Report 47). Minneapolis: University of Minnesota, National Center on Educational Outcomes.

Palincsar, A., & Brown, A. (1984). Reciprocal teaching of comprehension-fostering and monitoring activities. *Cognition and Instruction, 1,* 117–175.

Pellegrino, J., Chudowsky, N., & Glaser, R. (2001). *Knowing what students know: The science and design of educational assessment.* Washington, DC: National Academy Press.

Phillips, G. (1994). High stakes testing accommodations: Validity versus disabled rights. *Applied Measurement in Education, 7,* 93–120.

Pressley, M., Afflerbach, P. (1995). *Verbal protocols of reading: The nature of constructively responsive reading.* Mahwah, NJ: Erlbaum.

Sadler, D. (1989). Formative assessment and the design of instructional systems. *Instructional Science, 13,* 191–209.

Schon, D. (1983). *Educating the reflective practitioner: Toward a new design for teaching and learning in the professions.* San Francisco: Jossey-Bass.

Schultz, K. (2003). *Listening: A framework for teaching across differences.* New York, NY: Teacher's College Press.

Shepard, L., & Bliem, C. (1995). Parents' thinking about standardized tests and performance assessments. *Educational Researcher, 24,* 25–32.

Stansfield, C. (2002). Linguistic simplification: A promising test accommodation for LEP students? *Practical Assessment, Research and Evaluation, 8.* Retrieved from http://pareonline.net/getvn.asp?v=8&n=7

Stiggins, R., & Conklin, N. (1992). *In teachers' hands: Investigating the practices of classroom assessment.* Albany: State University of New York Press.

Stretch, L., & Osborne, J. (2005). Extended time test accommodation: Directions for future research and practice. *Practical assessment, research and evaluation.* Retrieved from: http://pareonline.net/genpare.asp?wh=4&abt=stretch

Tittle, C. (2005). Validity: Whose construction is it in the teaching and learning context? *Educational Measurement: Issues and Practices, 8,* 5–13.

Vygotsky, L. (1978). *Mind in society: The development of higher psychological processes* (M. Cole, V. John-Steiner, S. Scribner, & E. Souberman, Trans.). Cambridge, MA: Harvard University Press.

Zuriff, G. (2000). Extra examination time for students with learning disabilities: An examination of the maximum potential thesis. *Applied Measurement in Education, 3,* 99–117.

45

Assessment Frameworks for Teaching and Learning English Language Arts in a Digital Age

Julie Coiro and Jill Castek

The Internet has become increasingly central to our daily lives (Johnson, Levine, Smith, & Smythe, 2009), transforming the ways we access, use, and exchange information. To fully participate in a globally networked society, every student needs to develop strategies for locating, comprehending, and responding to text in ways that exploit the potentials of information and communication technologies (ICTs) (Educational Testing Service [ETS], 2003; International Reading Association [IRA], 2009; National Council of Teachers of English [NCTE], 2007). Making sense of digital information requires skills and strategies that are complex, and in some cases unique, to online reading and writing contexts (Afflerbach & Cho, 2008; Coiro & Dobler, 2007; Transliteracies Project, 2006). Thus, students' proficiencies in the new millennium cannot be determined solely on the basis of their literacy performance in non-digital contexts (Leu et al., 2005; O'Brien, 2006).

To date, existing assessments fail to measure the literacy skills, knowledge, and dispositions that are increasingly important for participation in a digital age (Assessment and Teaching of 21st Century Skills [ATC21S], 2009; IRA/NCTE, 2010). As a result, online literacy is not integrated into language arts standards and is rarely taught in schools (Hew & Brush, 2007). Often, it is viewed as an optional add-on rather than a vital component of literacy instruction requiring a fundamental shift in literacy pedagogy and assessment (O'Brien & Scharber, 2008). Due to the emergence of the Internet as today's defining technology for literacy and learning (Leu, 2007) and the rapid shift in literacy practices from page to screen (Lankshear & Knobel, 2006), a central question becomes: How can educators assess students' online literacy competencies, track progress over time, and identify strengths and weaknesses that can be addressed through instruction?

This chapter highlights research that suggests the Internet is reshaping reading, writing, and communication and sparking a transformation in the ways we teach and assess literacy and language arts. It is structured around the notion that educational assessments should draw on principles of evidence-centered design (National Research Council, 2001) to answer three essential questions: (a) What evidence is needed to represent proficiency in online literacy and language arts? (b) What situations or tasks can elicit such evidence? (c) How can this evidence be interpreted in meaningful ways? (see Figure 45.1).

The first section provides a rationale for the types of evidence we should be gathering about students' online literacy development. Illustrative examples of what these assessments might look like can be found in the latter sections of the chapter. However, assessments of online literacy and language arts are just beginning to emerge (see, for example, Coiro, 2009a; Leu et al., 2008), and their applications in classrooms are preliminary in nature. By drawing attention to contemporary research and principles of evidence-centered design, we intend to incite thinking that will provide a vision for future work in this area.

What Evidence is Needed to Represent Proficiency in Online Literacy and Language Arts?

In today's global knowledge society, print is no longer the dominant form of communication or expression (NCTE, 2007). Rather, the Internet and other ICTs have rapidly accelerated students' access to, and production of, a range of digital, nonlinear, multimodal, and interactive texts that are often unbounded in time and space (New Media Consortium, 2007). These dynamic online texts and their associated literacy practices require dynamic assessments that are sensitive to the diverse, multiple, and rapidly changing ways in which learners read, write, view, listen, compose, and communicate information in the 21st century (IRA/NCTE, 2010). The literature in this area suggests that language arts assessments in a digital age should reflect evidence of: (a) a broad range of richly intertwined print and digital language arts skills and practices, (b) an important set of dispositions toward participating in globally networked communities,

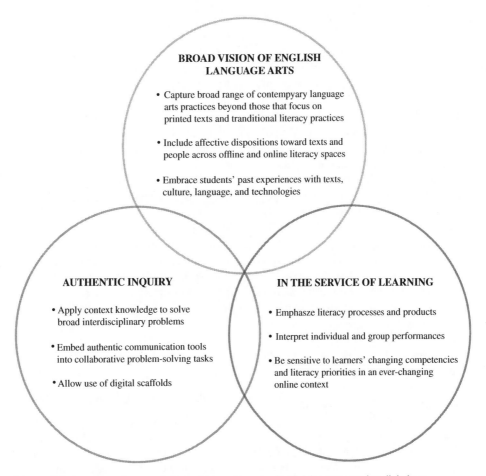

Figure 45.1 Assessment framework for teaching and learning English language arts in a digital age.

and (c) diverse perspectives about what counts as literacy in school classrooms.

Broad Range of Print and Digital Language Arts Skills and Practices Knobel and Wilber (2009) argue that three interlocking online literacy practices—participation, collaboration, and distribution—are challenging how schools traditionally define the ways readers and writers use and respond to texts. From these three practices emerge a whole host of additional language arts skills beyond reading, writing, listening, and speaking. These include, but are not limited to, the ability to review, critique, respond, tag, rate, remix, record, and collaboratively build on collective knowledge bases to generate new digital texts—while taking care to follow copyright laws and to be sensitive to how ideas might be perceived from diverse points of view.

Elsewhere, Churches (2009) outlines digital extensions to traditional classroom literacy practices associated with note taking, journaling, discussing, drafting, diagramming, displaying, presenting, and otherwise communicating with technology for informal and formal purposes. Each of these practices introduces skill sets that demand a broader range of assessment measures to inform teachers seeking to prepare students for success in a digital world. Importantly,

evidence from these assessments should move beyond rote recall or isolated skills practice to evaluate performance on tasks that blend information seeking, problem solving, and knowledge generation for authentic purposes (Shepard, 2000). In addition, educational assessments should occur within daily classroom activities and provide timely, contextualized, and useful information about what students can do and not just what they cannot (Tierney, 1998).

More specifically, authentic assessments should capture evidence in three key areas central to language arts performance in a digital age. First, authentic language arts assessments should be designed to capture students' ability to critique, evaluate, and synthesize multiple sources of simultaneous and often disparate information while applying a broad range of print and digital literacies (NCTE, 2007). Second, evidence should document students' ability to collaboratively generate and creatively produce print and digital information for many purposes and audiences (ATC21S, 2008; New Media Consortium, 2007). Third, assessments should elicit information about the level of fluency and efficiency with which students are able to apply these literacies across diverse print and digital contexts (Information Fluency, 2009; Leu, Kinzer, Coiro, & Cammack, 2004).

Dispositions Toward Participating in a Global Online Community Assessments of online literacy and language arts should also document students' evolving dispositions toward participating in globally networked communities (Coiro, 2009a; Popham, 2009). Positive dispositions, or attitudes and beliefs, are key dimensions of effective learning, particularly for students growing up in a digital information age (Johnston, 2005). In the context of language arts curricula, Web 2.0 technologies (such as open-source information and social networking sites) and emerging learning standards demand that online readers and writers be personally productive, socially responsible, and able to collaborate with other members of a globally networked community (e.g., Johnson et al., 2009). In addition, 21st-century learners are expected to be adaptable, imaginative, self-directed, emotionally resilient, and able to demonstrate effective oral and communication skills (American Association of School Librarians [AASL], 2007). Consequently, teachers require assessments that document important competencies such as strong interpersonal communication skills, an understanding of productive team dynamics, an appreciation of differences in cultural practices and work patterns, and the ability to respond appropriately to peer feedback (Afflerbach, 2007).

One important resource that can guide the instruction and documentation of such competencies is the *Standards for the 21st Century Learner in Action* developed by the AASL Learning Standards Indicators and Assessment Task Force (see http://www.ala.org/ ala/mgrps/divs/aasl/aaslproftools/standardsinaction/stan-dardsinaction.cfm). This document contains grade level benchmarks, action examples, and accompanying rubrics reflecting critical stages of development. These guidelines can help educators conceptualize, teach, and assess 21st-century learner dispositions such as emotional resilience, persistence, social responsibility, and personal productivity. Rather than suggesting one set of guidelines for all situations, we encourage educators to build on and adapt these ideas in ways that suitably address their unique educational contexts.

Diverse Perspectives of What Counts as Literacy in School Classrooms A third characteristic of literacy assessments for a digital age is that they reflect diverse perspectives about the knowledge and skills that are valued in the English language arts curriculum. As the literacy community seeks to more accurately reflect literacy as influenced by a wide range of cultural and personal histories, we are in need of assessment practices that preserve, respect, and make space for diverse interpretations about existing text while broadening the ways learners might creatively respond to text for academic and personal purposes (Cope & Kalantzis, 2000; IRA/NCTE, 2010; Moje, Willes, & Fassio, 2001). In other words, assessment practices should help students connect *who they are* to *what they do* in school (Gallego & Hollingsworth, 2000).

Specifically, future assessments of online literacy and language arts should honor and celebrate students' home culture and daily literacies (see Moll, Amanti, Neff, & Gonzalez, 1992). For example, O'Brien, Beach, & Sharber (2007) describe ways middle school teachers integrated multi-media and new literacies practices to build classroom community, increase motivation, and develop agency in meeting both school-based and personally relevant goals. Language arts assignments involved designing video games of the ideal city, populating it with characters, and writing narratives about the characters and their video gaming experiences; collaboratively writing radio plays produced using Garage Band; and using Comic Life (http://comiclife. com/) as a context for writing narratives with characters from popular science fiction stories or video games. While these media-rich activities helped students make connections across their home and school lives, struggling readers in particular perceived improvements in their own reading and writing abilities as a result of collaboration and participation. Documenting evidence of students' engagement in digital literacy experiences that transcend the boundaries of home and school may have the potential to shape adolescents' identities as social and literate individuals (see also Burnett & Wilkinson, 2005; Perry, 2006).

What Situations or Tasks Can Elicit Such Evidence?

A second consideration for designing assessments identifies a range of situations or tasks that elicit evidence of proficiency in online literacy and language arts. Recommendations in this area suggest that assessment be viewed as authentic and situated in classroom practice (Darling-Hammond & Snyder, 2000), while incorporating multiple measures and broader methods to document the strategies, thinking processes, and attitudes specifically associated with online literacy development. As online literacy practices become more prominent in school, it is critical that educators move beyond thinking about digital assessments as isolated tests and view these more as authentic opportunities for students to practice and apply the skills, knowledge, and dispositions they will need as readers and writers in a digital age. Performance-based learning activities can then be seamlessly integrated throughout the school day and paired with observational notes, self and peer checklists, and an examination of student work products. Examining such artifacts formatively for signs of development can help pinpoint students' strengths and weakness and guide future instruction. To that end, classroom embedded language arts assessment situations may include opportunities to incorporate: (a) authentic multidisciplinary problems to solve, (b) digital communication and workplace tools, and (c) embedded digital scaffolds.

Authentic Multidisciplinary Problems to Solve Literacy education in the 21st century must adequately prepare students for participation in a knowledge-based economy (Bereiter & Scardamalia, 2006). The ability to identify important problems, and then efficiently locate, critically evaluate, synthesize, and communicate potential solutions to those problems is a key resource for social and economic development (Leu et al., 2004). Collaborative online literacy experiences engage students in these inquiry-based processes as they negotiate meaning and construct new knowledge using online resources and networked communication tools. Moreover, visions of classroom instruction in the new millennium require learners to weave their knowledge of core subjects (e.g., science, math, history, and language arts), and appreciation of diverse perspectives, into the context of interdisciplinary issues such as global health, civic literacy, and economic stability (Trilling & Fidel, 2009). Consequently, valid assessments of online literacy and language arts should engage students in digital reading, writing, and communicating tasks contextualized in problem-based, interdisciplinary, real-world issues.

Authentic online projects such as those listed in the *Teacher's Guide to International Collaboration on the Internet* (see www.ed.gov/teachers/how/tech/international/guide_pg2.html) or sponsored by The Center for Innovation in Engineering and Science Education (CIESE; see www.ciese.org/collabprojs.html) encourage students to use ICTs to construct knowledge, share data, and negotiate meaning across disciplines and among learners who come from various cultural traditions and hold diverse points of view. As a result, students learn content and simultaneously develop skills that are vital to participation in an information age (Castek, 2008). Performance based scoring systems could be woven into these types of projects to track progress and offer feedback on students' developing knowledge, skills, and dispositions as they exchange ideas, respond to texts, and solve problems in authentic, online spaces.

Digital Communication and Workplace Tools Digital communication technologies have significantly shifted the way we interact in our daily lives and in the workplace (New Media Consortium, 2007). A wide range of social networking and information sharing tools (such as Facebook, Twitter, Skype, etc.) are emerging at a rapid pace. These applications have given rise to new means of communication, new places to communicate, and new avenues of interaction, thereby making it possible to connect with a wider and more diverse group of individuals than ever before (Johnson et al., 2009).

Consequently, language arts assessments should incorporate the information and communication tools used in the workforce and in students' daily lives (e.g., interactive blogs, wikis, VoiceThread, instant messaging, email, etc.). These applications have been used successfully in classrooms as forums for posing and answering questions (Charron, 2007), individual reflection (Richardson, 2006), higher-level thinking about content (Zawilinski, 2009), and cross-classroom collaboration (Boling, Castek, Zawilinski, Barton, & Nierlich, 2008). Unlike paper and pencil products, networked communication tools generate student work that can be archived in a searchable digital portfolio. Once catalogued, educators can examine students' writing development alongside their communication and collaboration

skills with ICTs. These assessment practices elicit tangible evidence of online literacy development and support teachers in addressing the skills required for communication and collaboration in a global society.

For some educators, online communication practices (e.g., instant messaging [IM] and texting) prompt concerns that non-standard writing forms might negatively interfere with students' use of standard conventions in formal academic writing. However, rather than simply correcting or dismissing these conventions as inappropriate, Jacobs (2008) and others (e.g., Helderman, 2003; Lee, 2002) argue it is important that students are able to communicate in both worlds (IM and academic writing) and to thoughtfully choose the formality of language that is appropriate for each. To guide teaching and assessment in this area, educators can engage students in discussions about the nature of their writing while developing: (a) a meta-awareness of the various ways we write for different purposes, audiences, and contexts (Jacobs, 2008), and (b) the ability to fluently 'code-switch' between formal and informal patterns of language use (see Turner, 2009). Turner provides examples of text convention charts and checklists that can be used to facilitate and document students' ability to translate writing conventions across multiple situations in ways that privilege both formal and informal writing contexts. Incorporating these practices for instruction and assessment into the language arts curriculum prepares students to adjust their use of written language (e.g., conventions, style, and vocabulary) to communicate effectively with a variety of audiences and for different purposes (see IRA/NCTE, 1996).

Embedded Digital Scaffolds In addition to engaging students in solving authentic problems, in part with online communication tools, future language arts assessment practices should begin to explore how digital scaffolds might be used to provide a richer picture of what all students know and can do. Multimedia enhancements such as text-to-speech reading aids, annotation tools, and scaffolds for summarizing, synthesizing, and reflection make it possible for academically diverse students to access online content (Anderson-Inman & Horney, 2007), solve real-world problems, and actively contribute to digital learning communities. Digital scaffolds accommodate the individual needs of diverse learners and reduce the chances that decoding and language differences impede learning (e.g., Edyburn, 2007; Proctor, Dalton, & Grisham, 2007).

In contrast to standardized tests that highlight areas where students fall short, future assessments need to make use of the wide range of digital tools that promote literacy success. Educators might, for example, explore the applications of emerging technologies such as supported e-texts (Anderson-Inman, 2004), cognitive rescaling tools (e.g., auto-summarizing features) (Edyburn, 2002), and tiered digital learning materials (Edyburn, 2007) that allow readers to alter the difficulty of text and formulate responses in multiple modalities. Other tools such as spell checkers, graphic organizers, concept maps, language translators, and word prediction software build on the strengths of academically diverse learners as they read, compose, and respond to texts. These digital scaffolds are especially supportive for diverse learners as they navigate the range and complexity of resources found on the Internet. In an age of rapidly emerging ICTs, digital scaffolds need to be made available during assessment and instruction to compensate for learning difficulties so all students can demonstrate their true language and literacy abilities.

How Can this Evidence be Interpreted in Meaningful Ways?

The third component of evidence-centered assessment practices is to ensure that valid evidence of students' digital literacy development, in all its complexity, is represented and interpreted in ways that improve teaching and learning. As the primary agents of assessment, teachers are responsible for translating evidence about students' existing language arts practices into meaningful instructional decisions (Johnston & Costello, 2005). To effectively inform teacher decision-making, assessment practices for online literacy and language arts should: (a) make visible information about students' online reading and writing processes and products, (b) inform interpretations of students' literacy and language development in both individual and group contexts, and (c) include opportunities for students and teachers to engage in productive literacy conversations about their progress and make contributions to the classroom community.

Online Literacy Processes and Products If teachers are to make informed decisions about how to support online inquiry and creative knowledge generation, assessments should be designed to capture both the processes that occur during these tasks as well as the resulting learning products. Thus, assessments should include reporting procedures to elicit multiple forms of data from which teachers can observe and document important developments and areas of challenge during literacy learning (IRA/NCTE, 2010).

In a classroom or lab setting where students use laptops, process and product data can be collected easily with online recording software such as Camtasia (see www.techsmith.com/camtasia.asp) or I Show U (see www.store.shinywhitebox.com/home/home.html). The software creates a video recording of students' actions and voices as they spontaneously engage in online reading and writing processes, just as if an observer were watching over their shoulder. Teachers, students, and peers can then play back the videos to better understand how students accomplish (or struggle with) tasks such as using search engines, constructing meaning and evaluating authorship across multiple sources, participating in IM exchanges, or collaboratively organizing and composing information in a shared document editor (e.g., Google Docs) or a social networking environment (e.g., Facebook or Ning). In addition, online tools such as Quia (www.quia.com) or Survey Monkey (www.surveymon-

key.com) can automatically compile student-generated responses for review.

Students might also be asked to think-aloud as they engage with these tasks to foster their own metacognitive awareness of the successes and obstacles they encountered along the way (see Kucan & Beck, 1997). Through dialogue and discussion, students may better understand and internalize their own strengths and set goals for online reading improvement. Reflection that takes place while students are engaged in the activity, and after completing the activity, promotes continuous learning in authentic contexts and is integral to the online inquiry process (Chappuis & Chappuis, 2007/2008).

Digital recordings can also provide a specific reference point for where in the online reading or writing process a group of students, or one student in particular, needs the most support (Coiro, 2009b). These challenging spots can then become the focus of future instruction. Over time, video recordings offer evidence of literacy development at certain points in the process, which might then be compiled in an online e-portfolio system (see, for example, Barrett, 2008) and explicitly linked to increases in the quality of students' associated literacy products over time.

Consider Digital Literacy Performance in Both Individual and Group Contexts In addition to documenting literacy processes and products, it will be important for language arts assessments to offer feedback about a student's individual contribution to an assigned online task as well as the quality of his or her working group's interactions and discussion (Johnston & Costello, 2005). By analyzing information from both types of data sources, teachers are able to attend to what students can do independently as well as how they contribute to group problem-solving and knowledge generation processes that are often embedded within authentic online literacy tasks.

As readers independently engage with reading and writing tasks, teachers might, for example, document evidence of a student's reading comprehension strategy use, dispositions toward online texts and tools, or use of appropriate discourses for communicating in a range of online contexts. Checklist assessments aligned to research-based criteria for particular literacy tasks are one effective way to help teachers (and students) determine individual strengths and areas of improvement (Afflerbach, Reutschlin, & Russell, 2007). Individual performance might also be documented across anticipated phases of an online reading or writing process. This information could then be used to estimate where a reader falls along an expected continuum of online literacy development and inform realistic next steps for instruction (see Coiro, 2007). Rich feedback about an individual's literacy performance supports teachers in identifying strengths and areas of need, and differentiating instruction accordingly (Riddle Buly & Valencia, 2002). Teachers can gather evidence of productive group work (e.g., attentive listening, progress toward a shared goal) through observational checklists, reflective progress reports, and students' self-assessments of their teammates and their own contributions to the project.

Include Opportunities for Productive Literacy Conversations

Finally, as we move into the next millennium, Tierney (2000) argues for a shift toward learner-centered assessment practices that "afford students opportunities to engage with teachers, caregivers, and stakeholders in meaningful partnerships involving genuine decision making" (p. 244). Thus, assessments of digital literacy development should be organized around students and teachers working together in literacy conversations to observe, reflect, and offer feedback on their progress and document learning over time (Serafini, 2001; Tierney, 1998). Productive literacy conversations are those that invite students to provide their own evidence of what they have achieved and to be involved in goal-setting activities that can directly inform future instruction (IRA/NCTE, 2010; Johnston, 2003). During these conversations, both teachers and students ask questions as part of an authentic inquiry process that engages them with "productive literacy practices and identities" (Johnston & Costello, 2005, p. 259) that inform literacy instruction.

Research also suggests student and teacher talk focus on evidence of online literacy development from multiple examples of student work in varied assessment tasks to better understand the complex literacies students are acquiring in ways not revealed in conventional standardized test scores of reading and writing (Afflerbach, 2007; IRA/NCTE, 2010). In addition, productive assessment conversations among groups of teachers provide a context for drawing on multiple sources of information to consider alternative solutions beyond the limitations of one's own assessment lens (Johnston, 2003).

Two Challenges for the Future of Online Literacy Assessment

In closing, as we look to the future, two points will continue to challenge progress in developing authentic and practical classroom assessments of English language arts in a digital age. The first issue is one of accessibility. It is vital that schools keep pace with the influx of new innovations and networking capabilities in ways that ensure students and teachers have equitable access to high-powered computers, high-speed networks, and the range of mobile and interactive whiteboard technologies that might be used to teach, monitor, and evaluate performance in online reading, writing, and communication skills. This will be especially challenging for districts situated in economically disadvantaged communities who struggle more often with issues of accessibility on a regular basis (e.g., Henry, 2007).

The second, and perhaps more pressing issue, is one of flexibility. Even with full access to equipment and networked connectivity, the ultimate challenge in assessing literacy in a digital age is that online texts, tools, and reading/writing contexts will continue to change rapidly as new technologies emerge (Leu et al., 2004). Yet, "the need for learners at all levels who can solve new problems, generate new knowledge, and invent new language practices will re-

main constant" (IRA/NCTE, 2010). To help learners realize their potential as citizens in a digital age, it is imperative that the literacy community, and its various stakeholders, continually reconsider and expand what it means to skillfully read, write, and communicate with ICTs. Subsequent revision and reconfiguration of online literacy measures will need to realistically keep pace in ways that document performance on a range of outcomes, not just those that cause direct improvements on conventional measures of print literacy.

As we venture forward, the journey will no doubt be challenging. Yet, it is a challenge that can no longer be ignored. For those who seek to venture forward, we believe practices that are grounded in evidence-centered design and driven by flexible solutions to address rapid and continual change in both technology and literacy hold much promise toward better understanding effective teaching and assessment practices of English language arts in a digital age.

References

Afflerbach, P. (2007). *Understanding and using reading assessment*. Newark, DE: International Reading Association.

Afflerbach, P., & Cho, B.Y. (2008). Identifying and describing constructively responsive comprehension strategies in new and traditional forms of reading. In S. Israel & G. Duffy (Eds.). *Handbook of reading comprehension research* (pp. 6–90). Mahwah, NJ: Erlbaum.

Afflerbach, P., Reutschlin, H., & Russell, S. (2007). Assessing strategic reading. In J. R. Paratore & R. L. McCormack (Eds.), *Classroom literacy assessment: Making sense of what students know and do* (pp. 177–194). New York: Guilford Press.

American Association of School Librarians (AASL). (2007). *Standards for the 21st century learner*. Retrieved October 1, 2009, from http://www.ala.org/ala/mgrps/divs/aasl/guidelines andstandards/learningstandards/standards.cfm

Anderson-Inman, L. (2004). Reading on the Web: Making the most of digital text. *Wisconsin State Reading Association Journal, 44*(2), 8–14.

Anderson-Inman, L., & Horney, M. A. (2007). Supported eText: Assistive technology through text transformations. *Reading Research Quarterly, 42*(1), 152–160.

Assessment and Teaching of 21st Century Skills (ATC21S). (2008, September 1). *Transforming education: Assessing and teaching the skills needed in the 21st century: A call to action*. Intel, Microsoft and Cisco Education Taskforce. Retrieved from http://www.atc21s.org/GetAssets.axd?FilePath=/Assets/Files/699792fd-4d41-44f2-8208-cbb3fccb6572.pdf

Barrett, H. C. (2008). Categories of e-portfolio tools. Retrieved October 1, 2009, from http://electronicportfolios.org/categories.html

Beach, R., & O'Brien, D. (2008). Teaching popular culture texts in the classroom. In J. Coiro, M. Knobel, C. Lankshear, & D. J. Leu. (Eds.). *Handbook of research on new literacies* (pp. 775–804). Mahwah, NJ: Erlbaum.

Boling, E., Castek, J., Zawilinski, L, Barton, K., & Nierlich, T. (2008). Collaborative literacy: Blogs and internet projects. *The Reading Teacher, 61*, 504–506.

Burnett, C., & Wilkinson, J. (2005). Holy lemons! Learning from children's uses of the Internet in out-of-school contexts. *Literacy, 39*, 158–165.

Bereiter, C., & Scardamalia, M. (2006). Education for the knowledge age: Design-centered models of teaching and instruction. In P. A. Alexander & P. H. Winne (Eds.), *Handbook of educational psychology* (2nd ed., pp. 695–713). Mahwah, NJ: Erlbaum.

Castek, J. (2008). *How do 4th and 5th grade students acquire the new literacies of online reading comprehension? Exploring the contexts that facilitate learning*. Unpublished doctoral dissertation, University of Connecticut, Storrs.

Chappuis, S., & Chappuis, J. (2007/2008). The best value in formative assessment. *Educational Leadership, 65*, 14–19.

Charron, N. (2007). "I learned that there's a state called victoria and he has six blue-tongued lizards!" *The Reading Teacher, 60*, 762–769.

Churches, A. (2009). *Bloom's digital taxonomy*. Retrieved October 5, 2009, from http://edorigami.wikispaces.com/Bloom%27s+Digital+Taxonomy

Coiro, J. (2007). *Exploring changes to reading comprehension on the internet: Paradoxes and possibilities for diverse adolescent readers*. Unpublished doctoral dissertation, University of Connecticut, Storrs.

Coiro, J. (2009a). Rethinking reading assessment in a digital age: How is reading comprehension different and where do we turn now. *Educational Leadership, 66*, 59–63.

Coiro, J. (2009b). Promising practices for supporting adolescents' online literacy development. In K. D. Wood & W. E. Blanton (Eds.). *Promoting literacy with adolescent learners: Research-based instruction* (pp. 442–471). New York: Guilford Press.

Coiro, J., & Dobler, E. (2007). Exploring the comprehension strategies used by sixth-grade skilled readers as they search for and locate information on the Internet. *Reading Research Quarterly, 42*, 214–257.

Cope, B., & Kalantzis, M. (2000). *Multiliteracies*. London: Routledge.

Darling-Hammond, L., & Snyder, J. (2000). Authentic assessment of teaching in context. *Teaching and Teacher Education, 16*(5-6), 523–545.

Educational Testing Service [ETS]. (2003). *Digital transformation: A framework for ICT literacy. Princeton, NJ: Educational Testing Service*. Retrieved December 15, 2006, from http://www.ets.org/Media/Research/pdf/ICTREPORT.pdf

Edyburn, D. L. (2002). Cognitive rescaling strategies: Interventions that alter the cognitive accessibility of text. *Closing the Gap, 21*(1), 10–21.

Edyburn, D.L. (2007). Technology enhanced reading performance: Defining a research agenda. *Reading Research Quarterly, 42*(1), 146–152.

Gallego, M. A., & Hollingsworth, S. (2000). Introduction: The idea of multiple literacies. In M. A. Gallego & S. Hollingsworth (Eds.), *What counts as literacy: Challenging the school standard* (pp. 1–23). New York: Teachers College Press.

Helderman, R. S. (2003, May 20). Click by click, teens polish writing: Instant messaging teaches more than TTYL and ROFL. *Washington Post*, p. B01.

Henry, L. A. (2007). *Exploring new literacies pedagogy and online reading comprehension among middle school students and teachers: Issues of social equity or social exclusion?* Unpublished doctoral dissertation, University of Connecticut, Storrs.

Hew, K. F., & Brush, T. (2007). Integrating technology into K-12 teaching and learning: Current knowledge gaps and recommendations for future research. *Educational Technology Research and Development, 55*(3), 223–252.

Information Fluency. (2009). *21st century information fluency*. Retrieved October 2, 2009, from http://21cif.com/

International Reading Association (IRA). (2009). *New literacies and 21st century technologies: A position statement*. Newark, DE: IRA. Retrieved September 16, 2009, from http://www.reading.org/General/AboutIRA/PositionStatements/21stCenturyLiteracies.aspx

International Reading Association & National Council of Teachers of English (IRA/NCTE). (1996). *Standards for the English language arts*. Newark, DE; Urbana, IL: Authors. Retrieved January 4, 2010, from http://www.reading.org/General/Publications/Books/bk889.aspx?mode=redirect

International Reading Association & National Council of Teachers of English (IRA/NCTE). (2010). *Standards for the assessment of reading and writing (Rev. ed.)*. Newark, DE; Urbana, IL: Authors. Retrieved January 4, 2010, from http://www.reading.org/General/CurrentResearch/Standards/AssessmentStandards.aspx

Jacobs, G. (2008). We learn what we do: Developing a repertoire of writing practices in an instant messaging world. *Journal of Adolescent & Adult Literacy, 52*(3), 203–211.

Johnson, L., Levine, A., Smith, R., & Smythe, T. (2009). *The 2009 Horizon Report: K-12 Edition*. Austin, TX: The New Media Consortium.

Johnston, P. (2003). Assessment conversation. *Reading Teacher, 57*(1), 90–92.

Johnston, P. (2005). Literacy assessment and the future. *Reading Teacher, 58*(7), 684–686.

Johnston, P., & Costello, P. (2005). Principles for literacy assessment. *Reading Research Quarterly, 40*(2), 256–267.

Knobel, M., & Wilber, D. (2009). Let's Talk 2.0. *Educational Leadership, 66*, 20–24.

Kucan, L., & Beck, I.L. (1997). Thinking aloud and reading comprehension research: Inquiry, instruction, and social interaction. *Review of Educational Research, 67*, 271–299.

Lankshear, C., & Knobel, M. (2006). *New literacies: Everyday practices and classroom learning* (2nd ed.). Buckingham, UK: Open University Press.

Lee, J. (2002, September 19). I think, therefore IM. *New York Times*, p. G1.

Leu, D. J. (2007, May). *What happened when we weren't looking? How reading comprehension has changed and what we need to do about it*. Keynote research address presented at the Annual Meeting of the International Reading Association, Reading Research Conference, Toronto, Canada.

Leu, D. J., Castek, J., Hartman, D., Coiro, J., Henry, L., Kulikowich, J., et al. (2005). *Evaluating the development of scientific knowledge and new forms of reading comprehension during online learning*. Final report presented to the North Central Regional Educational Laboratory/Learning Point Associates. Retrieved Oct. 13, 2009, from http://www.newliteracies.uconn.edu/ncrel.html

Leu, D. J., Coiro, J., Castek, J., Henry, L. A., Reinking, D., & Hartman, D. K. (2008). Research on instruction and assessment in the new literacies of online readingcComprehension. In C. C. Block, S. Parris, & P. Afflerbach (Eds.), *Comprehension instruction: Research-based best practices* (pp. 321–346). New York: Guilford Press.

Leu, D. J., Kinzer, C. K., Coiro, J., & Cammack, D. (2004). Towards a theory of new literacies emerging from the internet and other ICT. In R. B. Ruddell & N. Unrau (Eds.), *Theoretical models and processes of reading* (5th ed., pp. 1570–1613). Newark, DE: International Reading Association.

Moje, E. B., Willes, D. J., & Fassio, K. (2001). Constructing and negotiating literacy in a seventh-grade writer's workshop. In E. B. Moje & D. G. O'Brien (Eds.), *Constructions of literacy: Studies of teaching and learning in and out of secondary schools* (pp. 193–212). Mahwah, NJ: Erlbaum.

Moll, L. C., Amanti, C., Neff, D., & Gonzalez, N. (1992). Funds of knowledge for teaching. *Theory into Practice, 31*, 132–141.

National Council of the Teachers of English (NCTE). (2007). *21st-century literacies: A policy research brief*. Retrieved February 2, 2008, from http://www.ncte.org/library/files/Publications/Newspaper/Chron1107-ResearchBrief.pdf

National Research Council. (2001). *Knowing what students know: The science and design of educational assessment*. Washington, DC: National Academies Press.

New Media Consortium. (2007). *Social networking, The third place, and the evolution of communication*. Retrieved October 1, 2009, from http://www.nmc.org/evolution-communication

O'Brien, D. G. (2006). "Struggling" adolescents' engagement in multimediating: Countering the institutional construction of incompetence. In D. E. Alvermann, K. A. Hinchman, D. W. Moore, S. F. Phelps, & D. R. Waff (Eds.), *Reconceptualizing the literacies in adolescents' lives* (pp. 29–45). Mahwah, NJ: Erlbaum.

O'Brien, D., & Scharber, C. (2008). Digital literacies go to school: Potholes and possibilities. *Journal of Adolescent & Adult Literacy, 52*, 66–68.

Perry, T. B. (2006). Multiple literacies and middle school students. *Theory Into Practice, 45*, 328–336.

Popham, W. J. (2009). Assessing student affect. *Educational Leadership, 66*, 85–86.

Proctor, C. P., Dalton, B., & Grisham, D. L. (2007). Scaffolding English language learners and struggling readers in a universal literacy environment with embedded strategy instruction and vocabulary support. *Journal of Literacy Research, 39,* 71–93.

Richardson, W. (2006). *Blogs, wikis, podcasts, and other powerful web tools for classrooms.* Thousand Oaks, CA: Corwin Press.

Riddle Buly, M., & Valencia, S. W. (2002). Below the bar: Profiles of students who fail state reading tests. *Educational Evaluation and Policy Analysis, 24,* 219–239.

Serafini, F. (2001). Three paradigms of assessment: Measurement, procedure, and inquiry. *The Reading Teacher, 54,* 384–393.

Shepard, L. A. (2000). The role of assessment in a learning culture. *Educational Researcher, 29,* 4–14.

Tierney. R. J. (1998). Literacy assessment reform: Shifting beliefs, principles possibilities, and emerging practices. *The Reading Teacher, 51,* 374–390.

Tierney, R. J. (2000). How will literacy be assessed in the next millennium? *Reading Research Quarterly, 35,* 244–250.

Transliteracies Project. (2006). *Research in the technological, social, and cultural practices of online reading.* Retrieved October 1, 2009, from http://transliteracies.english.ucsb.edu

Trilling, B., & Fidel, C. (2009). *21st century skills: learning for life in our times.* San Francisco: Jossey-Bass.

Turner, K. H. (2009). Flipping the switch: Code-switching from textspeak to standard English. *English Journal, 98*(5), 60–65.

Zawilinski, L. (2009). HOT Blogging: A framework for blogging to promote higher order thinking. *Reading Teacher, 62*(8), 650–661.

46

Authentic Professional Development and Assessment for Language Arts Teachers Capacity for Change

Patricia Ruggiano Schmidt and Sunita Singh

In recent years, No Child Left Behind (2002) punctuated the importance of the language arts; teachers and schools were held accountable for student achievement. This legislation continues to cause great anguish among those who believe teaching and learning are processes that cannot be evaluated by test scores alone. Adding to this dilemma is the fact that language arts teachers are expected to meet the academic and social needs of a growing student population from diverse linguistic, cultural, ethnic, and economic backgrounds (Sleeter, 2001). This information seems especially challenging when perusing state language arts curriculums, typically written by educators from the dominant, mainstream, middle-class, European American cultures. These educational outlines usually feature goals and objectives, materials and resources that frequently ignore languages and cultures of those from under represented groups. Ultimately, this way of proceeding inadvertently disempowers and marginalizes many students (Cummins, 1996; Nieto, 2000; Gunderson, 2009).

Therefore, it is no surprise that strong diversity education programs have become necessary elements for teacher professional growth and development (Sleeter, 2008; Schmidt et al., 2009). Unfortunately, there is little research on the assessment of language arts teachers who participate in these programs (Fitzgerald, 2003; Howard & Aleman, 2008). Specifically, a review of the literature on teacher assessment has emphasized authenticity (Haertel, 1990; Tellez, 1996) and "teacher capacity" (Grant, 2008). Portfolio assessments, in particular, are considered authentic, since they often demonstrate "teacher capacity" to develop understandings of students and families, learn new pedagogical content knowledge, and cultivate an awareness of their own professional power. Portfolio assessments can include classroom observations by parents, administrators, researchers, and students, materials and resources created by the teacher, course evaluations, parent and teacher conference interviews, teacher self-evaluations, and any other information that might contribute to professional development.

Therefore, this chapter begins with brief descriptions of theoretical frameworks that support authentic teacher assessment as it relates to "teacher capacity." Next, it summarizes language arts teacher preparation and in-service experiences that address teacher capacity as a means for authentic assessment. Then it presents representative findings from programs that appear to demonstrate language arts teacher capacity for development and change. Finally, it concludes with recommendations for authentic assessment of language arts teachers.

Theoretical Frameworks Guiding Authentic Language Arts Teacher Assessment

Teacher Efficacy and Teacher Capacity   When analyzing authentic teacher assessment, teacher efficacy is a key concept. Bandura (1994) proposes that self-efficacy beliefs are "concerned with people's beliefs in their capabilities to exercise control over their own functioning and over events that affect their lives" (p. 80). Beliefs of humans are largely seen as being agents of their development, and these self-efficacy beliefs have a powerful impact on their actions. These beliefs help "determine how people think, feel, motivate themselves and behave" (Bandura, 1994, p. 71) and consequently affect the results of the actions of the individuals. In the case of teaching, such beliefs influence teacher and student outcomes (Tschannen-Moran, Woolfolk-Hoy, & Hoy, 1998). Similarly, teacher efficacy (Goddard, Hoy, & Hoy, 2000) revolves around the idea of "teacher capacity" for knowledge development, reflection, action, and self-evaluation. Also, teacher beliefs in their own abilities to accomplish instructional goals are internal processes related to teacher self-efficacy (Wolters & Daugherty, 2007). The following statement in *A Nation at Risk* (U.S. Department of Education, National

Commission on Excellence in Education, 1983), illuminates these ideas:

> Teachers should have a good grasp of the ways in which different kinds of physical and social systems work; a feeling for data and what uses to which they can be put; an ability to help students see patterns where others see only confusion; an ability to foster genuine creativity...; and the ability to work with other people in work groups that decide for themselves how to get the job done. They must be able to learn all the time...Teachers will not come to school knowing all that they have to know, but knowing how to figure out what they need to know... (p. 25)

Effective professional development can change teachers' understanding of the process of teaching and their expectations of success and therefore self-efficacy (Swackhamer, Koellner, Basile, & Kimbrough, 2009). Therefore, assessment of teacher efficacy should include teacher capacity for gaining self-knowledge, for community understanding, for gaining and implementing pedagogical content knowledge implementation, and awareness of professional power. It follows, then, that language arts teacher capacity will be demonstrated in the ability to learn about students' languages and backgrounds, in the ability to create learning environments that appreciate differences, and in the ability to make connections with the school curriculum, all of which encourage academic and social achievement. The sociocultural perspective guides teachers toward the development of such capacities.

Sociocultural Perspective The sociocultural perspective on classroom teaching and learning (Vygotsky, 1978; Rogoff, 1990; Gutiérrez, 2002) embraces the idea that teachers and children construct meaning through social interactions across and within cultural settings. Students become literate within the cultures of home, school, and community as they and their teachers construct the classroom culture and define language and literacy. Teachers who are guided by this perspective must also be aware of the power issues involved in language arts teaching and learning, and critical race theory assists in this recognition.

Critical Race Theory Critical race theory or CRT (Ladson-Billings, 1999; Nebeker, 1998), analyzes power relationships in society with the following principles: (a) societal structure has made race invisible, due to the realities of White privilege; (b) experiential storytelling and listening to the voices of those who have been discriminated against as part of the social order are legitimate; (c) meaningful social change can only occur when there is a radical change in existing social structures; (d) civil rights legislation seems to be de jure rather than de facto, thus maintaining White supremacy (Jenson, 2005), and finally; (e) educators must take action by beginning to change the social structure of schools through culturally relevant pedagogy or culturally responsive teaching (Ladson-Billings, 1995; Au, 2000). This type of teaching makes connections between a student's home and community and the required curriculum

and motivates students to see relationships that have meaning in their own lives (Schmidt & Ma, 2006; Schmidt & Finkbeiner, 2006).

Professional Development Programs for Today's Language Arts Classrooms: Problems and Possibilities

Professional in-service courses provided by school districts and teacher preparation programs at colleges and universities that offer rich learning experiences, assist teachers in forging positive relationships with diverse groups of people (Lazar, 2004; Rogers, Marshall, & Tyson, 2006). However, those professional development programs require enough time for reflection, and support (Fullan, 2004; Howard & Aleman, 2008), so that teachers may adapt and implement new instructional practices. Such programs use "teacher capacity" to examine the need for change, to participate in a process for change, and to see the results of change. Teachers are often transformed and begin to see their own power as advocates for diverse groups of children (Schmidt et al., 2009). Their experiences encourage them to implement culturally responsive language arts in a curriculum that connects home, school and community for more meaningful teaching and learning (Ladson-Billings, 1995; Schmidt, 2005a). In these programs, teachers, administrators, and/or researchers may videotape, observe, and model teaching; teacher volunteers may be paid for their time after school and become participants in research.

Long-term in-service programs, and university course work seem the most productive in the development of teacher capacity (Nir & Bogler, 2008), since they actually assist language arts teachers in making culturally compatible and dynamic connections between home and school (Noordhoff & Kleinfield, 1993; Schmidt, 2005a, 2005b). However, lifelong emotions and attitudes of present and future teachers, regarding cultural, linguistic and economic diversity may deter the preparation process (Willis, 2000; Sleeter, 2008).

Language Arts In-Service Program Strategies In light of this information and previous research studies (Britzman, 1986; Banks, 1994; Osborne, 1996; Schmidt, 1998a; Schmidt et al., 2009), there is evidence that teacher self-knowledge is the first and foremost consideration when attempting to help teachers understand diverse groups of students. One model for developing self-knowledge is the *ABC's of Cultural Understanding and Communication* (Schmidt, 1998b). It is a five-step process based on the adage "Know thyself and understand others." A brief description follows:

1. Teachers write autobiographies starting with earliest memories. Sharing their stories is not mandatory.
2. Teachers interview several parents and community members away from the school setting and ask questions regarding how and what to teach their children.

3. Teachers compare and contrast similarities and differences with their own stories and their parents' and children's stories.
4. Teachers analyze differences and reflect on similarities and differences.
5. Teachers create plans for incorporating community and family funds of knowledge into the required curriculum.

Also, it is clear that in-service must include authentic experiences with diverse groups of people (Cochran-Smith, 2004). The following research-based strategies assist in the professional development of language arts teachers:

1. Interview and listen to parent stories (Edwards, 1999, 2004; Rodriguez-Brown, 2009).
2. Live in the school community and/or frequent local establishments, such as grocery stores, parks, eateries, and religious centers (Noordhoff & Kleinfield, 1993).
3. Invite classroom visitors from diverse backgrounds to contribute to the curriculum. First hand experiences with diverse populations stimulate perspective sharing (Schmidt, 2005b).
4. Write reflective journals about research articles and resources (Greene & Abt-Perkins, 2003).
5. Observe and analyze videotaped lessons in colleagues' classrooms to assist in planning lessons and creating home/school/community connection activities, and discovering successful characteristics (Schmidt & Finkbeiner, 2006).
6. Support teachers with mentoring and modeling language arts lessons and units, so they will try new ideas and ways of proceeding (Whitcomb, Borko, & Liston, 2006).
7. Create portfolio assessment criterion. Portfolios usually include samples of self-evaluation, a goal-setting process, academic products, teacher-created tests, standardized evaluation, observations, attitude surveys, interviews, and any other applicable anecdotal records (Tellez, 1996; Fitzgerald, 2003).

When these kinds of strategies are implemented, authentic language arts teacher assessment seems possible. However, when searching for authentic professional development and assessment in diverse settings, there were few long-term descriptive studies.

Teacher Capacity and Language Arts In-Service Programs In the following section, brief descriptions of several programs are presented. The term "teacher capacity" is not stated in the programs, but teachers' actions and words indicated positive changes. Teachers changed in their understandings of community connections, pedagogical content knowledge (student assessment included), and awareness of professional power. These published (Reyhner & Garcia, 1989; Trueba, Jacobs, & Kirton, 1990; Moll, Amanti, Neff, & González, 1992; Edwards,

1999; Paratore, 2001; Schmidt, 2005; Izzo & Schmidt, 2006; Schmidt et al. 2009; Rodriguez-Brown, 2009) and unpublished studies (Schmidt, 2006; Singh, 2007 were selected, because European American teachers were given long-term authentic opportunities to meet and work with diverse groups of students and families. As a result, they gained new information and insights for classroom implementation of the English language arts.

Teacher Capacity: Understanding Self and Others The in-service program created by Trueba and his colleagues (1990) was guided by ethnographic principles and scholars. Teachers learned about Hmong cultural conflicts and struggles in schools and communities by meeting regularly with Hmong family members in a variety of comfortable community settings. They also shared their own life experiences and joyously discovered how to incorporate Hmong language and literature in their classrooms to support achievement in the English language arts.

Similarly, a 3-year ethnography (Singh, 2007) focused on in-service teacher assessment and provided evidence for culturally responsive teaching in a kindergarten classroom comprised of students from African American, Latino, Korean, Japanese, and Vietnamese backgrounds in an urban setting. This European American teacher personally connected with parents on a weekly basis to honor bilingualism and promote writing and speaking in English.

Other long-term projects have promoted intergenerational literacy. Teachers were taught how to work with families in urban and rural settings (Edwards, 1999; Paratore, 2001), and gained personal and professional knowledge. The findings demonstrated that parents improved their own English language arts while reading and writing with their children at home.

Finally, several long-term, in-service elementary and secondary professional development programs in urban and rural settings (Reyhner & Garcia, 1989; Moll et al., 1992; Schmidt, 2005, 2006; Izzo & Schmidt, 2006; Singh, 2007; Schmidt et al., 2009; Rodriguez-Brown, 2009) gave voice to several Native American, Hispanic, African American, Sudanese, and Vietnamese families. Teachers who visited homes and communities for family interviews as part of their in-service experiences, were provided information and opportunities for implementing diverse cultures and languages in the curriculum. The sharing of personal information blurred the boundaries between home and school and brought diverse visitors, games, stories, histories, and other artifacts into the classrooms and schools. The results included lively and meaningful learning of the English language arts. Rather than only talking about how to help parents learn to support their children academically, teachers used family and community knowledge and resources to make the curriculum more relevant.

The findings from this small group of studies were based on reported classroom observations, teacher and family interviews and anonymous surveys. The following representative teacher comments from study participants indicate that their professional development yielded positive behaviors.

> When I realized my parents couldn't read, how could I expect them to read to their children. That is when I came to know the devastating power of teacher assumptions. (Edwards, 1999, p. 18).

> I know that meetings in homes with my Sudanese parents show them that I respect them. I want them to know me and learn from them, so that I can better teach their children. This has to be one of my best years in teaching! (Schmidt et al., 2009, p. 245)

> I was nervous at first...but once we began the interview, it seemed that Ms. Lopez was really enjoying talking about her family, her children, and her life. I learned more than I expected. (Moll et al., 2005, p. 78)

> It's a two-way street. Hispanic families can teach the schools...and schools can teach the families. We need both for our children. (Rodriguez-Brown, 2009, p. 56)

> I never realized the importance of being seen in the neighborhood. I go to their sports events, but never to the stores or parks surrounding the school. Communicating with parents face to face, in their homes or on neutral ground, gave me more information and power as a teacher. Word is out and they expect me to call or visit and ask for help. (Salamone, in press)

As a result of self-examination (Schmidt, 2005b; Schmidt et al., 2009) and confidence gained from practicing various interview processes, teachers became comfortable with parent/teacher relationships and could see the value in learning about and from the community. Secondary and elementary teachers stated the following in interviews and surveys.

Teacher Capacity: Pedagogical Content Knowledge (Includes Student Assessment)
Previous research (Greene & Abt-Perkins, 2003; Schmidt & Ma, 2006) has analyzed culturally responsive language arts instruction and discovered specific characteristics in the planning of units of study: high expectations, use of community and family resources, cultural sensitivity, active teaching methods, teacher as facilitator, group and paired work, and student control of portions of lessons. Teacher assessment in culturally responsive ways is process oriented. Teachers maintain student portfolios that include samples of student work from the classroom and home, teacher notes regarding student class contributions and student focus and grade level information reflecting student gains on teacher created tests and standardized tests. Analyses of samples of teacher lesson plans, videotaped lessons, participant observations, and interviews demonstrated that when these characteristics were included, lessons seemed successful.

Teachers also changed priorities for student assessment. They created student portfolios, noted student focus of attention, analyzed student work, and compared weekly teacher created tests and annual standardized tests. Teachers became more attentive to individual student needs and ways to connect with student interests associated with academic and social achievement. Elementary and secondary teachers across several studies have expressed the following in these summary comments from participant observations and manuscripts:

> When the parents were invited to help in the selection process for school materials and resources, they gained an understanding of the English language arts and could support their children's learning. Teachers saw changes in the children and gradually the school refrained from automatically labeling Native American children in special education categories. (Reyhner & Garcia, 1989, p. 88)

> My goals for my students were to develop the skills of sharing, cooperating, and participating in a diverse social group and express themselves through a variety of media including, but not limited to visual arts, creative dramatics, music, and dance I capitalized on the diversity among my students and the characters in the story to build appreciation among my students for different cultures, races, and gender. (Singh, 2007, p. 117)

> High expectations...I heard people talking about it, but I didn't know what it meant until I saw what my kids can do when they are interested in an activity. I never had students working in pairs. I was afraid of losing control. I was afraid that they'd just goof off and not learn anything. I like that they are reading and writing together and there is that 'healthy hum' as they share ideas. The results of the state exams were the best this year and I didn't sweat it. 70% of the kids passed it easily and that is a record for this school. (Schmidt, 2005b p. 20)

Teacher Capacity: Awareness of Professional Power
The teachers that children need to succeed are those who have the capacity to self-evaluate, learn new information, implement new ways of planning and assessment, and use their professional power (Cochran-Smith, 2004). And that professional power, gained from authentic in-service often stimulates the need to advocacy. The teachers in these studies gained a greater awareness of injustice and a noticeable passion for institutional change. For example,

> I put in the note (for the principal), I said I want planning time so M [teacher for the Spanish-speaking children] and I can get together and she can tell me what she is doing so I can support during literacy. I also told her I won't be teaching the Latinos social studies and science because that was done during literacy time. There is no time in the afternoon to do that, they have all these specials and they have math everyday, and if I am going to give them playtime, when I am supposed to do social studies and science? I have to implement those during literacy time. (Singh, 2007, p. 250)

> The children aren't getting what they need from this school. The school doesn't understand the struggles of many families. Most of my parents work longer hours than I do and they can barely make it. I never really felt what they felt

until I got to know them. Now, I need to help other teachers learn. (Schmidt et al., 2009, p. 245)

We call the principal or assistant principal into our grade level meetings. We ask questions and get answers; we get what we need for our kids right away. The administrators can support many of our new ideas and initiatives, because we keep them informed. (Izzo & Schmidt, 2006, p. 171)

As teachers we need to gain better understandings of diverse communities, so our classrooms and schools can capture community "funds of knowledge" and make learning relevant. Then we will begin to meet the academic and social needs of our students. (Moll et al., 2005, p. 81)

Recommendations for In-Service or Professional Development Programs that Build Teacher Capacity

Authentic assessment and the concept of "teacher capacity" (Grant, 2008) were promoted in the longitudinal studies of language arts teacher professional development presented in this chapter. So, where do we go from here?

Research suggests that professional development workshops are fruitless district expenses if they are not long term (Goodlad, 1998; Fullan, 2004). Obviously, we believe that there should be a national commitment to programs that give time and sustained support to language arts teachers as they implement curriculum in classrooms with students from diverse cultural, linguistic, ethnic and economic backgrounds. Time is essential in allowing teachers to explore self-knowledge, learn to appreciate diversity, study communication opportunities, and create risk-free classroom environments that explicitly promote meaningful support for the English language arts.

Mixed Methods Language Arts Teacher Assessment Based on Teacher Capacity To begin remedying existing assessment procedures in language arts classrooms mixed methods appears to be the reasonable and authentic way to proceed (Blanton, Sindelar, & Correa, 2006; Grant 2008). Questions such as, "Do teachers have the capacity to learn? What evidence is there that they have changed and developed as professionals?" should guide assessment. We also propose that,

1. States consider required in-service coursework throughout the school year...coursework that includes the strategies used in this chapter (Raymond, 1994; Eisenman, Hill, Bailey, & Dickison, 2003).
2. Teacher professional organizations or teacher education programs could be paid to provide administrator approved coursework (Guskey, 2000).
3. No matter what the program, administrator support is a necessity (Mullen & Brad, 2006; Singh, 2007; Yendol-Hoppey, Jacobs, & Dana, 2009).
4. Administrators should not be the sole evaluators of teachers...other teachers, professors, parents, students, and community members should be allowed to as-

sess (Zeichner & Hoeft, 1996; Guskey, 2000; Foote, 2009).
5. Self-evaluation and goal setting by a teacher encourages professional growth (Broemmel, Swaggerty, & McIntosh, 2009; Dobson, 2009; Sleeter, 2009).
6. Teacher assessment of student progress needs to be individualized and valid (Colvin, Flannery, Sugai, & Monegan, 2009).

In conclusion, the children from diverse linguistic, cultural, and racial backgrounds are fast becoming the majority in our nation's schools. Therefore, we believe that infusing their talents through excellent educational opportunities should be a priority. Moreover, it is time for those who control society to support teachers who make the commitment to teach the English language arts to diverse groups of students. These teachers need time, knowledge, and resources for authentic professional development. And as they deepen their understandings of community connections, pedagogical content knowledge, and professional power, they should be authentically assessed for the positive changes they make for the students and families in their schools.

References

Au, K. H. (2000). A multicultural perspective on policies for improving literacy achievement: Equity and excellence. In R. Barr, M. L. Kamil, P. Mosenthal, & P. D. Pearson (Eds.), *Handbook of reading research* (Vol. 3, pp. 835–851). New York: Erlbaum.

Bandura, A. (1994). Self-efficacy. In V. Ramachandran (Ed.), *Encyclopedia of human behavior* (Vol. 4, pp. 71–81). New York: Academic Press.

Banks, J. A. (1994). *An introduction to multicultural education.* Boston: Allyn & Bacon.

Banks, J., & Banks, C. A. (1995). *Handbook of research on multicultural education.* New York: Macmillan.

Blanton, L. L., Sindelar, P. T., & Correa, V. I. (2006). Models and measures of beginning teacher quality. *Journal of Special Education, 40,* 115–127.

Britzman, D. P. (1986). Cultural myths in the making of a teacher: Biography and social structure in teacher education. *Harvard Educational Review, 56*(4), 442–456.

Broemmel, A. D., Swaggerty, E. A., & Mcintosh, D. (2009). Navigating the waters of teacher induction: One beginning teacher's journey. *The New Educator, 5*(1), 67–80.

Colvin, G., Flannery, K. B., Sugai, G., & Monegan, J. (2009). Using observational data to provide performance feedback to teachers: A high school case study. *Preventing School Failure, 3*(2), 9–104.

Cochran-Smith, M. (Ed). (2004). *Walking the road: Race, diversity and social justice in teacher education.* New York: Teachers College Press.

Cummins, J. (1996). *Negotiating identities: Education for empowerment in a diverse society.* Ontario, CA: California Association for Bilingual Education.

Darling-Hammond, L., & McLaughlin, M. (1995). Policies that support professional development in an era of reform. *Phi Delta Kappan, 76,* 597–604.

Dobson, D. (2009). Royal, warrior, magician, lover: Archetypal reflectivity and the construction of professional knowledge. *Teacher Education Quarterly, 36*(3), 149–165.

Edwards, P. A. (1999). School-family connections: Why are they so difficult to create? In W. Dorsey Hammond & T. E. Raphael (Eds.), *Early literacy instruction for the new millennium.* (pp. 73–90). Grand Rapids,

MI: Michigan Reading Association; Ann Arbor, MI: Center for the Improvement of Early Reading Achievement, University of Michigan; and Newark, DE: International Reading Association.

Edwards, P. A. (2004). *Children's literacy development: Making it happen through school, family, and community involvement.* Boston: Allyn & Bacon.

Eisenman, L., Hill, D., Bailey, R., & Dickison, C. (2003). The beauty of teacher collaboration to integrate curricula: Professional development and student learning opportunities. *Journal of Vocational Education Research, 28*(1), 85–104.

Fitzgerald, S. (2003). Teacher Evaluation. In J. Flood, D. Lapp, J. R. Squire, & J. M. Jensen (Eds.), *Handbook of teaching the English language arts* (2nd ed., pp. 478–490). Mahwah, NJ: Erlbaum.

Foote, M. Q. (2009). Stepping out of the classroom: Building teacher knowledge for developing classroom practice. *Teacher Education Quarterly, 36*(3), 39–53.

Fullan, M. (2004). *Leading in a culture of change: Personal action guide and workbook.* New York: Corwin Press.

Goddard, R. G., Hoy, W .K., Woolfolk Hoy, A. (2000). Collective teacher efficacy: Its meaning, measure, and impact on student achievement. *American Educational Research Journal, 37*(2), 479–508.

Goodlad, J. (1998). *Educational Renewal: Better teachers, better schools.* New York: Jossey-Bass

Grant, C. A. (2008). Teacher capacity: Introduction to the section. In M. C. Smith, S. Feiman-Nemser, D. J. McIntyre, & K. E. Demers (Eds.), *Handbook of research on teacher education: Enduring questions in changing contexts* (pp.127–133). New York: Routledge.

Greene, S., & Abt-Perkins, D. (Eds.). (2003). *Making race visible: Literacy research for racial understanding.* New York:Teachers College Press.

Gunderson, L. (2009). *ESL (ELL) literacy instruction: A guidebook to theory and practice* (2nd ed.). New York: Routledge.

Gutiérrez, K. (2002). Studying cultural practices in urban learning communities. *Human Development. 45*(4), 312–321.

Guskey, T. R. (2000). *Evaluating professional development.* Thousand Oaks, CA: Corwin Press.

Haertel, E. H. (1990). Performance tests, simulations and other methods. In J. Millman & L. Darling-Hammond (Eds.), *The new handbook of teacher evaluation: Assessing elementary and secondary school teachers* (pp. 278–294). Newbury Park, CA: Sage.

Howard, T. C., & Aleman, G. R. (2008). Teacher capacity for diverse learners: What do teachers need to know? In M. C. Smith, S. Feiman-Nemser, D. J. McIntyre, & K. E. Demers (Eds.), *Handbook of research on teacher education: Enduring questions in changing contexts* (pp.157–174). New York: Routledge.

Izzo, A., & Schmidt, P. R. (2006). A successful ABC's in-service project: Supporting culturally responsive teaching. In P. R.Schmidt & C. Finkbeiner (Eds.), *The ABC's of cultural understanding and communication: National and international adaptations* (pp. 161–187). Greenwich, CT: Information Age.

Jenson, R. (2005). *The heart of whiteness: Confronting race, racism, and white privilege.* San Francisco: City Lights.

Ladson-Billings, G. (1995). Toward a theory of culturally relevant pedagogy. *American Educational Research Journal, 32*(3), 465–491.

Ladson-Billings, G. (1999). Preparing teachers for diverse student populations: A critical race theory perspective. In A. I. Nejad & P.D. Pearson (Eds.), *Review of research in education* (Vol. 24, pp. 211–247). Washington, DC: American Education Research Association.

Lazar, A. (2004). *Learning to be literacy teachers in urban schools: Stories of growth and change.* Newark, DE: International Reading Association.

Moll, L. C., Amanti, C., Neff, D., & González, N. (1992). Funds of knowledge for teaching: Using a qualitative approach to connect homes and classrooms. *Theory into Practice, 31*(2), 132–141.

Moll, L., Amanti, C., Neff, D., & Gonzalez, N. (2005). In N. Gonzalez, L. C. Moll, & C. Amanti (Eds.), *Funds of knowledge* (pp. 71–88). Mahwah, NJ: Erlbaum.

Mullen, C. A., & Brad, J. W. (2006). Accountability-democracy tensions facing democratic school leaders. *Action in Teacher Education, 28*(2), 86–101.

Nebeker, K. C. (1998). Critical race theory: A white graduate student's struggle with the growing area of scholarship. *International Journal of Qualitative Studies in Education, 11*, 25–41.

Nieto, S. (2000). Placing equity front and center: Some thoughts on transforming teacher education for a new century. *Journal of Teacher Education, 51*(3), 180–187.

Nir, A., & Bogler, R. (2008). The antecedents of teacher satisfaction with professional development programs. *Teaching and Teacher Education, 24,* 377–386.

No Child Left Behind Act of 2001, Pub.L. 107-110,115 STAT. 1425 (2002).

Noordhoff, K. & Kleinfield, J. (1993). Preparing teachers for multicultural classrooms *Teaching and Teacher Education, 9*(1), 27–39.

Osborne, A. B. (1996). Practice into theory into practice: Culturally relevant pedagogy for students we have marginalized and normalized. *Anthropology and Education Quarterly, 27*(3), 285–314.

Paratore, J. R. (2001). *Opening doors, opening opportunities.* Boston, MA: Allyn and Bacon.

Raymond, R. C. (1994). Southeastern writing projects and the two-year college teacher. *Teaching English at the Two-Year College, 21,* 288–296.

Reyhner, J., & Garcia, R. L. (1989). Helping minorities to read better: Problems and promises. *Reading Research and Instruction, 28*(3), 84–91.

Rodriguez-Brown, F. (2009). *The home-school connection: Lessons learned in a culturally and linguistically diverse community.* New York: Routledge.

Rogers, T., Marshall, E., & Tyson, C.A. (2006). Dialogic narratives of literacy, teaching, and schooling: Preparing literacy teachers for diverse settings. *Reading Research Quarterly, 41*(2), 202–224.

Rogoff, B. (1990). *Apprenticeship in thinking: Cognitive development in social context.* New York: Oxford University Press.

Salamone, K. (in press). From pasta to poets: Creating a classroom community through cultural sharing. In P. R. Schmidt & A. Lazar (Eds.), *We can teach, We can learn: Culturally responsive literacy pedagogy.* New York: Teachers College Press.

Schmidt, P. R. (1998a). *Cultural conflict and struggle: Literacy learning in a kindergarten program.* New York: Peter Lang.

Schmidt P. R. (1998b). The ABC's of cultural understanding and communication. *Equity and Excellence in Education, 31*(2), 28–38.

Schmidt, P. R. (2005a). *Preparing educators to communicate and connect with families and communities.* Greenwich, CT: Information Age.

Schmidt, P. R. (2005b). *Culturally responsive instruction: Promoting literacy in secondary content areas.* Naperville, IL: Learning Point Associates.

Schmidt, P. R. (2006, November 30–December 1). *Envisioning new possibilities: Preparing literacy teachers for culturally and linguistically diverse classrooms.* Paper presented at the National Reading Conference, Los Angeles, CA.

Schmidt, P. R., & Finkbeiner, C. (Eds.). (2006). *The ABC's of cultural understanding and communication: National and international adaptations.* Greenwich, CT: Information Age.

Schmidt, P. R., & Ma, W. (2006). *50 literacy strategies for culturally responsive teaching, K-8.* Chicago: Corwin Press.

Schmidt, P. R., Gangemi, B., Kelsey. G. O., LaBarbera, C., McKenzie, S., Melchior, C., et al. (2009). In J. Coppola & E.V. Primas (Eds.), *One classroom: Many Learners* (pp. 227–250). Newark, DE: International Reading Association.

Singh, S. (2007). *Changes in literacy beliefs and practices of a kindergarten teacher: A three-year longitudinal study.* Unpublished dissertation, University of Illinois, Urbana-Champaign.

Sleeter, C. (2001). Preparing teachers for culturally diverse schools. *Journal of Teacher Education, 52*(2), 94–106.

Sleeter, C. (2008). An invitation to support diverse students through teacher education. *Journal of Teacher Education, 59*(3), 212–219.

Sleeter, C. (2009). Developing teacher epistemological sophistication about multicultural curriculum: A case study. *Action in Teacher Education, 31*(1), 3–13.

Swackhamer, L. E., Koellner, K., Basile, C., & Kimbrough, D. (2009). Increasing the self-efficacy of inservice teachers through content knowledge. *Teacher Education Quarterly, 36*(2), 63–78.

Tellez, K. (1996). Authentic assessment. In J. Sikula, T. Buttery, & E. Guyton (Eds.), *Handbook of research on teacher education* (2nd ed., pp. 704–721). New York: Simon and Schuster Macmillan.

Trueba, H. T., Jacobs, L., & Kirton, E. S. (1990). *Cultural conflict and adaptation: The case of Hmong children in American society.* New York: Falmer.

Tschannen-Moran, M., Woolfolk-Hoy, A., & Hoy, W. K. (1998). Teacher efficacy: Its meaning and measure. *Review of Educational Research, 68*(2), 202–248.

U.S. Department of Education, National Commission on Excellence in Education. (1983). *A Nation at Risk: The imperative for educational reform.* Washington, DC: U.S. Government Printing Office.

Vygotsky, L. S. (1978). *Mind in society: The development of higher psychological processes.* Cambridge, MA: Harvard University Press.

Whitcomb, J., Borko, H., & Liston, D. (2006). Living in the tension-living with the heat. *Journal of Teacher Education, 57*(5), 447–453.

Willis, A. I. (2000). Keeping it real: Teaching and learning about culture, literacy, and respect. *English Education, 32*(4), 267–277.

Wolters, C. A., & Daugherty, S. G. (2007). Goals structures and teachers' sense of efficacy: Their relation and association to teaching experience and academic level. *Journal of Educational Psychology, 99*(1), 181–193.

Yendol-Hoppey, D., Jacobs, J., & Dana, N. F. (2009). Critical concepts of mentoring in an urban context. *The New Educator, 5*(1), 25–44.

Zeichner, K., & Hoeft, K. (1996). Teacher socialization for cultural diversity. In J. Sikula, T. Buttery, & E. Guyton (Eds.), *Handbook of research on teacher education* (2nd ed., pp. 525–547). New York: Macmillan.

47

Assessing *Every* Child

Using Purposeful Language Arts Assessments in Diverse Classrooms

JENNIFER D. TURNER AND CHRYSTINE C. HOELTZEL

Every student has been raised in a culture and is cultured. Assessment is more than testing; it is based on a deep knowledge of a child's patterns of success and failure and an understanding of their worldview. (Hilliard, 1995, p. x)

Hilliard's words remind us that the way we think about language arts assessment must be restructured to fit the changing literacy demands of current classrooms (Edwards, Turner, & Mokhtari, 2008; Johnston, 2005). Language arts teachers are working with more students of diverse ethnic, racial, and linguistic backgrounds, (e.g., African American, Latino/a, Asian, and Native American) in their classrooms, and the diversity in our K–12 schools is expected to grow exponentially over the next few decades (Au, 2006). In addition to changing student demographics, language arts assessment must now address complex issues like socioemotional and relational aspects of literacy development because we recognize that literacy is more than a child's score on a test.

Currently, we use language arts assessment as a means of data collection, but we often neglect the purpose of that data collection. Purposeful assessment of students requires ongoing and comprehensive data collection that enables language arts teachers to accurately determine students' existing proficiencies, to identify potential areas of challenge, and to tailor instruction to address those strengths and needs (Afflerbach, 2007b; Stiggins, 2007). Clearly, the purposes of language arts assessment may vary depending on the audience, including teachers, parents, administrators, and policymakers (Afflerbach, 2007a), and in order to construct a comprehensive and continuous portrait of each individual learner, multiple assessments should be administered in consideration of those multiple purposes. Like Nutbrown (1999), we believe that "clarity of purpose is crucial if assessment….is to be properly understood, and if future assessment instruments are to be authentic" (p. 33).

In this chapter, we outline three purposes for classroom teachers' administration of language arts assessments that are well-established in the field: (a) assessment of learning; (b) assessment for learning; and (c) assessment of the learner. Specifically, we offer examples of assessments given for each purpose aimed at recognizing language arts proficiencies connected to diversity and culture. We also advocate that a fourth purpose of language arts assessment, assessment of the learners' social worlds, must be considered in order for language arts teachers to understand the rich insights and perspectives that can be offered by the caregivers in the home and community.

Purpose 1: Assessment of Learning

Assessment of learning does not typically coincide with theories of constructivist learning (Pryor & Crossouard, 2008) because most summative assessments do not measure active learning or distinguish how students construct their own understandings. Although summative assessments may not have tangible benefits for students, they are necessary to provide evidence of student learning. Afflerbach (2007a) believes summative assessments provide educators with a summary of student achievement. He argues that summative assessments can, "help us take measure of student achievement in relation to reading curriculum goals and district or state learning standards" (p. 49). High-stakes mandated tests like ones administered through the National Assessment of Educational Progress (NAEP) or through individual states are the most common summative assessments in public schools across the United States. They provide the educational community with students' proficiency levels in those districts. However, research has demonstrated that those tests are not sensitive to diverse populations (Artiles, Reschly, & Chinn, 2002; Hilliard, 1995), and this shift to a business-like model, where students are regularly assessed in order to place them into "appropriate" programs with one-size-fits-all curricula, instruction, and assessment, leaves little room for language arts educators' adjustments to meet students' needs.

Fortunately, an authentic assessment approach allows teachers to address real-world applications of students' evolving literacies (Frey & Schmidt, 2007). A more authentic, summative approach that honors the linguistic, cultural, and cognitive diversity of each learner allows language arts teachers to use assessment data to reflect the scope of students' cultural backgrounds and the curriculum being taught in the classroom (Bukowiecki, 2007). Although there is some debate about the purposes and definitions of portfolios and performance assessments, both forms of assessment can, in many circumstances, be considered authentic (Afflerbach, 2007a; Guthrie, Van Meter, & Mitchell, 1994).

Portfolio Assessments Portfolios are collections of student artifacts that provide evidence about the "range, depth, and trajectory of student performance" (Garcia & Pearson, 1994, p. 356). Researchers distinguish among four types of portfolio assessment: (a) showcase portfolio; (b) documentation portfolio; (c) process portfolio; and (d) evaluation portfolio (Valencia & Place, 1993). In particular, the documentation portfolio is a valuable summative tool because it details students' completed work over time (Afflerbach, 2007a) and offers insight into the process of students' development. Tierney and Clark (1998) argue that portfolios provide short and long term evidence of emerging patterns, are grounded in classroom practices, and offer rich depictions of student progress.

Portfolios can incorporate information from across contexts and sources such as work samples, completed artifacts, and audio/video examples. Kong and Fitch (2002/2003) illustrate how portfolios can turn assessment into a tool of learning for students by organizing and challenging them to critically engage in reading, speaking, writing, and listening around texts. Moreover, portfolios offer language arts teachers a chance to involve the student in the assessment process because portfolios require students' input and enable them to become navigators' of their own literacy growth. By involving the learner in the assessment process, language arts teachers are granting them ownership (Barrett, 2007). Specifically, portfolio assessments are important to diverse populations of students, because cultural resources can be celebrated, particularly if they include parent contributions such as homework samples, drawings, books read at home, and other home artifacts that illustrate students' achievement gains (Spinelli, 2008).

Performance-based Assessments Performance-based assessments are the collection of educational artifacts "that call for students to produce responses similar to those required in instructional environments" (Harris & Hodges, 1995, p. 182). These assessments allow for the examination of students' processes and help communicate instructional expectations to students, reflect authentic literacy tasks, and provide evidence of students' accomplishments in relation to learning objectives (Guthrie, Van Meter, & Mitchell, 1994). Typically, they require students to design, perform, or produce (Pennsylvania Literacy Framework, 2000).

The production of story boards or posters, and a student's ability to follow written directions are all examples of performances that can be used as assessments. Process-focused performance assessments consist of techniques such as "think alouds," where students communicate their mental processes in an effort to help them identify how they construct meaning from text. Although the above performance assessments enable language arts teachers to determine students' literacy understandings, we want to specifically highlight the use of dramatizations and student self-evaluations as two possible assessments to use with students with varying backgrounds.

Dramatizations. A dramatization in a language arts classroom is any performance or re-creation of text, such as a staging of *Lon Po Po: A Red Riding Hood Story from China* (Young, 1989), which would allow students to demonstrate their comprehension, oral reading fluency, or literacy understandings of the text. Researchers have demonstrated that dramatizations can be used with children in early childhood classrooms through secondary classrooms and beyond (Morrison & Chilcoat, 1998). A variation of dramatizations is curriculum-based reader's theatre (Flynn, 2004), which uses student and teacher-created scripts that specifically address state standards, curriculum, and interdisciplinary themes. Dramatizations can offer language arts teachers valuable opportunities to assess important reading and writing skills that would not necessarily be feasible through typical summative assessments.

Student Self-Assessments. Typically, student self-assessments are a process-driven evaluation system where students have the ability to use assessments to change their behaviors, set-goals, and redirect their learning efforts. Although that is often a distinction of a formative assessment, upon the completion of a unit, semester, or year, students can certainly reflect back on the learning that took place and assess their abilities in relation to their starting point. Researchers have found that students can accurately assess reading and writing learning such as their comprehension strategy use (Moore, Lin-Agler, & Zabrucky, 2005), as well as their own writing processes and final products (Andrade, Du, & Wang, 2008). Johnston (2005) supports the idea of incorporating self-assessments into a classroom assessment system because they give students control over their own learning and help to build resilient readers. Self-assessments, dramatizations, and portfolios provide language arts teachers with important evidence of learning.

Purpose 2: Assessment for Learning

Heritage (2007) defines formative assessment as, "a systematic process to continuously gather evidence about learning…where students are active participants with their teachers, sharing learning goals and understanding how their learning is progressing, what next steps to take and how to take them" (p. 141). Formative assessments should yield descriptive data that can be used to improve instruction and influence student learning (Afflerbach, 2007b) that target specific, finely grained learning goals rather than broad academic standards (Gallagher & Worth, 2008). Formative assessments contribute to classrooms with diverse populations because language arts teachers can "gather evidence about how students are approaching, processing, and completing tasks in a particular domain" (Garcia & Pearson, 1994, p. 357) and use that information to shape classroom practice. Many well-planned and well-executed assessments can sometimes serve as both an assessment of learning and an assessment for learning; however, formative assessments are important to teachers because the information gleaned impacts the instructional process.

Dynamic Assessments Dynamic assessment is a unique form of K–12 assessment with characteristics that include an application of students' learning processes and a test-teach-retest format (Macrine & Sabbatino, 2008; Spinelli, 2008). Although dynamic assessments can also function as an assessment of learning, they tend to be a more process-oriented strategy, because they inform classroom practice. One of the major distinctive attributes is that the examiner becomes a sort of mediator who attempts to elicit the student's "modifiability as a response to environmental efforts for change" (Tzuriel, 2000, p. 387). Research has demonstrated that dynamic assessments improve learners' level of performance and achievement on reading tasks (Tzuriel, 2000) by attending to the abilities rather than the disabilities of the learner (Tzuriel & Kauffman, 1999).

The evaluator is responsible for providing and removing support, as needed, to obtain information regarding the child's reading ability and assess both the processes and the products of learning. An example of using dynamic assessment for reading could include an assessment of a student's comprehension. After asking the student to describe the main idea of an expository text, if the student does not understand, the assessor may provide examples, pictures and supporting details to supply the needed background information. Then, the evaluator could remove the supports and assess the child's understanding of the material by having the child express the main idea of a new text. Dynamic assessments are valuable for students of diverse backgrounds because, when in the hands of teachers who are continually reflecting how bias operates, the assessments can be (a) less biased toward experiences, social practices, or literacy understandings (Laing & Kamhi, 2003); (b) more fair than conventional product-oriented methods (Macrine & Sabbatino, 2008); and (c) offer guided support with a mediator that interacts with the student (Spinelli, 2008).

Checklists and Rating Scales Checklists and rating scales are tools that language arts teachers can use in classrooms to identify the skills students are employing at any given time, and serve as a way to accumulate anecdotal evidence of embedded student learning by providing a means of recording student literacy processes, rather than outcomes. Checklists and rating scales provide informal assessment information that illustrates how a child performs in the classroom on a day-to-day basis. Like many quality assessments, checklists and rating scales can also assess student learning outcomes; however, they often function to provide teachers with valuable data to inform instruction. One major benefit of checklists is their versatility, because they can be used in a number of settings and for a number of purposes (Paratore & McCormack, 2005). Recorded student behaviors can provide important insight into why and how children act under certain conditions, which is particularly important in diverse classrooms. Checklists offer language arts teachers a closer view of "students' skills, strategies, and work as they unfold," (Afflerbach, 2007b, p. 269) as opposed to solely focusing on what is produced as a result of reading.

By using checklists, classroom teachers can determine children's individual assets and challenges in ways that reveal constructive information for guiding instruction. Furthermore, student checklists and rating scales that include rubrics help support student understandings of teacher expectations and foster self-regulatory behaviors (Massey, 2003). Romeo (2008) describes a checklist to assess student' writing, by keeping track of students' goal setting, to document students' progress, and to aid students in remembering to follow the steps of the revision process. Checklists and dynamic assessments are relevant for students with a wide range of backgrounds, because they are a form of authentic assessment, which focuses on the development of individual students instead of making comparisons among groups of students (Garcia & Pearson, 1994).

Purpose 3: Assessment of the Learner

Individual affective assessments help language arts teachers determine contributors and outcomes of students' reading success (Afflerbach, 2007a) by assessing learner attitudes, motivations for reading, and interests. Such assessments are an integral part of helping language arts teachers determine how children see themselves as readers (or non-readers). The educational system has primarily focused on the assessment of learning paradigm, guided by the premise that teachers should use curriculum to guide instruction and *then* assess to determine whether students' achieved proficiency in any part of the curriculum (Edwards et al., 2008). But a more current paradigm is needed to adapt to the changing climate of today's classrooms, since students come to classrooms with varying proficiencies that are not always valued by our educational system, and those proficiencies have a tremendous impact on students' literacy capabilities.

In order to reach students in diverse classrooms, language arts teachers must know their students in order to match students' prior knowledge with the content and curricula to be taught. Since the goal of instruction is typically to bridge the gaps in knowledge that exist, teachers must know what their students do not know, which is why assessment for learning becomes relevant. Knowing the student is as important as knowing content and gaps in learning. Williams and Bauer (2006) advocate for affective accountability, and it can be achieved by assessing both cognitive and affective characteristics of students. In turn, language arts teachers "become accountable to students and adjust the curriculum accordingly" (Williams & Bauer, 2006, p. 20). Language arts teachers, who apply affective assessment to student writing, can better understand and connect to curriculum content and student personal traits, qualities, and interests.

Affective Assessments Student's reading abilities and achievement are just one aspect of reading development that can be measured. Affective attributes can offer tremendous insight into the children's maturity as a reader (Guthrie & Wigfield, 2000). Assessing the "self" is an important part of the assessment process, which includes a reader's motivation, self-concepts, interests and attitudes (Afflerbach, 2007a; McKenna & Stahl, 2009). Afflerbach (2007a) contends that "successful student readers must be motivated, of positive attitude, of good self-concept, and capable of making accurate attributions for their performances" (p. 155). Among many ways to assess children's self-efficacy, instruments like motivation surveys, self-concept scales, reading attitude surveys, reader interest surveys, checklists, and other affective instruments may be used.

Reading Assessments. A few such measures exist to assess the learner's attributes toward reading and writing. Instruments like the *Motivation to Read* profile (Gambrell, Palmer, Codling, & Mazzoni, 1996), which is a 2-part assessment to evaluate students' beliefs about themselves as a reader, help educators ascertain students' interest in reading and their overall motivation to read. Another means of assessing students' motivation to read is the *Motivation for Reading Questionnaire* (Wigfield & Guthrie, 1997) that attempts to measure motivation specifically related to intrinsic and extrinsic motivational components and address students' specific motivational tendencies such as self-efficacy, compliance, and grades.

Reader interest and reader attitude are important affective qualities that have important implications for teachers' understandings of their learners. Language arts teachers often give students reading interest surveys that typically ask students about school reading interests, favorite kinds of books, reading habits, reading strategies, and special areas of interest. Two measures to assess children's attitude toward literacy are the *Elementary Reading Attitude Survey* (McKenna & Kear, 1990) and the *Writing Attitude Survey* (Kear, Coffman, McKenna, & Ambrosio, 2000). In both surveys, elementary children are instructed to read statements about reading and writing and circle the cartoon picture of Garfield that best corresponds to how they feel about those statements. Literacy teachers in middle school and secondary classrooms may want to adapt these instruments to assess older students, or they may want to use the "intergenerational conversation" approach (Bean, Bean, & Bean, 1999). Through intergenerational conversations,

adolescent students complete a chart that describes the kinds of literate practices that they engage in on a daily basis (e.g., reading magazines, doing homework, computer use, phone, television/movies) and talk about what those literate practices mean to them. Although Bean used intergenerational conversations to learn more about his daughters' literate practices, we believe that this approach has great potential for language arts teachers because rather than making assumptions about culturally-diverse students and their out-of-school literacy practices (e.g., minority students don't read outside of school), this tool can elicit first-hand information about students' multi-literate lives.

Writing Assessments. Many language arts teachers face the pressures of incorporating on-demand writing assessments into their daily practices because of the looming pressures of state standardized tests. Although we are not arguing for less attention to be paid to on-demand writing or other commonly assessed genres of writing, we assert that those forms of writing do not typically allow teachers to learn about their students. Through journal writing, reflective writing, and reading response logs, language arts teachers can informally learn about students' perceptions, backgrounds, interests, and identities (Davi, 2006). For example, a teacher could ask a student to "freewrite" on a relevant topic from a class text or to write a reader autobiography to communicate how he has been shaped as a reader.

Purpose 4: Assessment of the Learners' Social Worlds

According to Edwards, Pleasants, and Franklin (1999), children live in multiple social worlds "which affect them and all aspects of their development" (p. xix). Perhaps the two most critical worlds are family and community. Families are the child's first and most critical teachers, and parents, siblings, grandparents, and even extended family members (e.g., aunts, uncles) can provide language arts teachers with useful information about students' literacy strengths and needs (Edwards et al., 2008). When language arts teachers think of home literacy practices, they tend to think of traditional "mainstream" activities, such as helping with homework, parent-child bookreading, and actively participating in home-school events such as parent-teacher conferences and back-to-school night, and volunteering in classrooms (Edwards & Turner, 2010). Additionally, Anderson and Stokes (1984) identify nine domains of literate practices in the homes of culturally-diverse children that are often overlooked by teachers and schools: (a) daily living including tasks such as making shopping lists and paying bills; (b) entertainment, such as reading the TV guide or rules to a board game; (c) school-related activity; (d) religion, including reading religious texts and attending services; (e) general information, including miscellaneous literate activities; (f) work; (g) literacy techniques and skills, including those initiated by the child (e.g., coloring) and those initiated by the adult; (h) interpersonal communication, including writing letters or notes to family and friends; and (i) storybook time. Although several of these domains directly connect with mainstream home literacy practices, Anderson and Stokes argue that the other nontraditional domains also significantly contribute to the literacy development of culturally-diverse students. As a result, language arts teachers and schools who use purposeful assessments that illuminate students' social worlds can learn more about the home literacy practices related to these nine domains by positioning parents as the "more knowledgeable others" (Vygotsky, 1978) in the relationship with teachers and schools.

Furthermore, when language arts teachers gather data from students' families and communities, the purpose is not to assess their literacies in a judgmental or evaluative way (e.g., one family is less literate than another), but rather to inform. More specifically, language arts teachers should gather this information to gain new insights about the literacy practices and cultural discourses in the family and community, and to learn more about how these familial and cultural influences have shaped students' literacy development (Edwards et al., 1999). In so doing, language arts teachers can move beyond a deficit perspective, and use a "funds of knowledge" perspective (Moll, Amanti, Neff, & Gonzalez, 1992) to identify and interpret the wealth of resources within culturally-diverse families and communities.

Family Assessments

Parent Stories. Listening is a powerful form of assessment, but educators generally talk *to* parents rather than talking *with* them (Edwards et al., 1999). A critical tool that helps teachers learn to listen to parents is parent/family stories. Parent stories are "narratives gained from open-ended conversations and/or interviews between teachers and parents" (Edwards & Turner, 2010, p. 141). Eliciting parent stories through questionnaires (Edwards et al., 1999) and family interviews (Kidd, Sanchez, & Thorp, 2004) invites caregivers to share specific information about children's ways of learning and communicating, the family's routines and schedules, the interaction and relationships between parents and students, the family's perceptions about schooling, and their expectations, hopes, and dreams for their children. In contrast to traditional forms of assessment that primarily gauge students' development of school literacy, family stories serve as a critical tool for gathering information about students' out-of-school literacies by offering insight into the literacy practices situated within their homes and communities. Parent stories are a powerful tool for K–12 schools because "by using stories as a way to express the nature of the home environment, parents can select anecdotes and personal observations….to give teachers access to complicated social, emotional, and educational issues…that unravel the mystery of students' early literacy beginnings" (Edwards et al., 1999, p. viii). Teachers can then use the personal data derived from the parent stories to make classroom literacy instruction more congruent with their cultural knowledge and background (Edwards & Turner, 2010).

Parent Journals. Parent journals can also serve as a means of authentic assessment into students' home literacy lives. Shockley (1994) initiated communication with the families of her first-grade students by inviting them to write about their children and their home lives in dialogic journals. Through this writing, Shockley exchanged pertinent information with parents about their children's reading and writing skills, and learned more about the beliefs, expectations, and insights that parents had about their children. Similarly, Lazar and Weisburg (1996) asked parents enrolled in a college-reading program to write journal entries about their children and to share the journals with their children's teachers. They concluded that the journals were effective in enhancing home-school connections because the parents' entries revealed the students "purposeful use of print within the context of family life" (p. 228), and teachers were able to use this information to support the literacy development of their students both at school and at home.

Home-Community Assessments

Community Literacy Walks and Photo Journals. Afflerbach (1996) noted that "a critical contribution to…assessment…can be made by students themselves. Students' self-assessments often are an underutilized resource in reading assessment" (p. 202). Researchers have uncovered several methods for students to "read and write" their own cultural worlds through community literacy walks and photo journals. Community literacy walks are planned outings when teachers and students walk through the local neighborhood surrounding their school (Cancienne, 2009). As Orellana and Hernandez (1999) demonstrated in their classic study, children as young as first grade are aware of the environmental print in their communities, and have the capacity to make meaning of this print. Orellana and Hernandez walked with a group of 15 students in their urban community, taking pictures of local shops, visiting a Salvadorian market and a Guatemalan bakery, talking about the languages on the signs (e.g., a shop sign written in English, Korean, and Spanish) and critically discussing the print that held special value to them (e.g., street signs, graffiti, movie posters in a video store). After the literacy walk, Orellana and Hernandez encouraged the students to draw pictures and dictate stories about their experience, noting that several children who were reluctant to speak and write in class were highly engaged in these activities. Similarly, the teachers in a study conducted by Allen and her colleagues (2002) noted high levels of participation when they gave students cameras and encouraged them to take pictures of their homes, families, and communities and create photo journals. Both community literacy walks and photo journals are compelling assessment tools because (a) they provide an opportunity for language arts teachers to explore children's literate worlds and learn about the community at the same time; (b) they provide opportunities for students to critically read, interpret, write, and talk about their social worlds; and (c) these tools could easily be adapted for students in middle school and high school classrooms.

Conclusion

Amidst concerns about the low levels of literacy achievement amongst culturally-diverse students, questions abound about the "best" ways to assess their language arts development. In this chapter, we argue that the answer depends upon the purposes of that assessment. Assessment *of* learning provides teachers with evidence of the learning that occurred over a period of time; whereas assessment *for* learning enables teachers to use relevant student assessment data to revisit gaps in instructional content. By assessing the learner and the learner's social world teachers are better equipped to understand the rich, and sometimes undervalued, knowledge that students bring with them to school so they make appropriate instructional decisions that support students' literacy learning.

Based upon our belief that "assessment must serve students" (Farr, 1991, p. 95), we contend that purposeful assessment programs enable language arts teachers to gather student data, and use it to make instructional decisions, in light of four different purposes. First, purposeful assessments give language arts teachers a synopsis of students' learning through summative and formative (e.g., portfolios, performance-based assessments) measures. Second, purposeful assessments, including dynamic assessments, rating scales, and checklists, offer invaluable data to language arts teachers about students' ongoing learning, as it occurs within the classroom. Next, purposeful assessments help language arts teachers to gain a deeper sense of their students as readers, and to consider how personal traits and interests shape language arts development. Finally, purposeful language arts assessments that are rooted within a cultural ecological orientation towards assessment build upon students' experiences and values their social worlds, and should be embraced in culturally-diverse classrooms. By tapping into familial and community resources, language arts teachers can begin to understand how cultural characteristics, language, literacy environments, home-school connections, and other cultural resources play a part in students' literate worlds.

References

Afflerbach, P. (1996). Engaged assessment of engaged readers. In L. Baker, P. Afflerbach, & D. Reinking (Eds.), *Developing engaged readers in school and home communities* (pp. 191–214). Mahwah, NJ: Erlbaum.

Afflerbach, P. (2007a). *Understanding and using reading assessment K-12.* Newark, DE: International Reading Association.

Afflerbach, P. (2007b). Best practices in literacy assessment. In L. B. Gambrell, L. M. Morrow, & M. Pressley (Eds.), *Best practices in literacy instruction* (pp. 264–282). New York: Guilford Press.

Allen, J., Fabregas, V., Hankins, K., Hull, G., Labbo, L., Lawson, H., et al. (2002). PHOLKS lore: Learning from photographs, families, and children. *Language Arts, 79*(4), 312–323.

Anderson, A. B., & Stokes, S. J. (1984). Social and institutional influences on the development and practice of literacy. In H. Goelman, A. Oberg, & F. Smith (Eds.), *Awakening to literacy* (pp. 24–37). Exeter, NH: Heinemann.

Andrade, H. L., Du, Y., & Wang, X. (2008). Putting rubrics to the test: The effect of a model, criteria generation, and rubric-referenced self-assessment on elementary school students' writing. *Educational Measurement: Issues and Practice, 27*(2), 3–13.

Artiles, A. J., Reschly, D. J., & Chinn, P. C. (2002). Overidentification of students of color in special education: A critical overview. *Multicultural Perspectives, 4*(1), 3–12.

Au, K. H. (2006). *Multicultural issues and literacy achievement.* Mahwah, NJ: Erlbaum.

Barrett, H. C. (2007). Researching electronic portfolios and learner engagement: The REFLECT initiative. *Journal of Adolescent and Adult Literacy, 50*(6), 436–449.

Bean, T. W., Bean, S. K., & Bean, K. F. (1999). Intergenerational conversations and two adolescents' multiple literacies: Implications for redefining content area literacy. *Journal of Adolescent and Adult Literacy, 42*, 438–448.

Bukowiecki, E. M. (2007). Teaching children how to read. *Kappa Delta Pi, 43*(2), 58–65.

Cancienne, M. B. (2009). Walking and talking in student communities: Teachers explore their internal landscapes. *Curriculum and Teaching Dialogue, 11*, 149–157.

Davi, A. (2006). In the service of writing and race. *Journal of Basic Writing, 25*(1), 73–95.

Edwards, P. A., Pleasants, H. M., & Franklin, S. H. (1999). *A path to follow: Learning to listen to parents.* Portsmouth, NH: Heinemann.

Edwards, P. A., & Turner, J. D. (2010). Do you hear what I hear? Using the parent story approach to listen to and learn from African American parents. In M. L. Dantas & P. Manyak (Eds.), *Home-school connections in a multicultural society: Learning from and with culturally and linguistically diverse families* (pp. 137–155). New York: Routledge.

Edwards, P., Turner, J., & Mokhtari, K. (2008). Balancing the assessment of and the assessment for learning in support of student literacy achievement. *Reading Teacher, 61*, 682–684.

Farr, R. (1991). The assessment puzzle. *Educational Leadership, 49*, 95.

Flynn, R. M. (2004). Curriculum-based reader's theatre: Setting the stage for reading and retention. *The Reading Teacher, 58*(4), 360–365.

Frey, B. B., & Schmidt, V. L. (2007). Coming to terms with classroom assessment. *Journal of Advanced Academics, 18*, 402–423.

Gallagher, C., & Worth, P. (2008). *Formative assessment policies, programs, and practices in the Southwest Region.* (Issues & Answers Report, REL 2008–No. 041). Washington, DC: U.S. Department of Education, Institute of Education Sciences, National Center for Education Evaluation and Regional Assistance, Regional Educational Laboratory Southwest. Retrieved from http://ies.ed.gov/ncee/edlabs

Garcia, G. E., & Pearson, P. D. (1994). Assessment and diversity. *Review of Research in Education, 20*, 337–391.

Gambrell, L., Palmer, B., Codling, R., & Mazzoni, S. (1996). Assessing motivation to read. *The Reading Teacher, 49*(7), 518–533.

Guthrie, J. T., Van Meter, P., & Mitchell, A. (1994). Performance assessments in reading language arts. *The Reading Teacher, 48*, 266–271.

Guthrie, J. T., & Wigfield, A. (2000). Engagement and motivation in reading. In M. L. Kamil, P. B. Mosenthal, P. D. Pearson, & R. Barr (Eds.), *Handbook of reading research* (Vol. 3, pp. 403–422). New York: Erlbaum.

Harris, T. H., & Hodges, R. E. (1995). *The literacy dictionary: The vocabulary of reading and writing.* Newark, DE: International Reading Association.

Heritage, M. (2007). Formative assessment: What do teachers need to know and do? *Phi Delta Kappan, 89*(2), 140–145.

Hilliard, A. G. (1995). Culture, assessment, and valid teaching for the African-American student. In B. A. Ford, F. E. Obiakor, & J. M. Patton (Eds.), *Effective education of African American exceptional learners: New perspectives* (pp. ix–xvi). Austin, TX: Pro-Ed.

Johnston, P. (2005). Literacy assessment and the future. *The Reading Teacher, 58*(7), 684–686.

Kear, D. J., Coffman, G. A., McKenna, M. C., & Ambrosio, A. L. (2000). Measuring attitude toward writing. *The Reading Teacher, 54*(1), 10–23.

Kidd, J., Sanchez, S. Y., & Thorp, E. (2004). Gathering family stories: Facilitating preservice teachers' cultural awareness and responsiveness. *Action in Teacher Education, 53*, 153–167.

Kong, A., & Fitch, E. (2002/2003). Using book club to engage culturally and linguistically diverse learners in reading, writing and talking about books. *The Reading Teacher, 56*(4), 252–262.

Laing, S., & Kamhi, A. (2003). Assessment of language and literacy in African American children. *Language, Speech, and Hearing Services in the Schools, 34*, 44–55.

Lazar, A. M., & Weisburg, R. (1996). Inviting parents' perspectives: Building home-school partnerships to support children who struggle with literacy. *The Reading Teacher, 50*(3), 228–238.

Macrine, S. L., & Sabbatino, E. D. (2008). Dynamic assessment and remediation approach. *Reading and Writing Quarterly, 24*, 52–76.

Massey, D. D. (2003). A comprehension checklist: What if it doesn't make sense? *The Reading Teacher, 57*(1), 81–84.

McKenna, M. C., & Dougherty Stahl, K. A. (2009). *Assessment for reading instruction* (2nd ed.). New York: Guilford Press.

McKenna, M. C., & Kear, D. J. (1990). Measuring attitude toward reading: A new tool for teachers. *The Reading Teacher, 43*(9), 626–639.

Moll, L. C., Amanti, C., Neff, D., & Gonzalez, N. (1992). Funds of knowledge for teaching: Using a qualitative approach to connect homes and classrooms. *Theory into Practice, 31*(2), 132–141.

Moore, D., Lin-Agler, L. M., & Zabrucky, K. M. (2005). A source of metacomprehension accuracy. *Reading Psychology, 26*, 251–265.

Morrison, T. G., & Chilcoat, G. W. (1998). The 'living newspaper theatre' in the language arts classroom. *Journal of Adolescent and Adult Literacy, 42*, 2–14.

Nutbrown, C. (1999). Purpose and authenticity in early literacy assessment. *Reading, 33*, 33–40.

Orellana, M. F., & Hernandez, A. (1999). Talking the walk: Children reading urban environmental print. *The Reading Teacher, 52*(6), 612–619.

Paratore, J. R., & McCormack, R. L. (2005). *Classroom literacy assessment: Making sense of what students know and do.* New York: Guilford Press.

Pennsylvania Literacy Framework. (2000). Harrisburg, PA: Department of Education.

Pryor, J., & Crossouard, B. (2008). A socio-cultural theorisation of formative assessment. *Oxford Review of Education, 34*(1), 1–20.

Romeo, L. (2008). Informal writing assessment linked to instruction: A continuous process for teachers, students and parents. *Reading & Writing Quarterly, 24*, 25–51.

Shockley, B. (1994). Extending the literate community: Home-to-school and school-to-home. *The Reading Teacher, 47*, 500–502.

Spinelli, C. (2008). Addressing the issue of cultural and linguistic diversity and assessment: Informal evaluation methods for English language learners. *Reading and Writing Quarterly, 24*, 101–118.

Stiggins, R. J. (2007). Assessment crisis: The absence of assessment for leaning. *Phi Delta Kappan, 83*, 758–765.

Tierney, R. J., & Clark, C. (1998). Portfolios: Assumptions, tensions, and possibilities. *Reading Research Quarterly, 33*, 474–486.

Tzuriel, D. (2000). Dynamic assessment of young children: Educational and intervention perspectives. *Educational Psychology Review, 12*(4), 385–435.

Tzuriel, D., & Kauffman, R. (1999). Mediated learning and cognitive modifiability: Dynamic assessment of young Ethiopian immigrant children to Israel. *Journal of Cross Cultural Psychology, 30*, 359–380.

Valencia, S. W., & Place, N. (1993). Literacy portfolios for teaching, learning and accountability: The Bellevue Literacy Assessment Project. In E. Hiebert, P. Afflerbach, & S. Valencia (Eds.), *Authentic reading assessment: Practices and possibilities* (pp. 135–166). Newark, DE: International Reading Association.

Vygotsky, L. (1978). *Mind and society.* Cambridge, MA: Harvard University Press.

Wigfield, A., & Guthrie, J. T. (1997). Relations of children's motivation for reading the amount and breadth of their reading. *Journal of Educational Psychology, 89*(3), 420–432.

Williams, N. L., & Bauer, P. T. (2006). Pathways to affective accountability: Selecting, locating, and using children's books in elementary school classrooms. *The Reading Teacher, 60*(1), 14–22.

Young, E. (1989). *Lon Po Po: A Red Riding Hood story from China.* New York: Penguin Group.

48

Issues in the Assessment of Culturally and Linguistically Diverse Students with Special Needs

Janette K. Klingner, KaiLonnie Dunsmore, and Patricia Edwards

Recent research and policy changes highlight the need to examine the cultural and linguistic dimensions of assessment, particularly as part of a system for identifying students with disabilities. A considerable body of evidence substantiates that students of color, students living in poverty, and English language learners are disproportionately represented in special education (Artiles, Rueda, Salazar, & Higareda, 2005; Donovan & Cross, 2002). In addition, intervention research suggests that appropriate instruction can reduce the need for special education by accelerating students' literacy development (Scanlon, Vellutino, Small, Fanuele, & Sweeney, 2005; Blachman et al., 2004; Taylor, Short, Shearer, & Frye, 2007). Changes in legal policies at state and national levels around special education identification procedures have forced far greater attention on the instructional context and on the appropriateness and quality of intervention services. This has led the education community to confront more directly the culturally situated nature of assessment tools and practices and the close link between assessment, instruction, and educational goals when evaluating students' abilities.

In this chapter, we examine new directions for literacy assessment in a special education system that attends to the cultural basis of school-based cognitive development and learning (Rogoff & Chavajay, 1995). We describe recent changes in the assessment and identification of learning disabilities (LD), assessment in Response to Intervention (RTI) models, cultural and linguistic influences on test performances, problematic assessment procedures, and culturally and linguistically responsive assessment practices.

Changes in the Assessment and Identification of Learning Disabilities

The last decade has brought dramatic changes in how we assess students to determine whether they possess a learning disability (LD). In the almost 50 years since Samuel Kirk first used the term "learning disability" (Kirk

& Bateman, 1962) and Barbara Bateman described LD as "an educationally significant discrepancy between [an individual's] estimated intellectual potential and actual level of performance related to basic disorders in the learning process" (1965, p. 220), psychologists and other members of multi-disciplinary assessment teams have identified LD primarily by determining a student's potential, typically by administering an intelligence test, and comparing that with the student's academic achievement. Reading was by far the most common area of disability (about 80%). Yet, for various reasons, numerous researchers, professional groups, parents, and policy makers challenged the IQ-achievement discrepancy as the core of LD's definition and focal point of identification procedures (see Aaron, 1997, for a review of research challenging the validity of the discrepancy formula). In this chapter, we discuss concerns about LD identification procedures that inadequately assess diverse student populations. We also describe current assessment practices and highlight some promising directions for developing assessment and instructional tools that acknowledge the cultural origin of human cognition (Rogoff, 2003) and literacy practices more specifically (Cole, 1996).

Problems with the Construct of Unexpected Under-achievement as Assessed with IQ Tests Until recently, one of the fundamental principles of LD has been the belief that there are real differences between individuals with a demonstrated discrepancy between IQ and achievement and those individuals with a "flatter" profile, or, in other words, who are low in both IQ and achievement. The presumption has been that the instructional needs of students with "true" LD are somehow different than those of students who are at the lower end of normal distributions in IQ and achievement. Yet, this does not seem to be the case. As far back as in 1992, Fletcher, Francis, Rourke, Shaywitz, and Shaywitz compared five groups of children with varying IQ-achievement profiles and determined that differences among groups were minimal. They concluded their report by questioning the validity of segregating students according to IQ-achievement discrepancies.

Stuebing et al. (2002) conducted a meta-analysis of 46 studies to evaluate the validity of LD classifications based on IQ-discrepancy and the exclusion of students who are poor readers but who do not display this discrepancy. They found substantial overlap between IQ-discrepant and IQ-consistent poor readers, and noted that differences could be largely explained by the selection criteria used to form groups. In other words, students' membership in a given IQ-discrepant or IQ-consistent group did not predict how well they would respond to reading instruction. Stuebing et al. recommended doing away with IQ testing as part of LD identification procedures, and instead moving to a model that includes looking at how students respond to research-based interventions. Like other researchers who examined the validity of IQ-discrepancy classifications, Stuebing and her colleagues focused on reading and not other aspects of written or oral language.

Over this same time span, literacy intervention research was accumulating that indicated that appropriate instruction could reduce the number of students qualifying for special education, especially in reading. A number of studies found that adequate classroom instruction, which was differentiated in both material resources and instructional practices to support the individual learning needs of students, could effectively ensure that most students reached grade level achievement (Hiebert & Taylor, 2000; Cunningham & Allington, 2007; Taylor, Pearson, Clark, & Walpole, 2000). Other researchers provided evidence that specifically targeted interventions (within the classroom or provided by trained personal as supplementary to classroom instruction) could bring to grade level the majority of those students who continued to struggle with literacy difficulties (Blachman et al., 2004; Vellutino, Scanlon, Small, & Fanuele, 2006; Pinell, Lyons, DeFord, Bryk, & Seltzer, 1994). This research contributed to our understanding of the instructional context within which student literacy abilities are developed, supported, and assessed. In fact, Vellutino, Scanlon, Zhang, and Schatschneider (2008) emphasized that many students' reading disabilities have an *instructional* etiology that may or may not be in addition to a biological one.

At about the same time, the U.S. Department of Education, Office of Special Education Programs convened a panel of leading LD researchers to discuss LD identification procedures (Bradley, Danielson, & Hallahan, 2002). The panel agreed that the IQ-achievement discrepancy is not a valid way to identify students with LD, and concluded that the most promising method of identifying individuals with LD is to do away with IQ testing and instead to implement RTI.

Also at this time, the National Academy of Sciences convened a panel of experts to summarize the research related to the disproportionate representation of culturally and linguistically diverse students in special education. This group also concluded that IQ is ineffective in the identification of LD, and noted that the use of IQ tests with culturally

and linguistically diverse students is fraught with problems (Donovan & Cross, 2002). They recommended alternatives that do not involve the use of IQ tests, and promoted the widespread use of early screening, early intervening services, and RTI. They asserted that if early reading programs help culturally and linguistically diverse students receive more appropriate instruction, then the number of students who continue to struggle will decrease and will more likely be those who require a special education.

Response to Intervention With these initiatives and new research findings serving as a backdrop, Congress passed the Individuals with Disabilities Education Improvement Act (IDEA), in 2004. IDEA (2004) promotes RTI as way to identify students with LD and gives states the option of discontinuing the use of IQ-Achievement discrepancy formulas. IDEA also stipulates that schools should screen students and provide Early Intervening Services to all students who are not making progress, as part of general education, before a student is considered for possible special education placement.

Yet some of the assumptions underlying RTI are flawed, especially when applied with culturally and linguistically diverse students. For example, the idea of "research-based" tends to be applied with a one size fits all mentality, without considering issues of population and ecological validity (Klingner & Edwards, 2006). When students do not respond to interventions, educators seem too quick to assume the problem resides in the child, and not with the quality and appropriateness of instruction (Orosco & Klingner, 2010). It appears that there is not enough of a focus on the context for learning and improving instruction and educational opportunities for students. Also, educators seem to be relying on just one or two progress monitoring measures to assess students' response to instruction, rather than conducting comprehensive evaluations of students' strengths and areas of need. The most common progress monitoring tools (e.g., Dynamic Indicators of Basic Early Literacy Skills) may hold limited internal or external validity for the literacy skills being targeted by teachers or state assessment systems (Hoffman, Jenkins, & Dunlap, 2009; Shelton, Altwerger, & Jordan, 2009; Nelson, 2008). Although we have questions and concerns about RTI, particularly with culturally and linguistically diverse students, we believe that it provides an opportunity to move in new directions and address problematic past practices. In any case, the IQ-achievement discrepancy way of identifying LD is obsolescent.

Assessment in RTI. RTI is an assessment-based system. Yet creating the appropriate system is a challenge in culturally and linguistically diverse schools (Klingner, Soltero-González, & Lesaux, 2010). When considering how best to assess student learning, it is important to consider school contexts and to reflect about school-level models of appropriate assessment and instruction. Rather than simply focusing on individual students and emphasizing students' differences in relation to a majority culture norm, the goal should be to design assessment systems and effective learning environments tailored to the needs of diverse school populations.

All assessment data should be used expressly to support student learning, whether to inform constructive discussions about classroom-level instruction or student-level supplemental supports. It is important to consider the function of each assessment and not to use assessments for other purposes than those for which they were intended. There is no single best test or assessment strategy. Different assessments—even in the same language or literacy domain—capture somewhat different skills and knowledge. This is because of the assessment format, background knowledge required for the items, and the way the skill of interest is defined for measurement. All RTI assessment strategies should reflect the multi-dimensional nature of language and reading. Multiple assessments should be used to provide a comprehensive portrait of a given student's strengths and needs.

Screening batteries should sample from the entire range of language and literacy skills needed for academic success. While many screening batteries focus on print awareness, phonological awareness, and letter-word identification, they typically do *not* include measures of vocabulary knowledge, oral language proficiency, and/or listening and reading comprehension. This omission is particularly detrimental for linguistically diverse students, many of whom develop age-appropriate word reading skills but need support to further develop their language and comprehension skills.

Progress monitoring should include analyses of oral reading (e.g., Running Records, Qualitative Reading Inventory) in addition to measures of oral reading fluency. Writing should be analyzed as well, for example, using rubrics such as the 6+1 Writing Trait Model. Content expertise in literacy as well as language acquisition are required in order to analyze and interpret these assessments, but they can yield high validity and be done with a great deal of rigor and standardization (Lipson & Wixson, 2009). Progress monitoring should be used to adjust instruction to ensure that it meets the needs of individual students as well as of classrooms of learners. In other words, it can show which instructional approaches are most effective and which are not working. When most culturally and linguistically diverse students are not thriving, this is a systemic issue that needs addressing.

When any decision is being made about instructional support services for a given student, parents, as well as educators or support personnel with knowledge and expertise in learning to read in a second language and in how to distinguish between second language acquisition and learning disabilities, should be active members of the decision-making process. Parents can provide insights about the student's history and to ensure that efforts to provide culturally responsive assessment and instruction do not treat linguistic or ethnic groups as if they were homogenous.

Also, it is important to attend to the unique character-

istics and needs of adolescents (Fisher & Ivey, 2006) and recognize that broader cultural knowledge is uniquely constructed through the community-based activities of adolescence (Heath, in press) and multimodal forms of literate engagement (Bailey, 2009). It is particularly crucial that assessments attend to the identities, motivation, interests, and existing strategies of adolescent readers and writer to create a more comprehensive portrait informing instructional practices (Moje, Overby, Tysvaer, & Morris, 2008; Alvermann, 2002; Greenleaf & Hinchman, 2009).

Cultural Influences on Test Performance Any test performance is the result of a complex interaction between the task characteristics and the constraints inherent in the testing situation. Variance across cultural groups in test performance may be due to different interpretations of the nature of the task, the type of problem being solved, and the process used to find a solution (Goodnow, 1976). Cultural variation in assessment results may be due to differences in the situations in which various cultural groups typically apply their skills more than to differences in the actual skills (Cole & Bruner, 1971). Individual interviews can be helpful to determine why a student interprets a test item in a particular way (Solano-Flores & Nelson-Barber, 2001).

Because of how they are developed, standardized tests typically possess strong psychometric properties for some students, particularly those who speak English as their first language and are from mainstream backgrounds. Yet when used with culturally and linguistically diverse students, these tests lack the same levels of predictive and construct validity they show with English-only students (Abedi, 2002; MacSwan, Rolstad, & Glass, 2002). In other words, they tend to underestimate achievement. One potentially problematic aspect of test development is that test developers draw test items from a universe of information to which they assume test takers have been exposed. Yet children from diverse backgrounds might not have been exposed to this body of information, placing them at a disadvantage (Samuda, 1989). Rather, they have been exposed to different information. The reality is that assessments in the United States reflect the abilities, skills, knowledge, and language valued by U.S. "core culture" (Mercer, 1973, p. 13). Yet, this fact is not adequately considered when interpreting test results for students from diverse backgrounds. The evaluator's challenge is to figure out what a score on a given test means, and what can and cannot be concluded from assessment results.

Research in the neurosciences has more recently provided additional evidence of the needs to examine learning disabilities as a cultural as well as biological phenomenon and to develop assessment tools that attend to individual literacy development as a culturally situated process. "In general, genetic research comparing abilities and disabilities suggests that what we call 'learning disability' is merely the low end of the same genetic and environmental factors responsible for the normal distribution of learning ability. In other words, the abnormal is normal" (Kovas & Plomin,

2008, p. 14). This suggests that assessment tools for both regular education students and those identified with special needs should attend to literacy development as a culturally situated process, understanding that any genetic or biological differences are mediated through the instructional environment.

Similarly, efforts to map the brain during various aspects of reading (e.g., word retrieval, phonological processing, and comprehension) indicate differential patterns for students with phonological processing difficulties. However, longitudinal research and cross cultural variation suggest that it is difficult to extricate the cultural origins of difference from those of the biological when examining the etiology of disability (Katzir & Paré-Blagoev, 2006). Current views of brain development emphasize its plasticity and developmental responsiveness to environmental stimuli far beyond what was initially thought of as critical windows for language and literacy development (Miller & Tallal, 2006). In fact, functional magnetic resonance imaging (fMRI) of the brains of adults and children with dyslexia reveals differential patterns; significantly, such research also indicates that intervention or instruction can reduce or ameliorate these differences as the brain learns, over time revealing more "normal" patterns of brain activity (Gaab, Gabrieli, Deutsch, Tallal, & Tempe, 2007).

Developing protocols for using assessment data in ways that support student development and highlight the plasticity of the brain can be hindered by views of reading (dis)ability as a static phenomenon as opposed to a condition that may be experientially (or instructionally) constructed (Fischer, 2008). Through longitudinal attention to the instructional context of literacy learning as well as the cognitive profiles of students as evidenced on formal, standardized measures, work by Vellutino et al. (2006, 2008) contributes to our understanding of the ways in which assessments can under-examine the socio-cultural dimension of school instruction and practice. What we assess as "ability" is as much a function of the instructional and environmental context and access and opportunity as it is mental constraints. Psychometric assessment is itself, therefore, a cultural activity, although it has tended to portray itself as revealing dimensions of student ability distinct from cultural experience and practice.

Linguistic Influences on Test Performance
Numerous scholars have written about the potential for linguistic bias in assessments (Rogoff, 2003; Solano-Flores, 2006; Valdés & Figueroa, 1994). ELLs' test performance is affected by issues of language dominance and language proficiency. They may have only a surface level understanding of vocabulary on an exam and be confused by words with multiple meanings, referents, and pronouns. Assessments rely on particular linguistic forms that are familiar to some children but may be unfamiliar to others (Rogoff, 2003). Children who are familiar with the language and structure of a test are more likely to respond in ways expected by the examiner.

Test developers typically do not take into consideration all the ways language, dialect, and register affect students' understanding of test items. Addressing the language adequacy of test materials requires the use of sophisticated approaches to test development (Solano-Flores, Trumbull, & Nelson-Barber, 2002; Tanzer, 2005). Solano-Flores (2008) contends that "current ELL testing practices are limited in their effectiveness to produce valid measures of academic achievement because they are based on categorical, deterministic views of language and erroneous assumptions about the capacity of assessment systems to effectively communicate with ELL students" (p. 189). Problematic procedures include classifying ELLs into a few overly simplistic categories of language proficiency and treating ELLs as if they are more linguistically homogeneous than they are.

Problematic Assessment Procedures
In numerous studies of ELL testing practices over the years, researchers have found that psychologists tend to over-rely on the results of English-language testing, exclude native language test results, and give inadequate attention to language acquisition issues or classroom context as possible explanations for students' struggles (Figueroa & Newsome, 2006; Harry & Klingner, 2006; Klingner & Harry, 2006; Maldonado-Colon, 1986; Ochoa, Rivera, & Powell, 1997). For example, Harry and Klingner (2006) found that the psychologists in their investigation of disproportionate representation seemed to be overly influenced by teachers' informal diagnoses of children's problems, school personnel's impressions of the family, and external pressures for identification and placement in special education. They sometimes disregarded established identification criteria and placed students in special education programs for which they did not truly qualify, to "save" a child or to "protect" him. They apparently lacked understanding of cultural and linguistic influences on test performance. To address these problematic assessment procedures, we recommend shifting from a focus on finding out what is wrong with students to figuring out how best to help them. In other words, assessments in special education or as part of RTI should be used in more formative ways than in the past, or, in other words, to identify learning needs to improve teaching by making instructional adjustments (Shepard, Hammerness, Darling-Hammond, & Rust, 2005).

Culturally Responsive Assessment
All learning is cultural (Cole, 1996; Rogoff, 2003). Therefore, as Moje and Hinchman (2004) observed, "All practice needs to be culturally responsive in order to be best practice" (italics added, p. 321). Culture is not a static set of characteristics located within individuals but is fluid and complex, varying across contexts (Gutierrez & Rogoff, 2003). Children are socialized to learn in particular ways in their homes and communities. In order to provide valid measurements of what students know and can do, assessment practices must access student knowledge in ways that are consonant with how they

organize and understand subject matter, and with how they express their understandings.

Culturally responsive literacy assessments must go beyond examining the degree to which students have acquired basic components or sub-processes in reading and writing and also examine the ways that best support meaning making for *particular* students. We draw here upon the accommodation and incorporation principles of Wiley's (1996) framework as possible ways of developing and interpreting assessment practices in culturally diverse contexts (Klingner & Edwards, 2006). Embedded in each of these perspectives is an assumption that assessment is inextricably linked with instructional practice. That is, *what* and *how* we assess student learning is reciprocally related to the strategies and goals of instruction.

Accommodation, according to Wiley (1996), requires educators to deepen understandings of the communicative styles and literacy practices among their students and to account for these in their instructional and assessment practices. Several qualitative studies have shown that, even in impoverished conditions, homes can be rich in print and family members can engage in literacy activities of many kinds on a daily basis (Anderson & Stokes, 1984; Heath, 1983; Purcell-Gates, 1996; Taylor & Dorsey-Gaines, 1988). Assessment practices that *accommodate* the rich linguistic and cultural resources that students bring to literacy learning require tools and protocols that address the resources that students develop in home and community contexts to support goal-related literacy activities (Heath, in press; Moje & Hinchman, 2007). For example, Moje and colleagues have developed survey tools for examining adolescent's interests, skills, and experiences with literacy (Moje et al., 2008).

Incorporation (Wiley, 1996) involves studying community practices that have not been valued previously by schools and incorporating them in the curriculum. It also means surrendering a privileged position and acknowledging that much can be learned from diverse ethnic groups. Assessment tools explicitly developed to address how students define, value, and use literacy as part of their practices in and out of school "offer the potential for schooling to be adjusted to meet the needs of families" (Cairney, 1997, p. 70). These kinds of assessment tools provide the potential for the reflexive analysis that reveals not only what students know and can do but the conditions under which such behaviors are most likely to occur. These tools move beyond descriptions of individual capacities to broader examinations of the instructional context. For instance, Moll (2009) described how teachers learn to engage in new forms of assessment and instructional practices through involvement in their communities.

Conclusion

In conclusion, assessment practices should not be isolated from the goals of the literacy curriculum and associated assumptions about the meanings of literate practice in diverse communities (Klingner & Edwards, 2006). Assessments do not provide instructionally valid data if they are decontextualized from the practices within which literate knowledge and skills are constructed. Whether as part of RTI or another purpose, assessment results must be considered in relation to the sociocultural contexts in which instruction and assessment take place (Artiles, 2002; Gee, 2001). In this chapter we have tried to provide a framework for developing and using assessment data that moves closer to leveling the educational playing field for African American, Hispanic, and other culturally and linguistically diverse students in the United States.

References

Aaron, P. G. (1997). The impending demise of the discrepancy formula. *Review of Educational Research, 67*(4), 461–502.

Abedi, J. (2002). Standardized achievement tests and English language learners: Psychometric issues. *Educational Assessment, 8,* 231–257.

Alvermann, D. E. (2002). Effective literacy instruction for adolescents. *Journal of Literacy Research, 34*(2), 189–208.

Anderson, A. B., & Stokes, S. J. (1984). Social and institutional influences on the development and practice of literacy. In H. Goelman, A. Oberg, & F. Smith (Eds.), *Awakening to literacy* (pp. 24–37). Exeter, NH: Heinemann.

Artiles, A. J. (2002). Culture in learning: The next frontier in reading difficulties research. In R. Bradley, L. Danielson, & D. P. Hallahan (Eds.), *Identification of learning disabilities: Research to policy* (pp. 693–701). Hillsdale, NJ: Erlbaum.

Artiles, A. J., Rueda, R., Salazar, J. J., & Higareda, I. (2005). Within group diversity in minority disproportionate representation: English language learners in urban school districts. *Exceptional Children, 71*(3), 283–300.

Bailey, N. M. (2009). "It makes it more real": Teaching new literacies in a secondary English classroom. *English Education, 41*(3), 207–234.

Bateman, B. (1965). Learning disabilities: An overview. *Journal of School Psychology, 3*(3), 1–12.

Blachman, B. A., Schatschneider, C., Fletcher, J. M., Francis, D. J., Clonan, S. M., Shaywitz, S. E., et al. (2004). Effects of intensive reading remediation for second and third graders and a 1-year follow-up. *Journal of Educational Psychology, 96*(3), 444–461.

Bradley, R., Danielson, L., Hallahan, D. P. (2002). *Identification of learning disabilities: Research to practice.* Mahwah, NJ: Erlbaum.

Cairney, T. H. (1997). Acknowledging diversity in home literacy practices: moving towards partnerships with parents. *Early Child Development and Care, 127-128,* 61–73.

Cole, M. (1996). *Cultural psychology: A once and future discipline.* Cambridge, MA: Harvard University Press.

Cole, M., & Bruner, J. (1971). Cultural differences and inferences about psychological processes. *American Psychologist, 26,* 867–876.

Cunningham, P. M., & Allington, R. L. (2007). *Classrooms that work: They can all read and write* (4th ed.). Boston: Allyn & Bacon.

Donovan, M. S., & Cross, C. T. (2002). *Minority students in special education and gifted education.* Washington, DC: National Academy Press.

Figueroa, R. A., & Newsome, P. (2006). The diagnosis of LD in English language learners: is it nondiscriminatory? *Journal of Learning Disabilities, 39,* 206–214.

Fischer, K. W. (2008). Dynamic cycles of cognitive and brain development: measuring growth in mind, brain, and education. In A. M. Battro, K. W. Fischer, & P. Léna (Eds.), *The educated brain* (pp. 127–150). Cambridge, UK: Cambridge University Press.

Fisher, D., & Ivey, G. (2006). Evaluating the interventions for struggling adolescent readers. *Journal of Adolescent & Adult Literacy, 50*(3), 180–189.

Gaab, N., Gabrieli, J. D. E., Deutsch, G. K., Tallal, P., & Tempe, E. (2007). Neural correlates of rapid auditory processing are disrupted in children with developmental dyslexia and ameliorated with training: An fMRI study. *Restorative Neurology and Neuroscience. 25*(3-4), 295–310.

Gee, J. P. (2001). A sociocultural perspective on early literacy development. In S. B. Neuman & D. K. Dickinson (Eds.), *Handbook of early literacy research* (pp. 30–42). New York: Guilford Press.

Goodnow, J. J. (1976). The nature of intelligent behavior: Questions raised by cross-cultural studies. In L. B. Resnick (Ed.), *The nature of intelligence* (pp. 135–144). Hillsdale, NJ: Erlbaum.

Greenleaf, C. L., & Hinchman, K. (2009). Reimagining our inexperienced adolescent readers: From struggling, striving, marginalized, and reluctant to thriving. *Journal of Adolescent & Adult Literacy, 53*(1), 4–13.

Gutierrez, K., & Rogoff, B. (2003). Cultural ways of learning: Individual traits or repertoires of practice. *Educational Researcher, 32*(5), 19–25.

Harry, B., & Klingner, J. K. (2006). *Why are so many minority students in special education? Understanding race and disability in schools.* New York: Teachers College Press.

Heath, S. B. (1983). *Ways with words: Language, life, and work in communities and classrooms.* New York: Cambridge University Press.

Heath, S. B. (in press). Family literacy or community learning? Some critical questions on perspective. In K. Dunsmore & D. Fisher (Eds.), *Bringing literacy home.* Newark: Bringing Literacy Home.

Hiebert, E. H., & Taylor, B. M. (2000). Beginning reading instruction: Research on early intervention. In M. Kamil, P. Mosenthal, P. D. Pearson, & R. Barr (Eds.), *Handbook of reading research* (Vol. III, pp. 455–482). Mahwah, NJ: Erlbaum.

Hoffman, A. R., Jenkins, J. E., Dunlap, S. K. (2009). Using DIBELS: A survey of purposes and practices. *Reading Psychology, 30*(1), 1–16.

Individuals with Disabilities Education Improvement Act of 2004. Public Law 108–446.

Katzir, T., & Paré-Blagoev, J. (2006). Applying cognitive neuroscience research to education: The case of literacy. *Educational Psychologist, 4*, 53–74.

Kirk, S. A., & Bateman, B. (1962). Diagnosis and remediation of learning disabilities. *Exceptional Children*, (2), 73–78.

Klingner, J. K., & Edwards, P. (2006). Cultural considerations with response to intervention models. *Reading Research Quarterly, 41*, 108–117.

Klingner, J. K., & Harry, B. (2006). The special education referral and decision-making process for English Language Learners: Child study team meetings and staffings. *Teachers College Record, 108*, 2247–2281.

Klingner, J. K., Soltero-González, L., & Lesaux, N. (2010). Response to intervention for English language learners. In M. Lipson & K. Wixson (Eds.), *Approaches to response to intervention (RTI): Evidence-based frameworks for preventing reading difficulties* (pp. 134–162). Newark, DE: International Reading Association.

Kovas, Y., & Plomin, R. (2008). Genetics of learning abilities and disabilities: Implications for cognitive neuroscience and translational research. In J. Reed & J. Warner-Rogers (Eds.), *Child neuropsychology: Concepts, theory, and practice* (pp. 40–57). New York: Wiley-Blackwell.

Lipson, K., & Wixson, M. (2008). *Assessment and instruction of reading and writing difficulties: An interactive approach* (4th ed.). Boston, MA: Allyn & Bacon.

MacSwan, J., Rosltad, K., & Glass, G. V. (2002). Do some school-age children have no language? Some problems of construct validity in the Pre-LAS Español. *Bilingual Research Journal, 26*, 395–420.

Maldonado-Colon, E. (1986). Assessment: Interpreting data of linguistically/culturally different students referred for disabilities or disorders. *Journal of Reading, Writing, and Learning Disabilities International, 2*(1), 73–83.

Mercer, J. (1973). *Labeling the mentally retarded.* Berkley: University of California Press.

Miller, S. & Tallal, P. A. (2006). Addressing literacy through neuroscience. *School Administrator, 63*(11), 19–23.

Moje, E. B., & Hinchman, K. (2004). Culturally responsive practices for youth literacy learning. In J. Dole & T. Jetton (Eds.), *Adolescent literacy research and practice* (pp. 331–350). New York: Guilford Press.

Moje, E. B., Overby, M., Tysvaer, N., & Morris, K. (2008). The complex world of adolescent literacy: Myths, motivations, and mysteries. *Harvard Educational Review, 78*(1), 107–154.

Moll, L. C. (2009, October). *Mobilizing culture, language, and educational practices: Fulfilling the promises of Mendez and Brown.* Sixth Annual Brown Lecture in Educational Research, American Educational Research Association, Washington DC. Retrieved from http://cmcgc.com/aera/2009/aera.html

Nelson, J. M. (2008). Beyond correlational analysis of the Dynamic Indicators of Basic Early Literacy Skills (DIBELS): A classification validity study. *School Psychology Quarterly, 23*(4), 542–552.

Ochoa, S. H., Rivera, B. D., & Powell, M. P. (1997). Factors used to comply with the exclusionary clause with bilingual and limited-English-proficient pupils: Initial guidelines. *Learning Disabilities Research & Practice, 12,* 161–167.

Orosco, M., & Klingner, J. K. (2010). One school's implementation of RTI with English language learners: "Referring into RTI." *Journal of Learning Disabilities, 43,* 269–288.

Pinell, G. S., Lyons, C. A., DeFord, D. E., Bryk, A. S., & Seltzer, M. (1994). Comparing instructional models for the literacy education of high-risk first graders. *Reading Research Quarterly, 29*(1), 8–39.

Purcell-Gates, V. (1996). Stories, coupons, and the TV guide. Relationships between home literacy experiences and emergent literacy knowledge. *Reading Research Quarterly, 31,* 406–428.

Rogoff, B. (2003). *The cultural nature of human development.* New York: Oxford University Press.

Rogoff, B., & Chavajay, P. (1995). What's become of research on the cultural basis of cognitive development? *American Psychologist, 50*(10), 859–877.

Solano-Flores, G., & Nelson-Barber, S. (2001). On the cultural validity of science assessments. *Journal of Research in Science Teaching, 38*(5), 553–573.

Samuda, R. J. (1989). Psychometric factors in the appraisal of intelligence. In R. J. Samuda & S. L. Kong (Eds.), *Assessment and placement of minority students* (pp. 25–40). Toronto, Canada: C.J. Hogrefe.

Scanlon, D. M., Vellutino, F. R., Small, S. G., Fanuele, D. P., & Sweeney, J. M. (2005). Severe reading difficulties — can they be prevented? A comparison of prevention and intervention approaches. *Exceptionality, 13*(4), 209–227.

Shelton, N. R., Altwerger, B., & Jordan, N. (2009). Does DIBELS put reading first? *Literacy Research and Instruction, 48*(2), 137–148.

Shepard, L., Hammerness, K., Darling-Hammond, L., & Rust, F. (2005). Assessment. In L. Darling-Hammond & J. Bransford (Eds.), *Preparing teachers for a changing world: What teachers should learn and be able to do* (pp. 275–326). San Francisco: Jossey-Bass.

Solano-Flores, G. (2006). Language, dialect, and register: Sociolinguistics and the estimation of measurement error in the testing of English-language learners. *Teachers College Record, 108*(11), 2354–2379.

Solano-Flores, G. (2008). Who is given tests in what language by whom, when, and where? The need for probabilistic views of language in the testing of English language learners. *Educational Researcher, 37*(4), 189–199.

Solano-Flores, G., Trumbull, E., & Nelson-Barber, S. (2002). Concurrent development of dual language assessments: An alternative to translating tests for linguistic minorities. *International Journal of Testing, 2*(2), 107–129.

Stuebing, K. K., Fletcher, J. M., LeDoux, J. M., Lyon, G. R., Shaywitz, S. E., & Shaywitz, B. A. (2002). Validity of IQ-discrepancy classifications of reading disabilities: A meta-analysis. *American Educational Research Journal, 39,* 469–518.

Tanzer, N. K. (2005). Developing tests for use in multiple languages and cultures: A plea for simultaneous development. In R. Hambleton, P. Merenda, & C. D. Spielberger (Eds.), *Adapting educational and psychological tests for cross-cultural assessment.* Mahwah, NJ: Erlbaum.

Taylor, B. M., Pearson, P. D., Clark, K., & Walpole, S. (2000). Effective schools and accomplished teachers: Lessons about primary grade reading instruction in low-income schools. *Elementary School Journal, 101*(2), 121–165.

Taylor, B., Short, R., Shearer, B., & Frye, B. (2007). First grade teachers provide early reading intervention in the classroom. In R. L. Allington & S. A. Walmsley (Eds.), *No quick fix: Redesigning literacy programs in America's elementary schools, The RTI edition* (pp.159–178). New York: Teachers College Press.

Taylor, D., & Dorsey-Gaines, C. (1988). *Growing up literate: Learning from inner-city families.* Portsmouth, NH: Heinemann.

Valdés, G., & Figueroa, R. A. (1994). *Bilingualism and testing: A special case of bias.* Norwood, NJ: Ablex.

Vellutino, F., Scanlon, D., & Small, S., & Fanuele, D. (2006). Response to intervention as a vehicle for distinguishing between children with and without reading disabilities: Evidence for the role of kindergarten and first-grade interventions. *Journal of Learning Disabilities, 39*(2), 157–169.

Vellutino, F. R., Scanlon, D. M., Zhang, H., & Schatschneider, C. (2008). Using response to kindergarten and first grade intervention to identify children at-risk for long-term reading difficulties. *Reading and Writing: An Interdisciplinary Journal, 21,* 437–480.

Wiley, T. G. (1996). *Literacy and language diversity in the United States.* Washington, DC: Center for Applied Linguistics and Delta Systems.

49

Assessing the English Language Learner (ELL)

Lee Gunderson, Dennis Murphy Odo, and Reginald D'Silva

The Growth of ELL (ESL)

The number of human beings who speak a language other than English continues to increase in the United States, Canada, and Australia, for example, as the number of immigrants grows. In 2006, 34.70% of the population of Los Angeles, California, was foreign born; 25.50% of Miami, Florida; 39.60% of Vancouver, British Columbia; 45.70% of Toronto, Ontario; 28.90% of Melbourne, Australia; and 31.70% of Sydney, Australia (Statistics Canada, 2008). In the United States, the National Center for Education Statistics (NCES, 2004) reported that "The number and percentage of language minority youth and young adults— that is, individuals who speak a language other than English at home—increased steadily in the United States between 1979 and 1999" (p. 1). NCES added,

> Of those individuals ages 5–24 in 1979, 6 million spoke a language other than English at home. By 1999, that number had more than doubled, to 14 million. Accordingly, of all 5- to 24-year-olds in the United States, the percentage who were language minorities increased from 9 percent in 1979 to 17 percent in 1999. (p. 1)

The number of ESL students in U.S. public schools has almost tripled over the last decade (Goldenberg, 2006). In 2004 Crawford observed that one-fourth of the school-age students in the United States were from homes where a language other than English was spoken. The school-age population (K–12) will reach about 40% ESL in about 20 years (Center for Research on Education, Diversity, and Excellence, 2002). Between 1990 and 2000, the number of Spanish speakers increased from about 20 to 31 million (U.S. Census Bureau, 2001). The Census Bureau report also showed a significant increase in the number of speakers from other linguistic groups, particularly Chinese and Russian. Individuals at all ages enter school to learn the English skills they need to learn, gain employment and participate in society. Planning for their instruction is a

significant issue for teachers at all levels and assessment becomes central.

In this chapter we first define and differentiate terms such as ESL and ELL and describe the populations they represent. The use of assessment measures to place students into appropriate instructional groups is described and the distinction between interpersonal and academic language is reviewed. The use of assessment in the classroom and as a gate-keeping tool is addressed in addition to the appropriateness of the use of published measures to assess ESL students. The first issue addressed is terminology.

Defining ELL

Over the years students who speak a language other than English have been titled English as a Second Language (ESL) learners. However, English in some cases is not the second language (L2), but may be the third (L3), the 4th (L4), etc., language, and, as a result, members of this population have different linguistic resources to draw on. The term "English Language Learner" (ELL) has been adopted by educators, primarily in the United States, to describe better the notion that English may not be the L2. However, it is not a particularly good term because students who speak English as a First Language (L1) are also English language learners (Gunderson, 2008). The term "Teaching English to Speakers of Other Languages" (TESOL) is used outside of the United States. Students who learn English in environments where it is not the language of the community are referred to as English as a Foreign Language (EFL) students. The pedagogy related to EFL is different from ESL (ELL) because students are not immersed in English in the community and the major task of the teacher is to try to provide them English models (Gunderson, 2008, 2009). An added difficulty with the term "ESL" or "ELL" is that it does not adequately characterize the diversity of human beings it represents. Those who use the term "ELL" do so to describe those K–12 students who come from homes in which the language used for daily communications is not English and who must learn English to succeed in schools where the medium of instruction is English.

The ELL (ESL) Population

A serious problem with the ELL (ESL) conceptualization is that it does not adequately describe the underlying complexities of differences in age, motivation, literacy background, and first and second language achievement (Gunderson, 2008, 2009). Those classified as ELL or ESL vary in age from pre-school to senior adults. Many speak no English at all, while others vary in oral English proficiency. Many have never attended school, while others have earned high academic credentials in the language of instruction in their home countries. They are from diverse cultural backgrounds that vary in the way they perceive the importance of teaching and learning. Many are immigrants to an English-speaking country, while many ELL learners are born in an English-speaking country, but speak a different language at home (Gunderson, 2008, 2009). Indeed, in the Vancouver, Canada, school district 60% of the kindergarten students are ESL and 60% of this number are born in Canada (Gunderson, 2007, 2009). Many immigrant ESL students come from impoverished refugee backgrounds, others have high levels of education and socioeconomic status. Thus, ESLs or ELLs do not adequately represent the underlying complexity of the human beings in the category.

Assessment Issues in ELL

Instruction in mainstream classes, those typically enrolling students of different abilities but of the same relative age in the same classrooms, is based broadly on the notion that the acquisition of English is developmental and occurs over time as human beings grow into maturity. It is also thought that there is a relationship between language development and "grade level." Grade 1 students differ from Grade 7 students in systematic ways. Their teachers design instruction that is appropriate for their grade levels. ESL (ELL) students represent a more complex problem because their English and their cultural and learning backgrounds vary in many different ways, even in individuals who are the same chronological age (Gunderson, 2009). In addition, Cummins (1979a, 1979b, 1981, 1983, 2000) and Cummins and Swain (1986) argued there are two basic kinds of English a learner has to learn; "basic interpersonal communicative skill" [BICS] and "cognitive academic language proficiency" [CALP], the language of instruction and academic texts. BICS appears to take about 2 to 3 years to develop and CALP about 5 to 7. "Hello, how are you?" and "What is your name" represent BICS, while "Identify a current controversial world political issue and develop and defend your position" is an example of CALP.

Teachers are faced with the task of determining what learning activities and materials are appropriate for instruction and measurement of learning, while institutions such as universities and some governments are interested in determining whether or not an individual's English ability is advanced enough for them to either enter a post-secondary program or to have the skills necessary to be integrated into a society and, therefore, be eligible to immigrate. Thus, in some instances, assessment serves to guide learning by informing teachers of students' needs while in others it serves as a gatekeeper by excluding those who do not meet its standards.

Instructional Levels—Determining Appropriate Instructional Strategies

Language teachers have for some time opted to assess their students to ascertain their "level" of English language proficiency. The difficulty with the levels approach is that they do not really exist (Gunderson, 2009). A popular levels approach was developed in 1983 by the American Council for the Teaching of Foreign Languages (ACTFL). The assessment is a one-on-one assessment focusing primarily on oral language. Three levels of beginner, intermediate, and advanced are distinguished (see, ACTFL, 1983). A learner can be identified as a low beginner or a high intermediate, etc. The behaviors that determine inclusion in a particular group are usually described in an assessment matrix. The assessor asks a series of questions to elicit knowledge of vocabulary, syntax, and pragmatics. The following is an example of a matrix developed by Gunderson (2009) showing oral language "levels" and their attendant features.

0-Level English

a. Cannot answer even yes/no questions
b. Is unable to identify and name any object
c. Understands no English
d. Often appears withdrawn and afraid

Beginner

a. Responds to simple questions with mostly yes/no or one-word responses
b. Speaks in 1–2 word phrases
c. Attempts no extended conversations
d. Seldom, if ever, initiates conversations

Intermediate

a. Responds easily to simple questions
b. Produces simple sentences
c. Has difficulty elaborating when asked
d. Uses syntax/vocabulary adequate for personal, simple situations
e. Occasionally initiates conversations

Advanced

a. Speaks with ease
b. Initiates conversations
c. May make phonological or grammatical errors, which can then become fossilized
d. Makes errors in more syntactically complex utterances
e. Freely and easily switches codes

More elaborate approaches involve the assessment of English listening, speaking, reading and writing skills, e.g., the Canadian Language Benchmarks (CCLB, 2007).

The notion of levels is an important one for teachers because they are thought to predict a student's probability of succeeding within a particular teaching and learning environment. A beginner is different from an intermediate in various ways, and the instruction they are involved in is also different. Teachers often refer to ESL students as Level 1 or Level 5, depending upon their performance on an assessment measure. The notion of levels varies widely from jurisdiction to jurisdiction. In some cases there are 3, 4, 5, 8, or 10 levels, which are determined most often by locally developed informal assessment measures (Gunderson & Murphy Odo, 2010). Good assessment is essential to the design of appropriate instructional programs. The difficulty for classroom teachers is that there are few, if any, appropriate measures for them to use.

Classroom Assessment

Black and William (1998) reviewed more than 250 studies and found that there was a relationship between good classroom assessment and student performance. Most classroom-based assessment has been developed by teachers (Frisby, 2001; Wiggins, 1998). Unfortunately, most teachers report they are unprepared to assess and teach ESL students (Fradd & Lee, 2001). According to Pierce (2002), the majority of teachers employ assessments they remember they were involved in when they were in school: multiple-choice, cloze-like measures, matching, and true/false tests. This seems to have been the pattern for 50 years (Bertrand, 1994). Unfortunately, it seems, "... many teachers are unprepared for the special needs and complexities of fairly and appropriately assessing ELLs" (Ehlers-Zavala, Daniel, & Sun-Irminger, 2006, p. 24). Gunderson and Murphy Odo (2010) have recently reviewed the measures used by teachers in 12 local school districts to assess ESL students. The number of different measures and approaches in use was surprising. The Idea Proficiency Test (IPT) (see Ballard, Dalton, & Tighe, 2001a, 2001b) was the measure most often used for primary level ESL students. Other assessments mentioned were the Brigance, (1983) the Bilingual Syntax Measure (Burt, Dulay, & Hernández, 1976), the Woodcock Reading Mastery Test (Woodcock, various dates), the Woodcock-Munoz (Woodcock-Munoz-Sandoval, 1993), the Pre-IPT, the Comprehensive English Language Test (CELT; Harris & Palmer, 1986), informal reading inventories, the Waddington Diagnostic Reading Inventory (Waddington, 2000), the Alberta Diagnostic Reading Inventory, the SLEP, the Gap (McLeod & McLeod, 1990), PM Benchmarks (a system for placing students in leveled books), the RAD (Reading Achievement District—a local assessment measure), the Peabody Picture Vocabulary Test (PPVT; Dunn & Dunn, 1997), and a variety of locally developed listening, speaking, reading, and writing assessments. A serious difficulty is that most of these measures were not designed to provide

ESL instructional levels so different heuristics in different districts were developed to translate them into levels. The designation "beginner," for instance, varies significantly across districts as a result of the measures involved and the number of levels districts chose to identify. Two school districts reported the development and norming of tests for elementary and secondary students comprised of leveled passages taken from academic textbooks that were transformed into maze passages (see Guthrie, Seifert, Burnham, & Caplan, 1974). Scores from these measures were used to compute ESL levels; four in one case and five in the other. Interestingly, different metrics were used to compute instructional levels. So, for instance, a CELT score was used to determine ESL levels based on local intuition and experience. Most often the locally developed assessments involved one-on-one interviews in which students respond to tasks that require recognition of colors, body parts, school items, and the ability to answer simple questions (see, for example, Gunderson, 2009). There are also standardized assessments used by personnel at post-secondary institutions to make decisions concerning admissions to their programs.

Predicting Academic Success

The best known standardized English assessment measure is the Test of English as a Foreign Language (TOEFL) published by Educational Testing Service (ETS). The publisher notes:

> In fact, more institutions accept TOEFL test scores than any other test scores in the world — more than 7,000 colleges, universities and licensing agencies in more than 130 countries, to be exact. (ETS, 2009a)

There are different forms of the TOEFL. The classic paper-and-pencil form had standardized scores with 500 being the mean and 50 being the standard deviation. There are newer versions including a computer- and an Internet-based version that have different scoring criteria (see score comparison tables (ETS, 2009b)). The online version is based on a "communicative competence" model that requires learners to view clips of science lessons, for example, take notes, and respond to questions.

TOEFL scores are used by post-secondary institutions to screen students for admission to their programs. The criteria for admission to programs varies from institution to institution and among departments in institutions (see, for instance, University of British Columbia, 2009). There is evidence that TOEFL scores are not highly predictive of success in university (Al-Musawi & Al-Ansari, 1999), however, although they continue to be used to do so. ETS also produces the Test of English for International Communication (TOEIC) and the Secondary Level English Proficiency (SLEP), both standardized assessment measures. The primary users of the SLEP are secondary teachers. The SLEP "measures the ability to understand spoken English," and "the ability to understand written English" focusing on grammar, vocabulary, and reading comprehension (ETS, 2009c).

The International English Language Testing System (IELTS) is a test of English language proficiency developed by the University of Cambridge Local Examinations Syndicate (2009). There are two versions: individuals who want to gain admission to a university in an English-speaking country take the academic version, while the other version is appropriate for trade schools and other purposes. Scores range from 1 to 9 with 1 being zero-level English, while 9 indicates native-like ability. Different universities require different IELTS scores to be eligible for admission. Both ETS and Cambridge have international centers around the world where students can take these tests. ELL assessment issues and standardized testing are procedures relevant to large-scale achievement testing in the United States.

Large Scale or High-Stakes Testing

According to Abedi, Hofstetter, and Lord (2004), "Historically, English language learners in the United States were excluded from participation in large-scale student assessment programs; there were concerns about the confounding influences of language proficiency and academic achievement" (p. 1). However, the United States has seen a focus on large-scale assessments due to the accountability requirements of the No Child Left Behind Act of 2001 (PL 107-110). No Child Left Behind permits assessing ELLs in their first language for up to 3 years, but few states do. In 2005 a group of school districts sued the state of California to force it to allow Spanish-speaking students to take state-mandated tests in Spanish. Plaintiffs in Coachella Valley Unified School District v. California argued that the state "violated its duty to provide valid and reliable academic testing" (King, 2007). On July 30, 2009, "The First District Court of Appeal in San Francisco rejected arguments by bilingual-education groups and nine school districts that English-only exams violate a federal law's requirement that limited-English-speaking students 'shall be assessed in a valid and reliable manner'" (Egelko, 2009).

A lawyer for the school districts and advocacy groups stated,

> The court dodges the essential issue in the lawsuit, which is: What is the testing supposed to measure? If you don't have to evaluate the testing, California gets a free pass on testing kids (who) don't speak English, using tests that they have literally no evidence of their validity. (Egelko, 2009)

The ruling was that "The law does not authorize a court to act as "the official second-guesser" of the reliability of a state's testing methods." The difficulty is that English measures are neither reliable nor valid when ESL students are involved. In some cases, accommodations are made for them.

The procedures of providing ELL students accommodations during assessment sessions varies across jurisdictions, but includes such activities as lengthening the time allowed to take a test, allowing ELLs to be tested in separate rooms, allowing students to use bilingual dictionaries, the use of two versions of the test at the same time written in English and students' first languages, providing oral translations for students, and composing responses in first languages. In 1998–1999, 39 states reported using test accommodations (Rivera, Stansfield, Scialdone, & Sharkey, 2000). There is considerable controversy about providing accommodations, however. At the time of the writing of this chapter, accommodating students through the provision of L1 assessments has been judged not to be required.

ELLs, Assessment, and Technology

Advances in technology have made it possible for assessments to be administered as computer- or Internet-based measures. These developments have already taken place with measures such as the TOEFL (see above). An increasing use of technology to administer standardized and non-standardized assessments has raised interest in issues relating to mode-effects (e.g., computer displays versus print form) and familiarity with computers, which have significant implications for ELLs. There is evidence that performance in paper-based and computer-based modes of assessment may vary due to ethnicity or gender (Gallagher, Bridgeman, & Cahalan, 2002). In addition, familiarity with computers is known to influence performance in writing (Horkay, Bennett, Allen, Kaplan, & Yan, 2006) and mathematics (Bennett et al., 2008) high-stakes tests. These issues need to be taken into consideration with ELLs particularly immigrant and refugee students. A related problem has to do with access. Indeed, access to computer and/or to the Internet is widely varied and, therefore, creates systematic differences in access. These are all areas that need further research.

The State of the Art of ELL Assessment Research

As noted above, the category ESL or ELL is deceptive in that it represents millions of human beings who vary in age, first-language development, English achievement (both interpersonal and academic), educational backgrounds, immigration status, motivation, socioeconomic background, cultural views of teaching and learning, professional backgrounds, and social and academic aspirations. It is not, therefore, possible to review the breadth and depth of available research in this chapter. There are, however, some overall generalizations that can be made.

Generally, the assessment practices and approaches designed for and used with native English speakers have been adopted and used with ELL students. This phenomenon is especially apparent in jurisdictions such as the United States where high-stakes assessments have become so important. There are serious validity and reliability concerns associated with this practice. It is not clear that the notion of accommodation, one borrowed from special education, helps in either case. Leung and Lewkowicz (2008) argue that this "common educational treatment irrespective of differences in language backgrounds" (p. 305) is emblematic of the view that both treatment and assessment should be inclusive. It does not account, among other features, for cultural differences that can cause difficulties for ESL students (Fox, 2003; Fox & Cheng, 2007; Norton & Stein, 1998).

Overall, English proficiency is a significant variable in ELL assessment. In addition to the BICS/CALP distinction mentioned above, Bailey (2005) proposes that there is a language of tests that is a different "register" or "discourse domain." The use of such language creates a problem of "face validity." Is the test actually testing what it is designed to test or is it a test of the language of tests?

English as a Foreign Language (EFL) students around the world are assessed using many of the same measurements that are used to assess ELL students. EFL students are enrolled in programs in non-English contexts such as Japan where the language of the community is not English. They do not have ready access to native models of English that ELL students usually do. This is very much like the way students learn Latin in secondary school. It appears that EFL assessments are generally used to measure oral language ability such as the ACTFL mentioned previously.

Our review of the assessment procedures and methods in use in K–12 schools in 12 school districts raised several issues that related to ESL learners' assessment that were not found in studies such as Bertrand (1994), so we present them here. First, we found that there was a need for a measure that would discriminate students with language pathologies and/or learning disabilities from those who only needed English instruction. District members also expressed the need for a reliable measure to sort out secondary students' content knowledge and their linguistic knowledge. Lastly, they contended that assessment should be developed to isolate ESL students' specific areas of weakness so that teachers could more effectively use them to guide instruction.

Summary and Conclusions

The use ELL or ESL is unfortunate because it masks the underlying complexity of the human beings included in the category. ELL is inaccurate as a term because native English-speaking adults continue to be English language learners well into old age. Perceptions and pedagogical prescriptions are the most troubling aspects of the use of these terms. In article after article the ESL or ELL is used as though they represent a homogenous group of human beings. Pedagogical recommendations are made on the notion that they are a single group with the same skills and abilities. Of course, this is far from the truth. Our experience is that teachers use the term to represent all students who speak English as an additional language. In addition, they appear to perceive ESL students as human beings who have trouble learning to read (English). And this too, is far from the truth for some students, but not for others. ESL (ELL) is a term that should either be qualified when used or discarded as a general term.

The assessment of ELL/ESL/EFL learners is a significant foundational process for teachers to determine the appropriate teaching and learning programs for their students from kindergarten to the mature adult level. ELL assessment traditionally includes measures of listening, speaking, reading, and writing. There are three basic kinds of assessment instruments. The first is purely instructional in that it is designed to indicate the level at which students should be placed for instruction. The second type of measure is designed to provide an estimate of proficiency related to norm groups and involves scores such as percentiles and NCEs. The third is designed to provide predictive information concerning how well a student will succeed academically. Unfortunately, it appears that most measures are based on native English models. Another difficulty is that students' English proficiency has a profound effect on their ability to succeed on a test. It is often difficult for a student to succeed on a test when the language of the test is difficult or unknown to them. Some have noted that the language of tests is also unique.

Recently, assessment measures have been computerized and some have been put on the Internet. This raises serious questions of access, especially for students from countries where access is difficult or non-existent. For example, we have been told that the cost of taking an online test in a country like Zimbabwe is prohibitive.

Educators from many jurisdictions have borrowed the concept of accommodation from special education to make the assessment procedures fair to ELLs who differ in various ways from native English speakers. There is disagreement concerning the validity of test results as a result of accommodations since they are not often included in the norming procedures of the instruments. We have heard some opine that accommodation is not itself fair, and that the results of standardized assessment provide information about how well students will do in an English-speaking instructional setting.

It has been recommended that assessment measures be constructed that are written in different first languages. Some have argued that the number of first languages in schools would make this an expensive and impractical approach. In July 2009 the use of English-only assessment measures was upheld in a federal appeals court in California.

It is clear from a review of existing assessment practices that school-based personnel use a wide variety of instruments and procedures. It is also clear that there is the belief that it is important to identify a student's "English level" for instructional purposes, but there is little agreement on how many levels should be identified. The precise process for determining a level is somewhat fuzzy, but it involves the interpretation of a variety of scores from a variety of tests.

The research base concerning ELL assessment is not substantial. It focuses on measures originally designed for native English speakers. They do not do well generally on such measures. Indeed, they do not do well in school and a great number drops out, particularly from lower socioeconomic groups. The state of the art of assessment and instruction involving ELLs is extremely dire. The issues of ELL assessment needs urgent attention since ELLs are the most rapidly growing group in our schools.

References

Abedi, J., Hofstetter, C. G., & Lord, C. (2004). Assessment accommodations for English language learners: Implications for policy-based empirical research. *Review of Educational Research, 74,* 1–28.

Al-Musawi, N. M. &. Al-Ansari, S. H. (1999). Test of English as a foreign language and first certificate of English tests as predictors of academic success for undergraduate students at the University of Bahrain. *System, 27*(3), 389–399.

American Council for the Teaching of Foreign Languages (ACTFL). (1983). *ACTFL proficiency guidelines.* Hastings-on-Hudson, NY: ACTFL Materials Center.

Bailey, A. L. (2005). Language analysis of standardized tests: Considerations in the assessment of English language learners. In J. Abedi, A. Bailey, M. Castellon-Wellington, S. Leon, & J. Mirocha (Eds.), *The validity of administering large-scale content assessments to English language learners: An investigation from three perspectives* (pp. 79–100). Los Angeles: Center for Research on Evaluation/National Center for Research on Evaluation, Standards, and Student Testing (CRESSR).

Ballard, W., Dalton, E., & Tighe, P. (2001a). *IPT I oral grades K-6 examiner's manual.* Brea, CA: Ballard & Tighe.

Ballard, W., Dalton, E., & Tighe, P. (2001b). *IPT I oral grades K-6 technical manual.* Brea, CA: Ballard & Tighe.

Bennett, R. E., Braswell, J., Oranje, A., Sandene, B., Kaplan, B., & Yan, F. (2008). Does it matter if I take my mathematics test on computer? A second empirical study of mode effects in NAEP. *The Journal of Technology, Learning and Assessment, 6*(9), 1–40.

Bertrand, J. E. (1994). Student assessment and evaluation. In B. Harp (Ed.), *Assessment and evaluation for student centered learning* (pp. 27–45). Norwood, MA: Christopher-Gordon.

Black, O., & William, D. (1998). Inside the black box: Raising standards through classroom assessment. *Phi Delta Kappan, 80*(2), 141–148.

Burt, M. K., Dulay, H. C., & Hernández, E. (1976). *Bilingual syntax measure.* New York: Harcourt Brace Javonovich

Brigance, A. H. (1983). Brigance Comprehensive Inventory of Basic Skills II (CIBS II). North Billerica, MA: Curriculum Associates.

Cambridge University Press. (2009). IELTS catalogue. Retrieved July 14, 2010, from http://www.cambridgeesol.org/

Centre for Canadian language benchmarks (CCLB). (2007). Canadian language benchmarks. Retrieved August 10, 2009, from http://www.language.ca/display_page.asp?page_id=206

Center for Research on Education Diversity and Excellence. (2002). A national study of school effectiveness for language minority students' long-term academic achievement final report. Retrieved August 10, 2009, from http://www.crede.ucsc.edu/research/llaa/1.1_final.html

Cummins, J. (1979a). Cognitive/academic language proficiency, linguistic interdependence, the optimum age question and some other matters. *Working Papers on Bilingualism, 19,* 175–205.

Cummins, J. (1979b). Linguistic interdependence and the educational development of bilingual children. *Review of Educational Research, 49*(2), 222–251.

Cummins, J. (1981). Age on arrival and immigrant second language learning in Canada: A reassessment. *Applied Linguistics, 2*(2), 132–149.

Cummins, J. (1983). Language proficiency and academic achievement. In J. W. Oller (Ed.), *Issues in language testing research* (pp. 108–129). Rowley, MA: Newbury House.

Cummins, J. (2000). *Language, power and pedagogy.* Toronto, ON: Multilingual Matters.

Cummins, J., & Swain, M. (1986). Linguistic interdependence: A Central principle of bilingual education. In J. Cummins & M. Swain (Eds.), *Bilingualism in education* (pp. 80–95). New York: Longman.

Crawford, J. (2004). *Educating English learners: Language diversity in the classroom* (5th ed.). Los Angeles: Bilingual Educational Services.

Dunn, L. M., & Dunn, D. M. (1997). *Peabody picture vocabulary test.* San Antonio, TX: Pearson.

Educational Testing Service (ETS). (2009a). TOEFL® Internet-based Test (iBT). Retrieved August 10, 2009, from http://www.ets.org/portal/site/ets/menuitem.1488512ecfd5b8849a77b13bc3921509/?vgnextoid=f138af5e44df4010VgnVCM10000022f95190RCRD&vgnextchannel=b5f5197a484f4010VgnVCM10000022f95190RCRD

Educational Testing Service (ETS). (2009b). TOEFL® Internet-based Test (iBT). Retrieved August 10, 2009, from http://www.ets.org/Media/Tests/TOEFL/pdf/TOEFL_iBT_Score_Comparison_Tables.pdf

Educational Testing Service (ETS). (2009c). SLEP — Secondary Level English Proficiency. Retrieved August 10, 2009, from http://www.ets.org/portal/site/ets/menuitem.1488512ecfd5b8849a77b13bc3921509/?vgnextoid=e9d52d3631df4010VgnVCM10000022f95190RCRD&vgnextchannel=04dd197a484f4010VgnVCM10000022f95190RCRD

Egelko, B. (2009, July 30). Court says English-only tests ok in schools. The San Francisco Chronicle. Retrieved from http://www.sfgate.com/cgi-bin/article.cgi?f=/c/a/2009/07/30/BAIJ191KB0.DTL

Ehlers-Zavala, F., Daniel, M. C., & Sun-Irminger, X. (2006). Assessing English-language learners in mainstream classrooms. *The Reading Teacher, 60*(1), 24–34.

Fox, J. (2003). From products to process: An ecological approach to bias detection. *International Journal of Testing, 3,* 21–48.

Fox, J., & Cheng, L. (2007). Did we take the same test? Differing accounts of the Ontario Secondary School Literacy Test by first (L1) and second (L2) language test takers. *Assessment in Education, 14,* 9–26.

Frad, S. H., & Lee, O. (2001). Needed: A framework for integrating standardized and informal assessment for students developing academic language proficiency in English. In S. R. Hurley & J. V. Tinajero (Eds.), *Literacy assessment of second language learners* (pp. 130–148). Boston: Allyn & Bacon.

Frisby, C. L. (2001). Academic achievement. In L. A. Suzuki, J. G. Pomterotto, & P. J. Meller (Eds.), *Handbook of multicultural assessment* (2nd ed., pp. 541–568). San Francisco: Jossey-Bass.

Gallagher, A., Bridgeman, B., & Cahalan, C. (2002). The effect of computer-based tests on racial-ethnic and gender groups. *Journal of Educational Measurement, 39*(2), 133–147

Goldenberg, C. (2006, July). Improving achievement for English-learners: What the research tells us. *Education Week, 25,* 34–36.

Gunderson, L. (2007). *English-only instruction and immigrant students in secondary schools: A critical examination.* Mahwah, NJ: Erlbaum.

Gunderson, L. (2008, November). The state of the art of secondary ESL teaching and learning. *Journal of Adolescent and Adult Literacy, 52*(3), 184–188,.

Gunderson, L. (2009). ESL (ELL) literacy instruction: A guidebook to theory and practice (2nd ed.). New York: Routledge.

Gunderson, L., & Murphy Odo, D. (2010). A survey of ESL assessments used in 14 local school districts (manuscript in preparation).

Guthrie, J. T., Seifert, M., Burnham, N., & Caplan, R. (1974). The maze technique to monitor reading comprehension. *The Reading Teacher, 28*(2), 161–168.

Harris, D. P., & Palmer, L. (1986). *CELT examiner's instructions and technical manual.* New York: McGraw-Hill.

Horkay, N., Bennett, R. E., Allen, N., Kaplan, B., & Yan, F. (2006). Does it matter if I take my writing test on computer? An empirical study of mode effects in NAEP. *The Journal of Technology, Learning and Assessment, 5*(2), 1–50.

King, M. (2007, May 22). English-only tests, judge rules. Santa Cruz Sentinel. Retrieved from http://www.santacruzsentinel.com/archive/2007/May/22/local/stories/04local.htm

Leung, C., & Lewkowicz (2008). Assessing second/additional language of diverse populations. In E. Sohamy & N. H. Hornberger (Eds.), *Encyclopedia of language and education* (2nd ed., Vol. 7, pp. 301–317). New York: Springer.

McLeod, J., & McLeod, R. (1990). *NewGAP*. Novato, CA: Academic Therapy Publications.

National Center for Education Statistics (NCES). (2004). Language minorities and their educational and labor market indicators — recent trends (report #2004-009). Washington, DC: U.S. Department of Education, Institute of Education Sciences.

Norton, B., & Stein, P. (1998). Why the "monkeys passage" bombed: Test, genres and teaching. In A. Kunnan (Ed.), *Validation in language assessment* (pp. 231–249). Mahwah, NJ: Erlbaum.

Pierce, L. V. (2002). Performance-bases assessment: Promoting achievement for English language learners. *ERIC/CLL News Bulletin, 26*(1), 2–7.

Rivera, C., Stansfield, C. W., Scialdone, L., & Sharkey, M. (2000). *An analysis of state policies for the inclusion and accommodation of English language learners in state assessment programs during 1998–1999.* Arlington, VA: George Washington University, Center for Equity and Excellence in Education.

Statistics Canada. (2008). *2006 Census: Labour market activity, industry, occupation, education, and language of work place.* Ottawa, Canada: Statistics Canada.

University of British Columbia. (2009). Calendar: TOEFL and GRE Requirements. Retrieved August 10, 2009, from http://www.students.ubc.ca/calendar/index.cfm?tree=12,204,345,0

U.S. Census Bureau. (2001). Ability to speak English for U.S. residents ages 5–17, 2000. Retrieved December 18, 2006, from http://factfinder.census.gov/home/saff/main.html?_lang=en/

Waddington, N. J. (2000). *Diagnostic reading and spelling tests 1 & 2: A book of tests and diagnostic procedures for classroom teachers.* Strathalbyn, South Australia: Waddington Educational Resources.

Wiggins, G. (1998). *Educative assessment: Designing assessments to inform and improve students performance.* San Francisco: Jossey-Bass.

Woodcock, R. (Various dates). *The Woodcock reading mastery test.* New York: Pearson.

Woodcock, R., & Munoz-Sandoval, A. (1993). *Woodcock-Munoz language survey.* Itasca, IL: Riverside.

Section VII

Methods of Research on Teaching the English Language Arts

SECTION EDITORS
DAVID BLOOME, THANDEKA CHAPMAN, AND PETER FREEBODY

Section VII focuses on research methods, theoretical frameworks, and methodologies found in research concerning English language arts teaching and learning environments. The following chapters describe, analyze, and critique current research trends in the field of literacy education.

Bloome, Chapman, and Freebody assert that the previous emphasis on rigor and the enumeration of new approaches, methodologies, and methods, has shifted to a focus on complexity, multiplicity, and substantive engagement with the epistemological and ontological construction of teaching and teachers, learning and learners, and language and literacy. Through an analysis of the chapters in this section, Bloome et al. identify six ideas that mark an evolution in approaches to researching the teaching and learning of the English language arts.

Moss examines the use of ethnography in teaching and learning the English language arts. She describes the current and past research in ELA to discuss the possibilities and limitations of ethnographic research methods.

Willis explains the multiple relationships between critical theory and teaching ELA. She extends the lens of critical theory to current race-based legal theories that position race as the center of discussions concerning policy and practice in education.

Smagorinsky uses his experiences to call into question researchers' methodological choices in teaching and learning the English language arts. He asserts that researchers must create designs that fit the questions they are asking and the data they wish to collect concerning educational processes.

McNaughton highlights three distinct sets of child development studies to describe the different time frames for research. McNaughton provides a rationale for the use of the various time frames and explains what each of these sets of data provides to education researchers.

Liddicoat expresses the breach between the monolingual English-only researcher and the multilingual or non-English speaking participant. He details the problematic nature of conducting English-only research in a global context that does not value the multiplicity of languages found in schools, classrooms, and communities.

Gutierrez, Bien, and Selland advance the notion of using syncretic approaches to study conceptions of language and literacy in their research. They describe these approaches as an effort to seek "goodness of fit" between research methods and questions in an effort to provide more complex data and analysis in sociocultural education research approaches.

Chapman and Kinloch apply the constructs of "emic" and "etic" that originated in cultural linguistic research to current research they describe as intimate research. They explore various methodological approaches to research in teaching and learning English language arts to describe the ways in which researchers utilize insider perspectives and data specific to culture and context to present education research that resonates across the experiences of teachers and students in ELA.

Athanses highlights studies in K–12 ELA classes conducted by teachers practicing teacher inquiry. He draws on inquiry reports, studies of products and processes, and personal experiences with inquiry curriculum development, teaching, and research in preservice to pose questions concerning the nature of teacher inquiry.

Calfee and Chambliss emphasize the role of design in guiding the preparation, implementation, and reporting of data-based studies. The chapter has four sections: (a) framing a research question, (b) constructing a research design, (c) collecting and analyzing the data, and (d) making sense of the findings. They recommend a mixed-methods strategy as the most appropriate approach for dealing with the complex issues typical of research in the language arts arena.

Carter provides a brief description of Critical Discourse Analysis (CDA) and a review of its influences and histories. She emphasizes multiple approaches to CDA and foregrounds influences from European social theorists as well as Black scholars in the later 19th and early 20th centuries. Carter advocates for the use of CDA to examine power relations in teaching and learning the English language arts and to provide documentation of educational inequities that continue to persist in education settings.

Freebody interrogates the two sided nature of education research and policy, researching policy implementations, and influencing policy and legislation. He explores how conceptualizations of the scope and significance of language education and how different kinds of research designs yield different versions of education in the ELA and affect their applicability towards policy.

50

Complexity, Multiplicity, Timeliness, and Substantive Engagement

Methodologies for Researching the Teaching of the English Language Arts

*D*AVID *B*LOOME, *T*HANDEKA *C*HAPMAN, AND *P*ETER *F*REEBODY

In the last decade, a series of handbooks, textbooks, and special issues of journals dedicated to exploring methodology and methods in the social sciences and education have been published (e.g., Bloome et al., 2008; Cresswell, 2007; Dyson & Genishi, 2005; Green, Camilli, & Ellmore, 2006; Heath & Street, 2008; Kamberelis & Dimitriadis, 2004; Reinking & Bradley, 2007; Tashakkori & Teddlie, 1998; Willis et al., 2008; Yin, 2003). These have provided both the neophyte and the experienced educational researcher with valuable introductions and advanced discussions of the multiple research traditions, perspectives, and tools. As Smagorinsky (this volume) notes, unlike previous generations today's reading, writing, and literacy researchers are faced with a "virtually endless" array of approaches. The myriad approaches notwithstanding, discussion and debate of how to approach research on the teaching and learning of the English language arts continues to evolve. But where the emphasis had previously been on rigor and the enumeration of new approaches, methodologies, and methods, the current attention focuses on complexity, multiplicity, and substantive engagement with the epistemological and ontological construction of teaching and teachers, learning and learners, and language and literacy. These current foci are drawn from and implicit within the intricate learning experiences researchers are attempting to document. Teacher and student experiences and their questionable and contested learning outcomes compel researchers to ask complex questions that cannot be constrained by traditional quantitative and qualitative social science research models.

Evolving Toward Complexity, Multiplicity, and Substantive Engagement

A trend that can be noticed in recent methodological handbooks, texts, and journals is increasing emphasis on the use of multiple research traditions, perspectives, methodologies, and methods (Calfee & Chambliss, this volume). This direction is sometimes referred to as the use of complementary

approaches (see Green et al., 2006) or the use of mixed methods (Johnson & Onwuegbuzie, 2004). These two terms are not synonymous. The first refers to the principled construction of complementarities among differing perspectives about what counts as knowledge and how knowledge is generated. The second refers to the use of various methods (also described as tools and techniques), and how their use might be orchestrated within a particular research study or program of research. However, both directions share the initial focus on the learning contexts as the guiding principle for the research. The questions and methods are constructed to capture the experiences of English language arts classrooms, not to impose static research designs upon these sites and situations.

The chapters in this section reflect conversations concerning the trajectory of research in the field of English language arts and do not repeat what can be found in these handbooks texts, and journals. However, the chapters here do build upon the attention paid in these handbooks, textbooks, and journals to complementarity and mixed methods. Namely, there is growing recognition in the field of educational research generally, and in research on the teaching of the English language arts specifically, that the use of singular methodologies—regardless of how elegant their conduct and eloquent their rationale—are not up to providing the field with a sufficiently deep understanding of educational problems to allow educators and policy makers to address the needs of students and communities effectively (Gutierrez et al., this volume). Indeed, too often educational research has reified, reduced, and simplified the complex psychological, social, cultural, linguistic, and political nature of teaching and learning the English language arts. Too often, educational research has failed to take seriously what it means to locate teaching and learning in time and place. Students and teachers evolve and change over time as do the multiple layers of context in which they learn and teach. As a consequence, educational research has too often eschewed deep understanding of the complexity, multiple dimensions and layers (hereafter, multiplicity), and timeliness of educational problems in order to offer simple and simplistic policies, practices, and programs.

Similarly, in much of the educational research that has been used to inform educational policy and the professional development of teachers and in teachers' planning documents, patterns of practice are shared and debated in compact, idealized terms (e.g., teaching writing models, small-group writing session, inquiry-based projects, open classroom discussion, peer-tutoring mathematics worksheets). These idealizations might come from central or local policy documents, professional development experiences, teacher preparation programs, or from the cultural models of teaching and learning held by educators, parents, and others who too often look to program outcomes and ignore the learning journey. It is only through close, detailed research that embraces the complexity, multiplicity, and timeliness of teaching and learning can deep understandings be generated of how it is that features of everyday processes in classrooms (what teachers and students do together) provide or deny opportunities for and the take up of deep learning of academic discourses.

Each of the chapters in this section provides ways of approaching the complexity, multiplicity, and the need for substantive engagement in research on the teaching and learning of the English language arts. It is in this sense that the chapters in this edition of the *Handbook of Research on Teaching the English Language Arts* both build on and differ from the past edition. The chapters from the previous edition continue to inform and provide a base for our understandings of research perspectives, methodologies, and methods (as do the handbooks, textbooks, and journals noted earlier). But the field has evolved, and the optimism that a single perspective, methodology, or well-orchestrated use of methods, will provide the deep understanding needed by educators and policy makers to address trenchant educational problems is gone. Nor is there optimism that a simple parallel play of differing methods for different aspects will yield deep understanding. The notion that—if we could only be more rigorous, better orchestrate our research programs, better align theoretical framing with research questions and methods, employ more sophisticated software for data analysis and statistical modeling, etc.—no longer looks promising to those committed to sustainable and consequential change. Instead, educational researchers have begun to ask how can we theorize the logics-of-inquiry needed to capture the complexity, multiplicity, and timeliness of teaching and learning the English language arts. It is important to note that this is not a defenestration of what has come before, but rather an evolution grounded in our collective experiences in searching for substantive engagements that can lead to more promising educational policies and practices for teaching and learning the English language arts.

Additionally we recognize that the shift in education research is most often directly in conflict with the research required to receive government funding and influence

district policy initiatives. This shift epitomizes the age-old tensions between the academy and the public sphere of policy and large-scale implementation of practice. Thus research in English language arts remains a highly contested space for those researchers who bend and break methodological rules.

Reading Across the Chapters

The authors of the chapters in this section make clear that methodologies are not defined by the tools employed but by the epistemological and ontological assumptions researchers hold and by the theorizing that defines what teaching and learning the English language arts is (Calfee & Chambliss, this volume). They also make clear that such theorizing is not static but may evolve within a study (e.g., Athanases, this volume; Chapman & Kinloch, this volume; Gutierrez et al, this volume; Willis, this volume), over the course of a researcher's career (e.g., Smagorinsky, this volume), over decades as a field evolves (e.g., Carter, this volume; McNaughton, this volume; Moss, this volume; Smagorinsky, this volume; Liddicoat, this volume), as a function of concerted efforts to be more inclusive of diverse communities and histories (e.g., Willis, this volume; Carter, this volume; Gutierrez, this volume; Liddicoat, this volume), and as a function of the evolving interplay and tensions among research, policy, and practice (e.g., Freebody, this volume; McNaughton, this volume, Calfee & Chambliss this volume).

Reading across the chapters in this section, there are six ideas we highlight as marking an evolution in approaches to researching the teaching and learning of the English language arts. Not every chapter addresses all six, and each chapter considers important issues beyond the six listed below. These six ideas are not specific to a particular methodology or paradigm, although some are more prominent in some approaches to research than others. Before listing and discussing these six ideas, we note that when we invited these authors to write their chapters we did not envision these six ideas. They are ideas with long histories and are not, in and of themselves, new. What is new, however, is that they have moved to the center of discussion about how to frame methodologies for research in the teaching and learning of the English language arts.

1. Dialogic logics-of-inquiry. It is common place to look for coherence in a research study among the theoretical framing, the methodology, and the interpretation of findings. Without supplanting the importance of such coherence, the chapters in this section challenge the necessary linearity of such coherence. Athanases (this volume), Chapman and Kinloch (this volume), Smagorinsky (this volume), and Willis (this volume) argue that there is a dialectical relationship between theory and practice and among theory, methodology and data collection. Coherence may also involve a recursive relationship.

Coherence may also be defined as articulate and deep engagement in a "productive tension between convention and creativity, the aesthetic and the functional, acquisition, production, innovation, and critique" (Freebody, this volume). Liddicoat (this volume) adds another dimension to such a dialectic. He writes "A reflective research design is therefore one which considers how language, which is often the focus of investigation itself, positions the research participants, impacts on their identities and agent positions and (re)produces discourses of marginalisation or deficit." It will no longer do to treat the conduct of research as a procedural algorithm in which a theory yields a methodology that yields findings and interpretations. Instead, researchers need to reflect upon and respond to the relationships of theory, methodology, and findings, and the tensions that are created by difficulty in capturing the complexity, multiplicity, and timeliness of teaching and learning the English language arts in a substantive manner. Further, researchers need to push beyond single studies or even single programs of research, to look across cases, to look across time, and across research programs (McNaughton, this volume; Smagorinsky, this volume).

One way to describe the call for more dialogically oriented logics-of-inquiry is by analogy to Bakhtin's (1935/1981) concept of heteroglossia. For Bakhtin, the aesthetic and import of the novel derived from the multiple voices expressed. This included the voices of the various characters and narrators, but also the other voices implied from other novels, literary works, and from other sources including people's everyday lives. Every utterance of the novel reflects and refracts the past utterances of others from diverse locations. Similarly, the idea here is to recognize the "heteroglossia" involved in researching the teaching and learning of the English language arts, and to craft with it a coherence that will allow for substantive engagement.

2. The centrality of time. As McNaughton (this volume) notes, in attempting to understand language and literacy development, it is important to capture both historical change and individual change. In researching the teaching and learning of the English language arts, the time scales (cf. Lemke, 2000) involved may extend from a few minutes to decades; regardless, people and their contexts change over time. People do not exist in individual bubbles isolated from what is happening around them. They are complexly and multiply located in time. And while it may be difficult for any one study or program of research to capture both historical change and individual change over a significant period of time, as a field we need to recognize both dimensions and interpret our studies in a "timely" manner.

Time becomes a factor in the development of relationships during the research process. Researchers hesitate to enter a site for research without first building trust and rapport with the participants in ways that demonstrate their solidarity with the group (Willis, this volume). Teacher-research is often conducted as part of larger professional development projects that may occur over a significant amount of time (Athanases, this volume). Additionally, participant-researcher trust and study trustworthiness are strengthened and directly connected to time spent in the field.

3. Location matters. Although many classrooms may share some similar features, there are no generic classrooms. The particularities of each classroom matter as does its physical and social location within a school, within a local community, with a region, and a nation (Athanases, this volume). It makes a difference whether teachers and students are laboring under the nation-state policies of No Child Left Behind and Race to the Top or under the state policies of Literate Futures (Freebody, this volume). And, it makes a difference about how one location is related to another; how the classroom is related to the home and community (Moss, this volume). These locations and their relationships to each other serve as sites of knowledge reproduction and reconstruction. The context of learning is taken beyond the physical space of classrooms and shared with local community members, organizations, and resources (Chapman and Kinloch, this volume).

Although there has always been movement through immigration and various economically and politically driven changes, location may matter more so in contemporary educational research because of the increased pace of such movement and because of increased economic and cultural globalization. For many students, being in a place is always about the cultural and linguistic juxtaposition of where they are from, where they are now, and where they may be in the future (cf. Liddicoat, this volume). Additionally, students' connections between the school, home, and community are strained by the disparate locales they claim.

What constitutes the "local" is also influenced by people, events, and agendas that may be distant. It may often seem to teachers and students that people thousands of miles away want to manage what happens in their classroom; and, it may also be the case that teachers and students pull into the classroom ideas, frameworks, resources, etc., from distant places. The complexity and multiplicity of location affects what counts as knowledge, who has knowledge, the social, cultural, and linguistic identities of the teacher and the students (Moss, this volume), and re-framing traditional teacher-student roles in non-traditional learning spaces (Chapman and Kinloch, this volume). The local is no longer easy to define.

4. Language matters. Liddicoat (this volume) argues that there is an English monolingualism in research on the teaching and learning of the English language arts. Such monolingualism is not a technical matter to be solved by the hiring of translators, but rather is an epistemological bias. Too often, he argues, the knowledge and competence of students who are not native English speakers is under appreciated or overlooked. As importantly, the monolingualism of research studies frames the object of study in ways that distort what constitutes teaching and learning. Liddicoat argues that "the key issue in research design is not so much methodology as a reconceptualiation of what constitutes research practice in contexts of linguistic and cultural diversity."

Although not focused on the diversity of languages per se, Carter (this volume) and Freebody (this volume) raise similar issues. Language is both the object of study (the language teachers and students use in instructional conversations, the language of the literature they read, their writings, etc.) as well as the means by which research occurs (researchers ask questions, write field notes, conduct surveys, write up reports). For students and for researchers, language can constrain and control but it can also open up possibilities, liberate, and provide create potential. Carter (this volume) focuses attention on the analysis of talk and text by making visible the ways that language can constrain critical inquiry and negatively position students. Subtly (and sometimes not subtly at all), the wordings and ways teachers, students, and textbooks use language promote an epistemology and a world view that may privilege some at the expense of others (see also Willis, this volume). What is at issue here in research on the teaching and learning of the English language arts is not just the need to increased attention to such hegemonies but also the need to understand that such dynamics occur even when the topic of the study is focusing elsewhere.

5.   Knowledge is diversely located. Part of what is at stake in a research methodology is whose knowledge and whose histories count for generating a logic-of-inquiry (see Athanases, this volume; Carter, this volume; Freebody, this volume; Gutierrez et al., this volume; Liddicoat, this volume; Moss, this volume; Willis, this volume). This involves the knowledge students have and bring to the classroom and also the knowledge base employed by the field in constructing the logics-of-inquiry for research. For example, Carter (this volume) and Willis (this volume) argue that the roots of critical discourse analysis and of critical theory, respectively, do not lie just in European social theories. They point to intellectual histories of African American scholars and activists that also inform critical approaches. Athanses points to the knowledge teachers bring to researching teaching and learning and argues for "practice-based evidence" as part of the configuration in conceptualizing a logic-of-inquiry.

Action Research, teacher-led research, and students as researchers (Willis, this volume; Athanases, this volume; Chapman & Kinloch, this volume) are direct challenges to traditional modes of research. In these new amalgamations of research methods and methodologies the knowledge authority is placed inside the learning community, not in a distant physical space or with outside researchers. Teachers and students become the experts of their situations and are the motivated change agents to seek solutions to contemporary issues. The researcher becomes the facilitator and documenter of the process and outcomes rather than the primary tool of the research.

6.   Methodologies are motivated. By motivated we mean that they involve a particular way of seeing the world, a particular place from which to view the world, a particular language with which to characterize it, particular notions of epistemology and ontology, and a particular agenda. That methodologies are motivated do not make them pernicious nor does the notion of methodologies as motivated result in a limbo of relativity. Rather, to note that methodologies are motivated highlights the importance of a dialogic approach to conducting research, critical reflection on the limits of research, and the importance of looking across studies and programs of research.

Part of what is required in constructing a logic-of-inquiry on the teaching and learning of the English language arts is consideration of how the knowledge constructed in study travels. For example, Chapman & Kinloch (this volume) offer the construct of "fittingness," a process whereby potential consumers decide whether the knowledge from a research study fits their particular situation and how it might be adapted to their particular situation. What is at the heart of the concept of "fittingness" is a sense of respect and mutuality between the researcher and the people (the teachers and students) in the research study and with the consumers who might use the findings.

Willis examines the use of critical race theory as a framework for research in English language arts. This theory is unapologetically motivated by the centrality of race and racism, the researcher's epistemology, and the federal and local policies which affect the experiences of teachers and students.

Final Comments

Taken together, the chapters here raise a challenge to the field of research on teaching and learning the English language arts. How can we construct methodologies that capture the complexity, multiplicity, and timeliness of teaching and learning in a manner that allows researchers, educators, and the general public to have substantive engagement with what counts as knowledge, whose knowledge counts, when, where, and how? How can we construct a heteroglossic context for the conduct and use of research that has sufficient coherence to inform and move practice and policy forward without constraining the imaginations of teachers, students, and researchers? What does it mean to construct research in English language arts with such different approaches than what is being privileged in education policy?

As Freebody notes, research exists in the public sphere. What we do and how we do it is part of the public construction of civic society and culture. Like it or not, research has been incorporated into the public policy sphere and in controversial ways which hold serious consequences for teachers and students. Elmore (1996) has noted three "conceits" embodied in much educational policy and reform:

- the new policy automatically takes precedence over and replaces previous policies;
- policies emanate from a single level of a system and embody a single message about what educators should do differently; and
- policy can and should operate in more or less the same way in whatever settings it is implemented.

The question for researchers is: What type of research programs could begin to address these "conceits," could, perhaps, reveal them not only as "conceits" but as active obstacles to the reform of educational practice and policy in the English language arts? In order to be valuable to teachers and students and viable to policy makers, the field of English language arts requires that phenomena be studied in diverse and multiple ways that account for time, location, language, perspective, history, and innovative inquiry.

References

Bakhtin, M. (1981). *The dialogic imagination* (C. Emerson & M Holquist, Trans.). Austin: University of Texas Press. (Original work published 1935)

Bloome, D., Carter, S., Christian, B., Madrid, S., Otto, S., Shuart-Faris, N., et al. (2008). *On discourse analysis: Approaches to language and literacy research.* New York: Teachers College Press.

Cresswell, J. (2007). *Educational research: Planning, conducting, and evaluating quantitative and qualitative research.* Englewood Cliffs, NJ: Prentice-Hall.

Dyson, A., & Genishi, C. (2005). *On the case: Approaches to language and literacy research.* New York: Teachers College Press.

Elmore, R. F. (1996). Getting to scale with good educational practice. *Harvard Educational Review, 66,* 1–16.

Green, J., Camilli, G., & Ellmore, P. (Eds.). (2006). *Handbook of complementary methods in education research.* Mahwah, NJ: Erlbaum and AERA.

Heath, S., & Street, B. (2008). *On ethnography: Approaches to language and literacy research.* New York: Teachers College Press.

Johnson, R. B., & Onwuegbuzie, A. (2004). Mixed methods research: A research paradigm whose time has come. *Educational Researcher, 33*(7), 14–26.

Kamberelis, G., & Dimitriadis, G. (2004). On qualitative inquiry: *Approaches to language and literacy research.* New York: Teachers College Press.

Lemke, J. (2000). Across the scales of time: Artifacts, activities and meanings in ecosocial systems. *Mind, Culture and Activity, 7*(4), 273–290.

Reinking, D., & Bradley, B. (2007). On formative and design experiments: *Approaches to language and literacy research.* New York: Teachers College Press.

Tashakkori, A., & Teddlie, C. (1998). *Mixed methodology: Combining qualitative and quantitative approaches.* Thousand Oaks, CA: Sage.

Willis, A., Montavon, M., Hunter, C., Hall, H., Burke, L., & Herrera, A. (2008). *On critically conscious research: Approaches to language and literacy research.* New York: Teachers College Press.

Yin, R. (2003). *Case study research: Design and methods* (3rd ed.). Thousand Oaks, CA: Sage.

51

Research as Praxis

Documenting the Dialectical Relationship Between Theory and Practice

STEVEN Z. ATHANASES

…there is no such thing as teaching without research and research without teaching. One inhabits the body of the other. As I teach, I continue to search and re-search. I teach because I search, because I question, and because I submit myself to questioning. I research because I notice things, take cognizance of them. And in so doing, I intervene. And intervening, I educate and educate myself. I do research so as to know what I do not yet know and to communicate and proclaim what I discover. (Freire, 1998, p. 35)

Far from the common conception of a theory and practice divide in education, Freire (1998) frames teaching and research as intimately connected. He highlights the mutually informing nature of actions that include teach, notice, search, research, intervene, question, educate oneself, communicate, and proclaim. While these actions appear naturally linked for Freire, many teachers benefit from processes and tools that forge links to connect such actions. Among these processes is teacher inquiry. Grounded in Deweyan perspectives and reflective practice (Schön, 1983), teacher inquiry typically includes positioning practitioner as researcher rather than object of study, collaboration of participants in formal or informal inquiry communities, systematicity in gathering and analyzing data, and development of an inquiry stance of asking critical questions about practice and schools (Cochran-Smith & Lytle, 2009; Gore & Zeichner, 1991; Goswami, Lewis, Rutherford, & Waff, 2009; Valli et al., 2006). Some models and practices also foreground social justice as an inquiry goal (Fecho & Allen, 2003).

How has such inquiry been conducted by educators? How does inquiry serve teachers and their students? How might inquiry processes and products contribute to larger knowledge communities in education? These are questions I consider in this chapter. Though methods I discuss have been applied to practitioner inquiry beyond classrooms, I highlight studies in K–12 English language arts (ELA) classes conducted by teachers of those classes. I generally use the more specific term *teacher inquiry*, drawing on a

review of inquiry reports; studies of products and processes; and personal experience with inquiry curriculum development, teaching, and research in preservice. I highlight purposes and methods with ELA examples, raise issues, report innovations, and suggest ways to move ahead methodologically as a form of ELA research.

Dialoguing of Theory and Practice: How Teacher Inquiry Can Promote Praxis

Unlike much academic research arising from gaps in research knowledge or in theory development, teacher inquiry begins in practice. Inquiry often yields descriptions of practice and case studies, initiated in and often responding to a puzzling moment, event, or student (Ballenger, 2009; Gallas, 2003; Griffin, 2004). Puzzling moments lead the teacher to a focus or problem framing, followed by the collection of data that may include fieldnotes, interviews, taped discourse, and records of student work, interactions, and performance. The goal of such inquiry is development of new knowledge about a learner, a group of learners, or learning and teaching processes, and often for use in direct action. Often teacher inquiry moves from problem framing to specific designs for action to improve students' opportunities and achievement. Such work often includes baseline and exit data, generally in the form of student work, to frame actions or innovations designed to achieve results. Teachers who engage in multiple rounds of inquiry report a dynamic and dialectical tension between doing and reflecting on doing (Freire, 1998). Using analytic tools to examine artifacts of instruction and student behaviors and perceptions can promote conscious understanding to guide future actions and may lead to a kind of theory level of logical ordering and coherent framing to deeply understand a variety of similar situations (Korthagen, 2010). This theorizing also enables *praxis*, practice or action informed by knowledge and notions of change.

The notion of praxis began with Aristotle's work to

categorize three basic human activities, each with its own corresponding knowledge and goals. *Theoria*, or to view, spectate, or contemplate with clarity and dispassion, featured the theoretical, with the goal of truth. *Poiesis*, or to produce, featured the poetical, with the goal of making or creating. *Praxis* featured practical knowledge with the goal of action. Some definitions reduce praxis to application of theory, a unidirectional, top-down model of knowledge originating in contemplation and theory. However, many conceptions of praxis view theory and praxis as mutually informing, functioning in a recursive manner. Praxis, in such a view, is practice that is part of a system of critical reflection on action, in service of generating new knowledge and theory to again shape transformed action.

Many fields view praxis as actions textured with conscious thought. In fields as diverse as economics, political science, occupational therapy, theology, computer science, theatre, and curriculum theory, praxis signifies actions shaped by ideation, reflection, and planning. It is often informed by conceptual knowledge and, in some cases, prompted by concerns of social justice. Praxis in teacher inquiry is committed action informed by reflection, histories of educational ideas, nested contexts, and new knowledge constructed through systematic inquiry with data. One teacher researcher described how inquiry promotes theory and practice as mutually informing:

> Each shapes the other. My current understandings about how literacy is taught and learned shape decisions about my practice; my implementation of those decisions, aided by systematic reflection, further shapes my evolving theory. At times in this process, I have entered into a state of grace as theory and practice elegantly dialogued around me. At other times, I have limped along badly, aware of gaps and inconsistencies in the work of the classroom as it related to my theoretical understandings. (Fecho, 2004, p. 29)

Fecho's (2004) gaps and inconsistencies echo Freire's (1998) view of practice and theory as a dynamic, dialectical tension between doing and reflecting on doing. This tension, however, need not be as oppositional as depicted by Hegel's theory in which thesis faces antithesis in a cyclical manner. Praxis in teacher inquiry may yield Fecho's elegant dialoguing, or a dialectical union of reflection and action (Hoffman-Kipp, Artiles, & Lopez-Torres, 2003). When and how does teacher inquiry promote theory generation? Some argue that teachers' actions are always and already theory-driven and that reflection on praxis always constitutes theorizing. Others offer more complex analyses. Examination of one experienced teacher researcher's work illustrates the processes.

How an Experienced Teacher Used Teacher Inquiry to Theorize and Transform Practice

Through classroom inquiry in several U.S. locales, Gallas (2003) explored imagination and literacy. She began with a puzzling realization that a young student's reading comprehension problems appeared rooted in inexperience with imaginative play. For several years, Gallas drew on ethnographic methods that included collecting and analyzing fieldnotes and her own journal entries; audio- and videotaped (and often transcribed) classroom discourse and interviews with students; and children's writings, drawings, and other artifacts of work and play. Supported by a community of the Brookline Teacher Research Seminar (BTRS, 2004), Gallas especially examined transcripts in ways informed by a BTRS tenet that students were making sense, and it was the teacher researcher's job to understand what that sense was. Theoretical and empirical works shaped analyses and provided explanatory power: "Four approaches to literacy helped me clarify what I was seeing in my data" (Gallas, p. 62). For example, Gallas expanded her understanding of literacy acts to see them as parts of larger discourses and analyzed how discourse appropriation was intimately connected to children's engagement and developing sense of literate identities. She noted patterns in how students used texts and literacy tools, when and how students became part of a story, how they engaged in storytelling and drama, and how they learned to interact with books in imaginative ways. She especially reviewed data for examples of how imagination and embodied engagement with texts supported comprehension.

Gallas (2003) tapped other sources in featuring fidelity not to "the literature" but to understanding the role of imagination in literacy development. These included literary authors, social and psychological thinkers, verifiable and retrievable sources from wildly disparate fields. Also, a bank of classroom experiences was a key knowledge source in reviewing data: "This exchange was one I had seen before with these young writers; it is most probably one that other teachers of young children have also witnessed" (Gallas, p. 46). In this way, the more experienced teacher as researcher abstracts across time, events, and cases. Finally, Gallas explicitly examined ways she drew on life experiences, especially developing imagination in childhood, as yet another source as she worked to develop and refine a theory of imagination and literacy. Her culminating work, documented in a final section of her book, is an instantiation of how she used her developing theory to guide new action—ways she and her students engaged in praxis where imagination gets explicitly treated as tightly interwoven with literacy development. Gallas' work provides an exemplar for highlighting methods of teacher inquiry.

Methods, Knowledge Production, and Theory in Teacher Inquiry

Finding Focus and Problem Framing Because teacher inquiry often arises from puzzling students and events and from patterns in students' performance, an important puzzle, challenge, or problem generally shapes the inquiry once focused and framed. ELA inquiries range in focus. They include curricular concerns such as documenting children's growth in response to a curricular innovation. One such example was a study that used coding of children's story strategies to gauge cultural resources students brought to bear on narrative and how these evolved after curricular innovation in narrative writing (Heatley & Stronach, 2002). Inquiries include gender equity concerns such as diversifying writing genres primary students produce, and documenting impacts of such change on the writing and work habits of resistant boys (McPhail, 2009). Concerns of language and access play a role in inquiry conducted by Lew (1999) as she examined writing by a second language learner completed in 9th and 12th grades and interviewed the student about her perspectives on her writing, writing needs, and recommendations for teaching writing. Other classroom-based ELA inquiries respond to institutional concerns, such as Douillard's (2003) account of how she critiqued and challenged a district writing assessment for K–6 students by developing and testing a revised instrument. Through construction of clearer prompts and a more detailed scoring guide to capture dimensions of writing, Douillard worked with colleagues to test her new assessment tools and provided evidence of how the revised prompt provided greater task focus for students and the scoring guide captured nuances of writing in the sample responses of two of her students. Published reports of inquiry, however, often belie the complex process of finding focus.

Problem-framing in teacher inquiry may be clear and sudden or may require longterm reflection. One first-grade teacher reported how she was aware that she and other teachers avoided exploring the events of 9/11, assuming the issues were too frightening and complex for young children to handle (Burns, 2009). However, after a student raised questions about 9/11, the problem frame was clear: It was time to take action, informed by literacy models, to enable students to read, respond to, and discuss themes of war in a month-long unit, and it was time to study students' engagements with this innovation. Through analysis of students' writing, drawings, and transcribed discussions, Burns distilled themes of students' readiness to reflect on war, rehearse more peaceful stances, and learn to take actions in support of peace. Her new understandings from even a month-long unit offer teaching and learning principles to shape future actions for Burns and the readers of her report.

Fecho (2004) provides a book-length account of inquiry that likewise began in a surprising classroom event, but the problem framing evolved and expanded over time. As a White male teacher working with mostly African American youth in an urban school, Fecho was enthused to share with students Nikiki Giovanni's poem "Beautiful Black Men." However, students proclaimed resistance to what they felt was a stereotypical depiction and use of dialect and slang that "made fun of the way Black people talk" (Fecho, p. 13). The teacher's "anticipated love-in for this lyric from the 1960s became, instead, a spontaneous protest" (p. 14). Fecho later engaged students in conducting their own inquiries into issues of language and power, which enabled students and teacher to learn much about

these issues. The puzzling moment prompted the teacher's reflection and action, but the larger inquiry unfolded over many years and through close looking at focal students and their work, yielding theory development about the role of inquiry in exploring race, language, identity, and power among adolescents.

As work unfolds over time, teacher researchers have some periods of systematic data collection and analysis and others when demands of practice trump systematicity of inquiry or when a particular inquiry issue recedes or gets recast. Fecho (2004) notes that for many experienced teacher researchers, inquiry is not conducted through bounded studies but rather through an ongoing attention to often related and developing foci. It is not a tidy formula:

> We go into a meaning-making mode that includes past, current, and future discussions. We don't perceive the problem, go to the literature, collect the data, analyze them, and implement new practice.... Rarely is there one moment of epiphany where our purpose and direction come suddenly clear. Instead, our process is marked by a series of small "ahas"... (p. 29)

A bank of professional experience, however, may be tapped by more veteran teachers and often supported by artifacts of instruction, even when data collection is not formally underway.

Data Collection in Teacher Inquiry Opportunities for data gathering are the teacher researcher's affordances, accessed when adopting an inquiry stance (Cochran-Smith & Lytle, 2009). Classroom researchers coming from the outside must negotiate entry, build rapport and trust with participants, and hope that on classroom visit days, there will be adequate access to information as raw data. In contrast, teacher researchers enjoy privileged access to all forms of student work; immediate gathering of formal and informal student reflections; potentially longer term data collection that *being there* affords; and access to an emic perspective of student and classroom life through daily contact. These opportunities, however, yield rich data only for those teacher researchers who have methods and tools to gather relevant information and who manage to play ongoing dual roles of teacher and researcher. Student work samples and achievement data serve as primary data sources in much teacher inquiry. Field notes and classroom discourse data can be more difficult to collect for the practicing teacher. As already illustrated by the work of Gallas (2003), the BTRS (2004) nonetheless developed a culture of taping and transcribing discourse for seminar discussion and inquiry; such data figure heavily in the work of the group.

Analysis and Evidence in Teacher Inquiry When conducted with rigor, teacher inquiry yields practice-based evidence. This term flips the popular expression derived from policy and measurement that all teaching practice should be evidence-based. McNamara (2002) critiques how the phrase often means imported evidence, decontextualized from real classrooms, arguing that evidence needs to derive *from classroom practice*. Such practice often is immediate and necessarily responsive for the professional, viewed as praxis when tapping a knowledge base of effective practice and/or prior inquiry. Methodological adaptations and new standards may be needed for this particular kind of ELA research; nonetheless, nothing is more crucial than providing illustrations and evidence to support claims (Mitchell, 2003).

In a review of 25 reports in a UK pilot project designed to enable educators to take charge of and participate in teacher research, Foster (1999) found value for teachers but also several major and many minor problems. Some of these relate to other forms of research but still warrant discussion. First, projects had only sketchy information on research design and methods, often unclear foci, omission of how key constructs were defined, and especially little information on how qualitative data were analyzed. Second, amounts of data were extremely limited, often ambiguous, with qualitative data often decontextualized and unattributed, and cases presented without clarifying how they represented full samples. Third, lack of adequate evidence undermined claims and, in some cases, evidence lacked relevance to claims. Foster warned that a lack of critical scrutiny of teacher research projects can yield questionable claims that can, in turn, support questionable classroom practices. Zeichner (2009) echoed this concern, noting we need to beware of an uncritical glorification of teacher knowledge, as there is good and bad teacher research, just as with any kind.

The field of teacher inquiry can benefit from increasingly careful attention to data and evidence. Of particular importance is establishing trustworthiness and usefulness of the report, clarifying that it is more than mere story (McBride, 2003). This includes providing attention to what was done with artifacts to turn them into "data" that can be examined to assess claims. Some argue that all student work is data; more accurately, such work serves *potentially* as data. One set of analytic tools builds one set of understandings; selecting another leads to other findings (Erickson, 2004). M-CLASS teams, named for the group's multi-city project focused on multicultural teaching and teacher research in urban schools in the 1990s, worried about this—that their biases or partial stories would uncover semi-truths (Freedman, Simons, Kalnin, Casareno, and The M-CLASS Teams, 1999). Certainly, the myth of objectivity in scientific research was challenged significantly in the mid-20th century. Nonetheless, as Erickson points out, one does not merely *find* data; one must *construct* both data and their analyses together.

Various analytic tools have been used effectively in teacher inquiry (including studies cited in this chapter), and resources describing their use are available for teachers. Analyses in teacher inquiry may be guided by ethnographic methods including considerations of classrooms as developing cultures and the use of multiple perspectives in analyzing experience (Frank, 1999). Discourse analysis pro-

cesses and tools may include learning to frame and reframe conversations and learning to read conversations for power dynamics and for issues when clashes occur among students (and between students and teacher) related to race and other identity issues (Rex & Schiller, 2009). Rubrics of various kinds help to quantify degree of success in hitting achievement targets but need critical treatment of what they do and do not capture. Practice is helpful in coding larger patterns in student work that require repeated readings. A priori categories may play a role in examining certain features: quantity and fit of descriptive words in children's narrative; attention to knowledge sources students use to make sense of literary text; ways students warrant evidence in analytic writing. To analyze more global features of student work and thinking, many ELA teachers are well positioned, as this involves thematic exploration, analytic moves many learned through the discipline of literary analysis. When we compare and contrast two poems or find a thread of ideas across novels, we do some textual analysis, close looking at language and resources to construct meaning. Such attention is necessary in teacher inquiry in ELA, a language-rich subject area. It also is necessary in any inquiry where classroom discourse, open-ended questionnaires, or interviews play a role, as these language-based data sources require close analysis of connections among language units.

Clearly, data displays and textual representations of evidence are keys to strengthening knowledge claims for both the teacher researcher her/himself and others. Several challenges and insights from the M-CLASS (Freedman et al., 1999) are salient. Challenges included gaining critical distance from one's practice and the need to construct both teaching and research strands of a double narrative. Insights included research leaders guiding teams to be careful to use data and not memories for claims, and a team member reporting value in narratives but resisting gratuitous storytelling that did not address research questions.

Other Sources for Ideas and Explanatory Power Literature sources are vital for strong teacher inquiry. Teachers often resist academic research because it feels unrelated to K–12 classroom concerns, uses language inaccessible to K–12 teachers, and often positions teachers as the problem with education (Freedman et al., 1999; McNamara, 2002; Zeichner, 2009). Since inquiry foci often originate in classroom life, many who conduct teacher inquiry do not find it necessary to document where the problem comes from: "It arose in front of my eyes." Also, because many conducting teacher inquiry hold the goal of feeding new insights right back into practice rather than sharing it in public forums, they find it unnecessary to situate the work in larger educational conversations as recorded and published. While such a position is compelling, it risks perpetuating a kind of solipsistic effort, in a vacuum, unaware of parallel efforts in other classrooms, other labs, trying to reinvent the wheel.

Many teacher inquiry reports include few if any references and often with a mere nod: "I agree with Authors 1, 2, and 3 that students need to write frequently in order to develop." Some miss the potential of linking their inquiry to readings for creative leaps in thinking and for transformation of understanding (Hubbard & Power, 1999). Situating context-specific details in larger literacy ideas and conversations helps to make a case matter to larger communities (Dyson & Genishi, 2005). In this way, the writer abstracts from particulars. This enables moving from reporting *what happened* to reflecting on *what happens* (Moffett, 1968). As noted earlier in the Gallas (2003) example, some longer term inquiries also provide new ways of thinking about kinds of knowledge sources and literatures to be tapped for teacher inquiry.

Cross-Case Analyses and Cumulative Knowledge in Teacher Inquiry

Reports of cross-case analyses of teacher inquiry in ELA are rare, but their use can support the cumulative nature of knowledge production. Individual inquiries and case studies can promote theory-generation; however, cross-case analyses can add generalizations about teaching and learning phenomena. Two examples point to possibilities. Both include cross-case work on topical content and what was learned about it, as well as on the inquiry process itself. In one teacher education course, four preservice teachers managed systematic documentation and mostly quantitative analyses of varied approaches to journal writing they tested with elementary grade students (Radencich, Eckhardt, Rasch, Uhr, & Pisaneschi, 1998). In addition to reporting specifics of the four cases, the authors report both content and process themes across cases to inform future inquiry, particularly in the context of demanding teacher education experiences and timelines. A set of ideas emerged as potential guides for future teaching and inquiry. The authors caution that they cannot generalize from four highly contextualized cases, but their work offers promise for future cross-case studies. A second example approaches a multicase study: a set of cases sharing foci but designed to enable variation in topic and context (Stake, 2006). Freedman et al. (1999) include 6 M-CLASS cases from several U.S. cities, as well as cross-case analyses of processes and products of the full set of 24. Analyses emerge as a clustering of cases by three themes; a chapter per book section on cross-case issues per theme; and a final chapter on discoveries from teaching and inquiry in urban schools.

Future multicase studies of teacher inquiry might identify cross-case choice points in advance, or a "quintain," a common target or theme with, as Stake (2006) suggests, multiple related cases in varied contexts, elements that can support generalization across cases. Conducting multicase study may require a cultural shift and some professional retooling, but teacher inquiry and ELA research can benefit from such work to find ways to learn the uniquely situated nature of cases of phenomena but also commonalities that document trends and help build a professional knowledge base.

The Role of Research Colleagues

Conducting teacher inquiry is challenging for various reasons, including lack of time, institutional support, and career incentives/rewards for doing it. Still, many teachers engage the work and commit to going public with it, particularly if supported by communities of like-minded teacher researchers. Support, according to Loughran (2003), requires three conditions: (a) share and make research a collaborative venture; (b) develop confidence so it is safe to reveal even unsuccessful inquiry outcomes; and (c) communicate findings so others will identify with them, making reports ring true. Groups that support teacher inquiry in ELA document such practices. Some develop mechanisms to tap models and mentors. M-CLASS teams benefitted from university-based staff providing resources, instruction, and feedback on projects, as well as inquiry models to promote discussion of genre features (Freedman et al., 1999). Experienced BTRS members modeled processes for colleagues newer to inquiry, including methods for taping, transcribing, and analyzing student talk (Ballenger & Rosebery, 2003).

Many other groups have supported teacher inquiry (e.g., National Writing Project sites and lesson study teams); one focuses inquiry on a teaching and policy link (Rust, 2009). More university-schools collaborations on inquiry may support development of the knowledge base for teaching. It is noteworthy that several highly accomplished long-term inquiries were conducted by current and former K–12 teachers who hold doctorates. Perhaps extended academic time to study and ruminate enabled production of such theory-generating work. This fact suggests a need for institutional arrangements of various kinds to sustain the work, deepen it, and strengthen it methodologically. Partnerships of schools and university offer possibilities to support these efforts, but many issues need to be considered for their success, including commitments to joint activity and mutual support, as well as grasping and critiquing ways in which contextual issues and pressures impact processes and outcomes (Stronach & McNamara, 2002).

Conclusion

Developing as a movement, teacher inquiry took hold in recent decades (Cochran-Smith & Lytle, 2009). Reports of professional development values for teachers from conducting such inquiry are plentiful. However, Zeichner (2009) notes how "few seriously treat the knowledge that teachers generate through their inquiries as educational knowledge to be analyzed and discussed" (p. 108). As a professional practice and knowledge generating activity, teacher inquiry invites such analysis and discussion. Continued attention to methods and reporting, and a commitment to analysis across cases, can result in teacher inquiry as increasingly conscious and informed praxis.

Author's Note

The author thanks Lisa H. Bennett and Juliet Michelsen Wahleithner for critical feedback on an earlier draft of this chapter.

References

Ballenger, C. (2009). *Puzzling moments, teachable moments: Practicing teacher research in urban classrooms.* New York: Teachers College Press.

Ballenger, C., & Rosebery, A. S. (2003). What counts as teacher research? Investigating the scientific and mathematical ideas of children from culturally diverse backgrounds. *Teachers College Record, 105*(2), 297–314.

Brookline Teacher Research Seminar (BTRS). (2004). *Regarding children's worlds: Teacher research on language and literacy.* New York: Teachers College Press.

Burns, T. J. (2009). Searching for peace: Exploring issues of war with young children. *Language Arts, 86*(6), 421–430.

Cochran-Smith, M., & Lytle, S. L. (2009). *Inquiry as stance: Practitioner research for the next generation.* New York: Teachers College Press.

Douillard, K. (2003). Writing matters: Exploring the relationship between writing instruction and assessment. In A. Clarke & G. Erickson (Eds.), *Teacher inquiry: Living the research in everyday practice* (pp. 9–19). New York: Routledge Falmer.

Dyson, A. H., & Genishi, C. (2005). *On the case: Approaches to language and literacy research.* New York: Teachers College Press.

Erickson, F. (2004). Demystifying data construction and analysis. *Anthropology and Education Quarterly, 35*(4), 486–493.

Fecho, B. (2004). *"Is this English?" Race, language, and culture in the classroom.* New York: Teachers College Press.

Fecho, B., & Allen, J. (2003). Teacher inquiry into literacy, social justice, and power. In J. Flood, D. Lapp, J. Squire, & J. Jensen (Eds.), *Handbook of research on teaching the English language arts* (2nd ed., pp. 232–246). Mahwah, NJ: Erlbaum.

Foster, P. (1999). "Never mind the quality, feel the impact": A methodological assessment of teacher research sponsored by the Teacher Training Agency. *British Journal of Educational Studies, 47*(4), 380–398.

Frank, C. (1999). *Ethnographic eyes: A teacher's guide to classroom observation.* Portsmouth, NH: Heinemann.

Freedman, S. W., Simons, E. R., Kalnin, J. S., Casareno, A., & The M-CLASS Teams (1999). *Inside city schools: Investigating literacy in multicultural classrooms.* New York: Teachers College Press.

Freire, P. (1998). *Pedagogy of freedom: Ethics, democracy, and civic courage.* Lanham, MD: Rowman and Littlefield.

Gallas, K. (2003). *Imagination and literacy: A teacher's search for the heart of learning.* New York: Teachers College Press.

Gore, J. M., & Zeichner, K. M. (1991). Action research and reflective teaching in preservice teacher education: A case study from the United States. *Teaching & Teacher Education, 7*(2), 119–136.

Goswami, D., Lewis, C., Rutherford, M., & Waff, D. (2009). *On teacher inquiry: Approaches to language and literacy research.* New York: Teachers College Press.

Griffin, S. (2004). I need people: Storytelling in a second-grade classroom. In Brookline Teacher Research Seminar (Ed.), *Regarding children's worlds: Teacher research on language and literacy* (pp. 22–30). New York: Teachers College Press.

Heatley, G., & Stronach, I. (2002). Happily ever after: Plotting effective narrative writing with 10-year-old children. In O. McNamara (Ed.), *Becoming an evidence-based practitioner: A framework for teacher-researchers* (pp. 51–62). New York: Routledge Falmer.

Hoffman-Kipp, P., Artiles, A. J., & Lopez-Torres, L. (2003). Beyond reflection: Teacher learning as praxis. *Theory into Practice, 42*(3), 248–254.

Hubbard, R. S., & Power, B. M. (1999). *Living the questions: A guide for teacher researchers.* Portland, ME: Stenhouse.

Korthagen, F. A. J. (2010). Situated learning theory and the pedagogy of teacher education: Towards an integrative view of teacher behavior and teacher learning. *Teaching and Teacher Education, 96*(1), 98–106.

Lew, A. (1999). Writing correctness and the second-language student. In S. W. Freedman, E. R. Simons, J. S. Kalnin, A. Casareno, & The M-CLASS Teams (Eds.), *Inside city schools: Investigating literacy in multicultural classrooms* (pp. 165–178). New York: Teachers College Press.

Loughran, J. (2003). Exploring the nature of teacher research. In A. Clarke & G. Erickson (Eds.), *Teacher inquiry: Living the research in everyday practice* (pp. 181–189). New York: Routledge Falmer.

McBride, J. (2003). Working on the underbelly of the underdog: Listening for the ring-of-truth in a teacher-researcher's story. In A. Clarke & G. Erickson (Eds.), *Teacher inquiry: Living the research in everyday practice* (pp. 209–220). New York: Routledge Falmer.

McNamara, O. (Ed.). (2002). *Becoming an evidence-based practitioner: A framework for teacher-researchers.* New York: Routledge Falmer.

McPhail, G. (2009). The "bad boy" and the writing curriculum. In M. Cochran-Smith, & S. L. Lytle (Eds.), *Inquiry as stance: Practitioner research for the next generation* (pp. 193–212). New York: Teachers College Press.

Mitchell, I. (2003). Why do teacher research? Perspectives from four stakeholders. In A. Clarke & G. Erickson (Eds.), *Teacher inquiry: Living the research in everyday practice* (pp. 199–208). New York: Routledge Falmer.

Moffett, J. (1968). *Teaching the universe of discourse.* Boston: Houghton Mifflin.

Radencich, M. C., Eckhardt, K., Rasch, R., Uhr, S. L., & Pisaneschi, D. M. (1998). University course-based practitioner research: Four studies on journal writing contextualize the process. *Research in the Teaching of English, 32*(1), 79–112.

Rex, L. A., & Schiller, L. (2009). *Using discourse analysis to improve classroom interaction.* New York: Routledge.

Rust, F. O. (2009). Teacher research and the problem of practice. *Teachers College Record, 111*(8), 1882–1893.

Schön, D. A. (1983). *The reflective practitioner, how professionals think in action.* New York: Basic Books.

Stake, R. E. (2006). *Multiple case study analysis.* New York: Guilford.

Stronach, I., & McNamara, O. (2002). Working together: The long spoons and short straws of collaboration. In O. McNamara (Ed.), *Becoming an evidence-based practitioner: A framework for teacher-researchers* (pp. 155–168). New York: Routledge Falmer.

Valli, L., van Zee, E. H., Rennert-Ariev, P., Mikeska, J., Catlett-Muhammad, S., & Roy, P. (2006). Initiating and sustaining a culture of inquiry in a teacher leadership program. *Teacher Education Quarterly 33*(3), 97–114.

Zeichner, K. M. (2009). *Teacher education and the struggle for social justice.* New York: Routledge.

52

Policy and Research in the English Language Arts

Massive, Inclusive, and Artful Design Choices[1]

PETER FREEBODY

Language is the most massive and inclusive art we know.

Edward Sapir (1921, p. 189)

Societies have shown an abiding interest in how their citizens use language. Whether the outcomes of centuries-long attempts to educate and regulate language have been constraining or liberating, inclusive or just massive, and whether or not some notion of research has played a part, governing bodies have rarely regarded citizens' ways of using language as peripheral, as mere accompaniments to the real business of the social world (Lo Bianco, 2007). Because it concerns the calibre and range of what youngsters will come to value, and talk, listen, read, and write about, language education has been at the heart of educational efforts for centuries, speaking directly to the creation of both persons and a people—citizens, workers, members of families, communities, societies, and cultures.

This chapter begins with a long view from history, showing the longevity of policy's applications to language education and the conditions that have motivated those applications. It turns then to two recent, contrasting examples of policy interventions, and concludes by outlining some challenges facing researchers and educators interested in English language arts education. Of underlying interest here is how we conceptualize the scope and significance of language education, how different kinds of research designs yield different versions of education in the English language arts, and how each of these versions has, in turn, its own way of presenting language as amenable to transformation via policy.

The concept of the language arts is open-textured, covering a set of goals, materials, activities, and participation settings. Goals include the developing knowledge, skills, and dispositions that relate to social participation via oral and written language communication. Materials typically include materials drawn from valued everyday and literary, aesthetically- and functionally-motivated textual sources, multimodal texts, and digital and print texts, along with

increasingly complex combinations of these. Activities generally include reading, writing, listening, making, valuing, talking, and responding to these materials. Participation settings include personal, interpersonal, group, and intercultural communications, from intimate, to familiar, to general.

The term "policy" is taken here to refer to public decisions that name target practices to be institutionally regulated: it thus is made up of action plans, rationales for those plans, and ways of assessing progress and success. Target practices range from resource allocation and dissemination of system data to the adoption of materials in classrooms and the assessment of students' learning. Policy also articulates how compliance will be monitored and enforced, and how key target practices will be inter-related (e.g., how the outcomes of assessment regimes will determine resource allocation), and how implementing these decisions will serve broader, underlying values and ideological goals (e.g., providing equity of access and participation, passing on a cohesive cultural heritage). Potentially, research can speak directly and consequentially to the full range of these practices and their rationales.

This chapter is written at a high point in the story of policy interventions into the teaching and learning of the English language arts. The high point refers not only to both the overtness and reach of government interventions but also to the explicit use of certain forms of research to legitimate such interventions. Over recent decades three significant developments have brought us to this high point. First, the increasing diversity of learners' cultural and linguistic backgrounds has been recognized as presenting challenges to teachers, schools, and systems. Second, expectations have intensified that schools will provide increasingly complex communicational skills to meet the demands of contemporary vocational, civic, and personal life. Third, schools have been publicly singled out as especially accountable for the economic, moral, and cultural condition of a society. Finally, there has arisen a sense in the professional, bureaucratic, and public communities that there seems to be enough research evidence available in and around the topic of teaching and learning the English language arts to afford durable, perhaps even final, answers to the big educational questions of *what?* and *how?*

These developments are felt nowhere more keenly than in the practices and policies surrounding English language arts education. Regular waves of pressure to implement reforms in resource reallocation, pedagogy, and professional training have become part of the experience of educators in classrooms, regional offices, and state and national bureaucracies. The following discussion shows that versions of these three developments are evident in both the long and the short history of language, social life, and policy.

Regulating Future Citizens' Oral and Written Language: A Long View

In the West, the origins of democracy, literacy, and formal language education are associated with ancient Greece. In fact, the extent of the individual and collective reach of language education and the motivation for policy intervention are well illustrated by accounts of Athenian life in the 5th–4th centuries BCE. Decades of both the threat and the reality of war, most notably with Persia and Sparta, had shaken the Athenians' sense of cultural identity, an identity attached to a distinctive notion of the citizen, a member of the city-state who "had a right to debate, and a right to vote on, the decisions that affected his life and that of his city" (Stone, 1988, p. 9). Public dialogue and debate had become central to the Athenians' sense of how they were different from their neighbours and predecessors. In Athens at this time "speech became the political tool par excellence, the key to authority in the state … The art of politics became essentially the management of language" (Vernant, 1982, p. 49). Their use of oral and written language was the seed-bed for the Athenians' form of civic participation and democracy (Robb, 1994).

By 450 BCE debates about how to educate aspiring young Athenians in the oral and written skills of political and civic participation were underway (Harris, 1989; Thomas, 1994). The puzzling trial and execution of Socrates is partly explained by his critique of Athenian forms of governance. But he was also charged with "corrupting the youth of Athens" (Plato's *Apology*, Ap. 24, b8-c1) through his direct, disputative language education practices with his students and, more dangerously, their powerful fathers (Colaiaco, 2001). Undecorated, personally engaged debate about genuine moral problems Socrates saw as the only valid form of meaningful political and civic participation, and he taught essentially a form of philosophic rhetoric on that basis. It was as a language educator that Socrates was condemned.

Two thousand years later, in 1647, the first known law mandating schooling—the Ould Deluder Satan Law—was passed. It was about the English language arts. The Puritan authorities of Massachusetts instructed every community of 50 or more families to have a school and to employ a reading and writing teacher, to outwit the ways of the Evil One by the teaching of reading and writing (Monaghan, 2005). Here is the original rationale for the Ould Deluder Satan Law:

> It being one cheife project of that ould deluder, Satan, to keepe men from the knowledge of the Scriptures, as in former times by keeping them in an unknowne tongue, so in these latter times, by perswading from the use of tongues, that so at least the true sence & meaning of the originall might be clouded by false glosses of saint-seeming deceivers, that learning may not be buried in the grave of our fathers in the church & commonwealth. (cited in Monaghan & Barry, 1999, p. 2)

As with the Athenians, a sense of being surrounded by potentially menacing and benighted neighbors, and a commitment to the enhancement of their distinctive cultural and, in this case, religious citizenry led these communities to mandate a specific form of language and literacy education. From the earliest days of legally mandated schooling, writing, as "a tool for the attainment of learning", was to be a focus of instruction, not just reading (Monaghan, 2005, p. 38). Harvard College had been established 11 years earlier, and a notion of a religion-informed, active citizenry drawn from among the young men of the ruling and aspirational classes had motivated the law. It was a futures- and a participation-oriented policy.

The development of a competent, but, perhaps equally, distinctive kind of language user, for both ancient Athens and the Puritan communities of Massachusetts, was taken to play a key part in the maintenance of their special identities, both individual and communal, in the face of their inauspicious circumstances. Systematic education in those individual and collective resources that we group under the heading "Language Arts" has long been of interest to the political class and to public administrators. In the European tradition, they became objects of policy surveillance and regulation over 2000 years ago, and they have remained so (see Freebody & Zhang, 2008, for applications to early language arts education in China).

Research in Policy, Policy in Research: Examples from Literacy Education

Centuries after the Ould Deluder Satan Law, language arts education remains a target of policy, but research now accompanies rhetoric in policy formulations. Two recent policy interventions in literacy education are discussed here to exemplify the different roles that research can play in the formulation of and public rationale for policy.

No Child Left Behind (NCLB, signed into law in 2002) was a broad-ranging U.S. policy intervention whose bases were stated as follows:

> [The NCLB Act] will help close the achievement gap between disadvantaged and minority students and their peers. It is based on four basic principles: stronger

accountability for results, increased flexibility and local control, expanded options for parents, and an emphasis on teaching methods that have been proven to work. Test data will be reported by economic background, race and ethnicity, English proficiency and disability. Measuring progress by subgroups will demonstrate not just that overall student performance is improving, but also that achievement gaps are closing between disadvantaged students and other students. Holding schools accountable for the academic achievement of all subgroups ensures that no child is left behind. (U.S. Department of Education, n.d.)

This intervention operated with a clear definition of rigorous research as the warrant for regulations and guidelines about "teaching methods that have been proven to work" (National Reading Panel, 1999): replicated experiments with standardized or psychometrically defensible outcome measures (but see Camilli, Vargas, & Yurecko, 2003, on the inappropriateness of the analyses). Regulations and guidelines applied to many aspects of educational activity. Literacy education was a significant part of this blanket initiative, and guidelines relating to it were based in large part on issues established in the report of an earlier U.S. government sponsored expert review of research (National Reading Panel, 1999).

These initiatives, at the time of writing, have been reshaped and incorporated into the Race to the Top Program (U.S. Department of Education, 2009). This program also explicitly singles out "reading/language arts and mathematics, as reported by the National Assessment of Educational Progress and the assessments required under the Elementary and Secondary Education Act" as key indicators (U.S. Department of Education, 2009, pp. 6–7). The combination of terms is informative: First is the distinct-but-conflated status of reading and the language arts, signalling the special status of reading over and above writing, speaking and listening, and reflecting the priorities of No Child Left Behind; second is the embodiment of these in the previous assessment regimes; third is the naming of "reading/language arts and mathematics" at the same level of generality, in terms of systems' achievements, as "increasing high school graduation rates … and increasing college enrolment" (U.S. Department of Education, pp. 6–7).

Thus reading/language arts and mathematics, as assessed by standardized measures, are taken to reflect the highest order benchmarks of school and system well-being, comparable in terms of accountability and informativeness to graduation and continuation rates. On the matter of the evidence base for these initiatives, the National Reading Panel, No Child Left Behind initiative and the Race to the Top program, taken in tandem, intersected with debate and government intervention on the matter of what was to count as evidence (one outcome of which is the What Works database; U.S. Department of Education, 2010). So policy, in this instance, included not only a reference to supporting evidence, but an explicit indication of what kind of methodological and analytic choices would be taken seriously in policy debates.

A second kind of intervention, called Literate Futures (Luke, Freebody, & Land, 2000), inquired into literacy teaching in primary and secondary public schools in Queensland,[2] Australia, to locate a set of emergent issues that could form the bases of reform. The data for this study comprised observations in schools, interviews with several thousand teachers, principals, students, parents and interested community members, the analysis of policy documents, data relating to general educational achievement in schools, and analyses of demographic and economic features and projections of the regions across the state. The rationale for the recommendations rested to a significant extent on an analysis of "futures" based on demographic and labour-market trends. The relevant research literature was contextualized by the concerns that emerged from these data bases, rather than the other way around. Recommendations were made about: (a) student diversity, including a focus on regular "distance travelled" targets using a wide range of assessment data; (b) whole-school literacy plan to be developed by teachers, parents and other stakeholders; (c) the teaching of reading reshaped through "balanced, multi-method approaches" (Luke et al, 2000, p. 81); and (d) the incorporation of new technologies and multiple modalities into classroom work across the school years and curriculum areas.

These two policy formulations (discussed more fully in Freebody, 2007) embodied contrasting views of

- how teachers should implement the intentions of central policy, comparably, in all of the settings within a jurisdiction,
- the degree of agency and professionalism that can and should be exercised in those implementations,
- how clearly the future language and literacy demands on workers and citizens should be formulated and simulated in schools across a jurisdiction,
- how statutory bodies and central offices should mandate and monitor the use of certain teaching methods, and
- how definitive and generalizable the guidance should be that research provides regarding those methods.

No Child Left Behind and Literate Futures differed dramatically on these counts, not just on the extent and nature of their research base. The contrasts show that these debates revolve partly around optimal levels of specificity in the application of research findings (from experiments or elsewhere) to classrooms, and the relation of that to optimal degrees of professional, on-site adaptation by classroom, school and district personnel.

One of the minority statements to the U.S. National Reading Panel (1999) report clarifies this set of issues:

the Panel needed to assess the implications for practice growing out of research findings. As a body made up mostly of university professors, however, its members were not qualified to be the sole judges of the "readiness for implementation in the classroom" of their findings or whether the findings could be "used immediately by parents, teachers, and other educational audiences." Their concern, as scientists, was whether or not a particular line of instruction was clearly enough defined and whether the evidence of its experimental success was strong. What they did not consider in most cases were the school and classroom realities that make some types of instruction difficult—even impossible—to implement ... the work of the NRP is not of poor quality; it is just unbalanced and, to some extent, irrelevant. But because of these deficiencies, bad things will happen. Summaries of, and sound bites about, the Panel's findings will be used to make policy decisions at the national, state, and local levels. (Yatvin, pp. 2, 3)

Debates about NCLB and Literate Futures persist, but it is clear that the aspiration of these two policies was to improve language and literacy learning, and that both were predicated on an understanding of the importance of language arts education for equity and access of educational provision to traditionally disadvantaged, disenfranchised, and residualized groups. The debates generated indicate that this connection, so self-evident in most policy formulations, is in fact complex and multifaceted. The nature and extent of the connection between the English language arts and educational disadvantage may vary in extent and in kind from site to site. To inform policy strongly, clearly, and reliably, therefore, research on this connection itself needs to accompany more generically-oriented experimental research on what works in laboratory, classroom, or community settings.

We can observe that familiar distinctions among ways of doing research are associated with distinctive theorizations of language teaching and learning. For instance, there is an obvious connection between, on the one hand, the conduct of experiments that compare the relative merits of different ways of teaching and learning in the language arts and, on the other, a notion that features and uses of language are readily measurable individual attributes that are distributed evenly across all the possible clients of a school system or indeed a nation—reading levels, English spoken proficiency ratings, scores on standardized writing tests, and so on. Testing relative effects of different educational approaches (pedagogies, materials, and so on) via experimentation conceives of the teaching-learning contexts across a system as directly comparable in all of their key knowable features. Other research frameworks emphasize and document the nature of effective teaching and learning in terms of strategies for teaching (e.g., Langer, 2001), or the details of the linguistic aspects of the home-school interface and its implications for language learning in and out of school (e.g., Brice Heath, 1983), or the knowledge-building potential of particular interactional formats in different curriculum areas (e.g., Freebody, in press).

Some of the richest research in the English language arts presents some of the clearest challenges to policy makers, for instance:

• Murphy and Edwards (2005) conducted a meta-analysis of 49 studies examining the effects of various types of

small-group discussions on higher-level thinking and comprehension. They found that, in the most productive discussions, teachers *retained considerable control of text and topic while allowing students considerable interpretive flexibility and the opportunity to elaborate their ideas for extended periods of time*. Notably, this problem-solving basis for classroom discourse had strong effects for below- and average-ability students.

• Kuiper, Volman, and Terwel (2005) reviewed the literature on the use of the Web as an information resource by students from early schooling to Year 12, drawing together theoretical and philosophical as well as empirical studies. Two of their main conclusions were (a) the vast amount of information on the Web results in access to information, but *students generally lack the skills to decipher, weigh up, analyse, and compare that information with other sources* and (b) that there is an urgent need for empirical research on this topic.

• Gregory (2005) explored the ways in which young children use school language at home and home talk at school, observing the socio-dramatic play of children as they "played school" at home, compared with the way they talked about home during school. She found that students used cultural resources such as poetry to bridge home and school learning and that, in the home, older siblings acted as teachers to their younger siblings in both their action and their talk. Gregory argued that children need to enact these experiences, so that when they encounter them again they can link the appropriate language with the objects and feelings associated with those experiences, experiences often provided through socio-dramatic play with siblings and peers. Gregory argued that in order for schools and teachers to understand and build on the resources of home learning, *playful talk at home needs to be observed and understood, and teachers need to attempt to find out how school talk is mediated in home environments*.

How to legislate on such findings? How to guide strongly enough to avoid dilution and eclecticism in practice, while allowing professionals to adapt and re-enact the findings in diverse settings?

Conclusion

In her discussion of what we might learn from the rise of literacy in Ancient Greece, Rosalind Thomas commented on the

fascinating tension between the obvious fact that writing makes certain activities possible or easier, and that different potentials are seized upon by different communities. In some, writing means bureaucracy, control and oppression by the state, in others an enabling skill that frees an individual's creative potential. (2009, pp. 13–14)

Researchers in the English language arts have generally made choices in design and analysis that operate, however explicitly, on one or the other of these assumptions: Has an instance of research on the English language arts been designed to search for and highlight deficiencies that need to be regulated or controlled through a different kind of education? Or does it signal opportunities to enhance the efficacy, knowledge, breath of communicational repertoire, and creative potential of its young, to propagate language diversity? The choice of one or the other relates directly to choices about research method and methodology. These choices also both reflect and organize relationships among teachers, policy makers, and researchers, relationships of expertise, support, and power. There is much research operating on one or the other of these dispositions, and very little that, through design or analyses, theorizes, studies, or even acknowledges the fascinating tension between them. In diverse, dynamic, and increasingly globalized societies, even more so than in ancient Greece or Puritan Massachusetts, the key research is that which inquires into this double-edged nature of education in the English language arts, analyzing site by site, in the details of interactional and material features, how those potentially contradictory imperatives are acted out.

For the work of educational practitioners and policy makers alike, there is a need to re-chart continually the contents and boundaries of education in and around the language arts. Cultural and linguistic demographics, patterns of social exclusion and of civic participation, technologies of communication and knowledge production and access, and the communication demands of the curriculum and of the vocational, civic, and domestic environments toward which school students are headed, are all changing rapidly, simultaneously reshaping one another. There is therefore a need to view research into education in the English language arts as an ongoing, essential program that aims to renew our knowledge, practice, and policy, rather than to clinch definitive, timeless answers to the core questions of pedagogy and learning, regardless of how convenient to the administration and comforting to the community such answers may seem. The imperatives emerging from the experiences of teachers, students, and the communities served by schools need to reshape our continually research and policy agenda.

The English language arts embody the productive tension between convention and creativity, the aesthetic and the functional, acquisition, production, innovation, and critique. Education in the English language arts can entail an exploration of how the personal is, and can be, made public, and vice versa, or they can ignore that part of its reach; they can be inclusive and artful, a key zone in which youngsters come to see, articulate, and become part of what is noticed in a culture and what is not, or they can be simply massive, standardizing reading, writing, and smoothing over the sometimes uncomfortable interpretive possibilities of the business of the social world. The issue is that researchers also have these choices. Researchers need to make these choices with a focus on learners and

teachers; but also, in these times, researchers need to retain a lively understanding that the choices they make in design and analysis speak to policy makers. Motivating such an understanding is an awareness that policy makers will revert to ever-more sophisticated, intricate modes of regulation alone unless they can be informed by healthy research traditions that consciously live in the contested zone of expression and constraint.

Notes

1. The author is pleased to acknowledge the valuable input of his editorial colleagues, especially David Bloome and Thandeka Chapman, in the preparation of this chapter.
2. Queensland is a state whose area (1.74 square kilometres) is approximately 2½ times the area of Texas, and whose population (4.4 million) is about one-sixth that of Texas.

References

Camilli, G., Vargas, S., & Yurecko, M. (2003). Teaching children to read: The fragile link between science and federal education policy. *Education Policy Analysis Archives, 11*, 1–51.

Colaiaco, J.A. (2001). *Socrates against Athens: Philosophy on trial*. New York: Routledge.

Freebody, P. (2007). *Literacy education in schools: Research perspectives from the past, for the future*. Camberwell, Victoria: Australian Council for Educational Research.

Freebody, P. (in press). Socially responsible literacy education. To appear in F. Christie & A. Simpson (Eds.), *Literacy and social responsibility*. London: Equinox.

Freebody, P. & Zhang, B. (2008). The designs of culture, knowledge, and interaction on the reading of language and image. In L. Unsworth (Ed.), *New Literacies and the English Curriculum* (pp. 23–46). London: Continuum.

Gregory, E. (2005). Playful talk: The interspace between home and school discourse. *Early Years, 25*, 223–235.

Harris, W.V (1989). *Ancient literacy*. Cambridge, MA: Cambridge University Press.

Heath, S. B. (1983). *Ways with words*. Cambridge, UK: Cambridge University Press.

Kuiper, E., Volman, M., & Terwel, J. (2005). The web as an information resource in K–12 education. *Review of Educational Research, 75*, 285–328.

Langer, J. (2001). Beating the odds: Teaching middle and high school students to read and write well. *American Educational Research Journal, 38*, 837–880.

Lo Bianco, J. (2007). Contrasting and comparing minority language policy. In A. Pauwels, J. Winter, & J. Lo Bianco (Eds.), *Maintaining minority languages in transnational contexts* (pp 78–106), Basingstoke, UK: Palgrave-Macmillan.

Luke, A., Freebody, P., & Land R. (2000). *Literate futures*. Queensland, Australia: Department of Education. Retrieved August 24, 2009, from http://education.qld.gov.au/curriculum/learning/literate-futures/

Monaghan, E.J . (2005). *Learning to read and write in colonial America*. Boston, MA: University of Massachusetts Press.

Monaghan, E. J., & Barry, A. L. (1999). *Writing the past: Teaching reading in colonial America and the United States 1640–1940*. Presented at the Annual Convention of the International Reading Association, San Diego. Retrieved August 24, 2009, http://www.historyliteracy.org/download/Book5.pdf

Murphy, P. K., & Edwards, M. N. (2005, April). What the studies tell us: A meta-analysis of discussion approaches. M. Nystrand (Chair), *Making sense of group discussions designed to promote high-level comprehension of texts.* Meeting of the American Educational Research Association, Montreal, Canada.

National Reading Panel. (1999). Retrieved July 14, 2010, from http://www.nationalreadingpanel.org/Publications/publications.htm

Plato. (~389 BCE). *Georgias.* Retrieved August 24, 2009, http://oll.libertyfund.org/?option=com_staticxt&staticfile=show.php?title=766&chapter=93703&layout=html&Itemid=27

Plato. (399 BCE). *Apology.* Retrieved August 29, 2009, http://www.gutenberg.org/files/1656/1656.txt

Robb, K. (1994). *Literacy and paideia in ancient Greece.* Oxford, UK: Oxford University Press.

Sapir, E. (1921). *Language: An introduction to the study of speech.* New York: Harcourt, Brace. Bartleby reprint retrieved February 19, 2010, from http://www.bartleby.com/186/10.html

Stone, I. F. (1988). *The trial of Socrates.* Surrey, UK: Anchor Press.

Thomas, R. (1994). Literacy and the city-state in archaic and classical Greece. In A. Bowman & G. Woolf (Eds.), *Literacy and power in the ancient world* (pp. 33–50). Cambridge, UK: Cambridge University Press.

Thomas, R. (2009). Writing, reading public and private 'literacies': Functional literacy and democratic literacy in Greece. In W. A. Johnson & H. N. Parker (Eds.), *Ancient literacies: The culture of reading in Greece and Rome* (pp. 13–45). New York: Oxford University Press.

United States Department of Education. (n.d.). NCLB, cover page. Retrieved July 14, 2010, from http://www2.ed.gov/nclb/accountability/ayp/yearly.html

United States Department of Education. (2002). No child left behind. Retrieved August 24, 2009, from http://www.ed.gov/nclb/landing.jhtml

United States Department of Education. (2009). *Race to the top program, executive summary.* Retrieved February 20, 2010, http://www2.ed.gov/programs/racetothetop/executive-summary.pdf

United States Department of Education. (2010). *What Works Clearinghouse, practice guides.* Retrieved February 20, 2010, from http://ies.ed.gov/ncee/wwc/publications/practiceguides

Vernant, J-P. (1982). *The origins of Greek thought.* Ithaca, NY: Cornell University Press.

53

Ethnographic Research in Teaching and Learning the English Language Arts

Studying the Cultural Contexts of Teaching and Learning the English Language Arts

GEMMA MOSS

In an earlier review, Green and Bloome (1997) drew attention to the different ways in which ethnography has influenced research in education. They made a useful distinction between ethnography as practiced within anthropology and the rather different use of ethnography when adopted and deployed as part of educational research. Classic ethnography has traditionally been predicated on prolonged immersion in the research setting(s). It operates inductively using extensive periods of observation and participation to build a deep understanding of the relevant distinctions and categories that structure social life in ways that are familiar to community members but alien to the researcher. The classic ethnographer starts as an outsider and works their way in. This approach to research has led to the development of a range of procedures and research tools which have become core to the discipline. By contrast, it is more usual for education researchers to borrow more selectively from the tradition often in pursuit of more narrow and specific research purposes. To capture some of these distinctions Green and Bloome draw a contrast between "**doing ethnography**"—the traditional extended and open-ended engagement with a particular community; "**adopting ethnographic perspectives**"—a more closely focused study of certain aspects of community practices and social life, predicated on understanding the logic of that activity from participants' point of view; and "**using ethnographic research tools**"—adopting particular methods that derive from that tradition, such as participant observation, or open-ended interviews, but deploying them with more limited objectives in mind.

For education researchers, immersion in the research setting for an extended period is relatively rare, increasingly so in recent times. Indeed when contact is sustained with a particular community for a significant length of time it is more likely to have as its goal changing classroom practice in interaction with participants (Bloome, Power, Morton, & Otto, 2005; Hicks, 2002). In which case the researcher may well take an active part in modifying the setting they observe. In the light of Green and Bloome's distinctions the key questions for this article are: when and under what circumstances have researchers in the language arts turned to ethnography? How has this work fed into an understanding of the cultural contexts in which English language arts teaching and learning takes place? What lessons can be drawn for pedagogy in the English language arts classroom?

The Turn to Ethnography in the English Language Arts

The use of ethnography in the English language arts can be traced back to a moment in time when linguistics and social psychology were increasingly influential in education. In reflecting back on this period of intellectual activity, roughly from the mid-1960s to early 80s, Bernstein described this in terms of a "remarkable convergence" across a range of disciplinary fields on the concept of competence:

> The concept refers to procedures for engaging with and constructing the world. Competences are intrinsically creative and tacitly acquired in informal interactions. They are practical accomplishments. The acquisition of these procedures are beyond the reach of power relations and their differential unequal positionings, although the form the realizations may take are clearly not beyond power relations. (Bernstein, 1996, p. 55)

He saw this as a historically specific conjunction of ideas and pedagogic practices. An example of this kind of blending across different traditions can be seen in the UK in the writings of educationalists such as James Britton, Douglas Barnes, and Harold Rosen from the late 60s onwards. Their work helped focus English teachers' attention on the use of children's own language as a positive resource in the classroom. The spontaneous creativity of children's speech was counterposed to the dry formality of much teacher talk (Barnes, 1977). Capturing children's language at its most creative often seemed to necessitate stepping outside the confines of the classroom and turning away from its existing prescriptions for the well-crafted sentence or figure of speech. The turn in linguistics towards the study of children's early language in naturally occurring settings reinforced this sense of children's innate creative capacity. Often undertaken by the parent as researcher and facilitated by the advent of the portable tape-recorder, analysis of children's entry into language focused on their intentions, and their grasp for meaning which seemed to drive linguistic development (Halliday, 1975). Children's developing skills as readers and writers could be mapped onto this communicative imperative with function taking precedence over form. The concept of emergent literacy signals this same shift, allowing teachers to suspend or mitigate normative judgements that might otherwise be passed on children's texts based on their approximation to the formal features of standard written language.

Indeed, by extension the analysis of linguistic development through the study of naturally occurring speech became a resource for developing new modes of assessment for children's progression in reading, writing and the language arts more generally (Perera, 1985). Examining the natural course of progression outside school yielded the necessary course of progression inside the language arts classroom which good teaching could then reinforce as well as deliver. This kind of study of children's use of language, whether written or spoken, places children themselves and their activity at the centre of the classroom with teachers playing a facilitative role (Dyson, 2003). In Bernstein's terms this creates an invisible pedagogy which reshapes relations between the teacher and the taught even as it reorders the content of the curriculum (Bernstein, 1996).

Under these conditions what happens outside school, retrieved through observation or research, sanctions change in curriculum content. Such changes were intended to enhance children's sense of agency. In these ways the interests of professionals and academics interlocked. From the perspective of the early 21st century this point of convergence does indeed now seem a long way away. Since the mid1980s successive waves of government-sponsored reform have exerted much more centralised control over the school curriculum, defining and prescribing more tightly what its content should be, often through a relentless focus on the measurable outcomes any such interventions should deliver. This has created a new dynamic to the work of the school. Such moves have reinstated visible pedagogies that are much less permeable to cultural activity that lies outside the school (Bourne, 2000; Gutiérrez, 2000). The use of ethnography in language arts research has been coloured by these shifts in the larger landscape.

Studying the Cultural Contexts of Teaching and Learning in the English Language Arts

The switch from invisible to visible pedagogies has set new challenges for ethnographic research in English and the language arts. Ethnographic research is rooted in concepts of culture and community and the specifics of time and place. Researchers have used this to explore the boundaries between literacy and language practices at home and school and bring them into new relationship. This remains a central concern for work in this area. Yet this endeavour has also raised a number of questions for the field. Where should the focus rest, with which communities, which settings, which practices and which texts? These are political as well as logistical questions. They throw into relief different understandings of the purposes of education and its potential reach. They also map onto conflicting views of the ideal as well as actual relationships between education, social structure and agency.

These issues are contested within the field as much through the selection of the object of enquiry as through open debate. Take for example Dombey's study of the bedtime story (1992). Using recordings of the conversation that occurs as mother and child make their way through a picture book, Dombey argues that the talk that accompanies the reading matters as much as the voicing aloud of the words on the page. Her analysis of one such event shows that mother and child review the action of the story as it unfolds, ask questions about what will happen next and talk about why things are as they are. The analysis focuses on the democratic and creative potential of both spoken and written language. It demonstrates the pedagogic value of talk about text that actively engages children with exploring the narrative logic of the story world. The focus on the playfulness of this encounter and its intimacy acts as a riposte to didactic literacy pedagogies which prioritise decoding and accurate recall at the expense of other important aspects of learning to read. Yet, the data also captures practices which are specific to and much valorised by particular middle class communities. This potentially sets at nought those communities who do not already share this practice.

The title of Heath's article "What No Bed-time Story Means" (1982) highlights some of the tension points, suggesting as it does that the absence of the bed-time story matters. Heath proposes that in important ways literacy practices in "mainstream" homes dovetail with ideas about literacy learning that are prevalent in school. She argues that by contrast other communities experience no such continuities in practice as they enter school. This disadvantages their children whilst simultaneously privileging those whose practices operate seamlessly either side of the home-school boundary.

"What No Bed-time Story Means" derives from Heath's extensive and full-scale ethnographic research into the language and literacy practices of two distinct Appalachian communities, Roadville and Trackton, which culminated in the publication of *Ways with Words* (Heath, 1983). This was indeed the result of "doing ethnography" in the classic anthropological tradition. In the book Heath returns to the question of the apparent absence in the White working-class community of Roadville and the Black working-class community of Trackton of particular competencies and practices closely associated by middle-class communities with literacy learning. She turns this contrast on its head by revealing the presence of other no less important competencies these communities generate round literacy which schools overlook.

This takes the argument over home school boundary relations in another direction, towards the issue of whether and how schools recognise what communities already do. The book makes a strong case for teachers to identify and fully understand different ways of entering into uses of language and literacy, rooted in diverse community practices which children will bring with them into school. This acts as a challenge to normative judgements, which would otherwise create a picture of deficient communities. Once teachers recognise the "funds of knowledge" communities already deploy new connections can be built from home to school practices in ways that open up school learning to all (González, Moll, & Amanti, 2005).

These remain powerful ideas which continue to influence ethnographic research into the English language arts. Yet, they have not fully settled the issues of which kinds of literacy practices, which communities and which texts teachers should pay attention to, nor how they should use that knowledge in the classroom. In the research literature, arguments revolve around the extent to which co-opting out-of-school knowledge inside school acts as a powerful resource; how such knowledge can act as a bridge to other kinds of school-based literacy practices; and whether pedagogies formed across the boundary can act as levers to produce higher achievement or greater social equality? In the United States these arguments have played out most strongly round practices and texts associated with minority communities; in the UK they are as likely to play out around gender, new technologies or social class.

In one sense this is a framing issue: the kinds of research into home practices advocated by Dombey and Heath both have a point and a function, but they bring very different things into relationship through the sampling choices they made. The accounts they generate of particular local practices unsettle schooling in different kinds of ways, and do so with different strategic objectives in mind. Both Ladson-Billings' (1995) work on culturally relevant pedagogies and Gutiérrez's (2006) work on pedagogies for empowerment make explicit where they think priorities should lie. Both draw attention to what they see as shortcomings in some attempts to bring home and school into a different alignment, and in particular challenge approaches that do not really deliver for communities via this route. For Gutiérrez, this is partly a methodological issue. She argues that the research-base is often insubstantial, the engagement with the community insufficient:

it has become commonplace to study cultural communities even when we know very little about a community, its history, its shared and varied practices, and to carry out our work without the accompanied examination of the assumptions we hold vis-à-vis such communities. (2006, p. 225)

But there is also a hard edged politics to the case they make. Both insist that such approaches will only be enough if they lead to high achievement—and the record here is at best patchy (Ladson-Billings, 1995). In making this judgement, they are increasingly looking out to an educational landscape fundamentally shaped by performance scores and the verdict they pass on individuals, on teachers, on schools and on communities.

The Cultural Contexts of Teaching and Learning in the English Language Arts: Looking Towards the Future

In an interesting discussion on the contribution case studies and small-scale ethnographies make to knowledge about literacy, Brandt and Clinton (2002) comment on a significant weakness in the field that derives from its insistence on a focus on the local. They argue that the local is always intersected by larger shapes, and that to ignore this is to rob the analysis of proper depth. We simply end up looking in the wrong place for the wrong kinds of evidence. Championing the local is not enough to bring things right.

Where anyone is observed reading and writing something, it is well worth asking who else is getting something out of it; often that somebody will not be at the scene. Literacy objects can function as the medium through which the energies invested in literate practices in one context are organized into benefits for those in other contexts (just as benefits from other contexts might flow to individuals through the use and form of their literacy). We need perspectives that show the various hybrids, alliances, and multiple agents and agencies that simultaneously occupy acts of reading and writing. Agency is indeed alive and well in reading and writing but it is not a solo performance. (Brandt & Clinton, 2002, p. 347)

In the article they suggest that these more complex connections that link literacy here to literacy there can be traced through the materiality of literacy and its technologies: individual agency is not enough to subsume bigger forces elsewhere.

The Brandt and Clinton (2002) article has provoked considerable discussion amongst ethnographers of literacy (Street, 2003, 2004; Lewis, Enciso, & Moje, 2007). It has also brought general acknowledgement that there is indeed a limit to research at the local level:

for many people the literacies they engage with come from elsewhere and are not self invented; and there is more going on in a local literacy than "just local practice", [these] are all important caveats to deter [researchers] from over emphasizing or romanticizing the local. (Street, 2003, p. 2826)

Attention has turned to what dealing with the non-local, cast as the distant/the autonomous, might mean. This has set the scene for a re-run of arguments over structure and agency, and how far local action is constrained by forces outside itself or still finds room to re-make the social world. Much of the discussion then focuses on the tools available to make the distant appear and whether or how far this is necessary. However, in the context of this piece, I want to take this discussion another way and reflect on the limits of "the local" as a frame by which to count in or count out the object of study (see also Kell, 2006).

To put the local in place in research into English and the language arts, researchers often start either with a particular text or a particular community and then within this frame document the social interactions that instantiate reading or writing as meaningful exchanges in this case. The local is a distinct mode of operating – authentic and purposeful. By challenging the limits of the local, Brandt and Clinton's (2002) charge seems to rob such moments of their inner integrity. Yet as things stand in terms of the technologies and sites for literacy practices, and the settings in which literacy is learned, it is becoming increasingly hard to get a handle on "authentic" practices in this way (Kirkland & Jackson, 2009). Texts seldom belong fully to one community—hip-hop literacies provide an obvious example. Via the music industry and the Internet such texts have gone out well beyond the community boundaries that might once have generated and contained them. Even within the originating community (however that could be defined, taking into account differences of gender and class), hip-hop literacies do not stand for a single thing (Hill, 2008). Rather they take their place amongst a veritable cacophony of other practices both at the point they originate and as they continue to circulate. This brings them into a continuous process of dispute and challenge. Indeed, how disputes and challenges arise and are resolved may be more important to study and document than who really owns the practice or the space that is required to enact ownership (Moss, 2007)

Texts do not always align with particular communities, whilst particular communities are themselves divided by gender and class (Moss, 2007; Solsken, 1993; Stabile, 2000). How then should ethnographers of English and the language arts frame their enquiry?

I began this chapter by signalling the way in which over the last 20 years centrally-driven processes of education reform have altered relations between teachers and taught, and between schools, communities, and the state (Bernstein, 1996). These changes can be instantiated at the level of classroom practice (Moss, 2004). The attempt to bring practices from home into school have become immensely more difficult; rather a reverse process is underway in which homes as cultural sites are increasingly pedagogized by the state (Ball & Vincent, 2005). The relative success schools are able to demonstrate in terms of pupil performance now plays out in the public arena. If they do not meet the benchmarks set, teachers, schools, pupils, and communities can all variously be blamed. In this sense learning literacy in schools is shaped through the intertwining of the local and the distant, the autonomous and the ideological. Keep the focus too tight on patterns of social interaction in school classrooms or their relationship to home, and we risk missing something else: the economic ruin visited on whole communities through economic re-structuring that has reshaped expectations about what education should do for whom. Ethnographies of literacy learning need to keep these bigger shapes in mind as they navigate and the immediate and the small scale.

References

Ball, S., & Vincent, C. (2005). The 'childcare champion'? New Labour, social justice and the childcare market. *British Educational Research Journal, 31*(5), 557–570.

Barnes, D. (1977). *Communication and learning in small groups.* London: Routledge and Kegan Paul.

Bernstein, B. (1996). *Pedagogy, symbolic control and identity.* London: Taylor & Francis.

Bloome, D., Power, C., S., Morton, C., B., & Otto, S. (2005). *Discourse analysis & the study of classroom language & literacy events: A microethnographic perspective.* Mahwah, NJ: Erlbaum.

Bourne, J. (2000). New imaginings of reading for a new moral order: A review of the production, transmission and acquisition of a new pedagogic culture in the UK. *Linguistics and Education, 11*(1), 31–45.

Brandt, D., & Clinton, K. (2002). Limits of the local: Expanding perspectives on literacy as a social practice. *Journal of Literacy Research, 34*(3), 337–356.

Dombey, H. (1992). Lessons learnt at bedtime. In K. Kimberley, M. Meek, & J. Miller (Eds.), *New readings* (pp. 29–36). London: A & C Black.

Dyson, A. (2003). *The brothers and sisters learn to write: Popular literacies in childhood and school cultures.* New York: Teachers College Press.

González, N., Moll, L. C., & Amanti, C. (2005). *Funds of knowledge:Theorizing practices in households, communities, and classrooms.* Mahwah, NJ: Erlbaum.

Green, J., & Bloome, D. (1997). Ethnography and ethnographers of and in education: A situated perspective. In J. Flood, S. Heath, & D. Lapp (Eds.), *A handbook of research on teaching literacy through the communicative and visual arts* (pp. 181–202). New York: Simon & Shuster Macmillan.

Gutiérrez, K. (2000). Teaching and Learning in the 21st Century. *English Education, 32,* 290–298.

Gutiérrez, K. (2006). White innocence: A framework and methodology for rethinking educational discourse. *International Journal of Learning, 12,* 1–11.

Halliday, M. A. K. (1975). *Learning how to mean.* London: Arnold.

Heath, S. B. (1982). What no bedtime story means: narrative skills at home and school. *Language and Society, 11,* 49–76.

Heath, S. B. (1983). *Ways with words.* Cambridge, UK: Cambridge University Press.

Hicks, D. (2002). *Reading lives: Working-class children and literacy learning.* New York: Teachers College Press.

Hill, M. L. (2008). Toward a pedagogy of the popular: Bourdieu, hip-hop, and out-of-school literacies. In J. Albright & A. Luke (Eds.), *Pierre Bourdieu and literacy education* (pp. 131–161). London: Routledge.

Kell, C. (2006). Crossing the margins: Literacy, semiotics and the recontextualisation of meanings. In K. Pahl & J. Rowsell (Eds.), *Travel notes from the new literacy studies: Instances of practice.* Clevedon, UK: Multilingual Matters.

Kirkland, D., & Jackson, A. (2009). "We real cool": Toward a theory of black masculine literacies. *Reading Research Quarterly, 44*(3), 278–297.

Ladson-Billings, G. (1995). But that's just good teaching! The case for culturally relevant pedagogy. *Theory into Practice, 34*(3), 159–165.

Lewis, C., Enciso, P., & Moje, E. (Eds.). (2007). *Reframing sociocultural* research on literacy: identity, agency and power. Mahwah, NJ: Erlbaum.

Moss, G. (2004). Changing practice: The national literacy strategy and the politics of literacy policy. *Literacy, 38*(3), 126–133.

Moss, G. (2007). *Literacy and gender: Researching texts, contexts and readers*. Abingdon, UK: Routledge.

Perera, K (1985). *Children's reading and writing*. Oxford, UK: Blackwell.

Solsken, J. (1993). *Literacy, gender and work in families and in school*. Norwood, NJ: Ablex

Stabile, C. (2000). Resistance, recuperation, and reflexivity: The limits of a paradigm. In N. Brown & I. Szeman (Eds.), *Pierre Bourdieu: Fieldwork in culture*. Lanham, MD: Rowman & Littlefield.

Street, B. V. (2003). The limits of the local— 'Autonomous' or 'Disembedding'? *International Journal Of Learning, 10*, 2825–2830.

Street, B. V. (2004). Futures of the ethnography of literacy? *Language and Education, 18*(4), 326–330.

54

Analyzing Text and Talk Through Critical Discourse Analysis

STEPHANIE POWER-CARTER

This chapter provides a brief description of Critical Discourse Analysis (CDA) and a review of its influences and histories. The perspective here emphasizes multiple approaches to CDA and foregrounds influences from European social theorists as well as Black scholars in the later 19th and early 20th centuries.

CDA is an analytic approach that makes visible how language and various semiotic systems are implicated in social structures and social control, incorporating multiple disciplines and methodological approaches grounded in multiple histories (Wodak & Meyer, 2009). CDA can be characterized as having an overtly political agenda (cf. Kress 1990), examining how power and inequality are reproduced and enacted through text and talk in various social and political contexts (Van Dijk, 1993). Researchers using CDA are interested in understanding how discursive sources of power and dominance are reproduced, maintained, and transformed (Fairclough 1989, 1992, 2003).

CDA and related approaches (such as Critical Applied Linguistics cf., Pennycook, 2001) are becoming more widely used in research on the teaching and learning of the English language arts as researchers seek to better understand problems with language, literacy, and academic learning (e.g., Ivanic, 1998; Luke, 1995; Rogers, 2004; Sarroub, 2004). Particular attention has been paid to how some groups' literacy practices are marginalized and viewed as failing, while the literacy practices from dominant groups are viewed as high achieving (e.g., Carter, 2007; Kumasi, 2008). CDA is useful because many English language arts researchers see power relations as key to addressing educational inequities (see Bloome, Power-Carter, Morton-Christian, Otto, & Shuart-Farris, 2005, for further discussion of power).

Power relations are most effective when they are taken for granted, not questioned, and assumed to be "natural" without reasonable alternative. Gramsci (1971) called such extension and naturalization of power relations hegemonic. One agenda of CDA has been to make such "naturalized" and hegemonic power relations visible and thereby open to analysis, critique, and deconstruction.

CDA focuses on both micro and macro power relationships. Micro power relations involve local contexts (e.g., teacher-student interaction) within which a form of dominance or injustice occurs; macro power relations involve larger institutional and social contexts, and may be inscribed in particular laws and state policies. Both micro and macro level power relations are derivative of cultural ideologies and social, political, and economic structures. The distinction of micro and macro levels of power relations is a heuristic one. Power relations located at a macro level are experienced in everyday events (a micro level); and what people do in everyday events influences power relations at a macro level.

For example, consider the classroom discussion below from an ethnographic study on African American girls in a required high school British Literature classroom in the United States (see Carter, 2001). During this particular class they are discussing one of Shakespeare's sonnets, *My Mistresses Eyes are Nothing Like the Sun* (Sonnet 130). The teacher has engaged the students in discussing what the main idea is and, after several student responses, the teacher provides an "official" interpretation. She says:

> What we can read into it. Most of the sonnets before this had this most beautiful woman always being tall, long blonde hair, pretty big blue eyes and that was the universal beauty and that was Dante's beauty. From the Italians. So you had to be tall, slender, long blonde hair, pretty blue eyes, rosy checks. Uh so if you weren't that you were not, not attractive. Ugly. So if you're a-a tall brunette, not attractive, with brown eyes, you're still ugly according to the sonneteers. You're still not attractive. You're nothing.

The teacher's use of the phrase "read into it" suggests that she is asking students to do more than decode text; she is also asking them to read between the lines while perhaps also directing them toward a particular "reading" of the text. She uses the third person pronoun "we" to create a collective sense of identity and a shared, standard "reading" for which the students are accountable. The teacher describes the sonneteers' representation of beautiful women as "tall" "long blonde hair" with "pretty big blue eyes." She describes those characteristics as "universal beauty." Women without those characteristics are not only ugly, they're "nothing." Although this may not be the teacher's point of view about women's beauty, it is presented as a "universal" view of beauty and it derives from official and valorized literary texts.

The public, standard "reading" is problematic for students who are unable to attain these qualities, particularly, the African American girls. During interviews with the girls, they stated that they viewed the teacher as calling them ugly. And while this may not have been at all the teacher's intention, promulgating a raced definition of beauty (one prevalent in contemporary magazine and television advertisements as well as in the sonnets) marginalizes the African American girls both in terms of "beauty" and as readers (the way they read the sonnet is outside the standard reading.

A close examination of the sonnet shows that it can be read as arguing against the use of beauty as a criteria for the sonneteer's love. Yet, even in the dismissal it acknowledges what counts as "universal beauty" as he loves her in spite of not having those universal beauty characteristics. The characteristics of "universal beauty" are those of a particular set women of European descent.

There is a tense change during the discussion, from past to present tense. The teacher says, "according to the sonneteers you're still not attractive you're nothing." The tense shift suggests that certain dominant positions that support a particular view of beauty are also current. The Elizabethan sonneteers, white males of the European bourgeoisie, define "universal beauty" both then and now.

The brief analysis above illustrates how CDA makes visible how various linguistic and text based content and structures embed power relations at a macro level (sexist and racist concepts of beauty) within micro level contexts, how they valorize dominant ideologies (in this case about beauty, race, and gender relations), and marginalize and attack the personhood of some within local settings (the classroom) and in the broader society (Black women in general).

CDA Influences and Histories

The historical roots of CDA, in part, can be traced back to the Frankfurt School of the 1930s. Among the scholars associated with the Frankfurt School are Herbert Marcuse, Theodor Ardona, Max Horkheimer, Walter Benjamin, and Jurgen Habermas. The Frankfurt School is often credited with creating one of the first models of critical cultural studies (Kellner, 1989; see also Wiggershaus, 1994) and combined cultural and communication studies, textual analysis, and the analysis of social and ideological effects. An analysis of power was explicit in these studies as they argued that popular culture was used to manipulate the masses to become unreceptive and docile.

More recently, CDA has become associated with a group of European scholars (Teen van Dijk, Norman Fairclough, Gunther Kress, Theo van Leeuwen, Ruth Wodak, among others) that emerged in the 1991 following a symposium at the University of Amsterdam (see Rogers, 2004; Wodak, 2004). Building on a broad range of European social theorists (including the Frankfurt School), they sought an agenda that would make visible how discourse is produced, interpreted and reproduced; structured by dominance; highly contextualized; and socially and historically situated (Wodak & Meyer, 2009).

There are important variations among the perspectives taken by scholars employing CDA. Approaches vary with regard to the linguistic perspectives employed (systemtic functional linguistics, e.g., Kress & Hodge, 1979; applied linguistics, e.g., Pennycook, 2001; American models of grammatical and textual analysis, sociolingusitics, and literacy criticism, e.g., Gee, 1999, 2004), the interdisciplinary nature of the analysis (i.e., which set disciplines are employed; see Wodak & Chilton, 2005, for one set of interdisciplinary variations) and how discourse analysis is connected to various social theories and perspectives including history, ethnography, cultural studies, and social theories derivative of particular theorists such as Foucault, Bourdieu, and Bernstein (see van Leeuwen, 2005).

Although not labeled "Critical Discourse Analysis," the scholarship of Black scholars in the United States in the later 19th and early 20th centuries also provides a foundation for current iterations of critical discourse analysis. These scholars include W.E.B. DuBois, Ana Julia Cooper, Carter G. Woodson, Sojourner Truth, among others. Their experiences were informed by a unique social location rooted in a history of marginalization (DuBois, 1903). Their experiences in their everyday lives and as scholars were rooted in different epistemological understandings that were often ignored or invisible to dominant society. In their scholarship, they examined societal problems as well as how power and inequality were reproduced and enacted through text and talk in various social and political contexts.

For example, consider Sojourner Truth's "Ain't I A Woman Speech" at the 1851 Women's Rights Convention in Akron, Ohio. Sojourner Truth (1797–1883) was born a slave and became an activist and lecturer. The societal problem in which she focused was personhood. Personhood is a construct that examines "who and what is considered to be a person, what attributes and rights are constructed as inherent to being a person, an what social positions are available" (Egan-Robertson, 1998, p. 453). In her speech, in a mainly unfriendly and hostile environment, Sojourner Truth sought to challenge existing sexist and racist ideologies that positioned Black women negatively but that were nonetheless naturalized. The excerpt from her speech below was recorded in a manner that attempted to capture her use of African American language.

Excerpt from *Ain't I A Woman*

> Dat man ober dar say dat womin needs to be helped into carriages, and lifted ober ditches, and to hab de best place everywhar. Nobody eber halps me into carriages, or ober mudpuddles, or gibs me any best place! And ar'n't I a woman? Look at me! Look at my arm! [And here she bared her right arm to the shoulder, showing her tremendous muscular power] I have ploughed, and planted, and gathered into barns, and no man could head me! And ar'n't I a woman? I could work as much and eat as much as a man—when I could get it—and bear de lash as well! And ar'n't' I a woman? I have borne thirteen chilern, and seen 'em mos' all sold off the slavery, and when I cried out with my mother's grief, none but Jesus heard me! And ar'n't I a woman? (http://www.kyphilom.com/www/truth.html)

The talk in this excerpt situates Sojourner Truth in a particular historical contexts where women are positioned as "needs to be helped." Sojourner Truth acknowledges the complexities of power relations and how she has been positioned as a Black woman by the dominant group, noting that "Nobody eber halps me into carriages, or ober mudpuddles, or gibs me any best place!" Moreover, by posing the question "Aren't I a woman," she begins to make visible complexities of power relations among women and how most women from the dominant group did not even recognize her personhood, womanhood, or intellect. Part of what she is challenging is how "woman" is being defined and the underlying narrative of women's lives, including the raced nature of an assumed and taken for granted definition and narrative of "woman" and the relationship of women to men. Her use of Black vernacular also constitutes a critique of the location of knowledge. Assuming that the recording of her speech is reasonably accurate, she challenges the naturalized assumption that knowledge is located in and validated by the formalized language of professional and "educated" classes, and instead locates knowledge in the everyday experiences of Black women (which can be viewed as a precursor to some aspects of critical race theory, see Crenshaw, Gotanda, & Thomas, 1995, and to Black feminist theory, see Collins, 1990).

Final Comments

What counts as CDA is defined by its purpose: to examine how texts, language practices, and related semiotic systems structure power relations that result in social, civil, economic, and political inequities. The epistemological basis of CDA derives from many histories including European social theorists, Black scholars and activists, and others, who seek to make visible how discourses at both a micro and macro level privilege some at the expense of others, deny personhood to some, and do so in a manner that appears natural and common sense and unassailable. CDA challenges those discourses, reveals the linguistic and semiotic means by which they assert and promulgate, and creates opportunities to imagine alternatives.

In researching the teaching and learning of the English language arts, CDA provides a way to make visible the power relations implicit in the literary texts read and in class discussions. But CDA can also be a curricular component providing teachers and students with a framework for analyzing as well as a way of articulating how they have been marginalized or had their personhood attacked.

References

Bloome, D., Power-Carter, S., Morton-Christian, B, Otto, S., & Shuart-Farris, N. (2005). *Discourse analysis and the study of classroom language and literacy events: Micro-ethnographic perspective.* Mahwah, NJ: Erlbaum.

Carter, S. (2001). *The possibilities of silence: African-American female cultural identity and secondary English classrooms.* Unpublished doctoral dissertation, Vanderbilt University, Nashville, Tennessee.

Carter, S. (2007). "Reading all that white crazy stuff": Black young women unpacking whiteness in a high school British literature classroom. *Journal of Classroom Interaction, 41,* 42–54.

Collins, P. (1990). *Black feminist thought: Knowledge, consciousness, and the politics of empowerment.* Cambridge, MA: Unwin Hyman.

Crenshaw, K., Gotanda, N., & Thomas, K. (Eds.). (1995). *Critical race theories: The key writings that formed the movement.* New York: The New Press.

Egan-Robertson, A. (1998). Learning about culture, language, and power: Understanding relationships among personhood, literacy practices, and intertextuality. *Journal of Literacy Research, 30,* 449–487.

DuBois, W.E.B. (1903). *Souls of black folk: Essays and sketches.* Chicago: A.C. McClurg and Company.

Fairclough, N. (1989). *Language and power.* London: Longman.

Fairclough, N, (1992). *Discourse and social change.* Cambridge, UK: Polity Press.

Fairclough, N. (2003). *Analyzing discourse: Textual analysis for social research.* London: Routledge.

Gee, J. P. (1999). *An introduction to discourse analysis: Theory and method approaches to discourse.* New York: Routledge.

Gee, J. P. (2004). Discourse analysis: What makes it critical? In R. Rogers (Ed.), *Critical discourse analysis in education* (pp. 19–50). Mahwah, NJ: Erlbaum.

Gramsci, A. (1971). *Prison notebooks.* New York: International Publishers.

Ivanic. R. (1998). *Writing and identity: The discoursal construction of identity in academic writing.* Amsterdam: John Benjamins.

Kellner, D. (1989). *Critical theory, Marxism, and modernity.* Baltimore, MD: John Hopkins University Press.

Kress, G., (1990). Critical discourse analysis. *Annual Review of Applied Linguistics, 11,* 84–99.

Kress, G., & Hodge, R. (1979). *Language and ideology.* London: Routledge.

Kumasi, K. (2008). *Seeing white in black: Examining racial identity among African American adolescents in a culturally centered book club.* UMI Dissertation Services: Ann Arbor, MI.

Luke, A. (1995). Text and discourse in education: An introduction to critical discourse analysis. In M. Apple (Ed.), *Review of research in education* (Vol, 21, pp. 3–48). Washington, DC: AERA.

Pennycook, A. (2001). *Critical applied linguistics: A critical introduction.* Mahwah, NJ: Erlbaum.

Rogers, R. (2004). A critical discourse analysis of literate identities across contexts: Alignment and conflict. In R. Rogers (Ed.), *An introduction to critical discourse analysis in education* (pp. 51–78). Mahwah, NJ: Erlbaum.

Rogers, R. (Ed.). (2004). *An introduction to critical discourse analysis in education.* Mahwah, NJ: Erlbaum.

Sarroub, L. (2004). Reframing for decisions: Transforming talk about literacy assessment among teachers and researchers. In R. Rogers

(Ed.), *An introduction to critical discourse analysis in education*. (pp. 97–116). Mahwah, NJ: Erlbaum.

Truth, S. (1851). Ain't I a woman? Retrieved March 11, 2010, from http://www.kyphilom.com/www/truth.html

van Dijk, T. A. (1993). Principles of critical discourse analysis. *Discourse and Society, 4*(2), 249–83.

Van Leeuwen, T. (2005). Three models of interdisciplinarity. In R. Wodak & P. Chilton (Eds.), *A new agenda in (critical) discourse analysis*. (pp. 3–18). Philadelphia: John Benjamins.

Wiggershaus, R. (1994). *The Frankfurt School: Its history, theories, and political significance* (Michael Robertson, Trans.). Cambridge, MA: The MIT Press.

Wodak, R. (2004). Critical discourse analysis. In C. Seale, G. Gobo, J. F. Gubrium, & D. Silverman (Eds.), *Qualitative research practice* (pp. 197–213). London: Sage.

Wodak, R. (2005). Preface: Reflecting on CDA. In R. Wodak & P. Chilton (Eds.), *A new agenda in (critical) discourse analysis* (pp. xi–xiii). Philadelphia: John Benjamins.

Wodak, R., & Chilton, P. (Eds.). (2005). *A new agenda in (critical) discourse analysis*. Philadelphia: John Benjamins.

Wodak, R., & Meyer, M. (2009). Critical discourse analysis: History, agenda, theory and methodology. In R. Wodak & M. Meyer (Eds.), *Methods of critical discourse analysis* (2nd ed., pp. 1–33). London: Sage.

55

Emic Perspectives of Research

THANDEKA CHAPMAN AND VALERIE KINLOCH

The term "emic" is often used when describing qualitative research that focuses on the uniqueness of a culture or experience. Thomas Headland, noted linguistic, anthropologist, and student of Kenneth L. Pike, concluded that less than 30% of authors from 20 different research fields credited Pike in their discussions of emic and etic perspectives (Headland, Pike, & Harris, 1990). As can be expected, the terms "etic" and "emic" have been widely used and re-defined in the research literature from various disciplines. For this chapter, Pike's original articulations of emic research are used as a means to re-capture the original intent of the term and to apply it to current research in the field that resonates with emic forms of scholarship.

The body of scholarship highlighted in the chapter comes from various methodologies, diverse sets of assumptions, and often does not adhere to a rigid set of "scientifically-based" research processes. The focus on emic research transcends the paradigms of post-positive, interpretive, and critical research (Willis, 2007) or external, internal, or interactional categories of research (Bredo, 2006). Instead, the chapter focuses on the common experiences, questions, and concerns researchers encounter when conducting intimate projects on learning spaces, families, and students involved in teaching and learning in English language arts (TLELA). Additionally, the nature of TLELA settings as connected to the discipline of English, as a complex set of relationships and group dynamics among teachers and students, and as tied to all aspects of language and culture, lends itself to a cultural linguistic analysis similar to the scholarship cultivated by Pike. In this chapter the nature and possibilities of research focused on emic perspectives of culture and behavior are discussed using recent studies in TLELA to highlight the value of emic perspectives, the tensions inherent in doing this work, and the new challenges and possibilities that emerge.

Definition of Emic

Pike, a researcher from the field of linguistics, constructed the terms "etic" and "emic" by removing the first half of the words "phonetic" and "phonemic" to describe the interplay between what the researcher sees as parts of language, verbal and nonverbal, and culture that are reflected in other cultures and languages specific to a certain group: "To put it another way, the etic is the level of universals, or the level of things which may be observed by an 'objective' observer. The emic is the level of meaningful contrasts within a particular language or culture" (Barnard, 2000, p. 114). Pike credits previous scholars and mentors for their descriptions of the dualist interplay between the general and the specific that is imbedded in linguistics and cross-cultural research. It was only when framing this interplay through a theory of tagmemes or tagmemic theory, that he felt the need to label the process of linguistic and cultural analysis in these distinctive ways. Pike states, "Culture and language learning form an essential inseparable dyad for understanding in cross-cultural contexts" (Pike & McKinney, 1996, p. 40). In truth, because Pike thought of language as both verbal utterances and nonverbal behavior that elicited response, he would rail at a distinction between language and culture as two separate entities when they are so indelibly tied to one another.

As with other dialectical systems, the components of emic cannot properly be defined and discussed without an understanding of components of etic. Pike describes the principal differences, which are referenced throughout this chapter, between them:

- Creation versus discovery of a system: The etic organization of a world-wide cross cultural scheme may be created by the analyst. The emic structure of a particular system must be discovered.

- External versus internal view: Descriptions or analysis from the etic standpoint are "alien" in view, with criteria external to the system. Emic descriptions provide an internal view, with criteria chosen from within the system. They represent to us the view of one familiar with the system and who knows how to function within it himself.
- External versus internal plan: An etic system may be set up by criteria or 'logical' plan whose relevance is external to the system being studied. The discovery or setting up of the emic system requires the inclusion of criteria relevant to the internal functioning of the system itself.
- Absolute versus relative criteria: The etic criteria may often be considered absolute, or measurable directly. Emic criteria are relative to the internal characteristics of the system and can be usefully described or measured relative to each other.
- Non-integration versus integration: The etic view does not require that every unit be viewed as part of a larger setting. The emic view, however, insists that every unit be seen as somehow distributed and functioning within a larger structural unit or setting, in a hierarchy of units and hierarchy of settings as units.
- Sameness and difference as measured versus systemic: Two units are different etically when instrumental measurements can show them to be so. Units are different emically only when they elicit different responses from people acting within the same system.
- Partial versus total data: Etic data are obtainable early in analysis with partial information. In principle, on the contrary, emic criteria require a knowledge of the total system to which they are relative and from which they ultimately draw their significance.
- Preliminary versus final presentation: Hence, etic data provide access into the system- the starting point of analysis…. The final analysis or presentation, however, would be in emic units. (1967, p. 39)

Pike warns that confusing the distinctions between etic and emic perspectives may jeopardize the data analysis and findings and misrepresent the people and culture being explained.

Definitions In this chapter, the term "emic" is paired with the terms research, constructs, data, and perspective. Emic research or studies refers to research designs focused on specific localized contexts. Emic constructs refer to those components of emic units that can be assumed to contribute to context specificity—social, linguistic, race, location, political situations, etc. Emic data is the information researchers gather to articulate the events, perceptions, and behaviors identified in these specific contexts. Lastly, emic perspectives are those points of view held by the participants in their everyday lives and cultivated by researchers to document those same lives.

Transferability Goals of Researchers Conducting Emic Studies In the beginning of the chapter, emic studies are not referred to as unique, but as intimate research. The distinction between unique and intimate is worth noting. The definition of unique is something that is like no other, whereas the definition of intimate is a relationship of closeness and proximity, physical and emotional. Studies that focus on emic constructs highlight those aspects specific to particular contexts, but also desire the reader to draw parallels between his/her own experiences and those of the participants. Stake (1978/2000) describes this phenomenon as naturalistic generalization. When explaining the relationship between the general and the particular, Stake states that "naturalistic generalization, arrived at by recognizing the similarities of objects and issues in and out of context and by sensing the natural covariations of happenings" is "both intuitive and empirical" (2000, p. 22) and is often superior to other generalizations that can lead to over-simplifying events and people's perspectives. Naturalistic generalization is neither prescriptive nor universal, but contextualized by the educator reading or hearing the scholarship.

Intimate research captures often unknown programs and examples of successful teacher practice and student learning. The context(s) of the events and participants' experiences remain integral to the stories that the researcher relates to the public. Education researchers hope that documenting people's lives in this manner will inspire other educators to replicate good practice, alter or eliminate less-successful elements of their approaches to education, and show more of the possibilities for teaching and learning. Lincoln and Guba (1979, 2000) offer that readers' ability to make connections between themselves and the study, to transfer or translate the newly described situation to their own situations, is called "fittingness." Fittingness is the ability of the reader, once that she has ample description and information about the contexts of the study, to then relate those contexts to her own, given that only she knows the details of that context. Only the reader, who knows both her context and the published study, can properly transfer the findings or suggestions to a new setting. It is incumbent upon the researcher to provide the necessary emic analysis to the reader so that she can properly make those transfers.

Why TLELA Researchers Choose to Conduct Emic Studies

The nature of teaching and learning in English language arts is both a personal and community endeavor. Through the many components of and interactions with language, English teachers regularly ask students to take various risks in their classrooms. These risks range from sharing an analysis of an academic text to disclosing personal experiences, thoughts, and beliefs. Teachers ask students to establish textual, personal, and social connections with and across canonical and contemporary readings as well as with popular cultural forms. Then, they require students to critically explain and explore their identities in writing and in speech. Students become emotionally vulnerable to peers and teachers when asked to submit their writing for critique or defend their position during a class discussion. Reader Response theory and critical theory, two commonly used frameworks for teaching literature, require the reader to personally engage with the text. When a teacher invites students on a journey through time and space, she seeks to engage students beyond the acquisition and enhancement of academic skills into a deeper understanding of social, emotional, and political issues that reflect who they are or wish to become in the future. Researchers attempt to mimic these same personal relationships and ask participants to risk vulnerability in emic research so that they may document the intimate nature of teaching and learning in English language arts.

Nature of Methodologies that Highlight Emic Perspectives

Given the emic nature of TLELA, research methodologies that support the philosophies of teachers of English seem to make a reasonable pairing. A meta-analysis conducted by Juzwik et al. (2006) showed that over 75% of the reported studies conducted between 1999 and 2004 on teaching and learning writing were done using interpretive methods. While that does not qualify the studies as emic, it does draw attention to the increasing ways researchers have gravitated towards methods that may provide emic data. We believe that most qualitative methodologies that lend themselves to research require an analysis of emic constructs. However, it is up to the researcher to shape her study in the direction of such an intimate research design.

A number of issues and criteria affect the decision to focus on emic constructs. Researchers who collect emic data on participants' lives and perceptions appreciate the flexibility of the researcher as observer, participant, instructor, and learner: "Participants can be both subjective and objective, and observers [researchers] can be both subjective and objective" (Harris quoted in Headland, Pike, & Harris, 1990, p. 50). In this vein, the researcher takes on different forms due to what is required by the contexts of the research, the way that the study evolves, and the research questions. In TLELA, these studies may have one or more of the following goals:

- Understand how teachers and students make connections between art and life
- Describe/explain students' communities—small/large; close/distant; present/historical
- Describe/explain students' literacy practices
- Explore student identity
- Document the teaching of ELA—how and why teachers of ELA do what they do
- Provide examples of good practice

The adaptability of the research process and these research goals reflect various methodologies that align with ethnography and case study research in TLELA.

Ethnography

Lillis (2008) justly contends that ethnographic methods and an ethnographic methodology are not synonymous terms. She advocates for more research on writing to employ a full ethnographic methodology to express an emic perspective of the TLELA. Lillis suggests that "a lengthy or sustained engagement in participants' academic writing worlds, and the collection and analysis of a range of types of data in order to build holistic understandings" (p. 362) allow the researcher to create thick descriptions (see also Heath & Street, 2008) of participants, events, and contexts of these learning spaces. Her understanding of ethnography stems from Hammersley's features of education ethnography:

- Ethnography is concerned with the collection and analysis of empirical data drawn from "real world" contexts rather than being produced under experimental conditions created by the researcher; The research involves sustained engagement in the field;
- A key aim is for the researcher to attempt to make sense of events from the perspectives of participants; Data are gathered from a range of sources, but observation and/or relatively informal conversations are often key tools;
- The focus is a single setting or group of relatively small scale or a small number of these. In life history research, the focus may even be a single individual;
- The analysis of the data involves interpretations of the meanings and functions of human actions…. (Lillis, 2008, p. 358)

In addition to these features, which parallel the components of emic research detailed earlier, Heath and Street (2008) argue for the subjective, interpretive, and partial nature of ethnographic research. They contend: "The *emic* or locally held perspective of an individual, group, or institution, such as a school, can bring into its knowledge system that which has been established from an *etic* or comparative analysis" (p. 44). Education ethnographers use emic perspectives from participants to highlight the emic constructs particular to groups or individuals in teaching and learning settings.

Case Study

Similarly, case study research in education is often used to document the emic perspectives of the participants and the emic constructs of a group while allowing the reader to create naturalistic generalizations or fittingness. When discussing the role of case study research Stake (1978/2000) gives his opinion:

Its [case study's] best use appears to me to be adding to existing experiences and humanistic understanding. Its characteristics match the 'readiness' people have for added experience. As Von Wright and others stressed, intentionality and empathy are central to the comprehension of social problems, but so also is information that is holistic and episodic. The discourse of persons struggling to increase their understanding of social matters features and solicits these qualities. And these qualities match nicely the characteristics of the case study. (2000, p. 24)

Undoubtedly, "cases are constructed, not found" (Dyson & Genishi, 2005, p. 2); they contribute to what we know about and learn from what Stake (2000) refers to as "existing experiences" and "social matters." Case studies have holistic and episodic ventures that correlate with emic and etic constructs of individual studies. The emic constructs are the bounded systems around the case—those criteria, contexts, and events that are specific to that study. The etic constructs are the grand hypothesis or broader issues being targeted in the study (Stake, 1978/2000).

Role(s) of the Researcher According to Pike's tagmemic theory, etic and emic participant perspectives are two sides of the same coin that must be teased a part by the knowledgeable researcher. When the researcher analyzes etic data, those verbal and nonverbal behaviors that are clearly related to other groups or the greater society, she creates a type of cultural understanding across groups. When the researcher analyzes the data looking for independent emic data, she then creates a second type of understanding within the group. The third understanding results from removing the specific contexts surrounding the emic data and cross-referencing them with other non-specific emic data to confirm or disconfirm the possibilities for new etic data that can be generalized across groups. Thus, an emic data without its specific cultural context may also serve an etic analysis of the larger societal context (Pike, 1967).

The knowledgeable researcher, who understands the cultural contexts being observed and documented, is integral to the emic study. Pike and McKinney (1996) explain the dyad that is created by language and culture in contexts that are cross-cultural. To prevent misinterpretations and "cultural clash," they insist that "the individual who seeks to work successfully in a second culture context needs to gain an emic view of that culture" (p. 40). The researcher's ability to understand the insider perspective is only one aspect of conducting emic research. The researcher bridges academic explanations of behavior and perception to the documented events and lived experiences of the participants. Barnard (2000) asserts, "…they [the participants] might be unable to describe the emic system [constructs] which underlies their cultural understandings and practices. The discovery of that system is the task of the analyst, not the informant" (p.114). As highlighted in various educational studies, it is essential that researchers explain and translate the emic constructs of participants to other venues so that the lives of the participants may be better understood and acknowledged.

Goals and Overview of Small Studies

A wealth of scholarship in TLELA has embraced emic research. The shift from etic to emic research points to

ongoing interest for researchers to ground ethnographies and symbolic and interpretive observational approaches in local events, practices, and ways of life. Such a perspective encompasses sophisticated analyses of life patterns, unique relations of spatial-temporal conditions, and events of/within specified groups (participants) and communities (contexts). Important in such studies are the ways researchers rely on emic perspectives to document what they observe and learn without the imposition of etic, outsider and predetermined, often fixed, analytic categories.

There are educational projects on students' literacy practices (Mahiri, 1994; Dimitriadis, 2001), democratic engagements across contexts (Kinloch, 2009; Gustavson, 2008), school/non-school identities (Hill, 2009), and textual productions (Vasudevan, 2006). Additionally, a number of studies seek to understand how teachers and students make connections between art and life, describe students' communities (e.g., small/large; distant/close; present/historical), and document TLELA to determine how/why teachers do what they do (Fecho, 2004; Yagelski, 2000). The importance of adopting an emic perspective impacts what researchers observe and how they conduct observations indicative of what participants demonstrate through their own actions and life experiences.

Emic Perspectives and Literacy Research in Nonschool Contexts This latter point—that emic data can reveal participants' patterns of life and inform how researchers conduct observations—is reflected in representative literacy studies in nonschool contexts. Mahiri (1994), for example, describes the adaptive literacy practices of African American males participating in the Youth Basketball Association, in Chicago, Illinois. He observes how the youth engaged in a number of literacy activities: "close and extensive readings of certain texts—newspaper accounts of sports events, basketball card collections and associated guidebooks, and computer sport game screen texts and instruction books" (p. 143). In observing such practices, which he describes as "novel" and "alternative" reading rites because they often go unnoticed in schools, Mahiri recognizes relationships between participants and contexts. These behaviors and the contexts that make the reading both a viable literacy and an ignored competency may be classified as emic data specific to African American boys, but also an etic analysis concerning the nature of American boys' reading interests.

The recognition of interconnections between people and places, or participants and their familial, social contexts, is a significant factor in research that utilizes an emic perspective. In addition to his early research on adaptive literacy, Mahiri (1991, 1994) has conducted extensive studies on the literacy practices of urban youth in a variety of contexts and forms: high school classrooms, community sites, digital environments, and African American youth culture. Close documentation of their actions and practices—whether during their involvement with sports or activities around writing—can reveal the complexities of youth literacy experiences as situated within local contexts and around local knowledge (Kinloch, 2010; Jocson, 2005; Dyson, 2005).

Undoubtedly, there are tensions inherent with conducting emic research. As the research study evolves, careful decisions have to be made about how to intimately document people's lives, engage in in-depth analyses of observations, and how to conceptualize personal and public (e.g., community/family and school/society) relations. These considerations parallel critical researchers' concerns about participant-researcher relationships and the dissemination of research findings (see Willis this volume).

To conduct "critical" research, Morrell (2008) acknowledges the sophisticated ability of people to engage in meaning-making processes that locate their lives and literacies within frameworks that reject deficit models (e.g., at risk, struggling readers/writers/thinkers). In this way, Morrell, much like Mahiri and other scholars (Bartlett, 2007; Lee, 2007; Lewis, Enciso, & Moje, 2002; Street, 1984) understand literacy as a social practice situated within contexts and by contextual factors that attend to dynamics of culture, power, privilege, and politics. These critical frames echo emic constructs and etic analyses in that the issues and frames of reference being documented are specific to particular racial, social, and gender groups, but their characteristics of oppression are very similar in ways that critical researchers may see as resonating with multiple groups.

Critical research further calls for researchers to work with participants to reveal emic data, culturally specific events, behaviors, and attitudes, which have been overlooked or under-valued in past research. Research that allows researchers to collaborate with and learn from local participants, such as Lunsford, Moglen, and Slevin's (1990) work prompts questions such as, "Are there literacies we do not see?" to re-evaluate TLELA classrooms from multiple emic perspective. Such is the case with current research concerned with the cultural practices of children, youth, and adults in and out-of-schools (Black, 2005; Hill & Vasudevan, 2008). By using an emic perspective in critical research, researchers can learn about the interactive patterns that affect participants' literacy practices, events, and learning processes as embedded in local time-space configurations. Such research moves beyond providing decontextualized superficial descriptions of participants and their environments. Critical and emic research both acknowledge and investigate the ways in which particular acts/events influence participants' engagement with others and local social institutions (e.g., schools, community centers, writing groups, etc).

Kinloch (2007, 2009, 2010) relies on theories of critical pedagogy and postmodern geography to observe cultural productions and community engagements of African American high school students in New York City's Harlem community. Concerned with gentrification in the area, participants utilize mapping, video interviews, and community surveys to: document art forms; question meanings of community; capture current and past spatial-temporal conditions; and examine the community as text to produce creative, personal written and oral narratives on their lived experiences and knowledge of historical trends. The students as researchers draw on their lives and the lives of local residents to document their emic perspectives of gentrification.

Important in the work of other literacy scholars are the critical stories that emerge *from* the experiences of participants and *from* the stories that are shared with readers (Kirkland, 2009; Lunsford, 2009; Fisher, Purcell, & May 2009; Chapman, 2005). As Vasudevan (2006) observes, it is important to engage in a redefinition of the meanings of teaching and learning in working with young people. This redefinition means that taking the stories of young people pubic in ways that honor students' engagements with storytelling, multimodality, and spatiality, the researcher becomes the interpreter of the emic constructs in which students live. These interpretations contribute to how teachers can better understand and relate to students within and across contexts. These research examples, along with others (see Alvermann, 2002; Hull & Schultz, 2003; Morrell & Duncan-Andrade, 2002) offer an important rationale for using students' emic perspectives and behaviors to support TLELA.

Emic Perspectives and Literacy Research in School Contexts

Emic research on/with participants' interactions within local settings impacts what researchers know about TLELA. As Lee (1995a, 1995b, 2007) explains, researchers and educators can benefit from employing multiple dimensions of learning, which stem from emic data of students' lived experiences, to support educative collaborations between students and teachers. To demonstrate this point, Lee (2007) draws on student engagements with familiar repertories involving African American language, hip-hop and popular culture, and students' cultural knowledge from familial communities. Connected with her teaching and Cultural Modeling Project, these engagements support collaborations across dimensions of learning (i.e., social; emotional; cognitive). They reveal the effectiveness of *signifying* as a scaffold for the teaching and learning of skills in literary interpretation, which promotes students' cultural knowledge and academic learning. Given the ongoing drive of policy makers to standardize student learning in public schools across the nation, Lee's work is important because it reconfigures "the institutional contexts in which [students] practice their literacies" (Vasudevan & Campano, 2009, p. 331).

There are several other examples of transformative studies occurring within and across school space that are ethnographically based and that utilize emic constructs. Staples (2008) describes the negotiations with and around popular culture texts by African American youth in Youth Leadership (YL), an afterschool program at an urban high school. She engages in acts of teaching and learning as collaborative endeavors with youth. This approach allowed her to observe how they read critical media texts—film, television, the Internet, print media—as they re-defined their identities from disengaged learners (institutional label) to cultural critics (Staples' label). By encouraging participants to analyze media forms and media as texts, Staples sets the stage for additional work that, in her own words, "can show us the myriad possibilities for teaching and learning with adolescents who struggle with decoding skills, sociocultural understanding, and political resistance through inquiry and action" (p. 70).

Staples (2008) is not alone in her use of popular culture and media texts in a school setting as tools to motivate students to increase their critical capacities and re-define their identities. Hill (2009) turns his attention to "the ways that hip-hop-based education shapes and responds to students' lived experiences with hip-hop culture" (p. 2). He views the classroom as a space in which teachers can use hip-hop culture, language, and techniques to educate students and honor their identities that are cultivated from emic and etic contexts.

Questions that Researchers Are Asking and Larger Implications

Researching the impacts of emic constructs of culture, race, and locale, to name a few, in TLELA leads researchers to a host of complex questions that can further guide English language arts research and teaching agendas: How do participants see themselves, their school and community contexts, and researchers? What stories do they tell, ignore, and resist? In what ways do they see themselves and those around them reading, writing, questioning, participating, and/or resisting involvement in learning spaces? How do researchers, and what is our responsibility to, represent their stories/lives to readers? These questions, not meant to be exhaustive, are grounded in emic research involving contexts and specificity that support researchers' attempts to uncover etic analysis of common realities, conditions, and patterns as these things are connected to experiences in the world and to TLELA.

If researchers and educators of English language arts are to do this work, then Fecho's (2004) advice is important. He insists "that we immerse ourselves in looking closely at the transactions we make across cultures" (p. 157) by engaging in reflexive inquiry on classroom practices and interactions we have with students in situations of learning and teaching. Fecho's insistence is a crucial one to consider. Drawing on critical inquiry pedagogy, he examines ways for students to make their own meanings of texts and of the world while crossing cultural boundaries and using language to enhance critical literacy skills. Significant questions emerge from Fecho's study: How can educators make space for and encourage students to draw on multiple voices and identities to construct texts that are thematically and linguistically complex? How do researchers acknowledge the possible tensions between students' appropriation of mainstream discourse and their retention of familial discourses? How can an emic perspective reveal,

"the tensions our pedagogy places on students" (p. 110; see also Yagelski, 2000)?

The emic studies of Fecho (2004), Staples (2008), Hill (2009), and other scholars (Chapman, 2007; Gutiérrez, 2008; Gutiérrez, Baquedano-Lopez, & Turner, 1997) point to Cochran-Smith and Lytle's (1999) call for a more critical "ethnographic research tradition and a multi-disciplinary understanding of language, literacy, and pedagogy" (p. 16). Undoubtedly, literacy researchers are working to meet this call in their investigations of issues that affect people's learning processes. These studies include: the relevance of literacy and spoken word poetry in the lives of students of color (Fisher, 2007); the role of writing for students who craft, perform, and publish poetry (Jocson, 2008); and the value of stories of pain and progress etched onto human flesh (Kirkland, 2009). Such work points to expanded understandings of literacy and raises valuable questions: How do students conceptualize acts of literacy as they negotiate identities and participate in literacy activities? What can we learn from it?

As evidenced from the aforementioned review of literacy studies, educational projects that utilize an emic perspective can draw strength from Lee's (1993, 1995a) cultural modeling framework. Her framework advocates for an instructional design "that makes explicit connections between students' everyday knowledge and the demands of subject-matter learning" (Lee, Spencer, & Harpalani, 2003, p. 7). Utilization of this framework, for example, requires the researcher to focus on the common experiences, questions, and concerns she encounters when conducting intimate research in school and nonschool learning spaces and with students in TLELA. Doing so highlights the value of emic perspectives and presents new challenges for doing this work.

References

Alvermann, D. (Ed.). (2002). *Adolescents and literacies in a digital world*. New York: Peter Lang.

Barnard, A. (2000). *History and anthropology*. Cambridge, UK: Cambridge University Press.

Bartlett, L. (2007). Literacy, speech and shame: The cultural politics of literacy and language in Brazil. *International Journal of Qualitative Studies in Education, 20*(5), 547–563.

Black, R. W. (2005). Access and affiliation: The literacy and composition practices of English-language learners in an online fanfiction community. *Journal of Adolescent and Adult Literacy, 49*(2), 118–128.

Bredo, E. (2006). Philosophies of Educational Research. In G. Elmore & P. L. Green (Eds.), *Handbook of contemporary methods in education research* (2nd ed., pp. 3–31). Washington DC: American Educational Research Association.

Chapman, T. K. (2005). Expressions of "voice" in portraiture. *Qualitative Inquiry, 11*(1), 27–51.

Chapman, T. K. (2007). Interrogating classroom relationships and events: Using portraiture and critical race theory in education research. *Educational Researcher, 36*(3), 156–162.

Cochran-Smith, M., & Lytle, S. L. (1999). The teacher research movement: A decade later. *Educational Researcher, 28*(7), 15–25.

Dimitriadis, G. (2001). "In the clique": Popular culture, constructions of place, and the every day lives of urban youth. *Anthropology and Education Quarterly, 32*(1), 29–51.

Dyson, A. H. (2005). Crafting "The humble prose of living": Rethinking oral/written relationships in the echoes of spoken word. *English Education, 37*(2), 149–164.

Dyson, A., & Genishi, C. (2005). *On the case: Approaches to language and literacy research.* New York: Teachers College Press.

Fecho, B. (2004). *"Is this English?" Race, language, and culture in the classroom.* New York: Teachers College Press.

Fisher, M. T. (2007). *Writing in rhythm: Spoken word poetry in urban classrooms.* New York: Teachers College Press.

Fisher, M. (2008). *Black literate lives: Historical and contemporary perspectives.* New York: Routledge.

Fisher, M. T., Purcell, S. S., & May, R. (2009). Process, product, and playmaking. *English Education, 41*(4), 337–355.

Gutiérrez, K. D. (2008). Developing a sociocritical literacy in the third space. *Reading Research Quarterly, 43*(2), 148–164.

Gutiérrez, K. D., Baquedano-Lopez, P., & Turner, M. (1997). Putting language back into language arts: When the radical middle meets the third space. *Language Arts, 74*(5), 368–378.

Gustavson, L. (2008). Influencing pedagogy through the creative practices of youth. In M. L. Hill & L. Vasudevan (Eds.), *Media, learning, and sites of possibility* (pp. 81–114). New York: Peter Lang.

Headland, T. N., Pike, K., & Harris, M. (Eds.). (1990). *Emics and etics: The insider/outsider debate* (Vol. 7). London: Sage.

Heath, S. B., & Street, B. V. (2008). *On ethnography: Approaches to language and literacy research.* New York: Teachers College Press.

Hill, M. L. (2009). *Beats, rhymes, and classroom life: Hip-hop pedagogy and the politics of identity.* New York: Teachers College Press.

Hill, M., & Vasudevan, L. (Eds.). (2008). *Media, learning, and sites of possibility.* New York: Peter Lang.

Hull, G., & Schultz, K. (Eds.). (2002). *School's out! Bridging out-of-school literacies with classroom practice.* New York: Teachers College Press.

Jocson, K. (2005). "Taking it to the mic": Pedagogy of June Jordan's Poetry for the People and partnership with an urban high school. *English Education, 37*(2), 44–60.

Jocson, K. (2008). *Youth poets: Empowering literacies in and out of schools.* New York: Peter Lang.

Juzwik, M. M., Curcic, S., Wolbers, K., Moxley, K. D., Dimling, L. M., & Shankland, R. K. (2006). Writing into the 21st century: An overview of research on writing, 1999 to 2004. *Written Communication, 23*(4), 451–476.

Kinloch, V. (2007). "The white-ification of the hood": Power, politics, and youth performing narratives of community. *Language Arts, 85*(1), 61–68.

Kinloch, V. (2009). Suspicious spatial distinctions: Literacy research with students across school and community contexts. *Written Communication, 26*(2), 154–182.

Kinloch, V. (2010). *Harlem on our minds: Place, race, and the literacies of urban youth.* New York: Teachers College Press.

Kirkland, D. (2009). The skin we ink: Tattoos, literacy, and a new English education. *English Education, 41*(4), 375–395.

Lee, C. D. (1993). *Signifying as a scaffold for literary interpretation: The pedagogical implications of an African American discourse genre* (Research Report series). Urbana: IL: National Council of Teachers of English.

Lee, C. D. (1995a). A culturally based cognitive apprenticeship: Teaching African American high school students skills in literacy interpretation. *Reading Research Quarterly, 30*(40), 608–631.

Lee, C. D. (1995b). The use of signifying as a scaffold for literary interpretation. *Journal of Black Psychology, 21*(4), 357–381.

Lee, C. D. (2007). *Culture, literacy, and learning: Taking bloom in the midst of the whirlwind.* New York: Teachers College Press.

Lee, C. D., Spencer, M. B., & Harpalani, V. (2003). "Every shut eye ain't sleep": Studying how people live culturally. *Educational Researcher, 32*(5), 6–13.

Lewis, C., Enciso, P., & Moje, E. B. (2007). *Reframing sociocultural research on literacy: Identity, agency, and power.* Mahwah, NJ: Erlbaum.

Lillis, T. (2008). Ethnography as method, methodology, and "deep theorizing": Closing the gap between text and context in academic writing research. *Written Communication, 25*(3), 353–388.

Lincoln, Y. S., & Guba, E. G. (1979). *Naturalistic inquiry.* Newbury Park, CA. Sage.

Lincoln, Y. S., & Guba, E. G. (2000). The only generalization is: There is no generalization. In R. Gomm, M. Hammersley, & P. Foster (Eds.), *Case study method* (pp. 27–44). Thousand Oaks: Sage.

Lunsford, A. (2009). Literacy for life. *English Education, 41*(4), 396–397.

Lunsford, A., Moglen, H., & Slevin, J. (Eds.). (1990). *The right to literacy.* New York: Modern Language Association.

Mahiri, J. (1991). Discourse in sports: Language and literacy features of preadolescent African American males in a youth basketball program. *Journal of Negro Education, 60,* 305–313.

Mahiri, J. (1994). Reading rites and sports: Motivation for adaptive literacy of young African American males. In B. Moss (Ed.), *Literacy across communities* (pp.121–146). Cresskill, NJ: Hampton Press.

Moje, E. B. (2002). But where are the youth? On the value of integrating youth culture into literacy theory. *Educational Theory, 52*(1), 97–120.

Morrell, E. (2008). *Critical literacy and urban youth: Pedagogies of access, dissent, and liberation.* New York: Routledge.

Pike, K. (1967). *Language in relation to a unified theory of the structure of human behavior.* The Hague, The Netherlands: Mouton & Co.

Morrell, E., & Duncan-Andrade, J. M. R. (2002). Promoting academic literacy with urban youth through engaging hip-hop culture. *English Journal, 91*(6), 88–92.

Pike, K. L., & McKinney, C. V. (1996). Understanding misunderstanding as cross-cultural emic clash. In K. R. Jankowsky (Ed.), *The mystery of culture contacts, historical reconstruction and text analysis: An emic approach* (pp. 39–64). Washington DC: Georgetown University Press.

Schultz, K. (2003). *Listening: A framework for teaching across differences.* New York: Teachers College Press.

Stake, R. E. (2000). The case study method in social inquiry. In R. Gomm, M. Hammersley, & P. Foster (Eds.), *Case study method* (pp. 19–26). Thousand Oaks, CA: Sage. (Reprinted from *Educational Researcher*, 1978, 7, 5–8).

Staples, J. M. (2008). "Are we our brothers' keepers?": Exploring the social functions of reading in the life of an African American urban adolescent. In M. L. Hill & L. Vasudevan (Eds.), *Media, learning, and sites of possibility* (pp. 57–72). New York: Peter Lang.

Street, B. (1984). *Literacy in theory and practice.* Cambridge, UK: Cambridge University Press.

Vasudevan, L. (2006). Making known differently: Engaging visual modalities as spaces to author new selves. *E-Learning 3*(2), 207–216.

Vasudevan, L., & Campano, G. (2009). The social production of adolescent risk and the promise of adolescent literacies. *Review of Research in Education, 33,* 310–353.

Willis, J. (2007). *Foundations of qualitative research: Interpretive and critical approaches.* Thousand Oaks, CA: Sage.

Yagelski, R. (2000). *Literacy matters: Writing and reading the social self.* New York: Teachers College Press.

56

Research Designs for Empirical Research

ROBERT C. CALFEE AND MARILYN J. CHAMBLISS

In the second edition of the *Handbook of Research on Teaching the English Language Arts*, our chapter on research methods emphasized four points: (a) framing a research question, (b) principles of research design, (c) constructing a design using factorial techniques, and (d) interpreting findings. This chapter builds on the same foundational elements, updating several points and providing more recent citations. The area of experimental design has remained stable for decades, and so this plan seems sensible.

The previous chapter also included an extended example of the application of factorial design to a complex research problem in the literacy area—teaching argumentative texts to middle grade students. The current revision is considerably abbreviated, and we have shortened the illustrative material. We recommend that readers refer to the earlier version for additional detail.

A significant development since the earlier chapter, the entry of mixed-methods strategies, is a major addition to this chapter. While we mentioned this topic previously, it has become a significant design consideration in the past 10 years. The mixed-methods label first appeared in the mid-1990s (Jaeger, 1997), and the last decade has seen a virtual explosion of activity (Calfee & Sperling, 2010). The original idea was to combine quantitative and qualitative methods for investigating research questions, a departure from earlier practice in which individual problems were explored with one method or the other. Experimental design techniques were traditionally associated with quantitative approaches, while qualitative techniques were employed for in-depth exploratory investigations, often taking shape as case studies. The two strategies differed most obviously in the choice of outcomes, but they also employed different design arrangements and relied on different methodologies and epistemologies. Mixed-methods techniques will be woven throughout this chapter, reflecting their benefits in the literacy and language arenas.

Two key words in the title are *design* and *empirical*.

We set the stage for the chapter with a brief discussion of the concept of empiricism as an approach to knowledge. We next concentrate on design, where we address the four foundational elements of experimental design mentioned above. Throughout we call upon an abbreviated narrative from the example on teaching and learning argumentative text in the earlier chapter. We assume that a reader is familiar with basic concepts of social science and educational research. For additional detail, consult Berliner and Calfee (1996, especially chapters by Behrens & Smith, Jaeger & Bond, and Hambleton), Gall, Borg, and Gall (2006), Krathwohl (1997), Myers and Well (2003), Osborne (2008), and Alexander and Winne (2006, especially chapters by Nesbit & Hadwin, and Cooper).

Empiricism is a systematic approach to answering certain types of questions. Through the collection of evidence under carefully defined and replicable conditions, social science researchers seek to discover the influence of factors that affect human thought and action, and to understand when and why these influences occur. Nonempirical research spans a wide range of other approaches, including mathematical, logical, historical, and legal, many of which support empirical techniques.

The empirical tradition plays a significant role in creating and validating social and psychological theories about how people think and act. In language arts, for instance, data-based research has supported models that link reading and writing as social acts (e.g., Nystrand, 1989, 1997). No longer are readers and writers perceived as lost in their impenetrable thoughts, but instead as communicating with one another through both oral and written media.

Empirical research also searches for answers to practical questions. A high school English teacher seeks to improve her students' understanding of formal arguments. A middle school teacher aims to encourage his students toward more strategic comprehension. A remedial reading teacher wants to improve vocabulary instruction to help students do better on standardized tests. These questions support scholarship and conceptual analysis, but the primary goals are pragmatic.

Empirical research is disciplined (Cronbach & Suppes, 1969). It is distinguished "by the ways observations are collected, evidence is marshaled, arguments are drawn, and opportunities are afforded for replication, verification, and refutation" (Shulman, 1988, p. 4). The essential criterion for judging empirical evidence, from a research perspective, is *validity*; researchers must defend their interpretations of evidence against counter-interpretations.

Empirical research is sometimes equated with statistics and experimentation, in contrast to qualitative methods and naturalistic inquiry. We think this contrast is misleading for several reasons. First, it leads a researcher to concentrate on methodology rather than conceptualization. Second, it implies that the researcher must choose between what are often characterized as "hard" and "soft" approaches. Third, it overlooks the fact that virtually all significant educational problems call for a mix of methods, and all require rigorous conceptualization and creative design. Shulman (1988) advises novice researchers, "Become *skilled and experienced* in at least two methodologies ..., become *aware* of the rich variety of methods of disciplined inquiry..., [and] do not limit your education to methodology alone" (p. 16). Our notion of empirical research design will encompass a full range of systematic approaches directed toward both theoretical and practical questions. The most appropriate starting point for a research project is a problem: questions unanswered by a previous investigation, a pragmatic need, or a theoretical puzzle. Conceptualization and design focused on the problem should then determine the methods. Conceptualization represents the researcher's efforts to understand and analyze the structure of a research question. Design, the focus of this chapter, covers the variety of strategies for planning data collection in a way that generates valid answers to the research question.

Research Strategy: What Is the Question?

Novices tend to begin a research project by thinking, "I'd like to prove that...." Educators tend to advocate their favored positions and actions. "Spelling tests are bad (or good)." "English teachers should (or should not) know about linguistics." "Promoting student motivation is (or is not) a critical ingredient in a writing assignment." We can become passionate about these matters. Such hypotheses are entirely appropriate as starting points for inquiry, but developing a research problem requires a fundamental shift toward "I wonder what will happen...." A small switch, but with major implications. For instance, the earlier proposals now take shape as questions. Under what conditions are spelling tests bad or good? What are the effects of linguistic background on the thinking and behavior of English teachers? In what ways do higher or lower levels of motivation affect students' responses to different types of writing assignments?

The revised questions can open Pandora's box because they challenge the researcher to explore a universe of possibilities. No longer is the task to compare one condition with another. Rather, the investigator is led to think about a broad array of situations, outcomes, and individuals. Spelling tests come in many flavors, and may help with some tasks (new spelling tests) and interfere with others (writing assignments), for some students (compulsives) but not others (impulsives). How to grapple with the infinite possibilities? The simple answer emerges from the application of *design* principles as an essential tool for translating a question into a research study.

Framing an Answerable Question.   Empirical research begins with the formulation of a workable scientific question, one that can be answered by objective evidence. For instance, imagine yourself as the high school teacher mentioned at the beginning of the chapter. You want to help your ninth graders write well reasoned and coherent arguments. You are familiar with Toulmin's (1958) concept of argument, which has become important in your thinking. Toulmin proposed that all arguments have three basic parts: a claim or assertion, the English teacher's thesis statement; evidence offered in support of the claim; and warrants, which link evidence to claim. Complex arguments may also include qualifications, counterarguments, and rebuttals.

It took you a while to grasp Toulmin's notion of a "warrant." Claims, evidence, and even counterarguments and rebuttals seemed fairly straightforward. Toulmin described warrants as general statements, such as "If this evidence, then this claim." The relationships among claims, evidence, and warrants are clearest in simple arguments. Suppose the claim is that wolves often represent evil in folk tales. The evidence is that in well-known folktales, wolves terrorize and almost kill three little pigs, a little girl wearing a red coat and her sick grandmother, and a little Russian boy and his pets. The warrant fills any gaps in reasoning: Any character that terrorizes and almost kills innocent people and animals represents evil. Warrants become crucial when connections between evidence and claim are not obvious, when they need to be explained or defended against counterarguments.

After reviewing several written arguments, you have become convinced that focusing attention on warrants might help students reason more effectively in reading and writing. In addition to the Toulmin model, you want to explore the impact of social aspects of instruction on reading and writing (Spivey, 1997). Your experience suggests that students learn more effectively when they have opportunities to apply what they are learning; in learning about argument, this means that they have opportunities to critique a writer's ideas (Mathison, 1998) and to anticipate responses to their writing (Rubin, 1998), which you think could be supported through small-group activities.

You look over a list of questions that you have scribbled during your reading and thinking:

- What is the essence of a good argument?
- What do my students know about the concept of argument?
- How can I effectively teach students to comprehend, critique, and compose arguments?

Let's consider the researchability of each question. The first cannot be answered empirically because the answer requires value judgments—"good" is the fly in the ointment. The second and third questions, in contrast, both provide starting points for empirical study. Students' responses to "What makes this argument strong?" can provide evidence about thinking processes. Assessing student writing following different instructional approaches can inform the third question.

The key to evaluating a potential research question is to ask yourself, "Assuming that I collect evidence of some sort, and obtain a particular set of results, to what degree can I use the results to make a convincing argument in relation to the original question?" This exercise requires that you step outside your own convictions and become a self-critic. It also helps to find a friendly enemy along the way, someone interested in your problem, and willing to work hard at destroying your line of argument. Defending your interpretations against alternative explanations is an essential part of the research process, and is a significant theme in this chapter.

Finding Evidence.   Once a question has appeared on the scene, the researcher must decide what evidence might be relevant to the question, how to gather it, and how to analyze and interpret the data. It helps to know the territory: What do you already know about research on comprehension of argument texts, about comprehension and composition in general, about effective instructional practices, and so on? Another task is a review of the literature, which can seem a daunting task. By selecting a few best evidence papers as starting points and working backwards (Krathwohl, 1997, chap. 6; Slavin, 1986), you can shape the job into manageable proportions. You should also bring your professional knowledge and experience into the mix.

You must then reach decisions about *what* data to collect, along with *how* and *where* to carry out this task, and from *whom*. We will cover the *what* of data collection later as a design task, and a few fundamentals will set the stage for now. First, should you focus on numbers or "stuff" (observations, interviews, videos, documents, and the like) —quantitative or qualitative? In fact, you don't really have a choice. Empirical data are inherently qualitative, and it takes a uniquely human act—*measurement*—to assign numbers to observations. A student essay begins as stuff, but you can count the number of words, calculate the average sentence length, or ask a panel of judges to use rubrics to evaluate the work. Whether you decide to measure and how you decide to do it is a conceptual matter.

A second dimension to *what* is *how much*? A useful principle is *triangulation*, which means collecting diverse data for each construct in the study. If you are interested in student writing, then the starting point is to identify a variety of writing assignments appropriate to the research question. We will go into more detail about this task in the design section. You can look at different facets (length, coherence, mechanics) of each composition. You might also explore the value of artifacts (student notes and outlines) and indicators (e.g., ask students to talk about the compositions and how they planned and produced them). If this amalgam of information produces a consistent picture, then you have the basis for a strong argument. The *how* of data collection encompasses two overlapping strategies; the researcher can either *observe* or *intervene* with the intent of *describing* or *experimenting*. Imagine a young boy examining an ant hill. One moment he is the naturalist, observing the hectic activity in the insect community. Suddenly driven to intervene, he pokes a twig into the hole and watches the ants' responses.

To observe or to intervene? Most texts on research methodology separate these two approaches, one section on naturalistic approaches and a second on experiments. *Experimental*, *quantitative*, and *statistical* are often bound together in one package, and contrasted with *naturalistic*, *qualitative*, and *descriptive*. Fortunately, the joining of quantitative and qualitative methods is becoming more commonplace (Calfee & Sperling, 2010). Both approaches are clearly empirical, in the sense that they both rely on evidence. Moreover, the various strategies are independent; you can design a naturalistic investigation that uses quantitative methods, or an experimental study that employs qualitative assessments. Quantifying observations allows the researcher to employ statistical techniques for summarizing information and conducting inferential analyses (how closely related or disparate are two sets of evidence). The richness of qualitative information, on the other hand, may allow the researcher to delve into underlying processes and explore complex hypotheses. For instance, measuring the length of two sets of compositions may reveal substantial and trustworthy differences; students taught about warranting write substantially more than students without such instruction. Student interviews may resist quantification, but suggest to the researcher how instruction led students to write longer essays. For instance, suppose several students tell you something like this: "I knew that if I just wrote my main point and a few details you wouldn't like my paper, so I just rambled around—that's kinda what you mean by that warrant thing." The interview results may not yield what you hoped for, but they connect the quantitative information with the instructional treatment.

The *where* of data collection is frequently tied to the *who*. Traditionally, real classroom situations are contrasted with laboratory environments, the latter presumably unreal. More recently, collaboration between teachers and researchers has been contrasted with researcher-imposed designs (Freedman, Simons, & Kalnin, 1999). Simple contrasts may be misleading. Researcher-imposed designs implemented within either classrooms or laboratories are supposed to eliminate extraneous fluctuations in conditions, because the classroom can be a wild and crazy place. The practical value of researcher-imposed designs and laboratory findings is often questioned, whereas teacher designed, classroom based research seems directly applicable.

Neither stereotype stands up under close scrutiny. One can find examples of untrustworthy laboratory research and excellent instances of classroom-based investigations. The practical significance of a study depends on the quality of the research rather than the characteristics of the setting. An important bridge between these extremes is the *design experiment*, in which systematic variations are tried out in different classrooms through collaborations between teachers and researchers, using a range of quantitative and qualitative indicators to inform the teams (Brown, 1992; Collins, 1994). The design experiment technique, although still undergoing refinement, illustrates the merging of methodological distinctions that previously seemed contradictory.

Evidence is trustworthy to the extent that it holds up against attack from informed critics; research has much in common with law. Earlier we introduced validity as centrally important. Informed critics will value signs of research validity and dismiss research attempts that are invalid. Closely related is the concept of *control*. In social science research, control refers to the researcher's efforts to ensure the validity of the interpretations, the trustworthiness of the argument, the generalizability of the findings. An essential ingredient for adequate control is *design*, which refers to the steps in identifying the contextual factors that influence performance, planning the conditions of data collection so that these factors are adequately represented, and ensuring that the plan supports generalizability of the findings, so that you can argue that the findings are trustworthy, replicable, and broadly applicable. The concepts of *factors* and *factorial design* described later provide one strategy for establishing adequate control.

Setting the Stage. In this section we expand the earlier discussion of "teaching argument" into a research scenario to which factorial design principles can be applied. The scenario lays out starting points for where and who. Assume that you are developing a proposal for your masters thesis. Two teachers in your school employ distinctively different approaches to argument instruction—one quite traditional, the other quite innovative. The traditional teacher relies on lecture and discussion to cover thesis/support forms of argument. Her basic model is the five-paragraph essay, the claim or thesis in the introductory paragraph, three paragraphs of evidence or support, and a conclusion that summarizes the argument. The second teacher introduces students to several forms of argument, including counterarguments and rebuttals. She emphasizes the role of warrants in linking evidence to claims, which serves as a scaffold to help students identify and question their thinking, which she refers to as "metacognition."

Here you have the makings of a natural experiment.

The plan seems simple enough on first glance; your task as researcher will be to visit classrooms and document what you see. On reflection, however, you to realize that reality is more complex. For instance, your questions and your presence may influence both teachers and students. Such effects are not necessarily bad, but they show that research almost always entails some intervention.

You next consider a planned experiment, with one class assigned to an innovative treatment, the other to business as usual. This plan also seems simple enough at first. You need to construct materials for the innovative treatment, find out what happens in business-as-usual, identify measures to assess performance at the beginning and end of the study, and work out details of the statistical analysis, your advisor raises several questions. First, she warns that the two treatments appear to be *confounded*. She is not denouncing your ideas! Confounding is a technical term describing a condition where two or more dimensions or factors vary simultaneously. In your plan, the two treatments differ in several ways, including the goals (five-paragraph compositions vs. analytic essays), the reading materials (none vs. some), the teaching approach (lecture vs. small-group discussion), and student activities (individual vs. group assignments), to name a few. These contrasts co-vary; they change from one class to another, along with differences in the teachers and the students. If the results favor the innovative approach, what are the critical elements?

Confounding is serious enough, but your advisor raises other concerns. How can you be sure that the treatments will be implemented as you intend? What if the measures do not tap into critical instructional elements? You begin to understand that, even in a planned experiment, you still have to play the naturalist's role, documenting in detail what happens during instruction in the two classes. Your advisor has caused you to pause for reflection—her mantra is pay now or pay later.

Principles of Factorial Design

This section of the chapter develops the foundational concepts of research design. Any field of study evolves in stages or paradigms, beginning with careful examination of intuitive experiences and ideas and then increasingly careful collection of evidence. Data patterns emerge, often to transmute or vanish. Eventually the patterns lead toward formulation of theoretical ideas, which explain and enlighten the evidence. Along the way, investigators rely on informed guesses. Educational research is in the middle stage of educated guesses today. Educators do not yet have powerful theories and so must still rely on experience and hunches to guide much of their work. Disciplined planfulness is crucial, however, and hence the focus in this chapter on research design.

We first lay out three fundamental barriers that design techniques help surmount: *inadequate construct validity*, *confounding*, and *extraneous variability*. Then we discuss four fundamental principles of factorial design: the *concept*

TABLE 56.1
Technical Vocabulary for Factorial Design Terminology

FACTOR: A variation in treatment conditions, in person characteristics, or in instrumentation, that the researcher includes in the design to achieve control over the performance outcomes in a study; also referred to as an *independent variable.*

LEVEL OF A FACTOR: A particular choice or selection from possible variations in a factor.

MEASURE: Result of observation or measurement of performance under specified conditions; also referred to as a *dependent variable.*

TREATMENT FACTOR: Variation in environmental conditions under direct control of the researcher. *Amount of time allowed for revising a draft* is a treatment factor; *5, 10,* and *30 minutes are levels.*

PERSON FACTOR: Pre-existing characteristics of a person or group, identified by the researcher for selecting a sample for investigation. *Undergraduate major* is a person factor; *English, Engineering,* and *Political Science* are levels.

OUTCOME FACTOR: Facet used in designing a measurement package (e.g., test, observation, interview, or questionnaire). *Writing topic* is an outcome factor; *contemporary writing styles, earthquake preparation,* and *world conflicts* are levels.

NUISANCE FACTOR: A variation included in a design to ensure adequate control; not necessarily of conceptual or practical importance. *Class period* is a nuisance factor; *early* and *late morning* and *afternoon* are levels.

of design, the *elements of factorial design, connections among the elements,* and *integration around a theme.* We rely on a technical vocabulary that has evolved over the past several decades; the critical terms are shown in Table 56.1. This table should be helpful as you proceed through the chapter. As we lay out the factorial system, we will also present ways in which mixed-methods bridges can connect quantitative and qualitative approaches.

Three Barriers.   The construct validity of a research study, as for an achievement test, refers to the trustworthiness of various interpretations of the evidence; does the finding mean what you think it means, where "it" is the construct? Validity can be compromised in several ways, but most shortcomings arise from a failure to think through the path that leads from initial question to final interpretation. The concept of test validity offers a helpful metaphor.

As for an achievement test, the construct validity of a set of research findings depends not only on the data but on the interpretation. Is the plan of the study adequate? To what extent does the context allow generalization to other situations? To what extent do findings agree with other studies? What are the cost-benefit implications of various decisions springing from the study; when the decision is correct or when it is wrong? The more you know about the answers to such questions, the more secure will be the construct validity. One purpose of research design is to increase the chances of trustworthy outcomes. As Cronbach (1988) puts it, "Validators should do what the detached scientist does; [the key ingredient is] a vigorous, questing intellect...." (p. 14).

The second barrier, *confounding,* occurs when the effect of the primary factor cannot be separated from the confounded factor(s), in which instance the findings are significantly compromised. Confounding can arise in your study if you select two teachers, assigning each (and their students) to one of the instructional approaches. Suppose you find a striking difference in writing outcomes. The cause might be the teacher, the students, the program, or any combination of the three. Given these possibilities, the evidence is difficult to interpret with any confidence, and this difficulty is virtually impossible to repair after the fact.

Confounding is the major shortcoming of designs that contrast an innovative approach and a traditional method, the classical experimental-control technique. A quarter century ago, Cronbach (1963) pointed out the limitations of this design, but it is still commonplace in the empirical literature, and is viewed as the "gold standard" by the Department of Education (see National Research Council, 2002, for a discussion of federal policies in educational research). Any comparison between two groups is necessarily confounded, and hence subject to multiple interpretations. Our advice, if you are contemplating such a study, is to consider options. A more complex design can separate the confounded variables. Qualitative descriptions of classroom life under the innovation and the control group can often help untangle confoundings.

Uncontrolled variability, the third concern, occurs when unintended fluctuations obscure patterns in the data. Reducing or identifying extraneous variability is essential because of the critical importance of *variance* in educational research. On the one hand, systematic or explainable variance is the payoff from a study. You predict that performance under the novel treatment will differ from the traditional approach, presumably because of the treatment. You hope the difference will be large. On the other hand, unexplained variance is the gauge against which systematic differences are measured; large differences in student performance within the two conditions may completely obscure a treatment effect.

This chapter is not about statistics, but when designing a study it helps to understand the statistics game. Your job is to construct a design in which systematic variability is maximized and unexplained variability is minimized. Suppose, for instance, that writing scores (rated on a 1–10 rubric scale) for one approach range from 8 to 10, while they range from 3 to 5 in the other approach. This difference clearly passes the eyeball test. On the other hand, if scores range from 6 to 10 in the treatment group and 5 to 9 in the control group, the differences may be due to chance. In this second situation, however, suppose that many girls score 9 or 10 in the first group, while boys in both groups range around 5 to 8. Now you can tell a different story; the treatment makes a difference, but only for girls.

The concept of control encompasses the full range of methods employed to strengthen validity. Chief among these methods is design, although other techniques are also important. For instance, in order to generalize your findings to other situations, the data should be based on a *random sample* from some population of interest. This standard is difficult if not impossible to meet. Social science research typically relies on handy random samples. You call upon your professional network to gain access to a particular school. It is not a chance selection, but perhaps you can argue that it is typical of schools in the area. Some teachers cooperate with you, others do not. You may locate a purposive sample, selected because it meets conditions important for your hypotheses. Such constraints and decisions limit the generalizability of your findings. The important point is to *be aware* of these constraints, and to *document* them for yourself and your audience. The reader can then assess the degree to which nonrandomness compromises your argument.

A second nondesign control issue is the establishment of *uniformity* during data collection. A well constructed design provides control over certain variables, but others will be free floating. For instance, suppose your study spans a 5-week period. Consult the calendar—what coming events may influence instruction or assessment? If the critical posttest is scheduled on the day before a big football game, students may not give full attention to the task. What is happening in the lives of students and teachers throughout the study? If several students know that their family is moving in two months, they may not try their best. If one teacher is in the midst of a divorce and another is fighting with the Internal Revenue Service, this may not be the best time for them to take on a new program—nor, for that matter, to handle a traditional approach.

These scenarios illustrate the difficulty of establishing uniformity. You should nonetheless do your best to keep conditions constant, attend to discrepancies, and take care to document everything. Like randomness, complete uniformity is seldom attainable. Problems arise when you do not detect unusual happenings and fail to report them. Performance outcomes can fluctuate because of these events, and these fluctuations can cloud the picture if you ignore them.

The Concept of Design. A well-planned design can be critical for separating treatment effects from background noise. It is the best protection against threats to validity, confoundings, and extraneous variability. Textbooks on research design often stress the procedures and mechanics of the design task, including statistical methods like analysis of variance. We will start instead with the underlying principles of design, which apply equally to descriptive and experimental investigations, to quantitative and qualitative approaches.

Many human endeavors rely on the concept of design, sometimes through recognition and appreciation of naturally occurring patterns, more often through creation and construction. As Simon (1981) notes, design is the feature that distinguishes between the natural and the artificial, between happenstance and the artifices of humankind. All designs have three essential ingredients (Chambliss &

Calfee, 1998). First is a set of distinctive elements, what Simon calls "nearly decomposable components." Second are the linkages that bind individual elements together. Third is the theme that gives overall shape and meaning to the enterprise.

We turn next to the application of design principles in a research study. The elements include the factors that influence performance: treatment or environmental variations, differences between individuals, and various plans for assessing performance. The elements are linked by one of two relationships, crossing or nesting. The theme encompasses the overarching research objectives, as these are represented by specific questions and hypotheses. A design that covers these three domains should generate a data structure that informs your research questions in a well- controlled—i.e., trustworthy and generalizable—fashion.

Factorial Elements. A factor is a variable that the researcher defines and controls in order to evaluate its influence on performance. Some factors can be directly controlled; others spring from natural variations. Your study, for instance, provides several candidates as factors for inclusion in the design: argument type, instructional method, prior student experience with arguments, age and sex of students, teacher experience with the genre, and choice of a written or oral test. As suggested earlier, your best strategy at the outset is to cast a wide net—brainstorm, think divergently. The idea is not to create a shopping list of every conceivable variable, but to identify a range of factors that may substantially influence performance or inform your understanding of the phenomenon.

Novice researchers tend to identify one or two factors of central interest, and then rely on randomness to handle other effects. Such a strategy leaves too much to chance. Keep in mind the following principle: *If you ignore factors that influence performance, variability from these sources does not disappear; instead, it remains to cloud the picture.* In a well-controlled study, the researcher pins down important sources of variability, ensuring that systematic effects stand out clearly against background noise.

For practical purposes, we distinguish three primary types of factors: (a) treatment factors; (b) person or individual-difference factors; and (c) outcome factors. A fourth category, nuisance or control factors, is also useful in preparing a design.

A *treatment factor* is an environmental variation directly controllable by the researcher. Argument type and task might serve as treatment factors in your study. You decide to introduce students to two types of arguments: a simple version where all the evidence supports a single claim and a complex form where different facets of a claim are supported by different pieces of evidence. You arrange two types of classroom interaction: one in which students work together in small groups to analyze the two types of arguments, and another in which the teacher models the analysis through lectures. You have defined two treatment factors, each with two variations.

The primary goal in identifying factors is to assess the importance of each variation in its own right, the *main effect* of the variation. To what extent do students perform differently on simple and complex arguments? What is the effect when students work in small groups? Main effects are the primary goal from most studies, and it usually makes sense to include two or more primary factors in the design. In a *complete factorial design*, the research plan includes all combinations of the factors, which can increase the cost of the study, but not by much, and sometimes not at all. For instance, you could conduct two separate studies, one for each factor, yielding a total of four different conditions. If you combine the two factors, then two times two equals four, which is the same number of conditions as for two separate studies.

The real payoff from a factorial design is that you can also assess the *interaction* among factors. An interaction occurs when the effect of one variable depends on conditions associated with a second factor. For instance, simple arguments may not benefit from social interaction, but complex arguments may be more readily comprehended under this condition. Interactions are not bad, nor are they necessarily complicated. They often play an essential role in providing contextual information, in helping the researcher understand the conditions under which a treatment is more or less effective.

A *person factor* is an intrinsic characteristic of an individual or group. Age, sex, ability, and prior experience are examples. These factors guide the selection of teachers, students, and classes, either because of theoretical interest in the effects or to control extraneous variability. For instance, if you know that some students have learned about arguments while others are unfamiliar with the concept, then you should include student experience as a design factor. If some teachers understand the argument genre better than others, then you should include teacher understanding as a factor. Interactions can occur among person factors. Students with no prior instruction about arguments might benefit from a teacher who understands the argument genre, but having a teacher who understands the genre well might matter less for students with prior knowledge. Interactions can also emerge from combinations of treatment and person factors. For instance, more experienced students may not benefit from small-group interactions, while novices do better in a small group than when left on their own.

Outcome factors direct the choice of measures in an investigation. Like treatment factors, they can be directly manipulated by the researcher, although this opportunity is frequently overlooked. The tendency is to select an off-the-shelf instrument without thinking about its relation to the research questions. Your school probably administers a standardized comprehension test. Why not use this test to assess the relative effectiveness of the two programs? In making this decision, you face trade-offs. On the one hand, most standardized tests use rather vague expository passages, seldom in the argument genre, and they tap the students' ability to recognize rather than to produce.

Given such limitations, you should think about constructing measures that directly assess students' ability to handle argument structures, that demonstrate their ability to craft a persuasive text, and that reveal attitudes and confidence about these tasks. On the other hand, standardized tests are proven instruments with established reliability estimates, while your measure has neither established reliability nor validity. You might use a standardized test as an index of general student ability, and rely on your measure for a more focused look at students' composition of arguments.

Once you have chosen the factors for your design, you then need to decide on the levels for each factor. Sometimes the decision is straightforward; if sex is a factor, then male and female are obvious choices. For a factor like undergraduate major, the range of options is greater, and the selection requires more thought. If revision time is a treatment variable, the number of options is virtually infinite. Think first about the relation between this factor and performance. For instance, does performance increase steadily with time? Might it increase for a while and then decline? Beyond a certain point, further time might actually lead to a poorer outcome. Each factor in the design requires careful consideration along these lines.

Building a Factorial Design. The simplest way to construct a design from factors is to treat them like Lego blocks—simply snap the pieces together. This strategy works well as a start, but needs additional refinements. Two factors can be joined in either of two ways: crossed (every level of the first factor is combined with every level of the second factor) or nested (the levels of the second factor differ for each level of the first factor). The two plans are illustrated in Figure 56.1, where you can see the parallel between a matrix and a hierarchy. In a matrix, every level on the first dimension is combined with every level of the second dimension. In a hierarchy, the lower levels may have a common thread, but they do not connect to other points at the same level. When a set of factors is crossed, you can evaluate both the main effects of each factor and the interactions among them. When factors are nested, only the main effects of the primary factor can be evaluated, because the design does not include combinations of the two factors.

As illustrated in Figure 56.1, nesting may be required by the nature of two factors. When the researcher decides to vary text type, then different works are needed within each type. You could try to rewrite *Three Little Pigs* as a compare-contrast or argument, but the result would lose something in translation.

Factorial methods have two advantages. First, like Lego toys, they can combine large numbers of factors in simple but flexible ways. Second, factorial methods offer a strong defense against inadvertent confounding, because the effects of any two factors are independent of one another. This assurance has two caveats. First, each combination must include an equal (or proportionate) number of observations. For instance, suppose you divide a writing class into high and low achievers (the achievement factor) which

Crossed Design

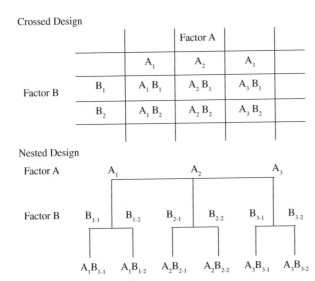

Figure 56.1 Two types of factorial linkage: Crossed and nested.

you cross with boys and girls (the sex factor). You are likely to find more high girls and low boys than the other two combinations; the design is partly confounded because the two person factors are correlated; the boys level is also low achieving, and contrariwise. This problem can be serious, and needs to be fixed. One approach is to divide boys and girls into two groups of equal size, using the achievement midpoint (the median), which reduces the confounding. Second, the factorial strategy offers no guarantee that a particular factor will not be confounded with other factors *not* in the design. Low-achieving may also mean from poor families, for instance, a problem that can be dealt with in a similar manner.

An important consideration in planning a design is deciding how to assign individuals or groups to various treatment combinations. The issue is generally discussed in research texts as the choice of a *between-subject* or *within-subject* plan, but it is better thought about as a decision about crossing versus nesting persons with other design factors. The decision to nest or cross persons with other factors reflects both practical and theoretical considerations. The researcher sometimes has little choice for practical reasons. For instance, individual-difference factors like sex or personality dictate that individuals be nested within the levels of a factor. A person is either male or female, impulsive or reflective. Treatment factors can generally be crossed with person factors, and sometimes it makes sense to do so. If a treatment combination takes only a minute or two to administer, and the student is available for an hour, the researcher should probably administer as many conditions as possible, which means crossing student with several factors.

Crossed and nested person designs provide qualitatively different information. If each student is tested under a single condition, the researcher cannot assess individual reactions to different combinations. When each individual is tested under several conditions, then performance contrasts are measurable. To be sure, the researcher must then attend to changes due to the testing itself. People improve with

practice and become fatigued over time. Several techniques (e.g., Latin-square designs, Myers & Well, 2003) permit control over such influences.

Theme. The final ingredient in a design is the conceptual framework that guides selection of factors and decisions about how to combine them. While we have placed this topic at the end of our list, it is of paramount importance. The thematic foundations of a research study require knowledge of the territory, experience in dealing with the issues, and a large dollop of intuition and art. On the other hand, the task can also be guided by a systematic strategy, for which Simon (1981) again offers counsel. Although some systems appear complex on the surface, Simon argues that all are fashioned around a relatively small set of separable components, each with a distinctive internal structure, each linked in simple ways to one another. We applied this notion earlier to the composing of a written argument and the planning of the sample study. It also applies more generally to the conceptualizing of virtually any research problem.

The key is to look for the joints that divide a complex system into a few simpler entities. Carving a turkey provides a metaphor. A turkey can pose quite a challenge to the novice carving the Thanksgiving bird. The trick is to find the joints, so the carver can divide a big job into a few relatively small ones. Think about *messes, lumps, chunks*. If you carve a problem into a lot of little pieces, you will be overwhelmed by the details. If you try to handle the problem as a whole, you will be confused by the apparent complexity. Human beings can most effectively handle a few items at a time; the key is to keep it simple—more to the point, make it simple.

How do you know when you have hit a joint in a conceptual domain? We suggest that when the technical language and relations in one chunk differ from those in another chunk, you have found a joint. The previous discussion about selecting treatment, person, and outcome factors illustrates the point; we talked differently about the choices within each of these domains. Locating the chunks, then, is the key to analysis of a complex question; it also lays the foundation for synthesis, for bringing the chunks back into relation to one another.

Let us apply this reasoning to the previous vignette. Your initial thinking about argument was fuzzy and complex. You saw the issues as one dimensional, and the best method seemed obvious. But then you were soon burdened by technical details of control. Looking for a few joints allows you to divide the big problem into manageable chunks that help with management of the details. You have already moved in this direction by focusing on two thematic areas: forms of argument and styles of integrated instruction. Both areas have a distinctive technical base; each can be considered as an entity in its own right.

You can then apply the divide-and-conquer principle to each of the two domains. For instance, how might you subdivide the complexities of instruction—pedagogical method, materials, and management? The answer is implicit in the question. Divide each big chunk into a handful of distinctive subchunks, and decide which are critical to your research question. The chunks will then need to be re-related to one another, but the capacity to assess interactions is inherent in the technology of factorial design.

Creating the Design

This section addresses ways in which the previous concepts and procedures apply to construction of a specific research plan. Here we move from divergent to convergent thinking, from strategy to tactics. Assume that you have identified two thematic issues: how well can students comprehend arguments that include warrants, and in what ways do opportunities for small-group interaction help support both comprehension and composition. You plan to use multiple-choice tests to assess comprehension and writing assignments to tap into productive competence. Your research questions are reflected in the design: What is the impact of small-group activities on students' ability to handle more or less complex arguments when they are assessed by recognition and performance tasks? You have created a learning model that describes your hunches about the underlying mechanisms at work under the various conditions, for students with more or less experience in dealing with arguments, from which you have ventured several expectations about the pattern of the results.

Now you need to formalize a plan of action. You have several options, which can be guided by a few principles. First, two thematic chunks—how students process arguments and how instructional approaches produce learning—need to be expanded into operational factors. Second, you should think about starting with two or three bite-sized investigations rather than putting all of your eggs into a single basket. Third, you need to keep the ultimate goal in mind, and take care not to drown in details. The factors selected for the design support the thematic foundations of the study, while ensuring that the design controls significant sources of extraneous variability. The following sections offer practical advice about refining the design and preparing the details of the research plan. We have selected a few items for emphasis and illustration.

Big Picture and First Steps.   The first word of advice is to keep your primary goals in mind, and keep moving in that direction—unless you have a good reason to change direction. You have shaped the elements of a plan; an image of the research problem is taking shape in your mind's eye. How should you proceed next? As noted above, one option is to proceed with a full-scale experiment. Another is to conduct a series of mini-studies. A third, returning to your first idea, is to pursue a naturalistic investigation based on observation, interview, and assessment. Our suggestion is that you keep in mind all levels of this continuum, but especially the middle. You can collect preliminary data while also refining your thoughts about the big picture. Immersing yourself in actual data will have both practical and theoretical benefits.

	Comprehension Processes	Method of Instruction
Treatments	Argument differences	Small Groups vs. Teacher Lectures Comprehension & composition
Students	Different levels of expertise	Different levels of expertise
Outcomes	Performance measures	Performance measures Transfer measures Statisfaction measures Field notes

Figure 56.2 Design for study of argument comprehension and social context of instruction.

You began the project with a literature review, which helped you shape a theoretical perspective. Refining a conceptual framework requires abstract thinking, but it also benefits from practical experiences. The challenge is to translate your ideas into concrete form. A graphic organizer may help you document your evolving plan. Figure 56.2 shows a midstream road map for moving from Post-It notes to the next step in your design. The matrix presents the two thematic elements as column headings; the rows show the factorial categories central to most research plans. The sketch provides a structure for capturing ideas; the entries in the figure are only illustrative. Creating the plan is a dynamic enterprise; use Post-Its, or record your thoughts on a word processor. Ask colleagues for comment and criticism. Be flexible; the one constancy in research design is change.

Our second recommendation is that, as your plans take shape, spend time in your research context (e.g., classrooms, teachers, and students), looking and listening, trying out your ideas and procedures and materials in realistic settings. What you see and hear will be guided—consciously or unconsciously—by the conceptual framework that fills the walls of your study area. Before the design is cast in stone, recheck the context. What are potential sources of evidence? What variations are especially critical? Where are you least certain and most confused? What questions should you pose to informants? What answers do you expect, and how can you follow up for clarification? These initial forays into the field, though tentative, should be guided by your design. You are still framing the research question. You are still developing instruments. The decisions springing from ongoing descriptive work can continue to shape the study.

Data Analysis   The design proposal was finally approved, you decided on your strategic course, came to know the territory, and the data are in hand. This chapter is about the role of design in the research enterprise, and we have neither the mandate nor space to say much about the tasks of data analyses. Some remarks about the connection between design and analysis do warrant attention, however. Whatever the nature of the evidence, one basic principle should be followed, whether the evidence is quantitative or qualitative, whether in the form of numbers, field notes, interviews, pictures, videotapes, or whatever. The principle is to *fully immerse yourself in the data*. This activity is commonplace when the data are qualitative and the design is a case study, but less so with a factorial design and quantitative data. Here the usual approach is to load the data into a statistical program and see what emerges—hopefully including some statistically significant findings.

This approach is a mistake for a variety of reasons, which we will not explore in detail. But here are some guidelines for an alternative strategy. One job is to *summarize*, where you move through the basic observations looking for eye-catching trends. For numbers, the search for trends falls under labels like *mean*, *variance*, and *correlation*. The usual tactic is to ask the computer for descriptive statistics. For the complex observations typical in qualitative analyses, the approach is to immerse yourself in raw observations, transcribing recordings, filling thick binders with Post-Its and multicolored highlightings. The researcher, following the tenets of grounded theory (Glaser & Strauss, 1967), is also looking for trends, springing from consistencies in the evidence, based on informed judgment and a search for consistencies. In an ongoing debate in *Educational Researcher* on epistemological differences between quantitative and qualitative analyses, Ercikan and Roth (2006) argued that the differences in methodology might not really be all that great; that all research is based on perception, all perception has both qualitative and quantitative aspects, and all types of methodological justification must lead to logical/reasonable conclusions (Chambliss, Alexander, & Price, in press).

Both tactics share important strategic components. The researcher dealing with numbers is now advised to explore the data, to study frequency distributions, prepare scatter-plots, and be on the lookout for unusual events. The field of *exploratory data analysis* (Behrens & Smith, 1996) includes a range of systematic techniques for tasks similar in many respects to the work of qualitative researchers. Likewise, the qualitative researcher can call upon computer programs like NVivo (www.qsrinternational.com) and QDA Miner (www.provalisresearch.com) to replace Post-It notes and highlighters for data management but, more importantly, to handle the tasks of classification and summarization. The new programs even provide the qualitative researcher with the capacity to count and to measure. The researcher exploring qualitative evidence is well advised to look for trends analogous to those found in statistical methods. Central tendencies—what are the typical elements in the data set? Variability—what deviations from typicality do you find? Correlations—in what ways do parallel trends seem to emerge? You may not be able to attach precise indices to these trends, but you can convince your readers of their existence. To be sure, arguments based solely on anecdotes rest on perilous ground.

Exploration and summarization can both be linked to design issues in factorial plans. We mentioned earlier that factorial designs allow the researcher to evaluate both main effects and interactions. To remind you, main effects reflect differences that emerge as you move from one level to another of a factor, such as the differences between males and females, or between writing by individuals versus small group assignments. Interactions describe patterns associated with factorial combinations; girls do better than boys when writing individually, while boys do better than girls in small group settings. Statistical procedures like analysis of variance generate indices for identifying reliable differences associated with main effects and interactions. An exact parallel does not exist for qualitative methodologies, but the researcher can still examine the evidence for such patterns and develop arguments to support various conclusions. In doing so, the researcher may find himself or herself falling back on numbers, as in the following example:

> In 70% of the small group protocols, boys expressed a competitive stance on the writing task, whereas girls voiced a more cooperative slant. These trends were supported in the interview data. When I talked with students after individual writing assignments, competitive, cooperative motivations were mentioned by only 15% of the students.

The notion of including both quantitative and qualitative evidence in the overall design of research studies has a long history, but has advanced in the past two decades in new and invigorating forms. Classic research methods textbooks began to emphasize a mixed strategy in the 1980s (e.g., Jaeger, 1988), usually by recommending that a primary method be complemented by secondary methods. For example, a large-scale survey of writing practice (quantitative) might provide direction for selection of a set of individual case studies (qualitative). Creswell and his associates (Creswell, 1994, 2003, Creswell & Plano Clark, 2007) expanded this idea, developing a taxonomy of mixed-methods combinations applicable to a variety of settings. These treatments tended to keep the two basic methodologies—quantitative and qualitative—at arm's length. The reasons for maintaining the separation are understandable. The two methods approach research problems from different epistemological stances—different ways of thinking about the nature of knowledge and the tasks of science. They tend to rely on different design strategies—case studies versus factorial designs and large-scale surveys. They obviously differ in the type of basic evidence upon which they rely—numbers versus words—although Ercikan and Roth (2006) point out many underlying epistemological similarities.

Even if an underlying logic could be used to integrate qualitative and quantitative approaches, quantitative and qualitative researchers differ in the language that they use to talk about their work. Calfee and Sperling (2010) liken the situation to the Tower of Babel, and propose an integrated model for mixed-methods research strategies. They acknowledge that epistemological differences pose a fundamental challenge to a genuine merger of the fields. Nonetheless, by proposing a bridging vocabulary, they show

how activities such as exploration and summarization can be connected within a study, not as parallel play, but as genuinely integrated endeavors. This approach begins during the framing of the research problem, where methods emerge as appropriate complements to the problem. They present illustrations from previous studies in the language-literacy field demonstrating the possibilities springing from an integrated approach, including connections with factorial design strategies. Greene (2001) has also argued for the power of integrating the two approaches, explaining that "Points of tension between the different methods…are juxtaposed and analytically blended into a dialectic synthesis. It is this synthesis in integrated designs that fulfills the fundamental mixed method purpose of understanding more fully" (p. 57). If a similar chapter is prepared a decade hence, the author may no longer preface the work by describing such designs as primarily within the purview of quantitative outcomes, but as a general strategy for research planning.

Interpretation

The study is complete. You have implemented the design, have completed the analyses, and the data are in the bag. Unfortunately, data do not answer questions; people do. For evidence to have meaning, you must deal with several more questions. How far can you trust the evidence; how far can you generalize the findings; how convincingly can you persuade others of your interpretation? You hopefully reflected earlier on your response to various outcomes—*before you collected the data*. The findings either support your expectations or they have surprised you.

Suppose the results turn out as you predicted. You show that students in the novel treatment for analyzing and composing arguments are more likely to participate vigorously in classroom discussions about one another's arguments and to prepare coherent arguments for their classroom assignments than those in the traditional approach. What does this result mean? Your argument appears straightforward; the innovative approach is superior, supporting your convictions about what students need to learn and how they can best learn it.

Suppose the results do not come out as expected? You may have difficulty imagining this outcome. Given all your planning, thinking, and work, how could this happen! But it does. The most frequent disappointment occurs when an innovative treatment produces little or no effect, when the *null hypothesis* (no difference) cannot be rejected. This result can come about for either or both of two reasons. First, the treatment may actually not be effective—hard for you to accept, but possible. Second, student performance may vary so widely that random fluctuations swamp the treatment effect. It is like a slot machine, which costs you on each play; you do not immediately notice the loss because sometimes you win and sometimes you lose. A well-conceived research design allows you to identify extraneous sources of variability in performance, so that you can tell whether you have won or lost.

At the core of interpretation is establishing the *validity* of the findings, ensuring that your argument holds up under close scrutiny. You are about the concept of validity as it applies to testing: Validity is the extent to which a test measures what it is supposed to measure. In fact, recent thinking (Messick, 1995; Kane, 2006; Lissitz, 2009) about validity has taken a different turn: "Validity is the strength of the argument that a particular test outcome means what the tester says that it means" (Lissitz, 2009, p. 742). Test theorists approach validity from two perspectives: internal validity and external validity (Campbell & Stanley, 1966; Cook & Campbell, 1979; Porter, 1997). Internal validity responds to the question, "To what degree can I trust the evidence that is within my grasp" External validity asks, "To what degree can I extend the findings to other situations?"

The matrix in Figure 56.3 links internal and external validity with the design perspectives from this chapter. The matrix looks in turn at factors controlled in the design and at uncontrolled or free floating factors. The cell to the upper left corresponds to the original notion of internal validity. The other three cells are variations on external validity.

The first test of validity, *conceptual clarity*, centers on the adequacy of the factorial design. Now that the data are in, how clearly can you tell what happened? To what degree do the factors appear as compelling representations of the constructs (the underlying concepts) that are incorporated in the conceptual framework and the research questions? To what degree can you make sense of patterns in the data? Complex interactions may have appeal when you first think about a problem, but they can also render interpretation difficult. To what extent did the treatments work as intended? Most significantly, to what degree might the study be replicated with some assurance of obtaining similar results? Secrest, West, Phillips, Redner, and Yeaton (1979) refine these points: "The essence of construct validity is that one has a good understanding of the conceptual meaning of the treatment…. It refers to our interpretation of the treatments, not the treatments themselves" (p. 17). For instance, you may discover that when you form small group writing teams, student exchanges do not play out as you intended. You imagined a *cooperative* enterprise, but qualitative observations reveal cooperation, along with competition and a lot of parallel play. This finding is not a failure—you have learned something from the results.

The second validity test, *situational stability*, is the degree to which the evidence allows you to project the basic findings with confidence to other contexts, based on the original design. What about the influence of factors that you decided to ignore; how do they appear to influence the outcome, directly or through interactions? If the sample of participants is too small or too homogeneous, then you may not feel confident about extending the findings. If the instruments are too specialized, you may be hesitant to recommend your results to others. Replication is again a key consideration; how confident do you feel that you would obtain similar results if someone else repeated the study, keeping the design intact, but with different samples of participants and in different contexts?

The next two categories go beyond the details of your original design to extensions of the underlying constructs. Researchers seldom limit their interpretive scope to a particular study. You are interested not just in the program that you have developed, whatever shape it may take in the final design, but in the concepts that undergird the program. Researchers aspire to broadly generalizable statements, and here the issue of external validity comes to the fore.

Figure 56.3 has two entries in this column. First is *conceptual match*. In going beyond the original conditions, while staying close to the original conception, how safe are you in projecting your results? A great deal depends on the clarity of the original conceptualization, and the degree to which the basic conditions can be implemented in a similar manner under variations in the specifics of the design. The argument program showed considerable promise on its first test flight. A colleague plans to implement the program in a different setting, but must modify it to fit local conditions. What are the boundaries? The small-group activity seemed to be a critical component. You developed a series of group planning guides with scripts and graphic organizers, which appeared quite effective in scaffolding students' efforts to lay out the claim-evidence-warrant trilogy in complex arguments. Duplicating the guides was expensive, and your friend is planning on a much reduced version. You provided a week of professional development before the start of the school year. Your friend is thinking about two hour-long after-school meetings. What should she keep and what can be jettisoned? Changes of this sort can be thought of as "dosage" issues, as changes in the intensity of the treatment. But as you can imagine, the changes also influence the conceptual structure of the program in ways that are difficult to assess.

Finally there is *situational match*, which is related to

what Cronbach (Cronbach, Glesser, Nanda, & Rajaratnam, 1972; Shavelson & Webb, 2006) labeled *generalizability*. Suppose a user wants to change the program and then implement it in a different situation; what are the chances that the results apply under these circumstances? Your program has been tried out under one set of conditions, with certain factors under control. The students are from middle-class backgrounds, the classes are relatively small, the teachers are experienced professionals, and resources are available for staff development and collegial interactions. Do the findings hold up in situations where these conditions do not hold? If the treatment is powerful, then the variation in program specifics and local contexts should not matter. An investigation should ideally provide linkages that inform judgments about the transferability of the findings.

The two dimensions in Figure 56.3 are represented by two binary levels; in fact, they are better thought of as end points on a continuum. Any effort to replicate a study necessarily entails changes of various sorts. Some will be obvious, others more subtle. Some will be well planned, others more accidental and incidental. Research depends on informed judgment, which depends in turn on continually wrestling with the conceptual issues. Interpretation is a form of pattern detection; fortunately, the human mind excels at this task.

Concluding Thoughts

Research is problem solving, and the problems are real. Empirical data are part of the process, though not always the most significant element. Educational and social science research are particularly demanding because the theoretical foundations are weak and researchers sometimes overlook the theoretical tools that are available (Suppes, 1974). But the times are a-changing, and rapidly. Cognition and social cognition, the practical emphasis on educating rather than

	Conditions Within Immediate Domain of Study (design remains constant)	Conditions Beyond Domain of Study (design changes; underlying concepts remain constant)
Factors Within the Design	CONCEPTUAL CLARITY (Affected by the design factors) * Clarity of concepts * Size and simplicity of effects * Inadvertent confounding	CONCEPTUAL MATCH (Affected by the replicability of underlying concepts) * Repeatability of plan * Interactions * Faithfulness to plan
Factors Outside the Design	SITUATIONAL STABILITY (Affected by the effect of factors in the situation) * Extraneous factors, direct and interactive * Reliability of measures * Size of sample; number of observations	SITUATIONAL MATCH (Affected by the degree of similarity between situations) * Presence of new conditions and contexts * Reliance on new tests * Different people and groups

Figure 56.3 Matrix displaying impact of design and context factors on internal and external validity of a research study.

training, and the challenge of helping every individual realize his or her full potential—the road ahead is exciting and demanding.

Educational and social science research nonetheless remains in the sleepwalking phase (Koestler, 1968). Even the best of our theories are more heuristic than formal, and we must often rely on experience and intuition. Success frequently depends on doing several things right rather than pursuing the one best answer (Slavin, 1986; Tyack, 1974). Cronbach (1975) paints a gloomy prospect for generalizable research in education, portraying a hall of mirrors with infinitely complex and intricate interactions. In fact, where research designs allow evaluations to be evaluated, the evidence suggests that simple interactions are fairly commonplace, most often in conjunction with substantial main effects. Complex interactions, however, are actually quite rare.

Although the tasks may appear daunting, we are optimistic about the enterprise. Researchers are well advised to bite off only as much as they can chew comfortably when first approaching a problem, while also avoiding taking merely baby bites. Whether as producer or consumer of empirical research, you might consider the divide and conquer strategy. A series of modest but well-designed studies is likely to be more informative than a single humongous effort. Critical experiments are rare in our business; a researcher has made a contribution if his or her investigation provides one or two insights—which may spring from a mistake that suggests what *not* to do. When you read a research report, it may resemble bowling; the investigator sets the pins, throws the ball, and counts how many pins fall. Reality is different. "Some of the most excellent inquiry is free ranging and speculative in its initial stages, trying what might seem to be bizarre combinations of ideas and procedures, restlessly casting about ..." (Cronbach & Suppes, 1969, p. 16). But threading through all the elements is one critical theme—design.

We have not recommended a fixed algorithm for planning empirical research, but the strategy exemplified in the earlier vignette often works quite well. First, learn as much as you can about the territory through a descriptive study. Your goal is often driven by person factors such as motivation and psychological processes. Then, move on to experiment and innovate; try out a series of instructional treatments, perhaps one or two chunks at a time. Innovations are difficult to implement, and success is more likely by proceeding in phases. Plan to assess the implementation and to examine in detail the full range of potential effects (positive and negative). You may not be able to complete an in-depth evaluation of every participant; a better mixed-method strategy is to select a few individuals for "thick" study, for contrast with the thinner data from the entire group.

Our main message throughout has been the essential importance of *design*—basic building blocks, linkages, and an overarching theme. We have focused on factorial designs because they are simple, flexible, and have been thoroughly studied for almost a century. The various components assume different shapes in different stages of an investigation, but if you build on them consistently, they provide coherence and unity for the effort. You will learn something from the experience, and will gain satisfaction from the enterprise—whether you take on the task yourself, or move through an investigation vicariously.

References

Alexander, P. A., & Winne, P. H. (Eds.). (2006). *Handbook of educational psychology* (2nd ed.). Mahwah NJ: Erlbaum.

Behrens, J. T., & Smith, M. L. (1996). Data and data analysis. In D. C. Berliner & R. C. Calfee (Eds.), *Handbook of educational psychology* (pp. 945–989). New York: Macmillan.

Berliner, D. C., & Calfee, R. C. (1996). *Handbook of educational psychology*. New York: Macmillan.

Brown, A. L. (1992). Design experiments: Theoretical and methodological challenges in creating complex interventions in classroom settings. *The Journal of the Learning Sciences, 2,* 141–178.

Calfee, R. C., & Sperling, M. (2010). *Mixed methods: Approaches to language and literacy research*. New York: Teachers College Press.

Campbell, D. T., & Stanley, J. C. (1966). *Experimental and quasi-experimental designs for research*. Chicago: Rand McNally.

Chambliss, M. J., & Calfee, R. C. (1998). *Textbooks for learning: Nurturing children's minds*. Malden, MA: Blackwell.

Chambliss, M. J., Alexander, P. A., & Price, (in press). Epistemological threads in the fabric of pedagogical research. *Teachers College Record*.

Collins, A. (1994). Toward a design science of education. In E. Scanlon & T. O'Shea (Eds.), *New directions in educational technology*. New York: Springer-Verlag.

Cook, T. D., & Campbell, D. T. (1979). *Quasi-experimentation: Design and analysis issues for field settings*. Chicago: Rand McNally.

Creswell, J. W. (1994). *Research design: Qualitative and quantitative approaches*. Thousand Oaks, CA: Sage.

Creswell, J. W. (2003). *Research design: Qualitative, quantitative, and mixed methods approaches*. Thousand Oaks: Sage.

Creswell, J. W., & Plano Clark, V. L. (2007). *Designing and conducting mixed methods research*. Thousand Oaks CA: Sage

Cronbach, L. J. (1963). Evaluation for course improvement. *Teachers College Record, 64,* 97–121.

Cronbach, L. J. (1975). Beyond the two disciplines of scientific psychology. *American Psychologist, 30,* 116–127.

Cronbach, L. J. (1988). Five perspectives on the validity argument. In Wainer & H. I. Braun (Eds.), *Test validity*. Hillsdale, NJ: Erlbaum.

Cronbach, L. J., Glesser, G. C., Nanda, H., & Rajaratnam, N. (1972). *The dependability of behavioral measurements: Theory of generalizability for scores and proWles*. New York: Wiley.

Cronbach, L. J., & Snow, R. E. (1977). *Aptitudes and instructional methods/A handbook for research on interactions*. New York: Irvington.

Cronbach, L. J., & Suppes, P. (Eds.). (1969). *Research for tomorrow's schools: Disciplined inquiry for education*. New York: Macmillan.

Ercikan, K., & Roth, W. M. (2006). What good is polarizing research into qualitative and quantitative? *Educational Researcher, 35,* 14–23.

Freedman, S. W., Simons, E. R., & Kalnin, J. S. (1999). *Inside city schools: Investigating literacy in multicultural classrooms*. New York: Teachers College Press.

Gall, M. D., Borg, W. R., & Gall, J. P. (2006). *Educational research: An introduction* (8th ed.). Boston MA: Allyn & Bacon.

Glaser, B., & Strauss, A. L. (1967). *The discovery of grounded theory: Strategies for qualitative research*. Chicago: Aldine.

Green, J. L., Camilli, G., & Elmore, P. B. (Eds.). (2006). *Handbook of complementary methods in education research*. Mahwah, NJ: Erlbaum.

Greene, J. C. (2001). Mixing social inquiry methodologies. In V. Richardson (Ed.), *Handbook of research on teaching* (4th ed., pp. 251–258). Washington, DC: American Educational Research Association.

Jaeger, R. M. (Ed.). (1997). *Complementary methods for research in education* (2nd ed.). Washington, DC: American Educational Research Association.

Kane, M. T. (2006). Validation. In R. L. Brennan, (Ed.), *Educational measurement* (4th ed.). Westport, CT: Praeger.

Koestler, A. (1968). *The sleepwalkers.* New York: Macmillan.

Krathwohl, D. R. (1997). *Methods of educational and social science research: An integrated approach.* Menlo Park, CA: Addison Wesley.

Lissitz, R. W. (Ed.). (2009). *The concept of validity.* Charlotte NC: Information Age.

Mathison, M. A. (1998). Students as critics of disciplinary texts. In N. Nelson & R. C. Calfee (Eds.), *The reading-writing connection/ninety-seventh yearbook of the National Society for the Study of Education* (pp. 249–265). Chicago: The National Society for the Study of Education.

Messick, S. (1995). Validity of psychological assessment: Validation of inferences from persons' responses and performances as scientific inquiry into score meaning. *American Psychologist, 50,* 741–749.

Myers, J. L., & Well, A. D. (2003). *Research design and statistical analysis* (2nd ed.). Mahwah NJ: Erlbaum.

National Research Council. (2002). *Scientific research in education.* R. J. Shavelson & L. Towne (Eds.). Washington DC: National Academy Press.

Nystrand, M. (1989). A social-interactive model of writing. *Written Communication, 6,* 66–85.

Nystrand, M. (1997). *Opening dialogue: Understanding the dynamics of language and learning in the English language.* New York: Teachers College Press.

Osborne, J. W. (Ed.). (2008). *Best practices in quantitative methods.* Thousand Oaks CA: Sage.

Porter, A. C. (1997). Comparative experiments in educational research. In R. Jaeger (Ed.), *Complementary methods for research in education* (2nd ed., pp. 521–586). Washington, DC: American Educational Research Association.

Rubin, D. L. (1998). Writing for readers. In N. Nelson & R. C. Calfee (Eds.), *The reading-writing connection/ninety-seventh yearbook of the National Society for the Study of Education* (pp. 53–73). Chicago: The National Society for the Study of Education.

Secrest, L., West, S. G., Phillips, M. E., Redner, R., & Yeaton, W. (1979). Introduction. In L. Secrest (Ed.), *Evaluation studies review annual, Vol. 4* (pp. 15–35). Beverly Hills, CA: Sage.

Shavelson, R. J., & Webb, N. M. (1991). *Generalizability theory: A primer.* Thousand Oaks CA: Sage.

Shulman, L. S. (1988). Disciplines of inquiry in education: A new overview. In R. Jaeger (Ed.), *Complementary methods for research in education* (2nd ed., pp. 71–116). Washington, DC: American Educational Research Association.

Simon, H. A. (1981). *The sciences of the artificial* (2nd ed.). Cambridge, MA: MIT Press.

Slavin, R. (1986). Best evidence synthesis: An alternative to meta-analytic and traditional reviews. *Educational Researcher, 15*(9), 5–11.

Spivey, N. N. (1997). *The constructivist metaphor.* San Diego, CA: Academic Press.

Suppes, P. (1974). The place of theory in educational research. *Educational Research, 3,* 3–10.

Tashakori, A., & Teddlie, C. (2003). (Eds.). *Handbook of mixed methods in social and behavioral research.* Thousand Oaks CA: Sage.

Toulmin, S. E. (1958). *The uses of argument.* Cambridge, UK: Cambridge University Press.

Tyack, D. B. (1974). *The one best system: A history of American urban education.* Cambridge, MA: Harvard University Press.

57

Child Development Studies Over Time

Stuart McNaughton

The study of language and literacy over time has a long history. The history of child development studies involves three distinct sets that are based on time. Each examines reading and writing and those activities more broadly conceived as literacy and language arts over different units of time. The sets of studies range from a long-term time perspective over multiple years, through a medium-term frame of weeks, months, and years, to a short-term or micro genetic frame of seconds, minutes and hours. The latter two in part owe their features to the older set of studies with the long time frame. So the longer term studies provide an historically and conceptually appropriate introduction for the other two sets.

Classic Child Developmental Designs

In 1972 Clay presented the results of an ongoing study into children's literacy development from the entrance to school. Initially over 1 year, the follow up of 100 children extended to a further 2 and 3 years. The design she used was a classic longitudinal design in which she repeatedly measured the same group of children over time plotting changes in specific knowledge such as alphabet knowledge, changes in cognitive strategies such as selective attention to highly informative cues, and changes in self-regulation such as self-corrections. She drew on a well-established design to provide the powerful demonstration that these components of development had a pre history (they were emergent before school) and that the developmental properties were best described as a growing orchestration or integration (Clay, 2001).

Her study drew on the early developmental studies such as the Fels Longitudinal study and Gesell's study at Yale (e.g., Gesell & Ilg, 1946), which asked questions about when changes occur and in what sequences, assuming that the phenomena being measured change in form and function over time. They used the obtained patterns to develop grand theories of development, in Gesell and Ilg's case a strongly maturational theory which introduced the idea of developmental readiness. Gesell and Ilg produced growth gradients which represented normative trends within which they could identify individual variations. These early studies using the classic designs provided for theorists such as Clay the methodological tools to apply to literacy.

The Development of Literacy? It goes without saying that literacy phenomena are developmental and hence studies which look at the attributes of change over time in form and function are important. Or are they? While it doesn't need arguing now, this view was not always obvious or accepted. When the idea of emergent literacy developed by Clay (1972) was proposed, it was counter to some developmental views of the time. There was a view that, because children needed to be deliberately taught to read and write at school, examining the attributes of reading and writing over time was not a proper domain for developmentalists. The proper study should be of organically changing aspects of psychological functioning, and hence studies which tried to capture written language development over time were not appropriate (Wolwhill, 1970). Interestingly, this view was despite Gesell and Ilg (1946) having produced growth gradients for "reading behaviour" from 15 months to 5- to 6-years to show that school skills are subject to the principle of developmental readiness, and never the sole product of training or drill.

Clay's (1972) time-based design helped to establish the developmental nature of literacy. Studies like Clay's provided an empirical context within which encompassing theories of development could be examined. For example, the longitudinal studies of Ferreiro and Teborosky (1982) interpreted the patterns of changes in writing as evidence for the epigenetic view of developmental change derived from the genetic epistemology of Piaget. The large waves of change in children hypotheses about the nature of the written system could be mapped onto general developmental stages.

Interestingly, the studies by Clay (1972) and further research reviewed by Sulzby and Teale (1991) helped establish an alternative theoretical view to the epigenetic account. Their studies also supported cognitive models of children as thoughtful and strategic. But in addition they provided a means for linking reading and writing to social contexts, notably family or schools. Comparisons between studies illustrated how development could take different forms under different conditions and hence led to theories that predicted multiple pathways of learning. The evidence enabled theorists to establish that socialisation conditions present both at home and at school were central to development, rather than peripheral and provided one foundation for more recent sociocultural theorizing (McNaughton, 1995).

The classic studies over time of this sort were not only longitudinal, there were also cross-sectional designs. The latter are studies in which change over time is captured by taking a slice at several different ages at the same point in time, thus providing a picture of how development changes over these ages, and hence, presumably, over time as children age. Cross sectional studies can also take a form in which only one or two ages are sampled, but these ages are repeatedly sampled over successive years or multiples of years giving a picture of how children of the same age but of different historical cohorts might be similar or different over historical time.

There are variants that are mixtures of the two, not surprisingly termed mixed designs, which provide ways of overcoming readily identified shortcomings of each (Overton & Reese, 1973). For example, longitudinal designs, especially over very long time frames, suffer from problems such as differential drop out and the use of measures that may become outdated. Although cross sectional studies provide a quicker means of plotting shifts over time, they rely on samples of cohorts and because of this do not represent any individual in change over time. They can conflate historical change with individual change. Mixed designs capitalize on the strengths of each to provide short-term longitudinal components which enable individual trajectories to be plotted but in a cross sectional format, which means that patterns of change over long time frames can be captured.

The classic designs using longer time frames that have an underlying developmental logic are critical to the study of language arts and continue to be sorely needed. They provide two sorts of important evidence. They yield basic evidence about the nature of development and learning over time. They also provide a means for plotting how wider socialisation changes, including systemic and policy changes at national levels might be associated with changes in children's literacy levels.

Unraveling the Developmental Threads In terms of the former, the recent analyses by Whitehurst and Lonigan (2001) and by Paris (2005) based on longitudinal studies have enabled important new models of development to be developed and tested. These theorists have provided further evidence to support models of development that are multi componential and assume parallel pathways for the development of components. In the Whitehurst and Lonigan model these are sets of "inside out" (such as sound and print units of knowledge and skills) and "outside in" (knowledge and skills relating to words, semantic units and textual structures) and in the Paris model the equivalent sets are "constrained" and "unconstrained" knowledge and skills.

The assumptions about the developmental relationships and changes are different in these contemporary models and more longitudinal studies are needed to plot conditional relationships and pathways over time using techniques such as structural equation modeling (Whitehurst & Lonigan, 2001) and growth modeling. These can help untangle which assumptions best represent the evidence by explicating the necessary and sufficient relationships between sets of skills and knowledge states. This will enable even better designs for instructional interventions. The need is not just for general theories of literacy but also in those components that have not been adequately mapped. For example, Pearson, Hiebert, and Kamil (2007) have argued that there is a pressing need for studies of growth in vocabulary but that these are dependent on better definitions and measures of vocabulary.

Systemic Changes The second contribution that these designs make is illustrated by cross sectional studies that monitor cohorts of children to examine how a system is performing. National data bases such as the National Assessment of Educational Progress, available since the early 1970s, have enabled long-term monitoring of achievement scores. It is possible to plot patterns of change, in the achievement levels of different groups of students at fourth and eighth grades and relate these to broad policy shifts. For example, Porter & Polikoff (2007) used the data bases to describe how Black students' performance in reading and writing has been consistently below that of White students, although there have been shifts. In reading there were large gains in Black students' scores during the 1970s and 1980s. But in the 1990s these gains were reversed and the gaps actually got larger. The picture from 2002 reflects a period of unprecedented federal spending and policy changes through the No Child Left Behind legislation and as yet there is little evidence 3 to 4 years into the programme that gaps have changed markedly (Porter & Polikoff, 2007).

Like the United States, Canada, and other countries, New Zealand also has a national monitoring project which samples a range of reading and writing and oral language tasks for students in year 4 (9-year-olds) and year 9 (14-year-olds) of schooling. Four yearly cycles provide evidence of students' strengths and weaknesses and how systemic changes such as policy initiatives might impact. From these cycles of assessments it is known that a major literacy strategy commenced in 1998 and focused on school years 1–4 was associated with a positive change in reading accuracy at year 4 (9 years). However, the sampling of tasks includes comprehension tasks and it also known that there has been little change in comprehension levels for those students most at risk in the system, Māori students (from the indigenous community) and Pasifika students (from recent immigrant or second and older communities from Pacific islands), despite the changes in decoding levels (Lai, McNaughton, Amituanai-Toloa, Turner, & Hsaio, 2009).

The Search for Explanations: Unraveling the Variability in Development Over Time

The second set of studies also uses time to study learning and development. Generically labeled "single case" (Hersen & Barlow, 1976), "time series" (Risley & Wolf, 1973), or "single subject" experimental designs (Neuman & McCormick, 1995), these designs use time as a means of identifying causes and hence identifying the means for altering learning and development.

The early foundations for these studies were in the radical behaviourism and operationalism of Skinner (1953) and Sidman (1960), who set out the epistemological bases for the designs. They proposed a disarmingly simple view of cause which equated establishing cause with methodological control. That is, if sources of variability in behaviour could be established so that rates and patterns of learning could be reliably altered under known conditions, then cause had been established.

The original methods, developed with nonhuman subjects, were designed to enable researchers to test and elaborate principles of reinforcement, punishment and stimulus control under tight experimental controls. The basic method involved systematically changing the contingencies of consequences (such as positive reinforcers) and antecedents (such as prompts and instruction) to behaviour, and then plotting the behavioural correlates of these systematic changes against time. If the experimenter could, through systematic replication, reliably and generally repeat the relationships between application and behaviour change, then a robust causal analysis was demonstrated (Sidman, 1960).

The basic methods were elaborated in real world settings using designs that enabled researchers to examine the sources of variability in classrooms and family and other applied settings (Risley & Wolf, 1973). The designs used the idea of baselines established by repeated measurement against which the effects of an introduced intervention could be compared. The core designs included "reversal designs" in which interventions were successively introduced and removed, and "multiple baseline designs" in which interventions were systematically applied in a lagged fashion across multiple subjects or behaviors.

Successive generations of researchers have taken these designs and shown how they can be applied to the language arts (Neuman & McCormick, 1995). They have provided analytic tools to guide the design of effective intervention procedures contributing to a range of productive long-term research programmes such as those of Whitehurst and col-

leagues (e.g., Whitehurst & Valdez-Menchaca, 1988) who developed the family and preschool language intervention programme of Dialogic Reading, and Brown's (1997) Reciprocal Teaching and, more broadly, Fostering a Community of Learners programmes.

Optimism and the Solving of Real World Problems There are two fundamental contributions the second set of studies have made to the range of research endeavors associated with the language arts. One is a commitment to optimism at being able to find and use causes of learning to make a significant difference. A second is the capability to study individuals and groups in ways that enable the identification of sources of variability.

The early applied behaviour analysts were associated with programmes in developmental and educational psychology and had a commitment to change. The optimism was expressed in Baer's (1973) contribution to a book on methodological issues in life span developmental psychology entitled "The Control of Developmental Process: Why Wait?." The applied behaviour analysts took literally Hume's argument in *A Treatise of Human nature* (1739) that one can't get an "ought" from an "is." That is, just because the state of the world is like it is, that is no reason to resign from attempts to change the world into what it ought to be, or perhaps could be.

Was this optimism warranted? As noted above, the portfolio of studies provides an impressive demonstration of their usefulness ranging from precise measurement of instructional effects to contributing to the design of large scale interventions. But there are weaknesses.

The single case designs are essentially quasi-experimental designs because they do not randomise assignment to experimental and control conditions. The single case designs control for issues relating to internal validity by the demonstration and precision of experimental control, but their believability is dependent on how reliably the treatment effect can be shown. In addition, even if internal validity is high there is the issue of external validity, how generalisable are the effects beyond as it were the single case.

Hence, the need to replicate systematically effects and processes is heightened because of the reduced experimental control (Raudenbush, 2005). McCall and Green (2004) argue that in applied developmental contexts, evaluation of programme effects requires a variety of designs including quasi experimental, but our knowledge is dependent on systematic across site analyses. Replication across sites adds to our evaluation of programme effects, particularly when it is inappropriate or premature to conduct experimental randomized designs. Such systematic replication is also needed to determine issues of sustainability (Coburn, 2003) and scaling up (McDonald, Keesler, Kauffman, & Schneider, 2006).

A recent series of large scale interventions that used single case design logic illustrates how the weaknesses in these designs can in part be overcome. The studies were designed to address a long-standing challenge for more effective teaching in a particular context of culturally and linguistically diverse students (Lai et al., 2009). An intervention model (The Learning Schools Model), which focuses on inquiry processes through which schools can fine tune instruction in reading comprehension, was tested in a systematic replication series across like and unlike clusters of schools (McNaughton & Lai, 2009). The design across three studies uses single case logic within a developmental framework of cross sectional and longitudinal data. The measures of students' achievement taken at Time 1 generated a cross section of achievement across school year levels (years 4–5–6–7–8), which provides a baseline forecast of what the expected trajectory of development would be if planned interventions had not occurred (Risley & Wolf, 1973). Successive stages of the intervention could then be compared with the baseline forecast and judgments about acceleration that are contextually valid could be made.

This design, which includes replication across cohorts, provides a high degree of both internal and external validity. The internal validity comes from the in-built testing of treatment effects. The external validity comes from the systematic replication across cohorts. A first study was with a cluster of urban primary schools serving culturally and linguistically diverse students from the poorest communities. The systematic replication involved a second cluster of like schools and then a third cluster of unlike (rural and small town) schools. The design has been employed in three studies over 5 years involving up to 10,000 students, over 250 teachers, in 48 schools. The Learning Schools Model has been shown to accelerate, reliably and generally, gains in reading comprehension over 3 years by between 0.5 to 1.0 year in achievement, over and above expected gains during that period.

Despite being quasi-experimental, arguably these designs are well attuned to the nature and vicissitudes of applied settings and are particularly useful in the early stages of developing interventions because of this. Schools are open systems. In school settings researchers have limited control over the many known and unknown influences on teaching and learning, even in the most structured randomised control designs. Over short and unpredictable time frames schools change in features, such as the demographic characteristics of both teachers and students. They change in instructional resources, professional capabilities and in curricula. As was found in the Learning Schools Model studies (Lai et al., 2009), school years are punctuated by summer breaks in which as yet not well-identified family and community practices have effects on achievement. The significance of only some of these potential influences is known, and examining interventions in precise single case studies is a useful tactic.

Of course, randomisation in large-scale experimental studies provides one way of controlling for these potential sources of constraints on replicability. But, even if randomising large numbers of schools is possible in large scale interventions, the logic of a randomisation exercise is flawed as a means for knowing better about the replicability and generality of the interventions in Sidman's (1960) terms. What we need to know better are the influences on variability in the effectiveness of an intervention, not account for that variability by reducing them to common error variance.

The optimism behind these studies needs to be tempered. There are sources of variability in learning which are very difficult for researchers to change. These are the sources to which Berliner (2006) recently referred when noting the limits to what educational psychological applications can achieve in creating more effective schooling. Public policy, economic and political processes are needed to control variability in such things as poverty, in housing and employment, in access to child care and to well-resourced schools, each of which are sources of differences in achievement between groups in the United States.

Microgenetic Studies: Strategies and Skills in Dynamic Change

The third set of studies employs a much briefer time scale than the previous two; typically the scale is of minutes, hours, and days. The idea of studying moment by moment changes in performance has a venerable history which includes Wundt's (1910) studies in the early 20th century of sensation and perception for which he perfected techniques to study reactions to stimulation over brief time periods.

The newer intensive techniques provide the means for developing and testing theoretical models for children's complex learning. The central theoretical question asked in these studies is about the processes by which children learn (Siegler, 2000). The basic idea is to observe periods of rapidly changing competence. Children who are on the verge of important developmental changes are provided with exposure to experiences that are predicted to be associated with change, and the course of children's behaviour is studied intensively.

The models of cognitive skill or expertise assume that moment by moment performance in discrete activities that have known and changing task parameters provide the sites of learning. This is where the dynamic properties of knowledge, strategies and self-regulation can be described and where change and adaptation occur. When engaging in complex learning tasks such as learning to decode narrative texts accurately and fluently, or comprehending an informational text (and thereby potentially acquiring not only new information but also greater skill), new forms of cognitive skill or expertise can emerge.

The method relies on the intensive study of performance in short bursts of real time. By sensitively measuring the properties of children's performance in relationship to task parameters such as difficulty level and features of the activity setting including sources of external or self-generated feedback, we are in a position to understand the nature of learning and the nature of change in skill. Brown (1997) also used this technique in her studies of communities of learners. Her analyses included studies of the conditions that promote spontaneous uses of explanations in classrooms and of children's' understanding and use of analogies in reading. In the latter case, 10-year-olds in a laboratory setting were given 4 mini passages to read over 6 days. The passages had analogies to be solved in reference to previous passages. Repeated measurement confirmed that increased problem solution occurred, particularly in the solution of what she termed "deep analogies."

Microgenetic studies have been significant in developing analyses of intertextuality as a social construction. That is, for understanding how children and teachers jointly construct ideas about connections between texts and how children learn within those constructions (Shuart-Fans & Bloome, 2004). For example, Bloome and Egan-Robertson (1993) analysed a 15-minute segment of instruction in a first-grade classroom. The intensive descriptions of types of linkages made by teachers (such as seeking the correct date to write or giving directions for homework) show how classroom activities are essentially cultural events in the sense of sites where rules and norms for dealing with texts are established and negotiated. This first grade analysis is consistent with Siegler's (2000) developmental view of these designs in that the transition to school marks a time of rapidly developing competence, the classroom conditions for which can be analysed in considerable detail.

The three sets of studies over time adopt different lenses to study changes in children's behaviour and to plot the course of development and learning. The lenses provide different contexts for understanding the nature of changes, from macro levels to micro levels. They provide for close description as well as experimentally based explanations. They are important tools in our methods for designing more effective conditions in which children learn.

References

Baer, D. M. (1973). The control of developmental process: Why wait? In J. R. Nesselroade & H. W. Reese (Eds.), *Life Span developmental psychology: Methodological issues* (pp 185–193). New York: Academic Press.

Berliner, D. (2006). Our impoverished view of educational reform. *Teachers College Record, 108*(6), 949–995.

Bloome, D., & Egan-Robertson, A. (1993). The social construction of intertextuality in classroom reading and writing lessons. *Reading Research Quarterly, 28*(4), 304–333.

Brown, A. L. (1997). Transforming schools into communities of thinking and learning about serious matters. *American Psychologist, 52*(4) 399–413.

Clay, M. M. (1972). *Reading: the patterning of complex behavior.* Auckland, New Zealand: Heinemann.

Clay, M. M. (2001). *Change over time in children's literacy development.* Auckland, NZ: Heinemann Education.

Coburn, C. E. (2003). Rethinking scale: Moving beyond numbers to deep and lasting change. *Educational Researcher, 32*(6), 3–12.

Ferreiro, E., & Teborosky, A. (1982). *Literacy before schooling.* Exter, NH: Heinemann.

Gesell, A., & Ilg, F. L. (1946). *The child from five to ten.* London: Hamish Hamilton.

Hersen, M., & Barlow, D. (1976). *Single-case experimental designs: Strategies for studying behavior change.* New York: Pergammon Press.

Lai, M. K., McNaughton, S., Amituanai-Toloa, M., Turner, R., & Hsiao, S. (2009). Sustained acceleration of reading comprehension: the New Zealand experience. *Reading Research Quarterly, 44*(1), 30–56.

McCall, R. G., & Green, B. L. (2004). Beyond the methodological gold standards of behavioural research: Considerations for practice and policy. *Social Policy Report, 18*(2), 1–9.

McDonald, S. K., Kessler, V. A., Kaufman, N. J., & Schneider, B. (2006). Scaling-up exemplary interventions. *Educational Researcher, 35*(3), 15–24.

McNaughton, S. (1995). *Patterns of emergent literacy: Processes of development and transition.* Auckland, New Zealand: Oxford University Press.

McNaughton, S., & Lai, M. K. (2009). A model of school change for culturally and linguistically diverse students in New Zealand: A summary and evidence from systematic replication. *Teaching Education, 20*(1), 55–75.

Neuman, S. B., & McCormick, S. (1995). *Single-subject experimental research: Applications for literacy.* Newark, DE: International Reading Association.

Overton, W. F., & Reese, H. W. (1973). Models of development: Methodological implications. In J. R. Nesxselroade & H. W. Reese (Eds.), *Lifer-span developmental psychology: Methodological issues* (pp. 65–86). New York: Academic Press.

Paris, S. G. (2005). Reinterpreting the development of reading skills. *Reading Research Quarterly, 40*(2), 184–202.

Pearson, P. D., Hiebert, E. H., & Kamil, M. L. (2007). Vocabulary: What we know and what we need to learn. *Reading Research Quarterly, 42*(2), 282–296.

Porter, A. C., & Polikoff, M. S. (2007). NCLB: State interpretations, early effects and suggestions for reauthorisation. *Social Policy Report, 21*(4), 3–15

Raudenbush, S. W. (2005). Learning from attempts to improve schooling: The contribution of methodological diversity. *Educational Researcher, 34*(5), 25–31.

Risley, T. R., & Wolf, M. M. (1973). Strategies for analyzing behavioral change over time. In J. R. Nesselroade & H. W. Reese (Eds.), *Life-span developmental psychology: Methodological issues* (pp. 175–183). New York: Academic Press.

Shuart-Fans, N., & Bloome, D. (eds.). (2004). *Use of intertextuality in classroom and educational research.* Greenwich, CT: Information Age.

Sidman, M. (1960). *Tactics of scientific research: Evaluating experimental data in psychology.* New York: Basic Books.

Siegler, R. S. (2000). The rebirth of children's learning. *Child Development, 71*(1), 26–35.

Skinner, B. F. (1953). *Science and human behavior.* New York: The Free Press.

Sulzby, E., & Teale, W. (1991). Emergent literacy. In P. D. Pearson, R. Barr, M. L. Kamil, & P. Mosenthal (Eds.), *Handbook of reading research* (Vol. 2, pp. 727–757). New York: Longman.

Whitehurst, G. J., & Lonigan, C. J. (2001). Emergent literacy: Development from pre-readers to readers. In S. B. Neuman & D. K. Dickinson (Eds.), *Handbook of early literacy research* (pp. 11–29). New York: Guilford Press.

Whitehurst, G. J., & Valdez-Menchaca, M. C. (1988). What is the role of reinforcement in language acquisition? *Child Development, 59,* 430–440.

Wolwhill, J. (1970). The age variable in psychological research. *Psychological Review, 77*(1), 49–64.

Wundt, W. M. (1910). *Principles of physiological psychology* (Trans E. B. Tichener). London: Swann, Sonnenschein.

58

Theory and Method in Research on Literacy Practices

Adaptations and Alignment in Research and Praxis

Peter Smagorinsky

When I began my doctoral studies in 1983, research conduct was relatively clear. The modal investigator in reading, writing, and language studies conducted research in order to identify best teaching practices, typically employing experimental designs to contrast two or more "treatments" to determine their relative effects. Hillocks (1986) describes a typical study of this sort:

> Troyka (1974) conducted a study with college freshman remedial composition students in twenty-five experimental classes (n = 172) and twenty-five control classes (n = 181). The experimental procedure involved what she called "simulation-gaming".... The control groups, on the other hand, were taught about using facts, reasons, incidents, and comparison and contrast, but in what appears to be a traditional presentational manner. (pp. 125–126)

Studies of this sort, designed to identify factors that contributed to higher writing scores as determined by such factors as the presence and detail of primary traits (e.g., in an argument, the presence of claims, evidence, and warrants), were de rigueur through the early 1980s. The researcher's task was to identify treatments for contrast, determine the variables to contrast across treatments, set up the experiment to control for other variables, construct appropriate pre-test and post-test tasks and counterbalance them in the design to avoid task and order effects, develop valid scoring rubrics and train raters to evaluate the essays reliably, persuade teachers to run the study, observe the instruction to corroborate the teachers' use of the different treatments, and run appropriate statistical tests to calculate the significance of differences in the students' change scores from pre-test to post-test and contrast the effectiveness of the experimental and control groups according to these change scores.

With a single paradigm dominating research, what mattered most was to construct experiments that produced significant differences between treatments while also meeting standards for validity and reliability. Even with so little under dispute to complicate research conduct, Hillocks (1986) only found 35 of over 500 studies conducted over a 20-year period that met the most basic standards within the experimental tradition, in particular the control of variables. Given that Braddock, Lloyd-Jones, and Schoer (1963) had found even fewer exemplary writing studies conducted from 1904 to1963 that met their standards for rigor, we can conclude that throughout the history of writing research, and perhaps literacy research more broadly speaking, studies have been plagued with problems of design, even when relatively few designs have been available to muddy the methodological waters.

In the years that immediately preceded the publication of Hillocks's (1986) review of writing research, a major methodological upheaval had begun as literacy researchers, often emerging from backgrounds in the humanities, began to reject experiments and statistics and argue in favor of studies that looked at qualitative features of literacy practices rather than those that could be reduced to numbers for statistical contrasts. Qualitative researchers argued for the value of studying smaller samples in greater depth, inquiring into why and how things happen rather than how often, focusing on the particular or typical rather than the general, humanizing research by emphasizing language rather than numbers, and otherwise studying processes rather than outcomes of education. Other investigators began studying literacy in community settings (Heath, 1983), in clinical environments (Flower & Hayes, 1980), in the workplace (Odell & Goswami, 1985), and in other settings outside the classroom, drawing on traditions beyond the experimental norm: anthropology (Heath, 1983), cognitive psychology (Flower & Hayes, 1980), sociolinguistics (Green & Wallat, 1979), and other fields that have since contributed to the expansion of possibilities in literacy research.

Many people found this new emphasis to be liberating. At the same time, it provided the basis for new realms of confusion, given that the open-endedness of research conduct and the novelty of the approaches provided few guidelines. The experimental tradition provided a certain algorithmic comfort in that its procedures were fairly standard, sequential, and tidy, even as it appears to have mystified the great majority of researchers whose work Hillocks (1986) found lacking. The newer qualitative methods, drawing on heretofore unaccessed traditions, provided little in terms of precedent or established procedures in literacy studies. And as the field undertook a "social turn" in the 1980s, each study's situated nature further defied the straightforward application of cookbook approaches to conducting research.

If my experiences as a reviewer of manuscripts for many journals is any indication, the field of educational research has never quite recovered from its move from one established focus and tradition to seemingly unlimited possibilities for research topics, the theoretical perspectives that motivate inquiries, and the methods available to guide investigations. Hillocks's (1986) exclusion of about 93% of experimental studies for methodological problems is actually lower than the percentage of articles that I recommend that editors reject in my role as reviewer, often on methodological grounds. Research method thus continues to perplex the field, even as methodology remains a common topic of discussion and dispute in books and journals.

My page allocation for this chapter will allow for a relatively brief effort to illustrate some studies in which authors have eschewed algorithmic conceptions of research design and conduct in order to adapt theory and method to inquiry. These examples demonstrate the protean nature of employing research methods in situated studies and the adaptive decision-making that is often required to get beyond the sorts of research recipes outlined in methods textbooks. This reflexive approach involves considerably more than picking a theoretical frame or paradigm and adopting its accompanying methodology. Rather, it requires an effort to adjust method to situation and engage in adaptations where appropriate in terms of design, conduct, analysis, and interpretation. I will next illustrate the adaptive nature of research conduct, first with my own use of protocol analysis and then a teacher research study by Fecho (2001).

Illustrations of Paradigmatic Adaptation and Alignment

Protocol Analysis from Two Perspectives My evolving use of protocol analysis illustrates the relation between theory and method (Smagorinsky, 1998). During my doctoral studies, I adopted an information processing approach from the field of cognitive psychology to investigate how people think as they write. I was impressed and influenced by Flower and Hayes's (1980 and many other publications) adoption of Ericsson and Simon's (1984/1993) argument regarding the clear and careful alignment between information processing theory and protocol analysis as an investigative method, a perspective I defended in a set of publications (Smagorinsky, 1989, 1994a, 1994b). I used that framework for my dissertation research (Smagorinsky, 1991), which employed a quasi-experimental comparison of

three instructional methods for teaching extended definition to high school juniors. I took a sample of students from each treatment and had them produce pre- and post-instruction think-aloud protocols. I conducted a statistical analysis of the extent to which the different means of instruction produced different effects in the types of thinking they engaged in. I interpreted the results in terms of the different patterns in cognition revealed through the protocols, which at the time I treated as "in-the-head" cognition that was responsive to the single external variable of instructional modes.

Following my dissertation I began to read more sociocultural perspectives on cognition that led me to question the interpretation of data as in-the-head phenomena responding to a single variable such as instruction as a one-to-one correspondence. These readings (e.g., Newman, Griffin, & Cole, 1989; Vygotsky, 1987; Wertsch, 1991) led me to see cognition as more intricately interwoven with the setting of activity, not only the immediate surroundings but the cultural and historical practices through which current performance takes its cues. The premises of the information processing paradigm became insufficient to me, leading me to conceive of the "task environment" that was recognized but unelaborated in information processing studies as the source of the cultural mediation that shapes cognition.

Yet, I still valued protocol analysis as an investigative method. I needed to re-theorize it, however, if it were to serve my inquiries from a sociocultural perspective. In all of my studies beginning in the early 1990s, I have taken a Vygotskian framework to understand not only cognition but its relation to the cultural practices that precede it and mediate it in the present. I have used protocol analysis as part of this effort, including studies of writing (e.g., Smagorinsky, Daigle, O'Donnell-Allen, & Bynum, 2010) and nonverbal composing both in English classes (e.g., Zoss, Smagorinsky, & O'Donnell-Allen, 2007) and across the secondary school curriculum (e.g., Smagorinsky, Cook, & Reed, 2005). In doing so, I have needed to change the theoretical terms on which I base its use.

From an information processing standpoint, protocol analysis provides a window into the mind (Hayes & Flower, 1983) and identifies cognitive processes so that researchers may develop models of cognition. These assumptions presume cognition to take place largely between the ears. From a sociocultural perspective, however, thinking is mediated by cultural tools that tie cognition to the setting of mentation; thinking is situated in settings and is inseparable from the particular tasks, purposes, addressees, genres of activity, and other factors of communicative importance. Further, since thinking is mediated by speech during the production of a think-aloud protocol, thinking develops through the process of articulation, making a protocol less a window into the mind than a vehicle for thinking itself. The cognition inferred is thus less amenable to the formation of transferable models than an occasion for understanding a situated utterance responsive to the social demands of the situation.

Through this ontological shift in the use of protocol

analysis, I have moved away from the construction of universal cognitive models and used the method to make inferences about the means of cultural mediation through which frameworks for thinking are internalized. These cultural schemata suggest that when I study cognition in relation to writing and other forms of composition, I need to situate that thinking within communities of practice that might be disciplinary, community-based, and otherwise originating in and mediated by specific forms of cultural practice. This shift has enabled me to continue using a methodological tool in which I have confidence, yet change the framework, focus of analytic attention, specific ways of using the method from controlled clinical setting to participants' chosen situated locations, and other factors that must be clearly outlined in any reports I fashion through which to share the findings.

Adapting Methods to a Practitioner Inquiry Action research—the study of one's own practice—has been used by classroom teachers since at least the 1950s. Various factors have helped to elevate teacher research to higher status in the last few decades: its embrace by university researchers as both a source of better teaching and insightful research (e.g., Cochran-Smith & Lytle, 1993); the availability of publication outlets through book publishers, journals, and the Internet (e.g., Gallas, 2003); explicit efforts on the part of the editors of research journals to publish and reference teacher inquiries that meet university standards for publication (e.g., Smith & Smagorinsky, 1998); the establishment of refereed journals dedicated wholly to teacher research (e.g., http://journals.library.wisc.edu/index.php/networks); the creation of awards to honor exemplary practitioner inquiries (e.g., the James N. Britton Award established by NCTE); the development of teacher research networks to support classroom inquiries and their inquirers (e.g., Brookline Teacher Researcher Seminar, 2004); the generation of reviews of teacher research in such areas as composition (e.g., Fecho, Allen, Mazaros, & Inyega, 2005); the identification of teacher research as a critical area of development by the National Writing Project and other national networks and organizations (http://www.nwp.org/cs/public/print/resource_topic/teacher_research_inquiry); the creation of online resource collections to assist aspiring classroom inquirers (e.g., http://carbon.ucdenver.edu/~mryder/itc_data/act_res.html); the formation of the Teacher as Researcher Special Interest Group in the American Educational Research Association; and other developments in the field that support the view that distance and disinterest are not requirements of systematic studies of classroom processes.

Practitioner inquiries cannot be conducted in the same manner as research done by an outsider such as a university researcher, who has considerable latitude in how to position herself in the classroom and attend to other details of method, and the time both to prepare for each stage of the research and to analyze it in relative peace and quiet. Teachers who wish to study their own teaching, in contrast, must add the research component to a day already replete with students, administrivia, grading, reporting, additional duties, and much else. The demands of teaching constrain research efforts at every level: planning, conducting, and analyzing. It is no surprise that much effective teacher research benefits from small communities of inquiry that provide support in not only the intellectual demands of conducting research but the emotional needs of those who take on what can be an onerous task (O'Donnell-Allen, 2001).

Because classroom research must be conducted on the fly, conventional research methods must be adapted in order to be applicable to the demands of simultaneously teaching and meeting other obligations in school and life, and studying one's own teaching. Producing teacher researcher that is publishable through refereed outlets often requires further, often extreme measures, such as taking leaves of absence in order to produce the writing (e.g., Gallas, 2003) or doing the writing as part of a dissertation that might only find time for refinement into publications through the luxurious provision of time available through a university position (e.g., Fecho, 2001).

I will next look at Fecho's (2001) teacher research study, recognized as exemplary through its receipt of the Alan C. Purves Award as the article published in the 2001 volume of *Research in the Teaching of English* most likely to have an impact on classroom practice. Fecho's study looks into issues of threat that arose through his students' critical inquiry into a cultural clash between their own Caribbean American community and that of neighboring orthodox Lubavitcher Jews. Fecho frames his study through a Freirean "post-structural view of literacy learning, one that sees language, literacy, culture, power, inquiry, and agency as being present throughout our daily transactions and possessing a productive potential despite the sense of threat often associated with them" (p. 12). To put this framework into action, he formed his classes into task forces that investigated issues of culture and power that they encountered in their daily lives, and for this article focuses on the conflict with the Lubavitchers explored by his Caribbean American students and the attendant reading they did to inform their analysis, which they produced as a written report.

To conduct this inquiry, Fecho (2001) needed to adapt research methods to his position as a practicing teacher, albeit one who wrote his account after leaving the classroom. He begins his method section by arguing that "teacher research, as a genre of academic research, can and perhaps should be conducted and reported differently from other genres of academic research." These differences are manifest in "the importance of the story of the question [and in] the way teacher research, so embedded in practice, develops its own sense of rigor and validity" (p. 17). Rigor and validity, he argues, must be conceived differently from the ways in which they have historically been treated in educational research, because the rigor of an investigation often relies on serendipity, i.e., on the teacher researcher's opportunism in collecting data while simultaneously teaching the class being studied. Validity is often a function of the teacher researcher's emic, or insider perspective on the classroom, and thus follows from the teacher's embedded understanding of what matters locally. Fecho further argues that

> Because their research grows out of their practice as much as it grows out of the discussions of the larger research community, teacher researchers find it facilitative and significant to tell in narrative form how their question and methods emerged. This description frequently links them to a dissonant or disconnecting event that focuses a generic question and sets the study into full gear. Responding to an immediate transaction within the classroom, teachers use their intimate knowledge of the context and history of that classroom to enact a study that responds to all three concerns. Telling the story of that moment when some event calls context and history into question seems not only useful but necessary. (p. 18)

Fecho (2001) thus links his critical theoretical perspective to his emic stance to provide a rationale for his research methodology, which did not rely entirely on a carefully prepared design but rather was enacted in situ as the opportunities to collect data emerged during his teaching. His data collection, he reports, included

> classroom transcripts conducted during self-evaluation discussions (CT), written self-evaluations (SE), compilations of student work (SW), my *ad hoc* audio journal (AJ), pertinent excerpts from the dialogue journal completed between student teacher Rachel Ravreby and me (DJ), and two student interviews that were the result of serendipity: A discussion was begun that we then agreed to tape (SI). (pp. 18–19)

His written report for the journal article consists of "vignettes created from the audio journal, the student self-evaluations, and the dialogue journal initiated by Rachel because these are the tools that were most conducive to representing the data that pertained to issues of threat" (Fecho, 2001, p. 19). This approach enabled Fecho to attend concurrently to both his teaching and his research, allowing him to dovetail his students' inquiry into his own by using students' work and drawing on a dialogue journal that was being kept with or without the research, and employing the audio journal to record his impressions in the catch-as-catch-can whirlwind of classroom teaching.

Fecho chose to report his findings through a series of vignettes, which he argues "honors the stories of my classroom by positioning them as central to the work. Also, my writing about my sense of these stories extends the meaning making, narrative process. My intent is to, as Ellis (1997) argues, use stories to provoke other stories and to put a human face on abstract and dispassionate research" (2001, p. 20). Thus, across the organization of his article, Fecho worked to align his theoretical perspective with his stance and investigative method, and, ultimately, to realize the confluence of these areas in the narrative mode of data presentation. His effort at transparency helped to substantiate his work for a readership that was not accustomed to reading a report with this orientation or form in an archival literacy journal.

Conclusion

In this chapter I have argued that complex studies cannot rely algorithmically on canned research methods. Rather, researchers need to adapt methods to epistemology and seek alignment across the whole of the study and its conduct and reporting. Given how infrequently a textbook approach can be uncritically applied to a new and interesting problem, it is thus incumbent on a researcher to provide the details of research conduct so that readers can fully appreciate the thoughtful adaptations made to produce the inquiry within the framework of antecedent scholarship. Without such details, reviewers and readers must infer a study's integrity, a risk that I do not recommend.

References

Braddock, R., Lloyd-Jones, R., & Schoer, L. (1963). *Research in written composition*. Champaign, IL: National Council of Teachers of English.

Brookline Teacher Researcher Seminar. (2004). *Regarding children's words: Teacher research on language and literacy*. New York: Teachers College Press.

Cochran-Smith, M., & Lytle, S. L. (1993). *Inside/outside: Teacher research and knowledge*. New York: Teachers College Press.

Ellis, C. (1997). Evocative autoethnography: Writing emotionally about our lives. In W. G. Tierney & Y. S. Lincoln (Eds.), *Representation and the text: Re-framing the narrative voice* (pp. 115–139). Albany: State University of New York Press.

Ericsson, K. A., & Simon, H. (1984/1993). *Protocol analysis: Verbal reports as data*. Cambridge, MA: MIT Press.

Fecho, B. (2001). "Why are you doing this?" Acknowledging and transcending threat in critical inquiry classrooms. *Research in the Teaching of English, 36*, 9–37.

Fecho, B., Allen, J., Mazaros, C., & Inyega, H. (2005). Teacher research in writing classrooms. In P. Smagorinsky (Ed.), *Research on composition: Multiple perspectives on two decades of change* (pp. 108–140). New York: Teachers College Press.

Flower, L. S., & Hayes, J. R. (1980). The dynamics of composing: Making plans and juggling constraints. In L. Gregg & E. Steinberg (Eds.), *Cognitive processes in writing: An interdisciplinary approach* (pp. 31–50). Mahwah, NJ: Erlbaum.

Gallas, K. (2003). *Imagination and literacy: A teacher's search for the heart of learning*. New York: Teachers College Press.

Green, J. L., & Wallat, C. (1979). What is an instructional context? An exploratory analysis of conversational shifts over time. In O. Garnica & C. King (Eds.), *Language, children, and society* (pp. 159–188). London: Pergamon Press.

Hayes, J. R., & Flower, L. S. (1983). Uncovering cognitive processes in writing: An introduction to protocol analysis. In P. Mosenthal, L. Tamor, & S. Walmsley (Eds.), *Research in writing: Principles and methods* (pp. 207–220). New York: Longman.

Heath, S. B. (1983). *Ways with words: Language life, and work in communities and classrooms*. New York: Cambridge University Press.

Hillocks, G. (1986). *Research on written composition: New directions for teaching*. Urbana, IL: National Conference on Research in English and Educational Resources Information Center.

Newman, D., Griffin, P., & Cole, M. (1989). *The construction zone: Working for cognitive change in school*. New York: Cambridge University Press.

Odell, L., & Goswami, D. (Eds.). (1985). *Writing in nonacademic settings*. New York: Guilford.

O'Donnell-Allen, C. (2001). Teaching with a questioning mind: The development of a teacher research group into a discourse community. *Research in the Teaching of English, 36*, 161–211.

Smagorinsky, P. (1989). The reliability and validity of protocol analysis. *Written Communication, 6,* 463–479.

Smagorinsky, P. (1991). The writer's knowledge and the writing process: A protocol analysis. *Research in the Teaching of English, 25,* 339–364.

Smagorinsky, P. (1994a). Introduction: Potential problems and problematic potentials of using talk about writing as data about writing process. In P. Smagorinsky (Ed.), *Speaking about writing: Reflections on research methodology* (pp. ix-xix). Thousand Oaks, CA: Sage.

Smagorinsky, P. (1994b). Think-aloud protocol analysis: Beyond the black box. In P. Smagorinsky (Ed.), *Speaking about writing: Reflections on research methodology* (pp. 3–19). Thousand Oaks, CA: Sage.

Smagorinsky, P. (1998). Thinking and speech and protocol analysis. *Mind, Culture, and Activity, 5,* 157–177.

Smagorinsky, P., Cook, L. S., & Reed, P. (2005). The construction of meaning and identity in the composition and reading of an architectural text. *Reading Research Quarterly, 40,* 70–88.

Smagorinsky, P., Daigle, E. A., O'Donnell-Allen, C., & Bynum, S. (2010). Bullshit in academic writing: A protocol analysis of a high school senior's process of interpreting *Much Ado About Nothing. Research in the Teaching of English, 44,* 368–405.

Smith, M. W., & Smagorinsky, P. (1998). Editors' introduction. *Research in the Teaching of English, 33,* 133–135.

Vygotsky, L. S. (1987). Thinking and speech. In L. S. Vygotsky, *Collected works* (Vol. 1, pp. 39–285) (R. Rieber & A. Carton, Eds.; N. Minick, Trans.). New York: Plenum.

Wertsch, J. V. (1991). *Voices of the mind: A sociocultural approach to mediated action.* Cambridge, MA: Harvard University Press.

Zoss, M., Smagorinsky, P., & O'Donnell-Allen, C. (2007). Mask-making as representational process: The situated composition of an identity project in a senior English class. *International Journal of Education & the Arts, 8*(10). Retrieved from http://www.ijea.org/v8n10/v8n10.pdf

59

English in the Era of Globalisation

Implications for Research Methodologies for English Language Arts

Anthony J. Liddicoat

Increasing globalisation and the increasing mobility of populations has become truisms in discussions of education, and their impact on educational systems and practices is widely acknowledged. As Luke notes:

> One of the consequences of economic globalisation is the relative permeability of borders and accelerated, though uneven, flows of bodies across geographical and political boundaries. New population demographics threaten the stability of large-scale educational systems as linguistic and ethnic monocultures. (2003, p. 133)

Such forces have changed the nature of teaching and learning and necessitate an increased engagement with linguistic and cultural diversity. In addition to processes of mobility, the use of technologies has disconnected communication and social networks from local contexts in ways that allow and even require individuals to develop affiliations and identities that cut across national, ethnic and linguistic lines (Gee, 2000a, 2000b; Lam, 2006). The consequence is that language practices are constituted transnationally. This is not simply a case of the integration of speakers of English as an additional language into wider patterns of English language communication but also involvement of people in complex multilingual contexts, such as those found in anime fan-sites (Black, 2007; Thorne & Black, 2009). This chapter aims to examine some issues which globalisation and increasing mobility have for research in English language arts and the considerations which researchers need to make in developing research designs for complex multilingual contexts. It will argue that the key issue in research design is not so much methodology as a reconceptualization of what constitutes research practice in contexts of linguistic and cultural diversity.

The Monolingual Habitus and Its Effects on Research

The Nature of the Monolingual Habitus Linguistic and cultural plurality has always been a reality. However, after

the rise of the idea of the nation state, such plurality ceased to be considered a normal feature of a nation and nation-states have often been understood in terms of linguistic and cultural homogeneity (see Hobsbawn, 1991). This underlying myth of the linguistic and cultural uniformity of the nation-state permeates the structures, forms and contents of school systems and has had an impact on the theory and methodology of educational research as has been demonstrated for example for various countries in Europe by Gogolin (1994), Kroon and Vallen (1994) and Vermes (1998). In the context of English language arts, Gutiérrez (2001, p. 564) has similarly noted that in curriculum "Language arts was characterised primarily by its focus on developing the *English* Language Arts to English speaking children." Bernhardt has observed in the research context that:

> first language reading research is almost exclusively "English-language based"; second language research is conducted likewise.... The overwhelmingly English-speaking North American/ British/Australian literacy industry that drives teacher education policy and academic publishing certainly plays a role. Further, the overwhelming numbers of English speakers in positions of academic power across the globe drive the agenda that focuses on English as the sole language of interest. (2003, p. 112)

Such comments reveal a potential conflict within English language arts between a tendency to equate English with language, seeing "English language" as the underlying construct, and seeing English as only a component of language.

Gogolin (1994) has termed this overwhelming orientation to a single language a "monolingual habitus"—that is a habit of mind in which existing linguistic and cultural diversity is rendered invisible in research practices. Within an English language context, Liddicoat and Crichton (2008) identify a number of characteristics of the monolingual habitus that have potential implications for the ways in which research around English are to be understood. These include:

- an emphasis on knowledge created in and communicated through English to the exclusion of knowledge associated with other languages;
- lack of attention to the linguistic and cultural context in which knowledge will be used;
- neglect of the "non-English" competences and capacities of learners;
- construction of learners' English second language as a deficit and of their English language learning as remediation;
- the "invisibility" of the linguistic and cultural context of English; and
- lack of consideration of knowledge and discipline practices as culturally and linguistically contexted.

The Monolingual Habitus and the Multilingual Learner

Budasch and Bardtenschlager (2008) have identified the prevailing monolingualism of educational practice as one of the key impediments to research into language practices among multilingual learners. In the research context, the monolingual habitus is manifested in research approaches which consider all learners as speakers of a particular language either without reference to the linguistic diversity of actual student populations, or by characterising students who are not speakers of the majority language as defective speakers of the language or as in deficit with reference to other students. In particular, notions of uniformity often render invisible diversity in the lived experience of students or reduce diversity to a series of overarching, static and undifferentiated categories of difference. Luke notes that "[M]uch of the literature on multiculturalism tends to treat all multilingual 'ethnicities' of a piece, without due attention to social class, location and history" (2003, p. 135). Bernhardt (1991) has observed that in descriptions of research methodologies learners of English are frequently treated as an undifferentiated whole and researchers fail to report (or to discover?) the internal complexity of the category "learners of English" except in terms of proficiency levels. The homogenisation of learners of English has frequently been deployed in both research and policy contexts to construct labelling of English learners as either "other" or as "deficit other." For example, in Australia it has been common practice to identify learners as either ESB (English-Speaking Background) or NESB (Non-English-Speaking Background) constructing a view of the learner (and in research, of the research participant) in terms of the presence of absence of English as the only relevant variables differentiating between groups. The result is to consider learners only in relation to English monolingualism as the uncontested linguistic norm and to view competence in other languages only as instances of an absence of or deficit in English. Similar issues occur with other group

labels such as LEP (Limited English Proficiency) or LOTE (Languages other than English) which construct aspects of multilingualism in terms of relationship to English as norm. As Luke notes. "In countries like the United States, United Kingdom, and Australia...literacy and language education continues to routinely categorise the multilingual subject as 'Other', as afterthought, exception, anomaly, and 'lack'" (2003, p. 135).

Such namings represent not only categorisations of people around their access to English but also construct the field of knowledge on particular ways—that research legitimately focuses either on those that have English or those that do not. Such labels draw boundaries between languages as inherent to the understanding of the phenomenon being investigated. The investigation of English as unitary object presupposes the exclusion of "not English" and with the consequent potential to segment the linguistic repertoires of the individual in ways which obscure the interrelationships of languages as an organic whole for the bilingual or multilingual individual. To speak more than one language is not to incarnate within oneself multiple equivalents to the monolingual native-speaker but rather to have a language capacity which is spread differentially over two or more languages according to experiences and needs (Hornberger, 1994, 2004). Where research focuses only on one aspect of the language repertoire of such individuals it takes something that is part of an integrated whole and treats it as if it existed only in isolation (Heinz, 2001). This means that access to English has the potential to become a discriminating factor which masks other features of the learner and potentially renders them unknown and unknowable.

The monolingual habitus therefore ignores the complex linguistic lifeworlds of learners or reduces the complexity to a deficiency. It also ignores the interrelations between the languages in the learners' linguistic repertoires in the linguistic and cultural practices in which they engage, including those involved in learning itself. As a result, linguistic and cultural diversity is constructed as external to the research context and without significance in understanding the research question framed in terms of language. In research methodologies in English language arts, the monolingual habitus is most noticeably present in research methodologies which use English as the sole vehicle for data collection without establishing whether the choice of English is in fact the most relevant language for some or all of the research participants to use or how the use of English positions learners within the context of the research project. Choice of language in any educational context, including in research design, "is about which identities students can take up in classrooms and which identity will be valued. Language choice is not solely an educational choice but is always a political issue linked to mechanisms of social control" (Gutiérrez, 2001, p. 566; see also Woolard, 1998). A reflective research design is therefore one which considers how language, which is often the focus of investigation itself, positions the research participants, impacts on their identities and agent positions and (re)produces discourses of marginalisation or deficit.

The focus on English is often the result of a default—English is the only language the researcher is able to assess the learner because the researcher does not have access to the language of the learner. However the decision by the researcher to homogenise the language practices of a group of learners to conform to the language practices available to the researcher is rarely problematised in discussions of research methodologies and, moreover, is not seen as needing to be problematised. That is, the convergence of language practices on the language of the researcher (in this case English) is naturalised and the removal of the language practices of learners themselves from the research agenda is masked by this process of naturalising English. Aspects of the learners' linguistic repertoire are a priori deemed irrelevant to the research process not because of a theorised position on the relationships between language practices exercised through different languages but because of their inaccessibility to the researcher. For Bernhardt (2003, p. 114) this reduction of what constitutes relevant research information is a grave flaw in research method: "When researcher deficiencies interfere with the ability to provide trustworthy data, the entire research enterprise becomes suspect."

An Ecological View of Language as the Research Context in English Language Arts

The Nature of Linguistic Ecologies An alternative to the monolingual habitus is the recognition that languages exist within linguistic ecologies. The concept of linguistic ecologies was pioneered by Haugen (1972), who uses the metaphor of the ecosystem to understand the roles and relationships of languages with the communicative practices and linguistic repertoires of communities and individuals. Haugen argues that language ecologies involve both psychological interrelationships—between languages known and used by individuals—and sociological interrelationships—between members of a society in which particular languages are used. The focus on "language" in language ecologies is however misleading as to the nature of such ecologies—it is not just languages that have such interrelationships but varieties of language (e.g. standard and non-standard varieties, regional and social dialects, etc.). That is, all differentiated linguistic codes used by individuals and/or communities are salient elements of a linguistic ecology.

The interrelationships that exist in the ecology influence which languages are used for which purposes, how languages are valued and how they relate to other value systems, what languages represent for users and communities, and the perceived viability of speaking particular languages in particular societies. This means that investigating only one language or one language variety purely in isolation from the other languages and varieties of the individual or of the society denies the interrelationships between languages and marginalises aspects of language repertoires.

One problem facing researchers in English language arts is the position of the English that is being researched in the linguistic ecologies which form the research context. Within educational systems, the interrelationships between languages are inevitably subjected to pressure as education is fundamentally a linguistic act and is intrinsically tied to and provides prestige for particular (standardised) language varieties. That is, English language education is a vehicle for the reproduction of Standard English in ecologies which may be characterised by multilingualism and/or multiple varieties of English. Outside school contexts, the standard language is only one component of the ecology, although in schooling it is often represented as the entire ecology or as the only valid member of it.

A second problem for the researcher lies in the symbolic load borne by English within its ecology. This symbolic load is potentially extremely complex. At one level, there is the symbolic capital which accrues to mastery of the variety of English privileged by the schooling system (see Bourdieu, 1982). This symbolic capital means that Standard English is frequently considered as an objective good and the acquisition of the variety can be enforced through schooling because it is so considered. However, Standard English may have other symbolic loadings within it ecologies. Languages are not simply codes to be deployed for communication, they are also markers of identity. This means that a particular language variety, such as Standard English, may be perceived as a language of assimilation, of disempowerment or of marginalisation or it may be seen as a threat to identity. In such cases, the acquisition of Standard English would not be considered an objective good and its place in schooling may effectively threaten the value seen in schooling delivered in and reproducing the status of that language. Fordham (1999), for example, reports that the African American high school students in her study actively resist the requirement to learn to speak and communicate in Standard English, through their adherence to African American vernacular English. She argues that the students' refusal to discontinue their use of vernacular English as the language of communication while at or in school, and their wholesale avoidance of the standard dialect in most other contexts is an act of resistance to an externally imposed norm. She sees language as a site of contestation where the language practices rewarded by schooling are seen as threats to identity, and a language variety is rejected because of the threat it poses that identity. She notes that rejection of Standard English does not necessarily equate with an inability to use the variety, as the students she investigated did use the standard when it was relevant to what they wished to achieve. Rather, the students did not view the standard as their language, but the language of another, alien group. Students who adopted Standard English in order to succeed therefore needed to maintain dual linguistic identities, adopting the standard when needed but otherwise rejecting it as a linguistic norm. The students' language practices were perceived by external others as in deficit—the students' failure to use Standard English was generally understood as incompetence and an inability to perform a culturally sanctioned task by the dominant, Standard English-speaking educational system.

Stroud and Wee (2007) similarly argue that the language practices of English language schooling in Singapore marginalise the multilingual identities of students and lead to negative stereotyping of Singaporean ways of speaking both in English and in other languages. In this case too, students resort to transgressive language use to protect and reaffirm their identities. Such studies reveal a fundamental tension in educational research between evaluations of language use seen from the perspective of a validated norm in isolation from other the language ecology and the symbolic load carried by languages in the ecology.

Recognising the Place of Language Ecologies in Research

Investigating language from an ecological perspective involves recognising the various impacts of context on what is being investigated and the ways in which inter-relationships between language, languages and contexts construct both the situation under investigation and the act of investigation itself. Such ecological understandings of language education have been recognised in some language education contexts, especially where education promotes the learning of an exogenous language. Mühlhäusler (2000) has articulated a number of characteristics of what he calls "ecological thinking" in relation to language education, which includes:

- giving consideration not just to system internal factors but wider environmental ones;
- being aware of the dangers of monoculturalism and loss of diversity; and
- being aware of those factors that sustain the health of language ecologies.

That is, the researcher needs to be mindful of conducting research on any one language, of the place held by that language in its linguistic ecology, of the interrelationships it has with other languages, and of the potential impact on the linguistic ecology of both the teaching of this language and the research conducted on it.

The challenge that globalisation poses for English language arts research is to develop research designs and methodologies which recognise the ecological nature of language and the potentially complex place of the English language within learners' language ecologies. As Luke argues:

> At issue is not whether and how we can recover English education as unitary field and profession, at best a theoretically and industrially vexed task. The question is how we might reinvent it in relation to an understanding of its own social and cultural complexity and dynamics. (2004, p. 87)

One way for research to engage with such dynamics is to recognise and make space for hybrid language practices available in learners own language ecologies and to validate these as part of an English language arts focus (Gutiérrez et al., 1999). For Gutiérrez (2001, p. 567), the concern for hybridity reflects a desire to put "language back into language arts." An example of a research focus on English language arts which emphasises language can be seen in Shopen (2009). Shopen reports a study of classroom interaction in which an indigenous teacher teaching in Australia's Torres Strait Islands used hybrid language practices to engage learners in sophisticated language practices. The teacher introduced the learners to a song in Kalaw Lagaw Ya, a local indigenous language, then in Torres Strait Creole. This was then followed by a game in which students rolled a dice to select a language–Kalaw Lagaw Ya, Torres Strait Creole, or Standard Australian English. The teacher would then give them a line of the song in a language other than that shown on the dice, and the students would reproduce the song in the language shown. In the case of Standard Australian English, this was an original creation as the song had not been presented in this language. The learners' discussion largely focused around how to represent local realities in English. The learners were engaged in complex linguistic and metalinguistic work which allowed them to draw on their entire language repertoire in constructing and communicating meanings. Most notably, non-indigenous Standard Australian English-speaking children in the classroom were involved in the hybrid language practices being established. The focus was thus on the hybrid language practices being constructed, not on English as a privileged language and other languages having only a supporting function. As Guttiérez et al. note:

> hybrid literacy practices are not simply code-switching as the alternation between two language codes. They are more a systematic, strategic, affiliative, and sense-making process among those who share the code, as they strive to achieve mutual understanding. (2001, p. 88)

The language practices described in Shopen's (2009) research exemplify this distinction and reveal ways in which learners' language repertoires can become fully engaged in learning and how such learning can be captured by a research approach which views language as ecological.

Gutiérrez's (2001; Gutiérrez et al., 1999) and Shopen's (2009) work involves a research approach in English language arts that focuses on *language* as the key entry point into diverse practices, and backgrounds *English* as the starting point. It is in fact this change of emphasis that is needed to re-situate English language arts research within the diverse communicative practices of the globalised era. Research in English language arts in the context of cultural and linguistic pluralism requires research designs that are sensitive to the highly contexted nature of English. Such research designs need to consider as part of an overall research approach and be sensitive to:

- the status of English as potentially only one component of the meaning-making repertoire of learners;
- the cultural and linguistic situatedness of English and of the knowledges and behaviours that are associated with literate practice in English;
- the political and social situatedness of English in the value systems of learners and the ways in which this influences language practices; and
- the interrelationships between languages and literacies which exist within learners language ecologies.

Such research designs provide a contextual framing in which other aspects of research design, such as particular methodologies, can be shaped and critiqued. They also provide for the possibility of constructing research which problematise monolingual and monocultural understandings of what constitutes English language arts.

References

Bernhardt, E. (1991). *Reading development in a second language: Theoretical, empirical and classroom perspectives.* Norwood, NJ: Ablex.

Bernhardt, E. (2003). Challenges to reading research from a multilingual world. *Reading Research Quarterly, 38*(1), 112–117.

Black, R. W. (2007). Fanfiction writing and the construction of space. *E–Learning, 4*(4), 384–397.

Bourdieu, P. (1982). *Langage et pouvoir symbolique* [Language and symbolic power]. Paris: Arthème-Fayard.

Budasch, G., & Bardtenschlager, H. (2008). *Est-ce que ce n'est pas trop dur? Enjeux et expériences d'alphabétisation dans un projet de double immersion* [Isn't it too hard? Stakes and experiments of the elimination of illiteracy in a double immersion project] [Electronic version]. *Glottopol: Revue de Sociolinguistique en Ligne, 11*. Retrieved July, 21, 2009, from http://www.univ-rouen.fr/dyalang/glottopol/numero_11.html

Fordham, S. (1999). Dissin' «the standard»: African American Vernacular English as guerrilla warfare at Capital High. *Anthropology & Education Quarterly, 30*(3), 272–293.

Gee, J. P. (2000a). New people in new worlds: Networks, the new capitalism and schools. In B. Cope & M. Kalantzis (Eds.), *Multiliteracies: Literacy learning and the design of social futures* (pp. 43–68). London: Routledge.

Gee, J. P. (2000b). Teenagers in new times: A new literacy studies perspective. *Journal of Adolescent and Adult Literacy, 43*, 412–420.

Gogolin, I. (1994). *Der monolinguale Habitus der multilingualen Schule* [The monolingual habitus of the multilingual school]. Münster, Germany: Waxmann-Verlag.

Gutiérrez, K. D. (2001). What new in the English language arts: Challenging policies and practices, ¿y qué? *Language Arts, 78*(6), 564–569.

Gutiérrez, K. D., Baquedano-López, P., Alvarez, H. H., & Chiu, M. M. (1999). Building a culture of collaboration through hybrid language practices. *Theory into Practice, 38*, 87–93.

Haugen, E. (1972). *The ecology of language.* Standford, CA: Stanford University Press.

Heinz, B. (2001). 'Fish in the river': Experiences of bicultural bilingual speakers. *Multilingua — Journal of Cross-Cultural and Interlanguage Communication, 20*(1), 85–108.

Hobsbawn, E. J. (1991). *Nations and Nationalism since 1780: Programme, Myth, Reality.* Cambridge, UK: Cambridge University Press.

Hornberger, N. H. (1994). Continua of biliteracy. In B. M. Ferdman, R. Weber, & A. G. Ramirez (Eds.), *Literacy across Languages and Cultures* (pp. 103–139). Albany: State University of New York Press.

Hornberger, N. H. (2004). The continua of biliteracy and the bilingual educator: Educational linguistics in practice. *International Journal of Bilingual Education and Bilingualism, 7*(2&3), 155–171.

Kroon, S., & Vallen, T. (1994). Das nationale Selbstverständnis im Unterricht der Nationalsprache. Der Fall der Niederlande [National self-understanding in the instruction of the national language. The case of the Netherlands]. In I. Gogolin (Ed.), *Das nationale Selbstverständnis der Bildung* [National self-understanding of education] (pp. 151–182). Münster, Germany: Waxmann-Verlag.

Lam, W. S. E. (2006). Culture and learning in the context of globalisation: Research directions. *Review of Research in Education, 30*, 213–237.

Liddicoat, A. J., & Crichton, J. (2008). The monolingual framing of international education in Australia. *Sociolinguistic Studies, 2*(3), 367–384.

Luke, A. (2003). Literacy and the other: A sociological approach to literacy research and policy in multilingual societies. *Reading Research Quareterly, 38*(1), 132–141.

Luke, A. (2004). The trouble with English. *Research in the Teaching of English, 39*(1), 85–95.

Mühlhäusler, P. (2000). Language planning and language ecology. *Current Issues in Language Planning, 1*(3), 306–367.

Shopen, G. (2009). Above expectations: Dialogic potential in Australian Indigenous primary schools. In J. L. McConnel-Farmer (Ed.), *The education of young children: Research and policy* (pp. 189–206). Yarnton, UK: Linton Atlantic Books.

Stroud, C., & Wee, L. (2007). A pedagogical application of liminalities in social positioning: Identity and literacy in Singapore. *TESOL Quarterly, 41*(1), 33–54.

Thorne, S. L., & Black, R. W. (2009). Second language use, socialization, and learning in internet interest communities and online gaming. *Modern Language Journal, 93*(4), 802–821.

Vermes, G. (1998). Schrifterwerb und Minorisierung als psychologisches Problem [The acquisition of writing and minoritisation as a psychological problem]. In I. Gogolin, S. Graap, & G. List (Eds.), *Über Mehrsprachigkeit* [On multilingualism] (pp. 3–19). Tübingen, Germany: Stauffenburg-Verlag.

Woolard, K. (1998). Introduction: Language ideology as a field of enquiry. In B. Schieffelin, K. Woolard, & P. Kroskrity (Eds.), *Language ideologies: Practice and theory* (pp. 3–47). New York: Oxford University Press.

60

Syncretic Approaches to Studying Movement and Hybridity in Literacy Practices

Kris D. Gutiérrez, Andrea C. Bien, and Makenzie K. Selland

This chapter discusses the logic of inquiry and affordances of syncretic approaches to the study of literacy. Syncretic approaches are defined here as the principled and strategic use of transdisciplinary perspectives for the theoretical and methodological treatment of the social practices of literacy learning (Gutiérrez & Stone, 2000). Of significance, a syncretic approach is contingent upon an expansive theoretical network that materializes from the goodness of fit between relevant theoretical constructs and the complexity of sociocultural phenomena. In our own work (Gutiérrez, 2008), it is the process of seeking a goodness of fit that allows the researcher to draw, in a principled way, from expansive theories of learning and development (Cole, 1996; Engeström, 1987, 2001; Rogoff, 2003), critical social theories (Luke, 2003), sociocultural and social practices views of literacy (Barton & Hamilton, 1998), including New Literacy Studies (Gee, 1996, 2005; Street, 1984, 2003), and multi-literacies approaches (Cope & Kalantzis, 2000) to link the particular to the larger social context of development.

In this chapter, we advance the notion of using syncretic approaches to the study of literacy and build on the work of scholars who have engaged syncretic conceptions of language and literacy in their research. One salient example is found in the work of Duranti and Ochs (1997) who proposed a notion of syncretic literacy to describe how "an intermingling or merging of culturally diverse traditions informs and organizes literacy activities" (p. 2). Hill (2001) takes up a similar approach to describe what she terms as syncretic linguistic practices which are "active and strategic efforts by speakers" who "draw on their understandings of historical associations of linguistic materials to control meaning and to produce new histories" (p. 243). More recently, new conceptions of syncretic literacies involve melding together distinct literacy practices that are generally incompatible or in tension with one another and promote the development of powerful literacies that challenge current models of academic literacy (Gutiérrez, 2008).

Cultural-Historical Approaches to Syncretic Literacies

Our work on syncretic literacies is anchored in cultural-historical activity theoretical approaches to learning and development as the central explanatory theory (Cole & Engeström, 1993; Engeström, 1987, 2001; Leont'ev, 1981; Sannino, Daniels, & Gutiérrez, 2009). Anchoring work in a central theoretical approach allows for the development of a coherent framework through the thoughtful integration of complementary theoretical and methodological tools. However, constructs are often under-theorized in literacy research, and theories, like the people who use them, have blind spots, making the need for approaches that extend, deepen, and sharpen our conceptions and methods more essential. A goodness of fit, then, is constituted by a complex, hybrid approach that opens up the possibility of illuminating these blind spots.

We argue that a syncretic perspective also can help account for the social and cultural organization of literacy practices, their histories, their complex and varied uses and meanings and, in this way, is consonant with a more powerful definition of literacy as a set of practices; where literacy is always situated in a sociocultural milieu mediated by proximal and distal influences. As we have previously noted, by focusing on the collective as well as on individual sense-making activity, we can document new forms of activity that can lead to rich cycles of learning—or what Engeström (1987, 2001) calls "expansive learning" (Gutiérrez, 2008, p. 152).

For example, while remaining anchored in cultural historical activity theoretical approaches to learning and development, we strategically blend theoretical and methodological tools from literacy, social and anthropological theories, cultural studies, and Critical Race Theory, for example, to conceptualize approaches to syncretic literacies and to examine literacy learning for students from non-dominant communities.

In this work, we argue that a syncretic approach to understanding literacy brings to bear a range of theoretical lenses that yields a repertoire of methodological tools to examine the mutual and interdependent relationship between the individual and the social world. As Engeström (2001) has argued, these theories challenge the Cartesian divide that separates the individual and her cultural means, focusing rather on multiple layers of influence. From this perspective, individual cognition and practice is imbued with the social, the historical, and the biological (Cole, Cole, & Lightfoot, 2009).

One of the affordances of these multiple layers of analysis is that it can help make visible the complex and situated nature of learning and allows examination of the social and cognitive consequences of our working theories, methods, instructional practices, and interventions. At the same time, by attending to historicity, individual practices are connected to their cultural and historical context, thus, linking the local with the global. In this way, literacy practices are not discretely circumscribed phenomena but instead occur as a part of laminated, overlapping, and interwoven social phenomena across time and space.

Like all methodologies, syncretic approaches also are organized around particular ideologies: particular ways of defining what counts as knowledge, how knowledge develops, and how knowledge counts (Apple, 1982, 1999; Green & Luke, 2006). Our own literacy research is oriented toward social problems and is animated by a commitment to do scholarly work that advances the field's understanding of the literacy practices of non-dominant communities, and that extends theories and methods that better capture the complexity of literacy learning and more nuanced understandings of a community's practices. One ideological tenet that has driven our work has been to push on prevailing conceptions of literacy that are narrow, monocultural, monolingual, and too often serve to fail students and place them at risk for school failure. The affordances of a syncretic approach are important even in cases where a robust theoretical approach to literacy learning is in place, as our most valued theories may not fully account for the additional developmental demands placed on youth from non-dominant communities. For instance, do our understandings of students' literacy practices account for the role of race and ethnicity in literacy learning? Consider that a race- and equity-sensitive orientation would begin by acknowledging the complexity of literacy practices in which the enabling and constraining properties of literacy at work are made visible. As an example, this approach would make evident how race is "languaged" and language is "raced," that is, it would theorize how race and racism are indexed in language (Alim, 2009).

Clearly, there is a need for a fuller theoretical explanation of the ways race, language, and literacy constitute capital in schooling environments. Such an explanation would be organized around a political economy that challenges approaches to literacy that rely on an essentializing monocultural and monolingual lens to define students'

linguistic repertoires and to design their educational futures (Gutiérrez, Ali, & Henríquez, 2010; Gutiérrez and Rogoff, 2003). Rupturing reductive notions of literacy, however, entails developing new conceptions of communities and their practices. For example, understanding students' literacy practices as static and bounded belies the stable and improvisational character of cultural practices and ignores the inherent hybridity in human activity. Such reductive views of students' literacy practices contribute to the limited capital their toolkit has in formal schooling environments, notably in reform pedagogies organized around autonomous forms of literacy (Street, 1984).

Following a syncretic approach, sociohistorical understandings of the language practices of dual language learners can provide more accurate and useful descriptions of people's socialinguistic practices, including their genesis and the sources of their mediation. Thus, rather than focusing on students' linguistic deficiencies, a cultural-historical approach would seek to know more about students' history of involvement with language and literacy practices (Gutiérrez, 2008). Further, consider the conceptual and methodological shifts required when a dynamic view of a community's literacies is employed: here the starting assumption is that literacy practices are both culturally-informed and culture-producing.

A dynamic and instrumental notion of culture is fundamental to accounting for the shifts in students' literacy practices over the past decade. Today's students are much more adroit in reading and talking about multimodal texts than conventional written texts, especially those valued in schooling environments, and their repertoires reflect engagement with a variety of media across time and space (Gee, 2004; Leander, Phillips, & Taylor, 2010). Their movement as border-crossers (Tuomi-Gröhn, Engeström, & Young, 2003) across virtual and geographical boundaries—across a range of activity settings—helps ensure that their language and literacy practices are the product of the intercultural and hybrid practices of which they are a part. Thus, understanding this hybridity is key to cultivating new learning and expanding students' literacy practices.

This more complex view is particularly consequential as the essentialism at work in literacy policies and practices belies the hybridity of students' everyday lives, including their linguistic practices. The emergence of new diasporic communities, the result of increased transnational migration have resulted in a variety of intercultural activities in which a wide range of linguistic practices become available to members of non-dominant communities. Life for 21st-century youth involves border-crossing and this movement is mediated by an array of hybrid artifacts, practices, and increasingly new technologies. Understanding the resulting "linguistic bricolage" (Pavlenko & Blackledge, 2004, p. 32) requires more nuanced conceptions and historical understandings of cultural communities and tools to account for what takes hold as youth, their tools, and practices travel across activity settings. Conceiving of learning as movement (Engeström, 2005; Gutiérrez, 2008) should invite the use of multi-sited ethnographies (Marcus, 1998) and expansive theories of learning and development to understand 21st-century literacies and the processes of identity formation involved with this movement. It should also motivate us to examine the consequences of intercultural exchange that could be leveraged to engage students in literacy activities that build upon difference rather than deficit.

To elaborate, a syncretic approach begins with recognition of a particular social problem as part of people's everyday experiences; acknowledgment of their complexity, historical location, and embeddedness in multiple levels of context; and the incorporation of research as part of a program for addressing the social problem. For example, with regard to literacy education, a syncretic approach pushes on extant theories of literacy that have not led to robust literacy instruction for all students or to the development of powerful literacies (Hamilton, 1997; Hamilton, Macrae, & Tett, 2009) that students could leverage in school settings and beyond, sociopolitical issues not withstanding. Acknowledging and foregrounding the sociocultural nature and complexity of language and literacy development go hand in glove with a principled and transdisciplinary logic-of-inquiry that more fully accounts for the multimodality of communication, especially pertinent in an age of expanding digital new media. In other words, fundamental to syncretic approaches, like other methodologies, are inherent connections between how the social phenomena under study is conceptualized (in this case, young people's literacy practices), the logics-of-inquiry framing the study, and the methodological tools employed.

Although a syncretic approach draws on different methods, it is distinct from approaches described as mixed methods and mixed methodologies. The term "mixed methods" refers to the use of multiple methods such as incorporating interviews, natural observations, and controlled experiments within a single study or program of research. These methods may derive from different traditions (e.g., qualitative research and quantitative research). Although thoughtful discussions are a part of mixed methods approaches (Johnson & Onwuegbuzie, 2004), a syncretic approach is not only about what tools to employ. Rather, it is about how to conceptualize and frame the phenomenon to be studied and then designing a logic-of-inquiry that is organized around a principled connection between the conceptualization and frame and the inquiry itself.

One instantiation of this approach is the social design experiment (Gutiérrez & Vossoughi, 2010) akin to Engeström's "change laboratory" (2004). In contrast to some design models, the social design experiment resists ahistorical approaches that do not account for a situated understanding of the social phenomenon or target community; social design experiments are open and dynamic systems that are subject to revision, disruptions, and contradictions and are co-designed (Gutiérrez & Vossoughi, 2010, p. 102); moreover, social design experiments in our work are concerned with social consequences and transformative potential (Engeström, 2004). In designing research that addresses social inequities in ways that "propel the potential for change in the participants, their practices, and their social context of development" (p. 102), the theoretical frameworks driving social design experiments must be as complex as the problems they attempt to address. Thus, the social design experiment is a hybrid environment organized around expansive conceptions of learning, literacy, and communities and seeks to answer questions such as: What new conceptions of literacy and methodological tools, for example, would best help us understand the complex and hybrid repertoires non-dominant students bring to schooling and learning experiences? What new arrangements would foster learning? What kind of learning ecology, tools, forms of participation and assistance, and ways of organizing learning will ratchet up development, as well as promote equity and transformative outcomes?

Studying Literacy Learning as Movement

Connecting individual practices to their cultural and historical context and connecting the local with the global is based on the premise that literacy practices are not discretely circumscribed phenomena but instead occur as a part of laminated, overlapping and interwoven social phenomena across time and space. Students exist and engage in literacy practices that are influenced by the historical and present-moment contexts unique to their experience. Thus, it is often more productive to study students' "movements across their daily routines" (Gutiérrez, 2008, p. 151) in order to understand how the tools and resources available to them—historically, culturally, and in the design of learning environments—are then taken up to constitute the practiced literacy.

One such social design experiment involved a study of the migrant program at UCLA—a program that brought high school students from migrant farmworker backgrounds to the university for an intensive 4-week summer residential program. This was a hybrid ecology that reframed the relation between home and school, between everyday and scientific knowledge and practices, and the local and the historical. Within this approach, individual and community literacies come in contact and work in tandem with institutional genres and conventions in the production of syncretic texts and a resulting sociocritical literacy (Gutiérrez, 2008). Enabled by its design and conceptions of literacy and learning as movement, syncretic literacy practices, characterized by a merger of familiar cultural forms and the conventions of academic literacy privileged in a university setting, leveraged both students' horizontal expertise and the vertical expertise valued in school settings (Engeström, 2003). Accounting for the relation between the horizontal and vertical, the everyday and the scientific, is not the norm in studies of the literacies of youth, particularly those from non-dominant communities.

Thus, a persistent limitation of previous literacy research involves the ways non-dominant communities have been studied, where communities have been examined as bounded entities, without accounting for the ongoing movement and flow occurring, especially in communities experiencing migration and transmigration (Gutiérrez, 2008; Hage, 2005; Marcus, 1998). However, studying people's movement and what takes hold requires new sensibilities, new tools, and a new imagination about communities and their practices as unbounded. Here the multi-sited ethnography would help us attend to the multiple influences on literacy practices and the ways those practices shape and are shaped by cultural mediators, both proximally and distally. Attending to the flow and diffusion of youth across settings makes visible the hybrid character of the practices of which they are a part, including the hybrid nature of literacy practices. The power of following youth in their daily rounds, across time and space, and across borders, for example, and the importance of developing compelling, evidence-based narratives about their literacies should involve what Marcus (2005) calls "methodological bricolage" (p. 2), the kind of bricolage invoked in the multi-sited ethnography or cultural-historical activity theoretical approaches in which a minimum of two activity settings is valued (Engeström, 2005). The methodological bricolage characteristic of activity theoretical approaches in particular is inherently transdisciplinary, as third-generation activity theory anticipates the need for attending to complexity, border-crossing, and hybridity (Engeström, 1999; Sannino, Daniels, & Gutiérrez, 2009). Of significance in the syncretic approach elaborated here, activity theory complements the fundamental principles of the multi-sited ethnographic approach and may help us better theorize and document new immigrant and diasporic communities by examining how cultural activity is influenced by local and distal sociohistorical and sociopolitical demands.

From this perspective, the production of principled, respectful, and nuanced understandings of 21st-century literacies is best served by syncretic approaches that draw on the most illuminating theories and productive methods to document youth and their literacy practices as dynamically constituted rather than essentialized products of bounded communities, and to study "cultural flows" (Hall, 2004, p. 9) and the mutual constitution of local, national, and transnational practices (Hall, 2004). If not, we are likely to reproduce narrow and essentialized accounts of youth and their literacy practices—accounts that are neither accurate nor useful in mediating the development of powerful literacies (Hamilton, 1997) for all youth.

References

Alim, H. S. (2009, February). *Race-ing language, languaging race.* Paper presented at CLIC Symposium on Race & Ethnicity in Language, Interaction, and Culture, UCLA.

Apple, M. (1982). *Cultural and economic reproduction in education: Essays on class, ideology and the state.* Boston: Routledge & Kegan.

Apple, M. (1999). *Power, meaning and identity: Essays in critical educational studies.* New York: Peter Lang.

Barton, D., & Hamilton, M. (1998). *Local literacies: Reading and writing in one community.* London: Routledge.

Cole, M. (1996). *Cultural psychology: A once and future discipline.* Cambridge, MA: Harvard University Press.

Cole, M., Cole, S., & Lightfoot, C. (2009). *The development of children.* New York: Worth.

Cole, M., & Engeström, Y. (1993). A cultural-historical approach to distributed cognition. In G. Salomon (Ed.), *Distributed cognitions: Psychological and educational considerations* (pp. 1–46). Cambridge, UK: Cambridge University Press.

Cope, B., & Kalantzis, M. (Eds.). (2000). *Multiliteracies: Literacy learning and the design of social futures.* New York: Routledge.

Duranti, A., & Ochs, E. (1997). Syncretic literacy in a Samoan American Family. In L. Resnick, R. Saljo, & C. Pontecorvo (Eds.), *Discourse, tools, and reasoning* (pp.169–202). Berlin: Springer-Verlag.

Engeström, Y. (1987). *Learning by expanding: An activity-theoretical approach to developmental research.* Helsinki, Finland: Orienta-Konsultit Oy.

Engeström, Y. (1999). Activity theory and individual and social transformation. In Y. Engeström, R. Miettinen, & R. Punamaki (Eds.), *Perspectives on activity theory* (pp. 19–38). New York: Cambridge University Press.

Engeström, Y. (2001). Expansive learning at work: Toward an activity theoretical reconceptualization. *Journal of Education and Work, 14,* 133–156.

Engeström, Y. (2003). The horizontal dimension of expansive learning: Weaving as texture of cognitive trails in the terrain of health care in Helsinki. In F. Achtenhagen & E. G. John (Eds.), *Milestones of vocational and occupational education and training. Volume I: The teaching-learning perspective* (pp. 153–180). Bielefeld, Germany: Bertelsmann Verlag.

Engeström, Y. (2004). New forms of learning in co-configuration work. *Journal of Workplace Learning, 16,* 11–21.

Engeström, Y. (2005). (Ed.). *Developmental work research: Expanding activity theory in practice, 12.* Berlin: Germany, International Cultural-Historical Human Sciences, Lehmanns Media.

Gee, J. (2004). *Situated language and learning.* New York: Routledge.

Gee, J. (2005). Semiotic social spaces and affinity spaces from the age of mythology to today's schools. In D. Barton & K. Tusting (Eds.), *Beyond communities of practice: Language, power, and social context* (pp. 214–32). Cambridge, UK: Cambridge University Press.

Gee, J. P. (1996). *Social linguistics and literacies: Ideology in discourse.* (2nd ed.). London: Taylor & Francis.

Green, J., & Luke, A. (2006). Introduction: Rethinking learning: What counts as learning and what learning counts. *Review of Research in Education, 30*(1), xi–xiv.

Gutiérrez, K. (2008). Developing a sociocritical literacy in the third space. *Reading Research Quarterly. 43*(2), 148–164.

Gutiérrez, K., Ali, A., & Henríquez, C. (2010). Syncretism and hybridity: Schooling, language, and race and students from non-dominant communities. In M. Apple, S. Ball, & L. A. Gandin (Eds.), *The Routledge international handbook of the sociology of education.* New York: Routledge.

Gutiérrez, K., & Rogoff, B. (2003). Cultural ways of learning: Individual traits or repertoires of practice. *Educational Researcher, 32*(5), 19–25.

Gutiérrez, K., & Stone, L. (2000). Synchronic and diachronic dimensions of social practice: An emerging methodology for cultural-historical perspectives on literacy learning. In C. Lee & P. Smagorinsky (Eds.), *Vygotskian perspectives on literacy research: Constructing meaning through collaborative inquiry* (pp. 150–164). New York: Cambridge University Press.

Gutiérrez, K., & Vossoughi, S. (2010). "Lifting off the ground to return anew": Documenting and designing for equity and transformation through social design experiments. *Journal of Teacher Education, 61*(1-2), 100–117.

Hage, G. (2005). A not so multi-sited ethnography of a not so imagined community. *Anthropological Theory, 5*(4), 463–475.

Hall, K. (2004). The ethnography of imagined communities: The cultural production of Sikh ethnicity in Britain. *ANNALS, AAPSS, 595,* 108–120.

Hamilton, M. (1997). Keeping alive alternative visions. In J. P. Hautecoeur

(Ed., P. Sutton, Trans.), *Alpha 97: Basic education and institutional environments* (pp. 131–150). Hamburg, Germany: UNESCO Institute for Education.

Hamilton, M., Macrae, C., & Tett, L. (2009). Powerful literacies: The policy context. In F. Fletcher-Campbell, G. Reid, & J. Soler (Eds.), *Understanding difficulties in literacy development: Issues and concepts* (pp. 176–192). London: Sage.

Hill, J. (2001). Syncretism. In A. Duranti (Ed.), *Key terms in language and culture* (pp. 241–243). Malden, MA: Blackwell.

Johnson, R. B., & Onwuegbuzie, A. (2004). Mixed methods research: A research paradigm whose time has come. *Educational Researcher, 33*(7), 14–26.

Leander, K., Phillips, N., & Taylor, K. (2010). The changing social spaces of learning: Mapping new mobilities. *Review of Research in Education, 34,* 329–394.

Leont'ev, A. N. (1981). The problem of activity in psychology. In J. V. Wertsch (Ed.), *The concept of activity in Soviet psychology* (pp. 37–71). White Plains, NY: Sharpe.

Luke, A. (2003). Literacy and the other: A sociological approach to literacy research and policy in multilingual societies. *Reading Research Quarterly, 38*(1), 132–141.

Marcus, G. E. (1998). *Ethnography through thick and thin.* Princeton, NJ: Princeton University Press.

Marcus, G. E. (2005, June 27–28). *Multi-sited ethnography: Five or six things I know about it now.* In Problems and Possibilities in Multi-sited Ethnography Workshop, University of Sussex, UK. Unpublished manuscript.

Pavlenko, A., & Blackledge, A. (2004). *Negotiation of identities in multilingual contexts.* Clevedon, UK: Cromwell Press Ltd.

Rogoff, B. (2003). *The cultural nature of human development.* New York: Oxford University Press.

Sannino, A., Daniels, H., & Gutiérrez, K. (2009). (Eds.). *Learning and expanding with activity theory.* Cambridge, UK: Cambridge University Press.

Street, B. V. (1984). *Literacy in theory and practice.* London: Cambridge University Press.

Street, B. V. (2003). What's "new" in new literacy studies? Critical approaches to literacy in theory and practice. *Current Issues in Comparative Education, 5*(2), 77–91.

Tuomi-Gröhn, T., & Engeström, Y., & Young, M. (2003). From transfer to boundary-crossing between school and work as a tool for developing vocational education: An introduction. In T. Tuomi-Gröhn & Y. Engeström (Eds.), *Between school and work: New perspectives on transfer and boundary-crossing* (pp. 39–61). Amsterdam: Pergamon.

61

Critical Approaches to Research in English Language Arts

Arlette Willis

The first decade of the 21st century brings with it a resurgence of interest in critical theorizing and innovative use of critical approaches in English language arts (ELA) research. Every researcher's epistemological point of view informs her theoretical framework, methods, and questions as well as guides data collection, analysis, and interpretation. The goal of critical theory, according to Fay (1987) is to "explain a social order in such a way that it becomes itself the catalyst which leads to the transformation of this social order" (p. 27). Critical theorizing is not a mystical understanding reached by only a select few. In fact, Gramsci (1971) has argued that everyone is a critical theorist: "participants in a particular conception of the world, has a conscious line of moral conduct, and therefore contributes to sustain a conception of the world, or to modify it, that is to bring into being modes of thought" (p. 9). Critical theories and methods have evolved over time to address "new theoretical insights and new problems and social circumstances" (Kincheloe & McLaren, 2005, p. 306). This on-going process of reconceptualization, or criticality, meets the ever-changing challenges and complexities of our world and lives in the world. A brief review of the epistemological "roots and routes" (Hall, 1984) of critical theorizing and current manifestations that inform ELA critical approaches follows. The chapter concludes with a discussion of applications of critical theorizing in qualitative ELA studies.

Epistemological and Theoretical Foundations

Critical theorizing is part of a vast history of ideas in the world and as such there is no definitive history of critical theory. There are several key moments in critical theorizing—used as a convenient means of understanding the ever-evolving nature of critical theory—but these do not form a comprehensive history. Most commonly, historical overviews of critical theory begin with Western European ideas. In this chapter, they are followed by the often-overlooked contributions of African American scholars and

social activists. Next, the contributions of Paulo Freire are reviewed because of their importance to ELA researchers that employ critical literacy and critical literacy pedagogy. The most recent moment, centering of racial/ethnic epistemologies, theories, and methods, follows.

Western-Eurocentric From a Western-Eurocentric point of view, critical theorizing begins with the thinking and scholarship of Kant, Hegel, and Marx that informs the ideas, thoughts, personalities, and writings associated with members of Das Insititut für Sozialforschung (Institute for Social Research), also known as the Frankfurt School. The initial focus of the Institute was "first and foremost to serve in the study and extension of scientific Marxism" (Wiggershaus, 1994, p. 35). Scholars from the Frankfurt School did not create or promote a unified notion of critical theory, but rather "they came to view their disciplines as manifestations of the discourse and power relations of the social and historic contexts that produced them" (Kincheloe & McLaren, 2000, p. 280). Individual scholars were advocates of select Marxist principles, others preferred to focus on the writings of Kant or Hegel, and still others sought to create new theories. Critical theorizing was interdisciplinary albeit it focused on the industrial corporate state (capitalism/economics) and politics. During this moment, social class was the primary, but not sole, unit of analysis.

Critical Theory (capitalized to reflect this particular moment) examined power and its relationship to economic and social class issues. The writings of Antonio Gramsci (1971), an Italian Marxist, shifted the focus to hegemony and ideology; later extending to culture, language, and society (Forgas, 2000). In addition, the writings of Frantz Fanon (1965, 1967) challenged traditional CT scholars to openly address issues of colonialism, ideology, imperialism, and racism.

Bronner (2002) reveals that Frankfurt School's emphasis among the first, second, third, and fourth generations (Pierre Bourdieu, Jacquez Derrida, Michael Foucault, Jurgen Habermas, and Stuart Hall, among others) highlights shifts in focus and units of analysis from primarily social class to culture, language, mass communication, media, etc. Scholarship will continue to evolve as subsequent generations advance CT. In general, however, early variations of CT did not address issues of race/ethnicity, gender, or sexual orientation in their critical projects.

Early 20th-Century African American In the Americas, social theorists also examined notions of hegemony, ideology, and power; particularly those who experienced colonialism, inequality, and oppression. African American scholars and social activists, Ana Julia Cooper, W. E. B. DuBois, and Carter G. Woodson, extended CT notions in the application and examination of race, gender, inequality, oppression, and power. Cooper (1892), for instance, argued that Black women faced both gender and race discrimination and held very little power. DuBois (1903/1995) compellingly argued that people of African descent in the United States lived with double-consciousnesses, "this sense of always looking at one's self through the eyes of others, of measuring one's soul by the tape of a world that looks on in amused contempt and pity" (DuBois, 1995, p. 3). Woodson (1933) clarified that in U.S. society, African Americans were coerced into replicating White thinking. Collectively, the scholarship of these social activists is antecedent to contemporary notions of critical theories (lower case to reflect expanded notions of criticality directly and expressly addressing race, class, gender, sexual orientation, religion, and their intersectionality).

Paulo Freire: Critical Theorizing and Critical Pedagogy
Latin American scholar and social activist, Paulo R. N. Freire (1921–1997) also fought against inequality, oppression, and power. Epistemologically, Freire's thinking was informed by several social theories, most notably the writings of Marx. He adopted Marx's dialectical materialistic epistemology that calls for "1) understanding the interrelated processes happening in the world; and 2) provide space for human intervention in the processes to change that world for better" (Au, 2009, p. 224). Freire's ideas are best captured in his notion and application of *conscientização;* a concept that expanded over time to reflect changes in history, culture, politics, and social circumstances. Initially, he declared:

> Every relationship of domination, of exploitation, of oppression, is by nature violent, whether or not the violence is expressed by drastic means. In such a relationship, dominator and dominated alike are reduced to things—the former dehumanized by an excess of power, the latter by the lack of it. (Leistyna, Woodrum, & Sherblom, 1996, pp. 339–340)

Freire extended conscientizaçã to represent, "awareness of the historical, sociopolitical, economic, cultural, and subjective reality that shapes our lives, and our ability to transform that reality" (Leistyne et al., 1996, p. 340). He believed that social transformation was possible through education (Freire, 1970). He created a venue for teachers to envisage their role as agents of social change by adopting and adapting a humanizing, critical pedagogy. Ideas that evolved from his work include critical literacy/ies and critical pedagogy. To him, critical literacy and pedagogy honor and respect humankind as well as the multiple cultures, knowledges, languages, and literacies of learners. The lifework of Freire also encouraged educators, teachers in particular, to develop their critical consciousnesses and to help develop critical consciousness in learners. There are numerous definitions, descriptions, and features of critical literacies however, epistemologically all reference CT and the influence of Freire's theorizing. Aronowitz and Giroux (1985), for instance, posit that critical literacy:

> would make clear the connection of between knowledge and power ... demonstrate modes of critique that illuminate how, in some cases, knowledge serves very specific economic, political and social interests ... function as a theoretical tool to help students and others develop a critical relationship to their own knowledge. (p. 132)

Anderson and Irvine (1993) suggests critical literacy encompasses "learning to read and write as part of the process of becoming conscious of one's experience as historically constructed within specific power relations" (p. 82). Shor (1999) describes features of critical literacy as an approach, discourse, pedagogy, social practice, means of self-discovery, and an avenue to promote justice and address inequity. He defines *critical literacy* as "language use that questions the social construction of the self... examine our ongoing development, to reveal the subjective positions from which we make sense of the world and act in it" (p. 2). Janks (2002) and Luke (2004) have extended definitions to address the complexities of the increase use and dependence on media and technology to communicate, local and global contexts, and the uses of New Literacies in classrooms.

McLaren (2000) characterizes critical pedagogy as "a way of thinking about, negotiating, and transforming the relationship among classroom teaching, the production of knowledge, the institutional structures of the school, and the social and material relations of the wider community, society, and nation-state" (p. 35). Apple, Au, and Gandin (2009) articulate that most projects "broadly seek to expose how relations of power and inequality (social, cultural, economic), in their myriad forms combinations, and complexities are manifest and are challenged in the formal and informal education of children and adults" (p. 3). As critical theory continues to progress, current manifestations also will change to reflect cultural, economic, historical, political, and social circumstances.

Critical Race/Ethnic Epistemologies and Theories

The 20th anniversary of Critical Race Theory (CRT) occurred in 2009. It marked a milestone in an intellectual movement that embraced and challenged the historical moment when it began. CRT called for the explicit acknowledgement of the lived experiences of people of color in the United States, and, now globally. It extended early Leftist attempts of White scholars, Critical Legal Studies (CLS) advocates, to move toward radical scholarship and explicated the "meaning of race, racism, and law to people of color and the world" (Onwuachi-Willing, 2009, p. 1501). Delgado (2009) shares the early beginnings of CRT by retelling three separate but interwoven stories about its origins from Harvard, Berkeley, and Los Angeles. He recalls how CLS attendees gave time, space, and audience to scholars of color, but "made few, if any, organizational changes" (p. 1514). Delgado opines that all three stories serve to inform a history of the early days of CRT as the historical moment and contexts (cultural, political, social) were pregnant with possibility for the theoretical orientation among legal scholars of color. CRT pioneers sought to "reexamine the terms by which race and racism have been negotiated in American consciousness, and to recover and revitalize the radical tradition of race-consciousness among African-Americans and other peoples of color" (Crenshaw, Gotanda, Peller, & Thomas, 1995, p. xiv). Proponents acknowledge that the concept of race is socially constructed and not a biological or scientific fact while simultaneously understanding that this construct operates as "fact" within the United States and reflects a history of oppression for people of color.

CRT is informed by Black feminist theory, critical theory, critical legal studies, feminism, liberalism, Marxism/neo-Marxism, post-structuralism, postmodernism, and neopragmatism. Race-conscious theories that emerged include: AsianAmerican Critical Theory (Chang, 1993; Liu, 2009); LaCrit (Solórzano & Yosso, 2001); Critical Indigenous/Studies (Bishop, 2005); Critical White Studies (Delgado & Stefancic, 1997; Frankenberg, 1993; Giroux, 1997; Roediger, 2001); Red Pedagogy (Grande, 2004); Tribal Critical Studies (Brayboy, 2005); and critical raced feminisms (Collins, 1990/2000), Chicana feminism (Delgado-Bernal, 1998) and Mestiaz consciousness (Delgado-Bernal, 2001, 2002; González, 2001), among others. These contemporary critical evolutions fill-in the gaps found in CT—gendered, race-centered, and sexual orientation—and interrogate intersecting oppressions of class, language, immigrate status/citizenship, and religion within multiple domains of power. Moreover, CRT demonstrates a need to adopt a more inclusive epistemological and theoretical stance; a multi-perspectival approach that accepts the intersectionality and fluidity of forces in contemporary research. A number of scholars (Ladson-Billings, 1997; Solórzano & Yosso, 2001; Tate, 1997) have adapted CRT for education. Scholars have applied its themes to education research and ELA researchers have apply CRT to studies of language and literacy.

In sum, the epistemological and theoretical moments of critical theorizing expose the complexity of criticality. Although there is no singular definition, history, theory, or method that is common to all criticality, there are shared characteristics that inform critical projects, summarized by Kincheloe & McLaren (1994):

all thought is fundamentally mediated by power relations that are social and historically constituted; that facts can never be isolated from domain of values or removed from some form of ideological inscription; that the relationship between concept and object and between signifier and signified is never stable or fixed and is often mediated by the social relations of capitalist production and consumption; that language is central to the formation of subjectivity (conscious and unconscious awareness); that certain groups in any society are privileged over others and, although the reasons for this privileging may vary widely, the oppression that characterizes contemporary societies is most forcefully reproduced when subordinates accept their social status as natural, necessary and that focusing on only one at the expense of others (e.g., class oppression versus racism) often elides the interconnections among them; and, finally, that mainstream research practices are generally, although most often unwittingly, implicated in the reproduction of systems of class, race, and gender oppression. (pp. 119–120)

Weis, Fine, and Dimitriadis (2009), more recently, have called for expanding critical research methods to become more imaginative and courageous, to account for "deep, local, and historic conditions within which cultures and movements grow and change and *at the same time* such evidence of the ways in which global lives carry across sites, bodies, capital privilege, culture, critique, and despair" (p. 439). The singular unit of analysis of the Frankfurt School has given way to more totalizing critiques that seek to account for intersecting, layered, and interrelated forces through transformative action. Criticality has retained CT's interdisciplinarity, but now draws on multiple critical theories and uses units of analysis that include gender, language, race, religion, and sexual orientation among others.

Critical Approaches in ELA Research

Approaches or methods of criticality are not reducible to a set of steps, guidelines, and criteria (Bronner, 2002; Quantz, 1992). Applications of critical approaches acknowledge the epistemological and theoretical positions that inform the question(s) posed, observations, data collection, development of categories, coding of units, links between categories, selecting compelling examples, framework for analysis and interpretation, and presentation of data. Critical theories inform qualitative research methodologies in case study, discourse analysis, ethnography, and narrative (autobiography, biography, counter/storytelling) inquiry. ELA researchers also use criticality to enhance understandings the effects of global and local contexts (historical, political, social) in language and literacy theorizing, research, and praxis.

Carspecken and Apple (1992) and Lamphere (1994) describe a body of research that exhibits general critical qualitative methods. Bloome and Carter (2005) define *critical discourse analysis* as "a set of approaches to discourse analysis focusing on power relations. The models of power, understandings of language, culture, and social processes, and foci of analysis, varies across approaches"

(p. 1). Critical ethnography draws on five reoccurring themes: knowledge, values, society, culture, and history (Quantz, 1992). Foley and Valenzuela (2005) believe that critical ethnography addresses issues of power, language, and truth. Madison (2005), however, characterizes critical ethnography as "critical theory in action" (p. 15). Critical policy analysis, according to Shaw (2004) consists of the following assumptions: single truth theory, researcher objectivity, and homogenization of participant experience. Edmonson (2002), whose body of work interrogates policies related to reading research, claims that "educational policy and educational practices are never objective, technical matters. Instead they are always evaluative and political" (p. 118). There is a long and troubling relationship between federal policies and literacy, underscored by power relations and class and racial discrimination and inequality. Critical literacy research has exposed and helped to demystify the ideological hegemony that sustains the reproduction of mainstream literacy research, practices, and recommendations.

CRT scholars draw from multiple racial/ethnic epistemologies to situate their work and ask questions that challenge preconceived notions about the beliefs, values, knowledge, and ways of making meaning held by people of color. Solórzano and Yosso (2002) argue CRT methodology is theoretically grounded research that: foregrounds race and racism in all aspects of the research process; challenges the traditional research paradigm, texts, and theories used to explain the experiences of people of color; offers a liberatory or transformative solution to racial, gender, and class subordination; focuses on the racialized, gendered, and classed experiences of students of color; and uses the interdisciplinary knowledge base of ethnic studies, women's studies, sociology, history, humanities and the law to better understand the experiences of students of color (p. 24).

CRT methods emphasize cultural and experiential knowledge through narratives and voice to examine race, racism, and power in society. Scholars produce their own narratives as counter-stories to the way culture, lives, and experiences of people of color that contradict or oppose the assumptions and beliefs held by many Whites. Inherent in the narrative forms are voice, or the ability of a group to articulate their experience in ways unique to them (Delgado and Stefancic, 2001). The process begins by collecting, examining, and analyzing a host of concepts, ideas, and experiences while using both theoretical sensitivity and cultural intuition. Next, counternarratives are constructed by gathering data, reviewing extant literature, drawing on their professional experiences, and reflecting on their personal experiences (Solórzano & Yosso, 2001, p. 476). Finally, several scholars have extended the use of CRT to include literary analysis (Brooks, 2009), personal stories (Aguirre, 2005), portraiture (Chapman, 2005), and a self-study of Whiteness (Marx & Pennington, 2003).

Critical theorizing rests on the hope of effecting positive change to create an equitable socially just society. As critical approaches continue to evolve, ELA researchers' applica-tions also will evolve as they address equity and injustices, challenge traditions in the field, resist the reproduction of ideas and values of privileged and dominant groups, improve pedagogy and curricula, and help to transform ELA processes to become more socially just.

References

Aguirre, A. (2005). The personal narrative as academic storytelling: A Chicano's search for presence and voice in academe. *International Journal of Qualitative Studies in Education, 18*(2), 147–163.

Anderson, G. L., & Irvine, P. (1993). Informing critical literacy ethnography. In C. Lankshear & P. L. McLaren (Eds.), *Critical literacy: Politics, praxis, and the postmodern* (pp. 81–104). Albany: State University New York Press.

Apple, M. W., Au, W., & Gandin, L., A. (2009). Mapping critical education. In M. W. Apple, W. Au, & L. A. Gandin (Eds.), *The Routledge international handbook of critical education* (pp. 3–19). New York: Routledge.

Aronowitz, S., & Giroux, H. (1985). *Education under siege*. South Hadley, MA: Bergin-Garvey.

Au, W. (2009). Fighting with the text: Contextualizing and recontextualizing Freire's pedagogy. In M. W. Apple, W. Au, & L. A. Gandin (Eds.), *The Routledge international handbook of critical education*, (pp. 221–231). New York: Routledge.

Bishop, R. (2005). Freeing ourselves from neocolonial domination in research: A Kaupapa Maori approach to creating knowledge. In N. Denzin & Y. Lincoln (Eds.), *The Sage handbook of qualitative research* (pp. 109–138). Thousand Oaks, CA: Sage.

Bloome, D., & Carter, S. (2005, February). Critical discourse analysis in and across educational contexts. A workshop presented at the annual conference of National Council of Teachers of English Midwinter Assembly for Research, Columbus, OH.

Brayboy, B. M. J. (2005). Toward a tribal critical race theory in education. *The Urban Review, 37*(5), 425–446.

Bronner, S. (2002). *Of critical theory and its theorists* (2nd ed.). New York: Routledge.

Brooks, W. (2009). As author as a counter-storyteller: Applying critical race theory to a Coretta Scott King Award book. *Children's Literature in Education, 40,* 33–45.

Carspecken, P., & Apple, M. (1992). Critical qualitative research: Theory, methodology, and practice. In M. LeCompte, W. Millroy, & J. Preissle (Eds.), *The handbook of qualitative research in education* (pp. 507–553). San Diego, CA: Academic Press.

Chang, R. S. (1993). Toward an Asian American legal scholarship: Critical race theory, poststructuralism, and narrative space. *California Law Review, 19,* 1243–1323.

Chapman, T. K. (2005). Expressions of 'Voice' in portraiture. *Qualitative Inquiry, 11*(1), 27–51.

Collins, P. H. (2000). *Black feminist thought: Knowledge, consciousness, and the politics of empowerment* (2nd ed.). New York: Routledge (original work published 1990)

Cooper, A. (1892). *A voice from the south*. Xenia, OH: Aldine.

Crenshaw, K., Gotanda, N., Peller, G., & Thomas, K. (Eds.). (1995). *Critical race theory: The key writings that informed the movement*. New York: The New Press.

Delgado, R. (2009). Liberal McCarthyism and the origins of critical race theory. *Iowa Law Review, 94,* 1505–1545.

Delgado-Bernal, D. (1998). Using a Chicana feminist epistemology in educational research. *Harvard Educational Review, 68,* 555–582.

Delgado, R., & Stefancic, J. (1997). *Critical white studies: Looking behind the mirror*. Philadelphia: Temple University Press.

Delgado, R., & Stefancic, J. (2001). *Critical race theory: An introduction*. New York: New York University Press.

Delgado-Bernal, D. (2001). Learning and living pedagogies of the home: The *mestiza* consciousness of Chicana studies. *International Journal of Qualitative Studies in Education, 14*(5), 623–639.

Delgado-Bernal, D. (2002). Critical race theory, Latino critical theory, and critical race-gendered epistemologies: Recognizing students of color as holders and creators of knowledge. *Qualitative Inquiry, 8*(1), 105–126.

DuBois, W. E. B. (1995). *The souls of black folks.* New York: Ginn and Co. (original work published 1903)

Edmondson, J. (2002). Asking different questions: Critical analyses and reading research. *Reading Research Quarterly, 37*(1), 113–119.

Fanon, F. (1965/1961). *The wretched of the earth* (Trans. C. Farrington). New York: Grove Press.

Fanon, F. (1967). *Black skin, white masks.* (Trans. C. L. Markmann). New York: Grove Press (original work published 1952)

Fay, B. (1987). *Critical social science: Liberation and its limits.* Ithaca, NY: Cornell University Press.

Foley, D. E., & Valenzuela, A. (2005). Critical ethnography: The politics of collaboration. In N. Denzin & Y. Lincoln (Eds.), *The Sage handbook of qualitative research* (3rd ed., pp. 217–234). Thousand Oaks, CA: Sage.

Forgas. D. (Ed.). (2000). *The Antonio Gramsci reader:* Selected writings 1916–1935. New York: New York University Press.

Frankenberg, R. (1993). *White women, race matters: The social construction of whiteness.* Minneapolis: University of Minnesota Press.

Freire, P. (1970). *Pedagogy of the oppressed.* New York: Continuum.

Freire, P. (1973). *Education for critical consciousness.* New York: Seabury.

Freire, P. (1993). *Pedagogy of the city.* New York: Continuum.

Giroux, H. A. (1997). Rewriting the discourse of racial identity: Towards a pedagogy and politics of whiteness. *Harvard Educational Review, 67*, 285–320.

González, F. E. (2001). *Haciendo que hacer* — cultivating a Mestiza worldview academic achievement: Braiding cultural knowledge into education research, policy, and practice. *International Journal of Qualitative Studies in Education, 14*(5), 641–656.

Gramsci, A. (1971). *Selections from the prison notebooks of Antonio Gramsci* (Ed. & Trans. Q. Hoare & G. Smith). New York: International Publishers.

Grande, S. (2004). *Red pedagogy: Native American social and political thought.* New York: Rowman & Littlefield.

Hall, S. (1984). Encoding/decoding. In S. Hall, D. Hobson, A. Lowe, & P. Willis (Eds.), *Culture, media, language* (pp. 129–138). Birmingham, UK: Centre for Contemporary Cultural Studies. (original work published 1973).

Hall, S. (1984). Reconstruction work. *Ten, 8*(16), 1–10.

Janks, H. (2002). Critical literacy: Beyond reason. *Australian Educational Researcher, 29*(1), 7–27.

Kincheloe, J., & McLaren, P. (2000). Rethinking critical theory and qualitative research. In N. Denzin & Y. Lincoln (Eds.), *Handbook of qualitative research* (2nd ed., pp. 279–314). Thousand Oaks, CA: Sage.

Kincheloe, J., & McLaren, P. (2005). Rethinking critical theory and qualitative research. In N. Denzin & Y. Lincoln (Eds.), *Handbook of qualitative research* (3rd ed., pp. 303–342), Thousand Oaks, CA: Sage.

Ladson-Billings, G. (1997). I know why this doesn't feel empowering. A critical race analysis of critical pedagogy. In P. Freire (Ed.), *Mentor-*

ing the mentor: A critical dialogue with Paulo Freire (pp. 127–142). New York: Peter Lang.

Lamphere, L. (1994). Expanding our notions of 'critical qualitative methodology': Bringing race, class, and gender into the discussion (response). In A. Gitlin (Ed.), *Power and method: Political activism and educational research* (pp. 217–224). New York: Routledge.

Liu, A. (2009). Critical race theory, Asian Americans, and higher education: A review of research. *InterActions: UCLA Journal of Education and Information Studies, 5*(2). Retrieved July 30, 2009, from http://repositories.cdlib.org/gseis/interactions/vol5/iss2/art6

Luke, A. (2004). Teaching after the market: From commodity to cosmopolitan. *Teachers College Record, 106*(7), 1422–1423.

Madison, D. S. (2005). *Critical ethnography: Method, ethics, and performance.* Thousand Oaks, CA: Sage.

Marx, S., & Pennington, J. (2003). Pedagogies of critical race theory: Experimentations with white privilege. *International Journal of Qualitative Studies in Education, 16*(1), 91–110.

McLaren, P. (2000). *Che Guevara, Paulo Freire, and the pedagogy of revolution.* Lanham MD: Rowman & Littlefield.

McLaren, P., & Giarelli, J. (Eds.). (1995). *Critical theory and educational research.* Albany: State University of New York Press.

Onwuachi-Willing, A. (2009). Celebrating critical race theory at 20. *94 Iowa Law Review,* 1497–1504.

Quantz, R. (1992). On critical ethnography (with some postmodern considerations). In M. LeCompte, W. Millroy, & J. Preissle (Eds.), *The handbook of qualitative research in education* (pp. 447–505). San Diego, CA: Academic Press.

Roediger, D. R. (2001). Critical studies of whiteness, USA: Origins and arguments. *Theoria,* 72–97.

Shaw, K. (2004). Using feminist critical policy analysis in the realm of higher education: The case of welfare reform as gendered educational policy. *The Journal of Higher Education, 75*(1), 56–79.

Shor, I. (1999). What is critical literacy? *Journal of Pedagogy, Pluralism, & Practice.* Retrieved from http:www.lesly.edu/Journals/jppp/4/shor.html

Solórzano, D., G., & Yosso, T. J. (2001). Critical race and LatCrit theory and method: Counter-storytelling. *International Journal of Qualitative Studies in Education, 14*(4), 471–495.

Solórzano, D., & Yosso, T. (2002). Critical race methodology: Counterstorytelling as an analytic framework for education research. *Qualitative Inquiry, 8*(1), 23–44.

Tate, W. (1997). Critical race theory and education: History, theory, and implications. *Review of Research in Education, 22*, 195–247.

Weis, L., Fine, M., & Dimitriadis, G. (2009). Towards a critical theory of method in shifting times. In M. W. Apple, W. Au, & L. A. Gandin (Eds.), *The Routledge international handbook of critical education* (pp. 437–448). New York: Routledge.

Wiggershaus, R. (1994). *The Frankfurt School: Its history, theories, and political significance* (Michael Robertson, Trans.). Cambridge, MA: The MIT Press.

Woodson, C. G. (1933). *The mis-education of the Negro.* Washington, DC: Associated Publishers.

Contributors

Lead Editors

Diane Lapp, San Diego State University
Douglas Fisher, San Diego State University

Section Editors

Peter Afflerbach, University of Maryland
Peggy Albers, Georgia State University
Donna E. Alvermann, University of Georgia
David Bloome, The Ohio State University
Thandeka Chapman, University of Wisconsin, Milwaukee
María E. Fránquiz, The University of Texas, Austin
Peter Freebody, The University of Sydney
Nancy Frey, San Diego State University
Jerome C. Harste, Indiana University
Douglas K. Hartman, Michigan State University
Wen Ma, Le Moyne College
Christine A. Mallozzi, University of Kentucky
Cheryl A. McLean, Rutgers, The State University of New Jersey
Lesley Mandel Morrow, Rutgers, The State University of New Jersey
Nancy Roser, The University of Texas, Austin
Robert Rueda, University of Southern California
Patricia Ruggiano Schmidt, Le Moyne College
Allison Skerrett, The University of Texas, Austin
Jennifer D. Turner, University of Maryland
Vivian Vasquez, American University
Karen Wood, University of North Carolina, Charlotte

Authors

Peter Afflerbach, University of Maryland
Peggy Albers, Georgia State University
Mary Ariail, Georgia State University
Steven Z. Athanases, University of California, Davis

Arnetha F. Ball, Stanford University
Richard Beach, University of Minnesota
Thomas W. Bean, University of Nevada, Las Vegas
Andrea C. Bien, University of Colorado at Boulder
Camille L. Z. Blachowicz, National-Louis University, Chicago
David Bloome, The Ohio State University
Fenice B. Boyd, State University at Buffalo, SUNY
Cynthia H. Brock, The University of Nevada, Reno
Robert C. Calfee, University of California at Riverside
Rebecca M. Callahan, The University of Texas at Austin
Jill Castek, University of California, Berkeley
Courtney B. Cazden, Harvard Graduate School of Education
Marilyn J. Chambliss, University of Maryland
Thandeka Chapman, University of Wisconsin, Milwaukee
Summer Clark, University of Maryland
Julie Coiro, University of Rhode Island
Mikel W. Cole, Vanderbilt Peabody College
Reginald D'Silva, University of British Columbia
Glenn DeVoogd, California State University, Fresno
Catherine Doherty, Queensland University of Technology
Susan Dougherty, Rutgers, The State University of NewJersey
KaiLonnie Dunsmore, Ball Foundation
Brian Edmiston, The Ohio State University
Patricia Edwards, Michigan State University
Linnea C. Ehri, City University of New York
Patricia Enciso, The Ohio State University
Kathy Escamilla, University of Colorado at Boulder
Douglas Fisher, San Diego State University
Peter J. Fisher, National-Louis University, Chicago
Tanya R. Flushman, Vanderbilt Peabody College
Dana L. Fox, Georgia State University
María E. Fránquiz, The University of Texas, Austin
Peter Freebody, The University of Sydney

Nancy Frey, San Diego State University
Meg Gebhard, University of Massachusetts at Amherst
Lee Gunderson, University of British Columbia
John T. Guthrie, University of Maryland
Kris D. Gutiérrez, University of Colorado at Boulder
Jane Hansen, University of Virginia
Helen Harper, University of Nevada, Las Vegas
Jerome C. Harste, Indiana University
Douglas K. Hartman, Michigan State University
Renee Hobbs, Temple University
Chrystine C. Hoeltzel, University of Maryland
Susan Hopewell, University of Colorado at Boulder
George G. Hruby, University of Kentucky
Glynda Hull, New York University
Radha Iyer, Queensland University of Technology
Robert T. Jiménez, Vanderbilt Peabody College
Valerie Kinloch, The Ohio State University
Brian Kissel, University of North Carolina at Charlotte
Janette K. Klingner, University of Colorado at Boulder
Melanie Landon-Hays, Utah State University
Diane Lapp, San Diego State University
Henry M. Levin, Teachers College, Columbia University
Rachael Levy, University of Sheffield
Cynthia Lewis, University of Minnesota
Anthony J. Liddicoat, University of South Australia
Allan Luke, Queensland University of Technology
Joyce E. Many, Georgia State University
J. R. Martin, University of Sydney
Miriam Martínez, The University of Texas, San Antonio
Ramón Antonio Martínez, The University of Texas, Austin
Jackie Marsh, University of Sheffield
Bronwyn MacFarlane, University of Arkansas at Little Rock
Maureen McLaughlin, University of Pennsylvania
Stuart McNaughton, The University of Auckland
E. Jennifer Monaghan, Brooklyn College of The City University of New York
Ernest Morrell, University of California, Los Angeles
Lesley Mandel Morrow, Rutgers, The State University of NewJersey
Gemma Moss, Institute of Education, University of London
Dennis Murphy Odo, University of British Columbia
Bill Muth, Virginia Commonwealth University

Nancy Nelson, University of North Texas
David O'Brien, University of Minnesota
Kate Pahl, University of Sheffield
Jeanne R. Paratore, Boston University
Julie L. Pennington, The University of Nevada, Reno
Kristen H. Perry, University of Kentucky
Stephanie Power-Carter, Indiana University
Ellen Pratt, University of Puerto Rico, Mayaguez
Timothy Rasinski, Kent State University
Sylvia Read, Utah State University
Michael RobbGreico, Temple University
Brian C. Rose, Vanderbilt Peabody College
Nancy Roser, The University of Texas at Austin
Deborah Wells Rowe, Vanderbilt University
Jennifer Rowsell, Brock University, Ontario, Canada
Patricia Ruggiano Schmidt, Le Moyne College
Caitlin Ryan, East Carolina University
Makenzie K. Selland, University of Colorado at Boulder
Timothy Shanahan, University of Illinois at Chicago
Marjorie Siegel, Teachers College, Columbia University
Sunita Singh, Le Moyne College
Allison Skerrett, The University of Texas, Austin
Peter Smagorinsky, University of Georgia
Dorothy Strickland, Rutgers, The State University of New Jersey
Thomas Swiss, University of Minnesota
Ana Taboada, George Mason University
Stacie L. Tate, American University
Shane Templeton, University of Nevada, Reno
Dianna Townsend, University of Nevada, Reno
Megan Tschannen-Moran, The College of William and Mary
Jennifer D. Turner, University of Maryland
Verónica E. Valdez, University of Utah
Vivian Vasquez, American University
Lalitha Vasudevan, Teachers College, Columbia University
Susan Watts-Taffe, University of Cincinnati
Allan Wigfield, University of Maryland
Arlette Willis, University of Illinois at Urbana-Champaign
Kelly Wissman, University at Albany, SUNY
Karen E. Wohlwend, Indiana University
Karen Wood, University of North Carolina, Charlotte
David B. Yaden, Jr., University of Arizona

Index